THEORIES
OF
LEARNING

Fifth Edition

GORDON H. BOWER
ERNEST R. HILGARD

Both of Stanford University

Prentice-Hall, Inc., Englewood Cliffs, N.J. 07632

Library of Congress Cataloging in Publication Data

BOWER, GORDON H
    Theories of learning.

    (The Century psychology series)
    Authors' names in reverse order in 3d and 4th eds.
    Bibliography:
    Includes index.
    1. Learning, Psychology of. I. Hilgard, Ernest
Ropiequet, (date)   joint author. II. Title.
BF318.H55 1981   153.1'5   80-19396
ISBN 0-13-914432-3

I dedicate this book to my students—past and present—
who have enriched my life with learning.   —G.H.B.

The Century Psychology Series

Printed in the United States of America

10 9 8 7 6

Acknowledgments for the use of copyrighted material
  appear on page 626.

Editorial/production supervision
  and interior design by Joyce Turner
Cover illustration: *Lavender Mist* by
  Jackson Pollock, 1950, 7'4" x 9'11". Courtesy
  National Gallery of Art, Washington, D.C.
Art Director: Lorraine Mullaney
Manufacturing buyer: Edmund W. Leone

Prentice-Hall International, Inc., *London*
Prentice-Hall of Australia Pty. Limited, *Sydney*
Prentice-Hall of Canada, Ltd., *Toronto*
Prentice-Hall of India Private Limited, *New Delhi*
Prentice-Hall of Japan, Inc., *Tokyo*
Prentice-Hall of Southeast Asia Pte. Ltd., *Singapore*
Whitehall Books Limited, *Wellington, New Zealand*

I

Behavioral-
Associationist
Theories

CONTENTS

III
Related Fields

PREFACE

Psychology seems to be constantly in a state of ferment and change, if not of turmoil and revolution. In attempting to understand mental life, thousands of psychologists are continually proposing new perspectives, ideas, phenomena, experimental results, and investigative methods at a pell-mell pace. The professional often feels that he is drowning in a torrential flood of information and loses track of whether he is in a mainstream or a side eddy; the new student doesn't know where to enter the waters or in which direction to swim. In such situations, a time-tested method for reducing the information overload is to examine the genesis of major, integrative perspectives and to study their development into the contemporary research scene. The historical perspective provides a major organizing scheme for student and professional alike, since many of the "big questions" about mental phenomena were posed long ago, and the answers to the questions advanced by the historically prominent positions serve as prototypes, of which contemporary hypotheses can often be seen as sophisticated progeny.

The aim of this text is to provide the student with an understanding of modern learning theory, its historical context and background. To this end we review the theories of learning expounded by the major "schools" of psychology—behaviorism, gestalt, cognitivism, information-processing—as well as the learning theories associated with major intellectual figures such as Thorndike, Pavlov, Guthrie, Hull, Tolman, Skinner, and Estes.

Each theory is expounded in terms of its historical setting and the scientific problems that the theorist was addressing. As theoretical ideas are introduced, the salient experimental evidence related to them is briefly surveyed. Each theory is expounded initially from a sympathetic perspective. However, each chapter ends with a critical discussion and evaluation of the evidence for the theory's claims.

Comparing this new edition with the fourth edition, the reader will note many changes in content. As before, the first chapter introduces the philosophical antecedents of psychology, contrasting the theories of mind advocated in philosophical Empiricism and Rationalism. Since these contrasting themes are powerful and recurrent, we have used them to reorganize the chapters of this new edition. The early chapters are examples of the Empiricist methodology: these are learning theories heavily influenced by associationism and behaviorism; included are chapters on Thorndike, Pavlov, Guthrie, Hull and the neo-Hullians, the Verbal Learning Tradition, Skinner, Estes, and Recent Developments in Behavior Theory. Following those are a contrasting set of examples of Rationalist theories: these are learning theories heavily influenced by ideas of organization and cognitive structure; included are chapters on Gestalt psychology, Tolman, Information-Processing theories, and Recent Developments in Cognitive Psychology. Following these two major sections are chapters surveying two related, important fields, the neurophysiology of learning, and applications of learning principles to education and instruction. Each chapter has been substantially revised and updated to show the contemporary relevance of the historical positions by citing current research that builds on the previous ideas.

Adoption of the Empiricism vs. Rationalism framework required recasting the form and focus of several chapters from the earlier edition. Thus, the chapter on Functionalism, which was always an inchoative maverick on the scene, has been rewritten as Human Associative Learning (Chapter 6) to emphasize its views on learning. It is grouped in the first set of chapters because the verbal learning tradition (the strongest modern issue from Functionalism) has always had an associationist cast. Since this book historically has been oriented around theorists rather than fields, the chapter on Mathematical Learning Theory has been rewritten so that it revolves around the theoretical writings of William Estes. More so than the efforts of others working in mathematical learning theory, Estes's stimulus sampling theory has the coherence and range that marks it as a global theory of learning in the tradition of Guthrie, Hull, and Tolman. Although each theory chapter mentions recent research of relevance to that theory, the two Recent Developments chapters survey research related to general issues addressed by a class of theories (behavioral vs. cognitive). Thus, Chapter 9 surveys recent developments in behavioral theories, including work on biofeedback control of involuntary responses, theories of Pavlovian conditioning, equilibrium theories of reinforcement, and applications of behavioral techniques to medical and psychiatric problems. Chapter 13 surveys recent work in cognitive psychology such as theories of short-term memory, depth of processing, imagery, episodic memory, semantic memory, story memory, and social learning. Chapter 15 on education has been thoroughly rewritten to emphasize the instructional techniques in education that have been suggested or supported by learning theory. We hope that with these changes, the text will provide a firm foundation for the student to understand and perhaps contribute to modern theories of learning or its applications.

Regrettably, the chapters on Piaget and Freud in the previous edition have been deleted from this edition, because a survey of teachers using the text indicated that those chapters were not being used in the typical course in learning theory.

This text can serve many instructional purposes and provide reading materials for a variety of standard college courses. It is tailored for a course (of one or two academic terms) on Learning Theory. Portions of the text will fit well into a course on History of Psychology (notably, chapters 1–7, 10–12). Instructors teaching learning classes who wish to emphasize phenomena or principles of conditioning and animal learning will find that a course can be built around Chapters 2–9, 11, and 14. If instructors wish to build their course around human memory and cognitive information processing, then the relevant material is in chapters 1, 6, 8, 10, 12, 13, and 15. Thus, the book should be viewed as a resource to be used in flexible ways. (We might note that for many years this text is more often cited and used than almost any other, as necessary for preparing for Ph.D. qualifying or certification exams in psychology.

Revising a comprehensive text is an extensive job, and we are pleased to acknowledge the help of several people. First, we were aided by Joyce Lockwood, who cheerfully endured the retyping of the several drafts of the manuscript. The manuscript was substantially improved by the high-quality copy editing of Larry Barsalou (a Stanford graduate student in psychology) and Robert Mony. The final shepherding of the manuscript into print was overseen by our production editor, Joyce Turner, and our editor at Prentice-Hall, John Isley. To all of them, we extend our sincere thanks.

G. H. B.
E. R. H.

I
THE NATURE
OF
LEARNING THEORY

It is no secret that psychology developed out of philosophy. The really fascinating and absorbing questions of psychology were not "discovered" by modern psychologists, but rather have been matters of deep concern to philosophers for many centuries. Philosophical psychology began as an attempt to deal with the nature of man; later, psychology split off to become the "science of mental life." The questions were: What is mind, consciousness, awareness? What is the relation of the mind to the body? How does the mind develop from birth? How does it acquire knowledge of the world? How does it come to know other minds? To know itself? What drives us to action? What is the self? What produces continuity of personal identity? These and many other questions have provided the intellectual underpinning of modern psychology.

MEMORY AND KNOWLEDGE

This is a book about *learning* and *memory,* which is a branch of modern psychology. The study of learning and memory came from two philosophical sources: the analy-

sis of knowledge (how we come to know things), and the analysis of the nature and organization of mental life. The first issue concerns what philosophers call *epistemology,* the theory of knowledge. The second issue concerns the nature and contents of our concepts, thought, images, discernments, reminiscences, and imaginations; the further question here concerns what operations, rules, or laws underlie these mental phenomena. The study of learning may be aptly called experimental epistemology, since learning and knowing seem related in the same way as a process is to its result, as acquiring is to a possession, as painting is to a picture. The close relation between the meanings of *learn* and *know* is obvious and can be found in any dictionary—say, the *American Heritage Dictionary:*

> *to learn* (verb): (1) to gain knowledge, comprehension, or mastery through experience or study. (2) To fix in the mind or memory; memorize. (3) To acquire through experience. (4) To become informed of, to find out.

> *to know* (verb): (1) To perceive directly with the senses or mind; apprehend with clarity or certainty. (2) To be certain of; accept as true

beyond doubt. (3) To be capable of, have the skill to do. Used with *know how* to do something. (4) To have a practical understanding through experience with something. (5) To experience, to be subjected to. (6) To have firmly secured in the mind or memory. (7) To be able to distinguish, recognize, discern. (8) To be acquainted or familiar with.

To *learn* means "to gain knowledge through experience"; but one of the meanings of "experience" is "to perceive directly with the senses," a meaning that appears initially in the definition of *know*. But *knowledge* is defined, among other things, as *learning* (erudition) and as familiarity or understanding gained through experience, and learning is defined as acquired knowledge. So we come full circle.

Consider the two further terms *memory* and *remembering*. *Memory* is the faculty of retaining and recalling past experiences, or the ability to remember, and *remembering* is defined as recalling an experience to mind or thinking of it again. These clearly form an interconnected cluster of concepts. More than that, in our everyday dealings, memory (or remembering) is one of the primary ways by which we know things and by which we support knowledge-claims. The status accorded in the law courts to testimony from firsthand witnesses attests to the evidential power-to-persuade of direct memories: "How do I know that John stole the money? Because I *remember* seeing him with his hand in the till." The existence of such memories constitutes a prima facie case for the knowledge-claim—unless other considerations enter to cause doubts. In fact, one of the earliest uses of the psychological study of memory was to undermine its validity for supporting knowledge-claims. These studies showed that many memories of remote events reported in testimony were inaccurate, distorted, and subjectively biased. These mistakes were especially likely in memories of emotionally laden crimes, fights, or disasters.

ALTERNATIVE EPISTEMOLOGIES

One of the most engaging issues within the theory of knowledge is the question of how concepts and knowledge arise, and what is the relation between experience and the organization of the mind. Two opposing positions on this matter are *empiricism* and *rationalism*. These have been constant combatants within the intellectual arena for centuries, and strong forms of them are still recognizable today in "scientific" psychology.

Empiricism

Empiricism is the view that *experience* is the only source of knowledge. Special emphasis is given to sensory experience, although some knowledge is derived from intellectual reflections regarding relations among experiences. Our ideas are derived from sense impressions, either as direct copies of sensory impressions (so-called simple ideas) or combinations of several simple or complex ideas. The sensory impression of an object (say, an orange) is decomposable into sensory qualities—sensations corresponding to its color, smell, size, texture, taste, and so on. These sensory qualities become connected (or "associated") in the mind because they occur closely together in time or in space as we interact with the object. The idea of an orange is complex, but reducible to inter-associations among simpler, more primitive ideas. Further "knowledge" acquired about oranges can be expressed by associating this complex of ideas to the other relevant ideas—for example, that oranges are fruits and are edible.

Empiricism has the following features: (1) *sensationalism,* the hypothesis that all knowledge is derived through sensory experience; (2) *reductionism,* the thesis that all complex ideas are built up out of a basic stock of simple ideas, and that complex ideas are in turn reducible to these simple ideas; (3) *associationism,* the thesis that ideas or mental elements are connected through the operation of association of experiences that occur closely together in time (contiguity), and (4) *mechanism,* the thesis that the mind is like a machine built from simple elements with no mysterious components.

Empiricism involves two basic learning mechanisms: (1) internal representations of simple ideas ("memory images") which originate by simply *copying* their corresponding sense impressions into the memory store; and (2) complex ideas are formed by connecting together in memory simple ideas that are experienced contiguously; they are connected by an associative bond. The memory that event A was followed immediately by event B is recorded in memory as an association from idea *a* to idea *b*. This is in effect copying into memory the fact of the co-occurrence of mental contents *a* and *b*. Such associations can record temporal or causal sequences of events, such as striking a match—lighting the match—heat—fire. Activating or reviving these associative sequences from memory is the presumed method by which the mind moves in thought from one idea to another. This method accounts for the order of succession in a chain of ideas during idle thinking or goal-directed thinking. To illustrate goal-directed thinking, suppose that the final event in a chain becomes a goal ("I want to eat ice cream"). Then thinking of that goal will call to mind an immediate precursor of it from the past ("Buy some at the shop"), and that thought in turn will bring to mind what must first occur in order to cause it ("Get money and go to the shop"), and so on. Thus, a goal-directed chain of ideas may unwind backward from effect to cause until it arrives at some action that can be performed now to initiate the thought-out sequence. Associative chains that reflect causal sequences can be used in

two basic ways: they may run forwards from *a* to *b* to *c* to *predict,* anticipate, or expect future events from the present event or action; and they may run backwards from *c* to *b* to *a* to *explain* why event *c* happened or to *plan* how to bring *c* about. Predicting, explaining, and planning are fundamental skills by which we deal with the world, and the associative theory suggests ways to do these things.

Empiricists included in their theory of mind the notion of "reflection," whereby the mind supposedly can call up from memory several ideas, compare them, and arrive at some conclusion which would be recorded as another association. The idea of reflection was needed to explain how we gain knowledge by abstraction, inference, and deduction. By "abstracting" the common, critical properties out from the varying, accidental, nonessential properties, we form a general concept of a type of thing from experience together with a set of its widely varying examples. In deduction, we bring into conscious reflection a logical consequence of other things we know. Thus, if we know that Bill is taller than·John, and John is taller than Pete, then upon reflection the mind can deduce (and store in memory) that Bill is taller than Pete. According to the empiricist doctrine, reflection is the only mechanism the mind has available to free itself from being a totally passive recorder of sequences of sensory impressions.

Empiricism and associationism as explanations of mental phenomena were greatly elaborated by such philosophers as Thomas Hobbes, John Locke, David Hume, James Mill, and John Stuart Mill. One development of particular interest concerned the laws of association-formation. Assuming contiguity of experienced events to be the necessary and sufficient condition for association-formation, the empiricists proposed that the *degree* of association (or amount of memory) would vary directly with the *vivid-*

ness of the experience, its *frequency,* its *duration,* and its *recency* (closeness in time) to the retention test. Such conjectures have generated much experimental research on learning and memory, and every learning theory deals with these factors in one way or another.

Associationism led to the experimental investigation of learning. The first experiments on human memory, by the German scientist Hermann Ebbinghaus (1885),[1] explicitly set out to test certain proposals of associationist doctrine; the first experimental monograph on animal learning, by Edward Thorndike (1898), was titled *Animal intelligence: An experimental study of the associative processes in animals.*

Developments within the American schools of psychology over the last seventy years have hardly altered the associationistic approach. Theories have become more precise, and much more detailed information has been accumulated. Also, the important roles of motivation, reward, and punishment in learning and performance have received greater systematic treatment than was accorded them in the classical associationist tradition. The behavioristic revolution, led by John Watson, substituted observable stimuli and responses for the mentalistic ideas and images of earlier times. But the associationistic cast of the "acquisition mechanism" (or learning device) remained. It is thus fair to say that empiricism and associationism formed the mold into which contemporary learning theory has flowed and jelled—perhaps even solidified. Unfortunately, there appear to be several flaws in the assumptions of classical associationism, considered either as an epistemology or as a means for reconstructing the contents of mental life. These flaws become apparent when we examine the opposing epistemological position, *rationalism.*

[1] References are cited in parenthesis by year. The reference list is at the back of the book.

Rationalism

Rationalism is the general philosophical position that reason is the prime source of knowledge, that reason rather than sense data, authority, revelation, or intuition is the only valid basis for knowledge, belief, and action. In their writings, rationalist philosophers such as Descartes, Leibniz, and Kant confront empiricism at almost every turn. Rationalists have an entirely different perspective on the role of "sense data" in our construction of reality. For the empiricist, our ideas are passive copies of sense data; for the rationalist, sense data are unstructured, undifferentiated chaos and only provide raw material to an interpretive mechanism that considers these raw data as clues regarding their probable source and meaning. The raw data can be interpreted only according to certain forms—more precisely, according to certain classes of innate perceptual assumptions with which the mind begins.

What are these forms, these interpretive assumptions? Different rationalist philosophers have considered different notions as "self-evident" truths. One example of an interpretive assumption is that events always appear to us embedded in a temporal-spatial framework: physical events (and even most things we call mental events) occur at a particular time and at a particular place—or, at least, we cannot prevent ourselves from interpreting them in that way. Kant and Descartes thought that our knowledge of space was simply the projection onto the world of the "self-evident truths" of Euclidean geometry with which we were born. Kant rejected Bishop Berkeley's earlier empiricistic attempt to *derive* the perception of depth (of objects in three dimensions) and of the perceptual constancies from empirical correlations between sensations on the two-dimensional retina and the sense of touch—for example, reaching the hand to the object in view. This issue still absorbs the interest of psychologists who study perceptual development (see T. G. R. Bower, 1965; E. J. Gibson, 1969), and recent evidence appears to favor the "innate" hypothesis of depth perception. That is, newborn infants appear to see objects in depth, and they perceive an object to be the same whether it is near or far from them, which changes its image on the retina.

Perceptual Organization

A general criticism rationalists have leveled against classical empiricism is that the empiricist theory of perception provides an inadequate account of the unitariness of percepts and the role relations play in creating perceptual unities. The rationalists claim that relations among elementary sense points are just as primary and psychologically vivid as the sense points themselves; we do not hear a series of tones but a coherent melody; we do not see a particular brightness but the ratio of reflectances between a spot and its surround; we do not see successive stills of an object's changing locations but its "continuous motion" through visual space. The color of an object "adheres" or sticks to its surface as an inalienable property of a unity: we do not sense "redness" and "apple," but rather the unity of "a red apple." Gestalt psychology, reviewed in Chapter 10, began as a revolt against the elementaristic and reductionist analyses of perceptual experience provided by classical empiricism. The Gestalters supposed that perceptual experience revealed "emergent" properties (e.g., apparent motion) not derivable from additive combinations of the properties of its elements (e.g., sequences of stills). Perceptions were said to become *organized* according to certain laws of segmentation, relational grouping, and simplicity; perceptual processes were said to seek out "good forms" and to impose such organizations and interpretations upon chaotic or amorphous "matter," to use Kant's term.

One example of an innate presupposition of the mind, according to Kant, is the notion of *causality* of events in time and space. The empiricist, David Hume, had earlier raised skeptical doubts about the concept of causality, arguing that "Event A causes B" was reducible primarily to "A is invariably followed by B." Kant argued instead that causality was just as basic or perceptually primitive an experience as temporal succession. Rationalists felt that the mind was preset to "project" causality into our interpretations of successive events in the world.

Modern experiments by Michotte (1954) and others suggest that people are strongly biased to ascribe causality to perceptual events related in tightly specified ways. For example, if people watch a movie depicting a red ball moving left to right and touching a resting black ball, which then moves left to right off the edge of the screen, they do not see the two objects as moving independently. Rather they have a powerful experience of causality, of the red ball "colliding with and launching" the black ball. The perception depends critically upon the timing of the beginning motions of the red and black balls and the correspondence of their two paths of motion. Depending on these factors, perceivers see the red ball variously as launching the black one, or picking it up and carrying it, or chasing it, or moving independently of it. Such experiments suggest that perceptual judgments of causality are just as immediate and finely tuned as are judgments of brightness or color. These issues will be clarified in our later discussion of Gestalt theory, but the important point now is that Gestalt psychology began as a brand of philosophical rationalism.

Mental Organization

As we shall see, rationalism has been somewhat successful in its attack upon the doctrine of associationism (Anderson &

Bower, 1973; DeGroot, 1965; Duncker, 1945; Mandler & Mandler, 1964). For one thing, it is clear that "associations" between ideas carry with them information regarding the *type of relation* involved. For example, in our mind a restaurant is associated with eating, a glutton with eating, a fork with eating, and a steak with eating. But the unadorned "associative link" of the classical doctrine does not explain our knowing that the relation between the first pair of ideas is that of *location* to action, the second pair of *actor* to action, the third pair of *instrument* to action, and the fourth pair of *object* to act. The mind requires a representation of knowledge wherein interassociated ideas are *labeled* according to their type of relation: for example, that *animal* is labeled as a superordinate of *bird,* that *canary* is a subordinate of *bird,* that *wings* or *feathers* are properties of *birds,* and that *sings* or *flies* are possible actions of birds. Such labeling seems necessary in order to conduct efficient searches through memory for information that meets certain requirements. For instance, it is not clear how the associationists' mental apparatus would answer any question of the form "What has relation R to concept X?" (e.g., "What is an instance of a bird?"). If associations are tagged with relational labels, then restricted searches and retrievals are possible. The way in which we use associations can be determined by instructions stating general goals ("Give me the opposite association of each word—up-*down*, left-*right*, tall-*short* . . ."); after a short while, these "determining tendencies" become unconscious, and automatically direct the associative process as it operates on the stimulus words (taking *heavy* into *light* and so on). Classical associationist doctrine has no way to represent the influence of these selective determining tendencies.

The associative theory of mind has been further criticized because it fails to explain how the mind imposes a structure onto incoming (sensory) perceptual data. That is,

the theory provides no restrictions or constraints on what could be associated with what; there were no inherent principles for determining the "belongingness" of items of experience (see Thorndike's treatment of "belongingness" in Chapter 2), no restrictions regarding "well-formedness" of input structures. The rationalists argued that "raw experience" together with associative learning principles are not sufficient to prevent the accumulation of a disorganized mass of accidental vagaries that collapse in a booming, buzzing chaos of overwhelming particulars. Rather, certain "constraints" must be imposed (as innate forms or principles) in interpreting events; only hypotheses of particular forms are acceptable by the human mind.

Language Acquisition: A Rationalist's Example

Nowhere is this hypothesis of innate constraints advanced more vigorously than in certain modern accounts of how children acquire their first language. Linguists such as Chomsky (1972), Lenneberg (1967), and McNeill (1970) argue that empiricist assumptions are inadequate in principle to account for the learning of the linguistic competence shown by every native speaker. The language learner must learn a fantastically complex and abstract set of rules for transforming strings of speech sounds into meanings, and vice versa. Modern analyses of linguistic competence illustrate just how abstract are the grammatical rules that children exemplify in their dealings with language—in judging whether utterances are grammatical, whether they are unambiguous, and whether two sentences mean the same thing. The problem for the empiricist is that this abstract and complex language competence seems to be learned more or less uniformly by all children at about the same early age with relatively little variation (ignoring dialects). The problem is compounded by the fact that recordings of adult utterances to preverbal children reveal many halts, slips, grammatical mistakes, fragmentary utterances, hems-and-haws, changing of sentences in mid-utterance, and utter nonsense. In short, from a grammatical point of view, the speech input to preverbal children is noisy slop. Moreover, the parent-as-trainer tends to react to a child's utterance according to its intention, use, or truth or falsity rather than its approximation to good grammar. A typical scenario is: "Daddy went store?" "No, he went to the office"; "Daddy office?" "Yes, that's right: Daddy office." Such episodes hardly seem optimal for the child to learn the rules of grammar.

The paradox is how our linguistic competence, which seems to be governed by this abstract set of grammatical rules, could ever be learned from such chaotic linguistic inputs. In rejecting empiricist accounts, Chomsky (1972) argues that the child must begin life innately endowed with a small set of *linguistic universals* as regards both some basic concepts and some basic principles. Examples of basic concepts would be the twenty-odd distinctive features of speech sounds (see Jakobson et al., 1963) out of which all known languages compose their vocabularies; or the grammatical concepts of subject and predicate. Examples of principles would be those that distinguish the deep logical structure of an utterance from its surface phonological, or sound, form (see Chomsky, 1972, for discussions of these terms). Similar components—concepts and rules—are found in all natural languages studied so far: they appear *universal* to human language. The theory is that these abstract principles of universal grammar are part of the child's innate endowment, that they provide an interpretive schema to which any particular language must conform. Chomsky states this argument as follows:

> . . . it seems that knowledge of a language—a grammar—can be acquired only by an organism that is "preset" with a severe restriction on the form of grammar. This innate restriction is a precondition, in the Kantian sense, for linguistic experience, and it appears to be the critical factor in determining the course and result of language learning. The child cannot know at birth which language he is to learn, but he must know that its grammar must be of a predetermined form that excludes many imaginable languages. Having selected a permissible hypothesis, he can use inductive evidence for corrective action, confirming or disconfirming his choice. Once the hypothesis is sufficiently well confirmed, the child knows the language defined by this hypothesis; consequently, his knowledge extends enormously beyond his experience and, in fact, leads him to characterize much of the data of experience as defective and deviant (1972, p. 91).

Chomsky proposes that the guiding metaphor for language acquisition should be not learning but *maturation,* rather like embryonic development of sense organs and limbs under the guidance of the genetic DNA codes within the embryo. The child's "speech apparatus" develops with appropriate triggering events and exposure to a language community, just as any biological organ requires an appropriate milieu for its development.

Chomsky makes no pretense of having discovered a full set of linguistic universals (Greenberg, 1962) or of having provided the details of how specific linguistic hypotheses are formulated (in what language?) and tested. He does argue, however, that such a framework has much more chance of advancing our understanding of language acquisition than the empiricist-associationist account, which has impressed him and other linguists as simply false.

Final Comments on Rationalism

Here, then, we have specific examples of rationalism and their persuasive force. As Kant (1781, p. 1) wrote: "Although all our knowledge begins *with* experience, it by no means follows that it all originates *from* experience." For real knowledge it is necessary to presuppose a certain framework of thought relationships over and above the raw sense data. You may ask, How did the mind come to acquire these innate structures that one is led to attribute to it? One can answer, "natural selection"—on the premise that the mind is the way it is because it helps the individual adapt to the way the world truly is (less fortunate innate endowments having been eliminated during biological evolution); or one can answer at a deeper level that the exact processes by which the innate organization of the human organism evolved are still a total mystery.

Rationalism, Empiricism, and Modern Learning Theory

The foregoing discussion of empiricism and rationalism provides some background for comparing modern learning theories. All behavioristic theories of learning are also associationistic: they include those of Thorndike, Pavlov, Guthrie, Hull, Skinner, and the school of functionalism. These schools developed out of the combination of associationism with hedonism.[2] Gestalt psychology and the newer information-processing approaches to psychology are clearly at the rationalist end of the spectrum. Tolman's brand of cognitive psychology straddles the fence on several important matters. Mathematical psychology, at least stimulus-sampling theory, is associationistic, although nothing inherent in the use of quantitative theories requires that orientation.

Let us now return to the central topic of this chapter—namely, learning—and note some of the important distinctions that

[2] In the seventeenth and eighteenth centuries, a great deal of thought was given to human interests, values, and motivations as reasons for action. This was connected with developments in utility theory (see Bernoulli, 1738; Bentham, 1789), which extended the doctrine of *hedonism*. Hedonism asserts that each individual is motivated by the desire for pleasures and by aversion from pain and deprivation. Modern learning theories like Hull's (Chapter 5) can be regarded as the offspring of the intellectual traditions of associationism and hedonism.

have grown up around this concept. Concept formation in science progresses by drawing distinctions and classifying cases, and so it is with the concept of learning.

CHARACTERIZATION OF LEARNING

Learning, as we noted before, is often concerned with the acquisition of knowledge. *Acquisition* refers to a *change* in "possession." At one time, the organism did not "possess" a given bit of knowledge; at a later time, it did. What caused that acquisition? At a minimum, something had to happen to the organism to change its state of knowledge. Typically we suppose that the organism had some specific experience that caused or was in some way related to the change in its knowledge state; either the world put some sensory information into it, or it may have tried out some action and observed the consequences, or it may have thought out a proof of a geometry theorem, or any number of other events.

What is the nature of the knowledge that the organism learns? This can be quite varied—as different as there are different ways of knowing and different contents to be known. The simplest knowledge in anyone's memory is merely a biographical "event record": an event of a particular description happened to me at such-and-such a time in such-and-such a place. This is frequently phrased as storage of a "copy" of sensory experiences, a metaphor so old that even Plato used it. One problem (among several) with the copy, or "image," theory of memory is that in remembering a scene, one usually sees oneself as an actor in the scene—which, of course, could not have been the sense impression one experienced on that occasion. Perhaps it is better to say merely that the organism can be conceived of as "storing a description" of the event that occurred. Typical events might be: "My dog Spot bit the postman,"

"Henry kissed Anne," or "The word *pencil* was presented to me by the experimenter." In the make-believe world of talking animals, Pavlov's dog might say to itself, "The bell was followed by food"; and the giant axon of a squid on a dissecting table might say, "Irritation of my nerve ending is followed by a hell of a shock." Suppose that such event descriptions or event sequences are stored in memory: although they are not profound items of wisdom, they are nonetheless bits of an organism's knowledge about its world.

So the experience causes a change in the organism's knowledge. Does it always change? Well, no; not always: we know the organism might have failed to learn for any number of reasons—perhaps it was not paying attention when the event occurred. So perhaps we had better relax the conditions to say that the experience *may* cause (probably causes) a change in the state of knowledge.

But Doubting Thomas asks, "How do you know that your subject has changed his or her state of knowledge?" Good question: how can you tell what somebody knows? Well, you could ask him or her, "Ahh, please, would you mind telling us what you know?" If the subject is a college professor, you will get no end of blather (sometime next week you'll have forgotten what the question was); if it's the giant axon of a squid, a deadly silence answers back. The question was poorly framed: you want rather to know whether the subject's knowledge about a *specific* event has changed as a result of a specific experience. So you try to frame specific questions—or specific "retrieval cues," as we say. You ask, "What did Spot do?" "Who kissed Anne?" "What word was presented to you by the experimenter a few moments ago?" "What event follows the bell?" "What follows axonal irritation?"

After asking the question, you wait for the subject to answer. What form does the answer take? He or she responds: she says

something, he nods his head, she licks her chops, or it generates a synaptic potential. Question, answer; stimulus, response. From the response, we *infer* whether or not the subject has available the specific information of interest—or, at least, we find out whether our question gains access to that stored information. The word *infer* is used advisedly; whether or not somebody possesses a bit of information is not uniformly guaranteed either by our having presented the information to him or by his saying that he knows it (he could be lying or mistaken or have misunderstood the question). So we infer someone's knowledge from inputs to him and outputs from him, and we *infer* learning caused by an experience because of before-to-after changes in his inferred knowledge.

We may summarize our discussion by the sequence of events charted in Table 1.1.[3] This isolates the important happenings within a single learning episode (called a *trial),* going from a possible pretest through presentation of the information to be remembered, and trace formation (or acquisition), through retention, to retrieval and utilization of the stored information. We speak of the *memory trace* as being whatever is the internal representation of the specific information stored at time 2 in Table 1.1. The experiencing and new knowledge state at Times 2 and 3 are usually classified as *perception,* whereas memory, or *retention,* of the perceived information is tested after the retention interval spanning Time 3 to Time *n.* In different experiments, this interval can vary from several seconds to several years; when this interval is varied, we are studying *forgetting.* What is forgetting? That's simply your failing to remember something on a current test when we had reason to believe

---

[3] Tables and figures have double numbers, the first referring to the chapter number and the second to the figure or table within the chapter.

TABLE 1.1. Flow chart of the important events within a learning episode ("trial") and inferred states of the subject's knowledge. The terms at the right are the labels psychologists use to refer to the theoretical processes going on at particular times during this sequence. S and E refer to the subject and the environment (or experimenter), respectively.

Time	Inferred States and Events	Psychologist's Labels
0	S's prior state of knowledge	} Pretest
1	E presents Event X to S	
2	S experiences Event X	Trace formation (Acquisition)
3	S's new state of knowledge	
.		
.		Trace retention
.		
n	S's "altered" state of knowledge	
$n+1$	E cues S to test S's knowledge	} Trace retrieval
$n+2$	S answers or responds	} Trace utilization

that you knew the information earlier. Different other events can be presented to the subject (are said to be *interpolated*) during the retention interval from time 3 to time n; if we vary these and notice how retention of the original target item is affected, we are said to be studying *interference* effects on retention.

At time $n + 1$ we test the subject's retention by presenting one or more *retrieval cues,* which act as questions whose purpose is to assess what the subject knows about the target event. *Trace retrieval* is the process by which the test cue gains access to the information the subject has stored about a given target item. The test cue can come in a variety of forms; it can even be systematically altered from the "natural" cue for the target information. At the simplest level we may ask a human subject

to describe or name the to-be-remembered event, or to recognize its recurrence. At a more complex level, say with propositional material, we may ask for meaningful paraphrases of the learned proposition, for use of it in an argument, or any of a number of other "behaviors" we take as illustrating comprehension of a statement.

We may present the same information repeatedly to the subject, and he or she may practice remembering it many times over. Successive repetitions of the same event are typically separated by several minutes and/or by presentations of other information to be learned. Learning refers to the overall change in the subject's knowledge from Time 0 on the first trial until Time n on the last trial of the experiment. Elementary conditioning experiments with animals may use several hundred trials, on each of which two events occur in temporal contiguity (for example, the sounding of a bell to Pavlov's dog, then its eating of food placed in its mouth). In such animal experiments, of course, the experimenter measures some response (like the amount of saliva) made to the retrieval cue (the bell). This response is considered to index the animal's knowledge of the temporal order of events (that the bell is followed by food). Behaviorists would not describe matters this way: they would say that it is the response itself which is learned to the bell and not some knowledge about the temporal order of events. But that is a matter to be discussed later.

The text surrounding Table 1.1 provides a preliminary characterization of learning events and their terminology. But the characterization is actually incomplete because there are other learning activities which seem not fully captured by the description in Table 1.1. The main class of these has to do with the learning of *skills*, perceptual-motor skills as well as intellectual skills. Examples of skills are typewriting, swimming, bicycling, piano playing, brushing your teeth properly, multiplying two-digit numbers quickly, and so on. Most skilled activities are a vast set of interrelated component responses. (In typing, for example, the sight of "M" on the copy to be typed gets translated into striking a particular key.) We may suppose that practice provides feedback information for all of these components. In the case of skills, we describe the person's (or animal's) knowledge in terms of her *knowing how* to do something rather than her being able to describe events to us. The remembering is exemplified in the performance. Even our common vocabulary for describing skill learning differs from that used for the "fact learning" of Table 1.1: there is no "target information" to be remembered, but rather a sequence of coordinated movements, usually done to some stimulus, and executed either well or poorly.

A Possible Definition of Learning

To return, then, to our beginning problem of characterizing learning, experimenters who deal with animals or nonverbal humans need some kind of working definition of learning that does not require verbal instructions, verbal questions, and verbal answers. They obviously have to observe some kind of overt behavior of the subject, presumably one that indexes the specific learning. Framing such a definition is difficult, but a serviceable one is the following:

Learning refers to the change in a subject's behavior or behavior potential to a given situation brought about by the subject's repeated experiences in that situation, provided that the behavior change cannot be explained on the basis of the subject's native response tendencies, maturation, or temporary states (such as fatigue, drunkenness, drives, and so on).

The definition allows an inference regarding "learning" only when a case cannot be made for another explanation. It does not state sufficient conditions for learning, since some cases of repeated experience with a situation do not produce observable changes in responses. Let us consider some of the behavioral changes that are excluded by this provisional definition.

Native Response Tendencies vs. Learning

Early writers within comparative psychology attempted to catalog and classify native or innate ("unlearned") activities into the reflexes (such as pupillary constriction to light), taxes (such as a moth's dashing into a flame), and instincts (such as a bird's nest-building). Such activities are characteristic of various species, and those more nearly idiosyncratic to one species are called *species-specific* activities.

Such species-specific behavior is said to be innate, meaning that its form is set down in the nervous system of all members of that species independent in some ways from experience. But it turns out to be very difficult to classify behaviors as *altogether* innate or altogether learned. One finds that the expression of many instinctive behaviors depends upon experience or learning (Hinde, 1966). For example, the development and expression of sexual behavior or of maternal behavior in monkeys depends critically upon the young monkey's having "normal" contacts with its mother and "normal" opportunities for play with age mates (Harlow & Harlow, 1966; Sackett, 1967). The development of the characteristic song of many species of birds depends upon the young bird's hearing that song during its early life (Marler, 1970; Nottebohm, 1970). For instance, the development of the song of the chaffinch or of the white-crown sparrow appears to be as follows: during its first springtime of life, the young male must be exposed to the singing of males of its species, although the young bird does not itself sing during this time. During the mating season the following year, the young bird (even if now in isolation) begins to sing; his initial songs are of poor quality and phrasing, but are nonetheless recognizable as the song dialects of the males of his species. A remarkable sidelight is this: by sheer practice alone, plus listening to himself, the young bird comes eventually to sing a very good reproduction of the older birds' song. The puzzle is how can this bird, in total isolation, improve the match between his singing and the model he heard a year ago? Apparently we must suppose that something like a memory record is made of a genetically selected song, and that the stored record can serve the following year as a template and an "interior tutor" for correcting the initial poor-quality productions of the young bird. But what an utterly astounding accomplishment for a mere bird-brain!

Another illustration of the in-between nature of species-specific behavior is *imprinting* (Hess, 1958; Lorenz, 1952). A young duckling, for example, is prepared instinctively to accept a certain range of mother figures, characterized by size, movement, and vocalization. Once such a mother figure has been accepted and followed about, only this *particular* mother will elicit following. The selected mother (who may be Professor Lorenz crawling on hands and knees) has become imprinted. Imprinting is a form of learning, but one closely allied to the preparedness of a particular kind of organism of a particular age. Except in fowls, there is little evidence of imprinting in the human or animal world.

Students of ethology, the study of natural behaviors of species in their natural habitats, have discarded the "innate versus learned" distinction as a too rigidly "either-or" affair. Behavior and its development are too complex to be simply assigned to such exclusive categories. Ethologists strive instead to analyze and understand the various components of a given species-specific pattern and how it develops out of experiential interactions. The innate constitution of the animal, like Kantian a priori forms, causes it to develop in certain ways, given the usual stimulation of its ecological niche. However, this normal development can be overridden by extreme variations in environmental conditions.

Maturation vs. Learning

Maturation is learning's chief competitor as a modifier of behavior. If a behavior pattern matures through regular stages, irrespective of intervening practice, the behavior is said to develop through maturation and not through learning. If training procedures do not speed up or modify the development of the behavior, such procedures are not causally important and the changes are not classified as learning. Relatively pure cases such as the swimming of tadpoles and the flying of birds can be attributed primarily to maturation. However, as indicated before, many activities are not as clear-cut, but develop through a complex interplay of maturation and learning. A convenient illustration is the development of language in children. Children do not learn to talk until old enough, but that development depends critically upon appropriate stimulation from their verbal community at the critical times. The "wolf children" found in the wilds or babies brutally locked in attics for years have no language and develop rudimentary and primitive forms only very slowly by patient tutoring (Itard, 1932; Lenneberg, 1967).

Fatigue and Habituation vs. Learning

It has been common practice to distinguish motor fatigue or sensory habituation from learning proper. When a motor act is repeated in rapid succession, there is often a loss in efficiency—it becomes slower and weaker in amplitude until eventually the subject may refuse to perform it. We say the response has suffered "fatigue" or that its performance shows "work decrement." The fatigue occurs faster, the greater the effort of the response, and recovery from fatigue occurs over a "rest time." In terms of performance curves, fatigue and recovery curves look very much like curves of experimental extinction and spontaneous recovery; however, common practice has been to apply the "learning" label to the latter but not to the former case. Why? Because fatigue, unlike extinction of a conditioned reflex, is presumed not to induce enduring and relatively *permanent* changes in the behavior. But a moment's reflection will show this defense is useless, since extinction effects can also be reversed —an extinguished response can be trained, and with little effort. So what is the crucial difference? There really is none as long as we remain solely at the behavioral level of measuring the elicited response. Other information has to be brought into the decision—namely, all those behavioral consequences that would be implied by the descriptions (for the human) that in the one case he stopped responding "because he was tired" versus, in the other case, he stopped "because he learned that food no longer followed the bell" (or whatever). From the response decrement alone we can not make this decision regarding hypothetical causes.

Consider a second kind of change, that called *habituation*. Simply presenting a stimulus produces a perceptual reaction (what Pavlov called the *orienting reflex*, or OR). This reaction can be recorded electrically throughout the nervous system. If the stimulus is repeated over and over in a monotonous series, the OR aroused by each presentation becomes weaker and weaker, eventually declining to an almost undetectable level.[4] Subjects are said to have *habituated* to that stimulus; they have "gotten used to it." Habituation displays many of the same functional properties we ascribe to learning (or to extinction): it dissipates with time (like "forgetting" or "spontaneous recovery"); it is easily disrupted or dishabituated by interpolation of a novel, interfering event; a recovered OR to a stimulus can be habituated again and again, and each time it habituates a little faster than before (like relearnings of a forgotten response); and habituation generalizes to other similar stimuli as a function of their similarity to the habituated stimulus. (Chapters 9 and 14 discuss habituation in more detail.) Thus, habituation displays many similarities to the laws of learning.

Do we want to call habituation learning? We equivocate: in some cases, Yes; in others, No. It depends on the complexity of

---

[4] Habituation is distinguished from sense-organ *adaptation,* such as that occurring within the retinal cells during light adaptation; or the differential bleaching of color pigments in the retina causing us to see different colors in succession as we stare continuously at a high-intensity yellow light (Cornsweet, 1970). In these cases, the reduced or altered responsiveness can be traced directly to changes at the receptor surface.

the stimulus to which habituation occurs. If it is an electric shock to a sensorimotor synapse in the spinal cord of a decerebrate (brainless) cat, we would rather label it sensory adaptation. However, if it is a more complex stimulus (a tone pattern or a picture) that requires higher brain centers for its discrimination, we would prefer to label it learning. In these latter cases, habituation seems to index (inversely) the development of an internal representation of the stimulus event or of its general class. Habituation of this kind seems to be a crude form of *pattern recognition,* which probably depends upon the organism's having learned or stored a replica or model of the habituated pattern. Once the model is formed, each incoming stimulus is compared to it, with dishabituation ("surprise") occurring in case the mismatch between the two is extensive enough. In fact, theories of cortical habituation (Sokolov, 1963, reviewed in Chapters 3 and 14) use just such concepts of internal models and mismatching processes. And surely, we would want to say that pattern recognition is a result of learning. So habituation is one of those cases that straddle the boundaries of our loose concept of learning.

Performance vs. Learning Factors

Learning is an inference from performance, and only confusion results if performance and learning are equated. The concepts of learning versus performance parallel the concepts of disposition versus actualization, of knowing how to do something versus actually doing it. Performance may be poor on a retention test for many reasons other than lack of earlier learning. The topic of motivation, or drive, is relevant here: motives, or drives, are a few of the psychological factors responsible for converting knowledge into action. A rat who knows how to thread her way through a maze to find food at a goal-box may nonetheless not do this if she is currently

stuffed with food. She must first be made hungry if she is to show us what she knows. Another illustration is provided by performance when a subject is ill or under the influence of drugs or intoxicants. The fact that performance of a learned act fails when the subject is drugged does not mean that he did not learn originally or that he has forgotten what he learned. When the normal state has been restored, the performance may return to normal levels without intervening training. Labeling of a drug, an illness, or food satiation as "performance reducers" instead of "unlearning" factors depends upon the *reversibility* of their action. The behavior returns when the subject "comes out from under the influence" of the drug or sickness. If, on the other hand, the original learned behavior could not be recovered after the immediate effects of the drug wear off, then we would say that that drug has had an *antimemory* effect; it either blocks the consolidation of a memory trace, or destroys the trace, or prevents its expression. In Chapter 14 we review just such literature regarding the anticonsolidation effects of certain drugs.

ISSUES THAT SEPARATE LEARNING THEORIES

While it is difficult to frame a definition of learning adequate to cover all diverse forms and exclude other causes of behavior change, the definition of learning itself is not a major source of difference between learning theories. Their differences are over issues of interpretation, not over definition. Everyone realizes that satisfactory definitions flow only from satisfactory scientific theories of the phenomena in question. Learning is one of those loose, open concepts that includes diverse subtypes. Some psychologists feel that we should stop using such a general label to gather together so many different kinds of effects of experience. However, learning is more like a chapter heading than a technical term in contemporary psychology, and the term continues to serve a useful function in non-technical contexts.

Let us turn now to some issues that have arisen in the formulation of actual theories. As indicated earlier, the major conceptual division within psychological approaches is that between empiricism and rationalism. A major thesis of empiricism is that learning occurs through contiguous association of events or ideas. This associationistic framework was accepted by almost all learning theories and theorists of the first half of this century: Pavlov, Guthrie, Thorndike, Ebbinghaus, Hull, Skinner, and Tolman. The only real opposition was to be found among Gestalt psychologists, information-processing theorists, and cognitive psychologists. Some recent work (Anderson, 1976; Anderson & Bower, 1973) attempts to synthesize these approaches.

A second division has been the basis of contention even within associationistic theories. This is the conflict between *stimulus-response* theories and *cognitive* theories. This division produced much controversy during the middle years of learning theory, from approximately 1925 through 1965. The stimulus-response theorists include the above associationists—except for Tolman, who was the first systematist of cognitive theory. We may begin by examining three kinds of preferences on which stimulus-response theorists tend to differ from cognitive theorists.

1. Peripheral vs. central intermediaries. Ever since the behaviorist John Watson suggested that thinking might be "merely" the carrying out of subvocal speech movements, stimulus-response (S-R) theorists have preferred to find response or movement intermediaries to serve as integrators of behavior sequences. Such movement-produced intermediaries can be classified as *peripheral* mechanisms (far away from the brain) or as *central* (ideational) intermediaries. The S-R theorists claim, for example, that a

hungry rat's run through a maze to a remote feeding box is held together in part by tiny, implicit, food-eating responses, such as chewing and salivation, that occur in anticipation of the goal as he runs through the maze. The S-R theorist may assume these miniature responses are occurring even when they are not observable. The cognitive theorist, on the other hand, more freely infers central (brain) processes, such as memories or expectations, as integrators of goal-seeking behavior. The differences in preference survive in this case because both kinds of theorists depend upon *inferences* from observed behavior, and the inferences cannot be directly verified in either case. It is potentially easier to verify tongue movements in thinking than it is to discover a revived memory trace in the brain, but in fact such verification is not offered with the precision necessary to compel belief in the theory. For example, no one has shown that thoughts of widely different content produce really different miniature movements of the tongue or vocal cords. Yet, we do react differently depending upon our thoughts. Under the circumstances, the choice between the peripheral and the central explanation is not forced, and favoring one or the other position depends upon other more general systematic preferences.

2. Acquisition of habits vs. acquisition of cognitive structures. The stimulus-response theorist and the cognitive theorist come up with different answers to the question: What is learned? The answer of the former is "habits"; the answer of the latter is "cognitive structures" or "factual knowledge." The first answer emphasizes the development of smooth-running sequences of responses; the second answer emphasizes factual knowledge, such as a child learning where the candy store is located. Clearly people acquire both kinds of knowledge—procedural (habitual skills) and factual knowledge. Among the controversial issues is whether both kinds of knowledge are reducible to just one kind—say, to complex habits as the S-R theorists claim. Thus, an S-R theorist would attempt to represent a bit of factual knowledge someone has (Chicago is located in Illinois) by noting that that knowledge makes available a large number of dispositions to respond to appropriate situations. Included here would be a set of habits to respond "Illinois" when a person is asked what state Chicago is in. But cognitivists argue that this identification involves a basic confusion, that our everyday concept of answering a question (by asserting a proposition) is a logical type completely different from our everyday concept of a response or reaction. Responses like a knee-jerk to a tap assert no proposition whatsoever, and the reflexive utterance of "Illinois" to a simple question does not constitute real evidence of knowledge. Such issues generate much debate. Putting aside the case for linguistically competent humans, a smaller issue is whether the knowledge that lower, non-verbal organisms have can be adequately represented in terms of stimulus-response habits. There the issue is harder to resolve. Curiously, Edward Tolman tested his cognitive expectancy theory of learning exclusively on animals, apparently believing that the case for a cognitive theory of human learning was already intuitively obvious.

3. Trial and error vs. insight in problem-solving. When confronted with a novel problem, how does the learner reach a solution? S-R theorists find learners assembling their habits from past situations appropriate to the new problem, responding either according to the elements that the new problem has in common with familiar ones, or according to aspects of the new situation that are similar to situations met before. If these do not lead to a solution, learners resort to trial and error, bringing out of their behavior repertory one response after another until the problem is solved. Cognitive theorists agree with much of this description of what learners do, but they add interpretations not offered by the S-R theorists. They point out, for example, that granting all the requisite experience with the parts of a problem, there is still no guarantee that learners will be able to bring these past experiences to bear upon the solution. They may be able to solve the problem if it is presented in one form but unable to solve it if it is presented in another form. In order for earlier learning to make an impact, the learners' current way of describing the problem must make contact with some description of a related problem they solved before, such contact producing "insight" into the current solution. The S-R theorist tends, by preference, to look to the past history of the learner for the sources of a solution, while the cognitive psychologist, by preference, looks to the contemporary structuring of the problem.

These three issues—peripheral versus central intermediaries, acquisition of habits versus acquisition of cognitive structures, and trial and error versus insight in problem-solving—give something of the flavor of the differences between these two major families of theories.

OTHER CRITICAL ISSUES

Some issues lie outside the conflict between the S-R and the cognitive theories. Thus, two S-R psychologists may differ as to the role of reinforcement in learning, and two cognitive theorists may differ regarding the interpretation of extinction. Four of these issues will suffice to alert us to some controversies within learning theory.

1. Contiguity vs. reinforcement. The oldest law of association is that ideas experienced together tend to become associated. This has come down to the present day as the principle of association by contiguity, although S-R psychologists describe the association as between stimuli and responses, not between ideas. Some theorists have accepted the principle of association by pure contiguity alone—for example, Guthrie (an S-R psychologist) and Tolman (a cognitive psychologist). Other theorists insist that learning does not take place through contiguity alone; rather, they say, there must be some sort of reinforcement, some equivalent of reward or punishment in order for associations to be formed.

2. Extinction of learned responses. After a rewarded response is well learned, it will extinguish if it occurs repeatedly without reinforcement. A variety of training conditions are known to systematically influence the persistence with which the organism continues responding during the extinction period. There are several plausible theories of extinction, and only occasionally can they be classified purely as S-R or cognitive. One plausible theory is that during extinction the animal simply learns to expect no reward, and stops responding because of that expectancy. An alternate theory suggests that nonreward is aversive (frustrating) and that it sets up active inhibitory processes which compete with performance of the formerly rewarded response. Both theories can be elaborated to handle the major findings regarding extinction.

3. Learning by jumps vs. small increments. The possibility that learning takes place at its most basic level in all-or-none fashion was early proposed by Guthrie, and it has received support from several sources. The alternative is, of course, that learning takes place gradually. Modifications in learning may take place even "below threshold," so that several trials may be necessary before the results of learning reach threshold and begin to be revealed in performance. This was Hull's position. The issue, then, is not one between S-R and cognitive psychologists; psychologists within either major camp can take opposing positions on this issue of all-or-none learning.

4. One or more kinds of learning? Theorists of varying persuasions have argued for recognition of different types of learning that follow different laws. Theorists such as Mowrer and Thorndike argued that emotional responses (of the autonomic nervous system) become associated on the basis of pure contiguity of their elicitation to a neutral stimulus, whereas instrumental responses (of the skeletal musculature) require the addition of a reward or punishment for associations to be formed. Hull, on the other hand, argued that the same reinforcement principle was at work in all learning situations.

This brief introduction suggests that what seem to be opposed points of view between S-R and cognitive theories may turn out to be based on differences in preference, each being possible of persuasive statement, and to a point justifiable.

The Plan of This Book

The chapters that follow are arranged into groups according to their affinity to stimulus-response, behavioral associationism (empiricism), or to cognitive-organizational theory (rationalism). The behavioral versus cognitive categories will serve to classify most theories of learning, although substantial bodies of research are independent of both. The work of B. F. Skinner and his followers is reviewed in the first section because Skinner is a behaviorist, and rejects cognitivism, not because he accepts S-R theory or associationism. The work on verbal learning is sometimes considered the remnant of work by the functionalists, but it is included in the first section because its unifying theory is associative learning. After reviewing in each section the major theorists and positions, the section concludes with a chapter reviewing recent developments in that class of learning theories. Following the two major sections on behavioral and cognitive theories, we end with two nontheoretical chapters, one reviewing research on the neurophysiology of learning, one reviewing applications of learning ideas in instructional (educational) psychology.

The chapters that follow present a variety of systematic positions with illustrative experiments that test their assertions. Something can be learned from each of them. Each has discovered phenomena that expand our knowledge about learning. At the same time, no one has succeeded in providing a system invulnerable to criticism. The construction of a fully satisfactory theory of learning continues as an uncompleted task. But this is in the nature of science. The only completed research field is a dead one.

SUPPLEMENTARY READINGS

General sources on the psychology of learning:

GAGNÉ, R. M. (1970). *The conditions of learning.* Rev. ed.

HULSE, S. H., DEESE, J., & EGETH, H. (1975). *The psychology of learning.* 5th ed.

KIMBLE, G. A. (1961). *Hilgard and Marquis' conditioning and learning.* 2nd ed.

KINTSCH, W. (1970). *Learning, memory, and conceptual processes.*

Contrasting points of view toward learning:

ANDERSON, J. R., & BOWER, G. H. (1973). *Human associative memory.*

ESTES, W. K., et al. (1954). *Modern learning theory.*

GOLDSTEIN, H., et al. (1965). *Controversial issues in learning.*

HILL, W. F. (1971). *Learning: A survey of psychological interpretations.* rev. ed.

KOCH, S., Ed. (1959). *Psychology: A study of a science.* Vol. 2.

The Annual Review of Psychology, appearing first in 1950, each year reviews critically the current experimental and theoretical literature on learning. The reviews are valuable not only as indexes to the literature but also for the trends in experiment and theory detected by the reviewers.

The psychology of learning and motivation: Advances in research and theory, edited by G. H. Bower, has been published annually in a series since 1967; each volume contains numerous chapters written by eminent learning theorists (of all persuasions) reviewing their own and others' research.

2

THORNDIKE'S CONNECTIONISM

For nearly half a century, one learning theory dominated all others in America, despite numerous attacks upon it and the rise of its many rivals. The preeminence of the theory of Edward L. Thorndike (1874–1949), first announced in his *Animal intelligence* (1898), was aptly assessed by Tolman:

> The psychology of animal learning—not to mention that of child learning—has been and still is primarily a matter of agreeing or disagreeing with Thorndike, or trying in minor ways to improve upon him. Gestalt psychologists, conditioned-reflex psychologists, sign-gestalt psychologists—all of us here in America seem to have taken Thorndike, overtly or covertly, as our starting point (1938, p. 11).

The basis of learning accepted by Thorndike in his earliest writings was association between sense impressions and impulses to action (responses). Such an association came to be known as a "bond" or a "connection." Because it is these bonds or connections between sense impressions and responses which become strengthened or weakened in the making and breaking of habits, Thorndike's system has sometimes been called a "bond" psychology or simply "connectionism." As such, it is the original stimulus-response, or S-R, psychology of learning.

While more recent versions of S-R psychology have reduced the prominence given to Thorndike's interpretations of learning, it must not be supposed that his views are of historical interest only, for they continue to influence much recent experimentation. Nearly a quarter of a century after Tolman made the statement just quoted, Postman, another active worker in the field of learning, had this to say:

> The picture of the learning process which Thorndike sketched more than fifty years ago is still very much on the books. No comprehensive theory of human learning can afford to ignore the heritage left to us by Thorndike (1962, p. 397).

CONNECTIONISM BEFORE 1930

Thorndike's theory changed very little between 1898 and 1930. During these years Thorndike devoted himself largely to applications of his established theory to problems of educational or social importance. Because of the stability of the concepts during these years, one can select any of Thorndike's many publications to serve as a guide to his theory. The major work, from which most of the quotations in what follows have been taken, is the three-volume *Educational psychology* (1913–1914), which represents the system at the height of its popularity.

Trial-and-Error Learning

The most characteristic form of learning of both lower animals and man was identified by Thorndike as *trial-and-error learning,* or, as he preferred to call it later, learning by selecting and connecting. In this paradigmatic situation, learners are confronted by a problem situation in which they have to reach a goal such as escape from a problem-box, attain some food, or win some money. They do this by selecting a response from a number of possible responses, performing that response, and then receiving some consequence or outcome. A trial is defined by the length of time (or number of errors) involved in a single reaching of the goal. Thorndike's earliest experiments were of this kind, done chiefly with cats, although some experiments with dogs, fish, and monkeys were included (1898, 1911).[1] When Thorndike began his early work, a very common explanation for animal "intelligence" was that the animal would "think through" or reason to a solution of a problematical situation. The literature of comparative psychology at that time was filled with anecdotes (about pet dogs and cats) which were presumed to show that animals would reason and deliberate before choosing that act which fulfilled their purposes.

Thorndike despised such theorizing about animal behavior; he viewed it as a shoddy kind of anthropomorphic projec-

tion of the layman's mentalistic concepts into the mind of the beast, giving one the smug satisfaction of having explained something when in fact only a fanciful analogy had been drawn. Like a true mechanist of his day, Thorndike sought to provide a *mechanistic* account of animal learning, one that could be stated in terms of elementary events and operations which were not more complex than the behavior they were supposed to explain. For instance, "deliberate reasoning" is not an elementary concept, but requires analysis into simpler terms. As Thorndike says (1898, p. 39), he began his work "to give the *coup de grace* to the despised theory that animals reason."

The typical experiment is one in which a hungry cat is placed in a confining box such as that shown in Figure 2.1, which is reproduced from Thorndike's very first paper (1898). Some sort of unlatching device—a loop of wire, a handle, a knob—would be mounted inside the box; when it was manipulated, the door would fall open, permitting the animal to escape confinement and get a bite of food just outside the door. In Thorndike's analysis, the interior of the problem-box constitutes the "stimulus situation"; to this stimulus situation, the animal would bring a repertoire of possible behaviors or responses to try out in attempting to escape from the box. Thus, typically the initial trials would be characterized by much irrelevant, unsuccessful behavior for the first several minutes—a great amount of clawing, biting, rubbing, meowing, thrashing about, and clinging to the ceiling—before the door latch would be tripped, in almost an "accidental" fashion. The performance score recorded on a given trial was the amount of time elapsed before the animal performed the correct response and escaped. Initially, these times were very large due to so much random, irrelevant behavior. However, on succeeding trials the time scores become

---

[1] When years only are given, the name of the author can be understood from the context.

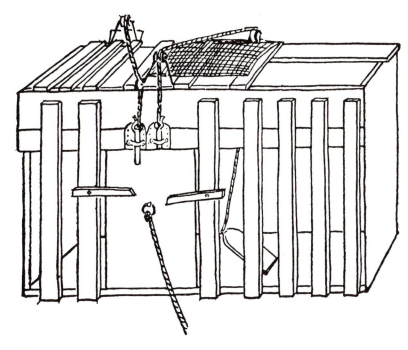

Figure 2.1. Drawing of one of Thorndike's puzzle-boxes. The animal would be confined inside. The door could be opened if the animal pulled on a latch mounted inside the box. (From Thorndike, 1898.)

smaller, but slowly and irregularly. This gradual learning is typically graphed as a "learning curve," with "time elapsed before successful response" plotted on the vertical axis and successive practice trials on the horizontal axis. Figure 2.2 shows data of five different cats from Thorndike's first report. Such response-time curves typically show large values initially, declining to small, relatively stable values near the end of 30 to 70 practice trials. While the curves in Figure 2.2 are for single subjects, more typical learning curves plot the *average* performance score of a group of subjects that are similarly treated over trials. This often produces much smoother, more gradual learning curves.

The gradualness of such learning curves suggested to Thorndike that the cat does not really "catch on" to, or "gain insight into," the method for escaping, but learns it instead by the gradual stamping in of correct responses and stamping out of incorrect responses. For Thorndike, the important point was that the gradual stamping in of rewarded responses and stamping out of unsuccessful ones was an automatic, *mechanistic* explanation for the change in the animal's performance from the early to the later trials of training. No great intelligence was required to mediate such mechanistic learning. After recounting his diverse experiments with several species of animals and many types of problem-boxes, he concluded that he had "failed to find

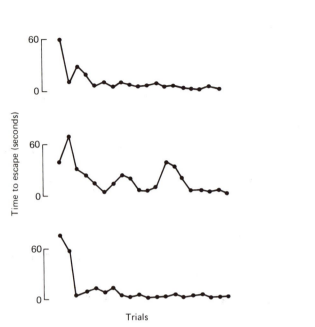

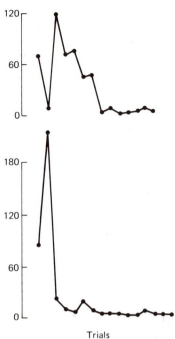

Figure 2.2. Trial by trial learning curves of five cats required to pull a loop of string to escape from a puzzle-box. The cats were trained about 10 trials a day. (From Thorndike, 1898.)

any act that even *seemed* due to reasoning."

The Early Law of Effect

Thorndike's main contribution to psychology was to formulate the so-called *law of effect*. The student should not be overly persuaded by the term *law*, since it reflects the usage of scientists of long ago. Today we would refer to it simply as a hypothesis or conjecture about the sorts of events that cause learning.

Thorndike formulated his mechanistic law of effect in the following terms:

> Of several responses made to the same situation, those which are accompanied or closely followed by satisfaction to the animal will, other things being equal, be more firmly connected with the situation. . . ; those which are accom-

panied or closely followed by discomfort to the animal will, other things being equal, have their connections with that situation weakened (1911, p. 244).

Rewards and nonrewards, or successes and failures, were thus proposed as mechanisms for selection of the more adaptive response. The principle bears much resemblance to the mechanism of natural selection by successful adaptation or survival of the fittest, which was the basis for Charles Darwin's theory of the evolution of species. Thorndike, as well as other comparative psychologists of his era, was influenced by the intellectual attractiveness of Darwin's analysis of species selection.

Thorndike saw that his law of effect added an important supplement to the familiar law of habit formation through repetition (the so-called law of exercise):

But practice without zeal—with equal comfort at success and failure—does *not* make perfect, and the nervous system grows *away* from the modes in which it is *exercised with resulting discomfort.* When the law of effect is omitted—when habit-formation is reduced to the supposed effect of mere repetition—two results are almost certain. By the resulting theory, little in human behavior can be explained by the law of habit; and by the resulting practice, unproductive or extremely wasteful forms of drill are encouraged (1913, p. 22).

Thorndike's interest in rewards and motives for learning, which grew out of his experiments with animals, continued as he turned his attention to learning as it occurs in schools. There arguments over punishment, promotion, grading practices, and other incentive devices were rife, even though academic psychologists had not yet awakened to the centrality of motivational concepts.

Thorndike's experiments on animals had a very profound influence upon his thinking about human learning. He became convinced, contrary to the then popular beliefs, that animal behavior was little mediated by ideas. Responses were said to be made directly to the situation as sensed. While he did not go so far as to totally deny ideation among animals, he was convinced that the great bulk of their learning could be explained by the direct connecting of acts to situations through the automatic action of the law of effect, unmediated by ideas. The similarity of the learning curves of human subjects learning many difficult associations (such as foreign vocabulary words) with those of animals led him to believe that the same essentially mechanical phenomena disclosed by animal learning are also fundamental to human learning. Although always aware of the greater subtlety and range of human learning, he showed a strong preference for understanding more complex learning in terms of simpler learning principles, and for identifying the simpler forms of human learning with that of animals.

Both theory and practice need emphatic and frequent reminders that man's learning is fundamentally the action of the laws of readiness, exercise, and effect. He is first of all an associative mechanism working to avoid what disturbs the life-processes of the neurones. If we begin by fabricating imaginary powers and faculties, or if we avoid thought by loose and empty terms, or if we stay lost in wonder at the extraordinary versatility and inventiveness of the higher forms of learning, we shall never understand man's progress or control his education (1913, p. 23).

Thorndike's pungent attacks upon the vacuousness of mentalistic accounts formed the background for the mechanistic S-R theories that were to dominate the study of human learning for many decades.

Objections to the Earlier Law of Effect

As noted previously, the law of effect refers to the strengthening or weakening of a connection as a result of its consequences. When a modifiable connection is made and is accompanied or followed by a satisfying state of affairs, the strength of the connection is increased; if the connection is made and followed by punishment or an annoying state of affairs, its strength is decreased. Thorndike thought of the strength of a connection in terms of the probability of the response occurring to the relevant situation. More probable responses would also occur sooner in a trial-and-error situation in which the subjects try out one response after another until they hit upon the correct one.

Two chief objections were made to the law of effect by its critics at the time of its early formulation. First, it was objected that satisfaction and annoyance were subjective terms, inappropriate for use in describing animal behavior. But Thorndike was ahead of his critics, for he had early stated what he meant by such states of affairs in operational terms:

By a satisfying state of affairs is meant one which the animal does nothing to avoid, often doing things which maintain or renew it. By an annoying state of affairs is meant one which the animal does nothing to preserve, often doing things which put an end to it (1913, p. 2).

These definitions prevent the law of effect from being circular, because the states of affairs characterized as satisfying and as annoying are specified independently of their influence upon modifiable connections. The law of effect then states what may be expected to happen to preceding modifiable connections that are followed by such specified states. Therefore, Thorndike had answered this first objection.

The second objection was that the backward effect of an outcome on something now past in time goes opposite to normal laws of causation. Since the stimulus-response event occurs before the reward (or punishment), how could the latter exert an influence upon the earlier event? The past is gone, whereas effects can be felt only in the present. The criticism, like the first, is logically faulty. The causal effect of the outcome upon the S-R connection is revealed in the probability of recurrence of the response when the situation next occurs; whether or not such an effect is observed in the future is a matter of observation and experiment, not something to be denied on logical grounds. This second objection does, however, raise a slight problem for psychological theory; if the rewarding or punishing outcome is delayed after the critical response, some mechanism must be postulated to maintain information about which response occurred in order for the outcome to strengthen that response selectively. Later theories of "delayed reward" explicitly provide some short-term memory mechanism to carry out this information-maintaining function. Thorndike did not recognize this as a critical problem, however.

Translated into familiar words, Thorndike's law says that rewards or successes

further the learning of the rewarded behavior, whereas punishments or failures reduce the tendency to repeat the behavior. So much would merely be a reassertion of common observations. But Thorndike went further and insisted that the action of consequences is direct, mechanical, automatic, and need not be mediated by conscious ideas. It is precisely with respect to these technical addendums to common sense that later critics from cognitive psychology were to attack Thorndike's statement of the law of effect—as we shall see presently. In this insistence on mechanical action, Thorndike's law of effect anticipates the reinforcement principle adopted in later conditioned-response theories. The later changes in his theory reduced the importance of annoyers relative to satisfiers (see the revised law of effect, below) and added some new phenomena, but the central importance of a modified law of effect persisted in Thorndike's final statements of his position.

Subordinate Principles

Thorndike was not a systematic theorist proposing a coherent set of interesting principles. Instead, he wrote prolifically about analyses of learning, identifying a number of significant variables, factors, or principles involved in typical learning situations. In the account below, we list several of these lesser principles that Thorndike described. Their uneven generality is apparent.

Exercise. In a short account of Thorndike's views, the impression may be given that repetition of a habit was presumed to increase its strength, on the premise that "practice makes perfect." Thorndike in his early writings referred to this as the *law of exercise.* This law has two forms: The *use* of a connection increases its strength; the *disuse* of a connection (not practicing it) leads to its weakening or *forgetting.* Only later did Thorndike recognize the subtle inconsistency between the principle of exercise (use) and his law of effect, at which time he reinterpreted "use" to mean "rewarded correct use."

Readiness. Readiness characterizes many of the circumstances under which a learner tends to be satisfied or annoyed. Thorndike recognized several forms of readiness: if a strong desire for an action sequence is aroused, then the smooth carrying out of that sequence is *satisfying;* if that action sequence is thwarted or blocked from completion, then such blocking is *annoying;* if an action is fatigued (tired out) or satiated, then forcing a further repetition of the act is *annoying.* Thorndike was trying to cover a number of cases with these generalizations. Examples of the first two rules are chains of consummatory behaviors, such as a child going to the refrigerator for ice cream. The desire for food brings into readiness the early responses of the action sequence; similarly, performance of the early steps of the action sequence enhances the subject's readiness for the next steps. (In this principle, Thorndike was *not* referring to the "reading readiness" idea familiar to educators. He discussed reading readiness in terms of how many basic skills a beginner had learned before receiving reading instruction.)

Response variation. In order for a response to be rewarded, it must occur. When learners face a problem, they try one thing after another. When the appropriate behavior is stumbled upon, success follows and learning is possible. Were the organism unable to vary its responses, the optimum solution might never be elicited. Even when a response to a given situation is found to yield some reward, there is still adaptive value to some variation around that response, since the reward may be larger or more frequent for other responses. Thus, Thorndike was recognizing that premature fixation of behavior could be maladaptive.

Differing salience of stimulus elements. Learners are able to react selectively to prepotent or salient elements in the problem or stimulus situation. That is, they can pick out the essential item from a complex pattern and base their responses upon it, neglecting other adventitious features that might confuse a lower animal. This ability to deal with the relevant parts of situations makes analytical and insightful learning possible. This selection of the critical element is described in terms of either attention or abstraction.

Associative shifting. Thorndike's *principle of associative shifting* is this: if a response can be kept intact through a series of gradual changes in the stimulating situation, it may finally be given to a totally new stimulus. The stimulating situation is changed first by the addition of some elements, then by the subtraction of others, until nothing from the original situation remains. Thorndike illustrates this principle by the act of teaching a cat to stand up at command. First a bit of fish is dangled before the cat while you say, "Stand up." After enough trials, by proper arrangement, the fish stimulus may be omitted, and the verbal signal will alone evoke the response. The general statement of the principle of associative shifting implies that we may "get any response of which a learner is capable associated with any situation to which he is sensitive" (1913, p. 15). This is similar to conditioning in which a conditioned stimulus ("Stand up") comes to substitute for an unconditioned one (the dangling fish). Thorndike, while noting the similarity, believed the Pavlovian conditioned response to be a more specialized case under the broader principle of associative shifting. Thorndike's principle also resembles what Skinner has called "fading" or "vanishing," whereby discriminative control of a response is shifted from one stimulus to a second. This principle is now in wide use in teaching-machine programs. An elementary example is that of children being taught to spell a new word by pairing the presentation of the spoken with the written word (which they copy). Initially, the child copies a visual word (say, pencil) while hearing and seeing it. Later, as he hears "pencil" the child sees only a part of the word (say, p - nc - l) and has to fill in the blanks. Over further trials, fewer visual letters are given as prompts (say, p - - - - l) as the word is spoken, and the child has to spell it. Eventually, the child learns to spell the complete word after just hearing it. Such educational applications, however, flowed from Skinner's ingenuity and were not part of Thorndike's many suggestions regarding practical problems.

Response by similarity or analogy. Responses to new situations are assumed to be based on assimilating the new to a previously learned situation, and giving a response based on the similarity or analogy of the two situations. Learners respond to a new situation as they would to some situation like it (later theorists called this "stimulus generalization"); or they respond to some element in the new situation for which they have a response in their repertory. Responses can usually be explained by old learning, together with inborn tendencies to respond; on this account, there is nothing mysterious about responses to novelty, since novel situations can always be decomposed into new arrangements of mainly familiar features and parts.

Let us elaborate further upon Thorndike's view of how learning transfers from one training situation to a second testing situation or new learning task. To some extent, all formal education is aimed at a kind of transfer *beyond* the classroom of knowledge and skills learned *in* school. Whether the proper way to achieve this

end is to teach more formal subject matter such as mathematics, or to give more attention to practical subject matter such as vocational training and civics, the problem is a central one for educators.

As an early educational psychologist, Thorndike interested himself in the problem. His theory began to take form in an experimental study done in collaboration with Woodworth (Thorndike & Woodworth, 1901), and was formally stated in his early *Educational psychology* (1903). As noted above, the theory proposes that transfer depends upon the presence of identical elements in the original task and in the transfer task which it facilitates. Either the stimulus elements of two situations or the response-components of two similar skills may be identical. In school subjects, either substance (ideas) or procedures (skilled actions) may have overlapping elements. For example, the ability to speak and write well is important both in the schoolroom and in many tasks of ordinary life. Hence mastery of these skills will serve in different pursuits, and transfer should result because of what the different situations require in common. The procedures of looking things up in diverse sources such as a dictionary, a cookbook, and a chemist's handbook have much in common, despite the dissimilar contents of the three kinds of books. If an activity is learned more easily because another activity was learned first, Thorndike thought it could only be because the two activities overlap. Transfer is always specific, never general; when it appears to be general, the fact remains that new situations have much of old situations in them.

To some extent, intelligence as measured by I.Q. tests may be thought of as a measure of an individual's general transfer capacity. That is, the test measures the ability to give right answers in relatively novel situations. Thorndike's theory of intelligence was, like his theory of transfer, a matter of the number of relevant specific connections. The more bonds the individual has that can be used, the more intelligent he or she is.

Besides the several principles of learning enumerated here, Thorndike also devoted much attention to how to improve the school learning of students. He stressed that students must be interested in the material and concerned about improving their performance. Interest was believed to arise because students regard the material to be significant for some personal goal; and interest was said to motivate their attentiveness to studying. These clearly are the first principles underlying most teacher-training courses, and they make good sense. They are not, however, distinctive recommendations unique to Thorndike's approach.

During the stable period of Thorndike's system, many changes in the psychological climate occurred, but these left him unruffled. The rise of behaviorism and the new importance attributed to the conditioned response affected him but little because the new enthusiasts were talking what was to him a congenial language. However, starting in 1930, he revised and elaborated upon his law of effect and began distinguishing it more clearly from the principle of exercise noted above.

CONNECTIONISM AFTER 1930

The revisions of his original hypotheses were reported by Thorndike in a number of journal articles and monographs with various collaborators, the main results being gathered in two large volumes under the titles *The fundamentals of learning* (1932a) and *The psychology of wants, interests, and attitudes* (1935). One series of experiments hit at the distinction between the principles of exercise vs. effect in modifying behavior. Another series of studies refined the law of effect and sought new evidence for it.

Disproof of the Law of Exercise

The type of experiment used to disprove the law of exercise involved situations in which a class of responses is repeated under circumstances that minimize rewarding effects. For instance, a blindfolded subject would be asked to draw a 4-inch line, and to do so hundreds of times over many days, but never with any feedback information from the experimenter regarding the accuracy of the drawings. Thorndike was here interested in whether the initially more frequent responses (such as line lengths between say, 4.1 and 4.6 inches long) would slowly "drain off" strength from the less frequent responses. Eventually the high-frequency responses would become ever more probable, and the low-frequency responses would be driven out. This was, he supposed, the implication of the law of exercise whereby a response to a situation is strengthened by its sheer occurrence; and since the probabilities over all responses must sum to 1.00, increasing the probability of one class of responses must decrease the probability of another class.

The results in this and several similar experiments by Thorndike were distinctly negative; the probability distribution of line lengths drawn on the twelfth practice day was in essentials the same as the distribution on the first practice day. Without information or rewarding feedback, there was relatively little change in the response distribution. In full contrast, if, each time after an attempt to draw a 4-inch line, the person is informed as to whether the product was too long or too short, the response productions improve rapidly until they are tightly distributed at about 4 inches (Trowbridge & Cason, 1932).

The line-drawing experiment shows that repetition of a *situation* without knowledge of the correct response produces little or no change in the relative frequencies of the several responses. However, Thorndike was well aware that some varieties of repetition ("exercise") are important, and they are precisely those simple stimulus-response connections in which subjects know or believe they are remembering correctly. For instance, a pupil who has been told to remember that the capital of Oregon is Salem is well advised to subvocally rehearse the sentence or pairings "capital of Oregon-Salem," even though the teacher is not standing by delivering a series of verbal reinforcements. Such implicit "exercise" of the connection is well known to promote long-term retention of the connection. Thorndike would explain the effect of this and similar kinds of rehearsal as due to an internal "confirming reaction" (or satisfier) that subjects supposedly experience after each S-R rehearsal, as though they were saying to themselves, "Capital of Oregon-Salem—right."

THE REVISED LAW OF EFFECT

Thorndike interpreted a number of experiments as showing that the effects of reward and punishment were not equal and opposite, as had been implied in earlier statements on the effects of satisfiers and annoyers. Instead, under several conditions, reward appeared to be much more powerful than punishment. This conclusion, if confirmed, would be of immense social importance in the fields of education and criminology.

One of these experiments was done with chicks (1932b). A simple maze gave the chick the choice of three pathways, one of which led to "freedom, food, and company"—that is, to an open compartment where there were other chicks eating. The wrong choices led to confinement for 30 seconds. Statistics were kept on the tendencies to return to the preceding choice if it had led to reward, and to avoid the preceding choice if it led to punishment.

Thorndike interpreted his findings as follows: "The results of all comparisons by all methods tell the same story. Rewarding a connection always strengthened it substantially; punishing it weakened it little or not at all" (1932b, p. 58).

The corresponding experiment with human subjects consisted of a multiple-choice vocabulary test. For example, a Spanish word was given with five English words, one of which was the correct translation. A second and a third Spanish word followed, and so on through a list, each word with alternative translations arranged in the same manner. Subjects would guess the translation word, underline it, and then hear the experimenter say *Right* (the rewarded response) or *Wrong* (the punished response). How did the subjects change their responses the next time through the list? As with the chicks, reward (*Right*) after a response led to increased repetition of the rewarded response to that stimulus word, but punishment (*Wrong*) after a response did not lead to a lessening of the probability of that response being repeated to that stimulus word. In six experiments of this general sort, Thorndike concluded that the announcement of *Wrong* did not weaken connections enough to counterbalance the slight increase in strength gained from the response simply occurring (1932a, p. 288). There were some statistical difficulties in Thorndike's interpretations of his data which caused him to underestimate the significance of punishment. In a later section, we shall take up some of these criticisms of Thorndike's interpretation of his results, as well as counterevidence.

Thorndike and his staff went on to collect a series of testimonials about the relative efficacy of rewards and punishments from published biographies and other sources, going back many years. The almost universal evidence of the greater beneficial effect of reward rather than punishment gave practical support to the findings of the experiments, which otherwise could be criticized as being too far removed from ordinary life (1935, pp. 135–44, 248–55).

As in the disproof of the law of exercise, Thorndike's repudiation of the principle of weakening by annoying aftereffects was not absolute. Only direct weakening was denied. According to Thorndike, punishments do affect learning, but indirectly. He proposed that their indirect effect comes chiefly from leading the learner to do something in the presence of the annoyer which makes him less likely to repeat the original connection.

> An annoyer which is attached to a modifiable connection may cause the animal to feel fear or chagrin, jump back, run away, wince, cry, perform the same act as before but more vigorously, or whatever else is in his repertory as a response to that annoyer in that situation. But there is no evidence that it takes away strength from the physiological basis of the connection in any way comparable to the way in which a satisfying after-effect adds strength to it (1932a, pp. 311–13).

The Spread of Effect

In 1933 new evidence was offered in support of the law of effect. This evidence was described as the *spread of effect* (1933a, 1933b). We will discuss the spread of effect in detail because it was a phenomenon discovered by Thorndike and uniquely promulgated by him. He used it to argue for the *automatic* influence of rewards, which was one of his postulates. The experiments purported to show that the influence of a reward acts not only on the connection to which it belongs, but on temporally adjacent connections occurring just before or after the rewarded connection. The effect diminishes with each step that the connection is removed from the rewarded one. The effect strengthens even punished connections in the neighborhood of the rewarded one. The experiments appear to support the automatic and mechanical action of reward or punishment. A characteristic experiment was one in which the subject was asked to state a number from 1 to 10 following the announcement of a stimulus word by the experimenter. The experimenter then called the subject's response *Right* or *Wrong,* these rewards and punishments conforming to some prearranged assignment of correct numbers to each word. In either case, the assignment of numbers from the point of view of the subject was arbitrary, and the subject's cue to repeat the number first given to the stimulus word or to change it on the next trial with that word came from the experimenter's reaction following each number. However, the word lists were so long that the subject could not recall very well on the second trial just what was done to each word during the first trial.

After the list had been read a number of times in this manner, the subject's responses were classified to find the number of times the response to a given stimulus word was repeated the next time that word was presented. Not only were the rewarded responses repeated more often than the others, but responses followed by *Nothing* (the experimenter said nothing) were repeated beyond chance expectancy *if* they occurred close in time to a response called *Right.*

The experiment by Tilton (1945) is an example. He repeated the spread of effect experiment with careful controls to determine what the empirical level of response repetition would be without the saying of *Right* or *Wrong* (i.e., the experimenter saying nothing following the subject's response). Tilton also arranged that a response to a stimulus called *Right* would be surrounded by other S-R pairings which were only called *Wrong,* and vice versa. He then proceeded to plot the spread of effect on either side of an isolated rewarded or an isolated punished response (Tilton, 1939, 1945). He found that the effects of

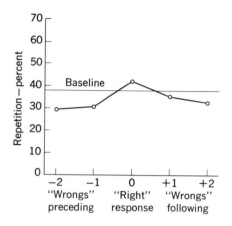

Figure 2.3. Gradient of effect around a *Right* response. Calling a response *Right* increases its repetition; calling a response *Wrong* decreases its repetition. The decrease from being called *Wrong* is less, however, when the response called *Wrong* is near an isolated Right. (From Tilton, 1945.)

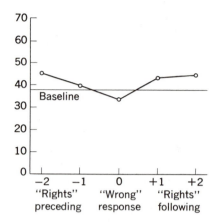

Figure 2.4. Gradient of effect around a *Wrong* response. Calling a response *Wrong* decreases its repetition; calling a response *Right* increases its repetition. The increase from being called *Right* is less, however, when the response called *Right* is near an isolated *Wrong*. (From Tilton, 1945.)

Right and *Wrong* are about alike, the announcement of *Wrong* decreasing repetitions about as much as *Right* increased them. A replotting of Tilton's results is shown in Figures 2.3 and 2.4.

Tilton's study shows that there is a tendency for punished responses in the neighborhood of reward to be repeated more frequently than such responses remote from reward. Their punishment (being called *Wrong*) suffices, however, even one step from reward, to lead to *less* repetition than would occur if the response were neither rewarded nor punished (Figure 2.3). Similarly, when a response called *Wrong* (punished) occurs in the midst of a series of rewarded responses, the neighboring rewarded responses are repeated less frequently than they would have been had they not been in the neighborhood of the punished response. Again, however, their reward (being called *Right*) is enough to lead to their repetition at a *greater* frequency than that represented by the neutral baseline (Figure 2.4).

The important point here for Thorndike is the apparent "gradient" of repetition probability for pairs occurring close in time to the isolated rewarded or punished pair. This continuous function was presumed to demonstrate the spreading of the automatic strengthening effect of a reward to temporally contiguous connections, and similarly for the spread of the weakening effect of a punishment.

The startling and counterintuitive nature of such results led to much experimentation, a good deal of which was an attempt to explain away the spread-of-effect gradients (such as Tilton's) as being caused by one or another artifact or contaminating variable in the task. And indeed a fair number of other factors—such as recurrent number-guessing sequences, nonrandom guessing habits altering the repetition baseline, and the influence of set or intention to learn—were shown to influence the spread-of-effect data and consequently to cast in doubt its original interpretation. The array of conflicting evidence on the issue was reviewed in a prior edition of this volume (Hilgard & Bower, 1966, pp. 28ff.) and by Postman (1962).

An Alternative Explanation

Weighing the evidence for one or another artifact, it now appears that the spread of effect is very likely the result of much simpler processes than Thorndike supposed. First, we might note that the spread of effect as a theoretical principle was evoked solely to explain the particular data collected under this rubric, and the old law of effect is actually logically independent of whether or not spread occurs. Second, we believe that the spread-of-effect data are probably the result of stimulus generalization among serial positions within a list, and may have nothing whatever to do with the spreading aftereffects of a reward. To illustrate this explanation, let's consider a small list of eight arbitrary items typical of a Thorndikean experiment and illustrated below (Table 2.1): on Trial 1, the list of words (*cup, scissors,* . . .) is presented, to each of which the person guesses a digit from 1 to 10, following

which the experimenter always arbitrarily says "Wrong" except for, say, the fifth item in the series. Following the first cycle, a second cycle through the series occurs, with the items being presented in the same serial order, and the subject making a Trial-2 guess, as listed in the last column. Our hypothetical data illustrate repetition of the response "3" to *pencil,* which had been directly rewarded on Trial 1 and also repetition of responses given to stimuli presented two steps before and after the rewarded *pencil*-3 connection. These illustrate spread of effects, of course.

The stimulus generalization explanation for such data might proceed as follows (suggested by Estes, 1969a). First, we conceive of this paired-associate task as the concurrent learning of many stimulus-response-outcome triplets (eight, in our example). Within any given trial of a stimulus-response-outcome (S-R-O) sequence, there is some likelihood that the subject learns any and all of the three pairwise associations, namely, S-R, S-O, and R-O. These are presumed to be learned independently. An index of an S-O association, for example, would be that the person

TABLE 2.1. Illustrative events on two trials of a Thorndikean associative learning task. *S* and *E* denote the Subject and the Experimenter, respectively.

Serial Position	Cue Word	Trial 1 S's Guess	Trial 1 E's Feedback	Trial 2 S's Guess
1.	cup	7	wrong	2
2.	scissors	9	wrong	1
3.	plate	5	wrong	5
4.	sky	6	wrong	6
5.	pencil	3	RIGHT	3
6.	book	1	wrong	1
7.	house	8	wrong	8
8.	chair	2	wrong	6

could later recall that to the word *pencil* the experimenter had said "Right" to the subject's response. Moreover, and relevant to the spread-of-effect issue, we may suppose that the person identifies the serial position of each item in a rough and imprecise way, but nonetheless enters this serial position into associations with the S-R-O events that occur at that position in the list. For the list illustrated above, this would mean that the person might associate (during Trial 1) an implicit "serial position 5" to *Right* as an outcome. This would be evident, for example, in his later ability to say after studying the list that a pairing approximately in the *middle of the list* had been called *Right* by the experimenter (note that the *Right* was a salient event, isolated among a series of *Wrongs*—which arrangement is necessary for spread-of-effect experiments).

The further assumption of Estes's theory is that the person's memory of the outcomes associated with a stimulus complex controls whether or not he will perform the response he remembers having made to that stimulus. If he remembers the response he made to *pencil* and remembers either that the response to *pencil* or to serial position 5 was called *Right,* then he will repeat the response he remembers having made. This is the basis for the repetition effect for connections followed by *Right.* If the person remembers that the outcome for a stimulus (or serial position) was called *Wrong,* then he will make a different response from that which he remembers having made on the prior trial. This is the basis for why *Wrong* will, other things being equal, reduce repetition of responses below an appropriate control baseline (which is response-repetition given a neutral event, neither *Right* nor *Wrong,* after the response on Trial 1).

To deal with the spread of effect, we need suppose only that the person's memory for the serial position that was correlated with a *Right* is imprecise, so that

"serial position $5 \rightarrow Right$" *generalizes* to neighboring serial positions 3, 4, 6, and 7, according to their distance from the correct location. Such stimulus generalization is a well-documented phenomenon, so it is not an unreasonable supposition. This principle suffices to explain the spread of effect. To illustrate, consider the S-R-O event "*book-1-Wrong*" that occurs in serial position 6 just following the *Right* in serial position 5. Suppose that the person remembers what she said—that is, the S-R event. If she recalls "*book-Wrong*" then she will not repeat the "*book-1*" connection (as Tilton's data show in Figure 2.3). If she forgets the *Wrong* for *book,* then she might recall, incorrectly as a generalization error, "serial position 6-*Right*" because serial position 6 is very similar to serial position 5. If this generalization or confusion occurred among adjacent serial positions, then the spread of effect would result as a *performance* factor (rather than a learning factor, as Thorndike had interpreted it). This essentially amounts to a strategy to "repeat S-R connections that you can remember having made to a context that was approximately serial position 5."

Several implications follow from this position generalization hypothesis regarding the spread of effect. First, if subjects are asked on Trial 2 to recall the response made on Trial 1 *and* whether it was called *Right* or *Wrong,* one finds that the probability of recalling the response made before is independent of which effect (*Right* or *Wrong*) followed it; however, there is a generalization spread in recalling outcomes, such that pairs called *Wrong* but in proximity to a pair called *Right* are likely to be later misrecalled as having been called *Right;* the opposite occurs for a pair called *Wrong* surrounded by pairs called *Right* (see Nuttin, 1949, 1953). This is exactly as expected by the generalization theory.

Furthermore, the spread of effect should be markedly reduced in magnitude if the stimuli are presented on Trial 2 in a new, scrambled serial order. Zirkle (1946) in fact found that the spread of effect was eliminated with rescrambling of the test list; the tendency to give an R to an S that had occurred close to an "S-R *Right*" connection did not increase unless that S recurred in the same or a nearby serial position as it had during Trial 1.

The illustration above has used a short list and assumed a fortuitous pattern of associations to explain the spread of effect; with long lists, these factors will have lesser effects. But it must be realized that the spread of effect was at best a small effect (reexamine Figures 2.3 and 2.4). That so much experimental effort went into deciding the "reality" of this effect illustrates the allure of a critical theoretical issue.

Belongingness

In addition to the revisions of the laws of exercise and effect, several new terms entered Thorndike's theoretical system as he revised it after 1930. One of these, *belongingness,* by its recognition of an organizational principle, made concessions to Gestalt psychologists. According to this principle, a connection between two units or ideas is more readily established if the subject perceives the two as belonging or going together. For example, if the person hears a repetitive series of sentences such as "John is a butcher. Harry is a carpenter. Jim is a doctor" and so on, the association "butcher-John" will be a much stronger one than is "butcher-Harry," despite the fact that "butcher" occurs closer in time to "Harry" than to "John." Obviously, the person is perceiving, grouping, and rehearsing the flow of words as subject-predicate constructions; his knowledge of syntax groups the words together in a manner differing from their temporal contiguity, and assigns the predicate of a sentence to the subject of the same sentence rather than to the next sentence. There are hun-

dreds of examples of this principle at work, illustrating how various perceptual variables (like temporal or spatial proximity) determine which units will be perceived and rehearsed together, and consequently connected. Thorndike recognized this belongingness factor without being very clear on how to accommodate it to his mechanistic system.

The other use of belongingness Thorndike recognized was that the reward or punishment which follows a stimulus-response event should be perceived as "belonging" to that S-R event, or interpreted by the person as being related to his response. For instance, if during learning of a paired-associate item, the subject were suddenly to be given a big payment by the experimenter with an offhand remark like "This is the wage I was going to pay you later," or if a shock were delivered to the subject but the experimenter said, "Oops, sorry; that was an accident of my equipment," then those rewarding or punishing events would not be seen as *contingent* on the person's response. Therefore, the response which precedes such an aftereffect without belonging will not have its associative connection altered very much by the experience. These belongingness effects clearly have to do with how the subject has perceived or grouped together units which are to be rehearsed as an associative unit.

Associative Polarity

While the principle of belongingness may be interpreted as something of a concession, the principle of *polarity* was emphasized as defying Gestalt principles (1932a, p. 158). Thorndike's principle of polarity stated that connections act more easily in the direction in which they were formed than in the opposite direction. If you have learned German vocabulary items by always testing yourself in the German-to-English direction, you are likely to fail in a test on the English-to-German direction. Thorndike's polarity principle says that associations can be unidirectional between two terms rather than necessarily bidirectional. He contrasted this with the *associative symmetry* view (which he attributed to Gestalt theory) that a connected pair of items forms a new whole or unit; according to this view, since the entire trace is revived by the recall cue, it makes no sense to say that an association could exist in one direction but not in the other.

The issue of associative symmetry is still current among contemporary workers in human learning. The resolution of the symmetry issue seems to depend on: (a) the subject's mode of rehearsal—Merryman (1969) has shown that subjects can be led to rehearse paired associates in such a manner as to form mainly unidirectional or mainly bidirectional associations, depending upon how they think they will have to use their pair knowledge during test trials; and (b) the *availability* of the two units as recallable responses (Horowitz et al., 1966). If we have assured a person's familiarity with each unit, specifically her ability to recall the unit by itself, then her recall of that unit when cued with the other member of the associated pair will be high. Given subjects' normal rehearsal methods, the two elements of a pair will tend to show associative symmetry to the extent that both units are equally available as responses per se. For instance, in our German-English illustration given above, the English speaker would be more familiar with the English than with the German word, and hence her recall in the two directions would appear asymmetric, but, according to Horowitz and associates (1966), only because of the different availability of the German and English words.

Stimulus Identifiability

Throughout his theoretical writings Thorndike continued to identify important factors in learning and to report new experiments demonstrating their importance.

Two factors worthy of mention are his notions of *stimulus identifiability* and *response availability,* since both of these relate closely to contemporary work. The principle of identifiability is that a situation is easy to connect to a response to the extent that the situation is identifiable, distinctive, and distinguishable from others in a learning series. Thorndike is here recognizing the issue of stimulus discrimination, or perceptual learning, that plays a large role in later theories of associative learning. He talks about stimulus identification as follows:

> Learning as a whole includes changes in the identifiability of situations as well as changes in the connections leading from them to responses. . . . Elements of situations which are hard to identify because they are hidden qualities or features are analyzed out into relief, and made identifiable by having attention directed specifically to them and by the action of varying concomitants and contrast (1931, pp. 88–89).

Thorndike thus recognized the importance of stimulus recognition to association formation; he also described the typical means by which the relevant distinctive feature is abstracted from a series of complex stimulus patterns—namely, by variation of irrelevant features and contrasting appearances of the relevant feature over many trials. These ideas, of course, have a quite modern ring to them.

Response Availability

> Consider now the principle of availability as get-at-able-ness of the response, which is that, other things being equal, connections are easy to form in proportion as the response is available, summonable, such that the person can have it or make it at will (1931, p. 89).

The kind of distinction Thorndike had in mind here was that some responses are overlearned as familiar acts (e.g., touching our nose, tapping our toes) which are readily executed upon command, whereas more finely skilled movements (e.g., drawing a line 4 inches as opposed to 5 inches long while blindfolded) may not be so readily summonable. In this matter, Thorndike was recognizing what today we would call *response differentiation,* the ease with which the person can distinguish two or more responses which are to be paired with corresponding stimuli. The terms *response availability* or *response learning* came to be used in the later literature to refer to acquisition of a complex chain of items— for example, to say the sequence *"HXDFR"* to a particular signal, or to write the German word *aufgang* as the equivalent of "exit" in English.

THORNDIKE AND SELECTED CONTEMPORARY ISSUES

It will help place the contribution of Thorndike into perspective if we examine two contemporary strands of research related specifically to his positions. We will consider some modern interpretations of the law of effect as applied to human learning, and the subject of learning without awareness. Thorndike's views on these topics stimulated much systematic experimentation and theorizing. In our opinion, the fates of time and scientific evidence have not smiled on Thorndike's earlier positions; yet, although later theorists have taken issue with Thorndike, it should be recognized that criticism is the highest form of flattery in the world of science. Insignificant theories are rarely criticized; they are simply ignored and allowed to die a quiet death from neglect.

Recent Hypotheses about Effect in Human Learning

Although Thorndike frequently demonstrated the role of after-effects upon human learning, he was somewhat unsuccessful in delving deeper into explaining *how* a reward had its influence in strengthening an

S-R connection. He was temperamentally opposed to the idea of the subject "thinking over" his past S-R reward experiences and consciously deciding how to respond on the next trial to that situation. Such an approach smacked too much of unscientific speculation for Thorndike's tastes.

The two hypotheses that seem today to be more in keeping with the facts about rewards in human learning were, surprisingly, formulated clearly by Thorndike himself: but he rejected them, using arguments which in hindsight seem fallacious. These alternate interpretations of why aftereffects strengthen S-R connections were dubbed the *rehearsal* and the *ideational* (or *informational*) *hypotheses* by Thorndike. Thorndike formulated the rehearsal hypothesis as follows:

> The next doctrine or hypothesis to be considered is that when a certain connecting has been followed by a satisfier, the individual concerned *repeats the connection* or something more or less equivalent to it. He thus strengthens the right connections himself by repetition. The wrong connections he may simply dismiss, or he may strengthen their negatives as by saying to himself *Four cross lines, don't turn head to left* (1931, p. 51).

Current research on human learning gives much support to this differential rehearsal viewpoint, especially in learning situations in which the learner is presented with many more items than she can learn and these vary in their importance or value when learned. For example, the person might be presented with a number of paired-associates to study and told for each one how much money she will receive if she can remember that pairing on a later cued recall test. In such a situation, recall will vary directly with the expected payoff for remembering a given item. However, it appears likely that this is largely due to more rehearsal time allotted by the subject to the high-payoff items to the detriment of the low-payoff ones (Atkinson & Wickens, 1971). If the person has strategic control over which items are entered into or deleted from a small set of items undergoing active rehearsal as the list of pairs are presented serially, then high-payoff items receive the highest priority in remaining in the active rehearsal set. It is this rehearsal which is alleged to be the causal variable promoting better learning of high-value items. Thus, amount of reward would have its influence not directly on learning but by way of instigating more or less rehearsal of items according to their value.

A similar rehearsal-like effect has been found for simple recognition memory for single pictures (of naturalistic scenes) that were presented as pairs for study but with different monetary values assigned to each picture of the pair (Loftus, 1972). For example, a given pair of pictures might have 9 points assigned to the left-hand picture and 3 points for the right-hand picture; these were the points to be earned if the subject could later recognize this picture from among a set of similar pictures. As expected, Loftus found that higher-valued pictures were remembered better than lower-valued pictures on a recognition test. The interesting and significant results came from recordings of concurrent eye movements as the subject studied the pair of pictures for 3 seconds. The significant variable proved to be the number of eye fixations on a given picture. Later recognition memory for a given picture increased directly with the number of eye fixations on it during the study trial. Valued pictures received more eye fixations, on the average. Significantly, however, there was no residual effect on memory of monetary value once the number of eye fixations was held constant. That is, for all pictures receiving, say, six eye fixations, the person's later recognition memory was equally good irrespective of how many points that picture was worth. The conclusion is that monetary value affects memory only through the intermediary of affecting the amount of visual processing of the picture. This may be analogous to rehearsal of verbal materials.

So rewards (anticipated or delivered) surely act in human learning by promoting differential exposure to and rehearsal of the connections to be learned. Of course, Thorndike did not deny this. He said:

> Such strengthening by repetition does, of course, occur in many acts of learning. Everybody must admit this. The question is whether it is the *essential* and general method by which satisfiers and annoyers following connections strengthen or weaken them, or only an accessory or occasional procedure (1931, p. 51).

From consideration of several experiments in which rewards had their usual positive effects but which precluded the subject's carrying out much conscious postreward rehearsal, Thorndike concluded that differential rehearsal was not an *essential* or necessary feature determining the influence of rewards. In this we must agree with him; one can observe effects of reward even when differential rehearsal is prevented, although permitting differential rehearsal magnifies the observed effects. The remaining issue is then how to interpret such reward effects as are found when rehearsal is minimized or equalized among conditions. We next take up the information hypothesis.

The Information Hypothesis Regarding Aftereffects

Thorndike's formulation supposed that satisfiers act directly to strengthen the S-R connections they follow. The main alternative to Thorndike's hypothesis supposes that the events in the stimulus-response-outcome sequence may be remembered simply by virtue of their occurring together (with "belonging"), and that the person's memory of the rewarding or punishing outcome causes him on the next trial to carry out the same response or to alter it according to whether he does or does not want that same outcome again. This viewpoint, given briefly in the preceding section explaining the spread of effect, has been promoted by Buchwald (1967, 1969) and by Estes (1969a). It was anticipated by Thorndike as the following lines demonstrate:

> The first of these theories declares that [aftereffects influence connections] by calling up ideas of themselves or some equivalents for themselves in the mind. For example, in our experiments in learning to choose the right meaning for a word [in foreign vocabulary learning], the person has these experiences: Seeing word A, response 1, hearing "Wrong"; seeing word A, response 2, hearing "Wrong"; seeing Word A, response 3, hearing "Right." When he next sees word A, any tendency to make response 1 or response 2 calls to his mind some image or memory or ideational equivalent of "Wrong," whereas any tendency to make response 3 calls to his mind some image or memory or ideational equivalent of "Right." So this theory would state. It would further state that such memories or ideas of wrong associated with a tendency must *inhibit* the tendency, and that such memories and ideas of right associated with a tendency must *encourage* it to act, and so preserve and strengthen it.
>
> In the same way this theory . . . would explain the learning of a cat [in a T maze] who came to avoid the exit S at which it received a mild shock and to favor the exit F which led to food, by the supposition that the tendency to approach and enter S calls to the cat's mind some image or idea of the painful shock, whereas the tendency to approach and enter F calls to its mind some representation of the food, and that these representations respectively check and favor these tendencies (1931, pp. 47–48).

The first paragraph of this quotation contains the essentials of the current Estes-Buchwald theory of how reward operates in human learning; the second paragraph contains the hypothesis, subscribed to by Kenneth Spence and Clark Hull in his later writings (see Chapter 5), that responses are selected by the anticipation of rewards or punishments consequent on the responses.

Having formulated this ideational theory of aftereffects, Thorndike rejected it on the basis of three arguments which appear, with the wisdom of hindsight, to have been inadequate. First, he said that his subjects rarely report introspectively recalling the *Right* or *Wrong* announcements of the experimenter from the previous trial. But he seems not to have collected any systematic data on such matters and relied merely on volunteered reports, which are often unreliable. More recent experiments which ask subjects to recall prior outcomes as well as to give correct responses find appreciable recall of the outcomes (Allen & Estes, 1972).

Second, Thorndike argued that some learned, skilled movements occur so very quickly that there simply would not be enough time to bring up an image of the outcome before firing off the response (e.g., a boxer flicking a left jab through a momentary opening in his opponent's defense). The criticism fails, however, if the alternate theory provides for direct S-R connections which can be fired directly by short-circuiting the usual deliberate intervention of S-O memories. Estes's theory has exactly such a short-circuiting option available to handle high-speed execution of habitual S-Rs. Third, Thorndike argued that the ideational theory would expect symmetrical effects of *Right* versus *Wrong*, since each was just an "informational stimulus," whereas in fact Thorndike had found that *Wrong* apparently had a much smaller effect in weakening connections than *Right* had in strengthening them. But Thorndike's conclusion can be faulted: he typically used an incorrect baseline for computing repetition effects (the correct baseline is the repetition probability when the subject's initial response is followed by neither *Right* nor *Wrong*); when the correct baseline is used, the effects of *Right* and *Wrong* appear more symmetrical (see the results of Tilton in Figures 2.3 and 2.4).

Having dealt with Thorndike's criticisms of the informational hypothesis, let us briefly review a few experiments on human learning which seem to support that hypothesis in contradiction to Thorndike's interpretation of the law of effect.

Buchwald's delayed-information experiment. An ingenious experiment by Buchwald (1967) tested a rather critical difference between the satisfier and information theories of reward. Consider the standard Thorndikean two-trial experiment in which words are presented and the subject guesses digits, as illustrated before in Table 2.1. Some of Buchwald's subjects received immediate feedback of *Right* or *Wrong* following each S-R event on Trial 1. However, a novel procedure was used with his other subjects; on Trial 1, they made guesses to each stimulus word but were told nothing (neither *Right* nor *Wrong*) at that time. But on the Trial-2 test which followed some minutes later, when shown a stimulus word, they were then told, "The response you made to this word on the previous trial was Right (or Wrong)." They then gave their Trial-2 response. Let us call this the delayed-information condition.

Thorndike's analysis expects that subjects receiving immediate feedback for their response on Trial 1 will show larger changes in response probability than will those subjects receiving very delayed information; for Thorndike, the satisfier or annoyer had to occur just after the S-R connection to influence its strength. But the Buchwald-Estes analysis predicts just the opposite result, that subjects receiving delayed information should show greater changes in response-repetition probabilities due to being told *Right* or *Wrong* than will the subjects receiving immediate feedback. To see the reasoning, consider the case where the stimulus word is *sky*. The subject's response is 4, and the experimenter immediately says *Wrong*. The possible connections formed here are *sky*-4, *sky*-*Wrong*, and 4-*Wrong* (the latter association is useless, since, with the typically large number of items, any specific response such as "4" would be often right and often wrong). On the next trial, in order to show an effect of *Wrong* in reducing repetition of *sky*-4, the person has to remember *sky*-4 and *sky*-*Wrong*, and use the latter to prevent his giving the response 4 to *sky*. To the extent that the

immediate-feedback subject forgets the *sky*-*Wrong* association, he will repeat *sky*-4 at the baseline probability. Consider now the case with delayed information; here the subject may remember that he said 4 to *sky* on Trial 1 and now is told before he responds on Trial 2 that this earlier response was wrong. He can therefore inhibit response 4 to *sky*. Clearly, the delayed-information subject need only remember his earlier S-R association in order to inhibit that R, whereas the immediate-feedback subject needs to remember both his earlier S-R association and the S-O association from the prior trial to inhibit that R to that S. Since they need to remember more to reject 4 to *sky* on the second trial, the immediate-feedback subjects are therefore expected to show less of an effect of *Right*-*Wrong* than the delayed-information subjects.

The results of Buchwald's experiment (1967) and of a replication (noted in Estes, 1969a) confirmed the predictions from the informational analysis: repetition of the Trial-1 response was increased for the delayed-*Right* over the immediate-*Right* condition, whereas repetition was reduced more for the delayed-*Wrong* than for the immediate-*Wrong* condition. The upshot, then, is a strong confirmation for the information hypothesis in contrast to Thorndike's interpretation of satisfiers as directly stamping in S-R connections which they follow.

Estes's "never-right" experiment. In the typical trial-and-error learning experiment, the stimulus, response and reward events typically occur together so that the learning of the S-R unit and that of the S-R-O unit are inextricably confounded. Estes contrived a situation "in which the subject could learn relationships between stimulus-response combinations and reward values without any possibility of a direct strengthening effect of the latter upon the former" (Estes, 1969a, p. 75). In the experiment,

TABLE 2.2. Design of "never-right" experiment. Alphabetic letters stand for distinct nonsense syllables, and digits represent the monetary points assigned. (From Estes, 1969a.)

Stimulus	Value Assigned	Informational Condition	Reward on Correct
a	1, 2	Random	1, 2
b	3, 4	Random	3, 4
c	1, 2	Never right	0
d	3, 4	Never right	0
e	1	Uniform	1
f	2	Uniform	2
g	3	Uniform	3
h	4	Uniform	4
$i, j, \cdots, p$	0	Uniform	0

the subjects were shown eight pairs of nonsense syllables over repeated trials; within each pair, one syllable (i through p in Table 2.2) had a value of zero whereas the other syllable (a through h in Table 2.2) was worth a certain number of points (1, 2, 3, 4) when chosen. The various assignments are shown in Table 2.2. The syllables are represented in the table by alphabetic letters. Syllables e through p are easily understood; they were uniformly paired with 1, 2, 3, 4, or 0 points, respectively, as indicated in the table. Now in order to win the indicated number of reward points, the subject had to first select the correct syllable (as contrasted to the 0-point alternative in each pair) and then indicate correctly how many points the chosen syllable was worth. For example, in a typical trial, syllable f (worth 2 points) might be presented along with syllable n (worth 0 points); the person could receive 2 points only if she chose f *and* said it was worth 2 points; any other sequence (e.g., f and a guess of 3 points) was penalized by receiving no points. The correct value for the chosen syllable was always displayed at the end of

the trial. This procedure obviously induces the subject to learn the payoffs associated with each syllable.

Along with these uniform-payoff syllables, four other stimuli, a, b, c, and d, have two different point values associated with them as indicated in Table 2.2. For the "random" stimuli, a and b, the experimenter decided in advance to say one or the other value on a random half of the trials regardless of the subject's guess; on the average, once the subject learned the two values associated with syllables a and b, she would receive reward half the time.

The critical items are c and d, the never-right items, which were also assigned two different point values. For a test card like c versus k, if the subject chose c and guessed any value other than 1 or 2, then she received no points and a value of 1 or 2 was indicated randomly as the correct value for that trial. But if the subject chose c and guessed 1 point, the assigned points were said to be 2 on that trial; if she had said 2 points for c, the experimenter would have said that 1 was the correct value for that trial. In either case, the subject received no reward on trials when she chose *c* or *d*; it was just that she was led to expect that *c* and *d* are "valuable" syllables (in comparison to the uniform-0 syllables), but that she had been unlucky in not guessing the correct value on these particular training trials.

It will be recalled that this unorthodox procedure was used to avoid the usual confounding between the learning of information about what outcomes follow given S-R events and the strengthening effect of that outcome on the S-R connection. The events surrounding the subject's choice of the never-right items give the subject information about possible reward magnitudes but never give her the "satisfaction" of receiving that reward.

The subjects were trained on this eight-item list until they completed two trials of choosing the correct syllable of each pair and correctly anticipating its value (or one of its two values). A first result worth noting is that the rate of learning (to choose the correct syllable) was the same for the random and the never-right conditions. Thus, obtaining the "satisfaction" of receiving points for one's choice promoted no faster learning of that choice than did receiving information about how many points one might have received had one guessed properly. The more critical results came from a series of test trials, in which the syllables used in training were recombined into various choice sets; the same point assignments were used, only they were not shown during the test series. The person was told to choose so as to maximize the points she would earn, which she was to be paid at the end of the test series. The variety of different test pairs is summarized in Table 2.3 along with the percentage in a direct choice pair. The marginal entry gives the average proportion of time that the row stimulus was chosen over all the competitors with which it was paired.

The information theory supposes that subjects will select that alternative which they anticipate will lead to the larger reward. Such is clearly upheld for the uniform items (see the marginal entries in the last column): frequency of choosing an item (*e* through *h*) increases directly with its assigned payoff. Even the random items appear to fall (in choice value) at about the average of the values for the corresponding uniform items.

The significant data for the information theory concern how the never-right items *c* and *d* are treated during the test series. The important result is that the never-right items seem to behave almost exactly like the randomly rewarded items with the same point values. For example, R(3, 4) and NR(3, 4) have about the same average preference, neither being preferred over the other (see the .56 of row 4, column 2, where .50 would indicate equality of preference for the two alternatives). NR(1, 2) is preferred to U1, but NR(3, 4) beats NR(1, 2) by about the same degree as R(3, 4) beats R(1, 2). Finally, averaging the two comparisons of random with never-right items, the mean preference is only .52 for the random conditions. In all respects, then, subjects appear to treat these two classes of items as equivalent in value or attractiveness.

The test data in Table 2.3 show that reward value is very effective in producing systematic differences in the responses selected; the subjects were acutely sensitive to relatively slight variations in reward values. Therefore, the absence of a difference between the random and never-right conditions makes all the more credible the informational analysis of reward effects. For items in these two conditions, the subject had equal opportunities to associate the same reward values with choice of the syllable. The only feature that differed between the two conditions is that for the never-right items the subjects in fact never received the satisfying aftereffect of any

TABLE 2.3. Choice proportions of row over column stimuli in the "never-right" experiment. Entries symmetrical about the main diagonal add to 1.00. R refers to Random payoff, U to Uniform payoff, and NR refers to Never Right items. (From Estes, 1969a.)

Stimulus	Reward Condition	a	b	c	d	e	f	g	h	Average
a	R (1, 2)	—	.02	.61	.05	.85	.19	0	0	.25
b	R (3, 4)	.98	—	1.00	.44	1.00	.95	.79	.05	.74
c	NR (1, 2)	.39	0	—	.01	.76	.04	0	0	.17
d	NR (3, 4)	.95	.56	.99	—	.95	.92	.74	.01	.73
e	U1	.15	0	.24	.05	—	.04	0	0	.07
f	U2	.81	.05	.96	.08	.96	—	0	.01	.41
g	U3	1.00	.21	1.00	.26	1.00	1.00	—	.02	.64
h	U4	1.00	.95	1.00	.99	1.00	.99	.98	—	.98

monetary payoff. Thus, the notion of "satisfiers" cannot be evoked to explain any direct strengthening of the subject's choosing a never-right syllable. Learning occurs and anticipated rewards have their appropriate selective function in performance, all without the aid of any direct satisfying aftereffects of a rewarded connection.

The conclusion of this and several other studies by Estes (1969a) is that the informational (or "ideational") interpretation of the law of effect is consistently supported. Learning of S-R, S-O, and R-O associations seems to proceed independently of the value of the outcome, O. The assigned value of the outcome influences performance; that is, the anticipation of a highly valued outcome provides facilitative feedback to energize an S-R connection. Anticipation of nonreward or punishment to a stimulus provides inhibitory feedback that blocks or prevents the S-R connection from firing the response. Along with such a theory, of course, one needs some ideas about what kinds of outcomes will be valued or what causes their relative values to change, depending on the subject's state. Such matters are usually discussed under the heading of "motivation."

Although the data confirming the information hypothesis have been presented only for experiments involving human verbal learning, the presumption is that a similar analysis of reward-punishment effects can be made for conditioning experiments with animals (see the earlier Thorndike quotation stating the ideational hypothesis). In fact, many theories of instrumental (operant) conditioning do make just this analysis of reward effects (e.g., Logan, 1960; Mowrer, 1960; Spence, 1956): contiguity of experience (with "belonging") between a stimulus and a response is presumed to suffice to strengthen the association between the two; rewards and punishments act to influence performance of the instrumental response by virtue of being anticipated just prior to occurrence of the response. These views, which have been arrived at after much sifting of experimental data, make central use of the distinction between learning (of an S-R connection) and performance—roughly, between *knowing how* to do something versus actually *doing* it. At the time Thorndike was working and thinking, this learning-performance distinction was neither well formulated nor believed to be critical. Later, Tolman (see Chapter 11) was one of the first major theorists to give the learning-performance distinction a central position in hypotheses regarding learned behavior.

Learning Without Awareness?

One final issue will be discussed because it stems from Thorndike's views and still excites the curiosity of modern experimentalists. This issue regards the alleged "automatic" action of a reward or punisher in influencing the S-R connection which it follows. Thorndike believed that aftereffects exerted their influence in this automatic fashion, acting to strengthen behavior whether or not the subject was consciously aware of the contingency between his response and the rewarding outcome. The ideational, or informational, theory would seem more compatible with the opposite view, that subjects would learn to expect rewarding consequences for a response and hence alter their performances according to these expectations.

This issue has been argued most vigorously in verbal conditioning studies. In a typical experiment, the subject is asked to do some verbal task, such as to free associate, or say simple words, or compose sentences (using one of six pronouns in conjunction with a list of verbs provided by the experimenter). Usually, some irrelevant pretext is fabricated to elicit the subject's cooperation in this task—for example, he is told that the experimenter is recording intonation contours in the subject's production of different phonetic combinations. The experimenter monitors the words spoken for a while, to establish a baseline rate for productions of a given kind; then she begins unobtrusively to say *good* or *umm-hmm* (indicating approval)

whenever the subject says a particular kind of word (e.g., a plural noun of any sort). Usually during this period, the subject's rate, or probability, of producing instances of the rewarded response class increases. In some experiments, the reward contingency may be terminated for a period, during which time the response rate drops back to the baseline rate. This basic experiment has been done many times with many different types of responses, different types and scheduling of reinforcers following the critical responses, and with variations in instructions.

The procedure in such experiments, with free-flowing speech, ill-defined response categories, and subtle, unobtrusive, symbolic rewards, is not conducive to high levels of conditioning. Roughly speaking, it is difficult for the subject to isolate and rehearse the relevant S-R-O events. There are indeed rather wide individual differences in sensitivity to the reinforcement contingencies, with some subjects conditioning very readily and others not at all. It turns out that this degree of conditioning correlates fairly well with the subject's "awareness" as measured by his self-reports on a questionnaire administered at the end of the conditioning session. The questionnaire probes for the person's knowledge of what was really happening in the experiment: "Was the experimenter saying anything? If so, what? When? Were you selecting your words according to any particular rule? What? Why? Did you notice yourself saying particular words more than others? If so, why? Do you feel as though the experimenter were trying to influence what you said? If so, how?" Such questions can vary from general and vague to detailed and leading, and experimenters have varied in the type and extent of questioning.

To illustrate how awareness of the response-reward relationship may relate to the extent of verbal conditioning, Figure 2.5 shows results from a plural-noun study by DeNike and Spielberger (1963) where

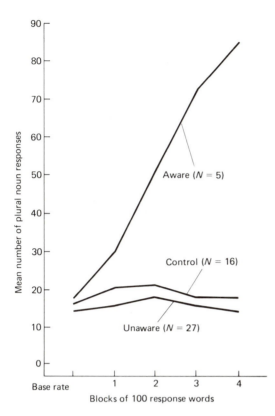

Figure 2.5. The role of awareness in the effectiveness of verbal conditioning procedures. Subjects who showed awareness of the experimenter's saying "Good" increased their production of plural nouns. Other subjects who were not aware showed no change in rate, but behaved just like the control group. (From DeNike & Spielberger, 1963.)

the experimental group was divided on the basis of their answers on the postexperimental questionnaire into aware and unaware subjects. Data on the two groups are plotted separately in the figure. The control subjects simply produced words without the experimenter's rewarding any responses and these subjects show a steady base rate of plural noun productions throughout the experiment.

The significant feature is the high level of conditioning for the aware subjects in contrast to the virtual absence of conditioning for the unaware subjects; the unaware subjects do not differ from the nonreinforced control subjects. Such results as these suggest that human subjects try to figure out what is going on in such experiments, and if they can get the right hypothesis (i.e., infer that the experimenter says "Good" whenever they say a plural noun), then they will "instruct themselves" to produce plural nouns if they want the experimenter to say "Good" to them. The most detailed formulation of this volitional hypothesis is given by Dulany (1968); a critical paper by Brewer (1974) argues convincingly that all human conditioning results can be readily explained with this volitional hypothesis.

The alternative position is that human learning *can* occur without awareness of reinforcement contingencies, although it may not be such a dramatic performance change as is produced by an explicit self-instruction to produce responses of a specific class. The proponents of this view such as Kanfer (1968) point to the less-than-perfect correlation between verbal reports of awareness and level of conditioning, or they emphasize cases in which the critical response rates change without much awareness apparent in the subject's reports. They take the position that the primary response (such as saying plural nouns) *and* the verbal self-reports are both to be viewed as dependent variables that are functionally related to a number of experimental variables, and that concurrent learning of the two types of responses (to say nouns *and* to describe the reward contingencies) could proceed independently but both be related to the same experimental variables.

Upon closer analysis, the verbal conditioning paradigm is quite ill-suited for settling this issue of awareness and learning, since the response to be influenced is normally under "volitional" control and since the response and its outcomes are both quite observable to the subject. The issue can be addressed more simply by studies in which the responses or their effects are not attributable to awareness for the simple reason that the action itself (or its outcome) is not observable. The former conditions have been arranged in experiments with human subjects by Hefferline and his associates (Hefferline & Keenan, 1963; Hefferline et al., 1959), and by Sasmor (1966). In these studies, very tiny, unobservable muscular responses, such as tension in a thumb muscle, detected by the experimenter through electronic amplification, were shown to be modifiable when these responses were made to produce a positive reinforcer (a monetary payoff) or avoid a noxious stimulus (the postponement of an aversively loud noise). The frequency of this unseen response increased and decreased appropriately during conditioning and extinction; and yet none of the subjects could identify verbally the exact behavior response that was producing the reinforcers. They were being conditioned without being able to state correctly what they were doing to cause the reinforcer to appear.

But interpretive difficulties still remain. The volitional hypothesis explains such results by noting that although subjects often guess incorrectly about what response is causing the reward to appear, they often have acquired some *correlated hypothesis* that causes them to alter the relevant movement. Thus, subjects in the tiny-thumb-tension experiments might believe that payoffs are delivered for slightly shrugging their shoulders, or imagining that they are writing a letter; these activities will cause correlated changes in tension in the muscles of the hand, which the experimenter records as conditioned miniature thumb movements.

It seems clear now that these two views are not so terribly different. Once one encounters the problems of measuring awareness, of specifying exactly how subjects

ever come to be aware of (or able to verbalize) the reinforcement contingencies, of specifying exactly how their describing to themselves the reinforcement contingencies leads to control of their overt responses—once all these issues have been squarely faced and answered, it then seems that the automatic S-R and the volitional interpretation are very similar except for differing emphases. This is not an infrequent happening in psychological theorizing. The question of whether rewards exert their influence in an "unconscious, automatic manner" turns out to be a rather poorly framed research question that has generated much experimentation and relatively little light. This judgment is not to denigrate the value of the verbal conditioning paradigm as a possible model for how reinforcement operates in all sorts of social settings involving verbal behavior, such as job interviews, psychiatric interviews, opinion polling, mental testing, personality testing, and psychotherapeutic sessions (see Krasner, 1962). For instance, studies illustrating how a psychotherapist selectively reinforces and punishes particular remarks of a patient, albeit often in an unwitting manner, are significant in revealing effective variables in interpersonal influence and attitude change within psychotherapy.

Thorndike: Educator with a Love for Facts

Thorndike taught in a school of education, training teachers, and so was constantly confronted with the challenge of using psychology to inform educational methods and policies. He was an empirical scientist in temperament; and, despairing of the vague philosophical issues surrounding many educational practices, he tried whenever possible to cast an issue into a form that would allow factual resolution. For example, Thorndike championed the ideas of educational measurement and clear statement of educational objectives. Thorndike gave great impetus to the scientific movement in education, arguing that educational practices be regulated according to verified outcomes of specific practices. His tremendous drive led to enormous output in fields as varied as handwriting scales, dictionary writing, methods in teaching arithmetic and spelling, intelligence tests, and vocational guidance. But the secret of his output was not only energy: the output stemmed also from his matter-of-fact conception of science, the notion that, in order to do something about anything, you have to know specifically what you are about.

This specificity approach helps you to roll up your sleeves and get to work. Consider, for example, all the complications involved in the teaching of reading. What is it that the child is to be taught? Philology? Grammar? Phonics? It took a Thorndike to propose a simple answer: "Words." With that answer, he proceeded to count the frequency with which each word occurs in samples of English texts, by tabulating millions of printed words from all manner of sources. He then arrived at the most common words. These are the words which must surely be understood. He made available lists and dictionaries to facilitate teaching the most needed words. A specificity theory like Thorndike's tells the educator where to look and how to measure in a baffling field such as schoolroom practices.

The specificity approach is also a source of weakness, and it has been the target of the most severe attacks upon Thorndike. The illustration above shows the kinds of criticisms Thorndike invites. Is language no more than words? Are the most frequent words really what we wish to teach? Perhaps we need to think of language as a means of expression, and therefore equip the child with the minimum set of tools necessary for adequate communication. The possibilities of this approach have been shown in the development of Basic English, wherein the central vocabulary of 850 words overlaps only in part with Thorndike's most frequent words. The approach of Basic English takes into account the organized character of language as an instrument for conveying meaning. Thorndike, true to association tradition, tended to think of language as a collection of words, which he then set out to treat quantitatively. As did all psychologists at that time and for some time later, Thorndike provided only a very superficial and inadequate analysis of language acquisition and language functioning. Part of the revolution in modern linguistics and psycholinguistics was the demonstration of complexities in language of a sort beyond the wildest dreams (or nightmares) of behavioristic psychologists.

Thorndike's objective, mechanistic bias pervaded his conception of the actions of rewards and punishments, and weakened somewhat his analysis of these phenomena. The notion that the law of effect works mechanically on all connections in the neighborhood of the rewarded one suggests that reward affects many activities other than the one intended. In hoping to show that the law of effect worked this way, he slighted the internal relationships between success and what the individual is trying to do; he overlooked the fact that satisfaction depends heavily on the learner's attainments relative to his level of aspiration. Although Thorndike did refer to the role of goals and interests in learning, he accorded them secondary status; his scientific preoccupations led him away from the internal relations of effort and success to the external relationship of any routine reward strengthening any connection that happened to be near it.

Thorndike's views about the role of learning by "understanding or insight" have also been controversial. He believed that understanding grows out of earlier habits, and the best way to program learners to have insight into a new problem is to teach them many connections relevant to the problem. Whenever situations are understood at once, Thorndike asserted, it happens by assimilation, by responding to those elements that the new situation has in common with the old situation, where old habits were appropriate. Thorndike's subordination of insight and understanding to drill and habit generated much debate in education. While he thought insight very rare in animals—perhaps rarer than it actually is—he did not deny insight in humans. He was not awed by it, and thought it best understood by the same associative laws as applied in other situations. Just as erroneous inferences are made because of habitual associations which throw learners off their course, so the insights of the genius are made by appropriate habitual associations and analogies. He had this to say of reaction to novel situations:

> There is no arbitrary hocus pocus whereby man's nature acts in an unpredictable spasm when he is confronted with a new situation. His habits do not then retire to some convenient distance while some new and mysterious entities direct his behavior. On the contrary, nowhere are the bonds acquired with old situations more surely revealed in action than when a new situation appears (1913, p. 29).

Although this comment is true enough, Thorndike's failure to describe the way in which past habits are utilized in problem solution, to consider what arrangement of elements makes a problem hard, what easy, when the same essential bonds are involved, is a genuine limitation. The difference is a real one for school practice. For instance, in this context it is possible to learn number combinations first (establish the "bonds"), then acquire some glimmer of understanding of number concepts, then comprehend arithmetic operations like addition in terms of sets, and then learn multiplication. In the end, you come out

at the same place, knowing the multiplication tables and knowing how to use them. However, it is not a foregone conclusion that the one method of teaching will be more efficient than the other, either for the students knowing precisely what has been taught or for their being able to apply it in new situations. Thorndike's preoccupation with bonds has insured that we turn to others, not Thorndike's followers, for a more careful appraisal of the role of meaning and understanding in normal learning.

SUPPLEMENTARY READINGS

Thorndike was a prolific writer. His bibliography appears in two parts in the *Teachers College Record:* for the years 1898 to 1940 in volume 41 (1940), pages 699–725; for the years 1940 to 1949 in volume 51 (1949), pages 42–45. The total comes to more than 500 items.

The following books contain his major contributions to learning theory, with much supporting experimental data:

THORNDIKE, E. L. (1911). *Animal intelligence.*

THORNDIKE, E. L. (1913). *Educational psychology: The psychology of learning.* Vol. II.

THORNDIKE, E. L. (1922). *The psychology of arithmetic.*

THORNDIKE, E. L., et al. (1928). *Adult learning.*

THORNDIKE, E. L. (1931). *Human learning.*

THORNDIKE, E. L. (1932a). *The fundamentals of learning.*

THORNDIKE, E. L. (1935). *The psychology of wants, interests, and attitudes.*

THORNDIKE, E. L. (1949). *Selected writings from a connectionist's psychology.*

The following biography of Thorndike is also recommended:

JONCÍCH, G. (1968). *The sane positivist: A biography of Edward L. Thorndike.*

3
PAVLOV'S
CLASSICAL CONDITIONING

Conditioned reflexes were first studied experimentally by the distinguished Russian physiologist, Ivan Petrovich Pavlov (1849–1936), who gave them their name. Although he did not begin his investigations of conditioned reflexes until he was fifty years old, he spent the rest of his long life in laboratory investigations of them, eventually with a research staff that numbered well over 100 professionals and assistants. His influence upon learning theory has been considerable outside the Soviet Union as well as within it; the prominent place of conditioned reflex concepts in American theories will become abundantly clear in the ensuing chapters presenting the views of Guthrie, Skinner, and Hull.

Pavlov's classical experiment is by now familiar to every student. When meat powder is placed in a dog's mouth, salivation takes place: the food is the *unconditioned stimulus* (US) and the salivation the *unconditioned reflex* (UR). Then some arbitrary stimulus, such as a light, is combined with the presentation of the food. Eventually, after repetition and the correct time relationships, the light will evoke salivation independently of the food: the light has become a *conditioned stimulus* (CS) and the

response to it is called a *conditioned reflex*. American psychologists have tended to use the words *conditioned response* (CR) instead of *conditioned reflex*, but the difference in terms is not very important.

Pavlov began his scientific career with investigations of heart circulation, then turned to the study of the physiology of digestion, for which we was awarded the Nobel Prize in 1904. The main work on conditioned reflexes began in 1899 with the publication of Wolfson's thesis, done under Pavlov's direction, entitled "Observations upon salivary secretion" (Pavlov, 1927, p. 412). The newly discovered reflexes were then called "psychic secretions" to distinguish them from the unlearned physiological reactions. Pavlov wrote two books on this work in the next quarter of a century; they were translated into English under the titles *Conditioned reflexes* (1927) and *Lectures on conditioned reflexes* (1928). At the time these books were written, Pavlov was already seventy-five, but he now became interested in psychiatry, and in the remaining years of his life spent a good deal of time making observations in mental hospitals and attempting to parallel some of his observations with experiments upon dogs in his laboratory. His later papers were collected and published in several volumes.

Anticipations of Conditioning

Modern experimental psychology developed under the influence of association theory, which had its origins in the work of the English empirical philosophers—Locke, Hobbes, Berkeley, Hume, Hartley, and the Mills. Ever since Aristotle, the laws of association have tended to be stated as those of temporal contiguity, similarity, and contrast of the elements to be associated. Over time, association by contiguity came to be considered the primary principle, and it was given apparent physiological form, as in this quotation:

> When two elementary brain processes have been active together or in immediate succession, one of them on reoccurring tends to propagate its excitement into the other (James, 1890, I:566).

If, as in this statement from William James, we emphasize contiguous events and state their association as one between brain states, we are not far from Pavlov's conception of the conditioned reflex.

The fundamental facts of conditioning were known before anyone attempted to do what Pavlov did—that is, to study exactly what happened and to vary the parameters that controlled the events. Whytt recognized "psychic secretion" over a century before Pavlov:

> We consider . . . that the remembrance or *idea* of substances formerly applied to different parts of the body produces almost the same effect as if these substances were really present. Thus the sight, or even the recalled *idea* of grateful food, causes an uncommon flow of spittle into the mouth of a hungry person; and the seeing of a lemon can produce the same effect in many people (1763, p. 280, as quoted by Rosenzweig, 1962).

PAVLOV'S EXPERIMENTS AND THEORIES

Some Empirical Relationships

Pavlov's contribution rests not so much on his discovery of the conditioned reflex or even on his theorizing about it, as in the care with which he explored numerous empirical relationships and thus determined the essential parameters and provided the background and terminology for countless succeeding experiments.

Reinforcement, extinction, and spontaneous recovery. The history of a simple conditioned reflex begins with its acquisition through repeated *reinforcement*—that is, the repeated following of the conditioned stimulus by the unconditioned stimulus and response at appropriate time intervals. Pavlov presented data from already conditioned dogs, so that the course of original acquisition is not commonly available from his data. However, comparable experiments show that the acquisition of a conditioned response follows an S-shaped curve, the initial portion of trials having few or no responses, then a rapid increase in responses, then some falling off in rate of increase. The curve of Figure 3.1 shows the initial acceleration, but the experiment was not continued long enough for the slowing down to occur as an asymptotic level of responding is achieved.

When reinforcement is discontinued and the conditioned stimulus is presented alone, unaccompanied by the unconditioned stimulus, the conditioned response gradually diminishes and disappears, a process that is called *experimental extinction*. Pavlov published numerous tables showing such extinction; the data from one of them are plotted in Figure 3.2. Note, however, that, after some elapsed time without further repetition of any kind, the conditioned salivation has returned; this is called *spontaneous recovery* of the extinguished reflex.

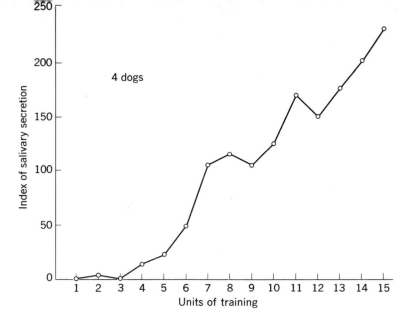

Figure 3.1. The course of acquisition of a conditioned salivary response. The salivation anticipated injection of morphine, which served as the unconditioned stimulus. Average results from four dogs. (Plotted by Hull [1934b, p. 425] from the data of Kleitman & Crisler [1927].)

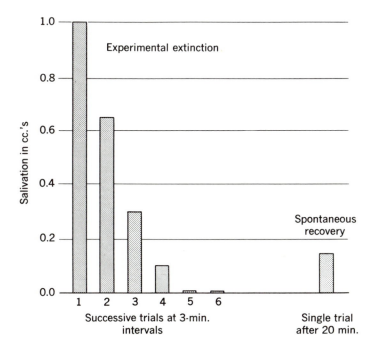

Figure 3.2. The course of extinction and of spontaneous recovery. The decreasing heights of the bars at the left indicate the fall-off in conditioned salivation as the conditioned stimulus (the sight of meat powder) was repeated without reinforcement. The bar at the right shows spontaneous recovery after a rest of 20 minutes. (From Pavlov, 1927.)

Pavlov's explanation of these effects will be discussed later.

Generalization of conditioning and extinction. In the process of conditioning, the response comes to be evoked by a broad band of stimuli centered around the specific conditional stimulus. The CR will occur on a test to a neighboring stimulus to an extent dependent upon the similarity of the test stimulus to the training stimulus. This is called *stimulus generalization*. Figure 3.3 shows an example: in this study by Hovland (1937), human subjects were conditioned to give a galvanic skin response (GSR, sweating of the palm) to a tone by pairing the tone with an electric shock. Following training, the subjects were tested with three tones varying in frequency (pitch) and lying differing distances from the training CS. This distance is measured by counting up the number of just-noticeable differences (JNDs) between the CS and

the test stimulus. Figure 3.3 plots the results, namely decreasing generalization of the CR to tone stimuli that are progressively more distant from the training CS.

Not only is there generalization of a conditioned response following training, there is complementary generalization of "non-responding" following extinction. Although first discovered by Pavlov, the effect can be illustrated much more clearly by another part of Hovland's (1937) experiment shown in Figure 3.4. In this case, subjects were first conditioned through intermixed trials to give a GSR to all of four pitched tones. Then an extreme tone was presented alone repeatedly without shock, so that the GSR to that tone extinguished (or became *inhibited*, as Pavlov would say). Thereafter, the subjects were tested without reinforcement with all four tones, yielding the results in Figure 3.4. This shows the lowest response amplitude to the extinguished stimulus (above zero JND), but progres-

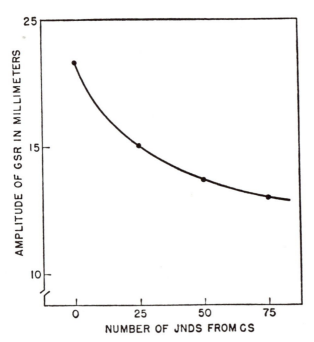

Figure 3.3. Stimulus-generalization gradient for the galvanic skin response conditioned to a tone of 1,000 cycles per second. (From Hovland, 1937.)

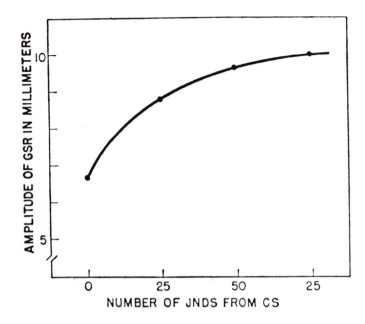

Figure 3.4. Gradient of generalization of extinction. GSR was conditioned to all tones and then extinguished to an extreme tone (at 0 on scale). Finally, tests were conducted with all tones. (From Hovland, 1937.)

sively less decrement (generalized inhibition or nonresponding) the farther the test stimulus is from the extinguished stimulus.

As we shall see farther on, Pavlov tried to explain generalization phenomena in terms of the spreading ("irradiation") of the positive effects of conditioning ("excitation") in the cortex between the neural action sites of the CS and the test stimulus. Similarly, the generalization of extinction effects to a stimulus was said to reflect spreading of inhibition around the cortical site of the extinguished stimulus.

Differentiation. A conditioned response that generalized to a wide range of stimuli would be quite maladaptive in situations that require a precisely tuned reaction sensitive to subtle or critical features of a stimulus situation. Consequently, *differentiation,* the complementary process to generalization, has great adaptive significance. Pavlov demonstrated repeatedly this process of differentiation, showing how initial generalization from a reinforced CS to a test stimulus could be overcome by contrasting

the two stimuli alternately over trials. That is, the subject receives a series of trials randomly alternating between presentations of the positive CS (called CS+) paired with the unconditioned stimulus and trials of the negative CS (called CS-) not paired with reinforcement. Eventually, after some fluctuations, the conditioned reflex occurs mainly to CS+ and little or not at all to CS-. The subject now *discriminates* between CS+ and CS-, whereas previously he had *generalized* his conditioned response between the two. Just as Pavlov discussed generalization in terms of underlying irradiation in the cortex, so he thought of differentiation as the corresponding *concentration* of excitation at the CS+ cortical site and of inhibition at the CS- cortical site.

Favorable Time Relationship Between CS and US

Conditioning depends upon the CS preceding the US slightly or occurring simultaneously with it. If the CS follows the US (so-called *backward* pairings), no excitatory (positive) conditioning results, though some inhibitory (negative) conditioning may result, depending on precise experimental arrangements. When the CS precedes the US by several seconds, it may terminate before the US (the so-called "trace" procedure); this usually results in poorer learning than if the CS continues into the US (called "delayed" conditioning). In either case, after acquisition the conditioned response begins to occur after the CS and before the US, with a latency proportional to the time interval between the CS and US. That is, the subject learns to withhold his response until a point just before the US is expected. The extent of conditioning varies in an inverted-U function with the CS-US interval. Figure 3.5 shows a typical curve, giving the number of conditioned responses during a series of unreinforced test trials, after training at differing CS-US intervals for cats conditioned to retract their forepaw. The CS was a tone and the US was a shock to the forepaw, eliciting retraction. The optimal interval for quick, phasic skeletal responses, such as the eyeblink or foot flexion, is typically about half a second. For automatic responses like salivation or the GSR, the interval causing optimal conditioning is longer, between 5 and 30 seconds depending on conditions. The explanation for the CS-US interval function, and

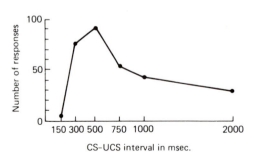

Figure 3.5. Total number of conditioned responses to extinction criterion as a function of the interstimulus interval. (From Wickens, 1973.)

its variation across response systems, is a matter for theories to address.

Uses of the Inhibition Concept

Pavlov used the concept of inhibition to refer to almost any decrement or loss in a conditioned reflex. He identified several decremental factors, naming each as some variant of inhibition. *External inhibition* referred to a temporary loss of a CR due to an extraneous distracting stimulus, as when a loud sound distracts the animal and reduces conditioned salivation to a light CS. *Internal inhibition* is a learned form of inhibition that is evoked by a stimulus paired with nonreinforcement under circumstances when the US is otherwise expected. For example, following conditioning, if the CS is repeated without reinforcement in the procedure called extinction, Pavlov would explain the waning of the conditioned response by saying that the CS now produces internal inhibition of the reflex. If a CS$^+$ is paired with reinforcement, in contrast to an alternate CS$^-$ presented without reinforcement, then the CS$^-$ is said to become associated with internal inhibition. If stimulus A alone is paired with reinforcement, and the stimulus compound A + B is presented without reinforcement, then stimulus B will become a *conditioned inhibitor,* meaning it becomes associated with internal inhibition. Pavlov thought of conditioned (internal) inhibition as a specific *antiresponse* force that is directed at stopping the specific response (e.g., salivation or eyeblink) from being elicited by the positive CS$^+$. As noted, Pavlov also believed that internal inhibition associated with a stimulus would generalize to similar stimuli.

Pavlov's Theories of Cerebral Conditioning

Pavlov was a physiologist, and so when he sought explanations for conditioning phenomena he appealed frequently to "higher nervous activity," by which he meant the physiological processes within the cerebral cortex. An early experiment in which conditioning was attempted in a dog whose cerebral cortex had been cut out convinced Pavlov that conditioned reflexes could not be formed in the absence of the cerebral cortex.[1]

Although many brain damage experiments were conducted and some anatomical localization of function was recognized, the main physiological processes described by Pavlov are *inferences* from behavior, not the result of direct studies of particular centers. For instance, when the "visual analyzer" or the "auditory analyzer" were mentioned, they were assigned only vague anatomical sites, and their properties were inferred primarily from the kinds of visual or auditory discriminations of which the animal was capable. Further, Pavlov referred to "pathological cortical cells" to explain deviant behavior, but did so without backing up his speculations with neurological observations. Contemporary neurophysiologists use modern electrophysiological, pharmacological, and other techniques for direct study of the brain, but at this point we are considering the theories Pavlov first enunciated years ago.

Association. Pavlov hypothesized that the connection between the excitation ("nervous arousal") produced by the conditioned stimulus and the center aroused by the unconditioned stimulus is the result of a kind of attraction or drainage of impulses from the first aroused center to the second, similar to the suggestion quoted above from William James. Presumably the direction of attraction is a matter both of time

[1] Experiments done much later showed, in fact, that relatively crude sorts of conditioned reflexes could be formed in dogs without their cortex; however, especially simple stimuli that require little processing, such as the flashing of a bright light, must be used. Such studies are reviewed in Chapter 14.

order (the conditioned stimulus arriving first and serving a signaling function) and of relative intensity (the unconditioned center, normally being more highly excited, attracts excitation from the CS center). What Pavlov called *conditioning* is what psychologists have called *association:*

> Thus, the temporary nervous connection is the most universal physiological phenomenon, both in the animal world and in ourselves. At the same time it is a psychological phenomenon —that, which the psychologists call association, whether it be combinations derived from all manner of actions or impressions, or combinations derived from letters, words, and thoughts. Are there any grounds for differentiation, for distinguishing between that which the physiologist calls the temporary connection and that which the psychologist terms association? They are fully identical; they merge and absorb each other (1955, p. 251; original date, 1934).

Irradiation, concentration, and reciprocal induction. Two fundamental nervous processes, excitation and inhibition, were hypothesized to manifest themselves in various ways; their interactions provide the basis for the operation of the cerebral hemispheres. Incoming impulses by way of afferent nerves and the lower brain centers finally reach some special cells of the cortex appropriate to the sensory system (analyzer) to which the afferent nerves belong. From these special cells the excitatory process irradiates to various other cells over a cortical area. This irradiation provides the basis for the generalization of conditioned reflexes among similar stimuli, through the overlap of the populations of nerve cells excited by the differing stimuli. The idea was that stimuli that are physically alike or psychologically similar will also activate neighboring places in the cerebral cortex. During discrimination training, irradiation was counteracted by the *concentration* of excitation back to the special cells of CS+ This differentiation through discrimination, in which the positive stimulus is reinforced and the negative one not, develops an inhibitory process associated with the negative stimulus that reduces the spread of excitation from the positive stimulus and concentrates it where it belongs. The inhibition to the negative stimulus also generalizes to similar stimuli, which can be demonstrated by showing that immediately after presenting the negative stimulus, the response to the positive one is also weakened. This is true in the early stages of the establishment of a differentiation; later, when both excitation and inhibition have been concentrated, *reciprocal induction* takes place. This phenomenon was rediscovered and renamed *behavioral contrast* in modern times (see Hilgard & Bower, 1966, pp. 514–18). In reciprocal induction, the effect of the positive conditioned stimulus becomes stronger when applied immediately or shortly after the concentrated inhibitory stimulus; the effect of the inhibiting stimulus likewise proves to be more pronounced when it follows the concentrated positive one. Thus the eventual cortical patterns are determined by the interplay of excitation and inhibition through irradiation, concentration, and reciprocal induction.

As noted earlier, the evidence Pavlov used in favor of his cortical theories was entirely behavioral; he never directly measured cortical electrical fields (it was not technically feasible at the time Pavlov was active), so his brain theorizing was purely conceptual and based on inferences from behavior. Hence, as the behavior of his dogs showed irregularities or great complexities, Pavlov merely complicated the presumed operations of irradiation and concentration of excitation and inhibition—for example, he stated that they waxed and waned in temporal waves and patterns following a conditioning session. By and large, the complexities of behavior that Pavlov described have not been securely replicated or accepted (see, for example, Loucks, 1933), and most psychologists regard Pavlov's brain theorizing as fanciful and lacking conceptual power for making novel predictions.

Types of nervous system. Pavlov hypothesized four types of nervous systems based on the presumed strengths of excitatory and inhibitory processes, how rapidly they shift, and whether they are balanced. These hypothetical types turned out to be coordinated with the ancient classification of temperaments that has come down from Hippocrates. Where excitation and inhibition are both strong, but equilibrated, two types arise. If the states are labile, the *sanguine* temperament results; if they are inert, then the *phlegmatic* temperament is found. If, however, excitation overbalances inhibition so that the processes are unequilibrated, then the temperament is *choleric*. Finally, when both excitation and inhibition are weak, whether the states are labile or inert, a *melancholic* temperament ensues.

While each animal has one or another of these temperaments, its actual character depends upon its experiences with the environment; thus character is "an alloy of the characteristics of type and the changes produced by external environment" (Pavlov, 1955, p. 260; original date, 1934).

Second signal system. While in his own work Pavlov did not give strong emphasis to the point, he recognized that the ability to use language greatly enlarged human potentialities, and later Soviet psychologists have developed these views extensively. The conditioned reflex mechanisms that human beings share with lower animals are grouped together as the *first signal system;* human language provides the *second signal system.*

> When the developing world reached the stage of man, an extremely important addition was made to the mechanisms of nervous activity. . . . Speech constitutes a second signalling system of reality which is peculiarly ours, being the signal of the first signals. On the one hand, numerous speech stimulations have removed us from reality, and we must remember this in order not to distort our attitude toward reality. On the other hand, it is precisely speech which has made us human, a subject on which I need not dwell in detail here. However, it cannot be doubted

that the fundamental laws governing the activity of the first signalling system must also govern that of the second, because it, too, is activity of the same nervous tissue (Pavlov, 1955, p. 262; original date, 1934).

In other words, if a flashing red light is a first signal for a CR, then the words "flashing red light" are a second signal that refers to the first signal, and which can enter into conditioned associations, too. Although recognizing some role for language, Pavlov did not develop these ideas experimentally or theoretically.

Pathological states. Pavlov was quite interested in investigating pathological behaviors. His initial discoveries of *experimental neuroses* in dogs were made quite by accident. A dog was taught to salivate to the presentation of a circle but received no reinforcement upon the presentation of an elongated ellipse. Then, over a series of trials, the radius of the ellipse was shortened, making it progressively harder to discriminate from the circle with which it continued to be contrasted. As the discrimination became exceedingly difficult, the dog's behavior became erratic, his discriminative performance became very poor, and he began to show signs of "emotional disturbance." Whereas he had formerly been trained to stand quietly in the restraining harness of the conditioning apparatus, he now began to struggle, moan, and bark. Eventually the dog became quite disturbed and resisted being taken into the conditioning laboratory. He had acquired what Pavlov called an experimental neurosis; Pavlov thought such disturbed states could be produced by a conflict within the cerebral cortex of the antagonistic forces of excitation and inhibition at closely adjacent sites.

Although difficult discriminations (involving reward versus nonreward) have not proved in later work to be the most reliable procedure, experimental neuroses of this general sort are easily produced in laboratory animals by placing rewarded approach behavior into direct conflict by punishing it. For example, a very hungry cat that has been trained to press a lever for a food reward can then be punished with a severe electric shock for pressing, with the result that it shows disturbed, conflicted behavior (see Masserman, 1943; Dollard & Miller, 1950). The study of such conflict and disrupted, neurotic behavior has been an interesting sidelight in the literature of learning theory.

This is not the place to go into Pavlov's views with respect to psychiatric pathology in any detail. He felt that the experimental neuroses in his animals were similar to neurasthenia in man, that persecution delusions corresponded to something like hypnotic states in the dog, that catatonic schizophrenia was a hypnoticlike state of inhibition, that manic-depressive reactions represented a derangement of relations between excitatory and inhibitory processes. Obsessional neuroses and paranoia he felt must be due to a pathological inertness of the excitatory processes of different motor cells.

Pavlov's leap from speculative brain physiology to confident statements about neuroses and psychoses appears much too pat to be taken seriously as scientific explanation. In summary, then, we find Pavlov accounting for a myriad of relationships on the basis of a clash of excitation and inhibition in the cerebral hemispheres, their irradiation and concentration, together with some characteristics of cortical cells, including their occasional inertness or pathological excitability.

DEVELOPMENTS AFTER PAVLOV

Pavlov was a centrally significant figure in the development of American behaviorism; behaviorists like John B. Watson (1916) took inspiration from Pavlov's work to use the conditioned reflex as the basic building block for their theoretical reconstruction of behavior. In Russia, Pavlov was an imposing, powerful intellectual giant who throughout his very long and active life heavily influenced the course of Russian psychology and physiology. A good deal of the research stemming from Pavlov's work concerned simple extension of the conditioning paradigm to new responses, new sorts of stimuli, new species of animals. With a little ingenuity, a psychologist can think of literally thousands of small problems to investigate, the results of all of which conceivably will be collated in some encyclopedia concerning all that is known about conditioning or learning of one or another species of organism.

Interoceptive Conditioning

One interesting development was the investigation of *interoceptive conditioning* within either human beings or higher animals. In interoceptive conditioning, the usual conditioning procedure is used, except that either the CS or the US (and UR), or both, involve stimulation of an internal organ such as the kidney, heart, or pancreas. It turns out that a fantastically large variety of internal organs can be conditioned to respond in the Pavlovian manner to a variety of internal signs. Bykov (1957) reports a number of such experiments. For example, a physiological stressor can be applied to a dog (as a US), producing hypertension as an unconditioned reflex, and this hypertensive response can become conditioned to any of a variety of either external or internal stimuli. Similarly, by use of drugs or special implanted electrodes, enhancements in normal activity can be reliably elicited from and conditioned in such organs as the pancreas (insulin release), the liver (glycogen uptake), the kidneys (urinary extraction), the bladder (urination), the heart, the stomach (flow of secretions), and the gall bladder, as well as in various and sundry endocrine glands (e.g., adrenals and salivary). It would seem that almost anything that moves, squirts, or wiggles could be conditioned if a response from it can be reliably and repeatedly evoked by a controllable unconditioned stimulus.

The fact that such interoceptive conditioning is possible is suggestive for interpretations of many so-called psychosomatic symptoms. For example, the man who becomes hypertensive when he thinks about a hated boss is understandable, as is the child who "gets sick to his stomach" at the thought of eating some food which earlier made him nauseous. Conceivably, the delicate balance in which our physiological systems maintain our inner milieu in constant equilibrium is coordinated in part by cross-conditional adjustments between the activities of interrelated organs or systems— i.e., a departure of one system from its equilibrium acts like an internal CS for an anticipatory adjusting CR in a compensatory system. In any event, these studies have shown that the organs inside an animal are just as conditionable as are those outside (albeit a bit slower because they have their "natural rhythms"). This generalization also includes special activities of brain cells themselves.

Inhibitory Conditioning

Pavlov proposed that, during experimental extinction, an active inhibitory process was building up and becoming associated to the nonreinforced CS, so as to overcome and impede the former positive response to the CS. He thought of this inhibition as becoming conditioned to the CS during extinction (or to the negative CS⁻ during differentiation training) and as being an *antiresponse* factor. American psychologists, especially Skinner (1938), looked at such data and questioned whether one really needs an active inhibitory concept: why would not simple *loss of excitation* account for all of Pavlov's data? Hearing no convincing answer, most psychologists held in abeyance their judgments on the utility of behavioral inhibition constructs.

In later experimentation, much evidence was found for existence of conditioned inhibitory factors in classical and operant conditioning. Some experiments by Rescorla (1969a) were particularly clear in demonstrating conditioned inhibition of fear or anxiety in dogs and rats. A necessary component of such demonstrations was an already conditioned response to some base stimulus to which was added an excitatory or an inhibitory stimulus, in order to assess the change in responding. In one demonstration by Rescorla (1966), dogs were first trained to avoid electric shock in a two-compartment shuttle-box by jumping back and forth across a middle fence. The shock was reprogrammed to start 30 seconds after each jump, with the shock coming on the side in which the dog was sitting. This contingency sufficed to keep the animals shuttling back and forth to avoid the shock. The number of crossings per unit of time was the measure of conditioning, and after much training the dogs settled into a fairly steady rate of responding. This was the baseline response to the shuttle-box situation which was then used to test later excitatory or inhibitory stimuli.

Following the avoidance training, the dogs received a phase of Pavlovian conditioning involving a tone and an electric shock. Each dog was penned into one side of the shuttle-box and given tones and electric shocks for several sessions. For one group, designated P for positive contingency, the 5-second tone was always followed by a shock. For a second group, called N for negative contingency, shocks occurred frequently and were unheralded by any stimulus, but a 5-second tone was *never* paired with, nor followed within 30 seconds by, a shock, so that for these subjects the tone served as a safety signal. For a third group, called R for random, the tones and shocks occurred independently of one another, at random times; for these subjects, the tone had no predictive validity for the occurrence of the shock.

Following these tone-shock sessions, the dogs were returned to the shuttle-box and continued their avoidance training. After stability of avoidance rates had returned, a series of probe-stimulus tests was given: the tone would be sounded for 5 seconds (not systematically related to the ongoing shock schedule) and shuttle responses recorded in 5-second periods for half a minute before and for a minute after the tone probes. The results averaged over several such tests are shown in Figure 3.6, showing average rate of barrier crossing in 5-second periods for six pre-CS (tone) periods, for the one tone period (marked CS), and for eleven 5-second periods following the tone period.

Group P (which had the "excitatory" conditioning of fear to the tone) almost doubled their response rate during the tone, while group N (which had the "inhibitory" conditioning of fear) reduced their response rate to about one-third the baseline. Group R which had no specific correlation between tone and shock showed no change in response rate to the tone. Following the tone probe, the response rates returned gradually to the baseline level of avoidance maintained by the shuttle-box shock schedule.

Thus, for group P the tone had become a reliable predictor of shock occurrence, conditioned to a fear reaction; when the probe tone elicited this anticipation of shock, that alone sufficed to kick off the shuttle-avoidance response. For group N, the tone had become a reliable predictor of absence of shock; it had become a safety signal, conditioned to inhibition of fear or relief from anxiety. Therefore, the probe tone reduced the dog's level of fear and thus reduced his rate of shuttle-avoidance, which is based on such fear.

There are more recent demonstrations of conditioned inhibition, using both classical and instrumental responses, so it is no

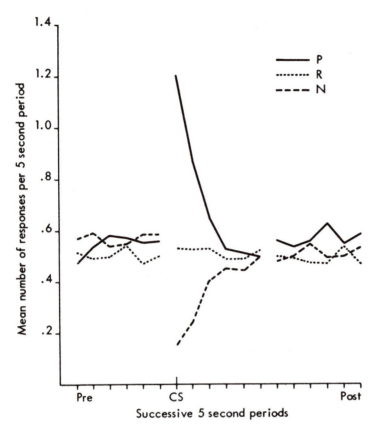

Figure 3.6. Mean number of responses per 5-second period in successive periods prior to CS onset, during the CS and the subsequent 30 seconds of differential conditioning treatment, and after the expiration of that period. (From Rescorla, 1966.)

longer possible to doubt the reality of such opposing or antiresponse factors that arise from negative correlations between the presence of a neutral stimulus (the CS) and the appearance of a reinforcing stimulus.

Inherent inhibitory effects of conditioning. What is even more remarkable is that later experiments have confirmed some of Pavlov's earlier observations that the positive conditioned stimulus (correlated with occurrence of reinforcement) comes to acquire certain *inhibitory* characteristics of its own. That is, as the conditioning experiment continues, the animal initiates pro-

cesses to the CS that oppose the CR and the UR. In a review of such paradoxical inhibitory factors in conditioning, Kimmel writes:

> The studies reviewed . . . support the conception that the acquisition of classical conditioning involves a distinctly negative component side by side with its more well-known positive characteristics. After the formation of an initial association of an excitatory nature, the CS gradually begins to develop inhibitory properties that result in attenuation and delay of the CR and even its ultimate total loss under continued reinforcement, as well as diminution of the UCR in the presence of the CS. This UCR diminution is revealed particularly by the technique of

omitting the CS and comparing the resulting UCR with UCRs observed (both before and after) when the CS is present (1966, p. 238).

The research reviewed by Kimmel mainly involved human subjects and noxious unconditioned stimuli like shock or an airpuff to the eye. In these cases, the person may come to steel herself or get prepared to receive the noxious US when the CS comes on, with a consequent reduction in UCR magnitude; the occasional US given without prewarning by the CS catches her unprepared, and elicits the full UCR it did at the onset of training. In this view of matters, the conditioned stimulus would come to evoke preparatory responses that reduce the effectiveness of the UCS, and these will often be in opposition to the excitatory CR. In fact, it now appears (Siegel, 1978; Schull, 1979) that there are a set of unconditioned stimuli (such as morphine injections) for which the unconditioned reaction goes in one direction (reduced sensitivity to pain) but the conditioned reaction goes in the opposite direction (increased sensitivity). Schull (1979) proposed that strong emotional stimuli that disrupt the internal milieu will set off compensatory reactions to counteract that disturbance; he further proposed that these compensatory processes can become conditioned. He proposed this as a mechanism for explaining *adaptation,* the lessening of an organism's response to a strong stimulus that is repeated many times.

Even with Pavlov's favorite salivary conditioning situation, there is evidence of inhibition in the gradual lengthening of the latency of the CR (its time of occurrence between the CS and US), with the CR sometimes totally disappearing, "receding" to that temporal point of the interval when the US is delivered. Pavlov (1927) mentioned such phenomena, which he called *inhibition of delay.* Sheffield (1965) and Ellison (1964) have replicated these effects in salivary conditioning with dogs. A usable

analysis of the situation proposed by Skinner (1937a) is that inhibition of delay results from the experimental subject's acquiring a more precise temporal discrimination regarding the time of delivery of the US (food) following the onset of the CS. The interval from CS-onset to US-onset may be conceived of as a stimulus continuum, with early-interval cues being associated with nonreinforcement while later-interval cues at the time of the US delivery become conditioned due to their reinforcement. This difference in reinforcement for early versus late CS-US interval cues may be conceived to set up two opposing tendencies. These are diagrammed in Figure 3.7. The early-interval cues (just after CS-onset) would become conditioned inhibitors, whereas late-interval cues would become excitors. The tendency to give the CR at any time within the CS-US interval would be given by the excess of the excitatory over the inhibitory tendencies graphed above that time in Figure 3.7. In this theory, the magnitude of the CR would be seen at its largest in case the customary US is either delayed or omitted on specific test

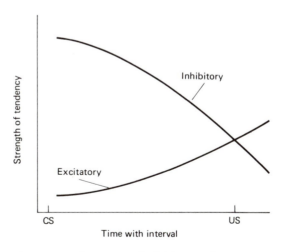

Figure 3.7. Illustration of inhibitory and excitatory tendencies associated to early vs. late portions of the time interval from CS to US.

trials. When this is done, a large CR appears at almost precisely the time when the US should have been delivered (see Ellison, 1964).

Second-Order Conditioning

The pairing of a neutral stimulus with an unconditioned stimulus results not only in its becoming a conditioned stimulus for the response but also in its becoming a reinforcing stimulus in its own right. Thus, what was formerly a conditioned stimulus (call it S1) can be used in a second pairing phase to condition another neutral stimulus (S2) to the same reflex. Pavlov (1927) first reported this phenomenon, which he called *second-order* (or *higher-order*) *conditioning,* since a first-order conditioned stimulus (S1) was being used to reinforce the response in pairings with a second-order stimulus (S2). A typical demonstration would involve teaching a dog to salivate to a light by pairing the light (S1) with meat powder (US); then, in a second phase, a tone (S2) would sound before the light (S1) but the combination would not be followed by meat powder. The temporal relationships and the four stages of conditioning are shown in Figure 3.8.

Higher-order conditioning is of considerable theoretical importance since it suggests a way to transfer reinforcing power as well as a response from one to another arbitrary stimulus without any primary reinforcement after the initial stage. This might explain, for instance, how symbolic rewards like money or verbal praise acquire their reinforcing value.

Although second-order conditioning was a theoretically useful concept, it was not subjected to intensive investigation until recent times in research by Rescorla and his colleagues (Holland & Rescorla, 1975; Rescorla, 1973, 1978; Rizley & Rescorla, 1972) and by Rashotte and associates (1977). Some experiments have studied second-order conditioning using fear based on electric shock; others have used food-anticipation indexed by the animal's preparatory responding. It appears that approximately the same learning principles apply to second-order as to first-order conditioning.

One interesting question concerns what the animal learns in second-order conditioning. Rescorla (1973) points out three possibilities: (1) the second-order stimulus (S2) causes the animal to expect the first-order stimulus (S1); (2) S2 causes the animal to think of the unconditioned stimulus

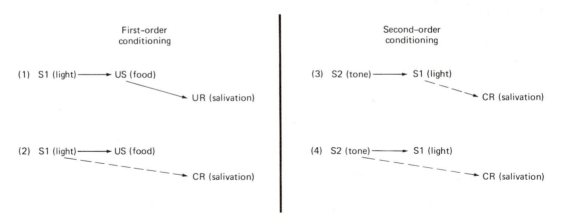

Figure 3.8. Illustration of first-order conditioning (light to food) and of later second-order conditioning (tone to light).

(US); or (3) S2 becomes directly associated with the response elicited by the US and by the first-order S1. Rescorla noted that evidence regarding the first alternative could be gathered by modifying the conditional properties of S1 *after* second-order conditioning of S2 to S1 had already been accomplished. In experiments by Rizley and Rescorla (1972), after S2 had been associated to fear in second-order conditioning, the first-order stimulus S1 was extinguished by presenting it repeatedly without shock. The question is, how would extinction to S1 affect the strength of conditioning to S2 that had been accomplished by pairing with S1? Rizley and Rescorla found no loss in the second-order conditioned reflex (to S2) due to extinguishing the first-order conditioned reflex (to S1), leading them to conclude that second-order stimuli do not operate by causing the animal to expect the first-order stimulus and thus to perform the first-order response in anticipation. This outcome was also obtained with rats in an appetitive second-order conditioning experiment (Holland & Rescorla, 1975). However, this outcome has not been obtained using pigeons undergoing second-order conditioning of food anticipation to visual stimuli to which they responded (Rashotte et al., 1977; Rescorla, 1978). In these latter experiments, extinction of the first-order stimulus following second-order conditioning led to substantial reduction in conditioned responses to the second-order stimulus. Current research is sorting out the procedural or species differences responsible for the differences in results.

A curious paradox arises from noting that the second-order conditioning procedure is very similar to the procedure by which S2 becomes a conditioned inhibitor. That is, S1 has been paired with the US whereas S2-then-S1 has not been reinforced with the US. How can the same procedure turn a neutral stimulus into both a positive CS for a response and a conditioned inhibitor for it?

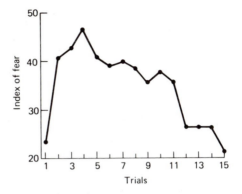

Figure 3.9. Progress of a second-order CS undergoing early conditioning followed by gradual extinction as it is differentiated from the reinforced first-order CS. (Adapted from Rizley & Rescorla, 1972.)

But the paradox is only apparent. The resolution is that the positive excitatory conditioning (that gives rise to second-order conditioning) proceeds rapidly over the first few trials of pairing S2 with S1, whereas negative inhibitory effects set in much more slowly (see Figure 3.9). Moreover, the development of conditioned inhibition to S2 depends upon the subject receiving many trials contrasting "S1-reinforcement" with "S2-S1-no reinforcement." Experiments of this type conducted by Rizley and Rescorla (1972), and Holland and Rescorla (1975), clearly show both phases. As Figure 3.9 illustrates, there is a brief acquisition phase of second-order conditioning of S2, then gradual loss of the CR to S2 over trials, as the nonreinforced second-order trials are contrasted with reinforced S1-alone trials. Eventually S2 acts as an active inhibitor. This is evident in that the conditioned response was larger to S1 alone than to test trials when S1 and S2 were presented together.

The recent development of powerful procedures for creating second-order conditioning provides psychologists with valuable tools for analyzing conditions of associative learning. Rescorla (1978), for example, has been able to show that the extent of second-order conditioning depends upon the similarity of S2 to S1 and upon the consistency with which S2 is followed by S1 versus S1' (where S1 and S1' are different stimuli conditioned to the same US). Rescorla has also investigated second-order discriminations in a procedure where one second-order stimulus is consistently paired with a positive excitatory CS and another second-order stimulus is paired with a negative inhibitory CS. These and related experimental arrangements promise to provide many new findings to inform our theories about association formation.

Classical and Instrumental Conditioning

Although some writers, especially physiologists, imply that learning and Pavlovian conditioning are essentially synonymous, this position is not generally held among psychologists. One kind of distinction that has arisen is between conditioning of the type studied by Pavlov, which has come to be called *classical conditioning,* and another variety that has come to be known as *instrumental conditioning,* or *operant conditioning.*

The distinction between classical and instrumental conditioning is that in instrumental conditioning the reinforcement on

a trial is made contingent (dependent) upon a critical response occurring, whereas in classical conditioning the reinforcement (US) is delivered independently of whether or not the subject responds to the signal. An initial example of instrumental conditioning was reported by two Polish psychologists, Miller and Konorski (1928), who taught a dog to lift its paw to a signal in order to get a food reward; they distinguished this training from the standard Pavlovian method. Hilgard and Marquis (1940) coined the labels *classical* and *instrumental conditioning,* which are currently popular. Other writers on learning have used different labels for the two types of conditioning; Table 3.1 gives some of these alternative labels.

As noted, in prototypical cases, classical conditioning and instrumental conditioning clearly differ in procedures, or in the scheduling of stimulus events. In classical conditioning, the US, or reinforcing stimulus, is contingent on presentation of the CS and is applied independently of any response the subject may make (although the subject herself may not think so). Also, the conditioned response that is measured is *usually* a fractional part of, or resembles, the unconditioned response elicited by the US. In instrumental conditioning, presentation of the reinforcer is typically contin-

TABLE 3.1. **Twofold classifications of learning proposed by different authors. (From Kimble, 1961, p. 66.)**

Author(s)	Term for Classical Conditioning	Term for Instrumental Conditioning
Thorndike (1911)	Associative shifting	Trial-and-error learning
Miller and Konorski (1928); Konorski and Miller (1937a)	Type I	Type II
Skinner (1937a)	Type S, or respondent	Type R, or operant
Schlosberg (1937)	Conditioning	Success learning
Hilgard and Marquis (1940)	Classical conditioning	Instrumental conditioning
Mowrer (1947)	Conditioning	Problem-solving

gent upon a specified response; for example, a hungry rat depresses a lever in order to get a bite of food. A discriminative stimulus may enter into this correlation: food may be given for a lever-press, for instance, only when a tone is sounding in the conditioning chamber, and not when the tone is off. (Skinner calls this a *discriminated operant.*) The operant response (the lever press) usually does not resemble the response to the reinforcing stimulus (eating and salivation).

The procedures differ somewhat in their obvious manipulable variations; for example, the CS-US interval is an inherent variable in classical conditioning, whereas the response-to-reinforcement interval (the so-called delay of reinforcement) is inherent in the instrumental conditioning paradigm. It is a remarkable fact that the dynamic laws of learning—acquisition, extinction, generalization, and so on—are very similar for the two types of learning situations; in most cases the term *reward* need only be substituted for the term *unconditioned* stimulus. Theorists like Hull and Guthrie denied that there was any real difference in the nature of learning in the classical and instrumental procedures. Other theorists (primarily Mowrer, 1947; Schlosberg, 1937; and Skinner, 1937a) believed that somewhat different response systems were typically implicated in the two forms of conditioning. Thus, behaviors were divided into those mediated by large skeletal muscles (such as movements of the limbs) versus those mediated by smooth muscles (such as the heart and glands) via the autonomic nervous system. It was conjectured that responses of this latter sort were involuntary, were elicited by unconditioned stimuli (for example, shock elicits arousal throughout the autonomic nervous system), and were conditionable only in the classical manner. On the other hand, skeletal responses are rarely under control of unconditioned stimuli, are "emitted voluntarily" rather than elicited by a US, and are condition-

able primarily by instrumental conditioning procedures. This was the standard "two-factor" theory which dominated learning theory in America for approximately thirty years after 1937. We shall have much to say about it in later parts of the book, the research surrounding it, and how it is being modified in the light of new conceptualizations. Suffice it to say that some persuasive arguments have been made against the distinction and that the theoretical distinction has generated much interesting debate (Terrace, 1973). But we are getting far ahead of our story.

Phylogenetic Comparisons

The conditioned reflex provided a usable methodology for the comparative study of forms of learning across many different species of organisms. In principle it can be a powerful tool in the hands of a comparative psychologist. Once a reliable unconditioned stimulus has been found and isolated, the technique can be used to investigate whether a given organism is at all sensitive to a given dimension of stimulus variation (for example, to discover if rats are color-blind), or whether the animal can learn conditional discriminations of a given complexity. Certain sorts of cross-species comparisons are prone to misinterpretation inasmuch as learned behavior is a function of many variables (temperature, drive level, naturalness of the testing environment, distracting stimuli, reward preferences) for which optimal values could well vary drastically across species. Therefore, comparative psychologists tend not to be so concerned with, for example, the relative "intelligence" of different animals in learning mazes of different complexities. They are rather concerned with how the behavior of a single species is affected by variation in several learning parameters; they are also concerned with whether organisms at a particular level of phylogenetic development are capable of showing one or another type of learning or learning phenomenon under the most optimal circumstances one can create for that animal.

Certainly since the days of Darwin, comparative psychology has worked on the implicit belief that there are various "levels" of learning abilities and different types or kinds of learning, ordered from simple forms (like habituation) to the complex (like learning verbal problem-solving). The belief, too, has been that these levels or types of learning are added progressively as one moves up the evolutionary scale, from simple one-celled organisms through various lower phyla to the primates and man. Comparative psychologists, particularly the Russians, as well as ethologists, have been patiently collecting and classifying such results for many years.

A review and theoretical perspective on that vast catalogue of data was completed by Razran (1971). He organized his presentation around an evolutionary hierarchy of learning types, summarized in Table 3.2. To indicate just briefly some of the learning types not yet discussed here, *sensitiza-*

tion refers to a great sensitivity (lower threshold) of a UCR due to its having been evoked recently; *configuring* refers to differentiation of specific patterns of compound stimuli; *eductive learning* is like predictive learning, which makes use of notions of object permanency; *symbosemic, sememic,* and *logicemic* are three stages of linguistic learning, from single words, to simple predications, to propositional connectives.

Arranging species in a scale from simple to more complex phyla, Razran attempted to show that more complex learning can be achieved only by organisms at a higher level in the evolutionary scale. This correlation comes about supposedly because evolutionary forces selected out variations in the species and so developed more highly structured organisms that can display higher forms of learning. A few of Razran's generalizations from the experimental studies are:

> Coelenterates are readily habituated but cannot be conditioned.
> Prevertebrate chordates and spinal mammals habituate, become sensitized, but likewise are not conditionable.
> Sensory preconditioning and learned stimulus configuring is possible only in birds and mammals.
> Eductive learning is possible with more intelligent birds and mammals (crows, magpies, dogs, and cats) but not in less intelligent ones (pigeons, chickens, ducks, and rabbits).
> Oddity and learning sets are largely primate behaviors, and symboling is an exclusively human achievement.

The general evidence clearly supports Razran's thesis of a hierarchical development of learning skills. Thus, not all organisms can be trained by classical conditioning techniques, although all seem capable of habituation. It is to Razran's credit that he undertook the painstaking job of collating and organizing the myriad facts available in the relevant Russian and English literature. The danger in such broad

TABLE 3.2. Evolutionary levels of learning according to Razran (1971, pp. 310—311).

A. *Reactive (Nonassociative)*
  1. Habituation
  2. Sensitization
B. *Connective (Conditioning)*
  3. Inhibitory (punishing)
  4. Classical
  5. Reinforcing (instrumental, operant, reward conditioning)
C. *Integrative (Perceiving)*
  6. Sensory-sensory learning (sensory preconditioning)
  7. Configuring
  8. Eductive learning
D. *Symboling (Thinking)*
  9. Symbosemic
  10. Sememic
  11. Logicemic

brushstrokes is that negative results are hailed as very diagnostic (e.g., that species X shows no learning of type Y); when in fact all we can conclude is that one or more attempts, with specific CSs, USs, and procedures, failed. The next topic to be discussed suggests that one must carefully sample the range of "ecologically valid" stimuli before reaching firm conclusions about what a given species can or cannot learn.

Equivalence of Associability

Psychologists have recently been interested in species-specific variation in what stimuli and what responses are readily conditionable (by classical or instrumental procedures) and which are difficult or impossible to condition. Previously, the standard position of learning theorists on this issue was what Seligman (1970) has termed the assumption of *equivalence of associability*. Roughly, it is the supposition that any stimulus the organism can perceive can be linked up to any response it can make, according to the standard laws of learning and with relative indifference to what is being linked to what. Some quotes from Pavlov suggest the position:

> It is obvious that the reflex activity of any effector organ can be chosen for the purpose of investigation, since signalling stimuli can get linked up with any of the inborn reflexes (1927, p. 17).

> Any natural phenomenon chosen at will may be converted into a conditional stimulus . . . any visual stimulus, any desired sound, any odor, and the stimulation of any part of the skin (1928, p. 86).

It is essentially this principle of equivalence of associability that accounts for the very arbitrary, almost barren and unnatural, choices of uninteresting stimuli and responses that learning psychologists have used routinely over the past eighty years. If the principle is true, then any stimulus or response lying conveniently at hand in the laboratory will do, since the same general laws should apply no matter what is used. Or so it was believed.

A number of learning theorists are now beginning to doubt this belief: certain critical data are appearing that clearly break the rule and do so with no dispute possible. Inklings of the matter came long ago, even in Thorndike's (1911) original puzzle-box investigations. Although his cats readily learned to pull strings and handles and to push buttons to escape the confining puzzle-box, Thorndike encountered inordinate difficulty trying to teach them to lick (wash) themselves in order to escape, despite the fact that coatwashing has a fairly high spontaneous rate. Seligman (1970) reviews many other examples. For instance, it is next to impossible to teach a hungry dog to yawn for a food reward or a rat to groom in order to get a reward, or to reduce a rat's "rearing on hind legs" by punishing it with a loud noise. Part of the laboratory folklore for many years has been that rats and cats will seldom learn or maintain lever-pressing avoidance responses, whereas allowing them to jump out of the apparatus to avoid shock is readily conditionable. Such matters can be passed off to one or another disturbing contaminant—a too-low initial response level, or incompatibility of the US-eliciting behavior with the response to be conditioned, or whatever. Scientists are rarely at a loss for post hoc excuses to salvage a cherished general principle.

Meanwhile, however, the evidence continues to grow that evolution has innately endowed certain species with an affinity or "preparedness" for connecting certain stimulus and response events and not others. The connections that are learned readily seem almost to have a clear evolutionary basis (e.g., fleeing to escape aversive stimulation); those for which the organism is "contraprepared" (to use Seligman's term) seem arbitrary and "unnatural." They are either unnatural in the sense of taking a response involved in one consummatory sequence (e.g., the courtship dance of mating doves) and trying to link it into a different motivation-reward system ("dancing" to get food to eat); or unnatural in the sense that a part of the organism's innate reaction to the reinforcing stimulus (or natural series of acts leading up to its consummation) is required to be eliminated and short-circuited in order to have efficient conditioned performance. Breland and Breland (1960) provided several striking illustrations of how their various animals kept intruding species-specific behavior patterns into the arbitrary operant conditioning tricks they were trying to teach them. To take an even further leap regarding species preparedness, Lenneberg (1967) has conjectured that the human child is naturalistically prepared or preprogrammed for language acquisition. All children learn language despite the typical absence of carefully arranged training contingencies. Lenneberg would suppose that language preparedness is a peculiarly human characteristic. However, this claim has been disputed by several investigators who have undertaken long-term projects to teach selected chimpanzees or gorillas to communicate symbolically with their human trainers. For example, Gardner and Gardner (1971) were the first to report training a chimp (Washoe) to communicate with them in American sign language. This manual language of the deaf was used rather than spoken utterances since chimps have only a crude vocal apparatus. Washoe learned to sign a name for visual objects, for arrangements of objects in relations ("orange in box"), and to sign to indicate her wants for food, water, play, and so on. Rather dramatic claims for the primate's language abilities have been advanced by sponsors of the several projects (Desmond, 1979).

Skeptics have countered that crucial aspects of "real" language are missing in the primate signaling data. For instance, the primates rarely sign spontaneously without prompting, rarely sign about objects that are absent, show only a rudimentary appreciation of the meaning of the signs, show little abstraction of sign use across situations, and show few, if any, syntactic constraints in generating strings of signs to compose a "sentence." Terrace (1979a, 1979b) has sharply criticized the primate language projects for inadequate data collection, and shoddy experimentation. He argues that, similar to demonstrations of extrasensory perception, demonstrations of true language in primates must be arranged with the utmost care to collect fake-proof, unquestionably solid evidence for important claims. In particular, double-blind tests should be used to insure that the "language of the chimp" is not all in the eye of the beholder (who knows what the chimp should be signing in a given context), and that the chimp's signing is not inadvertently prompted by well-meaning trainers. Terrace points out that current methods of reporting signing data are inadequate because they are strongly filtered through a sympathetic interpreter (the trainer) who knows what the chimp should be signing. The worry is that a random "babble" will nonetheless be seen by the sympathetic interpreter as communicating something sensible in a syntactically correct manner. The validity of Terrace's arguments, and ways to alter data collection in the primate projects to deal with them, are current topics of discussion and debate. Clearly, the attention given to the language-training projects indicates the scientific significance of the question of whether true language is mediated by neural mechanisms unique to the human brain.

To return to our earlier topic, a volume entitled *Constraints on learning* (Hinde & Stevenson-Hinde, 1973) reports and classifies numerous cases of supraprepared and contraprepared reactions depending upon the conditioning arrangement. As noted, the theme seems to be that a conditioning procedure is always introduced into a continuing stream of behavior which naturally occurs in a given motivational state like hunger and that the results of the conditioning procedure depend upon the way the to-be-conditioned response fits into things the animal would naturally be doing when hungry.

A study by Shettleworth (1975) is illustrative and noteworthy because she invested much time observing and recording the natural behaviors of her animals (golden hamsters) in a given test situation. By tracking the frequency and duration of twenty-four different response classes, Shettleworth could describe which ones increased as the animal became hungry and which ones decreased. With this information at hand, she then set out to condition instrumentally one or another selected response using food as reward for the hungry hamster, choosing responses that had comparable average spontaneous rates of occurrence before conditioning. Her results, depicted in Figure 3.10, reveal vastly different learning rates for six different responses. To identify briefly a few of the behaviors, "scrabble" refers to the hamster standing erect and scraping his forepaws against a wall of the test cage, "open rear" is rearing up on the hindlegs without touching a wall, "dig" and "wash face" are obvious, "scratch" of the body was done with the hind foot, and "scent mark" refers to the hamster pressing the scent gland in its flank against a wall with arched back and raised tail.

Importantly, the three behaviors that increased dramatically when rewarded with food were also the ones that increased somewhat when the hamster was made hungry and was anticipating eating; whereas the three behaviors (washing, scratching, marking) that conditioned poorly, if at all, were ones that had decreased when the hamster was hungry and expecting food. Also, the conditioned responses of these

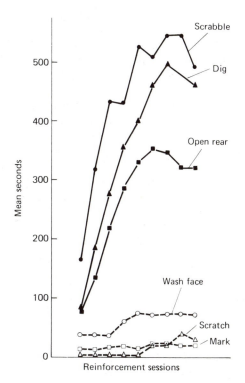

Figure 3.10. Mean time of a 20-minute session spent performing the rewarded response for groups of hamsters rewarded for one of six different behaviors. (From Shettleworth, 1975.)

latter forms that did occur became "unnaturally" abbreviated, almost as though the hamster's reason for scratching, for example, was shifting from "remove irritation of a flea bite" over to "get the food dispenser to operate." Shettleworth concludes that conditioning rates of different action patterns vary with how compatible the criterial response is in relation to those the animal would naturally perform when anticipating the reward being used. If the response to be conditioned is incompatible with those evoked by anticipation of the reward, then the arrangement creates conflict, interference, and low levels of conditioning.

Bolles (1970, 1972) had earlier analyzed

those cases where animals had failed to learn avoidance responses to painful stimuli, and had come to a conclusion similar to Shettleworth's. Bolles proposed that animals begin with a repertoire of innate defensive reactions to painful or threatening situations, which he called "species-specific defensive reactions" (SSDRs). For the rat frightened by shock, such reactions include fleeing, freezing, aggressively attacking some object, leaping up, circling about, and screaming. Bolles hypothesized that an animal will readily learn a specific escape or avoidance response to shock or fear if the response is one of its SSDRs (or closely compatible with one), such as fleeing or freezing, but will not readily learn a response that is not an SSDR. Bolles suggests that this perspective alters the traditional reinforcement analysis of avoidance learning. His analysis does not premise a direct association from the CS to an avoidance response; rather, the CS makes the animal frightened, which brings out a repertoire of SSDRs. The "correct" SSDR gets selected from among the others not so much because it removes the CS and reduces fear but because all the others are ineffective in the given experimental situation and are punished by continued shock.

Selective Association of Food Stimuli to Sickness

An apparent case of selective preparedness was demonstrated in experiments by Garcia and his associates (Garcia & Koelling, 1966). Thirsty rats drank saccharine-flavored water from a drinking spout that caused lights to flash and noises to sound with each lick. During the session, the rats were exposed to strong x-rays; this makes the animals feel sick and nauseated, but not until about an hour later. Subsequently, the rats were tested for their learned dislike (or conditioned sickness) to the light-plus-noise stimuli and to the saccharine-flavored water. It was found that the rats had acquired a strong aversion to saccharine-water but none whatever to the flashing light plus noise. The brain had picked out the novel saccharine taste rather than the "bright noises" to selectively associate to the unconditioned reaction of feeling sick.

It might be argued that for rats the saccharine taste is just a more salient stimulus than the light-noise combination. To rule out this simple excuse, Garcia and Koelling also ran a complementary experiment in which licking at "bright noisy saccharine water" was the CS, whereas a painful electric shock to the feet was the US. On a later test of the elements, the bright noise was now found to have acquired aversive properties, whereas the saccharine water had acquired relatively little association to the shock US. It thus appears that externally applied USs (the foot shock) are readily conditioned to external cues like flashing lights and buzzers, whereas internal UCRs like stomach upsets, nausea, and sickness become selectively associated to novel tastes. The basic results here have been replicated and extended by Domjan and Wilson (1972) and Revusky and Garcia (1970). Garcia has proposed in later work that this selective association of a novel taste to an induced sickness can occur over very long time delays (up to many hours), which is well beyond the range of CS-US intervals at which conditioning can be made to occur in the typical situation involving an arbitrary, phasic stimulus. When an animal becomes sick it is selectively biased, so to speak, to remember or "call to mind" the last novel thing it ingested, or distinctive eating place, and to associate that taste or eating place with its current sickness. In Seligman's terms, the taste-to-nausea connection is *highly prepared* by the innate wiring of the organism.

Later experiments have revealed several complications. First, the *novelty* of the feeding situation following illness is critical. Animals can learn to avoid external feeding cues followed by nausea (induced by a poison injection), but only if the feeding cues (such as a distinctive food trough for a rat) are relatively novel and are introduced into a testing situation to which the animal has been thoroughly habituated. Thus, after habituating rats for twenty-five daily sessions to eating wet bran mash from a given container and locale in a test cage, Mitchell, Kirschbaum, and Perry (1975) found that if the animals spent two sessions eating from a novel container and then were injected with poison, they would avoid eating from the novel container on following days. However, practically no avoidance of the novel container was produced if only ten habituation sessions had been given before the poisoning trials with the novel feeding trough. So the animal's ability to associate nausea differentially with an external feeding cue increases the more novel that cue is in relation to other feeding cues to which the animal has been habituated.

A second complication is that a bout of stomach sickness and nausea seems to make animals more shy of *any* novelty in taste or locale connected with eating. This general aversion, called *neophobia* (avoidance of new things), may go a long way in explaining some of Garcia's data that had appeared to show novel taste-to-nausea associations learned over extremely long CS-US intervals. If a bout of stomach nausea causes the animal to avoid any novel feeding situation, one need not invoke a specific association of a specific novel taste presented just before the nausea in order to explain the animal's aversion to the novel taste or feeding cues. For example, Mitchell, Kirschbaum, and Perry (1975) found that a single pairing of nausea with eating from a highly familiarized feeding container was sufficient to cause nearly complete avoidance of eating from a slightly familiarized (relatively novel) container over subsequent test days.

The discovery of neophobia in animals following nausea should not lead us to reject the whole idea of conditioning *specific* food aversions. Such specific aversions are legion (ask anyone what foods upset his or her stomach!). However, the neophobia findings do increase the experimental demands upon investigators who wish to demonstrate taste-specific aversions in conditioning experiments.

The facts reviewed in this section, showing different learning rates of different behaviors and selective association of internal versus external cues, clearly argue for abandonment of the assumption of equivalent associability. The facts themselves are not "explained" in any sense by saying that the organism is "prepared" or "unprepared" to make a given association, since that merely relabels the observation that the conditioning rate was fast or slow in particular cases. The more probable explanations are likely to be of an evolutionary-developmental type, which illuminate the adaptive significance of certain present biases on classes of events likely to be associated in the animal's natural environment.

ESTIMATE OF PAVLOV'S CONTRIBUTION TO LEARNING THEORY

Pavlov has had a major impact upon learning theory, particularly his systematic investigations, his theories of association, and his biases about what phenomena are worthy of investigation. He molded the *conditioning paradigm* of associations established by the pairing of stimulus events, and that paradigm has had a pervasive influence and seductive allure for the thinking of any student of learning.

Razran (1965) has summarized Pavlov's influence in paragraphs, which may be paraphrased as follows:

1. Pavlov stimulated an enormous number of experimental investigations using the paired-stimulus method, with all kinds of organisms, throughout their life spans and with a great variety of stimuli and responses. Razran estimated that by 1965 some 6,000 experiments had been performed using Pavlov's exact classical conditioning paradigm; these experiments had been reported in at least twenty-nine different languages, but most frequently in Russian and English.

2. Pavlov converted the general notion of associative learning by way of conditioning into a highly parametric area of study—that is, the quantitative influences upon conditioning interested him from the beginning. One illustration of this is the persistence of his terms to define the significant variables. In Kimble's (1961) glossary of terms relevant to conditioning and learning, thirty-one terms are attributed to Pavlov, and twenty-one others to all other psychologists combined.

3. Pavlov succeeded in getting the conditioned reflex adopted as the most convenient basic unit for all of learning. Although the desirability of this is a matter of some dispute, and other units compete with it (while some authorities question that there is any such basic unit at all), there is no doubt that it took a leading place for many years.

4. By introducing the notion of the second-signal system, unique to man, Pavlov prevented the system from being frozen at an unprofitable reductionist level, in which no distinction would be made between animal and human learning. Oddly enough, he accused the American psychologists of oversimplifying and of not being in tune with the complexity of actual events.

5. Pavlov's continuing interest in psychopathology, beginning in 1903 but evidenced particularly in his later years, opened up fruitful rapprochements between learning theory and psychiatry. Razran notes that of the six volumes in Russian reporting Pavlov's Wednesday seminars, three volumes, comprising 1,716 pages, are reports of clinical demonstrations in which he participated.

6. Even when the instrumental conditioning paradigm was introduced and studied, it was found that most of the parameters discovered in the classical conditioning paradigm still held. While there are some differences, the basic facts of reinforcement, extinction, generalization, and so on, are found to hold. Skinner, scarcely a Pavlovian, has found it possible to use many of Pavlov's terms in describing the functional relations within his variety of operant conditioning. While he went much farther than Pavlov in studying schedules of reinforcement, the first experiments on intermittent reinforcement were indeed done in Pavlov's laboratory. Because rewarded learning, which fitted the instrumental paradigm more nearly than the classical one, was characteristic of American studies of animal learning, Pavlov's work became more acceptable when it was found that most of the principles also held within instrumental conditioning.

Pavlov's Influence on Psychologists

Pavlov, in trying to make his studies purely objective, anticipated American behaviorism and later contributed to the behaviorist tradition in America. While he remained strictly within physiology, as he understood it, he was not unaware that he was dealing with essentially psychological problems, and in his Wednesday seminars he made many references to the writings of those psychologists he had read. He thought particularly well of E. L. Thorndike and felt that in some respects Thorndike's work had anticipated his own.

As far as his influence upon American psychology is concerned, by testimony of the American psychologists themselves, Pavlov ranks with Freud and Wundt as a major influence (Coan & Zagona, 1962). It therefore behooves the student of learning theory to know something about the man who is responsible for so many of the concepts of contemporary psychology, especially in the field of learning.

SUPPLEMENTARY READINGS

The following English sources cover most of Pavlov's major writings:

PAVLOV, I. P. (1927). *Conditioned reflexes*. Anrep translation.

PAVLOV, I. P. (1928). *Lectures on conditioned reflexes.* Gantt translation.

PAVLOV, I. P. (1941). *Conditioned reflexes and psychiatry.* Gantt translation.

PAVLOV, I. P. (1955). *Selected works.* Edited by Koshtoyants and translated by Belsky.

PAVLOV, I. P. (1957). *Experimental psychology and other essays.*

For shorter introductions to Pavlov's work, the interested reader can do no better than to read some of Pavlov's own summaries. His very early essay (1903) "Experimental psychology and psychopathology in animals" gives much of the later flavor; it can be found in Pavlov (1928), pp. 47–60, and in Pavlov (1955), pp. 245–70. A chapter by a devoted follower is Gantt, W. H. (1965), "Pavlov's system," in B. B. Wolman and E. Nagel, eds., *Scientific psychology* (1965), pp. 127–29.

Books that carry on the experimental tradition started by Pavlov, but make their own contributions, include:

BYKOV, K. M. (1957). *The cerebral cortex and the internal organs.*

GRAY, J. A., ed. (1964). *Pavlov's typology.*

KONORSKI, J. (1948). *Conditioned reflexes and neuron organization.*

LURIA, A. R. (1966). *Higher cortical functions in man.*

RAZRAN, G. (1971). *Mind in evolution: An East-West synthesis of learned behavior and cognition.*

For biographical material on Pavlov:

BABKIN, B. P. (1949). *Pavlov: A biography.*

FROLOV, Y. P. (1937). *Pavlov and his school.*

While much of the experimentation in American laboratories has departed from the classical conditioning paradigm, that there is still vigorous interest in it is shown by the following books:

BLACK, A., & PROKASY, W. F., eds. (1972). *Classical conditioning II.*

ESTES, W. K., ed. (1975). *Handbook of learning and cognitive processes: Vol. 2. Conditioning and behavior theory.*

GEIS, G. L., STEBBINS, W. C., & LUNDIN, R. W. (1965). *Reflexes and conditioned reflexes: A basic systems program.*

KIMBLE, G. A. (1961). *Hilgard and Marquis' conditioning and learning.* 2nd ed.

MACINTOSH, N. J., & HONIG, W. K., eds. (1971). *Fundamental issues in associative learning.*

PROKASY, W. F., ed. (1965). *Classical conditioning: A symposium.*

4

GUTHRIE'S
CONTIGUOUS CONDITIONING

In some respects, the system proposed by Edwin R. Guthrie (1886–1959) follows naturally from those of Thorndike and Pavlov. It is an objective stimulus-response association psychology, and uses the conditioned-response terms coming from Pavlov while being practical and relevant in the spirit of Thorndike. But in other respects, the interpretations of learning are very different. It is such similarities and differences which pose issues for learning theory.

GUTHRIE, THORNDIKE, PAVLOV, AND BEHAVIORISM

Thorndike accepted two kinds of learning: (1) selecting responses and connecting to stimuli according to the law of effect, and (2) associative shifting, wherein a response to one stimuli shifts onto another stimuli paired with it. For him associative shifting was a subsidiary principle, and by far the major burden was carried by selecting and connecting (or trial-and-error learning). For Guthrie, on the contrary, a conception like associative shifting became the cornerstone of his system. Guthrie did not accept the law of effect in Thorndike's

sense, and this was the basic cleavage between their systems.

Guthrie was an early behaviorist. Behaviorism as a school of psychology is usually thought of as originating with John B. Watson (1878–1958), who in 1913 announced the behaviorist position, and became its most vigorous spokesman for several years until his involvement in an adultery scandal forced him to resign from academia and take a job in commercial advertising. The behaviorists, then and now, had and have in common the conviction that a science of psychology must be based upon a study of that which is observable, physical stimuli, and the muscular movements and glandular secretions aroused by stimuli. The behaviorists have differed among themselves as to what may be inferred in addition to what is measured, but they all exclude self-observation (introspection) as a legitimate scientific method. (However, if studied as verbal behavior, much of what is called introspection can be saved for investigation.) Partly as a protection against an indirect use of introspection, behaviorists have tended to prefer experimentation on animals and infants. They conceive of themselves as biologists who happen to be interested in how organisms behave under various circumstances.

Watson's *Behavior: An introduction to comparative psychology* (1914) was the first book to follow the announcement of his new position. In it were his attempted refutation of Thorndike's law of effect and his substitution of the laws of frequency and recency in its place. He believed that animal learning, as in the maze or problem-box, could be explained according to what the animal had most often been led to do in the situation, with the most recent act favored in recall. Because the successful act was both most frequent and most recent (it occurs at the end of each trial in the puzzle-box), its recurrence on the next trial could be explained without recourse to an added principle of rewarding effects. This denial of effect was part of his program of getting rid of the residual subjectivity which he felt was implied in Thorndike's concepts of satisfiers and annoyers. While the frequency-recency theory did not survive telling criticism (Gengerelli, 1928; Peterson, 1922), it points up Watson's desire to find objective laws to substitute for those with even a tinge of subjectivism.

The behaviorist knows that other events intervene between measured stimuli and the response to them. In order to preserve a coherent position, these intervening events are posited to be much like the observed ones—that is, thoughts or expectancies are represented as *implicit* or *covert* stimulus-response sequences. In his early studies on rats' learning of maze habits, Watson (1907) had attributed great importance to *kinesthetic stimuli* as integrators of the maze-running habits involved. Because kinesthetic stimuli occur during the organism's movements, they fit well into a behavioral or response-oriented psychology. The unobserved processes inferred to be going on between stimuli and responses are said to be comprised of subliminal movements and movement-produced stimuli. This emphasis upon kinesthesis as the integrator of animal learning served Watson well when he theorized about human thought processes. He decided that thought was primarily a matter of implicit speech—that is, talking to oneself. Sufficiently sensitive instruments, he conjectured, would detect tongue movements or other movements that accompany thinking. Later technical developments indeed provided some support for these "miniature response" accompaniments to thinking (see reviews in McGuigan & Schoonover, 1973). Watson was thus able to hold to his consistent behaviorist position without denying that thinking goes on.

Watson later realized that the conditioned reflex of Pavlov might serve as a useful paradigm for learning (Watson, 1916). Because it grew out of the objective tradition within Russian physiology, it fitted his temper and he adopted it enthusiastically. In Watson's later writings, the conditioned reflex was central to learning, as the unit out of which habits are built.

Watson's general textbook, *Psychology from the standpoint of a behaviorist,* appeared in 1919. It was soon followed by other books written from an avowedly behavioristic standpoint. Among these was Smith and Guthrie's *General psychology in terms of behavior* (1921). Like Watson's book, it treated all of psychology from a behavioral viewpoint and made use of conditioning principles. It, too, stressed movement-produced stimuli as the substrate for much skilled action. Smith and Guthrie showed less concern than Watson for experimental and neurophysiological detail, but instead gave a plausible interpretation of ordinary experience from the behavioristic standpoint. Guthrie's later writings preserved the flavor of the Smith and Guthrie book.

Doubtless influenced by Watson, Guthrie

began to use the language of conditioning in his behavioristic psychology, but he chose to use what was learned from conditioned reflexes in a manner very different from Watson. Watson used the Pavlov experiment as a paradigm of learning, and made the conditioned reflex the unit of habit, building his whole system eventually on that foundation. Guthrie, unlike Watson, started with a principle of conditioning or associative learning, a principle which is not dependent strictly on the Pavlov kind of experiment. Pavlov, in fact, criticized Guthrie for his emphasis on the one principle of contiguity, without sufficient concern for the many complexities within conditioning (Pavlov, 1932). Guthrie (1934) replied, arguing that Pavlov's was a highly artificial form of learning, and what was found to occur within Pavlov's experiments needed explanation according to a more general principle.

CONTIGUITY OF CUE AND RESPONSE: THE ONE LAW OF ASSOCIATION

Guthrie's one law of learning, from which all else about learning was to be made comprehensible, was stated as follows: "A combination of stimuli which was accompanied by a movement will on its recurrence tend to be followed by that movement" (1935, p. 26).[1]

There is an elegant simplicity about the statement, which avoids mention of drives, of successive repetitions, of rewards or punishments. Stimuli and movements in simultaneous conjunction: that is all. This one principle serves as the basis for an ingenious and intriguing theory of learning.

A second statement is needed to complete the basic postulates about learning:

[1] Where the quotations from Guthrie remain unchanged between the 1935 and 1952 editions of his book, the earlier only will be cited.

"A stimulus pattern gains its full associative strength on the occasion of its first pairing with a response" (1942, p. 30). That is, learning should occur in one trial, in an all-or-none fashion.

This somewhat paradoxical statement, in view of the undeniable improvement in habits with practice, is a necessary adjunct to the theory, because it makes possible a number of derivative statements about learning and forgetting. We shall presently see how Guthrie explained gradual learning.

These postulates promote a kind of *recency principle,* for if learning occurs completely in one trial, that which was last done (was most recent) in the presence of a stimulus combination will be that which will be done when the stimulus combination next occurs. Equivalently, this principle says that retroactive interference (see Chapter 6) would be complete in one trial.

How could Guthrie demonstrate that more complicated forms of learning conform to these simple principles? His problem was to show that complex learning or insightful, purposive learning can, in fact, be derived from these basic principles along with auxiliary suppositions. It was Guthrie's task to show that each of these forms requires no new principles of explanation beyond the primary law of association by contiguity.

Why Strict Contiguity of Measured Stimulus and Response Is Not Essential

An important variable in standard conditioning experiments is the time interval between the conditioned stimulus and unconditioned response. As noted in Figure 3.5, the empirical results suggest a gradient, with a most favorable interval and less favorable intervals on either side of this optimal interval. The optimal interval varies from half a second to many seconds, depending on the response system conditioned and the measure of conditioning.

Guthrie was able to defend strict simultaneity of stimulus and response in the face of such data by proposing that the true stimulus being conditioned is not the stimulus as measured. An external stimulus will give rise to movements of the organism. These movements, in turn, produce kinesthetic stimuli. When associations appear to be made between stimuli and responses separated in time, it is because these intervening movements fill in the gap. The true association is between simultaneous events. (This analysis does not really *explain* the fact that a CS-US interval of intermediate length is optimal for learning —see Figure 3.5.) The same analysis would be used to explain how an animal learns to deliberately delay its response to a signal in order to get the reward; the signal cues off a *chain* of procrastinating behaviors that usher the animal directly into the point of reinforcement.

There is a strong preference for *movement-produced* stimuli as the true conditioners in Guthrie's system. They permit the integration of habits within a wide range of environmental change in stimulation, because these stimuli are carried around by the organism. As noted above, some of this preference dates from the early emphasis of Watson (1907) on kinesthesis as the basis of control of the maze habit, a position no longer tenable.[2] Such covert movement-produced stimuli provide ever-present explanations for conduct which cannot be inferred from external stimulus-response relationships. Unfortunately, they are a weak reed for a behaviorist to lean on.

Why Repetition Brings Improvement

Guthrie had two means for deriving apparent gradual improvement, one due to trial-to-trial variability in the exact stimuli

[2] Honzik (1936) found kinesthesis to be one of the least useful of several sensory controls of the maze habit.

present for response, the other due to the complexity of the total behavior lumped together as the "response" of interest. According to this second, or response complexity, argument, the reason practice brings improvement is that improvement and other forms of success refer to acts, to outcomes of learnings, rather than to the minutiae of *movements*. Guthrie believed that his interest in the small components of movement patterns, and the prediction of movements, was almost unique among learning theorists; others, he said, were interested in gross goal achievements and large-scale results of one sort or another. One difference between him and Thorndike was that Thorndike was concerned with his subject's scores on tasks—with words learned, pages typed, or correct responses attained. Guthrie was concerned only with the fine details of movements of the organism, regardless of whether they led to error or success.

A skill, such as getting the ball into the basket in a game of basketball, is not one act but many. It depends not upon a single muscular movement but upon a number of movements made under a number of different circumstances. Any one movement may be learned in any one trial, but to learn all the movements demanded by the complicated skill calls for practice in all the different situations: while near the basket and far away, on one side and on the other, with and without a guard nearby. Practice is necessary; but it produces its consequences, not according to a law of frequency, but according to the simple principle of the attachment of cues to movements. The more varied the movements called for in a given act of skill, and the more varied the cues which must become assimilated to these movements, the more practice is required. There is no mystery about the length of time it takes to learn to operate a typewriter: there are so many keys in so many combinations, calling for the attachment of a great many cues to a great many responses. It is concomitantly necessary to get rid of the faulty associations which lead to what, from an achievement point of view, is an error. This is done by having the correct behavior occur to the cue which previously gave rise to the faulty behavior. When finally all the cues lead to acceptable behavior, the task is mastered. The apparent contradiction between single-trial learning and the actual experience of painstaking fumbling before success is achieved is resolved when the skilled task is seen to be composed of a large number of habits.

As mentioned, even when an apparently simple response (like salivation) was to be learned to a simple CS like a bell, Guthrie invoked trial-to-trial variability in the precise stimulus to the animal—the dog might change her posture, open or close her eyes, have a flea-bite irritating her on some trials, hear a stray noise outside the lab, and so forth. Assuming these stimulus elements are active on some trials and inactive on others, that only active elements determine the response and can get conditioned on a given trial, the theory is able to derive a gradual learning curve for even a simple conditioning setup. These assumptions are precisely those which lie at the heart of Estes's *stimulus sampling theory,* which will be taken up in Chapter 8.

Associative Interference, Forgetting, and the Breaking of Habits

The fact of extinction is one of the findings of conditioning experiments that is in need of explanation. Because responses should remain faithful to their cues, Guthrie could not agree to extinction as a decay in habit strength due to mere nonreinforced repetition. According to him, extinction always is a result of associative competition or interference—that is, through the learning of a different, incompatible response to the stimulus situation.

His is an interference theory and hence requires no new principles, because the original learning and the interfering learning follow the same rules. His theory leads one to search for new stimuli present in extinction that were not conditioned during training, since these would serve to elicit responses other than the CR. As one example, during acquisition the CS is presented usually in the presence of stimulus traces of the US and UR from the just-prior trial; yet, these US and UR traces are typically absent during extinction, and hence the CS-without-US-trace forms a novel pattern that could evoke some response incompatible with the CR. And by the one-trial learning postulate, that pairing would suffice to condition the competing response to the CS.

Guthrie explained forgetting in the same way. If there were no interference with old learning, there would be no forgetting. Guthrie's position is but an extreme form of the retroactive inhibition theory of forgetting, to be discussed in Chapter 6. It has been shown, for example, that conditioned responses, even though in some respects they appear fragile, are actually quite resistant to forgetting (Hilgard & Campbell, 1936; Skinner, 1950; Wendt, 1937). The long-lasting character of most laboratory conditioned responses can be understood as intrinsic to learning that is highly specific to cues not confronted in the learners' daily life outside the conditioning situation. If learners lived in the conditioning situation, their responses would be subject to more interferences. Furthermore, in the typical conditioning experiment, the subject receives a large number of trials in associating a particular CS with a single US. Undeniably, much more forgetting of simple CRs would occur with less practice and concurrent learning of, say, twenty different CSs paired with presence versus absence of ten different USs. This more closely approximates the task complexity of multiple verbal associations which is known to lead to much forgetting.

If it is desired to break a habit (that is, to accelerate its replacement), it is only necessary to cause countermovements to occur in the presence of the cues to the habit. The problem of locating the cues and substituting counterbehavior often takes time, because many cues may lead to an undesirable habit.

> Drinking or smoking after years of practice are action systems which can be started by thousands of reminders. . . . I had once a caller to whom I was explaining that the apple I had just finished was a splendid device for avoiding a smoke. The caller pointed out that I was at that moment smoking. The habit of lighting a cigarette was so attached to the finish of eating that smoking had started automatically (Guthrie, 1935, p. 139).

Guthrie suggested three methods by which activities are commonly weakened:[3]

1. The first is to introduce the stimulus that you wish to have disregarded, but only in such faint degree that it will not call out its response. This is the method of breaking in a horse to the saddle by starting with a light blanket and gradually working up to full equipment, at no time permitting the horse to become so startled that it lunges or struggles. This is called the *toleration method,* because it presents the CS at just that level (the current threshold) the subject will tolerate without evoking the response, and then the critical stimulus is gradually raised.

2. The second is to repeat the full signal until the original response is fatigued, and then continue it, so that new responses are learned to the signal. The bronco-busting of western ranches followed essentially this technique. It is called the *exhaustion,* or *flooding, method.*

3. The third is to present the stimulus when other features in the situation inhibit the undesirable response. One illustration given by Guthrie is that of training a dog not to catch and eat chickens by tying a dead chicken about its neck. As it struggles to get rid of the corpse,

[3] Paraphrased from Guthrie (1935), pp. 70–73.

it develops an avoidance response to chickens at close quarters. Another example, illustrating maladaptive learning, is the disobedience learned by the child whose mother calls him when he is too occupied with what he is doing to obey. This is called *counterconditioning.*

These techniques for breaking unwanted habits have been picked up and applied with much ingenuity by modern psychotherapists in helping their patients overcome debilitating emotional and behavior problems. One example is called *systematic desensitization* (Wolpe, 1958) and is used to relieve (extinguish) a patient's severe anxieties or phobias regarding some situation. A typical case might be a businessman who wishes to overcome a debilitating phobia he has about riding on airplanes. With the patient, the therapist first identifies a hierarchy, or graded series, of situations ordered according to their psychological closeness to the dreaded event—in this case flying in an airplane. These might include distant situations that evoke little anxiety such as reading airplane travel brochures, holding a toy airplane, or seeing an airplane overhead; nearer things like driving to the airport, walking into the terminal building, approaching the check-in desk, talking to the stewardess, walking up to the door of the plane, going inside the plane, moving around or sitting inside the stationary plane, taxiing, taking off on short trips, going on longer trips, flying in turbulent weather, and so on. The items in this generalization hierarchy are rated by the patient according to how much anxiety they arouse.

In the second phase, the therapist teaches the patient the techniques of deep muscle relaxation—that is, how to relax all muscles completely, how to get the relaxation under nearly immediate verbal control (saying "relax" as a CS for a relaxation response pattern), and how to discriminate between when he is tense and when he is relaxed.

In the third phase, the fear aroused by the patient's *imagining* the various situations in his stimulus hierarchy is then extinguished by a combination of the toleration and counterconditioning methods. While deeply relaxed, the patient is asked to imagine the least fear-arousing situation in his hierarchy (for instance, ordering tickets). This is done in imagination for several extinction trials, then is repeated with the next higher fear-arousing item in the hierarchy, and so on. The patient moves on to the next item in the series only if he can remain thoroughly calm and relaxed while imagining himself in that situation. After several one-hour therapeutic sessions with this procedure, the patient eventually should be imagining himself in the phobic situation but feeling no fear.

Fourth, if possible, along with the imaginal counterconditioning in the therapist's office, the patient is also led through a graded series of real-life situations arranged in a fear hierarchy leading up to the formerly dreaded activity. For example, the therapist might accompany the patient to the airport, while he talks with a stewardess, sits inside a stationary plane, and so on. During these activities, the therapist would be urging the patient to remain calm and verbally reinforcing him for doing so. Even if these dry runs in the field cannot be arranged, the extinction of the fear in the imaginal situation still transfers substantially to the real-life setting, where the patient's fear will be lessened.

This procedure for extinguishing phobias is now one of the standard tools in the armamentarium of the behavior therapist. Wolpe (1958) and many others have reported high "cure" rates with the procedure applied to a variety of phobias, such as fear of heights, of animals, of public-speaking, of exam-taking, of being outdoors, of autos, of sexual encounters, and so on. The components of the clinical procedure have been much studied in the laboratory settings using the common localized phobias of college students—excess fear of snakes, spiders, public-speaking and so on. The procedure—which is undeniably successful in eliminating a high percentage of unwanted phobias—has two components: the fear is elicited at first by only a very weak cue for it, and the imaginal cue is also paired with deep relaxation. The relaxation "response" is presumed to be antagonistic to the anxiety reaction (it "reciprocally inhibits" fear). Therefore, in theory the weak cue becomes connected to the relaxation response. Because of stimulus generalization, the anxiety-inhibition conditioned to the weakest cue will also reduce the fear now aroused by the next cue in the hierarchy, and it, too, can then be overlaid or replaced by the antagonistic relaxation response. The idea is that if the cues are introduced in slow progression, one could optimally extinguish the phobic reaction throughout the stimulus hierarchy without an anxiety reaction once being experienced by the patient.

One may ask how the various extinction methods compare, say, in their effectiveness in reducing a CS-CR habit within a fixed number of trials or a fixed period of time. A study by Poppen (1968) provided an early comparison of various pure techniques, and combinations of techniques, in extinguishing in rats the fear evoked by a tone that had been paired with electric shock. Poppen found that the toleration-plus-counterconditioning technique was most effective, whereas the typical extinction procedure (simply presenting the CS briefly without shock) was the least efficient. Different neurotic phobias may succumb to different methods. Thus, Rachman, Hodgson, and Marks (1971) found that *flooding* was the most efficient method for reducing obsessional compulsions (such as handwashing); Bandura (1977b) found that encouraging the patient to respond overtly to the graded hierarchy of threatening stimuli led to faster extinction of snake phobias than did simply imagining those activities. These are just a few of the sequelae of Guthrie's speculation on how to break habits.

GUTHRIE'S VIEWS ON MOTIVATION, INTENTIONS, REWARDS, AND PUNISHMENT

Motives. The motivational state of the organism, its hunger, thirst, or state of comfort or discomfort, had no formal place in Guthrie's learning theory; the motivational state is important only because it determines the presence and vigor of movements that may enter into associative connections. The motive is important only for the stimulus-response sequences that occur, specifically the consummatory response sequences like eating, drinking, mating, and so forth. The movements that occur get associated to the coincident cues; if a hungry cat acts differently from a well-fed cat, its movements are different and so its learning may be different. It learns what it does; what it does is more important than what its motivational state happens to be.

Motives are, however, important in providing *maintaining stimuli,* keeping the organism active until a goal is reached. The goal removes these maintaining stimuli, and brings the activity to an end (Guthrie, 1942, p. 18). Guthrie believed that these maintaining stimuli tend to keep a series of acts integrated, and account for anticipation of goal objects (for example, food to satisfy hunger), for behavior characterized by intention or purpose.

Intentions. Conduct seems to be organized into sequences in which people (or lower organisms) make plans and carry them out, or at least start to carry them out. Guthrie was aware of this and discussed learning with and without intention

(1935, pp. 202–211). His position was to analyze planning in terms of S-R mechanisms.

He and Smith had earlier followed the lead of Sherrington and Woodworth in considering sequences of behavior as composed of preparatory responses followed by consummatory responses (Smith & Guthrie, 1921; Sherrington, 1906; Woodworth, 1918). Such acts appear from the outside to be intentional, for the earlier adjustments clearly are in readiness for the consequences that are to follow. These anticipatory responses or readiness reactions are said to be conditioned to maintaining stimuli.

The typical case is that of the hungry rat running down an alleyway to food at the end. The activity is maintained by the internal stimuli aroused by food deprivation to which running and eating behavior have been conditioned in the past. That is, the rat found food at some previous time in this situation after running while hungry. These internal stimuli, plus the stimuli from the runway (if it has been previously a path to food), maintain the running of the animal against competing responses, such as stopping to explore. Anticipatory salivation or chewing movements give directional character to the behavior. All this food anticipation is fulfilled if there is food at the end of the maze. Because the stimuli of hunger and anticipation are now removed, and the animal is removed from the maze, all the learning is intact for a new trial at a later time. This paradigm provides a way of talking about human intentions and purposes also.

> The essence of an intention is a body of maintaining stimuli which may or may not include sources of unrest like thirst or hunger but always includes action tendencies conditioned during a past experience—a readiness to speak, a readiness to go, a readiness to read, and in each case a readiness not only for the act but also for the previously rehearsed consequences of the act. These readinesses are not complete acts but they consist in tensions of the muscles that will

take part in the complete act (Guthrie, 1935, pp. 205–206).

This statement goes a long way toward the point of view which those with very different theories of learning accept. The only feature which keeps it within the bounds of Guthrie's theory is that all the readinesses, including the readiness for the "previously rehearsed consequences of the act," are said to consist in tensions in the muscles. This assumption, characteristic of the behaviorist position regarding cognitive events, remains in the realm of conjecture rather than of demonstration.

Reward. While Guthrie believed as everyone else does that rewards influence outcomes, his rejection of the law of effect and of the principle of reinforcement in conditioning was based on the position that nothing new is added to associative learning by reward except a particular sort of mechanical arrangement. This mechanical arrangement, which places reward at the end of a series of acts, removes the organism from the stimuli (internal as well as external) acting just prior to the reward. Hence, since the rewarded response is the last one to occur at the end of a trial, there is no further opportunity for competing responses to occur to the apparatus stimuli and to displace the final (correct) response. Instead of behavior's being strengthened by reward, reward protects it from new associations being formed to the *same* stimuli. The successful response was just as strong before the reward occurred, but, if there had been no reward, new behavior in the same situation would have been evoked, resulting in the displacement of the correct response by other, irrelevant responses becoming associated to the experimental stimuli. The act leading to the reward, since it is the last act in the problematic situation, is the one favored when the situation next repeats itself. Guthrie was very explicit about this. Of an animal's escape from a problem-box he said:

The position taken in this paper is that the animal learns to escape with its first escape. This learning is protected from forgetting because the escape removes the animal from the situation which has then no chance to acquire new associations.

[Of latch-opening followed by food.] *What encountering the food does is not to intensify a previous item of behavior but to protect that item from being unlearned.* The whole situation and action of the animal is so changed by the food that the pre-food situation is shielded from new associations. These new associations can not be established in the absence of the box interior, and in the absence of the behavior that preceded latch-opening (1940, pp. 144–45).

Although this is the fundamental position with respect to reward, and frequently reiterated in opposition to the law of effect and related interpretations, the action of reward is found to be somewhat more complicated when one examines the totality of Guthrie's system. The first (and primary) role of reward is to remove the animal from the problem situation and thus prevent unlearning. But by the principle of association, the animal also learns the activity that he carries on in the presence of the reward (chewing and salivating to food, for example), and this behavior tends to be evoked by renewed hunger and by any of the cues from the conditioning situation that may have persisted while the rewarded behavior was going on.

. . . There is one act, however, to which hunger may remain a faithful conditioner. That is the act of eating; and the faithfulness of hunger to this association derives from the fact that hunger dies when eating occurs. As Stevenson Smith and I pointed out in our *General Psychology,* elements of the consummatory response tend to be present throughout a series of actions driven by a maintaining stimulus (1935, pp. 151–52).

Not only do general movements of eating tend to be aroused by hunger contractions, but the specific movements demanded by the particular nature of the food are possibly in evidence. Hence when the rat runs the maze he is ready for whatever reward has been received in the past, sunflower seed or bran mash. This readiness is an actual muscular readiness . . . (1935, p. 173).

Here Guthrie states some aspects of the drive-reduction hypothesis, that rewards (at least eating) act by changing internal drive states (hunger cues are removed), and some aspects of the "anticipatory reward" interpretation of the action of reinforcement. Guthrie's interpretation of reward was at once ambiguous, provocative, and a source of frequent attacks upon his position. Some reinforcing events clearly are interpretable in terms of stimulus change following the critical response. For example, in human associative learning, the subject typically rehearses the correct response to each stimulus before the next item occurs, thus insuring that the correct response was the last one to the stimulus before it changed. Or, in an avoidance learning situation, animals learn more quickly the greater the amount of change in the frightening situation immediately after they respond (Bower, Starr & Lazarovitz, 1965). The problem with situations that involve stimulus change as reward is that they are easily interpretable with other theories. Thus, for example, a theory which supposes that avoidance responses are reinforced by anxiety reduction would also handle the results; the greater the change away from that CS directly conditioned to fear, the greater the loss of fear due to generalization to the post-CR stimulus; hence, the greater the fear reduction and reinforcement following the response. Thus, such results do not provide differential evidence in favor of Guthrie's reinforcement hypothesis.

Guthrie's hypothesis has suggested a variety of experimental operations that turn out to be not the least bit rewarding. We can arrange for certain radical changes in the environment to occur immediately after a rat depresses a lever, such as her receiving an electroconvulsive shock, or having the floor drop out from under her, or suddenly jiggling the box, or stuffing her in a black cloth bag; such events simply do not act as rewards, although psychologists have argued that Guthrie's theory predicts that they should. Guthrians argue that such abrupt events do not appear to act like rewards because they elicit competing responses that become conditioned to the situation and thus interfere with the instrumental response. But the crucial competing responses have rarely been measured to buttress such arguments. The essential untestability of the stimulus-change hypothesis of reward has led contemporary Guthrians to abandon it in favor of a *conditioned excitement,* or motivational interpretation of the action of rewards. We will discuss this theory later in this chapter.

Punishment. For Guthrie, the primary interpretation of punishment was the same as for any other bit of associative learning: organisms tend to do what they did before under the same circumstances:

> . . . Sitting on tacks does not discourage learning. It encourages one in learning to do something else than sit. It is not the feeling caused by punishment, but the specific action caused by punishment that determines what will be learned. To train a dog to jump through a hoop, the effectiveness of punishment depends on where it is applied, front or rear. It is what the punishment makes the dog do that counts or what it makes a man do, not what it makes him feel (1935, p. 158).

> What we can predict is that the influence of stimuli acting at the time of either satisfaction or annoyance will be to reestablish whatever behavior was in evidence at the time (1935, p. 154).

If Guthrie had stopped with statements such as these, it would appear that he treated reward and punishment in a symmetrical fashion. Certainly punishment changes a situation very strikingly, as reward does. Hence one might infer that all antecedent behavior would remain intact, being protected from new learning by the altered conditions of punishment as much as by the altered conditions of reward.

The symmetry in treatment of reward

and punishment, as implied in the foregoing quotations, is somewhat illusory, for "doing what you last did" refers to very different parts of the behavior cycle depending on whether the reference is to reward or punishment. The "what-you-last-did" that remains in your behavior repertory because of reward is what you did *just before* the reward appeared: "what-you-last-did" in the case of punishment refers to what you did *just after* the punishment started and at the time it ended with escape. Punishment produces *maintaining stimuli* that are relieved by a later movement that brings relief:

> . . . An animal on a charged grid, a barefoot boy on a hot pavement, a man sitting on a tack have as their goals mere escape from the intense stimulation that causes general tension and restlessness as well as specific movement. These stimuli continue to act as what Stevenson Smith and I called maintaining stimuli until some movement carries the subject away from the source of stimulation, or the source of stimulation away from the subject (1935, p. 165).

When these stimuli are removed, we have the circumstances defining reward in Guthrie's theory, and so, if that were the whole story, the prior behavior should remain intact. This kind of relief from punishment has come to be known as *escape learning* to distinguish it from the *avoidance learning* that occurs in anticipation of the noxious stimulus. To move from escape learning to avoidance learning, we require an anticipatory response, conditioned to some cue, so that the punishment is circumvented. Guthrie's system makes provision for anticipatory responses, and these can be used to explain avoidance learning. The animal merely makes the escape response to some cue present at the time of punishment—a cue which, fortunately, makes its appearance before the threatened punishment. Hence what happens at the end of a sequence of acts leading to punishment does something *in*

addition to and *other than* removing the organism from the scene; it also sets up some conditioned anticipatory responses.

This idea, that the avoidance response is an anticipatory form of the escape response elicited by the noxious stimulus, has implications of varying empirical truth value. One curious set of implications concerns a set of studies on what has come to be called "experimental masochism," in which it appears that a rat actively seeks to give itself a painful electric shock (see Gwinn, 1949; Brown, 1969). As always, its terminal behavior depends upon a particular training history. For instance, the animal is first trained to run down a long alleyway having an electrically charged grid floor to get to the safety box at the end. Then he is taught, when placed in the alley without shock on the floor, to run rapidly to the end-box in order to avoid a shock that comes on after a few seconds. In this second phase, when the subject gets shocked, he is in the process of running to the end-box, and the effect of the shock when it does come on is to impel him forward even faster into the safety box. Once this running pattern is established, the contingencies can then be altered as follows: if the rat will just sit still when placed in the start-box of the alleyway, he will receive no shock and will be removed from the box after 30 seconds; however, if he moves a short distance out of the start-box, he will step onto the electrically charged grill and "punish himself." Such training suffices to trap the subject into a vicious cycle: he has been taught to run before shock comes on, and to run when the shock hits him. Therefore, despite the change in contingencies from the experimenter's point of view, from the subject's perspective the contingencies (during "punished extinction") are the same as in avoidance training as long as he keeps on running. Rats may continue this self-punitive behavior for many hundreds of trials, as Guthrie's theory would predict, until on some random trial they happen to sit still in the start-box or happen to lurch back to safety rather than dashing forward when they step on the shock grill. Once these novel responses occur, "extinction" proceeds precipitously, perhaps in a trial or two—also as Guthrie would have predicted (see Dreyer & Renner, 1971).

However, it should be mentioned that, in apparent opposition to Guthrie's analysis of avoidance learning, one can train animals and people to make one response to avoid a noxious event but a different response to terminate that state of affairs if it should happen. For instance, in anticipation of a possible house fire, we buy fire insurance and check wiring insulation and the furnace; but if the house is actually burning around us, we run to the nearest exit or assist others to get out. Obviously we can discriminate between, and act differently to, the threat of our house burning down and the actual event. In less complicated surroundings, it has been demonstrated that a rat can be trained to make one response (rear up on its hind legs) to avoid a shock when a tone sounds; but if that fails, to make a different response (depress a lever in his chamber) should the shock come on and have to be terminated by the subject (Mowrer, 1947). Such discriminative avoidance is difficult for rats to learn, in line with Guthrie's argument, but the fact that they can learn the problem at all counters Guthrie's views.

In escape and avoidance learning the subject learns to respond actively to deter or terminate a noxious stimulus. In contrast, punishment is typically used to inhibit behavior that is strong because it is, or has been, rewarded. We may use punishment to try to stop the child's doing something she enjoys, to break a "bad habit." According to Guthrie, punishment of this kind can work only if it creates a kind of competition or conflict between the approach response to reward and the withdrawal reaction to the punishment.

Guthrie's position with respect to punishment has been aptly summarized by Sheffield:

> a. Punishment works only if the last response to the punished situation is incompatible with the response that brought on the punishment.
> b. Punishment works only if the cues present when the incompatible response is performed are present when the punished response is performed.
> c. Punishment that produces only emotional excitement will tend to fixate the punished response (1949).

The main point is that punishment is effective in conflict situations where incompatible responses occur to the punishing stimulus. An experiment by Fowler and Miller (1963) illustrates the differing effect of punishment depending on whether it elicited a response compatible or incompatible with the instrumental response. They trained rats to run down an alley to food; control animals received no shock, whereas experimental animals received a mild electric shock just before they picked up the food pellet. Some rats received the shock on their forepaws, which elicited a backward flinching response, supposedly incompatible with the forward running response; other rats received the shock on their hindpaws, which elicited a forward lurch, supposedly compatible with the forward running response. The results in terms of average running speed to the foodbox are shown in Figure 4.1. In comparison to nonshocked rats, those shocked on the forepaws showed slower running, whereas those shocked on the hindpaws showed *faster* running. Thus, these results provide dramatic support for Guthrie's view that the effect of punishment depends on how the response it elicits relates to the punished instrumental response.

To balance the perspective, however, it should be noted that the facilitation of per-

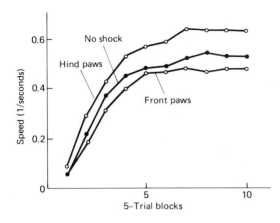

Figure 4.1. Speed of alley running in groups of rats shocked near the goal. The groups received either hind-paw or front-paw shock; controls received no shock. (From Fowler & Miller, 1963.)

formance by punishment such as found by Fowler and Miller (1963) is quite rare and depends on circumscribed conditions. In particular, their result obtained only when shock was introduced infrequently and gradually, starting at very weak levels and never advancing over trials to really strong intensities. When more intense shocks are used, the punished active response is usually suppressed. However, this is not necessarily inconsistent with Guthrie's theory, since intense shocks are more likely to elicit "freezing," which would suppress active responding. The real problem with testing Guthrie's theory becomes apparent; whatever the effect of punishment, Guthrie could always claim that it was due to the compatibility or incompatibility of the instrumental response to the *typically unobserved* reaction to the punishment. Attempts to measure these competing responses and to relate punishment effects to them (Dunham, 1971, 1972) have not supported Guthrie's position. Rather, it looks as though animals stop making the punished response because they want to avoid the aversive stimulation that is contingent upon it.

Neo-Guthrian Interpretations of Rewards and Intentions

Among the many contemporary experimental psychologists influenced by Guthrie, F. D. Sheffield has been not only one of the more persuasive defenders of the theory but a proponent of innovations in it. One of the more salient changes has been in Sheffield's reinterpretation of how reward operates to guide instrumental responses, especially in appetitive situations. Sheffield's account was first made available in 1954 in a mimeographed version of a colloquium speech, and later in publications (Sheffield, 1965). Let us consider the simple situation in which a hungry rat, say, is running through a T-maze for a food reward in one of the end-boxes, or is depressing a lever that delivers a bite of food. The first idea is that the proprioceptive stimuli from the critical response (lever-pressing) are in an optimal temporal relationship to the unconditioned response (eating), so that fractional parts of the consummatory response will become conditioned to these critical proprioceptive cues as well as to those precursor movements preceding the critical response (approaching the lever, rising up to press the lever, and so on). It is further supposed that when early components of this successful behavior chain are begun, they produce stimuli causing anticipation of consummatory activity; this anticipation produces "excitement" which feeds into invigorating the ongoing segment of the successful response chain, making it compete more successfully against interfering distractors. By the end of sufficient conditioning trials, the rat is attracted to perform the successful behavior chain because when he selects successful responses they produce stimuli that maximize the conditioned arousal of the consummatory response (anticipation of reward). Sheffield used these ideas to explain a great deal of the action of positive rewards on learning. It is significant that a similar account of reward effects was adopted by Spence (1956) and other Hullians in their concept of incentive motivation (which was the intervening variable affected by reward in Hull's system, see Chapter 5). Sheffield's ideas also influenced Mowrer (1960) in later accounts of his theorizing regarding reward effects.

Another innovator in the Guthrian tradition, W. K. Estes, has adopted somewhat the same hypothesis about how rewards influence instrumental responding. Estes writes:

> It is assumed that . . . response evocation depends upon the joint action of stimulus input from receptors and input from drive [motivational] mechanisms. . . . Originally these specific mechanisms are activated by unconditioned stimuli; for example, the mechanism associated with hunger is activated by the taste of food, the mechanism associated with pain by impinging traumatic stimulation. The result of activity of a drive mechanism is to generate what may be termed facilitatory or inhibitory feedback. . . . By associative learning . . . control of these positive and negative drive mechanisms is extended to stimuli which have preceded the original unconditioned stimuli. . . . The result of this combination of motivational and associational mechanisms is that after some learning experience the organism's behavior is continuously modulated by anticipations of rewards or punishments, behavior sequences leading to increases in positive feedback being preferentially selected and behavior sequences leading to decreases in positive feedback or to punishment being inhibited (1970, pp. 10–11).

If for "facilitative drive feedback" in Estes's statement one substitutes the phrase "excitement by conditioned arousal of the consummatory response," the similarity of the two formulations is heightened. The new addition by Estes is the notion of reciprocal inhibition between the general "positive" and "negative" drive centers. Thus, if while performing an appetitive response sequence the animal sees or hears a signal associated with anxiety, that will activate the negative or inhibitory drive mechanism, reciprocally inhibit the positive drive mechanism, and thus lower performance of any appetitive response while the anxiety signal is present. This type of effect, termed *conditioned suppression,* was first observed long ago by Estes and Skinner (1941), and has been much studied. Estes's assumption of reciprocal inhibition between positive and negative motives seems reasonable and appears to enable us to interpret a number of different results of punishment (see Estes, 1969b).

Controlling the Learning Process

It is part of the charm of Guthrie's writing that it was closely in touch with everyday life and provided amusing but cogent suggestions for meeting the problems of animal training, child-rearing, and pedagogy. This practicality is not a necessary characteristic of the system, for if one seriously attempted to provide evidence for the theory she would be buried in the midst of the precise movement correlates of measurable stimuli and the muscular tension accompaniments of preparatory adjustments. But the system was not intended to be taken seriously in that sense. As long as a convenient way of talking about things could be found without seeming to contradict the system, quantitative precision was presumed not to be essential. It was Guthrie's conviction that scientific laws, to be useful, must be approximately true, but that they must also be stated coarsely enough to be teachable to freshmen (1936).

Most of the practical advice Guthrie gave was good advice, and he succeeded in making it flow from the theory. Consider the following:

> The mother of a ten year old girl complained to a psychologist that for two years her daughter had annoyed her by a habit of tossing coat and hat on the floor as she entered the house. On a hundred occasions the mother had insisted that the girl pick up the clothing and hang it in its place. These wild ways were changed only after the mother, on advice, began to insist not that

the girl pick up the fallen garments from the floor, but that she put them on, return to the street, and re-enter the house, this time removing the coat and hanging it properly (1935, p. 21).

Why was this advice given? Behavior is in response to stimuli. Hanging up the coat and hat had been a response of the girl to her mother's pleading and the sight of the clothing on the floor. In order that the desired behavior be attached to its proper cues, it was necessary for her to go outside and come into the house, so that entering the house became the cue for hanging up the coat and hat.

The following represent the kind of suggestions that recur in Guthrie's writings:

1. If you wish to encourage a particular kind of behavior or discourage another, discover the cues leading to the behavior in question. In the one case, arrange the situation so that the desired behavior occurs when those cues are present; in the other case, arrange it so that the undesired behavior does not occur in the presence of the cues. This is all that is involved in the skillful use of reward and punishment. Students do not learn what was in a lecture or a book. They learn only what the lecture or book caused them to do.

2. Use as many stimulus supports for desired behavior as possible, because any ordinary behavior is a complex of movements to a complex of stimuli. The more stimuli there are associated with the desired behavior, the less likely that distracting stimuli and competing behavior will upset the desirable behavior. There would be fewer lines confused in amateur theatricals if there were more dress rehearsals, since the cues from the stage and the actors are part of the situation to which the actor responds. In other words, we should practice in the precise form later to be demanded of us.

3. To form an intentional habit, force yourself to always make the response and never let a slip-up occur. Then it will become so automatic as to occur without our effort. For instance, the advice works in teaching oneself to put on seat belts in an auto, or come to a full stop at stop signs while driving, and so on. Brook no excuses or interference with the desired routine.

Response Stereotyping in Learning

Guthrie performed relatively few experiments to test his ideas, but one he did carry out with Horton (1946) investigated *stereotypy* ("sameness" over trials) of an animal's learned response. Guthrie and Horton studied cats escaping from a puzzle-box who received tuna fish as a reward, with the door release operated by the cat rubbing against a pole in the center of the box. The release mechanism also caused a camera to photograph the cat at the moment of its successful contact with the pole. The animal was first habituated to the problem-box, taught to walk out the door to get fish, and then the door was locked and the pole and camera made operative. By examining the photographs of a cat performing the correct response over successive learning trials, Guthrie and Horton concluded that response stereotypy was the rule: a cat which rubs its left flank against the escape pole may do so time after time; another may nudge its head into the pole from the same position in the cage time after time. The published photographs were rather convincing. In agreement with Guthrie's theory of one-trial learning of specific movements, a cat seemed to learn some peculiar method of escape on the first trial and then repeated it more or less in that form trial after trial.

Critics noted several objections to the Guthrie and Horton experiment and interpretation. They tried to emphasize the substantial variability in a cat's behavior from trial to trial, and to explain the stereotypy in other terms. For example, if the behavior that succeeds is simple and easily learned, then any theory expects stereotypy of that prepotent and reinforced response. Another telling objection is that the physical nature of the successful response places certain constraints or limitations upon what kinds of things the cat could do to move the pole. The basic point can be made by drawing an exaggerated analogy.

The effect of this restriction in picture taking could be seen more clearly in an experiment that required the animal to stand on his legs and reach out of the upper corner of the cage in order to press a button to release the door and take the picture. In this way we further restrict the set of possible responses and achieve added stereotypy. On the other hand, other experimental situations could be constructed, which would reduce stereotypy. In either case, however, what is procured are data concerning responses defined in terms of effect (Mueller & Schoenfeld, 1954, p. 358).

The most serious objection to the Guthrie-Horton experiments is that it appears likely that they were not observing any *response learning* whatsoever. Rather, the "pole rubbing" behaviors of their cats were most probably a species-specific form of "greeting" behavior of practically all members of the *Felidae* family (including lions, tigers, jaguars, ocelots, and domestic cats). This sort of flank rubbing or head rubbing occurs spontaneously when a cat sees a loved object such as a friendly person. The "greeting rub" is typically directed at the love object (notice how your cat rubs against your shins); if the love object is too far away, then the rub may be directed at a nearby doorpost, piece of furniture, or to Guthrie and Horton's "escape pole." Moore and Stuttard (1979) performed a partial replication of the Guthrie-Horton experiment except that they never fed their cats near the problem-box nor let them escape by rubbing the center post. Nonetheless, Moore and Stuttard observed that their cats rubbed the center post (in stereotyped fashion) primarily when the human observer was visible outside the glass-windowed problem-box; however, the cats hardly ever rubbed the pole when a human or other fond object was not observable. Since Guthrie and Horton were always in view of their cats, it seems likely that they were eliciting only species-specific greeting reactions from their cats. Consequently, there probably was no

"response shaping by reinforcement" going on in their experiments. Thus, the chosen learning situation has a great deal to do with what aspects of behavior will be revealed. The problem-box of Guthrie and Horton, which at first appears to lay bare the primitive nature of learning, may in fact be a highly specialized situation poorly designed to show the behavior of the cat as it goes about learning.

Further Tests and Extensions

Guthrie's theory has not provoked much critical testing, either positively or negatively, perhaps because of its "slippery" appeal to unobservable movements and stimuli. Some experiments critical of Guthrie's idea of response learning have been done. Experiments reviewed by Lashley (1924) showed that animals tended to learn a large equivalence class of responses that achieve a certain end result rather than learning a rigid specific movement. A rat taught to run through a maze for food will, under altered test conditions, swim through the same maze when it is flooded, or roll on the floor (if inner-ear damage has upset its coordinated running), doing so unerringly to get to the goal-box. Or a person who has been conditioned to *extend* her resting index finger to a CS in order to avoid a shock to the fingerpad will now *flex* her finger to the CS when her hand is turned over; she has learned to "move away from" the shock pad, not to flex or to extend her finger (Wickens, 1938). Such experiments stand as testaments against ready adoption of Guthrie's claims of specific cue-muscle movement habits as the basis for all learned behavior. It might appear instead that any available response is called into service as needed to achieve a certain end result, such as getting to the food-box or avoiding the shock.

One notable effort to find evidence for Guthrie's theory was by Voeks (1948, 1950), who examined response repetition of humans learning a multiunit punchboard maze. In line with Guthrie's last-response conditioning rule she found that the better predictor of which response a subject would make at a given choice-point of the maze was the most recent response he had made there on the previous trials, *not* the most frequent response made there over the entire past series of trials. However, more extensive work on selective learning by Noble (reviewed in Noble, 1966) found that the best predictor of individual responses at each choice-point was that based on past reinforcements. That is, the most likely response was that which had been reinforced most frequently at that choice-point over previous trials. Reinforcement was a far better predictor of response selection than were frequency and recency.

In further work, Voeks (1954) studied classical eyeblink conditioning of humans under rigidly controlled stimulus conditions. She found that most subjects showed all-or-none learning in her situation, jumping from zero CRs up to a high percentage of CRs on one trial after training began. She came to this conclusion by examining trials after the subject's first CR, and noting that no subject increased his CR probability over these trials. Half her subjects gave CRs on every trial after their first one, and there were only a few lapses for the others.

How do Voeks's results compare with the many acquisition curves published for CRs? It is well known that curves for groups of subjects show characteristics very different from curves for individual subjects. Voeks has very convincingly shown, just as Guthrie had argued, that response acquisition may occur all-or-none in one trial for each individual and yet the group average learning curve will show a gradual slope. The accompanying learning curve (Figure 4.2) results, for example, when the probability of response is plotted as a group function for fifteen subjects, all of whom had jumpwise curves—that is, all of whom responded consistently with CRs after making their first CR. The form of the curve is determined solely by the trial on which the first CR happened to appear for different subjects. It was revealing facts such as these which motivated the modern development of all-or-none learning models in stimulus sampling theory (see Chapter 8).

Voeks predicted jumpwise curves of learning under the very uniform conditions of stimulation that she arranged, and her predictions were well borne out. However,

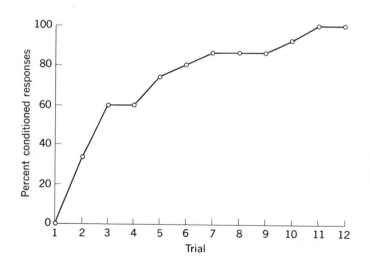

Figure 4.2. Misleading effect of combining individual learning curves. The group curve results from combining the curves of fifteen subjects, all of whom had jumpwise curves—i.e., a run of no responses followed by consistent responding. (From Voeks, 1954.)

not all individual conditioning curves are of this jumpwise type. For example, Hilgard (1931) and Cohen, Hilgard, and Wendt (1933) early published eyelid conditioning curves for individual subjects which showed rather gradual conditioning. Why the difference? It probably concerns the greater degree of control over extraneous stimuli in the extreme situation arranged by Voeks, for it is known that conditioning occurs more rapidly with less distracting variability in the conditions surrounding CS presentation. Also, Voeks used a very strong airblast to the eye as a US, and it is likely that many of her subjects learned what would today be classified as a "voluntary avoidance" response rather than a true conditioned response. Furthermore, to reduce variability of muscular kinesthesis at the time of CS presentation, Voeks had her subjects bite on a bite board and squeeze a hand dynamometer; but it has since been discovered that such heightened general muscle tone sensitizes many reflexes, particularly ones like an eyeblink. Finally, Spence (1956) showed that such jump-type conditioning curves would be implied by a theory (like Hull's) which assumed gradual accumulation of associative strength, a low degree of fluctuating variability in strength from moment to moment, and the assumption that CRs occur only when the momentary strength of the S-R habit exceeds some threshold for response evocation. Considerations such as these support alternative interpretations of Voeks's data.

Guthrie's ideas were extended by F. D. Sheffield (1961), a student of Guthrie's, who developed a theory to explain the learning of complex sequential tasks from demonstrations and practice. Central to Sheffield's extension was the concept of *sensory responses* ("images"), which are presumed to be completely central in locus and need not have motor components. Sensory responses are the internal representatives of external stimulus patterns:

> Such sensory responses are assumed to be subject to the learning principles of association by contiguity and are assumed to have cue properties as well as response properties. That is, a sensory response can not only be connected to a cue, but also is a cue to which other responses can be connected (1961, p. 14).

> The position taken here is that what is usually called "perception" refers to cases in which the immediate sensory stimulation is not only eliciting its innate sensory responses, but is also eliciting other sensory responses which have been conditioned to the immediate stimulation in past experience (1961, p. 15).

Sheffield uses the postulated sensory responses to discuss the student's learning of what things look like (e.g., the inside of a carburetor) and to represent the sequence of events and actions the student learns as she learns to take apart a carburetor and check it for flaws. Sheffield refers to the "cross-conditioning" of one sensory response to others, to represent sequences of expected events in the stages of taking apart a machine or putting it back together. These sensory response sequences, learned perhaps from observing a movie or demonstration, guide later behaviors.

Although the notion of conditioning of sensory responses in patterns and sequences was rather novel in the stimulus-response tradition, it seems in many respects almost exactly what the mentalist or cognitive psychologists had been talking about for years. Do we obtain any more "objectivity" by talking about *sensory responses* than about *images* or *ideas*? What is the gain from discussing the *conditioning* of a sensory response-produced cue or pattern to another sensory response if the theory is just the "association of ideas" in S-R dress? A fair evaluation is to note that Sheffield's paper provides one of the more detailed analyses of perceptual-motor skills—of their acquisition, internal representation, and use; and the analysis is valuable whatever one's predilections for a theoretical vocabulary.

In his final paper, Guthrie (1959) repeated the arguments for his system but added one important change—namely, he now emphasized the role of *attention* in selecting the stimuli that will be conditioned and that will control responding. His new rule is succinctly stated as "What is being noticed becomes the signal for what is being done" (Guthrie, 1959, p. 186). This makes the control of attention an important component in accounting for behavior. Guthrie also noted that when two cues are presented which elicit incompatible responses, the subject will engage in pronounced attentive behaviors, scanning the cues for a clue to decide which response to perform. This is similar to Tolman's idea of the vicarious trial-and-error (VTE) behavior of animals in conflict (see Chapter 11), and it anticipates the scanning model of choice behavior proposed by Estes (see Chapter 8). Guthrie presented no new evidence in support of his learning theory, but continued to argue that other results were interpretable within his system.

ESTIMATE OF GUTHRIE'S POSITION

Guthrie's Position on Typical Problems of Learning

By way of summary, we shall briefly state Guthrie's position on several representative problems of learning.

1. Capacity. Problems of capacity are not formally treated, although species differences are recognized and allowance is made for maturation as a determiner of many classes of acts (1935, pp. 18, 38). Presumably any response which the organism can make may become associated with any stimulus to which it is sensitive —this generalization about the possibility of learning is reminiscent of what Thorndike says about associative shifting. This presupposition

of equivalent associability now appears to be false, based on evidence reviewed in Chapter 3. If pressed, Guthrie could find a basis for differences in capacity both in the differentiation of movement and in the discrimination among proprioceptive cues. All animals are not equally versatile and equally equipped with receptors.

2. Practice. Practice assimilates or alienates cues to specific movements until a whole family of stimulus combinations comes to evoke a whole family of responses, which lead to the outcome socially described as successful performance. Because skill represents a population of habits, learning appears to accumulate with repetition, although basically each individual habit or atomic unit is learned at full strength in a single repetition.

3. Motivation. Motivation affects learning indirectly through what it causes the animal to do. Reward is a secondary or derivative principle, not a primary one as in Thorndike's system. Reward works because it removes the animal from the stimulating situation in which the "correct" response has been made. It does not strengthen the "correct" response, but prevents its weakening because no new response can become attached to the cues which led to the correct response. Thus there is a relative strengthening, because responses to other cues get alienated. We illustrated a few of the difficulties of this idea, and showed how reward effects are now being treated by the neo-Guthrians, Sheffield and Estes.

Punishment does several different things at once. In general, its effects for learning are determined by what it causes the organism to do, according to the principle that the best predictor of learning is the response in the situation that last occurred. We may distinguish four cases:

a. Mild punishment may be merely exciting, and enhance ongoing behavior rather than disrupt it.

b. More intense punishment may break up a habit by leading to incompatible behavior in the presence of the cues for it.

c. A continuing aversive stimulus acts like a drive, producing maintaining stimuli that keep the organism active until it finds relief. Then the consequence for learning is really like that of reward: the act that leads to safety is rewarding because it terminates the punishment, and, by removing the maintaining stimuli, protects from unlearning the activities carried on in the presence of those stimuli.

d. Stimuli that have previously accompanied the punishment produce behavior that formerly occurred following the punishment itself. Here we have an illustration of anticipatory response, essential to avoidance behavior. The cues to avoidance must earlier have been present at the time of punishment for this anticipation to occur. A problem with this view is explaining how organisms learn avoidance responses which differ from the escape response given to the noxious stimulus.

4. Understanding. Concepts like "insight" are handled in a derisive manner, although it is recognized that learning with foresight of its consequences may occur. Guthrie's tendency was to talk down such learning, however, just as Thorndike did, and to emphasize the mechanical and repetitive nature of most human as well as animal learning. Such learning with intention and foresight as does occur is explained on the basis of conditioned anticipatory or readiness reactions, based upon past experience and hence not contradicting association principles.

5. Transfer. Learning transfers to new situations because of common elements within the old and new. In this the position is rather like Thorndike's. Stress is laid, however, on the identity being carried by way of common responses evoked, the proprioceptive stimuli being sufficiently similar in the case of responses to a variety of stimuli to evoke common conditioned responses. The emphasis upon movement-produced stimuli thus represents Guthrie's supplementation to Thorndike.

Because of his principle of responses being conditioned to all adventitious contiguous stimuli, Guthrie expected rather little transfer and was, in fact, rather extreme about it. The only way to be sure to get desired behavior in a new situation is to practice in that new situation as well. To be able to perform in a variety of situations, you have to practice in a variety of situations.

6. Forgetting. Learning is said to be permanent unless interfered with by new learning. Hence all forgetting is due to the learning of new responses which replace the old responses. It may take place gradually for the same reason that skills may be acquired gradually: remembering depends upon many habits to many cues, and subhabits may drop out gradually as subcues become attached to new responses.

In contrast to Thorndike, Guthrie was an avowed behaviorist who made it a matter of some importance to get rid of subjective terms, to refer, for example, to inner speech instead of to thinking. The emphasis upon movement-produced stimuli was part of the older behaviorist tradition of Watson which Guthrie carried on. While he was an orthodox behaviorist in these respects, his was an informal behaviorism, with little of the brittleness of earlier Watsonianism.

Invulnerability of the Theory: A Cause for Skepticism

The uncertainty that exists in practically all learning experimentation makes the fact-minded psychologist suspicious of a finished system at this stage of our knowledge. While scientific truth must eventually have exceptionless validity—if its laws are truly lawful—the history of our most advanced sciences shows that their theories move by successive approximations, and the most advanced theories do not emerge full blown from the head of the theorist. Even as loose a system as Thorndike's went through revisions on the basis of evidence regarding the effects of punishment; as you will see in Chapter 5, Hull's system was continuously being revised to meet experimental fact. One of the sources of uneasiness about Guthrie's system lies in its assured answers to the problems of learning—answers that remained unchanged through more than forty years of active psychological experimentation. Experimental controversies finally become resolved as we learn more about independent variables that modify the measured consequences. No matter how these issues get resolved, Guthrie's system remains unchanged. Either the theory is a miraculously inspired one or it is not stated very precisely, and hence is not very sensitive to experimental data.

The Simplicity of the Theory May Be Illusory

Certainly much of the fascination of Guthrie's theory rests upon his apparent ability to explain a wide range of phenomena from the single principle of one-trial contiguous association. Parsimonious scientific theories are attractive. A painstaking search through Guthrie's writings for careful definition of stimulus and response, for distinctions between observables and constructs, for statements taking the form of predictions and those taking the form of *a posteriori* explanations, led critics to conclude:

> While the principles of conditioning which he expands seem to have a parsimony that would be desirable in a theoretical formulation of behavior, a closer analysis reveals that a formidable set of additional assumptions and constructs are required if his theory is to possess any real applicability to experimental data (Mueller & Schoenfeld, 1954, p. 377).

> It is undoubtedly true that many reviews of Guthrie in the literature have mistaken incompleteness for simplicity (Mueller & Schoenfeld, 1954, p. 368).

Guthrie was without peer in the use of anecdote and illustration to make pertinent comments about the activities of everyday life, including symptoms found in the psychological clinic. This complicated material he talked about in dramatically simple terms, and his theory makes this kind of talk possible. There is much to be learned from Guthrie's type of psychologizing, a type that is appealing enough to have led many promising young men and women to enter upon productive careers in psychology—a contribution to the field not to be overlooked.

At the experimental level, Guthrie's greatest contribution was to call attention to the large element of repetitiveness and stereotypy in behavior when the opportunities are favorable to such stereotypy. But Guthrie was at heart an associationist with a strong behavioristic bias. Although the associationist tradition will doubtless continue on, the particular set of behavioristic renditions of it given by Guthrie seem to have lost their appeal to succeeding generations.

SUPPLEMENTARY READINGS

The two following books, available also in more recent paperbound editions, give Guthrie's own theory:

GUTHRIE, E. R. (1935) (1952). *The psychology of learning.*

GUTHRIE, E. R. (1938). *The psychology of human conflict.*

His own shorter summaries, which show how little the theory changed over the years, can be found in the following three accounts:

GUTHRIE, E. R. (1930). Conditioning as a principle of learning. *Psychological Review, 37,* 412–28.

GUTHRIE, E. R. (1942). Conditioning: A theory of learning in terms of stimulus, response and association. Chapter 1 in *The psychology of learning.* National Society for the Study of Education, 41st Yearbook, Part II, 17–60.

GUTHRIE, E. R. (1959). Association by contiguity. In S. Koch, ed., *Psychology: A study of a science.* II: 158–95.

For a critical review of Guthrie's contributions from the point of view of the logic of science and system making, see:

MUELLER, C. G., JR., and SCHOENFELD, W. N. (1954). Edwin R. Guthrie. In W. K. Estes et al., *Modern learning theory.* Pp. 345–79.

5

HULL'S SYSTEMATIC BEHAVIOR THEORY

Clark L. Hull (1884–1952), greatly impressed by Pavlov's *Conditioned reflexes* when it appeared in 1927, published thereafter a long series of theoretical papers and books that in their totality comprise the best example of systematic theorizing in psychology during the first half of the twentieth century. Hull's theory is avowedly behavioristic and mechanistic, and studiously avoids reference to consciousness. Its central concept is habit, and it derives most of its information about habit from experiments with conditioned responses, primarily with animals. Complex behavior furthermore, is assumed to be derivable from what is known about more elementary forms of learning. Hull used the findings of conditioning experiments as his springboard, adopted Thorndike's law of effect, and tried to explain purposes, insights, and other phenomena difficult for earlier behaviorism to encompass.

THE BASIC ORIENTATION

Hull was a behavorist and he searched for a theory of behavior that explained how and why organisms made the responses they did. The current stimulating environment is only partly responsible for the behavior selected; we must recognize other influences such as the organism's history of prior training in this or similar situations, biological need-states created by deprivation of food, water, or the like, the organism's state of health or fatigue, injection of drugs, and so on. Hull subscribed to the view that the influence of these historical and/or deprivational variables upon a variety of behaviors could be summarized by one or another *intervening variables,* or theoretical constructs such as *habit strength* or *drive level.* We cannot observe drives or habits, of course; instead, they are theoretical constructs, inferred from either a history of inputs or a set of responses.

In everyday life people use terms like habit, thirst, or fatigue in meaningful ways, but the scientist must pay careful attention to the logic behind the use of such terms in a theory. *Thirst drive* is an example of an intervening variable: we know several things we can do to an animal to make it thirsty (feed it salted food, deprive it of water); and we know several things a thirsty animal is likely to do, such as work hard to get to water, drink a lot of fluids, and so on. Abstractly, if there were

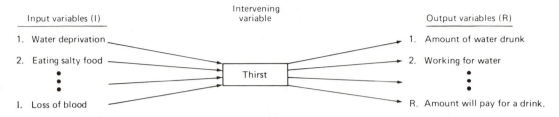

Figure 5.1. Illustration of an intervening variable that mediates the effect of *I* input variables upon *R* output variables.

I input variables causing thirst, and *R* output responses indexing thirst, there are in principle $I \times R$ empirical relations to be determined (see Figure 5.1). If, on the other hand, we postulate thirst as an intervening variable, and it proves to be unitary (that is, it produces the same types and levels of behavior no matter how the thirst is brought about), then the number of relationships to be determined is reduced to $I + R$—the *I* standing for relations from the inputs to thirst, and the *R* relations from thirst to the outputs. Whenever $I \times R$ is greater than $I + R$, then some economy is achieved by postulating intervening variables.

Since a given psychological state usually has multiple causes and multiple effects, the theoretical psychologist is practically forced to postulate intervening variables to mediate between cause and effect within the organism. Hull was much more open and explicit than were other learning theorists about the logic of his postulation of intervening variables. He thought such postulations were legitimate so long as the theoretical construct (like thirst) was anchored to manipulable input variables or histories, and to measurable behaviors. In his theory Hull postulated about eight intervening variables and specified their causal input variables; he then described how the several intervening variables combined to determine final behavior observed in conditioning and problem-solving situations. At different times Hull thought of these inter-

vening variables (like habit or thirst) either as mere fictions convenient for summarizing calculations in the theory, or alternatively as real neural or biochemical states and events in the nervous system (which is the layman's presupposition). For most purposes, it makes no difference whether one ascribes physiological reality to the intervening variables.

The 1943 Postulate System

Although Hull developed his theory over a number of years, his best statement was in his *Principles of behavior* (1943). He presented his postulates in quantitative form, with accompanying mathematical notation. We have paraphrased and recast them here to make them more comprehensible; for a fuller exposition, see Hull (1943), or Hilgard and Bower (1966).

As noted, Hull's basic goal was to break down the stimulus-response link of a learned response into a series of intervening variables that mediate the causal influence of the conditioned stimulus upon the response performed. With respect to a specific response like a conditioned eyeblink to a CS, the theory identifies certain positive factors leading the subject to make the response (namely, habit strength and drive) and certain negative factors that subtract from the response (namely, response fatigue and conditioned inhibition). The difference between these positive and negative factors for a given response determines

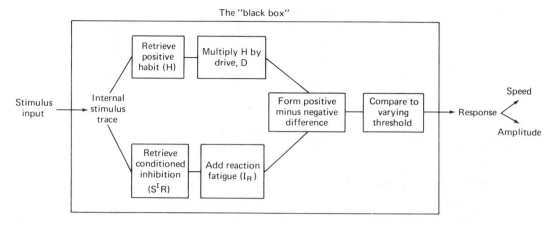

The "black box"

Stimulus input → Internal stimulus trace

Retrieve positive habit (H) → Multiply H by drive, D

Retrieve conditioned inhibition ($_sI_R$) → Add reaction fatigue (I_R)

Form positive minus negative difference → Compare to varying threshold → Response ⟨ Speed / Amplitude

Figure 5.2. Schematic summary of Hull's intervening variables and how they enter into determining whether a conditioned response will be given to a conditioned stimulus.

whether it will be performed and, if so, at what speed and intensity.

The sequence of calculational stages within Hull's theory is depicted in Figure 5.2. The external CS sets off an internal stimulus trace that lasts for a brief time; the stimulus arouses from memory one or more responses, each of which has a certain positive associative strength to that stimulus (habit, symbolized as H) and also a certain negative or inhibitory strength to that stimulus (conditioned inhibition, or $_sI_R$). The net positive strength is obtained by multiplying the habit strength by the organism's current drive level (motivational state). The total negative factor is obtained by adding the organism's temporary response inhibition (similar to its fatigue or "weariness" and denoted as I_R) to its conditioned inhibition. We then take the difference between the net positive and negative factors. This difference is the net strength, or *reaction potential,* in favor of that response. This reaction potential is then compared to a randomly varying threshold, with the response occurring if the reaction potential exceeds the variable threshold on this trial. If the response occurs, its speed and intensity (or amplitude) is greater as its net strength increases. In

case several responses are aroused by the stimulus, as in a choice-discrimination situation, the subject is assumed to choose that response which is momentarily stronger.

The *net response strength,* symbolized by $E,$ can be represented mathematically as follows:

$$E = (H \times D) - (_sI_R + I_R).$$

This equation applies to initial acquisition, during which habit (H) grows with reinforced trials while the inhibitory factors remain fixed; it also would apply to extinction, during which conditioned inhibition ($_sI_R$) would increase whereas $_sH_R$ remains fixed. Thus the equation describes both acquisition and extinction of conditioned responses within Hull's system. The reader will recognize that, in the abstract, Hull's theory is rather similar to Pavlov's ideas about behavior being determined by the subtraction of internal inhibition from excitation and to Guthrie's ideas of the conditioned response competing against interfering movements evoked by the CS. Also, determining action according to the difference between positive and negative factors is similar to economists' ideas that people choose that alternative course of action which will maximize their expected net utility (that is, the values gained minus those lost by a given choice). What is different is that Hull tried to specify in detail how various experimental variables had their impact upon one or another intervening variable, and he sought to confirm his hypothesis with experimental data.

Habit Strength and Its Causal Variables

Hull believed in association of stimuli to responses, and he used *habit strength* to denote the strength of a given association. Learning in Hull's theory consists of the growth of habit over a series of reinforced trials. Hull further assumed that the limit to which a habit strength would grow was higher the more favorable was the potency and timing of the reinforcement for that response.

Suppose we let M stand for the limiting strength of habit under given experimental circumstances. If we let H_n denote the strength of a habit at the beginning of the nth trial of the experiment, then another reinforced trial causes an increment (ΔH) to H_n as follows:

$$\Delta H = \theta(M - H_n). \qquad (1)$$

That is, the change in habit strength caused by a given reinforced trial is proportional to the difference between the current level of habit strength and the limit, M, which is the maximum strength that could be obtained with these learning conditions. θ is a fraction determining the rate of growth in habit per trial. Repeated conditioning trials under the same learning conditions corresponds to repeated application of Equation 1, which leads to the following general equation describing habit on any trial, n:

$$H_n = M - (M - H_1)(1 - \theta)^{n-1}. \qquad (2)$$

This equation says that habit strength increases as a concave function of the number of reinforced trials, n, starting from an initial value, H_1, on Trial 1 and approach to a limit M, since the fraction $(1 - \theta)^{n-1}$ decreases to zero as n is increased indefinitely.

In his 1943 postulates, Hull held to a strict reinforcement view of habit growth: a trial incremented a response's strength only if it was rewarded. In Hull's view, reinforcement acted in the same way in Pavlovian as in instrumental conditioning—namely, by providing a "satisfying" (or need reducing) effect following a response. In this view of Pavlovian conditioning, the food (US) which followed the bell (CS) was not only an unconditional *elicitor* of salivation but also a *satisfier* which would reward any ongoing response, including the salivation produced by the food. Especially when the salivary response occurred in anticipation, the food would act as a strong reward for the response. According to this view, then, learning in the Pavlovian as in the instrumental conditioning situations involved a reward, or satisfaction, principle. What differed between the two procedures was that the Pavlovian procedure used the US to *force* the correct response (salivation) to occur in proper contiguity to the CS, whereas no similar arrangement could be enforced for instrumental responses emitted at the subject's whim.

Hull went beyond the law of effect and hypothesized that all primary ("biological") reinforcers serve to reduce their corresponding drive (or need), and conversely, that any reduction of a drive would act as a reinforcing event. Thus, food reduces the hunger drive, breathing reduces a need for oxygen felt by the suffocating person, and so on. The evolutionary significance of drive reducers being reinforcers is clear: organisms that cannot learn to reduce their biological needs will not survive long enough to reproduce.

In his later writing, Hull shifted his position slightly and identified reinforcement with *drive-stimulus reduction,* which was assumed to be more like satisfaction of a craving than a need. There is a subtle distinction between cravings and biological needs. Most needs lead to cravings or appetities, but some do not—for example, during asphyxiation by carbon monoxide one does not experience a painful craving for oxygen. And we have many cravings that are not based on real needs—the obese person may eat when already full. Also, a craving can be reduced without a reduction of a biological need: a hungry rat will be rewarded by saccharine water, which is sweet but utterly nonnutritive; a hungry baby can be pacified by nonnutritive sucking on a pacifier. These would be examples of what Hull intended by drive-stimulus reduction rather than need reduction. In primary reinforcement, the two events (drive reduction and drive-stimulus reduction) are so closely associated that it does not matter very much which is assumed to be reduced. But needs may require time for their satisfaction (as in the time required to digest food) whereas incentives (including food) work promptly as reinforcers, more as stimuli might be expected to work. Furthermore, as secondary reinforcement came into greater prominence in reinforcement theories, the stimulus-reduction theory became even more attractive. This follows because secondary reinforcement value is attached to stimuli that can be introduced quickly and phasically.

Hull felt that reward variables affecting the level of performance should be reflected in the limit, $M,$ to which habit strength would grow under given reinforcement conditions (see Equation 2). Thus, for instance, since it was known empirically that instrumental performance was faster if learning occurred with a larger reward and slower if the reward was delayed following the response, Hull simply postulated that M in Equation 2 was an increasing function of the amount of reward given on a trial, and a decreasing function of the delay of reward on a trial. This amounts to assuming that the organism learns a stronger habit when the reward is large and delivered quickly.

Hull assumed that habit was permanent and that it never decreased (recall that nonreward just builds up conditioned inhibition to offset H during extinction). These two assumptions soon caused trouble; results soon appeared showing that following the training of animals with a large (or immediate) reward, shifting them to a smaller (or delayed) reward decreased their performance to a level appropriate to that smaller (or delayed) reward. The theoretical trouble was easily smoothed over by Hull's then assuming (1952a) that reward affected incentive motivation (dubbed K) rather than the limit of habit strength of the response, and that net positive reaction potential was habit multiplied by drive (D), both multiplied by incentive motivation (K). This views reward variables primarily as performance factors rather than learning factors, and M was assumed to have the same fixed value. Nonetheless, Hull stuck to his position that habit acquisition required some minimal amount of reinforcement in order to grow to its fixed limit.

The Role of Drive

The concept of drive was very important in Hull's theorizing. It had three distinct functions:

1. Without some drive there could be no primary reinforcement, because primary reinforcement requires the rapid diminution of some drive. Each need or drive state specifies a set of goal objects whose consummation would decrease the need; these consummatory acts serve as the normal means of primary reinforcement.

2. Without drive there could be no response, for drive activates habit strength into reaction

potential. Hull assumed that drive (D) multiplied habit strength (see Figure 5.2), so that a "zero-drive" state implied that no response tendency (E) could exceed the reaction threshold.
3. Without the distinctiveness of the internal stimuli provided by the various drives (so-called *drive stimuli*), there could be no regulation of habits by the need state of the organism, no way for it to learn to go to one place for water when thirsty and to another place for food when hungry.

The first of these conditions describes *which* types of goal objects will be reinforcing when the subject is in a particular need state, and describes *why* these particular stimuli will be reinforcing. The second condition attributes energizing potential to a drive; it goads the animal into action in the direction of need satisfaction. The third condition attributes to drives a discriminative or steering role in behavior.

Hull encountered some difficulties, however, in trying to get precise about this notion of drive. He thought of all drives from all sources as contributing to a general pool of energy, which was indexed by D, the energizer (multiplier) of all habits. Thus, a response trained under one drive (hunger) might still be energized and goaded to action during special tests conducted while the animal was operating under a different drive (say, thirst). He recognized the problem, however, that some habits were relevant to some drives but irrelevant or antithetical to others. For example, it did not seem right intuitively that aversive drives (pain, fear) should activate food-seeking habits. And when drive interactions began to be studied directly, it was found that hunger and thirst were intimately interlocked; a familiar example is that a thirsty man with a parched throat is not inclined to eat dry rolls unless his hunger has reached severe limits. Although Hull was cognizant of these problems (he felt some could be handled by the selective function of drive stimuli), he nonetheless went ahead and postulated a particular equation for pooling "relevant" and "irrelevant" drive strengths so as to come up with an effective multiplier index. But the equation he conjectured ignored the basic conceptual difficulties of his hypothesis of a generalized drive pool.

The Inhibition Postulates

Hull's notions about inhibition were gathered from two sources: the literature on fatigue caused by repetitive performance of motor reactions (Hull's I_R); and Pavlov's ideas about internal (conditioned) inhibition generated by nonreinforcement during extinction. For Hull, as for Pavlov, conditioned inhibition ($_sI_R$) was a *learned* form of active inhibition, a learned opposition to a specific response. There was even some attempt to maintain a drive-reduction interpretation of how the habit of "not-responding" came about. Supposing the reaction R were very effortful and generated much aversive drive (fatigue); stopping or quitting the response then would be reinforced by the immediate reduction in fatigue. Therefore, the conditioned inhibition would really be based on an associative habit for the "stopping of R." However, the drive interpretation of fatigue (I_R) is a mixed blessing, since if (I_R) is like a drive state it should enter into the general drive pool (D) as envisioned by Hull. Furthermore, I_R should multiply *its* habit $_sI_R$, as in the $H \times D$ formula. Instead, Hull assumed that I_R and $_sI_R$ simply add together to form an inhibitory composite that was subtracted from the excitatory potential for making the response. This was an inconsistency in treating positive and negative habits; Hull recognized it but did not rectify it.

Hull used these inhibition concepts to derive several phenomena of interest, by capitalizing on factors that increase the strength of I_R and $_sI_R$. For example, heavily massed trials with an effortful response produce the well-known phenomenon called *work decrement,* and a rest period following such massed elicitations produces some recovery of the motor response. Similar effects are found in nonreinforced extinction of simple conditioned reflexes. These were hardly surprising deductions, given the basis for postulating these principles.

Hull's specific inhibition postulates have fared rather badly in light of subsequent conceptual and empirical attacks (Koch, 1954; Gleitman et al., 1954). For example, Hull for some inexplicable reason related resistance to extinction to net response strength by postulating a mathematical formula ad hoc instead of deriving such a relationship from net strength and his postulates regarding nonreinforced trials and the buildup of $_sI_R$. No matter, since it is clear that an unelaborated inhibition theory could not begin to explain the increased resistance to extinction provided by partially reinforced training. Furthermore, the postulates as stated imply the absurd conclusion that conditioned inhibition for a response should eventually overtake the positive habit tendency for the response. For one thing, for on-off responses, "stopping" the response (say, halting at the end of a runway) is always in a closer temporal relation to reward (e.g., eating) than is the positive response (running), therefore "stopping" should be more favorably reinforced than the positive response. So on that ground conditioning should be impossible. Second, to mention another flaw, although Hull indicated a limit, *M,* on the growth of habit strength, the limit of growth of $_sI_R$ was just the prevailing level of the positive habit. But this means that as training continues and the positive habit reaches its limit, each trial builds up some fatigue and hence some should theoretically accumulate up to the current value of habit. Since performance reflects the difference between the positive and inhibitory tendencies, the above derivation suggests that learning curves should

increase and then, with continued practice, turn over and decrease—which is absurd. These deficiencies are perhaps small matters that could be patched up with closer attention to details of formulation of the inhibition assumptions or to the laws of chaining.

There were two other major conceptual problems with the inhibition postulates: (a) the fact that some relatively effortless responses (like eyeblinks, GSRs, pupil dilation) undergo relatively rapid extinction, whereas Hull's postulates would have predicted such responses to extinguish very slowly because they produce so little fatigue per trial; and (b) the notion of a "not-response" (underlying inhibition) was ill-defined, and seemed to lead into a tangle of conceptual puzzles. For any given *R,* what is its not-*R*? How many different not-*R*s is an organism performing at any one time? One? Five? Five thousand? It would seem better to identify extinction, as had Guthrie, with acquisition of particular competing (interfering) behaviors—although, to be sure, Guthrie was typically never very explicit about what these competing responses might in general be.

As these comments suggest, Hull's specific formulation of I_R and $_sI_R$ was not generally acclaimed, although the need for some kind of inhibitory construct was clearly recognized from the outset. For example, Spence (1936) gave a rather general, noncommittal formulation of inhibition due to nonreinforced responding in discrimination learning which better withstood the test of time. Amsel (1958, 1962) later identified frustration as the underlying basis for conditioned inhibitory factors in appetitive conditioning. We shall be meeting these terms later on.

The Final Behavior System

Hull's final book, *A behavior system,* appeared in 1952 just after his death; it contained some revisions of his postulates along with numerous applications. He attempted to explain a variety of more complex behavior, such as trial-and-error learning, discrimination learning, maze learning, and problem-solving.

We have already noted some of the differences between Hull's earlier and later postulates.[1] The first change is in the conception of primary reinforcement. While in the 1943 postulates, primary reinforcement depended upon need reduction (hence reduction in D), it came in 1952 to depend chiefly on the reduction of drive-produced stimuli.

The second important change is that the "goodness" of reinforcement had no influence upon habit strength, provided there is some unspecified minimum amount; what counts is only the frequency with which reinforced trials have occurred. This was basically, then, a contiguity theory of association formation.

The third important change is the addition of a number of nonassociative (nonlearning) factors affecting reaction potential. While some of these had been recognized in the 1943 book, they were now incorporated in a different manner, all as multipliers affecting reaction potential through the multiplication of habit strength. The constitution of positive reaction potential now becomes

$$E = H \times D \times V \times K$$

where V is the goodness of the evoking stimulus (a function of CS-intensity in a Pavlovian situation) and K is the incentive motivation based on the amount and delay of reward.

The new role for the amount of incentive (K) should be noted. In the 1943 version, the amount of incentive was assumed

to limit the maximum amount of habit strength that could be acquired. In 1952, the amount of reinforcement on the prior trial determined the vigor of response (reaction potential) on the next trial, while it did not affect habit strength. This enabled performance to shift up or down readily in response to changes in reward. While other changes in detail occurred, one is worth citing because it reflects a change in interpretation: this is the conception of the influence of delay in reinforcement. As a first change, delay in reinforcement now produced less reaction potential ($_sE_R$), while earlier it was assumed to cause less habit strength ($_sH_R$). But also the time intervals have shrunk: in the 1943 version, the primary gradient for a single reinforced response extended up to perhaps 60 seconds (1943, p. 145); in the 1952 version, it extended not more than 5 seconds (1952a, p. 131). The shortening of the gradient came about as secondary reinforcement gained more prominence for Hull as a theoretical mechanism for generating longer gradients of reinforcement. Hull was influenced by Spence's (1947) suggestion that all gradients may be generated through immediate secondary reinforcements or other intermediate mechanisms.

Derived Intermediate Mechanisms

Hull's system classifies as a *reductive* system, in that more complex phenomena are deduced on the basis of presumably simpler, more basic phenomena and relationships. In this sense more complex phenomena are "reduced" to the simpler through analysis. It is characteristic of all systems of this kind *that they intend to explain behavior that is superficially unlike the behavior from which the postulates are derived*. In other words, Hull did not intend merely to systematize the account of hungry rats pressing levers for food, from which most of the data for his later set of

---

[1] A critical exposition of the postulates can be found in the second edition of this book (Hilgard, 1956, pp. 127–50). Hull's own treatment of them is more thorough in his *Essentials of Behavior* (1951) than in *A behavior system* (1952a).

postulates derived. Rather, he intended to arrive at the basic laws of behavior, at least the laws of the behavior of mammalian organisms, including the social behavior of man. Many of Hull's most brilliant deductive accounts of complex phenomena were made in early papers, prior to the postulate systems.[2]

To bridge the gap between the simple laboratory experiments and the more familiar behavior of organisms adapting to a complex environment, he derived a few *intermediate mechanisms*. Once these mechanisms are available, they can be used as theoretical tools to explain many more varieties of behavior. We shall consider three of the mechanisms: the directive role of *anticipatory goal responses*, the *gradient of reinforcement* (originally called the *goal gradient*), and the *habit-family hierarchy*.

Anticipatory Goal Responses

Many of the stimuli present at the time the goal is reached are present earlier as well. These include the stimuli from the internal drive (what Guthrie called maintaining stimuli), environmental stimuli present both earlier and during reinforcement, traces from earlier stimuli persisting to the goal, and stimuli aroused by the animal's own movements. Hull assumed that all of these stimuli become conditioned to the goal response (eating and salivation) to a degree dependent on their trace availability at the time the goal response occurred. Hence in reactivating a sequence of acts leading to a goal, as in running through a maze, these stimuli conditioned to the goal response could elicit fractions of the goal response prior to reaching the goal. These fractional, anticipatory goal responses (r_Gs) are important integrators of chains

[2] For an introduction to the deductions available before 1940, see the summaries in Hilgard and Marquis (1940): maze learning, pp. 216–21; serial verbal learning, pp. 221–26; reasoning experiments, pp. 236–41; circumventing a barrier, pp. 242–43.

of behavior in Hull's system, and he made very ingenious use of them.

The fractional anticipatory responses give rise to stimuli (s_G). These response-produced stimuli can be assigned several functions. First, these s_G stimuli can become conditioned to differential responses and so aid in eliciting them. Thus, a rat can be taught more readily to turn left in a white maze and right in a black maze if the reward is qualitatively different in the two situations to be discriminated (e.g., food powder versus sucrose solution). The discrimination of which turn to make in which maze is helped by the different r_Gs leading to different s_Gs in the two situations, and the different s_Gs become differentially associated to the left vs. right turning responses. Second, the s_Gs can serve as the equivalents of "directing ideas," "purposes," or "intentions." In such illustrations, Hull referred to r_G as a "pure-stimulus act"—that is, an act that functionally provides a stimulus which maintains a steering role in guiding a chain of behavior. An illustration would be that of a child thinking or saying "Cookie" to himself as he assembles and goes through the complex steps required to pull up a chair and climb on it to reach the cookie jar.

Hull also hypothesized that conditioning of an appetitive r_G underlies the phenomena of positive secondary (or learned) reinforcement. If pairing a CS with a positive primary reinforcer causes it to become conditioned to r_G, then that CS will serve as a secondary reinforcer. Hull hypothesized that conditioned arousal of the r_G-s_G mechanism was innately reinforcing. The hypothesis explains most facts about secondary reinforcers—that they show acquisition, extinction, stimulus generalization, and partial reinforcement effects on their persistence, and vary with the magnitude of the reward on which they are based. A small logical problem with Hull's hypothesis arises from asking why r_G does **not** reinforce its own elicitation to the CS. If it did, then extinction of, say, a conditioned salivary reflex would be impossible. Clearly, that possibility has to be ruled out in the theory.

Hull also used the r_G-s_G mechanism in describing the further mechanisms of the goal gradient and the habit-family hierarchy, concepts to be met next. The important point, however, is that on the basis of a simple conditioning principle (namely, r_G becoming connected to earlier stimuli in an instrumental sequence), Hull derived a mechanism of wider generality (e.g., the directive role of s_G).

The Gradient of Reinforcement

A time interval of great importance in instrumental conditioning is the one between the occurrence of the critical response and the receipt of reinforcement. The measurement of the gradient is done in instrumental conditioning situations (e.g., lever-pressing or running down an alleyway for a food reward) or in a selective learning situation (e.g., a monkey presses a red or green panel, and receives a sugar pellet at some delay interval later). In such experiments, delaying the reward typically retards learning or degrades performance, and more so the longer the delay. Based on some early results from lever-pressing experiments with rats, Hull had conjectured a declining delay of reinforcement gradient that was fairly short, "possibly no more than thirty seconds and very possibly less than sixty seconds."

But all sorts of complications began to arise for this postulate, because in further experimentation it was found that the specific values of delay at which learning could not be produced depended critically upon the experimental arrangements, specifically on the nature of the stimulus changes correlated with the correct response and the nature of the activities induced in the subject during the delay interval. Spence (1947) pointed out how

the delay of reward gradient depended crucially upon the presence versus absence of secondary reinforcing stimuli following the correct response, particularly in selective learning. If the correct response immediately produces a distinctive stimulus associated with primary reward (regardless of its delay), whereas an error leads to a different stimulus, the former distinctive stimulus will act as an immediate satisfier reinforcing the correct response. For instance, an experiment by Wolfe (1934) used a T-maze leading to distinctively different goal-boxes with reward provided in the correct one after a 20-minute delay; despite this delay, conditions were still adequate for the operation of *immediate* secondary reinforcement for the choice response of turning into the correct end-box; therefore, rapid learning could still be shown at a 20-minute delay of reward. As a second example, in the lever-pressing situation proprioceptive traces from having pressed the lever were presumed to persist for many seconds and, being paired with later food reward, to thus be converted into secondary reinforcing stimuli which will occur immediately, of course, upon any later recurrence of the lever-press. Spence (1947) showed further that if one could eliminate external "stimulus props" or interfere with internal props as possible sources of immediate secondary reinforcement, then the "true gradient" of delay of primary reinforcement was around 5 seconds for a rat. This seems somewhat close to what one might expect for immediate memory of an earlier S-R event.

By combining recognition of a short primary gradient and secondary reinforcing stimuli scattered along the route of a maze or other route to a goal, Hull and Spence derived the *goal gradient,* whereby earlier components of a long chain of behaviors will be reinforced and strengthened to a lesser degree than will behavioral components closer to the goal (in time). One of the original applications of this principle was to account for the orderly elimination of errors by rats learning long multiple-T mazes. According to the principle, responses nearer to the goal would be more strongly reinforced than those farther removed, so that short paths would be preferred to longer ones, blinds (incorrect choices) nearer the goal would be eliminated more readily than blinds farther away, longer blinds would be more readily eliminated than shorter ones, and so on (Hull, 1932). The basis for the derivation is that a fixed difference in time between a correct turn at a multiple-maze unit and an incorrect turn there which must be undone is more discriminable the closer in time that unit is to the point of reward—rather like the Weber-Fechner law for discriminating two time intervals. The goal gradient principle was later applied to experiments involving the circumventing of barriers between the learner and a visible goal, with Hull proposing that the approach behavior to the perceived goal object should vary according to the goal gradient. That is, the nearer the learner came to the goal, the stronger should be its response-evoking power. This explained, for example, why animals had particular difficulty solving "long-way-around" (detour) problems when the animals are set down very near food that is just on the other side of a screen. In these problems, the animal must abandon the direct approach and in fact move away from the food in order to detour around the screen.

The Habit-Family Hierarchy

A third derived principle is that of the habit-family hierarchy. Because in the natural environment there are typically multiple routes between a starting point and a goal, the organism learns alternative ways of moving from a common starting point to a common goal position where it finds need satisfaction. These alternatives constitute a "family" of equivalent responses—called a habit family—because of an inferred integrating mechanism. The integration into a family is by way of the *fractional anticipatory goal reaction,* present as each alternative response is performed. The fractional anticipatory goal reaction provides a stimulus (s_G) to which the various overt responses are conditioned. Through the differential action of the derived gradients of reinforcement, some responses are less strongly conditioned to s_G than others. The starting responses of longer routes, for example, are more remote from reinforcement than the starting responses of shorter routes. Hence the latter are more strongly reinforced, and more strongly conditioned to s_G. As a consequence, the alternative behavior patterns are arranged in a preferred order. The less favored routes are chosen only when the more favored are blocked. It is this set of alternative habits, integrated by a common goal stimulus, and arranged in preferential order, that constitutes a *habit-family hierarchy.*

It was further deduced by Hull that if one member of a habit-family hierarchy is reinforced in a new situation, all other members of the family share at once in the tendency to be evoked as reactions in that situation (Hull, 1937). This makes possible the explanation of response equivalences and other appropriate reactions in novel or problematic situations, such as those found in reasoning experiments.

The principle was first applied to maze learning (Hull, 1934a) where it served chiefly to explain the tendency for the rat to enter early blind alleys that pointed in the direction of the goal-box, even though such blinds may not have been entered previously and so had never been reinforced in the maze situation. Goal orientation was taken to represent an inappropriate transfer of spatial habits acquired as the animal roamed about freely in an open field. Another application was in relation to the detour experiments (Hull, 1938). The amount of difficulty in turning away from a perceived goal beyond a barrier depends on the presence of habit-family hierarchies as well as upon goal gradients. In the usual experience of open space, the favored path is the straight line between the learner and the goal. The next-favored starting response is that making the least angle with the goal. The greater the angle the less favored is the starting response in that family of habits built up in previous experience. Hence, when blocked, the learner prefers a path which goes off at a right angle to one which requires that he turn his back on the goal. In some objective situations he may come to prefer a longer path over a shorter one, if the habit-family hierarchy proves to be misleading.

Hull's Quantitative Emphasis

Although our exposition has tended to minimize the matter, Hull became increasingly interested in later years with the *quantitative* aspects of his theory. He tried to scale or measure response strength in quantitative terms and to determine the precise numerical value of particular constants in the equations relating an intervening variable to an independent variable or dependent variables. Most notably, he tried to derive quantitative predictions for the results of new behavioral experiments beyond those involved in inferring the original postulate set. His final book (1952a) consisted essentially of one quantitative derivation after another concerning performance in a variety of experiments on serial chaining of responses, stimulus discrimination learning, latent learning, spatially oriented behavior in open fields, "detour" problems, incentive shifts, approach-avoidance conflict, motor skills, and many other situations studied by psychologists. Hull would start his derivations by taking his postulates and assigning certain initial hypothetical values to the many intervening variables of the theory, and then re-

strict himself to a very uncomplicated and unrealistic characterization of the behavioral situation, making up new rules for quantitative combinations as they were needed. Eventually, some final calculations of net reaction tendency were obtained which could be compared with some measure of the animals' behavior in the experiment being modeled. If he had predicted the correct *qualitative* (ordinal) trends in the data, he felt satisfied and said the "theorem had been verified." Hull would frequently summarize the successfulness of his theorizing in terms of the number of "confirmed theorems" or in like terms.

Despite Hull's love for the quantitative aspects of his theory, the consensus judgment of the subsequent generation of psychologists, even of those sympathetic to Hull, was that the specific quantitative details were the most arbitrary, least important, least interesting, and least enduring features of Hull's theorizing (see Amsel, 1965, for this viewpoint expressed by a neo-Hullian). By modern standards in mathematical learning theory, Hull did not have a tractable mathematical system. That is, he had far too many parameters to be measured and far too weak a measurement theory to really get much leverage on the quantitative details of his data. His mathematical derivations are also suspect in detail (see the discussion of cases by Cotton, 1955; Koch, 1954; or in the earlier edition of this book, Hilgard & Bower, 1966, pp. 170–180), since they typically involved a plethora of idealizing assumptions, arbitrary assignments of values to intervening variables, and ad hoc rules invented to handle special problems arising in each derivation. In such circumstances, it is doubtless wiser to consider Hull's theory at the informal, verbal level as we have done here, the concepts and interrelated ideas being of more enduring significance. We would be remiss, however, not to point out that it was the quantitative ambitions of Hull's program, and the arguments for it which he so persuasively stated, that set the stage for later developments in mathematical learning theory.

THE NEO-HULLIANS

For some twenty years, roughly between 1930 and 1950, Hull was a very important person in the Institute of Human Relations at Yale University, where he not only influenced successive generations of graduate students and colleagues in psychology, but also left his mark on colleagues in related fields of the behavioral sciences, particularly anthropology and psychiatry. The richness of his contributions is not fully represented in his published papers and books, as sets of *Seminar notes* and *Memoranda* from 1934 to 1950 fully attest.

Among those influenced more or less directly by Hull who have continued to write in the field of learning, Neal E. Miller (1959) and O. Hobart Mowrer (1960) have adopted styles of their own, and although remaining within the tradition of S-R reinforcement theory, they never did use Hull's more formal approach. Kenneth Spence perhaps represented a more direct continuation of Hull's general type of theorizing, but with reasoned alterations. His point of view is best presented in two books, *Behavior theory and conditioning* (1956) and a volume of collected papers entitled *Behavior theory and learning* (1960b). Spence, who was chairman of the psychology department at the University of Iowa for nearly twenty-five years, influenced a large number of students in his neo-Hullian tradition, among them Abram Amsel and Frank Logan. We shall now briefly discuss the contributions of these men.

N. E. Miller

Miller drew inspiration and major concepts from Hull's theory, but developed them informally and applied them to a wide range of behavioral phenomena. He was the foremost advocate for many years of the strict drive-reduction hypothesis of reinforcement, alternately attacking and defending it as an heuristic spur to progress in our conceptualization of what causes rewards to be reinforcing. Miller also developed the notion of *acquired drive,* referring to stimuli which through a conditioning process come to possess the functional properties of a drive. The best example of an acquired drive is *fear* or *anxiety.* In Miller's analysis (1951), fear is an innate response to painful stimulation, and as a response it can be conditioned to an antecedent stimulus.[3] But the fear response also has stimulating effects, which are twofold: first, these can serve as discriminative cues so that differential responses may be attached to them; second, when these fear stimuli become sufficiently intense, they act as driving, motivating stimuli which will energize particular responses instrumental in escaping or avoiding those unpleasant, aversive situations which are arousing the fear. Finally, when the conditioned stimuli arousing the fear response are removed, the fear drive is reduced, thus affording reinforcement for any instrumental responses just preceding the removal of the fear stimuli. This set of hypotheses became the basis for the analysis of avoidance conditioning that was to dominate that research area for several decades. Eventually, major emendations were required in the theory (see Bolles, 1972).

Another contribution of Miller (1944) was to elaborate and develop a precise formulation of *conflict theory,* beginning with some ideas of Lewin (1935). Consider two different places in space, *A* and *B,* and suppose that, with respect to each place ("goal")

---

[3] Incidentally, a problem for Miller was how the fear response was reinforced; to be consistent with his drive-reduction position, he had to argue that the onset of fear was reinforced by the later offset of the aversive painful stimulation—a position over which he and Mowrer were to disagree.

the subject has either an approach tendency, an avoidance tendency, or a combination of approach and avoidance to one or another or both places. The situation is so contrived that the organism is forced to make a choice, or at least behave preferentially with respect to the two goals. Miller proceeds to classify these situations and to indicate the behavior expected, given particular strengths of the approach and avoidance tendencies. Thus, for example, pure approach-approach conflicts are expected to be unstable and quickly resolved in favor of the stronger or more attractive alternative; avoidance-avoidance conflicts lead to stable immobilization at an intermediate point between *A* and *B*; and double approach-avoidance situations (involving two ambivalent choices) lead to oscillations, hesitations, false starts, beginning movement in one direction but then return, and so on.

The more frequently analyzed situation concerns Miller's theory of a simple approach-avoidance conflict, the components of which are diagrammed in Figure 5.3. Here the goal object is at once a source of attraction and repulsion, tempting the subject toward it but deterring her from full commerce with the goal. A typical experimental arrangement to study such conflict would be that involving a hungry rat trained to run down a straight alleyway to food reward, but after training, subjected to a series of painful electric shocks in the goal-box. Her approach tendency to the food is offset by her fear of shock at the goal-box. Both tendencies show a *goal gradient,* diminishing with distance from the source of attraction or repulsion.

Miller supposed that the avoidance gradient had a steeper slope than the approach gradient [4] and that the net tendency to approach the goal depended on the algebraic difference between the approach and avoidance tendencies. Under appropriate circumstances, such as those diagrammed in Figure 5.3 when the strength of avoidance exceeds that of approach at the goal, the theory predicts true *conflict* behavior. When placed at the start of the alleyway, the animal will run toward the goal, but then stop, move back and forth, advance some, retreat some, and generally oscillate around the equilibrium point, *E*. This equilibrium point is where the two gradients cross; it is stable in the sense that any deviation of the animal from the point *E* will bring to bear forces that will tend to drive her back toward *E*.

Miller listed a set of variables that should affect the strength of the approach tendency and another set that should affect the strength of the avoidance tendency. Variations in these should have predictable effects upon conflict behavior. For example, an increase in approach drive should bring the subject closer to the goal (the point *E* moves to the left), as should a lowering of

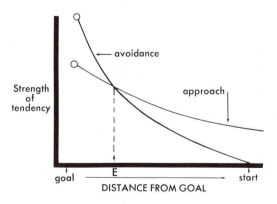

Figure 5.3.   Illustration of spatial generalization gradients of strength of approach and avoidance tendencies plotted against distance from the goal back toward the start of a straight alleyway.

[4] As Miller and Murray (1952) have shown, this assumption is in fact derivable from the idea that the net avoidance tendency is based on a learned drive (fear), which suffers generalization decrement over distance from the goal, whereas the approach tendency is typically based on an internal drive that is constant with only habit, *H,* revealing stimulus generalization.

the avoidance tendency, although in either case the subject should experience greater anxiety at the new points of equilibrium than was formerly the case.

Miller carried out an admirable series of studies confirming and extending this analysis of conflict (summarized in Miller, 1959). He also extended the same theory to analysis of the Freudian notion of displacement behavior (Miller, 1948b), in which a person selects a similar goal object (in Freud's theory, a "displaced love object") when she is ambivalent and full of conflict regarding choice of an original goal object.

Along with a colleague, John Dollard, Miller applied these hypotheses regarding learning, acquired drives, and conflict to the analysis of thinking, language, personality, neurosis, psychotherapy, imitation, and social behavior. Stimulus- response concepts were considerably liberalized in such analyses. For example, in their analysis of matched dependent behavior (a "copying" type of imitation), Miller and Dollard (1941) carried out something like a *cybernetic* analysis of several simple behavioral examples. One illustration was that of a student learning to sing on key, learning in particular to sing a musical note so as to match a voice teacher's sung note. The perceived discrepancy between the student's and teacher's notes was conceptualized as a graded cue motivating an appropriately graded, directional alteration in vocal response, so that the altered note sung by the student appeared closer to that of the teacher. This is a relational response guided by feedback of a relational cue. Reducing the discrepancy was conceptualized by Miller and Dollard as a secondary reward for the student's learning to match his sung note to a heard note. Such analyses, and similarly ingenious ones appearing in the book *Personality and psychotherapy* (Dollard & Miller, 1950), went a long way toward convincing psychologists that a liberalized version of the stim-

ulus-response-reinforcement approach was a viable and healthy alternative for learning theory.

Later, Miller turned his attention to analysis of the physiological and biochemical substrates of motivation and reward, areas in which he has also made significant contributions (1958, 1965). He was also at the forefront of research attempts to operantly condition many involuntary responses of the autonomic nervous system. Chapter 9 discusses these important attempts to produce visceral learning through biofeedback.

O. H. Mowrer

Mowrer, a colleague of Hull and Miller at Yale during the mid-1930s, was greatly influenced by them but also developed his own set of unique hypotheses. Among his many pursuits, Mowrer has maintained a constant interest in the interpretation of conditioned anxiety (conditioned drives generally) and conditioned reinforcement. An early position of his (Mowrer, 1947) was that two "principles of reinforcement" are required: (1) instrumental responses involving the skeletal musculature mediated by the central nervous system are reinforced and strengthened by drive reduction; (2) such emotions as fear, nausea, and so forth involving the smooth musculature (glands, viscera, vascular tissue) mediated by the autonomic nervous system are learned by sheer temporal contiguity of a CS to the elicitation of the emotional response. Thus, for example, the simple pairing of a buzzer with painful shocks was sufficient to associate fear to the buzzer, but some active avoidance response (like jumping across a barrier between two compartments) was reinforced because it reduced a fear drive. This was dubbed the *two-factor learning theory*, and was a view subscribed to by many learning theorists (including, for instance, Skinner) for a number of years.

Following Miller and Dollard (1941), Mowrer offered and researched a particular analysis of *punishment* that was to prove pivotal in later altering his conception of learning and habit formation. To illustrate this analysis of punishment, consider the case of a hungry rat who has been trained to depress a lever to obtain a bit of food, and who then begins to receive a painful electric shock every time he presses the lever. After a few presses and shocks, he slows his rate and eventually stops pressing altogether; punishment has suppressed the formerly strong behavior. But why? How are we to interpret this matter? Mowrer's interpretation was that the proprioceptive feedback stimuli of lever-pressing were in appropriate temporal contiguity to the shock, so that cues associated with the lever along with those response-produced cues of pressing it became conditioned to fear. On later trials, if the rat begins to approach the lever and rises up to press it, these incipient movements present him with a proprioceptive stimulus pattern which arouses anxiety. Those anxiety-provoking stimuli deter him from carrying through the incipient response; the way to escape these fear-arousing cues is to cease and desist from the punished act—to do nothing. Thus, whereas in the *active* avoidance situation the animal reduces fear and avoids shock by doing something like jumping out of the shock-box, in the punishment situation the animal reduces fear and avoids shock by doing nothing. This was to become the generally accepted analysis of how punishment operates to inhibit responses (Bolles, 1972; J. S. Brown & Jacobs, 1949; Dinsmoor, 1954).

But Mowrer thought over the asymmetry implicit in this position: as posited, positive rewards directly strengthen the habits of instrumental responses, whereas punishments operate indirectly, not by reducing the habit but by having the cues of beginning the response conditioned to fear, which inhibits the "putting through" of the response. He noticed (1956) that the asymmetry was unnecessary if one simply reinterpreted the notion of a *positive habit,* such as that of our hungry rat pressing a lever for food reward. Why not interpret positive habits in the same way as he had been interpreting punishments, except reverse the sign of the anticipated outcome? The proprioceptive feedback from making the correct response is in favorable contiguity to the positive reinforcement (drive reduction) so that it should acquire secondary reinforcing capabilities by contiguity conditioning. And by analogy to the way incipient punished responses are deterred, incipient rewarded responses should be pushed on through to completion, because their proprioceptive response pattern is conditioned to hope, to the anticipation of reward. In this conception, there is not a direct associative connection between the external stimulus and the instrumental response, not an S-R bond in the traditional sense. Rather, feedback stimulation from the correct response has become conditioned to a positive emotion (hope, or secondary reinforcement), which excites or feeds energy into the putting through of that response.

As noted in Chapter 4, this theory is similar to Sheffield's and, later, Estes's analysis of the role of reward in instrumental conditioning. However, since Mowrer excludes direct S-R habits, one is left wondering how the organism ever selects which responses to "begin incipiently." Mowrer (1960) proposes that the brain carries out a rapid *scan* over the central representations of a repertoire of responses, inhibiting those associated with fear and facilitating those associated with hope. But this mechanism has not been elaborated in detail. What is the scanning mechanism? What is scanned over? How many possible responses are there? Five, a hundred, a million? How does the device temporarily store the values of the anticipated reward for each scanned alternative and how does it then compare (or even discriminate) the many hundreds of values scanned? Moreover, how is this all to be done with the quick dispatch that characterizes well-practiced habits? These are the hard questions that Mowrer never really answered in his tentative feedback analysis. These are *not* problems for the particular formulations of anticipatory reward scanning by Sheffield and Estes; since they assume direct S-R connections, they assume that reward-scanning is involved in decisions in initial learning before correct habits have been selected and well learned.

Because of this conception of habit as the classical conditioning of a reinforcing emotion to some response-produced cues, Mowrer (1960) was quite concerned with systematizing the several classes of conditionable emotions as to their reinforcing aspects. Figure 5.4 shows the several possibilities considered by Mowrer, beginning with the primary reinforcing events of electric shock or eating for a hungry organism. The diagram is to be read as the flow of events in time (from left to right) within a conditioning trial. The cue *A* preceding shock (which brings about an *increment* in the drive of pain) will become conditioned

to a fraction of that drive increment, which fraction we call fear or anxiety. A cue *C* paired with onset of a positive reinforcer like eating by a hungry baby will become conditioned to the ensuing drive reduction; "hope" is Mowrer's name for the emotion underlying secondary reinforcement. The novel types of conditionable relations pointed out by Mowrer are exemplified by cues *B* and *D* in Figure 5.4. Cue *B* is one that signals the imminent termination of pain or drive reduction; therefore, on Mowrer's hypotheses, cue *B* will become associated with *relief* from pain. The validity of the phenomenon of relief, or reassurance that pain is about to stop, is subjectively apparent to anyone who has endured prolonged pain (e.g., of a dentist's drill). There is also an accumulation of behavioral evidence for such a relief effect, in particular evidence that frightened animals or animals experiencing shock can be reinforced by stimuli which have been associated with safety or with shock termination.

The other novel arrangement in Figure 5.4 is cue *D*, paired with the removal or withdrawal of a positive reinforcer. Examples would be cues that precede "taking

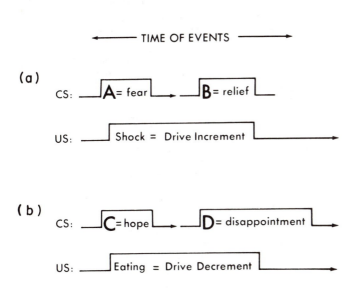

— TIME OF EVENTS —

(a)

CS: A = fear   B = relief

US: Shock = Drive Increment

(b)

CS: C = hope   D = disappointment

US: Eating = Drive Decrement

Figure 5.4. Various pairing arrangements for conditioning. (A) A cue *A* preceding a drive increment caused by painful shock will become associated with *fear*, whereas a cue *B* heralding the offset of pain becomes associated with relief from *anxiety*. (B) A cue *C* preceding a drive decrement caused by a hungry animal's eating becomes associated with *hope*, whereas a cue *D* preceding the removal of reward becomes associated with *disappointment* or *frustration*.

candy away from a baby" or withdrawing a licking tube of sugar water from a hungry rat. The idea is that such cues come to act as secondary punishers themselves.

Figure 5.4 has shown the expected "emotions" conditioned by various arrangements between neutral cues and the onsets or terminations of primary reinforcers. Once conditioned, these various stimuli can be made contingent upon some instrumental response so as to increase or decrease its frequency.

Figure 5.5 diagrams the six possible outcomes following occurrence of the instrumental response and assigns to these the labels which Mowrer uses. A *decremental reinforcement* in Mowrer's conception is one which reduces (decrements) a drive, having a positive effect on the prior instrumental response; an *incremental reinforcement* increases (increments) a drive, having an inhibitory or punishing effect on the prior response. It should be realized, of course, that these outcomes will have their specified effects on behavior only when the organism is in the appropriate drive state. Thus, an animal satiated on food cannot be rewarded by food or by stimuli *C* associated with food or punished by stimuli *D* associated with withdrawal of food. Similarly, an animal who is not frightened will not be reinforced by presentation of a cue *B* associated with relief from fear or pain.

Mowrer (1960) reviews evidence indicating the heuristic value of this symmetric classification system, and a fair amount has

appeared since. An example of an experiment showing punitive effects of cues (like *D*) paired with reward removal is a study by Stea (1964). During an initial disappointment conditioning phase, Stea would insert a drinking tube into the cage of a thirsty rat; after it had begun drinking from the tube, Stea would sound a tone and then withdraw the drinking tube from the cage (the tone preceded and followed the tube withdrawal by a few seconds). After a number of such trials, the second phase of the experiment began during which the rats received a number of free and forced trials to both arms of a T-maze, being rewarded with water from a dish on both sides. This established a baseline performance of equal preference for the two arms of the maze. In the third phase of the experiment, Stea now sounded the "disappointing" tone whenever the rat went to a particular side (say, the left side) of the maze to get its water. As a result, the animals developed a significant preference for the opposite side, where they avoided the disappointing tone. Control subjects receiving the same treatment, except that tone and water removal (or water presentation) were only randomly related in the first phase, showed no preference in the third phase for the nontone side. Thus, for the experimental subjects the tone has acquired negative value and acts like a punisher because it has been associated with the withdrawal of water, or with the frustration of a consummatory response.

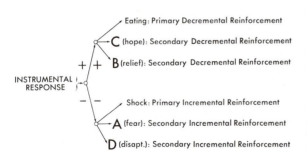

Figure 5.5. Mowrer's classification of the six types of reinforcers that may follow an instrumental response; those outcomes on the + + branches act as positive reinforcers (drive reducers) for the response; those outcomes on the − − branches act as negative reinforcers or punishments for the response.

Such a result is, of course, consonant with Mowrer's identifying cues of type *D* as punishers. Although such classification systems have their usefulness, they should not be viewed as proving the underlying drive-reduction view of reward on which Mowrer based his classification. Any simple hedonic conception of "pleasant versus unpleasant" activities could have been substituted for Mowrer's theoretically loaded terms "drive incremental" or "drive decremental" reinforcement. As a matter of fact, it now appears very likely that the drive-reduction hypothesis is empirically inadequate (see Hilgard & Bower, 1966, pp. 481–87 for our earlier discussion of its problems). However, this does not affect the classification system for reinforcers which Mowrer has proposed.

K. W. Spence

Kenneth Spence was assuredly closer to being Hull's collaborator and successor than any of the other learning theorists whom Hull influenced. Following Hull's death, Spence was clearly the leader of the tradition of Hullian theory, although he was constantly rethinking and altering significant parts of the theory. There was a reciprocal influence between Spence and Hull. Actually, Hull gained much from Spence, borrowing his ideas regarding discrimination learning, transposition, the use of intervening variables in theorizing, the notion of incentive motivation, the derived gradient of reinforcement, and many other hypotheses. In the following, we will merely touch on a few of Spence's contributions.

Discrimination learning theory. Spence's initial work (1936) was with a theory of discrimination learning, called the *continuity theory* for reasons to be explained shortly. In the simplest discrimination setup, called the "go–no go" type, the subject, usually an animal, is positively reinforced for responding in the presence of one stimulus (called the positive stimulus, conventionally denoted as S^+), and not reinforced for responding in the presence of another stimulus (the negative stimulus, denoted S^-). With differential training, the subject comes to respond promptly to S^+ but not to S^-; changes in the stimulus control changes in her behavior—she discriminates. A slightly different version of the experiment presents S^+ and S^- simultaneously, and the subject makes a preferential choice between the two stimulus patterns. Learning is revealed when the subject selects S^+ unerringly on such choice trials.

In his classic paper of 1936, Spence provided what was to become the "classical" or "traditional continuity" view of discrimination learning, a view which withstood many strong tests and many vigorous critics and provided a foil for most related developments in studies of discrimination learning. The basic approach asserted that analysis of discrimination learning should require no new concepts beyond the notions of simple conditioning, extinction, and stimulus generalization. It was assumed that cumulative effects from reinforced responding to the positive stimulus would build up a strong excitatory tendency at S^+. Similarly, it was assumed that conditioned inhibition would accumulate at S^- from the frustration consequent upon nonreinforced responses made in the presence of S^-. These excitatory and inhibitory tendencies established at S^+ and S^- are assumed to generalize to similar stimuli, with the amount of generalization decreasing with decreasing similarity. The net tendency to respond to any stimulus is then given by the generalized excitation minus generalized inhibition to that particular stimulus (see Figure 5.6). This simple theory has proven extremely serviceable and has provided good accounts of much that we know about discrimination learning (see G. A. Kimble, 1961, for a summary). Over the years, its inadequacies have been slowly unearthed—they often amount to incompletenesses rather than incorrect assumptions of the theory. A review of several of these failings was contained in an earlier edition (Hilgard & Bower, 1966, Chapter 15), and they will not be recounted here.

Transposition of relational responding. All theoretical approaches to discrimination learning begin by trying to specify, either formally or intuitively, what it is that a subject has learned in his discrimination training. How are we to characterize the subject's knowledge gained by this educative procedure? For behaviorists, this question gets translated into one about stimulus control of responses: what is the *effective stimulus* controlling the subject's discriminative performance? At one level of analysis, practically all theories answer this general question in a similar manner: the effective stimulus variable that comes eventually to control discriminative performance is that feature (cue, attribute, and so on) or set of features present in S+ and absent (or different) in S⁻. Such features are called relevant cues because their variations correlate with presence or absence of reinforcement for responding. Cues not so correlated are termed irrelevant.

But let us consider a problem where the relevant cues consist of different values along some ordered stimulus continuum (such as size, brightness, or heaviness). For example, suppose a monkey is trained to use size as a cue for securing a food reward. The setup may consist of simultaneously presenting two boxes between which the monkey is to choose; the one containing the reward has a top with an area of 160 square centimeters, whereas the other box, containing no reward, has a smaller top 100 square centimeters in area. The *relational* theory supposes that, in this situation, the subject would learn the relation "the *larger* area is correct." The *absolute* theory supposes that the subject has learned specific stimulus-response connections; in particular, that the reaching response is conditioned positively to the specific value of the rewarded stimulus (160) whereas the response is inhibited to the value of the nonrewarded stimulus (100).

Which mode of description of "what is learned" is better is more than a matter of taste, because transfer tests with new stimuli provide us with data for inferring what the subject has learned in the 160 versus 100 situation. If the subject had learned a relation ("choose the larger one of the stimuli"), then he should in some degree be able to transfer his response to this relation to new stimulus pairs differing from those used in training. That is, the relation he has learned is one that transcends the specific stimulus pair used to exemplify the relation. Thus, if we test the animal with the new pair 256 square centimeters versus 160 square centimeters, he should still choose the larger stimulus in this pair, namely, 256, in preference to 160, despite the fact that 160 was rewarded in the prior training series. The usual experimental result is that animals do choose the 256 stimulus in preference to the 160 stimulus. That is, they *transpose* the relation "larger" along the size continuum. Such studies are thus called *transposition experiments*.

This kind of transposition has been found with fair regularity in experiments, and it has been offered as evidence for the relational view of what the animal learns (Kohler, 1918). It was formerly thought that such a transposition was inconsistent with the absolute theory, since, on that basis, how could one ever predict that a new stimulus (256 square centimeters) would be chosen in preference to the one (160 square centimeters) that had been so often rewarded in prior training?

It was in this context that Spence published another classic paper in 1937 demonstrating that transposition and several related phenomena are perfectly predictable from an absolute stimulus theory of what is learned. All that is required, according to Spence, is the assumption that the generalization gradients of habit strength and inhibition around the specific S+ and S- values of training have a certain reasonable form. This view is best illustrated in Figure 5.6, which depicts a theoretical view of the situation established by the 160 versus 100 size discrimination training. The figure shows a habit gradient set up around the reinforced stimulus of training (160), and an inhibition gradient set up around the nonreinforced stimulus (100). The net tendency to respond to any size stimulus is given by the difference between the generalized habit and inhibition at that point. These difference scores are indicated in Figure 5.6. In a choice test between two stimuli, that stimulus having the larger net response tendency will be chosen. For example, for the training pair of 160 versus 100, the net tendency to respond to 160 is 51.7 and to 100 is 29.7; so in this pair, the 160 stimulus would be chosen.

A number of implications follow from this "absolute" stimulus theory. It does predict transposition over a short range of stimulus pairs close to the training pair; for example, from the difference scores shown in Figure 5.6, the animal would be expected to choose the 256 stimulus (which

has a difference score of 72.1) in preference to the 160 stimulus (difference score of 51.7). Thus, a stimulus near S+ but on the side opposite S- is expected to actually be stronger or more attractive than S+ itself. Examination of Figure 5.6 shows too that prediction of how the animal will choose on a given test pair of stimuli depends critically on how far the pair is from the training pair. As the test pair is moved above and away from the training pair, the theory first predicts transposition for near test pairs, then reversal of transposition (choosing the smaller) for pairs of intermediate distance (as in 409 square centimeters versus 256 square centimeters), and then random choices for test pairs very far removed from the training pair (as in, say, 900 square centimeters versus 1300 square centimeters). This decline in transposition with distance has indeed been found many times and it provides a difficulty for the relational view. Furthermore, according to Spence's theory, S+ and S- need not be simultaneously present for comparison in order to establish the conditions required by the theory to predict transposition in later pairwise tests. Single stimulus presentation of S+ and S- with reinforcement and nonreinforcement of responding should serve suitably to produce later transposition choices on paired tests. Transposition is found following such single-stimulus

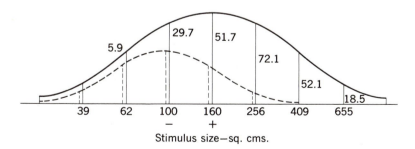

Figure 5.6. Hypothetical generalization gradient for habit (solid curve) around 160 (+) and inhibition (dashed curve) around 100 (−). The difference, habit minus inhibition, is indicated numerically at various points. The stimulus values are equally spaced on a logarithmic scale. (From Spence, 1942.)

training, although various procedural changes generally cause it to be somewhat less than that following simultaneous-presentation discrimination. Several other predictions are derivable from Spence's theory; for example, the test stimulus range over which transposition is observed should be less when S⁻ is even farther below the S⁺ of training. In general, the effects predicted by Spence's theory have been confirmed by experiments. A study by Honig (1962) is particularly clear in showing several of these effects within a single experiment.

Carrying matters a step further, Spence (1942) extended his theory to cover cases involving three training stimuli. In the *intermediate size* problem, the animal would be trained to choose the 160 stimulus from the triad consisting of 100, 160, and 256 square centimeters. Figure 5.7 depicts Spence's analysis of the situation in terms of his specific stimulus theory. An inhibition gradient is set up around both nonreinforced stimuli, with the two gradients being summated at points where they overlap. From this diagram, several implications are evident. First, the intermediate-size problem should be much more difficult to learn than a two-choice problem. This may be seen by comparing Figure 5.7 with 5.6, noting that the net differential reac-

tion tendency to S⁺ is much less for the intermediate size task. Second, learning to choose the intermediate stimulus should prove more difficult than learning to choose either of the end stimuli of the three (largest or smallest). This is true and is easily derived, although it is not shown in Figure 5.7. Third, there should be no transposition following training on the middle-size problem but there should be transposition after training on one of the end stimuli of the triad. In Figure 5.7, for example, following training on the middle-size stimulus, a test with the triad 160, 256, and 409 should lead to choice of 160, the specific positive stimulus of training. In fact, for any test triad, the preferred stimulus should be that one closer in size to 160. Spence (1942) reported data showing indeed that his subjects (chimpanzees) did not transpose the middle-size relation to the test triad (160, 256, 409) following training on 100, 160, 256.

Despite the attractive parsimony of Spence's theory and the evidence that can be marshaled for it, other results have continued to appear suggesting that it either is incomplete or is inadequate in some other way. Some of these studies, such as those by C. B. Smith (1956) and Riley (1958), have emphasized, at least for the brightness continuum, the importance of

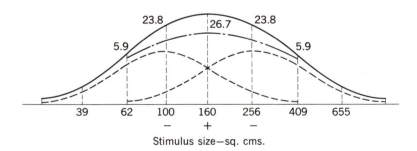

Figure 5.7. Hypothetical gradients following learning of the middle-size problem, where 160 was rewarded and 100 and 256 were nonrewarded. The inhibition gradients (dashed curves) around 100 are summated to yield a single net inhibition curve with a peak at 160. The difference, habit minus net inhibition, is indicated numerically at various points. (From Spence, 1942.)

the background contextual stimulation surrounding the focal stimulus patches to which the subject responds. Thus, a test patch of a particular brightness may be seen as lighter or darker depending on whether its surrounding background is darker or lighter, respectively, than the test patch. Riley, for example, showed that the decline in transposition on the "far tests" did not occur if the test-patch-to-surround-brightness ratio was kept the same in training and testing, although absolute intensity levels were changed for the tests. Moreover, in various follow-up experiments on the middle-size problem, transposition has often been found (contrary to Spence's result), although not in every instance.

A more comprehensive theory of transposition was proposed by Zeiler (1963). His theory assumed that the subject perceived each stimulus in relation to an internal norm or adaptation level (AL), a concept due to Helson (1964). The AL is like an average value of the stimuli experienced along the continuum of interest, such as size. The subject is presumed to learn to select that (positive) stimulus which bears a certain ratio to the current AL. By assuming that the AL changes according to the test set of stimuli, Zeiler shows how his theory explains most of the results on transfer following two- and three-stimulus problems.

As is often the case in the evolution of scientific explanations, the initial alternative hypotheses (relational versus absolute) are both eventually proved to be inadequate or insufficiently comprehensive. The new explanation, emerging dialectically, involves some novel concepts but also retains certain of the features of the previously competing theories. The transposition phenomenon engendered a controversy only in regard to the behavior of animals and possibly preverbal children. Spence himself restricted his theory's application to nonverbal organisms, believing that the human's use of symbolic language intro-

duces novel factors not covered by his theory. It is indeed true that humans learn and use relational concepts in abundance and our language is replete with relational or comparative terms which we use properly hundreds of times each day (*greater, above, farther, to the west of,* and so forth). Several investigators have been concerned with how transposition responding varies as the human child develops and becomes more proficient in the use of language. The general trend of the findings is that transposition improves with the mental age and/or linguistic proficiency of the child, although there have been a few discrepant reports (see Hebert & Krantz, 1965, for a review).

Continuity theory. One issue requiring mention is the manner in which Spence (in his 1936 paper) treated discrimination learning with respect to compounds or bundles of stimulus cues. The typical discrimination task involves multiattribute or multidimensional stimulus patterns. For instance, in a typical simultaneous discrimination task, a monkey might be required on a particular trial to choose between "a large white triangle on the left" versus "a small black square on the right." By convention, large and small are called the *values* of the size *dimension*. In this illustration, there are four binary (two-valued) dimensions, so there are $2^4 = 16$ possible stimulus patterns (and 8 complementary pairs). The experimenter will select the value of one of the dimensions as correct (e.g., triangle), so that choice of any pattern having that value will be rewarded. If triangle were correct, then shape would be called the *relevant* dimension, whereas size, color, and position would be *irrelevant* dimensions. The various values of the irrelevant dimensions are usually paired equally often with the reinforced value as with the nonreinforced value. For example, the triangle is on the left for half of the trials, and the square is on the left for the other half of the trials. With such arrangements, consistent choice of an irrelevant value (e.g., left) would result for half the trials in reward and for half in nonreward.

With this as background structure to the issue, the nature of Spence's learning and composition rules can now be stated. Roughly speaking, he assumed that every value of a stimulus pattern could be assigned a net reaction tendency for approach (its excitatory minus inhibitory tendencies), and that the total tendency to approach a given pattern was approximated by the algebraic sum of the reaction tendencies of the component values comprising it. When the subject was to choose between two patterns (habit bundles), she was expected to choose that one with the larger summated reaction potential. A further assumption was that, following response to a pattern with consequent reward or nonreward, at the end of that trial the reaction tendencies of each of the components of the chosen pattern were appropriately increased (if it was a rewarded trial) or decreased (if it was nonrewarded). Thus, the subject bases her selection on *all* perceived components of the chosen stimulus, and she learns (alters net habit strengths) with respect to *all* perceived components. Moreover, it was presumed that the changes in habit tendencies to particular cues occurred gradually, by the *continuous* accumulation of increments and decrements due to rewards and nonrewards. This is what earned it the title of *continuity theory.*

On this view, for example, a subject might begin with a set of habitual preferences for what prove to be irrelevant cues in the discrimination problem, so that a rat may show systematic position preferences in a maze before the automatic effects of differential reward gradually shape its responding into control by the relevant cue (say, the brightness of the maze arms). In this theory, differential approach tendencies accrue to the positive versus negative values within the relevant dimension, whereas the approach tendencies toward the two values within irrelevant dimensions tend gradually to become equalized (but with trial-to-trial variability in strengths due to favorable or unfavorable runs of rewarded correlations with the positive value). The animal comes to respond errorlessly when the habit differential favoring the positive over the negative value is sufficiently great to offset any and all combinations of habit differentials from the irrelevant cues; that is, the summated habit for any positive pattern (bundle) exceeds the summated habit for its complementary (opposite) negative pattern.

These sets of assumptions—regarding the composite determination of choice, and gradual learning with respect to all perceived components—were the core of the continuity theory. Almost all of these assumptions were denied by Spence's opponents, such as Krechevsky or Lashley or Tolman, who espoused a type of *hypothesis-testing theory* of discrimination learning. Details of the hypothesis-testing theory, particularly Levine's work on human discrimination learning, will be reviewed in Chapter 11 in Tolman. The key assumptions of hypothesis-testing theory are these:

a. The subject's response on a given trial is based on only one (or at most, very few) features of the total pattern. She "selectively attends" to only that one feature of the pattern.

b. The rewarding or nonrewarding outcome on that trial causes the subject to learn primarily only about that cue (hypothesis) that dominated her choice for that trial. Mainly, the outcome acts like information enabling confirmation or disconfirmation of a conjecture (hypothesis) regarding the correct solution to the discrimination task.

c. The solution tends to occur suddenly, "insightfully," in an all-or-none manner rather than by the gradual accumulation of strength.

There are differing forms of such non-continuity theories, varying according to their rules for altering the "attentional" process and the "S-R learning" process. There has been a very lengthy and productive history of research on the details of formulations of such discrimination theories. Partial summaries of the vast literature on the topic are contained in Sutherland and Mackintosh (1971), and Trabasso and Bower (1968). It is a credit to Spence's theorizing that his classic formulation (and experimental argumentation) held center stage for so many years in the analysis of discrimination learning. Few miniature theories for specific subphenomena in psychology have proven so robust and viable in the light of subsequent research.

Incentive motivation. Another area in which Spence significantly influenced Hullian theorizing was in conceptualizing the actions of rewards and nonrewards upon instrumental behavior. In 1943, Hull had originally assumed that habit strength, the primary associative factor in the theory, was affected by the conditions of reinforcement. Spence had argued, however, that reward should be conceptualized as having a motivating or energizing effect on habits rather than directly affecting the associative factor itself. In fact, in Spence's formulation (1956, 1960a), habit strength was assumed to be a function of the number of S-R contiguities (trials), whereas reward conditions (reward magnitude and number of rewarded trials) were assumed to affect reaction potential through an incentive motivational factor, K. It was assumed moreover that incentive motivation combined additively with drive, D, to comprise the full motivational complex which multiplied habit strength. Thus, dropping subscripts,

$$\text{Hull: } E = H \times D \times K - I$$
$$\text{Spence: } E = H \times (D + K) - I.$$

These different combination rules for D and K lead to somewhat different predictions. However, they can be decided only in conjunction with a strong theory of how to measure reaction potential; different measures of E, such as response speed, resistance to extinction, and preferential choice, yield different answers to the question of how D and K combine. The issue is not resolvable at present.

Spence was the first theorist to promote the idea of relating the incentive motivation construct K to the strength of the fractional anticipatory goal response (r_G-s_G). The r_G is viewed as a classically conditioned response which moves forward in the instrumental chain. Its early occurrence in the chain is presumed to channel excitement into performance of the response. This analysis seems plausible since variables which affect r_G amplitude (e.g., amount or quality of reward) or extent of r_G conditioning (e.g., number of trials, delay or probability of reward) are assumed also to have corresponding effects on the theoretical construct K. As indicated in Chapter 4, this is similar to the way Sheffield and Estes relate rewards to performance of instrumental responses.

There has been considerable disenchantment with this identification between r_G amplitude and incentive motivation. The arguments are summarized by Logan (1968). For one thing, one needs something like "incentive motivation" to account for how animals run to escape shock (see, for example, G. H. Bower, 1960), yet in such cases it is difficult to imagine what is the classically conditioned goal response whose anticipation is "exciting." Another argument takes literally the conjecture that r_G is a peripheral response, and then shows that direct attempts to manipulate r_G for food by using drugs which facilitate or inhibit salivation have not had the expected effect on performance of food-rewarded habits (see Lewis & Kent, 1961). Williams (1965) recorded salivation from dogs who had learned to press a panel to produce food on a fixed interval schedule, where the first panel-press after a given interval has elapsed is reinforced. Williams found that instrumental panel-pressing occurred long before salivation began, and the two response systems correlated poorly over time within a trial. What, then, provides the incentive motivation for the early panel presses before salivation begins? Ellison and Konorski (1964) observed a similar dissociation between panel-pressing and salivation: to a first signal, their dogs pressed a panel several times in order to produce a second signal that was followed (without further presses) by food several seconds later. They observed that to the first signal the dogs pressed but did not salivate; to the second they salivated but did not press. Such results indicate that salivation (an index of r_G-s_G), while correlated with the imminent delivery of food reward, has no vital connection to instrumental responding. In fact, it seems intuitive that instrumental activity should be most adaptive when it leads the animal out of a situation where it is not expecting reward into one where it does.

Hull and Spence conceived of K as generalized incentive motivation that energized all habits (see equation above). However, it is not clear that much is gained by adding the notion of generalized motivation to the basic idea that organisms can associate distinctive rewards with stimuli or responses that precede them. A number of experiments have shown, contrary to motivation theory, that instrumental responding for food is usually *depressed* if a Pavlovian CS for food is introduced during the running off of instrumental responding; the disruption is most likely when the response needed to get food is incompatible with the instrumental response (LoLordo et al., 1974). A critical experiment by Trapold (1962) studied enhancement of the startle reflex to a gunshot as a measure of generalized motivation, since earlier work by Brown, Kalish, and Farber (1951) had shown the startle reflex to be enhanced in the presence of a Pavlovian CS which elicited fear due to pairings with shock. Unfortunately, Trapold found that a Pavlovian CS for food not only produced no enhancement of the startle reflex, but actually decreased it, contrary to the general idea that food anticipation is motivating.

A more likely account of these findings is that animals do learn to expect specific reinforcers to specific stimuli and that these anticipations serve primarily a guiding role in selecting responses—that is, the r_G-s_G has a more important role in response selection than in providing motivation. An interesting experiment on this was reported by Trapold (1970) demonstrating the reinforcer specificity of the assumed r_G-s_G mechanism. Rats had to press one lever in the presence of a tone to receive a food pellet reward, and a different lever in the presence of a clicking noise to receive a sugar water reward (see Figure 5.8). This instrumental discrimination proceeded more quickly if prior to this lever training the animals had received Pavlovian pairings of tone-with-food pellet and clicker-with-sucrose; the instrumental discrimination was learned more slowly if the initial Pavlovian pairings had been reversed, with tone-sucrose and clicker-pellet. Such results suggest that the stimuli become signals for their specific, associated rewards, and that the different anticipations helped differentiate the tone from the clicker. The associative diagram is shown in Figure 5.8 for the case where the Pavlovian CS-to-reinforcer pairings are consistent with those operating in instrumental discrimination training.

The several results reviewed do not confirm the idea that anticipated rewards instigate a generalized motivational state. Moreover, the reward expectancy must be

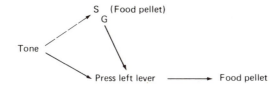

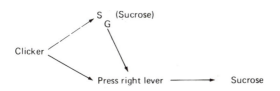

Figure 5.8. Diagram of consistent associative pairings in the Trapold (1970) experiment. The discriminative Pavlovian conditioning of Phase 1 establishes connections (dashed arrows) which help mediate the learning of correct instrumental responses to these cues in Phase 2.

specific to specific stimulus-response combinations. However, this does not force us to the view that animals initiate responses only after they have scanned over the responses and generated some anticipation of reward for each. Earlier we argued against Mowrer's response scanning theory of habit; a theory that relies on feedback from incipiently initiated responses to provide motivation or inhibition for that response does not have a way to let incentive motivation operate at the moment of choice. For example, assume a rat has had experience with a maze which has (to be absurd) 100 discriminably different alleyways leading off from one choice point, each associated with rewards of slightly different magnitudes or delays. Assuming equal experience with all alleyways (so that H's are equal), the r_G theory would have us believe that the rat can make his choice only by orienting to all alleyways in turn, getting a particular reading of r_G for each alley, storing that reading, withholding response until all re-

sponses have been scanned, then comparing the "r_G readings," and finally deciding upon that response with the highest reading. But this all seems a bit implausible. If 100-choice mazes strike the reader as too absurd, it should be recalled that at each moment in time throughout performance of a response chain, the organism may be conceived to be choosing from among a vast repertoire of possible responses. For instance, the micromolar theory of Logan (1960), which we shall meet later, supposes that for even the simplest qualitative response the animal is selecting its intensive characteristics—its speed, its amplitude, its forcefulness. As Logan (1968, p. 8) wrote, "It seems improbable that any organism has the time or resources to make momentary decisions on the basis of implicit monitoring of all possible courses of action." He then concludes, "At the present time, it appears preferable to conceptualize incentive motivation as specific to different S-R events and immediately given as a basis for choice *before* the choice is made" (p. 8).

In Logan's view, then, incentive motivation is specific to particular S-R events and is a major determiner of response selection. He supposes (see Logan, 1969) that incentive motivation is scalable upward or downward according to the joint actions of rewards and punishments. Rewards have positive incentive value, punishments have negative incentive value, and the net incentive for a given response depends on the difference between the positive and negative factors. Readers familiar with economics or value theory in philosophy will note that incentive motivation is being used here by Logan very much like the concept of subjective utility in those disciplines. Indeed, this is no accident, since Logan wants the theory about decision-making or response selection by lower organisms (see Logan, 1965) to be consistent with the way we view decision-making by intelligent humans; and utility theory was developed to account for (or normatively prescribe) the choices of "rational" men.

Abram Amsel

Abram Amsel, a student of Spence's, is a prominent contemporary worker within the Hullian tradition. Amsel has concentrated his efforts on an analysis of nonreward and extinction of instrumental behavior. Earlier interpretations of nonreward had assigned to it an essentially passive role. For example, Tolman supposed that nonreward served simply to disconfirm and weaken an animal's expectancy of reward. In Hull's earlier theory, nonrewarded trials were conceived as permitting inhibitory factors to build up without being offset by a corresponding increase in H or K. In contrast to this passive role of nonreward, Amsel's frustration hypothesis views nonreward of a previously rewarded response as an actively punishing and aversive event. In consequence, many of the effects of nonreward upon responding are now seen as analogous to the effects produced upon that same behavior by punishment.

In numerous papers (e.g., 1958, 1962, 1967), Amsel has developed and argued persuasively for this hypothesis; additional significant contributions to its development came from Wagner (1963, 1966) and Spence (1960a). We shall first state the hypothesis and then describe the kinds of experiments that have been adduced in support of it. The hypothesis is:

> The occurrence of nonreward at a moment when the subject is expecting a reward causes the elicitation of a primary frustration reaction (R_F). The feedback stimulation from this reaction is aversive and has short-term persisting motivational effects upon subsequent instrumental behavior. Fractional parts of this primary frustration reaction become conditioned in the classical manner to stimuli preceding its elicitation. Occurrence of this fractional response in anticipatory form is denoted $r_F \cdot s_F$. The cues, s_F, from

anticipatory frustration are principally connected to avoidance responses, but these connections can be modified through training.

Within the Hullian framework, the phrase "is expecting a reward" is translatable into statements about r_G, their mechanism for representing anticipatory reward. Recall that r_G is a learned variable differing in its amplitude with trials and with the characteristics of the reward (its amount, sweetness, and so forth).

The alleged motivational effect of frustrative nonreward may be seen in the intensifying or speeding up of responses occurring within a few seconds after the animal experiences nonreinforcement. The standard situation for studying this is a two-link runway. The rat is trained to run to a first goal-box for a reward; after a few seconds there, the entrance is opened to a second runway, which she traverses for a second reward. After training on this two-link sequence, omission of the first reward produces a momentary increase in subsequent speed of running down the second runway on that trial. The difference in running speeds in the second runway following nonreward versus reward in the first goal-box is taken as an index of the size of the frustration effect (FE). As Amsel's theory would predict, the factors that influence the size of the FE tend to be those which would make for stronger arousal of the r_G in the first link of the runway. That is to say, the greater the anticipation of reward, the greater the frustration produced by nonreward. A particularly important finding is that, with 50 percent rewarded and nonrewarded trials at the first goal-box, the FE does not appear during the initial trials but it develops gradually with training, presumably reflecting the further conditioning of anticipatory reward. A second important finding (Amsel & Ward, 1965) is that the FE to nonreward in the first goal-box diminishes and eventually disappears if discriminative cues are provided in the first runway (for instance, it is black or white) predicting reward or nonreward in the first goal-box. Thus, if no reward is expected, then nonreward is no longer frustrating. Third, it was claimed that the FE occurs when the amount of reward is merely reduced to a lower (nonzero) level, with the size of the FE graded according to graded reductions in the test reward below the amount customarily expected (G. H. Bower, 1962c). However, other evidence (Barrett et al., 1965) makes it appear that these graded efforts are in fact confounded with the temporary depressive effects upon running speed of the rat related to her having eaten more or less food in the first goal-box.

Wagner (1963) presents data to support the assumption that frustration may be conditioned and that it acts like an aversive drive-stimulus. Rats were run down a runway with half the trials rewarded and half nonrewarded in a haphazard order. A buzzer was presented just a moment before they looked into the empty food cup on nonrewarded trials. This procedure was presumed to associate the buzzer with the frustration reaction elicited when the rat looked into the empty food cup. Later, this buzzer was shown to enhance the startle reflex to a gunshot, a measure which has proved sensitive to acquired motivational effects of cues. Also, the buzzer could be used effectively to train and maintain a response which produced escape from the buzzer. The interpretation is that the escape response is reinforced because it terminates the buzzer, which is associated with aversive frustration. Research by Daly (1969, 1970, 1974) has shown particularly effective forms of learning presumably reinforced by "frustration reduction."

As applied to extinction of rewarded instrumental responses, frustration is presumed to act like punishment. Since extinction involves repeated frustration at the goal, the animal comes to anticipate frustration (the r_F-s_F mechanism) just as it

would anticipate with fear a painful electric shock at the goal. Anticipatory frustration initially produces avoidance of the goal, by evoking responses which interfere with continued approach to the place where frustration occurs. However, it is argued that partial reinforcement effectively trains the animal to tolerate frustration. In particular, the circumstances of such training result in the s_F cues becoming connected to approach rather than avoidance. Thus, extinction is supposed to be slower following partial reinforcement training because the normal means for arousing interfering (avoidance) responses has been temporarily preempted by the approach habit itself.

This hypothesis regarding extinction and partial reinforcement has received a fair amount of experimental support. There is little doubt that the conditions under which extinction occurs and their associated stimuli are aversive, and that the animal is reinforced by escaping them. For example, in a Skinner box animals will learn a new response to remove a stimulus that has been associated with extinction. Azrin (1964) has further shown that during extinction of a food-reinforced response, pigeons will learn a new response for which the payoff is a brief opportunity to aggress against (fight) another pigeon. Under neutral control conditions such fighting does not occur. The relevance of this observation to the frustration hypothesis is that such aggressive responses are known to be highly probable mainly when the bird is in pain or otherwise discomforting circumstances. These results are thus explicable if it is assumed that nonreinforced responses produce frustration and that frustration is aversive.

Another related fact is that tranquilizing drugs, which presumably reduce emotional consequences of frustration, will retard extinction and also partially release a response formerly inhibited by frustration. Additionally, Wagner (1966) has shown large transfer between training animals to resist the stress of punishment (electric shock) and training them to resist frustration for approach to a goal. In particular, if rats have been trained to continue approaching despite punishment at a rewarded goal, then the number of trials required to reach extinction is greater when food and punishment are stopped. Also, animals trained under partial reinforcement will continue responding longer once punishment is introduced at the goal. These results suggest that electric shock and nonreward have common properties, so that learning to withstand one of them transfers in some degree to the other. And this supports the interpretation of nonreward as a frustrating, aversive event.

The studies cited plus several others would appear to provide conclusive evidence that nonreward (when reward is expected) has an aversive effect much like a punishment. One should realize, however, that acceptance of that proposition does not logically entail belief in the particular interference theory of extinction which Amsel proposes. That theory says that anticipation of frustration at the goal is initially connected to avoidance of the goal (elicits responses interfering with goal-directed movement); by arranging circumstances so that the subject is induced to keep running under partial reinforcement training, the cues from anticipatory frustration become associated with approaching the goal rather than avoiding it.

One of the more convincing demonstrations that r_F-s_F can enter into associations with overt responses occurred in an experiment done in Amsel's lab by Ross (1964). Table 5.1 outlines the design of the experiment. During Phase 1, six groups of rats were trained in a short, black, wide box with either continuous (100 percent) or partial (50 percent) reinforcement using one of three responses: running, jumping across a gap in the floor, or climbing a wire-mesh wall to get to the food well.

These three responses had been selected by pretesting to be about equally difficult, and the animals did learn them at about the same rate. The crucial idea here is that during this Phase 1 training, the partial reinforcement groups are presumably having anticipatory frustration r_F-s_F conditioned to their approach response, whether that be running, jumping, or climbing. This presumption is tested in Phase 3 of the experiment.

Phase 2 of the experiment took the animals, operating under thirst for water rewards (rather than hunger), to a new apparatus and trained them with continuous reinforcement on a running response. The idea here was to use a situation quite dissimilar to that in Phase 1 so that differential transfer in Phase 3 can arguably arise from internal (mediated) rather than external stimulus similarity.

The critical phase is the third, during which the response learned in Phase 2 is extinguished. The question concerns how the various groups will rank order themselves in extinction. The data are shown in Figure 5.9 relating group mean running speed for the six conditions for the last block of acquisition trials and over 32 (8 blocks of 4) extinction trials. Amsel's theory predicts that during Phase 3 extinction the animals will be frustrated and begin to experience anticipatory frustration. What they *do* in the face of this anticipatory frustration depends upon what, if any, response they had been trained to make to it in Phase 1 of the experiment, *and* the compatibility of that response with the running response being measured during Phase 3. In particular, subjects who had had Phase 1 partial reinforcement with a running response (RP) should now show much superior resistance to extinction than their continuously reinforced mates (RC). Subjects trained in Phase 1 with a jumping response should show somewhat less of a partial reinforcement effect (JP versus JC). Paradoxically, the group receiving partial

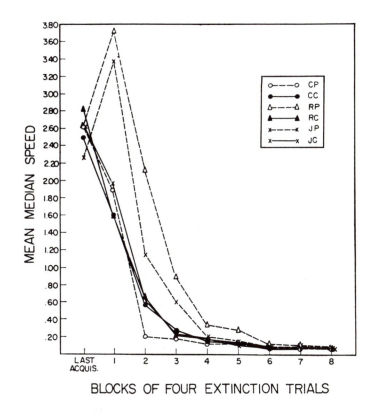

Figure 5.9. Data from the Ross (1964) experiment showing performance on last acquisition block and over all extinction trials. Data are plotted here as speeds; times were plotted in the original report. The symbols denoting groups refer to climbing, running, or jumping (C, R, J) under continuous or partial reinforcement (C or P). (From Amsel, 1967.)

TABLE 5.1.   Outline of the Ross (1964) experiment. (From Amsel, 1967.)

Phases of Experiment	(1) Preliminary Learning	(2) Acquisition Running Response	(3) Extinction Running Response
Apparatus	(A) Short, black, wide box	(B) Long, white, narrow runway	(B)
Motivation	Hunger	Thirst	Thirst
Experimental Conditions	*Running* Continuous (RC) Partial (RP) *Jumping* Continuous (JC) Partial (JP) *Climbing* Continuous (CC) Partial (CP)	*Running* Continuous Reward	*Running* Continuous Nonreward

reinforcement for a climbing response in Phase 1 are expected to be *less* resistant to extinction in Phase 3 than their continuously reinforced controls (CP versus CC). This was clearly the case for trial blocks 2, 3, and 4 during extinction. Amsel's theory predicts this "reverse" effect on the assumption that reintroduction of frustration cues in Phase 3 brings back the particular responses associated earlier to r_F-s_F, namely, climbing; and these responses are supposedly incompatible with running to the goal, thus hastening extinction of running in comparison to the continuously reinforced controls. Ross in fact observed a high incidence of "climbing" (up the wire-mesh walls of the runway) during extinction in Phase 3 by the CP rats, a response that was practically nonexistent during extinction of the other subjects.

The significance of this experiment is that it shows both positive and negative partial-reinforcement effects transferring from a training situation to a greatly altered test situation, and enables us to identify the response learned to anticipatory frustration as the critical mediating element. It shows that frustration aroused by nonreward when the animal is hungry and expecting food is very much like that aroused by nonreward when the animal is thirsty and expecting water. The result shows too that we cannot characterize the effect of partial reinforcement as teaching the animal simply to tolerate frustration and to persist responding in the face of frustration. Rather we must distinguish rather carefully exactly what response the subject has learned to make to anticipatory frustration and its relationship to the criterion response on which the subject's frustration tolerance is being assessed. Ross's experiment is of unquestionable significance for Amsel's theory. Because of its critical value, the experiment should be repeated to check its reliability.

Amsel (1967) later developed his frustration theory in discrimination-learning sit-

uations—for example, having the subject experience continuous reinforcement when run in a white alley and partial reinforcement when run in a black alley. This situation produces a *generalized partial reinforcement effect,* wherein resistance to extinction of the discrimination animal in his 100 percent alleyway is considerably greater than that of a control mate which had received continuous reinforcement initially in both alleyways. In some cases (see Pavlik & Carlton, 1965), a reverse partial reinforcement effect may be found in which the discrimination animal is more resistant to extinction in his continuously reinforced situation than in his partially reinforced situation. This would be expected in Amsel's theory if incentive motivation were higher in the continuously reinforced situation, whereas the frustration mechanism r_F-$s_F \rightarrow R$ is equally available to retard extinction in both situations.

Since it is one of the dominant conceptions of extinction, frustration theory requires critical analysis, because it clearly has a few failings. First, there is the suggestion in experiments by Levy and Seward (1969) that in the two-link runway no FE occurs if the rat is expecting different incentives (food and water) in the two goal-boxes—which is a most puzzling observation. Second, Amsel's extinction theory applies only to instrumental, appetitive responses, and leaves untouched extinction phenomena (such as partial reinforcement effects) in paradigms such as classical conditioning or instrumental escape conditioning (G. H. Bower, 1960). Partial reinforcement in classical defense conditioning (e.g., eyelid conditioning) enhances the CR's resistance to extinction, yet it is difficult to imagine what could be frustrating about not receiving an anticipated aversive stimulus. Third, Capaldi and his associates (reviewed in Capaldi, 1967) have been able to produce differential amounts of resistance to extinction by variations in the sequential pattern of reinforced and nonreinforced trials the animal experiences during the acquisition series—a set of facts with which Amsel's theory can make no contact. Furthermore, there is now ample evidence (see Robbins, 1971, for a review) for a partial reinforcement effect on extinction following even very short training series (five to ten trials), far too abbreviated to bring to completion the successive stages (of r_G conditioning, then r_F, and so on) envisioned by Amsel's theory. These latter points suggest that extinction is a process with multiple determinants, that Amsel's frustration hypothesis is probably one component of a viable explanation, but that for the total range of phenomena other mechanisms will have to be invoked. The currently most popular alternative is Capaldi's sequential hypothesis, which is a sophisticated elaboration of the early discrimination hypothesis. We shall be reviewing Capaldi's interesting work in Chapter 9.

Frank Logan

Frank Logan is another dominant figure working with the Hullian approach, and he has written extensively from that viewpoint (Logan, 1959, 1960, 1970; Logan & Wagner, 1965). He was Spence's student at Iowa and was at Yale during Hull's last years. He has made a number of contributions in both experimentation and theoretical work. His main concern (illustrated in his 1965 and 1969 papers) has been with determining how incentive motivation regulates behavior and how it is, in turn, regulated by the conditions of reward and punishment. His viewpoint in this regard was mentioned earlier in discussing the problems encountered by identifying incentive motivation with r_G amplitude.

Perhaps Logan is best known for developing the *micromolar* approach to behavior theory. This adopts a particular viewpoint of what it is that is reinforced, or what is learned, when we say that a re-

sponse is reinforced. The micromolar approach promoted by Logan (1956, 1960) begins with an argument for expanding the definition of response to include its intensive characteristics (its speed, amplitude, volume, and so on). In the classical view, exemplified by Hull's 1943 theory, response classes are defined in terms of their achievements—running down a runway or pressing a lever. The rule is to aggregate together all instances of behavior which achieve the same end result (e.g., getting the lever down); they are so aggregated because they are not differently reinforced by the experimenter. Variations in speed or amplitude of the response during training were taken to be indices of the strength of the response tendency. Hull formalized this idea in his reaction-potential construct E, which presumably determined the probability, speed, amplitude, and resistance to extinction of the response.

This classical approach runs into difficulties at several points, as Logan, among others, has pointed out. First, these various response measures frequently fail to be well correlated. During training, a measure such as response probability may improve monotonically with practice, whereas speed and/or force of the response may at first increase and then decrease over trials. One example is the lengthening latency of the CR in classical conditioning (mentioned in Chapter 3) as the animal learns to time the arrival of the unconditioned stimulus; a second is that forcefulness of lever-pressing first increases and then decreases during training, stabilizing at just above that minimal force required to operate the feeder. The second main difficulty of the classical approach results from the fact that one can differentially reinforce intensive characteristics of the response. Skinner (1938) was the first to show this experimentally, demonstrating in the free operant situation differential shaping of slow or fast rates of bar-pressing, weak or strong forces of bar-pressing, and long or short durations of bar-holding. The method is simplicity itself: simply reinforce only responses whose intensive properties fall within a specified criterion range, possibly advancing to stiffer criteria as the animal's performance follows along. It is clear that many skilled performances are differentiated in this way. It is also clear that through such differential reinforcement (e.g., of slow response speeds), the intensive properties of the response (a) may or may not increase monotonically with training, and (b) may be put in any relation to other intensive properties that we choose to reinforce (e.g., talking slowly and loudly, talking fast and softly, and so on).

Logan broadened the notion of differential reinforcement to include any variation in some parameter of reinforcement such as its amount, quality, delay, or probability. In conditions of *correlated reinforcement,* one or more dimensions of reinforcement are correlated with some intensive property of the observed behavior, such as its speed. The *terms function* specifies what reinforcement the subject receives for particular response speeds; it is similar to the terms of a contract between the subject and a reinforcing agent (the environment or the experimenter). A tremendous variety of terms functions are imaginable, only a few of which have been investigated. Examples in a runway situation might be: the faster the rat runs to the goal-box, the longer his reward will be delayed; or the faster he runs, the greater will be the amount of reward he receives; or reinforcement may be provided only when the speed falls in the interval x to y, and not otherwise, and so forth. In general, it is found that subjects adjust to such reward conditions, coming eventually to respond at a near optimal level (see Logan, 1960, for some results and a more detailed discussion).

To deal with the behavior of subjects under such conditions, Logan proposed the *micromolar* approach—that is, one which identifies different speeds as different responses, selectively influenced by differential reinforcement. Logan proposes essentially a utility analysis to deal with this approach, although he specifies the components of utility in terms of the intervening variables of habit, drive, incentive, and so on, of Hullian theory. The net utility (or E) of a particular response speed is given by its positive utility minus its associated negative utility. The main component of positive utility is incentive, which increases with the amount of reward provided for that speed and decreases with the total interval of reinforcement for that speed (total interval = duration of response + delay of reward following that response). The subject is viewed as learning through experience the incentive associated with each speed; however, the incentive for a given speed is influenced also by generalization of incentive learned for similar speeds. The main component of negative incentive for a particular speed is its effortfulness, fast responses requiring more effort. The profile of net utility across the speed continuum is then used to calculate the probability distribution of the various speeds. Generally speaking, the expected probability of a particular response speed depends on its net utility relative to that of alternative speeds. Thus, the sole dependent variable of the theory is response probability, but here, response refers to intensive properties of the behavior.

Suffice it to say that such a theory will account qualitatively for the more or less optimal performance subjects achieve under conditions of correlated reinforcement. Because incentive is specific to particular response speeds, the terms function gets mapped into the model's incentive profile, distorted somewhat because of generalization of reinforcement effects among similar responses. Thus does the model of the organism take account of and adjust its behavior in relation to the terms function.

Besides accounting for correlated reward

conditions, the approach also gives a creditable account of why Hull's conventional approach (called *macromolar*) worked when it did and failed when it did. Logan points out that almost all conditions of constant reward involve an implicit correlation between response speed and interval of reinforcement: the faster the rat runs to the goal-box, the sooner he gets the reward. The micromolar theory predicts that a particular response dimension will improve monotonically with practice only if some dimension of reinforcement improves with that response dimension. Thus, although speed of lever-pressing increases with practice because faster responses bring rewards sooner, the forcefulness of the lever-press does not increase because more forceful responses require more effort and bring no better reward. Logan has also shown how the micromolar theory implies the usual effects upon response speed of variations in drive, amount of reward, and delay of reward in constant reward situations. Many more details might be cited in connection with the theory, but we will not elaborate further.

The importance of the micromolar theory has been primarily that of conceptual housecleaning within learning theory. By virtue of Logan's analysis, several conceptual puzzles connected with the problem of how reinforcement shapes behavior have been unraveled and understood. The micromolar approach is general and applies to classical conditioning as well as instrumental conditioning, and it influences the way we talk and think about variables. For example, in cases of classical conditioning the micromolar theory says that the response amplitude learned will be that amplitude elicited by the unconditioned stimulus. This provides a direct interpretation of the fact that amplitude of the conditioned reflex correlates very highly with amplitude of the unconditioned reflex. Thus, the satiated dog that gives a feeble salivary CR has learned his response ampli-

tude just as well as the hungry dog that gives a large CR amplitude; the first dog is merely learning a smaller amplitude response. Similarly, the dog will tend to learn to salivate with a particular latency proportional to the CS-US interval. The micromolar approach has been quite useful too in interpreting the influence of various Skinnerian schedules of reinforcement upon rate of responding (see Chapter 7). At least some schedules may be viewed as more or less inexact terms functions which correlate probability of reinforcement with interresponse time. For example, variable interval schedules generate slow response rates, and this may be explained as due to the differential reinforcement of long interresponse times. Recent theoretical work by Shimp (1969) provides a utility sort of account of schedule performance, which supposes the animal to select among a set of interresponse times so as to maximize her momentary expected utility.

Moreover, the micromolar approach makes somewhat better contact than did the older approach with the learning involved in so many of our everyday performances. Reinforcing consequences typically depend not only upon whether a response is made but also upon whether it is made at the right time, at the right place, at the correct pace or intensity, and so on. In fact, it is difficult to imagine human situations in which the payoff does not depend in some way—such as in amount, delay, or probability—upon the skillfulness with which the response is made. The micromolar theory treats these temporal and intensive aspects of responding as part of what gets learned. In this respect, the treatment of the response is made more comparable to the conventional treatment of the stimulus, where we distinguish quantitative as well as qualitative variations. Just as an 80-decibel and a 50-decibel sound are different stimuli, so also a shout and a whisper are different vocal responses. In this manner, the descriptive level of our theory is brought more in line with the realities of many learning situations. The micromolar theory of Logan now provides us with the means of analyzing how the learning of differentiated, skillful responses occurs, where previously within the classical tradition no relevant theory had been articulated.

With this section, we close out the discussion of neo-Hullians and their contributions. Hullian theory has clearly been very successful in gaining the allegiance of many productive contemporary psychologists. The ones explicitly mentioned here are but a handful of a rather significant group of scientists working with a Hullian orientation. It is still to a rather high degree a theory based on animal-learning results and has not played a large role in current approaches to human memory. But that may be because of predispositions of the respective investigators and because different problems are being attacked in the main by the two areas. We turn now to our final remarks regarding Hull's position.

ESTIMATE OF HULL'S POSITION

Hull's Summary of Learning Mechanisms

Hull wrote extensively about many problems connected with learning. He maintained a Darwinian view—namely, that organisms evolved according to the ability of their nervous system to adapt their behavior to environmental demands. He conceived of learning as one of the major means by which organisms adapt. In his final book he listed and described eight *automatic* adaptive behavior mechanisms (1952a, pp. 347–50):

1. Inborn response tendencies provide the first automatic mechanisms for adapting to emergency situations.
2. The primitive capacity to learn is the second mechanism, "a slightly slower means of adaptation to less acute situations."
3. The antedating defense reaction, which is learned and then moved forward by stimulus generalization, provides the third adaptive mechanism.
4. The extinction of useless acts, negative response learning, is the fourth mechanism.
5. Trial-and-error learning is the fifth mechanism.
6. Discrimination learning is the sixth mechanism.
7. A second type of antedating defense reaction, depending on the persistence of stimulus traces (rather than upon generalization, as in the case of a perceived dangerous object), is the seventh mechanism.
8. The fractional antedating reaction (r_G), with its proprioceptive stimulus correlate (s_G), provides for the "automatic (stimulus) guidance of organismic behavior to goals." Hull ascribes particular importance to the mechanism when he writes:

> Further study of this major automatic device presumably will lead to the detailed behavioral understanding of thought and reasoning, which constitute the highest attainment of organic evolution. Indeed the $r_G \rightarrow s_G$ mechanism leads in a strictly logical manner into what was formerly regarded as the very heart of the psychic: interest, planning, foresight, foreknowledge, expectancy, purpose, and so on (1952a, p. 350).

How Satisfactory a System Did Hull Leave?

Hull's system had many points of superiority over other contemporary psychological systems. It was at once comprehensive and detailed, theoretical yet empirically quantitative. It is easy to locate faults within it because it is so carefully worked out, so explicit that its errors of incompleteness or inconsistency are easily brought into focus. A theory expressed solely in the ordinary literary language may sound very plausible because the gaps are glossed over through cogent illustrations (a charge leveled against Guthrie). A theory such as Hull's calls attention to itself whenever it jumps a gap. A severe critique by Koch

(1954) capitalizes on this relative explicitness of Hull's theory. In criticizing Hull's theory we must not lose sight of the fact that, with all its weaknesses, it was a major achievement.

We do well to think of Hull's system as really twofold. On the one hand, he embarked on a bold and comprehensive theory of behavior, a theory he hoped would serve as a basis for much of social science. On the other hand, he was experimenting with a very precise miniature system, with determinate constants based on controlled experimentation. He attempted to combine these two enterprises at once, and was not very skilled at distinguishing between what he accomplished on a large scale and what on a small scale, for he wanted the whole to be one system.

On the large scale, when dealing with behavior in free space, problem-solving, and ideas, Hull made skillful use of peripheral mechanisms, particularly the hypothesized r_G-s_G sequence. By interlocking these goal anticipations into other features of his system, particularly through the gradient of reinforcement and the habit-family hierarchy, he was able to make large-scale deductions of familiar forms of behavior. When moving on this large-scale level, the theory was very "molar" indeed, and almost no efforts were made to pin down precisely the kinds of anticipatory movements (chewing movements, bodily postures) that would serve as the tangible base for the important fractional antedating response. The large-scale deductions, built on r_G, do not require any one special theory of learning, so long as goal anticipation can be achieved by that theory.

When Hull was operating on a smaller scale and attempting to become precise and quantitative, he became highly particularistic, confining many of the later postulates and corollaries to the results of single experiments done with rats bar-pressing in a Skinner box modified so that a latency measure could be secured. Hull became so preoccupied with this quantification that he failed to distinguish between this exercise in miniature-system construction and the larger task on which he was simultaneously engaged. It would have been preferable to present the tentative generalization and then separately to offer the quantitative evidence as illustrative. But this is a stylistic defect of Hull as a system-maker, not a basic conceptual defect of the theory.

It must be acknowledged that Hull's system, for its time, was the best there was—not necessarily the one nearest to psychological reality, not necessarily the one whose generalizations were the most likely to endure—but the one worked out in the greatest detail, with the most conscientious effort to be quantitative throughout and at all points closely in touch with empirical tests. Furthermore, it may well be said to have been the most influential of the theories between 1930 and 1955, judging from the experimental and theoretical studies engendered by it, whether in its defense, its amendment, or its refutation.

Various objective estimates exist of Hull's influence upon psychology. For example, during the decade of 1941–1950 in the *Journal of Experimental Psychology* and the *Journal of Comparative and Physiological Psychology,* 40 percent of all experimental studies and 70 percent of those in the areas of learning and motivation referred to one or more of Hull's books or papers (Spence, 1952), while in the *Journal of Abnormal and Social Psychology* during the years 1949–1952 there were 105 citations of Hull's *Principles of behavior,* and the next most frequently cited book was mentioned but 25 times (Ruja, 1956).

Perhaps the most striking testament to Hull's influence is the talent and productivity of the large number of neo-Hullians whom he enlisted into the task of developing, extending, and applying his theory. Men such as Spence, Miller, Mowrer, Judson Brown, Grice, Amsel, Wagner, and Logan (and their students) have been dominating figures in American psychology over the years since 1940; they have significantly altered the intellectual landscape of learning theory. Their achievements and accomplishments are a tribute to the inspirational example set by Clark Hull and to the theoretical fertility of the system of concepts he molded together.

SUPPLEMENTARY READINGS

The four books which represent Hull's behavior theory are:

HULL, C. L., et al. (1940). *Mathematico-deductive theory of rote learning.*

HULL, C. L. (1943). *Principles of behavior.*

HULL, C. L. (1951). *Essentials of behavior.*

HULL, C. L. (1952a). *A behavior system.*

A review of the theory is:

LOGAN, F. A. (1959). The Hull-Spence approach. In S. Koch, ed., *Psychology: A study of a science.* Vol. 2.

A popular paperback explaining learning from a Hullian viewpoint is:

LOGAN, F. A. (1970). *Fundamentals of learning and motivation.*

A comprehensive textbook from the Hullian position is:

LOGAN, F. A., & FERRARO, D. P. (1978). *Systematic analyses of behavior: Basic learning and motivational processes.*

Spence's and Mowrer's views are set forth in these books:

MOWRER, O. H. (1960). *Learning theory and behavior.*

SPENCE, K. W. (1956). *Behavior theory and conditioning.*

SPENCE, K. W. (1960). *Behavior theory and learning: Selected papers.*

For a detailed and searching criticism of Hull's system from the standpoint of the logic of science, see:

KOCH, S. (1954). Clark L. Hull. In W. K. Estes et al., *Modern learning theory.* Pp. 1–176.

A rare opportunity exists to follow the course of Hull's thinking through excerpts from the 73 "idea books" that he left. The first of these was begun in October 1902, when Hull was only 18, and the last entry was made on April 21, 1952, 18 days before he died. They were intensely personal, and not intended for publication. As Ammons (1962) points out, it is instructive to compare the passages with the autobiographical sketch, which was of course intended to be read. The pertinent references are:

HULL, C. L. (1952b). Autobiography. In H. S. Langfeld et al., *A history of psychology in autobiography.* IV: 143–62.

AMMONS, R. B. (1962). Psychology of the scientist: II. Clark L. Hull and his "Idea books." *Perceptual Motor Skills,* 15: 800–2.

HAYS, RUTH (1962). Psychology of the scientist: III. Introduction to "Passages from the 'Idea Books' of Clark L. Hull." *Perceptual Motor Skills,* 15: 803–6.

HULL, C. L. (1962). Psychology of the scientist: IV. Passages from the "Idea Books" of Clark L. Hull. *Perceptual Motor Skills,* 15: 807–82.

6
HUMAN ASSOCIATIVE LEARNING

During the popular heydays of the major learning theories, the hot controversies between Hull and Guthrie and Tolman were fought out in *animal* learning laboratories. Most of the controversies surrounded theoretical interpretations of how rewards influenced learning and performance, how to conceptualize what is learned, and what were the critical ingredients for learning. These debates were carried into the animal learning laboratory because of the widespread belief that animal learning would be simpler to understand than human learning, that fundamental features of most learning phenomena could be studied with the lowly rat learning to navigate through mazes. Research proceeded on the premise that learning mechanisms were universal throughout the animal kingdom, and that simple conditioning principles discovered with lower animals would apply with only slight modifications to humans. There was enough suggestive evidence at hand to make this thesis plausible: for instance, classical GSR and eyeblink conditioning carried out with humans showed that variables of the conditioning situation such as the length of the CS-US interval had effects similar to those found with animal subjects.

THE HUMAN LEARNING TRADITION

Developing alongside this theory-dominated animal conditioning research was a body of research concerning associative learning in adult humans, specifically studies concerned with adults' acquisition of simple S-R associations and chains of associations. These were called studies of *verbal learning, sensory-motor learning,* or *skill learning.* We will review here the tradition of verbal learning, since it had a definite founder, a clear beginning, and definite paradigms, all of which have been lacking in the motor-skills research area. For reviews of the motor-skills literature, see Welford (1976) or the volume edited by Bilodeau (1966).

The verbal learning tradition began with Herman Ebbinghaus, dating from the publication of his treatise *Über der Gedächtnis (Concerning memory)* in 1885. Ebbinghaus began his work in the tradition of empiricism and associationism. He showed that associative learning processes, which had been topics of much speculation among philosophers, could be brought into the laboratory and measured. Considering the historical context, his achievements were remarkable: (1) He relied on objective instead of introspective reports of memory, using the relearning method and the savings score to infer retention where conscious recall failed; (2) he invented calibrated units (nonsense syllables), which supplied a limitless number of new learning materials for experimentation; (3) he challenged the established laws of association, particularly those of temporal succession, by introducing a quantitative study of remote associations; (4) he used statistical methods to summarize his findings and discuss the significance and relative magnitude of effects of several learning variables.

Ebbinghaus created a new experimental situation—namely, learning lists of nonsense syllables—in which a multitude of variables could be defined and their influence on "remembering" behaviors observed. The phenomena that Ebbinghaus discovered are still dealt with today, and his associative theories were extremely long lived. Verbal learning research has been long dominated by Ebbinghaus's work. Subsequent research has teased out the variables of verbal learning situations, measured them, and determined their laws. During the course of this research, the learning situation and paradigms underwent constant small modifications; in a sense, the task of empirical analysis was continually beginning anew. The three major verbal learning paradigms that have been studied most intensively are:

1. Serial learning. The subject learns to recite a list of items (syllables, words, digits) in a specified serial order. The recitation may be unaided or prompted serially; in the latter case, after each item-recall attempt the next item is presented as a cue for the following item in the series.

2. Free-recall learning. The subject tries to recite a list of items in *any order* she chooses, at any pace. The list of items may be presented only once or repeated several times, either in the same order or a randomly varying order for the items.

3. Paired-associate learning. The subject learns a list of discrete associations (pairs of syllables or words), denoted generically as *A-B*. The pairs are typically learned under instructions that *A* is to serve as the cue (prompt, stimulus) for recall of *B* (as the response). The responses may be either known and available (such as buttons on a keyboard) or items which themselves must be learned as units (such as foreign-language words).

These paradigms are partly defined by the units to be memorized (lists of single items versus pairs), and by the required criterion performance (e.g., ordered vs. unordered recall). The memories established by either procedure can be tested by recall, recognition, or reconstruction. Each paradigm can be used with large or small amounts of material, with short or long retention intervals. In addition, of course, the person may be learning several different lists in succession, so we can examine the influence of learning one list upon the learning or retention of another. As variables have been isolated and studied, a huge backlog of empirical information has accumulated about how humans learn in these situations. Many hypotheses have been proposed to integrate and account for the evidence on some particular question.

THEORY IN VERBAL LEARNING

During the years 1900 to 1930, studies of verbal learning were carried out largely by a group of psychologists calling themselves *functionalists* (see Chapter 9 in Hilgard & Bower, 1975). Functionalism was a loose confederation of methodological ideas, but the central goal was to perform a detailed experimental analysis of important psychological skills or tasks. Thus, the guiding idea was to dissect any given task, such as serial verbal learning, into a number of components or constituent skills, and to analyze these experimentally. The concern with empirical description led the researchers to avoid the global theories and their associated controversies that raged in the animal conditioning laboratories; instead, verbal learning researchers thought truth would be revealed by patient empirical analysis of specific learning tasks (see McGeogh & Irion, 1952).

The background theory of learning underlying verbal learning research was general associationism, supplemented in later years by some concepts from Hull's theory. Ebbinghaus started his work in the tradition of associationism. The basic idea was that remembering could be reconstructed in terms of connections (associations) among ideas, these connections were recorded into the mind (memory) by the contiguous occurrence of the two ideas in consciousness. This mental contiguity of to-be-associated ideas was allegedly caused either by the objective contiguity (in time or space) of the external events that arouse their corresponding ideas in the mind, or by the person thinking of (retrieving from memory) a second idea while considering a first one. Retrieval during this second mode of contiguity was characterized by there being a similarity or relatedness between the prompting idea and the mate it retrieves from memory. By whatever means it occurred, the contiguous experiencing of ideas *A* and *B* together in consciousness was presumed to establish an associative connection or bond between their internal representations. This association, or "line," from node *A* to node *B* could vary in strength, affecting the likelihood and speed with which *B* comes to mind when *A* is entered into consciousness. A given element may be associated with a number of different elements, denoted *A-B, A-C, A-D,* and so on. These will be ordered in strength at any one time. The stronger is the *A-B* association, the more likely it is to win out in competition with alternative responses. Learning consists in gradual strengthening of the association to the correct response, so that it will occur more surely than error responses to the stimulus. Before discussing how this theory was elaborated to deal with phenomena of the verbal learning laboratory, let us first note how this tradition dealt with the question of reinforcement in human learning, since that played such a central role in other learning theories.

Reinforcement in Human Learning

The typical verbal learning experiment is poorly designed to study motivation, reward, and the influence of these factors upon speed of learning or performance. The typical subjects are college students who are already sophisticated at motivating and rewarding themselves for learning practically any material set before them. The typical motivation for subjects to engage in the verbal learning task is provided by the experimenter's instructions and the subjects' desire to be cooperative and to work to earn their pay (or course credit points). The experimenter's instructions usually define the task, orient the subjects to it, initiate rehearsal of the material with intent to learn, define the criteria for adequate or correct performance, and sustain the subjects' performance throughout training. This has been called the *intentional learning set,* and it presumably exists as a pool of learning strategies that students have acquired through formal education by the time they reach college.

Much research has shown that the intention to learn has its main effect in initiating certain rehearsal or elaborative activities with respect to the to-be-learned material (see Postman, 1964). But if these same activities can be evoked by other orienting tasks, without the intention to learn, the subject will learn about the same amount incidentally. For instance, if subjects are asked to construct meaningful sentences for word pairs (for example, "pen-record" might be converted into a sentence like "My *pen* scratched a *record*"), they will thereby associate the pairs of words as indicated by their later ability to recall the second word when prompted with the first. This "incidental" learning is in no way improved if in addition sentence-generating subjects are also told to remember the material for a later recall test. What is important is what the subjects do with the material when they are exposed to it, not their intention to learn or the reason given to them for carrying out these elaborative activities.

The researchers in verbal learning have always adopted an empirical law of effect. They realized that the experimental situation is arranged so that the reinforcement that promotes learning is information about the correct response. Thus, a response followed by the experimenter's announcement of "Right" will increase in its probability to its stimulus; and informing the subject of the correct response has a similar effect. Thorndike assumed that the subject's response would be rewarded (cause satisfaction and strengthening) when it matched the response designated as correct, and would be nonrewarded or punished otherwise. The opposing viewpoint to Thorndike's law of effect is that information about the correct response is sufficient to promote learning, and that satisfiers after the correct response are irrelevant to learning. This view and evidence supporting it clearly has more to recommend it than does Thorndike's original view of reward in human learning. Of course, for the functionalist interested in dissecting the learning tasks, the viewpoint adopted on this reward issue was relatively immaterial. Probably because they were relatively unconcerned with issues of motivation and reinforcement, the functionalists' analysis of verbal learning tasks proceeded apace without becoming bogged down and entangled in the grand debates and controversies between the global theories (like the

Hull vs. Tolman debates) that raged from the 1930s to 1950s.

Let us turn now to elaborations of the basic associative theory developed by verbal learning theorists to explain basic phenomena revealed in studies of serial learning, of paired associate learning, of transfer of training, and of forgetting.

SERIAL LEARNING HYPOTHESES

Ebbinghaus investigated only serial learning and established many functional relationships. Included were the effects of list length on time to learn a list, the effects of different lengths of study time or number of study trials upon subsequent amount retained, and the effects of the duration of the retention interval on amount retained. In an associative analysis, a serial list, denoted *A-B-C-D-E* . . ., would be represented in memory by a chain of direct associations, *A* to *B*, *B* to *C*, and so on, so that seeing or thinking of item *A* arouses the *A-B* association and produces response *B*, which then arouses the *B-C* association and produces response *C*, and so forth. Ebbinghaus, however, observed that the learners themselves made frequent errors by recalling an item at an earlier position than was correct. Thus, after recall of *A* and *B*, the subject might next misrecall *D* or *E* instead of *C*. These anticipatory errors followed a distance gradient, with near errors being more likely.

The Doctrine of Remote Associations

These distant anticipatory errors led Ebbinghaus to postulate that the associative structure established during serial learning included remote forward associations as well as adjacent ones. These are depicted in Figure 6.1, where solid lines denote adjacent associations and dashed lines from each element to every following element in the series denote the remote

Figure 6.1. Diagram of adjacent and remote associations formed during the learning of a serial order of items.

associations. These remote associations could supposedly be activated at any point in the series, leading to anticipatory errors of decreasing degrees of remoteness. To reach perfect performance, the correct adjacent associations must be strengthened relative to the remote associations. Ebbinghaus believed that the existence of such remote associations (order errors) challenged the doctrine of association by simple contiguity, since stimulus A would not be present immediately contiguous with a remote item like C, D, or E. This problem was handled in a later refinement of the theory by Lepley (1934) and Hull (1935). They assumed that each stimulus item left a decaying stimulus trace which endured and was present when later responses in the series were evoked and reinforced. Therefore, associating these later responses C, D, E to the trace of stimulus A was a mechanism for producing graded strengths of associations to remote items in the series. The process is depicted in Figure 6.2.

Besides anticipatory errors, evidence of-

fered for the existence of remote associations by Ebbinghaus was that learning a first list resulted in some "savings" toward learning a new list derived from a previously learned one. If the original list is A, B, C, D, E, . . ., then a first-order derived list would skip every other item as in A, C, E, . . . and a second-order derived list would skip two items as in A, D, G, ... Using himself as the sole subject, Ebbinghaus found that, compared to a scrambled list, derived lists were somewhat easier to learn, and slightly more so the smaller the gap in deriving the remote list. This seems to be consistent with predictions of his doctrine of remote associations.

While Ebbinghaus's doctrine of remote associations led to much research, the ultimate judgment must be that it was incorrect and a misinterpretation of the data. First, the existence of order errors per se need not imply remote associations between items. One could just as well imagine that the items become associated to some internal representations of serial positions (for

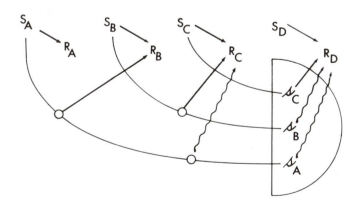

Figure 6.2. Stimulus-response representation of the series A, B, C, D, ... Presentation of each stimulus leads to its pronunciation. Traces of the stimuli (small s's) perseverate and become associated (wiggly lines) to more remote responses in the series.

example, the ordinal numbers "first is *A,* second is *B,* third is *C,*" and so on), and that order errors reflect stimulus generalization of responses among similar ordinal stimuli, as discussed in Chapter 2 regarding the spread of effect. This would explain the gradient of remote errors, as well as the fact that serial recall errors are somewhat likely to be backward (e.g., saying *B* after *E*) as well as forward. Second, the derived list method seems to have produced slight positive transfer for Ebbinghaus because he knew or could detect its principle of construction (e.g., skip every other item) and so could directly utilize his knowledge of the initial series to guess correctly on the derived list. Experiments by Slamecka (1964) that used derived lists of variable spacing between items avoided this problem, and his subjects showed no savings whatsoever. More seriously, Young, Hakes, and Hicks (1965) found that derived lists in fact created conditions of *negative transfer,* since in learning a derived list like *A, C, E,* . . ., the adjacent associations *A-B, C-D, E-F* acquired in the original list should be aroused, and will compete and interfere with the acquisition and performance of the new correct associates. Therefore, if familiarization with the items per se can be controlled (e.g., by using familiar words), then the derived list condition should produce negative transfer. As proof of this conjecture, Young and his colleagues indeed found considerable negative transfer (slower learning) of a first-order derived serial list compared to control subjects learning these items for the first time. Therefore, the derived-list methodology has fallen in disrepute, as has the doctrine of remote associations.

In later analyses of serial learning, researchers have distinguished between *item learning* versus *order learning.* The first refers to learners' ability to retrieve the items as unitary responses from memory, whereas the second refers to their ability to place the items retrieved into the correct serial order. Factors which affect item availability, such as the meaningfulness or familiarity, will affect item recall and will thus affect serial recall indirectly. In more recent studies of serial learning, this item-learning component is often circumvented by using familiar responses such as letters or digits; subjects may even know the exact item-set, so their only task on each trial is to remember a specified order of the items.

Serial Position Curve

One of the interesting facts about serial learning is that the ease of learning an item depends upon its position in the serial list. Figure 6.3 shows a characteristic serial position error curve; items at the beginning and end of the list are learned fastest, while items just beyond the middle are the most difficult. The relative shape of such serial position error curves seems to be invariant over changes in many variables that affect overall learning rate on the list, e.g., mean-

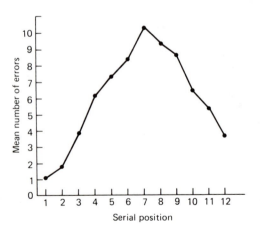

Figure 6.3. Errors at each serial position in the learning of a 12-item serial list of nonsense syllables to mastery. Errors include failures to respond. (From Hovland, 1938.)

ingfulness of the items, presentation rate, intertrial interval (McCrary & Hunter, 1953). The absolute number of errors varies with such factors, but the relative percentage of all errors that are attributable to errors at each position yields much the same curve. Because of the appealing simplicity of this invariance, many theorists have tried their hand at explaining it. Some of these efforts will be touched on in the subsequent discussion.

An early theory of the serial position curve was that of Lepley (1934) and Hull (1935) which made heavy use of the idea of remote associations and the acquisition of inhibitory connections to suppress these remote errors. These inhibitory factors were assumed to pile up most in suppressing responses in the middle of the list, and so most errors should occur at the middle positions. By some strange logic, it was assumed that inhibitory connections spanning adjacent positions (thus, the inhibition not to give E to B spans the pair C-D) caused errors at that interior position. The details are unimportant here since the basic premises of the hypothesis (i.e., remote associations) have been discredited as has the theory constructed on that basis.

An interesting second theory of the serial position effect was proposed independently by Jensen (1962) and Feigenbaum and Simon (1962). Jensen's exposition will be outlined here. It applies to the situation in which a subject is exposed to repeated trials through the same serial list, so that the end of the list is soon followed by the beginning of the list for the next trial. Jensen assumes that the items learned first (or best) are usually the ones to which the subject first attends, or in fact the first item or two in the list. These first learned items then serve as an "anchor point" for learning the remainder of the list. It is assumed that the subject learns most readily by attaching new items to previously learned items. This implies that items are learned around the anchor points both in

a forward and backward direction. The learning spreads out around the first one or two items in either direction. The order of learning for the data in Figure 6.3 can be predicted by folding the 12-item series around the anchor point of the first two items as follows (start in the middle!):

Serial
Position: 8, 9, 10, 11, 12, 1, 2, 3, 4, 5, 6, 7
Order of
Learning: 11, 9, 7, 5, 3, 1, 2, 4, 6, 8, 10, 12

The predicted order of learning is items 1, 2, 12, 3, 11, 4, 10, 5, 9, 6, 8, 7. The rule is to start with the first two items and then alternate successive items from the end of the series and away from the beginning of the series. This notion for predicting serial position difficulty appears quite valid; the average correlation between rank of predicted position difficulty and obtained errors was about .97 over some 70 serial position error curves that Jensen collated from the experimental literature. For example, for the Hovland data shown in Figure 6.3, Jensen's rule predicts the rank of error scores with only one slight misordering (items 6 and 9 are reversed from predicted). The fit of the theory is about as high as the reliability of the serial position curves obtained in different studies.

A problem with Jensen's approach is that it is basically a rule of thumb that describes serial position curves, but the underlying mechanism on which it is based—that is, attaching items to expanding anchor points—seems somewhat implausible. Furthermore, some tasks such as immediate recall of a series heard once (the familiar memory span test) yield neat serial position error curves like those in Figure 6.3, yet it is difficult to see how the anchor point theory really applies to a one-trial task (e.g., learning items at the end of the list as "near" the anchor point of the first item). Because the basic learning mechanism is somewhat vague and implausible, Jensen's theory has not been widely accepted despite its undoubted ability to predict relative serial position error curves.

Serial-position distinctiveness. An attractive recent theory of the serial position curve considers it to be a special case of the differing distinctiveness of positions along any ordered stimulus series. This theory say that some representation of serial position is an important stimulus component for the items of a serial list, and that the ends of the list are more discriminable or distinctive, and therefore better stimuli, than the interior positions of the list. Murdock (1960), Ebenholtz (1972), and G. H. Bower (1971) have articulated this theory and reviewed many studies showing that serial position curves arise whenever the subject must learn to assign different responses to stimuli that vary along a single dimension. An example would be learning to assign letters or names consistently to different lengths of lines, or shades of gray, or pitches of tones, or spatial locations of a dot, or intervals of elapsed time. In the typical experiment, these stimuli would be presented singly in random order, as in the paired associate paradigm. In each case, fewest errors would occur for assignments to the end stimuli and most errors to the interior ones. Bower (1971) pointed out that such results are predictable by assuming equal generalization gradients of responses associated to each stimulus position (see Figure 6.4); more errors occur in the middle of the series because generalized responses can be intruded there from similar stimuli on either side of the target stimuli. In contrast, the correct response is relatively dominant to the end stimuli since intrusion errors can generalize only from one side. This can be seen by simply adding up generalization tendencies for error responses at each stimulus in Figure 6.4. This theory is much like Spence's earlier theory regarding the difficulty of middle-size discriminations (see Figure 5.7, p. 116). Such

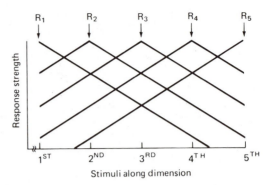

FIGURE 6.4. Strength of each response, R_i, associated to its corresponding stimulus, S_i, with generalization to similar stimuli spaced along the stimulus dimension.

theories handle the rote-serial learning results by supposing that the subject sets up something like "serial position markers" (e.g., first, second, . . .) to which she associates the successive list items, but the markers are more or less distinct and so the responses generalize between nearby position markers. Ebenholtz (1972) reports many experiments demonstrating the validity of positional learning as a dominant mode in serial learning.

To take matters one step further, Ebenholtz and Bower have suggested that the serial positional markers may be abstract and can be transferred to different sets of linearly ordered stimuli, either within the same sensory dimension or to a different dimension. For example, after learning to assign a set of nonsense syllables to lines of differing lengths, Ebenholtz's subjects showed positive transfer when the same responses were transferred and assigned in the *same order* as before to a set of gray patches varying in brightness. That is, the response learned to the shortest line was assigned to the darkest patch, and the remaining responses were kept ordered as learned previously. This transfer, done with college student subjects, may be simply explained by supposing that subjects are converting the stimuli of the set into some abstract codes such as "least, next to least, . . . , middle, . . . , next to most, and most," and then associating specific responses to these abstract codes. In any event, such a theory seems to have moved rather far afield from Ebbinghaus's original theory of remote associations.

PAIRED-ASSOCIATE LEARNING

In paired-associate learning (PAL), an explicit stimulus is provided for each response term. Normally a number of pairs are learned concurrently by the subject using the anticipation method—that is, the stimulus is presented, the subject responds, feedback is given. Paired-associate learning became increasingly popular because of its obvious face validity for the stimulus-response associationism that dominated human learning research in the years following 1940. The simplicity of PAL is only apparent, however, since the results rapidly become complex.

Following the program of constituent analysis, researchers in verbal learning have divided PAL into three component processes: learning to discriminate among the stimuli, learning the responses as units, and learning to associate the correct response unit to each stimulus. Modern theories of PAL deal with all three processes. An experiment by McGuire (1961) was exceptionally clear in illustrating these processes and, in addition, permits an assessment of the contribution of each factor to the performance of the complex behavior exhibited in PAL. Here we will touch on material relating to these component processes.

Discrimination Learning

Paired-associate learning clearly involves stimulus discrimination learning. In a classic paper, Eleanor Gibson (1940) recognized this and systematically applied to

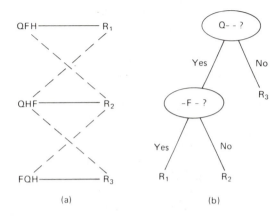

Figure 6.5. (A) Paired associate learning according to Gibson's habit-and-generalization theory and (B), according to EPAM's discrimination network. In A, solid lines indicate correct associations, whereas dashed lines indicate a few generalized error tendencies.

PAL Hull's theory of discrimination learning. This theory assumes that habit strength accrues between each stimulus and its correct response during each reinforced trial, that a response associated to one stimulus may generalize to other similar stimuli causing confusion errors or blocking of the correct response by the generalized one. Furthermore, because generalized responses are nonreinforced, the person will develop inhibition and suppress specific generalized errors at each stimulus to which they occurred. On this view, errors to a given stimulus cease when the correct response has a net strength (habit minus inhibition) exceeding the net generalized strength of each of the competing responses.

While the theory is reasonably complex, it does predict a number of well-known facts about PAL. First, there clearly is stimulus generalization during or after PAL. Thus, a response associated to a 3-letter stimulus like $Q\,F\,H$ will be found to occur to some extent to $Q\,E\,H$ or $Q\,F\,P$ or $Q\text{-}H$. Second, PAL proceeds more slowly the greater the similarity among the stimuli in the list. Thus, it will take longer to learn names to the stimulus set *QFH, QHF,* and *FQH,* which overlap in elements than to *ABC, DEF,* and *GHI,* which do not overlap at all. Third, in later work, Gibson extended the theory by assuming that subjects could be taught discriminating features of the stimuli so that positive transfer would be obtained when the same stimuli were associated with a second set of different responses. An experiment by Goss (1953) found such an effect of "predifferentiation" experiences in which subjects compared stimuli and noticed in what ways they differed; later PAL of new responses to these stimuli was more rapid than for control subjects previously exposed to different stimuli.

Later research has accepted the general facts about similarity effects on PAL but not dealt kindly with Gibson's particular formulation of the role of inhibitory factors in the process. Some later theories of stimulus discrimination in PAL proceed in a radically different manner from Gibson's early attempt. Thus, Simon and Feigenbaum (1964) developed the EPAM model which simulates PAL by developing a discrimination network or sorting tree during its experience in PAL learning (see panel B of Figure 6.5). Each node in the tree asks a test question of the stimulus ("Is the first letter a Q?") and is followed by two branches (to lower nodes) that are taken, depending upon the outcome of the test. Responses are stored at the bottom of the sorting tree and are retrieved and output when a stimulus is sorted to that terminal. Two stimuli are confused if they are sorted to the same terminal of the tree; confused stimuli can be distinguished by creating a new test node based on a distinguishing feature of one of them and entering this into the tree. Details of the EPAM model and its successor, SAL (Hintzman, 1968), are presented in Chapter 12 on information-processing theories. Suffice it to say that they account for the types of data mar-shalled for Gibson's theory, and then explain considerably more results besides.

Response Learning

Response learning refers to the acquiring of the nominal "responses" in the experiment as available units of memory. The nominal response in a PAL experiment may itself be a novel chain of elements such as a nonsense syllable or 3-digit number, and these must be learned as units. Typically, a majority of errors in such nonsense syllable experiments are failures to respond, or incomplete or garbled versions of the appropriate response terms. Thus, in learning the pairs 1-*QHJ*, 2-*QXJ*, and 3-*HJX*, the person may produce 1-*QJX* or 2-*QHJ*, and an error would be recorded. Clearly, the subject in such a task must learn several miniserial lists ("3 then *H* then *J* then *X*") and overcome confusions and interference among them.

The most potent factor controlling the response learning of nonsense syllables is how closely they approximate familiar letter sequences, specifically words. The more wordlike a nonsense trigram appears, or the closer it comes to matching statistics of real English words, the quicker it will be learned and given as a response in PAL. If the subject is prefamiliarized with a set of nonsense syllables, his later PAL will be facilitated when these units are used as responses. These effects of item learning occur not only in paired associates but also in serial learning and in free recall learning. Response learning effects are understandable simply as miniature serial learning tasks that are embedded within the overall task.

Association Formation

Association formation refers to the hooking up of discriminated stimuli with integrated response units. This process has served as a focus for much research. We will not review it here, but will merely point to two research topics surrounding association formation.

Incremental vs. all-or-none learning. A first topic concerns the time course of formation of an association over successive practice trials. If precise measurements could be made of the probability on each trial that a single stimulus evokes the correct response from a subject, what would this curve of response probability look like when plotted over successive practice trials? Would it increase gradually trial by trial or would it consist of one or more discrete jumps from one probability level to a higher one, each level being maintained for several trials? The answer is not obtainable directly since on a single trial for a single S-R pair we observe either a success or an error, but neither gives sufficient information to infer much about the underlying probability learning curve. Consequently, the attacks on this question have been indirect, examining implications of the gradual incremental view as opposed to the all-or-none discontinuous view of learning. Hull and the verbal learning researchers have generally championed the gradual incremental view; Guthrie, Estes, and the Gestalt psychologists have generally championed the all-or-none discontinuous view. For a review, see Restle (1965) or Bower (1967b). This issue will be taken up in more detail in Chapter 8 on stimulus sampling theory.

Mediators. A second issue surrounding association formation is the role of *mediators* in constructing a bridge from the nominal stimulus to the nominal response. A mediator is some bit of knowledge or some preexisting association that the subject comes up with to help her learn the *A-B* association. For example, to learn the pair *RZL-CAT* the subject might say she used the chain *R*-rat-cat or *Z*-hissing-*CAT* or *L*-leopard-*CAT*. Such mediators (also called

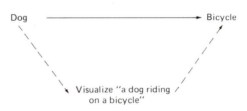

Figure 6.6. Two examples of mediators. The top mediator (dashed line) uses a selected letter-word associate to learn the pair *RZL-CAT*. The bottom shows use of an interactive image to associate a pair of nouns.

mnemonics) use a person's knowledge to find a link (see Figure 6.6). We know that pairs for which the subject can think of a mnemonic, or for which one is supplied, will be learned more rapidly than pairs without mnemonics. The learning not only of paired associates but also of single syllables or trigrams depends upon their triggering stray associations to so-called natural language mediators. Thus, nonsense syllables like *LUV* will be remembered as "LOVE with a spelling change," *CAF* as "cafe without the e," and so on. Prytulak (1971) found that nonsense syllables could be scored in terms of the ease of transforming them into familiar words; moreover, this measure of ease of word-making correlated very highly with the recallability of the nonsense syllables in verbal learning tasks. The results suggest that learning subjects convert a nonsense syllable into a "word plus a transformation," store this code in memory, and then decode it at the time of recall. If subjects remember the word but forget the exact nature of the decoding transformation, they may guess among plausible decodings during output. Thus, they might recall *LOV* rather than *LUV, CFE* rather than *CAF,* and so on. Prytulak noted a high frequency of these types of errors that would result from decoding a mediating word incorrectly.

These mediators occur presumably because it is easier to assimilate new material into something familiar plus a correction than to learn the novel combinations from scratch. Similarly, when adults learn *RZL-CAT* using the two partly familiar connections *R*-rat and rat-*CAT* (see Figure 6.6), they are telling us that priming, strengthening, and chaining old associations are more efficient for them than is learning the new associations directly fom scratch.

If adults are asked to learn pairs of meaningful words (say, DOG-BICYCLE), they will often make up a meaningful sentence linking the two concepts into a plausible and memorable interaction ("This DOG was riding on a BICYCLE"). Such mediators improve paired associate learning. Action sentences are better mediators than simple conjunctions ("A dog *and* bike are together"). Furthermore, subjects may also visualize imaginary pictures of the interaction, and this visualization can be shown to greatly enhance memory for the pairings. The benefits are somewhat greater when the subjects generate their own sentences or their own images rather than using one supplied by the experimenter (see Bobrow & Bower, 1969). These sentence-generating or image-generating techniques and their results on recall will be discussed later (see Chapter 13). They clearly form the central techniques of the set of mnemonic devices that have been commercialized in courses on memory improvement (Lorayne & Lucas, 1974). Mnemonic devices are strategies for deliberately recoding material-to-be-learned into a form suitable to be associated via

familiar concepts, typically with use of visual imagery. The techniques are quite effective (though less so than commercially advertised), and they have been somewhat researched in laboratory settings (Bower, 1970a; Cermak, 1975). Research on imagery and sentence mediators in associative learning has shaded into the theories of cognitive learning, and will be reviewed in Chapter 13. They seem rather far afield from the older conception that paired-associate learning concerned the establishment of S-R connections by methods analogous to classical conditioning. That older view was laid to rest quite some time ago.

This completes our brief review of functionalist analyses of serial learning and paired-associate learning. The next topics to be reviewed concern *transfer of training* and *forgetting* (or retention). Transfer of training refers to the effects of past learning upon the speed of learning some similar task, to which the earlier habits might be transferred. The transfer may be positive, negative, or neutral, and it depends on the amount and type of overlap in the structure of the two tasks. Because they are such rich domains of large effects, studies of the laws of transfer and forgetting in verbal learning have become the major and continuing enterprise of functionalist psychologists. We therefore review these two research areas in more detail, emphasizing historical developments.

STUDIES OF TRANSFER AND FORGETTING

Our historical review begins with a paper by McGeoch (1932), which provides an early functionalist's account of the conditions that affect transfer and the forgetting of verbal materials. McGeoch accepted two major laws of forgetting and transfer. The first is the *law of context,* which asserts that the degree of retention, as measured by performance, is a function of the similarity between the original learning situation and the retention situation. The second is the *law of proactive and retroactive inhibition,* which asserts that retention is a function of activities occurring prior to and subsequent to the original learning. Proactive and retroactive inhibition have been major topics of research for many decades, ever since the problem was first opened up by Müller and Pilzecker (1900).

The paradigm for retroactive inhibition is *A, B, A,* where the learning of material *B* is interpolated between the learning and the retention of material *A,* and interferes with the retention of *A.* The paradigm for proactive inhibition is *B, A, A,* where the learning of *B* prior to the learning of *A* interferes with the later retention of *A.* Both retroactive and proactive interference with learning are readily demonstrable, and the empirical relationships have led to a number of hypotheses. Studying the development of one of these hypotheses about retroactive inhibition will help us to understand not only retroactive inhibition but the manner in which functionalists construct their theories.

One set of problems concerns the *similarity* between the interpolated material and the material originally learned. E. S. Robinson (1927), arguing from some earlier results of his own and of Skaggs (1925), formulated a hypothesis later christened by McGeoch as the *Skaggs-Robinson hypothesis.* Robinson, following Skaggs, proposed relating the amount of retroactive inhibition to the dimension of degree of similarity between the original and the interpolated material or activity.

With the similarity dimension in mind, Robinson argued that the interpolation of identical material (material *B* the same as material *A*) would simply provide additional practice on material *A,* and hence lead to increased retention on the test trials during which retroactive inhibition is usually shown. Because retroactive inhibition with dissimilar materials was already an established fact, the natural conjecture is that starting with identity the amount of retroactive inhibition would increase gradually as dissimilarity was increased. Now, asks Robinson, what is likely to happen at the other end of the scale, as the original material (material *A*) and the interpolated material (material *B*) become *extremely* unlike? Presumably retroactive inhibition represents some sort of interference based on similarity between the original and interpolated activity. If there is very little similarity, there should be very little retroactive inhibition. Putting all these considerations together, it is reasonable to expect a maximum of retroactive inhibition at some intermediate point of similarity between materials *A* and *B.* Robinson formulated the whole generalization in words as follows: "As similarity between interpolation and original memorization is reduced from near identity, retention falls away to a minimum and then rises again, but with decreasing similarity it never reaches the level of obtaining with maximum similarity." He expressed this graphically as shown in Figure 6.7.

His own experimental test of the generalization was very simple. By the memory span method he studied the recall of the first four of a series of eight consonants as this recall was interfered with by the last four of the consonants. That is, the first four were considered to be material *A,* the last four material *B,* and the similarity and dissimilarity of materials *A* and *B* were controlled. Similarity was defined in terms of common letters in the two halves of the series. Maximum similarity means that the second four consonants were exactly the same in the same order as the first four; maximum dissimilarity meant that all the last four differed from the first four.

The results confirmed the hypothesis only partially. Starting with near-identity, retroactive inhibition increased as the interpolated material became increasingly dissimilar. This was part of the conjecture.

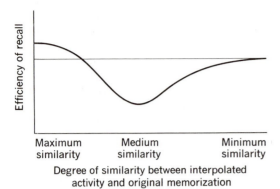

Efficiency of recall

Maximum similarity   Medium similarity   Minimum similarity

Degree of similarity between interpolated activity and original memorization

Figure 6.7. Similarity as a factor in retroactive inhibition. The curve is intended to show that retroactive inhibition bears a quantitative relationship to the degree of similarity between the interpolated activity and the material originally memorized. With maximum similarity, the interpolated activity provides positive transfer, hence increases the efficiency of recall. Maximum interference with recall is predicted to fall at some intermediate value of similarity. (From E. S. Robinson, 1927.)

But the decrease in the amount of retroaction (increase in recall) with maximum unlikeness was not found. In fact, with the materials totally dissimilar, retroactive inhibition was at a maximum.

Later investigators had no better luck than Robinson did in confirming his transfer curve. In fact, later analyses of verbal learning tasks began to uncover several distinct *sources* of "similarity" between two tasks as well as several distinct *kinds* of similarity. For example, in paired associate learning, the two successive lists of pairs may be schematized as S_1-R_1, then S_2-R_2; at least two sources of similarity are stimulus similarity (of S_2 to S_1) and response similarity (of R_2 to R_1). Second, the kinds of similarity may be in terms of overlap of common elements in nonsense syllables (e.g., *VAX* and *VAS* are said to be "formally similar") or in terms of semantic or associative meaning of two words (e.g., *elated* is somewhat similar to *high*, less to

low, and the opposite of *sad*). Recognition of these complexities spelled the demise of the Skaggs-Robinson hypothesis. In reviewing the history of studies of transfer and retroaction, Postman (1971, p. 1083) has this to say:

> In retrospect it becomes apparent that the Skaggs-Robinson hypothesis failed because it was essentially a nonanalytic formulation, which did not specify the locus of intertask similarity. The hypothesis lapsed into disuse as the analysis of similarity relations in retroaction, as in transfer, shifted to the investigation of stimulus and response functions.

Osgood (1949) proposed a more complex formulation of the relationships involved in transfer. His proposed mapping of similarity effects in paired associate transfer is diagrammed in the three-dimensional surface shown in Figure 6.8. What Osgood's surface states is that the amount of transfer in positive or negative directions is a function of shifts in similarity of *both* the stimulus conditions *and* the response required. Shifts in stimulus similarity are from front to back as noted on the right-hand margin, moving from identical stimuli (S_I) through similar stimuli (S_S) to neutral stimuli (S_N) that are far distant on a generalization gradient. Shifts in response similarity are represented from left to right, as noted along the back margin, with identical responses (R_I) being at the left, and moving progressively through similar responses (R_S), neutral responses (R_N), partially opposite responses (R_O) to directly antagonistic responses (R_A). For meaningful verbal materials, the "antagonistic response" was defined as the antonym, a word having the opposite meaning (e.g., *elated–sad*).

The best way to read the diagram is to read its edges first. The rear edge indicates that stimuli bearing *no* resemblance to those used in original learning do not result in any transfer effect, positive or negative, regardless of the degree of resemblance between the required responses and responses that have been used in earlier ex-

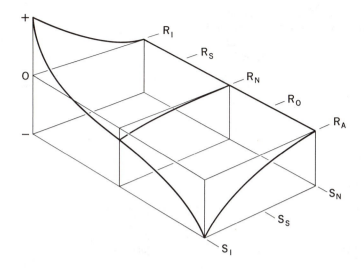

Figure 6.8. Osgood's transfer and retroaction surface. Vertical dimension, amount of transfer (+) or interference (−), with neutral zone represented by a plane (0). Left to right, amount of shift in response similarity between original task and new task, from identity (R_I) to antagonism (R_A). Front to rear, amount of shift in stimulus similarity between original and new task, from identity (S_I) to neutrality (S_N). (From Osgood, 1949.)

periments. The front edge indicates that with *identical* stimuli there will be maximum positive transfer with *identical* responses (for this is merely overlearning); whereas with directly *antagonistic* responses (opposite in meaning) there will be maximum interference, for the earlier responses will have to be completely unlearned or overcome. The left edge indicates that, with identical responses, shifts in stimulus similarity from identity to neutrality will result in decreasing transfer, but no interference in new learning. The right edge indicates that, for antagonistic responses, shifts in stimulus similarity from identity to neutrality will produce decreasing interference, but no positive transfer. The diagram is a surface, and yields a curve wherever it is cut by a vertical plane.

Although Osgood's surface represented an important systematic attempt to integrate a large range of transfer and retroaction phenomena, it soon became clear that it, too, was inadequate for a number of reasons. First, there never was any firm evidence that antagonistic responses were associated with more negative transfer than were unrelated responses, even in Osgood's own data. Second, although the verbal learning data give evidence of differences

in transfer between identical, similar, and unrelated stimuli (or responses), they have not shown a *continuous gradient* of effects as similarity is varied over the intermediate range (see Postman, 1971, p. 1054). This graded effect, of course, is implied by the smooth curves drawn. Third, the surface implies that transfer will always be zero when unrelated stimuli are used in successive tasks (see the rear edge of the surface in Figure 6.8). However, subsequent work has shown that this arrangement can produce positive transfer when the response term itself is novel and requires much learning. For example, in order for the subject to recite nonsense syllables as responses to neutral stimuli requires that the syllables be learned as integrated response units per se. Thus, a transfer design like *A-B, C-B* (dissimilar stimuli, identical responses) avoids the necessity of learning the second-list responses, and so can produce positive transfer on this account. (To keep straight the various transfer designs, refer to the illustrations in Table 6.1).

As a fourth complication with Osgood's surface, experiments using a design like *A-B, B-D* (the response in the first list serves as the stimulus in the second list) made it apparent that a so-called *backward* associ-

TABLE 6.1. Paired associate materials which illustrate different relations between an originally learned list (A–B) on the far left and an interpolated list to be learned. In each pair, the cue word used to prompt recall is the left-hand one.

$A \rightarrow B$	$A \rightarrow D$	$C \rightarrow B$	$C \rightarrow D$	$B \rightarrow D$	$A \rightarrow Br$
dog $\rightarrow$ pin	dog $\rightarrow$ shoe	card $\rightarrow$ pin	card $\rightarrow$ shoe	pin $\rightarrow$ shoe	dog $\rightarrow$ sky
cup $\rightarrow$ mat	cup $\rightarrow$ tree	book $\rightarrow$ mat	book $\rightarrow$ tree	mat $\rightarrow$ tree	cup $\rightarrow$ pin
desk $\rightarrow$ sky	desk $\rightarrow$ rug	car $\rightarrow$ sky	car $\rightarrow$ rug	sky $\rightarrow$ rug	desk $\rightarrow$ mat

ation was being established (from B to A) at the same time that the person was learning the forward association (from A to B). This backward association then intrudes and causes negative transfer in the A-B, B-D paradigm, although it causes positive transfer in the A-B, B-A design (one just reverses which items serve as cues and which as responses). As a fifth problem, the similarity relations treated in Osgood's surface deal with relations among individual items (pairs) across successive lists, and not with the overall structural relations between successive lists. But it is known that the greatest degree of negative transfer in verbal learning occurs when the stimuli and responses of the first list are simply *repaired* in new ways to compose the items for the second list. In symbolic notation, this is denoted as the A-B, A-Br paradigm (see last column of Table 6.1). Within the framework of Osgood's surface, this A-Br condition can only be represented as A-B, A-D with identical stimuli and different responses. Nevertheless, it is known that the A-Br paradigm produces much more negative transfer (largely due to competing backward associations) than does the A-D design.

As a sixth and final complication, Osgood's surface implies that negative transfer in the rate of learning a second list would be perfectly correlated with the amount of forgetting (retroactive interference) of the first list caused by the subject's learning of the second. While these two measures are frequently correlated, some discrepant cases are now well known. One of these discrepancies is that whereas A-B, C-D (unrelated stimuli and responses) serves as the baseline for defining zero transfer in second-list learning, it is clear that C-D interpolation causes extensive forgetting of A-B (or nonspecific interference) (Newton & Wickens, 1956). The forgetting of A-B by such C-D subjects is quite large compared to that of control subjects who learn A-B and then simply rest for an appropriate interval before a retention test. Adopting the C-D baseline, then, the C-D condition produces zero negative transfer but considerable retroactive interference. This observation, in fact, has been one of the reasons for recent doubts regarding the existence of retroactive interference specific to particular paired-associate stimuli (see Postman & Stark, 1969).

Quite clearly, transfer in paired associates is not a unitary process, but is rather composed of a number of distinct components which come into play during initial learning and transfer testing. As stimulus or response similarity is varied, different aspects or components of the transfer task

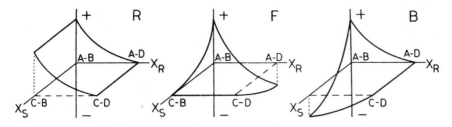

Figure 6.9. Component surfaces for response availability (R), forward associations (F), and backward associations (B). Degree of stimulus similarity is spaced along the X_S axis, and degree of response similarity along the X_R axis. The point of origin represents identity of both the stimulus and the response. Direction and degree of transfer are indicated along the vertical axis. (From E. Martin, 1965.)

will vary, although the net effort on performance may be unclear because different components contribute positive or negative effects which may cancel or nullify one another. Martin (1965) has published a more informed attempt to specify transfer surfaces for three different components carried over in transfer; this is shown in Figure 6.9. The three components of transfer considered are response learning (R, in the left-hand panel), forward associations (F, in the middle panel), and backward associations (B, in the right-hand panel). For response learning, the degree of positive transfer is high for identical responses, decreasing to zero for more dissimilar responses, and is independent, of course, of stimulus similarity. The surface for forward associations (F) is the same as Osgood's except that Martin suggests that the response continuum should extend only to unrelated responses (*A-B, A-D*); although antonyms are opposites in meaning they are associatively close to one another and this relation, more than their meaning opposition, dominates so as to produce slightly positive transfer when antonymic responses are used (see Postman, 1971). The results for backward associations (B) are rather symmetrical to those for forward associations except for an interchange of stimulus and response axes. In particular, interpolation of *C-B* following *A-B* learning pro-

duces maximal loss of the backward association from *B* to *A*, as indicated in the subject's failure to recall the first-list stimulus *A* when cued with the response term *B*.

Martin's hypothesis does not indicate specifically how these several factors will combine to determine the net transfer effect. It is clear, too, that even further factors have been identified which can influence transfer and forgetting, and these features are not depicted in Martin's surfaces. Thus, for example, a number of experiments have shown that there are some positive benefits from prior attentive exposure to the stimulus or the response terms since this serves to "predifferentiate" these items prior to the commencement of the criterion paired-associate task. To the extent that the subject has already learned to identify and discriminate among the stimuli, it is that much easier for him to continue discriminating while attaching particular responses to the predifferentiated stimuli. Although the normal *A-B, A-D* paradigm involves this predifferentiation factor, the competing response factor seems to override it and to determine net negative transfer in most circumstances.

Another factor missing in this transfer surface is what has been called *list differentiation*, the ability of the subject to identify the list membership of responses which he recalls. Thus during *A-D* learning following *A-B,* the person may intrude the *B* response, although he knows both responses, because he confuses the two lists. Or he may think of but withhold response *D* because he erroneously identifies it as coming from the first list. In like manner, following interpolation of *A-D,* if the person is asked to recall the first-list response, he may withhold *B* or intrude *D* if he is unable to distinguish which list the various responses occurred in. List differentiation as a process is closely analogous to remembering the time and context in which events occur, a topic of considerable interest in its own right (Anderson & Bower, 1972a; Hinrichs, 1970; G. H. Bower, 1972d). List identification will clearly be a factor in transfer, since confusions about list membership will increase with similarity of the stimuli or responses. Thus, for example, if the list-2 responses are digits whereas the list-1 responses are nouns, there would probably be perfect list differentiation and the subject would almost never intrude a digit response while trying to recall a list-1 noun.

Martin's hypothesis does encompass the massive negative transfer produced by the re-paired *A-Br* transfer task, since Figure 6.9 shows negative transfer for the forward association (at *A-D* in the middle panel) and negative transfer for the backward association (at *C-B* in the right-hand panel). What it fails to show is that the *A-B, C-D* paradigm produces zero negative transfer but nonetheless appreciable forgetting relative to a rest control condition. This is an issue we will touch upon later.

Let us retrace the evolution of these hypotheses (or guessed-at "empirical generalizations") regarding similarity effects in retroaction and transfer. First we have the early experiments demonstrating retroactive interference, and some that demonstrate the possible role of similarity as a factor. Next we have Robinson's somewhat crude dimensional hypothesis, leading to a series of experiments which reveal multiple sources and kinds of intertask similarities, requiring a generalization more complex than the Skaggs-Robinson hypothesis. At the same time these investigations of forgetting were occurring, a series of related experiments on transfer were being conducted, but as though the two phenomena had little in common. Presently Osgood offered his new synthesis, covering the data that had accumulated since Robinson's hypothesis was announced, incorporating in one stroke the results on transfer and on retroactive interference. But a series of analytical studies revealed that the Osgood surface was too simplistic, that there are even more components or independent factors involved in transfer. These more detailed analyses led to Martin's proposed *component transfer* surfaces for three of the important bits of learning that are now known to be carried over in transfer. Although Martin's proposals are the most adequate integrative summaries yet seen, it is clear that several isolable factors have still been ignored, and the weighting of the magnitude of the independent factors and their interactions in determining net transfer has been left for future specification. This sort of succession of hypothesized generalizations, with an interplay between data, analytical criticism, and theory, seeking a deeper analysis but a more revealing integration, is exactly what might be expected in a maturing functional analysis. This history also illustrates some of the potential frustrations of a functionalist approach; upon closer analysis, more and more variables or independent factors are discovered to influence the behavior under investigation, and the possibility of strong interactions between one variable and the functions obtained for other variables is a likely prospect. For example, the relating transfer function to response similarity probably varies in quantitative shape depending on whether one is dealing with "formal similarity" (overlapping elements of nonsense materials) or with "meaningful similarity" (e.g., synonymous words); and it is unclear yet whether the latter variable should be anchored to conceptual overlap of dictionary definitions of two words or to overlap of the associative hierarchies elicited by each word (see, for example, Deese, 1965).

The complexities of the behavioral phenomenon of transfer make some investigators despair (e.g., to say "nature couldn't be *that* complicated"), give it up as a poorly formulated scientific question, and move on to work on other issues in psychology with greater prospects of quick progress. The dyed-in-the-wool functionalist would argue that he was simply doing the yeoman's work of elucidating a phenomenon, and claim that no one is ever guaranteed simplicity in his findings and that, although the subproblems shift with the maturity of his analysis, the overriding phenomenon with which the area began (viz., transfer of training) is undeniably a central problem for all of learning theory. If it truly is a central issue, then, the functionalist would claim, it must be studied, analyzed, and understood with the only experimental and conceptual tools we presently have available. We must analyze and understand complexity because "that's the way the world is."

Analysis of Forgetting

The foregoing account of research on negative transfer and retroactive interference was carried out at the level of empirical description and generalization without much interest in theory. However, by far the most significant portion of the research of modern functionalists concerns the analysis of theoretical mechanisms of forgetting. The character of the functionalists' theoretical approach can perhaps be best appreciated by tracing the evolution of their ideas regarding forgetting. Most of this research has been done on verbal learning experiments with human adults. Of

course, animals forget too, even simple conditioned responses, and the study of forgetting in animals has become a major area of study (see Honig & James, 1971; Spear, 1978). To reduce the difficulty of the task of understanding, recent experiments on forgetting have concentrated on standard verbal learning situations to yield the main evidence.

If one asks the layman why he forgets things, he has a ready answer: he forgets things because he hasn't used them, or thought of them, for some time. He has forgotten the Spanish he learned in high school because he hasn't used it for the past ten years. But he remembers things he continues to use, such as the names of his friends.

The problem with this popular account is that it does not satisfy the scientists' curiosity regarding causal mechanisms. Lapse of time is not itself a causal variable, although causal events happen in time. If I leave an iron hammer outside, it will progressively rust with time. But it is not the lapse of time that rusts the hammer. Rather, it is the reaction of chemical oxidation that occurs in time.

We can give the layman's proposal a more neurological *sound* (if not sense) as follows: each learning experience establishes a neurological trace whose integrity is gradually obliterated by random neuronal noise that occurs at a fixed rate, eroding away the retrievability of the memory trace as the retention interval increases. Does this formulation buy us anything? The answer is "not really." Unless much more is added regarding relevant variables and their influence on the hypothetical process (and forgetting), the new proposal is worse than vacuous; it is dangerous because someone is likely to consider it seriously due to its apparent technical jargon.

A variety of substantive proposals concerning the causes of forgetting have appeared, differing considerably in their scope and the range of variables of which forgetting is said to be a function. For example, Freud supposed that some forgetting results from active repression of certain materials in the unconscious. A critical discussion of this hypothesis along with the conflicting data surrounding it may be found in an earlier edition (Hilgard & Bower, 1975); for a sympathetic reading of that conflicting literature, see Erdelyi and Goldberg (1979). Another conjecture, contributed by Gestalt psychologists and reviewed in Chapter 10, was that memories were multifaceted systems continually undergoing dynamic change, moving toward some better organization (or gestalt). This notion became translated in laboratory experiments into the question of whether a subject's recall of an asymmetric or incomplete figure or line drawing tends to move during a retention interval toward a "good" or "better" gestalt figure. Riley (1963), in his review of this extensive literature, concluded that there was little consistent support for the Gestalt idea. Recall of a figure pattern, more often than not, does tend to move toward cultural stereotypes but such trends as are found turn out more often to be explainable by verbal associations (to the original figure) or proactive interference from prior cultural learning than by Gestalt laws of perceptual organization.

The most serviceable theory of forgetting that has emerged from laboratory experiments is called the *interference* theory. This is closely tied in to the functionalists' analysis of negative transfer and interference. Currently, interference theory has far more adherents, because of more evidence in its favor, than any or all alternative theories of forgetting, so it is fair to call it the current dominating theme of experiments on forgetting. This is an association theory; that is, its basic primitive concept is the notion of an associative bond (functional connection) between two or more elements, the elements being ideas, words, situational stimuli and responses, or whatnot. As indicated earlier in our discussion of

transfer paradigms, the conventional notation uses letters $A, B, C \ldots$, to represent such elements or items, and the notation A-B to represent an associative bond between A and B established by some past training. It is presumed that these associative bonds can vary widely in their strength depending on the amount of practice. The experimental situation that best illustrates the theory is paired-associate learning, wherein the subject is taught a set (list) of pairs and then is tested later for retention. The theory applies as well to most other learning tasks, but the paired-associate task makes the expositional mechanics easiest to implement.

Interference Theory

The basic ideas of interference theory were first stated explicitly by McGeoch (1932), but through the succeeding years changes in the theory have gradually occurred. New concepts have been added, unsupported conjectures pruned away, and new experimental methods devised to measure more exactly the relevant dependent variables. The changing character of interference theory may be seen by comparing McGeoch's early statements with Postman's (1961, 1971) later formulations. In what follows, we shall indicate some of the changes and the shifts in emphasis.

The first principle of McGeoch's statement seems an absurd one for a theory of forgetting: it says that forgetting does not occur in an absolute sense. The strength of an association between two items, A-B, is established by training, and it is presumed to remain at that level despite disuse of the association. The cause of a measurable retention loss over time is not that the strength of A-B decays, but rather that alternative associations, A-C or A-D, have by some means (to be specified) gained strength in the absence of continued training on A-B. Thus, on a retention test, the subject may give C or D as the associate to

A, so we record a retention loss for the *A-B* association. The *A-B* association has not been lost or forgotten in any absolute sense; it is still there in memory, but *B* has been temporarily displaced, losing out in competition with elements *C* and *D* at the moment of recall.

On the basis of this theory, then, an association once learned is permanently stored, and forgetting is due to declining accessibility, a lessening probability of its retrieval from the storehouse. And this declining accessibility results from competing associations. Such an approach has at least the substrate required to account for the clinically puzzling instances of hypermnesia in which a person demonstrates exceptional recall, or believes his recall is genuine, of experiences from long before. Such heightened recall may occur in manic states, in the hours anticipating some emotionally exciting event (e.g., soldiers about to go into combat), in a hypnotic trance (see Reiff & Scheerer, 1959), or while following a line of free associations when on the psychoanalyst's couch (see Erdelyi & Kleinbard, 1978; Pascal, 1949; Stratton, 1919; Stalnaker & Riddle, 1932).

According to this theory, the *A-B* association may be tested by presenting one of the elements, say *A,* whereupon the subject tries to produce the associated *B.* We may think of *A* as a stimulus term and *B* as a response. As indicated in our earlier review of transfer, this suggests manipulating the degree of similarity of a test stimulus (call it *A′*) to the original training stimulus *A.* The principle of stimulus generalization predicts that *A′* is less likely to activate the *A-B* association in proportion as *A′* is dissimilar to *A.* Moreover, McGeoch suggested that we expand our conception of *A* to include any background contextual stimulation that is present when the *A-B* association is learned. Changes in such contextual stimuli have been found to result in poorer recall (Abernathy, 1940; Falkenberg, 1972; Pan, 1926). Thus, if the subject is tested for

recall in a different room than that in which he learned, or with a different type of stimulus-presenting device, or with the material presented on different backgrounds, or when he adopts a different posture, or whatever, his recall is poorer than when, during testing, precisely the original stimulating context is reproduced. Such results seem consistent with the analytic position of interference theory.

Earlier we mentioned that retention loss on a learned *A-B* association results from competition of alternative associations, *A-C,* at the moment of recall. If we ask where these conflicting associations come from, the logical answer is that they (or one similar to them, *A′-C*) come from learning either before or after the *A-B* learning but before the retention test. This analysis has led to the intensive investigation of situations in which the *A-B* and *A-C* learning is explicitly controlled. The two basic paradigms are called retroaction or proaction depending on whether the experimenter's interest is in retention of the first-learned or the second-learned material. These paradigms, together with the appropriate control conditions and some hypothetical recall data, are illustrated in Table 6.2. In the retroaction paradigm, the control group first learns the *A-B* associations, then rests, and later is tested for recall of *B* when given the *A* term. The experimental group learns *A-B,* then learns new pairs *A′-C,* and then tries to recall *B* when given *A.* The retroactive interference index calculated for the hypothetical data is 67 percent. The proaction conditions may be read similarly.

A variety of task variables can be studied in this context, and on the whole the recall results fall in line with what would be expected from interference theory (for reviews, see Slamecka & Ceraso, 1960; Postman, 1971). For example, retroactive interference increases with trials on *A-C* and decreases with trials on *A-B,* whereas proactive interference shows just the opposite functional relations, as expected. Consider just one ex-

TABLE 6.2. Recall results to illustrate forgetting due to retroactive and proactive interference.

	Retroaction		Proaction	
	Experimental	Control	Experimental	Control
List 1	A-B	A-B	A'-C	rest
List 2	A'-C	rest	A-B	A-B
Recall test	A-B	A-B	A-B	A-B
Percent correct recall	20	60	60	80
Effect	$\dfrac{60-20}{60}=0.67$		$\dfrac{80-60}{80}=0.25$	

ample, namely, the effect of the number of training trials on the *A-B* list (original learning, abbreviated OL) prior to *A-C* learning upon the relative dominance of the *A-B* and *A-C* associations. An experiment by Briggs (1957) illustrates the procedure and results (see Figure 6.10). Four different groups of subjects received 2, 5,

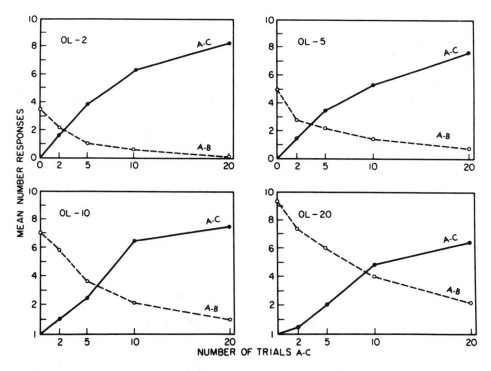

Figure 6.10. Relative response frequencies of the originally learned response (*A-B*) and the newly learned response (*A-C*) during learning of the new response as measured by modified free recall. The four graphs come from four different groups of subjects given 2, 5, 10, or 20 trials of original learning. (From Briggs, 1957.)

10, or 20 trials of *A-B* learning followed by 20 trials of *A-C* learning. The lists were ten paired adjectives. After intervals of 0, 2, 5, 10, and 20 trials of *A-C* learning, each subject received a modified free-recall test with the stimulus terms. On such tests the subjects were instructed to give whatever response first came to mind (including extra-list intrusions), and there was no feedback from the experimenter to indicate which response was wanted. Such a test assesses the relative dominance of *A-C* over *A-B*.

The curves in Figure 6.10 provide a graphic description of the frequency of the new *C* response and the old *B* response after varying numbers of *A-B* and *A-C* trials. At the beginning of second-list learning, the frequency of *B* recall depended directly upon the number of OL trials. During the course of *A-C* training, *B* responses decreased in frequency while *C* responses increased to a dominant role. After 20 trials of *A-C,* the amount of OL still exerted some influence, both in terms of a higher *A-B* recall frequency and a lower *A-C* recall frequency. This picture is exactly what one would expect from McGeoch's earlier ideas of response competition, since the modified free-recall test permits only one response.

McGeoch's hypotheses predict a perfect correlation between retention loss of *A-B* and the occurrence on testing of intruding associates, *C* or *D*. This correlation is not always found: on the *A-B* retention test following the *A-C* learning, the subject often is unable to respond with any associate. Two hypotheses were proposed to account for this and both probably have some validity. One notion that we mentioned earlier, proposed by Thune and Underwood (1943), is that the subject can discriminate the list membership (first or second) of associates that come to mind; to the extent that he does this, he will censor and reject response *C* when trying to recall the first-list response, *B*. This is plausible since it is known (Yntema & Trask, 1963) that subjects can judge with fair accuracy

which of two events has occurred more recently in the past. Another idea, first expressed by Melton and Irwin (1940), is that during the *A-C* interpolated learning, the first pair *A-B* is unlearned or extinguished. If so, then, when the test occurs soon after the *A-C* learning, *B* is temporarily unavailable as an associate.

The clearest evidence for *unlearning* comes from a recall method first used by Barnes and Underwood (1959). Using the *A-B, A-C* paradigm, the subject was asked on the later test to recall *both* list responses to stimulus *A* and to indicate their list membership. This is a noncompetitive recall situation, and failures are ascribed to unavailability of the responses. The results of Barnes and Underwood are shown in Figure 6.11. This shows that recall of *C* responses increased with trials of *A-C* learning but, more importantly, recall of *B* responses decreased with trials on *A-C*. Thus, as the *A-C* training is extended, the first-list associates become increasingly unavailable, presumably due to unlearning. A variety of follow-up experiments confirmed and extended these results, so that the concept of unlearning was widely accepted.

Postman and Stark (1969) challenged the validity of the associative unlearning concept. They noted that the *A-B, A-C* paradigm produced relatively little negative transfer when they tested the *A-B* pair by multiple-choice *recognition* (that is, recognizing that B_1 but not B_2 was paired with A_1).[1] Furthermore, although this paradigm produced the customarily large *recall* decrement for *A-B,* the forgetting was not

[1] Pair recognition shows strong RI in the *A-B, A-C* paradigm if the interfering response, *C,* is included among the distracting lures on the multiple-choice test for *A-B* (R. C. Anderson & Watts, 1971). However, this RI could be explained by response competition and loss of list differentiation rather than by specific unlearning of *A-B.* Nonetheless, it appears that recognition performance in the Postman and Stark experiment was too high in all conditions to reveal any effect due to associative unlearning.

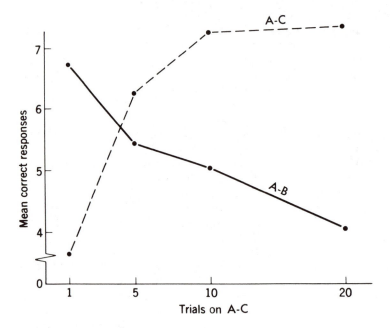

Figure 6.11. Mean number of responses recalled and correctly identified with stimulus and list in the *A-B, A-C* paradigm. Eight is the maximum possible score in each case. (From Barnes and Underwood, 1959.)

very much greater than that produced by an *A-B, C-D* paradigm. For these and other reasons, Postman and Stark suggested that retroactive interference was not being caused by stimulus-specific associative unlearning, but rather was due primarily to a suppression of the entire set of first-list responses, a suppression that develops during second-list learning and persists awhile into a later retention test for *A-B*. On this hypothesis, *C-D* interpolated learning would cause suppression of the *B* response set (as does *A-C* interpolation) and thus these items would be unavailable as responses on the *A-B* recall test. But if the *B* responses were made available as on the pair recognition test, then the person would show that he had not unlearned the *A-B* association.

Evidence for stimulus-specific unlearning was not long in coming following the Postman and Stark challenge. A spate of

experiments soon reported demonstrations of this effect (see Birnbaum, 1972; Delprato, 1972; Weaver et al., 1972). A typical one was that by Delprato (1972). He used a "within-list" design in which, across two lists, different items within the list learned by a subject exemplified an *A-B, C-D* relation and other items exemplified an *A-B, A-C* relation. The important point about such a design is that a factor like "suppression of first-list responses" should operate equally on all first-list pairs whether the corresponding second-list item is *C-D* or *A-C*. Therefore, any differences among items in recall of *A-B* could probably be attributed to stimulus-specific learning (i.e., learning *A-C* specifically weakens *A-B* in some absolute sense). Delprato's experiment showed exactly this result, with more forgetting on those specific pairs followed by *A-C* than those followed by *C-D*.

Furthermore, it was possible to prove

stimulus-specific unlearning even with pair-recognition testing (see Merryman, 1971). Apparently, recognition performance in all conditions in the Postman and Stark experiment was too high to provide a sensitive test of specific unlearning. Therefore, we can still retain the idea of stimulus-specific unlearning. However, there does seem to be something to the notion of a general loss of availability of first-list responses due to second-list learning. One may think of this loss of first-list responses as the unlearning of associations between general contextual stimuli and the first-list responses (see McGovern, 1964; Keppel, 1968). It has been proposed that this loss of availability to contextual cues can be studied in the multilist free-recall situation where there are no explicit cues for recall of each item on the list.

Proactive Interference and Spontaneous Recovery

Proactive interference is the decrement in recall of the second-list (*A-C*) material caused by prior learning of the first-list material (*A-B* or *D-B*). Proactive effects are minimal immediately after *A-C* learning, but they increase over a retention interval. It is almost as though the person became confused at the retention test between the two lists he had studied earlier. So one likely explanation of proactive interference is that it involves progressively more confusion between the two lists learned some time before; let us call this the "list-differentiation" idea. It is quite plausible that ability to discriminate between second-list items occurring *t* hours ago and first-list items occurring (*t* + Δ) hours ago will decrease as *t* becomes larger, a sort of Weber-Fechner law for time discrimination.

But a second explanation has been offered for this increase in proactive interference with an increase in the retention interval following *A-C* learning. This second hypothesis supposes, first, that the original

A-B associations are extinguished, unlearned, or inhibited during *A-C* learning, and, second, that these *A-B* associates spontaneously recover some of their prior strength over the retention interval. The analogy is to Pavlov's observation (see Chapter 3) that conditioned responses recover during a rest period after a series of extinction trials. Clearly, if the *A-B* associates spontaneously recover, they will compete with *A-C* recall, providing increasing proactive interference as recovery increases over time.

Several lines of evidence support this idea of *A-B* recovery following *A-C* learning. One is an earlier experiment by Briggs (1954), who studied the relative dominance of the *A-B* and *A-C* habits over varying retention intervals using the modified free-recall (MFR) test. In this experiment, subjects learned a first list of 12 paired adjectives (*A-B*) to a criterion of one perfect recitation, rested 24 hours, then learned a second list (*A-C*) to a once-perfect criterion, then received a final MFR test after either 4 minutes or 6, 24, 48, or 72 hours. At various stages during the course of both original and interpolated learning the subjects received an MFR test, in which they were asked to say whatever response first came to mind as they were shown each stimulus term. The results are shown in Figure 6.12. In the left panel is shown the relative frequency of first-list responses (*A-B*) as contrasted to preexperimental associates (*A-E*) from outside the list when tests were given after various levels of first-list performance, the criteria specified in terms of the percentage of pairs correct on the training trial just preceding the MFR test (0, 1/4, 2/4, 3/4, 4/4 of the list). As expected, extralist associates decline, whereas List-1 responses increase. After the 24-hour rest interval, the MFR test revealed some rise in extralist associates and loss of first-list associates (see the 0 point on List 2, the middle panel). Then during List-2 learning to various criteria, List-1 responses and extra-

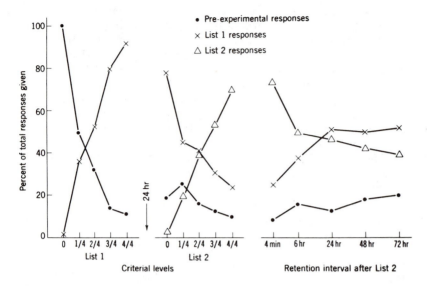

Figure 6.12. The left and center sets of curves are the acquisition and extinction functions when Lists 1 and 2 are learned successively in a retroactive-interference paradigm. Recall as a function of time from the end of List-2 learning is shown in the right-hand set of curves. (Adapted from Briggs, 1954.)

list associates declined, whereas List 2 responses increased.

The data of interest to the spontaneous recovery hypothesis are in the third panel (from separate groups of subjects), showing the relative percentages of *B*, *C*, or *E* responses at differing retention intervals. This graph clearly shows a gradual recovery over time of the *A-B* and *A-E* associates, with a corresponding loss of the most recently learned *A-C* associations. These curves are exactly what would be expected if *A-B* and *A-E* associates were recovering in strength following their unlearning during *A-C* training.

The problem with this interpretation, of course, is that the MFR test is a measure of *relative* response strengths of *B*, *C*, and *E*; Briggs's results could have been produced merely by a greater absolute loss in *A-C* rather than an absolute recovery in *A-B* or *A-E*. The obvious way to proceed is

to try to demonstrate absolute recovery of *A-B* in a noncompetitive recall situation, specifically the "modified modified free-recall" (MMFR) tests of the type used by Barnes and Underwood. That is, the subject is to try to recall both *B* and *C* responses when cued with stimulus *A*.

But the evidence for spontaneous recovery in studies of temporal changes using MMFR tests has been equivocal, particularly for longer retention intervals ranging from several hours to several days. However, the possibility remains that a small absolute recovery of *A-B* is being masked by progressively greater recovery of preexperimental associates (*A-E*), which are edited out by the subject in the typical MMFR test. If so, then recovery of *A-B* should be most likely in MMFR tests given at reasonably short intervals after *A-C* learning. In these conditions, positive evidence for absolute recovery of *A-B* has been

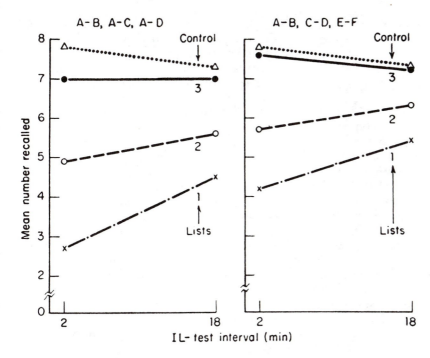

Figure 6.13. Mean number of paired associates recalled from the first, second, and third lists after 2 or 18 minutes' delay for subjects receiving either the *A-B, A-C, A-D* paradigm (left panel) or the *A-B, C-D, E-F* paradigm (right panel). Recalls of control groups who rested for an equivalent time following List-1 learning are also shown. (From Postman, Stark, & Henschel, 1969.)

obtained (see Postman et al., 1968; Postman et al., 1969). Figure 6.13 shows some recovery data from an experiment by Postman, Stark, and Henschel (1969, their Experiment III). The experimental subjects learned three successive lists, having either an *A-B, A-C, A-D* relation or an *A-B, C-D, E-F* relation for different subjects, and then received an MMFR test either 2 or 18 minutes after the final learning trial. Two control groups learned the *A-B* list, then were tested for its recall after a time interval equal to that occupied by the interpolated learning plus 2 or 18 minutes. Figure 6.13 shows significant absolute recovery over the retention interval for both first-list and second-list responses; the third-list response was not unlearned and shows a high level

of recall at both retention intervals. Significantly, the amounts of recovery are comparable for the *A-B, A-C* group and the *A-B, C-D* group. This fact suggests that this recovery of early list responses may be due to the dissipation over time of "response-set suppression" rather than to spontaneous recovery of stimulus-specific associative unlearning. That is, during interpolated learning the person may make available the responses being used in that list while selectively suppressing the entire set of responses used in earlier lists. But this suppression dissipates with time, allowing earlier responses to become progressively available for recall in MMFR tests. This issue of the source of recovery, whether of response availability or stimulus-response associations, is one currently under investigation.

The Magnitude of Proactive Interference Effects

One major shift in interference theory that has occurred consists in the powerful role assigned to proactive sources of interference in forgetting. In a major paper, Underwood (1957) employed the proactive idea to clear up what had been a major source of embarrassment to interference theory. Most of the earlier studies of retention had shown rather massive forgetting —about 80 to 90 percent—over 24-hour intervals. The claim that this was due to interference from casual interpolated learning seemed unconvincing since it was difficult to imagine much everyday learning that would interfere with nonsense materials learned in the laboratory. By collating various reports, Underwood determined that those studies reporting massive forgetting had used the same subjects under many list-learning conditions. The more lists a subject had learned, the more she tended to forget the last one when recall of it was measured the next day. Thus, proactive effects presumably accumulated over the lists learned earlier. If a subject learned only a single list of verbal material, then her recall was fairly high—around 75 to 80 percent after 24 hours.

A particularly apt illustration of massive proactive effects is provided by an experiment by Keppel, Postman, and Zavortink (1968). They had five college students learn and recall 36 successive lists (*A-B, C-D* relations) of ten paired associates at 48-hour intervals. Each test session began with a recall test on the prior list learned, followed by the learning of a new list to a criterion of one perfect recitation. The recall percentages are shown in Figure 6.14 plotted in successive blocks of three lists; this shows a dramatic decrease in recall from around 70 percent on the first list to around 5 percent on the last two lists. This illustrates the powerful effects that can be produced by proactive interference. It does not, of course, illuminate the mechanism underlying proactive interference in the *A-B, C-D, E-F* design. Presumably it is loss of availability of the final list's responses; if so, then there should be no cumulative proactive effects demonstrable in pair-recognition tests, or if the response words from successive lists came from distinguishably different (but memorable) semantic categories.

As noted, recall after 24 hours of a well-learned list is about 75 percent, when no interfering lists had been learned. Underwood and Postman (1960) attempted to account for the remaining 25 percent of forgetting observed by appealing to extraexperimental sources of interference. They point out that in learning arbitrary verbal associations or nonsense material in the laboratory, the subject probably has to unlearn the prior verbal habits which he shares with other members of his particular linguistic community. These prior verbal habits may be one of two types—letter sequence associations or unit (word) sequence associations. To give a transparent example, a subject is certain to enter the experiment possessing prior word associations like *table-chair* and *light-dark.* Suppose the learning task requires her to form the new associates *table-dark* and *light-chair.* During a rest interval, spontaneous recovery of the unlearned prior associates will produce a decrement in the probability of her recalling the associations learned in the laboratory. The experiments by Underwood and Postman plus related follow-up studies show some merits of this analysis. New materials that clash with prior verbal habits are forgotten more readily, usually being distorted in the direction of agreement with the prior habits. However, the evidence on this hypothesis has been somewhat conflicting, and it appears that a

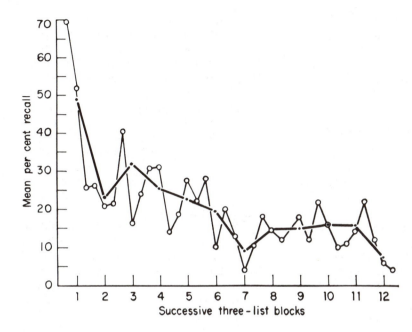

Figure 6.14. Mean percentage of recall of the immediately prior list at a 48-hour interval as a function of the number of prior lists, in blocks of three lists. The heavy black line averages larger blocks of nine lists. (From Keppel, Postman, & Zavortink, 1968.)

variety of complicating factors can enter to obscure the hypothesized relationship.

A powerful demonstration of proactive interference due to prior linguistic habits is to be found in a study by Coleman (1962). He took a 24-word passage of prose from a book and scrambled the words into random order. This order was given to a subject for brief study, and the subject then tried to reconstruct verbatim the serial order of the words he had studied. This reconstructed order was then given to a second subject to study and recall, and his reconstructed order was then studied by a third subject and recalled, and so on. The passage was successively filtered through 16 subjects. As it went from subject to subject, its recall (reconstructed order) was distorted more and more from the original jumble in the direction of sensible English sentences. One of Coleman's original passages and the sixteenth reconstruction of it is given in Table 6.3. The amount of change is dramatic, especially considering that each sub-

TABLE 6.3.   Change in recall of a passage as it moves through a chain of learners. (Adapted from Coleman, 1962.)

Original passage studied by first subject:	"about was good-looking way and treating made of that a him the quiet youngster nice he manners a them girls wild go with . . ."
Reproduction of sixteenth subject in the chain:	"he was a youngster nice quiet with manners good-looking and a way of treating them that made the girls go wild about him . . ."

ject was trying to reproduce verbatim the exact order of words he had studied. The change illustrates vividly the powerful effect of prior verbal habits in distorting recall of conflicting associations.

Interference with Meaningful Text

The laboratory studies of interference reviewed above have used "meaningless" materials, either nonsense syllables or random unrelated words. However, recent research provides extensive evidence that similar interference processes operate in the learning and forgetting of meaningful text materials, both at the level of single sentences and at the level of interrelated sets of sentences (text paragraphs). Although some doubts about interference processes had been raised by a few early nonanalytic experiments, recent positive demonstrations show retroactive interference or retroactive facilitation depending in a very lawful manner upon the exact arrangement of materials and the retention measure used for assessing losses (see J. R. Anderson & Bower, 1973; R. C. Anderson & Myrow, 1971; R. C. Anderson & Carter, 1972; Crouse, 1971; Myrow & Anderson, 1972).

We may illustrate the issues with recall of simple active declarative sentences of the form subject-verb-object (e.g., "The mechanic repaired the refrigerator"). We may view this proposition in either of two ways: the sentence establishes in memory a serial chain of associations between the successive words, or it establishes labeled functional connections between groups of semantic concepts which are aroused by these specific words. A variety of considerations suggest that the latter view is more nearly correct and more fruitful. We may now treat the semantic concepts corresponding to the subject, transitive verb, and object (call them S, V, O) as though they were terms in a "triplet" association-learning task, except that there are a tremendous number of syntactic constraints and semantic selectional restrictions which forbid certain word combinations (e.g., "Night the bounced running the" is literal nonsense).

Treating the concepts as terms in an associative triplet, we are then led to expect interference at this level if a given concept co-occurs with different concepts in new predications. Thus, following learning of S_1-V_1O_1, interpolation of S_1-V_2O_2 or S_2-V_1O_1 will lead to an associative loss between S_1 and V_1O_1, when the cueing is done in either direction. This loss would be assessed relative to a control interpolation symbolized as S_2-V_2O_2. An experiment by G. H. Bower (1978) demonstrated clear negative transfer and retroactive interference by subjects learning interpolated sentences bearing an *A-D, C-D,* or *A-Br* relation to the original sentences learned (see Table 6.1 for transfer conditions). The results were ordered exactly as predicted by paired-associate transfer results.

Further, interference evidently occurs at the level of conceptual learning. This can be demonstrated by using synonymous paraphrases, say of the V_1O_1 verbal construction. Suppose S_1-V_1O_1 is the sentence "The sheriff aroused the slumbering patient"; letting $P(V_1O_1)$ denote synonymous paraphrase of the verb phrase, then an S_2-$P(V_1O_1)$ sentence might be "The nurse awakened the sleeping sick person." It has been found that interpolation of such paraphrase constructions produces nearly as much retroactive interference as does use of the verbatim V_1O_1 paired with a new subject-noun, S_2 (see R. C. Anderson & Carter, 1972). Apparently, the cue V_1O_1 contacts a similar trace in memory as does its paraphrase $P(V_1O_1)$, and the S_2 associated with $P(V_1O_1)$ competes with recall of the S_1 associated earlier with the same predicate by use of the words V_1O_1.

Of course, this paraphrase effect could

be used to good advantage if one wished to facilitate conceptual (meaning) associations. Thus, a two-list experiment in which S_1-V_1O_1 in List 1 is followed by S_1-$P(V_1O_1)$ in List 2 will result in enhanced recall of the correct gist (meaning) to the S_1 cue of List 1, but probably with some loss in verbatim recall of V_1O_1. For the same reason, a paraphrased sentence $P(S_1)$-$P(V_1O_1)$ (e.g., "The policeman awakened the sleeping sick person") will be readily learned with high positive transfer following learning of S_1-V_1O_1. It is important to remain clear on this distinction between verbatim and gist recall, since it is possible to facilitate associations between general concepts (gist) at the same time one is interfering with verbatim recall.

A particularly striking example of the separation of these two levels was provided in an experiment by S. A. Bobrow (1970). He showed that if the subject and object nouns of a sentence were repeated as a pair in a second sentence, the association between them could be enhanced or not depending on whether the meanings of the nouns were maintained across the two sentence contexts. To illustrate, subjects learn to associate pairs of nouns like *pitcher* and *jam,* and do so using linking sentences as mediators. Suppose a sentence in the initial study list were "The milk *pitcher* was splattered with sweet *jam*." A sentence in the second list which preserved a similar conceptual meaning for the nouns would be "The lemonade *pitcher* was sticky with strawberry *jam*," whereas a sentence which totally altered the conceptual meaning would be "The baseball *pitcher* got caught in a traffic *jam*." The retention test, given at the end of the second study list, involved presentation of the subject noun (*pitcher*) for recall of the object noun (*jam*). As our intuition suggests, the subject-to-object association was greatly enhanced by interpolation of an identical or conceptually similar predica-

tion. But there was no accumulative learning when the meanings of the words were changed; performance was similar to what would have occurred if the *pitcher-jam* pair had been presented only once.

Although the illustrations above are for recall of single, isolated sentences, interference effects have been shown also for paragraphs, stories, "science lessons," and the like. In such experiments, one must attend carefully to what are the atomic assertions that relate concepts in the initial text, and how the specific predications about these concepts are altered in the interpolated learning. For example, Crouse (1971) and G. H. Bower (1974) have used short biographies of fictional persons as experimental passages. These comprise essentially a listing of life-history facts about the person. An interpolated passage which will produce little interference with the biography might concern, say, an art exhibit, whereas a passage causing maximal interference would be a second biography which systematically changes some of the facts contained in the first biography (such as names, dates, places, occupations, and so on). Bower found that specific facts which remained the same in the two biographies were facilitated in recall of the first biography whereas specifics which were changed (e.g., father's occupation) were forgotten, even though the subject was likely to remember to say something about the right general class of facts. That is, the subject might remember to say something about the father's occupation but would get the specific details wrong. This suggests, as mentioned earlier, that by appropriate interpolation one can selectively facilitate recall of the conceptual "macrostructure" of a passage while at the same time interfering with memory for the specific "microstructure" of the material. A later experiment by Thorndyke and Hayes-Roth (1979) is especially clear in showing these two effects—the learning of the macrostructure alongside interference with the microdetails of the passage.

SUMMARY COMMENTS

This brief tour through interference theory will suffice to indicate its major features. The main shifts that have occurred in it have been acceptance of the notions of unlearning and of response-set suppression, a new emphasis on proactive interference, and identification of a potent source of proactive effects in those prior language habits that conflict with the temporary verbal associations set up in a laboratory experiment. Increasingly, research is being directed at understanding interference and the forgetting of meaningful sentences and larger bodies of text. There have also been changes in the experimental techniques employed. For example, Barnes and Underwood's modified recall procedure mentioned earlier is now widely used because of the additional information it yields on what the person remembers. Pair recognition is used to assess associative learning, whereas free recall is often conceived as an index of pure "response availability." This is an active field of research and no brief discussion can do justice to the range of variables that have been investigated in relation to forgetting. For more comprehensive reviews, see McGeoch and Irion (1952), J. F. Hall (1971), Postman (1971), and Spear (1978).

Current studies of human learning and forgetting have continued in a highly analytical phase, with attention on progressively finer analysis of smaller aspects. As happens during analytical phases in other specialties, synthesis of the knowledge into a broader conception of the phenomena has been shunted aside. As a result, the possible uses of our scientific knowledge for solving practical problems have been only cursorily explored, and then in an often stumbling fashion. To mention just one major applied problem: educators or anyone engaged in training personnel would surely like to know how best to teach students something so that they will retain it for a long time. The laboratory work relating retention to the conditions under which training has occurred is clearly relevant; but it is often so far removed from the kind of task, background, and other variables that make up the applied situation that some ingenious extrapolation is required before the principles can be put to use. Writings by Gagné (1970), Staats (1968), and collections of papers edited by Hilgard (1964a) and by DeCecco (1967) represent a few attempts at reasonable extrapolations. The area of instructional psychology aims to improve instructional practices in schools by use of learning principles, task analysis, and skill training.

Characteristics of the Verbal Learning Tradition

Having reviewed research around selected topics in the verbal learning tradition, what may we say about the characteristics and orienting attitudes of the area's practicing researchers?

First, this functionalist tradition was committed to a firm environmentalism, believing that individual differences have largely arisen from differences in acquired skills and habits. They believed strongly in historical causation of current behavior; the cause of the person's present responses are to be found in her past training and how it is being transferred to the present situation.

Second, "mind" is considered as a collective name for a set of *dispositions* to behave in particular ways in particular circumstances. To describe a person's mind as bright or dull, retentive or forgetful, quick or slow is not to refer to some inner entity that causes individuals to act in certain ways; rather, it is to refer to their abilities and tendencies to act in these characteristic ways. This position is practically the same as the behaviorist's program.

Third, the verbal learning theorist prefers scientific concepts that are intersubjectively countable or measurable. Thus, the "meaningfulness" of a word will be identified with the average number of associates it evokes in thirty seconds, although this bypasses traditional definitions of meaning in terms of reference, use, or defining properties. Verbal learning theorists have a bias against mentalistic constructs such as imagery and nonverbal thinking. Insofar as possible, they assume that perceptual events are categorized, coded, and stored according to the verbal labels elicited by the events. Verbal learning theorists also oppose vague, heuristic constructs such as organization, structure, insight, and the gestalt properties of stimulus sets. Whenever possible, they translate the fuzzy and the mystical into simpler terminology of habit repertoires or stimulus patterns. Discontinuities in learning are believed to hide underlying continuities in habit acquisition.

Fourth, as noted, the verbal learning tradition has been firmly committed throughout to associationism, with a prolonged romance in midlife with Hull's S-R theory, since left behind in detail if not in spirit. Verbal learning theorists have tried to explain practically all phenomena uncovered in the verbal learning laboratory in terms of particular associative networks established between stimuli and responses, and the operation of simple retrieval rules such as cue similarity and response competition. The general tenets of associationism were criticized in Chapter 1 and shall be again in Chapter 13.

Fifth, the verbal learning tradition has been carried forward by a small group of psychologists, their students, and their students' students. Influential early functionalists (after Ebbinghaus) were Carr, Dewey, and Woodworth; they influenced McGeogh and Irion, who influenced Melton, Bilodeau, Underwood, Cofer, Osgood, and Postman, who influenced Keppel, Schulz, Spear, Martin, and so on. The research fervor for particular issues has been passed between generations, with many students of these scientists going on to productive careers in their own right. The dedication and productive energy of this group of researchers has earned them the gratitude of their scientific colleagues.

Modifications in Associationism

It is fair to say that associationism in the hands of modern verbal learning theorists is a different animal from the older British philosophical associationism, although it has evolved out of that philosophical tradition in response to critiques and empirical findings. Several of the criticisms are cited in Chapter 1 (under "Rationalism") and we will review a few of them here. First, while classical associationist theory said little about perceptual organization of sensory elements, it is now clear that the organization and "belongingness" of the sensory material greatly affects what the subject learns. Thus, when instructed to listen to a sequence of word pairs, *A-B, C-D, E-F* the hearer will segment the stream into pairs, and an element will become associated to the other members of its pair but not at all to elements of preceding or following pairs despite their objective temporal contiguity. Modern associationists accept such results but try further to show that the segmentation or grouping operation itself may be viewed theoretically as an attentional strategy or learnable higher-level response, which will show negative transfer, and so on.

A second point against classical associationism is that it did not recognize the many different *types* of associations that encode different types of relationships between two ideas. Labeling associations according to their type would permit efficient, relation-directed searches of memory and allow the direct retrieval of answers to questions like "What concept has relation R to concept X?" (e.g., "What's the superordinate category for *canary*?"). The retrieval of answers to such questions can be so fast that it is difficult to believe that individuals are somehow looking through long lists of associations in their memories trying to find an element on a list of superordinate names that is also on the list of associates to their concept of *canary*. Direct, relation-guided retrieval would seem more consonant with fast retrieval.

Related to the above is another complaint against classical associationism, which is that the classical theory does a poor job of explaining why the association retrieved can depend so much on the context in which a stimulus occurs. Thus, a red light means "stop" as a traffic signal but means "go through here" as a fire-exit sign. But this problem can be dealt with by assuming that retrieval cues always act within a patterned complex, that different goals or environments lead to different stimulus components in short-term memory (goal A or B or . . .), and that a specific stimulus (X) arouses different associations in the pattern $A + X$ than in the pattern $B + X$.

A further point not anticipated in classical associationism is that many of the associations observed (such as *RZL-CAT*) are not in fact direct ones but rather are mediated through a chain of more elementary associations. Thus, the temporal contiguity of *RZL* and *CAT* in the learner's experience has not resulted in her setting up an independent association, but rather has initiated a memory search for familiar associations which would solve the problem posed for her—namely, to unify arbitrary pairs of units. Of course, the notion of chains of mediating associations is within the spirit of modern associationism.

A third problem with classical associationism is that only simple ideas were as-

sumed to enter into associations, and associations were supposed to link only simple ideas, not chunks of ideas. Hull maintained a similar restriction. This restriction says that only "horizontal" links are permitted in theory (see Wickelgren, 1979b, for a discussion). This associative structure and two alternative ones are shown in Figure 6.15 for four interassociated ideas A, B, C, D. Panel A shows the classical hypothesis, that only direct element-to-element connections are permitted. (For this diagram, interpret the links as two-way associations.)

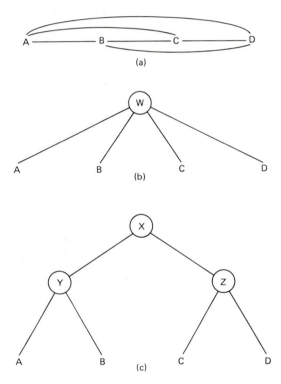

Figure 6.15.   Illustration of three types of associative structures for interrelating four items or properties, denoted A, B, C, D. (A) shows only horizontal associations. (B) permits vertical associations to the chunk node, W. (C) shows vertical associations outlining a hierarchy of two groups or chunks (Y, Z) that are grouped into the higher-level chunk, X.

Panel B shows a structure acquired by creating an abstract chunk or group node, *W,* into which each of the lower elements *A, B, C, D* has two-way links. Here, the ideas *A, B, C, D* are not directly linked to each other, but "communicate" with each other only through the chunk-node, *W.* The node *W* is abstract in the sense that it represents nothing except the co-occurrence of the four component ideas as a pattern or group; node *W* can also be thought of within an associative network as a switching terminal for shunting excitation arriving at *W* from a retrieval cue, say, cue *A,* out through the several pathways to *B, C, D,* thus to activate those ideas and bring them into consciousness. This terminology makes manifest that an associative network is basically a set of communication pathways, with nodes defined according to which other nodes (inputs) activate them and the nodes (outputs) to which they transmit activation.

Experiments by Ross & Bower (in press) and Arnold (1976) have supported the predictions of the vertical model in Panel B in preference to the horizontal model in Panel A. In the former study, adults studied many clusters of four or five slightly related words, then were tested for recall of each cluster by cueing with one or two words. The frequencies of the several recall patterns given one and two cues were fit quantitatively far better by the vertical model. Arnold (1976) came to a similar conclusion examining one-cue and two-cue recall of studied word-triplets as well as recognition of pairs and triplets. Thus, the evidence suggests the vertical model is preferable to the horizontal one. Anderson and Bower (1973), Estes (1972), and Wickelgren (1979) among others have also suggested the vertical association model.

Panel C in Figure 6.15 illustrates that chunk nodes (*Y, Z*) themselves can be grouped into a higher-order node (*X*), giving one the capability of hierarchically organizing base elements into groups.

Clearly we need a knowledge representation that permits any segmentation and grouping of elements, and also one that allows us to represent recursive grouping. This is required, for example, if the theory is to represent the person's memory for series of groups of elements. Such a representation is assumed in theories such as Lesgold and Bower's (1970), Estes's (1972), or Johnson's (1970) accounts of memory for chunked serial lists. Anderson and Bower (1973) also used a hierarchy of segmented idea units to represent complex sentences in memory. Thus, for example, in a simple declarative sentence, the noun phrase ("The old man") might correspond to node *Y* in Figure 6.15c, and the verb phrase ("petted the dog") might correspond to node *Z*; then, the top-level node *X* would be the internal code in memory permitting access to the conceptual structure established by the subject hearing and understanding the assertion "The old man petted the dog." These higher-level nodes like *X, Y, Z* can themselves enter into further associations. Thus the expanded associative theory envisions the growth of arbitrarily complex concepts encoded as associative configurations of elements, groups of elements, and groups of groups. These network formalisms underlie much of the developments in neo-associative theories of knowledge, concept utilization, and positional learning (Anderson & Bower, 1973; Kintsch, 1974; Norman & Rumelhart, 1975). These developments will be reviewed in Chapter 13.

Criticisms of the Verbal Learning Tradition

Critics of the verbal learning tradition have pointed to several shortcomings. First, it has used associationistic concepts of memory storage to understand its results, but has typically failed to specify the "executive monitor" which uses that memory base for answering questions or solving problems. As one illustration, verbal learning psychologists have proposed the idea that subjects edit their recall in a multi-list experiment when they are trying to recall a specific target list; as each item is retrieved, it is checked for a target list tag and is suppressed if it comes from the wrong list. But in a strictly associative theory, *what* carries out this editing function? How do we represent the program or routine that has been installed in short-term memory to guide this "generate-candidates-then-test" strategy for recall? How are those programs acquired? Typically, traditional verbal learning psychologists have bypassed such questions. Recent computer simulation theories such as J. R. Anderson's ACT model (1976) deal explicitly with these executive processes which use the associative memory.

A second common complaint is that the studies in the verbal learning tradition have nothing much to say about language learning. But verbal learning grew up during the "conditioning era" of psychology, was always intended to study basic associative learning in simplified arrangements, and was never aimed at bringing realistic school tasks directly into the laboratory. Many school tasks clearly do have large rote-learning components, and for these it appears that the results of the laboratory analogs apply as expected (for example, interference among similar biographies).

A third complaint of the critics is that verbal learning research is "crassly empirical," that it generates bushels of detailed data without revealing powerful, general principles or theories. To that criticism, the verbal learner would counter that science is first of all analysis and description of any phenomenon in all its myriad facets, and that "grand theories" are simply wasteful "grand delusions" unless one first has a secure empirical footing for theorizing. One should first try to figure out most of the variables that could influence some experimental phenomenon in order to make informed guesses about theory.

Verbal learners have proposed and researched a large number of theoretical hypotheses, although these tend to be local, tailored to a restricted domain, and have limited boundary conditions. But in terms of sheer hypotheses alive and well, the verbal learning psychologists can hold their own with others working on theories of animal learning. As global theories have lost their allure, as miniature hypotheses are being developed increasingly for specific learning tasks, the eclectic stance of functionalism has an increasing appeal for contemporary experimental psychologists.

SUPPLEMENTARY READINGS

The following books in the functionalist tradition may be recommended:

BILODEAU, E. A. (1966). *Acquisition of skill.*

HALL, J. F. (1971). *Verbal learning and retention.*

KAUSLER, D. H. (1974). *Psychology of verbal learning and memory.*

KLING, J. W., & RIGGS, L. A. (1971). *Experimental psychology.*

McGEOCH, J. A., & IRION, A. L. (1952). *The psychology of human learning.*

MELTON, A. W., ed. (1964). *Categories of human learning.*

OSGOOD, C. E. (1953). *Method and theory in experimental psychology.*

ROBINSON, E. S. (1932a). *Association theory today.*

SPEAR, N. E. (1978). *The processing of memories: Forgetting and retention.*

UNDERWOOD, B. J. (1966). *Experimental psychology.* 2nd ed.

WOODWORTH, R. S. (1958). *Dynamics of behavior.*

WOODWORTH, R. S., & SCHLOSBERG, H. (1954). *Experimental psychology.*

7
SKINNER'S OPERANT CONDITIONING

In a series of papers beginning in 1930, B. F. Skinner proposed a formulation of behavior which arose out of observations of animal performance in a type of experiment that he invented: the bar-pressing activity of a rat in a specially designed box called (by others) the Skinner box. Skinner believed that, in this setting, most of the important concepts of behavioral control could be examined and revealed. The success of his analytic procedures and demonstrations has appealed to several generations of "followers." What Skinner did was to isolate a few highly repeatable phenomena in conditioning—many of which Pavlov and Thorndike had studied and named before him—and then proceed to use these phenomena as a basis for concepts used in analyzing more complex forms of behavior. It is this collection of concepts, principles, and distinctions along with a particular philosophy of science and research strategy which characterizes the "Skinnerian" approach to psychology. Skinner's system was a thoroughgoing behaviorism, which is why it is reviewed in this section of the book. A basic faith is that complex behavior (neurosis, self-awareness, thinking, problem-solving), when properly analyzed, will be interpretable in terms of the complex interplay of elementary concepts and principles. This faith is very much like that which motivated Clark Hull's efforts or those of most other learning theorists. But whereas Hull was attracted to intervening variables and hypothetico-deductive theorizing, Skinner has rejected "theoretical constructs" as unnecessary. He has, for example, rejected a stimulus-response version of both behaviorism and associationism. Skinner has instead pursued either informal analyses (e.g., of cultural practices) or experimental analyses of various complex behaviors (e.g., reading).

Skinner is one of the most sophisticated and persuasive protagonists of the *behaviorist methodology* that psychology has ever seen. He rejects mentalistic or cognitive explanations of behavior, or explanations attributing behavior causation to inner psychic forces of any kind. Skinner argues that we understand a piece of behavior only when we have learned how to synthesize (train) that behavior from scratch, and how to predict and control that behavior. Mentalistic explanations are worthless, according to Skinner, because they do not tell us how to manipulate variables so as to synthesize or to control behavior. Such mentalistic explanations are incomplete, and their acceptance simply postpones doing a proper functional analysis of the behavior. A functional analysis of a given behavior means that we attempt to identify and isolate the environmental variables of which the behavior is a lawful function.

Although the early experimental work by Skinner was carried out with rats pressing levers for food pellets in a work chamber, the experimental base of the analysis has been gradually extended to other animals, to humans of all ages, and to situations and behaviors differing increasingly from the original base (e.g., to teaching machines and behavioral psychotherapy). Skinner has also defended a particularly compelling behavioristic position regarding the analysis of common-sense psychological terms such as *self, self-control, awareness, thinking, problem-solving, composing, will power,* and many of the psychodynamic concepts such as *repression, rationalization,* and other ego defense mechanisms. He has, in addition, propounded a particular analysis of *verbal behavior,* for the listener as well as for the speaker, which has been quite controversial. He has taken his ideas a step further in the analysis of the notions of *free will, inner determination,* and *social values,* and has discussed how one might arrange cultural practices by design so as to engineer a society that is "better" according to certain humanitarian values. For this reason, and for his popular books, *Walden two* and *Beyond freedom and dignity,* he is probably better known by the public at large than any other contemporary psychologist.

We cannot hope to review in one chapter Skinner's many contributions throughout a career spanning over forty-five years of scientific activities. We will tend toward the historical view, emphasizing Skinner's early collection of concepts and principles.

Later we shall delve briefly into the Skinnerian analysis of several complex skills. Skinner's early book, *The behavior of organisms* (1938), introduced the main ideas he was to apply with only slight variation to more complex cases over the next forty years. The first part of our review refers mainly to this historically significant book.

RESPONDENT AND OPERANT BEHAVIOR

A significant departure from traditional stimulus-response psychology within Skinner's system was the distinction between respondent and operant behavior. Since Watson, stimulus-response psychology had enforced the dictum "no stimulus, no response" by assuming the presence of stimuli when a response occurred even though no stimuli were identifiable. It was not doubted that stimuli were present to elicit such responses, if the experimenter only had means of detecting them. Skinner found this method of forcing facts both undesirable and unnecessary. He proposed that two classes of response be distinguished, a class of *elicited* responses and a class of *emitted* responses.

Responses that are elicited by known stimuli are classified as *respondents.* Pupillary constriction to light and salivation to lemon juice in the mouth serve as convenient illustrations of respondent reflexes. There is a second class of responses that need not be correlated with any known stimuli. These *emitted* responses are designated *operants,* to distinguish them from respondents. Because operant behavior is not elicited by recognized stimuli, its strength cannot be measured according to the usual laws of the reflex, which are all stated as functions of their eliciting stimuli. Instead, rate of response is used as a measure of operant strength in a given situation.

An operant may, and usually does, acquire a relation to prior stimulation. In that case it becomes a *discriminated operant;* the stimulus becomes an occasion for the operant behavior, but is not an eliciting stimulus as in the case of a true reflex. A simple illustration of an operant coordinated with a stimulus would be a reaction-time experiment as commonly conducted in the psychological laboratory. The correlation between stimulus and response may easily be changed, as by instructions to depress the key instead of lifting the finger from it. Most human behavior is operant in nature. The behavior of mopping a floor, driving a car, writing a letter, shows few respondent characteristics.

Although Skinner is a behaviorist, he is not an S-R psychologist. His notion of the operant refers to behavior that is avowedly *not* elicited by some stimulus, but is emitted. The S-R idea suggests a passive organism from whom a distinct stimulus triggers a specific behavior, and Skinner rejects that view as well as its mechanistic overtones for operant behavior. However, a discriminative stimulus is said to "set the occasion" for an operant, or to exert "stimulus control" over an operant, and that moves Skinner in the direction of the S-R theorists. But Skinner finds the concept of association to be unnecessary. The stimulus and response may be "associated" (occur together) in the world and be translated into a readiness to perform the response; however, the idea of an internal linkage between situation and response representations is just excess baggage, Skinner would claim.

Two Types of Conditioning

Related to the two types of response are said to be two types of conditioning. The conditioning of respondent behavior is said to be of "Type S," because reinforcement is correlated with stimuli. The conditioned stimulus (e.g., a tone) is presented together with the unconditioned stimulus (e.g., food) and thus comes to elicit the response (e.g., salivation). The reinforcing event that interests Skinner is the presentation of the unconditioned stimulus, not the response to it. Type S was the name Skinner gave to Pavlovian or classical conditioning, but this term has lost currency.

"Type R" was Skinner's name for instrumental or operant conditioning, and he believed it to be much more important. The letter R is used to call attention to the importance of the response term in the correlation with reinforcement. The experimental example he originally used was lever-pressing. For a hungry organism, this response may be strengthened by following it with food. Not the *stimulus* of the lever but the *response* of depressing it is correlated with reinforcement. The conditioned response does not resemble the response to the reinforcing stimulus; its relationship to the reinforcing stimulus is that the response causes the reinforcer to appear. In operant conditioning, reinforcement cannot follow unless the conditioned response appears; reinforcement is *contingent* upon the response. As noted in Chapter 3, this arrangement came to be called instrumental conditioning to distinguish it from the arrangements of classical conditioning (Hilgard & Marquis, 1940, pp. 51–74).

The laws of operant conditioning are similar to those of classical conditioning; both include a law of conditioning and a law of extinction. Skinner's law of operant conditioning may be compared to Thorndike's law of effect: *if the occurrence of an operant is followed by presentation of a reinforcing stimulus, the strength is increased* (Skinner, 1938, p. 21). Note that a reinforcing situation is defined by its stimulus; nothing is said about satisfying aftereffects or about drive reduction. Skinner suggested further (1938, p. 112) that conditioning of Type R may be limited to skeletal behavior, Type S to autonomic responses.

Positive and Negative Primary Reinforcers

A reinforcer is defined by its effects. Any stimulus is a reinforcer if it increases the probability of a response. The stimuli that happen to act as reinforcers fall into two classes (Skinner, 1953, p. 73):

1. Positive reinforcement occurs when a stimulus presented following an operant response, strengthens the probability of that response. Food, water, sexual contact, classify as positive reinforcers for appropriately deprived individuals.

2. Negative reinforcement occurs when removal of an aversive stimulus following an operant response, strengthens the probability of that response. A loud noise, a very bright light, extreme heat or cold, electric shock, are examples of *aversive stimuli*. Notice that the type of reinforcements are classified according to whether presentation or removal of a stimulus strengthens a preceding operant. An aversive stimulus is one for which the organism will learn something to escape it. As defined here, punishment is *not* negative reinforcement. Punishment is rather an experimental arrangement in which presentation of an aversive stimulus is contingent upon a designated response. We will discuss punishment from the Skinnerian perspective in a later section.

Skinner also recognized conditioned reinforcers based on the pairing of neutral stimuli with primary reinforcers. Conditioned reinforcement is also discussed in a later section.

Other psychologists have been interested in the question, Why is a reinforcer reinforcing? But this question has not been of much interest to Skinner. He is interested in why behavior changes, and finds reinforcers importantly involved. He rather tentatively accepts an explanation of reinforcement in terms of evolutionary and adaptive functions, but he does not find it of much help in the detailed functional analysis of what actually occurs (1953, pp. 81–84).

STUDIES OF OPERANT CONDITIONING

As noted earlier, to study operant conditioning, Skinner designed his special apparatus—a soundproof box in which a rat can depress a lever to deliver a pellet of food. The lever is connected with a recording system which produces a graphical tracing of the number of lever-pressings plotted against the length of time the rat is in the box. In this situation remarkably consistent and "lawful" results can be obtained. Modifications of the experiment can be introduced so that food is not delivered every time the lever is depressed. The consequences of doing this and of making other changes in the situation have been systematically explored. The "pigeon-box" is a corresponding arrangement for obtaining a response record as a pigeon pecks at a lighted plastic key mounted on the wall at head height and is reinforced by receiving grain.

The consequence of reinforcing the operant is an increase in its rate, or probability of occurrence per unit time. Since the animal usually remains continuously in the presence of the lever or response key, this is termed the *free responding*, or *free operant*, situation; discrete trials are not marked off, and since the response can occur at any time, response rate per unit time is the measure observed. Depending on the scheduling of reinforcements and many other factors, this response rate can vary over a large range, and one is interested in what will be the steady-state performance produced and maintained by particular reinforcement contingencies. We shall return to this topic later.

Regarding acquisition of this simple operant, Skinner offered the opinion that it would occur in "one trial" or instantaneously if the extraneous factors were eliminated and if the animal were appropriately prepared for the "one trial." For example, earlier experiences in the box would be used to habituate irrelevant exploratory or fearful behaviors, and earlier "feeder training" would condition the hungry animal to approach the food cup and eat at the sound of the food dispenser discharging a food pellet into the cup. If these behavioral components have been taken care of before the lever is introduced and connected to the feeder, then conditioning of lever-pressing is indeed very rapid, if not instantaneous. According to Skinner (as for Guthrie, see Chapter 4), lever-press conditioning typically appears gradual because it is a chain of many component behaviors, and "learning curves" reveal more about the "problem-box" and the conditions of prior preparation of elements of the response chain than they reveal about basic "laws."

Just as reinforcing an operant strengthens it, so nonreinforcement following the response is alleged to weaken it, and a prolonged series of nonreinforced responses results in a gradual lowering of response rate via the process called *experimental extinction.* The animal stops pressing because this action is no longer followed by reinforcement. Skinner, as did others, at first (1938, p. 26) thought that the number of responses emitted during extinction would be a measure of operant strength; however, his own studies of intermittent reinforcement led him to abandon that idea. In 1950, he came to realize, perhaps sooner than others, that we can differentially train an organism either to "resist" or to "desist quickly" in extinction, depending on how rewards and nonrewards are scheduled during training.

DISCRIMINATING STIMULI AND RESPONSES

Skinner has also done extensive research on stimulus discrimination. In behavioral terms, we say that an organism discriminates among two or more stimuli when it can learn to respond differentially (in different ways or with different rates) to each of the stimuli. Skinner refers to this as *stimulus control* since presentation or removal of a given discriminative stimulus controls the occurrence of a particular response pattern or its rate. A second kind of learning is *response differentiation,* in which the form of the response (its topography) or its intensity, amplitude, or latency is altered by differential reinforcement. Skinner presumes that the complexities of behavior can be understood according to stimulus discriminations and differentiated responses arranged into appropriate chains or patterns.

Discrimination of Stimuli

To illustrate Skinner's viewpoint, the standard lever-pressing experiment may serve to describe the purposes of discriminatory conditioning. Suppose that lever-pressing delivers a pellet of food in the presence of a positive stimulus, such as a light, and fails to deliver in the absence of this discriminative stimulus. The rat learns to respond only when the light is on. Skinner, like Spence and Hull, offers the usual analysis of discrimination learning in terms of reinforcement, extinction, and stimulus generalization. But Skinner notes that the light does not elicit the response in the sense that a cinder in the eye elicits tears or touching a heated pan elicits withdrawal. The difference between a discriminative stimulus as an *occasion* for a response and actually eliciting a response is clarified by an example. I reach for a pencil lying on the desk, but I reach only when the pencil is there and I want it, but I do not reach for it just *because* it is there. While the pencil does not elicit reaching, it has something to do with my reaching. If it were dark, I might grope for it because the discriminative stimuli would be lacking. The pencil does not elicit reaching in the light any more than in the dark. It is only the occasion for reaching given appropriate conditions (Skinner, 1938, p. 178).

Errorless discrimination learning. According to the classical view, discrimination is achieved by extinguishing generalized responses to the nonreinforced stimuli, S⁻. In Spence's theory, for example, the repeated frustration by nonreinforcement of responding to S⁻ causes the inhibition to become associated to S⁻.

Terrace (1963a), a student of Skinner's, devised a procedure for teaching a pigeon a perfect discrimination in such a manner that it never responds to S⁻ throughout the entire experiment; in other words, it never makes an "error." The studies use different colored lights on the pecking key serving as S⁺ and S⁻. The procedure involves (a) introducing S⁻ very early before the response to S⁺ is well conditioned, and (b) introducing S⁻ gradually, initially for very brief durations and at very dim intensities. Over successive trials, the intensity and duration of S⁻ stimulus trials are gradually increased to their full values. The method hinges in part upon certain peculiarities of pigeons such as the fact that they are initially unlikely to peck a darkened key. However, similar methods have been used with humans.

By using this simple procedure, Terrace showed that it is possible to achieve perfect discrimination without the occurrence of a single nonreinforced response to S⁻. In contrast, suppose that S⁻ is introduced, as it usually is, for the full duration and at full brightness after the pigeon has had several sessions of exposure to S⁺ and has become well conditioned. Under these conditions, the pigeon may emit several thousand responses to S⁻ before learning acceptable differential behavior. Thus, the difference produced by Terrace's simple procedure is truly enormous whether one thinks only in terms of ease of training a discrimination or also, by inference, of the amount of emotional frustration that the subject has been spared.

In a related experiment, Terrace (1963b) was able to show that an errorless discrimination learned to, say, red versus green key colors could be transferred to two new stimuli (a white vertical bar as positive and horizontal bar as negative) by a special method. The special method (see Figure 7.1) consisted in (a) first superimposing the vertical bar on the positive red key, and the horizontal bar on the negative green key, and (b) after several sessions of such superimposed conditions, gradually fading out (dimming) the red and green colors on the key, eventually ending up with only the vertical or horizontal bar on a dark key. By this procedure stimulus control is transferred from red versus green to vertical

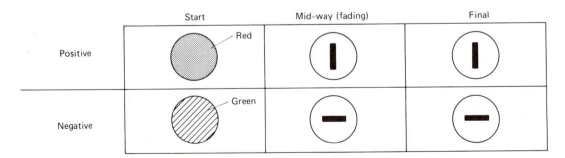

Figure 7.1. Illustration of pigeon-key stimuli used in shifting control of a red (+) vs. green (−) discrimination over to a vertical (+) vs. horizontal (−) line. The procedure is done gradually so that the animal never makes an error.

versus horizontal bars, and here, again, no errors occur in the course of the gradual transfer. It is of significance that Terrace was unable to train a vertical versus horizontal discrimination from scratch without errors (by manipulating brightness of S⁻). This suggests that if a difficult discrimination is to be trained, an optimal method is to train without errors another discrimination that is inherently easy for the subject (as colors surely are for pigeons), and then superimpose and fade into the more difficult stimuli. Terrace points out the relevance of his results to Skinner's claim that the optimal arrangement of programmed instructional sequences (in teaching machines) is the one in which the student never makes an error in answering questions during learning.

There are several intriguing byproducts of errorless discrimination performance that Terrace has emphasized by comparing them to what is obtained under the customary error-spotted procedure. First of all, the discriminative performance itself is far superior. Animals trained by the errorless method rarely respond to S⁻, whereas birds whose training routine is spotted with errors continue indefinitely to put out sporadic bursts of responses to S⁻. Second, observation reveals that the error-prone birds display a large amount of emotional behavior in S⁻, suggesting that it is probably an aversive stimulus for them, apparently because of the frustration generated by nonreinforced responding. In comparison, the errorless-trained birds in Terrace's study displayed relatively little emotional behavior in S⁻. Third, giving an injection of the tranquilizing drug chlorpromazine "releases" large quantities of responses to S⁻ in the error-prone trained birds but not in the errorless-trained birds. Presumably, the tranquilizer dispels some of the emotion that had been inhibiting responses to S⁻ for the animals trained with errors. Fourth, the errorless-trained birds do not show a *behavioral contrast effect*

(faster rates to S⁺ because it is alternated with S⁻), whereas the error-prone birds do: however, if an errorless-trained bird is induced to start making errors in S⁻ (say, by abrupt transfer from colors to lines mentioned above), then it begins to show contrast by increasing its rate of responding to S⁺. Fifth, a stimulus generalization gradient obtained following discrimination training shows a *peak shift* for the error-prone birds but not for the errorless birds. Peak shift refers to the fact that the peak (maximum) rate of responding is produced not at S⁺, but at a value displaced from S⁺ in a direction away from S⁻. Figure 7.2 shows this effect in Terrace's experiment (1964). The stimulus continuum is wavelength of light (corresponding to color changes to the human eye) measured in millimicrons. The S⁺ was at 580 and S⁻ at 540 millimicrons. Notice that the peak rate of responding during generalization testing is at 580 (the S⁺) for the errorless-trained birds, but is shifted over to 590 for the error-prone-trained birds.

What does it all mean? How is it best interpreted? A possible account might go as follows. Errorless discrimination is possible using Thorndike's principle of associative shifting, which in this instance is the same as Guthrie's principle of conditioning by sheer contiguity of the last response made before a stimulus terminates. Because of past extinction experiences with pecking at a homogeneous dark ground, the pigeon at the beginning of the experiment does not peck at the darkened key on the dark wall. Because the S⁻ color is presented initially dim and for short durations, the likely response to these S⁻ presentations is either withdrawal or just "sitting still," and this behavior is what gets conditioned to S⁻. This nonresponse then generalizes to brighter S⁻ colors. Behavioral contrast and peak shift are effects that depend upon the conversion of S⁻ into an aversive stimulus, and this is ordinarily achieved by the frustration generated by nonreinforced re-

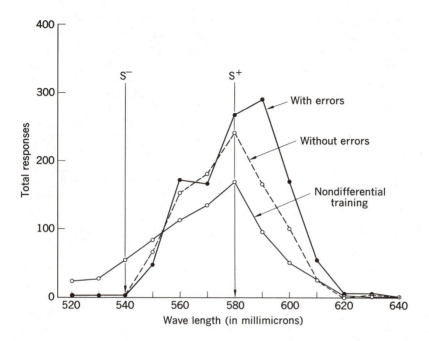

Figure 7.2. Generalization gradients obtained under three different conditions, relating response rate to variations in the wavelength (color) of a light projected on the pecking key. The lower gradient was obtained following simple conditioning at 580 millimicrons without a discrimination procedure. The other two gradients followed discrimination training on 580 millimicrons as S⁺ and 540 as S⁻, one procedure involving errors to S⁻, the other none. A peak shift appears in the former gradient because responding to 590 millimicrons was greater than to 580, the S⁺ of training. (From Terrace, 1964.)

sponding to S⁻. Since the errorless procedure produces relatively few nonreinforced responses, relatively little frustration is evoked or aversion conditioned to S⁻, and so contrast and peak shift do not occur in this case. In line with this reasoning, Grusec (1965) found that errorless-trained birds did show peak shift if they received electric shocks in association with S⁻, thus converting it into an aversive stimulus.

Not everyone accepts the special status and properties of errorless discrimination learning. Rilling (1977) has argued that an *error* is an arbitrarily defined piece of an entire response chain (i.e., closing the key switch), and that earlier parts of the chain may be regularly occurring to S⁻ without

being recorded. Therefore, he argues that we should not accord such special status to recorded errors. Furthermore, *errorless learning* is arbitrarily defined (most birds given the "errorless procedures" make some errors). Consequently, Rilling sees no reason to draw a sharp qualitative distinction between error-prone and errorless learning. The research of Rilling and his colleagues argues further that:

> The behavior of subjects with few errors is not fundamentally different from the behavior of subjects with many errors, except for the difference in errors. [Many byproducts of discrimination learning] have all been obtained independently of whether the discrimination was

acquired with or without errors. Therefore, a theoretical classification based on the distinction between learning with errors and learning without errors is not useful (Rilling, 1977, p. 475).

Rilling and his colleagues found that their errorless-trained birds did show significant aversion to S⁻ in that they would work to turn off S⁻ and replace it by a dark key between trials. Errorless-trained birds would also attack a "victim bird" restrained in the operant conditioning chamber during S⁻ more than they would during a neutral stimulus before conditioning. If attack is considered a sign of emotion ("anger"), then the errorless pigeons are somewhat emotional during S⁻, possibly frustrated just by the absence of S⁺ in a context where S⁺ often occurs. Also, investigators have often found behavioral contrast when the S⁻ was a blackout of the chamber, where no responses occurred to S⁻. Thus, the uniqueness of the effects due to Terrace's errorless procedures have now been called into question.

Whether or not errorless discrimination training causes qualitative shifts in phenomena, the practical significance of the procedure still stands. It shows that the conventional extinction procedure can be sidestepped in establishing a discrimination and that the performance thus obtained is better than the ones usually established. Terrace's procedure brings out a point of view concerned with optimality, asking questions regarding the best arrangement of training conditions, one that permits the subject to achieve some criterion of good performance. Possible goals here would be to devise training sequences to optimize the skillfulness of the eventual performance achieved, the speed of effecting a given change in performance, the production of a desired change with a minimum of errors, or a minimum of frustration or difficulty, and so forth. Such research yields results of practical relevance to educators,

psychotherapists, and others whose concern is with practical behavioral engineering.

Differentiation of a Response: Shaping

Response differentiation refers to reinforcement of certain properties of a response such as its speed, duration, or forcefulness. For example, Skinner (1938) trained some rats to press and hold down the lever for a long time in order to get reward; he trained others to press the lever with a forcefulness above a certain criterion. Similarly, as we will see in our later analysis of performance on a DRL schedule, we can train the subject to respond selectively at a fast or slow rate. The principle is that of operant reinforcement, but it is applied at the level of intensive variations of the response (what Logan calls micromolar responses, reviewed in Chapter 5). For example, in differentiating a forceful lever-press, one first reinforces any lever-presses, thus providing a distribution of variable forces. One then establishes a low force criterion, and rewards only those presses which exceed that criterion. The effect of this restriction is to extinguish weaker presses and strengthen forceful presses, so that the entire force distribution shifts to higher values. The experimenter's criterion may then be increased again, and again, and thus gradually "shape" the animal's lever-presses to higher values. An upper limit, of course, can also be imposed such that forces above that limit are not reinforced; and responses of different forces can be conditioned to several differential stimuli (Notterman & Mintz, 1962). The relevance of such results to the learning of complex human skills is obvious. For example, our social community shapes up a particular speed and loudness to our speaking in particular settings (e.g., whispering at funerals, shouting at baseball games), and severe deviations from that norm are punished.

Another type of shaping occurs when a new qualitative response or novel sequence of behavioral components is assembled into a unitary performance. This makes use of the notion of *chaining,* which played a role in Skinner's analyses.

Response Chains

Skinner (1938, 1953), argues that most complete acts are in fact a sequence of movements in which each segment provides feedback stimuli (external and internal) which become discriminative for the next segment of the response. Thus the act may be thought of as a chain of small $S^D \rightarrow R$ units. Even the simple lever-pressing response can be conceived to be a chain. In their discussion of chaining, Keller and Schoenfeld (1950, pp. 197–208) cite the six links in Table 7.1 as illustrative. In this chain each response produces the discriminative stimulus for the next response. The chain may be elaborated more or less for analytic purposes.

Does the chain operate as a unit? The well-conditioned rat makes the transitions so smoothly that it seems to be giving one response, not six. But the independence of the units of the chain can be tested experimentally.

1. If we eliminate only the stimulus for the final units of the chain (the pellet), as is done in one form of extinction, the earlier links of the chain are gradually weakened, but the last ones are unaffected. That is, the rat will still seize and eat a pellet exactly as before.

2. If we now eliminate both the fourth and fifth links in the chain (the apparatus noise as well as the pellet), and carry out extinction, we can find out more about the chain. Reintroducing the noise after extinction again reinforces bar-pressing. Hence, during conditioning, the stimulus of the fourth link (the apparatus noise) has become a conditioned reinforcer. Furthermore, the extinction of the preceding links in the chain has not extinguished the reinforcing properties of the fourth link.

This kind of functional and experimental study isolates units of the chain that preserve some independence from the whole; these units are part of a chain and their distinctiveness as units is not entirely arbitrary. It would be possible to record the separate responses, and not only the final one. The unit appropriate for experimental study turns out, in fact, to have a measure of arbitrariness about it. It is a matter of convenience whether to measure one response of the chain, or six responses, or many more than that; evidently, some selectivity is exercised by the experimenter. This is always true: *all* description is partial description.

This analysis of chaining suggests not

TABLE 7.1.   Listing of the stimulus-response components in the response chain of bar-pressing and eating. (From Keller & Schoenfeld, 1950.)

Operant Number	Discriminative Stimulus	Response of the Rat
1	Bar location	Approach of rat to front of box
2	Visual bar	Rising on hind legs; placing paws on bar
3	Tactual bar	Pressing of bar, thus activating food magazine
4	Apparatus noise	Lowering foreparts to food tray
5	Visual pellet	Seizing of pellet by teeth and paws
6	Pellet in mouth	Chewing of pellet

only laws for "breaking down" established chains, but also a means for training the organism to new chains, stringing together novel sequences of behavioral components much as one might string together differently colored beads to create novel designs in a necklace. The basic rule is to develop the chain one S^D-R unit at a time, starting from the reinforcement and working backward. The "reinforcement" for learning the next response in the chain is presentation of the S^D for the rest of the chain. If the exact response form does not occur initially at any appreciable rate, then reinforce any behavior which *approximates* the form desired; then when that variation occurs, require an even closer approximation to the form desired before giving reinforcement. Through successive approximations, the shaping method permits the finally learned behavior to be very different from that originally emitted.

> Animal trainers are well versed in this method. As a sort of *tour de force* I have trained a rat to execute an elaborate series of responses suggested by recent work on anthropoid apes. The behavior consists of pulling a string to obtain a marble from a rack, picking the marble up with the forepaws, carrying it to a tube projecting two inches above the floor of the cage, and dropping it inside. Every step in the process had to be worked out through a series of approximations, since the component responses were not in the original repertoire of the rat (Skinner, 1938, pp. 339–340).[1]

There have been a number of demonstrations of all sorts of novel and complex skills taught to various animals by means of

[1] For other accounts of animal training, see Breland and Breland (1951) and Skinner (1951). It is doubtful whether the best way to build up a response chain *ABC* is *always* to proceed from the reinforcement backward, adding new elements to the front end as in training *C*, then *BC*, then *ABC*. In many circumstances, it is just as appropriate to build up a chain forward, inserting a novel element between the penultimate response and reinforcement, as in the training sequence, *A*, then *AB*, then *ABC* to get reinforcement.

shaping by successive approximations. Skinner believes that this is the way most of our complex skills have been synthesized.

SCHEDULES OF REINFORCEMENT

The reinforcement of operant behavior in ordinary life is not regular and uniform. The fisherman does not hook a fish with every cast of the line, and the farmer does not always receive a beautiful harvest from his planting, yet they continue to fish and to plant. Hence the problem of maintaining or strengthening a response through *intermittent reinforcement* is more than a laboratory curiosity. Skinner has explored extensively two main classes of intermittent reinforcement, now called *interval schedules* and *ratio schedules*.

Fixed interval schedules are arranged using a clock: reinforcement is provided for the first response to occur after the lapse of a designated (fixed) interval of time, measured from the preceding reinforcement or from the onset of a "trial stimulus." Typical intervals studied range from 30 seconds to 10 minutes or so. This arrangement, earlier named "periodic reconditioning" or "periodic reinforcement" (both archaic now), virtually controls the number of reinforcements delivered per hour to the animal. Fixed interval (or FI, as it is abbreviated) schedules produce lawful and orderly results. A first result found by Skinner (1938) was that his rats tended to put out an approximately constant number of responses per reinforcement (about 18 to 20 lever-presses in one study). Thus the average rate of responding, expressed as responses per minute, would be about twice as high when the animal is working on a 2-minute FI (abbreviated FI 2') as when he is working on a 4-minute FI. A second finding was what is called the *FI scallop*, which is schematized in the upper left panel of Figure 7.3. The FI scallop is indicated by a zero rate of responding immediately after

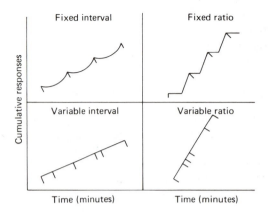

Figure 7.3. Example of cumulative response records on four standard schedules of reinforcement. A downward tick indicates delivery of a reinforcer.

temporal discrimination becomes sharper, but there are rather clear limitations on how closely a time interval can be estimated. This scalloping can be eliminated by *variable interval* (VI) schedules (shown in lower left panel of Figure 7.3) in which a range of intervals from very short to very long are used in a random, variable order. In VI, average performance depends mainly on the arithmetic average interval, varying in inverse proportion. The pause after reinforcement tends to be eliminated in VI, especially if very short intervals are included in the set. Under such schedules, the average performance is remarkably stable and uniform. A realistic illustration of such stability is found in Figure 7.4. Because of the stability and reproducibility of VI performance, it tends to be used as a baseline in assessing behavioral effects of diverse variables that may be introduced into the situation (drive level, punishment, drugs, and so on). Responses trained on VI schedules are also unusually resistant to extinction; it is not unusual, for instance, to observe pigeons responding more than 10,000 times during extinction following VI training. Resistance to extinction depends roughly on the mean and maximal interval in the VI program.

a reinforcement, then a gradual acceleration to a high response rate just near the time at which a reinforcement becomes available. The FI scallop develops gradually with continued exposure to a given FI, and is a clear indication of time discrimination. That is, on an FI, reinforcement is not available right after a reinforcement; but as "subjective" time goes by since the previous reinforcement, the animal's response becomes increasingly likely to be reinforced. With continued training, the

The other major class of reinforcement schedule is *fixed ratio* (abbreviated FR), in

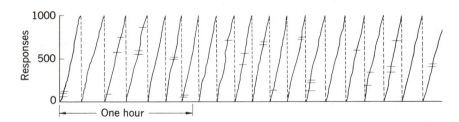

Figure 7.4. Responses within variable interval reinforcement. The curves are of the pecking responses of an individual pigeon reinforced at intervals ranging from 10 seconds to 21 minutes, but averaging 5 minutes. Each of the sloping lines represent 1000 responses; the pen resets to zero after each 1000. The whole record represents some 20,000 responses in about 3 hours, with an average of 12 reinforcements per hour. Each reinforcement is represented by a horizontal dash. (From Skinner, 1950.)

which reinforcement is provided for the *n*th response after the preceding reinforcement. Typical values of *n* are in the range of 10 to 200, although ratios as high as 1000 or more can be achieved with responses that are relatively effortless. Typically, an animal is not placed directly onto a high-ratio schedule, but rather is gradually worked up to it from lower ratio requirements to prevent early extinction.

Responding on ratio schedules tends to be very fast (called "bursts" in laboratory jargon), because the faster the animal responds the sooner he gets the reward (or the higher is his rate of reinforcement per unit time). Notice the illustration in the top right panel of Figure 7.3. As with the FI scallop, responding within an FR segment tends to be two-valued: a long pause after reinforcement followed by an abrupt shift to a very high response rate that is maintained until the ratio requirement is fulfilled and reinforcement is attained. The pause after reinforcement is longer with larger ratios, and is affected by many variables (emotion, drive level, drugs, and so on), whereas the terminal response rate seems relatively fixed and insensitive to such variables. The pause after reinforcement is likened by Skinner to "abulia," the inability to expend effort. An analogy would be the student who has just finished a term paper, perhaps in a burst of speed as the deadline approaches, and then finds it difficult to start work on a new assignment. In fixed ratio performance, response-produced feedback accumulated by the current response count becomes a discriminative predictor of reinforcement for the organism. A variety of experiments (e.g., Mechner, 1958) shows that animals can use their response count on lever *A* as a discriminative stimulus for switching over to pressing lever *B* in order to get a reinforcer made available by completion of the count on *A*.

As with the fixed interval, the pause after reinforcement on FR may be eliminated by adopting a *variable ratio* schedule, in which the ratio varies randomly from small to large. Because the probability of reinforcement for any response is approximately constant independent of the count, a uniform rate of responding ensues. Notice the performance schematized in the lower right panel of Figure 7.3. The rate is typically high because fast bursts of responses tend to "run into" reinforcement quicker, and so are preferentially reinforced. For example, on such schedules a pigeon may respond as rapidly as five pecks per second and keep up this rate for hours.

The possible variations in schedules of reinforcement are almost unlimited. Reward can be scheduled according to the passage of time, the number of responses, or some combination of these; schedules can be arranged in sequences with or without associated cues, and so on. Ferster and Skinner investigated the long-term effects of about twenty such schedules in their book *Schedules of reinforcement* (1957). It is difficult to summarize briefly the tremendous catalog of systematic data which Ferster and Skinner collected, although the asymptotic performance maintained by a given schedule is typically easily understood in terms of familiar concepts of stimulus discrimination and of reinforcement strengthening the specific momentary *rate* of response (or interresponse time) which prevailed at the moment reinforcement was delivered.

To illustrate just a few examples of schedule-induced performances, let us consider two schedules, DRL (differential reinforcement of low rates of responding) and a "tandem" schedule where a fixed interval requirement is followed by a fixed ratio requirement for reinforcement (abbreviated tandem FI-FR). First, on a DRL schedule, say of 10 seconds, a response will be reinforced only if at least 10 seconds have elapsed since the last response. If the response occurs too soon, the timer is reset and another wait of at least 10 seconds must occur before a response will be rewarded. DRL schedules generate *timing behavior;* the animal typically learns to go through a variety of rituals, which eventuate in a response at around the criterion time. The usual analysis of DRL performance as well as other schedule performances (see Morse, 1966; Shimp, 1969) treats the time between successive responses—the interresponse time or IRT—as the unit of analysis, as Logan (1960) does in his micromolar theory. That is, most schedules are presumed to impose a contract or "terms function," relating the differing probabilities of reinforcement to the different IRTs. On a 10-second DRL schedule, all IRTs less than 10 seconds have a zero probability of being reinforced, whereas IRTs greater than 10 seconds have a probability of one of being reinforced. This reinforcement probability, along with other factors, affects the "strength" of each IRT, and the animal is viewed as choosing (following each response) which IRT will be the next one she will emit. Without going into details, such theories expect animals to adjust their IRT selection to the DRL schedule, since only IRTs exceeding the criterion time are reinforced.

Consider next the performance on a tandem FI-FR schedule. Suppose the initial FI component is long, say 6 minutes, after which the first response terminates the FI component and, without any external stimulus change, begins a fixed ratio, say a small one of 5 responses, after the completion of which reinforcement occurs, and the program resets to the long FI component. Now, on a simple FI 6' schedule, a hungry pigeon might average, say, 100 responses per 6-minute interval (just to pick a hypothetical figure for illustration). But when the small FR 5 is added as a requirement at the end, as the tandem FI 6' FR 5 does, the response rate does not simply go up to 105 per 6-minute interval; rather it increases almost threefold, to around 300 responses per 6-minute interval. How are

we to understand such a huge effect on behavior of what appears to be a trivial change in the requirements for reinforcement? Again, we must attend carefully to the differences between the FI 6' and the tandem FI 6' FR 5 schedules in terms of the momentary rate of responding that is likely to prevail at the moment of reinforcement. A simple FI schedule differentially reinforces long IRTs, since the longer one waits after his prior response the more likely it is that the interval has timed out. The small ratio requirement tacked onto the end of the fixed interval alters matters: now reinforcement is most likely when a burst or run of fast responses occur, since they will meet the FR 5 requirement. The result is that "bursts" of 3 to 8 responses get strengthened as a unit. Thus, in the FI 6' portion of the tandem schedule, the bird still shows an FI scallop ("timing"), except that now when he responds he does so in bursts of key-pecks. The result is thus a large increase in the overall rate of responding when it is counted according to single pecks.

These are just a few examples of schedule-induced performances and how they can be reasonably analyzed in terms of reinforcement of different IRTs. Just as one can examine the performance of a single operant maintained by a given schedule, so can one examine *preferential choice* between two schedules, each correlated with a different response key. Herrnstein (1970), using response strength constructs somewhat like those of Hull, has shown how the percentage choice between two concurrent variable interval schedules (each associated with two different keys) comes to match the relative rates of reinforcement for pecking on the two keys.

It is worth noting that the reliability and regularity of long-term schedule performance is striking. The performance is also highly repeatable—that is, one can shift the animal temporarily to other schedules, but when he is shifted back to the original schedule he eventually attains nearly the same steady-state ("asymptotic") performance as he had before. It is because of this "recoverability" of the steady-state performance induced by a given schedule that the favored experimental procedure for Skinnerians is to run each of a few animals through all experimental conditions repeatedly in blocked sequence (see Sidman, 1960). In this way, for example, one might map out a complete function for each individual subject relating the independent variable (say, size of the fixed ratio requirement) to a dependent variable (say, the average pause after reinforcement in steady state). The procedure has a great deal to recommend it when one is dealing with steady states rather than acquisition ("transient") phenomena. Sidman (1960) provides the most persuasive arguments for use of this research strategy throughout *all* behavioral studies, not simply studies of schedules.

A further behavioral technique of widespread usefulness is what Ferster and Skinner (1957) call *multiple schedules.* The organism can be trained concurrently to respond appropriately to several different schedules, each occurring many times during an experimental session in random alternation with the other schedule components and each associated with a distinctive discriminative stimulus, such as differently colored lights back-projected onto the pigeon's pecking key. Skinner has trained a pigeon to as many as *nine* different performances (key-pecking patterns) controlled successively during the same session by nine different stimuli. For example, in a three-component multiple schedule, a pigeon might have an FI 1' when the key was green, an FI 2' when the key was white, and an FI 4' when the key was red, these three components occurring in random order each for 8 minutes. Because the animals tend to behave discriminatively and appropriately to each schedule component, one can in this way plot out a functional

relation for each individual, say relating responses per reinforcement to length of the FI. The procedure has much to recommend it. The problem with the method, clearly recognized by all, is that results must be interpreted cautiously when there are clear *interactions* between the several schedules that are successively controlling the response. An interaction means that performance on schedule A depends on schedule B with which it alternates within an experimental session. Although such interactions are themselves a topic of interest (in behavioral contrast phenomena), they do call into question the interpretation of the functional relations observed by use of multiple schedules.

Conditioned Reinforcement

The principle of conditioned reinforcement is simply this:

> A stimulus that is not originally a reinforcing one . . . can become reinforcing through repeated association with one that is (Keller & Schoenfeld, 1950, p. 232).

That is, through conditioning, a stimulus acquires the power to act as a reinforcer. This is often referred to by the phrases *secondary reinforcement* or *acquired reward.* Consider, for example, the acquisition of reinforcing power by the light in the following experiment. When a rat presses a bar, a light comes on. After 1 second, a pellet of food falls into the tray, reinforcing the bar-pressing. The light remains on for 2 seconds after the food appears. Several groups of animals are conditioned in this way, for 10, 20, 40, 80, and 120 reinforcements, respectively. After conditioning, the rate of responding is extinguished to a low level by having the bar press not turn on the light or deliver food. Then the contingencies are changed so that pressing the bar now turns on the light for 1 second, but does not deliver food.

Under these circumstances responses again appear, showing that the light has acquired reinforcing properties. The number of responses emitted in a 45-minute period increased with the number of prior pairings of light and food (Bersh, 1951).

Other experiments suggest that the light will acquire secondary reinforcing properties only if it appears *before* the reinforcing stimulus, and is thus either part of a chain or a discriminative stimulus for the consummatory response (Schoenfeld et al., 1950; Webb & Nolan, 1953).

The following summary of conditioned reinforcement shows its systematic importance in operant behavior:

> 1. A stimulus that occasions or accompanies a reinforcement acquires thereby reinforcing value of its own, and may be called a conditioned, secondary, or derived reinforcement. A secondary reinforcement may be extinguished when repeatedly applied to a response for which there is no ultimate primary reinforcement.
> 2. A secondary reinforcement is positive when the reinforcement with which it is correlated is positive, and negative when the latter is negative.
> 3. Once established, a secondary reinforcement is independent and nonspecific; it not only will strengthen the same response which produced the original reinforcement, but will also condition a new and unrelated response. Moreover, it will do so even in the presence of a different motive.
> 4. Through generalization, many stimuli besides the one correlated with reinforcement acquire reinforcing value—positive or negative (Keller & Schoenfeld, 1950, p. 260).

An important consequence of the development of secondary reinforcement is the emergence of a class of *generalized reinforcers* (Skinner, 1953, pp. 77–81). This generalization comes about because some secondary reinforcers tend to accompany a variety of primary reinforcers. Money is a convenient illustration, because money provides access to food, drink, shelter, entertainment, and thus becomes a generalized reinforcer for a variety of activities. The so-called social needs (need for attention, need for affection, need for approval) lead

to the kinds of persistent behavior best understood as a consequence of intermittent reinforcement, and the kinds of reinforcement sought are the generalized ones implied in the words *attention, affection,* and *approval*. Language behavior, such as calling objects by their correct names, tends to be reinforced by the generalized reinforcement from the listeners, who show in indirect ways whether or not they understand and approve. According to Skinner, eventually generalized reinforcers are effective even though the primary reinforcers on which they are based no longer accompany them (1953, p. 81).

OTHER INFLUENCES AFFECTING OPERANT STRENGTH

In the effort to remain descriptive and positivistic, Skinner has attempted to avoid the postulating of intermediaries not observed in his experiments, and to deal instead with a procedure that he calls *functional analysis*. A functional analysis is concerned with the lawfulness of observable relationships and the manner in which these relationships are modified under specified conditions. We have just reviewed one very important class of events in the functional analysis of behavior: reinforcements and how their scheduling affects operant strength. Drive, emotion, and punishment are also determinants of response rate in conditioning studies; how Skinner handled these classes of events will become clearer in the following sections.

Drive

Hours of food deprivation are important in determining the rate of responding of an animal reinforced by food. The independent variable actually plotted is exactly that—hours of deprivation. Is it necessary to say anything further? Is it necessary to talk about physiological needs, or hunger?

Let us first cite some typical experimental results and then return to these questions.

Eight rats learned to press a lever for food on a fixed interval schedule. They practiced daily but received the main portion of their food rations on alternate days. The correlation between responding and hours of deprivation showed up in high vs. low rates on successive days. Two subgroups were created and matched according to their response rates during conditioning. They were now extinguished on alternate days, one group when their hunger was high, the other when hunger was low. The high-hunger group yielded nearly double the responses of the low group on successive daily periods, although the two extinction curves show similar curvature (Skinner, 1950, pp. 201–2).

Does deprivation affect the strengthening effect of each reinforcement, or does it merely affect the rate of responding during extinction? In a test of these relationships, rats were trained with reinforcement after various durations of food deprivation, from $\frac{1}{2}$ hour to 47 hours. Various subgroups of animals received training amounting to 1, 10, and 30 reinforcements, respectively. Then the strength of conditioning was tested by resistance to extinction, at a common level of deprivation (23 hours). Resistance to extinction correlated with the number of prior reinforcements, but *not* with the level of deprivation during training (Strassburger, 1950).

These studies suffice to illustrate the kinds of relationships between drive and operant conditioning that are open to investigation. In a narrative account of the results we tend to move back and forth between describing the rats as "deprived of food" or as "hungry." The two expressions are operationally equivalent, though when we assign the results to "hunger" instead of to "hours without food," we tend to imply a theory. This leads us back to the problem of the status of "drive" as a concept.

Skinner is quite clear that he means by "drive" merely a set of operations (such as the withholding of food for a certain number of hours or reducing an organism's weight to a certain percentage of its "normal" weight) which have an effect upon rate of responding. He is interested in the lawfulness of these effects under various circumstances. He objects to most of the current psychological uses of "drive" by arguing for the following assertions (1953, pp. 144–46):

A drive is not a stimulus.
A drive is not a physiological state.
A drive is not a psychic state.
A drive is not simply a state of strength.

By these negatives he makes it clear that he does not accept the stimuli from stomach contractions as the prototype of drives, nor does he accept physiological needs, or pleasures or pains, or desires or wishes. For the purposes of the systematic study of behavior, the word *drive* is used only to acknowledge certain classes of operation which affect behavior in ways other than the ways by which reinforcement affects it. Skinner does not believe inference to an intermediary (intervening variable or hypothetical construct) to be necessary in order to carry out the functional analysis. The main arguments against Skinner's rejection of "drive" have been marshaled by N. E. Miller (1969), and the logic of such "intervening variables" was discussed in Chapter 5. Miller points out the parsimony of postulating an intervening variable like thirst or hunger when one must summarize a large number of input-output relations, relating a number of thirst-inducing independent operations (t) to a number of thirst-related behaviors (b). There are in principle $t \times b$ input-output functions to be determined. Postulating an intervening variable of thirst can reduce this number requiring determination to $t + b$ functional relations, showing how thirst (the intervening variable) is functionally related to the t independent variables and the *b* dependent variables. Miller set forth ways of testing this formulation, and laments that we have far too few successful tests of the "unitariness" of the plethora of intervening variables which psychologists postulate.

Emotion

Just as drives are inappropriately classified as stimuli, so according to Skinner, emotions are often unwisely classified as responses. Weeping at a bruised shin or over the loss of a game is ordinarily said to be an emotional response, but weeping because of a cinder in the eye is not. This way of treating emotion is rejected in favor of referring to it as a *relationship* between a situation and a response, in many ways like drive.

An example of this view of emotion is in the study of *conditioned suppression* or the *conditioned emotional response* (abbreviated CER), a phenomenon first demonstrated by Estes and Skinner (1941). It is known that painful electric shock causes a cessation or suppression of appetitive behaviors like eating or drinking or of instrumental responses reinforced by such consequences. What Estes and Skinner found was that a formerly neutral stimulus that is paired repeatedly with shock can then exert this same suppressive effect upon any ongoing appetitive behavior. A typical experiment uses a hungry rat trained to lever-press for food reinforcement on a variable interval schedule which generates a very steady rate of response. Then a series of Pavlovian conditioning trials are given, during which a tone comes on for 5 minutes and terminates with electric shock. Later, after the animal has returned to lever-pressing steadily on the VI schedule, the tone is sounded, say, for 5-minute periods. During the tone, the animal will often "freeze," reduce his pressing rate, crouch, and show signs of a conditioned

emotional response; objectively, the tone has suppressed lever-pressing. Once the tone-shock event terminates, the rat will soon resume lever-pressing. These tone-on and tone-off periods can be repeatedly alternated throughout the experimental session. Eventually the animal presses the lever at a high rate when the tone is off, and relatively little when the tone is on. The degree of suppression is typically reported in terms of a "suppression ratio," such as the drop in the response rate caused by the tone divided by the tone-off baseline rate. This index varies from 0 to 1 as the tone-controlled suppression of response rate varies from nil to total suppression.

Most psychologists interpret the outcome as due to *motivational* competition between conditioned anxiety and appetitive motives (Estes, 1969b; Stein, 1964). Moreover, the conditioning of anxiety by the tone-shock pairings is conceived of as a Pavlovian or classical conditioning paradigm. Therefore, the suppression ratio provides a convenient technique for studying classical conditioning, and it has been much exploited for that purpose (Kamin, 1965, 1969a; Rescorla, 1969b). Indeed, for many purposes, the suppression ratio can be treated as though it were "drops of saliva" in salivary conditioning.

Conditioned suppression is just one example of "emotion," and needless to say, there are many others. An emotional reaction that has been much studied (e.g., Ulrich & Azrin, 1962) is *reflexive aggression,* or fighting in animals elicited by pain caused by an electric shock or a physical blow (Azrin et al., 1965) or even by the frustration resulting from nonreinforcement of a response previously receiving positive reinforcement (Azrin et al., 1966). This seems to be a widespread response, found throughout many species; the aggression is not aimed discriminatively, but rather hits any available target, including "innocent bystanders."

Punishment

In punishment procedures, an aversive event is made contingent upon a response which typically has some prior source of strength. Skinner noted that the arrangement of contingencies in punishment is just the opposite of reinforcement (although the *effects* are not opposite). He distinguished two types of punishment: (1) the presentation of an aversive or unpleasant stimulus like a shock, and (2) the removal of a positive reinforcer. The second form of punishment is familiar in the form of penalties, detention, or banishment where the subject loses something valuable or some enjoyable privilege is taken away.

Skinner's views on punishment have undergone revision over the years. Some early studies by him (Skinner, 1938, p. 154) using a mild punisher (the lever slapped upward against the rat's paw when it was pressed) came to the conclusion that punishment was a relatively ineffective means to produce any permanent change in behavior. It was claimed that punishment did have a suppressive effect on behavior while it remained in force, but that when punishment was removed the former response "recovered" and was emitted nearly as much during extinction as was a nonpunished response. This interpretation that punishment is relatively ineffective in altering behavior has been widely quoted and used for various liberalizing arguments in practical applications of behavior modification. The prescription was to use only positive reinforcement since punishers were ineffectual and had only bad side-effects.

But the interpretation, in retrospect, is rather odd. By this strange logic, one might also claim that positive reinforcement is ineffective, is "only temporary with no lasting effects," because the response extinguishes when reinforcement is withdrawn. Later studies and analyses of punishment by Azrin and Holz (1966) show how very effective punishment can be in suppressing appetitive behavior, how it varies in a lawful way with the parameters of punishment, and also how behavior recovers after punishment is removed and reinforcement is continued. Azrin and Holz summarize their extensive investigations in the following set of statements:

> Let us summarize briefly some of the circumstances which have been found to maximize its effectiveness: (1) The punishing stimulus should be arranged in such a manner that no unauthorized escape is possible. (2) The punishing stimulus should be as intense as possible. (3) The frequency of punishment should be as high as possible. (4) The punishing stimulus should be delivered immediately after the response. (5) The punishing stimulus should not be increased gradually but introduced at maximum intensity. (6) Extended periods of punishment should be avoided, especially where low intensities of punishment are concerned, since the recovery effect may thereby occur. Where mild intensities of punishment are used, it is best to use them for only a brief period of time. (7) Great care should be taken to see that the delivery of the punishing stimulus is not differentially associated with the delivery of reinforcement. Otherwise the punishing stimulus may acquire conditioned reinforcing properties. (8) The delivery of the punishing stimulus should be made a signal or discriminative stimulus that a period of extinction is in progress. (9) The degree of motivation to emit the punished response should be reduced. (10) The frequency of positive reinforcement for the punished response should similarly be reduced. (11) An alternative response should be available which will produce the same or greater reinforcement as the punished response. For example, punishment of criminal behavior can be expected to be more effective if noncriminal behavior which will result in the same advantages as the behavior is available. (12) If no alternative response is available, the subject should have access to a different situation in which he obtains the same reinforcement without being punished. (13) If it is not possible to deliver the punishing stimulus itself after a response, then an effective method of punishment is still available. A conditioned stimulus may be associated with the aversive stimulus, and this conditioned stimulus may be delivered following a response to achieve conditioned punishment. (14) A reduction of positive reinforcement may be used as punishment when the use of physical punishment is

not possible for practical, legal, or moral reasons. Punishment by withdrawal of positive reinforcement may be accomplished in such situations by arranging a period of reduced reinforcement frequency (time-out) or by arranging a decrease of conditioned reinforcement (response cost). Both methods require that the subject have a high level of reinforcement to begin with; otherwise, no withdrawal of reinforcement is possible. If non-physical punishment is to be used, it appears desirable to provide the subject with a substantial history of reinforcement in order to provide the opportunity for withdrawing the reinforcement as punishment for the undesired responses (1966, pp. 426–27).

As a consequence of many such studies, the effects of punishment came to be interpreted by Skinnerians (see Azrin & Holz, 1966; Dinsmoor, 1954, 1955) in terms similar to those of Mowrer and Miller described in Chapter 5. The punishing aversive stimulus is assumed to convert the proprioceptive feedback from the punished response into a "conditioned aversive stimulus," so that when the response begins to occur later, the feedback from the incipient movements are aversive, and therefore the response is interrupted. There has been some disenchantment with this viewpoint (see Herrnstein, 1969; Schoenfeld, 1970), but this is not the place to detail those developments.

LABORATORY TECHNOLOGY

The source of substantive principles in one area of scientific knowledge may become a method or technology for another. Thus the transistor is of interest to the physicist for what it tells about solid-state physics, but it is a technological boon to the person constructing hearing aids or pocket-sized radios. Operant conditioning, similarly, has been very useful as a reliable methodology of controlling behavior. Associated with operant conditioning methods are a different set of experimental designs emphasizing behavioral analysis of individual subjects.

Single-Subject Research Designs

Traditional research design emphasizes comparison of a group of subjects receiving experimental treatment to an untreated control group. The variability of a treatment effect across subjects is what motivates the usual concern with sample statistics and significance tests of a null hypothesis; the aim is to prove that on the average the treated subjects performed differently from the control subjects. Skinner and his followers have down-played group statistics and concentrated instead on controlling the behavior of single organisms as they are cycled through the several experimental treatments of interest. The operant conditioners have developed three different research designs that can be used for studying the effectiveness of treatments within a single subject—the reversal design, multiple baselines, and multiple schedules.

Reversal design. The idea here is to evaluate a learning or reinforcement condition by applying it for awhile to see how contingent behavior changes above the baseline rate, and then remove the reinforcement condition to see if the behavior reverts ("reverses") to the baseline. The method is schematized in the top half of Figure 7.5 for, say, a problem child in primary school who rarely does math problems in her workbook when directed. During initial baseline recording, the child completes about two short addition problems per 30-minute math period. Then a point system is instituted, where she receives 1 point for each math problem completed correctly, and the opportunity to convert her points into equivalent tangible rewards (say, of candy) at the end of each math lesson. This reward program increases the rate of working problems for several days. Then in the reversal phase, the point system and back-up reinforcers are removed and no other reinforcers are substituted for each math problem. This results in a rapid fall-off in the number of

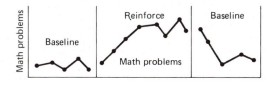

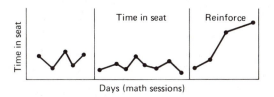

Days (math sessions)

Figure 7.5. Top panel alone depicts the three phases of a reversal design, wherein a reinforcement system increases a child's rate of math problem-solving. The bottom panel, in conjunction with the top, illustrates multiple baselines, with the two different responses reinforced at different points in the experiment.

problems being worked per day, returning to near the original baseline. In this case, for practical reasons, the teacher would reinstate the reinforcement system for math work to return it to a high rate. The logic of the design is that by the reversal we can be somewhat assured that our treatment was in fact responsible (causal) for the behavior change, rather than the change being caused by extraneous factors like the passage of time. The paradigm is: treatment in, behavior comes in; treatment out, behavior goes out. The reversal design is not always appropriate (e.g., a clinician would not revert a neurotic symptom removed by some behavioral treatment), but it is a simple, powerful tool when appropriate and when the behavior of individuals is reliable enough.

Multiple baselines. Another way to rule out extraneous influences in evaluating the effectiveness of some reinforcement treatment is to record several different behaviors (*baselines*) from a single subject, and to introduce the reinforcement contingen-

cies singly and separately at different times for each baseline behavior. The general procedure is schematized by comparing the two panels of Figure 7.5. Suppose this problem child also spends a lot of her time during the math lesson out of her seat, walking around the classroom, sitting with other children at their desks, and so on. Suppose the teacher wants the child to work at her own desk and not disrupt the other students. He decides to measure the time the child is sitting at her desk during the 30-minute math lesson. This is in a low range through the first two phases of the experiment, and remains unaffected when reinforcement is instituted for completing math problems. The fact that in the second phase the reinforced behavior (at top) increases whereas the other behavior (lower panel) does not indicates that the reinforcement is effective, and that its influence is specific to the behavior that produces it. This also means that the two response measures are approximately independent, in that one behavior changes its rate, whereas the other remains unaffected. The third phase in Figure 7.5 (lower panel) shows what happens when social reinforcement (attention and praise from the teacher) is made contingent on the child sitting in her seat and working. The increase in sitting-in-seat indicates that the social reinforcer is effective for that behavior. Multiple-baseline designs such as this can be used with as many behaviors as the experimenter wishes to record and track. If the behavior to be changed is undesirable, then use of a multiple-baseline design is advantageous, since it permits strong causal inferences (about treatment effects) even without reversal of the behavior change.

Multiple schedules. As noted earlier, a multiple schedule refers to circumstances where several different stimuli occur within an experimental session, each associated with a different reinforcement condition. For instance, different reinforcement schedules might be in force as the key in a pigeon box is lighted with red, yellow, or green lights in random order, each component on for, say, 5 minutes. Because the animal responds to each component according to its schedule, the arrangement permits the experimenter to plot out a complete parametric function for each subject singly. Thus, during one (asymptotic) session, the experimenter might be able to plot a steady-state rate of responding to a stimulus as a function of, say, the reinforcement rate in that stimulus, or its rate relative to the overall average reinforcement rate. Thus, in a single subject at one session, a complete behavioral function can be obtained.

Field Observation Procedures

Because of their frequent interest in applying learning principles to practical goals in field settings, Skinnerian psychologists have developed a range of techniques for reliably observing and recording problematic behaviors to be modified. Psychologists are often called in to deal with children or adults with adjustment problems in work situations, family interactions, classrooms, day-care settings, or mental hospital wards. Psychologists have to devise some way to measure unobtrusively the rate of occurrence of some relevant behavior in that setting, and then devise a program to alter that behavior towards more desirable goals without totally disrupting that environment. We will mention such behavior assessment procedures later in Chapter 9 when we review applications of behavior modification ideas. But this is assuredly one of the more concrete and valuable contributions of Skinner and his followers to applied psychology.

Uses of Stable Baseline Responding

The repeatability and stability of performance data are among the most attractive features of the Skinnerian approach to

experimental analysis. The behavioral analyst typically arranges controlled circumstances where many thousands of responses can be observed and where average response rates become very stable and reproducible. Also, the subject may be shifted repeatedly among many reinforcement conditions and typically recovers the same performance levels upon return to the same reinforcement condition. The regularity and stability of the steady-state behavior of single organisms attests to the refinements of experimental controls, constancy of motivation, and the controlling power of the reinforcement contingencies. It should be understood, of course, that such enviably regular data is gathered in steady state, usually after an animal has had many hours (or thousands of trials) of training to adjust to each reinforcement condition. In contrast, many other psychologists are interested in *learning*, in the process that generates a change or transition from an initial to a terminal response rate, and this transition often occurs quickly. Moreover, it may never be exactly repeatable since the animal's habits will transfer to help him should he be required to relearn the same task. For many practical concerns, however, interest may center on how some treatment affects asymptotic performance (or motivation), not transitory learning, hence free operant methods are in wide use.

One use that interests experimental psychologists is in animal psychophysics. It is possible, by using operant methods, to produce visual sensitivity curves for pigeons that show the course of adaptation to darkness with all the precision of experimentation with trained human subjects (Blough, 1961). A whole range of perceptual phenomena can be investigated with animals, including visual illusions, adaptation level effects, size constancy, and so on (Blough, 1966).

Another widespread use has been in the testing of drugs. Because the response rates that are recorded in the standard operant-conditioning situation are very sensitive to the influence of drugs, these methods become useful for calibration experiments in pharmacology. Thus, for example, most of the new drugs and medications that we receive today have already been screened through extensive animal testing (typically in operant-conditioning tasks), to check for undesirable side effects on behavior. The technologies of behavioral control are also widely used by physiological psychologists, whereby they assess reinforcing or motivating effects of electrical or chemical stimulation of the brain, behavioral alterations (e.g., overeating) caused by neurological damage (e.g., hypothalamic lesions), and so on.

The wide applicability of the technologies associated with stimulus control and reinforcement contingencies is recognized by many who are testing theories departing widely from those of Skinner. Thus much of the contemporary work in animal learning and motivation makes use of the Skinnerian technology. A volume edited by Honig (1966) shows the many uses that have been made of the method in the study of a variety of psychological and physiological topics. It is a fair statement that the Skinner box has displaced the maze as the favorite apparatus among American students of animal behavior.

Programmed Instruction

Skinner in 1954 announced and embarked upon a series of investigations and inventions designed to increase the efficiency of teaching arithmetic, reading, spelling, and other school subjects, by using a mechanical device expected to do some things much better than the usual teacher can do them, while saving the teacher for tasks that the teacher can do better. An early form of the device presented number combinations for the teaching of addition. The child punches her answer in a kind of adding-machine keyboard; if the answer is correct, reinforcement of a correct answer is signalled by having the machine move on to the next problem. This is functionally the same as following the student's response with the teacher's announcement of *Right*. Skinner early pointed out that no teacher can be as discriminating and fast-responding a reinforcer as the machine, for the teacher cannot be with every child in a class at once, commending proper responses and correcting erroneous ones. Furthermore, the teacher may not be as skilled in determining the proper order and rate of presentation of problems as has been determined by empirical studies of the content material.

Skinner's devices, and others modeled after them, soon came to be called *teaching machines* or *autoinstructional devices*, and the materials that became the basis for instruction came to be called *programs*. Some of them began to appear as programmed books (e.g., Holland & Skinner, 1961).

An important summary paper by Skinner in 1958 catalyzed the interest that had been mounting, and *programmed instruction* became a major educational and commercial enterprise that flourishes today. (Programmed learning will be discussed in greater detail in Chapter 15.) The important educational issues for Skinner were the following: (1) first, get a clear, detailed, objective specification of what it means to "know" the given subject matter; for Skinner, this typically consists of a detailed list of stimulus-response connections typically formulated in terms of questions and answers or topics and comments; (2) next, write a series of stimulus (question) → response (answer) *frames* that expose the student to the material in graded steps of increasing difficulty and that frequently retest the same fact from many different angles; (3) require that the learner be active—for example, require that a response be composed for each frame in the program; (4) provide immediate feedback for each response (answer); (5) try to arrange the questions such that the correct response is very likely to occur and be reinforced; thus, errors are avoided and learning is not usually accompanied by frustrating or punishing failures; (6) let each student proceed through the teaching program at her own pace; and (7) provide plenty of backup reinforcers (praise, merits, tokens) for diligent and effective work on the program.

While Skinner believed that the rationale for his proposals was derivable from the principles of operant conditioning, his theoretical interpretations have been the subject of some controversy. Whatever the verdict may be with regard to the essence of programmed instruction, there is no doubt that the upsurge of interest since the 1950s was due to Skinner, and there is no doubt either that he arrived at his methods through an attempt to generalize to education what he had learned through the study of operant conditioning in the laboratory.

Training the Retarded

Psychologists trained in Skinnerian techniques have also been at the forefront of work in educating mentally retarded (mild or severe) and handicapped persons. To assign a retarded person's problems to a "neurological disorder" is of no help in remedying the situation. The Skinnerian orientation focuses on specific behavioral deficits, asks what specific response chains are to be trained (e.g., to dress oneself), what smaller units these can be broken into, and how these small pieces of behavior can be trained separately. Thus, a retarded child may be taught the rudiments of counting by getting her to (a) attend to the teacher and to work on the task, (b) point to simple objects displayed on a screen, (c) pair off two sets of objects to check whether they have the same number, (d) name the numbers as she wiggles her fingers (number labels are on each

finger left to right), (e) pair fingers with objects in a set to be counted, also counting aloud, (f) pair off successive numerals (provided on blocks) with objects to be counted, and (g) count aloud, later silently, as she pairs numerals with objects. The reader may be surprised at how many steps there may be in the training plan, but many steps are often needed to break down the skill to be learned, and to make use of aids as half-way crutches. By such skill programming, disadvantaged people are now trained to perform simple and even complex tasks that formerly they appeared unable to achieve (see reviews by Birnbrauer, 1976; and by Lovaas & Newsom, 1976). Of particular concern in training retarded or psychotic children is their poor language ability, which frequently is nil. Many educational programs therefore explicitly set out to teach a disadvantaged child at least the rudiments of receptive (listening) and productive (talking) language.

Verbal Behavior

Language most clearly distinguishes human behavior from that of other mammals. Knowledge of how we acquire language, and how we use it, is essential to an understanding of human learning. Skinner has long been interested in verbal behavior. As early as 1936 he produced a phonograph record composed of chance groupings of speech sounds, which because they were chance were inherently meaningless. The record, called a "verbal summator," was used to study the words "read into" sounds by the listener. It was a kind of projective technique, similar in the auditory field to the inkblots used in the visual field (Skinner, 1936). Within the next few years Skinner reported studies of word association, alliteration, and other kinds of sound patterning.[2] His William James Lectures,

[2] Skinner (1937b); Cook and Skinner (1939).

delivered at Harvard University in 1948, appeared in revised form as a volume entitled *Verbal behavior* (1957), in which he approached verbal behavior as an empirical problem.

The main point of the analysis is that speech sounds are emitted (and reinforced) as are any other bits of behavior. Some speech utterances make requests or demands upon the hearer and get reinforced as the hearer complies. A child's utterance of "Milk, please" is reinforced when the parent complies and provides the requested commodity. This function (called the *mand function*) appears early in the language behavior of the child. A second function is concerned largely with naming discriminative stimuli (the *tact function*). A naming repertoire comes about in the "original word game" which the child constantly plays with her parents and others in her verbal community: "What's that?" "It's a car." "Is this a car?" "No, that's a wagon." And so on and on. Because objects and events are multifaceted, acquisition of a tact typically requires discrimination, wherein the same tact is reinforced to the relevant feature despite variation in irrelevant features. Thus the tact *red* comes to be controlled by the color of red apples, red cars, red dresses, and so on. This is really an elliptical way of talking: the utterance "red" actually is controlled by a complex of stimuli including the object (or our "memory" of it) and a request to name its *color* rather than its shape or palatability, and so on. Abstracting or generalizing means that a tact has come under the control of a single property of a whole class of complex objects. Thus, the concept of *sharp object* may be learned by experience with razor blades, knives, and so on. Moreover, acquisition of a new rule such as "Sharp objects can cut you; you should avoid them" will mediate immediate changes in responses to a range of stimuli which elicit the same label. Moreover, those avoidance responses will occur to new stimulus patterns (e.g., broken glass, sabres) which are labeled "sharp" by the community.

A third term introduced by Skinner is *autoclitic behavior,* which was his label for verbal behavior that is a comment upon or a description of other verbal behavior by ourselves (1957, p. 315). The speaker is commonly talking in part about her own role when she emits autoclitic behavior: "I was about to say . . . ," "I don't believe that . . . ," "John did *not* do . . . ," or "I hesitate to say that . . ." are example frames in which autoclitics occur. Thus, autoclitics can comment upon other verbal responses they accompany, or can specify the strength of that behavior, or can identify the effect on the speaker of the fact stated (as in "I was delighted that . . ." or "Happily, he . . ."), or negate the truth of another assertion.

Ordering of words is another large class of autoclitic phenomena. Traditionally called grammatical rules, these make use of what Skinner termed partially conditioned autoclitic frames (1957, p. 336). Following learning of such possession frames as "The lady's dog," "The lady's car," and "The man's car," the first appearance of the dog with the man can be tacted as "The man's dog" by tacting the objects and their relation using the possessive frame. It is proposed that similar word-position frames apply to the ordering of tacting adjective-noun relations and actor-action relations. These are, of course, the basis for predication, which is a primary function of language. Braine (1963) and Staats (1968) have developed this view that the information about syntactic structure primarily concerns the grammatical properties of *locations* within sentence frames (e.g., the first position in an English declarative sentence is often a determiner, the second a noun, and so on). Thus, the syntactical relation between words provided by a novel ordering ("The lady's cat" versus "The cat's lady") controls the right interpretation because of contextual generalization of the function of words filling certain slots in the frame. This permits some degree of generative productivity in the sense that it allows the child to understand novel combinations and orderings of words. Braine (1963) reported several positive experiments with children, as did Staats (1968). Premack (1969) and Gardner and Gardner (1971) have utilized these principles in building a sizable linguistic repertoire of manual signs in chimpanzees functioning as communicative signs to their trainers.

However, Skinner's book *Verbal behavior* has not been very influential in most analyses of human language. This may have come about because it was not well received by professional linguists, and was given a renowned and relentlessly negative review by Chomsky (1959). Largely due to Chomsky's linguistic analyses, modern studies of grammar and language have developed quite extensively beyond the relatively imprecise suggestions of Skinner. Also, the notion of contextual generalization was criticized as being unable in principle to account for most forms of linguistic productivity (Bever, Fodor, & Weksel, 1965a; 1965b). These arguments were accepted by most psychologists studying language, and so other performance models of syntax learning are being pursued presently. There have been several attempts to resurrect Skinner's analysis of verbal behavior as a performance theory that would repay serious experimentation (MacCorquodale, 1969; Segal, 1977; Winokur, 1976). Skinner's account of syntax and its acquisition is undoubtedly the weakest part of his analysis, whereas grammatical analysis is the strong suit of modern linguistics.

Some Functions of Verbal Responses

According to the behavioristic position, verbal behavior consists of responses under stimulus control and with stimulus consequences. But these behaviors can perform a variety of services for the organism. Many S-R psychologists (Dollard & Miller, 1950; Skinner, 1953; Staats & Staats, 1963) have been concerned with stipulating a few of these functions.

Let us note just a few of the roles of verbal responses in an S-R analysis. Verbal labels and utterances can be used as discriminative stimuli for our own and for others' behavior (as when we shout, "Run, fire," or "Stop it"); they can be used as reinforcing stimuli for our own or for others' behaviors ("Right" or "Wrong"); and used to provide anticipatory incentive or motivating stimuli (as when we say "I'll be paid tomorrow for this work" or "I'm being paid now for the work I did yesterday"). Also, sequences of cue-producing responses which parallel some external event sequence can be verbally rehearsed to strengthen the chain, thus "remembering" an external event sequence or a verbal proposition. Also, chains of cue-producing responses (words or sentences) are selected and utilized in relevant ways to solve problems.

A typical S-R analysis of problem-solving is that given by Staats and Staats (1963, p. 204) in interpreting an experiment by Judson, Cofer, and Gelfand (1956). Their subjects had been given Maier's two-rope problem to solve; the situation is a bare room with two widely separated ropes hanging down several feet from the ceiling. The subject's job is to tie the two ropes together. The ropes are too far apart for the subject to hold one and reach the stationary other one. However, the other rope could be reached by stretching if it were swung in motion as a pendulum. The solution therefore requires tying any available object on the end of one rope and setting it in pendulum motion in the direction of the other rope; this enables the person to grab both ropes at once and tie them together.

In their experiment, Judson, Cofer, and Gelfand showed that solution of this two-string problem could be facilitated if sub-

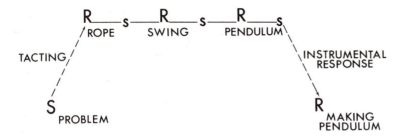

Figure 7.6. Schematic representation of a problem-solving sequence. The problem situation is tacted, then a verbal chain occurs, leading to an implicit stimulus that controls occurrence of the correct response, which solves the problem. (From Staats and Staats, 1963.)

jects were first taught a verbal serial list in which the words *rope-swing-pendulum* appeared in that order. In their reconstruction of this experiment, Staats and Staats use the diagram in Figure 7.6, and they identify three aspects of the overall behavior. First is the discriminative "tacting" (labeling) of the problematic situation in terms of a relevant stimulus (attending to and saying "rope"). Second is the running off of the verbal response sequence which was learned earlier, *rope-swing-pendulum;* this was made available to experimental subjects by the prior verbal learning task, whereas it is less available to the control subjects. Third are the instrumental behaviors of making a pendulum that are cued off by the implicit cue of saying *pendulum.*

The solution to the problem may fail if any one of these three components is lacking: the person may attend to irrelevant features of the problem situation; or he may notice the rope but not think of it as usable for a pendulum; or he may run off the verbal chain, but not know what *pendulum* refers to or how to make one. These components are identified in rather gross fashion here; they surely require a much finer functional analysis (e.g., *why* does the person, after saying *pendulum,* stop and construct one rather than continuing on with his verbal associative chains?); but Staats and Staats believe that this finer

analysis can be pushed through, and they illustrate the matter with many hypothetical cases (see also Staats, 1968). However, from the viewpoint of others working on complex problem-solving (e.g., Newell & Simon, 1972), this type of analysis is far too simplified, ignoring the vast amount of fruitless searching among irrelevant possibilities and ignoring the means for directing the search process along paths ("associative chains") likely to lead to success. This issue is discussed in more detail in Chapter 12.

Self-Attribution and Self-Awareness

Probably more than any other behaviorist, Skinner has been concerned with how individuals come to know themselves, how they become aware of their feelings and of other private happenings going on inside their own skins. For Skinner, "being aware of certain feelings" is a special kind of readiness to verbalize or act upon a complex of stimuli (internal and external) which are discriminative for that feeling. Thus, when I say, "My tooth aches," I am labeling a particular internal stimulus; when I say, "I am courageous," I am repeating an earlier judgment (e.g., about specific acts) made about me by myself or by others.

In discussing the "original word game," we mentioned how the child learns tacts (verbal labels) for objects and events through discriminative reinforcement provided by a verbal community. The same community can train a child to describe her own behavior; for instance, a child might be trained to report "I've wet my pants" or "I hit the cat" or "I'm eating a lot." The problem arises when the community tries to teach the child to label private events, internal stimuli, or feelings. Private events exclusively affect the experiencer; how, then, is the community to know when to point and name the event?

In teaching a child to describe pain, for instance, an observer must teach her the label at a time when it is likely that the critical stimuli are impinging on her. The verbal community identifies these critical times on the basis of observable stimuli affecting the child (e.g., she bumps her head) or from her behavior (e.g., crying and holding her head). A description like "That's painful" or "That hurts" may thus be established in the child's repertoire by the observer's saying, "Ouch, that's painful; I know it must hurt," when he sees the child bump her head and cry; later, the child will imitate and use that description for similar bumps and bruises. Once established, this verbal response will generalize to a large class of painful events which produce similar internal stimuli. Skinner identifies two other, minor ways to learn descriptions for private events. One is when I have learned to describe my overt behavior (e.g., my own talking), but that behavior then becomes covert; following a covert verbal sequence I can then say, "I've just been thinking that . . ." or something similar. Another way to learn descriptions for private events is through metaphorical extensions or analogies, as when we quickly understand and apply expressions like "butterflies in the stomach" for fright, "churning insides" for anger, and "pinpricks" or "ginger ale bubbles" for a foot that has fallen asleep. But these are minor

methods that cover few cases; the main means of learning self-descriptive terms is by the parent's inferring what is happening inside the child and then labeling it.

These resources of the community for teaching the child a self-descriptive repertoire are relatively meager compared to those used in training the finely tuned, discriminative labeling of publicly available stimuli. But then the result is frequently inadequate. The individual as well as the community typically have faulty or inadequate knowledge of her internal states. For example, a person may never learn to label her neck muscles as "tense" or her palms as "sweaty"; similarly, the community never knows when to trust a reported "headache" or "upset stomach" when that is used as an excuse with obvious instrumental value (as in malingering). Internal identifications we have not been taught remain as ones we are unable to make and are "unaware of." One potential of research on biofeedback of physiological measures like the electroencephalogram (EEG, or "brain waves") and electromyograph (EMG, or "muscle tension") is that these make public some gross measures of what otherwise are exclusively private events or states; responses involving these systems can now be labeled and consciously controlled through differential reinforcement keyed to the amplified feedback (Kamiya, 1969; reviewed in Chapter 9).

Significantly, in original training, a child learns to label her own feelings or emotional reactions partially on the basis of the same observable evidence that the community itself uses—namely, the impinging external stimuli (the situational context) and her own reactions to them, or the duration or intensity of her behavior. In fact, when the internal events, feelings, or attitudes are vague, amorphous, and unclear, a person's self-descriptions may rely more than usual upon these external circumstances or her responses. This has been illustrated in a classic experiment by Schachter and Singer (1962); these investigators were able to evoke such widely disparate emotional feelings as euphoria and bitter anger from subjects in the same physiological state of drug-induced arousal depending on whether they were placed with a stooge ("fake subject") who displayed euphoria or one who displayed rage reactions. Because the subjects experienced unexplained symptoms of arousal, they looked to their environment for clues to interpret their arousal, and that interpretation was happiness or anger accordingly as the other subject appeared to be happy or angry.

This line of analysis forms the basis for *self-perception theory,* which is presently a leading theory among social psychologists working on attitude change (Bem, 1967, 1972; Jones et al., 1971). The cornerstone of Bem's theory is that a person's attitudes correspond to her self-perceptions. The two main assumptions of self-perception theory are as follows:

> 1. Individuals come to "know" their own attitudes, emotions, and other internal states partially by inferring them from observations of their own overt behavior and/or the circumstances in which this behavior occurs.
> 2. To the extent that internal cues are weak, ambiguous, or uninterpretable, the individual is functionally in the same position as an outside observer, an observer who must necessarily rely upon those same external cues to infer the individual's inner states (Bem, 1972, p. 2).

This kind of theory has proved useful in interpreting the results of numerous attitude-change experiments done originally to support cognitive dissonance theory—for example, that subjects who are induced to role-play and argue against their initial opinion on some topic will consequently shift their true opinion drastically in the direction of the position they role-played. The references cited may be consulted for

information relevant to these hypotheses. But it is interesting that the hypotheses currently salient in social psychology derive in part from Skinner's behavioristic analysis of private experience.

Personality and Psychotherapy

Traditional psychodynamic theories of personality such as Freud's assume that the person possesses a set of personality traits, motives, and basic conflicts that are enduring and persistent over time and across different situations. Behavior, whether normal or disturbed, is alleged to be a symptomatic expression of these underlying traits and motives. When the inner conflicts and anxiety become too intense to deal with, the mental apparatus "breaks down" and expresses the inner turmoil in terms of an irrational, neurotic symptom.

Skinner (1953 and elsewhere) specifically rejects this interpretation. For him, motives, wishes, or desires are not explanations of behavior. To explain that a man spends an excessive amount of time cleaning and grooming himself neatly because he "has a compulsive need or wish for cleanliness" is to explain nothing at all. It merely moves the question back a step: *Why* does he have it? *What* determines that wish? To go beyond such useless "motive explanations," Skinner proposes that we analyze the observable events, conditions, situational variables, and past history which regulate the behavior in question.

For Skinner, behavior is to be accounted for in terms of the present stimulus complex and the past training history of the person with respect to similar situations. The past history provides the person with a large fund of information, skills, and values (analyzable in objective terms). Mental-trait descriptions of a person are relatively useless, first, because they correlate very poorly with how a person actually behaves across a range of social settings (see

Mischel, 1968), and second, because the trait description suggests no independent variables we can manipulate to control the behavior.

According to Skinner's analysis, then, a neurotic is someone who has learned to behave in ways that are personally, legally, or socially disapproved, and therefore considered deviant. Because neurotic behavior is learned, it can be unlearned or replaced by behavior that is better adjusted. The simple way to do this is to arrange contingencies such that undesirable behaviors cease receiving rewards and desirable behaviors begin receiving rewards. Simple as that sounds, the practice is in fact often difficult to implement due to frequent difficulties in identifying reinforcers that are sustaining the deviant behavior, in measuring the problematic behavior, in getting the contingencies to be applied consistently, and so on. Major credit goes to workers in behavior modification for routinely solving these difficult problems in field settings. The therapeutic outcomes are typically spectacular and beneficial. We postpone until Chapter 9 discussion of these and other applications of operant behavior modification techniques. In some ways they are the most impressive practical accomplishments of the behaviorist movement.

Impressive as are the applications of operant techniques, however, it is a mistake to suppose that their success "proves" that all of Skinner's approach to psychological phenomena is correct. They do show what benefits can be reaped by behavioral analysis, judicious use of reinforcement contingencies, and techniques of stimulus control; but then the empirical law of effect or the facts of stimulus discrimination have never been in dispute within learning theory. Such applications are typically designed to be helpful for individual problems rather than analytic and helpful in deciding among different theoretical interpretations.

ESTIMATE OF SKINNER'S SYSTEM

Skinner's Position on Typical Problems of Learning

The existence of textbooks written from the Skinnerian standpoint makes possible a summary of this position in relation to several problems.

1. *Capacity.* The behavioral repertoire of an individual organism must be carefully assessed and taken into account in shaping any specific behavior. A deficit in someone's behavior is often attributed to a deficiency in her training or environment. The belief is that behavior is very moldable and that (within limits) almost anyone can with proper training be shaped to some proficiency in any behavior. Regarding individual differences, Skinner argues for direct assessment of target behaviors, and against personality trait descriptions like *aggressive, lazy,* or *retarded.* A trait name does not refer to any unit of behavior suitable for study through the functional analysis that he recommends (1953, pp. 194–203). Thus, Skinner would reject most personality tests, saying that they provide useless characterizations of the person. Intelligence tests might be useful for educational decisions, since they sample directly the problem-solving skills they purport to measure; but the tests do not tell us how to *remedy* specific educational disabilities or deficits.

2. *Practice.* Something like a simple law of exercise (practice under conditions of contiguity of stimulus and response) is accepted as sufficient for Type S (Pavlovian) conditioning. The conditioning that occurs under Type R (operant), however, depends upon repeated reinforcement. Maximum conditioning may occur in a single trial for the single-unit operant; however, this is difficult to achieve experimentally. Usually, the accumulation of strength with repeated

reinforcement depends upon a population of discriminated stimuli and a chain of related operants, more or less after the manner of Guthrie's interpretation of the acquisition of skill with practice.

3. *Motivation.* Reward or reinforcement is necessary to increase operant strength. Punishment has a diverse range of effects, although typically it suppresses the response. The common usage of human motivational terms like *interest, apathy, happiness, depression,* and so on, refers typically to the consequences of effective or ineffective reinforcement contingencies. Internal drives are generally viewed by Skinner as relatively useless explanatory constructs, similar to personality traits. Skinner recognizes the effects of explicit deprivation variables on strength of operants reinforced by that restricted commodity, but he claims that nothing is added to a functional analysis by talking about a "drive" intervening between deprivation operations and changes in strength of operant responses.

4. *Understanding.* The word *insight* seldom occurs in Skinner's books. Keller and Schoenfeld identify insight with verbal description of learning contingencies, which typically produce subsequent behavior change under the stimulus-control of that verbal description. Problem-solving typically involves tacting (labeling) the problematical situation properly, then activating an appropriate verbal rule or response sequence leading up to a mediated cue for the solution behavior (as in the Staats and Staats analysis of the two-string problem). The emergence of the solution is to be explained on the basis of (1) similarity of the present problem to one solved earlier, or (2) the *simplicity* of the problem (F. S. Keller & Schoenfeld, 1950, p. 60). The technique of problem-solving is essentially that of manipulating variables (internal or external "hints" or stimuli) which lead to emission of the response. It is possible to teach people to "think" or "be creative" by these methods (Skinner, 1953, pp. 252–56).

5. *Transfer.* Skinner used the word *induction* for what is commonly called generalization in the conditioning literature. Such induction is the basis for transfer. As do others, he recognizes both primary and "secondary" or "mediated" generalization. The reinforcement of a response increases the probability of that response or similar ones to all stimulus complexes containing the same elements. Included is feedback stimulation from verbal labels; thus, an overt response will occur to a novel object if some property of it controls a verbal label which in turn controls the overt response. Therefore, having learned to shoot a revolver at soldiers in green uniforms in a particular fire zone, a man will also fire a rifle at any new soldier he sees in a green uniform in the same place. This general interpretation of transfer is, in spirit, very similar to Thorndike's.

DIFFICULTIES FOR SKINNER'S POSITION

As psychology advances, it is expected that new phenomena will be uncovered and new concepts invented in such manner as to raise questions about specific historical positions. This has occurred with several of Skinner's earlier ideas over the ensuing years, and a balanced evaluation of Skinner requires mention of these difficulties.

Doubts about the Operant-Respondent Distinction

The operant-respondent distinction proposed by Skinner and several others was to dominate learning theory for some thirty years. It was called *two-factor theory,* and it laid claim to a number of correspondences. Responses of glands and internal organs (*respondents*) were distinguished (by hypothesis) by being (a) elicited by innate, unconditioned stimuli, (b) controlled by the autonomic nervous system, (c) usually "involuntary," (d) characterized by minimal response-produced feedback, and most importantly (e) able to be classically conditioned but not operantly conditioned. In stark contrast, responses of striated, peripheral muscles (*operants*) were distinguished by being (a) sometimes emitted without identifiable stimuli, (b) controlled by the central nervous system, (c) under "voluntary" control, (d) characterized by distinctive proprioceptive feedback, and (e) able to be operantly conditioned but not classically conditioned.

This conceptual cleavage and set of correspondences came under increasing scrutiny, criticism, and reformulation (see Rescorla & Solomon, 1967; Staddon & Simmelhag, 1971; Terrace, 1973). Specifically, it now appears likely that some visceral responses mediated by the autonomic nervous system can be successfully altered by operant conditioning techniques (see N. E. Miller, 1969). Thus, for example, a thirsty dog can learn to salivate or to withhold salivation in order to get a drink of water, or a rat can be taught to make intestinal contractions to an external signal when such contractions are followed by a positive reward. These important findings concerning the operant conditioning of allegedly involuntary respondents will be reviewed in Chapter 9. The present conclusion is that such data indicate the operant-respondent distinction may have outlived its usefulness. Terrace, a Skinnerian himself, argues persuasively for modifying two-factor theory.

Let us examine other evidence often cited for the operant-respondent distinction. At one time it was felt that Pavlovian CRs were distinguished by being similar to their unconditioned response; this is the *substitution* idea, that the CS comes to substitute for the US in eliciting a *common*

response. If so, then operant conditioning would differ from Pavlovian conditioning in that the operant CR need not resemble the response to the reinforcing stimulus. But resemblance of the CR and UR turns out not to be a critical characteristic of operant-respondent conditioned responses. For example, a thirsty rat can be trained to lick at a dry water spout (an operant response) with the contingent appearance of the occasional water drop serving both to reward the response and to elicit further licking (like a respondent reflex). As another counter example to the resemblance criterion, in several Pavlovian conditioning preparations, the initial physiological reaction to the unconditioned stimulus may be counteracted by a compensatory reaction, and it is this compensatory reaction that comes to be evoked as a conditioned response to the CS. For example, Siegal (1978) found that while an injection of morphine reduces pain sensitivity in rats, a CS paired repeatedly with morphine causes an increase in pain sensitivity (other physiological indicators show similarly opposite patterns to the CS and US).

A further observation is that classical and instrumental processes overlap considerably. A close analysis of classical conditioning (e.g., the salivary conditioning paradigm) reveals that various skeletal ("operant") responses become associated to the conditioned stimulus, such as orienting to the food well, anticipatory chewing movements, ducking the head down to the food dish, and so on—all of these in addition to the salivary flow that Pavlov measured and emphasized (see Zener, 1937). Similarly, in instrumental conditioning, it is clearly established that components of the response elicited by the reinforcer become conditioned and occur in anticipation of it. Thus, as a dog begins to press a lever several times to get food, it will also start to salivate (see Shapiro, 1961; D. R. Williams, 1965). Thus, both operant and respondent behaviors seem to be conditioned in either type of experiment.

The main difference between instrumental and classical conditioning then reduces primarily to that of the *experimental procedure,* the way in which reinforcements (read "unconditioned stimuli") are scheduled. But there are intermediate procedures and undecidable test cases. A nice example is what is called conditioning of *superstitions,* a phenomenon first reported by Skinner (1948b) which he discussed in terms of operant conditioning. Suppose that a hungry pigeon is adapted to eating from a grain hopper in an enclosed box; the feeder is then operated periodically (say, for 3 seconds every 30 seconds) throughout several long experimental sessions. Although reinforcement (feeder presentation) is not contingent upon any particular behavior, the pigeon nonetheless eventually acquires some ritualistic, stereotyped chain of responses which it emits between reinforcements; different animals pick up different superstitions. This is explained as follows: when reinforcement is first delivered, the pigeon is behaving in some way, so this "operant" will be strengthened. It is then more probable that this same behavior, perhaps with small elaborations, will be in progress when the next reinforcement arrives. If so, it is strengthened even further; if not, some other behavior will be strengthened. Eventually the pigeon gets "trapped" into a particular operant sequence, which occurs and is reinforced at just that frequency which will maintain it. Conspicuous superstitious behaviors for a pigeon might include items like "turning sharply to one side, hopping from one foot to the other and back, bowing and scraping, turning around, strutting, and raising the head" (Skinner, 1953, p. 85). There have also been many demonstrations of the learning of "superstitions" by human adults exposed to random, noncontingent reinforcement (Wright, 1960), so there is little doubt regarding the effect.

Skinner interpreted the superstition experiment to mean that whenever a reinforcement is delivered to an organism, it strengthens whatever operant behavior is in progress at the time. The strengthening effect occurs regardless of whether or not the prevailing operant is truly instrumental in causing the reinforcer; from the organism's viewpoint, temporal contiguity between response and reinforcement is the important factor. Temporal coincidence is interpreted as causality. It is as though the organism believed its superstitious actions were producing the reinforcer.

Staddon and Simmelhag (1971) repeated the superstition experiment with pigeons with similar findings except they came to a different interpretation. They observed that the superstitious behaviors the pigeons emitted during the interval between reinforcements resembled the species-specific reactions pigeons make while eating or anticipating eating. These were mainly pecking at the empty cup (where grain was dispensed) or at the wall or floor nearby. Immediately after a reinforcement, which signaled a fixed delay prior to the next reinforcement, each pigeon would perform some variable behavior; but as time for reinforcement approached it would return to its routine of pecking near the grain dispenser. Staddon and Simmelhag believed that rather than strengthening particular ongoing operant responses, the fixed-interval reinforcements were giving rise to timed food anticipation, with the terminal behavior simply resembling eating. However, it is not clear how this analysis applies to or explains human superstitions such as rain dances or the like; there, the occurrence of the needed rain does not produce dancing, but rather just the mental review and belief that the dancing causes rain.

Curiously, Pavlov (1927) also studied and reported on a similar timed reinforcement arrangement with his dogs, except that he recorded salivation. Every so many minutes (say, 5 minutes) the dog in the experimental stand would be fed, and this cycle was repeated often. Pavlov found that the animal learned eventually to salivate near the expected time for arrival of the food. Because Pavlov thought the sheer passage of time since the last reinforcement became a conditioned stimulus for evoking conditioned salivation, he referred to this arrangement as *temporal conditioning,* a form of classical conditioning.

But since the schedule of events in the superstition experiment and in temporal conditioning are identical, why should we call one "classical" and the other "instrumental" conditioning? Because of the types of responses recorded in the two experiments? But we have just said earlier that many so-called respondents (like salivation) can be conditioned by use of operant reinforcement; similarly, some skeletal responses (like the eyeblink and the knee jerk) can be conditioned according to the classical conditioning routine. Thus, the response systems do not necessarily dictate different laws of learning.

The classical and instrumental conditioning may even be pitted against one another by rewarding the subject for withholding a response to a signal, but in a situation in which the rewarding US elicits the response which is to be withheld. An example of this contingency, devised by F. D. Sheffield (1965) and called *omission* training, is to reinforce a hungry dog with food only if he does *not* salivate to a signal. Shapiro & Herendeen (1975) have found successful operant conditioning with this procedure. Their dogs learned to "keep their mouth dry" in order to get food. By the end of training, the dogs were withholding salivation and being fed on about 80 percent of the CS trials. A two-factor theorist might argue either that 80 percent reinforced trials are insufficient to sustain a classical CR or that the classical CR that does develop will be weak and will oscillate through small acquisition-extinc-

tion cycles in tracking the occurrence and nonoccurrence of the US across trials. But Shapiro and Herendeen ran controls which excluded such explanations. First, yoked control animals receiving the same sequence of food and nonfood trials as their experimental mates earned nonetheless showed a high level of salivary conditioning, so the 80 percent reinforcement schedule was rich enough to sustain a very good classical CR when the negative-response contingency was not in force. Second, trial-by-trial analyses revealed that animals trained with the negative-response contingency were increasingly likely *not* to salivate to the signal the longer was the preceding run of trials on which they were reinforced for not salivating. This is just the reverse of the sequential effect expected by the law of classical conditioning. It would thus appear that classical conditioning is not a necessary consequence of CS-US pairings in time; nor is the "last response" performed to the CS (salivation) the one that is strengthened, which is what Guthrie would have guessed.

The view that seems to be suggested by these considerations (see Terrace, 1973) is a return to the one-factor theory of reinforcement advocated originally by Hull. That is, classical conditioning involves the same principle of reinforcement ("reward learning") as does operant conditioning, except that the recorded response and its means of initial elicitation differ in the two cases. There are several ways to conceive of how food as a reward could strengthen anticipatory salivation in Pavlovian conditioning. First, one could simply say (as Hull did) that eating food both elicits and simultaneously reinforces ("rewards") salivation. Second, we could suppose that the anticipatory CR is differentially reinforced because it makes the following US more rewarding (than if the CR had not occurred). Thus, on this hypothesis, anticipatory salivation enhances the taste, palatability, and rewarding value of the food which follows.

This view, proposed earlier by Perkins (1955), has much to recommend it, especially in those cases where the preparatory act reduces the unpleasantness of an aversive stimulus. Perkins also shows how this assumption, of appropriate preparatory responses enhancing reward values, can explain the learning of *pure observing responses;* these are special responses that have no obvious utility other than to provide information that prepares the animal for upcoming reinforcing events (see G. H. Bower et al., 1966). A third view of Pavlovian conditioning is the *expectancy learning* idea that does not require reinforcing a response of salivation. Due to the CS-US pairings, the CS acquires the ability to make the subject think of or expect the US; and in most cases, expecting a US causes a reaction, often one that resembles the response to the US itself, although it need not. But this clearly fails to account for the Shapiro and Herendeen (1975) findings.

Whatever the correct formulation of Pavlovian conditioning, clearly Skinner's strict dichotomy of response classes and laws for respondent and operant conditioning seems amiss. His earlier position on these important issues is no longer tenable. Some further complications for Skinner's position will be discussed.

Preparedness

As reviewed in Chapter 3, increasing evidence is refuting the *equipotentiality* postulate to which Skinner and other learning theorists have implicitly subscribed (which justified the use of such arbitrary responses as a lever-press by a rat). This assumes that any response the organism is capable of can be attached to any discriminable stimulus for any reinforcing stimulus; and the learning of the three-term contingency depends only on the independent identities of the three terms, not

their relation of natural fittingness or belongingness. Evidence reviewed by Seligman (1970) shows counterexamples; a stimulus may elicit innate responses which strongly compete with the one to be learned; or a given species-specific response (e.g., yawning in a dog) may occur only to specific stimuli and not be conditionable to other stimuli; or a reinforcer may recruit a set of instinctual activities which compete with the arbitrary operant which is to be established in the three-term contingency. For example, Breland and Breland (1960) reported many cases of instinctive behavior closely linked to food which began to intrude in advance of food delivery, interfering with the correct operant response and delaying reinforcement. Seligman proposes a classification of S-R-S contingencies in terms of whether individuals of a given species are *prepared* or *contraprepared* to make those attachments. An illustration of a prepared connection is the relating of an intestinal upset and nausea to an earlier novel taste, whereas the animal is contraprepared to relate that same upset to a flashing light. Another illustration is "autoshaping" of keypecking in pigeons, a topic to which we now turn.

Autoshaping

When Skinner first tested pigeons in his conditioning chamber, he chose as the response, more or less arbitrarily, the pigeon's pecking of a lighted key mounted at head level on a wall above the food tray. Reinforcement was provided by a few seconds' access to a tray of grain at which the pigeon pecked and ate. The choice of keypecking turned out to have been a fortunate one for gaining rapid conditioning. However, in retrospect that choice has also complicated detailed analyses of operant conditioning.

The complication is provided by the fact that pigeons are *highly prepared* to peck distinctive lighted objects when they are anticipating food reinforcement; pecking is an innate, species-specific action pattern recruited by food-foraging in pigeons. In a classic study, P. L. Brown and Jenkins (1968) found that hungry pigeons could be trained to peck a lighted response key simply by the experimenter illuminating the key for a few seconds before food delivery. The reinforcement need not be made contingent on keypecking at all in order to condition the keypecking. This phenomenon, called *autoshaping* since the animal shapes itself to responding, is quite reliable, powerful, and has been much studied since then. It appears that the auto-shaped keypeck is an example of a Pavlovian CR. The keylight coming on just before the pigeon is allowed to peck at grain converts the keylight into a CS for pecking at food; and the pigeon's innate repertoire takes over from there, causing it to peck a lighted spot that makes it "think of" food. Autoshaping proceeds more rapidly the more the spot of light on the key resembles a kernel of food. Conditioning of keypecks by the autoshaping procedure also conforms to most of the laws of Pavlovian conditioning. It is even possible to get second-order conditioning in the autoshaping situation (Rashotte et al., 1977). D. R. Williams and H. Williams (1969) were unable to train their pigeons to refrain from pecking the lighted key in order to obtain food (the omission training procedure mentioned previously). If the pigeon refrained from pecking the lighted key, it would be fed in a few seconds; but if he pecked the key, the light went off and he missed the food on that trial. The pigeons in the Williams and Williams experiment were unable to restrain themselves from keypecking on most of the trials. This indicates that the Pavlovian component of the autoshaping setup was stronger than the operant reinforcement component.

The autoshaping phenomenon has made investigators attend more closely to species-specific reactions to the reinforcer and how those relate to the response required to obtain reinforcement in the operant conditioning experiment. They note that the so-called operant response often has components that closely resemble the form of the respondent behavior elicited by the reinforcer. An example reported by Moore (1973) is that the exact manner in which pigeons strike the key differs, depending on whether they are pecking to get food or water rewards. The keypeck for food resembles the staccato bursts of grabbing kernels of grain; the keypecks for water resemble the scooping, swiping movements of gathering up water in the lower part of the beak. These are subtle effects.

The existence of Pavlovian components in the prototypic "operant" of the pigeon's keypeck has introduced conceptual complications not anticipated within Skinner's principles of operant conditioning. Autoshaping is neither a disproof nor an embarrassment to Skinner's system; it rather points up a complicating twist on what was originally considered to be simple—the nature of the response.

Undermining Intrinsic Interest

A frequent question that parents and teachers pose to psychologists is whether explicitly rewarding an activity that a child (or adult) should be interested in for its own sake (such as reading) will undermine the child's intrinsic interest in the activity. The question is important in raising the possibility of undesirable side effects of explicit operant rewards. These fears received some backing in a study by Lepper, Greene, and Nisbett (1973) of preschoolers' interest in drawing pictures with Magic Marker pens, a novel activity they found moderately interesting and fun to do. Some children drew pictures in a lab room knowing that they would earn a desired toy prize if they drew enough pictures for the experimenter, and all received the toy. Control children could draw pictures if they wanted to but no prize was mentioned or given to them. Later, in play periods in their regular classroom, the rewarded children were observed to spend *less* time than the controls drawing with the marker pens, and they rated it as a less interesting activity than other alternatives. Lepper and colleagues initially suggested that an extrinsic reward "overjustifies" engaging in an interesting task, and so reduces its intrinsic interest. A later interpretation is that the rewarded children come to think of the marker-pen drawing as something to be done "only for pay," and so they do not engage in it when a reward is not forthcoming.

Although several experimenters have replicated the Lepper finding, Feingold and Mahoney (1975) and Reiss and Sushinsky (1975) did not find the negative aftereffects of reward on children's connecting dots in a follow-the-dots picture book. A critical difference appears to be whether the child's "interest" is tested (without external rewards) in the same setting as the rewarded training setting. The Feingold and Mahoney, and Reiss and Sushinsky studies used very similar settings for training and testing, and obtained no after-depression of interest for the rewarded subjects, perhaps because the subjects somehow still believed they would get some kind of reward (if only praise) for their efforts. On the other hand, Lepper and colleagues observed their children in the classroom, with no "experimenter" present, which was quite different from the lab setting where the reward session had been conducted. In a direct test of this generalization hypothesis, Lepper, Greene, and Sagotsky (1978) found that rewarded subjects retested in the lab room with the experimenter attending (with no promise of reward now) showed no reduction below controls in rate of engaging in a formerly rewarded activity, whereas rewarded children did show the negative effect when observed in the free classroom situation; there, they engaged in

the target activity less than control subjects.

Lepper suggests that a teacher or parent should not use external rewards to promote a desired behavior unless the rewards are clearly needed to induce interest. This suggests caution in installing token economies or extrinsic systems for an entire class or group of people for every task without regard for whether a particular person needs the rewards to motivate his or her interest in the task. However, this issue is still not fully resolved and is likely to be a source of continuing debate and experimentation. But it does suggest certain strictures on an unvarnished interpretation of operant strengthening via external rewards.

Learning-Performance Distinction

Skinner has always considered reinforcers as strengthening operants directly, and has had little use for the learning-performance distinction which has been central to other learning theorists. But this issue clearly comes to the fore when it can be shown that someone has learned something quite well and knows how to do it, but does not perform for lack of reinforcement. For example, Bandura, Grusec, and Menlove (1966) had children observe a child model in a film perform a series of novel aggressive acts, and then the model received either rewarding, neutral, or punishing consequences in the film from a "teacher." When the child was later allowed to perform in the same situation, the frequency of aggressive responses imitating those of the model varied directly with the reinforcement of the model shown in the film. However, when incentives were offered in a second test for reproduction of the model's behaviors, the differences in imitation virtually disappeared between subjects exposed to differently rewarded models. Apparently, the children had learned the same amount from observing the model's behavior; they performed more or less of that behavior depending on whether they expected to be reinforced for it. Although Skinner can make this distinction (e.g., in terms of two levels of learning, one regarding the behaviors, and a controlling one regarding the consequences of that behavior), the fact is that he frequently does not, so that learning and performance concepts are rather confusedly intertwined in his discussions. Other psychologists are coming to the conclusion that reinforcement affects mainly performance (by means of "incentive motivation" or "anticipatory reward") rather than learning.

Observational Learning

Behaviorists like Skinner believe that people only learn responses; only those behaviors they have performed in some overt or covert manner. Cognitive psychologists believe that information about perceptual events can be learned by observation without the implicit verbalization or recitation of words (or other discriminating responses) referring to the observed events. How do these theories explain how someone observes a model perform, stores that information, then uses it to guide her later performance? The differing approaches between cognitive and behavioral theories show up in their analyses of how perceptual information is "remembered" over a retention interval before the organism is allowed to respond on the basis of that information. To consider a simple example, in "delayed matching to sample," a pigeon in a Skinner box first sees a red or a green sample color on a key it must peck, then has a short delay, followed by the lighting of two keys, one red and the other green, with reinforcement provided if it pecks the color which matches the sample color shown earlier in the trial. During the retention interval, how does the pigeon "remember" which sample color was presented? A standard Skinnerian reply

would suppose that each sample color becomes gradually converted into a discriminative stimulus which immediately starts the animal running off two different chains of ritualistic behaviors which "code and carry" the discriminative information over time so that it is available to guide the delayed choice (if chain 1 is in progress, choose the red key; if chain 2, choose the green key). But this claim of adventitious mediating chains has rarely been substantiated by observation; often the discriminating animal simply seems to sit during the delay interval, or at least behave similarly during the two types of delay intervals (see D'Amato, 1973). Apparently she just "remembers" the sample color as a central event, rather than remembering in her peripheral musculature. Thus, remembering stimulus information causes trouble for the behaviorist, so does observational learning, a phenomenon to be reviewed in Chapter 13.

Chomsky's Critiques

Perhaps the most effective critiques of Skinner's systematic position and his extrapolation of it to human affairs have been provided by the linguist Noam Chomsky, first in his critical review of Skinner's book *Verbal behavior* (Chomsky, 1959), and later in a similar critical review of Skinner's *Beyond freedom and dignity* (Chomsky, 1971). Chomsky attacks Skinner on a number of different fronts. First, he argues that knowledge of a multitude of input-output (or S-R) relations provides no explanation for behavior in any sense; rather, our task should be to understand the internal structure, states, and organization of the device (organism) that produces this set of input-output relations. To restrict one's theoretical enterprise to observable stimuli and responses is, for Chomsky, to place unwarranted fetters on the development of the science, and to condemn it to be a "monumental triviality" (Arthur Koestler's description of "behaviorism"). "By objecting, a priori, to this research strategy [postulating a theory of internal structure], Skinner merely condemns his strange variety of 'behavioral science' to continued ineptitude" (Chomsky, 1971, p. 19). At issue here is whether behavior is to be the subject matter of psychology or is to be taken only as evidence for the operation of the cognitive system.

Second, Chomsky adopts the standard lines of arguments of cognitive psychologists against the objectivity or validity of Skinner's concepts of stimulus, response, reinforcement, and response strength. Is any and every sensory event presented in the environment a stimulus, or just those to which the subject attends and reacts? What makes two stimulus patterns equivalent or similar? How can a "mediating pure stimulus act" be defined in objective terms? What responses are equivalent? Is the response not better defined as an action directed at a place? How do we distinguish topographically different responses which "mean" the same thing (e.g., proper names versus definite descriptions) and so are interchangeable instances of an operant class, from topographically identical responses which "mean" entirely different things depending on the context (e.g., answering "Yes" to "Did you kill George?" vs. "Are you innocent of killing George?"). Similarly, regarding reinforcements, recent evidence with human subjects (Dulany, 1968; Estes, 1969a) suggests that reinforcements function largely as informational events rather than as response-strengthening events, and that a given event (e.g., electric shock, a blast of hot air) can be assigned positive or negative reinforcing value depending on the instructions given to the person. Further, research on hypothesis-testing behaviors by humans (e.g., M. Levine, 1970) suggests that reinforcers serve as information, confirming or disconfirming entire hypotheses which are equivalent

to a full battery of specific S-R connections. Also, as will be noted in our review of the theory of reinforcers in Chapter 9, there seems no noncircular way to identify reinforcers that will be effective for all occasions and for strengthening any response. So there are some difficulties with Skinner's position just at this most elementary level.

Third, Chomsky comes down very hard on Skinner's casual attempts to extrapolate his concepts from the relatively restricted "rat-in-a-Skinner-box" domain to the processes and phenomena of human mental and social life. He argues that in Skinner's analysis of common-sense terms such as *want, intend, like, plan,* and *persuade,* those concepts are rather inadequately translated into the three-term contingencies countenanced by Skinner's system. Chomsky's claim is that when Skinner's extrapolations are interpreted literally (in the original laboratory meanings of the terms), they are clearly false; and when these assertions are interpreted in Skinner's vague and metaphorical way, they turn out under analysis to be merely a poor substitute for common-sense usage.

Because Chomsky is a linguist, he is particularly astute at showing the absence of clear reference of Skinner's allegedly scientific terms when he is discussing speech behavior. To take just one example, Skinner discusses verb endings (tense markers) by saying that for the speaker the past tense suffix *-ed* is controlled "by that subtle property of stimuli which we speak of as action-in-the-past" (Skinner, 1957, p. 121), whereas the *-s* in *The lady walks* is under the control of such specific features of the situation as its "currency," meaning "present tense." As Chomsky says (1959), "No characterization of the notion of 'stimulus control' that is remotely related to the bar-pressing experiment (or that preserves the faintest objectivity) can be made to cover a set of examples like these [Chomsky lists about seven or eight] in which, for example, the 'controlling stimulus' need not even impinge on the responding organism." Chomsky provides a number of criticisms of the specific examples of verbal behavior analyzed by Skinner.

Fourth, Chomsky argues that the behavioristic approach to language analysis *must* fail because it proposes to analyze only so-called surface features of utterances, whereas most regularities in language are revealed only when the grammatical "deep structure" is extracted by some complex syntax analyzer within the person. The deep structure of a sentence is something like the logical propositions which it asserts. The same surface string of words may have different deep structures. Thus the phrase *They are eating apples* (and thousands of phrases like it) is grammatically ambiguous since it has two possible deep structures, depending on whether *eating* is interpreted as a verb (so *they* means *agent*) or as an adjective (*eating apples* as contrasted to *cooking apples*). Another example is *Time flies,* which is three ways ambiguous depending on whether *time* and *flies* are independently interpreted as nouns or verbs (as in *The official timed the flies*). The deep-structure analysis is also important in illuminating the underlying similarity of a set of surface strings which are otherwise quite distinct. Thus, the passive-voice sentence *The boy was bitten by the snake* has a different surface form but the same deep structure as the active-voice sentence *The snake bit the boy*. The two surface forms are derived, according to Chomsky (1957, 1965), by two different *transformations* from the same deep structure or logical proposition. In the same manner, the sentence *Harold and Maude like to attend funerals and burials too,* is derived by successive "deletion transformations" from the full conjunction *Harold and Maude like to attend funerals, and moreover, Harold and Maude like to attend burials.*

Chomsky argues that these similarities and regularities among surface utterances cannot be understood without the speaker's or listener's having tacitly acquired a well-developed theory of English grammar enabling him to perform something like these translations. Chomsky and his colleagues (Bever, 1968; Bever et al., 1968) have argued that theories of language which deal only with the observable ("surface") features of the utterance cannot in principle provide an illuminating explanation of our linguistic abilities (e.g., in detecting ambiguities, in recognizing similarities of underlying forms, in generating recursive embeddings of subpropositions, and so on). Rather we must postulate more abstract concepts and assign to the language understander an "internal grammatical theory" which is tacit and exceedingly complex.

This is hardly the place to discuss these claims in detail. The main idea to be gotten across is the profoundly disturbing nature of Chomsky's arguments against the behavioristic account of language and, by implication, the behavioristic account of mental life. Chomsky was partly responsible for the rise of cognitive psychology (and psycholinguistics) to a position of prominence. In later commenting on his review of *Verbal behavior,* Chomsky had this to say:

> Rereading this review after eight years, I find little of substance that I would change if I were to write it today. I am not aware of any theoretical or empirical work that challenges its conclusions; nor, so far as I know, has there been any attempt to meet the criticisms that are raised in the review or to show that they are erroneous or ill-founded.
>
> I had intended this review not specifically as a criticism of Skinner's speculations regarding language, but rather as a more general critique of behaviorist (I would now prefer to say "empiricist") speculation as to the nature of higher mental processes. . . . I do not see any way in which [Skinner's] proposals can be substantially improved within the general framework of behaviorist or neobehaviorist, or, more generally, empiricist ideas that has dominated much of modern linguistics, psychology, and philosophy. The conclusion that I hoped to establish in the review—was that the general point of view is largely mythology, and that its widespread accep-

tance is not the result of empirical support, persuasive reasoning, or the absence of a plausible alternative (1967, p. 142).

Although MacCorquodale (1969, 1970) later attempted to answer Chomsky's critique, the answers simply did not register as effective or persuasive; furthermore, the tide in psycholinguistics had long since turned to a cognitive-mechanism approach to theorizing about linguistic competence and performance. It is a truism today that experimental psycholinguistics is a branch of linguistics and cognitive psychology, not an extension of behavioristic learning theories (see Clark & Clark, 1978, for a representative presentation of psycholinguistics).

THE CLASH WITH TRADITIONAL VIEWPOINTS

Skinner's "fresh start" approach to psychology has made it difficult for him to use the data collected by others outside the operant conditioning camp, and he rejects on principle the sorts of theoretical constructions to which other learning theorists are prone. Skinner and his followers have felt no responsibility for the task of coordinating their work closely with that of others studying learning (and the indifference is regrettably often mutual). For instance, in his most systematic book, *Science and human behavior* (1953), Skinner used no literature citations at all, and of those writers with some place in learning theory, he mentions by name only Thorndike, Pavlov, and Freud. His writing rarely refers to the experimental work of others, and certainly none done outside the operant-conditioning methodology.

This insularity is carried forward in pages of the *Journal of Experimental Analysis of Behavior* (*JEAB*), which is essentially the house organ of the operant-conditioning movement. As an index of what literature is being taken into account, one analysis of the papers cited in the bibliography of *JEAB* articles showed that nearly 40 percent of citations were to work previously published in *JEAB*, whereas a comparable specialized journal, the *Journal of Verbal Learning and Verbal Behavior*, showed less than 20 percent self-citations (see Krantz, 1971). Moreover, proportionate citations to *JEAB* articles in other journals devoted to analyses of conditioning and learning actually fell somewhat over the years surveyed. This tends to create two isolated camps or "schools," the operant conditioners versus the remainder of learning psychologists, who go their separate ways, tilling their independent soils.

Why is there this isolation, particularly the rejection of most of the rest of psychology by the operant conditioners? Krantz (1971) has proposed that strongly different experimental methodologies separate the two camps. The Skinnerian (see Sidman, 1960) argues that traditional experimental design (in learning studies), using trial-by-trial data averaged over trials and over different subjects, "destroys, confounds, or omits the significant data of moment to moment rate changes in a single organism's behavior" (Krantz, 1971, p. 62). In the conventional experimental design, a single subject receives typically a few learning trials in only one condition; as noted in an earlier section, in operant conditioning, a single subject may receive thousands of "trials" on any one experimental condition (reaching "steady-state behavior," as they say) before being switched to another value of a schedule variable or to a different experimental condition where he will again receive thousands of trials. A single subject may thus be successively cycled through nearly all values of the independent variable (e.g., mean VI length), his successive steady-state behaviors "tracing out" the functional relation as it exists for him. But the conventional design would use different subjects at the different values—the so-called "between-subjects" design.

This procedural difference is quite transparent in statistics (Krantz, 1971) on the relative usage of between-subjects versus within-subjects designs in *JEAB* and the comparable *Journal of Comparative and Physiological Psychology* (*JCPP*); for the years 1967 and 1969, only about 3 percent of *JEAB* articles used a between-subjects design, whereas 89 percent of *JCPP* studies did so; on the other hand, only 6 percent of *JCPP* studies used an exclusively within-subject design, whereas about 90 percent of *JEAB* articles did. (These percentages do not add to 100 because of mixed designs.)

Sidman (1960, p. 53 ff.) sees these two design strategies as incommensurate. The key to use of the within-subject design is *reversibility* of a behavioral phenomenon, particularly steady-state behavior. Reversibility means that a particular steady-state behavior under specified contingencies can be recovered over and over again after the subject has been shifted temporarily to other conditions and then returned to the original contingencies. Other psychologists may shy away from within-subject experiments because of general "transfer" effects, suspecting that the subject's behavior in a condition will depend on earlier conditions experienced and their order. The typical remark is that performance on later schedule parameters is "confounded" by general transfer effects, with unknown contaminating influences.

Sidman's reply is, first, to assert that such transfer effects are rare in steady-state experiments; and second, that if they exist, then they are themselves important objects for study. Irreversibility or transfer from one to another learning condition cannot be gotten around by running independent groups on the separate values of the independent variable and plotting a curve through the group average. As Sidman says:

> . . . [T]he function so obtained does not represent a behavioral process. The use of separate groups destroys the continuity of cause and effect that characterizes an irreversible behavioral process.

If it proves impossible to obtain an "uncontaminated" relation in a single subject [because of interactions], then the "pure" relation simply does not exist. The solution to our problem is to cease trying to discover such a pure relation, and to direct our research toward the study of behavior as it actually exists.

> . . . [W]here irreversibility is met, there is no individual curve that can answer the questions one may put to the group curve, or vice versa. The student should not be deceived into concluding that the group type of experiment in any way provides a more adequately controlled or more generalizable substitute for individual data.
>
> If my point strikes home, it should lead the student to re-evaluate much of the supposedly systematic data of experimental psychology. . . . When this is done, the student may find that he must abandon many of psychology's cherished generalizations. He is also likely to find himself faced with a choice. For the two types of data represent, in a real sense, different subject matters (p. 53).

It may be noted that the split between the two methodologies depends on the focus of interest—in particular, whether transitional (and transitory) behavior is of primary concern, as when the animal is *acquiring* a new skill or *extinguishing* an old habit; or whether asymptotic steady-state behavior is of central concern. The older learning theories tended to concentrate on acquisition and its rate, whereas operant conditioners are much more concerned with the steady-state behavior maintained by given contingencies. Their methodology rather resembles that of the psychophysicist who tests a single subject repeatedly. Similar thousand-trial designs are now common in studies of human memory (e.g., Atkinson & Shiffrin, 1965) and information processing (e.g., Sternberg, 1969). Therefore, there is really no reason for methodological segregation of these fields any longer.

The main division thus remains theoretical preference—or, rather, a preference for theorizing on one side versus a lack of sympathy for theoretical efforts on the other. This comes down to the matter of deciding what are the proper goals of a scientific psychology. And here we come again to the empiricism-rationalism schism of antiquity (see Chapter 1). There is a fundamental opposition between scientists who believe that progress is to be made only by rigorous examination of actual behavior resulting in the formulation of a few generalizations, versus those who believe that behavioral observations are interesting only insofar as they reveal underlying laws of the mind that are only partially revealed in behavior. Is psychology to be the science of the mind or the science of behavior? Is physics the science of physical things or the science of meter readings? Is science pursued for an understanding of the way things work or for controlling their workings? Is astronomy any less a science because astronomers can not do experiments on or control heavenly bodies? Do behaviorists confuse the subject matter of the field with the evidence available for drawing inferences about this subject matter? Skinner opts for behavior as the subject matter; cognitive psychologists who form the current opposition (e.g., Neisser, 1967; Rumelhart, 1978) suppose that one uses behavior as *evidence* for the operation of cognitive processes. This contemporary clash between alternative views illustrates how very fundamental are these essentially historic and philosophic assumptions.

SUPPLEMENTARY READINGS

The following books contain Skinner's own accounts of his work:

FERSTER, C. B., & SKINNER, B. F. (1957). *Schedules of reinforcement.*

HOLLAND, J. G., & SKINNER, B. F. (1961). *The analysis of behavior: A program for self-instruction.*

SKINNER, B. F. (1938). *The behavior of organisms.*

SKINNER, B. F. (1953). *Science and human behavior.*

SKINNER, B. F. (1957). *Verbal behavior.*

SKINNER, B. F. (1968). *The technology of teaching.*

SKINNER, B. F. (1969). *Contingencies of reinforcement.*

SKINNER, B. F. (1971). *Beyond freedom and dignity.*

SKINNER, B. F. (1974). *About behaviorism.*

A collection of Skinner's experimental and theoretical papers, selected by him as representative of his contributions, is found in:

SKINNER, B. F. (1972). *Cumulative record.*

A retrospective appraisal of some of Skinner's work, along with some autobiographical material, is:

DEWS, P. B. (1970). *Festschrift for B. F. Skinner.*

Two autobiographical volumes by Skinner are *Particulars of my life* (1976), and *The shaping of a behaviorist* (1979).

Skinner's novel *Walden two* (1948a), also available as a paperback, is worth reading, along with *Science and human behavior* (1953) for a comparison between the scientific system and its imaginary application in an experimental utopia. His *Beyond freedom and dignity* (1971) argues for the application of "behavioral technology" to the ills of society. It had a very controversial reception among intellectuals and social critics. The ethical implications of Skinner's analyses of free will, behavior modification, and social controls are the subject of an illuminating book by F. Carpenter, *The Skinner primer: Behind freedom and dignity* (1974).

For the methodological positions of Skinner, an inspiring and closely argued book is by M. Sidman, *Tactics of scientific research* (1960). For illustrations of various applications, a useful source is W. K. Honig, ed. (1966), *Operant behavior: Areas of research and application.* Note also W. K. Honig and J. E. R. Staddon, eds. (1977), *Handbook of operant behavior;* T. Verhave, ed. (1966), *The experimental analysis of behavior: Selected readings.*

8

ESTES'S STIMULUS SAMPLING THEORY

The introduction of the experimental method for the study of learning in the 19th century established a tradition of quantitative methods for recording, processing, and describing behavioral data. Response tendencies were commonly measured according to their amplitude, latency of response, or relative frequency of occurrence. Since the mid-1950s one trend has been toward framing hypotheses regarding learning that are based on the quantitative details of behavioral data. These *mathematical models* of learning seek to predict the exact numerical details of experimental results. A major historical impetus to this trend came from the writings and theoretical work of Clark Hull. Hull argued forcibly for the development of quantitative theories in learning. His own work in this respect was mainly programmatic and yielded few genuinely quantitative predictions of numerical data. However, the type of program for which Hull argued appeared in significant form after 1950 under the banner of mathematical learning theory. William K. Estes, whose work we review here, was a leader in this field. The early developments are reviewed in the *Handbook of mathematical psychology* (Luce et al., 1963,

1965), and in a textbook, *Introduction to mathematical learning theory* (Atkinson et al., 1965).

One important point to stress at the outset is that there is really no such thing as mathematical learning theory. This term denotes a particular kind of approach to theory construction rather than a single, specific set of postulates that could be properly called a theory. The use of mathematics is freely available to theorists of all persuasions. The mathematics involved is indifferent to the content of the psychological ideas expressed by it. That is, a diversity of substantive hypotheses about learning and behavior can be stated and analyzed in mathematical terms. Mathematical learning theory as a field is occupied by a loose confederation of workers, with different substantive ideas, whose only common bond is their use of mathematics as a vehicle for precise statement and for testing their hypotheses against data.

In overview, work in mathematical learning theory has concentrated around the experimental situations exploited by Hull, Skinner, and the functionalist tradition—namely, classical and instrumental conditioning, selective learning, and a major emphasis on human learning under laboratory conditions. By and large, too, most of the theoretical work has been predominantly in the vein of stimulus-response associationism. However, this primarily reflects the background and predilections of workers in the mathematical idiom, since cognitive hypotheses can be and often have been represented in mathematical form.

Rather than review mathematical learning theory in its entirety, this chapter concentrates on the work of one man, William K. Estes, who has been a stellar leader in that field since 1950. Estes enunciated a form of mathematical learning theory called *stimulus sampling theory*. It has been the most extensive and coherent continuing work in the field, it serves as a prototypical example of a mathematical learning theory, and so it well deserves its special treatment in this chapter.

BACKGROUND OF STIMULUS SAMPLING THEORY

Stimulus sampling theory (SST) started as a form of stimulus-response associationism, when Estes tried to formalize many of the ideas of Guthrie. The basic idea is that organisms learn by attaching new adaptive behaviors to stimulus situations where they formerly had mainly inappropriate behaviors. The conditions of reinforcement define what is adaptive in a given situation. Estes accepted the empirical law of effect, that reinforcers strengthen and guide behavior, although he did not believe that rewards operate by providing "satisfaction" or "drive reduction" after a correct response. In his earlier papers, in the 1950s, Estes favored a Guthrian interpretation of reinforcement—that is, reinforcers were stimuli which somehow insured that the correct response would be the last one to occur to the critical stimuli on a given trial. Later, for various reasons, Estes

switched to the belief that organisms were learning internal representations for external events and event sequences, and that associations formed between these event representations. The "event" in question can be either a stimulus (S), a response (R), or a reinforcing outcome (O). On this view, an organism experiencing an S-R-O sequence will learn associations for all pairs of elements, S-R, R-O, and S-O. Earlier, in discussing Estes's revisions of the law of effect, we illustrated how these associations interact to enable the organism to select an adaptive response. Roughly speaking, the stimulus-outcome connection provides "good" or "bad" feedback that either facilitates or inhibits a specific stimulus-response connection. But we are getting far ahead of our story. For most of the mathematical developments of stimulus sampling theory, it makes no difference how one interprets the empirical law of effect.

The Statistical View of Performance

Stimulus sampling theory explicitly treats learning and performance as a probabilistic (or stochastic) process. A *stochastic process* is simply a sequence of events that can be analyzed in terms of probability. Familiar examples are a sequence of coin tosses or rolls of dice. In a learning experiment—say, a rat learning to turn left in a T-maze—the sequence of his left or right responses over successive trials may be viewed as a probabilistic process. Think of it as a sequence of coin tosses, except that because of learning the coin becomes progressively more biased and likely to turn up the "correct" side. Our rat in the T-maze will produce over trials a sequence of correct (C) and error (E) responses, such as ECEECECCC . . . (all the rest C). We would have one such sequence for each of our N subjects in the experiment, and every one will differ from every other. Viewed in this microscopic way, an impressive amount of variability exists within an animal's responses from trial to trial, as well as between animals. If behavior is causally determined, how then do we account for all this variability? The deterministic approach assumes that the animals really differ in their genetic makeup and prior histories, and that these factors determine an animal's choices and sensitivity to reinforcement. The variable behavior by an animal across trials would be explained by positing variation in the external stimulus situation, in the animal's momentary attention to certain stimuli, to fluctuations in his motivation, to variations in his accessing of relevant memories, and so forth. The determinist argues that if all these effective causes were known to us at the moment of the animal's choice, then his choice would appear to be completely determined and, hence, predictable.

A defensible alternative approach, however, assumes that because behavior is determined by so many variable and unmeasurable causes, the best prediction of behavior we can offer in practice is a probabilistic one. Rather than saying "He will turn left this trial," we say "There's an 80 percent chance he will turn left." That is like our saying of the toss of a fair coin that there is a 50 percent chance it will turn up heads. Thus, we can characterize our prediction of what is going to happen for a single subject by stating for each trial the probability that each of the several responses should occur.

The main dependent variable of statistical learning theory is the probability of various responses of a subject at any point in time, given her particular learning theory. For our T-maze illustration, in the theory we would let p_1, p_2, p_3, . . . represent the subject's probability of making a correct response on Trial 1, on Trial 2, on Trial 3, and so on. The subscript on p_n denotes the trial number, n. Unlike a series of coin tosses, however, in a learning experiment the trial sequence of probabilities changes; in fact, the probability of a cor-

TABLE 8.1. First five trials of a hypothetical learning experiment. Correct or error responses have been generated in a row for each subject by comparing new random numbers to the theoretical probability of a correct response over the five trials.

Trials	1	2	3	4	5
Theoretical Prob. of C	(p_1) .50	(p_2) .60	(p_3) .65	(p_4) .70	(p_5) .75
Subj. 1	E	C	C	E	E
Subj. 2	C	E	C	C	C
Subj. 3	E	E	C	C	C
Subj. 4	C	C	E	C	C

rect response should increase over trials to nearly 1.00. The first five trials of a hypothetical learning experiment are depicted in Table 8.1, where we have the probabilities of the correct response being $p_1 = .50$, $p_2 = .60$, and so on.

A learning theory like stimulus sampling theory describes the effective events that promote learning. If a theory is sufficiently explicit and simple in its application to a given learning situation, then it allows one to develop a mathematical model to describe the changes in the subject's behavior over the course of the learning trials. A statistical learning model consists of assumptions about how the subject's probability of a correct response changes from trial to trial as a result of the outcomes she experiences on each trial. Given this representation of learning and performance as a trial sequence of response probabilities, then the theorist can predict any of a large number of descriptive statistics of the subject's data such as her total errors, her trial of last error (before an errorless performance run), and so on. Deriving predictions for such statistics from a statistical model consists only of mathematical work within the probability calculus, which itself has no psychological content or significance.

The variability in performance among different subjects can be treated in several ways. One way is to assume that the subjects really differ in learning rate and initial response tendencies, and so these aspects of the mathematical model are estimated and fit separately to each individual. A far more convenient approach is to assume that within a given experimental setting true individual differences are negligible, and that variability among different subjects is just that normally expected in different samples from a common sequence of probabilities. To illustrate, refer to Table 8.1 where we have generated four different sequences (hypothetical "subjects," one in each row). This was done by entering a random number table and deciding for each subject and each trial that the subject made a correct response if the next two-digit random number was less than the value of p on that trial. For example, on Trial 2, the value of p_2 is .60: the first random number encountered for that trial was 37, which is less than 60, so a C is entered for Subject 1 on Trial 2; the second random number was 83, the third 71, and the fourth 53, leading to decisions of E, E, and C responses for Subjects 2, 3, 4 on Trial 2. Hypothetical responses were similarly determined on Trials 3, 4, 5.

Inspection of the four subjects' sequences *suggests* large differences. Were we prone to jump to conclusions, we would say that Subjects 2 and 4 are fast learners, that Subject 1 is a slow learner, that Subject 3 seems to have caught on to the correct behavior suddenly after her initial poor beginning, and so on. Yet these are just superstitious *fictions* within us, the observers, because we know for a fact that these four subjects' responses were generated from the same underlying probabilities. (With more trials the variability between subjects appears even more extreme.) Thus, the assumption of common response probabilities

still generates much variability between samples ("subjects"). Therefore, one should not conclude that there are real individual differences here unless there are rather overwhelming differences. In practice, this fact has allowed the mathematical learning theorist to pool together the data from a group of homogeneous learners, assuming they are just different samples from a common underlying probability process; then the theorist tries to use the mathematical model to predict aspects of the pooled data. Of course, the model could be fitted to each subject's data separately, but that is much more work and considerably less impressive because so many unknown model parameters must be estimated.

With this as background on the stochastic approach to learning, let us now consider the substance of stimulus sampling theory.

BASIC ASSUMPTIONS OF STIMULUS SAMPLING THEORY

The Representation of the Stimulus Situation

As noted, SST is a formalization of Guthrie's approach to stimulus-response associationism. The stimulus situation is represented as a population of independently variable components or aspects of the total environment, called *stimulus elements*. At any moment on an experimental trial, only a sample of elements from the total population is active or effective. The less variable the experimental conditions, the less variable are the successive trial samples of stimulus elements.

Two sources of random variation in stimulation may be identified: the first arises from incidental changes in the environment during the experiment (extraneous noises, temperature fluctuations, stray odors, and so on); and the second arises from changes in the subject, either from changing orientation of her receptors (what she is looking at or listening to), from changes in her posture or response-produced stimuli, or from fluctuations in her sensory transmission system. When verbal stimuli are presented to human subjects, variability may occur due to different implicit associations or interpretations aroused by the material upon different occasions (see Bower, 1972d). There is no commitment to any fixed amount of such stimulus variability; that is to be estimated by the theory. Thus, in simple learning situations in which the experimenter is applying the same stimulus (say, the sound of a bell) at the onset of each trial, this is represented simply as a potential population of N stimulus elements.

On each trial, only a sample of the N elements will be active or effective. Figure 8.1 illustrates the drawing of a trial sample of stimulus elements. If we think of the stimulus elements as N marbles in an urn, various sampling schemes are possible, but two simple ones have been most widely employed in theoretical discussions. One scheme supposes that each stimulus ele-

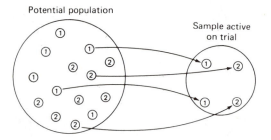

Potential population

Sample active on trial

Figure 8.1. Illustration of the process of drawing a random sample of stimulus elements (small circles) to be active on a given trial. The potential population contains 14 elements, and the sample contains 4 elements, so θ is 4/14, or .29. The 1 or 2 label on each element indicates whether it is associated with response A_1 or response A_2 at the start of this trial. In the population, the proportion of A_1-connected elements is 6/14 or .43.

ment has probability θ of being sampled, independently of how many other elements are sampled. According to this scheme, the number of elements in the sample will vary randomly from one trial to the next, with the average sample size consisting of $N\theta$ elements. The second scheme supposes that a fixed number of elements are drawn at random without replacement from the N elements of the population. If we let s represent the fixed sample size, then each element has an overall probability of s/N of appearing in the sample. The special models obtained when it is assumed that $s = 1$ are called pattern models. They have been much investigated, and will be reviewed later.

Response Connections and the State of the System

We have noted how the stimulus situation and trial sample are represented. To make contact with performance, the theory assumes that each stimulus element is conditioned to (connected to) one response. Response alternatives are denoted by subscripts like A_1 and A_2. In a two-choice experiment, for example, some elements would be connected to response alternative A_1 and some to the other alternative, A_2; in a free-operant situation, A_1 might be "pressing the lever" and A_2 would denote any behavior other than lever-pressing. It is supposed that the conditional connection between a single stimulus element and a response is unitary and at full strength, not varying in degree. According to this approach, we can characterize the subject's dispositions at any moment in our situation by listing the various stimulus elements and the relevant response currently associated with each element. Such a listing is the theoretical *state of the system* as it characterizes an individual at this time. Throughout the course of learning, the elements will be changing their associations for this subject; alternatively, we would say that the state of the system is changing trial by trial.

Since the probabilities of the various responses depend on the state of the system, we have to calculate the state of the system as trials progress. Can we find a useful way to represent the state of the system so that these calculations can be simplified? Indeed we can, and the reason for this is that the sampling schemes mentioned above assign an *equal* sampling probability to each element. Because of this assumption, we do not need to know *which* elements are associated with which responses in order to predict response probability. All we really need to know is *what proportion* of the stimulus elements are associated with each response. For example, in a two-response experiment, we could let p denote the proportion of elements associated with response A_1 and $1 - p$ denote the remaining proportion of elements associated with response A_2. In this case, our description of the state of the system reduces to the single number, p. And calculations of this single number are considerably easier to follow than would be calculations on the changing listing of associations for all the elements.

Performance and Reinforcement Rules

Performance on any trial is determined by the elements which are experienced, or "sampled," on that trial. The probability of any response is assumed to be equal to the proportion of sampled elements on that trial that are connected to that response. If a sample of size 10 contains 5 elements connected to A_1, 3 to A_2, and 2 to A_3, then the probabilities are 0.5, 0.3, and 0.2, respectively, that the response will be A_1, A_2, or A_3. If the number of elements is large so that the statistical law of large numbers applies, this performance rule has the effect of setting the probability of response A_1 equal to p, the proportion of

A_1-connected elements in the population. It is usually assumed that this is the case.

Having drawn a stimulus sample and responded, the subject then receives some reinforcing outcome. It is these outcomes that change the conditional connections of the elements sampled on a trial, thus altering the state of the system. In theory, if r response classes have been identified, then $r + 1$ theoretical reinforcing events are defined, denoted E_0, E_1, E_2, . . . , E_r. It is supposed that exactly one of these reinforcing events occurs at the termination of the trial. Events E_1, E_2, . . . , E_r refer to reinforcement of responses A_1, A_2, . . . , A_r, respectively, whereas E_0 denotes that none of the responses was reinforced. If a trial terminates with reinforcing event E_k, then all elements sampled on that trial become conditioned to response A_k if they were not already so conditioned. For example, if an element connected to A_1 is sampled on a trial when reinforcement E_2 occurs, then this element switches its conditional connection from A_1 to A_2 in an all-or-none manner. Finally, E_0 denotes a null event; occurrence of E_0 means that none of the responses was reinforced, so no change occurs in the conditioned connections of the sampled elements.

Let us comment on these conditioning assumptions. First, these axioms describe changes in the connections of stimulus elements over trials, and this is what learning is considered to be. By these rules, successive practice trials result in the attachment of the rewarded, or "correct," response to progressively more stimulus elements sampled from the population, occurring at the expense of detaching "error" responses from these same elements. The exact description of this process is given below. Conditioning of response A_1 is achieved at the expense of removing associations from alternative responses, and no special postulates regarding extinction are needed. Extinction is by interference in the sense that the probability of some reference response

A_2 declines while the likelihood of a competing response A_1 increases. Second, we note that following Guthrie, SST assumes all-or-none conditioning of the sampled elements to the reinforced response. Third, this representation of reinforcing events is theoretically neutral. For particular applications, one must take substantive assumptions about the relationships between the hypothetical reinforcing events and the actual trial outcomes—for example, food reward for a rat turning left in a T-maze, the unconditioned stimulus or its absence in classical conditioning, information about the correct answer in verbal learning, and so on.

Derivation of Basic Learning Equations

The state of the system, it will be recalled, is given by the fractions of stimulus elements conditioned to the various response alternatives. The assumptions of the theory permit us to derive how these proportions will change from trial to trial as a result of the reinforcing events. To simplify, imagine that we are dealing with a dog learning to salivate to a bell; salivation will therefore be our A_1 response and not salivating will be our A_2 response. The population of potential stimulus elements corresponding to the sounding of the bell (CS) is represented by analogy in Figure 8.2 as a bowl full of white (A_2) marbles. On Trial 1 with the bell, a sample of five stimulus elements occur, no salivation occurs to the bell; then the food US occurs, forcing salivation (A_1) to occur at the end of the trial, thus connecting the sampled elements to salivation. In our analogical model, we paint the five sampled "bell" marbles black to reflect their switchover to now being connected to salivation (A_1). These five A_1 conditioned (black) marbles are then returned to the bowl and mixed up with the white ones. On the second trial with the bell CS, a new random sam-

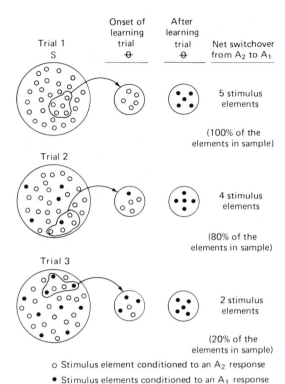

Figure 8.2. Estes's model of how stimulus elements change from the unconditioned state to the conditioned state. (From Hergenhahn, 1976.)

ple of five stimulus elements is drawn, consisting (by chance) of one black (A_1) and four white (A_2) marbles. The performance rule of the theory would say that the probability of a conditioned salivary response to the CS (bell) sample on this trial is one out of five, or .20. The food US is given at the end of the trial, resulting in the connecting of the sampled elements to the salivary response. The number of white marbles switched over to black at the end of Trial 2 is seen to be 4. The Trial-2 sample of marbles is returned to the larger bowl, and the marbles are all mixed up again in preparation for Trial 3. The CS sample on Trial 3 by chance has three A_1

and two A_2 elements, so the probability of a salivary CR to the bell is 3/5 or .60, and the US at the end of the trial results in conditioning (switching over) only two (white) elements to the A_1 response.

If we look at the number of A_1-connected elements in the total population at the beginning of each trial in Figure 8.2, it is 0, 5, and 9; for Trials 1, 2, and 3, and it will be 11 at the start of Trial 4. Since there are 32 elements in the CS population, this means that the proportion of A_1-connected elements at the beginning of the four trials are $p_1 = 0/32 = 0$, $p_2 = 5/32 = .16$, $p_3 = 9/32 = .28$, and $p_4 = 11/32 = .34$. While the total number of A_1-connected stimulus elements is increasing trial by trial, the size of the increase becomes less and less over trials. A learning curve which increases in large steps during the early training trials and then in progressively smaller steps over later trials is said to be *negatively accelerated*. Figure 8.3 below illustrates several such learning curves,

which start at $p_1 = .20$. Most empirical learning curves have this negatively accelerated shape to them.

The sampling and conditioning process depicted in Figure 8.2 can be described mathematically. Let p and $1 - p$ denote the proportions of elements connected to responses A_1 and A_2. Since these proportions will be changing over trials, we use a subscript to denote the trial number in question. Thus, p_n will denote the proportion of A_1-connected elements at the moment of evocation of the response on the nth trial. p_n may also be interpreted as (a) the probability that any randomly selected single element in the population is connected to A_1, and as (b) the probability that the response on trial n will be A_1.

Suppose that each trial ends with a reinforcement for response A_1; that is, an E_1 reinforcement terminates the trial. We wish to calculate p_{n+1}, the probability that an element is conditioned to A_1 at the beginning of the next trial, $n + 1$. Recalling

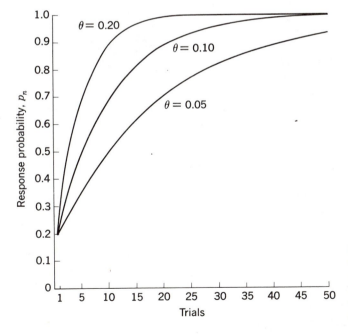

Figure 8.3. Graphs of the function p_n described by Equation 2, where $p_1 = 0.20$ and the learning rate, θ, has the values of 0.05, 0.10, and 0.20 for the three curves.

that θ is the probability that a stimulus element is sampled on any given trial, the learning equation may be written as follows:

$$p_{n+1} = (1 - \theta)p_n + \theta. \qquad (1)$$

This equation may be interpreted term by term: with probability $1 - \theta$ the element is not sampled, so its probability of being connected to A_1 remains the same as it was before, namely, p_n. The other possibility is that with probability θ the element is sampled, and the E_1 reinforcing event occurring on that trial conditions the element to A_1 with certainty.

Let us note a few mathematical facts about Equation 1. First, p_{n+1} will be greater than or equal to p_n, so an E_1 reinforcement increases the probability of an A_1 response. Second, p_{n+1} is a linear (straight line) function of p_n. From this fact comes the name *linear model,* in reference to a system of such equations. Third, an E_1 reinforcement increases p to an eventual limit (or asymptote) of unity. That is, when $p_n = 1$, then Equation 1 will give $p_{n+1} = 1$. If a consistent series of E_1 events were given, corresponding to repeated applications of Equation 1, p would increase from some initial value and approach an asymptote of unity. Thus, Equation 1 implies that consistent E_1 reinforcements would eventually lead to consistent occurrences of A_1 responses. If we wish to predict the learning curve, we simply trace out the trial-by-trial effect of applying Equation 1 to the initial value p_1 from which the process begins on Trial 1. To calculate p_n for a consistent sequence of E_1 events, we would repeatedly apply Equation 1. That is, p_2 is calculated from p_1 by Equation 1. Then p_3 is calculated from p_2 using Equation 1 again, and so on. The result of doing this is the following general expression:

$$p_n = 1 - (1 - p_1)(1 - \theta)^{n-1}. \qquad (2)$$

This expression gives p_n as a negatively accelerated function of the practice trial, n. The limit of p_n is 1, since the fraction $1 - \theta$ decreases to zero as it is raised to higher powers. Some graphs of this function are shown in Figure 8.3. For these curves, $p_1 = 0.20$ and θ is 0.05, 0.10, and 0.20 for the three curves. The curve rises faster for larger values of θ. Recall that θ is the probability that a stimulus element is sampled; when θ is low, there will be much trial-to-trial variability in the composition of the stimulus sample; when θ is high, most elements will always be present, so one sample will vary little from another. We see in Figure 8.3 how this stimulus variability affects the rate of learning. The retarding influence of increased stimulus variability upon learning was first noted by Pavlov (the phenomenon of external inhibition). Later experiments by Wolfle (1936), E. J. Green (1956), and Burke, Estes, and Hellyer (1954) give results interpretable in terms of θ variations.

Elimination of Interfering Responses and Extinction

Equation 1 describes the increase in the probability of an A_1 response on a trial when it is reinforced. But what is happening to the probability of an A_2 response as a result of this trial? Clearly the probability of an A_2 response will be going down, since the probabilities of the two responses must sum to one. (Due to the way the responses have been defined, one and only one can occur per experimental trial.) For example, if a reinforcement for a left turn in a T-maze increases a rat's probability of turning left (A_1), then it must reduce her probability of turning right (A_2) since on each trial she makes only one response. Stimulus sampling theory applies the same "choose one response" analysis to the CRs in Pavlovian and instrumental conditioning situations as well as to explicit choice situations.

Equation 1 implies a second equation which describes the decrease in the probability of an A_2 response due to an E_1 trial when the opposite (A_1) response is reinforced. Similarly, Equation 2 implies another equation describing the lessening probability of an A_2 response during a series of A_1 reinforced trials—namely:

$$p\ (A_2 \text{ on Trial } n) = 1 - p(A_1 \text{ on Trial } n)$$
$$= (1 - p_1)(1 - \theta)^{n-1} \quad (3)$$

According to Equation 3, the probability of an A_2 response starts at $1 - p_1$ on Trial 1, and declines to zero as practice with A_1 reinforcement continues. This occurs since $(1 - \theta)^{n-1}$ becomes smaller as n increases.

If, as observers, we had been concentrating on and recording A_2 behavior, we would note that A_1 training eliminates A_2 responses from the situation. This is the "interference" idea of Guthrie, adopted by Estes in SST: the connecting of one response to the stimulus elements of a situation occurs only by disconnecting all alternative responses to those elements. Thus, when we say we are "conditioning" response A_1 to a situation where it formerly did not occur, we could just as properly say that we are "extinguishing," or eliminating, all the other responses the organism makes to that same situation. Thus, Equation 3 can be thought of as an *extinction curve* for response A_2, and in fact empirical extinction curves (see Figure 3.2, p. 51) often have the shape described by Equation 2.

Recall that for a two-choice situation with responses A_1 and A_2, we defined E_1 as a reinforcement for A_1 and E_2 as a reinforcement for A_2. The effect of an E_1 reinforcement on the probability of an A_1 response was given in Equation 1. If we were to reinforce A_2 on a given trial, that would decrease the probability of an A_1 response by the following formula:

$$p_{n+1} = (1 - \theta)p_n + \theta \cdot 0 = (1 - \theta)p_n. \quad (4)$$

The stimulus sampling interpretation of Equation 4 is as follows: the probability that a stimulus element is connected to A_1 at the start of trial $n + 1$ is just the probability that it was connected to A_1 before trial n (p_n) times the probability that it was not sampled ($1 - \theta$) and conditioned to A_2 on trial n. An E_2 reinforcing event decreases p_n the way an E_1 reinforcing event decreases $1 - p_n$. If a series of E_2 reinforcers were to occur, then p_n would be reduced close to zero.

We may collect our critical equations as follows:

$$p_{n+1} = \begin{cases} (1 - \theta)p_n + \theta & \text{if } A_1 \text{ is reinforced on trial } n \\ \text{or} \\ (1 - \theta)p_n & \text{if } A_2 \text{ is reinforced on trial } n \end{cases}$$

These equations are the core of the *linear model*. We note that they are difference equations, expressing how a variable (p_n) changes its values from one discrete point in time (Trial n) to the next point in time (Trial $n + 1$).

APPLICATION OF SST TO SELECTED ISSUES

Response to Stimulus Compounds

One standard question is whether we can predict the probabilities of the various responses to a compound of several stimuli given knowledge of how the individual elements of the compound are connected to the responses. If one set of elements, denoted S_1, is connected to response A_1, and another set, denoted S_2, is connected to A_2, how are we to predict response probability to a compound or test pattern consisting of n_1 elements from S_1 and n_2 elements from S_2? The assumption of SST is that the response probabilities are determined by the proportions of stimulus elements in the sample connected to the various responses. In the test situation described above, the probability of response A_1 is expected to be $n_1/(n_1 + n_2)$, and of A_2, $n_2/(n_1 + n_2)$. Further, let S_3 be a third set of stimulus elements with a random one-half of the S_3 elements connected to A_1 and one-half of the elements connected to A_2. If the test compound consists of n_1 elements from S_1, n_2 from S_2, and n_3 from S_3, then the expected proportion of A_1 responses is

$$p = \frac{n_1 + \frac{1}{2}n_3}{n + n_2 + n_3}.$$

The $\frac{1}{2}n_3$ term in the numerator is the expected number of A_1-connected elements of the n_3 drawn from the S_3 stimulus set.

An experiment by Schoeffler (1954) provides a test of these predictions. The three sets of stimulus elements were identified as different sets of 8 small jewel lamps in a 24-lamp display in front of the subject. Subjects were first trained to move a switch in one direction (A_1) when elements of the S_1 set were presented, and to move it in the opposite direction (A_2) when elements of the S_2 set were presented. The S_3 lamps never were presented during this preliminary training, and the theory presupposes that these elements start off (and remain) randomly connected, half to A_1 and half to A_2. Following this preliminary training, subjects were tested for their response to different combinations of the S_1, S_2, and S_3 elements (lamps). During the test series, subjects were told to respond as they thought appropriate and there was no information feedback concerning the "correct" response.

The test combinations used and the results obtained are shown in Table 8.2 along with the predictions from three different combination rules. To illustrate how Table 8.2 is to be interpreted, consider the fifth test pattern (row 5) consisting of 8 bulbs of the S_1 set, 4 randomly selected bulbs of the S_2 set, and all 8 bulbs of the S_3 set. To this combination, the average rela-

tive frequency of response A_1 for the group of subjects was 0.62.

The column of predicted values labeled Averaging Rule uses the formula derived from SST above. For example, for Test 6 consisting of 8, 2, and 8 elements from S_1, S_2, and S_3, respectively, the predicted value is

$$p_5 = \frac{8 + \frac{1}{2} \cdot 8}{8 + 2 + 8} = \frac{12}{18} = 0.67.$$

This predicted value is identical with the 0.67 value observed. In fact, except for the second test pattern, the predictions of the averaging rule are uniformly close to the observed values.

The *neutral-elements rule,* an alternative suggested by LaBerge's work (1959), applies the averaging rule with the exception that S_3 elements are presumed to be neutral and to contribute to neither A_1 nor A_2. For instance, in Test 6, the neutral-elements hypothesis deletes the 8 S_3 elements and predicts $p = 8/(8 + 2) = 0.80$. From Table 8.2 it is seen that in Tests 5 through 8 where the two sets of predictions differ, the neutral-elements rule is consistently inferior to the averaging rule.

The last hypothesis, labeled Majority Rule in Table 8.2, assumes that the response is determined by whichever conditioned elements are in the majority in the sample. This rule, which at first thought seems plausible, is discredited by these data.

There are many other sets of data of this general type, in which the averaging rule is tested by its predictions about response proportions to novel combinations of conditioned stimuli. By and large, the averaging rule has fared quite well throughout these various tests, and it seems an excellent working assumption to handle these kinds of problems.

Some explanation is required of how SST interprets stimulus-compounding results in simple conditioning experiments

TABLE 8.2. **Proportions of A_1 responses, observed and predicted, to each of nine test patterns (rows). Composition of the test patterns is indicated by the column entries under S_1, S_2, S_3. See text for explanation of predictions. (From Schoeffler, 1954.)**

Test Pattern	No. of elements from			Observed $p(A_1)$	Predicted by		
	S_1	S_2	S_3		Aver. Rule	Neutral Elements	Majority Rule
1	8	8	0	.54	.50	.50	.50
2	8	4	0	.79	.67	.67	1.00
3	8	2	0	.81	.80	.80	1.00
4	4	2	0	.63	.67	.67	1.00
5	8	4	8	.62	.60	.67	1.00
6	8	2	8	.67	.67	.80	1.00
7	4	2	8	.54	.57	.67	1.00
8	8	0	8	.73	.75	1.00	1.00
9	8	8	8	.54	.50	.50	.50

where a single response like salivation or bar-pressing is recorded. In such experiments, the test combination of $S_1 + S_2$ usually produces a greater CR than does either stimulus alone. To handle this and other results of conditioning experiments, SST supposes that each conditioned stimulus always occurs together with a randomly variable set of background stimuli which are not conditioned to the CR. Therefore, the compound CS trial has a higher proportion of conditioned elements in the sample relative to the nonconditioned background elements $(n_1 + n_2/n_1 + n_2 + n_b)$ than does the single CS trial $(n_1/n_1 + n_b)$. Thus, the CR is expected to occur to the compound more than to the single S_1. Thus, by postulating nonconditioned background cues in those situations, this apparent "superadditivity" is consistent with Schoeffler's averaging rule.

Probability Learning

A considerable portion of the early experimental work in SST was carried out in the probability-learning situation. In its simplest arrangement, the task for the subject is to predict on each trial which one of two events is going to occur. After she has made her predictive response, the actual event is shown. An example experiment would have a subject predicting whether a left or right lamp will light on each trial; her prediction of left (A_1) or right (A_2) is followed by the experimenter turning on the left lamp (E_1) or right lamp (E_2). The common feature of these experiments is that the events occur in a random sequence, and there is usually no information available to help the subject predict perfectly which event will occur. The label *probability learning* describes this fact about the situation.

We let A_1 and A_2 denote the subject's two predictive responses and E_1 and E_2 the two events, E_i meaning that response A_i was correct on a given trial. When the subject is informed after her prediction that E_1 was the correct event, we assume that she ends the trial by rehearsing A_1; thus the E_1 (or E_2) event determines what was reinforced, and is independent of which predictive response was made. Note carefully that it does *not* matter whether the subject's predictive response is confirmed (or "rewarded") by the corresponding E outcome. Rather, conditioning depends only on the E event at the end of the trial, not its correspondence to the subject's predictive response.

Suppose that π denotes the probability that the reinforcing event E_1 occurs on Trial n, and $1 - \pi$ is the probability of an E_2 on Trial n. If an E_1 event occurs, p_n is assumed to increase; if an E_2 event occurs, p_n is assumed to decrease. The average change in the A_1 response probability is obtained by weighting the increase in Equation 1 by π (the likelihood of an E_1) and the decrease in Equation 4 by $1 - \pi$ (the likelihood of an E_2 event). This yields the following:

$$p_{n+1} = \pi[(1 - \theta)p_n + \theta] + (1 - \pi)[(1 - \theta)p_n]$$
$$= (1 - \theta)p_n + \theta\pi. \qquad (5)$$

Over many trials Equation 5 leads to the following learning curve:

$$p_n = \pi - (\pi - p_1)(1 - \theta)^{n-1}. \qquad (6)$$

This equation says that as training proceeds, the probability of the subject predicting an E_1 comes to match π, the objective probability of an E_1 event. That is, the $(1 - \theta)^{n-1}$ term goes to zero as n grows large, leaving $p_n = \pi$. A typical experiment might have trials of repeated races between two horses, Ned (A_1) and Jack (A_2), and the human subject tries to predict for each race which horse will win. If Ned wins, say, three-fourths of the races against Jack, then Equation 6 implies that subjects will eventually come to predict on three-fourths of the trials (races) that Ned will be the winner.

The matching of response probabilities to reinforcing event probabilities is not an obvious prediction. Moreover, it violates the economists' principle that people should always choose that option with the higher expected value, since that principle dictates 100 percent choice of the more frequently winning side. But probability matching falls out from the SST assumptions that reinforcing events E_1 and E_2 have symmetric effects on increasing p_n and $1 - p_n$.

This matching prediction has been tested many times and is usually found; moreover, the theory's predictions are fairly accurate regarding the shape of the learning curve. Experimenters have also investigated learning using many different means for scheduling the E_1 and E_2 reinforcing events. Just to illustrate the range, the probability of an E_1 event can be constant (as in Equation 6), or can vary over trials, can vary according to the response on Trial n or according to the response or reinforcing event that occurred a few trials back. No matter how the E_1/E_2 sequence is generated, the theory predicts, and one observes, probability-matching of the subject's eventual proportion of A_1 responses to her eventual proportion of E_1 reinforcing events.

Variants of Probability Learning

This probability-matching result has been pursued in a variety of ways. Binder and Feldman (1960), for example, have shown that the matching principle predicts response frequencies on tests with single stimulus components that in previous training had been parts of stimulus patterns. To illustrate, suppose we let a, b, and c represent three component stimuli. To the pattern ab we train response A_1; to the pattern cb we train response A_2. We unbalance the frequencies so that the ab pattern occurs, say, four times as frequently as the cb pattern. Binder and Feldman found that a later test to b alone resulted in approximately 80 percent A_1 responses and 20 percent A_2 responses.

This result may be interpreted in SST by noting that when the *b* element occurred (within the training patterns), four out of five times response A_1 was reinforced. Hence, the probability that *b* is connected to A_1 would come to match this 4/5 relative frequency of E_1 to E_2 reinforcements.

Another line of work investigates probability matching in elementary interaction situations involving two subjects at once. The two subjects work concurrently on probability learning tasks in lock-step trials. On each trial, each subject makes one of two responses and receives reinforcement for one of these. The new wrinkle is that the probabilities of the reinforcing events on each trial depend upon the response of both subjects on that trial. The reinforcement schedules for the two subjects are interactive in the sense that the probability of an E_1 event for subject *A* depends on subject *B*'s response as well as *A*'s. Special mathematical techniques are required to apply the model to such situations, since both *A*'s and *B*'s behaviors are changing over trials. When applied to a variety of such interactive conditions, the asymptotic predictions come quite close to the obtained data (see Suppes & Atkinson, 1960). As before, the prediction is that both subjects will eventually match their A_1 response frequency to their E_1 event frequency.

Several generalizations of the probability-learning experiment and theory have been investigated. In one procedure (Suppes et al., 1964), the subject's response and the reinforcing event vary over an entire continuum on which there are, in principle, an infinite number of response alternatives. In the task employed, the subject tries to predict where a spot of light will appear on the edge of a large circle before him. Suppes's generalization of the linear model to this situation appears to do a fairly good job of accounting for the mean response distributions. In a second variation (Suppes & Donio, 1967), discrete choice trials are eliminated. The situation is so arranged that the subject is always in either an A_1 or an A_2 "response state." For example, the subject might hold a toggle switch which he has to keep pushed to the left or the right side at all times. The subject is free to switch between response states at any time. The reinforcing events might be, for instance, left and right lamps which flash briefly at random intervals, with one point scored if the subject has his response switch on the same side as the lamp that flashes. In this situation, the primary dependent variable is the proportion of time the subject is in the A_1-response state. The setup, resembling a free-operant situation in many respects, has such independent variables as the time rate at which reinforcements are delivered and the proportion (π) of the reinforcements that are given on the A_1 side. The major prediction which has been confirmed is that the proportion of time that the subject spends in the A_1 state will converge asymptotically to π, the proportion of A_1 reinforcements, and this asymptote will be independent of the time rate at which E_1 or E_2 reinforcements are given.

A third variation of the standard probability learning task, studied by Neimark and Shuford (1959) and L. R. Beach and colleagues (1970), requires subjects to make trial-by-trial estimates of the probability that event E_1 either will occur on the next trial or has occurred over the past series of trials. Much like the average proportions of A_1 predictive responses, these probability estimates begin at around chance and then converge with continued practice to π, the true E_1-event probability. In further work, Reber and Millward (1968) showed that subjects could be brought rapidly to event-matching in their A_1 predictions by initially having them, rather than predict individual trials, merely *observe* a rapidly exposed series of E_1/E_2 events. What was important was simple exposure to the probabilistic information series rather than "rewards" and "punishments" for overt predictive responses.

Sequential Statistics

Our discussion shows that the model predicts the mean learning curve and the limiting value of the average response proportions as trials increase. Part of the power of learning models is that they permit us to predict much more than just these mean response curves. In principle, predictions may be derived for any feature of the data we care to examine.

An important source of information about the learning process is provided by *sequential statistics.* These gauge the extent to which a subject's response on trial $n + 1$ is influenced by his responses and/or reinforcing events on one or more prior trials. The immediate history of events for a subject on trials $n, n - 1$, and so on, has a large effect upon his response probability on trial $n + 1$. Sequential statistics enable us to examine these effects. For instance, we expect A_1 response probability to increase on the trial following an E_1 event, and decrease following an E_2 event.

Stimulus sampling theory can predict most one-trial dependencies observed in data. The discrepancies of the model's predictions from peoples' sequential choices appear when we examine response dependencies stretching over several trials. As one example, the model predicts that during a run of E_1 events the subject's probability of predicting E_1 should increase monotonically. But on the contrary, in early trials of an experiment the results often show the opposite pattern, with the human subject becoming increasingly likely to predict E_2 the longer has been the current run of E_1 events (and vice versa for E_2 runs). It is as though the subject believed that the E_1 run made an E_2 event increasingly due to occur in order to even out the series' proportions. This odd belief is called the *negative recency effect,* or the "gambler's fallacy," and it is indeed a firmly entrenched belief of most of us regarding real-world events.

A second set of discrepancies arises from the fact that subjects appear to be testing out hypotheses regarding the event series. That is, the typical subject has an implicit faith in the notion that the E_1/E_2 event series the experimenter is showing him has a systematic though complex pattern; hence, he constructs, tries out, and evaluates a series of hypotheses regarding local trial-by-trial regularities in the event series. Examples of such hypotheses would be the belief that the events are scheduled for double alternation (as in 22112211), or that only runs of a length of two or four identical events are being used (as in 111122112222). In a truly random reinforcement schedule, these beliefs in local regularity amount to little more than elaborate superstitions, though, for all that, they are nonetheless persistent. In Chapter 12, we consider a computer simulation model by Feldman (1961) which is designed to deal with this hypothesis-testing approach to the probability learning situation.

Do these discrepancies mean that the SST account of probability learning is fundamentally incorrect, as N. H. Anderson (1964) has argued? Some psychologists have thought so, and have tried to develop models for how people learn systematic sequences (see Myers, 1970; Vitz & Todd, 1967). An alternative theory proposed by Estes (1972a) is to identify the stimulus elements with memories or traces of the past sequence of outcomes and responses just before Trial n, and to suppose that these *sequence trace stimuli* can become conditioned in the standard manner to predictive responses. Thus, for example, in a series in which events alternate, the subject would associate the stimulus trace of an E_1 on the prior trial with making a current A_2 response, and the trace of a prior E_2 with a current A_1 response. This general approach has proven fruitful in accounting for many of the discrepancies between the standard SST model and sequential statistics observed in probability-learning experiments.

Spontaneous Recovery and Forgetting

The phenomena of spontaneous recovery and forgetting have been recognized for a long time. Pavlov was the first to report facts regarding spontaneous recovery (see Figure 3.2). Following experimental extinction of a conditioned response (CR), the CR showed some recovery if the dog was removed from the apparatus and allowed to rest in his home cage for a while before being returned to the experimental situation and tested. The CR had "spontaneously recovered" without any special reconditioning by the experimenter. Later studies have shown that the amount of recovery increases with the length of the rest interval between sessions. Pavlov and others have also performed experiments in which the CR is repeatedly extinguished over consecutive daily sessions. They report that the amount of recovery of the CR becomes progressively less as the extinction sessions proceed; eventually, the CR recovers not at all.

The salient facts about forgetting and spontaneous regression are markedly similar (see Ebbinghaus, 1885). The amount forgotten increases with time that has elapsed since the end of practice, and the amount of session-to-session forgetting becomes progressively less as daily practice on a task continues. Estes (1955a) pointed out the close relationship of spontaneous recovery and forgetting. The similarities of their functional laws are indeed apparent, as is shown below.

Estes (1955a) proposed to interpret spontaneous changes in response probabilities as due, to some extent at least, to random changes in the stimulating environment from one experimental session to the next. In our previous discussion of stimulus sampling theory, it was assumed that the stimulus population was fixed and that random samples from this population were effective from trial to trial. Estes proposed to expand this representation by assuming that at any given time only a portion of the total stimulus population is available for sampling, the remainder not being available at this point in time. Over time, different stimulus elements become effective or available for sampling, whereas previously available elements may become temporarily unavailable. The type of factors Estes presumably has in mind can be illustrated by day-to-day fluctuations in the temperature and humidity of the experimental room, changes in the subject's internal milieu, in his postural sets or attitudes, in the sensitivity of various receptors, and the like. Such fluctuations in subtle stimuli are practically beyond control. There need be no commitment in the theory regarding the magnitude of these changes; the amount of such change is to be estimated by inference from the change in behavior.

It is clear that if such random stimulus changes do occur, then they help account for spontaneous changes in response probabilities between experimental testing sessions. Regression or "forgetting" would occur if available elements conditioned to the response are replaced during a rest interval by elements, previously unavailable, which have not been connected to the response. Spontaneous recovery will occur if those elements to which the CR has been extinguished (by the end of an extinction session) are replaced by elements previously conditioned to the CR. These two schemes are illustrated in Figure 8.4, where are shown the "available" and "unavailable" sets of cues at the end of session n and beginning of session $n + 1$.

The top panel depicts the case producing forgetting. At the end of the acquisition session all the *available* stimulus elements have been conditioned to the CR

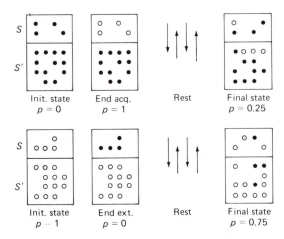

| Init. state
$p = 0$ | End acq.
$p = 1$ | Rest | Final state
$p = 0.25$ |

| Init. state
$p = 1$ | End ext.
$p = 0$ | Rest | Final state
$p = 0.75$ |

Figure 8.4. Hypothetical picture of stimulus fluctuation producing forgetting (top panel) or spontaneous recovery (bottom panel). The sets of available (S) and unavailable (S') elements are divided graphically into two boxes. Stimulus elements are represented as dots. Open dots indicate elements conditioned to some reference CR; solid dots indicate elements connected to incompatible behaviors. (From Estes, 1955a.)

(open dots) whereas none of the unavailable elements have been. Over a rest interval, the elements interchange progressively more between the two sets, resulting in a final state like that shown at the top right. This means that if the animal were to be retested at this interval, his probability of a CR would have dropped to about one-fourth, a case of clear forgetting. How much forgetting occurs depends on several factors, such as the extent of previous conditioning of the elements unavailable during this last training session. Several such forgetting curves are shown in the top panel of Figure 8.5, depicting less forgetting the more sessions of training one has had before the retention interval.

The bottom panel of Figure 8.5 depicts the converse case, of spontaneous recovery of an extinguished conditioned response. Here, assume that at the end of several acquisition sessions all stimulus elements have been sampled and conditioned to the

CR (open dots). An extinction session causes all available stimulus elements to lose their connections to the CR (or become connected to a response incompatible with the CR). Over a rest interval, the still-conditioned elements that were formerly unavailable now become available when a new testing session is given. In this case, the extinguished CR would recover from $p = 0$ at the end of extinction to a value of $p = \sqrt[3]{4} = .75$ at the delayed recovery test. The extent of recovery depends on the extent of conditioning of the unavailable elements at the end of the acquisition series. The bottom curves in Figure 8.5 show spontaneous recovery curves following a first, second, and third extinction session.

The hypothetical curves in Figure 8.5 are similar to those observed in experiments. The top panel demonstrates that the theory predicts less forgetting the greater the number of distributed retraining sessions. Similarly, the bottom panel shows the prediction of less recovery with more distributed extinction sessions.

We thus see that the fluctuation theory of stimulus change accounts for the usual shapes of forgetting and recovery curves, and for their progressive changes as retraining or extinction is continued. Estes (1955a, 1955b) uses the theory to interpret a number of other facts related to forgetting and distributed practice. In addition, Estes (1959a) has shown how the theory applies to experiments on forgetting involving retroactive and proactive interference. In terms of the model, the interference studies are not very different from the study of spontaneous recovery of a CR that has been conditioned and then extinguished (i.e., elements connected to a response differing from the first one learned). G. H. Bower (1967b) gives more explicit illustrations of how some findings of interference studies may be interpreted in these terms. The fluctuation theory has also been applied to experiments on verbal short-term memory (see Estes, 1971; Bower,

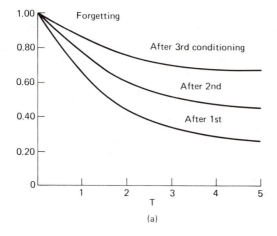

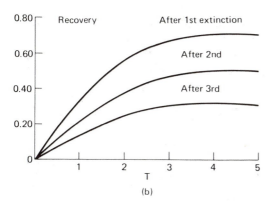

Figure 8.5. (a) Forgetting curves following 1, 2, or 3 conditioning sessions. The proportion of conditioned elements in the available set at the end of the conditioning session is unity, whereas conditioning of unavailable elements increases with training.

(b) Spontaneous recovery following 1, 2, or 3 extinction sessions. The proportion of conditioned elements in the available set at the end of the extinction session is zero, whereas level of conditioning within unavailable elements decreases with continued extinction. (From Estes, 1955a.)

1972d; L. R. Peterson, 1963), in which single verbal items are forgotten over brief intervals of several seconds filled with rehearsal-preventing, interpolated activities. In this case it is supposed that the verbal item is associated to "background contextual stimuli," which are progressively altered during an interpolation interval before the retention test for the single item (see Falkenberg, 1972). The primary results in short-term memory studies seem interpretable in terms of this fluctuation theory. In summary, then, the concept of random stimulus fluctuation has been a very fruitful hypothesis, considering how many and diverse are the kinds of phenomena that it explains.

Other Response Measures

As we have seen, the sole dependent variable of SST is response probability. But experimenters frequently describe their subject's performance in terms of other measures such as response latency (or speed), response rate, or response amplitude. Much as Hull did with his reaction potential construct, SST sets out to relate these other measures to its primary dependent variable, response probability. However, instead of simply postulating a particular relation between response probability and these other measures, the strategy in this case has been to derive this relationship by some hypothesis about how responses occur. By this means, it is possible to detach the assumptions about response properties from the remaining assumptions about learning and so test them separately.

Let us consider a very simple probability model for response latency. At the start of a trial, we present a signal, start a clock, and record the time elapsed before the subject performs some designated act. To be specific, suppose the act in question is getting a rat to run several steps down a straight alley (which has a food reward at the end) and interrupt a light beam outside the starting compartment. The latency measure is the time from the opening of the starting gate until the rat interrupts the light beam a few inches beyond the start-box. An elementary model of this process supposes that in each small unit of time (of length h seconds), the animal either performs the necessary act or does something else. We let p denote the probability that he performs the act in the next small unit of time if he has not already done so. The latency is then just the number of timed units of length h that pass before the act is performed. This is rather like the times you would have to flip a coin before it comes up heads. One can show that on the average, the response will occur in $1/p$ intervals, and so the average latency will be h/p.

This simple response model thus leads to an inverse relationship between average latency and response probability; as probability increases, latency decreases. In a learning experiment where we expect p_n to be changing over trials according to the learning function in Equation 2, the aver-

age latency L_n will decline over trials. The two right-hand panels of Figure 8.6 show two empirical curves that were fitted by this function. The bottom right curve is the average starting latency over trials of a group of rats learning to run down a runway for food reward. The top right is the average duration that rats held down a lever in a Skinner box when reward depended on pressing, then releasing, the lever.

The top left panel of Figure 8.6 gives the average rate of lever-pressing (in responses per minute) of the same group of rats working for consistent reward in a free-operant Skinner box. To interpret the free-operant situation in terms of the response model, assume that each response resets the clock to zero and that h/p is the average time until the next response. If

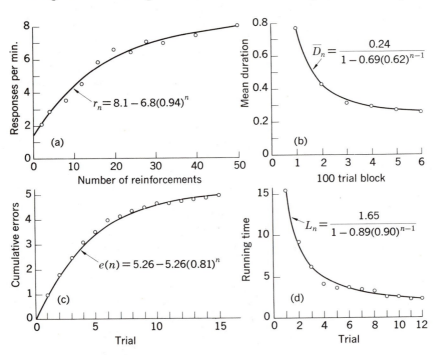

Figure 8.6. Four kinds of simple acquisition functions derived from statistical learning theory. Curves A, B, C, and D, respectively, represent rate of bar-pressing versus number of reinforcements, mean bar-press duration per 100-trial block, mean cumulative errors versus trials in T-maze learning, and median running time versus trials in a runway experiment. (From Estes, 1959a.)

the average time between responses is h/p, then the average *rate* of responding is the reciprocal, p/h. Given the theoretical equation for p_n as a function of the number of reinforcements n, the curve in the upper left panel may be fitted to the data.

We thus have seen how a probability theory can make contact with other measures of learned performance. Response amplitude, such as amount of a salivary CR, has not been specifically considered in the literature of SST, although a model that makes amplitude proportional to p_n is easy to devise. In this case, learning curves of CR amplitude would be expected to look like the response rate curve in the upper left panel of Figure 8.6. In another vein, Bower (1959, 1962a) has developed probability models to describe vicarious trial-and-error (VTE) behavior of subjects just before they make a choice. The role of this behavior in guiding the eventual choice was emphasized by Tolman (see Chapter 11).

Although the simple latency, or rate, models introduced above appear adequate for fitting mean response curves in simple acquisition, they are easily shown to be inadequate at a more detailed level of quantitative testing. For example, the elementary model implies that when p_n reaches unity, all responses occur in exactly time h, which is absurd. Moreover, the relative-frequency histogram of observed response times seldom has the shape implied by the simple model. Discussions by Bush and Mosteller (1955) and McGill (1963) show some of the detailed issues involved in predicting exact latency distributions. A fair amount of work in mathematical psychology is centered on the problem of predicting reaction-time distributions across a number of experimental conditions.

In the examples of verbal learning discussed so far, the retention measure has been response recall, and SST treats this case directly. However, an alternative retention measure is *recognition memory:* following exposure to a series of verbal items, such as words or nonsense syllables, the subject might be shown a long list of items, some old and some new, and be asked to check off the items she recognizes as having been presented in the study list. Memory is shown by the subject's ability to discriminate between old study items and new distractor items. Students will recognize this method as similar to true-false items on exams. Later in this chapter we discuss one way to interpret recognition memory for single items within SST.

Stimulus Generalization and Discrimination

No account of a learning theory is complete without at least brief mention of how it handles the issues of stimulus generalization and discrimination. Although there is an extensive literature on these topics in SST, we will merely indicate the outlines of the approach here.

SST conceives of stimulus generalization along the lines of the identical elements theory of Thorndike. A response associated with stimulus population S_1 will generalize to a test stimulus S_2 to the extent that the S_2 population shares common stimulus elements with the S_1 population. The situation for two stimuli is illustrated abstractly in terms of Venn diagrams, in Figure 8.7, where solid dots represent stimulus elements associated with a particular CR whereas open dots represent unconnected elements. The sets labeled S_1 and S_2 contain totals of 20 and 16 elements, respectively, and they share a set of 8 common elements (in the intersection subset marked I in Figure 8.7). The figure shows the state of the system following training on S_1 which has brought the performance of the CR to 75 percent. Assuming homogeneous mixing of the elements among all subsets of S_1, this means that about $8(.75) = 6$ elements of the intersection set I will be associated to the CR. When we then test for

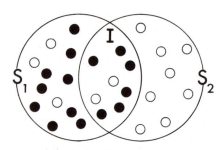

Figure 8.7. Illustration of two overlapping sets of stimulus elements. Solid dots represent elements associated to same reference CR. The index of stimulus generalization is provided by the proportion of elements that a given set shares with another.

generalization at S_2, the probability of the CR will be the proportion of conditioned elements (solid dots) in the entire S_2 set, which would be $6/(8 + 8) = .375$ in this example. The proportion of generalized CRs depends on the product of two factors: (1) the level of conditioning of the CR to the training stimulus, which level will be denoted as $p(S_1)$, and (2) the proportion of the S_2 (test) population of stimulus elements which it shares with S_1, which will be denoted here as s (s for similarity of S_2 to S_1). For the illustration above, $p(S_1) = .75$, $s = .50$, and so the CR probability to the generalized stimulus is $p(S_2) = sp(S_1) = (.75)(.50) = .375$, as illustrated numerically above. The similarity coefficients vary from zero (disjoint sets) to unity (complete overlap). But these coefficients are never observed directly; rather, they must be estimated from the ratio of the observed proportions $p(S_2)$ and $p(S_1)$, or by the ratio of *rates* of responding (see the earlier discussion relating free-operant rates to response probabilities). But once the $p(S_1)$ coefficient is estimated, it may be used to predict generalized responding for any conditioning level, $p(S_1)$, and be based on any kind of conditioned response.

This same set-theoretical analysis of the stimulus is used even when SST is dealing with simple one-dimensional stimuli like the loudness or pitch of a pure tone, the spatial position of a dot on a line, or any of hundreds of other quantitative as well as qualitative dimensions (see Atkinson & Estes, 1963; Carterette, 1961; LaBerge, 1961).

In simple *discrimination learning*, presentations of S_1 and S_2 occur in random alternation with, say, response A_1 reinforced to S_1, and either with A_1 not reinforced to S_2 or some other response A_2 reinforced to S_2. Assuming the usual laws of conditioning and extinction, inspection of Figure 8.7 suggests that the unique or distinctive elements of S_1 and S_2 will become readily associated to A_1 and to A_2, respectively. But problems arise with respect to the common elements in the intersection set, I. These common elements causing stimulus generalization also are responsible for failures to discriminate, making responding to S_1 a weighted mixture of the correctly conditioned unique elements and the "confusedly conditioned" intersection elements. In order to attain perfect performance according to such a model, the confusing common elements must be rendered nonfunctional (habituated or adapted out) by selective attention. This approach, dealing with selective attention to relevant cues, is exemplified in models proposed by Lovejoy (1968), Restle (1955), Sutherland and Mackintosh (1971), and Zeaman and House (1963). Selective attention to relevant cues is also the dominant theme in hypothesis-testing models of discrimination learning such as those of M. Levine (1970), Restle (1962), and Trabasso and Bower (1968). These will be discussed later in this chapter.

Motivation

Mention should be made of the conceptualization of motivation in SST. In an early, important statement, Estes (1958) attempted to handle the effect of drive level upon performance by assuming that deprivation (such as withholding water) causes certain intraorganismic sources of stimulation to become active (such as a dry mouth or stomach pangs); furthermore, the relative weight of these drive-stimuli in the total stimulus complex was assumed to increase with the duration of deprivation. By supposing that these internal drive-stimuli could themselves become associated to instrumental responses, Estes was able to account for many of the well-known facts relating motivation to performance. Also, the drive-stimulus approach has a natural way to handle findings regarding *drive discrimination,* in which an animal learns to respond discriminately depending on the type or intensity of drive level he is currently experiencing. The illustrations above have been of internal drives such as hunger and thirst, involving deprivation of food or water. But it is clear that the theory applies just as well, if not better, to externally induced "drives" from noxious stimulation such as electric shock, loud noises, bright lights, temperature extremes, and the like. These are clearly instances in which the drive-inducing operation con-

sists of increasing the intensity of a source of stimulation, which would be connected to some instrumental response. Estes's approach was to interpret the internal drives from deprivation in a fashion analogous to our intuitive interpretation of such external drives.

Responding to various deficiencies in this early formulation, Estes (1969b) proposed a second hypothesis regarding the role of internal drives in performance, and this was discussed earlier in Chapter 4. It is supposed that response evocation depends *jointly* upon input from discriminative stimuli and input ("facilitatory feedback") from a positive drive. Initially, the drive mechanism is activated only by a combination of internal conditions resulting from deprivation and an external unconditioned stimulus (e.g., taste of food). For example, the taste of food activates the drive mechanism (see panel *A* of Figure 8.8), which generates feedback elements that facilitate and maintain the consummatory behavior until the internal deprivation conditions have been materially altered. It is supposed that activation of this drive mechanism can be conditioned in the usual manner to external stimuli preceding the

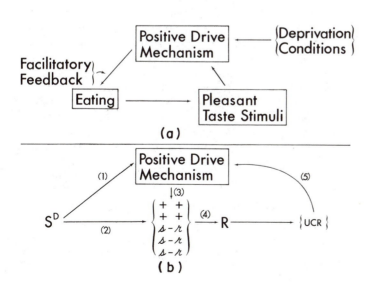

Figure 8.8. Illustration of facilitatory feedback from positive drive amplifier elements. Panel *A* shows how internal deprivation conditions and unconditioned taste stimuli combine jointly to activate the positive drive mechanism, which provides feedback to maintain eating. Panel *B* illustrates the situation in instrumental conditioning after the discriminative stimulus has become associated both to responses and to activation of the positive drive mechanism.

unconditioned response (which innately activates the drive mechanism). Thus, in the learning of instrumental appetitive responses, the discriminative stimulus (S^D in panel *B* of Figure 8.8) becomes associated not only to the reinforced response (link labeled 2 in Figure 8.8) but also to activation of the positive drive mechanism (link 1). This provides facilitatory input via link 3 (symbolized as $+ +$ in panel *B*), which summates with the association of the stimulus elements to the instrumental response, thus evoking the response (link 4). Due to the reinforcement contingencies, this response produces the reinforcer (say, food), which elicits consummatory behavior, which in turn activates the positive drive mechanism again (link 5); this further conditions the drive activation to the external stimuli of the reinforcing environment (strengthening link 1). Estes (1969b) makes further assumptions regarding noxious stimuli and their negative drive mechanisms, and how these determine escape and avoidance learning. It is also assumed that the negative and positive drive mechanisms exert mutually inhibitory influences on one another. In this way, Estes explains the phenomenon of *conditioned suppression* wherein a stimulus that evokes fear (due to its past association with pain) will suppress responding for appetitive rewards (see Chapter 7).

As noted in Chapter 4, this theory of drive, its conditioning and its joint facilitation of S-R associations in generating performance, is remarkably like the Hullian theory of *incentive motivation,* in which anticipation of reward (by means of r_g) to discriminative stimuli is presumed to generate excitement which feeds in to facilitate or invigorate ongoing instrumental responses. What the Estes theory does (as did· Sheffield's [1954], before that) is to eliminate the separate status of the drive (*D*) and incentive motivation (*K*) constructs in Hull's theory. Also, the assumption of reciprocal inhibition between positive and negative drive centers carries matters a step further.

SMALL-ELEMENT MODELS

As we have seen, the earlier versions of SST represented the experimental situation as a very large set of *N* stimulus elements, only a sample of which affect the subject on any one trial. With a large population of stimulus elements, the assumption of all-or-none conditioning of the sampled elements leads to gradual change in the proportion of the population elements connected to the response.

A classic paper by Estes (1959b) showed that rather different learning models follow from SST if one supposes that the number of stimulus elements (representing a situation) is small, say, one or two. It turned out that in many experiments these *small-element models* fit the data more closely than did the large-element model discussed previously. In his theoretical paper, Estes proposed changing a few crucial assumptions. First, he assumed that exactly one random stimulus element of the few available is sampled on a given trial. The sampled stimulus element is best thought of as the total configuration or pattern of stimulation effective on a trial. Second, at the outset of training the stimulus patterns will probably be in a neutral state, not conditioned to any experimental response. If such a neutral pattern is sampled, it will produce only random guesses among the response alternatives. Third, reinforcement is assumed to produce conditioning on only some of the trials and not on others. Specifically, the reinforcing event on a given trial is assumed to cause either (1) complete, all-or-none conditioning of the sampled pattern (an event having probability *c*), or .(2) failure of any conditioning on that trial, so that a sampled neutral pattern remains neutral at the end of the trial (an event having probability $1 - c$). In small-element models, c is going to play somewhat the same role as θ did in the large-element models.

Let us note how these assumptions apply in a specific case. In fact, let us go to the radical extreme of assuming just *one* possible stimulus element to see what happens. To be concrete, suppose that a given Pavlovian eyeblink conditioning situation were to be represented by a single stimulus pattern which is sampled on every trial, and this pattern begins in a neutral state, not conditioned to the eyeblink. This means that the initial probability of a CR here will be zero. During the early trials of conditioning, the CS produces no conditioned responses but the occurrence of the airpuff (the unconditioned stimulus) at the end of the trial may result in conditioning of the CR to the stimulus pattern. With probability c the reinforcement is effective in causing conditioning on any given trial, whereas with probability $1 - c$ it fails to cause any conditioning. For a single subject, on some one trial the conditioning "takes"—that is, the US results in conditioning of the single stimulus pattern to the CR. Hence, on the very next trial that subject's CR probability jumps to $p = 1.0$, since by assumption the single stimulus

pattern for the situation is always sampled and it is now conditioned. The learning curve for a single subject, then, would look like one of those step functions in Figure 8.9, jumping from $p = 0$ up to $p = 1$ in one trial. Since the US continues to occur after the CR, it is assumed that the subject will stay conditioned (at $p = 1.0$) and so will continue to give CRs.

The model assumes that the trial of effective conditioning for different subjects is given by a random waiting time; with probability c, conditioning occurs with the very first trial of the US; with probability $(1 - c)c$, it fails to occur on the first but then occurs on the second trial, and so forth. Again, the process is like flipping a coin until the first Head shows up, with the probability of Heads equal to c. Such a process implies that the cumulative probability that conditioning has occurred by trial n increases with trials.

Suppose that we pooled together the data from a large number of subjects, and also pooled data over blocks of trials. Then the *group average* learning curve would appear smooth like that in Figure 8.10. But we realize this group average learning curve is misleading, and is an artifact of pooling together many individual step

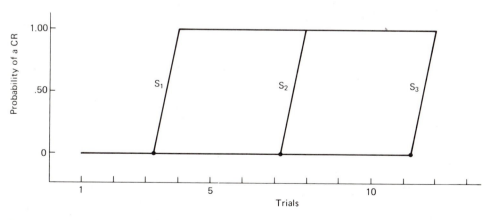

Figure 8.9. Illustration of step-function learning curves for three different subjects who differ on their trial of learning.

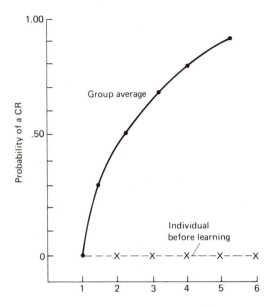

Figure 8.10. Illustration of learning curve for individuals before their point of effective conditioning (lower horizontal line) compared to group average proportion of conditioned responses which pools individuals who have learned the association with those who have not yet learned it.

functions like those in Figure 8.9. The contrast is shown vividly in Figure 8.10 where we compare the group average curve to that for individuals over trials before they were successfully conditioned. The reason the group average rises smoothly is that as training continues, progressively more subjects have been conditioned, and thus contribute their $p = 1$ rather than $p = 0$ to the group average.

A remarkable fact is that the group average learning curve predicted by the one-element model is identical to that predicted by the linear model and the large-element model of SST. The models differ in that the linear model and the large-element model assume that each individual subject has a gradually increasing learning curve whereas the one-element model says that each subject will exhibit a step func-

tion and that the smooth curve arises only from averaging across subjects. The difference between the models can be tested by appropriate analyses of the data. If the one-element model is appropriate, and if the subject ends training always giving a conditioned response (i.e., $p = 1$), then we should find no improvement in her performance before the trial of her last error (or failure to give a CR). This failure to improve prior to the last error is called *response stationarity;* it is expected because the subject begins in a nonconditioned (neutral) state, and the fact of an error on some later trial means that she has not yet left that nonconditioned state by that trial (otherwise, she would not make an error). A number of experiments were analyzed in this manner by Suppes and Ginsberg (1963) and Bower and Theios (1964), and many of these show the expected step functions. In many respects, this is the strongest evidence for the conclusion that the one-element model fits a given set of data.

Fitting the One-Element Model to the Data

The allure of small-element models is that they are mathematically simple, and it is therefore possible to derive a large number of predictions from them for a single set of experimental results. The predictions are often impressively accurate. To illustrate the range of successful predictions that are possible, let us apply the one-element model to an unpublished experiment by G. H. Bower on an elementary paired-associates learning task. Thirty college students learned a list of 20 pairs in which the stimulus member of the pair was a Greek letter and the response was the digit 1 or 2. Response 1 was assigned to 10 of the 20 stimuli selected at random. The 20-item list was gone through repeatedly in random order, using the method of anticipation until each subject gave three consecutive perfect recitations of the whole list of associates.

To represent this task in the model, we consider the stimulus member of each pair as a single pattern that is always sampled when that stimulus is presented. The pattern is considered to be in one of two states: either connected to the correct response, or prior to that, in a guessing state wherein the probability of a correct response is $p = 0.50$ (recall there are two responses). On each trial, following the subject's response with probability c the feedback information is effective in conditioning the correct response to the stimulus pattern if it is not already so conditioned; with probability $1 - c$ the reinforcement is ineffective and the state of the stimulus pattern remains as it was at the start of the trial. Items begin in the guessing state on trial 1 and stay there until their reinforcement is effective; once that happens, they remain conditioned so that the subject will respond correctly thereafter.

This model is to be applied to the trial-by-trial sequence of correct responses and errors that a subject gives to a particular stimulus item. With 30 subjects each learning 20 items, there are 600 such subject-item sequences of data. In principle, the theory could be applied by estimating a value of c for each of these 600 sequences.

However, to reduce computational labor, we will assume that all sequences reflect the same value of c. Proceeding on this assumption, it is found that a good estimate of c is 0.20. This means that, on the average, $1/c = 5.00$ reinforcements were required before an item was learned.

The observed and predicted results will be compared by means of two graphs and a table of statistics. First, Figure 8.11 shows the mean proportion of correct responses over successive practice trials. The initial trial is a pure guess, and the success rate starts at the a priori value of 0.5. Figure 8.12 is a histogram of the relative frequency of the total errors per subject-item sequence before learning. It shows, for example, that 17.3 percent (104 cases) of the 600 total sequences had zero errors, 25.0 percent (150 cases) had exactly one error, 18.2 percent (109 cases) had exactly two errors, and so on. Following the initial increase between zero and one errors, the predicted distribution follows an exponential decline for the proportions of sequences having more and more errors. Predictions for the distribution of the trial of the first correct response, and trial of the last error are similarly close to the data. Table 8.3 gives a summary of various pre-

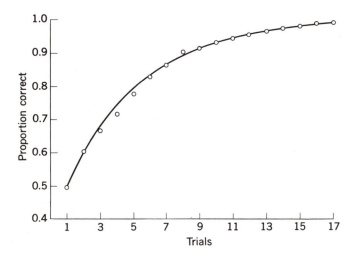

Figure 8.11. Observed and predicted mean proportions of correct responses over trials. Predictions derived from the one-element model. (Data from G. H. Bower, unpublished.)

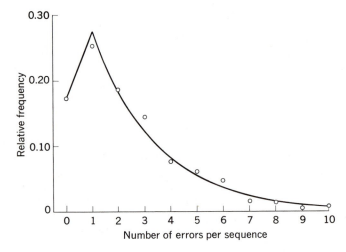

Figure 8.12. Probability distribution of the number of errors per subject-item sequence before learning. (Data from G. H. Bower, unpublished.)

TABLE 8.3. **Mean values of various statistics for the paired-associate experiment. The standard deviations refer to the statistic listed on the line above. Statistics presented are averages per subject-item sequence.**

Statistic	Observed	Predicted
Total errors	2.50	2.50
Standard deviation	2.34	2.50
Trial of first correct	1.92	1.84
Standard deviation	1.20	1.12
Trial of last error	4.18	4.17
Standard deviation	4.06	4.50
Prob. of error after an error	0.42	0.40
Total runs of errors	1.44	1.47
Runs of one error	0.85	0.87
Runs of two errors	0.33	0.35
Runs of three errors	0.13	0.15
Runs of four errors	0.08	0.06
No. pairs of errors:		
one trial apart	1.06	1.03
two trials apart	0.85	0.82
three trials apart	0.65	0.65
four trials apart	0.51	0.51

dictions of the model. The last ten entries refer to sequential statistics. To explain two examples, a run of exactly two errors is counted once whenever a trial sequence of the form ". . . CEEC . . ." is encountered in a subject-item protocol. A pair of errors three trials apart (i.e., on trials n and $n + 3$) is counted once whenever a trial sequence of the form ". . . EXXE . . ." occurs where the Xs may be correct or error responses.

The derivation of the theoretical predictions for such statistics is simple but lengthy and would serve no useful purpose here (see Atkinson et al., 1965; or G. H. Bower, 1961a). Though a variety of other statistics of the data could be calculated and predicted, the sample provided is sufficient to illustrate the accuracy of the model in this instance. Comparison of the observed and predicted values reveals that the model is astonishingly accurate. In fact, the fit of the theory in this case is probably as close as psychologists can ever expect to get in studies of learning. This is the more impressive because only one parameter c had to be estimated from the data before the predictions could start.

The close degree of correspondence between the obtained data and the predictions of a specific model as we have illustrated it above is nice to have, but more generality of a model across experiments is demanded. Similar accurate fits of the one-element model to paired-associates data have been reported in several publications (Bower, 1961a, 1962b; L. Keller et al., 1965; Kintsch, 1964; Suppes & Ginsberg, 1962). In addition, analyses of response times in several experiments have shown results in line with this model; that is, (a) no differences in speeds of correct and incorrect responses, and relative constancy of these, over trials prior to the last error on an item, and (b) abrupt increases in speed of the correct response after the trial of the last error. These results are consonant with the assumption of a guessing

state before conditioning occurs on or soon after the trial of the last error in a subject-item sequence.

In related work, Restle (1962) and Bower and Trabasso (1964) have used a slightly modified version of the model to account for an elementary form of learning to identify concepts in a discrimination task. In that work, the subject was assumed to be testing out various hypotheses regarding the solution to the problem. The "guessing" state corresponds to the subject's testing out irrelevant (incorrect) hypotheses, and the "conditioned" state corresponds to the subject's using the correct hypothesis for classifying the stimuli. This research area was extensively cultivated with mathematical models (see Trabasso & Bower, 1968) and a second generation of better models appeared. Papers by Chumbley (1969), Falmagne (1970), and M. Levine (1970) use the basic hypothesis-testing theory, but suppose that the subject gradually learns to reject hypotheses that have been tried and discarded, although he may forget that a given hypothesis was rejected some time ago. The correct hypothesis becomes increasingly likely to be selected because incorrect hypotheses are being increasingly eliminated as training proceeds. Developments in models of concept identification have become quite compatible with the information-processing approach to cognition (see Gregg & Simon, 1967), an approach to be discussed in Chapter 12.

The results confirming the one-element model in paired-associate learning have in common the fact that only two response alternatives are involved. Somewhat similar confirmatory results have been found in the case of recognition memory in which the subject says whether or not he has seen a particular stimulus (e.g., nonsense syllable) before in the preceding series (e.g., Bernbach, 1965; Kintsch & Morris, 1964; Olson, 1969). It is understood, of course, that paired-associate learning can be a complex tangle of processes involving stimulus discrimination, response learning, associative mediators, strategic guessing, and the like; and to the extent that these arise in the experiment, the strict one-element model will be violated.

Stages of All-or-None Processes

A fruitful approach to developing models for more complex learning situations was enunciated by Restle (1964a). He proposed that complex learning tasks could be analyzed into stages of components (parts), and suggested that we think of each stage of learning as an all-or-none process. This is in the spirit of Guthrie's earlier proposal. The stages of learning differ according to the content of the specific task being learned. In paired-associate learning, for example, one stage might consist of learning the response term as a unit, another stage might arise from confusion (generalization) errors between several stimuli in the list of pairs being learned. The latter stage would be overcome when the correct response became associated to a discriminating feature of the stimulus.

Other examples of multistate models have been proposed to deal with the relation between backward and forward associations in paired associations, the relation between recall and recognition of paired associates, the learning of emotional and instrumental responses in avoidance conditioning, the learning of one or both stimulus dimensions in two-dimensional concept formation, and so on.

As pointed out before, in these applications a given learning task is conceived to involve several stages, with each stage being a unit of learning which supposedly the subject acquires in an all-or-nothing fashion. When the simple all-or-none (one-element) process is used to describe each state, then the multiprocess model conjoins end-to-end several all-or-none processes. The all-or-none process is used as a basic building block. The conjunction of several

all-or-none processes yields a model which, in its gross properties, resembles a "continuous improvement" notion of learning. However, in comparison with the continuous linear model discussed earlier, the stage models generally are favored in respect to both their accuracy of fitting data and the relative ease with which theoretical derivations can be carried through.

This strategy of using all-or-none building blocks seems to have been fairly successful and fruitful. A number of models of this kind seem to operate effectively. The question of validity always centers around the cogency and sharpness with which a theory identifies the various subparts of the task with their associated parameters, and how convincing the data are in supporting the proposed partitioning into subtasks. In some cases, at least, specially designed experiments or data analyses can produce strong evidence favoring the task analysis proposed by a particular model (see G. H. Bower & Theios, 1964; Restle, 1964a; Trabasso & Bower, 1964).

RECENT DEVELOPMENTS

The field of mathematical learning theory has developed and expanded along many lines, infiltrating many branches of theoretical work in learning theory. It is impossible to review or summarize these extensive developments here. To a large extent, Estes has changed in a direction closer to cognitive psychology and away from his Guthrian S-R beginnings. This is shown, for example, in his recent views of how rewards operate to guide learning. His theory was discussed in Chapter 4, where it was assumed that organisms form associations among internal representations of events, such as stimulus-to-reward associations. For Estes, these interevent associations need not rest on stimulus-response connections. We noted earlier how this view enabled him to explain results which created difficulties for the view that reinforcers are satisfiers that serve only to strengthen S-R connections. One extension of Estes's ideas about reward has been to deal more explicitly with decision-making by subjects in preferential choice situations. This has led to what is called the scanning model, which will be described next.

The Scanning Model for Decision-Making

Hitherto we have been describing the subject as though her responses were simply a matter of stimulus-response connections. In many cases, this seems to be a serviceable approach to analyzing behavior. However, there are clearly other instances in which circumstances conspire to induce the subject to make a more deliberative choice. Such circumstances are typically arranged in studies of decision-making, and they are easily mimicked in the learning laboratory in studies of preferential choice. In the typical preferential choice experiment, the subject may be repeatedly offered a choice between two alternatives, A_1 and A_2 (or, more typically, a set of different pairs), each associated with a different rewarding outcome or set of outcomes. The subject's asymptotic choices reflect her particular "preference ordering" among the two or more rewards being compared. With N response-outcome alternatives, there are $N(N + 1)/2$ pairs that can be presented for choice, each varying in left-to-right orientation. Stimulus sampling theory now has a problem: it has to decide how to represent the stimulus situation to which the subject is responding on each trial. One alternative is to suppose that each of the $N(N + 1)$ different arrangements of choice stimuli is a distinct pattern and that the subject acquires $N(N + 1)$ distinct habits to respond left or right, each associated with its distinct arrangement. But that representation seems unparsimonious, if not silly. The preferred alternative is to suppose that each stimulus alternative represents a set of stimuli to which "approach" responses are connected. Then presentation of stimuli j and k for preferential choice corresponds to presentation of an analyzable compound, $S_j + S_k$. The scanning model presumes to describe the way in which the subject considers the alternatives and decides upon one of them.

As indicated earlier, Estes's approach to this situation treats the rewarding outcomes as informational stimuli, the representations of which can become associated with prior stimuli or responses that are temporally correlated with these reward magnitudes. For example, in a verbal discrimination task in which choice of nonsense syllable A_1 is followed by receipt of 5 points whereas choice of syllable A_2 (with which A_1 is compared) is followed by receipt of 3 points, the theory supposes that the person learns the response-to-payoff associations A_1-5 and A_2-3. This learning could be indexed by the person's ability to verbally predict or anticipate the points or value of each alternative response.

Given this knowledge of the payoffs, the subject is presumed to decide between A_1 and A_2 in three substages within a single, deliberative choice trial. First, she rapidly *scans* over the available responses A_1 and A_2, considering each in turn, and for each response she generates a prediction of the rewarding outcome ("points") to be obtained were that response to be chosen on this trial. Following this, she temporarily stores this predicted outcome. Second, she quickly *compares* the value or utility of the outcomes so predicted by the scanning process. Finally, she *chooses* that response with the highest predicted value. These sets of assumptions are the core of what Estes (1962, 1976) calls the *scanning model*. Thus, in the choice comparing A_1-5 points with A_2-3 points, the subject will eventually always choose the A_1 side once she has acquired the response-reward associations. The only cases where perfect preference will fail to be achieved are those in which the sensory *discrimination* between the rewarding outcomes is imperfect (e.g., a rat probably cannot reliably discriminate 5.02 grams of wet mash from 5.05 grams) or in which the outcomes themselves are complex "commodity bundles" or composite packages of many subcomponents about which evaluations fluctuate. Humans, of course, increase the discriminability of different quantities of reward by counting behavior, which produces a very discriminable stimulus (e.g., the words "eleven" vs. "twelve" pennies).

Consider the case in which the outcomes following each choice are probabilistic. To be concrete, let us suppose that the person is confronted with the choice situation diagrammed in Figure 8.13. Choice of alternative A_1 is followed by a win of $w\phi$ on a random proportion π_1 of the trials, whereas it is followed by loss of $x\phi$ on the remaining $1 - \pi_1$ proportion of the trials. Similarly, choice of A_2 wins $y\phi$ with probability π_2 and loses $z\phi$ with probability $1 - \pi_2$. If the subject begins from total ignorance, then we may presume that through repeated experiences she gradually learns the outcomes which can follow each response and she also learns the probabilities π_1 and π_2. That is, this situation really has two smaller "probability learning" tasks contained within it—namely, learning the different outcome probabilities following A_1 choices, and, independently, learning the outcome probabilities following A_2 choices. We may suppose that both of these component learning processes are described by something like the small-element pattern models described earlier.

Given this learning background, how ought the subject to choose? The scanning model attempts to predict this asymptotic choice probability from knowledge simply of the objective probabilities π_1 and π_2, and the payoffs w, x, y, z, all of which are under the experimenter's control. Let us consider a few special cases of how the scanning model operates. First, if every outcome that follows A_1 is favored over every outcome that follows A_2, then A_1 will obviously be the asymptotically dominant choice. Second, consider the symmetric case in which the wins and losses for the two alternatives are equal (i.e., $w = y$ and $x = z$) and their payoff probabilities differ. Asymptotically, the events within each choice trial go as follows: the subject generates a predicted win or loss for A_1 and similarly for A_2. This produces the four possible prediction pairs shown in Table 8.4. In the row of each prediction pair is also written the expected probability of that pair (based on the assumption of asymptotic probability matching of the two components), and the indicated decision given that predicted pair of outcomes for this trial. The decision rule is to choose the unique winner if there is one; if a tie occurs, the person should rescan her mem-

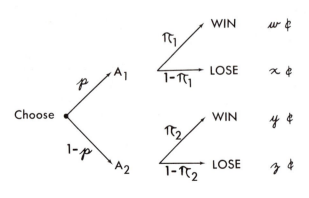

Figure 8.13. Illustration of a choice situation with probabilistic payoffs and penalties.

TABLE 8.4. Possible prediction pairs for winning $w¢$ or losing $x¢$, their joint probabilities asymptotically, and the decision in the four cases.

Row	Predicted Outcome for This Trial A_1	A_2	Probability of This Prediction Pair		Decision
1.	Win w	Win w	π_1	π_2	(Rescan)
2.	Win w	Lose x	π_1	$(1 - \pi_2)$	A_1
3.	Lose x	Win w	$(1 - \pi_1)$	π_2	A_2
4.	Lose x	Lose x	$(1 - \pi_1)$	$(1 - \pi_2)$	(Rescan)

ory, making a new independent pair of predictions for the two outcomes, and continue this until she generates a unique winner. This amounts to supposing that the subject continues scanning until she lands eventually in row 2 or row 3 of Table 8.4. Therefore, the expected asymptotic probability that she will choose A_1 will just be the likelihood of the row 2 prediction pair divided by the sum of the row 2 and row 3 probabilities:

$$P(A_1) = \frac{\pi_1(1 - \pi_2)}{\pi_1(1 - \pi_2) + \pi_2(1 - \pi_1)}. \quad (7)$$

Table 8.5 shows some predictions compared to observed proportions of A_1 responses in experiments by Atkinson (1962), by Siegel (1961), and by Friedman, Gelfand, and Padilla (1964). In each experiment, subjects received 200 to 400 trials on a two-choice probability learning task, with a 5¢ payoff for each correct prediction and a 5¢ penalty (loss) for each incorrect prediction (Friedman, Padilla, & Gelfand used only "points"). Different groups in each experiment corresponded to different values of π_1 and π_2 as shown in Table 8.5. The predictions are obtained a priori by simply substituting the values of π_1 and π_2 into Equation 7. Note that the asymptotic

response probabilities in the Siegel experiment (as in groups 3 and 5 in Friedman, Padilla, & Gelfand) exceed probability matching, which is a frequent finding when symmetric payoffs are used. The fit of the model's predictions are quite good in all cases.

The cases reviewed suggest the usefulness of the scanning model in predicting asymptotic choice probabilities in uniform ("riskless") situations as well as in probabilistic schedules with symmetric payoffs and losses. In further experiments involving multiple alternatives, such as pairing A_1 versus A_2 and A_3 versus A_4, but presented with differing frequencies, Estes (1976) found that subjects were also sensitive to the sheer frequency of winning for each alternative over trials, not to its *relative* frequency of winning per opportunity. Estes was able to fit a number of choice results assuming that the subject primarily scanned her memory of winning events, so that choices were biased toward the more frequently winning option.

In any event, we may conclude that the scanning model provides a viable approach to a process theory of decision-making. It has been used successfully for predicting individual behavior of animals and humans in situations ranging from paired as-

TABLE 8.5. Asymptotic probabilities of A_1 responses, observed and predicted in twelve conditions studied by Atkinson (1962), by Siegel (1961), and by Friedman, Padilla, and Gelfand (1964).

Exp.	Group	π_1	π_2	$P(A_1)$ Observed	$P(A_1)$ Predicted
Atkinson	1	.60	.50	.60	.60
	2	.70	.50	.69	.70
	3	.80	.50	.83	.80
Siegel	1	.75	.25	.93	.90
	2	.70	.30	.85	.85
	3	.65	.35	.75	.77
Friedman, Padilla, and Gelfand	1	.80	.80	.47	.50
	2	.80	.50	.81	.80
	3	.80	.20	.94	.94
	4	.50	.50	.48	.50
	5	.50	.20	.82	.80
	6	.20	.20	.47	.50

sociates to probability learning. It has been applied with success to two-person games in which payoffs depend on the joint actions of the two players (see Estes, 1962). It has been shown to follow logically from an earlier model for the VTE behavior of a subject at a choice point (see Audley, 1960; G. H. Bower, 1959). All in all, the basic notions contained in the scanning model have proved to be exceedingly simple, elegant, and powerful in bringing orderliness into a range of data regarding choice behavior.

Recognition Memory and Statistical Decision Theory

Bower (1972d) extended stimulus sampling theory to account for results on item-recognition memory. In the basic experiment, the human subject is given a series of verbal items to study (e.g., XQH, VQX, MHT) and is later tested for his ability to discriminate from memory whether or not certain test items were shown. Thus, pre-sented with XQH, the subject should say, "Yes, Old," and with VQH he should say "No, New." Measures of recognition memory are indices of discriminative accuracy, of the subject's ability both to say "Old" to old (studied) items and "New" to novel distractors. In such recognition-memory experiments, several factors are known to improve memory—the amount of study given to the items, a short retention interval, meaningful words as materials, and the dissimilarity of the novel distractors from old presented items. Other factors are known to increase the subject's *response bias*, his tendency to guess Yes when in doubt about a test item; these factors include the percentage of old items in the test series, the payoffs for identifying Olds versus News, and the penalties for missing Olds versus News. A usable model of the subject's decisions in recognition memory is *statistical decision theory* (also known as *signal detection theory*) (see Green & Swets, 1966), but unfortunately it has no foundation as a theory of learning.

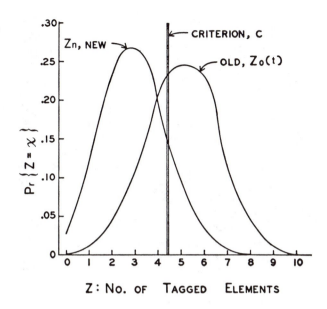

Figure 8.14. Probability distributions of sampled elements associated to a list-context tag for new and old test items. (From Bower, 1972d.)

Bower showed how stimulus sampling theory would imply a model for recognition memory that was practically like signal detection theory. One first assumes that presentation of a given experimental item like VQX gives rise to a sample of internal stimulus elements which become associated at that moment to the experimental context (call this a *context tag*). As time passes, when we re-present the same old item (VQX), the new sample of stimulus elements will overlap progressively less with the former sample that had been associated to the context tag. The overlap, in fact, can be described by Estes's fluctuation model set forth earlier. For any fixed retention interval and study condition, there will be some probability distribution of the number of elements in the test sample (from an Old item) with an association to the context tag. Such a distribution is shown to the right in Figure 8.14 for a sample of size 10 and overlap of .50 of the first and second examples from an old item. The other distribution, marked New in Figure 8.14, is the average probability that a sample activated by a novel distrac-

tor (e.g., VQH) will have certain numbers of context-associated elements. These are context associations to elements of a novel pattern acquired because this distractor overlaps (shares elements) with several patterns that were in fact presented earlier.

Suppose a test item gives rise to exactly three stimulus elements with context tags: Is it an Old or a New stimulus? Examining Figure 8.14, one sees that the likelihood is higher that such a sample comes from a New rather than an Old item, so one should decide "New distractor" in this case. Suppose, on the other hand, that the test item gave rise to a sample containing six elements with context tags; then Figure 8.14 says that "Old" is the more optimal response.

These cases exemplify a decision rule, which is this: set a criterion C and decide Old whenever the number of tagged elements in the test sample exceeds C, and decide New otherwise. With this decision rule, the proportion of Old decisions to Old items is the total area of the Old distribution above the criterion point; the proportion of Old decisions to New items (so-called *false positives*) is the area of the New distribution above the criterion. The criterion *C* is a response-bias factor that can be set by the subject to adjust his overall guessing style: if he sets *C* at a high value, say *C* = 9 in Figure 8.14, he will reject all New items but will do so at the expense of missing (failing to recognize) many Old items; if he sets *C* at a low value, say *C* = 2, he will say Old to most Old items but at the expense of falsely saying Old to many New distractors.

Each choice of a criterion *C* yields a certain percentage of Old decisions to Old items and, at the same time, to New items. As we vary the criterion, these two quantities vary together, and trace out a curve like one of those in Figure 8.15. These curves plot the probability of an Old judgment to an Old item (hits) against the probability of an Old judgment to a New item (false positives). The curves increase smoothly from the origin to the point (1,

1). These curves are called *memory-operating characteristics,* and they are routinely observed in recognition-memory studies when conditions influence the subject's setting of his response criterion at different places. A simple method to do this is to vary (with the subject's knowledge) the proportion of Old to New items across different test blocks. The greater the percentage of Old to New test items, the lower the subject should set his criterion, so as to accept more dubious test items as Old (because that is a rational bet).

Such variation in testing procedures will yield radically different percentages of Old recognitions (hits) and false positives. Yet, one would not want to claim that such procedures affect memory for Old items, nor do they affect the subject's discrimination of Old versus New items; rather, the theory alleges that such test procedures affect only where the subject sets his decision criterion *C*. Thus, all pairs of points (of hits vs. false positives) that fall along a given operating characteristic are said to exhibit the same discrimination of Old versus New items (or memory), differing only in whether the subject is adopting a high or low criterion. In these terms, the subject's amount of memory for an Old item depends on the distance between the average of the Old distribution and the New distribution in Figure 8.14. A large average distance would occur at a short retention interval, after a high degree of item learning, or when the New distractors are quite dissimilar and overlap very little with the Old items. A large average distance between the two distributions also leads to a higher hit rate and lower false-positive rate, which are considered to be standard indications of good memory discrimination. Figure 8.15 shows a family of curves calculated for the case where the average scaled distance between the Old and New distributions is decreasing (from 2.46 down to .38) as the retention interval increases.

The reason for going through these deri-

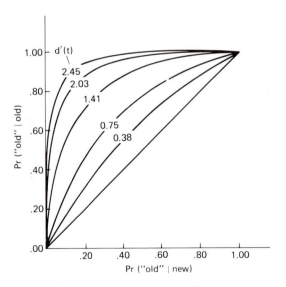

Figure 8.15. Memory-operating characteristics for differing values of memory discrimination, measured by *d'* at retention interval *t*. (From Bower, 1972d.)

vations is that the statistical decision theory appears to be the favored analysis of recognition memory at present. It is supported by many empirical studies and has helped interrelate Yes-No recognition indices, familiarity ratings, and multiple-choice tests of recognition memory (see Bower, 1972d for a review). Bower showed how the decision theory ideas could be cast within the framework of stimulus sampling theory, and extended these ideas to explain results on list discrimination, and judgments about the temporal recency of experimental events. Significantly, in order to derive the statistical decision theory, only the *response axiom* of SST had to be modified. Rather than setting the probability of an Old decision equal to the proportion of sampled elements with context tags, the assumption was altered so that the number of tagged elements in the sample had to exceed an adjustable criterion in order to produce an Old decision. It is characteristic that several interesting extensions and applications of SST have been achieved by slightly altering one or another assumption of the theory.

Estes's Hierarchical Associations Theory

The behavioristic view of learning is response oriented: what the organism learns is how to respond in specific stimulus situations. Estes (1972b, 1973) has recently shifted to an alternative memory-oriented viewpoint. Estes proposes that organisms store and retrieve memories of sequences of events (stimuli or responses), and that these memories can be manifested in many ways, not just by some specific conditioned response. Estes proposed a specific form for representing information about events in the organism's memory—namely, by the use of *control elements*. A control element is like a neural cell in memory that stands for the conjunction of two or more subunits; a control element represents a grouping or chunking of two or more other

memory elements by the perceptual coding system. Such chunk units were already introduced in Chapter 6. Control elements can enter into associations with other units in order to build up complex associative structures. The idea of a hierarchy of chunks is easily illustrated; the letters *t, o, d, a, y* are individual units with corresponding memory-control elements (indicating, for example, how to recognize and write each letter); similarly, the letter groups *t o* and *d a y* form memory-control units (for words); and finally, the grouping *today* has a corresponding memory-control element. The diagram in Figure 8.16 illustrates the several levels of groupings (control elements) in the hierarchy. If you think of each line between elements in Figure 8.16 as an association, you have most of what Estes intends with his associative hierarchies. Associative hierarchies such as those in Figure 8.16 have been discussed in the literature on human serial learning for some time (e.g., Johnson, 1970), ever since the idea of chunking was introduced by G. A. Miller (1956). The novel feature of Estes's use of the concept of chunking was to give it an explicit associative interpretation, and then use it to reformulate and explain some basic phenomena of conditioning (as well as human serial learning).

Figure 8.17 illustrates the associative

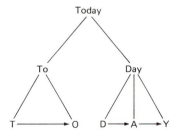

Figure 8.16. Illustration of a chunked memory structure representing a person's memory of the word pattern, TODAY.

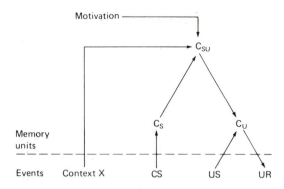

Figure 8.17. Illustration of Estes's theory of how the CS, the experimental context, and a motivational source combine into an associative configuration to excite the US-UR unit, leading to an anticipatory CR.

structure Estes supposes is established in a simple classical conditioning situation, where a CS is paired with a US in a specific experimental context (e.g., in a specific lab room). The symbol C_U stands for the control element representing the unconditioned stimulus (US) and the unconditioned response (UR) made to it; the top level control element C_{SU} represents the events of the CS being followed by the US in context X and (possibly) with the presence of some motivational source facilitating the activation. The basic idea is that the links in this associative structure pass along excitation to one another, causing units receiving excitation to fire. Thus, when the CS occurs in a context similar to X, the two sources of excitation along with a motivational source summate at the unit C_{SU}, which causes that excitation to be transmitted down the associative pathway to the control element, C_U. Arousal of element C_U is sufficient to cause a fraction of the UR to occur in anticipation of the unconditioned stimulus. If some one of these sources of input to C_{SU} is absent, then the activation may not suffice to elicit the response.

If an extinction series follows acquisi-

tion of CS-US, then the new event sequence is CS-no US (denoted $\overline{U}$), and so the organism sets out to establish that associative structure. He does so by setting up the inhibitory connection shown in Figure 8.18 between $C_{\overline{U}}$ and C_U. This develops simply due to the occurrence of a new event (namely, no US) at a time and place where formerly a different event (the US) was expected. Now, when the CS plus context activates the top level control element and excitation spreads to C_U and $C_{\overline{U}}$, the latter inhibits the former and so only $C_{\overline{U}}$ passes excitation to its subunits, resulting in behavior incompatible with the former UR and CR.

Estes (1973) applied this associative theory to several other phenomena of conditioning such as second-order conditioning and sensory preconditioning; but the theory has not yet been tested in detail against a range of data from classical and operant conditioning experiments. Estes has developed it mainly as a model for serial-order learning with humans. But one appeal of the hierarchical association model is that it attempts to treat conditioning phenomena using learning concepts derived mainly from research on human memory.

As mentioned, Estes (1976b) developed his theory largely to deal with serial learning. In the prototypic case the sub-

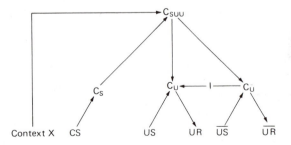

Figure 8.18. The associative structure Estes supposes is set up to reflect inhibition of a former CR as a result of extinction.

ject might be exposed quickly to six grouped letters (e.g., *VT/XS/BZ*), then be distracted by counting for a few seconds, then try to recall the letters in serial order. Ignoring the phonetic composition of the letters' names, we can see that Figure 8.19 depicts a memory structure established by the subject upon seeing and pronouncing the letters to himself. The top node, or control element, labelled LIST, divides into the three groups, and each group divides into its pair of letters. Estes assumes further that each letter unit, when stimulated, sets up a persisting *reverberatory loop of activation*, so that the hypothetical subject would be repeating something like "Vee, Vee, Vee" to himself, but also cycling a bit later with "Tee, Tee, Tee." This reverberatory loop of activation is for Estes what others have called short-term memory. If the six letters' reverberatory cycles fire off in perfect timing, then the memory system will experience just repeated cycles of *VT XS BZ, VT XS BZ,* and so on. But if there should occur any random perturbation in the timing of the reverberatory cycles for the individual letters, then two or more letters may switch their temporal order in this short-term loop. Switches of letters by one position are more likely than switches of two or three positions. As time passes, the migration of a letter's position

in memory increases. Because of the grouping of the letters into three segments with control elements, elements within a group are more likely to switch positions than are elements across a group. Whereas this reverberatory loop idea was adopted by Estes in order to reflect short-term memory for order information, representation of serial order in long-term memory requires associations between the elements at a given level (see *Today* in Figure 8.16).

These predictions and many others about serial-order memory have been confirmed in a series of experiments by Estes (1972b) and Lee and Estes (1977). The model has been particularly successful at predicting the gradients of positional confusion errors in ordered recall. In this theory, a subject will forget and *omit* a letter in recall if its phonetic subfeatures (not shown below the letters in Figure 8.19) become intermixed (by perturbations in the reverberatory process) with subfeatures of an adjacent letter. Such intermixing would create nonsensical (unrecognizable) phonetic jumbles, so no response would be given at that position in recalling the series. Thus, failure to recall an item would stem from mixing up the order of item subfeatures. This model also explains the fact that serial errors will be especially likely with phonetically confusable letters. Thus, a string of sound-alike letters such as *VTBDZC* produces many more order errors than will different-sounding letters such as *VXAGLI*.

A point in favor of Estes's model for order learning is that it has survived a number of detailed tests. For our purposes here, it represents a model for human learning which has also been extended to deal with conditioning. The sense of Estes's hierarchies of control elements is very much the same as the *duplex ideas* of British associationism, and the *higher-order memory nodes* of a theory proposed by Anderson and Bower in their book *Human associative memory* (1973). In fact, Ander-

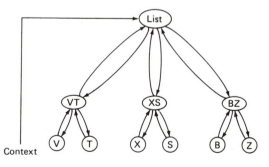

Figure 8.19. Memory structure Estes assumes to represent a serial list of six letters segregated into three perceptual groups.

son and Bower propose a specific *propositional interpretation* for their associational structures. They came to their views while trying to represent and explain what people remember from reading sets of factual assertions; but they noted how their associative networks were compatible with those of Estes's hierarchical theory. Both of these developments bring associationism into closer contact with topics central to modern cognitive psychology.

CONCLUDING COMMENTS

We have traced only a few lines of development in the evolution of stimulus sampling theory, emphasizing its Guthrian beginnings and its more recent liberalization in Estes's hands. Stimulus sampling theory has been the dominant approach within mathematical learning theories. We will note how mathematical theorizing has expanded and diffused throughout learning theory, and then conclude with a few comments on Estes's latest directions.

Range of Applicability of Mathematical Learning Models

Starting from a modest beginning in 1950, mathematical learning theories have been applied to an increasingly broader range of experiments. The specific ideas may vary from one application to another, but a common method of theory construction runs throughout. The range of behavioral phenomena investigated by these methods includes the traditional provinces of learning theory plus a few newly opened territories. We will list a sample of situations or phenomena for which mathematical models have been formulated and tested: classical conditioning, operant conditioning, stimulus generalization, mediated generalization, discrimination learning, partial reinforcement and extinction, rote serial learning, paired-associate learning, free verbal recall, short-term or immediate memory, attitude change, impression formation, concept identification of simple and complex sorts, probability learning, recognition memory, signal detection and recognition in psychophysics, imitation learning, avoidance conditioning, VTE and latency in choice situations, memory-search tasks, stimulus-compounding, correlated reinforcement and interresponse time distributions, paired-comparison choices, information integration, parametric investigations of drive, CS intensity, CS-US interval, and variations in reinforcement in conditioning situations, two-person interaction games, reaction time, spontaneous recovery and forgetting, retroactive interference experiments, and so forth. This list is representative but hardly exhaustive. Practically every domain of learning research has been infiltrated to some degree by quantitative theorizing.

The depth of the various applications differs considerably, some consisting only of a model for a single experiment, some amounting to a major line of continuing research. Some applications are of the quasi-quantitative variety in which it is shown that derivations from some general assumptions account for the major qualitative trends observed. Frequently a mathematical model simply leads to a reworking of data derived from some classical experimental situation, or leads to investigations of slight alterations of the standard situations. In its better moments, this reexamination of a familiar situation in terms of a mathematical model can bring to light new regularities in the data that had never before been suspected. For example, data analyses guided by the small-element learning models have shown the existence of performance plateaus or step functions in situations where it was previously thought learning was a continuous and gradual improvement in performance.

Mathematical learning models have been applied to resolve optimality questions about educational programs (see Atkinson & Paulson, 1972; Crothers, 1965; Restle, 1964b; Smallwood, 1962, 1971). The types of questions investigated include (1) how best to allocate study time to different independent materials in order to maximize the total amount the student learns in a fixed time; (2) the optimal rate for a teacher to present materials in a course in which understanding the nth unit requires that the student have learned the first $n - 1$ units; and (3) the best way in which to divide a large group of students into smaller tutorial classes so as to minimize the total cost (in teachers' plus students' time) of teaching particular material. When such problems are clearly formulated (often with simplifying conditions), a learning model can be used to calculate the value of different programs, and thereby tell us which programs teachers should use if they wish to optimize certain goals.

Mathematical modeling is a method or technique for formulating substantive theories, not a theory in its own right. In general terms, it is fair to say that mathematical models have guided psychologists into more intensive analyses of learning data. The models have shown us the rich information that can be gathered from learning data by carrying out more refined analyses. They have also demonstrated that valuable understanding sometimes arises from suitably sensitive comparisons of several well-formulated theories on data derived from very elementary experiments.

A wholesome side effect of the work in mathematical models has been the realization that such theories *can* yield predictions of data of an accuracy that is on a par with the accuracy of the best physical theories. The many instances now available demonstrate that numerical accuracy of a learning theory is possible in a restricted domain. Such demonstrations are important in helping us to establish realistic standards for our theories.

The ideas of stimulus sampling theory

are still current, although they are not a dominating force. Most of the early work in SST was done within the response-oriented approach to learning, which today seems to have lost popularity to the event-memory view of learning. Estes himself has shifted orientation in this regard. The contrast is shown, for example, in Estes's early treatment of probability learning as response conditioning (Estes & Straughan, 1954) versus his later treatment (Estes, 1976) of it as storage of event frequencies and their later retrieval and comparison ("scanning") in guiding decisions. Similarly, although it was Estes's initial paper that inspired the small-element learning models within SST and the notion of discrete stages of learning acquired in all-or-nothing steps, most of the later theoretical work has used different theoretical rationales to justify the particular multistage model under investigation. Often these theories are couched in terms of information-processing concepts. A possible reason for the decline in popularity of probabilistic learning models is that they show their descriptive power primarily by fitting data from multitrial experiments. But if one is more interested in the internal processes that mediate the effect of particular kinds of experiences upon memory, a single-trial memory experiment is often the most efficient way to collect relevant data. Here experimental (often verbal) materials are encoded once under one or another arrangement, and the subject is later cued for her memory of those materials. Such one-trial memory experiments simply do not provide the kind of data for which mathematical learning theories could show their best features.

What is perhaps remarkable is how easy it is to translate ideas from the abstract terms of stimulus sampling theory into other theoretical idioms, such as those of memory or information processing. Estes himself has been especially adept at showing how many of his ideas can be cast in terms of sensory memory concepts, with subjects conceived to store and retrieve information about events and their features, with learning occurring at several different levels. As another example, Bower (1972d) showed how notions of encoding variability could be translated into SST, and how SST easily led to statistical decision theory as a way to explain item-recognition memory, recency judgments, and the like. The availability of such translations suggests that the basic ideas of stimulus variability, of time fluctuation of stimulation, and of event associations are viable concepts necessary for explaining certain phenomena, regardless of whichever theoretical vocabulary is used for their formulation.

Although stimulus sampling theory has relatively few adherents as a total theory today, the basic ideas of the theory have been assimilated into a common stock of useful theoretical constructs. Estes, his colleagues, and sympathizers continue to carry forth significant contemporary work using these ideas to interpret phenomena of perception, simple and complex learning, and decision-making. Stimulus sampling theory is probably the most significant and consistently rational attempt at a global quantitative learning theory that we have ever had. The creation, development, and continual transformation of these ideas has been largely inspired by one man, William Estes, and his colleagues. The influence and impact he has had on this generation of learning psychologists is immense, and stands as testimony to the genius of the man himself.

SUPPLEMENTARY READINGS

Elementary introductory textbooks that introduce quantitative descriptions of basic psychological concepts are:

GREENO, J. G. (1968). *Elementary theoretical psychology.*

RESTLE, F. (1971). *Mathematical models in psychology: An introduction.*

More advanced textbooks are the following, with the first providing the most material on learning:

ATKINSON, R. C., BOWER, G. H., & CROTHERS, E. J. (1965). *Introduction to mathematical learning theory.*

COOMBS, C. H., DAWES, R. M., & TVERSKY, A. (1970). *Mathematical psychology: An elementary introduction.*

RESTLE, F., & GREENO, J. G. (1970). *Introduction to mathematical psychology.*

A text that stresses mathematical techniques of derivation with several classes of models is:

LEVINE, G., & BURKE, C. J. (1972). *Mathematical model techniques for learning theories.*

A collection of readings pertinent to the development of stimulus sampling theory is:

NEIMARK, E. D., & ESTES, W. K., eds. (1967). *Stimulus sampling theory.*

The standard compendium of authoritative articles is the three-volume work (with associated volumes of readings):

LUCE, R. D., BUSH, R. R., & GALANTER, E., eds. (1963, 1965). *Handbook of mathematical psychology.* Vols. I, II, III.

9

RECENT DEVELOPMENTS IN
BEHAVIORAL THEORIES

Research on the learning process continues at an accelerating pace, and has expanded in a number of directions. Several thousand psychologists and scientists in related fields are doing research that can be roughly classified as investigations of learning. It is next to impossible to cover the full range of phenomena under investigation. Indeed, this chapter merely touches upon a selected sample of recent developments. In some respects, research on learning has become more applied, with the development of related behavioral technologies as one consequence. For example, a number of psychologists are engaged in applying learning principles to the acquisition of language, to educational programs for teaching children various intellectual skills, to the modification of undesirable thoughts and behaviors of psychoneurotic patients and of problem children in classroom settings, to the efficient training of complex skills for military or industrial personnel, and to schoolroom behavioral management and the training of retarded children in simple skills. At the end of this chapter, we will review a few of these applications of behavior modification tech-

niques to problems of personal adjustment, academic skills, and job-related motivation. Chapter 15 discusses some of the work on programmed instruction, an important area of behavioral technology. Such behavioral engineering has immediate practical goals, and while not irrelevant to theory, it can be carried on without becoming distracted by unresolved theoretical issues. The value of learning research lies in its development of techniques of behavioral control, in the general frame of reference it provides and the concepts to be used in analysis, and, finally, in the factual knowledge obtained as the product of particular investigations.

The main trend in nonapplied ("pure") research in learning has been away from the large, comprehensive theories of the 1930s and 1940s toward the deeper experimental and theoretical analyses of the salient phenomena of learning. There has been intensive investigation of particular experimental tasks and paradigms which tap some kind of learning ability, with the consequence that the empirical mapping of many phenomena is now quite thorough. Many theoretical developments have stemmed from correcting earlier theoretical misconstructions, and from an increase in the definiteness, clarity, and precision of theoretical explanation.

In this chapter we will review a few of the prominent lines of recent research and theorizing in learning from the behaviorist point of view. The major conceptual division within research on learning lies between the behavioristic and the cognitive approaches. The prototype of the former research is a study of lower animals learning a simple response in a simple experimental arrangement for a biological reward, the experimenter describing the model subject and the results in terms of the stimulus-response-reinforcement concepts of modern behaviorism. The prototype of the latter, cognitive research, is a study of college sophomores reading a narrative story for comprehension, and later reconstructing its gist, with the experimenter describing the model subject and results in terms of cognitive information-processing concepts, semantic networks, reconstructive strategies, and the like. The student should understand there is wide variation in topics and subjects investigated within the behavioral and cognitive areas. This chapter reviews some new work in the behavioral tradition, although some applied work with human subjects will be very much in evidence here. Chapter 13 will review recent research in cognitive-organizational theories after the historical traditions have been discussed in Chapters 10, 11, and 12. Chapter 13 will review mainly recent trends in human learning research. There are increasing efforts to build bridges between theories in the behaviorist and cognitive areas (Anderson & Bower, 1973; Bandura, 1977a; Staats, 1964, 1975), and indeed some of the more fascinating work of the present and future promises to lie in this direction.

The first three-quarters of this chapter deals primarily with "animal conditioning" and reviews new work on operant conditioning of autonomic responses, new ideas about habituation and sensory preconditioning, changing conceptions of reinforcement and nonreinforcement, and new developments concerning selectivity of stimuli and responses in learning. The last quarter of the chapter reviews a few uses of behavioral-conditioning principles in psychotherapy, personal adjustment, and job settings. The treatment of these major topics must necessarily be brief and selective, but it should provide some perspective on modern developments in learning theory.

ELEMENTARY CONDITIONING PROCESSES

Voluntary Control of Involuntary Responses

One of the oldest distinctions in philosophical psychology is that between voluntary and involuntary responses: voluntary responses are those that we consciously will and control; involuntary ones are those that occur unconsciously, automatically, without our willing. Innate reflexes—the breathing of air, the pumping of the heart, the blinking of the eye to an air puff, the wetting of dry food in the mouth by saliva, the digestive processes set in motion by food in the intestines—these and a host of other responses are involuntary and unwilled. It is just as well that such routine processes are carried on automatically outside of conscious awareness. Their automaticity is in fact an enormous convenience, since our attention can then be disengaged from seeing that all these matters are taken care of. Volitional behavior, on the other hand, is that which is conscious, is willed and purposive, is an expression of one's intentions. It also uses up our attention or processing capacity.

Understandably, behavioral psychologists have been opposed to assigning conscious volitions and intentions to their animal subjects; and with animal subjects, the notion of volitional control could not be identified with the subject's verbal descriptions of his acts and their motives. Instead, the voluntary-involuntary distinction has become translated in behavioral psychology into a distinction between two distinct "response systems," each presumed to be learned and governed according to two different principles of learning. This is the distinction, explicated clearly by Skinner (see Chapter 7), between operant and respondent behavior, and their corresponding laws of conditioning. Operant responses involve the large skeletal muscles, innervated by the central nervous system, which are used to operate instrumentally upon the environment. Respondents are typically innate reflexes that involve smooth muscles of the glands or viscera, that are innervated by the autonomic nervous system, and are often involved in maintaining the homeostasis or equilibrium of the internal vital processes. Skinner and others proposed that such respondents could be learned *only* by the law of classical (Pavlovian) conditioning, by pairing the neutral stimulus to be conditioned with an adequate stimulus for eliciting the reflex; operant responses, on the other hand, could be learned *only* by the law of operant (reward) conditioning, by making some reinforcement contingent upon occurrence of the response to be conditioned. Although voices were often raised against this two-factor theory, the fact is that it maintained a position of prominence within learning theory for 30 years or so.

Within two-factor theory, there was a way to explain how a person could acquire "voluntary" control over a bit of respondent behavior—namely, by use of an intermediate operant response which either innately or through Pavlovian conditioning had come to control the respondent. For example, a person can learn to control his GSR (sweating of palms) either by tensing the muscles of his legs and torso on cue, or by saying to himself a word (e.g., *shock*) that he has earlier paired with an electric shock, thus evoking a galvanic skin reflex (GSR). Thus, were it to the person's advantage (say, to fake a lie detector test), he might learn *operantly* to control his GSR by saying "Shock" to himself or by moving some striated muscle group that causes his GSR to increase.

Everyone saw that in order to contradict the two-factor hypothesis, it would be necessary to show that respondents, such as heart-rate changes, visceral movements, or glandular secretions, could be learned according to the law of operant conditioning. Moreover, the demonstration had to be done in such a manner that an explanation in terms of an "operant mediator" was not plausible. It was this latter requirement that stymied the obvious projects. How to rule out intermediate instrumental behavior? The solution to this problem required the confluence of several significant technologies which became available during the 1960s.

First, the drug curare (or *d*-tubocurarine) can be used to knock out the skeletal musculature. Curare acts to block the action of acetylcholine at the neuromuscular junctures of the striated musculature. In adequate doses, the entire musculature loses tonus, becomes flaccid and immobile; drugged animals cannot even breathe, so must be kept alive by artificial respiration. Curare was used on poison arrows of primitive hunters because it killed by paralyzing the respiratory apparatus. A human who is given curare and respirated is fully conscious and aware of what is happening about him; he can learn, think out, and remember solutions to language puzzles given to him (see Leuba et al., 1968). He cannot talk or move while under the drug, of course, but he can report these events several hours later when the drug wears off.

So a prospective preparation for our critical experiment would be a curarized animal. But a second problem arises: since such animals are totally immobile, how are they ever to be rewarded when their viscera perform the right trick? The technological solution was to use electrical stimulation to pleasure centers of the brain (ESB) by means of implanted electrodes. Thus the appropriate preparation would be an animal (typically, a rat) having permanently implanted electrodes of proven rewarding quality, immobilized with curare, kept alive by artificial respiration, and with one or more electronic devices attached for recording some respondent activity such as cardiac, vasomotor, or visceral responses. This preparation is shown in

Figure 9.1 from DiCara (1970). Such are the artificial "ideal preparations" occasionally needed to answer scientific questions.

By the late 1960s, this preparation had begun to be studied by Neal Miller and his associates at Rockefeller University (Miller, 1969). They tried to condition operantly various visceral responses. To illustrate the procedure, consider the way one would try to condition an increase in the heart rate of an animal. The heart rate of a rat is around 400 beats per minute, but its moment-by-moment rate fluctuates considerably; the momentary rate can be estimated by setting a digital counter to count the number of beats in successive 5-second intervals. Suppose we wished to operantly condition our animal to increase its heart rate when a tone sounds, but to

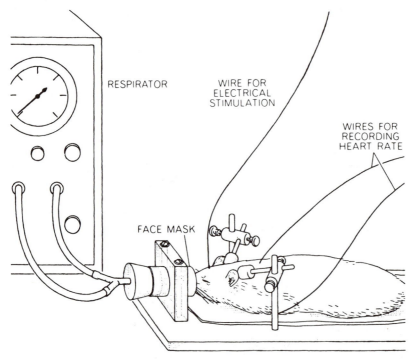

Figure 9.1 Illustration of a curarized rat fitted with a face mask connected to a respirator and with an electrode in a reward center of its brain. (From DiCara 1970.)

maintain a normal rate when the tone is off. The method of shaping and response differentiation can be used. Following recording of baseline heart rate to the tone, conditioning might begin by turning on the tone for 2 minutes every 4 minutes and delivering a rewarding ESB at the end of each 5-second observation interval during which the momentary heart rate is above a criterion rate. The criterion for reinforcement is initially low (say, 1 percent higher than the base rate); but over trials the criterion for reward is advanced to more extreme settings as the animal learns to increase its heart rate during the tone in order to get the ESB reward.

That is the general procedure. Perhaps the major result to report is that the procedure succeeds; that is, animals can learn reliably to change cardiovascular and visceral responses that are instrumental in getting rewards. The research being done on this presently is accomplishing several further ends. First, much research has aimed to establish the generality of the result with a variety of response systems. The list of visceral responses that have been successfully conditioned operantly in the curare preparation includes heart-rate increases or decreases, changes in blood pressure, control of blood vessel diameter (e.g., the vessels in the tail or ear of a rat), contractions of the large intestine, salivary secretion, and rate of formation of urine by the kidneys. This list is not exhaustive and doubtless will increase with further research. Second, there has been a concern to show that such conditioned operants follow pretty much the same laws as does any other learned response—that such responses show acquisition, extinction, retention, transfer, stimulus generalization, and discrimination. Third, much of the research has been concerned with establishing that these procedures produce true associative learning and not just sensitized responding, and that the learning changes are highly specific to the particular re-

sponse reinforced and not just a *general* arousal or relaxation pattern of the entire autonomic system. The way the first issue was answered, for example, was by modifying the rate of the response in opposite directions to two different discriminative stimuli. Thus a rat might be conditioned to *increase* the rate and intensity of its intestinal contractions above normal when a tone sounds, but to *decrease* them when a light comes on. The opposing responses to differential stimuli would seem to rule out explanations of results based on general sensitization of one class of responses due to the rewarding ESB or other, nonspecific artifacts. The second issue, the specificity of the learning changes, has been assessed by monitoring several different visceral response systems such as heart rate and intestinal motility. ESB reward would be made contingent on changes in one of these responses but not contingent on the other response; yet this other response system would be observed for correlated changes. An example of such results is shown in Figure 9.2 from an experiment by N. E. Miller and Banuazizi (1968). The graph shows heart rate plotted over approximately 500 training trials for two groups of animals, half rewarded (during the S^D or time-in stimulus) for speeding up their heart rate and half rewarded for slowing it down. During training, appropriate changes in heart rate occur for these two groups. Figure 9.2 also illustrates that rewarding a different response, intestinal contractions, has no effect upon the nonreinforced response, heartbeat. Thus the response changes are quite specific to that system on which reward is contingent, and do not reflect a generalized "autonomic" arousal. A *tour de force* on this specificity issue was performed by DiCara and Miller (1968), who trained rats to produce on cue relatively greater vasoconstriction (blanching) of the skin on their left ear than on their right ear (or vice versa). Such results show much greater specificity of sym-

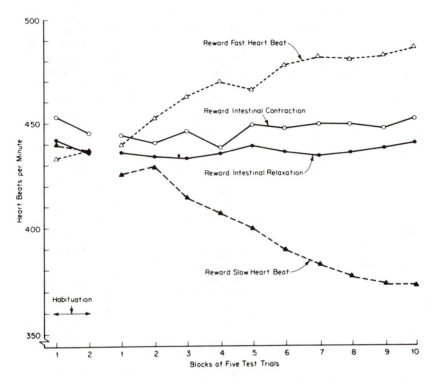

Figure 9.2. Rewarding increases or decreases, respectively, in heart rate produces changes in the appropriate directions, but rewarding a different response, intestinal contractions, produces no changes in heart rate. (From N. E. Miller & A. Banuazizi, 1968.)

pathetic nervous system actions than we would have believed possible before now.

Some Replication Problems. These results were produced at Miller's Yale laboratories through the late 1960's, and some of the major findings were replicated elsewhere (Fields, 1970; Hothersall & Brener, 1969). Thereafter, between 1970 and 1975, the research program began to experience difficulties replicating the basic findings with the curarized preparation, particularly the cardiovascular alterations (see Miller & Dworkin, 1974). The reasons for this are unresolved. The problem is that cardiovascular measures change in response to many other physiological systems, such as respiration rate, level of carbon dioxide in the blood, bladder distension, body temperature, and so on. It is difficult to control all of these in the curarized preparation. For example, the early curare experiments with rats respirated them with a face mask which pumped air in and out of their lungs. But minor movements of the rat's trachea, soft palate, or nasal passages could obstruct the passage temporarily, leading to changes in carbon dioxide in the blood, and consequent heart-rate changes. In later experiments, steady respiration has been guaranteed with an air tube inserted in the trachea. In these later experiments from Miller's laboratory, operant learning of cardiac responses in the curarized preparation has been a will-o'-the-wisp phenomenon, appearing or not in frustratingly inexplicable ways. Most researchers in the field, however, believe that operant conditioning of autonomic responses in the curarized animal is probably a real but variable phenomenon.

The difficulty of producing reliable results with the curarized rat should not blind us to the fact that successful operant conditioning of autonomic responses has been repeatedly demonstrated with non-curarized animals and people. As one illustration, an early experiment by Shapiro et al. (1964) using the human palmar GSR (a measure of sweating) produced reliable GSR increases in people rewarded for increases, and GSR decreases in others rewarded for decreases. Shapiro and Surwit (1976) review the many hundreds of cases of successful autonomic conditioning using operant contingencies. Such results are of practical clinical significance. On the other hand, results from the curarized preparation are of theoretical significance in ruling out skeletal muscles as mediators of the autonomic changes.

Biofeedback and Clinical Applications

Along with these laboratory studies with animals have been many concerted efforts to apply operant conditioning with biofeedback to alleviating problems of medical patients. By now there have been many hundreds of limited clinical tryouts of biofeedback conditioning with many different medical symptoms. Although frequent reports of success are trumpeted to the world, the fact is that the successes have not always been carefully controlled against powerful placebo effects; notably, when the proper controls are implemented, the results are often mixed. Early attempts by Miller and his associates to teach human patients with essential hypertension to lower their blood pressure had only weak and sporadic success, possibly because the patients were allowed to practice only a few minutes every few days when they were hooked up to the biofeedback machinery in the lab. Later work suggested that a persistent symptom may need to be monitored and worked at on a full-time continuous basis, which requires a portable apparatus that patients can wear.

Some of the more dramatic therapeutic changes in blood pressure have been produced by Brucker (1977) and N. E. Miller and Brucker (1978), who treated a form of hypotension in paraplegics or wheelchair-bound quadriplegics. In many of these patients, their broken spine has disrupted their normal mechanism for controlling blood pressure when they are in an upright position; when standing (say, on crutches), their pressure falls, they become dizzy, and faint. To avoid fainting, they are confined to a tilted wheelchair that keeps their legs up. Using continuous monitoring and feedback of blood pressure, Brucker helped several patients learn how to elevate their blood pressure so that they were able to be upright without fainting. The gain in comfort for these patients was very significant.

Biofeedback has also been used to rehabilitate muscular dysfunctions that may follow a stroke or spinal injury. Such patients may have little use of their hands, arms, legs, or ankles; and passive movement of the limbs by a physical therapist is of limited value. But electrodes can be placed on partially paralyzed muscles of such disabled limbs and biofeedback training can proceed (see Basmajian et al., 1975; Inglis et al., 1976). The patient tries by various "acts of will" or commands to move her limb, and the electromyograph (EMG) signals via a tone the extent to which her partly paralyzed muscle is being activated. Initial efforts may produce no overt movements, but the sensitive electrodes can pick up muscle potentials and amplify those signals to provide the crucial feedback the patient needs in the early stages. By successive shaping, the patient comes to generate larger electrical potentials in the muscle, then in a group of related muscles, then to move her limb ever so slightly, then farther movements, and then to guide and control the movements. In many cases the rehabilitation has been very impressive clinically, far outstripping the recovery expected for such cases with traditional physiotherapy methods.

Other clinical uses of muscle biofeedback have been the following:

1. Treatment of tension headaches by feeding back EMGs either from the frontalis (forehead) muscles or the back of the head-neck muscles, teaching the patient to relax (Budzynski et al., 1973);

2. Treatment of spasmodic torticollis (where the muscles on one side of the neck spasm for very long periods, locking the head over on that shoulder) by feeding back to the subject minor fluctuations in the EMG of the neck muscles, and reinforcing the spasmed muscles for relaxation (Brudny et al., 1974); and

3. Treatment of scoliosis, which is severe lateral curvature of the lower spine (it becomes almost S-shaped), by giving continuous feedback to the patient via a portable monitor and tone concerning the uprightness of posture (Dworkin, 1979).

The successes in these cases and many others attest to the fact that biofeedback will have a significant role in rehabilitative medicine. The techniques require careful, controlled testing and evaluation in practical settings (see Blanchard & Young, 1974, for discussion of problems concerning clinical evaluation of biofeedback).

Psychosomatic illnesses. If autonomic responses and movements of the viscera can be learned because of their instrumental values, the physical symptoms of psychosomatic illnesses may now be understood (see Miller & Dworkin, 1977). Psychiatrists refer to these social benefits as the "secon-

dary gains" of the psychosomatic symptom. For example, a child who is allowed to stay home from school because of a stomach upset and who is reinforced for avoiding an unpleasant situation at school may learn to have "genuine" stomach upsets whenever she wishes to avoid other unpleasant or anxious situations. The same analysis might apply to psychosomatic heart palpitations, fainting spells, headaches, and so on: since sick people are catered to, the symptom is rewarded by social attention and escape from unpleasant tasks.

A missing link in this psychological account is to specify why one particular symptom is chosen over another. Dworkin and associates (1979) advanced a hypothesis to explain the natural learning of essential hypertension. If a person who is in an unpleasant or frightening situation increases his blood pressure, this will stimulate the carotid sinus, which inhibits the reticular activating system of the brain, which in turn ultimately decreases the unpleasantness of the situation. In brief, an elevation of blood pressure would be reinforced by its indirectly creating reduction of aversiveness of a situation. (Other people might learn to take a barbiturate or tranquilizer in similar circumstances, with the calming of the reticular formation acting as the reward.) In support of this hypothesis, Dworkin and associates (1979) found that artificially raising a rat's blood pressure made it less responsive to and less afraid of a painful electric shock; but this effect was eliminated if the nerves from pressure receptors in the carotid sinus and aortic arch were cut surgically. Therefore, blood pressure elevation reduced aversiveness only when that change could inhibit the reticular formation. This is the kind of detective work needed to make plausible the theory of natural reinforcers for particular psychosomatic symptoms.

Of course, identifying a possible historical cause for a symptom does not solve the therapeutic problem, of getting the patient to abandon that symptom in favor of more adaptive, prosocial coping behaviors. For that task, too, behavior therapists have an armamentarium of methods for replacing maladaptive with adaptive habits.

Homeostatic mechanisms. Given the learnability of autonomic responses throughout the body and internal organs, one may suppose that they are playing a significant adaptive function in helping to maintain *homeostasis,* a stable and viable internal environment. The body has many physiological subsystems that must adjust to one another's changes; since most physiological functions (e.g., basal metabolism, breathing capacity, cardiac and kidney functioning) change markedly over the human life span, plasticity or adaptability of the various subsystems is required to keep the whole system in balance. It has been proposed that instrumental learning of autonomic functions may be involved in many of these homeostatic adjustments (see DiCara, 1970; Miller & Dworkin, 1978).

The idea that behavior is involved in homeostasis is quite familiar. A homeostat needs a *control loop* whereby deviation of the internal environment from its optimal setting causes some corrective action which reduces the internal discrepancy (see Figure 9.3). Thus, a thirsty animal drinks to restore water balance, a chilly person puts on woolen clothes to warm her body core, and a fish will swim to that stream location with just the optimal temperature and oxygen content. These are instrumental responses that directly reduce the discrepancy from optimum and so they are reinforced. That such drive reducers are biological reinforcers has obvious significance for the survival of the fittest in evolution.

Figure 9.3 illustrates a control loop in which a skeletal response is reinforced and learned because it restores homeostasis by way of its impact upon an intermediate

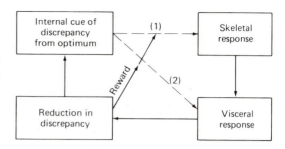

Figure 9.3. Diagram of the control loop in homeostatic control of some physiological function such as temperature regulation. Learned connections are indicated by dashed lines. (From Miller & Dworkin, 1978.)

visceral response. For example, some patients with paroxysmal tachycardia (the heart suddenly beats too rapidly) learn to control this "internal discrepancy" by taking a deep breath (see link 1 in Figure 9.3) which stimulates the vagal inhibitory reflex, breaking up the tachycardia and restoring normal heart rate. The relief from the alarming fear of the tachycardia rewards the deep-breathing activity.

Direct learning of a glandular, visceral or cardiovascular response to restore homeostasis is shown in link 2 of Figure 9.3, and this must be the dominant method by which our physiological subsystems adjust to and regulate one another. It is plausible that such visceral learning via reward occurs.

This homeostatic-loop idea suggests an interesting perspective on what have heretofore been considered *paradoxical* conditioned responses. Six of these have already been identified, and they are listed in Table 9.1. In standard lore of classical conditioning, the response elicited by the unconditioned stimulus is supposed to be transferred to the conditioned stimulus. But in these paradoxical cases, the response to the CS is just the *opposite* of the UCR, and hence could not be a simple matter of CS substitution for the chemical US. Thus,

TABLE 9.1. **Examples of paradoxical conditioned responses. When the chemical (left column) is injected as the US in a conditioning situation, the initial physiological reaction (middle column) is countered by a compensatory reaction (right column). This compensatory reaction becomes associated to, and elicited by, the CS.**

Agent (US)	Physiological Effect (UCR)	Learned Response (CR)
glucose	hyperglycemia	hypoglycemia
insulin	hypoglycemia	hyperglycemia
morphine	hyperthermia	hypothermia
morphine	analgesia	hyperalgesia
atropine	inhibits salivation	excess salivation
epinephrine	decreases gastric secretion	increased gastric secretion

the UCR to an insulin injection is a lowering of blood sugar (hypoglycemia) with concomitant weakness, whereas the conditioned response elicited by a mock injection in the former insulin situation is an increase in blood sugar. Similarly, injection of morphine causes high body temperatures and insensitivity to pain (analgesia), whereas the eventual conditioned response to a fake injection is the opposite, a lower temperature (the addict's "shakes") and greater sensitivity to pain (see Siegel, 1978).

These paradoxical conditioned reactions seem in fact to be compensatory or corrective reactions undertaken to eliminate a discrepancy created by the drug used as the US. For example, the immediate effect of injected insulin is to lower glucose levels in the blood; this causes the pancreas to release an enzyme that destroys insulin so that the glucose level can rise back to normal. Probably this pancreatic response is what becomes conditioned; the result, when a mock injection occurs, is that the pancreas releases its insulin-destroying enzyme, reducing the insulin level below normal; hence, the normal amount of glucose is not metabolized, and hyper-

glycemia results. Thus, if we view the US and its effects within the total homeostatic system, the paradoxical conditioned responses are in fact normal corrective or compensatory responses in a feedback loop adjusting to the disturbance caused by the US. Interestingly, the compensatory nature of the conditioned responses in these experiments suggests that instrumental reward might be shaping the learning, where the compensatory response is directly linked to the mechanism that restores homeostasis.

This area, relating homeostatic adjustments in biological subsystems to rewarded learning, is fascinating and promises new insights into the role of evolution in pre-wiring specific homeostatic settings for physiological subsystems. It appears that these settings are less prewired than we had originally thought. Rather, it appears the brain has general capabilities to learn whatever homeostatic settings optimally balance the several systems, such that a species fits easily into its environmental niche; however, these capabilities have most certainly been constrained to some extent by evolution. Further research along these lines should yield rich dividends.

Neuronal Conditioning

Concomitant with these demonstrations of the operant conditioning of visceral and cardiovascular responses, there also began to appear reports of the operant conditioning of neuronal responses in the brain, measured either by macroelectrodes recording from populations of brain cells or by microelectrodes recording the firing of just a few neurons. Olds (1965, 1969) was one of the first workers to report altering the spontaneous firing rate of single cells in the motor cortex of rats by delivering an electrical stimulus to brain sites that serve as a reward whenever the firing rate of the cortical neurons went above a preset criterion; in other series, a reduction of the spontaneous firing rate of the cell would be rewarded, resulting in the appropriate changes. Similar procedures have been used with several measures of neuronal responsivity, including theta waves recorded from the hippocampus (Blask, 1972), EEG spindles in the sensorimotor cortex (Wyrwicka & Sternman, 1968), the firing rate of single units in the motor cortex dissociated from a muscle group which they usually control (Fetz & Finocchio, 1971), and the amplitude of selected components of the evoked cortical response to a flash of light (Fox & Rudell, 1970).

The significance of such results is still in question—again, because of something like the old mediation argument. The neuron from which the recording is taken may not be the one that learns, but rather either (a) one involved in carrying out efferent commands to the motor system (i.e., most successful neuronal conditioning has been done with units in the *motor* cortex), or (b) one that receives sensory feedback from a motor operant that is controlled by the usual reinforcement contingencies. Thus, a monkey may alter a component of its evoked response to a light flash by defocusing its eyes, staring at a dark corner, or squinting; therefore, in reinforcing the monkey "for altering its visual evoked response," the experimenter may in actuality only be reinforcing "squinting" in an exceedingly indirect manner. Again, the use of curare preparations can help rule out some of these mediation arguments; but then the counter-argument just moves the locus of control inward and asserts that efferent commands are being recorded, reinforced, and learned.

At some point in such discussions, someone is almost sure to notice that such procedures are rather like reinforcing the curarized animal for thinking certain thoughts, and it is an accepted commonplace of private introspection that certain thoughts (e.g., daydreams or fantasies) can be increased in their frequency because of their pleasant consequences. A cogent and careful discussion of these issues of methodology, interpretation, and significance of the neuronal conditioning work is given by Black (1972). He concludes that such work is important for illuminating brain processes and brain-behavior covariations, and that the mediation question is not nearly so critical as a generation of psychologists had been led to believe. It was relevant only in the earlier fight between two-factor and one-factor reinforcement theorists.

Biofeedback and Control of Brain Waves

It is perhaps not a coincidence that the involuntary responses are the ones that we ordinarily do not see or feel, whereas the voluntary responses of large skeletal muscles are out in the open for our continuous inspection. It seems likely that it is the absence of continuous information about internal responses that causes them to be beyond our volitional control. After all, we ordinarily learn responses and learn to guide our behavior by observing what we do, seeing its consequences, and making appropriate adjustments. Knowledge of the response and its consequences is carried in what are called *feedback stimuli*, and they are exceptionally important in learning skilled movements. As one illustration, our normal speech can be seriously disrupted if an electronically controlled delay of about half a second is interposed by means of earphones between our speaking a word and hearing ourselves speak it. We begin to stammer, stutter, and slur our speech in a totally disorganized manner.

The thesis of the biofeedback movement is that many internal behaviors could be made more discriminable, and hence learnable or controllable, if their activity were to be fed back to the conscious person through amplifiers. A novel application of this hypothesis attempts the modification of brain waves. The initial work along these lines was done by Kamiya (1962, 1969), who sounded a tone as a feedback stimulus to a human subject whenever his scalp EEG showed an amount of *alpha-wave activity* above a criterion baseline. Alpha is a brain wave of about 8 to 10 cycles per second, which is correlated roughly with the subjective state of detachment, unconcern, or inner contemplation. Nonalpha, or the blocking of alpha, is caused by the person's either going into a light sleep (brain waves get even slower) or becoming very alert and attentive to some outside stimulus (brain waves become faster, more desynchronized). Kamiya found that after several minutes to several hours of correlation of a feedback stimulus with presence versus absence of alpha activity, most subjects learn to discriminate presence versus absence of their own alpha without the external tone. Furthermore, if subjects were asked to produce alpha (or to produce nonalpha) or were given rewards for doing so, it was reported that they could produce alpha (or nonalpha) at a rate in excess of the normal baseline. There is also evidence that by use of similar feedback techniques subjects can

learn to discriminate and to control other types of EEG patterns such as theta waves.

Studies of the EEG and its control have also been done with experienced practitioners of meditation according to Zen or Yoga discipline (see Kasamatsu & Hirai, 1966; Anand et al., 1961). During both forms of meditation, the practitioners show almost continuous alpha waves (normally associated with a state of relaxed alertness) if they are not disturbed. If an external sensory signal is presented, the Zen monks show nearly unvarying blocking of alpha ("arousal") to the signal; the remarkable report is that this blocking or cortical arousal response does not habituate with repeated trials for the Zen monks as it does for ordinary subjects. The Yogins, on the other hand, are almost totally unresponsive electrically to sensory stimulation, continuing in the alpha state. There are known to be a variety of other physiological changes during transcendental meditation, the changes reflecting a general slowing down of metabolic processes (see Ornstein, 1972). The suggested inference from the EEG observations is that *one* of the things Zen monks and Yogins learn to do in their years of meditation practice is to maintain the alpha state. The second inference is that one may be able to hasten training in meditation (where the novice is trying to achieve an ill-defined meditative state) by providing EEG feedback to shape more frequent attainment and improved maintenance of the alpha-wave state.

Promises and doubts about alpha control. These EEG feedback techniques have been hailed as a powerful new tool for helping individuals to expand their range of consciousness, to learn more about altered states of consciousness and how to produce them. These are fashionable topics in the human potential movement. For example, this enthusiasm is seen in the following quote from E. E. Green et al.:

The importance to our culture of this now developing technology for enhancing voluntary control of internal states can hardly be overstated. . . . Without stretching the imagination, the long-range implications and the effects for society of a population of self-regulating individuals could be of incalculable significance (1970, pp. 1–2).

This goal of obtaining greater self-control over one's internal processes (brain states) appears laudable, but some caution is surely needed in assessing and placing in perspective the findings on alpha control. A thorough critique of the alpha feedback literature and its interpretation can be found in a review paper by Plotkin (1979).

First, the evidence to date suggests that alpha control may be little more than inexplicit control of eye movements or eye-focusing. The most alpha that can be produced occurs when you are relaxed with your eyes closed in a dark room. If you open your eyes in dim light, alpha activity is blocked; the reduction in alpha activity is greater with greater visual scanning of the room or with greater emotional tension. Most of the earlier successful demonstrations of alpha control are deficient in several respects: first, they typically did not control or measure eye movements (or even whether the subject's eyes were opened or closed); second, there usually was no control for the upward drift in the baseline level of alpha activity as the subject relaxes over time by adapting to the initial arousal (and low alpha) caused by being hooked up to the experimental apparatus; third, the early experiments mainly demonstrated a difference in amount of alpha activity during the instructed alpha-on periods versus the alpha-off periods of the experimental session. But a simple difference can be produced not by enhancing alpha to above the normal baseline during alpha-on periods but by reducing alpha to below the baseline (by visual scanning) during the alpha-off periods. It might be further objected that people already know a variety

of mental tricks which will either enhance or reduce alpha activity, at least to a limited extent. To produce nonalpha, just scan your visual environment. To increase alpha, just relax, defocus your eyes and stare fixedly into the distance; then imagine that you are staring at a blank wall or that your eyes are covered with halves of ping-pong balls which produce diffuse nonpatterned light. Thus, by instructions alone, most people are able to produce large differences in amount of alpha activity. Without such instructions, one can suppose that telling the person to learn to "keep the tone on" (which means to produce alpha, say) is similar to giving him an ill-defined trial-and-error problem to be solved. He will cast about until he strikes upon some mental act he does which turns on the tone and keeps it on. Has he learned to "enter a different state of consciousness"? Has he learned to control his brain state? Or has he simply learned that what turns the tone on is defocusing his eyes and staring at a blank wall?

Evidence for this less flattering conclusion comes from a well-controlled experiment by Paskewitz and Orne (1973), who tried to train many subjects over many days to enhance their amount of alpha activity. They found, first, that if subjects were tested in a dark room and told to keep their eyes open, then no alpha enhancement could be produced above the baseline drift. If tested in a lighted room, they could learn to show a difference in alpha between "on" versus "off" periods. However, the most alpha activity obtained this way was barely half as much as was recorded before training when the subjects were told merely to relax and close their eyes. That is, training of alpha never came close to producing the alpha occurring simply with eyes closed. Second, the alpha difference achieved by subjects trained in the light completely disappeared when these subjects were tested in the dark (with eyes open in both conditions). It thus appears that the opportunity for scanning over a visual field is a necessary prerequisite for producing an alpha difference through such training. And clearly, it is a mistake to label this practice as training for deeper awareness of one's brain states or different levels of consciousness. The latter, flamboyant talk just leads to the muddled linguistic absurdity that every activity is correlated with a unique brain state or altered state of consciousness. But surely this is just a peculiar restatement of the standard brain-behavior hypothesis and of little interest.

The mixed successes of alpha biofeedback techniques are interpreted differently by the believers and nonbelievers in its powers. The believers say that the real learning of alpha control and the benefits from it can become manifest only with extensive diligent practice, and that brief laboratory attempts are useless. While not denying that the alpha feedback *situation* can produce a pleasantly detached, meditative euphoria, the nonbelievers claim that the effect has little or nothing to do with the brain waves per se but rather with the social demands and expectations of the typical subject in altering verbal reports of her subjective state. The same "subjective buzz" can be produced by giving fake or random tone feedback independent of the person's alpha so long as she believes that her alpha is controlling the tone (Plotkin, 1976, 1979). The social expectations of the subject are of paramount importance to her subjective experiences. For example, if the tone were to feedback real information about alpha but the subject were misled into believing that the tone was measuring some obscure physiological nonsense (e.g., the oxygen-carbon dioxide conversion ratio) which she should try to control, then the euphoric buzz of meditation is not part of the experience, regardless of whether or not the person comes to control her alpha waves. The social-demand hypothesis also has a ready

explanation of why the best subjective changes seen by the believers occur with long-term subjects who are committed to learning alpha control and to experiencing its altered state of meditative drifting. The more dedicated and the longer the credulous subject persists in training, the greater the social demand and personal expectation that she will experience the desired euphoric buzz, and the greater her discomfort from reporting a failure. A sensible position is that alpha waves are correlated with "bland quiescence," but how the person interprets and reacts to that state varies enormously with social demands and personal expectations. Thus, it should be possible to make quiescence extremely aversive by suggesting to the subject that it is a sign that she is "losing her mind."

Similar interpretive difficulties have arisen for studies attempting to reduce epileptic seizures through biofeedback control of EEG rhythms. Thus, Sterman (1973) found that his epileptic clients had fewer seizures over several weeks of EEG feedback training during which time they were rewarded for EEG rhythms of 12–14 cycles per second. Kaplan (1973) found similar reductions in seizures of epileptics by rewarding brain waves in the 6–12 cycles per second range. However, Kaplan attributed the technique's success, not to specific EEG rhythms, but to the patients' learning of muscle relaxation throughout their bodies. Such relaxation is known to oppose epileptic seizures.

Despite these critical results about EEG biofeedback, it should be noted that this research has been significant in altering our conceptions of self-control, awareness, and the nature of private events. Perhaps internal reactions, including our emotions and other affective moods, are normally difficult for us to control because they are usually not observed and discriminated as such; they are vague and undifferentiated stimulus patterns. If one were to make such internal reactions discriminable through feedback—to "expand one's inner awareness"—this should increase the possibility of self-labeling and self-control of these emotions. Although such procedures would not appreciably alter the relationship between stimulation and physiological effect, they could alter the relation between that physiological effect and the emotion associated with it. In the extreme; one can envision a stoical training regime whereby one is able to decide cognitively how he will react to what ordinarily would be an emotionally upsetting event.

An intriguing hypothesis is that we can control only those behaviors that we can discriminate (technically, we can discriminate a behavior if its occurrence can serve as an S^D for later behaviors such as labeling). In other words, if you cannot discriminate when you are or are not doing some "act," or if you cannot discriminate something else that controls the first act, then you cannot learn to control that act. One can cite two visceral responses that have immediately discriminable effects—namely, urination and defecation—which are uniformly and successfully controlled in most children through social reinforcement. Our thesis, that discrimination implies control, could be advanced even for skeletal responses. The intuition behind the hypothesis can be appreciated if you try to teach a small child to wink with one eye, or try to teach yourself to wriggle your left ear (a trick Neal Miller learned in order to prove the point): the best procedure is to stand in front of a mirror and watch yourself carefully, shaping by self-reward any small movement in the correct direction.

To return to the larger issue, we may finally ask whether the Zen meditator or the ear wriggler or the good golfer or painter is expanding his awareness and reaching a higher state of consciousness. Perhaps it is better to talk about most such matters of "awareness" in terms of skills—perceptual skills, motor skills, skills in describing one's internal states, and the like—that are taught to individuals by societies which apply highly discriminative contingencies. But these are matters for more general discussion than is feasible in this textbook.

CONCEPTIONS OF REINFORCEMENT AND NONREINFORCEMENT

The Relativity of Reinforcement

The law of reinforcement, or law of effect, is one of the more important principles in all learning theory. It is a rule for shaping behavior by the use of rewards (reinforcers). We train a rat to press a lever by giving it a bit of food when it does so. Because of the central significance of the principle, there have been attempts to state it in a general yet precise way. One commonly accepted formulation is this: a learnable response followed by a reinforcing event (stimulus, state of affairs) will receive an increment in its strength or probability of occurrence. Critics of the law of effect have argued that this formulation is not an empirical law but rather a definition of a reinforcing event. Let us see. If a reinforcer is defined as something that strengthens a response, then by substitution in the statement of the law, it becomes: a learnable response followed by something that strengthens a response will receive an increment in its strength! But this is just vacuous circularity. Surely there must be more to the principle than the trivial tautology that "a rose is a rose is a rose."

The question of whether or not the law has any empirical content was considered by Meehl (1950) in a key paper entitled "On the circularity of the law of effect." Meehl concluded that the law does have empirical content, and that its content concerns the *transituational generality* of a reinforcer. If I find that scratching a dog behind its ears will reinforce its behavior of lifting a paw to shake hands, then the law of effect makes the prediction that ear-scratching can also be used to reinforce other sorts of canine responses—hand-licking, tail-wagging, ball-rolling, stick-retrieving, and so forth. The law of effect is used in a "definitional" mode in the initial discovery of ear-scratching as a reinforcer; but it is used in an empirical, predictive manner when testing ear-scratching as a reinforcer for later responses. Meehl's reformulation of the law of effect is: all reinforcers are transituational. An equivalent, and more understandable, version is: a reinforcer can be used to increase the probability of *any* learnable response.

Meehl's analysis resolved the circulatory charge, and psychologists went on their way satisfied with this formulation of the general law of effect. One implication of Meehl's or Thorndike's statement of the law of effect is what may be called an "absolutist" classification of events as reinforcing or not reinforcing. That is, given a particular state of the subject (his conditions of deprivation or past training), we can roughly divide stimulus events into two lists: those that act upon him as reinforcers and those that do not. A list of reinforcers commonly contains biological items such as food, water, and sexual contact for appropriately deprived individuals, together with learned (secondary) reinforcers such as money, praise, social approval, attention, dominance, the spoken exclamation "good," and a variety of manipulation-curiosity-novelty satisfying types of activities. Given such a partial listing, some psychologists were challenged to try to guess what all these reinforcing things have in common—what is the common essential ingredient that makes them all reinforcers? A plausible idea, for example, was Hull's conjecture that all primary reinforcers serve to reduce drives or biological needs, and that secondary reinforcers such as praise derive their value from having been associated with many instances of drive

reduction, perhaps during the child's early rearing. This conjecture, as well as others like it, has been extensively researched and argued pro and con. G. A. Kimble (1961) gives a useful summary of this evidence for the interested student.

Premack's principle. In this context, Premack (1959, 1965) offered a useful reappraisal of reinforcement and the law of effect which increases these concepts' generality. As with many useful insights, Premack's argument stems from noting an implicit assumption contained in previous formulations of the law of effect. This implicit assumption is that the response or activities which are to be reinforced are neutral or of no intrinsic value to the subject. But suppose that we take an opposite viewpoint, that the organism engages in a variety of activities (including eating, manipulating, playing, and so on) that vary in their intrinsic value for it. Imagine further that by some means we have ordered these activities in a ranking from most to least preferred, in the order $A, B, C, D, \ldots$.

Given this ranking of activities (considered in this general sense), what is now an appropriate way to formulate the law of effect? Premack argues that the only sensible formulation ties the reinforcement relation to this preference ordering: a given activity can be used to reinforce those of lesser value but not those of higher value. In our $A > B > C > D$ ranking, we can use B to reinforce C or D, but B will not reinforce A. But acceptance of this point commits us to a relativity view of reinforcement. A given event or activity can be used to reinforce some responses but not others. C can reinforce D but not B, even though B is learnable, as we would find when we made A contingent upon B. Thus, not all reinforcers are transituational; a given reinforcer cannot be used to strengthen any learnable response whatever. Rather, an activity will reinforce only those activities of lesser value, not those of higher value.

An important question is, does this revision of the law of effect now make it completely circular? If Meehl's transitational idea is altered, is there any empirical content left to the law of effect? We can avoid the circularity, but it now requires two observations (rather than one) to make an empirical prediction. If we find that activity R reinforces A and that A reinforces Z, then the law predicts that R will reinforce Z. That prediction has empirical content and could possibly be false, and so would test the proposed law. Readers familiar with logic will recognize this as a test of the *transitivity* assumption about the reinforcement relation. So the law is testable even if we could find no independent way to assess value or preference.

A central issue is whether we can find an independent way to assess a subject's preference ordering for a set of activities. With human subjects, a verbal estimate of liking or attractiveness would probably serve as a valid index, though a slight hitch arises from the fact that people are occasionally unaware (unconscious) of what kinds of events can reinforce their behavior. But suppose that we wish to have some index of wide application, one that could be used with animals, or nonverbal mental defectives, and so forth. The search for an index of such generality constitutes a real challenge. Premack (1959) first proposed that a generally valid index of value would be response rate (or momentary probability) in a free-operant situation in which the commodity or activity is freely available to the subject. This is a plausible index: the more a person likes an activity, the more often he engages in it when it is freely available with no constraints attached.

To illustrate by a concrete example, suppose the values of four different activities are to be assessed for a kindergarten child: playing a pinball machine *(PB)*, looking at a movie cartoon *(M)*, eating small chocolate candies *(C)*, and hammering on a wooden pegboard *(H)*. The as-

sessment would consist of measuring how frequently (by count or by total time so spent) the child engages in each activity in a standard test room in which opportunity for engaging in each activity is introduced singly and separately. Suppose that the independent rates for a particular child come out in the rank order $PB>M>C>H$, from highest to lowest. Thus, we would predict that the opportunity to play with the pinball machine can be used to reinforce or increase the rate of either the M, C, or H activities; M can reinforce C or H but not *PB;* and C can reinforce H but neither M nor *PB*. The contingent test situation would involve one activity freely available; when it is performed, the other activity becomes available for a brief time and then turns off. For instance, in the $M>C$ test, candy would be freely available at one location. When a candy has been eaten, a movie projector in another part of the room would turn on, showing, say, a 30-second segment of a cartoon. A reinforcing effect would be inferred if the rate of candy eating increased above its baseline rate when this contingency was introduced. Premack (1959, 1963, 1965) has presented data from children, monkeys, and rats indicating that predictions of this sort are generally accurate.

In some cases, we know that the relative value of two activities or commodities can be altered by altering relevant conditions of deprivation. Thus, I can alter your relative preference for eating versus sleeping by depriving you of food or sleep, respectively. Therefore, we should be able to reverse the reinforcement relation between two activities by altering motivation. Premack (1962) demonstrated this effect in rats using water ingestion and running in an activity wheel. The ingestion rate was altered by water deprivation, and the running activity by depriving the rat of access to an activity wheel in an otherwise confining living quarter. When deprived of water but not of activity, water ingestion would reinforce running but not vice versa. When deprived of activity but not water, running would reinforce drinking but not vice versa. Thus, the reinforcement relation was reversible.

Premack's theory has the advantage of being operational, of generating novel experiments, and of describing many social activities used as human reinforcers. Acceptance of Premack's probability-differential view of reinforcement makes it misguided to search for some essential property of absolute reinforcing events (e.g., drive reduction) without considering the activity to be reinforced.

The difficulties with Premack's probability-differential theory of reinforcement have slowly come to light. They are summarized in papers by Timberlake and Allison (1974) and Timberlake (1980), who propose a more general theory to handle all results consistent with Premack's theory as well as other results that disconfirm his theory. Timberlake (1980) calls this an *equilibrium* theory of learned performance, while earlier, Timberlake and Allison (1974) called it the *response-deprivation* theory of reinforcement.

Equilibrium Theory

Let us return to the simple two-activity assessment procedure—say with a rat freely choosing either to run in a running wheel or to drink from a saccharin bottle. Suppose we let W and S stand for his baseline rate of doing these two activities, expressed in terms (say) of average durations of the two activities per one-hour in the choice situation. The experimenter can institute a contingency, say by restricting access to the saccharin bottle and only making it available for 15 seconds after the animal has run in the wheel for 15 seconds. Will the rat learn to increase her wheel-running to get the saccharin bottle? Premack's theory implies that this contingency will increase the rate of the instrumental re-

sponse (W here) only if S exceeds W in the free-choice baseline. In contradiction to this prediction, however, it is found that animals will learn to increase W to get access to a restricted contingent activity S even when S has a *lower* baseline rate than does W (see Timberlake, 1980). In other words, subjects will increase their rate of doing a highly valued thing if it lets them do a low-valued thing at near its desirable rate. One can think of the animal as wanting to wheel-turn and drink saccharin at stable rates W and S, and any contingency which disturbs that equilibrium will lead her to adjust her rate of the instrumental response so as to move the new rates, W' and S', in the direction of their former baseline values.

The general points of the equilibrium theory can be diagrammed as in Figure 9.4, which plots the two response rates on the two axes; to keep terminology straight, the instrumental response is whichever one is freely available (such as running) and whose performance causes brief access to

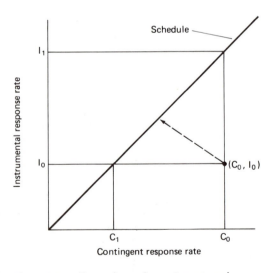

Figure 9.4. Illustration of contingent and instrumental response space with a 1-to-1 contingency schedule. The baseline rates of the two responses is the point (C, I).

the contingent response (such as drinking). The 45-degree line in Figure 9.4 depicts the commonly used 1-to-1 ratio schedule, wherein 1 unit of instrumental responding gives the subject access to 1 unit of contingent responding. Different schedule ratios would lead to lines of more or less slope. The baseline rates for the two responses are plotted as a point (I_0, C_0). After the 1-to-1 contingent schedule is imposed, the baseline rate of the instrumental response, I_0, will produce only a rate, C_1, of the contingent behavior, which is considerably less than the desired rate, C_0. In order to obtain the contingent response at rate C_0 on the schedule, the subject would have to increase his instrumental response rate up to I_1, considerably above its desirable baseline rate, I_0. Equilibrium theory states that some compromise will be worked out, so that the subject performs the instrumental response somewhat more to increase his receipt of the contingent response above C_1. The arrowhead indicates a possible equilibrium path (all such points fall on the line between the intersections indicated). This is the standard case in which the animal learns to perform a less-desired response at a higher rate and is rewarded by access to a more-desired activity. The theory also predicts that the greater the deficit from C_0 created by the schedule, the greater will be the change in the rate of instrumental responding.

The reverse schedule is shown in the top panel of Figure 9.5. Here the baseline point (dot) indicates that in the free-choice situation the instrumental response occurs at a higher rate than the contingent response. The schedule now dictates that if the subject continues to perform the instrumental response at rate I_0, the subject will be *forced* to perform the contingent activity at the rate, C_1, which is considerably above her desired rate of C_0. Such a forced contingency is really just a *punishment* contingency in disguise; analogously, the prototypic punishment forces the subject to

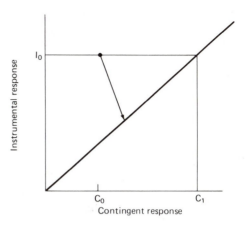

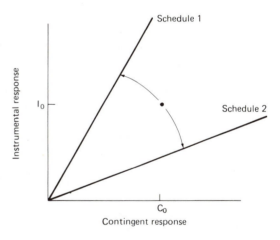

Figure 9.5. (Top) Response space for an excess of instrumental responding, analogous to punishment. (Bottom) Reversing direction of change of instrumental responding by lowering the ratio schedule.

take more of some noxious state such as shock (contingent activity) than she wants. The equilibrium theory predicts that the instrumental response decreases when such contingencies are imposed. Thus, for example, if a rat in a motor-driven running wheel is forced to run more than she optimally chooses when she drinks saccharin water at her base rate, then she will decrease her drinking rate (see a review by Allison, 1976). This is despite the fact that for some other response or schedule, running in the wheel might be reinforcing for a rat.

The two predictions above do not distinguish the Timberlake-Allison equilibrium theory from Premack's probability-differential theory. However, several distinguishing cases have been identified. One was noted before, where a low-probability contingent response—say, wheel-running—is restricted by the schedule and the only way for the animal to obtain baseline access to it is to increase her rate of performing a high-probability response—say, saccharin drinking. Premack's theory expects no increase in instrumental responding in such arrangements, whereas recent experiments clearly show substantial increases, as predicted by equilibrium theory. A second distinguishing prediction for equilibrium theory is that one should be able to decrease a lower-probability response by making a higher-probability response contingent on it through some schedule. The requisite schedule needs only to force the subject to perform the contingent high-probability behavior at a higher rate than is preferred. This arrangement is now known to reduce the rate of the instrumental response.

A conclusive demonstration in favor of equilibrium theory is illustrated in the bottom panel of Figure 9.5. This shows, for one and the same baseline, that whether response A will reinforce response B, or vice versa, can be reversed merely by changing the ratio of the contingent schedule. In Schedule 1, the baseline instrumental response rate, I_0, will lead to a lowering of the contingent response, so the instrumental response will increase according to the equilibrium prediction. However, the Schedule 2 ratio is such that the baseline instrumental response rate will lead to an enforced excess of responding to the contingent activity; therefore, the equilibrium theory predicts that the instrumental response rate should decrease under such a schedule. The implication is that whether a given contingent activity reinforces or punishes a given instrumental activity depends on their scheduled ratio (exchange rate). By reversing which activity is considered instrumental and which contingent, the reader can derive the implication stated above—that is, for any two responses A and B, whether A will reinforce B or B will reinforce A depends on the ratio of the contingency. (The statement for punishment is just the reverse.) Several experiments demonstrating such reversibility by schedule changes have been reviewed by Timberlake (1980) and Timberlake and Allison (1974). They provide very dramatic evidence for the equilibrium theory.

Remaining Problems for Equilibrium Theory

The equilibrium analysis has clearly brought us a long way from the empirical law of effect with which we began. We have had our horizons and intuitions about reinforcement relations expanded considerably. On close inspection, many practical reinforcement procedures used in home or school environments operate on something like the equilibrium principle: depriving a child of opportunity for some activity, even a mildly valued one like drawing pictures, is often used to motivate and contingently reward the child for some educationally relevant behaviors.

Several difficulties are yet to be solved by equilibrium theory. One is the problem of generality; another, the validity of response rate as an index of preference. The problem of generality arises when we notice that in almost all human learning studies the reinforcing operation is "information about what is the correct response." Through her motivating instructions, the experimenter or teacher has made being correct a reinforcing event for the subject, so that nothing else need be added to promote learning. The effectiveness of this operation probably depends upon a long history of cultural training in which being correct has been associated with parental praise and approval. For instance, in the case of very young preschool children, instructions and information are sometimes not enough; material rewards (trinkets, gold stars, candy) must be added if the children are to be kept working at difficult learning tasks. In any event, it is unclear how or whether such reinforcement by mere information is, or can be, covered by equilibrium theory. The same can be said for vicarious or observational learning (see Chapter 13).

The other problem is the general validity of the response-rate index of preference. It is difficult to get comparable measures on independent rates of different activities; it will not do just to let the calculated rates depend on arbitrary units imposed upon the behavior by the recording system. Conceived in a general sense, our activities or interactions with goal objects vary in multiple ways—in duration of each contact, rate of interaction during contact, time between contacts, and so forth; and it is not at all clear how to combine these features into a single index. Consider, for example, the difficulties of getting comparable measures by which to arrange in rank order the four activities of reading a book, blinking your eyes, playing the piano, and sleeping. Other problems arise in connection with the rate index (e.g., it can be differentially trained by reinforcement), and this specific proposal seems to be threatened by endless troubles and unavoidable limitations.

A third minor problem is that equilibrium theory assumes no interactions among different activities. Thus, for example, the theory would be unable to explain any result showing that the relative preference between two alternatives (say, vanilla or strawberry ice cream) reverses if a third element is added to the choice set (say,

strawberries). But such context effects have been found in some human preference judgments (see Tversky, 1977; Tversky & Sattath, 1979).

The difficulties mentioned are relatively minor and do not detract from the appeal of the equilibrium theory. Looking backward to Meehl's and Thorndike's earlier formulations of the law of effect, we seem to have made some progress in formulating reinforcement relations in a more general and valid way.

Nonreward and Extinction

Along with developments in the contemporary conception of reinforcement and the law of effect, there have also been changes in the interpretation of nonreward and extinction. Almost all of this theory stems from work on nonreward and extinction with animal subjects, although it is presumed that similar ideas apply to at least some types of human learning. Certain earlier interpretations of nonreward of a previously rewarded response had assigned to it an essentially passive role. As will be seen in Chapter 11, Tolman supposed that nonreward served simply to disconfirm and weaken an $S\text{-}R\text{-}S_g$ expectancy. Thorndike gave little systematic consideration to nonreward, and as best we can tell, he thought of it as essentially a neutral event. In Hull's theory (Chapter 5), nonrewarded trials are believed to permit inhibitory factors to build up without being offset by a corresponding increase in reaction potential. Hull's ideas about extinction were worked out only in very sketchy fashion and were never really adequate to a very wide range of data on extinction.

In the last 20 years, a number of hypotheses have been proposed regarding nonreward and extinction. Most of these hypotheses have aimed at explaining the increased resistance to extinction in animals trained with a partial reward schedule. That is, a rat rewarded on only, say, 30 percent of its runs down a straight alley will persist longer in running to the goal-box during extinction than will another animal trained with 100 percent rewarded trials. This simple fact, embellished with many ancillary results, has constituted a perennial challenge to theorists. Not that explanations do not abound; it is sorting them out with critical experimental tests that has proved a demanding, though also informative, task. In Chapter 5 we also reviewed Amsel's frustration theory of nonreward and how partial reinforcement increases resistance to extinction. In this section we review Capaldi's *sequential patterning* theory of nonreward and how it explains extinction phenomena.

The Sequential Hypothesis

Capaldi's theory (1966, 1967) of the partial reinforcement extinction effect is a sophisticated elaboration and refinement of two earlier ideas: (1) the *discrimination,* or *generalization,* hypothesis, which supposes that subjects will persist in responding as long as they cannot discriminate the extinction series from an unfortunate run of nonreinforcements embedded within the training series; and (2) the *stimulus aftereffects* hypothesis (V. F. Sheffield, 1949), which supposes that reward (R) and nonreward (N) events on one trial set up distinctive stimulus traces which persist over the intertrial interval and are part of the stimulus complex at the time the next response occurs. The stimulus aftereffects hypothesis supposes that during partial reinforcement training, persisting stimulus traces from nonreinforced trials (denoted S^N) become conditioned to the next response because of frequent NR transitions (i.e., a reinforced trial following a nonreinforced trial), and therefore the S^N stimuli that arise and prevail during extinction will maintain responding.

Capaldi elaborates these ideas in several directions. First, he supposes that a run of

k consecutive nonreinforced trials sets up a distinctive stimulus trace, denoted S^{N_k}. S^{N_k} stimuli ($k = 1, 2, 3, \ldots$) form a stimulus continuum along which there will be generalization of habit strength from a run length experienced and conditioned during training to other run lengths experienced during extinction. When a string of k N-trials terminates with a reinforced trial, an increment in habit strength (see Hull, Chapter 5) accrues between S^{N_k} and the instrumental response, with the asymptote of that habit being higher the greater the amount of reward provided on that trial. Second, Capaldi supposes that extinction can be conceived of as the presentation of a sequence of stimuli $S^{N_1}, S^{N_2}, S^{N_3}, \ldots,$ and is formally like testing for stimulus generalization: an animal will respond to S^{N_k} during extinction if S^{N_k} has sufficient habit strength either established during training or borrowed by generalization from neighboring N-lengths involved in training. In this view of matters, the significant variables characterizing a partial reinforcement training schedule are (1) the particular S^{N_k} stimuli which occur during training, and (2) the frequency with which they occur and are reinforced during training. These factors will determine the *habit profile* associated to the set of S^{N_k} stimuli at the beginning of extinction; that habit profile and its generalization of response tendencies to other S^{N_j} encountered during extinction jointly determine the resistance to extinction produced by a given training schedule.

In order to illustrate these notions, let us examine the 8-trial sequence in Table 9.2. Let us suppose that this sequence is repeated four times, for a total of 32 acquisition trials; after the first cycle, later cycles may be conceived to begin with an S^R stimulus on Trial 1 due to carryover from the R on Trial 8 of the prior cycle. The four rewards cause conditioning of the instrumental response to three patterns: S^R (on Trials 1 and 6), S^{N_1} (on Trial 8) and S^{N_3} (on Trial 5). After four cycles through

TABLE 9.2. Illustration of stimulus aftereffects analysis of an 8-trial sequence of rewarded (R) and nonrewarded (N) trials.

	1	2	3	4	5	6	7	8
Reward event	R	N	N	N	R	R	N	R
Stimulus trace from prior trial	S^R	S^R	S^{N_1}	S^{N_2}	S^{N_3}	S^R	S^R	S^{N_1}
Conditioning on this trial?	+	−	−	−	+	+	−	+

this series, the animal would have had seven reinforcements on S^R (recall that Trial 1 of the first cycle was not preceded by an R), and four each on S^{N_1} and S^{N_3}. The profile of the three habits and their separate generalization tendencies to other S^{N_R} stimuli are illustrated in Figure 9.6. The habit strength above S^R is higher than that above S^{N_1} and S^{N_3} because of its having had more reinforced trials. The S^{N_k} stimuli are spaced logarithmically along the axis, and the habit generalization gradients are assumed to be linear on that log scale. In this illustration, it may be seen that generalized habit from S^R alone would have been too weak to sustain performance at $S^{N_{50}}$ (on the fiftieth extinction trial), but the generalization of habit established at S^{N_3} would do so. In general, resistance to extinction produced by given training conditions depends upon the summated habit strength that is generalized to the right in this graph. The greater the N-length which can still evoke the instrumental response, the greater is the number of extinction trials for which the response persists.

This is a somewhat novel perspective on

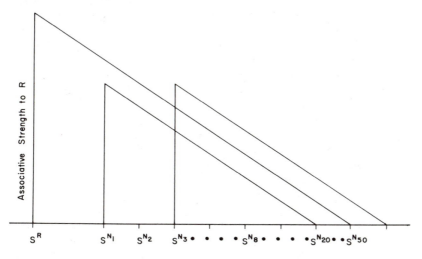

Figure 9.6. Plot of habit profile to the three reinforced sequential patterns illustrated in Table 9.2 and the generalization of these habits to other run lengths of *N* trials.

reinforcement schedules; it fits in very well with current sequential pattern models of probability learning such as those of Estes (1972a) and Myers (1970). But the obvious payoff for this novel perspective is that it can account for a range of experimental results comparing resistance to extinction following training on the hundreds of variants of partial reinforcement schedules. The range of results is reviewed in Capaldi's papers (1966, 1967) and cannot be reiterated here. One bit of supporting data, for instance, is that with a small number of training trials resistance to extinction is higher with more frequent occurrences of short N-lengths and fewer occurrences of long N-lengths (holding number of N trials constant), whereas with many training trials the most persistence occurs for those schedules having the longer N-lengths. Capaldi has also extended the hypothesis to handle the effects of other goal-box events, such as different confinement durations in a nonrewarded goal-box, different magnitudes of reward, and different delays of reward. His treatment explains the fact that animals trained with a large reward on every trial will extinguish faster than those trained with small reward because S^{large} is farther from S^N on a generalization gradient than is S^{small}. On the other hand, under random reward-nonreward schedules, greater persistence occurs for animals receiving the large reward because S^N is conditioned to a greater extent by the large reward on NR transitions. The transitions are shown to be important since animals receiving repeated cycles of SNL trials (small reward, then nothing, then large reward) proved to be much more resistant to extinction than those receiving the reverse sequence LNS (see Capaldi & Capaldi, 1970; Leonard, 1969).

A novel technique introduced by Capaldi (1966) is *intertrial reinforcement* (ITR), during which the animal is placed directly into the goal-box of the runway and rewarded. The ITR event functions within Capaldi's theory to establish the stimulus trace to be S^R for the next running trial regardless of whether the prior *running* trial had been N or R. The ITR, in other words, is one way to interject a different stimulus just before a given trial. Several ingenious experiments were done with ITR. Consider the five-trial schedule RNNNR that is repeated several times, and let an ITR event be interposed for different groups of subjects after either the first, second, or third N event of the cycle. A control group receives no ITR. The prediction from the sequential hypothesis is that the controls will be most resistant to extinction, next will be the group receiving ITR after the first N trial, next those receiving it after the second N trial, while the poorest persistence will obtain for the group receiving ITR after the third N trial. This ordering is predicted because the ITR cuts short the N-length which can be conditioned by the R on Trial 5 of the cycle. The control subjects experience S^{N_3} on Trial 5, and it becomes associated with the reinforced response. The subjects receiving ITR after the first N trial will then have S^R on Trial 3, then S^{N_1} on Trial 4, then S^{N_2} on Trial 5 (see Table 9.2 above). The subjects receiving ITR after the third N trial will have S^R on Trial 5. The groups thus differ in the longest N-length that becomes conditioned to the response, and their resistance to extinction increases the longer the N-length that has been conditioned.

One point at which Capaldi's theory deviates from the earlier aftereffects hypothesis of V. F. Sheffield concerns the time decay of information about the reinforcing event of the prior trial. Sheffield had assumed that R or N events set up relatively short-term stimulus traces which decay away after a few minutes. The problem with that idea is that it has no way to explain partial reinforcement effects that have been obtained with widely spaced trials, say one trial every 24 hours. Capaldi assumes, on the contrary, that a trace of the prior R or N event persists indefinitely until it is modified or replaced by the next event to happen in the goal-box of this situation. Clearly, for Capaldi, the prior R or N stimuli are now available in something like a *memory* which is reactivated when the animal is placed back in the stimulus situation of the maze. Thus, an alternative way to discuss the theory is to say not that S^N is a persisting stimulus from a prior N trial (say, 24 hours ago), but rather that S^N is a stimulating effect from the subject now recalling the N event from the prior trial. This memory interpretation is in some ways more heuristic than the stimulus trace interpretation. In any event, what is needed is some theoretical mechanism ("information carrier") that is instantaneously responsive to the most recent reward outcome, that encodes that information in a discriminative manner (this is where the r_g mechanism fails), and which retains that discriminative information over time until the next trial. This temporal retention is required because most of the usual partial reinforcement phenomena (see Capaldi & Capaldi, 1970) occur whether the training trials are massed (one trial every 15 seconds) or widely spaced (one trial per day). Of course, the construct of a memory for an event (the substrate of the S^R or S^N) is what is somewhat foreign to the spirit of S-R behavior theory.

Capaldi (1967) applies his hypothesis to explain a wide range of different phenomena of scheduling, including the speeded up relearning and extinction that occur with multiple blocks of acquisition and extinction trials, the effects of patterned schedules and their discrimination (e.g., double alternation), the effects of varied magnitude and varied delay of reward, contrast effects due to shifts in reward magnitude, the effects of differing intertrial intervals (conceived as components of the stimulus complex), and so on. The theory has also been applied with considerable success to human probability learning and to resistance to extinction in that context; and a mathematical model casting the main constructs of the hypothesis within the framework of statistical learning theory was developed and tested (Koteskey, 1972). The consensus of researchers is that the sequential theory is the best one currently available for predicting the resistance to extinction produced by most reinforcement schedules. Surprisingly, it does not use any concepts of inhibition, frustration, or competing responses; instead, responses stop during extinction because the S^{N_k} stimuli become sufficiently remote on a generalization gradient from those conditioned to the response during training. A theoretical problem that remains is to combine the sequential hypothesis in some creative way with the concepts of frustrative nonreward and inhibition (these are simply undeniable effects) so as to produce a more general and complete theory of nonreinforcement and extinction.

INFORMATIONAL VARIABLES IN CONDITIONING

A view that is gradually becoming accepted is that in order to produce effective conditioning, even of the simple Pavlovian variety, more is required than simple temporal contiguity of the conditioned stimulus (CS) and the unconditioned stimulus (US). Rather, evidence is accumulating that, in order to become conditioned, the CS must impart reliable information about the occurrence of the US; it must be a useful predictor of the time, place, and quality of the US. Moreover, even if a given CS is predictive, it still may not become conditioned to the US if its usefulness has already been preempted by another redundant stimulus which is a better predictor or which has had a longer history of successfully predicting the US. These remarks are in regard to conditioning of excitation to cues predicting the US, but they also hold true for conditioning of inhibition to cues predicting the absence of the US in a situation in which the US otherwise occurs.

The basis for these conclusions is contained in a remarkable series of papers by Rescorla and Wagner (for reviews, see Rescorla, 1972; Rescorla & Wagner, 1972; Wagner & Rescorla, 1972) studying classical conditioning, using typically the "conditioned suppression" or conditioned emotional response (CER) paradigm. They also develop a simple but intuitively compelling theory to knit together the diverse range of results they and other investigators have turned up. The basic notion is that the effectiveness of a reinforcement in producing associative learning to a prior stimulus depends not upon that reinforcement itself but upon the relationship between the reinforcement and the outcome that the subject anticipates. Thus one and the same US occurrence can have either no effect or a strong conditioning effect depending on whether the organism expected it. The principle that applies to excitation due to expecting a US also applies to inhibition due to omission of the US. And if the subject anticipates a given US on a given trial due to past learning with respect to one CS, then the reinforcing effect of the US on that trial is altered with respect to other simultaneously present stimuli. The theory can be stated more precisely:

> Consider a situation in which a compound stimulus, AX, is followed by a given reinforcer, US_1. The equations below describe the theoretical change in conditioning to the component stimuli, A and X, as a result of a single such trial. V_A represents the associative strength, or amount of conditioning to A, and is presumed to be monotonically related to such dependent measures as probability of response or latency of response.
>
> $$\Delta V_A = \alpha_A \beta_1 (\lambda_1 - V_{AX}) \qquad (1a)$$
>
> $$\Delta V_X = \alpha_X \beta_1 (\lambda_1 - V_{AX}) \qquad (1b)$$

> The parameter λ_1 represents the asymptote of conditioning supportable by the applied US_1; it is US-dependent and is subscripted to indicate that. The α and β are learning-rate parameters dependent, respectively, upon the qualities of the CS and the US (Rescorla, 1972, p. 11).

Study of these equations brings out a number of salient points. The change in conditioning of a given cue depends largely on the difference between the potency of the US (λ) and the associative strength to the stimulus *compound,* denoted V_{AX}. As a first approximation, it is supposed that $V_{AX} = V_A + V_X$—that is, the strength of the compound is just the sum of the strengths of its components. Thus, the smaller is the difference between λ and V_{AX}—the better the US is predicted—the less will be the change ΔV_A resulting from another pairing of AX with the US. The Vs in this equation can be negative, representing the case of conditioned inhibition. These equations are similar to the linear operators used in stimulus sampling theory (see Chapter 8) to describe trial-to-trial learning changes. We now consider the application of this model to several cases of experimental interest.

Blocking. Suppose that stimulus A alone has already been conditioned to the US, so that $V_A = \lambda$. Assuming that V_X begins at zero strength, we now introduce the compound stimulus AX paired with the same US. But since $V_{AX} = V_A = \lambda$, the incremental Equation 1b for ΔV_X equals zero. The prediction is that no conditioning will occur to cue X. This result, originally suggested by Pavlov's work on the overshadowing of one cue by another, has been much researched recently (Kamin, 1969b). It is called the *blocking effect* because prior acquisition of the A-US association blocks later learning of the X-US association in the AX compound. The effect was at one time claimed by selective attention theories (see Trabasso & Bower, 1968); however, it seems due instead to the "unsurprisingness" of the US following A in the AX compound. If the shock intensity used as the US is increased between the A training and the AX training, a higher value of λ would now prevail, so that Equation 1b expects (and one now finds) some learning (V_x) to occur to cue X during the AX training. This learning is assessed when cue X is presented by itself after the AX training. Suppose on the other hand that the US intensity is lowered when AX is presented. This lowers λ in Equation 1b so that ΔV_X will be negative for awhile, until $V_A + V_X$ declines to the new λ value. This means that V_X will be negative or inhibitory when assessed in combination with some other excitatory stimulus, B. This result has been obtained by Rescorla (1972a).

Concurrent training of other stimuli. Consider again the case where compound AX-US trials occur; alternating with AX trials are trials on which A alone occurs, and for different subjects A alone is either paired with the US or is not so paired. The model predicts that the group receiving concurrent A-US trials will show much less conditioning to cue X than the other, unpaired group. Why? Because the A-US trials cause V_A and hence V_{AX} to be large, thus by Equation 1b reducing the increment ΔV_X, the conditioning of cue X.

Extinction by continued reinforcements. By judicious selection of a stimulus schedule, one can *extinguish* a prior habit to cue A by pairing the compound AX with the US! To illustrate, suppose the shock intensity supports a λ of 1.0, and we begin by pairing cue A with the US, applying Equation 1a until, say, the value of V_A increases to .5. At this point we now give a block of single cue X-US trials sufficient to bring $V_X = 1$. We now proceed to give a few AX-US compound trials interspersed among many X-US trials. On the AX-

US trials, we will have $V_{AX} = V_A + V_X$ $= .5 + 1.0 = 1.5.$, so that Equation 1a yields $\alpha\beta(-.5)$; hence, ΔV_A will be negative. So pairing A with a stronger cue X on AX-US trials has the effect of *weakening* V_A, the associative strength of cue A. This kind of prediction has now been confirmed several times by Rescorla (1972a) and Kamin (personal communication, 1972). It shows the utter inappropriateness of the simplistic doctrine that temporal contiguity of a CS and US is all that is necessary and sufficient to obtain strong conditioning.

CS-US correlations. Earlier experiments by Rescorla (1968) had shown that conditioning of a CS (say, a tone) to a shock depended on the probability of the US in the presence of the CS relative to the probability of the US in the absence of the CS (when the rat was merely sitting in the experimental chamber). The higher the *correlation* between CS and shock, the better the conditioning. For a given US probability to the CS, discriminative conditioning to the CS was made poorer by increasing the US probability in the absence of the CS. In the extreme case where shocks never occurred when the CS was on but occurred often in its absence, the CS was converted into a conditioned *inhibitor* of fear; it became a signal for safety rather than fear. These results, apparently showing the effect of the CS-US correlation, are consistent with the conditioning equations above. Identify A with the background stimuli of the conditioning box, and let X denote the brief tone interjected into the situation, thus making up conceptually an AX compound. The greater the shock rate to A alone (in the absence of the tone), the greater V_A will become; consequently, by arguments similar to those above, the less will cue X become conditioned through pairing of the compound AX with a particular shock rate. Furthermore, if the shocks occurring in the absence of X (the tone) are always preceded by a second cue, B (a clicking noise), then B in the BA compound picks up some of the conditioning, depleting it from A (the background alone), with the result that cue X in the compound XA can now acquire some associative strength in its pairings with the US. So, all these results fit together neatly.

Inhibition. Equations 1a and 1b can describe acquisition of inhibitory properties if negative Vs are interpreted as inhibitory for the response in question. If stimulus A alone is conditioned to a US, and then extinguished ($\lambda = 0$), V_A will increase, then return to zero, but will not become inhibitory. But suppose after A is conditioned, we select a neutral cue X and present the stimulus compound AX without reinforcement. In this circumstance, both A and X will lose strength, until the combination $V_A + V_X$ equals zero. That would occur when $V_A = -V_X$, with both differing from zero. So, comparing the outcome of extinction to AX versus A alone, in the former case (but not the latter) we expect component A to retain some excitatory strength ($V_A > 0$) when it is tested alone, whereas X will have become a conditioned inhibitor. In neither case will A have become an inhibitory stimulus. The conditioned inhibitory power of X would be revealed by its ability to decrease responding when added to a different excitatory stimulus (say, B), in BX test trials. Both of these predictions, residual excitation for A and inhibition for X following extinction to AX, have been confirmed experimentally (see Wagner & Rescorla, 1972). Moreover, as Equation 1b predicts, the greater the strength of conditioning of A in original training, the greater the inhibition acquired by X during nonreinforced trials with AX. Incidentally, the fact that X becomes inhibitory during nonreinforced trials to AX makes implausible a theory which explains the blocking of X in reinforced trials to AX as due to the

animal not "paying attention" to the added redundant cue, X. The attention theory cannot have it both ways.

Inhibitory blocking. Previously we have discussed blocking or alteration of excitatory conditioning. It is also possible to arrange to block the learning of inhibitory properties by a cue (Suiter & LoLordo, 1971). In a CER situation, cue A is first made a conditioned inhibitor in the sense that A occurs without shock in a background situation where shocks otherwise occur frequently. Once A is established as a safety signal, cue X is now introduced in the compound AX paired with the absence of shock in a background of otherwise frequent shocks. However, later tests reveal that cue X does not acquire inhibitory properties in this procedure. Its learning has been blocked by the presence of the redundant inhibitory cue A. This is consistent with Equation 1 if the Vs and λ are given a negative (inhibitory) sign.

Generalization enhancement. Traditional learning theory has an age-old dictum which says that the optimal way to train an S-R connection is by direct reinforcement of that response to that stimulus. By tradition, reinforcement of the response to a similar stimulus should never produce greater performance levels to a target stimulus than does direct training with the target stimulus itself. It appears that we shall have to abandon this commonsensical dictum, since Rescorla (1976) has found clear and predictable counterexamples, cases where training to a *generalized* stimulus enhances performance more to a target stimulus than does reinforcement to the target stimulus itself. This paradoxical outcome and the circumstances that produce it are predicted by Equations 1a and 1b.

To start the derivation, let us acknowledge that a frequent way to conceptualize similarity of two stimuli is in terms of common or shared stimulus elements (see Thorndike's or Estes's representations of similarity, Chapters 2 and 8). Thus, we may represent a simple stimulus like a high tone as a compound of stimulus elements, denoted *AX,* and another stimulus like a low tone as another compound, *BX.* Here, *X* denotes the common elements, whereas *A* and *B* denote those elements unique to the two stimulus sets. Now imagine that in conditioning the high tone to a shock US, Equations 1a and 1b apply to the separate *A* and *X* components of that stimulus. With repeated reinforcements of *AX,* V_A and V_X will increase together until their sum equals λ asymptotically. At this point, V_A and V_X will each be, say, about one half of λ.

If we were to continue reinforcing *AX* from this point, their strengths would not change according to Equations 1a and 1b. But suppose instead that we gave trials with the generalized stimulus (the low tone, denoted as *BX*) paired with shock? Since *B* begins at low strength, the combination *BX* has strength far below λ; so by the analog of Equation 1a, V_B will increase, and by Equation 1b, V_X will also increase during a block of reinforced trials on *BX.* This increase in V_X should be manifested when we test the subject again on the original training stimulus, *AX.* On such a test, the compound strength V_{AX} ($= V_A + V_X$) will be higher than before, higher even than if the subject has just had extended training on *AX* alone. In an experiment, Rescorla (1976) found just this result, wherein training on a generalized stimulus (following initial learning) produced greater conditioned responding to a target stimulus than did extending training on the target stimulus itself.

A further prediction is that the increment in responding to *AX* produced by interpolated *BX* reinforcements will be greater the smaller the contribution of the *X* component (V_X) to the original *AX* performance. One way to reduce V_X is to carry out original training using discrimination trials between *AX+* and *BX-*. By Equations 1a and 1b, such discrimination training will lead to a high value for V_A, a near-zero value for V_X, and a negative (inhibitory) value for V_B. If, following discrimination, we give a block of reinforced trials to *BX* (the former negative stimulus), large changes should now occur in V_X and V_B by Equation 1, since they began the block at such a low level. Again, this large change in V_X should be revealed by final tests with the target stimulus, *AX.* Rescorla (1976) found just such results: the enhancement in *AX* responding induced by interpolated *BX* reinforcements was greater when *BX* had been formerly used as a negative or nonreinforced stimulus. The reader should remember that the notations *AX* and *BX* are being used here theoretically to represent what experimentally are simply two stimuli—namely, a high-pitched and a low-pitched tone. But in conjunction with the Rescorla-Wagner theory in Equation 1, the "common elements" view of similarity predicts these paradoxical results.

In nearly concurrent work, Blough (1975) proposed a more general framework for combining the Rescorla-Wagner theory with the common-elements view of generalization along a stimulus continuum. Blough assumed that a one-dimensional stimulus continuum (such as the wavelength of light) could be represented as a sequence of overlapping sets of hypothetical stimulus elements, with a normal (bell-shaped) probability distribution of sampling elements near the center of the presented stimulus (indexed by the point of the physical stimulus). Blough used a generalized form of Equation 1 applied to the conditioning of each hypothetical stimulus element of each presented stimulus set. He applied this theory to fit data collected on steady-state discriminative responding by pigeons to colored lights along a wavelength continuum. His data showed generalization of excitation and inhibition, and behavioral contrast (an effect introduced in Chapter 7). Behavioral contrast was evidenced by exaggerated "shoulders" of greater or lesser responding near an "edge" along the stimulus continuum at which the reinforcement rate abruptly shifted from a low to a high value. Blough's results are depicted in Figure 9.7. Keypecks at wavelengths below 597 nm were reinforced on an average of one out of twelve trials, whereas keypecks at wavelengths above 597 nm were reinforced on an average of one out of three trials. While in general Blough's pigeons adjusted their responding to a stimulus in graded fashion depending on its reinforcement rate, an interesting aspect of the data in Figure 9.7 is the shoulder and trough to either side of the edge between the high- and low-reinforcement zones. These are contrast effects in performance analogous to those on edge-enhancement (so-called Mach bands) in sensory psychophysics (see Ratliff, 1965), and they follow in this case from Blough's generalization of the Rescorla-Wagner model. The theory fits all these generalization gradients in quantitative de-

tail. Interestingly, it achieves its theoretical uniqueness by combining ideas from several distinct areas—stimulus sampling theory's representation of a stimulus continuum, the theory of nearby interactions among stimuli from sensory psychophysics, and the Rescorla-Wagner theory of conditioning of elements within compounds. The theory achieves a most impressive fit to a range of orderly results.

Expectancy, Surprisingness, and Conditioning

Equations 1a and 1b provide an economic description of many important results in conditioning (see the papers cited for other results). It is clear that the effectiveness of a reinforced pairing depends upon the strength of other cues presented simultaneously in the compound. However, scientists are rarely content with descriptive equations; they want to dig deeper in order to understand the psychological processes or mechanisms that underlie the phenomena described by the equations. There have been a few theoretical conjectures about the mechanisms underlying Equation 1.

The basis of a good theory was presented in Kamin's (1969b) original paper. In discussing the blocking effect (described above), Kamin conjectured that animals learn a lot only about unexpected events, ones that surprise them; if the subject can already predict what is going to happen (as she can in the second phase of the blocking paradigm), then she is not surprised by the US, and she learns nothing new regarding predictors of it. In this hypothesis, the degree of expectancy of the US (or its nonsurprisingness) is the sum of its predictabilities from the total aggregate of cues preceding the US on a given trial. The term $(\lambda - (V_A + V_X))$ in Equation 1 thus indexes the surprisingness of the US on an AX trial; and clearly, learning increases with this difference.

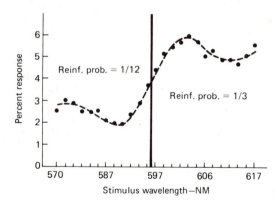

Figure 9.7. Relative response rates of three pigeons to key lights varying in wavelength. The vertical line separates the high and low reinforcement stimuli. Note the trough and peak to the left and right of the edge. (From Blough, 1975.)

To explain these matters, Wagner (1978) used several ideas from current information-processing theories of memory to propose a theory to rationalize the notion of surprisingness and Equation 1. First, expectancy is coordinated in Wagner's theory with the CS causing a representation ("idea") of the US to be retrieved from the animal's long-term memory (LTM) and made active in short-term memory (STM). (See the theories of STM and LTM in Chapter 13.) Wagner assumes that if the idea of an event is already active in STM at the time that event occurs, then no rehearsal (recirculation) occurs for the CS-US aggregate of events, and therefore no new learning or strengthening occurs for the events of this trial. If, on the other hand, the CS does not retrieve the idea of the US and enter it into STM, then occurrence of the US will be surprising, and the US-idea injected into STM will now be rehearsed with the CS so that a CS-US association forms.

While plausible, Wagner's theory that STM mismatch determines rehearsal (or consolidation) intensity has been difficult to test in a discriminating way, and only indirect evidence has been accumulated. Terry and Wagner (1975) have shown presumptive evidence that an unexpected US (shock) is maintained for a longer time in STM than is an expected US, which suggests greater rehearsal in the former case. Similarly, Wagner, Rudy, and Whitlow (1973) found that an expected Pavlovian event interfered less with new learning of a temporally adjacent Pavlovian episode than did unexpected events. Their experiment involved an episode to be learned (*A*-US), followed immediately on each trial by an expected event or an unexpected one. Learning of the *A*-US correlation requires that this dual event be rehearsed and maintained for a while in STM. But if a surprising event soon intervenes, it demands attention and gets priority with the rehearsal mechanism; thus, the consolidation

of the critical *A*-US learning process on that trial will be terminated sooner by an unexpected than an expected posttrial event. These were the results obtained, and they are quite similar to some found with surprising events in human memory. However, one would prefer a more direct test of the rehearsal assumptions.

As a further test of Wagner's hypothesis, Terry (1976) found that conditioning of a cue *A* to a US was much retarded if, just before *A*, a pretrial US was briefly delivered (US-*A*-US). In theory, this should have retarded learning because the pretrial US would cause the US to be represented already in STM at the time the real US occurs, and so no rehearsal of *A*-US will occur at that point. Extensive control experiments seemed to rule out distraction caused by the pretrial US as the explanation for the slowed rate of learning.

Habituation and Short-term Memory

Perhaps the best evidence for Wagner's theory comes from experiments on the *habituation* of a reflex to an unconditioned stimulus. As noted in Chapter 1, habituation refers to a gradual loss in responsiveness to a US that is repeated often and close together in time. If we assume that a US presentation causes an idea of the US to be activated in STM and to be maintained for a while (possibly being associated to the background cues), then a later US presentation would evoke a weaker amplitude of unconditioned response (UR), according to Wagner, because the idea of the last US may still be active in STM. This is Wagner's model of habituation and it fits the data rather well. It would explain why the UR diminishes more with repeated *massed* presentations of the US, why there is partial recovery of the UR over time (recovery is partial because of background conditioning of the UR), why interpolation of novel stimuli may release a habituated US-UR connection, why altering the background cues (e.g., the testing room) will release habituation of a reflex. and why changing the US eliciting a given UR (say, from food powder to a weak acid in order to elicit salivation) will release habituation of the UR. Wagner's theory also accounts for the phenomenon of the conditioned diminution of the UR (see Chapter 3, and Kimmel, 1966); this means that following CS-US pairings, the UR to the US will diminish when preceded by the CS, but will still be very large if the US occurs unexpectedly without the CS. This is predicted on the assumption that following conditioning, the CS causes an idea of the US to be activated in STM, so that when the US is actually presented it receives less reaction and processing. Whitlow (1975), an associate of Wagner's, published several further tests of the STM theory of habituation. Congruent with earlier results on habituation, Whitlow found that when pairs of tones were sounded, the UR (vasoconstriction) to the second tone was greater when it differed in pitch from the first tone. But the Same-vs.-Different tone effect decreased with time; it also decreased when a distracting light and vibrator stimulus were interpolated in the interval between the tones. These effects suggest that the Same-vs.-Different tone effect depended on short-term memory for the first tone, and that it was forgotten if either a distractor or a long interval occurred before the second tone. This is as expected by Wagner's theory of habituation.

This completes our brief review of Wagner's theory. The theory is important in tying together several distinct areas—short-term memory, rehearsal processes, habituation, interference and consolidation, and differential conditioning of elements within a compound of signaling stimuli. The range of the theory in encompassing a variety of phenomena is attractive. We can look forward to rigorous testing of these ideas in the future.

LEARNED HELPLESSNESS

Throughout this book we have worked on the implicit assumption that the term "learning" refers to the organism acquiring knowledge about regularities of events in its environment, learning that the presence or absence of event *A* is temporally correlated with the presence or absence of event *B*. In Pavlovian conditioning, the events are presentations of the CS and US, with the direction of the event correlation (positive or negative) being translated into an excitatory or inhibitory expectancy. In operant conditioning, the events are the occurrence of the instrumental response and the presentation of a reinforcer or punishment. Learning consists in the mapping of these event contingencies into the subject's brain as expectancies which then modify his performance.

However, a series of experiments by Seligman and Maier and their coworkers suggests an essential presupposition which the subject must have in order for any such learning to occur. The critical presupposition is that the subject must believe that the critical events are correlated and that they can be learned by proper attention and recording of them in memory. What Seligman and Maier have demonstrated (Maier & Seligman, 1976) is the converse proposition, that when reinforcing outcomes are independent of an organism's responses, it learns just that fact—that it will get the same outcomes whether it responds or not, and so responding is useless. This type of learning is metaknowledge; it is a second-order belief about response-outcome sequences—namely, that outcomes are independent of responses and therefore unlearnable.

While the possibility that organisms can learn that outcomes appear independently of instrumental responding strikes the layman as common-sensical, it turns out to be a novel form of knowledge for learning theory. Moreover, this knowledge operates in a peculiar manner. Once acquired, the belief in noncontingency tends to have widespread, even devastating, effects upon the subject in future learning situations. The effects are motivational, cognitive, and emotional, as we will discuss below.

One paradigm experiment was performed by Seligman and Maier (1967); it involved two phases for different groups of dogs. During Phase 1, the dog was restrained in a hammock and given many unpredictable, painful shocks. Some dogs could escape the shock by performing a panel-pushing response; other dogs received the same shock as the first dogs except they could do nothing to escape or control the shocks. During this first day, the escape subjects were presumably learning that the shock is controllable through their responses, whereas the inescapable-shock subjects learned that their responses have no influence. During Phase 2, on the next day, each dog received shock escape-avoidance training in a two-way shuttle-box, where prompt responding to a tone CS by jumping over the barrier between compartments was always followed by termination of the CS and avoidance of an impending shock. In this situation, subjects who received escapable shocks in Phase 1 quickly learned to avoid the CS. Similarly, control subjects not shocked during Phase 1 readily learned to avoid. In contrast, animals that received inescapable shocks in Phase 1 were practically "helpless" during Phase 2; they did not often jump to the other side to escape when the shock came on; rather they sat still, took the shock, and whined. They did not learn to escape or to avoid. These animals were severely debilitated, seemingly unable to help themselves deal with their traumatic situation. Because their inability to act depended upon a history of exposure to noncontingent, inescapable shocks, the phenomenon was named *learned helplessness* (LH for short).

Subsequent research has shown that something like the learned helplessness effect can be produced in many species, including humans, and that it occurs for various forms of appetitive reinforcers as well as for aversive stimulation. Interestingly, LH learned in one situation with one reinforcer will transfer to a second situation with a different reinforcer. For example, Hiroto and Seligman (1975) found that after being exposed to a long series of unsolvable anagram problems, human subjects in a second task failed completely to learn simple hand movements to escape and avoid a noxiously loud noise.

Maier and Seligman (1976) classify LH effects into three categories: motivational, cognitive, and emotional. The motivational deficit is most apparent; LH animals are very slow to *initiate* any active responses to get rewards or to escape or avoid punishment or frustration. They appear rigidly listless; they seem to give up and just wait for whatever event their environment has programmed for them. As the human subjects in Thornton and Jacobs's (1971) experiment on LH reported, they felt that they "had no control over the shocks, so why try."

The cognitive deficit of LH is more subtle but appears under proper analyses. Exposure to uncontrollable reinforcers or punishments creates difficulty for learning even when later responses do succeed; the LH animal or person is poor at perceiving that he has just now controlled the punishing event on a successful trial. This deficit was apparent in the early work showing failure of avoidance learning by LH dogs. If one of these dogs chanced to escape or avoid during the second phase of the experiment, he did not learn from that success experience (as normal animals did) that responding eliminates shock and that he can control it. His earlier LH experiences, that any form of responding was useless in eliminating shocks, seemingly gave rise to massive *proactive interference* with his now learning that responding can control outcomes. In later experiments, this cognitive deficit was also revealed by a changed ability of human subjects after LH treatments to estimate their degree of response-control over whether or not a red light would flash on a trial.

The emotional deficits of LH subjects are clinically interesting, and mimic those we associate with the hopeless, discouraged, or completely thwarted individual. The LH dogs seem very afraid, withdrawn, passive, depressed, and neurotic. The animals receiving inescapable shocks that cause learned helplessness also have very severe physiological stress reactions. Recent work relates learned helplessness to the failure of an animal's normal methods for *coping* with stress. This topic is of sufficient interest to warrant a brief digression.

Coping with stress. Animals have a complex range of internal reactions to stress. But how devastating and debilitating a given stress is psychologically depends markedly on whether the animal can prepare itself for the stressor and whether the animal thinks it has a way to *cope* with the stress when it arrives. The same factors have been identified as important in determining the severity of humans' reactions to their conditions of social or personal stress. Experiments by Weiss (1971a, 1971b) illustrate these effects with rats that received frequent electric shocks over many hours while strapped down on a table. If the shocks occurred often and at random, unexpected times, most of the rats soon developed severe stomach ulcers. If occurrences of shocks were signaled by a warning tone, fewer ulcers appeared. The fewest ulcers developed when not only did the warning signal occur but the rat could also perform a simple response to avoid or escape the shock. So the availability of a coping response appears to be a large factor in reducing the amount of psychological stress caused by a given physical stress. Of course, precisely this kind of coping has been discouraged in animals receiving the learned helplessness treatment. However, if performance of the coping response itself involves conflict (e.g., if it sometimes leads to further shock), ulceration then occurs again (Weiss, 1971b). Weiss found that the LH-stressed animals ate and drank less in and out of the stress situation, defecated frequently, lost weight and were listless. Weiss has also studied the physiology of these stress reactions, finding that animals with an available coping response to relieve stress had, during a period of shocks, lower corticosterone levels in the bloodstream and elevated levels of norepinephrine (a biochemical transmitter) in the brain than did controls without a coping response. In humans, drugs that elevate norepinephrine at the synapse are associated with activation and a euphoric mood, whereas mental depression is associated with depressed norepinephrine levels much like those of the helpless animal during stress.

Clinical depression and learned helplessness. In extrapolation to the psychiatric setting, Seligman (1975) has considered learned helplessness as an analog of human clinical depression, and has investigated many suggestive parallels between neurotically depressed patients and LH subjects in the laboratory. Thus, for example, depressed people differ from nondepressed people in judging their degree of response-control over events. Recently, the LH theory for humans has been modified by the addition of two factors: (1) whether the subject is told (or led to believe) that success or failure of her responses in a given task is a matter of skill or a matter of luck; and (2) whether she feels that what happens to her is largely under her control ("internal") or under the control of her environment ("external"). For relevant evidence, see a paper by Abramson, Seligman, and Teasdale (1978).

The research on learned helplessness is interesting for its novelty of conceptual approach and for its clear applications in clinical psychology. Most psychologists have intuitive or formal theories about hopelessness and discouragement in humans, which are closely linked with ideas about coping skills, about training of courage under stress, and about ways for overcoming depression (see Beck, 1976). Therapists are understandably interested in how to cure people of helplessness, or how to prevent them from becoming helpless when their environment briefly becomes noncontingent. These topics have been studied (Seligman, 1975); the "cures" get the patient to engage in some form of overt guided practice or participant modeling with successful performance of the coping response; the "preventive inoculation" uses healthy doses of contingent response-controllable training before and interspersed among increasingly longer bouts of noncontingent (or inescapable) aversive events.

The learned helplessness theory has met with some resistance among S-R theorists because they have no simple explanations for how an animal acquires trans-situational knowledge about event contingencies. Thus, S-R theory might envision that a dog receiving inescapable shocks would learn that responses A, B, and C which he has tried do not allow him to terminate the shock early. However, S-R theory envisions no mechanism that would enable the dog to conclude that *all* responses will be ineffective, or that shocks terminate independently of any response. Moreover, S-R theory can imagine no mechanism which will transfer such a hopeless attitude to new situations so that it would hinder learning with new responses and contingent reinforcers.

The competing theories to LH that have been offered (Black, 1977; Levis, 1976) have relied heavily upon the notion of super-stitious learning of responses during the inescapable-shock phase of the helplessness experiment. These responses then compete or interfere with active learning of the escape or avoidance response the experimenter records in Phase 2 of such experiments. (This is an example of proactive interference, see Chapter 6.) Thus, for example, if the animal by chance is crouching and freezing when the inescapable shock terminates in Phase 1, that response pattern will be reinforced and will occur more probably during the next shock; at that time, freezing would also be ongoing when shock terminates, and thus conditioning of the incompatible freezing "snowballs." If crouching and freezing are learned, then they will compete with running to escape and avoid shock in the second phase, and thus the LH effect would be observed. Such a view would predict that animals receiving the LH treatment would do well or poorly in the second phase depending on how compatible crouching and freezing were with the response required for reward in the second phase. Exactly these results were reported by Weiss and associates (1975); prior inescapable shocks *facilitated* subsequent learning of a minimal response requiring a rat to crouch and poke its nose through a hole, but interfered with its subsequent learning of a larger, more complex movement.

While plausible, the competing motor response hypothesis has not been very helpful in explaining all results. Maier and Seligman (1976) consider this and several other alternative hypotheses, and argue their case for the learned helplessness theory. The theory of learned helplessness is really a cognitive theory, concerned as it is with an animal's beliefs about the controllability of outcomes in a general class of tasks. Because it is a cognitive theory, learned helplessness theory fits neatly into other cognitive trends in theorizing about learning and motivation.

BEHAVIOR MODIFICATION

One of the most significant developments in recent years in psychology is the advancement in applications of behavior modification methods to many problems of social and personal adjustment. Some of these were briefly mentioned in Chapters 3 and 7, where we touched on systematic desensitization and contingency management methods. Behavior modification methods derive from learning principles and have by now been applied to a wide variety of behavior problems, from neuroses to problems of adjustment in educational classrooms, home, and work settings. Let us first notice how a behaviorist conceives of maladjustment such as mental illness or neurosis.

What is a neurotic, according to the behaviorists' view? Why do we classify a person as being abnormal or mentally sick? Learning theory (Bandura, 1969, 1971a; Mischel, 1971) suggests that this judgment is based on a social comparison, that compares the behavior in question to the norms of the social group. The neurotic has learned to behave in ways that are personally, legally, or socially disapproved and considered deviant. Of course, whether a given behavior is judged to be deviant, (whether it shows evidence of "craziness") depends on the social norms of the group doing the comparison (e.g., some forms of murder are approved during wartime).

The assumption of the behavioral approach is that people learn neurotic habits; they learn to be strange, even miserable. The function of psychotherapy, in this view, is to remove or replace the deviant behavior which is causing the misery. That behavior is alleged to be controlled by certain social stimuli and reinforcement contingencies. To eliminate deviant behaviors (or to replace them with approved behaviors), the therapist is to find the controlling stimuli or reinforcers, and remove them or alter them so that the de-

viant behaviors are extinguished or so that approved behaviors are strengthened in their place. The immediate goal of therapy should be to change the deviant behavior directly.

This general strategy is now called *behavior modification* or *behavior therapy,* and it is becoming a dominant approach to disturbed behavior in clinical psychology (Bergin & Garfield, 1971; Leitenberg, 1976). It is now being used successfully to treat all kinds of behavioral disturbances in all kinds of populations and institutional settings. Some examples of problems treated are depression, phobias, obsessions, drug-addictions, mutism, withdrawal, hyperactivity, self-injury, echolalia, bedwetting, eating disorders, temper tantrums, stuttering, excessive vomiting, insomnia, social deficits in autistic children, hostile attacks, and bizarre speech. The list is hardly exhaustive. Similarly, behavioral treatment programs are used in individual and group psychotherapy, in management of entire psychiatric wards, in prisons, in homes for juvenile delinquents, in institutions for mentally retarded children, for deaf-mute children, and for mentally disturbed children, in normal nursery schools, in primary schools, in the home setting, and so on. The simple procedure is to so arrange contingencies as to cease rewarding undesirable behavior and start reinforcing desired behaviors. Prosaic and banal as that sounds, the fact is that in specific situations identification and manipulation of the relevant variables can be an exceedingly subtle matter requiring some technical sophistication. A frequent problem is that important social agents— for example, those around a child—are not aware that they are subtly reinforcing the deviant behavior, most commonly with solicitous "attention" to the person when she behaves in the deviant manner. An autistic child may bang her head repeatedly against the wall. When she does this, the ward nurse runs and hugs her, partly to prevent her injuring herself. But if the nurse's reinforcing behavior is rescheduled so that she ignores the child when she bangs her head but pays attention to her and hugs her when she is not banging her head, then the frequency of head-banging extinguishes to zero. There are numerous similar examples in the behavior modification literature.

Characteristics of Behavior Modification Programs

The salient features of behavior therapy as a mode for treating disorders stem from its firm roots in behavioristic learning theories rather than from the intrapsychic, psychodynamic model popularized by Freud and psychoanalysis. Deviant behavior is not to be explained by appeal to underlying motives, conflicts, and personality traits, but by the person's habits acquired through her social experiences and reinforcement history. The goal of behavior therapy is specified in terms of creating new learning, by either teaching new prosocial behaviors that formerly were lacking or by replacing (or eliminating) antisocial or deviant behaviors. This contrasts with the goals of psychodynamic therapy, which are to help the client achieve insight into her unconscious conflicts, to make her feel whole again, to stimulate psychic growth.

Behavior therapists treat maladjustment or neurosis as a behavior disorder that is aversive to the client or to those around him. Their primary concern is with the *specific problematic behaviors,* not with some abstract trait description of the person. Consequently, behavior therapists devote much time to assessing objectively the problematic behavior before and during the therapy. In many instances, the therapist wants to assess the client's problem behavior directly in her usual social environments, wherever the problem occurs. To this end, behavior modifiers have developed a range of techniques for observing and recording problem behaviors in field settings. They are often dealing with people in ongoing work or family situations, or students in a nursery school or classroom. They have therefore had to invent ways to measure unobtrusively the rate of some target behavior in that setting, and then to find some way to modify that behavior without totally disrupting the environment.

The steps of a behavior modification program are roughly these:

1. Specify the problematic behavior as objectively as can be done, especially noting the situations when the problem behavior occurs frequently and when it occurs rarely.

2. Devise a way to measure the rate or frequency of the problem behavior (this will vary depending on its nature).

3. With the help of the client and any relevant supporters, decide upon the goals or objectives of the behavior modification program specified in behavioral terms.

4. Devise an intervention plan to alter the target behaviors, increasing those which are desirable and decreasing those which are undesirable; this is typically done by a mutual contract with the client, which spells out the desired behaviors and the reinforcement contingencies in terms the person can understand and can agree to.

5. After the intervention plan is set going, continue to record the problem behavior and keep monitoring the execution and progress of the plan; if it is not succeeding in changing the problematic behavior, then alter the plan or change some of its parameters (e.g., reward values); keep experimenting until the desired behavior comes about.

6. Once the problem behavior has changed to meet the initial goal, begin to phase out the intervention plan, building the behavior so that it can be maintained indefinitely by contingencies in the client's natural, social environment.

7. After phase-out, recheck for relapses in the client's problematic behavior over many months or years, and give booster treatments if relapses occur.

Any given case may use only a subset of these steps, but in principle all of them should be used. For each step in the process, a battery of techniques and advice is available to help the practicing behavior modifier. The first problem noted above, specifying the problem behavior objectively, is often a major stumbling block because lay persons are not accustomed to this way of characterizing someone's behaviors. For instance, parents or teachers will come to a behavior therapist complaining about a child who is aggressive or uncooperative or sloppy or inattentive, and ask the therapist to "fix it." But these labels describe trait inferences, not behaviors. So the behaviorist requires that the parent, teacher, client, and himself specify the problem in terms of frequencies of *behaviors-in-situations* (which are what led to *inferences* about aggressiveness or uncooperativeness). Then, each of these behaviors-in-situations may be observed, recorded, and perhaps become a target for change in the intervention program.

The problems of measuring and recording the rate of some target behavior have been much discussed; the variety of field circumstances often creates difficulties that require some ingenuity to overcome. The common measures taken are: time before a target behavior occurs; its duration when it occurs; its frequency per unit time or per opportunity to engage in it; its frequency during a specified recording interval; the frequency of time samples during which it occurs; or some derivative consequence of the behavior (e.g., "weight gained" is derivative from bites of caloric food). Techniques exist (see Kazdin, 1975) for time-sampled recordings of multiple behaviors from multiple subjects (say, several children in a classroom), and for checking reliability of the scoring. Use of one of these behavioral measuring techniques is necessary for any behavior modification program; the techniques themselves

are one of the tangible products of such behavioral technology.

The *intervention plan* is that spot in the program where specific learning principles are brought in to shape up desired behavior or extinguish (or replace) undesirable behavior. The most common technique is operant reinforcement: arrange contingencies to stop rewarding undesirable behaviors and begin rewarding desirable ones. The change may be very simple, as in scheduling a teacher to show approval (smiling, nodding, patting on back) to her students when they are paying attention to her and not when they are inattentive. The reward system may be made quite elaborate; the teacher could dispense tokens (poker chips, points) of differing value for desirable behavior, with the tokens exchangeable for various backup reinforcers like toys, play time, or candy. The rewards are tailored specifically to the client. Thus, a woman may reward herself with some pleasurable activity (e.g., reading a favorite book, skydiving, bathing in a hot tub) only if she has kept the number of cigarettes smoked that day below her target number. The Premack principle is routinely used by behavior modifiers in selecting rewards. The rewards are made contingent upon the desired response occurring, which is why such programs are said to involve *contingency management*.

Behavior modification therapists discovered early that the best contingency manager is the client herself, if she will cooperate in her behavior-change program. Thus, the client will be enlisted and trained on how to monitor and record her own target behavior (e.g., number of hallucinations per day, number of calories consumed), to plot these on a graph, and to reward or punish herself depending on whether she has met her goal for the day. Clients typically are involved in designing the behavior-change contract, stipulating what they should do or not do to get specified rewards. They also are often involved in decisions about changing the contingencies. This training in self-monitoring, self-regulation, and self-reward is therapeutic and beneficial insofar as it has continuing influence long after the client leaves the behavior therapist. Later, in Chapter 13, we will discuss the theoretical rationale behind such self-regulatory processes.

Familiar Behavior Modification Techniques

Let us briefly mention a few behavior modification methods and give some examples. Each has been used extensively in counseling or clinical settings.

Shaping. The target behavior is trained up gradually by adding more links to the chain or parts to the task. An example might be training a retarded child to dress herself more and more, by pulling on her slacks and blouse, buttoning up, putting on shoes, tying laces, and so on. Shaping also involves gradually advancing the criterion for reward as the target behavior is pulled along. Thus, a child might be required to study for increasingly longer times to earn TV privileges; a weight lifter must lift progressively more weight over weeks; a smoker fewer cigarettes every few days to earn his rewards.

Extinction. All rewards that might be maintaining some maladaptive behavior are removed, thereby decreasing its rate. For example, a child's temper tantrums can be decreased by having the parents isolate and ignore him when he has a tantrum; or a problem child in a classroom may be ignored completely as long as he is behaving badly. Extinction is also used extensively to reduce fear or anxiety; thus, a person with a phobia of harmless spiders or snakes may be exposed gradually to pictures

and actual situations involving the feared object that are increasingly threatening but which are shown to be harmless. This gradual reality-testing is called the *toleration* method, and its rationale was discussed earlier in Chapters 3 and 4. The procedure can be carried out in the imagination of the client, without external props.

Reinforcing incompatible responses. This technique eliminates a maladaptive response by combining nonreinforcement for that response with reinforcement for an alternative, prosocial response that competes explicitly with the maladaptive one. Thus, aggressive play between children may be decreased by the nursery teacher explicitly rewarding (by attention and approval) only peaceful, friendly play. A person who bites her fingernails may be trained to clench her fists and cross her arms in front of herself whenever she thinks of biting her nails. A phobic person may be trained, through deep-muscle relaxation, to remain calm as she is exposed to progressively more threatening interactions with the feared object or activity. This technique, called *desensitization,* relies upon a counterconditioning principle (see Chapters 3 and 4) that claims relaxation is incompatible with anxiety.

Modeling. Typically the client may not know how to perform the desired response. In such cases, he can learn by observing a competent model who sets an example and performs the target response correctly. The client then tries to imitate or match his own behavior to that of the competent model. Such imitation-by-observation is a basic form of learning, and we will discuss it later (see Chapter 13). Thus a shy, non-assertive man may observe a forthright person asserting herself when provoked by a social insult; the nonassertive man then might try to duplicate the assertive voice, body language, and content of the assertive woman he observed. Or a child frightened of a large dog might lose her fear by observing a friend playing and frolicking with the dog. The modeled behavior may then be practiced overtly or covertly (in imagination) by the learner. In overt practice, the learner tries to duplicate and practice some or all of the desired behavior in a safe setting (such as in the therapist's office or at home in front of a mirror). In covert practice, the learner tries to visualize herself in detail performing the desired behavior in the target situation of concern (such as asserting herself with an overbearing colleague at work). Often covert rewards (of success) are visualized to follow the new desired response. The goal of such behavioral rehearsal is to promote transfer of the new behavior to the real-life situation.

Punishment. An undesirable response may be inhibited by making punishment contingent on it. Thus, in a token economy, specific misbehavior may be penalized by loss of tokens or points. In a nursery school, disruptive aggression may be penalized by isolating the child in a dull "cooling-off room" for a while. An alcoholic wishing to abstain may take antibuse, a drug which causes him to become nauseous if he drinks alcohol. A smoker who wishes to quit may be forced to puff cigarettes rapidly in a small closet for 10 or 15 minutes until she almost becomes nauseated and ill from the excess smoke and nicotine. An obese person trying to lose weight may penalize himself by foregoing an evening snack when he exceeds his target calorie intake during the day. The punishment contingency in such cases may be reinstated in imagination at the time of the punishment; the person says to himself "I'm depriving myself now because I over ate at dinner." Covert, imagined punishment is often used to supplement other techniques for suppressing unwanted behavior. Behavior therapists are ambiva-

lent about the use of punishment in clinical settings: some believe punishment can be very effective in suppressing behavior; others believe it is ineffective and that in intense forms, it has undesirable side effects (e.g., the client resents and dislikes the change-agents). All agree that occasional uses of punishment in life-threatening cases have received bad press in the media and tarnished the public image of behavior modification techniques. Consequently, most avoid use of strong punishment in their programs for reasons of public relations—because the media has *punished* them for using it!

Stimulus control. Behavior prompted by cues can be controlled by controlling the cues. Thus, a smoker whose smoking is chained to drinking coffee may be asked (when he is trying to quit smoking) to refrain from drinking coffee. The over-stressed person may be sent away on vacation, the heroin addict may be sent to a detoxification center or told to avoid his addicted friends. In each case, the person is avoiding environmental cues that promote the problematic behavior. Furthermore, the client may have to be taught to discriminate appropriate from inappropriate situations for a behavior, which is a form of stimulus control. Thus, a supervisor may have to learn to criticize subordinates only in private and not in public; a shy person may have to learn what cues in another person's demeanor suggest she is interested rather than uninterested in talking; a juvenile delinquent may have to learn to discriminate that fighting is bad in school but all right in the boxing ring, that art work is welcome on paper but not on walls of buildings. Standard methods exist for training discrimination; for example, high-lighting and modeling appropriate situations for response, and contrasting these to inappropriate occasions, with rewards and nonrewards being delivered discriminatively for proper behavior.

The behavior modification techniques indicated are quite familiar in the abstract. The ingenuity of the behavior specialists has been in adapting and applying these principles to the complexities of actual cases. Often, when first presented, an emotional problem has no solution obvious to common sense. Perhaps because of the layman's tendency to overgeneralize about personality traits of the problem client, the case may be presented as a thoroughly global, confused, pessimistic and self-defeating picture. The skill of the behavior modifier is to cut through those layers of misguided impressions, pessimistic conclusions, and frustrations, and to redefine the problem as one of inappropriate behavior, as one for which positive programs can be undertaken. The effect of such affirmative actions, coming upon a long-standing scene of interpersonal frustration and hopelessness, is most therapeutic: the renewed hope for real change galvanizes the client and those helpers around him into taking positive steps to improve the situation. The frequent result of the behavior modification program is not only that the client changes for the better but also that his relationships with those helpers around him (e.g., parents, teachers, peers) improve immeasurably.

Range and Evaluation of Behavior Modification Practices

Behavior modification procedures have infiltrated and influenced practically every aspect of the mental health community, from casual self-improvement or personal adjustment courses for normal people to intensive, radical therapy with severe psychotics or pathologically disturbed people. The first author, for instance, routinely teaches a seminar in which normal college students learn and use behavior modification techniques to change some behavior of their own and that of a cooperative friend. The behaviors are items of concern to college students—improving study habits, concentration, social skills, swearing less, drinking or smoking less, saving money, losing weight, exercising more, reducing test anxiety, reducing fears of the dark, eliminating fears of hypodermic shots, stopping nail biting and nervous tics, reducing depression and loneliness, and so on. The problems sound small but are in fact of great personal concern. Such courses in behavior modification are quite common on college campuses, and the techniques are being widely disseminated. Similarly, such courses are often given to staffs of psychiatric clinics, hospitals, school counseling offices, juvenile detention homes, prisons, and institutions for the mentally retarded and emotionally disturbed. Furthermore, most clinical psychologists and psychiatrists are now trained in use of behavior modification techniques along with more traditional psychodynamic procedures. Behavior modification procedures have been applied to every psychiatric problem, and research comparing different methods is routinely reported in such journals as *Behavior Therapy, Behavior Research and Therapy,* and the *Journal of Applied Behavior Analysis.*

Is behavior therapy effective? That global question divides into many subissues: which alternative therapies should be compared; which therapies should be applied for which psychiatric complaints; how should improvement be evaluated and when; and so forth. The complexities of these issues are analyzed in a volume by Kazdin and Wilson (1978), who point out why global evaluation is difficult (for example, "behavior therapy" does not designate a single, uniform type of treatment). However, with due qualifications and hedges, it is nonetheless fair to conclude that behavior therapy is quite effective in improving the mental health of patients both on absolute grounds and relative to competing, nonbehavioral therapies. The distinctive features of behavior therapy are these:

1. Translation of the problem into behavioral terms, and setting behavioral objectives for treatment.

2. Emphasis on learning new behavior to improve the present problem rather than trying to uncover past causes for the present behavior.

3. Emphasis on explicit intervention in the patient's life, prompting her to alter her social environment, to arrange new reinforcement contingencies; deemphasis on taking medication, shock treatments, or brain operations.

4. Focus on assessing, changing, and monitoring the behaviors that constitute the problem; the motto is "the symptom is the problem, so cure the symptom."

5. Use of whatever therapeutic techniques seem called for, modifying those that are not proving effective in a given case (the therapist is accountable for helping the client).

6. Use of paraprofessionals or nonprofessionals from the patient's social support system to help in her change program; the goal is to change the problem behavior in the actual environment where it occurs, not in the therapist's office.

These features contrast with the layman's conception of treatments for mental illness; behavior therapy is indeed far from psychoanalysis. The stereotypical scenario of psychoanalysis has the patient freely associating upon the psychoanalyst's couch, trying to uncover repressed, unconscious conflicts and gain insight into the roots of remote traumas in his life. Psychoanalysts hope that such insights will cure the patient of whatever behavioral symptom brought him into analysis. The behavior therapists confront and argue against psychodynamic psychotherapists at virtually every step—in their theory of mental illness, their methods of assessment (Rorschach cards vs. situation-behavior inventories), and in content and methods of psychotherapy. The current trend and evidence seems clearly on the side of a liberal-ized (cognitive) behavior therapy. The increasing status of behavior therapy versus traditional psychodynamic therapy has clearly been one of the major revolutions in psychology, one bolstered and supported by behavioristic learning theory. More recent movements call for a synthesis of the behavioral, cognitive, and psychodynamic approaches to neurosis and therapy (Goldfried & Davison, 1976; Wachtel, 1977). This is clearly the direction for future development.

CONCLUDING REMARKS

It is out of the question to attempt an integrative summary that will neatly wrap up all the topics discussed in this chapter, along with accompanying prognostications of the future. We do not know how to do this, and we doubt whether it can be done in an intellectually honest, and yet satisfactory, manner. The analytical trend of modern experimental psychology has succeeded almost too well in breaking up the study of learning into many subfields and specialties. These specialties pursue their particular problems eagerly and penetratingly, but almost independently of one another. The behavioral modifications produced by experience (learning) constitute a vast subject matter. Specialization within it is to be expected, even required, if investigators are to uncover the myriad facts out of which a complex science it built. Regretfully, the day of the complete generalist in psychology has for quite some time gone into eclipse.

The topics of this chapter represent just a few of the many strands in contemporary research within behaviorist-associationist theories. One of the interesting developments to which we have devoted some space is the practical applications of learning principles to human clinical problems, as in use of biofeedback in behavioral medicine or behavior therapy in treatment of psychoneuroses. While these are engineering applications of basic principles, the clinical test situations have proven intriguing in their own right and have also been very worthwhile in feeding corrective information back to the basic theories and experimentation. A second trend, partly presaged in this chapter, is a strong movement of conditioning theories toward a cognitive, stimulus-stimulus brand of associationism, and away from stimulus-response theory. This trend, suggested in these early chapters by such phenomena as sensory preconditioning, short-term memory in animals, autoshaping (or sign tracking), and the Rescorla-Wagner theory of association, will be described more fully in the following chapters on cognitive learning theories. In recent years, psychologists working on learning have become more sympathetic to cognitive theory and less attracted to S-R theory.

Examination of the section headings of the current chapter—voluntary control, reinforcement, the law of effect, extinction, laws of Pavlovian conditioning, habituation—may at first glance suggest that the same old problems are being currently worked upon which have occupied psychologists almost since their profession was first recognized. A critic could interpret this in a depreciative manner to mean that no progress has been made in the solution of these problems, since they are still with us. The observation may be correct but the interpretation is not. Each of the terms we use has considerable scope and is merely a convenient chapter-heading label that is helpful in classifying and pigeonholing the volume of research knowledge, laws, theories, and small-scale hypotheses that have collected around a particular class of behavioral phenomena which presumably reveal fundamental processes or capabilities of some organism. As our techniques for manipulating and controlling behavior develop, we acquire the

means for generating genuinely novel behavioral patterns, some of a type never before encountered in just this form. As this is done, the range of an older term is simply extended to cover the new phenomena.

In a fundamental sense, the global problems of a particular science rarely change and the notion that they can be solved turns out to be inapplicable and naive. To cite an example, "understanding the nature of matter" was a problem set for physics by Aristotle, and it still remains today as a major problem for modern physics. But thousands upon thousands of small subgoals have been set and passed, advances have been made, and these in turn have generated and will continue to generate without limit further subgoals, questions, and searches for answers. Science is an enterprise that continues without end, because each good answer is sure to raise even more probing questions. What is true in the physical sciences applies also to the study of memory, or motivation, or forgetting, or any of the classical problems of psychology.

The science-game is infinitely more complicated than chess though it shares the same elements of skill, strategic planning, and fun. A general problem generates many subproblems, each in turn generating further subproblems, expanding quickly into an enormous tree of small issues, none of which ever really terminates. There are few criteria for evaluating the worth or importance of getting a partial answer to a given subproblem because the goal of the entire enterprise is never sharply defined. At best, the goal is envisioned in terms of "understanding" the problem or satisfying our curiosity. Many branches of the search tree are explored vigorously for a while and then abandoned for lack of satisfaction to the investigator, either because the results are understood too little or too well (until new doubts are raised).

How does one evaluate progress in such

an ever-shifting search tree? The only relevant criterion that comes to mind is the logical depth of the search—the number of subproblems that have been more clearly defined and investigated, or perhaps supplanted or bypassed in order to investigate more "fundamental" problems, and so forth. By such criteria, there has been a fair degree of progress in the research on learning. We are loaded with problems that we do not know how to solve and their numbers seem to multiply daily.

SUPPLEMENTARY READINGS

The following textbooks and edited collections provide detailed summaries of many developments in behavior theory.

BLACK, A. H., & PROKASY, W. F., eds. (1972). *Classical conditioning. II: Current theory and research.*

BOWER, G. H., ed. *The psychology of learning and motivation.* Annual volumes.

CATANIA, A. C. (1979). *Learning.*

ESTES, W. K., ed. (1975–1978). *Handbook of learning and cognitive processes.* Volumes 1–5.

HONIG, W. K., & STADDON, J. E. R., eds. (1977). *Handbook of operant behavior.*

LEITENBERG, H., ed. (1976). *Handbook of behavior modification and behavior therapy.*

LOGAN, F. A., & FARRARO, D. P. (1978). *Systematic analyses of behavior.*

MACKINTOSH, N. J. (1974). *The psychology of animal learning.*

O'LEARY, K. D., & WILSON, G. T. (1975). *Behavior therapy: Application and outcome.*

RACHLIN, H. (1976). *Behavior and learning.*

II

Cognitive-Organizational Theories

IO
GESTALT THEORY

During the first quarter of the century in America, the quarrels within academic psychology lay chiefly inside the framework of association psychology. Structuralism, functionalism, and behaviorism were all members of the association family. They are all examples of the working out of an *empiricist* methodology of science, whereby the accumulation of facts was supposed to lead one to the proper conception of nature. This complacency was disturbed by the new Gestalt doctrine which influenced the early American learning theories chiefly through the appearance in English of Wolfgang Köhler's *The mentality of apes* (1925) and Kurt Koffka's *The growth of the mind* (1924). Gestalt theory had been developing in Germany since it was first announced by Max Wertheimer in 1912, but these books, and the visits of Köhler and Koffka to America about the time of their publication brought the new theory vividly to the attention of American psychologists. Gestalt theory is one of the few examples of a *rationalist* theory in psychology. Gestalters begin with certain rather abstract ideas, concerning the nature of perception and thinking and the structure of psychological experience; they then proceed to *interpret* familiar observations in terms of these novel concepts as well as to arrange striking *demonstrations* of the operation of the alleged organizing forces to which their theory refers.

It must be remembered that Gestalt psychologists were primarily interested in perception and in problem-solving processes. Learning was viewed as a secondary, derivative phenomenon of no special interest; what was learned was a product of and determined by the laws of perceptual organization; what was performed depended on how the mind, using its current problem-solving processes, analyzed the structure of the present situation and made use of traces of past experience. It is easy to see why, with this orientation, Gestalters mainly did experiments on perception but relatively few studies of learning per se. Nonetheless, we will here give prominence to the learning studies they have done.

The strong conditioning and animal learning bias of early American psychology forced the Gestalters to undertake their discussions and controversies in America within the arena of animal learning and the special problems of interpreting it which were engaging the imaginations of psychologists at that time. Therefore, from its very first importation to America, Gestalt psychology was forced to defend itself on alien scientific territory.

For instance, Koffka's and Köhler's books had an important effect upon early American learning theory because of their detailed criticism of trial-and-error learning as conceived by Thorndike—a thrust at the very heart of the currently popular theory. The vigorous attack on Thorndike (and upon behaviorism) was supported by Köhler's well-known experiments on apes, described in detail in his book. Köhler's book brought the notion of insightful learning into the foreground, as an alternative to trial and error. He showed how apes could obtain rewards without going through the laborious processes of stamping out incorrect responses and stamping in correct ones, as implied in Thorndike's theories and as displayed in the learning curves of Thorndike's cats. Apes could use sticks and boxes as tools; they could turn away from the goal of the activity in order to adopt a means to the end.

Köhler's Insight Experiments

Köhler's experiments with apes were done from 1913 to 1917, on the island of Tenerife off the coast of Africa. His book about these experiments (Köhler, 1917) appeared in English in 1925 and immediately was widely read and quoted. Two main series of experiments interested American psychologists in Köhler's accounts of insight. These were the box problems and the stick problems.

In the single-box situation, a lure, such as a banana, is attached to the ceiling of the chimpanzee's cage. The lure is out of reach but can be obtained by climbing upon and jumping from a box which is available in the cage. The problem is a difficult one for the ape. Only Sultan (Köhler's most intelligent ape) solved it without assistance, though six others mastered the problem after first being helped either by hav-

ing the box placed beneath the food or by watching others using the box. The problem was not solved by direct imitation of others. What watching others use the box did was to lead the observer to attempt to use the box as a leaping platform, but sometimes without making any effort whatsoever to bring it near the lure. When the problem was mastered, a chimpanzee alone in a cage with box and banana would turn away from the goal in order to seek the box and to move it into position. This "detour" nature of insightful behavior is, according to Köhler, one of its important features.

The box-stacking problem, requiring that a second box be placed upon the first before the banana can be reached, is much more difficult. It requires both the inclusion of the second box into the pattern of solution, and a mastery of the problem of building a stable two-box structure. While the emphasis in secondary accounts of Köhler's work is usually upon the intelligence his apes displayed, he himself was at pains to account for the amount of apparent stupidity. In the box-stacking experiment, for example, he believed that the apes had shown insight into the relationship of one box upon another, but not into the nature of a stable two-box structure. Such physical stability as was achieved in later structures was essentially a matter of trial and error.

The stick problems required the use of one or more sticks as tools with which to rake in food out of reach beyond the bars of the cage. The beginning of insight occurs as the stick is brought into play, although often unsuccessfully, as when it is thrown at the banana and lost. Once it has been used successfully, it is sought after by the chimpanzee and used promptly. The most dramatic of the stick-using experiments was in a problem mastered by Sultan, in which eventually two sticks were joined together after the manner of a jointed fishing pole in order to obtain a banana which could not be reached with either stick alone. The process was a slow one, and the first placing of the sticks together appeared to be more or less accidental. Once having seen the sticks in this relationship, however, Sultan was able to "get the idea" and to repeat the insertion of one stick into the end of the other over and over again in order to reach a distant banana.

Köhler's interpretation of such performances by his apes was that they were intelligent attempts at problem-solving; that confronted with a problem, the animal could survey the relevant conditions, perhaps think through the probable success of a given act, then test it out as a possible solution to the problem. Köhler was particularly concerned with the way his apes might suddenly "see" the instrumental value of a tool (the stick as an extended arm) as a means to the goal. Because of these perceptual interpretations of the "Eureka!" experiences, they were dubbed *insight* experiments and the repetition of the successful act following insight was called *insight learning*.

Although the attack by Köhler and Koffka was chiefly upon Thorndike, it came at a time when American psychology was in the grips of a confident but somewhat sterile behaviorism. It is hard to see at this historical distance why such a common-sense and familiar notion as intelligent problem-solving (insight) should have created such a stir. But at the time, Watsonian behaviorism had, in fact, won support for a fairly hard-boiled view of learning, according to which the organism was played upon by the pushes and pulls of the environment and reacted in ways essentially stupid. The behaviorist doctrine was to avoid attributing higher mental processes to animals or men unless forced to do so as a last resort. Therefore, the return to a more balanced view, represented by the insight experiments, gave new hope to teachers and others who saw thinking and understanding returned to respectability. Insight was not a new discovery—it was a return to a conception

laymen had never abandoned. Nobody uninfluenced by peculiar doctrines would ever have denied insight as a fact—yet it took Köhler to restore it as a fact in American psychology. It was, in some respects, time for a change, and Köhler's experiments dramatized release from the negatives of Thorndikian and Watsonian thinking.

That the more enthusiastic reception for the new learning theories should have come first from the educators is not surprising.[1] There had already been a rift growing between Thorndike and the more progressive group within education, who, under Dewey's leadership, had made much more than Thorndike of the capacity of the individual for setting and solving his own problems. The child should learn by understanding the structure of a problem, not by rote repetition of an incomprehensible formula. The new insight doctrine fitted nicely their slogan of freeing intelligence for creative activity.

The visible opposition between Köhler and Thorndike was over insight and trial and error—that is, over intelligent learning as contrasted with blind fumbling. But the opposition between Gestalt psychology and association psychology goes much deeper. In order to understand this opposition, it will be necessary to examine Gestalt views in greater detail.

There are a number of variants within the Gestalt movement and among those strongly influenced by Gestalt conceptions. Köhler and Koffka were closest to Wertheimer, the official founder of the school. This chapter is devoted to their treatment of learning. Lewin, while originally from Berlin and definitely within the ranks, broke new ground. All four of these men, originally German, eventually settled in America, where they all have since died. They were the leaders of what is historically Gestalt psychology.

---

[1] It was an educator-psychologist, R. M. Ogden, who translated Koffka (1924).

The fullest and most systematic treatment of the problems of learning from the Gestalt viewpoint is found in Koffka's *Principles of Gestalt psychology* (1935). It was written after a period of acclimatization to America, and so meshes somewhat better than earlier writings with the concerns of American psychologists. Most of the direct references will be made to this source.

THE PRIORITY OF PERCEPTION IN GESTALT THEORY

Gestalt psychology had its start and achieved its greatest success in the field of perception. Its demonstrations of the role of background and organization upon phenomenally perceived processes are so convincing that only an unusually stubborn opponent will discredit this achievement. The primary attack upon association theory was an attack on the *bundle sensation theory*—the theory that a percept is composed of a bundle of sensation-like elements, bound together by association.

When Gestalt psychologists turned later to problems of learning, the concepts brought to the study of learning were those which had succeeded in the field of perception, and the arguments previously used against unstructured sensations were turned against the reflex. Despite the attention which Köhler's ape experiments received, Gestalt psychologists can be fairly said to have been only moderately interested in learning. This does not mean that their few experiments are without significance; it means only that they have considered the problems of learning secondary to the problems of perception. Perhaps in America the shoe was on the other foot, and in its preoccupation with learning American psychology had for too long been neglecting the relationship between the two fields.

The starting point for the Gestalter's treatment of learning is the assumption that the laws of organization in perception are applicable to learning and memory. What is stored in memory are traces of perceptual events. Since organizational laws determine the structuring of perceptions, they also determine the structure of what information is laid down in memory. In the case of trial-and-error learning in which the learner is confronted with some problem (e.g., to escape from the puzzle-box), Gestalt theory assigns great importance to the way the subject structures or "sees" the problem situation and how salient the correct action is within that structure. The ease or difficulty of the problem is thus largely a matter of perception. In this sense, Köhler's apes were presented with perceptual problems; if they literally "saw" the situation correctly, they had insight.

Laws of Perceptual Organization

Below we shall describe a few of the laws of perceptual organization as first proposed in a classic paper by Wertheimer (1923, translated and reprinted in 1938). He describes certain stimulus variables that determine how we group together certain stimuli, and thus how we structure or interpret a visual field in a certain way. Wertheimer mentioned a number of subsidiary factors, but we shall illustrate here only the factors of figure-ground, proximity, similarity, common direction, and simplicity. There were various attempts by the Gestalters to formulate a more general law stipulating the common features of these subsidiary laws of grouping. This more general formulation was called the law of *Prägnanz* (translatable not as "pregnant" but as "compact and significant"). This law simply says that psychological organization (read "perceptual groupings") tends to be "good gestalts" or "good figures," as determined by the subsidiary laws, and that this organization has the properties of regularity, simplicity, stability over time, and so on. Although Köhler and Koffka tried to explain the operation of this law of *Präg-nanz* in terms of dynamic distributions of fields of energy in the brain, subsequent generations have considered such explanations as relatively unenlightening (see Madden, 1962) and they will not be repeated here. However, we will try to show with each perceptual law an illustration of how it has been or could be used in a learning experiment.

1. *Figure-ground relationships.* The most primitive distinction the human perceptual system makes is between figure and background. Thus, the words on this page stand out as figures against the background of the surrounding white space. The figure is what you focus attention on; it stands out and is more noticeable or salient than the background. Typically, a visual figure is defined by contours or discontinuities of a different brightness or color with respect to the background. In some cases, what is figure and what is ground in a given scene is ambiguous, and the perceiver may organize it one way, then switch to seeing it another way. A familiar example of an ambiguous figure is the Necker cube in Figure 10.1 for which the front face switches into the back wall as the viewer spontaneously reorganizes it. Another reversible fig-

Figure 10.2. Reversible figure and ground. Note that either the light portion (the goblet) or the dark portion (two profiles) can be perceived as a figure against a background.

ure is Figure 10.2 that can be seen as two faces in silhouette or as a wine goblet.

The relevance of figure-ground to learning studies is that people learn primarily about the figure they focus in attention, and not about the background. What becomes an important figure can often be influenced by instructions to human subjects. If subjects are told to learn pairs of words presented on differently colored flash cards, they typically learn relatively little about color, because they have not paid attention to color and have not rehearsed it as "belonging to" the word pair on each card. Similarly if a subject organizes an ambiguous picture like Figure 10.2 as a wine goblet, she will fail to recognize this figure if on a later test trial she organizes the picture as silhouette faces. That is, her memory of that early experience is not of the "raw, unanalyzed" picture, but rather of a figural interpretation of a wine glass. This failure of recog-

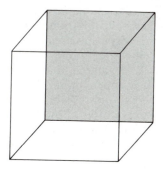

Figure 10.1. Necker cube. An illusion devised in 1832 by the Swiss naturalist L. A. Necker. Note that the tinted surface can appear as either the front or the rear surface of a transparent cube.

nition memory with altered perceptual interpretation of a stimulus was shown for pictures by Rubin (1921), by Wiseman and Neisser (1971), and for ambiguous naturalistic sounds by G. H. Bower and Holyoak (1973). The point is that it is *perceptually interpreted* objects, not raw stimuli, that are learned, and so the similarity of perceptual processes during learning and during retention becomes critical.

2. *The law of proximity.* Elements of a field will tend to be grouped together according to their nearness or proximity to one another. The closer together two elements are, the more likely they are to be grouped together. A few illustrations are given in Figure 10.3 using dots. In (a), the dots are perceived in groups of three, as *abc/def/ghi*, rather than another grouping like *ab/cde/fgh*. In (b), we group the dots as three rows of three dots rather than as three columns of dots. In (c), we aggregate the dots into groups *a/bcd/efghi/jklmnop* on the basis of their relative proximities.

These illustrate the proximity factor with visual stimuli distributed about in space. But we may also define proximity with discrete auditory stimuli distributed in time. In tapping on a drum, one will notice auditory groups emerging as a result

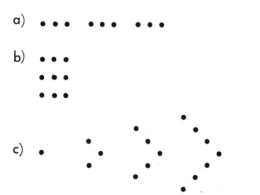

Figure 10.3. Illustrations of proximity as a grouping factor.

of alternating short and long time intervals ("proximities") between taps. These groupings elaborated into complex hierarchies of groupings within groupings, form the basis for musical rhythms.

These illustrations with dots and drum taps demonstrate the law with relatively neutral or meaningless stimuli. But this factor of proximity is in constant use when we communicate in reading, writing, or talking. We *hear* ("organize") speech as a series of distinct words with pauses between words and sentences, even though a spectrogram shows an almost continuous flow of sound (which *is* the way we hear an unfamiliar foreign language). In reading, spaces are used between words in order to se-gr-eg-at-et-he-wo-rd-si-nt-ou-ni-ts, and reading is very disrupted when this familiar segregation is broken. Strings of familiar letters or acronyms may not even be recognized if they are presented rapidly to the subject grouped into novel units.

Examples of the use of this grouping factor occur in research on memory by G. H. Bower and Winzenz (1969) and Bower and Springston (1970). The latter experimenters had subjects (college students) immediately recall a number a 12-letter series read to them according to a particular pause structure. With dashes to indicate temporal pauses, a typical series for recall might be *IC–BMF–BIJ–FKCO*. An important feature of such recall is that the pause-defined groups tend to behave as all-or-none units in recall; that is, the person tends to recall either all of the chunk or none of the chunk. This means, for example, that the *J* in the third chunk is much more closely tied (or associated) to *B* and *I* than it is to the *F* which follows it in order. Bower and Springston (1970) showed also that recall of a letter series was also much better if the pauses segregated it into familiar acronyms. Thus, the former series was better recalled if presented according to the pause structure *ICBM–FBI–JFK–CO* in which the pause-defined ("perceptual") groups correspond to familiar acronyms the person already knows.

You have met this law of grouping before in the guise of Thorndike's principle of belongingness. Two events would become associated only if they belong together, and one of the determinants of this belongingness of *A* with *B* is that the two occur close together in time or space. For example, suppose a student is told to learn from sight the following material:

CUF–NUX
PEL–JER
DEQ–PEM
SOQ–RIL

It will be found on later tests that he treated these as pairs, rehearsing and associating *CUP* to *NUX,* and *PEL* to *JER,* and so on. However, he has not formed associations from *NUX* to *PEL* or from *NUX* to *JER,* despite the fact that all these elements are spatially proximate to one another. The latter pairings are not seen as belonging together. This illustrates the fact that the paired-associate learning procedure capitalizes on more than the law of proximity for defining the groups to be learned, and for setting them off from one another.

3. *The law of similarity.* The law of similarity states that items similar in respect to some feature (shape, color, texture, and so on) will tend to be grouped together, provided this is not overridden by proximity factors. A few illustrations of this factor are given in Figure 10.4. Panel (a) is organized into successive triplets of black and white dots. Panel (b) is seen as successive columns of white and black dots in alternation. These similarity factors can be put into opposition or supplementation to the groupings suggested by proximities of the elements. Panel (c) shows opposition of the two factors in which spatial proximity clearly wins; these are seen as spatially segregated pairs with black and white dots al-

Figure 10.4. Illustration of grouping by similarity (of brightness and size in this instance).

ternating in their left-right order. Panel (d) shows "addition" of the two factors, both suggesting the same groupings.

A similar factor operates in the perception of auditory groups, say of tones differing in pitch. Thus two notes (C and F) played in pairs will be heard as CC/FF/CC/FF rather than as C/CF/FC. This factor also contributes to the perception of musical rhythm.

This factor is utilized constantly when we read or speak. For example, at a cocktail party, we can pick out and listen to a particular speaker against a noisy background because of the similarity of the speaker's voice quality from one moment to the next. Our shadowing or following of a spoken message becomes exceedingly difficult if the voice quality is constantly altered (e.g., by splicing in on a tape recorder a different voice for each word in the message). A similar result occurs with reading WhErEaLlThElEtTeRs (where all the letters) within a word are usually about the same size and color, making for ease of grouping.

A learning experiment by G. H. Bower (1972a) illustrates the potency of this similarity factor in promoting chunking of letter groups in recall. College students were shown flashcards on each of which were printed 12 equally spaced letters which in fact comprised four familiar acronyms. The letters varied in size, on some cards the large and small groupings corresponding to the acronym series, on other cards not corresponding. An example of a corresponding series is YMCAusaIBMgi, whereas a noncorresponding series of the same letters would be YMcauSAIbmgi. Each series was shown for only a few seconds before the subject was asked to recall it from memory. As expected, when successive letters of an acronym were presented in the same size, they tended to be seen together as a group, and to be recognized and recalled as the familiar group that they were. In the noncorresponding cases, however, subjects tended to adopt the groupings (by size similarity) into unfamiliar chunks, and so recalled the string more poorly. Thus, for instance, in the above illustration, the person would tend to recall the letters *SAI* as an all-or-none unit (albeit poorly) rather than overcoming the perceptual groupings to recall *USA/IBM* as units. A similar effect on recall was produced by only varying the *colors* of the successive letters on the card. The first four letters might be red, the next three yellow, the next three brown, and the last two blue. If the acronyms of different lengths were also arranged in this order, first the acronym of length 4, then two of length 3, finally the acronym of length 2, then the letters of a given acronym would be of the same color, which aided their utilization and boosted their recall. But if the order of acronym lengths conflicted with the colors, recognition of familiar abbreviations was poorer and recall of the briefly shown series was much worse.

4. *The law of common direction.* A set of points will tend to be grouped together if some appear to continue or complete a lawful series or extrapolate a simple curve. This is best illustrated with some examples as shown in Figure 10.5. Consider panel (a) for instance. By a measure of physical proximity, the dots comprising lines *A* and *B* are closer together than the dots comprising lines *A* and *C*. And yet our eye tends to assign *A* and *C* to the same group—namely, as parts of the simple line *AC,* and *B* is just an appendage sticking off this line. However, by moving line *A* closer to *C,* as in the right-hand figure of panel (a), the organization is now altered so that *A* and *B* go together to make up a line unit, whereas *C* now becomes the appendage. In this latter case, *B* is an *extrapolation* of the curve (line, rule) begun in part *A*.

Panel (b) is simply a set of dots arranged in a saw-toothed line by a "directional interpretation" of the dots. But alternative views are logically possible; for example, the second row of dots could have been organized as three sets of dot pairs in a row. But they are not; common, simple direction of the dots dictates the saw-toothed organization.

In panels (c) and (d), the principle of good continuation is illustrated somewhat differently. Panel (c) is seen (organized by our perceptual system) as a wavy curve (*AD*) cut by a line (*BC*); but we logically could have seen it as the wave-plus-line *AC* attached to the line-plus-wave *BD*. In the same manner, panel (d) is organized as a series of square teeth intersected by a continuous wavy line, whereas it logically could have been seen as a top half *C, D, G, H, K, L* drawn above the bottom half *A, B, E, F, I, J, M.* The factor of common direction or "common fate" determines the former natural descriptions of these drawings.

Panel (e) illustrates a point similar to that in panel (a)—namely, that our eye pairs line segment *A* with *C* because one is a regular, smooth continuation or extrapolation of the other, whereas segment *B* or *B¹* alters the direction of the curve, putting a "kink" or discontinuity in the curve.

It is relatively easy to demonstrate the learning effects due to the factor of good continuation. One elementary demonstration is by Kaswan (1957), who tested subjects' ease of "associating together" pairs of geometric figures, *A* with *B*, where segment

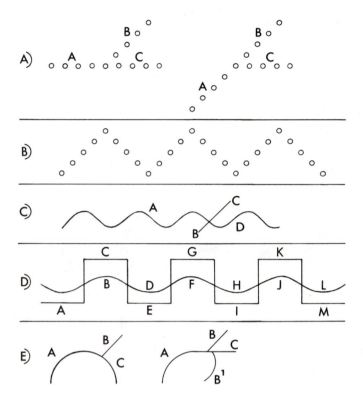

Figure 10.5. Illustrations of common direction or good continuation.

B either was or was not a good continuation of segment *A*. After seeing many different *A-B* pairs, the subject was tested by presentation of part *A* of each pair and asked to recall (in drawing) part *B*. Looking, for instance, at panel (c) of Figure 10.5, the subject would be shown segment *A* and have to recall the part it was paired with, either *D* (if it had exemplified good continuation) or *C* (if it had not). As expected, Kaswan found that pairs exemplifying the good continuation principle were learned and recalled much better than pairs not exemplifying this principle.

This demonstration incidentally raises the issue of whether the responses in the continuation and noncontinuation cases convey the same amount of information, given the stimulus as a recall cue. Given extrapolation of the cue, there are no more than a few good continuations, or possibly only one, to produce in response to a cue segment, but there are literally an infinite variety of possible noncontinuations. Perhaps the important feature is that, for good continuation pairs, the stimulus constrains the possible responses to one or a small number.

The principle of good continuation can be shown with alphabetic or numerical materials, whenever there is some possibility of inducing a *rule* for extrapolating a series of items. This kind of extrapolation is involved in letter-completion problems of the sort often found on intelligence tests. A few letters are given in a series, generated by some periodic rule by cycling through the alphabet (forward or backward); the person is to infer what the rule is and apply it to generate the next element. Thus, the series *abcbcdcdede* has a period of three, and cycles through the forward alphabet; the series therefore would be completed by the letter *f.* Similar problems of inducing a generating rule occur with mathematical series; thus, the series 1, 3, 7, 13, 21 is recognized as the series $n^2 + n + 1$ and has 31 as the next successor.

Also illustrating good continuation in the learning context are experiments by Restle and Brown (1970) on the learning of serial patterns, in which subjects learn to predict recurrent periodic sequences of digits such as 3454543. It is shown that subjects conceptually break the sequences down into "runs" (like 345) and "trills" (like 454), and learn the pattern as an organized hierarchy of such parts or subsequences. A run of numbers as in the musical scale is defined by continuation of a series of elements in a given direction.

5. *The law of simplicity.* This law says that, other things being equal, the person will see the perceptual field as organized into simple, regular figures. That is, there will be a tendency toward the *good gestalts* of symmetry, regularity, and smoothness. Again, this notion is easier to illustrate than to describe in words; Figure 10.6 shows a few examples. For instance, our eye tends to divide the figure of panel (a) into an ellipse (*AC*) overlapping with a square (*BD*), although another logically possible decomposition is *AB* (an ellipse with a chunk missing) abutting to *DBC* (a square with an interior arc). Similarly, in panel (b), the figure on the left appears as two overlapping icicles, whereas the figure on the right appears as a diamond inscribed inside a long icicle; yet the latter is logically (though not psychologically) decomposable into the same two overlapping icicles oriented differently. In panel (c), the pressures toward simplicity persuade us to structure the design as "a circle in front of a triangle," inferring the occluded triangle rather than describing the matter as "three small spurs at 4, 8, and 12 o'clock on a circle."

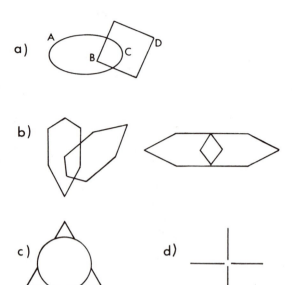

Figure 10.6. Some illustrations of figural simplicity as a factor in perceptual organization.

In these cases, and hundreds of others of the same general type, figural simplicity is an overriding principle dictating the way in which the picture will be "parsed" or decomposed into constituents. Pictures are always ambiguous in this sense of having multiple logical decompositions; they are also ambiguous insofar as a two-dimensional array can be the projection of a large variety of three-dimensional objects and relations. But the Gestalt principle of simplicity (or good gestalt) goes a long way toward prescribing which decomposition or which interpretation of the ambiguous picture will dominate.

Another demonstration of the law of simplicity is shown by the blind-spot experiment schematized in panel (d) of Figure 10.6. Everyone has a blind spot in each eye; it is that spot on the retina from which the optic tract emanates. A point stimulus projected precisely on this spot is not seen; it is a blind spot. With this as background, the crucial observation can be explained.

Suppose we have discovered that when a person stares at a certain spot to one side of the figure in panel (d), his blind spot is located in space precisely at the intersection of the four lines of the figure. If the figure in panel (d) is now presented to the person in such a way that its center is located at his blind spot, he will "fill in the gap" and see the lines in peripheral vision as a complete cross. Other figures with gaps yield similar perceptions of closed, complete figures. The person fills in the gap with the redundant, predictable extrapolation of the simplest description of the figures. This is sometimes referred to as the phenomenon of *closure*. The principle is that closed areas or complete figures are more stable than unclosed areas or incomplete figures.

These principles of perceptual organization can be put to use in the art of *camouflage* (Wertheimer, 1923), wherein a particularly significant figure is hidden or buried by extending and supplementing its lines so that attention is totally distracted from the original shape. In this way we make a particular parsing of the pattern unlikely. A simple example of such a transformation of the letter *F* is shown in panels (a), (b), and (c) in Figure 10.7. The *F* is totally hidden or "embedded" in the hourglass figure (c) on the right. On the other hand, if the lines are added but not touching the ends or continuing the lines of *F*, as in panel (d), the *F* still stands out as a distinct unit.

The Wholist Nature of Perception

Gestalt psychologists emphasized that the perception of form emerged from the relationships among the parts of the form, and in this process the parts might lose their former properties and take on new properties determined by the form of the whole pattern. The camouflaging of the *F* in Figure 10.7c is a simple example; the lines of the *F* are simply assimilated into another form and appear as bands on the hourglass figure. Another example is the tones comprising a musical melody. Played in isolation, each tone has a certain sub-

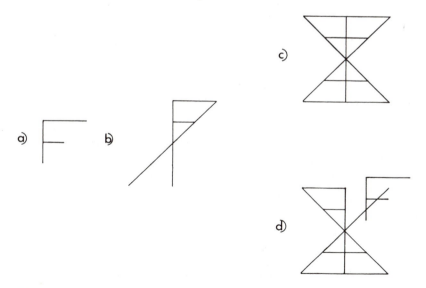

Figure 10.7. Example of successive stages in camouflaging a shape, the letter *F*.

jective pitch and loudness; but in the context of a melody the subjective pitch or loudness of the tone depends on the relation to its neighbors. The same note will sound utterly different when played in two different melodies. Similarly, a melody itself is an auditory form defined by the relationships (ratios) between successive tones, not by the absolute tones, since the same melody can be transposed and played in almost any musical key or octave by any instrument. Perceptual forms are said to "emerge" out of particular arrangements of elements, and to have properties not predictable simply from the properties of the elements. An example of an emergent physical property would be the liquid nature of water composed of hydrogen and oxygen gases; an emergent psychological property is the apparent motion (or the *phi phenomenon*) created by rapidly showing a discrete series of overlapping still photographs (of continuous movements) as is done at the cinema.

Such examples illustrate the idea that the attributes of the parts, insofar as they can be defined, depend upon their relations to the system as a whole in which they are functioning. This *wholist* view of perception has largely been accepted in modern perceptual theories, where it is labeled as *context-determined* or *top-down processing.* The point is that aspects of the entire pattern may be hypothesized before specific parts can be identified. An example is shown in Figure 10.8. The facial features (nose, ear, lips) recognizable in the context of the face would not be identified as such out of context. Modern theories of form perception use information from the complete pattern to constrain interpretation of the parts.

To make the discussion relevant to learning, the determination of part properties by wholist features is easily arranged in human memory experiments. The difficulty of remembering a list of words for free recall is known to depend upon the relation-

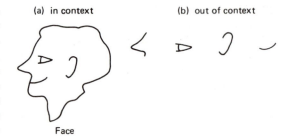

(a) in context (b) out of context

Face

Figure 10.8. Illustration of the identifiability of line drawings as facial features in context or out of context. (From Palmer, 1975.)

ships among the words. For instance, if a simple rule describes a set of words, then remembering of that set is enhanced considerably. An example of one such rule would be that all words on the list rhyme with *frog.* That is a *retrieval rule* that the knowledgable learner can use to generate at recall the candidates from the list of items to be learned. Thus, an item like *smog* has become easy to remember (compared to its difficulty in a random list) because of a whole-list property—namely, its presence in a list of words that rhyme with *frog.* For more subtle examples of wholist properties that facilitate recall learning, see papers by G. A. Miller (1958) and Whitman and Garner (1962).

THE SPECIAL PROBLEMS OF LEARNING

The general point of view of Gestalt psychology is expressed in the statement that the laws of organization apply equally to perception and to learning. There are, however, special problems within learning upon which Gestalters especially elaborated their ideas. They were most at ease in discussing human memory rather than animal conditioning experiments, and so most of the following illustrations deal with human memory. An initial problem is how to represent a memory—that is, how to conceptualize the way past experiences persist into the present. This is the concern of their trace theory, to which we now turn.

The Trace Theory

The Gestalt conception of a memory is not very different from that of Aristotle, who believed that perception stamped in a corresponding memory trace. Gestalters hold that the neural processes active during perception can endure in a subdued form as a trace. Thus, information is stored in substantially the same form, by the same neural processes, as in the original perception. As Köhler describes the matter:

> Neural events tend to modify slightly the state of the tissue in which they occur. Such changes will resemble those processes by which they have been produced both in their pattern and with respect to other properties (1938, p. 236).

Recall or remembering involves the reactivation of a given memory trace; in effect, it is a revival of the same perceptual processes that corresponded to the original perception. The trace continues to exist as an active process in the nervous system; but it is of too low an intensity to enter consciousness. In recall, a cue selects out and amplifies the intensity of a particular trace to raise it over the threshold of consciousness.

The empirical phenomenon of association, or *coherence* of elements *A* and *B* in memory, is viewed by Gestalters as a by-product of *A* and *B* becoming fused into a single unit, a unitary percept. The elements *A* and *B* do not remain as independent, separate, neutral facts connected by an indifferent bond like a piece of string between two distinct objects. Rather, *A* and *B* become organized or fused into a single object, a unit, a chunk. The laws of organization help prescribe how these units will be formed and how easily they can be formed. The ancient laws of association delineated by philosophers—contiguity, contrast, similarity, cause-effect, and so on—were seen as corresponding to Gestalt laws governing the formation of organized units—namely, proximity, similarity, good continuation, and closure.

Solomon Asch (1969; Asch et al., 1960) has produced several compelling demonstrations of the role of perceptual relations in promoting coherence of two items in memory. He has collected evidence regarding figure-ground, constitutive, and part-whole visual relations. In the figure-ground experiment, the person was exposed to a set of ten nonsense shapes paired with ten colors. There were several conditions corresponding to different relations between the color and the shape with which it was paired. Four of these conditions are illustrated in the top panel of Figure 10.9. The frame represents the flash card on which the form was shown. In case (a), the color (C) was seen as belonging to the surface of the figure against a white background (W), whereas panel (b) shows the figure as white against a colored background. In case (c), the color is seen as belonging to the outlined contour of the nonsense shape, whereas in case (d) the whole card is colored and the shape is outlined in black (B). After exposure to ten such figures, each subject was given a memory test: a duplicate of each contour, drawn in black on a white background, was to be matched to one of ten colored patches identical to the colors used in the exposure series. The results were that when the color was presented as belonging to the figure—was its surface or contour color as in panels (a) and (c)—matching on the memory test was about twice as good as when the color belonged to the background rather than to the figure, as in panels (b) and (d). In this manner, Asch established that coherence of an attribute and object in memory was controlled by its coherence in perception. These results were replicated and extended by Arnold and Bower (1972).

Another relation, illustrated in the mid-

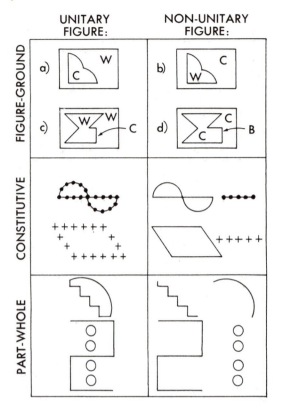

	UNITARY FIGURE:	NON-UNITARY FIGURE:

FIGURE-GROUND

CONSTITUTIVE

PART-WHOLE

Figure 10.9. Examples of unitary and nonunitary relations between perceptual items. (Adapted from Asch, 1969.)

dle panels of Figure 10.9, is the *constitutive* relation, in which a given form is composed or constituted of another set of smaller forms. For example, Figure 10.9 shows a sort of figure-eight constituted of black dots, and a rhombus constituted of small pluses. The pluses and the dots are the *modes* in which the larger forms are expressed. As in the previous experiment, a subject would be exposed to a set of nonsense forms expressed in particular modes, and then later would be given a memory test to assess the coherence in memory of the form with its mode. The control condition involved nonunitary presentation of the same two forms: the form (e.g., rhombus)

would be shown on the left in outline paired with a line of pluses (the mode) on the right of the study card. The two groups would be compared on a matching test in which each outlined, larger form was to be matched up with its paired smaller form (the mode). Again, subjects exposed to the unitary figures, in which the two shapes were related as "form X composed of mode Y," showed about twice as much coherence in memory of the shape pairs as did control subjects exposed to the nonunitary pairs.

A similar effect was produced by the part-whole relation, of which two are illustrated in the bottom panel of Figure 10.9. As can be seen, a unitary picture would be divided into two subparts, separated horizontally to make up the nonunitary control pairs. Subjects who had studied the unitary pictures nearly always recalled the subparts together accurately, whereas control subjects were likely to recall only one subpart or to mispair subparts when several were recalled. So again, perceptual unity of subparts made for unity of these subparts in memory.

The significant point here is that the simple law of association by contiguity is inadequate to handle these several illustrations. Asch and his predecessors have emphasized the *relation* between two elements or features as a means for cementing them together into a unit or chunk. Temporal or spatial contiguity (*A* before *B*, or *A* beside *B*) is not by itself a particularly compelling or salient relation; it is rather a necessary condition for other, more useful relations to be manifested. This emphasis goes counter to the elementarism of some forms of associationism which regarded relations not as primary facts but as decomposable into nonrelational facts occurring in contiguity.

The examples above use visual geometric stimuli to illustrate unitization effects in memory. However, similar types of effects can be shown with verbal or linguistic materials. As one example (Asch, 1969), two nonsense syllables can be more quickly associated together if they are pronounced together, blending and fusing like a two-syllable word (e.g., JATPIR or FUBNOL) instead of being treated and pronounced separately in cyclic pairs (e.g., JAT–PIR). As a second example, a list of three-word clichés (e.g., Happy New Year, ham and eggs, kick the bucket) will be better recalled (and coherently recalled) if they are presented as the set of familiar clichés they are than if all the words are scrambled and presented in unfamiliar triplets. The cliché is a unitary chunk for purposes of memory; it is recalled in all-or-none manner. As a final example of unitization, many mnemonic devices for improving one's memory require the learner to associate two items by imagining the two in some kind of unique relation, typically some vivid interaction. For instance, to remember a list of errands in which I am to buy milk after I buy a pair of shoes, I can associate *shoes* with *milk* by imagining my shoes filled with milk and myself drinking the milk from the shoes. Such bizarre elaborations demonstrably improve our memories (Bower, 1970a; Paivio, 1971). Gestalters would claim that such elaborations improve memory because they serve to relate and organize the two items (*shoes* and *milk*) into a single conceptual or imaginal unit, and association is a byproduct of relating. Without some such hypothesis, it is difficult to understand why adding supplemental material to a complex of elements to be associated should facilitate rather than compete with formation of associations between the critical elements.

Forgetting

After exposure to learning materials and after perception has laid down a unitary trace in memory, how does forgetting occur? Gestalt psychologists pointed to two separate aspects, or causes, of forgetting, one concerned with difficulties of trace retrieval at the time of testing, and the other concerned with the decay and disintegration of the trace by virtue of its contact with interfering traces. We will discuss each of these problem areas in turn.

Forgetting as retrieval failure. It was Höffding (1891) who pointed to a particular problem previously overlooked by association theories—namely, the question of how perception of a current stimulus can selectively retrieve past memories of specific relevance to that stimulus. From the vast file of memories we carry about with us, how does the present situation make contact with that specific memory which is appropriate to the occasion? Suppose stimulus objects A and B become associated, which means that some neuronal processes a and b have (in Gestalt theory) become fused into an interdependent unit ab. Due to changes in the prevailing psychological milieu, the later presentation of stimulus A is a different event than before, giving rise to a somewhat different perceptual process, a'. The question is how a' selectively retrieves the trace ab rather than any of thousands of alternatives; this hypothetical gap between presentation of A and retrieval of the trace ab is called the *Höffding step*, since he was the first to discuss this problem.

It is important to recognize that this was a problem with classical associationists. They gave explicit attention to association but relatively little to stimulus recognition. Höffding pointed out that stimulus recognition, retrieving a from a', would seem to be psychologically prior to activation of an a to b association. Associative recall will surely fail unless the cue is recognized as something about which something has been learned.

Höffding suggested that a' made contact with the a in the ab memory trace on the basis of *similarity;* because a' was more similar to a than to traces of other stimuli, the trace *ab* would be retrieved rather than some other one. The Gestalt psychologists picked up this idea and argued further (e.g., Koffka, 1935) that it was their version of the law of similarity that explained how *a* and *a'* became grouped together at the time of retrieval.

A basic problem with this similarity approach to retrieval is that it is essentially vague and unrevealing. Stimuli or situations have multiple descriptions; so between any three situations *A, B, C*, there can be a multitude of similarities and differences—on some dimensions of description, *A* is closer to *B*; on other dimensions, *A* is closer to *C*. The problem thus becomes one of weighting the various components of similarity so as to come out with unambiguous predictions. Without independent assessment of "psychological distances," ex-

planations of phenomena in terms of the similarity of the cue and the trace tend to be post hoc rather than predictive before the fact.

Some illustrations of retrieval cues of differential effectiveness are shown in Figure 10.10 for four different examples of inputs to be learned. For each input pattern, two different cues are illustrated. In each case, the top member of the two would be the more effective retrieval cue for recall (reproduction) of the original input pattern. The first two panels, with geometric patterns (a) and (d), show that the better retrieval cue is not necessarily the one which physically overlaps more with the input pattern; for example, cue (c) overlaps more with input (a) than does cue (b). Rather, the difference is that in (b) and (e), the cue is a relatively *articulated* sub-

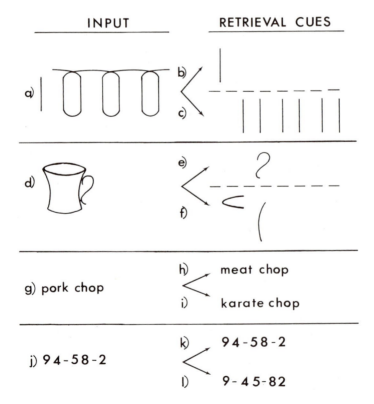

INPUT	RETRIEVAL CUES

Figure 10.10 Illustrations of "good" and "bad" retrieval cues for inputs of geometric forms, verbal phrases, and grouped-digit series.

part of the input pattern; in other words, the good cue would correspond to a distinctly articulated but integral part in the description (memory representation) of the original pattern. On the other hand, the poorer retrieval cues (c) and (f) comprise only noninformative fragments that would not have been distinguished and articulated in the initial description, or "encoding," of the input patterns into memory. In fact, patterns such as (c) may themselves become organized into new patterns (e.g., pair of vertical bars) whose descriptions are completely at variance with the description of the input pattern. Thus a simple similarity notion for retrieval requires considerably further specification of the representation of the input and probe as interpreted stimulus events. G. H. Bower and Glass (1976) showed that "good" subparts of nonsense figures were about five times more powerful than "poor" subparts as retrieval cues to prompt memory of a list of figures the subject had studied earlier.

The third panel illustrates the point with verbal memory. A subject may be shown a series of phrases, with the word to be remembered in capital letters (CHOP), whereas the other context word (*pork*) is explained as simply a possible aid to remembering the capitalized word. Later the person receives a recognition test for the words to be remembered (capitalized words). A new context word placed alongside the word to be remembered biases its *semantic* interpretation (meaning) to be either the same as or different from the input meaning. Although the subject is instructed to concentrate his decision on whether or not he has seen the word form to be remembered (e.g., CHOP) before in the experimental list, the context word has a strongly controlling effect upon his recognition memory (see Light & Carter-Sobell, 1970). Specifically, the CHOP studied in the context *pork* CHOP is not recognized at all well when tested in the context *karate*

CHOP. The word CHOP is encoded or interpreted differently in the two contexts. In this case, the similarity of relevance to the recognition decision is similarity of meaning rather than identity of the physical grapheme CHOP. Tulving and Thomson (1971) find similar effects even when the word to be remembered does not appear to have obvious multiple meanings; it is as though different context words selectively emphasize different semantic features of the word to be remembered. Thomson and Tulving (1970) also show that this encoding at the time of input drastically alters the ability of certain other words to cue recall of the words to be remembered. For instance, in example (g) of Figure 10.10, following study of a list of such pairs, if the person is tested with the cue "food" or "something to eat," he would quickly recall CHOP; but a cue like "a striking blow" (related to "karate CHOP") would not elicit recall of CHOP. Thus, the interpretation of CHOP at input determines what stimuli will or will not serve as effective retrieval cues for the memory of that event. This refers to a phenomenon known as *encoding specificity,* which will be discussed more fully in Chapter 13.

The fourth panel of Figure 10.10 illustrates how the grouping of an indifferent series of digits is part of its characteristic description or representation in memory. If a series like 94582 is grouped at input (by temporal pauses) into a 2-2-1 structure, that string of underlying digits will be recognized far better on a later recognition-memory test if the test series is grouped precisely in the same way as the input series (see Bower & Winzenz, 1969). The input series is not coded and stored by the person as a string of digits; rather it is represented as a sequence of chunks or groups, and these chunks are not re-presented when the test series has an altered group structure.

These last are just a few examples of the role of retrieval in memory; they illustrate how the Höffding step can slip and fail. While Gestalt psychologists did not specifically work on this problem, they did point to its significance, and to the role of stimulus recognition in associative recall. These were problems that had been neglected in earlier stimulus-response associationistic theories; researchers have subsequently turned increasing attention to just such problems, as is attested by recent references in this chapter.

Forgetting as trace disintegration. The Gestalters also applied their ideas on perception to the disintegration or modification of memory traces. The same dynamic laws of organization that are alleged to impose structure upon the elements of a perceptual field would also tend to transform incoherent and poorly organized traces over time into traces exhibiting better organization. There were thus autonomous "forces" acting upon memory traces slowly transforming their contents into a form more closely resembling a good gestalt—a simple, well-organized, and stable structure. If the trace transformation were too extreme, then all semblance of the initial trace would disappear so that a retrieval cue could not make contact with such an altered trace; in operational terms, the person would be said to have forgotten the original event. On the other hand, if the autonomous transformation were not too extreme, recall or reproduction of the trace should reveal systematic and progressive distortions in the direction of better organization.

This particular hypothesis was first proposed and researched by Wulf (1922), a Gestalt psychologist. He showed subjects a set of geometric forms that were incomplete or irregular in some way—in Wulf's terms, they deviated in some way from an obviously "better figure" which was simpler, more regular, more symmetric. Wulf had his subjects reproduce (draw) the memorized set of figures at successive weekly intervals, and tried to score their drawings for progressive and systematic distortions. He claimed to have found evidence for the progressive alterations of the reproductions (i.e., memory traces) in the direction of the good gestalt figures.

Because of the striking nature of such a finding and the hoopla made over it by the Gestalters, there was a flurry of experiments directed at the issue over the ensuing years. There were also attempts to extend the basic result from geometric forms to recall of thematic stories (Bartlett, 1932) and to the spreading of rumors within a social group (Allport & Postman, 1947). The later experiments using Wulf's design uncovered an unending series of complications and problems in performing and interpreting such experiments—complications in identifying a subject's reproduction with his memory, complications due to multiple reproductions (in making his *n*th reproduction of a figure, the subject is actually trying to remember his previous reproduction of it), complications due to verbal encoding (labeling) of the input figures in terms of familiar objects ("looks like a *bowtie*"), and so on and on. A good definitive review of the research on the issue, as well as a methodological critique of many of the experiments, was written by Riley (1963). His conclusion was that the mass of empirical evidence on the issue is largely *against* the Gestalt position. There are, to be sure, distortions in people's memory for geometric forms (or stories or rumors), but they seem to be predictable not so much by biases toward Gestalt good figures as by either (a) assimilation of memory of an input figure to a common cultural stereotype (an effect explicable in terms of associative interference), or (b) fusion and confusion of two or more figures in the list being memorized, so that hybrid reproductions occur by the piecing together of fragments of several figures, or (c) assimilation of the input form to that corresponding to a common label (e.g., "bowtie") used at the time of input, which coding distorts the reproduction of the form in a relatively constant manner over varying retention intervals. The upshot, then, is that Wulf's Gestalt analysis of such changes in memory has been replaced by a more refined and more firmly supported associative analysis of the phenomena.

Another view on forgetting expressed by Gestalt psychologists (e.g., Köhler, 1929, 1941) was that a trace could become distorted through its interactions with a mass of related traces similar to it. The idea was that a trace *A* will be more distorted by traces *B, C, D* . . . , the more similar are the perceptual processes underlying *A* and the other traces. This was their basic way of explaining why associative interference in forgetting experiments was related to the similarity of the interfering material to the material to be remembered. Experiments by von Restorff (1933) and Köhler and von Restorff (1935) demonstrated this similarity effect upon memory for a single item within a list. Von Restorff showed that part of the difficulty of learning a list of nonsense syllables (e.g., paired-associates) stems from their homogeneity; they are all undistinguished and equally confusable with one another. However, if one item is made to stand out perceptually by being presented in red letters or in a different type font, or is of different materials (e.g., digits instead of syllables), then that unique item will be remembered better than the other items. A variety of ways can be used to distinguish an item from the rest of a homogeneous list of items to be learned, and they all produce some enhancement in memory for the distinguished item. This has been called the *von Restorff effect* in honor of its discoverer.

How is the von Restorff effect to be explained? She and Köhler thought of the unique item as standing out like a figure against a ground of all the homogeneous items. Being thus distinguished, the trace laid down for the unique item would be isolated from the traces of the rest of the items, and therefore not be distorted by interactions with those traces. Accounts of the von Restorff effect by stimulus-response associationists have proceeded along similar lines, using concepts of stimulus generalization and associative interference. That is, because the stimulus of the isolated pair is unique, it will be confused less with other stimuli in the list, reducing generalized errors to the unique pair. As a further factor, it has been found that unique items have an advantage in memory because they are typically attended to and rehearsed more fully than are the homogeneous control items (see Rundus, 1971). Also, in free-recall tests it can be said that the distinguishing feature of the unique item (e.g., red letters) can serve as a unique retrieval cue for the word, whereas the physical characteristic of the homogeneous background items (e.g., black letters) is connected to multiple interfering responses. Regardless of how associative theorists analyze the von Restorff effect, the original experiments were motivated by testing of some Gestalt ideas regarding forgetting.

Rote Memorizing versus Understanding

One of the basic tenets of Wertheimer and other Gestalt psychologists was that rote memorization—the learning of senseless material by repetitive drill—was an inefficient and rarely used mode of learning in real-life situations. Instead, they claimed that people learned most things in everyday life by understanding or comprehending the meaning of some event or by grasping the principle underlying a sequence of episodes. Rote memorization is a last-resort, inefficient strategy adopted in those few cases (e.g., learning the psychologist's lists of nonsense syllables) when meaning and natural organizing factors are absent.

Research by Katona (1940) published in his book *Organizing and memorizing* provided several illustrations of the differing properties that characterize tasks learned by rote versus those learned by understanding a principle or rule. Katona's experiments were designed so that it was possible to commit the same material to memory with or without understanding, and then to test for later retention or for transfer to a new, similar task.

To illustrate, subjects might be asked to study and learn the number series 81644936-2516941 or the letter series *REKAEPSD-UOL*. Half the subjects would learn the series by rote; the others were given various hints that a principle or rule underlay the generation of the series (e.g., think of squared numbers, or backwards words). Those subjects who "figured out" the rule for generating the series—who "understood its meaning," to use Katona's terms—were able to reproduce the series better than their rote-memory companions both on an immediate and on a delayed retention test. Furthermore, once a student had grasped the principle generating the series, he was able to transfer his problem-solving set to new tasks involving similar problems. Thus, having "solved" the problems illustrated above, the subject would readily learn (exhibit "positive transfer" to) a new series such as 256225196169144 or *YRTSIMEHC-OIB*. Throughout a variety of problem-solving tasks and learning procedures, Katona illustrated his points relating learning-with-understanding to more rapid learning, superior retention, and superior transfer of learning to similar tasks.

The basic results in Katona's type of experiment are indisputable. At issue is how to characterize the outcomes scientifically. It appears in retrospect that the subject who has the rule (either because he discovered it himself or was told it) has a very much simpler description or representation of the series to be memorized. That is, the series is essentially characterized as a simple transformation or rearrangement of something that is already familiar and well-known (e.g., "spell *LOUDSPEAKER* back-

ward"). By thus making use of known material, the total number of *new* things (associations) to be learned is much smaller than if the problem is attacked at the level of rote memorization. By the same token, a series learned by a rule will be better retained weeks later because there are fewer elements and relations to remember and they are better organized than in the case of rote memory. What is varying in these two cases is the internal description of the stimulus series to be learned: one description is succinct, compact, meaningful; the other is long, clumsy, meaningless. Although Katona would not have agreed with exactly this characterization of the issue, the experiments do serve to illustrate the Gestalt concern with how the current organization of the perceptual field makes contact with older memories.

In the ensuing years there have been many further demonstrations that getting the person to learn (or "see") a rule or principle for generating the material results in much faster learning than does treating the material as a collection of independent, unrelated items. For a recent review of some of this material, see G. H. Bower (1970b, 1972c). The basic fact that understanding promotes learning and retention has never been doubted. What was in doubt is the interpretation of understanding (what does it denote for a behaviorist?) and whether the relation of understanding to learning has the revolutionary significance that it was once thought to have. Unfortunately, Gestalters and S-R psychologists became embroiled in disputes over educational practices (recall that Thorndike, an educationist, had proposed "stamping-in" drills), and were seemingly at loggerheads over whether to advocate teaching by drill or by understanding. Although the issue is still somewhat alive today in schools of education, the controversy has become resolved for psychologists by their getting an increasingly better representation of what is learned in differing cases, so that conflicting prescriptions can be avoided. In tasks that have underlying principles, one obviously teaches the simplest representation of the problem and rules for generating the solution; but if there are many such tasks with differing principles and procedures, then some repetitive drill is required to learn these higher-level descriptions well.

Problem-Solving and Insight

We will now review briefly the work of the Gestalters on productive thinking, problem-solving, and insight. It will be recalled that Köhler's experiments with apes were controversial because he supposed that when confronted with a problem the ape would often try implicitly to "think through" the problem's solution "in his head" before responding overtly. Insight might be characterized as implicit problem-solving activity which is successful. Based on his analysis of photographic evidence of the problem-solving behavior of apes, Yerkes (1927), following Köhler, had laid out the following sorts of behavioral criteria for insight:

> In acts which by us are performed with insight or understanding of relations of means to ends, we are familiar with certain characteristics which are important, if not differential. The following is a partial list of features of such behavior. It is presented here with the thought that the comparative study of behavior with insight, in different organisms, may reveal common characteristics.
>
> (1) Survey, inspection, or persistent examination of problematic situation. (2) Hesitation, pause, attitude of concentrated attention. (3) Trial of more or less adequate mode of response. (4) In case initial mode of response proves inadequate, trial of some other mode of response, the transition from the one method to the other being sharp and often sudden. (5) Persistent or frequently recurrent attention to the objective or goal and motivation thereby. (6) Appearance of critical point at which the organism suddenly, directly, and definitely performs the required adaptive act. (7) Ready repetition of adaptive response after once performed. (8) Notable ability to discover and attend to the essential aspect of

relation in the problematic situation and to neglect, relatively, variations in non-essentials (Yerkes, 1927, p. 156).

Subsequent analysis of problem-solving by primates and other mammals showed it was a rather complex assemblage of past habits joined with various learned strategies for trying hypotheses. For example, an experienced ape is more likely to achieve insightful solution of a problem than is an inexperienced one. Prior experience with using sticks as tools or boxes as ladders to climb upon enables a chimpanzee to solve later problems using these component skills (Birch, 1945). The difference between association theories and Gestalt theories lies in the implication of association theories that the possession of the necessary past experience somehow guarantees the solution. While Gestalt theorists would agree that past experience will facilitate solution, they object to explanations in terms of the non-insightful use of previous experience without taking organization into account. More is needed than the necessary amount of information. Just knowing enough words does not enable one to write a poem. Thus prior experience alone does not solve the problem.

A second fact that became readily apparent in subsequent research is that some experimental arrangements are more favorable than others for promoting insightful solutions. Both hypotheses inherent in the organism and perceptual structuring in the environment contribute to organization. Insight is more likely when the problematic situation is so arranged that all necessary aspects are open to observation. Moreover, solution occurs more quickly if all the parts which need to be brought into relationship are simultaneously present in perception; for example, it is harder for an ape to learn to use a stick which lies on the side of the cage opposite the food than to learn to use one which lies on the same side as the food (Jackson, 1942).

A significant development concerning insight research was by Harlow (1949) on *learning set* in monkeys. In an early study, Harlow trained monkeys on a large number of object-discrimination problems, each involving just six trials where the choice of a given object of a pair was rewarded with a raisin. Each problem involved a different pair of common objects such as a cup, a box, a comb, a shoe. Harlow observed over the series of some 350 problems that the monkeys were becoming much faster learners. His results are shown in Figure 10.11, which gives the monkeys' percent correct responses within the six trials while learning some new pair of objects before being switched to still another new set of objects. The early discriminations (Problems 1 through 8) show gradual improvement within the six trials on a problem; with the accumulation of experience, however, the monkeys become very adept at solving later problems. In the last block of problems plotted in Figure 10.11, the monkeys show virtually one-trial learning, with choice of the rewarded object jumping to around 97 percent following the first trial. Similar learning set results have been reported for all varieties of species with many varieties of rules for reinforcing choices.

The importance of Harlow's learning-set experiments is their demonstration " . . . that animals can gradually learn insight" (Harlow, 1949, p. 56). Thus, there need not be a fundamental opposition between theories stressing gradual versus insightful learning. Harlow proposed that with practice the animals gradually learn to eliminate extraneous hypotheses that lead to errors. Thus, a monkey would learn not to pay attention to the left-right position of the rewarded object, not to choose an object that was nonreinforced, and so on. The animal would gradually acquire the strategy: "If the object chosen is rewarded, choose it next time; if the object chosen is not rewarded, shift to the other object the next time." The dominance of this strategy over errorful hypotheses would explain the very rapid intra-problem learning demonstrated by the trained monkeys. However, the quick learning ability is specific to a particular rule—namely, that a particular object of a pair is always rewarded. If the reinforcement rule is drastically changed—for instance, responses to alternating positions now are reinforced regardless of the objects' locations—then the object-trained monkeys will show very slow learning once again. Levine (1965, 1969) developed a specific hypothesis-testing theory that accounts for most of these learning-set results. In historical perspective, however, the work on learning sets and the hypothesis-testing view of discrimination learning

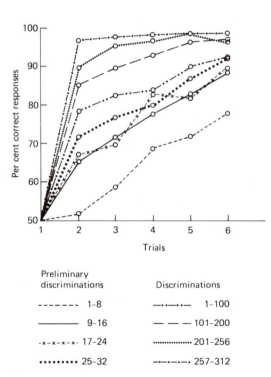

Preliminary discriminations	Discriminations
- - - - - - - 1-8	—··—··— 1-100
———— 9-16	— — — 101-200
-x-x-x-x- 17-24	·············· 201-256
········ 25-32	—·—·—· 257-312

Figure 10.11. Gradual improvement in monkey's ability to solve discrimination problems as found by Harlow. Although performance is relatively poor on early discrimination problems, later problems tend to be solved in just one trial. (From Harlow, 1949.)

were a thematic development from early
Gestalt views of problem-solving by insight.

Productive Thinking

Wertheimer lectured on thought processes for many years, but published only
a few fragmentary papers during his life-
time. He had, however, completed the manuscript of a small book just before his
death. This was edited by his friends and
appeared under the title *Productive thinking* (1945, 1959). In it a number of his experimental studies are summarized in his
characteristic way, with penetrating qualitative analysis of simple situations serving
to illustrate the differences between his approach and other approaches to which he
was objecting.

The two chief competing alternatives to
adopting the Gestalt approach to thinking
and problem-solving were said to be formal
logic, on the one hand, and association theory, on the other. Both of these alternatives
were believed to be too limited to encompass what actually happens when an individual confronted with a problem finds a
sensible solution.

The distinction is made throughout between a blind solution in which the learner
applies a formula, and a sensible solution
in which the learner understands what she
is doing in relation to the essential structure of the situation. The blind solution is
often an unsuccessful application of the
formula to a situation not seen to be inappropriate. Experiments are cited, for example, in which schoolchildren are taught
to find the area of a parallelogram by dropping lines from two corners perpendicular
to the base, thus converting the figure to a
rectangle, whose area can be found. Children who could do the examples perfectly
were baffled, however, when a parallelogram was presented in a new orientation,
so that the "correct" steps of the procedure
led to confusing results. They had learned
the solution according to a blind procedure.

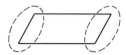

Figure 10.12. Troublesome parts in a child's
attempt to apply the rectangle method to a
parallelogram. (From Wertheimer, 1959.)

By contrast, the solution of a 5½-year-old
child is reported:

> Given the parallelogram problem, after she
> had been shown briefly how to get at the area
> of the rectangle, she said, "I certainly don't know
> how to do *that*." Then after a moment of silence:
> "This is *no good here*," pointing to the region
> at the left end; "and *no good here*," pointed to
> the region at the right [Figure 10.12]. "It's
> troublesome, here and there." Hesitatingly she
> said: "I could make it right here . . . but. . . ."
> Suddenly she cried out, "May I have a scissors?
> What is bad there is just what is needed here.
> It fits." She took the scissors, cut vertically, and
> placed the left end at the right [Figure 10.13]
> (Wertheimer, 1945, p. 48).

Another child, given a long parallelogram cut out of a piece of paper, remarked
early that the whole middle was all right,
but the ends were wrong. She suddenly
took the paper and made it into a ring.
She saw that it was all right now, since it
could be cut vertically anywhere and made
into a rectangle.

In cases such as these, the solutions appear in an orderly way, in line with the
true "structure" of the situation. It is this
structural approach which Wertheimer emphasizes. Children readily grasp such structural solutions unless they are badly taught

Figure 10.13. Child's solution of parallelogram
problem with a scissors. (From Wertheimer, 1959.)

A-figures   B-figures

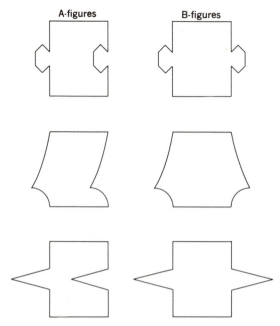

Figure 10.14. Applicability of solution of parallelogram problem to new figures. It is possible to change the A-figures sensibly so that they form rectangles. It is not possible to change the B-figures in this way. The ability of school children to solve the A-figures and to reject the B-figures is said to depend on something other than the familiarity of the figures. (From Wertheimer, 1959.)

in an atmosphere of blind repetitive drill. Given figures such as those on the left in Figure 10.14 and those on the right, they can easily sort out the unsolvable ones from the solvables. It is futile to argue, says Wertheimer, that these distinctions are made on the basis of familiarity, as the associationist seems to believe. Children make the distinction because they perceive the essential nature of the solution. The structural features and requirements of the situation itself set up strains and stresses which lead in the direction of improving the situation—that is to say, to solving the problem.

The implications of Wertheimer's point of view for teaching are fairly clear. It is

always preferable to proceed in a manner which favors discovery of the essential nature of the problematic situation, of the gaps that require filling in, so that, even at the cost of elegance or brevity, the proof is "organic" rather than "mechanical" (Duncker, 1945).

ESTIMATE OF GESTALT THEORY OF LEARNING

Gestalt Theory and the Typical Problems of Learning

Gestalt psychologists saw a somewhat distorted emphasis in conventional treatments of learning, so that the problems typically emphasized are not the most natural selection of problems from their standpoint. However, we can summarize the Gestalt position on learning as follows:

1. Practice. Our memories are allegedly traces of perceptions; association is a byproduct of perceptual organization. The laws of perceptual groupings also determine coherence of elements in memory. Repetition of an experience builds cumulatively on earlier experiences only if the second event is recognized as a recurrence of the earlier one. Successive exposures to a learning situation provide repeated opportunities for the learner to notice new relationships so as to provide for restructuring the task.

2. Motivation. The empirical law of effect, regarding the role of rewards and punishments, was accepted by Gestalt psychologists, but they differed from Thorndike in interpreting it. They believed that aftereffects did not act "automatically and unconsciously" to strengthen prior acts. Rather, the effect had to be perceived as *belonging* to the prior act—a position also emphasized by Thorndike. Motivation was viewed as placing the organism into a problem situation; rewards and punishments acted to confirm or disconfirm attempted solutions of problems.

3. Understanding. The perceiving of relationships, awareness of relationships between parts and whole, of means to consequences, are emphasized by the Gestalt writers. Problems are to be solved sensibly, structurally, organically, rather than mechanically, stupidly, or by the running off of prior habits. Insightful learning is thus more typical of appropriately presented learning tasks than is trial and error.

4. Transfer. The Gestalt concept most like that of transfer is *transposition.* A pattern of dynamic relationship discovered or understood in one situation may be applicable to another. There is something in common between the earlier learning and the situation in which transfer is found, but what exists in common is not identical piecemeal elements but common patterns, configurations, or relationships. One of the advantages of learning by understanding rather than by rote is that understanding is transposable to wider ranges of situations, and less often leads to erroneous applications of old learning. For comparison, see Spence's *S-R* analysis of transposition in Fig. 5.6.

5. Forgetting. Forgetting is related to the course of changes in the trace. Traces may disappear either through gradual decay (a possibility hard to prove or disprove), through destruction because of being part of a chaotic, illstructured field, or through assimilation to new traces or processes. The last possibility is familiar as a form of retroactive inhibition. Traces which continue to exist may at a given moment be unavailable because of momentary failure in the Höffding step.

In addition to such forgetting, there are the dynamic changes which take place in recall, so that what is reproduced is not earlier learning with some parts missing, but a trace distorted in the direction of a good gestalt.

General Aspects of Gestalt Theory

In discussing Gestalt psychology solely as a theory of learning, some of its more general features have been sidestepped, especially its philosophical orientation and its relation to biology. The objection to association learning theory is part of the wholistic emphasis within the general theory, and is coherent with the Gestalt opposition to atomistic explanations according to connections between parts. The

objection to sensations as elements of perception (the bundle hypothesis) is carried over in the objection to stimulus-response connections as elements of habits.

The *phenomenological* standpoint, often stated by Gestalt psychologists as opposed to the prevailing *positivistic* position, is not easy to characterize satisfactorily. Phenomenal observation is more subjective than behaviorism, and less analytic than the introspection recommended by Titchener. The recommended variety of observation is naturalistic and appreciative rather than analytical. For example, Köhler's later accounts of insight depended upon such a phenomenological description of events.

The interpretation of Gestalt psychology as a *field theory* rests largely on the evidence assembled by Köhler in his *Physische Gestalten* (1920), showing the relationship between Gestalt laws of organization and well-established principles in physics and biology.

As we mentioned, Gestalt psychologists were primarily concerned with perception and cognitive (problem-solving) processes. Their approach to learning and memory therefore emphasized a combination of these factors in learning situations—how memory mirrored perceptual organization and how problem-solving abilities were brought to bear in understanding a learning task, or in reconstructing a vague memory, or in transferring a learned principle to a new situation. These emphases were appropriate antidotes and challenges to the S-R associationism that prevailed in America.

Gestalt Psychology in the Present

The ferment created by the introduction of Gestalt psychology to America in the late 1920s and early 1930s largely subsided by the 1950s. Yet much remains valid in what the classical Gestalt psychologists taught. There were always several features to their writings: an experimental or demonstrational part in which one or another psychological phenomenon would be shown; then a polemical, almost philosophical part in which the ancient elementarism of Titchener's (or Watson's) analyses was flogged to death; and finally, some relatively incomprehensible field theory of the phenomenon would be advanced. In sensory psychology, the Gestalters easily proved their points, their data were accepted and explained in less inflammatory terms, and their approach to the area moved forward. So in the domain of sensory perception, the demonstrated phenomena of Gestalt psychology were absorbed into the mainstream. In the area of learning, following publication of Katona's experiments in 1940, relatively little experimental work was done from the Gestalt viewpoint. None of the Gestalters went into the study of conditioning and animal learning, which were the research areas dominating the interests of learning theorists during the period 1930–1960.

In the 1960s there was a resurgence of interest in the Gestalt approach to human learning. One of these research lines, by Asch and his associates, was reviewed earlier, and concerns the way perceptual organization influences coherence of elements in memory. Those demonstrations, along with related work by Bower and associates, kept in the forefront the idea that associating is the relating of elements, and that contiguity is simply a precondition within which other relations operate. Another idea that has proved very useful in analyses of human learning is the notion of unitization, or the "chunking" of discrete elements into an integrated unit.

In the late 1960s the organizational viewpoint on human learning acquired several strong advocates (Bower, 1970c; Mandler, 1967, 1968; Tulving, 1968). This is reviewed more fully in Chapter 13. The organizational view of memory strongly resembles certain premises of Gestalt psychology, particularly those explored by Katona. Most of the research in this area of verbal learning was done on *free recall,* an experimental setup in which the subject is exposed to a large set of items (e.g., common nouns) and then is asked to recall as many of them as he can in any order. On first glance, it is not obvious how a stimulus-response-association theory can even begin to analyze performance in the free-recall task (although see a model by J. R. Anderson, 1972, to illustrate how this can be done). Nonetheless, the organizational theorists (e.g., Mandler, 1968) suppose that the free-recall subject tries to relate the individual items together into subjective units or chunks, which then serve as effective groups that cluster together in his free recall. Recall is limited by the constant number of chunks and the number of items that can occur in a chunk (although a memory unit can contain other chunks —allowing the embedding of chunks within chunks; Mandler, 1967). The chunks typically adopted for word lists are semantic categories. Indeed, Tulving (1962) finds very high correlations between the amount recalled and measures of subjective organization in the recall protocol. Procedures which try to facilitate or interfere with stable organization of the list items produce corresponding increments or decrements in amount recalled (Bower, Lesgold, & Tieman, 1969). In case the number of subjective units proves to be larger than the optimal number, it is supposed that the person recategorizes his chunks into a smaller number of superordinate categories which is within the memory limit (see Mandler, 1968). In recall, then, the person is presumed to have immediate access to the superordinate categories or chunks, which he unpacks into their subordinate units during recall. This is an efficient recall strategy when the material clearly allows it, as Bower, Clark, Winzenz, and Lesgold (1969) have shown. We will not discuss further the organizational factors in memory. The amount of later research on the topic led to a research review volume, *Organization of memory,* edited by Tulving and Donaldson (1972).

The ideas of Gestalt theory still live in learning theory. Along with the emphasis on perceptual factors in memory and organizational factors in free recall, J. R. Anderson and Bower (1972b) have contrasted a Gestalt with an "elementaristic" analysis of how a person might learn and recall meaningful sentences. The issue is whether memory about a proposition can be decomposed into a number of quasi-independent associative relations, or whether the entire proposition organizes all its elements into a single chunk which is recalled in an all-or-none manner. The evidence, however, is conflicting and does not clearly support either the multiple-associations or the unitary chunk ideas (see the review in J. R. Anderson, 1976).

In general, Gestalt psychology had a stimulating and salutary effect on the study of learning and memory. Its ideas about human learning came to be appreciated and exploited in the early 1970s. Similarly, Gestalt studies on thinking and problem-solving, particularly the work of Duncker (1945) and Wertheimer (1945, 1959), were appreciated once again by scientists such as Allen Newell and Herbert Simon (1972), who worked on computer simulation of human problem-solving. Thus, the influence of a small band of German Gestalt psychologists lived on long after their deaths. They were, in fact, the intellectual forefathers of much of what is today called cognitive psychology, which is now a dominant viewpoint in American experimental psychology.

SUPPLEMENTARY READINGS

The books by the "big three" of Gestalt psychology are as follows:

Koffka, K. (1924). *Growth of the mind.*

Koffka, K. (1935). *Principles of Gestalt psychology.*

Köhler, W. (1925). *The mentality of apes.*

Köhler, W. (1929, 1947). *Gestalt psychology.*

Köhler, W. (1940). *Dynamics in psychology.*

Wertheimer, M. (1945, 1959). *Productive thinking.*

For a sympathetic yet critical account of Gestalt psychology, the following is pertinent: Prentice, W. C. H. (1959), "The systematic psychology of Wolfgang Köhler," in S. Koch, ed., *Psychology: A study of a science.* Vol. I: 427–55.

A good collection of readings, including many translated classic papers formerly available only in German, is:

Henle, M. (1961). *Documents of Gestalt psychology.*

I I

TOLMAN'S
SIGN LEARNING

The theory of Edward C. Tolman (1886–1959) was called purposive behaviorism in his major systematic work, *Purposive behavior in animals and men* (1932). Later he (and others) called it a sign-gestalt theory, or an expectancy theory. These later terms all emphasize the *cognitive* nature of the theory, which distinguishes it in certain respects from the stimulus-response theories of Thorndike, Guthrie, Skinner, and Hull. The designation *sign learning* provides a satisfactory short name, abbreviating sign-gestalt.

Tolman was a behaviorist, but one cast from a completely different mold than Watson, Pavlov, or Guthrie. Tolman was concerned with how behavior theory was to make contact with such notions as knowledge, thinking, planning, inference, purpose, and intention. He was a sort of layman's behaviorist, often describing an animal's behavior in terms of its motives, bits of knowledge (cognitions), expectations, intentions, and purposes, in much the way an intelligent layman would describe another person's behavior. Tolman's major influence was in opposing and partially counteracting certain restrictive premises adopted by his more strictly behavioristic predecessors and contemporaries. He was not a

systematist, but rather a very astute observer of animal behavior and critic of the prevailing S-R reinforcement theory of his day. The measure of his success is how much his opponents' theories (notably Hull's, see Chapter 5) were forced to acknowledge and deal with the phenomena and conceptual distinctions drawn by Tolman.

Despite some shifts in vocabulary, Tolman held firm to his main tenets during his career. His main beliefs were that behavior should be analyzed at the level of actions, not movements; that behavior was goal directed, or purposive; and that behavior was docile and varied according to environmental circumstances in pursuit of a given goal. Let us elaborate briefly on these principles.

BEHAVIOR AS GOAL-DIRECTED ACTIONS

Tolman argued that behavior was best described in terms of actions with a purpose and goal. We say someone is buying a record, drinking a soda, dialing a telephone number, and so on, without bothering to mention the movements. The achievement of some goal or end state, not the sequence of muscle twitches bringing that goal about, should be the psychologist's unit of analysis. In effect, this is the level of behavioral description of the layman's common language vocabulary for actions.

The *docility* of behavior simply means that it is adaptable to changing circumstances and that the way some end will be achieved will vary depending on the means available. If you can't drive to the market, you can take a bus, hitchhike, bike, or walk. The behavior chosen is not a reflex response to the goal, but varies adaptively according to the limitations of the situation. This means in particular that an organism can use its knowledge of paths in space, of tools, of obstacles to put together a completely novel and inventive solution for getting to an obstructed goal.

As noted, behavior appears to be goal directed, as a getting towards something, or a getting away from something. Current behavior is guided by what the subject believes will be its outcome. The cat is trying to get out of the box, the carpenter is pounding a nail, and the actress is trying to evoke an emotional reaction from her audience.

This question of whether behavior should be described in terms of purposes or in terms of movements is called the *molar* (large-scale)—as against the *molecular* (small-scale)—issue in learning theory. Like most complex phenomena (e.g., rainbows, football games), an organism's behavior can be described at several different levels (as can a corresponding stimulus situation). For example, a sentence uttered by an actor in a play may be described in terms of movements of his tongue, oral cavity, diaphragm, and vocal cords; or it can be described in terms of the sequence of phonemes emitted, or the words said, or the meanings or ideas conveyed, or the prosodic expertise of the delivery, or the function of the line in the playwright's de-

velopment of a character or of the plot, and so on. A similar set of onion layers characterizes the possible analyses of what a listener in the audience is "doing." It is pointless to ask, "But which of these various things is he *really* doing?"; clearly, in one sense, he is doing all of them. Rather, the issue is which level of analysis will prove more fruitful for answering particular questions of interest. Tolman clearly came down on the side of using molar descriptions of behavior, referring to its supposed *purposes*. What was upsetting about this program to the other comparative (animal) psychologists of that time was that it seemed anthropomorphic (projecting human traits onto lower animals) and unparsimonious (the purposes immanent in behavior were to be *derived* from simpler conditioning principles rather than taken as basic postulates at the outset). It also resembled teleological and vitalistic explanations then current in biology, some of which were clearly fallacious, had been roundly discredited, and were thence automatically suspect among biologists at that time. It was because of these surplus meanings that Tolman's brand of purposive behaviorism received a critical hearing from the other behaviorists of his day.

Tolman argued for a view of humans and animals that emphasized the organism's deliberative reflection about problems, its internal representations of the environment, how these representations could be used to solve problems, and so on. These cognitive processes are familiar in our intuitions of our mental life. It is therefore somewhat surprising for students to discover that Tolman looked for evidence of such cognitive processes in rats, the subjects of nearly all his experiments, rather than in humans where cognitive explanations of learning come so easily to mind. But the significant bias in the 1930s to 1950s was to study the learning of lower animals, since the field was dominated by the behaviorists, who were averse to making mentalistic attributions to the animals being investigated. Perhaps Tolman felt that his ideological adversaries had to be met on their own ground and that if cognitive processes could be demonstrated with lower animals, then the argument for his theory's applicability with humans would be won by default.

Tolman's writings spanned some 30 years; they are discursive, anecdotal, and filled with interesting ideas and observations. His theoretical constructs changed in form and content over the years, so it is not easy to summarize succinctly his systematic theory. We will here present the main ideas stemming from the later, more mature years of Tolman's theorizing.

TOLMAN'S LEARNING CONSTRUCTS

Expectancies and Cognitive Maps

Tolman's basic belief was that organisms acquire knowledge about their environment, about where important goals are located in it, and about how to get from one place to another. The unit of knowledge was the relation between two or more stimulus events (as in Pavlovian conditioning) or between a stimulus, a response to it, and another stimulus that followed the response. These latter, three-term units arise in instrumental learning; each is called an *expectancy*. These three-term expectancies, written within parentheses as $(S_1\text{-}R_1\text{-}S_2)$, refer to the organism's learning that in situation S_1, giving response R_1 will soon be followed by stimulus S_2. The best way to remember the process is to think of some sentence such as: "When this *doorbell button* (S_1), is *pushed* (R_1), I expect to hear the *ringing doorbell* (S_2)." This three-term associative unit, prior to acting now, is the expectancy. If ringing the doorbell becomes a goal (Tolman would say that S_2 becomes *positively valenced*), then the expectancy is

activated. I *push* the button only if I want to ring the doorbell; I may have the expectancy as a bit of knowledge without doing anything about it.

The basic learning assumption in Tolman's theory is that knowledge is acquired as a simple result of the animal's exposure and attention to environmental events. No reward is necessary—just contiguity of experienced events. Tolman assumed that an $(S_1\text{-}R_1\text{-}S_2)$ expectancy was strengthened every time the objective events S_1, R_1, and S_2 occurred in sequence; similarly, it was weakened whenever S_1 and R_1 occurred but were not followed by S_2. This latter weakening, or loss of a specific expectancy, was Tolman's view of the extinction process. During extinction, the maze-running animal learns to stop expecting a reward following R_1 and learns rather to expect an empty goal-box. For many purposes, we can treat the expectancy in Tolman's theory rather like we treated the S-R habit in Hull's theory. For example, expectancy is the construct used to explain effects of training, stimulus generalization, transfer, response competition, and the like. An interesting feature is that a sequence of expectancies can be *integrated* into a larger unit. In a two-unit T-maze, for example, a rat would first learn that at the first choice-point, a right turn leads to the stimuli of the second choice-point, to which a left turn leads to food. With repetition, the animal telescopes this chain of expectancies, all of which are activated at the start of the maze. Thus, he expects food to eventuate as he starts out on the correct path.

Tolman also believed in a thought process he called *inference*. The idea is this: if an animal already has an expectancy (S_1-R_1-S_2), and we then teach her another event connection S_2-S^*, then she will *infer* a new expectancy (S_1-R_1-S^*). Inference was the process by which new rewarding events at a goal-box (S_2-S^* pairings) could work their way back to affect any subsequent response selection.

If an animal is allowed to explore a territory, it will acquire a large number of bits of S_1-S_2 and S_1-R_1-S_2 connections. Tolman believed that the animal's knowledge about an environment came to be organized into a sort of *cognitive map* of that area rather than a simple unconnected listing of local stimulus-response pairs. He characterized this organization of knowledge in the following way:

> '[The brain] is far more like a map control room than it is like an old-fashioned telephone exchange. The stimuli which are allowed in are not connected by just simple one-to-one switches to the outgoing responses. Rather, the incoming impulses are usually worked over and elaborated in the central control room into a tentative, cognitivelike map of the environment. And it is this tentative map, indicating routes and paths and environmental relationships, which finally determines what responses, if any, the animal will finally release (1948, p. 192).

Tolman believed that sophisticated animals could use their knowledge of the spatial layout of objects and paths to find their way to a desired goal much the way you would use a city map to find your way around. Other things equal, the shortest path to the goal would be preferred. The idea of cognitive maps is appealing and has attracted much recent research, which we will touch on later in this chapter.

Learning vs. Performance

In Tolman's system expectancies are the bits of knowledge the organism learns. But we never carry out every action of which we are capable. In fact, a given bit of knowledge usually lays dormant in memory until it becomes needed to get some desired goal. Tolman was one of the first psychologists to draw a sharp distinction between learning and performance. We may know how to do something but not perform that act until properly motivated. A person may learn where a drug store is located near her new apartment, but not use that knowledge until she needs a prescription filled.

For Tolman, an expectancy (S_1-R_1-S_2) was converted into an action whenever the "goal" of that expectancy (S_2) became strongly and positively valenced. For example, if a thirsty animal had experience moving through a maze to a goal-box where it drank, the valence of the goal-box would be greater the more often the animal had drunk there, and the thirstier he was at present. If the animal were momentarily satiated on water, then the goal-box with water would have no value or valence for him. This valence notion closely parallels the Drive × Incentive motivational complex used in the theories of Hull and Spence. Similarly, the manner in which valence converts an expectancy into a "reaction tendency" for Tolman is like the way motivation converted habit into response strength ($_sE_R$) in Hull's theory. Tolman would relate "reaction tendency" to the usual performance indices of response latency, and choice dominance in competition with other courses of action. In these matters, Tolman did not differ much from Hull.

Tolman also assumed a principle of secondary reinforcement. Thus, if S_2 is a valenced stimulus, and if a neutral S^* is paired with S_2, then S^* was presumed to become valenced or valued. Further, in the sequence S_1-R_1-S_2, giving rise to a corresponding expectancy, if S_2 became highly valenced, then it was assumed that the earlier stimulus, S_1, would acquire valence also. This is recognizing the fact that stimuli that lead to valued events become valued subgoals, too. Thus, if inserting a poker chip (S_1) into a slot machine produces a grape (valenced S_2) for a chimpanzee, the chimp will soon value poker chips, and will learn new behaviors to get them.

A few comments are appropriate regarding these basic assumptions of Tolman's theory. First, we have paraphrased here an attempt by MacCorquodale and Meehl

(1953) to be precise about what Tolman was writing in his discursive and informal manner. Second, some of the assumptions of the system as outlined are little more than direct translations of empirical phenomena into the vocabulary of Tolman's theory (e.g., stimulus generalization and secondary reinforcement). Such translations are not to be interpreted as suggesting that Tolman in any sense "discovered" these psychological principles; they were known long before he began his systematic writings. (The same remark applies to many of Clark Hull's theoretical postulations, considered in Chapter 5.) Third, enumeration of the several principles does not do justice to the reams of psychological experimentation and evidence that lie behind them; this we try to sketch in the next section. Fourth, the enumeration does not mention many of the informal, more programmatic suggestions that were scattered throughout Tolman's writings and that provided a valuable stimulus for research into particular areas. Again, we can briefly mention only a few of these auxiliary hypotheses in the next section.

EVIDENCE RELEVANT TO TOLMAN'S VIEWS

Sensory-Sensory Associations

One prominent difference between stimulus-response and cognitive theorists was in the units that could be associated: S-R theorists believed that all learning (at least all that could ever be revealed) was describable as the attachment of responses to stimuli, whereas cognitive theorists like Tolman argued for direct associations between sensory elements, for S-S units in memory. Apparent simple test cases, such as humans' learning of stimulus word-word associations, were discounted as irrelevant on the belief that people would implicitly respond to—or name—the stimuli, so that

the stimuli would be associated indirectly via responses. For such reasons, the question of sensory conditioning was believed to be decided most surely by experiments with lower animals. Thus was invented the *sensory preconditioning* experiments to be described.

Sensory Preconditioning

In sensory preconditioning, two neutral stimuli, S_1 and S_2, are paired together for many trials, and then one of them, S_2, is paired with a biologically significant US until S_2 evokes a conditioned response (see Figure 11.1). In the final critical phase, the S_1 stimulus is tested for its association to the CR. If S_1 now evokes the CR to some degree (in comparison to control subjects for whom the stimuli were unpaired in Phase 1 or 2), then it is presumed that sensory preconditioning has occurred. The explanation is that S_1 becomes associated to S_2, then S_2 becomes associated to the US, and when S_1 is finally tested, S_1 retrieves a representation of S_2, which retrieves the idea of the US, which causes the CR to occur.

Brogden (1939) performed an early sensory preconditioning experiment yielding successful results. His dogs received 200 simultaneous pairings of light and buzzer, then received leg-flexion conditioning with one of these cues paired with shock to a foot. Tests with the other stimulus produced significantly more responding from experimental dogs than from control ani-

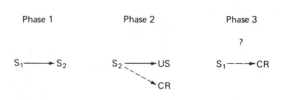

Figure 11.1. Three phases in a sensory preconditioning experiment. The third is the test phase, checking whether S_1 elicits the CR.

mals. However, the sensory preconditioning effect was quite small and short-lived in Brogden's experiment and others done about that time. Consequently, the sensory preconditioning effect was easy for S-R theorists to ignore.

Later experiments found that Brogden's procedures were not optimal. In particular, better sensory preconditioning occurs if S_1 precedes S_2 by a few seconds, and if the number of S_1-S_2 pairings is relatively small before habituation sets in. With such parameters in the conditioned suppression technique, recent investigations (Prewitt, 1967; Rizley & Rescorla, 1972) have found quite reliable sensory preconditioning effects. The effect can be produced whether S_1 and S_2 are in the same or in different modalities. Thus, there is no doubt that associations between neutral, nonmotivational stimuli can be formed in animals in the absence of obvious responses to the two stimuli. Thus, a major strong prediction of S-R theory was disconfirmed.

Short-Term Memory in Animals

Another line of evidence suggesting sensory conditioning comes from the ability of animals to remember a stimulus over brief retention intervals. This short-term memory ability in animals is being investigated more in recent times. An early technique was the *delayed reaction,* in which an animal observes the experimenter placing a reward at a distinctive location (which varies every trial), then after an interval the animal would be released, and the experimenter notices whether it chooses the correct location immediately. If successful, the animal is presumed to have retained some representation of the event over the retention interval. However, the delayed reaction procedure has lately fallen into disuse because it does not insure that the animal carefully attends to the "baiting" of the reward location nor does it easily rule out the possibility that the

animal remembers the reward location by simply holding a "pointing posture" like a hunting setter toward a bird in the field.

For such reasons, the preferred procedure is *delayed matching to sample,* and the steps within each trial are illustrated in Figure 11.2. On the front panel of a pigeon's or monkey's cage three keys are

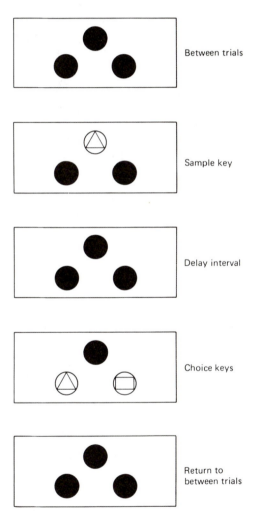

Between trials

Sample key

Delay interval

Choice keys

Return to between trials

Figure 11.2. Sequence of stimuli on three response keys within each trial of a delayed matching to sample experiment. Events occur in a top-to-bottom cycle.

mounted onto which stimulus forms will be back-projected. By gradual training, the animal is trained to respond (peck or push) on any key lighted with a shape. Then the animal is taught to peck at the center sample key (when it is on) in order to initiate presentation of the choice keys on the side. Responses to the choice key whose shape matches the sample shape on this trial are rewarded, whereas errors to the wrong shape are nonreinforced by return to the between-trials situation. The sample stimulus (triangle or square in Figure 11.2) is randomly alternated over trials, as is the location of the correct choice key. Thus, the animal must truly remember the sample stimulus on a given trial and choose its matching mate. Initial training on matching is with no delay and just two stimuli, but as the skill is acquired more stimuli may be introduced and the delays lengthened.

Figure 11.3 shows some typical short-term memory data from an experiment on pigeons by Roberts (1972). In different trial blocks, his pigeons were required to peck the sample key 1, 5, or 15 times be-

fore the sample was removed, initiating a delay of 0, 1, 3, or 6 seconds before the choice. Clearly the animals forget over the brief interval. Also, their initial levels of performance improve with more repetitions of the sample stimulus, but this does not affect forgetting rates, as is shown by the parallel decline in the curves.

For comparison to the pigeons' STM forgetting function, Figure 11.4 shows a similar STM function for humans obtained by Hellyer (1962). These subjects read a nonsense trigram (like CJM) presented 1, 2, 4, or 8 times in rapid succession before they counted backwards from 3 to 27 seconds and then attempted recall. Verbal memory improved with number of repetitions in much the way the pigeons' memory for the sample stimulus improved with the number of times they pecked on it before it was removed on a trial. The correspondence of the sets of curves is remarkable.

The theoretical question is, how does the animal retain a representation of the sample stimulus over the delay interval to cue his later choice of the matching stim-

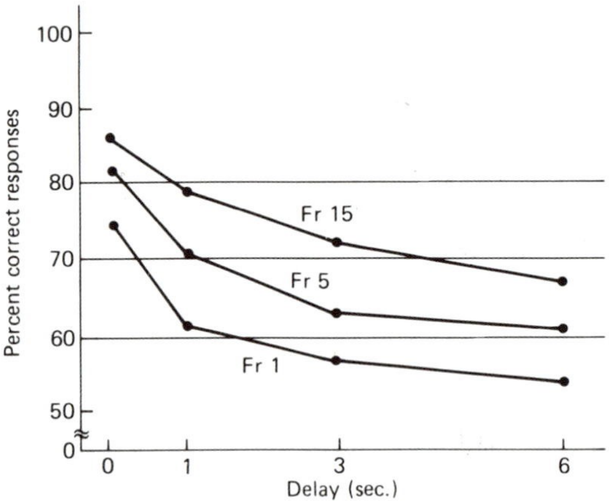

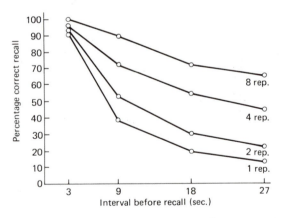

Figure 11.3. Percent correct matching to sample at delays of 0 to 6 seconds for pigeons that pecked the sample key 1, 5, or 15 times before the retention interval. (From Roberts, 1972.)

Figure 11.4. Percentage of correct recalls as a function of the duration of retention interval filled with counting backwards. The curves differ according to the number of consecutive presentations of the target item before the retention interval begins. (From Hellyer, 1962.)

ulus? Two S-R explanations are possible. The first says that the animal learns a set of "adjunctive" behavior chains (e.g., go to the left or right side of box during the delay interval), each triggered by a specific sample stimulus, and that these chains carry the memory of the sample stimulus over the retention interval. This view explains why delayed matching is a slowly acquired skill requiring much practice. However, it fails to explain anything else. For example, monkeys may learn to do delayed matching with 25 or more different stimuli, and it is implausible to hypothesize so many conveniently available response chains. Also, they will perform adequately on test trials with novel sample stimuli. Furthermore, searches for the mediating response chains (D'Amato, 1973) have proven singularly unrevealing. Mostly, animals seem to remember without "externalizing" that memory in their peripheral musculature throughout the retention interval.

An alternative S-R explanation is to say that pecking the sample stimulus sets up and strengthens a temporary S-R tendency (e.g., "peck triangle" in Figure 11.2), which is available and activated on the choice test. Since over trials, the "peck triangle" and "peck square" habits would be reinforced approximately equally often, the strengthening of the correct sample habit within a given trial would have to overcome any disadvantage (e.g., a stronger incorrect habit) created by past trials. Therefore, requiring more pecks to the sample key, as Roberts did in his experiment, should strengthen the habit for the correct response on that choice trial (which was the actual finding in Figure 11.3).

A critical problem with this later S-R account is that animals also readily learn conditional matching and cross-modal matching tasks nearly as well as the simple matching task described in Figure 11.2. In these tasks, a sample stimulus informs the animal that some associated, second stimulus will be correct on the choice trial.

Thus, a red sample light might signal that the triangle will be reinforced on that choice trial, whereas a green sample light signals that the square will be reinforced on that choice trial—or a high- or low-pitched tone might signal that the triangle or square will be reinforced on that choice trial. D'Amato and Worsham (1972) found that the performance of monkeys was just as accurate in conditional matching as in standard delayed matching to sample. Such results cannot be explained in terms of conditioning an approach response to the sample stimulus within a given trial.

Such results are more simply explained in terms of sensory associations. Within each trial, the animal must set up a temporary association, "current sample → triangle," and activate this memory to guide her choice. If it is a conditional match task, then the choice depends on further equivalence rules acquired and stored in permanent memory—namely, rules of the form "If current sample → red, then choose triangle." On this analysis, the task may be difficult because the subject at the time of the test has associative interference between different "current sample → X" memories. Basically, she must discriminate the most recent sample from earlier ones. Since discrimination over time follows Weber's law, with a given difference being less discriminable the longer the base interval, errors caused by confusions between this trial's sample and earlier trials' samples will increase with longer within-trial retention intervals. This is, of course, the standard forgetting function in delayed matching. Also, confusions of this trial's samples and earlier ones will increase the closer in time are successive trials, and this is true. Therefore, this theory of discrimination of time tags on sensory associations seems to give a neat account of many relevant facts of delayed matching to sample (for details, see D'Amato, 1973). Many other results on short-term memory in animals would seem to be explained along similar lines. From our present perspective, however, these sensory associations violate S-R theory.

Goal Learning as an Alternative to Response Learning

Stimulus-response theories imply that the organism, goaded along a path by internal and external stimuli, is learning the correct movement sequence which can be elicited under appropriate conditions of drive and environmental stimulation. In traditional S-R theory, the organism is supposed not to have, at the time of response selection, any representation of the goal; all that the organism "knows," according to a strict Watsonian interpretation, is that certain responses have particular strengths in particular situations. Reinforcement conditions are not represented in the subject's knowledge of the situation; rather, they are merely reflected in the relative strengths of particular S-R connections.

The alternative possibility propounded by Tolman is that organisms learn goals ("rewards"), so that they come to know what stimuli will follow particular S-R combinations. Thus, Tolman's S-R-S formulation ascribes to the subject an internal representation of the goal, or the next stimulus in the sequence. During the learning of a response sequence such as running a complex maze, the learner is following signs to a goal, is learning his way about, is following a sort of map—in other words, is learning not movements but goal routes. Many learning situations do not permit a clear distinction between these two possibilities. If there is a single path with food at the end and the organism runs to it faster at each opportunity, there is no way of telling whether its responses are being stamped in by reinforcement or whether it is guided by its increasingly stronger goal valence and expectation of food.

Because both stimulus-response and expectancy learning so often predict the same

behavioral outcome, it is necessary to design special experiments in which it is possible to favor one theory over the other. Three situations give strong support to the expectancy alternative. These are experiments on reward expectancy, on place learning, and on latent learning.

1. Reward expectancy. One of the earliest and most striking observations on reward expectancy was that of Tinklepaugh (1928). In his experiment, food was placed under one of two containers while a monkey was watching but was prevented from immediate access to the containers and food. A few seconds later, the monkey was permitted to choose between the containers and he invariably demonstrated his memory by choosing correctly. This is the standard delayed response situation. The behavior which is pertinent here occurred when, after a banana had been hidden under one of the cups, the experimenter, out of the monkey's view, substituted for it a lettuce leaf (a less preferred food). Upon turning over the correct container and finding the lettuce leaf instead of the preferred banana, the monkeys would show "surprise" and frustration, would reject the lettuce leaf, and would engage in definite searching behavior, as though looking for the expected banana. Somewhat the same sort of behavior was found by Elliott (1928) when the food in the goal-box of a rat maze experiment was changed from bran mash to sunflower seed. More systematic experiments were carried out later with chimpanzees (Cowles & Nissen, 1937). There is little doubt that animals have some sort of expectancy for specific goal-objects. Under those circumstances, other goal-objects produce signs of behavior disruption. Such behavior means that the sign-learning theory is appropriate; it does not, of course, mean that other theories may not attempt to deduce the behavior from other principles. As noted in Chapter 5, Hull's theory tried to represent reward expectancy in terms of the fractional anticipatory goal response (r_G). The experiment by Trapold (1972) reviewed in Chapter 5 is just one recent example of effects due to anticipation of different rewards. Moreover, Amsel (1958, 1962), a neo-Hullian, introduces his hypotheses about *frustration* by considering it to result from a discrepancy between an expected and obtained reward for responding. So the later Hullians basically accepted Tolman's notion that the organism has some representation of the expected reward at the time it responds.

2. Place learning. Experiments on place learning were designed to show that the maze learner is not moving from start to goal according to a fixed sequence of muscular or turning movements, such as would be predicted from the idea that responses are to be defined with reference to the exact musculature involved. Tolman believed rather that the animal is capable of behavior which is varied appropriately, according to altered orientations of herself or of the maze in relation to the environment; it is as though she knows where the goal is. For example, a monkey who has been rewarded for choosing a black triangle in preference to a white square when they are presented alternately to the left or right in a horizontal row will continue to choose the black triangle when the objects are presented in a novel vertical array, one above the other on the panel. The organism has learned to "approach black triangle" rather than to "choose right to the configuration of white left-black right."

There are several subtypes of experiments revealing such place or goal learning. The first subtype of the place-learning alternative to response learning leaves the form of the path intact but interferes with the movement sequences in getting from start to goal. In one experiment, rats that had learned to run a maze were then given cerebellar lesions; although they were now unable to move through the maze except by small circling movements, they nonetheless were still able to make their way through the maze without error (Lashley & Ball, 1929). They could not have been repeating sequences of kinesthetic habits learned earlier. In another study, rats were able to demonstrate what they had learned by running through the correct path after having been trained in swimming through the maze (MacFarlane, 1930). Still later, it was shown that rats that had been merely drawn repeatedly through a water maze on a raft to the goal, repeatedly observing the correct sequence of turns at signaled choice-points to a food-rewarded goal, were then able to run through the maze almost errorlessly when finally given a chance to perform. They had apparently learned the correct sequence of signs or cues to follow leading to the rewarded goal-box, all this without any overt running movements at all.

The second subtype of place-learning experiment sets a movement habit against a spatial habit and determines which is the more readily learned. Tolman and his collaborators (Tolman et al., 1946, 1947) arranged an elevated maze in the form of a cross, as shown in Figure 11.5. The response-learning group was started in random alternation from either S_1 or S_2, always finding food by turning to the right; that is, food was at F_1 when the start was S_1 and at F_2 when the start was S_2. The place-learning group, by contrast, always went to the same place for food. This meant that if running to F_1, a right turn would be required when starting from S_1, but a left turn when starting from S_2. In this experiment the place-learning group was much the more successful. The eight rats of the place-learning group all learned within 8 trials, whereas none of the response-learning group learned this quickly, and five of them did not reach the criterion in 72 trials. Under these circumstances (an elevated maze with many extramaze cues), it was clearly demonstrated that place learning is simpler than response learning.

However, other experimenters soon found conflicting results (e.g., Blodgett & McCutchan, 1947, 1948), discovering "response" learning to be sometimes faster, sometimes slower, or sometimes equal to "place" learning depending on the presence and distinctiveness of extramaze cues relative to left-right positional cues. Some resolution of the conflicting literature was provided by Restle (1957), who suggested that subjects can learn to respond with respect to either sort of cue ("place" or "response"), and that the relative learning rates depend on the relative salience or distinctiveness of the two types of cues in the total maze situation. For example, one can reduce the distinctiveness of place cues (e.g., by having the arms of the maze radiate in a V at angles progressively less than 180°). Such manipulations have the desired effect in slowing acquisition of subjects

who are required to learn with respect to the manipulated cue. Restle carried the analysis further with a mathematical model of discrimination learning which permitted quantitative assessment of the "salience" or "distinctiveness" of the place and/or the "response" cues. A significant prediction that was confirmed was that when subjects learn a problem in which place and response are always correlated and redundant (e.g., in Figure 11.5, the subject always starts from S_1 and always finds food at F_1), their learning rate will be the sum of the learning rates for subjects learning by place alone and for subjects learning by response alone. That is, learning rates are higher for problems with redundant relevant cues. Furthermore, Restle showed that in a conflict test given following "place + response" learning, when the two modes of responding are placed in opposition, the percentage of animals choosing the place alternative on the test trials was

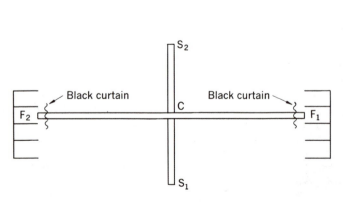

Figure 11.5. Maze used to test the relative ease of learning either a response which brings reward or the place at which reward is found. By starting irregularly at S_1 and S_2, but finding reward at the same food-box each time, one group of rats turns now to the right, now to the left, to find food always at the same location. These are the place learners. By starting at either S_1 or S_2, but always finding food as a result of turning the same way (say, left), another group is taught always to make the same response, but to find food at different places, depending upon the starting point. Place learning, under the conditions of the experiment, is found to be easier than response learning. (From Tolman et al., 1946.)

predictable from the earlier estimates of the relative saliences of the place and response cues—with the more salient cue receiving the predominant choices. Altogether then, Restle's analysis seemed to have satisfactorily resolved the place-versus-response controversy, and showed how in some respects the controversy was misguided or at least based on too simplistic an analysis of what is (or can be) learned.

The third subtype of place-learning experiment involves the use of alternative paths when a practiced path is blocked. An early form of the blocked-path experiment is that of Tolman and Honzik (1930a), which is said to demonstrate inferential expectation, or insight, in rats. The main features of the arrangement are as follows. There are three paths (1, 2, and 3), in that order of length from shortest to longest and hence in that order of eventual preference (Figure 11.6). In preliminary training, when path 1 was blocked at A, a preference was established between paths 2 and 3 for the shorter of these paths. Only when path 2 was blocked also did the rats run to path 3. A familiarity with all paths and a preference for them in the order 1, 2, 3 was established in preliminary training. An important feature of the maze design, crucial for the test, was that paths 1 and 2 had a common segment leading to the goal. Previously the block in path 1 had been placed at A before this stretch of common path; then the rat, after backing up from the block, ran to path 2. Now in the critical test trial, the block was placed farther along path 1, so that it fell in the common path, at point B. The question was whether the rat, in backing out again, would choose the second preference, path 2, and be frustrated, or would "infer" that path 2 was also blocked. What the rats did, predominantly, was to avoid path 2, and to take the path ordinarily least preferred, the long path 3, but the only one open, given the current block at point B. Again the hypothesis is supported that the rat

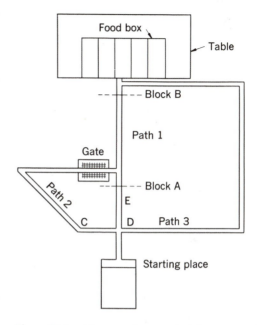

Figure 11.6. Maze used to test insight in rats. The paths become established as a hierarchy according to length, path 1 preferred to path 2, path 2 to path 3. If path 1 is closed by block A, the rats run by path 2. If path 1 is closed by block B, the rats run by path 3 if they have "insight" that the barrier closes path 2 as well as path 1. (From Tolman & Honzik, 1930a.)

acted in accordance with a "map" of the situation, and not according to blind habit, or according to the automatic performance in hierarchical order of habits elicited by choice-point stimuli.

The Tolman and Honzik experiment was criticized by other experimenters, who showed that the results, while reproducible, were easily disturbed by the manipulation of experimental variables such as alley width or enclosure of the alleys, which theoretically should not affect the animal's "reasoning ability"—see Evans (1936), Harsh (1937), Keller and Hill (1936), and Kuo (1937). A successful repetition was reported in an alley maze by Caldwell and Jones (1954), and an ingenious variation was introduced by Deutsch and Clarkson

(1959) with confirmatory results. Later experiments with higher primates have repeatedly demonstrated such insightful inferences (see Menzel, 1978).

3. Latent learning. In addition to the experiments on reward expectancy and on space learning, a third variety of experiment bears importantly on sign learning: the latent-learning experiments. These show that an animal can learn by simply exploring a maze, without food reward, so that, when reward is later introduced, performance is better than that of rats without this exposure, and is sometimes as good as that of rats with many previously rewarded trials. The "latent learning" consists of knowledge of the maze, not revealed in choice of the shortest path from entrance to exit until the rat is motivated to make that choice. The experiments, beginning with those of Blodgett (1929), were critical of the hypothesis that reinforce-

ment was necessary before any associative learning could occur at all. This popular hypothesis had been propounded by Thorndike, by Pavlov, and by Hull.

Following up the work started by Blodgett (1929), Tolman and Honzik (1930b) studied the effect of introduction of reward in a rat-maze experiment after the animals had been allowed to wander through the maze for ten trials without food. The control group, fed each day in the maze, reduced their error and time scores much more rapidly than the nonfed group. But when food was introduced for the latter group, they improved abruptly; their performance was just as good as that of the always-rewarded group. Thus, the nonfed group had apparently profited as much by its earlier trials as the fed group. Since this profiting did not show in earlier performance, the learning taking place is said to be latent. The results for error elimination are shown in Figure 11.7 There

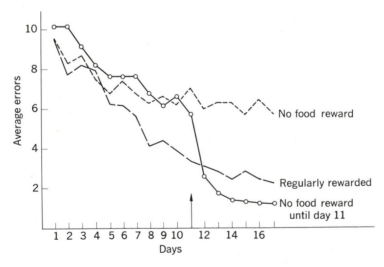

Figure 11.7. Evidence for latent learning in the maze. With no food reward there is some reduction in errors, but not as great a reduction as with regular food reward. Despite the higher error scores prior to the introduction of food, the group rewarded only from the eleventh trial immediately begins to do as well as the group that had been regularly rewarded. The interpretation is that some learning went on within the first ten trials, which did not show in performance until the food incentive activated it. (From Tolman & Honzik, 1930b.)

were three groups: two control groups, one rewarded throughout, the other nonrewarded throughout, and the experimental group, nonrewarded until the eleventh trial. On the twelfth day, the experimental group, having been fed but once in the maze, made as few errors as the group that had received food in the maze each of the preceding days.

Several comments about this experiment are required. The maze used was a 14-unit, multiple-T type (Stone & Nyswander, 1927), arranged with doors between each unit to prevent retracing. Even without food at the end, the rat still progressed through the maze (the error-door was locked); according to a last-response theory such as Guthrie's, learning conditions were ideal. The rat had no opportunity to unlearn what it last did in each segment, which was, of course, to go through the correct door to the next one. The results are critical of Guthrie's theory not because the rat shows latent learning but because it does not show *enough* learning when there is no food at the end of the maze. The Guthrie explanation is not sufficient, because the fed rats learned much better than the unfed ones in the early trials.

Reinforcement theories, in their older form, were also at a loss to explain latent learning. In the older forms of law-of-effect theories, the presumption was that reinforcement worked directly upon response strength, so that all that was learned should be revealed in performance. But this appeared to be contradicted by the instances of latent learning; as Tolman had conjectured, some learning (i.e., knowledge of the maze) might occur and be available without being *used* until motivational or reward conditions make it profitable.

In their defense against latent-learning experiments, reinforcement theorists usually made much of the decrease in errors during nonrewarded trials in latent-learning experiments (notice the declining error curves for the first ten days in Figure 11.7).

This decrease was taken as evidence that *some* reinforcement was present before reward was introduced. For example, since an incorrect choice in the maze resulted in the rat's bumping its nose against a locked door, perhaps correct choice responses became relatively stronger simply because incorrect choices were mildly punished. But such defenses could really only account for *that much* gain by reinforcement; any previously concealed gain, shown when reward was introduced, remained unaccounted for. As noted in Chapter 5, however, habit strength ($_sH_R$) in Hull's later theory is acquired independently of the magnitude of reinforcement, such that this difficulty no longer holds. Under minimum values of incentive magnitude, K, habit strength will be "latent," and will only be revealed in reaction potential when incentive motivation is created by introducing the food reward. Examples of minimum incentives that can be present without, say, food reward include exploration, return to home cage, and so on. But this change in Hull's theory was forced partly to handle the latent-learning results.

Tolman's explanation is that the nonreward situation was a good one for learning the spatial relations of the maze. Every unit had one dead end and another end with a door. The last thing done in each case was to go through the door. Recency (which is accepted as favoring expectancy growth) would strengthen the cognition that the door was the way from one segment to the next, though under nonreward conditions there were no reasons for the rat to show what it "knew." The substitution of the food at the end of the maze, a highly demanded goal-object, led the rat to use its cognitive map, to take the turns which led from one unit to the next. Hence the sudden reduction in errors. Although latent learning was in dispute for some time, and many of the maze results with rats were inconsistent, the net upshot was that latent learning was a real phenomenon. It is especially easy to show with higher primates, as we shall see later (Menzel, 1978).

Direct Alteration of Goal Valence

Tolman believed that animals could combine several bits of knowledge to infer what they should do in a choice situation. Knowing the way to a distinctive maze location and then learning that food is there, the animal at the entrance to the maze will *infer* that if she goes to that distinctive location she should find food. The latent-learning experiments reviewed above are relevant to this inference process, as are experiments in which, following learning, the incentive at the end of the maze is radically changed.

There have been several tests of this sort. A classic experiment is by Tolman and Gleitman (1949); they first familiarized rats with a T-maze that had food rewards in both distinctive end-boxes, making the attractiveness of the two maze arms equal. Then, on a critical day, the animals were placed directly into one of the distinctive end-boxes and given painful electric shocks. On the crucial free-choice tests which followed, the animals now predominantly chose the maze arm leading to the other end-box, avoiding the arm leading to the shocked end-box. Since the differential goal-box cues were not perceptible from the choice point of the maze (they were hidden behind curtains), the animal, in choosing, must have "remembered" that one maze arm led to that place where she had been shocked, and so avoided that arm and chose the other.

A second sort of experiment of this type is called *latent extinction*. The first such experiment was done by Seward and Levy (1949), and the literature on the topic was reviewed by Moltz (1957). In these experiments, animals are first trained on a simple instrumental response—say, depressing a lever in order to operate a food-dispensing

mechanism or running down a runway to receive food in the goal-box. After the performance is well established, the subject is given direct exposure to the goal situation without reward; the lever might be removed from the cage and the experimenter might operate the food-dispensing mechanism many times without actually delivering any food, or the animal might be placed directly in the goal-box of the runway repeatedly without any food being there. Such experiences inevitably result in extinction of the last part of the behavior chain established earlier; the animal stops going to the food-well when the dispenser clicks. But the critical observations occur when the animal is placed again in the first part of the runway, or when the response lever is reinserted in the cage. Invariably, that initial response has now been seriously weakened, often not occurring at all. The rat in the start-box is no longer so eager to run down to the end-box because she now "infers" that it will be empty of food; or in the lever-pressing type of experiment, the animal is not very eager to press the reinserted lever to sound the dispensing mechanism because she infers that the noise of the mechanism is no longer associated with food (the originally valenced object).

These are common-sense results; their unique property is that they imply that the strength of an instrumental response sequence can be altered without *that response* occurring and receiving the altered conditions of reinforcement. The rat did not press the lever, then get the dispenser sound and fail to receive food. Only the final link in the chain was broken; yet, the influence of that event was "passed back" to earlier members of the behavior sequence. Such results create difficulties for an S-R reinforcement theory which supposes that responses can have their habit strengths altered only when they occur and are then explicitly punished or nonrewarded. The results seem to call for two assumptions; that at the start of a behavior sequence, organisms have available some representation of what goal they expect to achieve at the end of the response sequence; and that that goal expectation can be altered by direct experience with the goal situation without execution of the prior response sequence leading up to it. These, of course, are exactly the assumptions made in Tolman's theory. It was results such as these which forced Hull and Spence to greater reliance on r_G, the anticipatory goal response, as a theoretical representation of the organism's goal expectation.

Reinforcement and Expectancy Confirmation

Tolman was opposed to the law of effect; he believed that learning about the correlation between events went on as a result of experiencing them together and that coincident rewards or punishments were unnecessary. Tolman did concede that motivation and reward might have an indirect effect upon what is learned by virtue of the fact that they partly determine which stimuli attract the subject's attention or are emphasized. Thus, a hungry rat is likely to attend to stimuli near the place where it is fed, and so learn more about that location than it would were it not fed there.

This emphasizing or informational function of reward is also apparent in studies of human verbal learning (e.g., Atkinson & Wickens, 1971). Subjects give preferential rehearsals to verbal items that they are told are valuable to remember, and this boosts their memory at the expense of less-valued items. In such cases, the "reward" acts as an informative signal, helping the subject select out particular events to be attended to, rehearsed, and learned.

If a given expectancy was run off and the goal or outcome was as expected, the expectancy was said to have been confirmed and so increased towards 100 per-

cent; if an unexpected outcome occurred, the original expectancy was disconfirmed and so decreased. Tolman and Brunswik (1935) argued that such rules enable the organism to learn about the probabilities of events in its environment. Brunswik (1939) performed an early version of the probability learning experiment with rats in a T-maze (see Chapter 8), and reported that the subjects learned eventually to match their percentage choices for one side to the percentage reinforcements given on that side.

The early work with probabilistic (or partial) reinforcement was occurring at the time Tolman was theorizing (Skinner, 1938; Humphreys, 1939). In this work it was found that a subject reinforced for, say, 50 percent of its responses proved to persist responding for much longer during extinction than would another subject reinforced for 100 percent of its responses. This so-called partial reinforcement extinction effect created a long-standing dilemma for S-R reinforcement theory, since how could a response reinforced only part of the time ever come to be stronger and more resistant to extinction than a response reinforced all the time during training? A variety of ingenious solutions to this puzzle have been proposed and researched over the years, several of which are discussed throughout this volume. But one of the prominent hypotheses suggested by Humphreys, Tolman, and others was the *discrimination hypothesis* suggested by the early probability-learning experiments. The hypothesis, in brief, is that expectancies and behavior change at a faster rate the greater the discriminability of the change of conditions between the training and testing series. This hypothesis reached its most refined statement and elaboration in the theorizing of Capaldi (1967) discussed in Chapter 9. The discrimination hypothesis was a most congenial one for Tolman, and the partial reinforcement extinction effect (or its variants) never proved a thorn in his side as it did for the S-R reinforcement theorists who were his contemporaries.

Provisional Expectancies as Hypotheses

In Tolman's view, prior to solving a learning problem, the learner is actively trying out various hypotheses regarding the nature of the (S-R-S*) relationships existing in the problem environment. A given hypothesis conjectured about the correct solution to a discrimination problem might be considered as a provisional expectancy. When the situation is not yet structured and path-to-goal relationships are not yet known, behavior would still be "systematic," based on these provisional hypotheses or guesses.

The initial evidence for this view was provided by Krechevsky (1932a, 1932b, 1933a, 1933b), a colleague of Tolman's. Krechevsky found that prior to learning a four-unit maze (with light versus dark cues plus left-right position cues at each choice point) his rats adopted systematic modes of response which they would "try out" for a while, then switch to a different systematic pattern. For instance, an animal might begin by consistently trying a "turn left" hypothesis, follow it for ten trials or so, then shift to an "alternate positions in successive maze units" mode for a while, finally hitting upon a "go to the dark side" hypothesis, which was correct. Krechevsky called these systematic modes of attempted solutions *hypotheses,* and contrasted them with "blind, random, trial and error" which was commonly supposed to be the prediction of the Thorndikean position for trial-and-error learning. Krechevsky showed convincingly that averaging time or error scores across groups of individuals tends to conceal the systematic nature of each individual's mode of attack. It was supposed that, rather than gradually stamping in the correct response, the effect of reinforcement was to consistently confirm the correct hy-

pothesis, whereas nonreinforcement was used as an informative signal for abandonment of a provisional but incorrect hypothesis. The correct solution would be hit upon all at once, when the animal abandoned a hypothesis based on an irrelevant cue and then selected the correct hypothesis based on the relevant cue. The solution to the problem was sudden and apparently "insightful," much as Gestalt theorists had predicted. These experiments and associated ideas furnished the opening shots in a long-standing but fruitful controversy over continuity and discontinuity in discrimination learning by animals, with the hypothesis experiments furnishing initial evidence for the discontinuity hypothesis.

The clearest statement of a hypothesis theory has been made by Restle (1962) and Levine (1965, 1969, 1970), and the clearest evidence for it has been collected by Levine (summarized in Levine, 1970) using human adults learning simple concept identification problems. A typical set of stimuli in one of Levine's experiments is shown in Figure 11.8. The stimulus patterns here vary in four binary dimensions: shape (X or T), size (large or small), color (black or white), and position (left or right). Each card contains a pattern alongside its full complement—for instance, a large black X on the left versus a small white T on the right. The experimenter elects to say *Right* whenever the subject selects that pattern having a particular property—for instance, those having the T shape. The subject's task is to learn always to select the correct pattern as each pair is shown.

Hypothesis theory supposes that a learning problem such as this is representable by saying that the subject at the outset of training entertains a small population of possible hypotheses (Hs) regarding the solution (e.g., one H would be "choose the left pattern"). The subject presumably selects an H and responds to the card according to that H; if his response is correct or if he

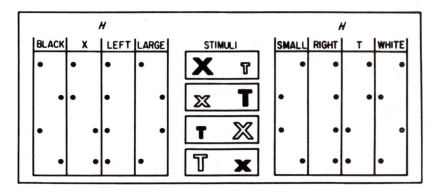

Figure 11.8. Eight patterns of choices (left or right dots in columns) corresponding to each of the eight hypotheses (H) when the four stimulus pairs are presented consecutively without feedback. (From Levine, 1970.)

is given no feedback regarding the correctness of his choice, he continues using the same H for the next trial. If his response is called *Wrong*, then it is assumed that he samples a different H from the pool of hypotheses. This "win-stay/lose-shift" strategy for H selection will guarantee eventual solution if the correct H is available in the subject's repertoire, since all incorrect hypotheses eventually lead to errors and are discarded, whereas only the correct hypothesis leads to consistently correct responses.

Levine assesses hypothesis behavior in humans by the use of test blocks of nonfeedback trials (the experimenter says nothing) interspersed among feedback trials when the person is told *Right* or *Wrong* for his response. It is assumed that nonfeedback trials cause no change in the subject's H, simply preserving the status quo for another trial. The arrangement of feedback (F_i) trials and nonfeedback trials (assessing H_i) is shown in Figure 11.9. Here F_1 denotes the initial feedback trial, H_1 the initial hypothesis as assessed, F_2 the second feedback trial, H_2 the hypothesis assessed following F_2, and so on. The cards in the test block are so arranged that each of the eight different, simple hypotheses

can be uniquely identified by the pattern of choices to the test cards. In Figure 11.8 for instance, with the sequence of four test cards as shown, the sequence of choices "left, left, right, right" would indicate that the person was testing out or holding a "choose X" hypothesis during that test block. Another eight of the possible $2^4 = 16$ response sequences (not shown in Figure 11.8) would not correspond to any of the simple one-attribute hypotheses, and would be denoted by Levine either as more complex Hs or as random behavior. Importantly, the technique permits the experimenter to inspect the subject's hypothesis behavior (if any) throughout the course of concept acquisition, relating the subject's current hypothesis to his prior hypothesis and the most recent feedback received.

In such conditions, adults' behavior conforms almost exactly to the postulates of H-theory. First, most of their test blocks (over 95 percent) reveal the use of systematic, simple Hs, with occasional lapses likely the result of stray "oops" errors, as Levine calls them. Second, subjects tend very much to follow the "win-stay/lose-shift" strategy for H-selection following a feedback trial. That is, if a response is called correct on a feedback trial, then the

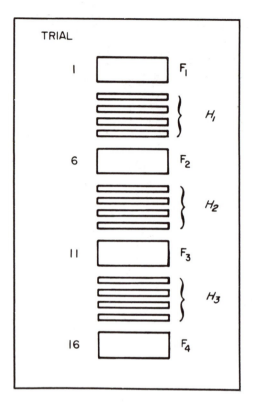

Figure 11.9. Schema of a 16-trial problem showing the feedback trials (F_i) on which the experimenter says *Right* or *Wrong* and the blank trials from which the hypotheses (the H_i) are inferred. (From Levine, 1970.)

next hypothesis will very probably be the same as the hypothesis on the just-preceding trial. Third, the correct H is eventually selected and typically maintained "all at once," and one can notice that it was never used prior to the trial on which it was selected. All of these are the sorts of results that Krechevsky was claiming to find for his rats learning their mazes back in 1932. One may take issue with the restrictive arrangements of Levine's experiments or note some opposing data from lower animals regarding the continuity position. But it is undeniable that the hypothesis-testing approach propounded by Krechevsky and

Tolman has had very strong experimental support and theoretical devotees (see Trabasso & Bower, 1968). The theory is still very much on the books.

Vicarious Trial-and-Error Behavior

Another set of observations cited by Tolman as consonant with his approach concerned so-called vicarious trial-and-error (VTE) behavior of animals at a choice point. This behavior, studied by Muenzinger (1938) and Tolman (1939) among others, is the hesitation, vacillation, and comparison of alternative stimuli by an animal at a choice-point before he "commits himself" to one or the other choice. This active scanning over and comparing of discriminative stimuli appeared to Tolman to support the view that the animal is considering each choice-stimulus in turn, generating expectations, and comparing them before choosing.

G. H. Bower (1959, 1962b) and Spence (1960b) later provided mathematical descriptions of choice-point behavior in terms of a random walk, with the organism orienting to each of the discriminative stimuli in turn and approaching or not approaching them with measurable probabilities. Bower showed how such a model fit the probabilistic structure of rats' VTE behavior during learning of a simple discrimination.

Later, Mowrer (1960) and Estes (1962, 1969a) developed the idea of a "response-scanning" or "stimulus-response scanning" mechanism to account for selection of rewarded responses and inhibition of punished responses. The thought was that in an instrumental conditioning situation, the organism internally scans through a limited repertoire of responses (either incipiently or entirely centrally). If the anticipated outcome for a response is negative (e.g., is associated to punishment and fear), then that response is inhibited. If the anticipated outcome for a scanned response is a high positive reward, then positive facilitative feedback is provided to "push" that incipient response on through to completion. These ideas arose earlier in our discussions of Estes's theory of reward (in Chapters 2 and 8) and in the Sheffield-Estes theory of incentive motivation (in Chapter 4). But clearly the notions of stimulus scanning, prediction of rewards, comparison of anticipated outcomes, and so forth, are all ideas that Tolman would have found quite congenial to his "cognitive" account of the components of decision-making.

Related Systematic Ideas

As intellectual climates change, ideas formerly expressed in one form tend to turn up in others, and may be unrecognized. As we have emphasized throughout this chapter, Tolman anticipated many of the later significant developments in learning theory.

Thus, *decision processes* have become very interesting in contemporary psychology, growing out of the theory of games as proposed by von Neumann and Morgenstern (1944). As the theory has been adapted by psychologists (Edwards, 1954, 1962), increasing interest arises in *subjective probability* and *subjective utility*, terms rather similar in meaning to Tolman's notions of expectancy value and object valence. The importance both of probabilities and of risk was explicit in the paper by Tolman and Brunswik (1935), in which their separate views were harmonized. Pointing this out does not mean that the ideas in decision theory came historically from Tolman and Brunswik. It is rather that if related ideas appear in new forms, with appropriate experimental and mathematical procedures, there is no special point in pushing for the earlier ideas, except to point out that they had a measure of validity. Rotter (1954), in a book designed to provide a theory for clinical psychology, evolved an expectancy-reinforcement theory, with many points of con-

tact with Tolman's views. His basic formula for *behavioral potential* makes it a function of *expectancy* of reinforcement and the *reinforcement value* of the expected reinforcement. The expectancy of reinforcement is close to Tolman's means-end readiness, and the reinforcement value corresponds roughly to valence.

A *structural model* proposed by Deutsch (1960) and used to explain a great variety of experiments represents a kind of thinking about psychological problems quite consonant with that of Tolman. Even though Deutsch proposes a "machine" type of model, in which such a machine has memory storage and feedback mechanisms, it can show insightful behavior of the order of Tolman's rats (Deutsch, 1954). In fact, one of the more ingenious experiments is a repetition, with changes, of the Tolman and Honzik (1930a) experiment, as reported by Deutsch and Clarkson (1959).

Some experiments with a Tolman-like interpretation (though not designed particularly in relation to his theory) were presented by Lawrence and Festinger (1962) to test predictions based on Festinger's concept of cognitive dissonance (Festinger, 1957). This is a type of motivational theory deriving from the level of aspiration experiments of Lewin, with which Festinger had been earlier associated (Festinger, 1942). The interpretation can be thought of as Tolman-like because of the inference to cognitive processes in rats.

The finding of the Lawrence and Festinger experiments is that animals who have been induced to perform an effortful response under insufficient reward conditions (e.g., small, infrequent, or delayed rewards relative to the effortfulness of the response) will reveal greater resistance to extinction of that response than will their more amply rewarded confreres. The interpretation is that the occurrence of an insufficient reward following an effortful performance induces a momentary state of cognitive dissonance, which is unpleasant to the animal. One method to reduce that dissonance is to seek out intrinsic attractions in the activity or the insufficient goal situation itself, which will justify the action just taken. Thus a man who moves a long distance to take a disappointingly low-paying job may begin to justify his staying with the job because he "likes the work" or "is getting good experience" or "the community is a great place to live." In a series of inventive experiments, Lawrence and Festinger (1962) showed the viability of this cognitive dissonance analysis of what was influencing rats to continue performing an insufficiently rewarded response during an extinction series. As Festinger (1961) has summarized the theory, "we come to love those things for which we have suffered." The results of Lawrence and Festinger are problematic for any theory that attempts to explain a response's resistance to extinction in terms of some response strength measure that increases the more favorable is the reward condition prevailing during acquisition. Yet this was the predominant theory for many years and was promulgated by Thorndike, Hull, and their followers.

Logan's theory of classical conditioning. As indicative of the current trend toward cognitive formulations, it should be noted that Frank Logan, a prominent Hullian theorist, has advanced a new theory of classical conditioning and incentive learning centered upon a sensory-sensory contiguity principle of association (Logan, 1977, 1979). He explicitly acknowledges that this was Tolman's basic thesis regarding conditioning. In Logan's view, the cognitive association of CS to US is established in one trial, and then begins to decay over time. Successive trials of CS-US pairings establish multiple traces, which are somewhat unique but also similar along a generalization gradient. A later CS presentation may call forth one of these memories by generaliza-

tion, in which case a representation of the US may become activated (as an expectancy). Thus, "learning is cumulative memory," to quote Logan. Once retrieved, whether a particular CS-US memory will produce a conditioned response depends in Logan's theory upon several motivational factors: the intensity dynamism of the CS (analogous to V in Hull's system), dynamism of the anticipated US intensity, and the prevailing disposition ("drive level") to make the response in question (to the US). Using further assumptions, Logan (1977) shows mathematically how his theory accounts for standard results on classical conditioning, effects of CS intensity, US intensity, drive level in appetitive conditioning, time discrimination, and other such matters. Logan handles extinction following acquisition by assuming two processes: first, that there is a decrease in the expectancy that the US *will* occur following the CS; and second, when the US fails to occur when it was expected, there is an increase in the expectancy that the US *will not* occur following the CS. This latter expectancy is Logan's equivalent of inhibition. A rule stating how these tendencies compromise enables Logan to deal both with extinction and with steady performance under partial reinforcement.

In discussing extinction and partial reinforcement, Logan appeals to ideas rather like Capaldi's (see Chapter 9). Acquisition of conditioned responding occurs when the CS is presented in the context of the stimulus following rewarded trials. In contrast, extinction trials occur in the context of prior nonrewarded trials, and this is a source of generalization decrement for retrieving the CS-US memories (expectancies). Hence, extinction occurs rapidly following continuous but not partial reinforcement training.

Logan calls his a hybrid theory, and he acknowledges combining ideas from a number of diverse sources—from Tolman, Spence, Capaldi, Estes, Rescorla, and Wagner. The mixture seems to have impressive power, and many classical conditioning phenomena are described by the theory. Furthermore, he believes that classical conditioning underlies incentive motivation for instrumental responses; specifically, feedback stimuli from the correct response become classically conditioned to, and thus lead to an expectancy of, the reinforcer (see Logan, 1979). In addition, instrumental learning still requires the assumption that stimulus-response associations are acquired and used in guiding operant responding. In many respects, Logan's theory is rather like that of Estes (1969) in supposing that both S-S and S-R associations are needed to support instrumental responding. This is another example of convergence in contemporary theorizing.

SPATIAL MEMORY AND COGNITIVE MAPS

Tolman used the alluring term *cognitive map* to characterize his rats' knowledge of the spatial layout of their mazes. Unfortunately, Tolman and his students did not develop much theory about cognitive maps. They did test the prediction that when an original goal-path is blocked, the animal should take the next available alternative or shortest detour around the barrier, a prediction which has been generally supported. Recent experiments on rats (Olton, 1979), chimpanzees (Menzel, 1973, 1978), and humans (Gould & White, 1974; Moar, 1979, 1980) have begun to explore systematically the way the organism learns and utilizes information about the layout of objects in space around her. We will briefly review some of the work reported by Olton on spatial memory in rats. Following that, we will review the work by Menzel on chimpanzees.

Reinforcement theory is based on the idea that reward for a response stamps it in, making stereotypy (behavioral fixity) a

likely eventuality. However, behavioral stereotypy is not always the most adaptive mode of adjustment to a given environment. Olton points out that rats are similar to many other species in having natural food-foraging strategies for finding scarce food widely scattered over the terrain. Once food is found at one spot and consumed, the rat should forage elsewhere and not return to this spot for some time. This strategy might have evolved over many generations, as this species adapts to its specific environment. But that strategy implies that rats will show great *variability* of behavior in exploring a space over which food has been placed.

For many years, experimenters have been trying to teach stereotyped response habits to rats learning to find food in a maze, and they have been puzzled by the large amounts of "spontaneous alternation" and exhaustive exploration the animals showed before they settled down to doing what the experimenter wanted them to do. The animals appeared to be exploring and learning about the spatial layout of the maze arms, and were initially disinclined to believe that food would be found consistently at the same location. Even if no food were available, rats would still learn to explore a complex maze systematically, patrolling its various alleyways every trial, rarely returning to an arm previously visited on that trial (see Uster, 1976; Uster et al., 1976). Of course, to conduct such efficient patrols, the rat must have learned the maze layout and must remember his travels on previous trials.

A dramatic demonstration of this short-term spatial memory in rats was arranged in an experiment by Olton and Samuelson (1976). This used the radial-arm elevated maze shown in Figure 11.10. A pellet of food is hidden at the end of each arm, and the rat is allowed to explore until it finds all eight pellets. Optimum performance would be to visit each arm once without repeating. Rats quickly learn to perform very

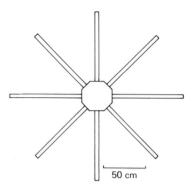

Figure 11.10. A radial-arm elevated maze. A food reward was hidden at the end of each arm, and the animal runs until he finds all the food. (From Olton, 1979.)

ing locations in the complex maze. Thus, the rat was shown capable of locating herself in a field from a novel perspective never seen before and still finding her way to the goal. Their performance here is much like what people do in using their maplike knowledge of a new town to get to a familiar destination from a novel starting point. They notice the direction to familiar landmarks, move to those, orient in the direction of signs closer to the goal, and continue combining patches of familiar routes as chunks until they weave their way to their destination. Such performances have not yet been explained by a complete theoretical model, although a few researchers in artificial intelligence (e.g., D. V. McDermott and B. J. Kuipers) have begun addressing the issue of how local route information is integrated into a maplike structure. The acquisition, representation, and use of spatial information in performance promises to be an area of research growth and interesting ideas. As one illustration, we will review the research of Menzel on area map-learning by chimpanzees.

Cognitive Maps in Primates

It is unfortunate that Tolman and his followers chose the lowly rat as their subject to demonstrate higher-order learning and inferential reasoning, since the rat's abilities seem rather limited. Had they chosen to work with monkeys or chimpanzees in their native field environment, they would have quickly uncovered hundreds of examples of intelligence in the use of tools, in using spatial knowledge, in negotiating through social relations with stronger adversaries, and so on. A number of psychologists and ethologists have observed chimpanzee colonies in the wild or in a large "experimental" field for many years, and have gathered a rich collection of astute observations on intelligent and social behaviors of these animals (Van Lawick-

well in this task, eventually choosing an average of 7.9 different arms in the first 8 choices. Clearly, they can remember where they have just been within each trial cycle, and avoid those places. Olton and Samuelson (1976) demonstrated that the rats were not achieving this high level of performance by using intramaze cues (from food odors or previous odor trails) nor from systematic movements (e.g., always turn left coming out of an arm). Rather, the rats depended upon extramaze visual cues they could see from the elevated arms, and they simply "checked off" in memory those places they had visited on a given trial. Later tests, reviewed by Olton (1979), show even more spectacular short-term memory for spatial locations visited by rats. Clearly, such performances are just the opposite of the response stereotypy usually emphasized in learning experiments; but then, repeated visits to the same place are nonreinforced in this radial-arm maze.

Other experiments by Olton show that following familiarization with a complex maze with reward given consistently at one location, the rat will go with few errors via a shortcut to that goal location when she is tested by being placed at novel start-

Goodall, 1971; Menzel, 1973, 1974, 1978). We will describe a few of the observations by Menzel on a group of chimps as they became familiarized with a new one-acre outdoor enclosure in which they were allowed to explore for only a few hours each day.

Chimps are initially frightened of unfamiliar terrain, so at first the group hovered around the building near where they entered the field. Gradually, the group explored more of the territory and became familiar with it. Older males would explore new territory more quickly than females or younger males. The animals moved in a group and stayed near trees or other high structures, or near bushes and cover. After familiarizing the chimps with their field, Menzel would introduce each day some new toy (like a teddy bear or doll) at different locations. Within a very few minutes after their release into the enclosure, the chimps would spot the new toy, make a beeline for it, explore it, and play with it. The detection of a novel object implies, of course, a thorough familiarity with the old objects of the field.

Menzel then gave the chimps a version of an Easter-egg hunt, which he called the Traveling Salesman Problem. One experimenter carried a chimp around while a second experimenter would show the chimp where he was hiding eighteen pieces of preferred fruit. Figure 11.11 illustrates a map for four different chimps of the locations of the eighteen hiding places on a given trial; the numbers in the circle tell the order in which these hiding places were shown to that chimp. After this observation trial, the chimp was released at the entrance to the field. The remarkable fact is that the animal would run directly to the various hiding places, eat the food, then run to the next, and so on. The paths of the four animals on their best trial is shown by following the arrow from *s* (start) in Figure 11.11. The animals remembered most (15 to 18) of the hiding places;

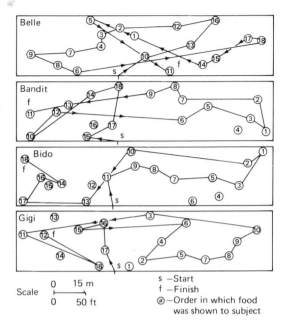

Figure 11.11. Maps showing four chimps' performances on an "Easter-egg" hunt. The numbers in the circles tell the order in which the chimps were exposed to the food being hidden. The arrowed path from the start (*s*) indicates their order of visiting the food drops. Food circles not touched by the line were not searched. (From Menzel, 1973.)

and control observations proved that they did not do it by smell or by random sighting of the food while roaming about. Moreover, they used a fairly efficient route in picking up the food, achieving something like a least-distance path. The order of visiting the food places was determined by their closeness in space, not by the temporal order in which the hiding places were shown to the chimps. The path is analogous to that of the traveling salesman who must visit customers in eighteen different towns and wants to drive the least distance possible. The salesman, of course, does slightly better because he has a real map to look at and can mark on it (an external memory aid) all places to be visited.

But chimps have only their mental (cognitive) maps and must remember the target places shown but once. Also, the chimps had multiple trials over several days with different hiding places; undoubtedly earlier patterns intruded and interfered slightly with memory for the current pattern of food locations.

The chimps seemed to pick up local landmarks as a way of remembering the hiding places: as the food was shown being hidden, the chimp would look about for any prominent object nearby (e.g., a tree, a bridge) and at a specific local cue (the brown cactus plant), as if associating the food to these landmarks. These then guided the chimp's later Easter-egg hunt. The errors made were due to confusion of local signs (e.g., looking behind an adjacent fencepost), much as a human would make small mistakes. In other tests, Menzel showed that, other things being equal, the chimp would go first to the nearer food, to the more preferred food, and to that side of the enclosure with the larger number of food drops on it.

In a later experiment on remote observation, chimps were held at the entrance as they watched an experimenter walk about the enclosure, and hide several pieces of fruit, signaling each hiding place by waving the fruit at them just before he hid it. Even in this remote-observation situation, the chimps performed remarkably well in running to the food when released later.

In a final experiment, the location of a single piece of fruit in the enclosure was indicated to the chimp by the experimenter pointing in its direction, or taking a few steps in its direction, as the chimp watched the experimenter. This social signal served to orient the animal; when released after several seconds, the chimp would take off running in the direction pointed out by the experimenter, and invariably find the food. In another experiment, the experimenter hid in the enclosure a large and a small pile of food on each trial (out of sight of the chimp); then he signaled to the chimp the direction of the large pile by pointing and walking fifteen paces toward it, and indicated the direction of the small pile by pointing and walking only five paces toward it. After a few trials to learn the significance of the two signals, the animal when released would immediately search in the long-pointing direction where the big pile of food was located; after finding that, the chimp would then go in the indicated direction to the smaller pile of food. Later projects were planned to test the chimps with more symbolic cues such as motion pictures or still photographs of the direction of the food from the entrance.

Such experiments reveal that educated chimpanzees have remarkable memories and are capable of planning goal-paths in space. These results depend, however, upon the animals being thoroughly familiar with a specific locale, much as they would learn their natural habitat. They were always very curious about exploring any new object introduced into a familiar terrain. (This frustrated Menzel's attempt to study chimps' ability to maneuver around novel obstacles to food—the chimps would become absorbed in exploring the novel obstacle and would not bother about the food!) In their everyday foraging and social interactions, the animals revealed that they could plan, use tools, use communicative social signals, and get around obstacles. For instance, if one chimp knows where a banana is hidden but another dominant animal is between him and the banana, he will figure out a way to detour around the stronger animal, perhaps lure him elsewhere, and then snatch the prize. The intelligent planning of the actions and interactions is striking and compelling. Tolman would have enjoyed watching such creatures.

As a theory, Menzel believes that chimps build up something like a cognitive map as they become familiar with the enclosure, locating all large landmarks and nearby local cues relative to one another. They then associate food with specific cues for locations on this map, and calculate how to get to these spots. An interesting question that remains is how the various local exposures to different parts of the space are integrated. Later research has focused on the human ability to build up a cognitive map from restricted exposure to a new city or building (Gould & White, 1974). In historical perspective, however, such observations on primate map-learning and use are the most striking evidence for Tolman's cognitive map theory.

FINAL COMMENTS ON TOLMAN'S INFLUENCE

While few recent experiments have shown their direct origin in Tolman's theory, a few contemporary developments can be traced back to Tolman and his influence. He clearly posed for standard stimulus-response theories many of the enduring problems with which it has struggled—for example, the distinction between learning and performance, latent learning, goal anticipation and incentive motivation, hypothesis-testing behavior, sharpening of the characterization of "what is learned," and so forth. Stimulus-response theorizing developed and matured well beyond Watson, Thorndike, and Pavlov because of the vigorous challenges provided by cognitive theorists who frequently were the first to call attention to some new problem area regarding learning. This was entirely wholesome, and in our time has led to a kind of coalescence of the competing learning theories in a synthesis of a sort not envisioned by the original protagonists. That cognitive theories of animal learning have recently come into vogue is indicated, for example, by a recent volume entitled *Cognitive processes in animal learning* (Hulse et al., 1978).

We may ask what kinds of scientific contributions are likely to endure. A global system, unless it is very successful in grouping together a number of well-established empirical facts (Newton's law, Einstein's relativity theory), is less likely to endure than a single well-established relationship (Archimedes' principle, Ohm's law, the Weber-Fechner law). Tolman's system was not tight enough to endure, and there is no "Tolman's Law" to give him immortality; perhaps the latent-learning experiment is as uniquely his as the nonsense syllable is uniquely Ebbinghaus's. Some of these less dramatic contributions, as they work their way into the stream of science, may be enough to win a rightful place in the history of science for the person who made them.

The hope, however, is for something more than this, and that is for the march of science (in our case, psychological science) to be evident either in firm factual relationships upon which future theories are built, or in the introduction of new paradigms which give science a fresh look, as emphasized by Kuhn (1962). In retrospect, Tolman's contribution may have been of this latter kind, giving a new cast to behaviorism by insisting that it be open to the problems created by cognitive processes, problem-solving, and inventive ideation. The sort of program Tolman envisioned seems now to be coming to fruition in modern cognitive psychology.

SUPPLEMENTARY READINGS

The only major book on Tolman's system is:

TOLMAN, E. C. (1932). *Purposive behavior in animals and men.*

Fortunately, his shorter writings have been assembled in book form:

TOLMAN, E. C. (1951). *Collected papers in psychology.*

A final summary and overview of his theorizing was published in the chapter:

TOLMAN, E. C. (1959). Principles of purposive behavior. In S. Koch, ed., *Psychology: A study of a science*. Vol. 2.

An interesting little book on motivation that was retitled because of World War II (but remains a book on motivation despite its title), is:

TOLMAN, E. C. (1942). *Drives toward war*.

For a thorough review of Tolman's position, with some suggestions as to possible steps in systematization, see:

MacCORQUODALE, K., & MEEHL, P. E. (1954). Edward C. Tolman. In W. K. Estes et al., eds., *Modern learning theory*. Pp. 177–266.

I2
INFORMATION-PROCESSING THEORIES OF BEHAVIOR

A recent technique in psychological theorizing involves the formulation of theories in the form of *programs* that run on high-speed computers. The aim of the enterprise is to get such a programmed computer to go through a series of actions that in some essential ways resemble or simulate the cognitive or behavioral actions of a real subject performing some task. This chapter explores and hopes to clarify this brief introductory statement; primarily we will be reviewing some of the theories and models that have been formulated in this manner.

The historical antecedents of this theoretical technique are diverse, although many of the modes of thinking have been imported into psychology from engineering. Perhaps an appropriate way to begin is with a discussion of the age-old art of *robotology*. People have long been fascinated by the similarities between the "behavior" of machines and the behavior of living organisms. All the analogies are there, implicit in our natural-language descriptions of what machines do. Robotology consists in the deliberate design of machines that mimic the behavior of living organisms. From a leisurely beginning, recent successful advances have made this enterprise nothing short of spectacular. It is now widely recognized that machines can be designed to perform many sorts of tasks previously done exclusively by humans. Indeed, the machine may often exceed the performance capabilities of the human it replaces. The effect of this engineering feat is apparent in the present concern about automation and the possible obsolescence of the human worker of the future.

During the 1950s a few behavioral scientists began to construct robots that were supposed to embody directly different principles about behavior. Included among these hardware models are W. R. Ashby's *homeostat* (1952) that seeks and maintains a favorable homeostasis of its "internal milieu," Walter's *Machina speculatrix* (1953) that imitates the actions of an animal foraging about its environment in search of food or shelter, Walter's (1953) and Deutsch's (1954) learning machines which mimic the maze learning of rats, Hoffman's machine (1962) that displays most of the phenomena of classical conditioning, and several others to be mentioned later.

One may ask whether these robots are

to be considered seriously. What is their logical status? Are they to be viewed as serious explanations of behavior, or merely as amusing, but idle, curiosities? The prevailing consensus is that a machine which accurately simulates relevant aspects of some organism's behavior indeed constitutes a genuine explanation of that behavior. The idea is that the abstract principles involved in designing the machine—its functional components and their organization—could in fact be the same as those describing the design and functioning of the living organism. In designing and building a machine to simulate certain behaviors, one is, in effect, working out a physical embodiment of a theory about how that behavior is produced by that organism. Getting the machine to work and to simulate some interesting behavior is a way of demonstrating that the theory is internally consistent and that it has specified a sufficient set of mechanisms. Running the robot through one or another task is logically equivalent to deriving theorems about behavior from the theory that is modeled by the physical realization. Conversely, it is claimed that we have a fairly complete understanding of a piece of behavior when we know how to build a machine that would behave in just that way.

The distinction here between an abstract theory and a particular mechanical model of it is similar to the logician's distinction between an axiom system and various realizations of it. The theory or axiom system has the top logical priority; the particular physical realizations of it are secondary. In this sense, it is psychologically irrelevant what hardware is used to realize our robot, whether it be cogwheels, relays, vacuum tubes, transistors, electrochemical processes, or neurons (although the neurophysiologist is concerned with the actual hardware). All proper realizations of the theory will carry out *isomorphic behaviors* —that is, they will display a parallelism or point-to-point correspondence in the be-

havior path that they trace out over time. If two systems show this kind of functional parallelism, this point-to-point correspondence in critical features, then we shall say that one system is a *simulation* of the other. If the correspondence is sufficiently extensive, then we have some reason to believe that the two systems are different realizations of the same theory. In scientific practice, this means that a theory about behavior could be tested by constructing a machine designed in accordance with the theory, and then seeing whether this machine simulates the behavior of interest.

But having reached this point in the argument, we can begin dispensing with the actual hardware altogether. This paring away can be done simply by attending to what are the essential as opposed to the irrelevant features of the system to be simulated. This clearly is determined by one's goals. As an example, suppose that our goal were to simulate the behavior of a rat learning a maze. Then it is clearly immaterial whether our robot looks like a rat, or moves on wheels rather than legs, or, for that matter, merely informs us (by some means) what it would do if it had legs to run with. It would seem that all that a psychological explanation would require is that our robot be equipped with (a) a pseudosensory system whereby it receives stimulus information from its environment, possibly with additional elements sensitive to its "internal drive" states, (b) a central network of learning, storage, and decision-making mechanisms, (c) some way for the central mechanisms to deliver or sustain commands to a motor system (actual or imaginary), and (d) a means for relaying back to the sensory system the effects of its motoric actions. These components are essential; the rest of the rat's natural accoutrements would appear to be just excess baggage from a logical point of view. Nonetheless, even agreeing to this functional caricature of the rat-as-learner does not carry us very far. The major work still lies ahead, in specifying the design and organization of these components, their "rules" of operation, and how they are interconnected.

But we may now dispense with the physical machinery entirely. The robot is just a physical embodiment of a particular explanatory theory; putting it through its paces corresponds to making various deductions from the theory. But there are alternate ways to make deductions from a theory. If the theory is simple enough, specifying only a few parts that perform simple functions, then deductions can be made either verbally, in symbolic logic, or with mathematics. But if the theory is complicated, then verbal deductions become tedious and error-laden, whereas mathematical ones often cannot be pushed through at all. In these cases, we can have recourse to a high-speed computer.

By this approach, we would program a computer so that it goes through the same steps that we would if we were making a verbal deduction from the theory. The computer does the job for us in a short time and it makes no errors. When programmed to operate according to our theory, the computer then becomes just another realization of that theory. It is, however, an inexpensive and efficient realization, since it saves us time and labor. But to realize a behavioral theory in the form of a computer program is not to imply that the theorist conceives of the organism as computerlike. The computer is being used here *merely as a tool for making deductions*. And the fact that a theory is realized as a computer program does not tell us what type of theory it is, or lend any special credibility to it. Any theory that is sufficiently well specified can be realized as a computer program.

The foregoing passages outline some of the arguments for stating theories in the form of a computer program. The strategy itself is noncommittal about the types of theories or concepts that are programmed. It is a historical accident that most theories realized in this way have in fact had a distinctly cognitive bias. This results from the aims of the particular theorists involved; often those aims have been to simulate human higher mental processes—thinking and problem-solving. However, a good deal of work has been done also on programs to simulate learning. In this chapter we review some of the problem-solving programs as well as those directly concerned with learning. We have no hesitation in including discussion of the problem-solving programs, since they illustrate important concepts common to the general approach, and they demonstrate how past learning can be utilized in novel and ingenious ways to solve problems.

INFORMATION-PROCESSING CONCEPTS AND MODELS

Each new theoretical approach usually creates its own descriptive language, or jargon, and so it is with the computer-simulation approach. The jargon is that of "information processing," and it derives from the ways computer scientists generally describe what their machines do. Stimuli, data, instructions—the generic name is "information"—are *input* or *read in* to the computer; after more or less whirling, the computer *outputs* (*reads out*) some particular end result, usually by printing it or displaying a picture on a cathode ray tube. Between the input and output, the computer is described as performing a series of instructed manipulations on the input data. These manipulations may consist of altering or transforming the mass of data, calculating something from it, comparing it to something else, using the result to search for something previously stored in the computer, evaluating what is found at intermediate stages, making decisions about it, and so on. Each of these manipulations may require a short series of instructions in the computer program, called a *subroutine*.

It is convenient to refer to subroutines in terms of the functions they perform with the information input to them. And from this, it is an easy step to begin referring to the subroutine as representing an *information-processing mechanism*. Thus, the computer-simulation theories of behavior may be generally described as postulating the existence within the organism of an array of information-processing mechanisms, each of which performs a certain elementary function, and these processes are assumed to be organized and sequenced in some particular way.

It is perhaps apt to describe most research in the information-processing (IP) area as a concerted effort toward the experimental synthesis of complex human behaviors. Some typical sorts of behaviors that are simulated include the reasoning of a chess champion in selecting his next move in a chess game, the generation of hypotheses by a subject solving a concept-formation task, the selection of stocks and other securities in which an investment broker can wisely invest his or his client's capital, and so forth. The models attempt to portray and understand human behavior utilizing rational capabilities to the utmost. Therefore, in conception and goals, IP models are separated by a wide gap from the traditional stimulus-response approach with its emphasis upon progressively finer analyses of simpler and smaller parcels of behavior. In revolt against this analytic tradition, the IP theories have attempted to synthesize these complex behaviors, to construct models whose capabilities equal those of humans.

To synthesize a complex piece of behavior (e.g., such as proving a theorem in symbolic logic), the theorist must specify many processes as well as a complex organization of all these processes. Additionally, many conditional decision rules must be specified which stipulate how the model is to be switched one way or another in

its search depending in the outcome of previous calculations. How are we to gather information about the performance capabilities of such a complex system? As mentioned earlier, we could arduously follow through its operation step by step using paper and pencil. But to shortcut this, the system is programmed as a sequence of instructions to be carried out by the computer. By running the program on a computer and having the computer print out its actions, we learn about its capabilities. First of all, we learn whether the system has been specified in sufficient completeness so that it will run at all; possibly more parts have to be specified or internal contradictions removed. Second, we can see whether the synthetic behavior it prints out displays the particular features we aimed to duplicate. Third, we can determine from different runs how the behavior of the entire program changes when we modify selected parts of it.

Computers are programmed by writing a usually long sequence of instructions which are to be carried out either on some input information or on information stored in the memory banks of the machine. The total sequence of instructions is called a *program*. Such programs have to be written in a precise format using some standardized language that the computer can "understand." The FORTRAN and ALGOL languages are in common use for programs that carry out ordinary numerical calculations. Figure 12.1 shows the flow chart of a simple program. As data, we have the weights of 12 people; the program is to calculate their average weight. We let $x(I) = 1, 2, \ldots , 12$ represent the 12 numbers. These 12 numbers are punched onto IBM cards and given to the computer. In the program, SUM is our label for a memory cell which we use as a temporary working space. The sequence of instructions is depicted in Figure 12.1. The main component is the "loop," which adds $x(I)$ to

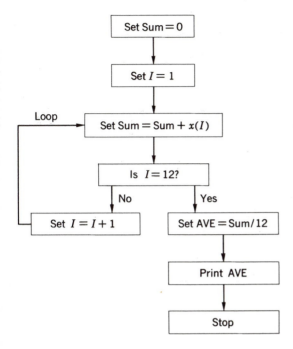

Figure 12.1. Flow chart depicting the steps involved in calculating the average of 12 numbers labeled x(1), x(2), . . ., x(12). A loop is used to calculate the sum of the numbers starting with x(1). On each pass through the loop, the index *I* is increased by + 1; after x(12) has been added to the sum, the program exits from the loop, calculates the average value, and prints it out.

SUM and increases *I* by 1. This loop is executed 12 times, and then the program goes on to the division and printout operations.

A Simple Simulation

Although this example illustrates numerical calculation, a slight variant of the program that has psychological content would use a loop to search a memorized list of elements, checking to see whether it contains a critical target item. This task has been studied extensively by Sternberg (1969) and others as indicating how short-

term memory is searched. The operative program for simulating performance in this "Sternberg task" is illustrated in Figure 12.2, where we have broken it down into small steps. The typical trial begins by loading a small list of digits or letters into short-term memory; these elements are denoted $x(1)$, $x(2)$, . . . , $x(N)$ in Figure 12.2. For the moment, think of $x(1)$, $x(2)$, . . . , $x(N)$ as N different storage cells in memory that hold the items of the list, say, the letters Q, W, F, G. We then give the probe letter (e.g., T), and the subject is to decide as fast as he can whether the probe is a member of the memory set. Since we are interested in the time he takes to make this decision, in our model we set up an internal clock called RT to keep track of the time, and we start this clock at zero when the probe is presented. The operative program retrieves an element from the memory set (an operation which takes time r), compares this element to the probe (which comparison takes time c), responds Yes if it matches the probe, but continues on to scan the next element of the list if the current $x(I)$ mismatches. The query "Is $I = N$?" is used to decide whether the complete memory list has been scanned. If it has not, then the index is updated and the next element on the list is fetched; if the whole list has been scanned without finding an element matching the probe, then the program exits by printing a No response.

This flow chart diagrams the step-by-step operations in doing the task, and attaches time charges to the various operations (which explains the frequent instruction to set the new RT equal to the old RT plus some constant). This program exemplifies what is called a *serial self-terminating search*. It is *serial* in the sense that the elements of the list are retrieved and compared to the probe in series, one at a time, rather than simultaneously (in parallel or all at once). It is *self-terminating* in the

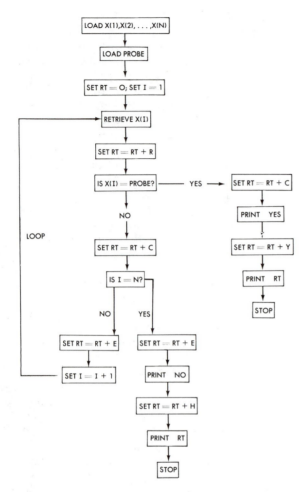

Figure 12.2. Flow chart depicting a simulation model to predict reaction times in the Sternberg "memory-searching" task. The subject is to decide whether or not a given probe item is a member of a prescribed set of items in memory, denoted x(1), x(2), . . ., x(N).

sense that the process stops (exits from the scanning loop) as soon as it obtains a match to the probe stimulus rather than scanning *exhaustively* through to the end of the list regardless of whether an earlier match was obtained. Assuming a random (uniform) distribution of positive probe locations within the list, the *average* location will be at $(N + 1)/2$ in a list of length N. With a self-terminating search, this $(N + 1)/2$ will then be the average number of fetch-and-compare operations carried out on positive probe trials. The equations implied for average reaction times on positive probe (Yes) and negative probe (No) trials will be:

$$RT(\text{Yes}) = (r + c)\frac{(N + 1)}{2} + e\,\frac{N}{2} + y$$
$$= \frac{(r + c + e)}{2}N + y + \frac{r + c}{2'}$$

and

$$RT(\text{No}) = (r + c + e)N + h. \qquad (1)$$

In each case, the reaction times are expected to increase as a straight line (or proportionately) as list length N is increased. The model programmed in Figure 12.2 expects the slope of the No line (the coefficient multiplying *N*) to be exactly twice the slope of the Yes line.

These are quite definite predictions from the process model in Figure 12.2. Though they serve to illustrate the approach, these particular predictions regarding the slopes are not always correct. Instead, the actual data (see Sternberg, 1969) often show *equal* slopes for the Yes and No lines. This could be produced by a model which scans exhaustively through all the memory-set items before exiting with the answer. This would require modifying the program diagrammed in Figure 12.2 so that it remembers any match encountered in its scan, but nonetheless completes the list scanning before responding Yes. Sternberg proposes essentially this model for his data; much experimentation has concentrated around this memory-search task and these kinds of models.

Subroutines and Task Hierarchies

Now, the entire program in Figure 12.2, starting from the initializing statements, could be given a name (SCANLIST) and then treated as a unitary *subroutine* for embedding within any larger program that requires such a function. Furthermore, the *x*(*I*) could also be the names of entire lists of symbols rather than single elements; then an instruction like "For *I* = 1 to *K*, SCANLIST *x*(*I*)," would essentially result in *K* successive calls to the subroutine in Figure 12.2, checking the different lists for a specified probe. The important point is to see that SCANLIST has now become an automatic routine that can be used repeatedly as a component process in solving other problems. This whole process, of making a program a component embedded within a larger program that may be embedded within a larger program yet, is *hierarchical* in nature. Looking at matters "from the top down," in order to do program ("job") *A*, we call in subroutine *B*; but *B* can call in subroutine *C*, and so on

and on, until single, simple instructions are encountered. Once *C* "completes its job assignment," it passes its result back up to *B*, which may then do some more manipulations (e.g., collate results from several subroutines) before passing its results back to *A*, which is the top-level executive program controlling or supervising the entire hierarchy. Such a hierarchical program is rather like the form of control and work allotment within a hierarchical business or governmental organization.

Figure 12.3 shows a schematic of a three-level hierarchy of a problem-solving or work-allotment program. To illustrate, suppose you want to attend a concert or other public event (goal *A*). To do so, you have to purchase tickets (subgoal *B*) and get yourself to the concert hall at the right time (subgoal *C*). To purchase tickets, you have to write a check and a letter (subgoal *D*) and mail it to the ticket office (subgoal *E*). Once you get the tickets, you must get to the concert hall at the correct time. You get dressed or otherwise prepared to leave home at the right time (subgoal *F*), walk or drive to the concert hall (subgoal *G*), then walk in and take your seat on time (subgoal *H*). By finishing subgoal *H*, we have simultaneously satisfied the next higher subgoal *C* (getting to the concert hall on time), and put ourselves in a position to satisfy the highest goal *A* (to listen to the concert). Once that is completed, the next goal is loaded into the processor to be achieved—for instance, to find a coffee house for an after-concert drink.

Diagrams such as Figure 12.3 have an intuitive appeal to psychologists interested in analyzing behavior into its components and their organization. The subgoals and activities can be broken down into as fine and minute detail as the scientist desires, yet the "location" of a given component can be seen in terms of where it fits into and how it functions in the overall organization of the performance. The interpretation of arrows in Figure 12.3 and their

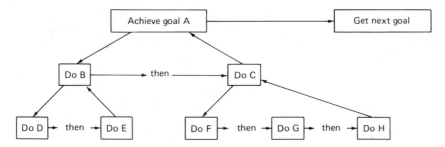

Figure 12.3. Schematic drawing of a three-level hierarchical program in which achieving particular goals depends upon achieving a set of subgoals, which means doing a set of component activities. The arrows indicate the direction in which information and control passes through the system.

direction is important. They indicate the direction of the flow of *control* by the central processor of the various activities; roughly speaking, the arrow mimics the brain shifting its "attention" and its processing effort to the activity at the tip of the arrow. This hierarchical analysis of psychological tasks derives directly from concepts of hierarchical computer programs, and it was imported into psychology by Simon, Newell, and other scientists working in computer simulation. A popular and accessible account of these ideas and their utility for psychological theory is *Plans and the structure of behavior* by G. A. Miller, Galanter, and Pribram (1960).

To return to the SCANLIST program in Figure 12.2 for the Sternberg task, it should be noticed here that the computer is being used as a symbol-manipulating device as well as a numerical calculator. For example, it fetches and compares two symbols for a match, as well as adding increments to the reaction-time counter. Within the IP literature, in fact, computers are viewed primarily as general-purpose symbol-manipulating devices. Mirroring this view, several list-processing languages have been developed to serve as convenient vehicles for formulation and expression of IP ideas into computer programs. Of the several list-processing languages available, LISP is the most often used in present IP work.

To illustrate just one of these languages, the basic objects of LISP are atoms (symbols) and "S-expressions," which are parenthesized lists of symbols or names of lists of symbols. The operations that can be performed in LISP include adding or deleting a symbol on a particular list, reshuffling several lists, combining two lists into a single one, naming a list, examining the words on a list to find matching words, describing the properties of a list and attaching this property list onto the first list, erasing a list, copying a list, and so forth. Such basic processes presumably form a natural language for the IP programs. In themselves, such small-scale operations appear not to impute any intelligence to the basic machinery that does it. However, when tens of thousands of such small-scale operations are cascaded within an organized program, the net performance characteristics of the machine change qualitatively into truly "intelligent" behavior, frequently of a variety unanticipated by the designer of the program.

SIMPLE LEARNING PROGRAMS

Most of the IP programs have dealt with simulations of complex problem-solving by human adults, and have not dealt in any systematic way with simulations of simple conditioning situations. This is partly due to their authors' greater interest in thinking, and partly their belief that simulation of simple conditioning did not sufficiently show off the advantages of simulation theorizing. However, we will briefly consider some examples of computer-simulation models of simple conditioning.

Pavlovian conditioning. Let us make up a simple simulation model of Pavlovian conditioning to illustrate several points. First, we would store in the computer's memory a list of innate reflexes, specifying how one or another unconditioned stimulus (US) elicits a particular unconditioned response (UR). When one of these is used in a Pavlovian experiment, we will also attach to the reflex a number between 0 and 1, reflecting the amplitude of the reflex. For a food US, this number would increase with the state of food deprivation (hunger) of the animal, and the amount of food given as the US.

Second, we would represent presentation of other (neutral) stimuli as alphabetic symbols A, B, C, . . . , so that over time and multiple trials in a conditioning experiment the symbol sequence might be A, C, US-UR, B, D, C, US-UR, E, F, C, US-UR, B, X, C, US-UR. We want a mechanical device to inspect such sequences and to infer which stimulus reliably predicts the US-UR event. This, of course, is the prototypic problem of induction—to detect regularities or correlations among events in an input stream. In the sequence illustrated, C is noted to regularly precede occurrence of the US-UR, so it would probably correspond to the conditioned stimulus (the CS) which the experimenter arranges to precede the US. All other stimuli fluctuate unreliably between trials with the CS and US. But how did you induce that C regularly precedes the US? By what rule or mechanism? Recall that the organism experiences the events just one at a time, extended over time, and does not have the

visual record as we have written it down here.

A simple rule is to have the organism inspect each input symbol and tabulate for it what symbol immediately preceded it and what symbol immediately followed it in the sequence. Such a tabulation would reveal that symbol C is regularly followed by the US-UR, and similarly, that the US-UR is regularly preceded by symbol C.

We also need a simple rule for performance, and it is this: as each stimulus symbol occurs, we look up in memory the tabulation of its successors; if it has regularly preceded the same US-UR event, then we have the computer print out that UR as an "anticipatory response" to that symbol; otherwise, it prints out nothing. The anticipatory UR would be the analog of the conditioned response in the simulation model.

To lead to realistic learning curves, we would need to have a continuous measure of "strength" of the conditioned association from the neutral CS to the UR. A possible learning rule would be this: for each trial, increment the strength of the CS-US connection by a fraction of the difference between the current strength of the connection and the strength of the US-UR being measured. By appropriate choice of the incrementing fraction, the standard curves of Pavlovian conditioning and extinction could be generated.

Although such an artificial learning system would simulate Pavlovian conditioning in standard circumstances, the aim of theorizing is to propose a system that will predict results obtained under many different conditioning situations. In this respect, the learning model briefly sketched can be quickly shown to have its failings. For example, as now stated, it will not learn if the predictive CS occurs two or more time intervals (or symbols) before the US. Also it does not take account of the intensity of the CS, nor the discriminability of the CS from the background stimuli in the situation. Nor does it account for the observation that the conditioning of CS_1 precedes more slowly if its trials are alternated with those of a second CS_2 that is being associated to the same US. Each such unpredicted result suggests some revision of the original model; the hope is that the revisions would dwindle as more results are considered and explained. Failing in that, the original model would be thrown over in order to start afresh. We will not attempt to revise our tutorial model here, since it has served its purpose.

Trial-and-error learning. A simple simulation model for trial-and-error learning is easy to construct. To a given stimulus situation, the organism is conceived to have a repertoire of responses, labeled R_1, R_2, . . . , R_n. It is often convenient to define one of these response classes by exclusion—that is, R_n is "everything else" other than the responses of central concern. Each response R_i to a stimulus has stored with it a strength, V_i, which determines the probability of its choice on that trial according to the formula:

$$p_i = V_i / (V_1 + V_2 + \cdots + V_n). \quad (2)$$

A response is selected each trial by use of a random number table so that response R_i will be selected with probability p_i on this trial. If a response occurs and it is reinforced, then its strength is increased by multiplying it by a reward factor β_1 which is greater than one and depends on the value of the reinforcer. If a response occurs and is not reinforced, its strength is decreased by multiplying it by a nonreward factor β_2 which is less than one but greater than zero. (These are the assumptions of Luce's [1959] response-strength learning model.)

If such a system is given multiple trials with R_1 reinforced and the other responses nonrewarded, it will soon train itself to invariably choose R_1. Having demonstrated

that the model can learn under some standard circumstances, we would proceed to test it by varying the experiment to check crucial assumptions. For instance, how would it handle partial reinforcement or probability learning or choice between different amounts of reward? Pursuing answers to such questions, of course, is what the explanatory game is all about.

Elements of a Learning System

Even these simple learning systems have several distinct parts. These are depicted in Figure 12.4 below. The model of the subject operates in some *task environment* such as a maze or a game of Tic-Tac-Toe. That task environment has certain objects and it defines certain actions and reinforcing contingencies. Relevant aspects of this task environment usually come to be represented in the subject's memory. The *Instance Selector* is whatever causes different cases or trials or instances of the task to be presented repeatedly to the subject. This is controlled by the experimenter in the typical laboratory experiment and is often trivial—for example, the experimenter randomly presents the stimulus patterns to be classified. In some circumstances, the instances can be selected by the learner herself in a sophisticated manner so as to optimize her speed of learning. The *Perfor-*

The task environment

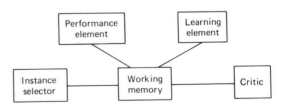

Figure 12.4. The four components of a learning system that adapts to some task environment. (Adapted from Buchanan, Mitchell, Smith, and Johnson, 1978.)

mance Element in Figure 12.4 is responsible for producing some response of the system to each new stimulus or instance. The *Critic* analyzes the response of the Performance Element in comparison to some standard of achievement: it evaluates the adequacy of performance, may localize the cause of errors, and may recommend repairs for how to improve the next performances. The *Learning Element* translates the recommendations of the Critic into specific changes in the parameters or rules used by the Performance Element. The task information and the subject's learning is usually represented in some manner in the *Working Memory,* and learning consists of altering the subject's knowledge about the performance required in the task environment. The Working Memory is the medium through which the several elements communicate their results to one another, and it contains past knowledge as well as the new knowledge emerging in this task environment.

These components are easily identified in our elementary model of trial-and-error learning. The task environment might be the T-maze, the left-right choices, and the rule that left choices are rewarded. The Instance Selector simply places the subject in the same choice situation every trial, represented here in terms of input of a single symbol. The Performance Element selects a left or right response by converting the relative strengths of the responses to probabilities, choosing a response by generating a random number. The Critic notes whether the response was rewarded or not, and recommends increasing its strength if rewarded and decreasing it if nonrewarded. The Learning Element computes the changes in strength according to this advice. Different learning systems handle these several functions in various ways, and some are done so automatically as to be hardly noteworthy. The elements provide a convenient framework for organizing and comparing different proposed learning systems, no matter how complex the task environment in which they operate.

Initial Developments

The years 1955 to 1960 marked the major beginnings of modern information processing models. Near the start of this period, Newell, Shaw, and Simon (1958; Newell & Simon, 1956) were beginning their work on the Logic Theorist, a program to simulate the way a student proves theorems in symbolic logic. At the same time a group of scientists at the Massachusetts Institute of Technology began work on automatic pattern recognition. Personnel in the Carnegie Mellon-MIT-Stanford University axis worked cooperatively and exchanged ideas and techniques during this formative period.

Since that time, there has been a fast proliferation of programs for models that perform a variety of intelligent tasks. Minsky provides an early review (1961a), as did a collection of early basic papers edited by Feigenbaum and Feldman (1963). This chapter is necessarily a limited review of what is going on in this rapidly expanding field. We shall select for discussion some of the work on models for pattern recognition (perceptual learning), problem-solving, and learning. Each system we shall review is in fact a very long and complex set of detailed instructions in a functioning program. This means that a brief description of each can merely touch upon the highlights of what a particular model does, and explain, in general terms, how it accomplishes this end.

A convenient, though frequently indefinite, classification of IP models divides them into those dealing with *psychological simulation* and those dealing with *artificial intelligence.* The distinction hinges primarily on the expressed intent of the theorist. If his intention is that the model mimic step by step the processes he believes a person goes through in performing a task, then he is engaged in simulation of human behavior; if his intention is to design an efficient program that will perform some complex task, regardless of how a person might do it, then he is engaged in artificial-intelligence research. A radar-linked computer that calculates the trajectory of an approaching missile and fires off a countermissile to detonate it is an example of an artificially intelligent machine. What is wanted here is that the machine outperform the person, not simulate behavior exactly. This distinction between the two research areas is not always clearcut, however, and the principles used in constructing efficient automata are usually worth study, if only to see where or how a person falls short. Also, the principles incorporated in an artificially intelligent program to solve problems often derive from observation and introspection about how a person solves that problem. A human is far and away the most versatile, general-purpose problem-solver on this earth, so a model of a human is often a good place from which to start in designing an artificially intelligent automaton. We may illustrate the problem of simulation by considering pattern recognition.

PATTERN RECOGNITION

The central question is how to build a model, or write a program, or program a machine, that will display some human capabilities for classifying and discriminating the flux of environmental energies bombarding the sensors. One of the most basic skills is the classification of single units of input. To classify is to sort a series of things into separate classes, or what we may call *bins*. Each bin has a name, and all things sorted into a given bin are given that name. The bin is an "equivalence" class; things sorted there must possess one or more features in common which constitute the cri-

teria for equivalence, though they may at the same time differ in a number of aspects irrelevant to the current classification. For example, in identifying printed and handwritten letters of the alphabet, a child in elementary school learns to give one name, "A," to all the objects in Figure 12.5. After perceptual learning, the identifying label is *invariant* under a variety of transformations in size, shape, orientation, and alteration by extraneous cues in the external stimulus. The problem is to get a machine to do the same good job of classifying these inputs that a competent and careful child can do.

In a trivial sense, the problem of pattern recognition is solved if the stimulus objects are reduced to a constant, standardized format before being given to the machine. For example, business machines are in use that "read" alphanumeric characters (the alphabetic letters plus the numerals 0 to 9) by a light-photocell scanning process. The scanner reads a character by matching the standardized input to one of a number of *templates,* or character prototypes, that it has in store. The input is identified as that template which best matches it. But the input to such devices must be printed in a standardized type font with a fixed orientation, size, and location. Such sensing machines are of practical use in banks (reading checks, account numbers,

Figure 12.5. Sample of variations in handwriting of the capital letter A. The problem is to program a machine that discards irrelevant variations and identifies all these patterns as the letter A.

and so on), in business firms, and in post offices (for sorting mail). However, they have almost no significance as solutions to the invariance problem outlined above.

A beginning step toward solution of the invariance problem is to write a program that carries out some simple cleaning-up and preprocessing on the stimulus input before it is fed to the decision machinery of the pattern recognizer. Such crude preprocessing might consist of smoothing out local irregularities, filling in small holes, dropping off excess curlicues, centering the stimulus on the receiving display, changing it to a standard size and orientation, and so on. Following such preprocessing, we might then try out the template-matching method in order to determine whether the whole system can now correctly identify all the stimuli. Figure 12.6 shows this method and illustrates one of its main disadvantages. The difficulty at this point is that even after preprocessing, a sample input may still match a wrong template better than the right template. In Figure 12.6b, for example, the *A* template incorrectly produces a better match to the input *R* sample than it does to the two *A* samples.

An alternative attack on these difficulties is to supplement the preprocessing with a variety of other information-extracting procedures that may be called *feature checking*. For example, a capital *A* usually has two mostly vertical lines, and one mostly horizontal line, is generally concave at the bottom, and so on. Such features together identify *A* rather than some other element. The feature list gives a standardized profile of an input and decisions may be made on the basis of this profile. The number and nature of such features are usually stipulated in advance by the model-builder. However, it is important to note that we have just pushed the problems with templates down a level, since we are now assuming templates for features.

Given a profile of features for the stimulus, there are two general schemes that can

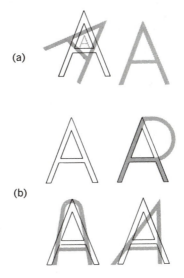

(a)

(b)

Figure 12.6. (A) The match of the unknown letter (grays) to the template (black outline) will not succeed if the unknown is wrong in size, orientation, or position. The program must begin by adjusting the sample to a standard size and orientation, as shown on the right. (B) Incorrect match may still result even when sample (black) has been converted to a standard size and orientation. Here the sample letter *R* matches the *A* template more closely than do the other samples of the letter *A*. (From Selfridge & Neisser, 1960.)

be used in coming to a decision about how to classify it: a *serial processor* and a *parallel processor*. To illustrate the serial processor, we use Selfridge and Neisser's (1960) example:

> . . . [A] program to distinguish the letters *A*, *H*, *V*, and *Y* [see Figure 12.7] might decide among them on the basis of the presence or absence of three features: a concavity at the top, a crossbar, and a vertical line. The sequential process would ask first: "Is there a concavity at the top?" If no, the letter is *A*; if yes, then: "Is there a crossbar?" If yes, the letter is *H*; if no, then: "Is there a vertical line?" If yes, the letter is *Y*; if no, *V* (p. 245).

A serial processor of this kind (called a *sorting tree*) is very efficient if the decision

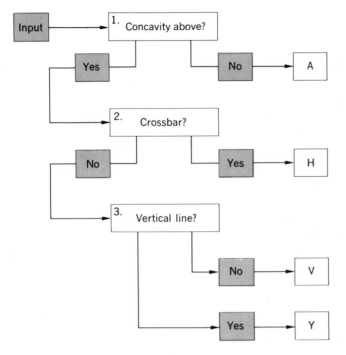

Figure 12.7. A sequential-processing program for distinguishing four letters *A*, *H*, *V*, and *Y*, employs three test features: presence or absence of concavity above, crossbar, and a vertical line. The tests are applied in order, with each outcome determining the next step. (From Selfridge & Neisser, 1960.)

at each node (question) of the tree is almost certain to be correct.[1] But consider its behavior when the input data are noisy (sloppy) and each feature identifier is unreliable and uncertain in its output. If one feature is incorrectly identified, then the stimulus will be shunted off in the wrong direction through the sorting tree, and subsequent features that are correctly identified may not suffice to compensate for the misidentification of the initial features. This serial processor places too great a reliance upon the correctness of identifying each single feature. Any single feature causes it to overcommit to a particular decision. Perhaps a better decision process is

one that pools together all of the feature information simultaneously; pooling many unreliable components can yield a total system whose reliability greatly exceeds that of any of its constituent parts. Most parallel processors do just this, whereas a serial processor must be outfitted with multiply redundant tests to achieve a similar result. We turn next to a parallel processor having this property.

In parallel processing, all the questions are asked at once, and all the answers can be presented simultaneously to the decision-maker (see Figure 12.8). Different combinations identify the different letters. One might think of the various features as being inspected by little demons, all of whom shout the answers in concert to a decision-making demon. From this concert comes the name Pandemonium for parallel processing (Selfridge & Neisser, 1960). A parallel processor of this nature is much less dependent on the reliability of the separate feature detectors. The combination of many

[1] Careful inspection shows that Selfridge and Neisser's illustration does not use the features in the most efficient way. A more efficient tree asks first for presence of a crossbar, yielding the pairs (*H*, *A*) and (*V*, *Y*), and then asks for presence of a vertical line, which discriminates the elements within each pair. The tree in Figure 12.7 would be said to contain a *redundant* feature.

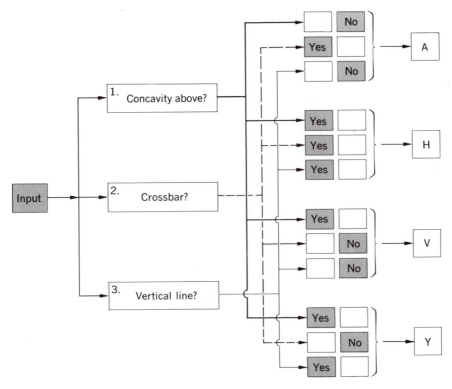

Figure 12.8. Parallel-processing program uses the same test features as does the sequential program in Figure 12.7 but applies all tests simultaneously and makes decisions on the basis of the combined outcomes. The input is a sample of the letters. (From Selfridge & Neisser, 1960.)

unreliable components may still give an overall reliable performance. Additionally, an important aspect of the parallel processor is that the features contributing to a particular pattern can be differentially weighted (by "amplifiers"), determining how loud the feature demons shout. Such differential weighting of the features by their importance cannot be done with the above serial processor. For example, using the parallel processor, the weight of the "concavity above" feature to the *A* pattern could be adjusted to make its absence three times as important as the absence of the "vertical line" feature. These weights can be adjusted in trial-and-error fashion with experience until a maximally effective

combination of the weighted features is achieved. Features that uniquely suggested the correct response are increased in weight, whereas features that suggested errors or random responses are decreased in weight. An alternative scheme is based on accumulating a large record of past patterns; the weight assigned to a given feature in calculating its contribution to, say, the *A*-pattern hypothesis, is the probability that, over past instances, the correct answer was *A* when that feature appeared. The sum of the probabilities of features contributing to each pattern is taken, and the pattern name with the largest sum is chosen as the identification of the input.

Since the mid-1950s, many hundreds of

pattern-recognition programs have been constructed in diverse stimulus domains to discriminate patterns. The tasks include discrimination of many varieties of single visual objects such as handwritten letters, faces, caricatures of common objects, and histology slides of cancerous vs. noncancerous tissues. The models perform with varying degrees of success, depending on the difficulty of the set of patterns to be discriminated and the availability of useful stimulus features for distinguishing them. Many programs (e.g., Uhr & Vossler, 1963) even develop their own critical features of the stimuli. By generating new features of the stimuli and evaluating their discriminating power, the models demonstrate a form of *perceptual learning;* they come to notice discriminating aspects of the stimuli that even the designer of the system may have missed. Models have also been written to deal with recognition of spoken words —for example, the numbers zero to nine spoken by different people. In this latter instance, the input to the program is a digitalized representation of the speech spectrogram that gives a moment-by-moment resolution of a complex speech sound into the amplitudes of the various frequency components.

Most of the research on pattern recognition has been concerned with solving the criterion task of discriminating the patterns, not with simulating the way an organism performs the task. We will illustrate two theories of pattern learning. The fact that the designers tested these theories against data from psychological experiments attests to their interest in psychological validity.

The Elementary Perceiver and Memorizer (EPAM)

The Elementary Perceiver and Memorizer (EPAM) is a pattern-recognition model developed by E. A. Feigenbaum and H. A. Simon. Their aim was to develop a model that simulates human behavior in a variety of discrimination tasks that involve associative learning. Included among these tasks would be paired-associate learning, rote-serial learning, recognition learning, immediate or short-term memory tasks, and learning to read text, naming objects or pictures, forming concepts, and the like. In principle, the stimuli could be given directly to the program in any form— visual or auditory. In fact, however, the present version of EPAM has no perceptual processor, so the programmer has to analyze the stimuli into distinctive features, punch this information onto IBM cards, and only then will EPAM be able to deal with the "stimuli."

Because of the comprehensive goals of the model, it is complicated and lengthy. The basic model (Feigenbaum, 1959) has undergone extensive testing and modification. The version to be discussed below is that described in a paper by Simon and Feigenbaum (1964). We consider its application to paired-associate learning. Specifically, suppose the model is learning a list of nonsense syllable pairs (*REH-GIJ, RUZ-FOT,* and so on). One part of the program simulates the experimental task—that is, it imitates a paced memory drum which exposes first a stimulus member, then the stimulus-and-response members together, repetitively cycling through all pairs in the list. The model's task is to anticipate (print out) the correct response when the stimulus is shown.

EPAM learns by building up a sorting tree, or discrimination net, that makes possible differentiation among the stimuli and responses. The sorting tree is a serial processing system much like that displayed previously in Figure 12.7. Stored at terminal nodes of this sorting tree are compound "images," which are more or less complete representations of the S-R pairs. In general, neither the features used for sorting nor the information stored in the image is complete—that is, no more information is stored than is minimally needed to get by on the task at hand.

Two learning processes, image-building (familiarization) and discrimination learning (tree-growing) are postulated. When a stimulus S in view is sorted to a terminal node, it is compared with the stimulus image, S', residing there (from past experience). If no image is there, then part of S is copied as the image at that node. If an image is already there, a comparison of S and S' is made; if differences in detail only are detected, S' is changed or augmented to match S better. Thus is the S' image of S grown. If a positive difference (not just a lack of detail) between S and S' is detected, then the discrimination learning process takes over and constructs two new branches from the former terminal node, with S and S' separately as the images of the new terminals. To illustrate, suppose that we can arrive at a current terminal node by tests on the first letter R, and the current image at this node is R—H (see Figure 12.9). Later RUZ is sorted to this node. In comparing RUZ to the image R__H, the program notes a difference in detail in the second position (not serious) and a positive difference (Z versus H) in the third position. It would then set up

a third-letter test at this node as shown in Figure 12.9. With this new node added to the tree, the stimuli REH and RUZ are no longer sorted to the same node and confusion errors between them will be avoided.

Although the sorting (recognizing) is done on the stimulus member of the pair, both the stimulus and response syllables are represented as a compound image S'-R' at the terminal node. The response image, R', is retrieved when S gets sorted to and makes contact with the stimulus image S'. The response image R' contains information enabling the program to locate another terminal node R'' in the net, and R'' will, after learning, contain the images of the three letters of the response syllables (G, I, J) and the information required to produce them (print them out). Eventually, then, presentation of stimulus REH causes the machine to print out GIJ and it has learned.

One virtue of this system is that it treats the nominal stimulus-and-response terms in comparable fashion—namely, as images to be built up in the sorting tree. Also the S-R pair to be associated requires no special representation as it is simply a compound image constructed from two simpler images. In addition to the recognition and

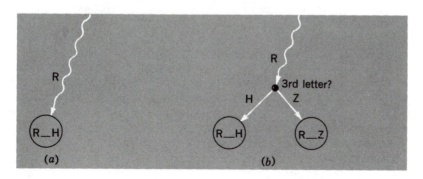

Figure 12.9. An example of how a formerly terminal node in EPAM's discrimination net will be elaborated to differentiate previously confused stimuli. (A) By first-letter tests on R. one arrives at a terminal node bearing the image R-H. (B) Later, when RUZ is sorted to this node, causing a confusion error, a new test is added, based on the third letter and two lower nodes are sprouted from this terminal.

learning processes mentioned above, EPAM has a higher-level executive routine that oversees and "runs the show." Part of its job is to keep the central processes in contact with the environment (e.g., "stop processing the last item; respond to the new S that has just appeared in the drum window"), to schedule where and how it shall distribute the processing effort and time at its disposal, since image-building and net-growing take processing time. It uses feedback about its current performance on an S-R pair to decide, roughly speaking, what is the matter and what part of the knowledge structure needs more polishing. These executive macroprocesses are responsible for some of EPAM's more interesting predictions—for instance, they allow it to predict serial position curves in rote-serial learning (see Feigenbaum & Simon, 1962) and to account for the effect on serial learning of segmenting the series into groups of varying sizes (see Gregg, 1972). There are many more details to EPAM, but this sketch is not intended to do more than describe the basic processes it uses.

Simon and Feigenbaum (1964) have put the EPAM model through a variety of simulated learning experiments and compared its trial-by-trial output with that of human subjects. It shows several similarities to the data. Like human subjects, EPAM takes longer to learn a list in which the stimulus items are highly similar (many common letters). It displays positive or negative transfer in learning a second list depending on the stimulus-response relations of the two lists, in much the same way that the human data depends on these relations (see the reviews of work on transfer and retention in Chapter 6). It shows the beneficial effect of prior familiarization with the stimulus-and-response terms before these are used in a paired-associate learning task. The model shows stimulus-confusion errors and retroactive interference to a degree depending on the similarity of stimulus items in the original

learned list and the interpolated list. The simulation of the data is sometimes fairly accurate in a relative quantitative sense—that is, the ratio of trials to learn under condition *A* to that for condition *B* is about the same for the model as for the human data. In an early paper, Feigenbaum and Simon (1961) showed that EPAM exhibited an interesting form of mediation (chained associations) seen in the training of reading. In Phase 1, EPAM learned to associate acoustically coded properties of the spoken word *kahr* with symbolic pointing to a visually coded picture of a car. In Phase 2, it learned to associate the visual word *car* with the acoustic pattern *kahr*. When later tested with the visual word *car* and required to point at a picture, it selected the car picture. This is a simple example of mediated transfer, and is of the elementary sort that most stimulus-response analyses would predict.

Hintzman (1968) has developed a series of models (dubbed SAL for Stimulus and Association Learner) based on the adaptive development of a discrimination net. The initial model (SAL-I), which simulates paired-associate learning, begins with essentially the same assumptions as EPAM except that net growth ("learning new discriminators") is considered to be a probabilistic process. In order to fit experimental results, Hintzman introduced three further assumptions in SAL. First, it was supposed that even after perfect mastery of an item the program can still learn further descriptors about that item (i.e., growth of the net could occur on correct-response trials as well as on error trials). This enables the theory to handle a variety of effects such as the effects of overlearning in reducing retroactive interference. Second, it was supposed that the "response" stored at the terminal node to which a stimulus is sorted could be a *list* or push-down stack of responses that have been reinforced to stimulus patterns sorted to that terminal. The rule for placing new responses on this push-down stack may be illustrated with respect to the terminal node denoted $R\_\_H$ in Figure 12.9. This node was arrived at only by tests on the first letter, R. Suppose response A1 is attached to this stimulus terminal. A later pair RUZ-A2 will be sorted to this same terminal and an error (A1) will occur. But suppose that a new discriminator is not learned on this occasion; then Hintzman's SAL-III model would store the new response A2 in the top of a push-down stack attached to the terminal node $R\_\_H$ (with the old error A1 placed in the second slot in the stack). This assumption of a temporally ordered response hierarchy at "confused" stimulus terminals turns out to have a number of salutary implications that accord with details of verbal learning experiments (e.g., that pair recognition suffers far less interference than paired-associate recall). A third assumption of SAL-III is that, over time, responses residing at lower positions on a push-down stack will "spontaneously rise," and in so doing "push out" more recent responses and cause them to be forgotten. This assumption, akin to the notion of spontaneous recovery of unlearned associations (see Chapter 6), enables SAL to account for several important facts regarding temporal changes in proactive and retroactive interference over a retention interval.

Hintzman's work is exemplary insofar as it utilizes relatively few assumptions, carefully delimits the range of phenomena to be explained, then proceeds systematically to explore the consequences of the simulated model in relation to a large number of different experimental results. The outcome is perhaps one of the most impressive examples we have of a simulation model being fit to a wide range of experimental results in learning. The EPAM and SAL models are surely not perfect nor complete theories, and they have been effectively criticized (see J. R. Anderson & Bower, 1973, Chapter 4). However, they are also clearly the sorts of serious models that a theoretical psychologist likes to have in his portfolio in trying to understand the nature of learning.

Concept Learners

Psychologists have for many years carried out investigations of concept learning, with many early ones falling within the framework of experimental tasks analyzed initially by Hovland (1952). Stimulus objects or patterns are characterized according to a list of attributes, each with a number of values. For example, geometric patterns can differ in the attributes of size, color, shape, orientation, and so on. If there are n attributes with v values each, then there are potentially v^n patterns in all. A concept can be defined by a division of this set into two parts, with the patterns in one part belonging to class A and the remainder belonging to the complement class $\bar{A}$.

To illustrate, the universe of patterns might be four-letter nonsense strings; in each letter position ("attribute") any of three letters ("values") can appear. If the attribute-values are (X, Z, T), (P, M, K), (J, W, R), and (B, T, S), then $XPJB$ and $ZPRT$ are elements of the universe while $XZTP$ and $XPTW$ are not. For convenience, in the following we use abbreviations such as $3J$ to indicate the J at position 3. In Hovland's initial scheme, concepts were defined by specifying one attribute-value (e.g., $2K$) or several attribute-values with a logical connective between them. In a *conjunctive* problem (e.g., $1X$ and $2P$), patterns containing both $1X$ and $2P$ go into class A; otherwise, into the alternative class $\bar{A}$. In other words, $1X$ (as is $2P$) is separately necessary but not a sufficient condition for class A. Several varieties of logical connectives are available besides these: exclusive disjunction ($2M$ or $4S$ but not both), implication ($4S$ or not $2M$ or both), and biconditional (1*X* and 2*P*, or not 1*X* and not 2*P*).

E. B. Hunt (1962) and Hunt, Marin, and Stone (1966), following early notions of Hunt and Hovland (1961), developed an information-processing model that learns or solves such concept problems. Although the initial model used several strategies that humans apparently also use (e.g., having a bias for conjunctive solutions), it contained features which humans quite certainly do not show, such as perfect memory for many previous patterns, perfect rationality, errorless checking and validation of a hypothesis.

The program proceeds roughly as follows: as successive instances of the *A* and $\overline{A}$ class are shown to the machine, they are stored away on two separate lists in memory. The model learns a concept by growing a sorting tree (serial processor); the sorting tree and the concept labels, *A* and $\overline{A}$, stored at its terminal nodes are then sufficient to classify all further instances. For example, a tree for the inclusive disjunction (2*M* or 4*S* or both) is shown in Figure 12.10a, and one for exclusive disjunction (2*M* or 4*S* but not both) in Figure 12.10b. The nodes of the tree ask a question about an attribute-value; depending on how an input pattern "answers" this question, it is shunted by the left or right branch to a lower node.

Hunt's concept learner is an algorithm embodying a wholist strategy, which looks for common features of objects classified similarly. Given the current lists of *A* and $\overline{A}$ patterns, it looks for one or more characteristics always present in one list but not in the other. If such features are found, they are made the first node of the sorting tree and the problem is solved. This alone suffices if the concept is the affirmation or denial of either one element (e.g., 2*M*) or a conjunction of elements. If no such feature is found, then a first node is composed of that feature which occurs most frequently in the positive instances. This node pro-

duces two new pairs of sublists—namely, lists of positive and negative instances which do or do not have the first feature. Treating each pair of sublists as a separate problem, the program uses the wholist strategy again (returns to the beginning) on each subproblem, and from there constructs a second and third node for the sorting tree. The reader may verify that two such recursions will suffice to solve any two-element concept—for example, the disjunctions in Figure 12.10. The recursion continues, or the decision tree grows, until all patterns in memory have been correctly classified.

In Hunt's program, the tree-growing routines will eventually come to a solution in the sense of correctly sorting all members of its *A* and $\overline{A}$ list. The decision tree it grows is not guaranteed to be the simplest in a logical sense but, in fact, it was so in most of the simulated runs of the program. Hunt, Marin, and Stone (1966) report results of several experiments on the model's behavior. The main evidence offered for considering this as an initial candidate for simulation of how people solve concept problems is that the rank order of difficulty in solving concepts of different logical types turns out to be about the same for the program as for most people. At best, this is a weak constraint and not a very demanding test for a reasonable model to pass. The difficulty of acquiring a given concept is roughly correlated with the length of the logical statement required to define it. For example, "2*M*" is easiest, "2*M* and 4*S*" is next, "2*M* or 4*S* or both" is next, and "2*M* and 4*S*, or not 2*M* and not 4*S*" is hardest. A somewhat more convincing result is that a subject's trial-by-trial classifications of patterns (while learning) were predicted better by the model than by the responses of another subject going through the same problem.

The deficiencies of the model considered as a simulation are its large memory, its rationality, and its reliance upon a wholist

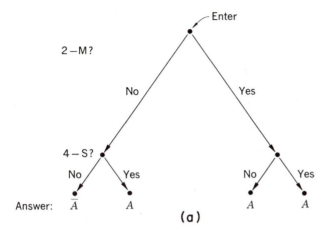

(a)

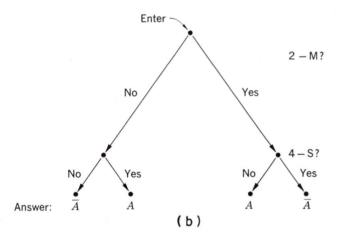

(b)

Figure 12.10. Examples of optimally efficient binary sorting trees for classifying stimuli. (A) the *A* concept is "2*M* or 4*S* or both." The first node asks whether the input pattern has an *M* in the second position; the second node asks whether it has an *S* in the fourth position. (B) the *A* concept is "2*M* or 4*S* but not both."

strategy. Humans have error-prone memories, are not always rational, and have flexible search strategies that are easily modified by instructions or by a small amount of practice on problems of one type (e.g., Haygood & Bourne, 1965). A more realistic model incorporating short-term memory considerations has been proposed by G. F. Williams (1971). Her model assumes two memory stores: a short-term buffer for stimulus values to which it has recently attended, and a long-term memory that holds evaluations of stimulus dimen-sions which the subject has tested and re-jected as irrelevant. The information in these two stores is assumed to interact; earlier decisions about what is irrelevant help determine the current hypothesis, which serves to focus attention and thus determine what new stimulus attributes are entered into the short-term buffer; the buffer information, in turn, is used to de-velop a new working hypothesis when the current one is shown to be incorrect. Stim-ulus dimensions which have been tested and found irrelevant have their "strengths" in long-term memory reduced almost to zero, from which they gradually recover (i.e., their irrelevance is forgotten). Williams programmed these focus and memory processes along with Hunt's earlier ideas regarding the way the subject selects a new hypothesis following an error. The model makes a number of strong trial-by-trial predictions regarding how the subject's hypothesis is altered depending on the nature of the mismatch between his current hypothesis and the pattern which he classifies incorrectly. Williams demonstrated the plausibility of her model in two experiments using practiced subjects who knew that the correct hypothesis involved a conjunction of two attributes (other concept rules can be handled by modifying the algorithm for constructing new hypotheses). In some respects, Williams's model is the most realistic one yet produced for the class of simple logical concepts which psychologists have studied in this tradition.

However, the fundamental deficiency of all such models stems from their restriction to only the Hovland type of concepts—that is, the format of attribute-value descriptions where the concepts are defined by logical operations on attribute-value pairs (*not* x, b *and* c, d *or* e). Such description spaces are simply not rich enough to represent many of the concepts that people learn and use. For example, relational and metric notions, such as "x is *above* y," "x is *longer than* y," cannot be represented in these terms, nor can so many of our concepts that are defined by relations among their parts. The concept of the letter *E*, for instance, requires a listing of its parts (three horizontal short lines, one vertical long line) in certain relations to each other (horizontal lines above one another and parallel, their left ends making contact with vertical line, and so on). Richer description spaces are provided in later programs such as that of Winston (1970) to be discussed, where objects and visual

scenes are described in terms of properties and relations among parts.

The Segmentation Problem and Perceptual Learning

Another problem is that many of the programs are developed for identifying single, isolated characters presented one at a time. But this is unrealistic for most circumstances. For example, cursive handwriting flows on continuously, and a major problem in analyzing it (for secretaries, paper graders, and computers alike) is finding a correct *segmentation*—that is, determining where are the boundaries at which one character stops and another one starts. This seems a trivial task for us most of the time because it is such an overlearned skill; but the problem shows up when we have to decipher an unfamiliar, nearly illegible hand. The same problem arises in speech recognition, where only an experienced listener can hear the pauses between word segments or between sentences. However, an acoustic recording of fluent speech reveals only a reasonably continuous stream of sound. The puzzle is how the speech-analyzing mechanisms can manage to segment this nearly continuous stream into phonemes, words, and phrases. The segmentation problem is very severe for character recognition programs, since without a segmentation routine they will never be able to analyze a complex pattern into its constituents. A machine that knew how to classify single alphabetic letters would, in the absence of a segmentation program, treat each two- or three-letter word as simply a novel pattern to be learned as a whole unit. A segmentation program would divide the word into letters, describe and recognize these individual objects, and describe their relationship to one another in the input word. With such capabilities, the system would be able to perceive (describe) an infinite variety of scenes, all novel in one or another detail, using a relatively small vocabulary plus a few relations (much as many thousands of printed words are generated out of 26 letters plus a "right of" spatial relation).

One of the very early programs that dealt with this segmentation problem in an effective way was the program MAUDE (Gold, 1959), for automatic decoding of Morse code. Morse code is based entirely on discriminating the temporal durations of beeps and silent periods. In principle, a dash is to be three times as long as a dot; silent spaces between dashes or dots within a letter should be as long as a dot; silent spaces between letters should be three times as long; and silent spaces between words should be seven times as long as a dot. In practice, human code senders vary in producing these durations, and this variability is the source of confusion. The most difficult job in decoding is to separate the within-letter spaces from the between-letter spaces. MAUDE uses contextual informa- tion to decide this. Since no Morse charac- ter is more than five dots or dashes long, it is assumed that the longest of six con- secutive spaces is a between-letter space and that the shortest is a within-letter space. The other four spaces of the six are classified according to whether they are above or below a threshold duration (con- tinuously adjustable to the particular sender). If the tentative spacings do not make a permissible code letter in Morse, then the longest space is reclassified as a between-letter space. Similar processes are used to distinguish dots from dashes. In performance, MAUDE's error rate is only slightly higher than that of well-trained code receivers.

MAUDE dealt with the segmentation problem for only a limited domain of in- put. More significant programs from a psy- chologist's viewpoint are those of Guzman (1968) and Winston (1970), which analyze and describe visual scenes comprised of solid blocks in various relations. Figure 12.11 illustrates the type of block scenes that

Figure 12.11. Illustration of cluttered block scene analyzed by Guzman's SEE program. (From Winston, 1970.)

Guzman's SEE program would analyze. It consists of a variety of lines, angles, surfaces, and objects (cubes, bricks, wedges), arranged in various overlapping relations. Guzman's program tries to isolate out objects and identify which surfaces belong together. The reader should appreciate how difficult a job this is for scenes like Figure 12.11. Even assuming the program can identify simple objects like wedges, blocks, and pyramids, cluttered scenes present three further problems: first, any object may appear in any orientation and perspective, so that it projects a novel two-dimensional image to the viewer; second, objects occlude and partly cover up others, and so objects must be identified even though their regular features are covered by other objects; third, such occlusion means that the program must decide which features go with which objects.

Guzman's SEE program proceeds by first identifying various types of *vertices* between surfaces, each vertex type suggesting a particular sort of linkage of the surfaces into one or more objects. Figure 12.12 shows nine of the common vertices along with their names. To illustrate, the *arrow* provides evidence that the two regions bounded by the small angles are adjacent

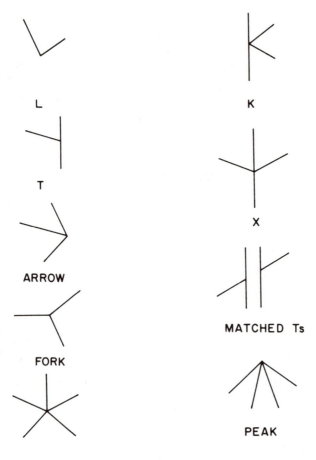

Figure 12.12. Illustration of nine common vertices used by Guzman's program in segmenting block scenes. (From Winston, 1970.)

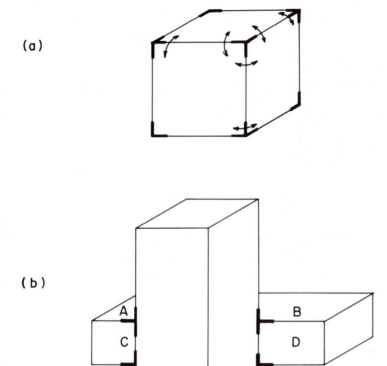

(a)

(b)

A   B

C   D

Figure 12.13. Examples of critical vertices (darkened) involved in identifying a cube (A), and one block occluding a second block (B). (Adapted from Guzman, 1968.)

sides of one object. The *fork* suggests that the three pairs of sides are adjacent at each of the three edges like the corner of a block. For an example of how these vertices are used to characterize an object, look at the solid cube in Figure 12.13a. The critical vertices have been identified by heavy darkening. The corner facing closest to us is a *fork* vertex, with three *arrow* vertices below and to the right and left of the *fork*. The remaining three corners are *L* vertices. The *fork* and *arrows* provide the requisite information for segmenting this figure. Noticing these vertices and how they are connected, the SEE program will link together particular surfaces and decide which represent different sides of the same objects; these tentative link-

ages are indicated by the curved arrows in Figure 12.13a. The program decides that this is a cube by adding together the successive constraints suggested by each vertex and its interconnections. To take a second example, the *T* and *matched-T* vertices are important in suggesting that one figure is occluding another which extends behind it. This is seen in Figure 12.13b, which shows such a scene with the relevant *T* vertices emphasized. By a set of "good continuation" heuristics, the SEE program will identify the left- and right-hand *T*s and thus aggregate together surface *A* with *B*, and surface *C* with *D*, and identify these as surfaces of a brick lying down which is occluded by the standing brick.

These brief descriptions cannot do justice to the range of heuristics SEE uses to segment and identify objects in a scene as jumbled and chaotic as that shown in Figure 12.11. Although SEE isolates surfaces and objects, it does not provide a very powerful *description* of a scene in terms of relations among identified objects. A program by Winston (1970) does just this, by imposing certain intelligent assumptions upon the visual world it is seeing (e.g., that blocks rest upon a table or other blocks rather than being suspended in midair). Winston takes the output of SEE as the input to his program, which then recognizes particular geometric relations between objects (such as *above, in front of, is supported by, abuts*) as well as properties of single objects. Winston's program builds up particular sorts of structural descriptions of a scene, represents these in terms of a particular formalism, and then tries to identify particular configurations with concepts and scenes with which it is familiar. Concepts are represented inside

the memory as labeled relational networks; these serve as the "class prototypes" in memory for such concepts as *angle, arrow-vertex, T-joint, rectangle, triangle, wedge, brick, house, tent,* and *arch.* Figure 12.14 illustrates a fragment of the representation of intermediate-level concepts such as a *wedge* and an *arch.* The structural description of a wedge states that it comprises (to the eye of the viewer) three surfaces, two of which are a kind of rectangle whereas the third must be a triangle. This latter feature, of course, distinguishes a wedge from a brick. Thus, when shown a wedge, the lower-level program will first identify lines, edges, angles, and surfaces, and then rectangular and triangular surfaces, gradually building up a description of the scene. When this description is matched in memory to the set of known objects (concept descriptions), the best match occurs to the *wedge* concept. The same process applies to the *arch* concept illustrated in Figure 12.12b.

(a)

(b)

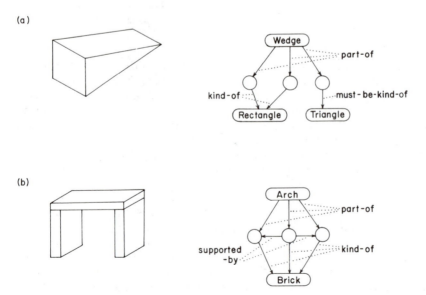

Figure 12.14. Relational graph structures that characterize the concept of a wedge and an arch. (Adapted from Winston, 1970.)

Learning Higher-Order Concepts from Examples

In Winston's program, higher-order concepts are constructed out of relations between lower-order concepts. For example, a *stack* or *tower* is a set of rectangles aligned and supporting one another; a *tent* is two wedges that abut in a particular way; a *table* is a brick supported by upright bricks or wedges ("legs") at four corners, and so on.

Winston was interested in the problem of teaching the machine complex geometrical concepts like *arch, table, house, arcade,* and so forth. He developed a program that would learn from exposure to a series of instances and noninstances of the concept being taught. An initial positive instance leads to a hypothesized description of the concept—say, the concept of a house (see Figure 12.15). Viewing the scene in Figure 12.15, Winston's program would describe a house as a wedge supported by a brick. The next three panels of Figure 12.15 show a series of training patterns containing what Winston calls near misses—that is, configurations that are close to a house but differ critically from it in one or another respect. When the machine is told that the configuration in panel (b) is "not a house," it describes the difference between panels (a) and (b), selects some specific difference as critical, and attaches to its revised concept of a house that the wedge *must be* (emphatically) supported by the brick. Similarly, panel (c) informs the machine that the top object *must be* a wedge and not a brick, and panel (d) informs it that the bottom object *must be* a brick and not a wedge. These emphatic ("must be") markers are attached to the final concept description (Figure 12.16), and must be satisfied if the machine is to classify any new pattern as a house.

Winston's program brings up several in-

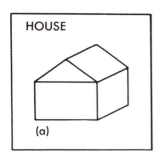

HOUSE

(a)

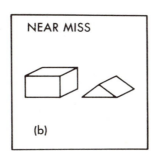

NEAR MISS

(b)

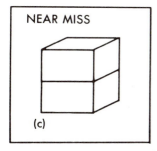

NEAR MISS

(c)

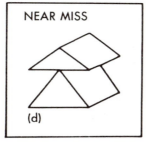

NEAR MISS

(d)

Figure 12.15. An example of the concept of a house and three "near-miss" negative instances. (From Winston, 1970.)

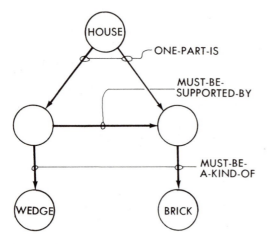

Figure 12.16. A description of the concept of a house in terms of labeled relations among primitive concept nodes. Roughly, this says that a house has two parts, one part must be a kind of wedge and one a kind of brick, and the wedge must be supported by the brick. (From Winston, 1970.)

teresting points. First is the question of how the concept learner assigns priority to given differences (between his current hypothesis and an instance which violates it). In reality, there are typically many differences; as experienced concept learners, we have tended to learn general strategies regarding what are likely to be important rather than irrelevant differences, and to use the high-priority differences to modify our earlier concept hypothesis. A second matter suggested by Winston's approach is the issue of optimal teaching sequences: given that we can specify the final form of a concept description, we should be able to arrange for presentation of a series of near misses which will most efficiently guide the learner to the correct concept. Child psychologists concerned with how the child develops certain Piagetian concepts (of conservation of mass, of volume, size, causality, time) have been quite interested in this matter of optimal training sequences.

Elementary concept-learning leads to sophistication and eventual expertise. Just as would a child, Winston's concept learner becomes more expert at chunking and describing scenes of the blocks world. One result of this expertise is that novel, complex scenes now provoke a relatively compact description by the model. For example, consider the scene in Figure 12.17, composed of a tent to the left of a house, both sitting on top of an arch. There are at least seven simple objects (bricks and wedges) in that scene, and they exhibit many interobject relationships. Before the system learns the intermediate-level concepts (of *tent, house, arch*), all of these parts and myriads of relationships would have to occur in the description of the scene. However, *after* the system has learned these concepts, they can be used as units to simplify the overall description to something approximating our English proposition "a tent to the left of a house both supported by an arch." Of course, following the system's exposure to this scene, the scene (or rather, its description) would be stored in memory like any other concept, and perhaps given an internal name (e.g., "Bill's architectural creation"). A later re-presentation of the scene would

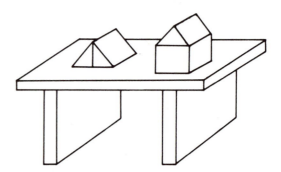

Figure 12.17. Example of a complex scene composed of familiar intermediate-level concepts (parts) in specifiable relations. Such scenes evoke a hierarchical description from Winston's program. (From Anderson & Bower, 1973.)

then lead to recognition memory—that is, the system would recognize that it has seen that scene before. On this account, then, recognition memory of individuals or individual scenes (or places) does not differ in essentials from classifying a pattern into a particular category.

Winston's program represents some of the more advanced and psychologically interesting work being done on scene analysis. It deals with an essentially static environment of toy blocks. The heuristics of Guzman's and Winston's programs are used in the "hand-eye" projects at Stanford and MIT, and the "robot" project at the Stanford Research Institute. We will touch on these projects in a later section. Progress continues on problems of mechanically analyzing naturalistic scenes such as photographs of cluttered living rooms, gardens, forests, hillsides, and so on. Advanced pattern-recognition programs are being developed to extract and use optical information such as linear perspective, texture gradients, and shades to come up with useful descriptions of complex visual scenes. A set of papers on these topics was edited by Hanson and Riseman (1978).

Speech Perception

Another successful line of research concerns speech recognition. The goal is to get a computer to "listen" to almost any speaker saying almost anything and have it print out (say, in English) a reasonable guess at her utterance. As noted before, speech flows smoothly with successive phonemes blending into one another, so the segmentation problem is very severe. To make matters worse, the blending of successive phonemes is so great that the sound of a given phoneme varies according to what phonemes are being said just before or after it. (An analogy would be if the vowels *a, e, i, o, u* were printed slightly differently depending on what consonant letters were printed before and after them.)

The only way to deal with all these problems is by strong use of *context* and of expectations about what should be said at given places in an utterance. An impressive speech-recognition system is Hearsay II (Reddy et al., 1973), which analyzes a speaker's utterances as she announces her moves in a chess game. Several sources of information are combined in Hearsay II: the analysis of the speech spectrogram to pull out major phonetic features, the combining of clusters of features into likely words, and strong expectations of the class of words to be heard at a given point in an utterance. These expectations are produced by the program's knowledge of chess and grammar (e.g., after "The white _____," expect a noun like *pawn* or *queen*). Its chess knowledge enables the program to anticipate the name of a specific move and hence its announcement, rather than some other move. The success of speech-recognition programs depends to a large extent on how well they can predict what is about to be said; to the extent that expectations reduce the number of alternative words that could be heard at any given point in the utterance, the amount of stimulus information needed to identify the word correctly can be correspondingly reduced. Although Hearsay II's performance to date in recognizing speech has been very impressive, one realizes how enormous is the future task of extending the model to understand conversations over many content areas, and to deal with unexpected remarks.

Perhaps more than any other program, Hearsay II brings into prominence the notions of combining sensory-data analysis with context-determined expectations. A program that works upward, using the sensory input to suggest pattern hypotheses, is dubbed a *bottom-up processor;* one that works downward, using strong expectations (hypotheses) to guide the search for evidence in the sensory array, is called a *top-down processor.* Most successful programs use bottom-up and top-down processes in combination to synthesize a final hypothesis about the pattern to be recognized. Hearsay II, for instance, combines information from four or five distinct sources—its knowledge of chess movements and names of chess pieces, its knowledge of grammar and phonetic sequences, and its knowledge of acoustic features and their relations to phonemes. Such complex syntheses of information sources are needed to deal with complex tasks. Speech recognition is a good illustration of the vast difference between the intuitive "simplicity" of a psychological ability and the scientific reconstruction of that ability. Many cognitive skills seem simple because they have been overlearned and practiced over many years; as a result, they have become "automatic" and are performed out of awareness. It is often just those skills that are most routine and automatic that are so difficult to reconstruct in a theoretical model.

Our review of programs dealing with pattern recognition has been brief but illustrates the main trends. In language, work on individual character recognition has been replaced by work on continuous speech recognition; in vision, the trend is towards more complex scene analysis, which is cast in terms of deriving structural descriptions of the parts and their interrelations in the scene. The structural description must be economical (for storage in a finite memory), selective of relevant features, but also rich enough to support all sorts of visual problem-solving and reasoning (e.g., solving geometric analogy problems). The present emphasis in research is on the difficult problems of segmentation, identification of relations, and the building of hierarchical descriptions, although the identification of particular objects still remains a standard component of all scene analysis programs.

These examples from pattern recognition have introduced us to other issues: for instance, is Hearsay II or Winston's program a simulation or a piece of artificial intelligence? Just because a program solves some of the same problems that confront the human brain does not mean that one is an accurate simulation of the other. Other criteria of fittingness to actual data are required. The "psychological reality" of several of the programs has not yet been put to really rigorous tests. What psychologists clearly need is some methodology for experimentally testing many of the very ingenious hypotheses and heuristics suggested by such programs as those reviewed.

Sequential Pattern Learning

Visual patterns have their information distributed simultaneously in space. We will now consider patterns that are laid out in time, in a temporal series. We will consider two programs, one that deals with probability learning, one with the series-extrapolation task of I.Q. tests. Both programs attempt to model the subject's attempt to arrive at a hypothesis about sequences of events.

Probability learning. Feldman (1961, 1962) proposed an early model to simulate the behavior of subjects in the binary experiment known as *probability learning*. Such experiments were described earlier in Chapter 8. In them, the subject tries to predict successive members in a sequence of binary events (e.g., C or P) that are shown to him one at a time. The sequences are constructed randomly (e.g., 70 percent C and 30 percent P events), although subjects frequently believe the sequence is lawful and orderly and try to discover its pattern. The traditional account of behavior in this situation is that given by stochastic learning models, which suppose that the subject's probability of predicting C increases or decreases trial by trial depending on whether the C or P event occurs. It will be recalled from our review in Chapter 8 that these models have trouble accounting for sequential patterning in the subject's responses.

Feldman's model supposes that in this situation the subject is trying to discover local patterns (or trying out sequential hypotheses) to explain the event sequence and to extrapolate (predict) the next member of the series. To get information relevant to these notions, Feldman had his subjects "think aloud" and state their reasons trial by trial for the predictions they made. A subject's protocol consisted then of the sequence of his predictions and the reasons he gave for each. Feldman's model attempts to account for the sequence of reasons, since the subject almost always made a prediction that was consistent with the reason he gave. The model is tailored specifically to simulate a particular subject, and details of the program vary for different subjects.

The program proceeds by the testing out of hypotheses that attempt to explain the event sequence. The trial-by-trial cycle for the model is as follows: use the current hypothesis to predict the next event; the next event occurs, and it is explained by an explanation hypothesis; a prediction hypothesis is developed, and is used to predict the next event; the next event occurs and the cycle repeats.

Each hypothesis consists of two components: an event-pattern hypothesis and a guess-opposite component. The event-pattern hypothesis is selected from a list of pattern hypotheses such as "progression of Cs," "alternation of two Cs and two Ps," and so forth. The patterns are placed on this list by the theorist after examining what types the subject said he used. The guess-opposite component may be either "on" or "off": if the pattern hypothesis is a progression of Cs and this component is off, the model predicts C; if the guess-opposite component is on, the model predicts P, the opposite of the pattern.

Various rules are employed whereby feedback from the event sequence is used to select, alter, or maintain the current hypothesis. If a hypothesis predicts correctly, it is retained for another trial. If it predicts incorrectly, it is likely to be replaced temporarily. In this case, the events from the last three or four trials are used to select the plausible candidates from the pattern-hypothesis list. If several candidates are plausible, the program chooses that pattern hypothesis which has been used most often in the past. The circumstances for modification of the guess-opposite component are more complicated and cannot be easily summarized.

Feldman (1962) published the outcome of fitting the model to the behavior of one subject. His procedure was to continually revise the model until it gave a good fit. Feldman summarizes the process as follows:

> The completion of the model was a lengthy task involving the iterative procedure of proposing a detailed model, testing the model against the data, modifying the model, testing again, and so on. During this procedure, almost every part of the model originally proposed was modified or replaced (p. 342).

A unique feature of Feldman's model assessment was his use of *conditional prediction*. If the model's prediction of the subject's hypothesis on Trial n proved incorrect, then the model was set back on the correct track by replacing its "predicted" hypothesis with the subject's actual hypothesis. The supposition was that the model is strongly path dependent, in the sense that if it is "off" on Trial n, it will get progressively farther off from the data if it is not set back on the track.

These two methodological points, models tailored for individuals and contingent predictions, are novel to Feldman's work. Suffice it to say that by using these techniques, Feldman demonstrated that his model was able to predict his subject's protocol with a high degree of accuracy.

Series extrapolation. The program by Simon and Kotovsky (1963) attempts to solve a sequential pattern-learning problem familiar to all of us from various IQ tests. The Simon and Kotovsky program attempts to infer the rule generating successive letters in a short series. In the Thurstone Letter Series Completion Test, the subject is shown a letter series and asked to supply the correct next letter of the series. Examples are *cadaeafa_*, *atbataatbat_*, and *wxaxybyzczadab_*. Such series vary in difficulty, and some are sufficiently hard so that an appreciable proportion of college students fail them. The Simon-Kotovsky simulation program supposes that subjects solve such problems by developing a "pattern description" of the sequence and then using this description to generate the next member of the series. The model subject is assumed to have certain cognitive equipment to begin with, notably, the forwards alphabet, the backwards alphabet, the concept of "next successor" on a particular list, and the ability to store a pointer to a starting symbol and to detect and produce cycles through a list (e.g., in the simplest instances, a repetitive cycling through the list (*b*, *a*) yields the series *bababa* . . .).

A standard format is used to state pattern descriptions, and the main job of the program is to discover a suitable pattern description. It first identifies periodicities in the sequence by looking for letters or relations that repeat at regular intervals. For example, *axbxcx* has period 2 based on the "next" relation in the forwards alphabet starting at *a* and with letter *x* repeating at the end of each cycle of two; *qxapxboxc* has period 3 in which the first element of each triplet uses the backwards alphabet starting at *q* and the third letter of each triple uses the forwards alphabet starting at *a*. The relation repeating at period 3 is "next successor" of the corresponding element in the prior triplet. If this simple periodicity cannot be found, then the program looks for a relation that is interrupted at regular intervals; for example, in *aaabbbcccdd_*, the relation "same letter" is interrupted in periods of 3. Once a basic periodicity has been identified, the program makes a further analysis to uncover the details of the pattern, by detecting the relations—"next successor" or "same"—that hold between elements within a period or between corresponding elements in consecutive periods (as in the *qxa* . . . example above).

If such a generative rule is found, then it is used to extrapolate the next element. Several variants of the model differing in their power—that is, in the richness of relations they can detect and use—were run and compared with the performance of college and high school students doing the same problems. A weak variant of the model did less well than the poorest subject, whereas a powerful variant did nearly as well as the best subject. There was considerable agreement among the subjects as a group and the program in ranking the problems in order of difficulty. Problem difficulty seemed correlated with the load on the subject's, and the model's, immediate memory. To solve the hard problems, the subject had to keep track in memory of her place on two separate lists (e.g., the forwards and the backwards alphabet), while for all easy problems she needed to keep track of her place on only one list.

Simon (1972) has shown how his representation of serial pattern processing is consistent with other approaches which try to relate the structural complexity of a series pattern to the person's ability (a) to remember and reproduce a short sequence or to learn a cyclically recurring sequence (Glanzer & Clark, 1962; Restle, 1970), and (b) to judge, rate, or rank-order the psychological complexity of different sequences (Vitz & Todd, 1969). The basic measure of sequence complexity is the length of the internal code needed to describe the serial pattern in some appropriate representation.

Simon argues that various theoretical approaches to serial pattern learning agree in supposing that subjects learn lawful sequences by inducing pattern descriptions which use the relations of "same" and "next successor" (in familiar numeric or letter "alphabets") between symbols, iteration of subpatterns, and hierarchic phrase structures. These are no more complex than what is needed to understand the relations between words in a sentence.

PROBLEM-SOLVING PROGRAMS

Much of the theoretical work in IP models has been directed at producing programs that reason and solve difficult intellectual problems of specific kinds. The goal for psychologically oriented research has been to get the computer to solve hard problems in humanlike ways. From a learning perspective, problem-solving is important since it reveals transfer of the person's skills in perceiving or representing the problem situation, in canvassing alternatives, and in retrieving from memory rules and procedures that succeeded on similar problems. Also of interest is the change in a person's strategies of attacking a complex problem as she solves it repeatedly.

Research in problem-solving (Bourne et al., 1979; Duncker, 1945) has identified three areas of importance: the first concerns how a person sees, interprets, or represents a problem statement to herself and comes to understand what it is about; the second concerns the procedures used in seeking a solution once she believes she understands the problem; and the third concerns the way she compares a generated solution to the solution criteria and decides whether a sufficient match occurs so that work can stop. The early simulation models bypassed the first, and in some ways more difficult, issue of how the subject interprets the problem; they concentrated instead on the second issue. The problem is

given to the program in a well-structured form, and the programmer ensures that the problem is interpreted correctly by the model before it is set to work on it. Later researchers have also begun to deal with the fuzzier issues of problem interpretation and representation and have constructed some special programs for them (Simon & Hayes, 1976). Language analysis programs, attached to so-called question-answering systems, are aimed at correctly interpreting problem statements (or questions); these systems can be especially powerful when they have a well-defined semantic domain within which the problems are stated—for example, a schematic picture of a scene or an electric circuit diagram (see Coles, 1968; and Winograd, 1972). The representation of the problem space is of crucial importance, since it is well known that a given problem can be difficult or easy depending on how it is represented internally. Although valuable discussions of this issue exist (Amarel, 1968; Nilsson, 1971), no general procedures or rules have been devised for concocting a good representation of a problem in order to make its solution transparent.

It is probably fair to say that the Logic Theorist program of Newell, Shaw, and Simon (1958) set the basic mode for many of the problem-solving programs that followed in the ensuing years. The Logic Theorist (LT) was designed to find proofs for theorems stated in the propositional calculus of symbolic logic. Such problems have a standard format. Some "givens," A, are provided, an end statement or theorem, B, is conjectured, and the problem for the theorem-prover is to try to transform the givens into the end statement. This has to be done by using the axioms of the system and the permissible transformation rules of the language (substitution, replacement, chaining, and detachment). As any student of logic can attest, theorem-proving is often a difficult and provocative task, and one in which failures are common. Since the axioms and transformation rules can be applied to the givens in a tremendous variety of sequential permutations, the problem is to select a path that leads to the given theorem.

A useful distinction may be made at this point between *algorithms* and *heuristic* methods of searching for an answer. An algorithm is a procedure or set of rules that is guaranteed to lead eventually to the solution of a given kind of problem. It is like a flawless, infallible recipe. Many algorithms exist in mathematics, such as rules for solving a set of linear equations, for inverting a matrix, for doing long division, and so on. But there are many more problems for which no algorithm is known, and some efficient strategy is needed to guide the search for a solution. Proving theorems in mathematics or the propositional calculus are examples.[2] To set out on a blind or even on a systematic search through all proper logical sequences that can be generated by the rules of the game, checking for one sequence that proves the theorem, would take a tremendously long time and be terribly inefficient. One could generate logical consequences of the givens for years in this manner without ever coming across a sequence that proves the theorem.

What obviously is needed is some means for directing the search toward a particular goal, one that has ways of detecting when it is getting close and what must be done to move still closer to the answer. In the Logic Theorist program, Newell, Shaw, and Simon used some *heuristics* to aid and guide the search process. Heuristics are rules of thumb telling one how to search

in ways that are probably fruitful or efficient. When successful, these can reduce the search time considerably, though there is no guarantee that they will always be successful. In LT the main heuristic was "working backwards" from the theorem to be proved. One or more propositions, A', are sought which imply the theorem B by a simple transformation of A'. A subproblem is then set up, to deduce one of these A' statements from the given, A, by a simple transformation. If it cannot do so directly, then it works backwards from A' to another proposition A'' that implies A', and then tries to deduce A'' from the given, A. A number of subproblems may be generated in moving backwards each step; these are stored on a list of subproblems to be worked on. They are then edited by special routines which delete those that look nonprovable and promote those that look simple to prove and that are "similar" in a special sense to the given. LT works on the subproblems in order, seeking a proof. If one subproblem fails to yield a proof within a time limit, it goes on to try the next. If it runs out of subproblems to work on and can generate no more, then it gives up and fails to solve the problem. A great deal more than this goes on in the LT program, and the paper cited should be consulted for the richness of detail needed.

In one experiment with LT, the first 52 theorems of *Principia mathematica* (a standard classic in symbolic logic by Whitehead and Russell, 1925) were given to LT in the order they appeared. If LT proved a theorem, it was stored in its memory for possible later use. With this order of presentation, LT proved 38 (73 percent) of the 52 theorems. About half were solved in under a minute of computing time on a small computer. Most of the remaining theorems took from 1 to 5 minutes each to solve. The amount of time to prove a given theorem increased sharply with the number of steps necessary to the proof.

---

[2] Algorithmic proof procedures have been developed for theorems in the propositional calculus (Wang, 1960, 1965) and in the first-order predicate calculus (J. A. Robinson, 1970) based on "resolution principles." However, those mechanical algorithms are exhaustive techniques that seem to be a very far cry from the heuristic methods used by a student in proving a theorem.

Other experiments showed that LT's ability to prove a given theorem depended on the order in which the theorems provided critical intermediate results for proving some of the more difficult theorems.

In discussing LT's performance as it was studied in several experiments, Newell, Shaw, and Simon (1958) point out numerous "human" characteristics of the model's problem-solving behavior. By way of summary, they say:

> We have now reviewed the principal evidence that LT solves problems in a manner closely resembling that exhibited by humans dealing with the same problems. First, and perhaps most important, it is in fact capable of finding proofs for theorems—hence incorporates a system of processes that is sufficient for a problem-solving mechanism. Second, its ability to solve a particular problem depends on the sequence in which problems are presented to it in much the same way that a human subject's behavior depends on this sequence. Third, its behavior exhibits both preparatory and directional set. Fourth, it exhibits insight both in the sense of vicarious trial and error leading to "sudden" problem solution, and in the sense of employing heuristics to keep the total amount of trial and error within reasonable bounds. Fifth, it employs simple concepts to classify the expressions with which it deals. Sixth, its program exhibits a complex organized hierarchy of problems and subproblems (p. 162).

It became clear very early that the advent of LT—more specifically, the methodology, aims, and strategies involved in the LT program—heralded a new era of conceptualization and theorizing about complex mental processes—thinking, problem-solving, and the like. With rare exceptions (Duncker, 1945; DeGroot, 1946; Bruner, Goodnow, & Austin, 1956), previous psychological discussions of thinking and problem-solving had been characterized by serious vagueness and a baffling recognition of the incompleteness or insufficiency of any particular hypothesis, mechanism, or theory to account for the multiple richness of the phenomena. The behavior of the LT program constituted a big step in the right direction: it was completely and precisely specified, and the sufficiency of its mechanisms was determinable. It brought a new technology for theory construction to the study of complex human behavior, an area, it should be remembered, that had been scarcely touched by the behaviorists.

Since the time of the Logic Theorist, many other simulations models have been developed for many formal reasoning tasks —solving calculus problems, constructing proofs in geometry, understanding algebra word problems, discovering interesting theorems in number theory. Most of these have not been tested to see if they directly simulate human ways of solving problems in these areas. Another line of research on reasoning programs is focused on those that play challenging games, a topic to which we turn now.

Game Players

The programming of a computer to play board games such as checkers or chess against an opponent shares many of the features found in programs that prove theorems. The arrangement of the pieces on the board at any moment constitutes the givens. The objective is to transform the givens into a winning final position by a sequence of moves permitted by the rules of the game. The permissible moves of the game play the same role as do the rules of inference in constructing logical arguments. Of course, in games, the program plays against an adversary who must be assumed to be at least as rational as the program.

The basic unit for analysis is the individual move. The program, having an internal representation of the board and the location of all the pieces, looks ahead several moves—my move, his possible countermoves, my next move, his next possible countermoves to that, and so on. How far ahead it looks is called the *depth* of its search. The *search tree* of possibilities can get very large if very many alternatives are considered at each move. The programs have to trade off the number of alternatives examined at each move for depth of search along particular branches of the tree. In general, programs that search deeply on a few promising alternatives are more successful. Various heuristics are used to decide which alternatives one or two moves ahead warrant a deeper search.

Once a search tree of alternatives at a given move has been constructed, the program has to evaluate the various branches to discover their worth and to decide upon a move. The ultimate consequences of playing the entire game, to "win, lose, or draw," are usually too remote and too indeterminate to be of much help in evaluating a particular move. Thus, some *evaluation function* is needed that is sensitive to subgoals regarding a single, local move. Experts at the game can usually tell us a few generally desirable criteria to use in local evaluations in particular types of games, such as those that have a bearing on board control, piece advantage, king-

piece exchange ratio, back row control, and so forth. In Samuel's checker-playing program (1959), a checker position was evaluated by computing a weighted average of the values of several such local characteristics. Each hypothetical position generated in a search tree was so evaluated.

In making a decision, the machine selects that move which has the highest value, where the value has been calculated by a *backwards minimax* procedure. Figure 12.18 shows a very simple search tree involving only two moves at each level (the computer may consider 10 to 20 moves at each level) and a search going only three levels deep (my move, his countermove, my next move). Each node on the tree represents a hypothetical state of the game. At the deepest level, the eight positions anticipated are scored by the evaluation function, with high positive scores indicating good positions for myself. Since I would choose the maximum scoring move on my second move, the value attached to the node above is the larger of the two lower scores. As to my opponent's move, we as-

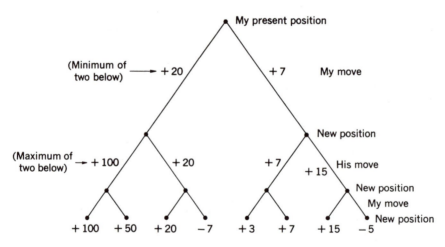

Figure 12.18. A search tree of moves three levels deep, where only two moves are considered at each level. The positions at the deepest level searched are scored by the evaluation function. The score on a node at level 2 is the maximum of the scores on its two lower branches; the score on a level 1 node is the minimum of the score on the two lower branches.

sume he would try to hold my gain to a minimum, so his choice would cause the minimum value to be attached to the node above. Backing up to my present position, the + 20 branch is clearly a better move for me than the + 7 branch, so that should be my choice.

This type of tree search and minimax backing-up analysis is done at every move of the game. Samuel's program for checker playing includes a variety of others features for improving the game it can play. Several are learning routines: one routine provides move-by-move feedback and correction of the weights assigned to the different subgoals in the evaluation function; the other involves a rote memory (on accessible magnetic tape) for all board positions previously encountered, searched, and evaluated. This omnibus memory helps reduce the search tree at each step to just those few branches that should be searched in greater depth.

Samuel performed many explorations with this program, trying different heuristics and self-improvement learning routines. The machine was trained by having it play checkers against human players and against published championship games from checkers books. The program improved its performance remarkably, eventually to the point where it could usually beat its human opponent. In the summer of 1962, a match was arranged between a former checkers champion, Mr. Robert W. Nealey, and the program. The machine won handily. At the conclusion of the game, Mr. Nealey commented:

> Our game . . . did have its points. Up to the 31st move, all of our play had been previously published, except where I evaded "the book" several times in a vain effort to throw the computer's timing off. At the 32-27 loser and onwards, all the play is original with us, so far as I have been able to find. It is very interesting to me to note that the computer had to make several star moves in order to get the win, and that I had several opportunities to draw otherwise. That is why I kept the game going. The

machine, therefore, played a perfect ending without one misstep. In the matter of the end game, I have not had such competition from any human being since 1954, when I lost my last game (Feigenbaum & Feldman, 1963, p. 104).

Since that time, Samuel (1967) has revised the scheme for evaluating positions and the attendant learning routines. The linear polynomial function of the prior work was abandoned in favor of a complex nonlinear evaluation process that involves hierarchical refinements of rough evaluations from many significant subpatterns or aggregations of "features" of given board positions. This new position evaluation function leads to many improvements in the checker playing of the program.

Samuel's program performs well because it searches over possible moves in an exhaustive and deep fashion, and it has an experienced way of evaluating anticipated outcomes. Programs that play passable chess (Greenblatt et al., 1967) have also been constructed along similar lines. While these programs play reasonable games, detailed studies of expert board-game players suggest that the experts spend much less time canvassing a broad range of alternatives, but rather quickly recognize portions of the board configuration that look promising and then spend a lot of time analyzing possible move sequences within those significant portions. Research by Chase and Simon (1973) with chess masters, and J. S. Reitman (1976) with masters of the Japanese game of Go find that experts are much better than novices at *perceiving* significant board configurations of pieces (such as "His Bishop is attacking my Queen"). These researchers suggest that through experience with many thousands of games the masters have built up in memory a vast store of significant chess (or Go) patterns which act like chunks—large units for perceiving and thinking about the game and its development from a given point; they also can remember which chunks (parts of the board configuration) have had promising or successful development in the past. The chess master's perception of a chess board has been likened to the way a skilled reader recognizes words as chunks in strings of letters. To simulate the chess master's perception, Simon and Barenfeld (1969) have written a computer program that will scan its (hypothetical) eyes over pieces arrayed on a chess board, notice significant piece configurations, spend time looking at the important patterns (as do human players), and then represent the current board situation for itself in terms of chunks of significant patterns. W. Reitman and Wilcox (1978) have similarly implemented a pattern-recognition and inference system that plays Go at a respectable amateur ranking. These later studies are significant in showing that the initial impulse to use the power of the computer for searching exhaustively over game moves was a misguided approach; rather, expertise seems to lie in the master's ability to perceive or recognize hundreds of familiar significant patterns, and to aggregate chunks at one level into a higher level to trigger a given strategy for searching moves from the current board position. The chess master and Go master represent high orders of perceptual learning within a restricted domain.

The General Problem-Solver

One of the most ambitious research programs on mechanical problem-solving is the General Problem-Solver (GPS), started by Newell, Shaw, and Simon (1959; Newell & Simon, 1961). GPS is a continuing project: since its conception in 1957, the program has existed in seven different operating versions, each version designed to handle a slightly different set of difficulties. Usable versions are given in books by Ernst and Newell (1969) and Newell and Simon (1972). GPS was intended to be a core set of processes that could work on and solve a variety of problems involving different subject matters such as proving theorems in logic, proving trigonometric identities, and solving word puzzles. In setting up its operation on any particular problem, a "task environment" is to be provided by specifying for the machine the objects to be encountered and the transformation rules (moves) of the particular game.

The premises and the goal must be stated in comparable terms so that GPS seeks to transform the premises (or starting point) into the goal. It uses *means-ends analyses,* generating subproblems to work on, and builds up a tree of subproblems. There are general routines for comparing two expressions and detecting differences between them. If differences are detected, GPS then seeks some transformation that reduces these differences. Figure 12.19 gives a summary of three goals (or subgoals) and the associated methods GPS uses for working on them. The goals often occur recursively within a loop. Starting with the goal of transforming object A (premise) into object B (conclusion), the program may find one or more differences. If so, it sets up the goal of reducing the most important difference. This then goes to the goal of finding an operator (allowable transformation) which can be applied to the premises. If it cannot be so applied, then it sees whether A can be transformed into something to which the first operator can be applied. Part of the task environment supplied to GPS with the problem is an operator-difference table giving the permissible transformations that are relevant to reducing particular kinds of differences.

Because pursuit of each goal often leads to a proliferation of subgoals within subgoals, the GPS program has an executive routine that monitors the generation of new subgoals, evaluates them on multiple criteria, and then discards them or decides the order in which they will be worked on.

GPS involves considerably more processes and heuristics than this brief descrip-

Goal I: Transform object A into object B

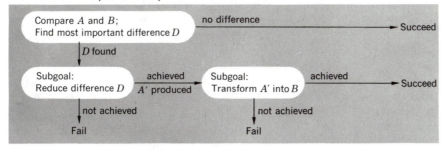

Goal II: Reduce difference D between object A and object B

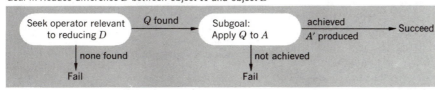

Goal III: Apply operator Q to object A

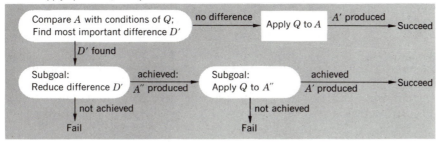

Figure 12.19. A summary of the major goals of GPS and the associated methods used to achieve them. The goals of transforming object A into B leads to the subgoal of reducing one or more differences between them. To reduce a given difference, a relevant operator is found. The next subgoal is to apply the operator to A. If that cannot be done, then the next subgoal is to see how A differs from something to which the operator can be applied. At this point the sequence will repeat at this lower level. (From B. F. Green, Jr., 1963.)

tion conveys. It proves theorems, of course. Of perhaps greater interest to psychologists is the attempt by Newell and Simon (1972) to fit "thinking aloud" protocols taken from subjects who are encountering and solving logic and crypto-arithmetic problems for the first time, after only minimal training on the rules of the game. The subject is asked to think aloud, to say what she is looking for or considering at every step of the way while proving a theorem. Similarly, the internal workings (reasonings) of the computer program are printed out as it proceeds step by step to solve the problem. Analyzing numerous protocols, the authors point out a number of similarities in what the program and the subject are doing at various points along the construction of the proof. Newell and Simon conclude that the program's point-by-point behavior is a fairly accurate simulation of some of the significant features of the subjects verbal output and sequence of rule selections.

It is clear nevertheless that the General Problem-Solver is still very far from attaining the general capabilities of the human adult. It requires that the goal be described in exactly the same way as the givens of a problem. From this common description, it then tries to transform the givens into the goal. This constitutes a restriction, of course, on the class of problems it can attempt to solve. For example, the Letter Series Completion task has goals not describable in this manner, and it is clear that GPS would have no way of handling these or similar problems. In brief, GPS does not work on ill-defined problems for which the goal is not well specified (e.g., to write a suspenseful story).

Robot Projects

Perhaps of most interest to psychologists are the integrated *robot projects* that have been developed at Stanford, MIT, and the Stanford Research Institute (SRI) over the past decade. The SRI robot appears the most ambitious of the several projects (see Fikes & Nilsson, 1971). It consists of a motor-driven cart with the following components:

a. a television camera for taking a picture of its visual environment, a range-finder for triangulating the distance to any point from the robot, and a "cat whisker" that acts as a tactual sensor; these all relay afferent or sensory information to

b. a computer holding a variety of programs for analyzing the afferent information, for planning out action sequences which will achieve certain effects upon its realistic environment, and

c. a set of motors that can turn the cart, drive it forward or backward, and a set of bumpers that can be used to push boxes and other objects over a smooth floor.

The realistic environment provides a rich arena for learning and a source of problems that can be posed for the robot to solve, as well as a fantastic number of engineering problems for the designers to solve. Let us consider just one problem to illustrate the nature of the system.

Consider Figure 12.20, which shows a

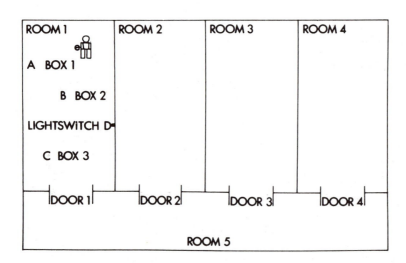

Figure 12.20.   Room plan for the SRI robot. (From Fikes & Nilsson, 1971.)

schematic environment of five interconnected rooms with the robot in room 1 along with three boxes and a light switch. A first issue is to represent in the robot's memory information about the spatial layout of its environment. Some of this is relatively permanent information, such as where doors are and what rooms connect with other rooms. Included in this permanent information are also a number of physical laws about the environment (e.g., that an object in one place is not in another place) and rules of motion (e.g., that the robot cannot run over a box without moving it, or it cannot get into a room by going through brick walls, and so on). Some of the information in memory is transient, such as the current location of the robot and the boxes. This information is acquired from the robot's video picture, which is analyzed by quite sophisticated scene analysis programs (see Tenenbaum & Barrow, 1976). The outcome of this transient analysis, together with the stable facts about the environment, are said to comprise the robot's current model of its world, call it M_0 (for initial model). For convenience, these facts are represented in terms of statements in the predicate calculus of logic. Thus, for example, the initial model (see Figure 12.20) would include the following statements regarding the locations of objects:

$$M_0: \begin{cases} \text{ATR } (e) \\ \text{AT (box 1, } A) \\ \text{AT (box 2, } B) \\ \text{AT (box 3, } C) \end{cases}$$

These statements say that the robot is at point e, box 1 is at point A, and so on. Suppose that the robot is now given the problem of gathering together the three boxes. This goal is translated into a statement in the predicate calculus, to find a location x such that all three boxes are at x. A problem-solving program called

STRIPS is the component that actually plans out the sequence of operators (steps or "motor commands") which the robot is to perform to achieve the goal-state. STRIPS proceeds rather like GPS, using mainly the means-ends heuristic (for reducing differences), except that it has more powerful deductive capabilities than GPS. Beginning from its current world model, M_0, STRIPS searches for a sequence of operators that will produce a new world model within which the goal statement is true. For the robot, the operators correspond to *action routines* whose execution causes the robot to take certain actions. Some of the action routines available to the SRI robot are as follows (consider the location constants to be two-dimensional vectors):

1. go to $_1(m)$: robot goes to coordinate location m;
2. go to $_2(m)$: robot goes *next* to item m;
3. push to (m, n): robot pushes object m next to item n;
4. turn on light (m): robot turns on light switch m;
5. climb on box (m): robot climbs up on box m;
6. climb off box (m): robot climbs off box m;
7. go through door (d, m, n): robot goes through door d from room m into room n.

Each such operator has a set of *preconditions* that must be true of the world model before it can be applied. For example, the preconditions of *climb off box* (m) are that m is a box and that the robot is on m. Also, carrying out an action causes the world model to change; these changes are handled by an *add* list and a *delete* list corresponding to each action. The add list gives the new facts made true by the effect of the action on the world, whereas the delete list gives the prior true facts that have been canceled by the effect of the action. Two simple examples of add and delete lists for operators are the following:

1. PUSH (*k*, *m*, *n*): robot pushes object *k* from place *m* to place *n*.

    precondition: AT (*k*, *m*): object *k* is at place *m*

                 ATR (*m*): robot at place *m*

    add list: AT (*k*, *n*): object *k* at place *n*

                 ATR (*n*): robot at place *n*

    delete list: AT (*k*, *m*): object *k* at place *m*

                 ATR (*m*): robot at place *m*

2. GO TO (*m*, *n*): robot goes from place *m* to place *n*

    precondition: ATR (*m*): robot at place *m*

    add list: ATR (*n*): robot at place *n*

    delete list: ATR (*m*): robot at place *m*

STRIPS uses a theorem prover to try to show that the goal follows from the initial world model, M_0. If it cannot do this at once, like GPS it extracts from the uncompleted proof the difference between M_0 and the goal, and seeks an operator relevant to reducing this difference. If one is found, a subgoal is set up to prove that the preconditions of that operator (what must be true if it is to be applied) are satisfied by the current world model. If so, then the operator is applied, the world model is updated (to M_1) by the add and delete lists of that operator, and the next step is to see whether M_1 satisfies the goal. If not, then the program takes the difference and applies the same routine again, and again in recursive fashion. If the precondition of a desired operator is not satisfied by the current world model, a subgoal will be set up to find an applicable operator which will imply a model that will satisfy the preconditions. This is, of course, the same sort of subproblem as the overall problem, and it illustrates the hierarchy of goals, subgoals, and models that may be generated by the search process. STRIPS evaluates particular continuations or lines of search by taking account of such factors as the number of subgoals remaining to be solved, the complexity of the differences among and types of predicates of these subgoals. It selects for development that search line having the better evaluation.

To return to the initial problem, the robot has been commanded to push to-gether the three boxes (or has been given another goal which requires this as a subgoal). It might first determine to push box 1 from place *A* to place *B* near box 2. But a precondition for applying a PUSH (box 1, *A*, *B*) operator is that the robot be at place *A*. So a GO TO$_2$ (box 1) operator must be used to satisfy this precondition. Having moved behind box 1 and pushed it to box 2, the robot then applies a similar operator sequence to push box 3 to box 2, thus achieving its goal. Although this description is quite brief, the amount of problem-graph searching the robot (computer) does to achieve the task is quite large. But it must be remembered that the robot is rather like an uneducated baby in its initial performance of such tasks.

Once it has carried out the task and similar ones several times, it will have learned a rather general subroutine for collecting together various objects. The subroutine, somewhat like a human's, would be generalized over such particulars as how many objects are to be collected, what the objects are, and where they are located relative to the robot's initial position. Fikes, Hart, and Nilsson (1972) have investigated how to generalize or abstract successful *action sequences* away from irrelevant particulars while capturing the relevant variables of each case. For example, if one object is fixed, such as the light switch in Figure 12.20, then the pile of other objects must be collected around the stationary object.

The SRI robot has been tried out on a wide range of tasks, the programs revised and tried out again on harder tasks, and so on in successive cycles of refinement. The robot solves a number of problems. To list just a few of these in reference to the arrangements of Figure 12.20: it can go to a fixed location in another room; it can remove any pushable box that is blocking a doorway it has to go through; it can go to a specified room and push a box from there to another room; it can turn on the light switch by moving the tallest box to beneath the light switch then climbing up on it, and so on. It can perform a surprising range of effective actions, and its capabilities are expanding. An interesting and instructive movie is available from the Robot Project at SRI that illustrates the varieties of problems the robot solves and which provides some explanation of the scene analysis routines and the planning carried out by the STRIPS problem-solving program. This project and the "hand-eye" projects at MIT and Stanford University have been very active in proposing substantive problems and achieving interesting results in the artificial intelligence field.

These robot projects are interesting to learning psychologists because they attack all of psychology's problems in an integrated endeavor—the robot must learn to see, learn to classify objects, learn to move and turn, learn sequences of moves, learn a cognitive map of its environment, plan and carry out efficient goal-directed actions, and learn to generalize over a cluster of action-sequences having a common goal. All of this occurs in a semirealistic environment. A successful learning theory should be able to help in the synthesis of such a general-purpose robot.

Intelligent Planners

As problem-solvers, STRIPS and GPS are inelegant; they must investigate a given plan for solving a problem in *minute detail*. For example, if you asked it to decide whether you can see a movie tonight, STRIPS would have to worry about whether you could reach into your wallet to get money or whether your eyes are functioning properly. Neither program produces an overall strategic plan of the problem before launching into the tedious details of a specific solution attempt. If there are many applicable actions (operators), each with many preconditions, the search at the level of detail will become quickly bogged down. What is needed is a facility for planning a solution

at more general levels of abstraction, ignoring all the standard details, and attending to only the most essential preconditions. A program by Sacerdoti (1974) called ABSTRIPS (for abstract STRIPS) constructs robot-action plans in just this way. The preconditions of an action operator can be rank ordered in terms of their likelihood of being a problem; thus, in our movie example, having money to pay for a ticket would be considered more problematic than being able to get the money out of your wallet. The initial plan in ABSTRIPS is formulated just to take care of the most critical preconditions of the needed actions. If this succeeds, ABSTRIPS then uses this initial plan as a skeleton to be fleshed out by subplans designed to achieve those preconditions (of the skeletal actions) at successively lower levels of importance. This seems a more realistic simulation of the human tendency to plan at a general level before worrying about the details.

ABSTRIPS works well on problems for which the subgoals can be achieved independently without interaction, so that the overall problem is solved by adding up the contributions of the solutions to the independent subproblems. Unfortunately, many real problems are "nonadditive" in the sense that one subgoal impacts upon or prevents a precondition for another subgoal. One example occurs when you have just enough money to purchase a movie ticket, but you do not have enough to buy a bus ticket and a movie ticket. Another example is shown in Figure 12.21: the initial state of three boxes is that box *C* is stacked on box *A* with box *B* standing alone, and the goal state to be achieved is the stack with *A* on top, then *B,* then *C* on the bottom. Standard subgoals for a program might be to get *B* on *C,* and *A* on *B.* But if the program works on either of these subgoals first and separately, the most direct way to achieve either subgoal precludes the possibility of achieving the other subgoal without some backing up. (For instance, the

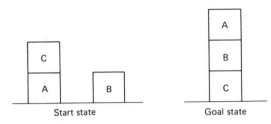

Figure 12.21. The problem is to transform the start state into the goal state in three moves without undoing any actions. This problem has nonlinear subgoals.

B-on-*C* subgoal can be achieved directly from the starting state by putting *B* on *C*, but that buries *A* in the wrong place.) Sacerdoti (1975) has programmed a more refined problem-solver that can solve such nonlinear problems by attending to interactions between subgoals and resolving conflicts between goals. For example, the program notes whether one action results in a state that prevents another needed action from occurring. If its subgoals are to paint the ceiling and paint the ladder, it will notice that painting the ladder first makes it unuseable for painting the ceiling, so the program orders the subgoals to deal with this. With many such elaborations, Sacerdoti's program was able to solve a range of challenging nonlinear problems. Fahlman (1974) has also designed an intelligent planner for solving nonlinear problems in geometric constructions. While these programs seem eminently worthy of psychological testing, there are presently no detailed comparisons of these planning theories' predictions with observed details of problem-solving behavior of humans. A beginning for such comparisons is contained in work by B. Hayes-Roth and F. Hayes-Roth (1979) on the way people plan a day's worth of errands and odd jobs before they go about a city. We may expect observations of everyday planning to become a more popular area for psychological study.

KNOWLEDGE SPECIALISTS

The foregoing efforts—GPS, STRIPS, and ABSTRIPS—explore powerful reasoning or problem-solving methods, but the methods are very general. Thus, Newell and Simon believe that *means-ends analysis* is of sufficient generality that it will arise in many different domains, whether proving logic theorems, finding a way home, or solving various puzzles. A countertrend that has become popular in artificial intelligence subscribes to the view that problem-solving is seldom a general skill, that an expert problem-solver performs well in her specialty because she has a large fund of knowledge about specific problems in that domain rather than an especially powerful reasoning method. This view was intimated in the Chase and Simon (1973) studies of the pattern-recognition abilities of chess masters. From this perspective, the way to simulate problem-solving is to pick a specific applied problem (such as medical diagnosis), extract from a specialist the relevant knowledge she has about problems, write this into the program as a set of rules for classifying specific cases, and let the program try to classify some problem cases. Next analyze the errors of the program, add some more rules or patterns, specialize others, and cycle again through the test-then-evaluate phase. Eventually, with enough help from several experts, enough experience with test cases, and enough theoretical ingenuity in managing and synthesizing multiple sources of evidence, one should develop a fairly expert problem-solver in a specific domain.

Just this strategy has been followed by E. A. Feigenbaum and his collaborators in the Heuristic Programming Project at Stanford University (Feigenbaum, 1978). With the help of experts, these computer scientists have developed and revised programs that solve difficult realistic problems in a number of specific domains. One program (PUFF) diagnoses medical patients for possible pulmonary (lung) disorders. The input to the program is a series of medical tests and measurements including, for instance, the air-flow rate and volume when the patient breathes into a tube. Also, relevant historical data are considered, such as age and amount of smoking. PUFF considers the data and comes up with a diagnosis that specifies whether the lungs or airways are normal or restricted, and if restricted, the likely disease type (such as bronchitis or emphysema). PUFF arrives at its diagnosis by classifying the many input measurements in several passes, using about 55 IF-THEN rules garnered from experts. The rules basically state that *if* a certain pattern of medical measurements is obtained, *then* certain inferences or advice is warranted. The inference rules can be arranged in a network to arrive at a conclusion in stages. For example, some initial medical measurements may suggest that other measurements be taken before diagnosis proceeds. The 55 rules in PUFF were arrived at by a pulmonary physiologist and a computer scientist going over about 100 patients, some normal and some with various pulmonary disorders; the physiologist had to make verbally explicit the many sources of information he considered and the rules of probabilistic inference he used. After that training set of 100 cases, PUFF was "tested" by comparing its diagnoses with those of expert physiologists on 150 new cases. The agreement was around 90 to 100 percent, depending on the strictness of the criterion for matching. That is a most impressive performance, since the program here is matching the diagnoses of expert clinicians in a difficult task environment.

Another successful "expert" program is MYCIN (Shortliffe, 1976), which diagnoses blood infections and meningitis infections and prescribes drug treatments. MYCIN acts as a consultant to a physician who types in medical test results as they are required. Like PUFF, MYCIN's knowledge is contained in a large number of rules that suggest probabilistic relations between a set of medical symptoms and a disease. A typical rule is this:

IF:
1. The site of the culture is blood, and
2. the gram stain of the organism is gramneg, and
3. the morphology of the organism is rod, and
4. the patient is a compromised host

THEN:
There is suggestive evidence (.6) that the identity of the organism is *Pseudomonas aeruginosa*.

Such rules were garnered from medical pathologists, each rule with a "certainty factor" attached. The MYCIN program tries to trace out backwards inference chains from each of several bacterial diseases to the observed medical symptoms and calculate the strength or probable validity of each chain of reasoning. The program may identify several harmful bacteria and prescribe specific antibacterial medications for each. The program can print out the chain of reasoning that leads to each conclusion. The trace enables the program's expert tutor to add to or modify the rules when the program is coming to unwise decisions. After training MYCIN with many cases, its decisions on a new set of cases were judged to be as good as the experts' 90 percent of the time.

The most impressive project of Feigenbaum's group is DENDRAL and its complement, META-DENDRAL. DENDRAL is a program that lists the molecular structures of plausible chemical compounds that could have caused a specific mass spectrogram. A mass spectrometer shoots a shower of electrons at a chemical compound, causing the molecules to break at particular bonds; this procedure creates fragments that have a certain mass or molecular weight. The mass spectrogram is a bar graph of the relative abundance of each molecular fragment plotted against the fragment mass. From these data and a theory of how molecules break up into fragments, the skilled chemist can make an accurate guess about the molecular structure of the unknown compound. DENDRAL was devised to simulate the educated hypotheses of such a skilled chemist. A large number of fragmentation rules were elicited from chemists and tried out. The typical rule shows how a given compound, characterized by a particular molecular structure, is likely to break apart. A simple rule for a nitrogen atom linked to a chain of three carbon atoms is:

$$(N–C–C–C) \rightarrow N–C//C–C$$

where the break is indicated by the slash, and the N–C fragment to the left would have its mass recorded. This rule may apply to several places on a large molecule.

Using the mass spectrogram as input data, one part of DENDRAL generates a large set of plausible molecular structures, then uses its knowledge of the data and specific constraints by means of fragmentation rules to reduce the number of plausible structures. Each plausible structure left over is then evaluated by simulating the mass spectrogram it would produce and comparing this with the one observed. After so evaluating a small set of plausible structures, DENDRAL then prints out a ranking of the top four or five candidate molecular structures for the unknown molecule. DENDRAL has been programmed with only enough rules to deal with restricted classes of chemical compounds (those of special interest to the designers). Within that domain, DENDRAL's performance in interpreting spectrograms is usually faster and more accurate than expert human performance—a truly remarkable achievement.

In refining the DENDRAL program to deal with new cases, the chemists were often forced to rethink or hypothesize new constraints on fragmentation or atom migration across fragments; in doing so they made some genuine discoveries in the-oretical chemistry. As a later development, META-DENDRAL was designed to make up its own molecular fragmentation rules to try to explain a set of basic data, pairing known molecular structures with their mass spectrograms. To restrict the search for useful rules, a weak set of constraints was stated at the outset, including, for example, those which state that double bonds and triple bonds do not break apart, only fragments larger than two carbon atoms appear in the data, and so on. Given a molecule-spectrogram pair (about 100 mass numbers), META-DENDRAL would generate a number of rules to break up that molecule so as to produce that spectrogram; then it would test and revise these as it dealt with more and more molecule-spectrogram pairs. It eventually would settle upon a coherent and very predictive set of fragmentation rules—in fact, many that had been suggested by the experts in building DENDRAL. When set to analyzing the spectrograms of a new family of complex ringed molecules for which the mass spectral theory had not yet been developed, META-DENDRAL discovered rule sets for each chemical subfamily. Moreover, the rule sets were judged by experts to be scientifically valid, and they have entered the arena of theoretical chemistry (for a summary, see Buchanan & Mitchell, 1978).

META-DENDRAL is a "learner" in the most creative sense of that concept. Beginning with relatively weak constraints about the form of the rules it is seeking, it induces more specific rules by using data in a cycle of "generate-test-evaluate-refine," progressively refining and modifying its rules of fragmentation. The designers of the program did not know in advance just what rules the program would discover. The fact that META-DENDRAL taught itself to be an expert tells us something about how input data can constrain the class of acceptable theories. Its success also tells us something about the efficiency of rule-generation and rule-evaluation mechanisms.

Information-Processing Theories of Behavior **399**

The practical success of such knowledge-engineering projects suggests that expertise is based on large quantities of relevant knowledge that are organized for efficient use and not necessarily on profound methods of reasoning. None of the general-purpose problem-solvers like GPS or STRIPS has any hope of ever achieving the successes of MYCIN or DENDRAL. Of course, their designers had different goals in mind.

These specialist programs are all written as rule-based inference systems. Their operating knowledge is contained in a large number of IF-THEN rules called *productions,* which say that if some antecedent conditions arise, then some consequent actions or decisions can be made. Productions are similar to stimulus-response pairs, except the stimulus condition can be a complex pattern, and the action can be a series of internal actions or state changes as well as overt responses. Productions may also contain variables and functions (for example, "if age is less than 30 years"), whereas S-R links were not conceived to be so general.

Many recent simulation theories are being written as systems of productions. The basic idea is that a set of rules (situation-action pairs) exist in long-term memory, that data enter into short-term memory, and these active data select and cause certain productions to fire, perhaps causing external responses or the addition of new data to short-term memory. The system runs in a series of *recognition-action* cycles, whereby data are recognized by some production which fires an action, which initiates the next cycle, and so on. Such a model seems appropriate to deal with the flow of thought or sequences of behavior, where the context plus the event of the last idea (or action datum) activates the association to the next thought or action. Productions seem a natural way to represent and model mental *procedures* such as adding two three-digit numbers in your head. It also gives a means for explicating the processes underlying habitual modes of thought such as seen in psychiatrically depressed or paranoid patients. In separate works, Newell (1973) and J. R. Anderson (1976) have suggested that production systems form a natural medium for models of cognitive processes.

LANGUAGE-PROCESSING PROGRAMS

Humans acquire most of their useful information not by doing but by being told. Most formal schooling is based on imparting information by instruction, by telling it to the pupil. Most of our knowledge of everyday affairs comes from reading or listening to news reports or gossip. The medium for all this learning is language; psychologists who study learning should therefore be interested in the details of how people learn from being told about things. It has been said that the one capability of human beings that sets them apart from other animals is their competence in using language—reading or listening to it, understanding it, using it for thinking and inference, and producing it in speech and writing. Modeling of these capabilities is currently the most formidable project confronting those at work in the simulation and artificial intelligence fields. The magnitude of this problem has resulted in its breakup into many splinter disciplines, each attacking a different aspect of the general problem. There are good general reviews of the chief issues and lines of research by Simmons (1970) and in books edited by Borko (1967), Minsky (1968), Schank (1975), and Simon and Siklossy (1972). We shall touch briefly on four of the splinter areas.

Mechanical Translation

After giving the computer text in one language (e.g., Russian) the machine is to output an acceptable translation of it in another language (English). Because of the multiple meanings and usages of a given word in both languages, a simple dictionary-search program produces nothing but gibberish. Some syntactic and semantic (meaning) analysis is required, and this is exceedingly difficult to supply. About 1968 or so, a conference of experts on machine translations came to the conclusion that all efforts based on syntactic analysis and word-for-word substitution had failed, and that this approach should be abandoned. Obviously before one can translate, one must first correctly understand what is being said in the source language. But this itself is a vast problem, so efforts have been directed to designing programs which understand. The basic notion (e.g., Schank, 1972) is to have a conceptual base ("meaningful understanding") into which statements are translated and from which other statements are output. If the input and output are in different surface languages, then translation is occurring. One of the better programs which does this sort of translation (between English and French) is one by Wilks (1973).

Information Retrieval

A person places a request for all available documents on some particular topic (e.g., "simulation of learning by machines"). The ideal machine, having a large file of documents and their indexed listing, determines what the request is about and which documents are relevant to it, retrieves them from the files, and delivers them (or a list of their references). Besides that of understanding the request, the problem here is to design a suitable classification and indexing system, since titles of papers seldom indicate the range of topics discussed in the article. Another approach is not to store indexed titles of documents, but rather to take as one's data base the entire text itself. For instance, early versions of the PROTOSYNTHEX program of Simmons and associates (1966) began with the text of the children's Golden

Book encyclopedia in memory, and requests were answered by retrieving relevant sentences from memory. The program first found the sentences in memory having the most words in common with the request, then performed some syntactic analysis to see whether the common words were in the right grammatical relationship to each other. If they were, then the selected text would be output as the answer. The problem with this approach is threefold: first, the request and the relevant target sentence in storage may be expressed in different paraphrases, so that literal word-matching fails to identify the answer; second, words can be quite ambiguous in having several meanings, and again simple word-matching will not necessarily select textual passages relevant to the requester's intended meaning (e.g., a request for information relevant to "banking" may retrieve facts about airplane flying, constructing raceways, or financial transactions); third, questions typically ask for inferences or deductions from a data base rather than for a simple spitting out of information from the store. Programs which can interpret questions and set up inferential procedures to compute answers are called question-answering systems. In many ways, they are the most interesting programs to psychologists.

Grammar Induction

This is an area of logic concerned with the learnability of grammatical rules of a language. The model makes this determination from word sequences which it judges to be grammatical or ungrammatical. The word sequence may or may not be accompanied by some environmental situation to which the "sentence" refers. The task is supposedly a model of the one facing children who must learn words and the grammatical rules of their language community from being exposed to many thousands of utterances. The induction task is very difficult because the sentence data alone are usually not extensive or crucial enough to distinguish among a large set of equivalent grammars. Further, few methods of induction are strong enough to arrive at a proper grammar just by generalizing from a sample of utterances. This work on pure syntax appears not to be yielding useable, practical results.

A more promising approach is to induce a grammar from input *pairs* consisting of a surface sentence together with a structural diagram of its meaning in some conceptual (or perceptual) base. J. R. Anderson (1975, 1976) and others have shown formally that simple grammatical rules are learnable when the induction program has access to such surface-meaning pairs. Moreover, in laboratory experiments, Moeser and Bregman (1973) have shown that artificial miniature languages composed of a few grammar rules and nonsense syllables as "words" are learnable by adults only if the utterances of the novel language are paired with the perceptual situation to which they refer. Furthermore, the nonsense words must refer consistently to parts of the perceptual field, and the syntactic organization of parts of the sentence should reflect properties of the perceptual organization of the visual field. However, later work suggests that learning can be speeded just by marking the constituents of the word sequence by pauses or intonation.

In related interesting work, Hamburger and Wexler (1975) and Wexler and Culicover (in press) have set forth an induction algorithm that will learn a small set of meaning-preserving transformations of sentences. For example, if the model receives at one time an active sentence ("John caught the fish"), a corresponding passive sentence ("The fish was caught by John"), and a meaning structure for both, the algorithm will figure out the general form of the active-to-passive transformation. This is not a simple task, since the great variety of sentence forms encountered requires that the algorithm come up with

intermediate concepts of grammatical constituents, such as "verb phrase," "noun phrase serving as direct object," and so on. The work of Wexler and his colleagues is tied closely to developments in theoretical linguistics, and has uncovered important principles of the learnability of different grammatical distinctions and rules.

Understanding and Question-Answering Programs

The two areas of understanding and question answering will be treated together because one of the standard tests of understanding a sentence is that one be able to answer questions requiring use of the information in that sentence. However, much of the research has kept these two emphases somewhat distinct, possibly to the detriment of progress in the overall area. The better understanding programs appear to be precisely those that have a powerful inference and question-answering component along with a realistic semantic-pragmatic basis (Winograd, 1972; Schank, 1975a).

The basic components of all such systems are diagrammed in Figure 12.22. The user (or the environment) inputs statements which are either facts, questions, or commands. These statements are usually made in a restricted subset of English, with particular kinds of grammatical complexities disallowed. A translator or parser tries to convert the input statement into a coded version that is understandable and useable by the internal processes of the program. This is *the* primary difficulty, of course. Parsing is the procedure by which different elements in a statement are grouped together in a logical "deep structure" and then assigned to some meaning and role in the utterance. To illustrate, an ordinary sentence like "The man who was angered by it called the polluters up" involves a complex set of syntactic relations. The use of the definite article *the* signals that the speaker has a particular man and particu-

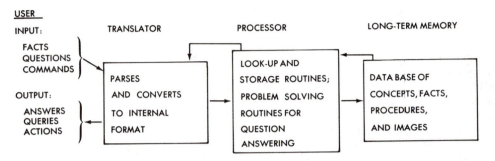

USER

INPUT:

FACTS
QUESTIONS
COMMANDS

OUTPUT:

ANSWERS
QUERIES
ACTIONS

TRANSLATOR

PARSES

AND CONVERTS

TO INTERNAL

FORMAT

PROCESSOR

LOOK-UP AND

STORAGE ROUTINES;

PROBLEM SOLVING

ROUTINES FOR

QUESTION

ANSWERING

LONG-TERM MEMORY

DATA BASE OF

CONCEPTS, FACTS,

PROCEDURES,

AND IMAGES

Figure 12.22. Major components of a fact-retrieval and question-answering system.

lar polluters in mind. Moreover, we know that the main verb is *called up* despite the fact that these two words are well separated in the surface sentence. In addition, we know that *called* is to be attached to *man* rather than to the pronoun *it,* which is closest to the verb. We know that the phrase beginning "who . . ." is a relative clause modifying "the man" and that the relative clause is a passive construction that extends to the main verb. The relative clause itself is an embedded proposition, saying that "something angered the man." Moreover, we know that the use of *it* in the relative clause probably refers to some adverse effect of the act of polluting (done by the polluters), which has angered the man. Thus, at a *conceptual* level the sentence is saying something like "Some persons or institutions polluted something, which caused the man to become angered, which caused him to telephone those persons or institutions"; presumably, he telephoned to complain to them about their polluting. Although an English speaker has the tacit knowledge to perform such parsing tasks effortlessly and to infer and fill in all the needed pieces of information and their connections, it has proved inordinately difficult to program a computer to do it for a wide or general range of sentences. The more successful syntax parsers are the ones programmed by Woods (1970), who was able

to realize something close to a Chomskian transformational grammar in an augmented recursive transition network, by Marcus (1977), which is similar, and by Riesbeck (1975, 1978), which is based on production rules using content words for building meaning representations from sentences.

A basic problem for syntactic parsers is that it does not suffice to simply look up the various meanings and grammatical parts of speech of the words in a sentence and then select combinations according to their fit to a host of standard grammatical frames. That approach quickly "explodes" into multiple parses of most sentences. As one example (cited in Quillian, 1968), an early parser written by Kuno and called the Harvard Multiple-Pass Syntactic Analyzer gave 120 different parsings to the definitional sentence "A *whip* can be a stick with a cord or leather fixed to the end of it, used to give blows in driving animals, etc., or as punishment." How can a dumb syntactic analyzer see 120 different parsings in that sentence, whereas we see only one? Because words have multiple meanings and syntactic form classes depending on their use in the sentence. For example, the word *fixed* in the definition can be a verb or an adjective and can mean *repaired, altered, drugged, bribed, arranged,* or *attached;* and *stick* can be a noun, verb, or adjective, and has even more meanings. The meanings of words *multiply* in the sentential combinations, leading to the absurd proliferation of multiple interpretations of the sentence.

Clearly what is needed is some way to combine the meanings of the various words in a way that makes sense. That, of course, is what various semantics-based parsing systems attempt to do. In semantics-based parsers, such as Quillian's (1968), Schank's (1972), or Winograd's (1972), the general idea is to allow the context of the discourse as well as the meanings of the various words to act jointly along with a syntax analyzer to determine the most likely parsing and interpretation of the sentence. Winograd's parsing system is rather like Woods's in that it is written as a sequence of programs (one for each major grammatical group) that can recursively call one another during parsing. The advance of Winograd's system over Woods's is that there is a continuous interaction between grammatical evaluation and semantic evaluation (checking for meaningfulness of a tentative parsing). Winograd's system also differs in that much of the knowledge it has in long-term memory is not stored as simple facts but rather as procedures (or rules) for proving or inferring certain consequences. For instance, instead of directly storing a universal fact like "All humans are mortal," Winograd's system would store this as a labeled "theorem" whose interpretation is roughly: "If I should ever wish to prove that X is mortal, then this can be done by proving that X is a human." The value of this representation is that it enormously facilitates inferences, such as the sophomoric logical syllogism "if Socrates is human, then Socrates is mortal."

In some of the more powerful question-answering systems (e.g, the QA-3 system of C. C. Green & Raphael, 1968, and C. C. Green, 1969a, 1969b), the translation goes from English into symbolic expressions in the predicate calculus. The facts that the system knows are then treated as a set of axioms, whereas a question to be answered is treated as a theorem to be proved by applying rules of inference to the axioms (the fact base). For example, if it knows facts such as IN (Bill, car), and IN (car, garage), and HAS (Bill, jewels), then QA-3, through certain inferences permitted by IN and HAS predicates, can prove that the jewels are now in the garage. The query "Where are the jewels?" would create a program to find an X such that IN (jewels, X) is true. Green's QA-3 system uses J. A. Robinson's (1970) resolution principle in mechanically deriving the theorem (answer to question) from the axiom system (the set of facts known). Although resolution techniques are powerful derivational tools in logic, they clearly are very inefficient and bear no resemblance whatsoever to the way people reason from a fact base.

As indicated, one of the most impressive language programs was written by Winograd (1972). Winograd's system handles discourse regarding a "toy world" comprised of a tabletop supporting wooden blocks and pyramids of various sizes and colors, and a large box in which objects can be placed. The discourse program drives a "mechanical hand" which can pick up blocks and move them about. The program has a number of primitive predicates for describing its visual world, and the actions it can perform with respect to that block world. Its approach to solving block-manipulation problems uses the PLANNER language, which allows easy formulation of recursive subgoals much as is done in the STRIPS program discussed earlier. Thus, given the command to GRASP (block B1), Winograd's program will first check for certain preconditions: "Is the hand already holding B1? Is B1 graspable? Is the hand holding something else? If so, get rid of it by finding a clear space on the table and putting the unwanted object there. Is the top of B1 cleared off so the hand can grasp it? If not, clear off the top of B1. How? By finding some clear space on the table, and. . . ." This sort of recursive programming of action routines to solve block manipulations is done with impressive efficiency.

Winograd's program is exemplary in combining several sources of information to come up with a correct parsing and understanding of a sentence. The three sources are (1) syntax rules and expectations, (2) semantic-meaning rules for deciding what combinations are sensible, and (3) the deductive-inference component, which figures out the referents for obscure expressions. The work of these three components is coordinated, and they pass their partial results or analyses back and forth while arriving at an interpretation of a sentence. For example, after the program has just picked up a small wooden block from a table filled with blocks, pyramids, and boxes, the next sentence it sees is this: "Find a block that is taller than the one you are holding and put it into the box." The system must figure out that this is a command to do something, know what block is being held, and know that "it" refers to the block (if any) the deduction-component decides is taller than the block being held at the moment. The syntax component tells us that "that is taller . . ." is a restrictive relative clause modifying the leading noun phrase, and the semantics and deduction parts figure out what comparison operations are called for by ". . . is taller than . . . ," and carries out the set of comparisons needed to find a taller block on the table. Winograd's program was particularly efficient in figuring out the referent in context for pronouns like *one* or *it*, which can refer to objects, attributes, actions, or episodes. The program makes sensible interpretations partly because it has knowledge about the block-world situation confronting it; as a result, many expressions that would ordinarily be ambiguous lose their ambiguity in this restricted context. Winograd's program showed what could be done if a program operates in a miniature world where everything has a definite name and place and follows simple rules or physical laws.

In carrying out a series of actions and subgoals along the way to carrying out a command, Winograd's program will store an explicit record of the sequence of intermediate-level events. This record comes in very handy in disambiguating anaphoric or pronominal references, wherein later sentences refer back to earlier events in an opaque way. For example, after the program is told early on to pick up and move a block and subsequently to count the number of objects on the tabletop that are not in the box, it is then asked: "Is at least one of them narrower than the one I told you to pick up?" The problem here, which Winograd's program solves, is to understand that the pronoun "them" refers to the objects enumerated just previously. It also has a record of which block it was told to pick up earlier. Retrieving the block's measurements, the program then compares these to the blocks that are not in the box, finds a narrower one, and so outputs the answer, "Yes, the red one." This short-term event memory thus enables the program to resolve ambiguities of references and to answer questions regarding why or how some state of affairs came into existence. In brief, the program can recite its autobiography. In addition to these components, Winograd's program has a rich variety of inference-making capabilities; this allows it, for instance, to answer complex questions regarding a visual scene.

Conceptual Dependency Analysis

A most interesting approach to language understanding has been developed by Roger Schank (1972, 1975a) and his collaborators (Schank & Abelson, 1977). Schank believes that conceptual-meaning analysis should be of primary concern in writing programs for parsing, understanding, and answering questions. He has attempted to develop a system of basic concepts that underlie action verbs, a set of rules for indicating how different conceptual categories (like ACTOR, ACT, OBJECT, ATTRIBUTE) can depend upon one another, and methods for mapping sentences into and out of these meaning structures.

The basic terms at the conceptual level are: *conceptualization* (that is, a complete thought), *physical objects* (called Picture-Producers, PPs), *locations, times,* and *acts.* Schank also postulates a number of conceptual rules such as these: *PPs perform acts, PPs have attributes, acts have objects, acts can have instruments and direction, acts can cause other conceptualizations.* An example is: "John went to town on his bicycle," where "John" is the actor, "went" is the name for an underlying primitive action called *Physical transfer,* "to town" is the direction of the transfer, and "bicycle" is the instrument used in the action.

Conceptualizations can also relate to one another. One important relation is causality, wherein one thing causes another. In many languages, the causal relation between two conceptualizations is sometimes compressed into a single word called a "causative verb." Thus, "John *killed* a mosquito" can be unpacked conceptually as "John did something which CAUSED the mosquito to change its state of health from alive to dead." By such meaning analyses, Schank hopes to explicate the closeness of meaning of terms like (kill, die), (buy, sell), (teach, learn), (cause, result), (convince, persuade), and so on. Moreover, Schank believes that his "conceptual rewriting" of sentences makes it easier to draw out implications of given statements. Thus, if we learn that John killed a mosquito, we may ask (or be prepared to learn) when and where this event took place, what means or instrument he used to do the deed, what caused him to act that way, and possibly what consequences follow.

Schank has promoted the idea that understanding a sentence implies that we can easily pull out inferences from it. The hypothesis is that when a person learns a given fact, at the same time she also acquires automatically a swarm of implications from that fact. This is important not only for answering questions about information implied by the sentence but also for determining how to interpret later sentences in a text. An early program by Reiger (1975), one of Schank's collaborators, was capable of drawing up to 18 varieties of inference from a single assertion. Reiger's program would generate successive waves of inferences forwards and backwards in time from the event described in the sentence. To illustrate, if Reiger's program hears "John socked Bill because Bill jilted Mary," it would make inferences such as this: John has a hand, John's fist made contact with Bill's body, Bill broke a romantic agreement with Mary, this caused Mary to become unhappy, John likes Mary, Mary's unhappiness distresses John, John wants to punish Bill because Bill's actions caused Mary's distress, Mary's unhappiness preceded John's socking Bill, Bill is probably hurt, Mary will probably feel better to see that John has avenged her, Mary will probably be grateful to Bill now, and so on. As each type of inference is drawn, Reiger's program could ask: What caused that? What should happen next? What physical or psychological conditions were needed for that to occur? Reiger's program simply fills out a lot of the things we would "know" or guess about once we had heard that statement. Unfortunately, this involves a vast number of implications. Most of these implications are not warranted by the dictionary meaning of the words in the assertion, but are suggested by our extralinguistic knowledge about human affairs and the physical situation. The relevance of Reiger's program for the learning theorist is that it spells out in detail one conception of "what is learned" once a person takes in a simple fact.

Causal chaining in text. Schank (1975b) argued that not all these implications are triggered off by the assertion; rather only those inferences are drawn that are needed to link up this sentence to later events in the discourse. Thus, if following the socking event, the next sentence is "Mary thanked John," Schank supposes that the listener builds an inferential bridge to link the earlier socking incident to the thanking incident. This would go through the "revenge" inferences about how pleased Mary was to see Bill punished. Schank proposes that the reader is aware of only those particular inferences that link statements into causal event chains and these are what the reader will later remember having made while reading the text. Thorndyke (1976) has reported psychological evidence supporting this conjecture.

The notion of causal chaining of events was generalized by Schank (1975b) to predict what would be critically important and memorable events in a short narrative story. By connecting one event to another, by noticing how the first either *enables* or *causes* the second event to occur, the reader would extract the skeletal action sequence in the story. Consider the simple narrative and its abbreviated causal chain in Figure 12.23. The events are linked by enablement or causal relations, and occur in the story in this order. According to Schank, this is the backbone of the story, and mainly these facts will be remembered. If we were to elaborate details around any single node (for instance, John's difficulty in fetching the mower or routine happenings while mowing the lawn), Schank's hypothesis says that these details will not be on the main event chain and so will be quickly forgotten by the reader. In experimental work, J. Black and Bower (1980) found that such causal event chains were very accurate predictors of which statements within short narratives would be remembered by groups of college readers.

It takes only brief consideration to notice that a large percentage of the inferences needed to link text statements together are supplied by extralinguistic information, by the reader's knowledge about the social and physical situations, and about the events being described. Thus, we can connect getting out the mower because we know that that enables the action of cutting the grass which is John's desired goal. And, we understand the phrase "get out the mower" not because of any purely linguistic rules, but because we are familiar with the situation and can analyze the text into the components of goal-action-enabling conditions.

Understanding Goals and Plans

In later work, Schank and Abelson (1977) have concentrated on analyzing narratives describing human episodes in terms of the character's goals, the probable plans it leads to, and the actions that the plan motivates. A text that describes parts of this goal-plan-action sequence can be understood by inferring other parts, which then help connect the disparate pieces of text. Often these connections would be obscure if we did not understand the goal and plan underlying them. Consider several examples:

1. Willa was in Paris and was hungry.
   She took out the Michelin guide.
2. Mary saw a storm coming up.
   She shut the windows of the house.
3. Junky Jack was desperate for a fix.
   He got a gun and went to a liquor store.

Think for a moment in detail how you understand such vignettes. In (1), you know Willa is not going to eat the Michelin guide, but rather this is instrumental to finding a nearby restaurant. In (2), you know that storms do not directly cause window-shutting, but that a normative goal

Narrative

John wanted to mow his lawn.

He got out the mower.

The sun was hot.

John removed his shirt and shoes.

He pushed the mower for 10 minutes.

Then the mower ran over his bare toe.

It cut his toe.

John went to the doctor.

He closed the cut.

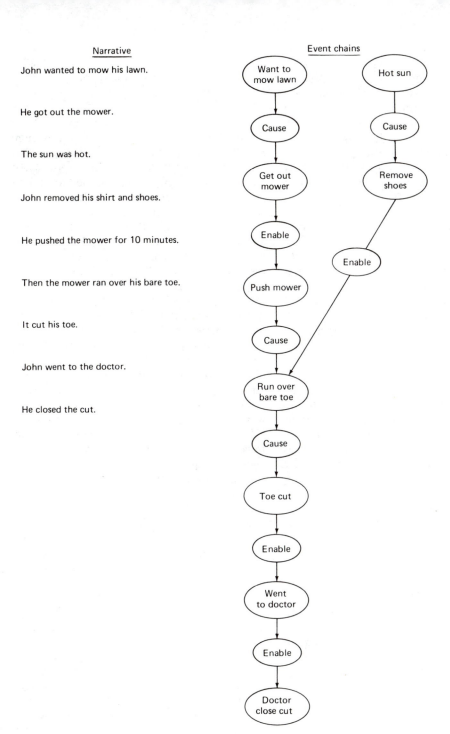

Figure 12.23. A simple event narrative and its analysis into dependent causal chains according to Schank's system.

of Mary (namely, having dry rooms) is threatened by the storm, and the window-shutting avoids the rooms' getting wet. In (3), you know Jack is not going to get a fix with his gun or at a liquor store, but most probably he will use the gun to hold up the store for money and use that to buy a fix. We know that in part because of our knowledge of liquor stores, of why desperate people get guns, and of the "liquor store hold-up" script, which is almost a cliché of modern American crime. Schank and Abelson (1977) and their student, Wilensky (1978), developed a program that "understands" a number of such simple vignettes. It does this by inferring a goal for the character, and assuming that each action has some part in a plan for achieving that goal. The range of situations and complicated motivational entanglements that Wilensky's program can understand is very impressive. The program does this by using a strong set of inferences about human motives, how motives complement or conflict with one another, how plans are designed to overcome obstacles towards achieving a goal, and how actions acquire their significance by their role in the character's plan.

If a particular goal-plan sequence has been used repeatedly by a person in a standard situation, Schank and Abelson suppose that it becomes routinized for her into a conventionalized activity they call a *script*. A script refers to a stereotyped sequence of events or activity such as eating in a fancy restaurant, having a medical checkup, placing a long-distance call at a pay telephone, attending a lecture, and so on. Through direct and vicarious experiences, people in Western cultures have learned more or less routine action plans to achieve their goals in these and many hundreds of other stock situations. Our background knowledge about such routine activities is called in to understand texts that refer elliptically to that activity. Consider this minimal vignette:

> John went to an Italian restaurant.
> He ordered lasagna.
> He liked it so he left a big tip.

Readers have considerably more knowledge about what went on than is stated. This excess knowledge becomes apparent when you answer questions about the story: Did John enter the restaurant? Did he sit down? Read a menu? Talk to a waiter or waitress? Did he eat? What? Did he pay for it? We answer such questions readily by using our knowledge of prototypical events in the restaurant script. Schank and his associates (1975) have written a program, SAM, that uses scripts to fill in the connections missing between the stated lines in such texts. Experiments by G. H. Bower, Black, and Turner (1979) found that in remembering such script-based stories, people were particularly prone to recall those events of the script that were not stated but were strongly implied by the script-events that were stated in the text. For example, in reference to our earlier text, you might believe after a few minutes that the text stated that John ate lasagna or that he paid the bill. Thus, there is clear psychological evidence for the filling-in processes postulated by SAM.

In a related development, Lehnert (1978), a colleague of Schank's, wrote a sophisticated question-answering program that was adept at giving humanlike answers to queries about script-based vignettes such as the John-ordering-lasagna one above. Lehnert's program first analyzes the question into one of six categories, and then calls up different algorithms for memory search and answer construction depending on the type of question. Thus, simple WHY questions about actions are often answered by looking up the stereotyped subgoal served by that action in the script: for instance, "WHY did John read the menu? Because he wanted to order."

Several of Lehnert's answer methods are very ingenious. One is the notion of a *ghost path* of what might have happened, since later questions often refer to this. Suppose we altered our former vignette so that after John ordered lasagna he was told that there was none left; instead, he ordered veal scallopini. The order-lasagna-then-fail-then-reorder-veal is what Lehnert calls an "interruption-resolution" pair. Whenever one is encountered in the story, the program constructs a hypothetical sequence (or ghost path) of events that normally would have occurred had the interruption not occurred. In the present case, this ghost path would contain events like John's getting and eating lasagna. Later, we ask Lehnert's program "How come John didn't eat lasagna?" The event of the question is not to be found in the computer's memory of the actual event chain, but "John eats lasagna" is matched in the ghost path generated from the interruption point. When this match is found, the program backs up to the interruption that created this ghost path and gives that as an answer. In this case, the answer is "Because the restaurant was all out of lasagna, he ordered veal scallopini." This is approximately the answer that people give to such questions about failed expectations. Lehnert's program matches characteristics of human question answering in many respects, and is an achievement in the simulation of natural language processing.

The reader should not misunderstand the goals of projects like Schank's SAM or Lehnert's question answerer. They are interested in people's general capabilities of filling out text with underlying inferences about situations, and their abilities in interpreting questions, and finding or deducing answers. They believe that the best research strategy for testing their general ideas is to model understanding and question answering in a very restricted domain such as restaurants, bus rides, car accidents, diplomatic visits, terrorist acts, or whatever. The restaurant script is a sort of toy world or microcosm for experimenting with ideas

about how to build humanlike understanding systems. Such a research strategy is familiar in other sciences (such as the geneticists' efforts with the genes of flies or intestinal bacteria), where a few convenient preparations are investigated intensively on the premise that the results will generalize to a wide range of cases. Thus, in discussing how SAM knows that "John ate the lasagna," we are at the same time discussing general mechanisms for solving one of cognitive psychology's most significant goals—the construction of a model of human understanding.

DISCUSSION AND EVALUATION

Now that we have described several information-processing models that have relevance to behavior theory, it may be helpful to discuss some of the advantages and accomplishments of this approach as well as a few of the problems connected with it. We take up the latter first, since we prefer to end the section in a positive, forward-looking vein. The main problems are those of communication and evaluating goodness of fit.

The Communication Problem

The gap in communication between computer simulators and experimental psychologists is serious, but it is one which seems to be closing over time. Despite the obvious contributions of the developments in computer simulation, psychologists have been slow to adopt the techniques of simulation placed at their disposal. One obvious reason for the communication gap has to do with the differing backgrounds, skills, and languages of experimental psychologists and computer scientists. Simulation programs are comprised of exceedingly long sequences of instructions, with an almost dumbfounding welter of complex details. These programs are all wrapped up and coded in a special language adapted to communication with a computer, not with a psychologist who understands nothing of LISP. As W. R. Reitman notes:

> . . . [T]he description of a recent version of the Newell, Shaw, and Simon General Problem-Solving program (GPS) runs to more than 100 pages and even so covers only the main details of the system. Furthermore, the discussion assumes a knowledge of an earlier basic paper on GPS and a knowledge of Information Processing Language V (IPL-V), the computer language in which it is written. Finally, the appendix, which simply *names* the routines and structures employed, takes another 25 pages. Unless one is familiar with similar systems, a thorough grasp of the dynamic properties of so complex a model almost certainly presupposes experience with the running program and its output (1964, p. 4).

Acquiring facility with one or more of the list-processing languages is difficult and time-consuming, especially so for older scientists who are very pressed for time by their usual research commitments. In place of a prolonged apprenticeship with a model's program and the computer, the ordinary experimentalist is dependent upon an intermediary to interpret the program for him. Because of the incompleteness of an "outsider's" knowledge of the program, he is unsure what the psychological assumptions in the theory are, or fails to grasp the importance and critical nature of one or another feature in the overall performance, such as the way a particular subroutine is coded.

But these problems are apparently being alleviated over the years, and for three reasons. First, new generations of graduate students in psychology are being trained in computer science, so that they can write simulation programs and understand those written by others. Second, the simulation theorists themselves (e.g., Gregg & Simon, 1967) have been rather vocal on the point that most simulation models are basically very simple in character, and that their length results only from necessary but psychologically irrelevant instructions for "housekeeping." Going along with this approach, published articles announcing new simulation programs frequently contain large sections flow-charting and describing the strategies, processes, and their basic operation, all in terms comprehensible to any psychologist. In principle, such program descriptions could be translated into a running program by any experienced programmer. A third reason for the narrowing of the communications gap is that the concepts and metaphors of information processing have by now thoroughly infused theoretical psychology, and have even become familiar pieces of jargon (see, for example, J. R. Anderson & Bower, 1973; P. H. Lindsay & Norman, 1972). The information-processing language—of programs, subroutines, conditional decisions, recursive subproblems and subgoals, searching through locations, associative memories—has been largely taken over, especially by cognitive psychologists, as an analogy to the way the mind works. Because psychological theories are increasingly being formulated in the idiom of information processing, the description of simulation programs is now in a vocabulary familiar and comprehensible to psychologists. Perhaps more than any other indicator, this wholesale adoption of information-processing metaphors within theoretical psychology reflects the major impact of the computer simulation movement.

Evaluating Goodness of Fit

The other major problem associated with computer *simulation* theories (which purport to be models of humans) lies in evaluating the goodness of fit of the model to the data. First, for the complex models such as GPS or EPAM, practically no *general* theorems can be proved regarding specific features of their behavior in particular situations. They differ in this regard from mathematical theories (at least those where explicit solutions can be obtained). Such general theorems are usually explicit equations of the form: "if the data statistics x_1, x_2, have known values, then the data statistics x_3 and x_4 should have the values $x_3 = f_1(x_1, x_2)$ and $x_4 = f_2(x_1, x_2)$." In the case of most information-processing theories, the results of a single simulation run may be relatively uninformative about the *general* characteristics of the behavior the program can display. Hence, many simulation runs must be made, usually under slightly varying circumstances or model parameters, in the hope that one can infer some general properties of the behavior it exhibits by examining this sample of results. Newell and Simon note the issue as follows:

> . . . [W]e can study the model empirically, exploring its behavior under variations of parameters and so on. But to date there is no body of theorems and general means of inference that allow us to derive general properties of the program given in symbolic form. Almost no interesting theorems, in the accepted mathematical sense of the word, have ever been proved about particular programs (1963, p. 375).

The accumulation of knowledge about a program's specific capabilities by this method is often slow. In consequence of this slow accumulation the theorist often cannot answer specific questions about her model until she has run her program under just those specific conditions. Thus, information feedback to the questioning experimentalist is often much delayed.

In lieu of general theorems, there are two favored methods for testing the validity of a simulation model of problem-solving. One is by getting the program to "handle" a number of *special cases* satisfactorily, much as Winograd's program correctly resolves particular referents for *it* or *one* in specific discourse contexts. Another favored testing method is to directly compare the step-by-step statements of the subject while thinking aloud and the cor-

responding "reasonings" produced by the computer program. Comparison with a single computer trace from the program will obviously not do if the program involves many probabilistic elements and, as a consequence, displays quite variable behavior over different runs. However, in the programs employing this "protocol-fitting" method (Feldman's binary choice machine and GPS), few or no probabilistic elements are involved; the same trace, therefore, is always obtained, given the same starting state and sequence of experimental events.

Despite its several advantages, the thinking-aloud technique also has some drawbacks. Often the subject's remarks have to be edited, "content analyzed," and coded in terms comparable to the computer's trace. Also, it must be assumed that the subject skips over or omits telling us about a number of processes that he must be running through. But which ones? It may be plausibly argued that the format and content of the subject's thinking-aloud statements are determined in part by incidental, selective reinforcements by the experimenter. For example, in one published protocol (Feldman, 1961), it would appear that during the early trials the subject was learning what kinds of thinking-aloud statements were acceptable to the experimenter. The effect of casual reinforcement (through facial expression, tone of voice, and so on) upon behavior in such ambiguous situations is well established (see Krasner, 1958). If pressed, an S-R theorist might argue that the content of the thinking-aloud statements could be considered as rationalizations of the more primitive effects of automatic selection of responses according to habits (productions?) established by past experience. Of relevance here is a disturbing experiment by Verplanck (1962) showing that by subtly reinforcing a subject's motor responses and the content of his verbal rationalizing of them, these two responses could be shaped almost independently of each other, even to the point of putting them entirely out of phase.

Skinner (1969) provides an illuminating perspective on several processes in problem-solving, including the person's ability (or inability) to verbalize all the steps he is "thinking through." Skinner also makes a very useful distinction between "rule-governed" behavior, which is mediated by explicit (verbalizable) rules, and behavior shaped by a long history of reinforcement contingencies which may be "unconscious, automatic, and unverbalizable." An example is the oft-cited discrepancy between the way grand masters actually play chess and the way they say that they do it; a program based on their prescriptions alone would be very amateurish. As has become obvious in later studies (e.g., Chase & Simon, 1973), chess masters have stored a vast fund of unverbalizable "situation-action" knowledge that they have accumulated in playing thousands of chess games. The older game-playing programs had largely rule-governed processes of search and evaluation, and little of significant pattern recognition. However, in principle, nothing prevents adding a large chess-pattern memory to the chess-playing programs (Simon & Barenfeld, 1969), much as Samuels did with his checkers program.

Ericson and Simon (1978) have presented a useful analysis of the validity of thinking-aloud protocols (which incidentally was a procedure recommended by John Watson), the inferences they warrant, and the way they are used to test simulation theories of cognitive processes. These researchers distinguish the several types of introspective reports in use according to *when* the report on the target mental activities occurs (either during, soon after, or a long time after the mental activity) and the *specificity* of instructions regarding what exactly the subject is to report (for example, give a "moment-by-moment account" versus a "general summary" of your activities). They point out that introspective reports of what

the subject is attending to or what rule she is using are very accurate when taken at the time, whereas later "retrospection" relying on memory creates difficulties. Ericson and Simon also argue that in using thinking-aloud protocols to test a simulation theory (say, of proving theorems in logic), the theorist uses the introspective report as an indicator of what problem-step (or statement) is in the subject's current focus of attention, but that the subject's comments do not explicitly contain the causes of this thought. We may think of thought as a sequence of jumps like a child hopping across a brook on dry stones; by analogy, the thinker can report her overall goal and subgoals and describe the "stone" she has just stepped on, though she may be rather inaccurate about (or simply unaware of) the processes that underlay why she took this exact step at this time. Ericson and Simon argue that a simulation theory can be validly tested by noting only the problem-states the person enters (analogously, the stones she landed on), disregarding her inability to comment validly upon why particular steps were taken. The problem-solving theory does explain those steps, but we do not require that the subject be able to report the causal mechanisms for her moves.

On the surface, the problem of validating a simulation theory would seem less severe with language processors: a program either parses a sentence correctly or not, finds a proper referent for a pronoun or not, answers a question properly or not. If it fails any one test, it requires modification. But the matter becomes sticky when it is realized that the programs by necessity must deal with a small but representative sample of words and limited syntactic input constructions. It is not a valid objection to show that the program fails to deal with sentences that use words it has not been taught, since that objection is easily overcome by adding to the program's vocabulary. Usually language programs are written to deal with sentences of certain syntactic types, and exemplars of those types may be used repeatedly in developing the program. The fact that the final program deals with just those examples is of little interest; rather some class of generalization tests or cases must be presented to allow the reader to evaluate the power and range of syntactic or semantic variants the language-understanding program can deal with.

Accepting the several methods of testing simulation models, a common feature is that the model is typically compared with the protocols of only one or two suitably selected subjects (usually bright, articulate ones). The program may in fact be written after the fact to simulate one particular subject's problem-solving protocol; and the model usually differs in small details when fitting it to different individuals. The argument is that individuals really differ, often considerably, and only invalid conclusions can issue from ignoring this fact. In constructing a model, one puts in various general processes or assumptions but then leaves it open with respect to a fringe of possible specific processes or their parameters which may be altered to model a particular subject. Hopefully, only these fringe processes will have to be changed to make the model fit other subjects. In a way analogous to factor analysis, the worth of the modeling enterprise depends on the weight of the common factors (general processes) relative to the specific or unique factors which are altered to produce the fits with different subjects. At present, the theorists have to admit that these relative weights are unknown.

Advantages in Simulation

Let us conclude this section by mentioning a few of the accomplishments, benefits, and advantages of the simulation approach. First of all, the simulation approach has been a strong antidote to the predomi-

nately analytic trend that has generally characterized experimental psychology. The job of a scientist is only half done when he has carried through a thorough, analytic breakdown of a behavioral phenomenon. An equally important, and often neglected, part of his job is to show how to reconstruct or synthesize the behavior from his analytic units. If the behavior is complex, then there is all the more reason to demand a synthesis (a model) that can be proven sufficient unto the phenomena it purports to explain. The computer is a tool for helping us prove that our theory specifies enough parts, together with sufficient detail concerning their exact rules of operation to make it behave. There can be no hidden or implicit assumptions in the model; if it is not explicitly written in the program, the computer prints back "Garbage!" and throws you off, a sobering lesson in the necessity of explicitness and completeness. Theorists find programming their theory of a phenomenon a revealing exercise; it often brings forth several aspects of the program they had not considered, or that are soon proven not to be workable.

A second point that we have learned is that the higher mental processes are neither so mysterious nor so complicated as to defy exact modeling, as had been formerly believed. Newell and Simon state this conclusion clearly:

> The first thing we have learned—and the evidence is by now quite substantial—is that we can explain many of the processes of human thinking without postulating mechanisms at subconscious levels which are different from those that are partly conscious and partly verbalized. The processes of problem solving, it is turning out, are the familiar processes of noticing, searching, modifying the search direction on the basis of clues and so on. The same symbol-manipulating processes that participate in these functions are also sufficient for such problem-solving techniques as abstracting and using imagery. It looks more and more as if problem solving is accomplished through complex structures of familiar simple elements. The growing proof is that we

can simulate problem solving in a number of situations using no more than these simple elements as the building blocks of our programs (1963, p. 402).

The general position that problem-solving involves organized sequences of only elementary processes is not itself a testable proposition. Rather, it is an orientation or strategy for undertaking the theory-constructing enterprise. In one sense, it is true that every complex process is eventually understood in terms of sequences of elementary (familiar) operations. So this position really reflects a confidence that the higher mental processes will eventually be understood by the rational methods of science.

A third benefit, as mentioned before, is that the computer and information processing are providing exceedingly alluring metaphors and analogies for psychological interpretations (see Newell, 1970). Programmed machines are said to detect, identify, compare, and classify stimuli; to store and retrieve information; to learn and to answer questions; to think, solve problems, and decide which strategies to use, and so on. Because we can see mechanically how these processes are carried out in a computer program, we are lured into believing (a) that these terms have lost their mentalistic cast, and (b) that we now understand how real organisms do the things to which we give the same names. The first belief is undeniably valid, and it accounts for information-processing concepts being the accepted vernacular within modern cognitive psychology, totally replacing the stimulus-response terminology which formerly dominated discussions in experimental psychology. We will describe this influence in the following chapter on contemporary cognitive psychology. Whether such information-processing analogies produce real understanding is a matter over which there is still lively debate. (Some of this debate arises from differing perspectives on what it means to "scientifically understand"

some phenomenon.) For example, a theorist like Skinner claims that the "Inside Story" of computer simulation tells us

> nothing new about behavior. Only when we know what a man actually does can we be sure that we have simulated his behavior. The Outside Story must be told first (1969, p. 295).

Skinner has some extreme views on what scientific understanding consists of. The alternative viewpoint, that situation-action correlations are only to be understood by rational theories about hypothetical information processing internal to the organism, is clearly the dominating theme in cognitive psychology. This shift in the paradigm of theoretical psychology was noted (and encouraged) in an overview by Newell (1970) on the relations between research in experimental psychology and artificial intelligence. He claims that computer simulation is just one way of doing theoretical psychology. After reviewing a number of uses of symbolic models in experimental psychology, he suggests that "a shift in the Zeitgeist in psychology has taken place toward a view of man as information processor" (p. 376). Later he writes

> . . . [I]f one looks at where the excitement has been over the last ten years in psychology—the places where rapid growth is taking place and which people talk about when asked "what's new"—a substantial fraction of these turn out to be connected to this shift towards information-processing models (p. 378).

A fourth benefit of unusually great importance is that the work on simulation has brought the study and explanation of complex cognitive process within practicable reach. It has redressed the unbalanced trend of behaviorism toward the finer analysis and study of smaller units of behavior under artificial conditions. The argument had been that more complex behaviors—thinking, language, and problem-solving—could be more easily understood only after simple behaviors under especially simplified conditions were better understood (e.g., rote learning, rats learning mazes, and so on). After some 40 to 50 years without striking advances in our understanding of the capabilities of the human mind, this argument began to have a hollow ring. It is one that certainly causes disillusion and discouragement in many students upon their first contact with a formal course in psychology. But the computer simulation technology has given us a tool for dealing with complexity in our theories, and has provided new impetus to the study of man's capabilities for thought. At the conclusion of a review of papers on simulation theories, Shepard cogently remarks:

> . . . [T]he start that is so admirably exemplified by many of the papers assembled by Feigenbaum and Feldman establishes a new direction in which those who aspire to precise, rigorous formulations may still find their way back to the heart of psychology—to the study of those processes that make man unique among known physical systems. Owing to the great complexities inherent in the problem, progress is bound to be slow—perhaps painfully slow. But, unless the goal itself is relinquished, what other alternative do we have? (1964, p. 65).

SUPPLEMENTARY READINGS

The following texts provide useful summaries of research in artificial intelligence.

BODEN, M. H. (1977). *Artificial intelligence and natural man.*

FEIGENBAUM, E. A., & FELDMAN, J., eds. (1963). *Computers and thought.*

HUNT, E. B. (1975). *Artificial intelligence.*

MINSKY, M., ed. (1968). *Semantic information processing.*

NEWELL, A., & SIMON, H. A. (1972). *Human problem-solving.*

NILSSON, N. J. (1971). *Problem-solving methods in artificial intelligence.*

SCHANK, R., & COLBY, K. M., eds. (1973). *Computer models of thought and language.*

SIMON, H. A., & SIKLOSSY, L., eds. (1972). *Representation and meaning: Experiments with information-processing systems.*

WATERMAN, D. A., & HAYES-ROTH, F., eds. (1978). *Pattern-directed inference systems.*

WINSTON, P. H. (1977). *Artificial intelligence.*

I3

RECENT DEVELOPMENTS
IN COGNITIVE THEORIES

Contemporary psychology has witnessed an increasing convergence of the historically distinct theories of learning. In large part this is because the behaviorist movement has lost much of its revolutionary fervor, and it finds fewer vociferous advocates on the current scene. The behaviorists seem more willing to accept the phenomena of interest to cognitive psychologists, and willing to liberalize their theories to deal with sensory imagery, sensory-sensory conditioning, hypothesis learning, observational learning, decision-making, and biases in processing of information for learning.

The lines of demarcation between the historical positions have softened, faded, and become all but indistinguishable. The debates have subsided. Increasingly, experimentalists talk the same language and listen to one another. There is an increasing unity of language and understanding among experimentalists working on learning. It is not uncommon for an experimentalist to operate within many of what were formerly considered to be somewhat differing theoretical orientations, ranging from Hullian theory to computer simulation. Each empirical subarea has its special phenomena to captivate interest, and one can soon learn the necessary vocabulary of

concept equivalences to permit moving among subareas.

In this chapter we shall review a few of the prominent lines of recent research and theorizing that take a cognitive perspective on learning. The topics are a selected sample, and books on cognitive psychology (e.g., Glass et al., 1979; Neisser, 1967, 1976; Wickelgren, 1979a) may be consulted for fuller coverage. First we shall consider cognitive psychology's critique of S-R conditioning theory and its accounts of human memory. Then we shall take up a number of topics and theories in contemporary cognitive psychology.

CRITIQUE OF S-R CONDITIONING THEORY

In Chapter 9, we reviewed the work on sensory preconditioning and on cognitive maps (Menzel, 1978; Olton, 1979). According to those findings organisms acquire knowledge about spatial layouts and event regularities in their world that is apparently not reducible to stimulus-response bonds. The insistence that all knowledge is reducible to stimulus-response associations seems to have been a mistake promulgated by the earliest founders of behaviorist learning theory. In their zeal to be objective and to banish dreaded mentalistic "ideas" from psychological theorizing, the early behaviorists *operationalized* knowledge (the product of learning) in terms of behavioral responses. However, this identifies (confuses?) the knowledge a person has about some event with the performances (behaviors) he may use to indicate that knowledge. But we know that if I teach you a new fact (say, "The population of Chicago is now 3,400,-000"), you can demonstrate your knowledge of that fact or use it in many different ways, supporting many different performances. Yet, these responses per se bear no similarity to one another. The basic problem is that conceptual knowledge seems not to be reducible to specific responses to specific stimuli.

We have mentioned throughout this volume several of the criticisms of the S-R conditioning theory of behavior. It is appropriate to summarize these criticisms briefly here in one place. However, let us state the specific version of S-R theory we are criticizing. It has the following three assumptions:

A1. The only elements required in a psychological explanation can be put into one-to-one correspondence with potentially observable elements. These elements must be observable stimuli or responses, or must be derivable from them. (Examples of derivatives would be mediating responses, covert responses, response-produced stimuli, and the like.)

A2. The elements mentioned in assumption A1 become connected or associated if and only if they occur contiguously in objective time or space.

A3. All observable behavior can be explained by concatenating the associative links mentioned in assumption A2.

These three assumptions were dubbed the *Terminal Meta-Postulates* of S-R theory by Bever, Fodor, and Garrett (1968), and we will abbreviate them as TMP. While various subsidiary factors, such as drive level, incentive, and so on, are often conceptualized as affecting the "strength" of relevant S-R connections, the main theoretical entities that compose and make the behavior "go" are the S-R connections.

Refutations of the TMP. The TMP can be refuted. Basically, any human performance will refute the TMP if, to explain the performance, we must postulate internal control elements or storage elements that are neither stimuli nor responses. In this category is almost any performance controlled by "lengthy computations."

There are many such counterexamples. A simple one is this: people can learn to discriminate or generate symbol strings in which the first and last elements match. Thus, if we were restricted to letters, strings like *XX* or *XYX* or *XYZPX* would be positive instances, whereas *XY* or *XXY* or *XXXYXY* would not be. The rule is easily described, but how is successful performance to be characterized in S-R terms? The stimuli are letters, as are the responses. But how do we say in S-R terms that the first letter of the string must match its last? We clearly need the notion of an *abstract variable* as well as the ability to select out the first and last elements of a series. The rule could be stated something like this: "If first letter is variable U and last letter is variable V, and U = V, then it is a positive instance." In this rule, U denotes a dummy local variable that is to be filled in by (or bound to) the first letter on this trial, and then compared to the binding for the last letter on this trial. But the idea of a local variable like U or V is itself neither a stimulus nor a response, but rather a logical place-holder in a simple computation. Thus, performance exemplifying such a first-to-last matching rule violates the TMP.

Bever and associates (1968) and Anderson and Bower (1973) describe some stronger examples of human rule-governed performances that violate the TMP. An example is discrimination of *mirror-image* strings, wherein the person learns to categorize or generate symbol strings of any length depending on whether its last half is the mirror image of its first half (e.g., *abccba*). A human subject can be "programmed" to do this; given any short string, say *xyz*, she can repeat it from memory forwards and then backwards. A problem here is that introducing a symbol early in a positive string commits one to having its mate at an indefinitely later point in the sequence, and this commitment and others must be remembered as many intervening symbols are generated; however, with practice, subjects could generate extremely long strings. Mirror-image strings can be generated by a push-down stack memory, a device that stores symbols and retrieves them on a last in-first out principle. Thus, to generate *xdccdx,* the memory would generate an *x* and store a token of *x* on the stack, then generate a *d* and store a token of *d*, then generate a *c* and store a token of *c*, and finally empty the three tokens from the stack and thus generate the last three symbols in the order *cdx*. The entities and operations just described all violate parts of the TMP. For example, the *c* and *d* tokens stored in the push-down memory are not "responses" in the standard sense, since standard responses are discrete time-limited events, not internal representations that reside for indefinite periods on pushdown stacks in memory.

The mirror-image example simply highlights the difficulties that "remote contingencies" create for a surface-oriented view of sequential behavior. Of course, many rules of grammatical utterances (e.g., the sentence subject and verb must agree in number) require the speaker-hearer to keep track of just such remote dependencies. And to keep track of these seems to require that we postulate elements that are neither responses nor stimuli.

Types vs. tokens. A given element (*type*) may appear in many different contexts, each occurrence called a *token* of that type. Thus, the word "occurrence" has three tokens of the letter *c*, two *r*'s, two *e*'s, and so on. In order to represent patterns or series of recurring elements, our memory must be able to create an indefinite number of tokens to stand in for a type in a given context, with each token pointing to its parent type. Without such distinctions between different tokens of the same type, our memory would not be able to spell words like *door* or *titillate*, and would confuse different contexts using the same type. Figure 13.1 illustrates the problem. Suppose the person wants to remember the sequences red-blue-green and yellow-blue-brown. The problem with the associative diagram in Figure 13.1a is that it also generates incorrect strings like red-blue-brown. The lower diagram, Figure 13.1b, illustrates associations among tokens in which the first and second sequences use different tokens of the blue concept. This associative structure will now permit errorless serial performance.

Labeling of associative relations. People can quickly make specific associations to a stimulus word, such as *opposite of* X, an *instance of* Y, and so on. These would be aided if associations between concepts were labeled according to their type, and if this relation could direct the specific search for an answer. This conflicts with the traditional view, which allowed only unlabeled, homogenous associations.

The functional response unit. Behaviorists have a most difficult time specifying unambiguously the response unit that S-R theories should focus on. Even in the simple Skinner box, the response unit can be characterized at a molar level (key-pecking) or at a micromolar level (different momentary rates of interresponse times), or in terms of micromolecular muscle patterns, or in terms of sequences of patterns

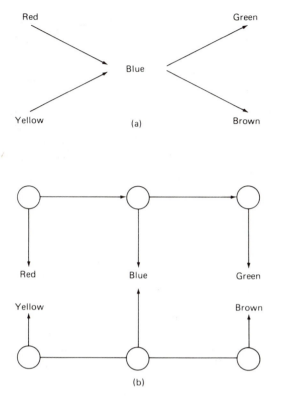

Figure 13.1. Associative diagrams to record two event series, red-blue-green and yellow-blue-brown. (A) This panel does not use the type-token distinction and so the two series will be confused. (B) This panel uses the type-token (circles) distinction, and so keeps separate records of the two contexts for the concept "blue."

of interresponse times (see Shimp, 1975). It seems the response is not such a theory-neutral datum.

Actions vs. responses. A long philosophical tradition (e.g., Goldman, 1970; Taylor, 1964) argues that the concept of a response (or reaction or movement) is a logical type that differs from the usual notions of *intentional action* by which laymen talk about behavior. This philosophical distinction parallels that between voluntary and involuntary responses, between willed and forced (or automatic) actions. The distinc-

tion is important because society does not hold people accountable for their involuntary responses as it does their voluntary ones. Similarly, verbal utterances like "My cat is calico colored" are never treated as reactions such as knee jerks or onion tears. Thus, it is senseless to ask whether a reaction is true or meaningful or pragmatically appropriate in a social setting, although we routinely ask this about verbal utterances. The argument is that we cannot properly characterize what someone is doing by referring only to her muscle movements. Rather, we commonly describe the apparent goal or intention of an action, and individual movements acquire their significance by virtue of their role in that plan. The reader might imagine describing (or listening to) the plays in a football game at a level of individual colorless movements versus intentional actions that fit into apparent plans. In contrast to S-R behaviorists, Tolman and the cognitive psychologists generally have sided with the laymen and philosophers on this issue, accepting the premise that intentional actions are the proper units of analysis for learning theory.

Problems with the law of effect. The law of effect has had a long, checkered career, and many of the controversies surrounding it were discussed in Chapters 2 and 9. For human learners, rewards apparently motivate performance; and they promote learning largely because they inform the subject about what she should attend to, rehearse, and learn (see research by Estes cited in Chapter 2). Thorndike's early viewpoint, that contingent rewards and punishers automatically and unconsciously strengthen or weaken responses, seems not to be true for human subjects. Humans learn few contingencies they remain unaware of (see Brewer, 1974); when contingencies have an impact on human behavior, the person usually figured them out and responded to get the rewards offered. Learning is more likely a conscious cognitive process than a direct unconscious process. On the other hand, once an emotional reaction has been strongly conditioned, a person's verbal description of it or realization of its senselessness may not diminish its arousal. Thus, a snake phobic may be unable to control his panic even though at the verbal level he "knows" the snake on his lap is harmless.

Problems with contiguity. The TMP assumes that elements may enter into association only if they occur contiguously in objective time and space. We are now aware of a large number of counter examples to this premise. First are the many demonstrations of belongingness in which elements appear objectively contiguous but are not associated because the "perceptual encoders" do not organize them together as a group. Second are the *blocking* and *overshadowing* results (Chapter 9) in which CS-US contiguity is not sufficient to create any association between them if the CS is presented only along with a stronger predictor of the US. Third, we now have many cases where two events that are not objectively contiguous nevertheless become associated because mental representations of them are brought together in "mental contiguity." One example of this is the conditioned bait shyness studied by Revusky and Garcia (1970), where the animal associates a novel taste with nausea that occurs several hours later. Analogous learning created by mental pairings of distant events has been studied in the human learning laboratory by Jacoby (1974). The reader should understand that the difficulties cited for the simple contiguity principle refer to assumption A2 of the TMP; they are also problems for an S-S or cognitive theory that used only A2 as its learning principle.

Need for higher-level nodes. In Chapter 6 we noted some alternative conceptions of associations that involve only basic ideas in horizontal connections, as opposed to abstract chunks of elements in vertical or hierarchical relationships. In building a memory system, the designer needs some economical way to refer to clusters of interrelated elements. This is achieved by chunk nodes (or patterns) that gather groups of base elements. Thus, in recording into memory the chunked series (ZPH) (BXT), it is convenient in theory to have a single memory unit that represents the whole string (S), units to represent the groups (G_1 and G_2), and then units to represent the letter-tokens themselves. Thus, the series would be represented hierarchically as $S \rightarrow (G_1, G_2)$, $G_1 \rightarrow (Z, P, H)$, $G_2 \rightarrow (B, X, T)$. Chunk nodes permit the memory system to treat these groups as units, recognize them when they occur in other contexts, output them as integrated units, and modify or expand upon them. Typically, more complex concepts (e.g., a *strike* in baseball) are built up out of relations among many simpler concepts (e.g., pitch, homeplate, height of the batter's knees, and so on). If all these are to be represented in a person's memory (since we do know and talk about such concepts), it is enormously economical to use a single unit (token) to refer to a complex concept (such as a pitch in baseball). But to do so requires that *vertical* associations to chunk nodes be permitted (see Figure 6.15) as well as *horizontal* associations between elementary ideas, objects, or properties.

This brief listing of some difficulties with an S-R conditioning theory of behavior is neither complete nor exhaustive (for more, see Anderson & Bower, 1973 or Brewer, 1974), but it exposes students to the historically important ones. We noted earlier also that S-R theory seemed unable to deal with elementary facts of human memory. Chomsky (1959) and others have argued forcibly that S-R theory is unable to handle the myriad regularities of our common abilities with language. For these reasons, many modern investigators of learning have abandoned a strict S-R conditioning theory, and have taken up either a very liberalized version of it (e.g., Bandura, 1971a, 1977a; Staats, 1968, 1975) or cognitive theory. In the following sections, we will discuss the major themes and orienting beliefs of modern cognitive psychology, paying particular attention to work on human memory.

COGNITIVE PSYCHOLOGY

Cognitive psychology is concerned with how organisms *cognize*—gain knowledge about—their world, and how they use that knowledge to guide decisions and perform effective actions. Cognitive psychologists try to understand the "mind" and its abilities or achievements in perception, learning, thinking, and language use. To this end, they postulate theories about its inner workings. Most cognitive psychologists follow the information-processing approach described in Chapter 12 and view the human brain as a kind of computer; like a computer, the mind has many distinct levels of organization (feature analyzers, pattern recognizers, sensory memories, conceptual memories), and at one level we can treat it as a symbol-manipulating system. A mental symbol system can internally represent the environment, construct patterns of symbols (e.g., propositions) of any complexity to represent scenes or events in the world, can store these symbol structures in memory with one or more designators, can retrieve a structure by use of a proper designator key, and can manipulate or transform these symbol structures in the activity we call thinking.

The basic components of an information-processing system are the *sensory receptors* that receive inputs from the environment, *effector units* that produce responses, a *memory store* that holds data structures or action programs, and a *central processor* wherein occur the major mental activities—thinking, judging, and making decisions.

A typical diagram of the human cognitive system is shown in Figure 13.2, with arrows between components suggesting the flow of information and control. The diagram is best understood by moving through it as though a stimulus were being learned or evaluated for some judgment. An environmental stimulus event is registered briefly in sensory buffers and then undergoes a recognition or classification procedure which attempts to match the input to known patterns (or rules) in memory or tries to describe the incoming pattern in terms of elementary concepts (e.g., "Here comes a man riding a bicycle"). If attention is directed to the event, then its internal description is kept active in short-term memory for a while. *Short-term memory* (STM) is the activated part of the concepts in memory, and it corresponds roughly to what we mean by consciousness (however, information can be in short-term memory and not be in consciousness). As the stimulus description enters STM, an active "program" deals with the event, perhaps by judging it, naming it, rehearsing it, or learning it if it is relevant and ignoring it if it is not.

The *working memory* on the right in Figure 13.2 maintains information about the local context, but this information is not in the focus of active memory nor in the distant recesses of long-term memory. The working memory builds up and maintains an internal model of the immediate environment as well as what has been happening over the past few minutes. This model is the framework within which the more rapid changes of the perceptual world before us are taking place, causing us to update our current model of the world around us.

The cognitive system developed in human history through evolution. But this development also occurs within each person's life; the cognitive system acts as an instrument of adjustment and as an aid in guiding purposeful action. Cognitive systems serve these purposes by acquiring information about the world, and then constructing action plans based on the contingencies in this information. These action plans are like computer programs that

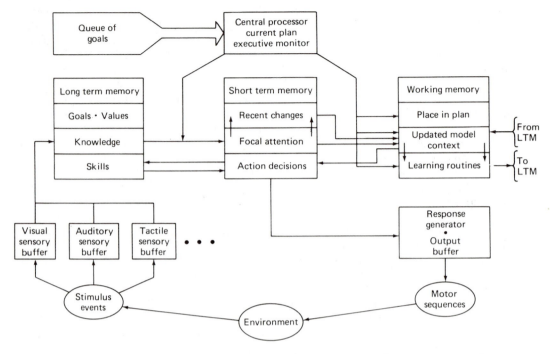

Figure 13.2. Diagram of the principal components of the perception and memory system. Arrows indicate the direction of information flow and control among the components. (From Bower, 1975.)

reside in memory and which can be called into working memory to guide the actions taken in response to the active contents of STM. Hence, the cognitive system is able to program itself to adapt and act successfully in its environment.

Information in Long-Term Memory

The *long-term memory* (LTM) is the repository of our more permanent knowledge and skills—it contains everything we know that is not currently in active memory. The information in LTM is of three kinds: sensory-perceptual knowledge, procedural-motoric knowledge, and propositional knowledge (or beliefs).

Sensory-perceptual knowledge. Sensory-perceptual knowledge is represented in analog form in our sensory information store. It is used in classifying sensory patterns and in storing memories of sensations of things. When these information structures are activated internally, they are responsible for the experience of generating images and of manipulating them in imagination. Along with images of objects, this store also holds cognitive maps of the layouts of objects in space for various locales.

Procedural-motoric knowledge. Procedural-motoric knowledge is knowledge of *how* to do something, from motor skills (bicycling) to intellectual skills (solving linear equations) to speech production. One approach represents these skills in memory in terms of a hierarchy of *productions* (rules). A production is like a generalized stimulus-response rule, only more powerful (see Chapter 12, p. 399). A production, symbolized as "conditions → actions," has one or more conditions that must be true of the contents of STM for it to be selected and executed. When a production is executed, one or more actions occur, and these may be either overt responses or internal ones such as continuing a mental calculation or retrieving something from LTM and making it active in STM.

A single production, as a condition → action pair, may be thought of as a simple instruction. Sequences of productions then are like stored computer programs that accomplish some result, such as searching the memory for an answer to some question, calculating the product of two double-digit numbers, memorizing a letter series, baking a cake, or whatever. Experimental instructions to human subjects can be thought of as causing the subject to create a sequence of productions that acts like an internal program enabling her to carry out the experimental task. The condition side of productions may refer either to sensory events (either afferent or efferent) or to ideas (patterns of active concepts) in STM. When executed, the production may then activate other ideas or transform those in consciousness. In this way, productions can be used to describe the flow of associated ideas through consciousness, either during goal-directed planning or during wish-fulfilling fantasies. Importantly, productions provide the *control structures* needed by any cognitive theory, since productions are responsible for carrying out successive moves or transformations in thinking, problem-solving, and planning. For example, the control structures oversee the planning process by monitoring its progress, deciding when to abandon one line and take up another, and so on. These decisions can be triggered by relatively simple conditions (e.g., too much time elapsed). Mechanisms for overseeing and guiding the operation of the cognitive system have traditionally not even been recognized, let alone spelled out in S-R theory. An attractive feature of

contemporary theories such as Anderson's (1976) ACT model is that it tries to stipulate the control processes in detail. In a human learning experiment, an example of a controlled process is the subject's selection of a memorizing strategy to use in solving the learning problem described to her by the experimenter.

Propositional beliefs. The third type of information in memory is declarative, including our beliefs about ourselves and our world, our knowledge of concepts and word meanings, our knowledge of general facts and of specific objects, events, and episodes. A *belief* is a proposition with a subjective truth value or credibility attached to it, such as "I believe that Buddha visited Persia." A *value proposition* involves a primitive predicate of the form "I value X," where X is a concept or a belief or possible state of affairs. Certain states of affairs become recurrently valued as a result of deprivation. In this way, biological motives enter the system.

In cognitive theories, propositional information is usually represented in terms of semantic (or conceptual) networks. A proposition states a relationship between preexisting concepts, such as "John kissed Mary" or "John bought a car." The premise in theories like ACT is that incoming stimulus events are analyzed by the perceptual system, which then delivers a propositional description of that input to memory. Thus, the "coin of the realm" going in and out of memory are propositions. Propositions are abstract, structured, and have a truth value. They can be represented in terms of networks of labeled associations among tokens of preexisting concepts. We will return to these semantic networks later in the chapter.

Learning Strategies as Procedures

Cognitive theories distinguish the passive recording part of memory from the active memorizing strategy the learner may be applying at the moment to deal with her experimental task, part of which may require that she record some materials into long-term memory. If the memory is a kind of library, passive memory is the actual placing of a new book onto the library shelf; the learning strategy would be analogous to the library's policy of handling and indexing new books for the card catalog before shelving them. The investigation of learning strategies is a relatively recent development (see O'Neil, 1978; and the discussion of mediated verbal learning in Chapter 6). When exposed to experimental materials, whether human subjects learn anything or if so, how much and what parts, can be shown to vary critically with the cognitive strategies they use in dealing with the materials. Some strategies (e.g., semantic elaboration of words) may produce large amounts of memory as an incidental by-product of the processing; other strategies may create relatively little memory regardless of the subject's intent to learn. Human beings may acquire a battery of different learning strategies or skills that they can apply as circumstances, motives, and materials require. Furthermore, there will probably be large differences in learning abilities among people, depending on the particular strategies or specific skills and knowledge they have acquired before they are compared on some test.

Memory Development in Childhood

Newborn infants demonstrate moderate memory for auditory, tactual, and crude visual patterns (as indicated by their later *lack* of interest in a familiar test pattern). From this starting point, learning abilities steadily increase throughout childhood. Developing memory ability has been investigated intensively by child psychologists (see Flavell, 1976) and has been well described in outline form. We will note a few of the main points.

First, memory improves because the conceptual system can "pull itself up by its bootstraps"; the more objects, patterns, concepts it recognizes as units in memory, the easier it is to learn new things about these concepts and relations among them, or to use them in new configurations. (Recall that a proposition is a new configuration of existing concepts.) The more concepts a child has, the more likely he is to understand new instances of any one concept and not be confused by events. Conceptual development occurs by specialization (or differentiation) of broad categories, and by generalizing over distinct subcategories. The richer, more differentiated a child's conceptual network, the more descriptors her brain automatically provides for new events fitting into known categories; this process results in more connections of the new event into preexisting concepts of memory. By hypothesis, such multiple connections should improve memory for events so connected. This unintentional "learning by understanding" goes on most of our conscious life, and it can be boosted by deliberate strategies. The processes just described are similar to Piaget's notions of assimilation and accommodation (Piaget, 1954).

In addition to this developing conceptual system, the child from 2 to 6 years of age appears to be acquiring concepts of time, the past, memory, forgetting, and his fallibility; during this time children also begin to acquire memory strategies for retaining important information. A child of about 3 to 4 probably does not understand the difference between instructions to look at something as opposed to memorize it. Only with experience does she come to understand that "memorize these pictures" means "do something with them now so that you will be able to reproduce their names later." As they mature, particularly as they enter formal schools, children acquire primitive learning methods, and then increasingly sophisticated ones. Some strategies that children use to remember the names of a collection of pictured objects might be as follows (in increasing sophistication):

1. Attend to the pictures one at a time. Stare at them.

2. Name each picture once as it is presented.

3. Name each picture singly and repeatedly.

4. Repeatedly name the pictures in sequence.

5. Group the pictures into similar categories (animals, toys, foods).

6. Visualize mental images of previously presented pictures.

7. Make up and rehearse meaningful sentences relating each picture to the one that follows it.

8. Make up an overall story that weaves through successive objects to be remembered.

Children who use more advanced strategies tend to remember more. Generally, older or more educated children use more advanced strategies. A child can improve her recall if she is taught a more sophisticated strategy and is induced to use it. Mentally retarded children use relatively primitive strategies and their performance can be improved by explicit training with more advanced learning methods. The techniques of mnemonic training for adults and the aged will be discussed later in this chapter.

Thus, children's memory improves in part probably because they acquire memorizing skills and learn which strategy should be selected for optimal results, depending on the materials and the criterion memory task. Along with these developing skills, Kreutzer, Leonard, and Flavell (1975) also found from interviews that children acquire increasingly sophisticated knowledge about memory (they call it *metamemory knowledge*)—about their own frailties, about immediate versus long-term memory, about what makes things hard to learn, which memory performances are difficult (e.g., verbatim vs. gist memory), and ways to learn, to test oneself, and uses of external reminder aids or stratagems (e.g., asking Mother to remind you). A fascinating ability that children develop in the 4-to-7 age range is discrimination of when something has or has not been learned well enough for later recall. At early ages, children grossly overestimate their up-coming memory performance on some study task and typically do not study nearly long enough to recall adequately. As they gain feedback from their successes or failures, they gradually come to use implicit self-testing to help them discriminate when they have learned enough to stop studying and are ready to be tested. This skill develops into adulthood so that we often have immediate "feelings" of knowing or not knowing the answer to some question, even before we have taken the time to search memory. In fact, Hart (1965) found that people could predict with fair accuracy whether they would be able to recognize an answer (to a question) that they had been unable to recall. This "feeling of knowing" of a blocked answer is rather like the familiar "tip of the tongue" experience (see Brown & McNeill, 1966).

The foregoing discussion has been a brief tour around the fringes of cognitive psychology's view of the mental apparatus, types of knowledge in memory, the distinction between control strategies versus the structural components of the mental apparatus, and the development of memory in children. We will return to several of the topics mentioned, and review some of the relevant ideas and data.

A MODEL OF SHORT-TERM MEMORY

For the past 20 years, a vast amount of empirical knowledge has accumulated from studies of immediate memory, where a human subject's recall of information is tested within a few seconds after he has studied it. If only one or two verbal items are involved, then he usually shows perfect immediate recall. Moreover, he will show perfect recall over an interval of 30 to 60 seconds, provided he is not distracted. But if he is distracted by some means—say, by having to respond to other material—then his ability to recall the first material drops off precipitously within the space of a few seconds. Such phenomena are familiar to most of us; after looking up a telephone number or street address, we forget it if something distracts us before we have written it down or used it. Figure 13.3 below shows some measurements of this effect in the laboratory. In this particular experiment by L. R. Peterson and M. J. Peterson (1959), the subject was briefly presented with a nonsense trigram (e.g., *CHQ*), and then was given an arithmetic problem (successively subtracting three from a random number) before being asked to recall the trigram. The curve shows the decreased probability that the trigram was correctly recalled after intervals of up to 16 seconds devoted to successive subtracting.

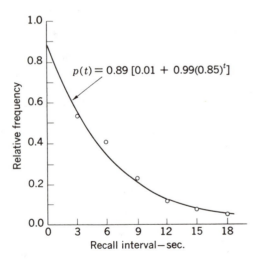

Figure 13.3. Percentage of correct recalls of a nonsense trigram after varying intervals of distraction by successively subtracting threes. The equation fit to the data points (open dots) is derived from Estes's stimulus fluctuation theory. (From Peterson and Peterson, 1959.)

Phenomena of this general type have stimulated much experimental research. In appearance, the findings seem to imply an STM of extreme fragility, lasting only a few seconds when distracting material is presented. But what is the functional use of this STM system in the overall economy of the mind? What relation does it have to our LTM? How are we to describe its operation? What are its laws? These and other questions have inspired some interesting theoretical conjectures and a spate of experimentation.

With a growing body of systematic results, it was not long before theories were put forth to explain the results. The alternative and predominant approach has been to treat STM as a separate memory store, or information-holder, distinct from LTM. The early formulations of this two-store model were by Broadbent (1957), Waugh and Norman (1965), and G. H. Bower (1967a). The most extensive and systematic statement of what was to become the standard "dual-memory" theory was given by Atkinson and Shiffrin (1965, 1968).

Figure 13.4 shows a simplified block diagram of the memory stores assumed in the Atkinson-Shiffrin buffer model. (It is just a slight variant of the system diagrammed in Figure 13.2.) A stimulus item input to the perceptual system is first analyzed, then identified, and if attended to (by the control processes), an internal code for it is entered into the active STM. The STM is of limited capacity, holding at most only a few items of information. If the items in STM are to be retained, the control processes initiate some sort of mnemonic activity such as rehearsal. For verbal materials, such rehearsals doubtless consist of subvocally going over the names of the items refreshing their activation in STM. In addition, it is usually assumed that each rehearsal cycle may transfer into more permanent LTM information about the item's presence on the list to be memorized. The STM can be thought of either

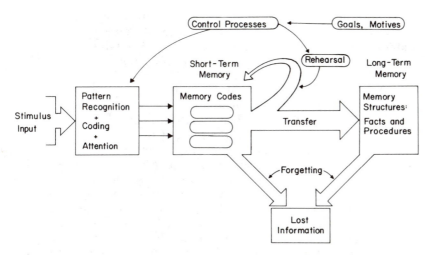

Figure 13.4. Diagram of storage components and control processes that are commonly assumed in modern theories of memory. See text for explanation.

as the set of rehearsal-activated nodes in memory or as a place in which occurs active, subvocal rehearsal of the material; because this going-over of material takes time and the STM has a limited capacity, there may only be time enough to go over a few items (say, three or four words) before the next items arrive to be dealt with. A distracting task like doing arithmetic requires attention and also enters new material into STM, thus limiting the amount of processing effort left over for rehearsal of the previous material to be remembered.

Thus, a to-be-remembered (TBR) item eventually becomes replaced or lost from the STM because the STM must deal with newly arriving information. The greater the demands of the interpolated task (e.g., the greater its difficulty), the more attention it takes away from rehearsal, and the sooner the TBR material will be removed from STM. In circumstances involving homogeneous interpolated material, it is commonly supposed that each interpolated item (e.g., each successive step in subtracting by threes) has some fixed probability of

causing an item in STM to be displaced or removed from STM. This formulation leads to an exponential loss of items from STM as time passes or more distraction occurs.

This picture of learning and forgetting is somewhat like a customer service queue (see G. H. Bower, 1967a; J. S. Reitman, 1971). Customers, representing TBR items, arrive periodically at the service counter and demand immediate service from a limited supply of clerks (rehearsal slots). An early customer may have his service interrupted if a new customer arrives before his service has been completed, and his server (rehearsal slot) is elected to take care of the new arrival. A customer who receives satisfactory service corresponds to an item that has been transferred to LTM before being bumped out of STM. A customer whose service is interrupted is presumed to leave dissatisfied; this event corresponds to an item in the model that is bumped out of STM before sufficient information about it can be transferred to LTM, so relatively little will be learned about it.

This sketch assumes forgetting from

STM proceeds primarily by displacement. But this view needs correcting on two counts. First, the probability that an item in STM will be disrupted by an interpolated item increases the greater the similarity of the two. Second, even without further inputs, if a person's attention can be diverted elsewhere, old items in STM seem to fade in strength to some degree.

To illustrate the operation of STM in concrete terms, let us follow through an illustrative example. (1) Visual presentation of the letter *L* in a letter list to be memorized in serial order would be identified as a familiar letter (pattern) and be coded if possible as the vocal name *ell;* (2) this pronunciation code, *ell*, would be rehearsed subvocally in STM along with several other letter items from the input list to be memorized; and (3) the memory structure established in LTM might be a factual proposition of the form *"L* was presented in the most recent list." To the extent that this structure is successfully built up, it is retrieved and used when the experimenter later asks the subject to name the letters presented on the most recent list he had studied. So much for the preliminaries. Let us now go somewhat deeper into the details and the research surrounding them.

Coding. The memory code is the temporary "name" or internal representation assigned to the stimulus item and deposited in STM. For vocal subjects dealing with verbal materials, this is most often the sound of the name of the stimulus or of a verbal description of it or (if it is a familiar picture) a label for it. The effect of this vocal naming is to convert a visual stimulus into an internal articulatory form. The number of items that can be rehearsed in STM is greater for letters that can be spoken quickly, and greater for fast talkers. If, however, the speech apparatus is otherwise engaged or inoperative at the time the stimulus to be remembered is visually presented, then this visual-to-articulatory conversion cannot occur and the presented stimulus appears to be retained in terms of its physical (visual) properties. As a second example of nonverbal coding, deaf persons dependent on manual sign language will use manual coding when they are to remember visually presented letters. In any event, the form of this internal representation of a target item determines (1) what other kinds of materials will interfere with or cause forgetting of the target, and (2) the kinds of confusion errors the person will make when he misremembers the target item. If he has coded an item according to its sound, then sound-alike materials will interfere and errors in recall are likely to sound like the target (e.g., he will recall *T* when it should have been *P* or *V* or *B*). If articulatory coding is prevented so that the person is forced to encode visually presented letters in terms of their visual characteristics (Kroll et al., 1970; Salzberg et al., 1971), then greatest interference is caused by interpolated material that is visually similar to the item to be remembered (e.g., *R* is visually but not acoustically similar to *P*). In like manner, for deaf persons using manual signs to encode items to be remembered, greatest interference will come from interpolated materials that involve signs that are manually similar to the item to be remembered (Locke & Locke, 1971).

The memory codes in STM are quickly available to retrieval. This quick retrieval from STM is studied in the task devised by Sternberg (1969, see Chapter 12). The subject hears a small set of one to six "target" items to place in her STM, and then hears a "probe" item; she is to decide whether the probe matches one of the target items. It is presumed that in this task the subject stores in STM the codes of the target items, and then, when the probe occurs, scans for a code that matches it. In this view, reaction time for probes will increase linearly with the number of items in the memory list (provided the list is shorter than STM capacity), and this is the standard finding. The more complex the items (e.g., nonsense syllables rather than letters), the more "space" they take up in the limited-capacity STM, requiring the overflow from big lists to be retrieved from LTM, all making for slower reaction time in the Sternberg task (Cavanaugh, 1972).

Intentional forgetting. If a person wants to forget something in STM—or rather, wants not to remember it—he has merely to stop rehearsing it and its memory code will fade away. A number of studies have been done on this "directed forgetting," and the procedure works rather well (see Bjork, 1970; Epstein, 1972). For example, in a free-recall situation in which single words are presented every 2 seconds to be learned, with the whole list to be recalled later, the person may be informed at some point during input that he is not responsible for the earlier items (he can "forget" them) and will have to recall only those that will follow (Bruce & Papay, 1970). A variety of follow-up tests, among which is an unexpected request for the subject to now try to recall items he was told earlier to forget, suggest that the "forget cue" is a signal to the subject to dump out of STM (to stop rehearsing) all those items he does not have to remember, so that they receive less total rehearsal and are therefore learned less than they normally would have been. The subject is able to edit his recall for only those items that occurred after (rather than before) the "forget" cue. Moreover, the data suggest that when recalling the terminal sublist, the subject can "set aside" the memory traces of those earlier items so that they do not compete with the items to be recalled.

Surprising events. Another way to cause forgetting of an item or an input series (for free recall) is to follow it with a high-priority item to which the subject can be expected to pay special attention. The high-priority item preempts storage space in STM, with the result that later items in the list (1) are somewhat less likely to be entered into STM, and (2) if entered, are likely to bump out the earlier memory codes of lesser priority—namely, those that entered just before the high-priority item. Experiments by Ellis et al. (1971) show both such decremental effects on recall of the immediately preceding (and several following) names of common object pictures in a list in which the special high-priority item was a photograph of a nude. Their results are shown in Figure 13.5, the critical item is recalled much above normal, while items immediately before and after it are depressed in recall. Tulving (1969) observed only a prior item decrement by putting into a list of unrelated words to be remembered the name of a famous person which the subject had been especially urged to recall. These effects may be interpreted as resulting from either rehearsal prevention or rehearsal enhancement. Monetary payoffs yield similar effects; if the person is told during study of an item that its later recall will be worth a lot of money, he will concentrate harder (rehearse more, maintain that item in STM for a longer time) and remember it better. The payoff affects the assignment of a priority and amount of rehearsal to the item, and that rehearsal in turn affects the strength of its memory trace laid down (see, for example, Atkinson & Wickens, 1971; Loftus, 1972).

Overt rehearsal. We have implied that various mnemonic effects are due to differential rehearsal of the appropriate material. A simple way to operationalize rehearsal processes is to have the subject "think aloud" as she is studying the list (Rundus & Atkinson, 1970; Rundus, 1971). If the subject is presented with a list of 20 unrelated words which she is to free-recall, and if the items occur singly at a leisurely 5-second rate, her moment-by-moment rehearsals might look like the protocol in

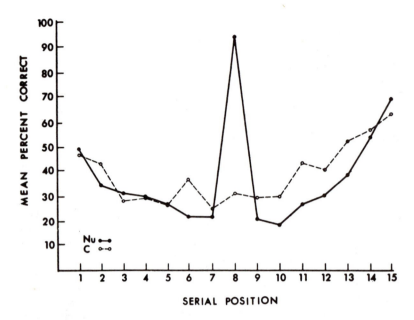

Figure 13.5. Percentage recall of names of pictures according to their serial position in the list. The "critical" list (solid curve) contained a photograph of a nude in serial position 8, whereas the "noncritical" list (dashed curve) used only the familiar, unemotional pictures. (From Ellis et al., 1971.)

Table 13.1. During each 5-second interval, she is overtly rehearsing about four tokens (covert rehearsal could be much faster). As each new word occurs, it is entered into the ongoing rehearsal set, others are dropped, and earlier ones may be picked up again in later rehearsals. Of the many descriptions one might give of such a protocol, perhaps the simplest statistic is just the number of times a given item (say the k-th item in the list) receives a rehearsal. Thus, in the hypothetical protocol in Table 13.1, the item that occurred in the first position (*dog*) received 8 rehearsals, the second (*rug*) also received 8, the third (*book*) received 1, and so on.

The dashed curve in Figure 13.6 shows the average number of rehearsals received by each of the 20 successive items in a study list; this is averaged over 25 subjects, each performing 1 trial on 11 different free-recall lists. The values are given on the right-hand ordinate of the graph, and vary from

a mean of 12 rehearsals for the first item to 2 rehearsals for the twentieth and last. Immediately following presentation of the list of words, the subjects free-recalled as many of them as they could in any order they wanted. The probability of recall of the word in each serial input position is graphed in the solid line labeled $P(R)$.

Several features of this serial position curve can be noted. First, the last few items of the list are well recalled—a so-called recency effect—and the theory supposes that these most probably were in the twentieth rehearsal set (see Table 13.1) and were retrieved from STM when recall was requested. Second, the initial items in the list are better recalled than the middle items—a so-called primacy effect. Of interest here is the fact that the number of rehearsals of an item correlates with its probability of recall, at least for items up to about serial position 14 (STM enters to enhance recall of later items). This corre-

TABLE 13.1. Hypothetical Example of Overt Rehearsal of Items During Input of List for Free Recall; Procedure Devised by Rundus & Atkinson (1970).

Item Presented	Items Rehearsed (Rehearsal Set)
1. dog	dog, dog, dog
2. rug	rug[1], dog, rug[2], dog
3. book	book, rug[3], dog
4. pen	pen, pen, rug[4], dog
5. ship	ship, rug[5], pen, dog
6. wall	wall, rug[6], wall, rug[7]
7. key	key, ship, wall, rug[8]
8. bag	bag, key, ship, wall
. .	.
. .	.
. .	.
20. hair	hair, sock, paper, hair

lation is quite strong even if one considers only items whose last appearance in a rehearsal set was four to seven items back, before recall commenced.

The standard *two-store* interpretation of such results is that the earlier "primacy" items are well recalled because they have a high strength in LTM (due to their extra rehearsals), whereas the later "recency" items are well recalled because they are in STM. An implication is that recall of these recency items is more fragile, more easily disrupted. This is true; if a distracting arithmetic task is interpolated for 30 seconds between list input and recall, the items in STM are removed and the "recency effect" in recall is wiped out. But the level of the primary effect is not much disturbed

by such interpolation. A further implication comes from the slight downturn in the rehearsal curve for items at the end of the list. If these items have lesser strength in LTM due to the fewer rehearsals, then a similar downturn should be detected in long-delayed recall of such lists. Such a delayed recall downturn was found by Craik (1970). The contrast between poorer long-term recall but excellent immediate recall of end-of-list items dramatizes the dissociation expected by the STM-LTM models.

Two-Store Theory and Levels of Processing

The evidence favoring the two-store memory models has been reviewed by Atkinson & Shiffrin (1968, 1971) and Glanzer (1972). The general approach is bolstered by findings which suggest that some experimental variables may affect memories in one store but not those in another. By introducing "control processes" that affect mnemonic activities, the approach also has the flexibility to deal with a range of instructional, strategic, and motivational influences. In the ensuing years, however, the two-store model has come under increasing criticism and experimental attack; consequently, it has been modified to deal with new considerations. Let us review a few of these countering considerations.

First, the layout of the "boxes" in Figure 13.4 seems askew, inasmuch as it doesn't show that information in LTM is always used for pattern recognition during initial perception and coding; that is, the diagram in Figure 13.4 suggests that LTM is entered only much later. This has been handled by diagrams like the earlier Figure 13.2, where sensory information directly activates LTM; in this conception, STM is not a "place" distinct from LTM but rather just a state of heightened activation for those "idea nodes" in memory corresponding to the perceived categories of experience. Second, the Atkinson-Shiffrin theory was largely about the control of verbal rehearsal of

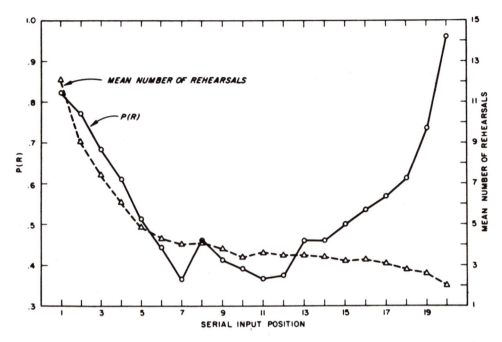

Figure 13.6. The mean probability of recall, P(R), and the mean number of rehearsals of an item as a function of its serial input position. (From Rundus, 1971.)

linguistic or nameable stimuli. It recognized that nonverbalizable stimuli leave behind traces that decay from STM, but it said little about these traces. Third, the STM-LTM models were for the most part relatively vague about what exactly was the "information" being transferred from STM into LTM. It could not be the presented word "dog," for example, since that is already known. Anderson and Bower (1973) argued that the information was best conceived as a proposition stipulating the context in which a familiar item occurred —e.g., The word "dog" occurred in the third position of the second list in this experiment." The STM-LTM theories were similarly vague about how newly arriving information in STM is first compared to that stored in LTM, so as to assess what is old, redundant, and can be ignored versus what is new, significant, and must be rehearsed and learned. This sifting and selec-

tion among the input elements to determine what is already known and what is new would seem to require much more interaction between the two memory stores than what is envisioned in the separate boxes of Figure 13.4.

Levels of processing. Perhaps the most serious challenge to the Atkinson-Shiffrin theory has come from the "levels of processing" framework proposed by Craik and Lockhart (1972; Craik, 1973). The basic idea is that STM or LTM result not so much from the "place" in the mind where an item is stored but rather from the *type of processing* it receives. This is diagrammed in Figure 13.7. Craik and Lockhart proposed that perceptual processing of a word like *dog* can be thought of as progressing through a series of stages, from the surface sensory features of the visual or auditory stimulus, to its pronunciation or

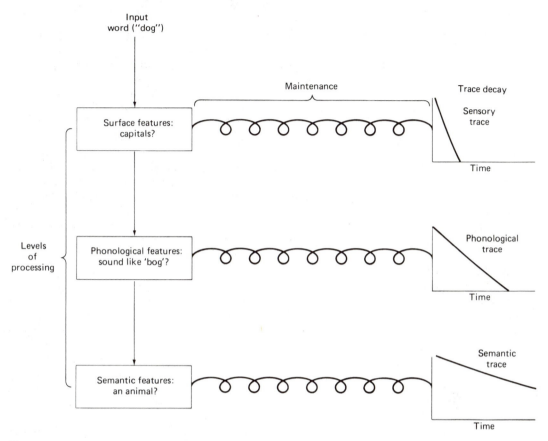

Figure 13.7. Illustration of three levels of processing of the word *dog*—visual, phonological, and semantic. The trace can be maintained at any given level. The memory trace established by superficial processing decays fastest (top right), whereas the trace from semantic processing decays slowest (bottom right).

sound, to its semantic or associative meaning. They proposed that a control process can be set to maintain processing at one exclusive level and prevent processing at a higher level. They further proposed that processing a word at a given level leaves behind a memory trace of that kind (sensory, phonological, or semantic), and that the rate of loss of a trace is slower the "deeper" or more semantic it is. These different decay rates for the three different memory levels are shown to the right in Figure 13.7.

Craik and Lockhart (1972) offered two forms of evidence for their point of view.

First, in diverse incidental learning experiments, it was demonstrated that subjects show better recall and recognition memory for a word the "deeper" the level of processing they are required to perform on it during the study trial. Thus, having the subject categorize a word semantically ("Is it a flower?") produces higher delayed recall than having him categorize its superficial visual properties ("Is it printed in capital letters?") or its phonological properties ("Does it rhyme with *bank*?").

The second sort of evidence cited by Craik and Lockhart tends to show that repetition of an item per se does not improve the memory of it so long as the repetition continues at the same depth of processing. This directly contradicts the earlier assumptions that verbal rehearsal alone caused information transfer to LTM. Craik and Lockhart distinguished two forms, *maintenance rehearsal,* which is superficial recycling of the material and does not promote LTM, and *elaborative rehearsal,* which promotes LTM by connecting the material-to-be-learned into existing associative structures in memory (via sentences or images). They conjectured that rehearsal time in the typical experiment promotes LTM only to the extent that it increasingly involves elaborate rehearsal.

Craik (1973) reviewed the evidence that variations in amount of maintenance rehearsal ("superficial sounding out") would not improve LTM for the words. A classic experiment of this kind was done by Woodward, Bjork, and Jongeward (1973). They presented single words in the context of a directed forgetting experiment. A word would be presented briefly and then, after an interval from 0 to 12 seconds, a green or red mark would occur, signalling subjects either to remember or to forget the word they had just studied. The subjects presumably maintain the word in a rehearsal state until this signal occurs. After such presentation of a short list of words, subjects would free-recall all the "remember" words in that list. After presentation of many such lists, subjects were unexpectedly asked to free-recall *all* the words from all the prior lists. The startling findings of the Woodward study was that free-recall probabilities of words were constant and independent of the delay time (rehearsal time) before the signal to remember or forget the word. "Remember" words were better retained than "forget" words, as expected, but the recall level in both cases was not affected by simple maintenance-time during study of an item. This kind of result—no effect on recall of phonological recycling

of a word—has been found repeatedly. A curious contrast in the Woodward et al. study was that performance did improve as a function of rehearsal interval when memory was tested by *recognition.* After the final free-recall test, the subjects were presented with a master list of words and had to check those that had been presented earlier. On this test their recognition of an item was better the longer had been its interval of maintenance rehearsal. Thus, although maintenance rehearsal did not help an item's free recall, it was contributing something to LTM to support recognition. This contrast has also been replicated in several experiments.

A possible interpretation of this contrast is provided by the theory of free recall and recognition memory proposed by Anderson and Bower (1972a). In that theory, recognition memory for an item depends upon the person establishing in LTM an association between the item and the idea of the experimental (list) context in which the item was presented. On the other hand, free recall of a set of items depends to a large extent upon the subject finding or establishing associations between items on the list, so that in recall the person can associate from one list item to the next. In these terms, maintenance rehearsal (recycling of a single word in a given context) will strengthen the word-to-context association, but not associations between list items. In fact, the single-item rehearsals prevent the subject from thinking about interitem connections needed for free recall. We know from other studies that free recall is greatly facilitated by instructing the subject to relate each item to as many others on the list as she can.

Criticisms of levels of processing. The levels of processing framework has itself come under increasing experimental and theoretical attack (see Baddeley, 1978; D. L. Nelson et al., 1979; T. O. Nelson, 1977). First, the notion of *depth of processing* has been attacked as too vague and circular, since there is no independent measure by which to order different processing tasks along the depth continuum. Second, it has been shown that a given orienting task (e.g., "What rhymes with this word?") does not restrict the memory trace of that item to that exclusive feature. For example, word pairs which are to be learned by imagery or semantic associations nonetheless will interfere with one another if they share common first letters or common sounds (see D. L. Nelson et al., 1979). Also, words encoded individually for rhyming sounds will nonetheless cluster in free recall by semantic categories—that is, the subject will recall from the list all words referring to animals, then foods, then vehicles, and so on. Third, it has been demonstrated empirically that repeated processing of an item at the same depth will improve its free recall if those repetitions occur at spaced intervals (T. O. Nelson, 1977). Craik has argued that the separate presentation of the same item and orienting task is not the same as maintenance rehearsal and, therefore, that the T. O. Nelson results are not relevant. However, the improvement in recognition memory in the Woodward (1973) study directly contradicts the idea that maintenance rehearsal leads to no learning. Fourth, whether a phonetic or semantic orienting task prepares the subject better for a later memory test depends on what the memory test is. For example, if the subject must estimate from memory how many words in the list rhymed with *bag, pen* and so on, she is considerably more accurate if she encoded the words in terms of their sounds rather than their meaning. So performance levels depend on whether the question on the memory test is compatible with the word attributes selected by the orienting task (see Morris, Bransford, & Franks, 1977).

Another serious problem is that within each of the levels identified by Craik and Lockhart (1972) an enormous variety of orienting tasks can be devised, and the levels idea by itself does not help in ordering their effect on memory. This issue has been pursued within the semantic level by Johnson-Laird and associates (1978) and B. H. Ross (in press). In the Johnson-Laird study, subjects classified each word in a list according to whether or not it had *all* three properties of being *liquid, consumable,* and *natural.* Thus, *cider* and *water* have all three properties, *beer* has two properties, *pie* has one of these properties, and *paper* has none. Later free recall of a word increased the greater the number of properties it had. The theory proposed by Ross for these and related results is that each semantic question the subject actively asks of the item provides a further association and retrieval route for its later recall. Ross also proposed that a true or false response to a question should *not* matter. Furthermore, during the orienting task, the subject goes through the property questions in order for each word and stops processing each word as soon as she can reach a decision on the overall question asked. Ross found, as had Johnson-Laird, that when the decision required was "*Yes if all* three properties," recall increased the greater the number of properties the word had. In addition, Ross found that if the decision was "*Yes if any* of the three properties," then recall was *poorer* the more properties the word had. Supposedly, for the *any* decision, the more true properties a word has, the sooner the questioning process stops and a decision is reached for that word; therefore fewer associations are established to support its later recall. Finally, if the subject is *forced* to indicate whether or not *each* property applies to the word, then her later recall is constant and independent of the number of positive properties the word has. Ross's findings support his hypothesis that it is the *total* number of decisions, and not just the number of *true* decisions, that is the crucial factor in these experiments. Thus, it appears that questions activate semantic associations—e.g., "*water* is *natural*"; and the several question properties are available in memory later to cue the subject to recall the list words, with more cues promoting more reliable recall. But in none of this theorizing has the levels of processing framework been of help.

These and other criticisms of the levels of processing framework have led to its gradual modification and elaboration to a point where it has disintegrated as a coherent theory (see the volume by Cermak & Craik, 1978). The facts uncovered within the levels framework are now being explained within the dual-memory framework by two factors: (1) the degree of elaboration of the to-be-remembered material (where "depth" is translated as "much semantic elaboration" of material); and (2) the correspondence between attributes emphasized during encoding and those helpful for answering the later memory test. These are familiar principles, and they are readily incorporated in the two-store memory models. Glanzer (1978), for instance, showed that results from the levels of processing experiments could be accommodated within a two-store theory like that of Atkinson and Shiffrin. As is often the case in psychology, criticisms of and challenges to a dominant theory lead to eventual counterarguments, refinements, and evolution of the dominant theory itself.

ORGANIZATION AND MEMORY

In reviewing Gestalt theory in Chapter 10, we discussed the role Gestalt theorists assigned to organization as a determinant of memory and recall. We reviewed several findings concerned with the coherence in memory of elements organized together by various conditions of grouping. The Gestalt view was that the perceptual or conceptual groupings of the material would become the "psychological units" in memory and recall.

This theme was echoed in a seminal paper by G. A. Miller (1956) in which he suggested, among other things, that immediate reproductive memory would be limited in terms of the number of chunks of elements rather than the number of single elements. Thus, a list of 7 two-syllable words is remembered just as well as one of 7 one-syllable words or of 7 single letters, because they are all treated as single units. The psychological unit is that amount of material which the person already knows (e.g., a word or cliché). The conjecture was that immediate recall was limited to about 7 or so chunks. The limit of 7 chunks is a statistical average, not an invariant number. In this view, a person learns a longer list—say of 14 unrelated words—by *organizing* the lower-order units into 7 or fewer higher-order units. Learning, then, was to be viewed as a matter of segregating, classifying, and grouping the elementary units into a smaller number of richer, more densely packed chunks.

This hypothesis, along with several others, motivated research on *free recall* and later on mnemonic devices. In free recall, as exemplified in the Rundus experiment reviewed above (see Figure 13.6), the subject is exposed to a list of words and then tries to recall as many of them as he can in any order. What is "free" about free recall is the order in which the person recalls the items from the set to be remembered. Such latitude permits us to attribute any systematic stereotypy and patterning of the subject's recall to the organizational processes the subject uses to learn the material. It may be noted that free recall does not obviously fit the standard stimulus-response paradigm, since there is no specific stimulus, only the unhelpful injunction from the experimenter to recall the word list just presented.

Starting with seminal papers by Bousfield (1953), Tulving (1962, 1966, 1968), and

G. Mandler (1967, 1968), free recall has been intensively studied as a test situation for revealing organizational processes in memory. A book edited by Tulving and Donaldson (1972) reviews and evaluates many branches on a large research tree regarding this topic. Investigations of free recall have shown repeatedly that subjects systematically group words together during recall despite the fact that these words were presented far apart during the input of the list. The subject's groupings most often tend to be on the basis of the words' similarity of meaning—i.e., their semantic associations. If the list is composed of words from several semantic categories (e.g., animals, cities, vegetables, cars), the words belonging to a given category will be especially likely to be grouped together during recall. On this hypothesis, the effect of repeated practice on a list of words is to increase the size and stability of these "subjective groups," which are sets comprised of several list words each. If the subject is forced to change his groupings every time he studies the list (by having him form mental images to represent varying quartets of list items), then improvement in his recall of that list is seriously retarded (see Bower, 1970b). It appears that interitem grouping of list words is both necessary and sufficient to promote free-recall learning: simple exposure to a list of words without instructions to learn promotes very little free recall (Tulving, 1966), whereas having the person simply sort the list words into categories on the basis of meaningful similarities promotes as good incidental recall later as when he is told to learn the words during sorting (G. Mandler, 1967). Such results suggest the view that learning is accomplished by *organizing* the materials.

As noted earlier, the *constant chunk hypothesis* is that average immediate recall cannot exceed a constant number of chunks (four to eight—the hypothetical number varies from one theorist to another). If the number of chunks becomes too large, they will have to be grouped in turn into a hierarchy of higher-order units. Figure 13.8 shows a hypothetical hierarchy of subjective units. The words of the list are indexed as W_1 through W_{27}. The nodes marked B_i are internal names, nodes, or codes in memory which stand for the word groups they dominate in the hierarchy; the A_i nodes stand for a collection of B_i nodes. This is the presumptive memory structure.

The important thing about such a hierarchy is that the top node can serve as the name held in STM for the complete information structure in LTM. Thus, list N could be retrieved by cueing the subject with "List N" (or having him cue himself); this cue can then be "associatively unpacked" in terms of chunks A_1, A_2, and A_3; the A_i can be unpacked in terms of the B_i, which then lead to generation of the words on the list. Johnson (1970) provides the most explicit model and tests of how a hierarchical memory structure could be retrieved. Johnson's tests involved *serial* recall of chunked (grouped) letter series, but his general model can be applied to unordered, free recall.

A hierarchy can be a powerful retrieval scheme, since it can readily span a number of elements (27 or 3^3 in the small hierarchy shown in Figure 13.8). Moreover, Bower and associates (1969) showed that free-recall subjects greatly benefited from having their word lists "preorganized" for them in a hierarchical fashion revealing the semantical hierarchies available in the carefully constructed word lists. The subjects appeared to use the hierarchical tree as a retrieval plan, starting at the top and unpacking successive levels in recursive fashion. Although these are interesting demonstrations of the power of hierarchical organizations in memory, they in no way prove that this is what subjects are in fact doing while they are learning lists of allegedly unrelated words. Regarding that issue, the jury is still out. Computer simulation

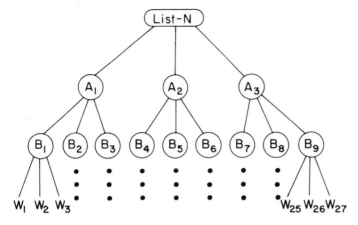

Figure 13.8. Illustrative hierarchy of higher-level chunks, encompassing into groups the 27 list words indexed $W_1, W_2, \ldots, W_{27}$. B_i indexes groups of W words; A_i indexes groups of B groups. The top node, List N, stands for the entire list in memory.

models of free recall (J. R. Anderson, 1972; Bower, 1972c) are explicitly *not* hierarchical in their basic character. However, the failures of Anderson's model seem related to its lack of hierarchical clustering. The papers cited should be consulted for details.

Mnemonic Devices

With the growing interest in organizational factors in memory, it was perhaps inevitable that psychologists would turn to the analysis of mnemonic devices. Mnemonic devices are those which enable the person to enrich or elaborate upon the material to be learned, all with the aim of helping her to remember it better. They typically help the person to classify and organize the material. There are a variety of mnemonic devices, varying according to the types of materials and recall requirements for which they are appropriate, and a number of semipopular books describe many of these (e.g., Furst, 1958; Lorayne & Lucas, 1974; M. N. Young & Gibson, 1966). One mnemonic device that has been analyzed extensively (Bower, 1970b) is the "pegword" method for learning ordered lists of items such as shopping lists, errands, historical events, sets of laws in psychology,

and so on. The technique is briefly illustrated in Table 13.2. The person first learns a list of rhyming pegwords, pairing concrete images with the first 20 or so integers. In learning a new list of items, the person then uses successive pegwords as imagined pegs upon which to hook the successive items of the list. As the first list word occurs (*cigar*), the person is to call to mind her first pegword, and form a mental image of some vivid scene of interaction between the two objects. Examples are shown in the right-hand column in Table 13.2. The images may be as bizarre as one wishes—their effectiveness seems independent of that aspect. This same procedure for imaginal pairing is followed for each of the list words in turn. To revive the list in memory, the person needs only to go through her already well-learned list of pegwords, and as she considers each one in turn she tries to recreate or recall the imaginal scene elaborated around that pegword image; from this remembered scene, she can usually name the desired item ("cigar").

This and similar schemes are exceedingly effective, at least in comparison to normal free recall of subjects not taught to use any special tricks. Recall might be improved by a factor of two or three times as much as normal. One of the main reasons

TABLE 13.2. Illustration of First Four Pegword Images and Their Use in Learning the First Four Items on a Shopping List.

Pegword	List Word	Mnemonic Image
one—bun	cigar	bun smoking a cigar
two—shoe	butter	spreading butter on shoe sole
three—tree	chicken	chicken sitting up in a tree
four—door	nails	hammering nails into front door
•	•	•
•	•	•
•	•	•

the device works so well is that the person has a systematic *retrieval scheme;* she knows how to cue herself with the items (the pegwords) to which she has explicitly associated the list words as they were presented. The usual free-recall subject, on the other hand, simply does not know how to remind herself of all the list words she knows. We know that if we give the ordinary subject various hints, especially semantic clues ("One of the list words was a dairy food"), she can recall a great deal more than she can free-recall on her own (Tulving & Pearlstone, 1966; Tulving & Psotka, 1971). The advantage for the pegword user, therefore, is partly the result of her knowing how to systematically cue each of the words from each input-list position. The second advantage of the pegword method undoubtedly stems from its deployment of mnemonic imagery. Since mental imagery has become a topic of recent concern in research on human memory, we will briefly review some of that research.

Mental Imagery

Mental imagery, or the "pictures of the mind's eye," was one of those introspectionist concepts that John Watson and other radical behaviorists found no use for in an objective psychology. Not that they denied the subjective experiences people describe as "having images"; rather, they argued that "public behavior" had to be analyzed first in its own right rather than only as an index of the subjective counterpart—which, in the behaviorists' lexicon, might just be excess baggage anyway. In any event, and for whatever reason, human memory came to be viewed through the somewhat distorted lenses of "verbal-motor habits" (see Watson, 1924b; Hull et al., 1940). In their classic and monumental survey of the field of human learning, McGeoch and Irion (1952) did not even mention the topic of mental imagery or imagination or visualization.

The tide has clearly turned, and mental imagery is now a popular research topic. This turnabout has been caused by growing acceptance of the cognitive view in memory research and rejection of the strict behaviorist view. Sustained and effective arguments have been given (Bower, 1972b; Cooper & Shepard, 1973; Paivio, 1971; Richardson, 1969) for recognizing mental imagery (or the "imaginal system") as one of the primary modes of representation of information in memory; and a variety of features have been suggested for distinguishing the imaginal from the verbal-symbolic mode of representation. For example, the imagery system seems specialized for dealing with information presented simultaneously, in parallel, from sources distributed about in space, whereas the verbal system would appear specialized for dealing with information presented sequentially, in series, from sources distributed over time. In brief, the imagery system (particularly *visual* imagery) represents information as distributed in space, whereas the verbal system deals best with information distributed in time.

A large number of learning experiments have now been done indicating that imaginal or pictorial representation of information usually facilitates memory, by factors ranging from 1.5 to 3 or so. For example, students told to concoct mental images so as to learn arbitrary pairs of concrete words will recall about 1.5 to 2 times more paired associates than will uninstructed controls. In extensive studies examining various attributes of words and how a person's learning of the words varies with these attributes, Paivio (1971) and his associates have found that the concreteness of a word's referent (or the vividness of the imagery it arouses) is the most powerful predictor of the word's memorability. This generalization held true in a variety of verbal learning tasks, even when the imagery value of words was compared to other measures such as meaningfulness, number of associations, familiarity, emotionality, and semantic-differential ratings. Moreover, standard verbal learning results that historically have been attributed to verbal factors like word meaningfulness may in actuality be due to an imagery effect (see Paivio, 1971, for examples), since imagery correlates fairly highly with a word's meaningfulness or the number of associates it elicits.

Why are pictures, then images, and then concrete words remembered in that order, with all remembered so much better than abstract words? The current conjecture is what is called the *dual-trace hypothesis* (Bower, 1972b; Paivio, 1971). It supposes that there are two distinguishably different forms of representation, the imaginal and the verbal, and that concepts within these systems are usually closely connected, much like equivalent words in two languages. When a word to be remembered is shown, the subject enters a memory trace of that event in his verbal store. If it is a concrete word, then the corresponding nodes (concepts) in the imaginal system are activated, the person "experiences the corresponding imagery," and a trace of the event is laid down in the imagery system. So a word (or word pair) that is imaged or a picture that is named has the advantage of having two, redundant copies of the memory trace laid down. The redundancy prolongs memory in comparison to abstract items, since it is assumed that the second, imaginal trace is likely to survive after the initial, verbal trace has decayed. That is, not only are there two traces, but the one in the imaginal system seems more resistant to forgetting.

Although this is not a particularly revealing hypothesis, it has led to a lot of supportive research (e.g., Paivio, 1971; Paivio & Csapo, 1972). It has also guided a large number of practical efforts to use imagery, pictorial representations, and special audiovisual aids in boosting learning in primary schools (Jensen & Rohwer, 1970; Rohwer, 1970). It now seems reasonably certain that all efforts at audiovisual instruction, plus teaching the pupil techniques of mnemonic elaboration and imagery of materials to be learned, are likely to maximize the amount of learning obtainable within the least time, and with the least repetitive drill and difficulty. However, much theorizing and research is still going on to further clarify the relation between imagery and language, particularly the role imagery has to play in conceptions of semantic meaning.

DISTORTIONS IN LEARNING CONTINGENCIES

Association doctrine outlines a mechanism by which the organism detects and learns correlations between events in its world. The association from A to B is assumed to track the relative frequency of event B following event A. As such, associative strength is a measure of predictability or expectancy of B given A. In this view of matters, association learning provides the foundations for organisms to become "intuitive statisticans" and to induce mechanically and with reasonable accuracy the regularities of events of their world.

In recent years, this view of humans as accurate intuitive statisticians has begun to crumble as many of their systematic errors, biases, and shortcomings have come to light. Some of these failings have been demonstrated in research by Tversky and Kahneman (1971, 1973, 1978; Kahneman & Tversky, 1971, 1973). The failings of interest in this discussion are those showing a strong impact of the subject's prior beliefs upon her ability to learn event correlations that disconfirm those beliefs. The evidence shows that if the person begins the learning series with a strong prior belief that two events are correlated (though imperfectly), it takes almost overwhelming evidence to convince her that this is not the case.

Classic experiments on this topic are those by Chapman and Chapman (1967, 1969). The Chapmans puzzled over why clinical psychologists persisted in using several personality tests such as the Draw-a-Person test (DAP) long after research had proven the tests to be invalid. The clinicians argued that in their experience the tests were quite valid and that certain responses of patients on the test were quite reliable signs of certain psychiatric illnesses. For example, clinicians believed that when patients drew pictures of people, those with paranoid tendencies would em-

phasize or distort the eyes, those with dependency problems would emphasize the mouth or make childlike drawings, those with homosexual tendencies would draw feminine males or figures of uncertain sex, and so on. These are illusory correlations, however, since the DAP has been shown repeatedly to be invalid.

The Chapmans hypothesized that the illusory correlations arose and persisted for two reasons: (1) beliefs about the covariation between a picture-sign and a psychiatric illness are frequently based on semantic associations or common-sense theories (e.g., eyes reveal suspicion, dependent means childlike) rather than accurate observation of covarying events; and (2) such beliefs survive actual experience with the relevant data even though that should disconfirm the belief. Their experiments provide ample confirmation for these hypotheses. First, laymen when asked to guess what body parts are suggested by psychiatric labels such as paranoia, dependency, impotence, overwhelmingly mention the same clues as the clinicians had alleged to have "seen" as significant signs on the DAP test. Second, naive students were shown 45 DAP drawings from mental patients which were *randomly* paired with six frequently mentioned psychiatric diagnoses (suspiciousness, dependency, and so on). Following their perusal of the picture-diagnosis pairings, the students were asked to guess which features of the DAP drawings had been associated most frequently with each diagnosis. These estimates of covariation by the students exposed to a *random* series virtually duplicated those of the experienced clinicians; that is, they asserted that suspiciousness in the picture series was usually indicated by a drawing which exaggerated or distorted the eyes, and so on. Similar results were obtained for responses to the Rorschach ink-blot cards as for the DAP test. The Chapmans postulated that the illusory correlations were due to semantic associations that were shared by the students and experienced clinicians. More generally, we may conclude that if people believe two events (such as a DAP sign and a personality trait) are correlated though imperfectly, that belief is exceedingly persistent and hard to shake. In fact, people are likely to come away from exposure to massively *disconfirming* evidence with their faith even *stronger* than before.

In a further experiment, the Chapmans (1969) showed that if semantically salient and popular signs (e.g., anal erotica, genitalia) were available in a card series to use in psychiatric diagnosis of homosexuality, naive observers would usually select and use them despite there being a different sign (seeing "monsters" in a particular Rorschach card) that was a perfectly valid cue for the diagnosis. That is, the false belief in the validity of a particular sign-to-diagnosis relationship was so powerful that it masked and prevented the learning of a true correlation that was present.

The results in the Chapmans' experiments are reminiscent of those on blocking and overshadowing in Pavlovian conditioning for which the Rescorla and Wagner model was appropriate (see Chapter 9). In that arrangement, a neutral stimulus *A* consistently paired with a US does not acquire associative strength if it has always been accompanied by a second stimulus *B*, which had previously been learned as a predictor of the US. To spell out the analogy to the Chapmans' learning situation, the prior belief that a given sign (*B*) is related to a particular psychiatric diagnosis (the US) can mask the learning of a real correlation between another sign (*A*) in the patient's pattern and the diagnosis. As presently formulated, the Rescorla-Wagner theory expects extinction of the preferred cue to occur as the subject is exposed to a random series of sign-sign pairings. The theory clearly needs some mechanism to account for increased resistance to extinction of associations established under probabilistic US schedules. A characteristic of most human beliefs is that sign-symptom

correlations are imperfect, and therefore some "failures" should be expected. Of course, just such a discounting rule prevents the discrediting of false beliefs.

Persistence of social stereotypes. The Chapmans' results have been replicated in several different settings, and the findings have been extended in several directions. As one extension, Hamilton and Rose (in press) demonstrated that racial stereotypes about blacks, Mexican-Americans, Asians, and Caucasians appear as biased memories in an analog to the Chapmans' frequency estimation task. Hamilton had his college-student subjects read a long series of race-to-trait pairings (e.g., black-shy, Asian-soft spoken, and so on) which overall were completely random in character. Later, when subjects estimated the frequency of particular pairings, they *overestimated* those pairings conforming to cultural racial stereotypes (e.g., Asians are quiet, Mexican-Americans are quick-tempered). Apparent frequency of a race-trait pairing seemed to be estimated from the strength of their association in memory, or—in what amounts to the same thing—by implicitly generating a sample of traits from the concept of that race in memory. Traits already associated with the stereotype thus have a starting bias. Hamilton and Rose note the pernicious influence of this mechanism for the persistence of unfair and invalid stereotypes (racial, sexual, religious, or otherwise). Even with "liberal-minded" college sophomores (of all races) and exposure to truly random race-trait pairings, the racial stereotypes which they know (but reject intellectually) nonetheless exert a subtle, unconscious influence on a measure of memory.

Such results as these question the accuracy of the "intuitive statistician" view of humans. The results showing bias were obtained in laboratory conditions optimal for learning and for disconfirming beliefs. In the real world, differences enter which probably would attenuate even further the impact on wrong beliefs of disconfirming data. First, in real life the cases of sign-to-diagnosis (or A-to-B) events occur sporadically spread over time, and are not concentrated within a few minutes' exposure. Second, in real life there is often a long lapse between a sign (*A*) and a later diagnosis (*B*), so contiguity rarely operates. In such a case, the person's memory for the sign (*A*) may be distorted so as to be consistent with the expected diagnosis (*B*). Third, and most critical, the coding or interpretation of the signs themselves (*A* and *B*) are often ambiguous, slippery, subject to pressures to be consistent with prior expectancies. Thus, whether the mouth in the drawing is judged to be really exaggerated depends on whether the patient was classified as dependent; whether that child's talking back to his teacher is interpreted as "aggressive" or "asserting his rights" depends on whether he is Mexican-American or Caucasian. That is, people's implicit theories cause them to perceive ambiguous data in a way that confirms their theory. Cognitive psychologists have long proposed, investigated, and explained how expectations influence perceptual classification. Thus, if from one sign (*Mexican-American*) the perceiver infers *aggression*, then that concept rather than an alternate one (*assertiveness*) will be activated and readied to "fire" when the perceiver sees the child talking up to his teacher. The category which thus fires off is the one the perceiver uses to classify, react to, and remember the event. The account here is similar to the one cognitive psychologists give of how people use context to interpret ambiguous words (*pork/karate*-CHOP) or pictures (see Figure 10.2 of the goblet vs. profiles).

Confirmation bias. Alongside the factors mentioned which diminish the impact of negative evidence, psychologists have uncovered a further *confirmation bias* that people commonly follow in testing their beliefs. When trying to test a particular hypothesis ("Do most Irishmen drink too much?"), people look predominately for positive confirming evidence (by going to pubs in Dublin) whereas logically they should search hardest for falsifying evidence (by visiting New Year's parties in America, or monasteries in Ireland). These tendencies have been noted repeatedly in laboratory studies, even when supposedly logical scientists are given various hypothesis-testing tasks (e.g., Mahoney, 1976). Assuming personnel interviewing is similar to hypothesis-testing, Snyder and Cantor (1979) have shown how interviewers' preconceptions about the job a candidate is applying for (librarian or car salesperson) influences the personal questions asked by the interviewer (the real subject) and influences the interviewer's recollection of random or ambiguous trait information given about the applicant. Interviewers asked questions that would mainly elicit information congruent with their stereotype of the job-filler (e.g., quiet vs. boisterous), and they mainly remembered applicant information that fitted their stereotype for the job. This is another example of the operation of the confirmation bias.

The confirmation bias, along with the low salience of critical events, the persistence of false beliefs, and the theory-driven interpretations of ambiguous events, suggests a dismal picture of humans as veridical scientists or information processors. The limitations of people's rationality, induction, and judgment seem inextricably bound up with the way memory operates; we have a number of heuristics or rules of thumb for helping us learn and make decisions about our environment, but the rules of thumb are not logical algorithms and they have frightening deficiencies. The nature, extent, and implications of these deficits are being explored intensively. A volume by Nisbett and Ross (1979) reviews and summarizes much of this work, which is significant in altering traditional views of human rationality.

EPISODIC VS. SEMANTIC MEMORY

As is perhaps becoming apparent to the student, investigators of human memory like to propose distinctions between various types of memories—short term versus long term, acoustic versus visual, imaginal versus verbal, and many more. These are helpful classifications in delimiting the domain over which empirical generalizations may be true; they are also quite heuristic in suggesting new questions to investigate as well as new answers to old questions. Most often such distinctions evolve gradually out of a body of experimental work, when the investigators realize that they are dealing with memory phenomena that differ in critical properties from those ascribed to other regular memories.

Tulving (1972) initially summarized and stated such a distinction now prevalent in memory research—namely, that between *episodic* memory and *semantic* memory. To quote Tulving,

> Let us think of episodic and semantic memory as two information processing systems that (a) selectively receive information from perceptual systems or other cognitive systems, (b) retain various aspects of this information, and (c) upon instructions transmit specific retained information to other systems, including those responsible for translating it into behavior and conscious awareness. The two systems differ from one another in terms of (a) the nature of stored information, (b) autobiographical versus cognitive reference, (c) conditions and consequences of retrieval, and probably also in terms of (d) their vulnerability to interference resulting in transformation and erasure of stored information, and (e) their dependence upon each other. In addition, psychological research on episodic memory differs from that on semantic memory in several respects (1972, p. 385).

Thus, episodic memory records information about temporally dated events which have particular sensory attributes, and which always have autobiographical reference. Examples would be that I remember just having heard thunder, or I remember seeing a bear in Yellowstone Park last summer, or I remember that the word *rug* appeared next to the number 14 in the list of pairs I just studied. A specification of semantic memory is as follows:

> Semantic memory is the memory necessary for the use of language. It is a mental thesaurus, organized knowledge a person possesses about words and other verbal symbols, their meaning and referents, about relations among them, and about rules, formulas, and algorithms for the manipulation of these symbols, concepts, and relations. Semantic memory does not register perceptible properties of inputs, but rather cognitive referents of input signals. The semantic system permits the retrieval of information that was not directly stored in it, and retrieval of information from the system leaves its contents unchanged, although any act of retrieval constitutes an input into episodic memory. The semantic system is probably much less susceptible to involuntary transformation and loss of information than the episodic system. Finally, the semantic system may be quite independent of the episodic system in recording and maintaining information since identical storage consequences may be brought about by a great variety of input signals (Tulving, 1972, p. 386).

Typically, semantic memories are in LTM, have lost all autobiographical reference or information about their mode or context of learning, and would be said to constitute part of our permanent knowledge. Examples of semantic knowledge are verbal relations like "Lions are mammals," "*Man* means *male human*"; facts like "Chicago is in Illinois"; laws like "A physical object cannot be located in two places at once"; and inference rules like "If object A is with object B, and A is located at place C, then B is also located at place C."

It takes little reflection to note that nearly all laboratory research on memory has been largely concerned with episodic memory. The subject is exposed to a series of discrete events (presentations of words or pictures in a list), and later is tested for the verbatim *accuracy* of his reproduction or identification of it. Most often the cue for reproduction refers to the temporal-spatial context of the events to be recalled, as in "Recall the names of the pictures you just saw in the experimental list." Of course, in encoding or learning events, the person may make use of knowledge in his semantic store. For example, if in a list of paired associates the subject sees the pair *robin-bird,* that is already a preestablished relation in his semantic memory. In this case, then, he need only tag this old, known relation with the new autobiographical information that it was presented in a particular experimental context.

Although the episodic-semantic distinction is widely recognized, the popularity of the distinction seems to rest more on its intuitive appeal than on solid evidence of different memory functions or processes. Once we grant that information in memory can vary in its content and strength (surely innocuous assumptions), it is not clear that much more is implicated in the episodic-semantic distinction. First, theories such as those of J. R. Anderson and Bower (1973), J. R. Anderson (1976), or Norman and Rumelhart (1975) always record new information (episodic or otherwise) into memory by linking it into the same semantic network, possibly with a context-of-acquisition noted. So in these explicit theories there is no *qualitative* distinction between a memory for an episode versus one for a general rule. Second, substantial interactions occur between so-called episodic and semantic memories, calling into question the idea that these are distinct or independent memory stores. As one simple example, if I repeatedly ask you a simple semantic question ("Is Cleveland in Ohio?"), you will answer increasingly faster, suggesting that the asking episode is altering the speed of access to the semantic information. Conversely, if I teach you many new facts about a familiar concept like Cleveland, it appears that you become slightly slower in answering a question about a previous "semantic" fact you knew about it (see J.

R. Anderson, 1976, Chapter 8). Although the episodic-semantic memory distinction is appealing, considerations such as these raise questions about whether it is fundamental to basic processes.

Context, Recency, and Frequency Judgments

Whether or not the episodic-semantic distinction is regarded as fundamental, any memory theory must recognize that stimulus events will be recorded into memory along with some description of their context of occurrence. This context contains not only the perceptual characteristics of the item's physical mode of presentation but also such incidental matters as *where* and *when* it was said or done and *by whom.* We may think of these contextual elements as features associated to the internal representation of the event, features that are potentially retrievable when the person is asked to remember or recognize the event (see J. R. Anderson & Bower, 1972a). Experiments have indeed shown that subjects automatically record all sorts of such incidental information; for instance, they can remember whether a word was presented visually or auditorily, whether it was spoken by a male or female voice, whether it was presented as a word or a picture, whether it was presented on the left or right display screen, and so on (see Light et al., 1973). Of special interest is that subjects can also judge how *recently in time* a given event occurred. Since such recency judgments obviously involve remembering, the main theories to explain recency judgments have been concerned with memory (see Hinrichs, 1970; Ornstein, 1969). One model that does a reasonably serviceable job supposes that presentation of an item establishes an association to a set of contextual elements and that the strength of this association declines systematically over time as other events are interpolated. When the item is re-presented for test, the person assesses the item's strength in memory, and on this basis decides on a recency-of-experience judgment for it. On this theory, one expects that items that are presented several times to strengthen their memory trace will, as a consequence, tend to be judged as having occurred more recently than weaker, once-presented items. This model has certain obvious flaws, and attempts to rectify it have been proposed (Flexser & Bower, 1974; Linton, 1975). The basic idea is that the item retrieves an associated context in which it occurred and, by one means or another, the person can figure out from this context how long ago the item occurred.

Another type of information available from episodic memory is the *frequency* with which an event has occurred in a given context, or the frequency with which events of a general class or type have occurred. An example of the first type would be the judgment that the word *dog* appeared three times scattered throughout an input list of words; an example of the second would be the judgment that there were approximately six animals mentioned in the input list. People are fairly accurate in these sorts of judgments regarding event memories whether or not they know during the study trial that such frequency information will be tested. The prevailing hypothesis regarding how frequency judgments are implemented in episodic memory is that subjects try to retrieve and count the different local contexts in which the test item has occurred (see J. R. Anderson & Bower, 1972a). Something like this counting process occurs for small frequencies (say, six or less), but a "retrieval sampling-plus-estimation" procedure is used for higher frequencies (e.g., comparing frequencies of occurrence of gasoline stations versus delicatessens in America).

One of the significant applications of this context-retrieval technique has been to the issue of deciding how repetition of an event improves its recall. There have been essentially two alternative proposals regarding why repetition enhances memory. One view is that a second presentation makes contact with and *strengthens* the trace of the initial presentation of the item, and recall reflects this enhanced memory strength. The other is that the second presentation lays down further information about the initial event, information detailing the context of its occurrence. Recall then improves because the person has more access routes to the event information or because the event information has been "multiply copied" in connection with several retrieval cues. An experiment by Hintzman and Block (1971) provides striking evidence for the latter view. They found that subjects could retrieve differential and veridical information about the successive repetitions of a single item. Following presentation of a 100-item list, for instance, subjects would be able to remember accurately that the word *dog* appeared twice, that its first occurrence was visual and was in the initial fifth of the input list, while its second occurrence was auditory and was in the third fifth of the input list. Such discriminative information could not be provided by a mechanism which deals with repetition by simply incrementing a "habit strength" for the word *dog*. It is instructive to point out that this very question of how the memory deals with repetition could not even have been clearly posed, let alone answered, within the framework of S-R behaviorism with its emphasis on verbal habits. This illustrates the type of questions of concern to memory theorists today.

Encoding and Retrieval Conditions

Current conceptions of memory have begun to recognize the powerful role of stimulus cues in retrieving our memories for events. Modern theorists are coming to believe that a memory for an event is like a locked treasure chest that requires just the right "key" (or retrieval cue) to unlock it and reveal its contents. To pursue the analogy further, the key for the lock depends on what the person thinks about the event as she experiences it. That is, the setting of the lock's tumblers is determined by the encoding operations the person performs on the item. This locked-chest analogy captures a general belief that is stated by Tulving and Thompson (1973, p. 269): "Specific encoding operations performed on what is perceived determine what is stored, and what is stored determines what retrieval cues are effective in providing access to what is stored."

The powerful influence of cues on recall was shown in early studies by Tulving and Pearlstone (1966) and Tulving and Psotka (1971). Following exposure to a list of categorized words (trees, foods, cities, and so on), subjects were unable to recall very many until given the category names as cues, at which point they recalled large numbers of the list words. The presumption is that subjects thought of these category names at the time they studied the list words, thus priming the category-to-instance associations; consequently, the category cue activated these associations during the recall test.

Tulving and Thompson (1971, 1973) have tried to control the way in which a word is encoded during study by presenting it in the context of another word. Thus, a to-be-remembered word like IRON might be presented in the context of a word like *clothes.* Tulving and Thompson assume that presentation of the pair *clothes*-IRON causes IRON to be encoded and stored in a specific manner; a later test condition will retrieve that episodic memory only to the extent that it overlaps with the interpretation of IRON that was stored. This is called the *encoding specificity principle,* or ESP for short. To illustrate, IRON may not even be recognized as having been on the list if it is tested by itself or in the pair *ore*-IRON but it would be recognized in the context *clothes*-IRON or *steam*-IRON. Furthermore,

IRON would be recalled to the cue of *clothes* or *pressing board,* but not to a normatively strong associative cue like *metal* or *ore.* An examination of these several conditions reveals circumstances in which a word (IRON) may be recalled to an encoded cue (*clothes*), but when presented alone may not be recognized as having occurred on the list. This finding, that a word can be recalled but not recognized, seems paradoxical until one compares the differing retrieval conditions in terms of the ESP.

Beyond the encoding specificity principle itself, the reason that a word may be recalled to a cue after it has just failed to be recognized may be related to a "priming" principle. *Priming* means that presentation of a word increases its availability as a response to a related stimulus. Thus, if presentation of the word IRON on the recognition test primes its availability as a response, then some recall to its cue of *clothes* will be expected for this reason. However, Bowyer and Humphreys (1979) found that priming effects were not large enough to explain all the frequency of recalls following recognition failures. Apparently, something like the ESP must be invoked.

The semantic interpretation. J. R. Anderson and Bower (1974) claimed that many of the ESP results could be interpreted in terms of different semantic features or concepts being aroused by different contexts at study versus testing. Thus, in the context of *clothes,* the grapheme IRON arouses the concept of the iron used in pressing clothes, not the metal ore. This aroused concept is what becomes associated to the list context. In order for a later test item to be recognized, it must retrieve a concept which is associated to the list context. This retrieval path may fail if the test context is *ore*-IRON or IRON itself, because these may invoke a semantic interpretation different from the one experienced during study. Several experiments where the meaning is explicitly biased differently during study versus testing (such as *strawberry/traffic*-JAM, or *pork/karate*-CHOP) have confirmed these predictions (Light and Carter-Sobell, 1970).

While the semantic interpretation hypothesis seems reasonable, it is somewhat strained to deal with ESP results that play on just slightly different meaning attributes of a word. Thus, the word PIANO is best retrieved by the cue *something heavy* after having been studied in the sentence "The man lifted the PIANO"; on the other hand, it is best retrieved by *something with a nice sound* after having been studied in the sentence "The man tuned the PIANO." But if the output cue does not match the input context, then cued recall is very poor (see Barclay et al., 1974). In these examples, the sense of PIANO does not change, although the property that is activated differs in the two cases. Thus, the semantic hypothesis must be generalized to deal with bundles of activated semantic features at input, and must note the extent to which the feature bundles aroused by the retrieval cues overlap with those at input. Such a theory can produce post hoc explanations for particular findings but leads to few surprising predictions.

A distinct upset for the semantic interpretation theory of ESP came when Watkins, Ho, and Tulving (1976) found significant context effects in recognition memory for pictures of faces. Their subjects were shown adults' portraits in the context of a verbal description (e.g., "This man works for the Mafia," "This man loves cats," and so on). They were later tested for face recognition with the face alone, the face plus its correct description, or the face with a description that had been paired with a different face in the study list. Recognition memory for the face was best when tested in the presence of its original paired description, and worst with a different description. The result is similar to the familiar experience of not recognizing an acquaintance one meets unexpectedly in a strange place. The effect in this case can not be explained by postulating different meanings of the face according to the different descriptions. However, it is reasonable to suppose that the subject tries to find some features in the face to suggest or justify the description (e.g., the sinister, hooded eyes of the Mafia character). If so, then a changed description of the face during testing (e.g., "cat lover") may cause the subject to sample different features of the face, with the resulting lower level of recognition memory. This interpretation is close to that given by Watkins, Ho, and Tulving (1976).

Memory gestalts. One motivation behind much of the work on encoding specificity was a desire to show that compound patterns may have emergent Gestalt ("wholist") properties, and that constituent elements of these patterns may not be recognizable when removed from the context of these patterns. A familiar example is that people may fail to recognize brief, mid-melody phrases played out of context whereas they are able to sing the complete melody. Watkins (1974) showed a similar effect with words. Following study of paired-letter clusters like SPANI-EL, EX-PLO-RE, and LIQUE-FY, subjects made many errors when asked to recognize the final letter clusters (EL or RD, RE or DE, and so on); however, they were able to recall at a high level the final letters when cued with the initial clusters (SPANI- and EXPLO-). Clearly, storing the whole word in memory as a chunk disguised the final letter cluster so that in isolation it could not be discriminated from unpresented clusters.

These examples dramatize the fact that cued recall of one part of a whole can exceed its recognition when there are strong part-whole relations and when the parts are unequal in retrieving memory for the whole. At issue is whether these cases are just peculiar exaggerations, or whether they point to a general phenomenon—namely, that the memory trace of any item is fundamentally altered by being encoded with its context as part of a new whole. The encoding specificity principle advances the latter claim, which is quite congruent with Gestalt theory. On the other hand, the J. R. Anderson and Bower (1974) theory tries to explain results on the basis of associations of constituent elements. It is noteworthy how the themes of old-style elementaristic vs. wholistic intuitions or biases keep playing through these modern controversies like a refrain. The historical perspective helps the student identify these themes in current research and use them as organizing principles.

SEMANTIC MEMORY

As noted earlier, semantic memory includes our knowledge of word meanings, of our language, of procedures for doing things (e.g., "action recipes"), and strategies for solving problems; it also includes our factual knowledge about the world, its individual events, personages, places, and laws. The domain is simply too vast to begin to enumerate exhaustively. In most studies of semantic memory, certain questions are of central concern. One question concerns the way in which the information in memory is organized. A second issue concerns how the mind gains access to particularly relevant information and retrieves it in the course of answering a question. Another issue concerns how already known information is used for detecting redundancy in newly arriving inputs in order to decide what is really novel and should be recorded in memory. A further and critical issue is how we would try to represent, in our psychological theories, the information which a person has regarding a particular domain of concepts. The decision on how to represent the subject's knowledge has

implications regarding his behavior in answering questions or drawing inferences or performing effective actions with respect to that domain.

There are currently two major methods for representing semantic knowledge, both of which are exemplified in current computer simulation programs. One supposes that most knowledge can be represented as a *labeled graph structure,* wherein the points or nodes represent universal concepts ("dogs") or particular individuals ("Spot") and the links between nodes represent labeled semantic relationships between the concepts or individuals. We shall further elaborate this notion below. The second approach, represented largely in T. Winograd's (1972) program for language understanding (see Chapter 12), tries to represent concepts in terms of inference rules (productions) and decision routines ("To decide if X is a *Republican,* first check to see if he has properties $p, q, r, . . .$"). Knowledge is represented generally in terms of action recipes or procedures for how to bring about some consequence or make some decision. Thus, a simple universal statement like "All men are mortal" would be encoded in terms of a small program encoding a procedure—to wit, that should one ever wish to find out whether X is mortal, it is sufficient merely to prove that X is a man.

Psychologists have been more attracted by the former representations, those using networks of labeled semantic relationships, on the belief that action recipes are easily "written" from static knowledge of what is the case and what the person wants to achieve. (Here again are the echoes of the Tolman-Guthrie debates on knowledge versus action.) Networks of labeled relations among semantic concepts are not really all that different from the earlier notions of the British associationists regarding how complex ideas were to be built up by associating simpler ideas together. What differs in the modern accounts is, first, the notion of the labeling of the association with the logical (or semantic) type it exemplifies; and, second, the notion that a complex idea need have no direct correspondence to an observable stimulus or response, and yet can still be represented as a single unit in memory, a unit about which further information can be predicted. We have met these ideas before, in this chapter and in Chapter 6. For a detailed discussion of these philosophical points and their ramifications throughout associationistic psychology, see J. R. Anderson & Bower (1973, Chapters 2 and 4).

One elementary approach to representing concepts and meanings in terms of graph structures can be illustrated by a semantic memory model developed by David Rumelhart, Peter Lindsay, and Donald Norman at the University of California at San Diego (see Rumelhart, Lindsay, & Norman, 1972; Lindsay & Norman, 1972; Norman & Rumelhart, 1975). First, the model distinguishes between concepts and events. A concept corresponds roughly to an idea; a concept is introduced into the system by way of definitions which give its relations to other concepts in the system. Typically, we mention the type or more general class to which the concept belongs, we mention one or more distinguishing properties of the concept, and perhaps we list several examples or instances of the concept. Thus, Figure 13.9 shows the simplest, graphic information defining the concept of a *bird*: it is a kind of animal, has feathers, has wings, can fly; examples of birds are robins, canaries, and so on. The number of properties, superordinates, and subordinates can be extended indefinitely (see Barsalou, in preparation). The elementary graph in Figure 13.9 exemplifies two aspects: that the relations are directional and that they are labeled. For example, we know that the relation of *bird* to *animal* is one of subordinate class (or "subset of").

A realistic memory, of course, contains many thousands of such concepts, each with

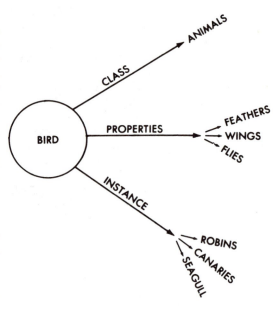

Figure 13.9.   Illustration of a labeled graph defining the concept of *bird*. The labeled associations point to properties, to supersets and to subsets of the concept.

very many connections, so that the actual topographical representation would look like a huge wiring diagram. But a fantastic amount of information is inherently encoded in such graph structures. To see just a hint of this, consider the fragment of a semantic network surrounding the concept of a *tavern* as shown in Figure 13.10. This graph implicitly encodes the information that a tavern is a kind of business establishment (as is a drugstore), which has beer and wine, and Luigi's is an example of a tavern. It also gives some properties of beer, wine, and Luigi's. This is only a fragment, of course, and much more information could and would be in a realistic memory. But notice how very many questions one is enabled to answer with just this fragment. For example, it can answer questions that require chains of subset relations, such as that "Luigi's is an estab-

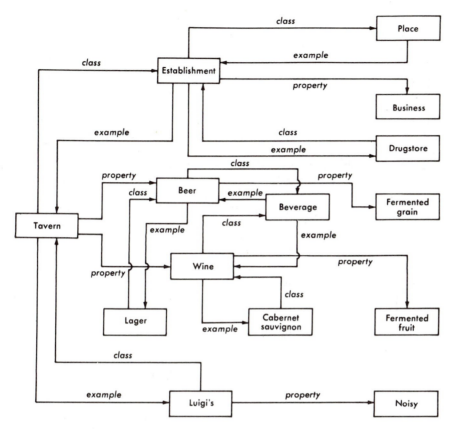

Figure 13.10. Fragment of a semantic network surrounding the concept of *tavern*. The linkages between concepts are labeled according to their type. (From Lindsay & Norman, 1972.)

lishment" or that "A drugstore is a place." It can also read out the properties or classes that any two concepts have in common. Thus, if we ask the system to compare the similarities and differences of *wine* and *beer,* it would quickly find that the similarities are that they are both beverages sold at taverns, but one is made from fermented grain while the other is made from fermented fruit. The number of factual relationships derivable and possible questions that can be answered increases exponentially as the number of encoded predicates or "bits of knowledge" increases.

Concepts and their definitions in terms of class, examples, and properties are quite serviceable for many purposes, but still further distinctions and rules are needed for building up second-order concepts from more elementary ones. Rumelhart and associates (1972) provide a set of such rules for forming second-order concepts, including rules of *qualification* (lamb → *young* sheep), *quantification* (crowd → *many* people), *location* (*under*water, *after*noon), and conjunction (ham *and* eggs). For encoding complete events, they use the notion of a *proposition*; the event is action based, denoting a scenario with agents, actions, and objects. For representing such events, Rumelhart and associates use the Case Grammar of the linguist Charles Fillmore (1968) as the formalism of their syntactic deep structure. Some of the major distinctions in Case Grammar are illustrated in Figure 13.11, which shows the proposed encoding of the event of the police rapidly chasing bank robbers with a car yesterday down Baker Street. The action centers around the main verb *chased*, which requires an agent (someone who performs the action), an object, and implicitly a means or instrument of the action. The act itself can be modified by an adverb of manner, such as *rapidly,* and time and location information can also be attached to the event. Linguistic propositions which we hear would have a similar encoding to that of actual events. Of course, most propositions we hear do not fill in so many details—they are elliptical or shortened in many ways by reference to earlier parts of an ongoing speech or dialogue.

Perceptual Encoding and Learning

We have indicated the form in which information is to be recorded into memory—that is, as propositions. Clearly, a necessary prerequisite for this to happen is that the sensory-perceptual system have routines for converting patterned stimulus sequences into propositions, by categoriz-

ing, interpreting, and putting them into a "declarative" framework. The solution desired is depicted in Figure 13.12, wherein an input first undergoes pattern recognition and is then fed to a linguistic or nonlinguistic analyzer (or both) that extracts the meaningful proposition(s) immanent in the input. Perceptual propositions are not coextensive with verbal labels, since it is presumed that nonverbal humans nonetheless have perceptual propositions. A visual stimulus might give rise to a perceptual proposition that would be described in words as "A blue triangle presented on a card before me." Several programs exist in artificial intelligence (e.g., Winston, 1970, 1977) for converting elementary blocks scenes to propositions. Although these programs clearly have only crude capabilities now, the goal of their operation is to convert sensory scenes into meaningful propositions. Language learning is conceived in part as the subject learning correspondences between words and perceptual referents, and between syntactic strings of words and perceptual propositions (see J. R. Anderson, 1976).

The language parser in Figure 13.12 is the part of the process that has been most worked on in artificial intelligence and psycholinguistics (see J. R. Anderson, 1976;

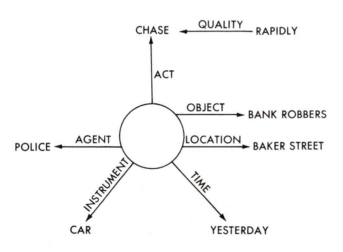

Figure 13.11. A graph structure depicting Case Grammar relations among various nouns and the main verb. This graph is encoding in memory the event of the police rapidly chasing bank robbers in a car yesterday down Baker Street.

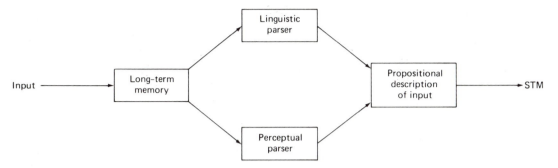

Figure 13.12. Components in translating a stimulus event into an internal propositional representation. Speech or writing is analyzed by the linguistic parser, whereas nonverbal stimuli are analyzed by the perceptual parser.

Marcus, 1979; Norman & Rumelhart, 1975; Schank, 1975a; T. Winograd, 1972). An array of methods has been tried for identifying word stems and endings, for analyzing input sentences into clauses and grammatical constituents, for identifying operative concepts and their relations, and for deciding what are the logical, atomic propositions expressed in the surface sentence. Automatic parsing of natural language by computer has become an advanced science in its own right. Suffice it to say that the output of the parser will be one or more propositions expressed, for example, as conceptual Case Grammar arguments of an action concept such as the CHASE proposition shown in Figure 13.11.

In such a theory, "learning" consists of simply recording the relevant fact into the conceptual network. Thus, the learning of a new proposition like "John is a thief" consists simply of establishing an association labeled "is a" (or "subset of") from my preexisting concept of John to my concept of thief. If I had no concept for John, then I would set up a new node in memory to represent this new concept to which further information would be attached.

Insofar as possible, new information structures such as those shown in Figure 13.11 are assumed to be "anchored into" the already known concepts of memory

(such as police, Baker Street, and so on): the new propositional information or event is simply a new set of temporary, labeled connections between these preexisting concepts. Once such a proposition is encoded and learned, the person can later use it to answer various questions. Questions typically specify *part* of the desired information, and leave blank the elements which are to be filled in by the answer. Questions such as, "What happened on Baker Street yesterday?" or, "How, where, and when did the police chase the bank robbers?" are rather like compound retrieval cues by which we probe the system for desired information. Most retrieval systems operate on a "pattern-matching" or similarity principle. The question is first analyzed into its Case Grammar format with some empty slots (with question marks), and then memory is searched for the best-matching memory structure that can be found for the probe. Particular linkages between concepts in memory will be retrieved and used only when the relations among the concepts are the same as in the probe question. Thus, in answering questions about whom the police chased yesterday, the system will pass over facts about police and chasing that did not happen yesterday, and will also discard retrieved instances where the police might have been the objects rather than the agents of the chasing action (e.g., wild lions were loose and chasing policemen down Baker Street yesterday). If the original propositional information has been recorded ("learned") successfully, if the question probe stipulates sufficient retrieval cues, and if the memory search proceeds rapidly and efficiently enough, the simulation model should come up with the right answer to the question. At present, the system that has been most implemented and tested for psychological plausibility in this respect is one by J. R. Anderson (1976); however, it would take us too far afield to go into details of his theory and the range of psychological evidence he uses to enhance its scientific credibility.

Two further matters require brief mention. First, it is understood that in such representational systems, entire propositions, once encoded, can now be treated as units in their own right, so that predications or comments can be made about them. For example, the system may record that *"John regrets that* such-and-such is true," that "such-and-such *is false,"* or that "something happened *just in the nick of time."* Also, propositions can enter into propositional *conjunctions,* by the use of connectives like *and, then, while,* and *causes.* Thus, a sequence of events, as contained for instance in a story, would be recorded in memory as a chain of propositional events of the general form, "event 1, then (event 2 while event 3) cause event 4, then event 5. . . ."

The second matter is the issue of inference and deduction in question-answering. Very often in discourse we are asked questions for which we do not have answers directly stored; rather, we must interpret the question and then try to infer the answer from other things we know. Thus we can answer the query, "Did Aristotle have a liver?" by retrieving the relevant facts that Aristotle was a human, and all humans have a liver, and by then applying the logical rule that a property true of a whole class is true of each member of the class. Similarly, if asked whether any part of the country of Chile is cold, we might retrieve the fact that the high Andes Mountains run through Chile and that the tops of mountains are usually cold; so even if Chile is near the equator, it still probably has some very cold locations. In this last illustration, the inference is starting to look more like "problem-solving," where a number of different facts have to be retrieved and their combination evaluated in order to come up with an answer. (For more discussion of question-answering, see Chapter 12.) Although each of us has developed a varied and complex repertoire for solving such inferential problems, psychologists still do not understand fully how to write a program to simulate the way a person does this.

Memory Search

Psychologists did much research in the 1970s studying the time it takes people to answer elementary questions such as "Is a *canary* a type of *bird*?" or "Does a *robin* have skin?". Most college students know subset relations between restricted domains of animals, and it is likely that the subject will answer some questions about remote concepts by using *chains of subset relations.* That is, the person might infer that a *salmon* is an *animal* not because he knows exactly that proposition but because he combines the two facts, a *salmon* is a *fish,* and *fish* are *animals.* An illustrative hierarchy of animal concepts and properties is shown in Figure 13.13, where vertical arrows denote subset associations. Questions involving inferences that require combining of facts or subset links were presumed to take longer to answer than questions involving simply accessing a single fact (a single link in Figure 13.13). It was hoped that the study of question-answering times would reveal the organization of the myriad

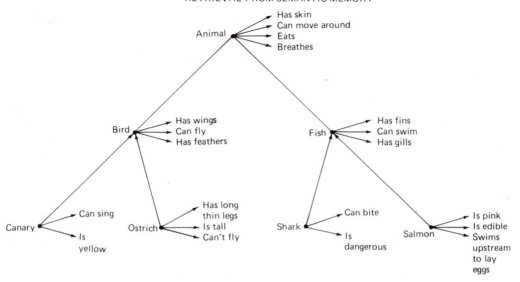

Figure 13.13. Illustration of a three-level hierarchy of animal concepts (points), with properties associated at specific concepts. The upwards-pointing arrows are *subset associations* and mean that the lower concept at the base of the arrow is a subset of the upper concept at the tip of that arrow. (From Collins and Quillian, 1969.)

facts in subjects' LTM and the process by which selected facts are retrieved for answering questions. Conjectured organizations like the one shown in Figure 13.13 could therefore be secured with data on question-answering times.

It is now generally conceded that, after a promising start, this program of research into semantic question-answering ran into insurmountable problems and came to an eventual stalemate. It appears now that conceptual families or domains are not neatly, logically, and economically organized, with properties stored only at the most general level of the hierarchy to which they apply (as Figure 13.13 illustrates). Rather, depending on a person's learning experiences, properties may be stored and cross-referenced at varying levels and strengths. The best predictor of people's reaction time to verify a true "subset"

statement or "property" statement is simply the normative frequency with which that concept or property is given as a constrained associate to the subject-concept by a population of similar subjects (see Glass et al., 1974). Production frequency is just a measure of associative strength, a concept that is incorporated in most current models of memory search (J. R. Anderson, 1976; Collins & Loftus, 1975). However, this approach permits practically no novel predictions beyond the general correlation between subject-to-predicate associative frequency and true reaction times.

The theories differ in the search processes they propose. The currently most popular theories assume that to verify the truth of a statement like "A *canary breathes,*" the two concepts are activated in memory and the activation spreads out blindly like an electrical current from each source along each of the associative paths leading from it. All nodes receiving activation just pass it along, spreading it among its out-paths. The processor is looking for an *intersection* of the two activation waves at some node (e.g., perhaps at the node labeled BIRD in Figure 13.13). An intersection represents some kind of connection between the subject (*canary*) and predicate (*breathes*) concepts, and so it must be evaluated to see if the series of connecting links are of the right type needed to answer the question. This path checking is needed to discard spurious connections. For example, *canary* and *is tall* would also intersect at the BIRD node in Figure 13.13, but one does not want the system to automatically say "True" to such intersections.

One implication of such a model is that false statements in which the subject and predicate have many common properties or spurious connections (e.g., "A *canary* is a *robin*") will take longer to reject than unrelated concepts because several spurious intersections must be examined closely before the overall statement can be rejected. The fact that closely associated subject-predicate sentences are slow to reject is considered evidence for the spreading activation theory of question answering. However, other models, which suppose that questions are answered by examining the overlap of semantic properties aroused by the subject and predicate concepts, can explain this effect as well (see Smith, 1976 for a review). It has proven difficult to devise definitive tests of the several competing theories of semantic memory organization and search using subjects' common knowledge. Perhaps a better strategy is that followed by J. R. Anderson and Bower (1973) and J. R. Anderson (1976) who taught subjects novel facts interrelated in a specific manner, and then tested their question-answering times for inferences of a known length in the associative network. Such experimentally constructed networks seem to yield clearer answers than the natural-istic semantic materials which contain much idiosyncratic variation and have basically unknown and uncontrolled organizations.

Learning from Text and Discourse

As noted earlier, theories of semantic memory such as J. R. Anderson's ACT model attempt to describe the learning of simple statements or factual assertions. Thus, a simple assertion like "John was unhappy" supposedly is analyzed by a person's language parser and recorded into memory by establishing associative links between preexisting concepts of *John* and *unhappy*. The basic unit of thought is presumed to be the subject-predicate (S-P) construction, which is usually interpreted to mean that the subject concept is a subset or member of the set of things described by the predicate. Thus, "Fido bit John" means that Fido is a member of the set of "biters of John." Complex propositions are represented in ACT as just more complex configurations of subject-predicate constructions.

As semantic theories have begun to describe successfully the way unrelated sentences are recorded into and retrieved from memory (as Anderson has attempted with ACT), psychologists have begun to study more complex phenomena such as the way people learn and remember *coherent sequences* of sentences or text.

There has been a long-standing fascination in experimental psychology with memory for meaningful texts, but the time has not been ripe for doing much with it as a scientific topic. Classic studies, for example, were carried out by Bartlett (1932), who described the distortions in his subjects' reconstructions of a somewhat anomalous Indian folktale, "The War of the Ghosts." Bartlett challenged the nonsense syllable tradition of Ebbinghaus that prevailed in his time (and until the 1960s), and pointed out fascinating interpretive distortions that occurred in reconstructive memory. Thus, for example, Bartlett noticed that some of his subjects during recall would regularize or conventionalize strange or unconventional parts of the story, would reinterpret the motives of the characters according to Western stereotypes, would focus and elaborate upon some striking detail, and so on. Although Bartlett's book and his observations were widely read and cited, psychologists working on verbal learning did not have the analytic tools at that time to deal with people's memory for text. They felt that the understanding of and memory for text presented formidable problems, and therefore considered text learning to be a problem for the future. Thus, what is surely a major issue for any theory of human memory—how people learn from discourse—was essentially postponed for many decades.

Later work relating associative-learning theory to psycholinguistics (e.g., J. R. Anderson & Bower, 1973; Kintsch, 1974) has put the central problem of learning from text back onto the active research agenda; and in recent years interest in developing theories of text understanding and text memory has increased enormously. Scientists from many disciplines—psychology, education, linguistics, and computer science—have made important contributions. Several books devoted to text memory (e.g., Freedle, 1979; Just & Carpenter, 1977; Kintsch, 1974; Meyer, 1975; Schank & Abelson, 1977) have appeared, as have articles in journals such as *Discourse Processes, Cognitive Science,* and the *Journal of Educational Psychology.* Several theoretical models have been constructed to describe how people understand and remember different kinds of texts and narratives (e.g., Kintsch & van Dijk, 1979; Thorndyke, 1978).

A text is a sequence of sentences. However, texts have a coherence and structure that makes them far more than an arbitrary sequence. One of the continuing jobs for researchers in this field is to describe the structure or organization of good text, and to say what makes it coherent. A useful hypothesis by Kintsch (1974), elaborated in Kintsch and van Dijk (1979), is that a necessary condition for coherence (though not a sufficient one) is that successive sentences share the same ideas (concepts or referents). That is, the propositions of a coherent text are interconnected; they refer frequently to the same things or ideas, and introduce new ideas only gradually. Thus, texts can be analyzed for coherence according to their patterns of concept repetition. An example of this concept repetition analysis is shown in Table 13.3. The text shown there is a long sentence composed of eight propositions; these are shown in predicate-argument notations to the left in Table 13.2. (A sentence often contains two or more propositions or basic relations.) Thus, the first proposition says that turbulence forms; the second says that this turbulence-formation is located at an edge; the third says that this edge is part of a wing, and so on. The diagram to the right in Table 13.2 connects those propositions which share a common idea. For example, Proposition 4 is connected to 1 through the common idea of "turbulence"; Proposition 8 is connected to 7 through the idea of "aircraft." The connections between all shared ideas result in the graph structure to the right in Table 13.2. This procedure can be extended to any length of text, and the resulting graph structure may become quite complex.

Let us suppose that the first few propositions of a paragraph contain its major topic. If so, then later mention of these topical concepts are subordinated to their earlier mention. Thus, a connectivity graph can be drawn with the main topic (first) proposition at the top and the other propositions fanning out below it as a set of subordinate qualifications, modifications, or details. It is then possible to define the level of a proposition as its distance in the connectivity graph from the main topic

TABLE 13.3 Sample Text Base and Text (From Kintsch, 1975).

Propositions	Connections and Levels
1 (FORM,TURBULENCE)	
2 (LOC:AT,1,EDGE)	
3 (PART OF,WING,EDGE)	
4 (GROW,TURBULENCE,STRENGTH)	
5 (LOC:OVER,4,SURFACE)	
6 (PART OF,WING,SURFACE)	
7 (CONTRIBUTE,TURBULENCE,LIFT,AIRCRAFT)	
8 (SUPERSONIC,AIRCRAFT)	

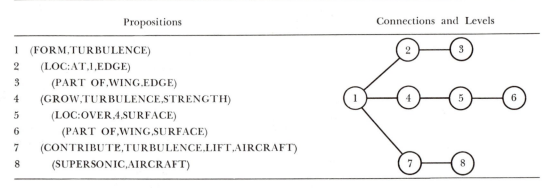

Text

Turbulence forms at the edge of a wing and grows in strength over its surface, contributing to the lift of a supersonic aircraft.

proposition. For instance, in the graph in Table 13.2, if we put Proposition 1 at level 1, then Propositions 2, 4, 7 will be at level 2, Propositions 3, 5, 8 at level 3, and Proposition 6 at level 4.

The level of a proposition in a text predicts whether a reader will judge it to be important; level also predicts whether the proposition will be remembered. In line with this prediction, Kintsch (1974, 1975) has found that the subject's probability of recalling the gist (meaning) of a proposition decreases the greater its logical distance from the main topic proposition. The effect is shown in Figure 13.14, which presents a graph of college students' gist recall of different 70-word paragraphs excerpted from *Scientific American* articles. Recall dependencies between propositions also seem to follow the connectivity graph; thus, a detail proposition (say, at level 4) will rarely be recalled alone without being accompanied by the higher-level (level 3) proposition connected to it. Further, thinking of the proposition at one level is known to "prime" the subject's readiness to retrieve from memory propositions directly connected to it in the graph structure. Thus, the level of a proposition in the connectivity graph is a major determinant of its recall.

This level variable also seems to predict subject's judgments of relative *importance* of the propositions to the "overall meaning" of the paragraph (see Bower, 1976). It also predicts the likelihood that the proposition will appear when the reader is asked to summarize briefly or write an abstract of the full paragraph.

The connectivity graph seems to work reasonably well because it is correlated with the usual topical organization of paragraphs. Thus, if a student outlines a text as he was taught in grammar school into main topics, subtopics, sub-subtopics with details, that organizational chart turns out to be similar to the levels in the connectivity graph formed according to the shared concepts hypothesis. For alternative conceptions of text structure, see Meyer (1975) and Thorndyke (1978).

Kintsch and van Dijk (1979) proposed a more general model for text memory that hypothesized a mechanism to explain why

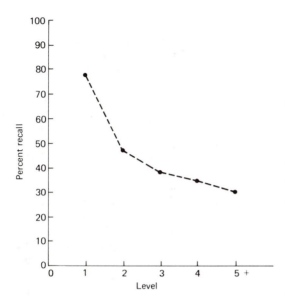

top-level propositions are better recalled (see Figure 13.14). Propositions that are central to the text and contain concepts that are frequently mentioned are as a result kept active longer in the reader's STM. Thus, these propositions are accorded extra rehearsal and learning time and become highly recallable for that reason. Kintsch and Vipond (1978) extended this hypothesis to predict the "comprehension difficulty" or "readability" of particular texts. Holding constant the familiarity of the words, they used different texts that introduced new ideas per proposition at varying rates. Kintsch and Vipond found that the rated difficulty of a text and the time subjects required to read it for understanding increased directly with the text's average rate of introducing new ideas. The Kintsch-Vipond reading model is an exact formulation of a principle long known to reading instructors—namely, that "redundant" or "slow paced" material is easier to read and

remember. This result also follows from Anderson's ACT or similar learning models, since more idea-sharing between successive propositions implies that *fewer* new associative linkages must be formed in order to record the text's information into memory.

Kintsch and van Dijk (1979) readily acknowledge that in processing a text, the reader or listener is doing many more things than just noting whether successive propositions share ideas. The reader is also abstracting the overall gist of the text in a form almost like an outline. Kintsch and van Dijk admit that the shared concepts hypothesis will not suffice for a full understanding of coherence relations within texts. For example, a sequence of sentences can enumerate different predicates about the same concept, yet the text will appear incoherent if the predicates are unrelated or contradictory. A second problem is that two sentences may be closely related and coherent, yet not share any concepts. For example, "John went to the restaurant. The steak was great. The waitress got a big tip" is a sensible sequence, yet no concepts are *explicitly* repeated. Readers understand the sequence because they can *infer* the deleted parts using their knowledge of the restaurant *script*. (This script idea was discussed in Chapter 12.) Thus, the script enables inferences about the ideas shared between these elliptical sentences: it was John who ate the steak and tipped the waitress who brought him the steak, and so on.

One of the major issues on the research agenda is specifying how readers use their knowledge of the situation a text is about to make plausible inferences; the computation of these inferences is necessary to fill the literal gaps in a textual description of the situation. This is an issue currently being addressed within restricted knowledge domains by schema theory (Thorndyke, 1978) and by Schank and Abelson's (1977) theory of scripts, plans, and goals.

Space does not permit a review of this work here; the references cited should be seen for some reviews (see also Bower, 1976, 1978c). Research on text understanding and memory has become a major focus of theoretical and experimental concern in cognitive psychology. We may expect such text research to have significant yields for our understanding of human learning of complex material. It should also contribute to instructional training in educational settings.

The Future of Global Models of Long-Term Memory

It is not possible in a brief survey to provide the full rationale, intuitive evidence, and motivation underlying the work on models of semantic information processing and text memory. The books by J. R. Anderson and Bower (1973), Kintsch (1974), Norman and Rumelhart (1975), or J. R. Anderson (1976) should be consulted for the underlying rationales. However, several comments are appropriate regarding the significance of these theories. First, they are theories which for the first time bring learning research into rather direct and fruitful contact with research in linguistics and psycholinguistics. It has always seemed that any sensible reconstruction of human memory must be able to make some reasonable remarks about how language is used to learn and to remember propositions, episodes, stories, plays, factual materials, and the like. But S-R theory and the verbal learning tradition have not built sturdy bridges from their laboratory base to the problem of the understanding of language; the persuasive and devastating criticisms of those older accounts made by the linguist Noam Chomsky, and by his associates, were reviewed in Chapter 7. Psycholinguistics as an intellectual movement was largely born out of Chomsky's critiques as well as his systematic insights about language. While psycholinguistics has been a most vigorous research area, it has remained largely divorced from the more traditional research on human memory (for reviews see Clark & Clark, 1978; G. A. Miller & McNeill, 1969; or Slobin, 1971). These new theories of semantic memory reviewed briefly above provide common grounds of contact and mutual interest between psycholinguistics, artificial intelligence, and the experimental psychology of memory. This is exemplified, for example, in the books by Anderson and Bower (1973) and Anderson (1976), which review and combine research work in these several areas. They propose a theory of an operational system for cognition (realized as a computer simulation program) which (1) carries out a linguistic analysis of sentences given to the system, (2) provides a means for looking up what is already known about the newly arriving information so as to decide what parts of old memories can be reused in recording the new information, (3) provides a mathematical description of the process by which new informational structures such as that in Figure 13.11 are acquired, and (4) describes and experimentally tests a plausible retrieval mechanism whereby a question or retrieval probe gains access to information that is relevant to constructing an answer. Practically all of the experimental evidence cited by Anderson and Bower as favoring their model comes from their own and others' research on memory for propositional materials, on confusion errors in sentence-recognition memory, on difficulties people experience in comprehending sentences and in verifying sentences against pictures or known facts, and on distortions of memory for thematically related textual materials. However, they also make very explicit efforts to show how their theory stems from the associationist tradition in psychology, how the theory would operate in standard verbal learning tasks, and how it encompasses the standard results supporting the interference theory of transfer and forgetting. The significance of the Anderson and Bower work was its detailed and serious attempt to bring together these two research areas and two traditions (associative memory and psycholinguistics), and to assess their respective contributions to understanding human memory.

Theoretical work on models of long-term memory is still in the formative, searching stage (see J. R. Anderson, 1976, and Freija, 1972, for reviews). Without doubt this is an area that will undergo a tremendous upswing in scientific activity within the next decades, and the modest theories now being tentatively offered will soon be outdistanced. The new work is important, however, because it represents the "coming home" finally of the prodigal psychologist to the tough but fascinating problems of understanding how the human mind uses its linguistic knowledge and intellectual skills in learning and remembering. Such problems cannot be avoided indefinitely; the promise of recent models of semantic memory and question-answering is that they are at least leading us once again into these paths, to ask the significant and fundamental questions. The road is rocky and progress is difficult; but we have the assurance that we are studying fundamental processes of the intellect. The development of performance models for language comprehension and memory, and their utilization, constitutes a major problem for cognitive psychology in the coming decades.

SOCIAL LEARNING THEORY

A book such as this one which reviews different theoretical approaches must give the impression that the present theoretical scene is seriously fragmented into a multitude of warring camps, all in contention for dominance. But that impression is terribly misleading; indeed, nothing could be further from the truth. Although disagreement exists within almost any collection of scientists, among learning theorists the disagreements usually concern not basic findings or fundamental principles but rather the interpretation to be placed upon certain facts. Within the contemporary scene in learning theory, disagreements are not over fundamentals except for the major division that still remains between Skinnerian behaviorists and cognitive psychologists. These two approaches involve somewhat different methodological orientations, different commitments regarding the proper subject matter of psychology, and different restrictions on what kinds of theories are admissible. This distinction was discussed in our review of Skinner's position (Chapter 7), and of the behavior modification movement within clinical and educational psychology which has derived its impetus from operant conditioning concepts. The reader may have gotten the impression that modern cognitive psychology (see P. H. Lindsay & Norman, 1972; Neisser, 1967) deals only with human memory and perceptual processes and not with other factors such as motivation, reward, and contingency management of behavior. But this is not true. Social learning theory, a systematic position advanced by Bandura (1969, 1971a, 1971b, 1977a; Bandura & Walters, 1963) and many others (Mischel, 1968; N. E. Miller & Dollard, 1941; Rotter, 1954; Staats, 1968, 1975), tries to provide a more balanced synthesis of cognitive psychology with the principles of behavior modification. It is a selective distillation of what is probably a "consensus" position of moderation on many issues of importance to any theory of learning and behavior modification. Social learning theory not only deals with the usual set of learning principles but also adds several new ones, and attempts to describe in detail how a set of social and personal competences (so-called personality) could evolve out of the social conditions within which this important learning occurs. It also deals rather explicitly with techniques of personality assessment (Mischel, 1968) and behavior modification in clinical and educational settings (Bandura, 1969; Krumboltz & Thoresen, 1969; Watson & Tharp, 1977).

Although the social learning theorist accepts the usual injunctions of the behaviorist against invoking psychodynamic "inner causes" of disturbed behavior, he tempers the injunction with a counteremphasis on the role of cognitive-symbolic functioning in acquiring new behaviors and in regulating the frequency and occasions of their appearance.

> A valid criticism of the extreme behavioristic positions is that, in a vigorous effort to eschew spurious inner causes, it neglected determinants of man's behavior arising from his cognitive functioning. Man is a thinking organism possessing capabilities that provide him with some power of self-direction. To the extent that traditional behavioral theories could be faulted, it was for providing an incomplete rather than an inaccurate account of human behavior. The social learning theory places special emphasis on the important roles played by vicarious, symbolic, and self-regulatory processes (Bandura, 1971a, p. 2).

As is well known, the traditional theories of learning had placed great emphasis on learning by direct experience, by the application of reinforcement contingencies to practiced responses. This is wrapped up in the notions of "learning by doing," of response differentiation, and of the shaping of complex behavior chains by successive approximation. Social learning theory accepts such shaping principles although it tends (much as did Tolman) to see the role of rewards in this process as both conveying information about the optimal response in the situation and as providing incentive motivation for a given act because of the anticipated reward. And in contrast to the learning-by-doing emphasis, social learning theory holds that a large amount of human learning is done *vicariously,* through *observing* another person

making the skilled responses (or reading about it or viewing pictures of it) and then by trying to imitate the response of the model. By this means, the observer can often learn and some time later perform novel responses without ever having made them before or having been reinforced for them (since they have never occurred before). It is obvious that many human skills (e.g., pronunciation of foreign words) could not be acquired at all without this observational learning, and that most other skills, such as driving, which *could* be learned laboriously (though dangerously) by reinforcing successive approximations alone, are in practice taught more efficiently through verbal instructions and demonstrations by a model performer. Although these teaching techniques are used routinely and are familiar to all of us, the reader should realize how very discrepant they actually are from the paradigm of training recommended by exclusive use of operant reinforcement procedures.

Observational Learning

In a fertile series of research papers and books, Bandura (1962, 1965, 1969, 1971a, 1971b, 1977a) has pointed out the ubiquity and efficiency of such observational learning in humans and has emphasized its unique features not found in the standard paradigms of shaping and instrumental conditioning. He has also carried out an admirable series of studies, mostly with young children, that throw light on the variables that influence such observational learning.

In the typical experiment, a kindergarten child (the subject) sits and watches some person (the model) perform a particular behavioral sequence. Later the subject is tested under specified conditions to determine to what extent his behavior now mimics that displayed by the model. His behavior is compared with that of control subjects who have not observed the model.

A number of factors can be varied in this situation, and many have been shown to affect the extent of imitative behavior performed by the subject. We list a few of those studied by Bandura:

A. Stimulus properties of the model
  1. The model's age, sex, and status relative to that of the subject are varied. High-status models are more imitated.
  2. The model's similarity to the subject: the model may be either another child in the same room, or a child in a movie, or an animal character in a movie cartoon, and so on. Imitation induced in the subject decreases as the model is made more dissimilar to a real person.
B. Type of behavior exemplified by the model
  1. Novel skills are compared to novel sequences of known responses. The more complex the skills, the poorer the degree of imitation after one observation trial.
  2. Hostile or aggressive responses. These are imitated to a high degree.
  3. Standards of self-reward for good versus bad performances. The subject will adopt self-reward standards similar to those of the model. Also, the subject will imitate the type of moral standards exhibited by an adult model. Techniques of self-control can be transmitted in this manner.
C. Consequences of model's behavior
  1. Whether the model's behavior is rewarded, punished, or "ignored" (neither reinforced nor punished) by other agents in the drama is varied. Rewarded behaviors of the model are more likely to be imitated.
D. Motivational set given to the subject
  1. Instructions given to the subject before he observes the model provide him with high or low motivation to pay attention to and learn the model's behavior. High motivation might be produced by telling the subject that he will be rewarded commensurate with how much of the model's behavior he can reproduce on a later test. Under minimal instructions, learning is classified mainly as "incidental."

2. Motivating instructions may be given after the subject views the model and before he is tested. This aids in distinguishing learning from performance of imitative responses.

This listing of variables in the observational learning situation is hardly exhaustive, and is intended only to show the range of possibilities. A wide range of behaviors can be transmitted under these conditions by the model, and the fidelity of the subject's mimicry (even under incidental learning conditions) is often remarkable.

As mentioned above, the model's behavior is more often imitated when the model has been rewarded rather than punished. Bandura was able to show that this reward-punishment variable affected the subject's *performance* of imitative responses but not his *learning* of them. After the observation trial, attractive rewards were offered to the subjects if they would reproduce the model's responses. This increased the display of imitative responses and totally wiped out the differential effect of having seen a rewarded versus a punished model. Thus it was found that the observer had learned the "bad guy's" responses even though he did not perform them until the incentive to do so was offered.

Mechanisms of Observational Learning

The mechanisms required for such observational learning have been rather extensively analyzed by Bandura and his associates. A volume (Bandura, 1971b) describes the research, but it can be briefly noted and contrasted to the Skinnerian view (see Gewirtz & Stingle, 1968). The operant-conditioning analysis of modeling relies on the standard three-term paradigm S^d-R-S^r, where S^d denotes the modeling stimulus (e.g., the model touching his left ear), R denotes the overt matching response performed by the observer, and S^r denotes the reinforcement provided by some agent for matching ("imitative") responses. As Bandura says about this paradigmatic reconstruction:

> The scheme above does not appear applicable to observational learning where an observer does not overtly perform the model's responses in the setting in which they are exhibited, reinforcements are not administered either to the model or to the observer, and whatever responses have been thus acquired are not displayed for days, weeks, or even months. Under these conditions, which represent one of the most prevalent forms of social learning, two of the factors (R → S^r) in the three-element paradigm are absent during acquisition, and the third factor (S^d, or modeling stimulus) is typically missing from the situation when the observationally learned response is first performed. . . . Skinner's analysis clarifies how similar behavior that a person has previously learned can be prompted by the actions of others and the prospect of reward. However, it does not explain how a new matching response is acquired observationally in the first place . . . such learning occurs through symbolic processes during exposure to the modeled activities before any responses have been performed or reinforced.[1]

In his analysis of observational learning, Bandura emphasizes four interrelated subprocesses. The processes and some of the variables affecting them are shown in Figure 13.15. First are *attentional* processes: the model stimulus must be attended to by the subject if she is to learn from the model; a number of factors are known to influence this attention, including, for example, the past functional value of attention to models of a particular type and competence. Included here are sensory abilities of the observer as well as stimulus distinctiveness of the model and her modeled actions. Second are *retention* processes, and the study of these has been the special province of researchers on human memory. If the model's behavior is to exert influence upon the observer's behavior at a much later point in time, then the model's be-

[1] Albert Bandura, *Social Learning Theory* (1971), p. 6.

havior as a stimulus event has to be coded, symbolically represented, and retained over that interval.

To elaborate on this latter point, observational learning in humans involves two representational systems—an imaginal and a verbal one. During exposure to modeling stimuli, sequences of corresponding sensory experiences (images) occur and appear to become associated or integrated by mere contiguity. (See F. D. Sheffield's [1961] analysis of the learning of "perceptual blueprints" mentioned in Chapter 4.) Later, the revival of the integrated sensory experiences will guide the observer's behavior in imitation. The abundant research on mental imagery in human memory lends special credence to this form of cognitive event sequences. The second representational system, verbal coding, can be designed to be of varying levels of efficiency. At the simplest level, once verbal labels ("names") are available to the subject, she can describe to herself the model's behavior as it unfolds, and can then rehearse and learn these verbal descriptions. Their later recall can serve as cues for directing or guiding the subject through the imitative responses. An experiment by Bandura, Grusec, and Menlove (1966) manipulated this factor by having children view a model (shown in a film) under three different conditions. In one, the subject verbalized aloud the sequence of novel responses performed by the model. In another, the subject was instructed merely to observe carefully. In the third, the subject was required to count rapidly while watching the film, and this presumably interfered with her implicitly verbalizing and learning the model's behavior. A later performance test, under either high or low incentive for imitation, showed the three groups ranked in the order in which we listed them in their ability to imitate the model's behavior. That is, subjects who described in words the model's behaviors learned best, and those who had to engage

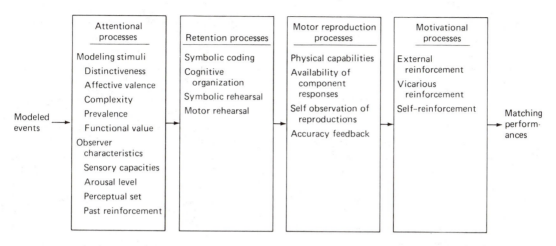

Figure 13.15. Component processes governing observational learning in Bandura's social learning analysis. (From Bandura, 1977a.)

in the interfering counting task during observation learned the least.

Related experiments by Bandura and Jeffery (1973) and by Gerst (1971) pretrained subjects to use a special vocabulary for verbally coding complex perceptual events. In the Bandura and Jeffery experiment, the subject learned a verbal name for each of several two-component movements describing the model person's path in moving a stylus through a visual maze; the criterion task required the subject to learn and reproduce a sequence of 12 movements (6 two-link movements). In Gerst's study, subjects were taught labels for components of the manual sign language of the deaf, and were then compared to nonpretrained subjects in their ability to learn from a visual demonstration of hand signs how to reproduce a set of signs. As would be expected, subjects who had been taught a special verbal code for specific components of the movements of the model easily segmented the criterion modeled sequence into these components, labeled them, rehearsed the labels, and were far superior to untrained controls in their later ability to reproduce the model's criterion performance.

None of this is surprising, especially not to researchers who study the role of cognitive representations in human memory. The experimental situation is really not much different from the typical laboratory study in verbal learning where a subject observes verbal items exposed by a memory drum and later recites them back (and if they are familiar patterns—words—they are more easily acquired than if they are unfamiliar nonsense). To a large extent also, variables similar to those found to influence verbal learning will apply to learning by observation (e.g., competitive sources of control, proactive and retroactive interference, complexity of the material, and so on). That is, if the subject is exposed to a "cast" of several models performing several different actions, we can well expect her (as does the paired-associate learner) to become confused in remembering which model did what performance with what consequences.

To return to Bandura's analysis of imitative learning in Figure 13.15, the third subprocess he emphasizes is *motoric reproduction* skills. A child or adult may know "cognitively" and roughly what is to be done (can "recognize" a correct performance) but nonetheless be relatively un-skilled at the performance itself. Skilled acts like auto driving, ballet dancing, or golfing typically require many small com-ponents; even though the sequence of acts may be communicated by observation, the fine motor coordination required within the components themselves may be absent in the novice, so that the entire perfor-mance appears quite amateurish. Often the relevant parts of the skilled movement (e.g., tipping a shoulder while swinging a golf driver) are not conspicuous to the casual observer or even to the performer himself, and considerable motor practice with feedback of results is needed to grad-ually shape the motor skills. But to soften this point, it is known that with some motor skills such as basketball shooting, driving, and dart throwing, covert "cogni-tive rehearsal" or "imaginary practice" can often produce significant improvements in actual performance (for a review, see Rich-ardson, 1969).

The fourth subprocess in Bandura's analysis of observational learning is the role of *reinforcement*. He treats the antici-pation of reinforcement as a motivational factor determining expression of cognitions and behaviors learned earlier. A person will tend to perform or inhibit a vicari-ously learned response to the extent that he believes he will be rewarded or punished for performing the act. Reinforcement may also alter the level of observational learn-ing by affecting who or what the observer will attend to (e.g., stimulus properties of attractive, prestigious models) and how actively he codes and rehearses the modeled behavior. This conception of reinforcement is rather like that adopted by most modern learning theorists with the conspicuous ex-ception of the Skinnerians; they would still hold to a "direct strengthening" view of reinforcement, and would account for "in-centive motivation" in terms of the dis-criminative-stimulus character of verbal "anticipations" of reinforcement.

As a final word on the topic, it is impor-tant to point out that in a practical sense an optimal training program for trans-mitting many behaviors to human beings would use the observational method in conjunction with differential reinforce-ment. By having the person observe a model, we increase the initial probability that a response pattern resembling the one desired will occur. After it occurs, the re-sponse can be further refined or differenti-ated and its rate stepped up by reinforce-ment. For some finely skilled performances, once the activity has been initiated, more benefit derives from actual practice in the skill than from further observing of the model. The division and order of allot-ment of time for observing a model versus practicing with reinforcing feedback will surely have different optimal arrangements depending on the nature of the particular task performance to be shaped. Such ques-tions concerning what is optimal would seem, at present, to have no general an-swers, and each must be worked out under appropriate field conditions.

This combination of techniques has also proven most effective in overcoming neu-rotic phobias in clinical practice. Much research has examined techniques to help patients overcome extremely debilitating fears of snakes, rats, or spiders. In the model-ing situation the client watches another person carry out increasingly bold ap-proach responses to a live snake; this ex-posure by itself moderately reduces the client's fear and also increases his ability to approach the feared object. However, the most effective procedure involves the model verbally encouraging the client to follow along. with her bold responses step by step, so that the transfer of the model's actions to the client occurs in small, progressive steps that result in increasingly bold inter-actions with the feared object. This *partici-pant modeling* technique has proven very effective in overcoming severe phobias in clinical patients.

We have discussed observational learning in some detail not only because of the intrinsic interest of the topic but also because it highlights one of the differences between social learning theory and a straightforward operant-conditioning analysis of the same phenomenon.

Motivation in Cognitive Theories

Motivation is primarily concerned with how actions are activated and selected. Cognitive theorists suppose that most external or internal instigators to action are mediated through the person's cognitive system. Common motivators include strong environmental stimulation (heat, cold, shock) and bodily conditions such as hunger, thirst, and sexual arousal. The cognitive theorist would point out that the impelling, "motivational force" of these conditions for humans is largely modifiable through the cognitive system. Thus, ascetics or hunger-strikers starve themselves and yet report little of the urgency for food we associate with extreme hunger. Also, people can be taught simple relaxation, distraction, and self-coping routines that will enable them to endure levels of pain that were formerly intolerable (see Meichenbaum, 1977). Experimental subjects who have fasted for a day and who then agree to a request to continue fasting for further experimentation will later report feeling less hunger, will have less free fatty acids in their blood (normally an index of hunger), and will eat less when they are eventually allowed a few snacks. A volume edited by Zimbardo (1969), *The cognitive control of motivation,* reviews many experiments in which indices of motivated behaviors are systematically manipulated by cognitions regarding social commitment, dissonance, and self-esteem. The point of such studies is that humans are not passive pawns of their biological drives or of external stimulation but can control their reactions to those forces.

Given the comforts of our affluent society, compelling external forces rarely move us. Instead, we are more often motivated by cognitive representations in which we strive to bring about desired outcomes or avert difficulties. The cognitions of future outcomes provide the largest single source of motivation for human action. Reinforcement and punishment, given or promised, affect behavior largely because they create expectations that particular actions will produce desired outcomes. These anticipated outcomes provide incentive motivation for the indicated actions in much the way envisioned by Hull and Spence.

Emotional reactions. Many human emotions are connected with anticipated gains or losses, or result from the appraisal of some personal event. Thus, expectation of a gain or success creates pleasant excitement and euphoria; anticipation of harm or danger creates anxiety. Appraising an event as causing the loss of something valuable creates feelings of sadness or depression. Anger results from appraising a noxious social event as deliberately intended harm toward oneself or a loved one. Relief results from the removal of fear or an uncomfortable situation. Cognitive psychologists believe that emotions are largely influenced by *cognitive appraisals.* The cognitive appraisal system is a set of rules, perhaps unconscious but nonetheless modifiable, for interpreting a range of social events as good or bad, happy or sad, threatening or harmless. For example, a severely depressed person often has internal cognitive rules which cause him to overreact to social events in self-depreciating and self-defeating ways. Thus, he will interpret a compliment as an expression of pity towards himself, overgeneralize any of his small failures as showing serious inadequacy, and leap to self-denigrating conclusions from neutral evidence (see Beck,

1976). He knows how to snatch defeat from the jaws of victory.

One advantage of conceptualizing emotions in this way is that it suggests therapeutic techniques for alleviating depression, shyness, unhappiness, and anxiety. A basic procedure is to attack the inappropriate thoughts of the patient in order to demonstrate the illogicality of the inferences, and to suggest substitute rules that will lead to more realistic and less disabling appraisals. This form of cognitive restructuring is frequently used in behavior modification programs (Beck, 1976; Ellis & Harper, 1973; Meichenbaum, 1977).

Self-Regulatory Processes

A second source of cognitive motivation lies in goal-setting and self-reinforcement. Self-motivation results from setting goals and defining standards by which people evaluate their behavior. People will commit themselves to a particular goal and evaluate their performance in relation to the goal. They will reward themselves with self-satisfaction if they attain their standard, but be dissatisfied and perhaps even punish themselves if they fail to attain it. These self-evaluations give goading force to the goals people set for themselves. The self-regulatory system enables a person to work towards behavioral goals, including even the goal of becoming independent of others' control.

Social learning theorists have written and researched many aspects of self-regulation (see Bandura, 1977a, 1977b). One task is to describe how children learn the components of self-regulation. These components include the setting of standards to be achieved, monitoring one's performance, evaluating it according to its approximation to the standard, and rewarding one's standard-attaining performance. By better understanding the components of the process, skills in self-regulation can be taught to children or adults who are deficient in

some respect and who wish to gain better control over their own behavior.

One much-studied issue is how children acquire evaluative standards. Mostly this occurs by imitation of the standards modeled by family, peers, and prestigious figures in the media. Children also acquire moral and ethical standards through their parents' or teachers' examples; they also learn through modeling how to justify their standards through moral appeals or arguments.

Psychologists have also studied how a person should set goals in order to motivate optimal achievement. All agree that it is best to have a clearly specified goal that is of moderate difficulty. Goals that are too hard or too easy to attain are neither motivating nor reinforcing when attained. Second, in order to attain a difficult and distant goal, one should set for oneself a series of small, immediate subgoals that lead up to that distant goal. Thus, an overweight person attempting to lose weight is advised to set small "proximate subgoals" (such as keeping track of and reducing the number of calories eaten for each half day) instead of setting a distant, difficult goal (such as losing 10 pounds in 5 weeks).

Self-regulation seems to be at the heart of several phenomena investigated under other names. For example, the *achievement motivation* of an individual refers to the extent to which she habitually sets very high performance standards for herself and willingly deprives herself of personal rewards until she attains them. A second phenomenon of self-regulatory processes is the role of "knowledge of results" in typical laboratory studies of learning and performance. Knowledge of performance reinforces and motivates only when the subject has set standards to be attained and can evaluate her own performance. The standards are typically specified by the experimenter's instructions. External reward systems (such as the nursery teacher's gold stars) are as powerful as they are because they induce subjects to set goals for themselves and evaluate their performance in accord with standards of their "trainer" (Locke et al., 1970).

Within the self-regulation literature there is considerable discussion concerning the interpretation of self-reinforcement (Bandura, 1977a; Rachlin, 1974). To outward appearances, a person depriving himself of a freely available reward whenever his behavior falls short of his present standard seems to contradict the hedonistic principle of animal behavior. Bandura and Mahoney (1974), however, showed that pigeons and dogs could be trained to deny themselves "freely available" rewards until after they had done an appropriate amount of "work" to earn them. The training regimen essentially punished or nonreinforced the animal whenever he ate the available food before he had earned his reward by prior instrumental responding. Once established with partial punishment, the work-to-eat routine persisted long after the punishment was removed. Thus, the animal *appeared* to forego immediate pleasure, and forced itself to work first to deserve its reward. Presumably, a child learns self-control techniques and continues to use them in order to gain similar backup reinforcers from her parents or social environment. After many years, the self-control procedures work automatically, with no back-up reinforcers except self-praise and "self-respect."

Once established, a self-reinforcement system typically produces two outcomes following a relevant action; a self-evaluation and an external outcome (perhaps a self-administered reward or penalty). These outcomes usually work together in enhancing or suppressing the behavior; thus, a student will praise herself and go out to a movie if she studies longer than her chosen goal time. The praise and the movie serve as incentive motivation before and during the studying behavior. Self-censuring and external penalties similarly motivate behaviors which avert such censure and penalties in the future. One issue being debated is whether the self-administered praise or reproof really strengthens or weakens behavior, or whether they work mainly by frequently prompting or reminding the person of external rewards he has promised himself for high achievements.

In some cases, self-evaluation conflicts with external outcomes, as when one truly devalues some action for which one's colleagues reward one, or when one values actions that the social group ignores or punishes. In these cases, self-evaluation often wins out in determining the regulation and persistence of the behavior. Some forms of self-regulation are so powerful that the behavior can become partially disengaged from social reinforcement systems. Thus, a poor, unrecognized artist who is convinced that his paintings meet the highest artistic standards, will sneer at the work of his more successful peers, and consider it vulgar commercialism. Strong-willed, self-controlled individuals are admired for their courage and independence if their works are prosocial (e.g., eccentric inventors and poets), but feared for their single-mindedness if their actions are antisocial (e.g., psychopathic killers, sadistic dictators). Bandura (1977a) has analyzed the personal and social conditions that can create and maintain antisocial or dehumanizing behavior. His analysis is especially relevant in dealing with aggression and criminality.

Efficacy Expectations and Performance

Tolman's expectancy theory and decision theory were focused exclusively on the organism's expectancy that a given action will lead to a given consequence. To the extent that an outcome contingent on an action is desired and expected, that action will be selected and activated. However, Bandura (1977a, 1977b) has noted another expectancy that is missing from Tolman's theory—namely, the organism's conviction that it can successfully execute the behavior required to produce the outcomes. Bandura calls this behavior *efficacy expectation,* since it consists of a prediction of how effective or competent one's behavior will be. Efficacy expectations differ from *outcome expectations,* which refer to the person's estimate that a given behavior will lead to certain outcomes. Figure 13.16 illustrates the locus of the factors entering into the two expectancies. Such expectancies can be clearly differentiated in verbally fluent people. Thus, a person may know and report that a reward will reliably follow a given behavior (a positive outcome expectancy) but have severe doubts about his ability to perform that behavior effectively (low efficacy expectation). These expectations can also be reversed. The efficacy expectation is similar to Hull's habit variable, $_sH_R$, which denoted the extent to which the organism knew how to perform response R in situation S. However, Bandura imputes more properties to this efficacy expectation construct than Hull did to $_sH_R$.

Like other constructs, efficacy expectations are anchored in terms of what external conditions affect them, and what influences they in turn have on performance. People have efficacy expectations regarding huge numbers of responses in various circumstances. A person's set of efficacy expectations is much like a long, personal list of beliefs about competencies and incompetencies. Regarding performance effects, Bandura assumes that the person's perceived sense of efficacy (mastery) of a given behavior affects whether he will use that behavior in coping with difficult situations; it influences how much effort he will expend on the behavior or how long he will persist with it in the face of obstacles and frustrations. The stronger the efficacy expectation, the longer and more effortful the behavior that will be tried. If the persisting behavior eventually succeeds, the efficacy expectation for that behavior in situations of that type will increase. If the behavior is performed poorly and fails or is given up prematurely, its efficacy expectation for that situation will decrease. In this way the efficacy expectation for a given response in a given situation adjusts itself according to the subject's experiences with that behavior.

Bandura has cited many factors that influence a person's efficacy expectation for some behavior. These are reproduced in Figure 13.17. The four major sources of knowledge about efficacy of a given behavior in a given situation are (1) past accomplishments of one's own behavior, (2) observing others' successes or failures with the behavior, (3) verbal persuasion by self or others, and (4) changes in one's emotional arousal in the target situation. Figure 13.17 lists many procedures that exemplify particular sources of self-efficacy knowledge. Most procedures in Figure 13.17 refer to behavior-therapy techniques commonly used to overcome fear. The techniques have been extensively researched, and they vary considerably in effectiveness. Bandura suggests that the performance-based therapy procedures such as participant modeling (top in Figure 13.17) are more effective than verbal persuasion or emotion-reducing techniques (desensitization) because a successful performance provides a more reliable source of evidence

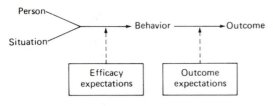

Figure 13.16. Point of reference of efficacy expectations as compared to outcome expectations. (From Bandura, 1977a.)

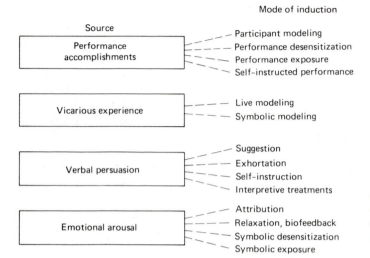

Efficacy expectations

Mode of induction

Source

Performance accomplishments
— Participant modeling
— Performance desensitization
— Performance exposure
— Self-instructed performance

Vicarious experience
— Live modeling
— Symbolic modeling

Verbal persuasion
— Suggestion
— Exhortation
— Self-instruction
— Interpretive treatments

Emotional arousal
— Attribution
— Relaxation, biofeedback
— Symbolic desensitization
— Symbolic exposure

Figure 13.17. Major sources of efficacy expectations and the sources through which different modes of influence operate. (From Bandura, 1977a.)

on which to change one's efficacy expectations. Thus, the best basis for predicting that you will be able to touch a live snake is the knowledge that you actually just did it instead of imagining it.

In research by Bandura (1977b), patients undergoing treatment for snake phobia gave ratings of efficacy expectations at various times before, during, and after treatment. Patients were unusually accurate at estimating how far they would be able to go in a graduated series of approaches and interactions with a snake. This estimate was the measure of efficacy expectation. Groups of subjects received several different kinds of treatment for their phobia, such as imaginal desensitization, modeling, or participant modeling. The groups differed markedly in the degree of change in approach behaviors to the snake. Further, these behavioral changes were paralleled by similar changes in their posttreatment estimates of efficacy in approaching the snake. The correlation between changes in efficacy expectations and in approach behavior was high and nearly identical in all groups. The three thera-

peutic programs influenced the changes in efficacy expectations and in behavior in a parallel manner. Thus, it is plausible to claim that behavior-change procedures are effective only in so far as they first modify efficacy expectations. Critics of the theory would argue that the changed efficacy expectations are just a correlated index of overt behavior changes brought about via reinforcement but are not themselves causes of those changes. Bandura (1978) has supported this research with many further investigations. He has also strongly defended his theory against critical attacks. The theory is currently receiving close scrutiny and is generating much research. We may expect to see significant developments in efficacy theory in the coming years.

CONCLUDING REMARKS

We have reviewed a number of features of social learning theory, using as an example the work of its leading spokesman, Albert

Bandura. Social learning theory is a hybrid; it is a form of cognitive behaviorism that analyzes the learning, motivation, and reinforcement of social behavior in terms of cognitive events mediating the impact of external events. For example, what is critical about reinforcement contingencies is how the person understands and represents them subjectively, not their objective parameters. In many respects, social learning theory is compatible with more liberalized versions of behaviorism. A salient feature of Bandura's work is that he eschews peripheral response mechanisms and readily admits central cognitive processes (coding, imagery, symbolic representations, problem-solving) into his theoretical accounts of observational learning, self-regulation, standard-setting, self-efficacy, and planning. He illustrates through example and experiment how such cognitive processes control the influence of reinforcement contingencies in controlling actions and determine how people think out and evaluate alternate actions, or change their self-concepts. The principles are applied with ingenuity to a wide range of social behaviors such as competitiveness, aggression, sex roles, deviancy, and pathological behavior (see Bandura & Walters 1963; Bandura, 1969, 1977a). In broad outline, social learning theory provides the best integrative summary of what modern learning theory has to contribute to the solution of practical problems. It also provides a compatible framework within which to place information-processing theories of language comprehension, memory, imagery, and problem-solving. These theories, for their part, fill in the details of the "representational systems" and "symbolic processes" that are referred to in applications of social learning theory. For these reasons, social learning theory may provide a basis of consensus for much of the learning research in the next decade.

SUPPLEMENTARY READINGS

An annual volume of new theoretical and experimental work is edited by G. H. Bower; these volumes cover major areas in learning theory and have been published regularly since 1967.

BOWER, G. H., ed. *The psychology of learning and motivation: Advances in research and theory.* Vol. 1 (1967) through Vol. 13 (1979), and continuing.

For recent theory and research on human memory, the following books are appropriate:

ANDERSON, J. R., & BOWER, G. H. (1972). *Human associative memory.*

ANDERSON, J. R. (1976). *Language, memory, and thought.*

BANDURA, A. (1969). *Principles of behavior modification.*

BANDURA, A. (1977a). *Social learning theory.*

CROWDER, R. (1976). *Principles of learning and memory.*

ESTES, W. K., ed. (1975–1978). *Handbook of learning and cognitive processes.* 5 vols.

LINDSAY, P. H., & NORMAN, D. A. (1972). *Human information processing.*

MELTON, A. W., & MARTIN, E., eds. (1972). *Coding processes in human memory.*

NEISSER, U. (1976). *Cognition and reality.*

NISBETT, R., & ROSS, L. (1979). *Human inference.*

NORMAN, D. A., & RUMELHART, D. (1975). *Explorations in cognition.*

SCHANK, R., & ABELSON, R. P. (1977). *Scripts, plans, goals, and understanding.*

STAATS, A. W. (1975). *Social behaviorism.*

WICKELGREN, W. A. (1979). *Cognitive psychology.*

III

Related
Fields

14

NEUROPHYSIOLOGY OF LEARNING

Nothing is more certain than that our behavior is a product of our nervous system. The proposition is almost more tautological than factual. This being the case, one may wonder why theories of learned behavior have not been more explicitly neurophysiological in their content, constructs, and referents. There are many historical reasons for this long-standing divorce between neurophysiology and behavior theory, and we will not attempt to discuss the cleavage here. For one thing, during the period from 1930 to 1960 when most of the leitmotifs in our current approaches to learning were developing, it was felt that neurophysiology had very little that was relevant to offer on the psychological issues of the day. But with the explosion of neuropsychological research in the last two decades, this bias is fading away. Second, the major theories were never intended to describe the specific, actual events as they go on in the nervous system of their model learner. The tactics have been, and still are in large measure, those of descriptive behaviorism supplemented by intervening variable theorizing. The description of generic S-R relationships lies at one level: if you do such-and-so to your subjects, they will behave in such-and-so way. The such-and-so in each instance may be replaced by a rather long listing of what are believed to be the relevant variables. At another level of theorizing, one simply postulates the existence within the organism of certain primitive mechanisms that carry out particular functions or that are governed by a particular set of rules. The behavioral implications of the postulated mechanisms plus their rules of operation are then derived for varying sets of boundary conditions under which the model organism is to be observed.

Levels of Discourse

Such psychological theories operate at a completely different level of discourse than do physiological theories, and what are primitive notions at one level are exceedingly complex mechanisms when viewed from the other. To consider just one example, a computer program to simulate fact retrieval and question-answering by humans must have differing components for (a) storing facts, (b) analyzing and interpreting questions, (c) searching memory for matching structures, (d) retrieving matching structures and composing acceptable answers. But even this brief characterization ignores the really difficult problems of inference and deduction which are inextricably tied up with question-answering. Computer programs to simulate such activities (see Chapter 12) postulate a series of information-processing and storage mechanisms, and an organized sequence of operations carried out on a data base by a set of processes (the program). But now, imagine the task of trying to understand what the program is doing (or attempting) in terms of a moment-by-moment listing of the electrical charges on all the thousands of transistors or in terms of the field alignment of all the millions of magnetic-core storage units in the computer. Imagine that we had similar information about the physiological states of the *twelve billion neurons* in the human brain, each with up to *five thousand* synapses. (The number of possible interconnections exceeds the number of atoms in the universe!) This vast amount of information and its fantastic complexity would utterly dumbfound us; we could not hope to begin creating much order out of such vast quantities of particulate information. Rather, we would need some very powerful theories or ideas about how the particulate information was to be organized into a hierarchy of higher-level concepts referring to structure and function (e.g., for the computer, the notion of a "bit," a "word," a "register," an "address," an "instruction," and so on). Many psychologists feel that their task is to describe the functional program of the brain at the level of flow-charting information-processing mechanisms. What is important is the logical system of interacting parts—the model—and not the specific details of the machinery that might actually embody it in the nervous system. The hardware embodiment is irrelevant to the main scientific question, which is whether the theoretical system gives an adequate explanation, description, or prediction of the primary facts relevant to it. If

it does so, then psychologists, by and large, are satisfied with the theory and are willing to leave it at that. In fact, they claim that their theories, when substantiated, place strong constraints on what will be acceptable neuropsychological theories of behavior.

Neuropsychologists, on the other hand, are not satisfied to leave matters at that level. They are, in fact, dedicated to finding out about the specific hardware that evolution has tucked into our skulls. They wish to discover the actual machinery and how it works in getting an organism around in its everyday commerce with its environment. This is an exceedingly difficult goal because both the nervous system and its behavior are complicated, and neither will be understood with any completeness for a long time. In this chapter we are concerned with learning; and the ability to store information about its history is perhaps the most remarkable capacity of the nervous system. It is also one of the least understood capabilities of nervous tissue.

An act of learning or an act of remembering probably involves many different parts of the nervous system. A performance of even the simplest conditioned response may fail because the organism does not see the stimulus, or does not attend to or register it with his sensory system; he may fail because he forgets how to interpret its meaning, because he never learned it at all, because he is momentarily unable to execute the motor units involved, or because he is no longer motivated to do so or is just not in the mood. This is a loose way to characterize the complex tangle of variables involved in whether and how often a learned act will be performed. It shows, too, the problems of delimiting the research area called the neurophysiology of learning. For example, should receptor physiology be included, since the retina has to transduce a photic signal before it can become a cue for a learned response? Should the study of muscle action be included, since muscles execute the learned performance? By convention such topics are excluded from the learning area because these structures are presumed to function similarly whether or not learning is involved. It is usually assumed that a light flash is coded at the retina in an invariant manner whether the light flash is neutral or produces an expectation of reward or punishment due to past learning. Because of this functional distinction, the physiology of the receptors and effectors is usually not considered relevant to the study of learning; their normal operation is a necessary but not a sufficient condition for information storage.

The main search for learning structures, on the other hand, is directed inward from these peripheral structures to the central nervous system, to the brain in particular. The main question, of course, is what normally happens in the brain during learning. What processes and encoding are involved in storing information in the brain in a relatively permanent manner? Once stored, how is access to this information or retrieval of it achieved to guide later performance? What anatomical structures are involved and how do they operate? Can other structures substitute for them when the original ones are put out of commission? What gets changed during learning, and what is the nature of the change? How does it persist and what, if anything, destroys it? These and many others are the global questions that instigate brain research. Of course, none of them has yet been answered to anyone's satisfaction. Each poses a very large and complicated puzzle, and at any given moment we have only a few pieces of the puzzle before us to aid us in inferring its nature.

Technical Developments

Research into the neurophysiology of learning has been slavishly dependent upon the development of techniques for probing inside the brain. Until about the time of World War II, the technique most commonly used was *ablation,* in which a part of the brain is destroyed or cut out. The technique was refined by development of stereotaxic surgery, whereby an electrode could be lowered into a precise spot inside the brain and there cause a small lesion by cauterizing the brain cells. Following ablation, the animal is observed for behavior deficits in one or more learning tasks. The hope is to infer whether the ablated brain structure is implicated in some way in the performances observed; but this inference is not definitive and it usually requires supporting evidence from other methods. Other techniques that yield information about the brain include electrical recording of the activity or artificial stimulation of selected components of the brain. On the electrical recording side, there are devices for amplifying and faithfully recording or displaying the tiny, rapidly changing electrical signals, which act as the "voices" of neural cells. Such amplifiers have made it possible to record a full range of electrical activity in the nervous system, from the gross electroencephalogram (EEG) obtained from the outer skull case down to the subminiature level which uses microelectrodes to record the activity of single neurons. Laboratory computers are also routinely used now to help the electrophysiologist record and detect regularities and lawful relations in certain forms of "noisy" EEG records in which the significant electrical events are often obscured by random electrical activity of no importance. On the stimulation side, the main techniques being currently exploited are those permitting direct electrical or chemical stimulation of a localized area of the brain of an intact animal that is awake, moving about, and behaving normally. Small bipolar electrodes may be implanted permanently in the animal's brain, with the animal living indefinitely with them in place. To stimulate the indicated brain structure, the wire tips of the electrodes protruding from the skull are connected to a source of electrical energy. Similarly implanted cannulae or tiny hypodermic needles may be used to inject chemical solutions or implant crystalline chemicals into a part of the brain. A technique has also been developed to provide for continuous sampling and measurement of various neural chemicals from the brain. Called the *push-pull system,* it involves two cannulae implanted side by side in the brain; a neutral "bathing" solution is slowly "pushed in" one cannula, while the solution plus the dissolved neural chemicals (from structures around the cannulae tips) are "pulled out" of the other cannula by a suction system. Neurally acting drugs can also be injected in tiny amounts, and their metabolites or other byproducts can be collected after varying times, thus providing a picture of the time course of uptake and activity by the drug. The existence of many such techniques creates conditions that have indeed been exceptionally favorable for an expansion of research in neurophysiology.

The specific topics to be reviewed in this chapter are a selected sample of those cultivated mainly within the last 35 years. The work on attention, reward, and motivation is included because of the central influence of these factors upon learning and performance. In each case, our intention will be to give some idea of the type of findings relevant to each topic, describing these in relatively nontechnical language so that results may be understandable to readers unfamiliar with neurophysiology.

MOTIVATION, AROUSAL, AND ATTENTION

Motivation and learning are intimately related, no matter what position one takes with respect to the role of drive in habit acquisition and in the performance of learned acts. Hence we turn first to neurophysiological knowledge about drive, reward and punishment, arousal and attention, before turning to the more strict learning topics of memory and association.

Motivational Mechanisms in the Brain

Extensive physiological research has investigated the neurological mechanisms involved in the common biological motives. Most work has been done on thirst, hunger, and sex. The story is, of course, far from complete, but at least some headway has been made. We will briefly review some of the evidence on the neural mechanisms in the brain subserving these consummatory activities.

Hunger. The study of hunger is by far the most difficult because of its many complex features. Organisms, in addition to being simply hungry for food in general, also regulate the amount of specific kinds of food they eat, and they do this according to their body's special requirements for carbohydrates, proteins, fats, minerals, and vitamins. A variety of diet-selection studies have shown that animals can detect their specific deficits and regulate their intake of appropriate substances with incredible accuracy. Recent studies have begun to clarify some of the mechanisms underlying this adaptiveness of diet selection. It has been found by Garcia and Koelling (1966) that a novel taste can become selectively associated with an internal physiological aftereffect (e.g., nausea or stomach sickness) at very long delays of several hours. This same type of association has been proposed to explain dietary selection by an animal with a particular dietary deficiency (see Rozin, 1965, 1967; Rozin & Kalat, 1972). The taste of a food rich in the needed substance is followed later by a beneficial internal effect; this results in that taste sensation's becoming a "good taste," which is then selected repeatedly by the animal.

Along with this enhanced understanding of selective subhungers, there is also rather extensive knowledge about the regulation of *how much* food in general is consumed. Multiple factors are involved, psychological as well as physiological. Popular concerns with overweight and health have motivated many studies of obese humans, and much is known about this topic. Obese people have more fat cells ready to absorb nutrients. As a result, they have a lower metabolic rate, so they burn up calories more slowly and gain more weight per calorie eaten than do slender people. Also, obese people seem to have a stronger conditioned release of insulin when they see (or think about) palatable food than do slender people. This anticipatory insulin release is similar to a Pavlovian conditioned response, and may underlie some of the intense "appetite" aroused in obese people by food stimuli. Based on such results, a treatment for obesity now being attempted is to extinguish the conditioned insulin release by pairing food stimuli with a drug that inhibits insulin release. This is alleged to reduce the urgent appetite or craving the patient feels when he thinks of his favorite foods.

Much research has centered on brain mechanisms that underlie feeding in animals. The primary neural structures involved either lie within, or are fibers passing through, the *hypothalamus,* which is located at the base of the brain directly behind the throat. The hypothalamus is a small nub of tissue in the human brain about the size of the tip of the little finger. It is phylogenetically a very old part of the brain. A number of biological functions seem to be regulated through the hypothalamus. One of these is regulation of hunger and feeding. The *ventromedial nucleus* close to the midline of the hypothalamus appears to contain fibers involved in stopping eating or detecting satiety. That is, its normal functioning seems to produce cessation of eating after the animal has consumed a sufficient amount to remove any deficit. This ventromedial nucleus may be destroyed by a localized electrolytic lesion; it is coagulated, or "burnt out," by a strong electric current delivered through an implanted electrode. When this is done, the animal for a time appears unable to stop eating. She overeats by large amounts (hyperphagia) and soon becomes very obese, perhaps more than doubling her normal weight. The overeating appears to be caused by the absence of an appropriate "stop" mechanism, not from an increased hunger drive. Hyperphagic animals will not work very hard to get their food, and they will not tolerate much adulteration of the food with bitter quinine before they reject it, whereas normally hungry animals will both work hard and tolerate quinine in order to get something to eat. Schachter (1971) has noted a number of parallels between hyperphagic animals and severely obese humans in their eating patterns.

At one time, the research story seemed simple. It was felt that the ventromedial nucleus integrated signals from the mouth, stomach, and certain nutrients (e.g., glucose) circulating in the bloodstream or cerebrospinal fluid; these stimulated the nucleus and its resulting activity, through some unknown means, terminated eating. Thus, if this structure were artificially stimulated by an electric current (by means of an implanted electrode) while a hungry animal was eating, the animal would be inhibited from further eating while the current was on (Wyrwicka & Dobrzecka, 1960). Learned responses rewarded by food were similarly inhibited by electrical stimulation of the ventromedial nucleus.

Recent research has complicated the picture (see Grossman, 1975). A first complication is that hyperphagia and obesity have been produced by minute lesions in other brain structures which give rise to fibers that pass through or nearby the ventromedial nucleus. Kapatos and Gold (1973), for instance, produced hyperphagic rats by selective lesions in the ventral noradrenergic bundle located along the pons and midbrain, which sends fibers near the ventromedial nucleus of the hypothalamus. A second complication is that it appears that the liver has crucial roles in signaling the brain when to start or stop eating, and the ventromedial nucleus and vagus nerve seem to be implicated in receiving and sending these signals. Liver function partly controls metabolism, the breakdown and utilization of food (nutrients) as energy. Normally, adipose tissue (what laymen call "fat") absorbs food fat and other nutrients during the absorptive phase after a meal, and then (like a sponge) releases these nutrients for energy conversion as needed during fasting, between meals. According to Friedman and Stricker (1976), the best explanation for the obesity produced by ventromedial lesions is that the lesions reduce metabolism, thereby putting the animal's body continually in the absorptive phase; the adipose "sponge" continually soaks up nutrients, never gives them back out, the muscle cells scream for energy, and so the animal eats more, although she is lethargic and unmotivated.

The "start" mechanisms for eating appear to lie in (or pass through) the lateral areas of the hypothalamus, one on either side of the midline. Destruction of the lateral hypothalamus on both sides (bilateral ablation) produces an animal that refuses to eat (or drink), and if special measures are not taken, it will starve to death in a cage filled with food. Teitelbaum and Epstein (1962) report that such animals go through several stages while being nursed back to recovery. For several days after the bilateral ablation, the animals (rats) refuse to eat or drink, and spit out substances placed in their mouths. They are kept alive by tube-feeding a nutrient liquid directly into their stomachs. After several days, they still refuse to drink but will eat highly palatable (sugary) foods. Later, they may eat regular lab food, though they still refuse to drink water. Still later, normal drinking may return in some animals.

Whether or not and how much an animal will recover seems to depend on the completeness of the original destruction; the larger the lesion, the less the likelihood of significant recovery.

Thirst. This ablation work seems to implicate the lateral hypothalamus in starting both eating and drinking. The two functions have been manipulated separately by localized electrical and chemical stimulation. Electrical stimulation in this area can cause a satiated animal either to eat or to drink depending on the precise location of the electrode. Injection of a tiny amount of a salty solution into this area of the brain will cause excessive drinking in a satiated animal; injection of pure water causes a thirsty animal to stop drinking. In the case of each of these kinds of stimulation, it has been shown that learned habits rewarded by food or water can be regulated (turned on or off) by the stimulation. A fair amount is known about the mechanisms involved in naturally occurring thirst and drinking. Water losses cause an increase in the concentration of electrolytes in the blood, with a resulting increase in its osmotic pressure. This in turn draws more water out of the cellular stores of the body. A set of neural cells lying in the vascular bed of the lateral hypothalamus puts out "thirst" signals when water is needed. These cells—called osmoreceptors—respond to an increase in osmotic pressure of the blood surrounding them. A minute injection of saltwater directly into this area mimics the effect of prolonged dehydration by raising the osmotic pressure in the tissue surrounding these osmoreceptors. One influence of these osmoreceptors is on the pituitary. The pituitary secretes an antidiuretic hormone that causes the kidneys to increase their reabsorption of water, and increase the concentration of urine excreted. The kidneys release angio-tensin, which causes the blood vessels to constrict so that blood pressure rises. Angio-tensin also stimulates the hypothalamus to send "drinking signals" to the cortex.

An interesting line of research begun by Grossman (1960) investigates differential chemical specificity of the feeding and drinking centers in the lateral hypothalamus of the rat. Grossman found that injection of certain chemicals (adrenergic drugs such as adrenaline) into the lateral hypothalamus greatly increased food consumption but did not increase the drinking of water. Injection of other chemicals (cholinergic drugs like carbachol) produced the opposite effect—increased drinking with no increased eating. Many other chemical effects of this kind have been reviewed by N. E. Miller (1965) and Grossman (1967). Of interest here is the fact that the adrenergic drugs used by Grossman (adrenaline and noradrenaline) have been identified as the neural transmitter substance for the sympathetic nervous system, whereas the transmitter for the rest of the nervous sysem is acetylcholine, a cholinergic substance. The selective sensitivity to adrenergic and cholinergic drugs by the drinking and eating centers suggests another basis for the functional differentiation of these drive systems despite their anatomical overlap in the hypothalamus.

Sexual behavior. Finally, we consider the brain centers involved with sexual behavior. In lower animals, sexual behaviors are closely correlated with circulating sex hormones in the blood stream—androgen (specifically testosterone) released by the male's testes, and progesterone and estrogen released by the female's ovaries. The manufacture and release of these gonad hormones is regulated in turn by pituitary hormones. The sex hormones appear to influence sexual behaviors by multiple pathways, but one set of influences occurs in the preoptic area of the hypothalamus, proximal to the pituitary. Ablations in some areas produce a complete loss of sexual behavior, whereas ablations in other areas

have produced exaggerated sexual behavior. In male rats exaggerated sexual activity has been produced by electrical stimulation in the anterior dorsolateral region of the hypothalamus. The electrical stimulus elicited persistent mounting of a female and produced an excess number of ejaculations, far beyond the satiating requirement of a normal male. Earlier work by Fisher (1956) in which testosterone was injected into the hypothalamus of the male rat produced similar results (see also Davidson, 1966). When the hormone was applied in one area (lateral preoptic), exaggerated male sexual behavior was elicited from both male and female rats. When injected in a slightly different area (medial preoptic area of the hypothalamus), both male and female rats would engage in "maternal" behaviors such as building a home nest and retrieving baby rats from outside the nest. These behaviors normally appear only in female rats after giving birth to a litter. When the testosterone hormone is delivered to a site between these two areas, mixed behavior may result: a male rat may alternate between nest-building and mating with an available female. Similar enhancement of sexual behavior in female cats has been reported by Michael (1962), who implanted small paraffin pellets containing estrogen into the hypothalamus. This caused the female to become sexually receptive ("in heat") for a period of 50 to 60 days, as the drug was absorbed very slowly. Though she was sexually receptive, the female cat's vagina and uterus were not in an estrous condition; she would be described as in heat behaviorally but not physiologically. Further, use of radioactively labeled hormones as tracers has shown that hypothalamic regions are implicated in taking-up estrogen from the bloodstream. From such results, it seems safe to conclude that sex drive and receptivity can be induced by direct hormonal stimulation of the hypothalamus.

Reliable sexual responsiveness to electrical stimulation was also reported by Caggiula (1970). Electrical stimulation to the posterior hypothalamus of male rats produced stimulus-bound copulation; if a receptive female were present, the male would readily mount and copulate when the brain stimulation was initiated and would continue, possibly through several ejaculations, as long as the brain stimulation was applied. Caggiula also showed that male rats receiving such brain stimulation would readily learn and perform a bar-pressing response reinforced by access to a receptive female. But the copulatory behavior was not a simple reflexive reaction. Rather, it depended on the convergence of appropriate external supporting stimuli (i.e., a receptive female had to be present to elicit the behavior) and brain tissue that had been appropriately primed through the body's standard supply of sex hormone. If the male rat was castrated, the frequency of sexual behavior "elicited" by the electrical stimulation gradually dwindled over a period of days (presumably as the remaining endogenous sex hormone was metabolized), and eventually the brain site was "sexually inert." Replacement of testosterone would, presumably, bring back the electrically controlled sexual behavior.

In concluding this brief sketch of neural drive centers, it is worth remarking that important structures for each drive system are found in the hypothalamus. In addition to the functions mentioned above, the hypothalamus is known to control other behaviors (e.g., aggressiveness) and to regulate various physiological functions (e.g., regulation of body temperature). Also, as we shall see, electrical stimulation in this area often produces either rewarding or punishing effects. The effectiveness of the rewarding brain shock to these sites can be enhanced or diminished by increasing or decreasing, respectively, the levels of hunger, thirst, or sex drive (e.g., Hoebel & Teitelbaum, 1962). Indeed, the hypothalamus might be called the motivational center of the brain. It now appears plausible

that a remarkable range of psychologically significant variables have their eventual impact upon this small, well-packaged nub of neural tissue.

Reward and Punishment by Brain Stimulation

The significance of the hypothalamus has been enhanced by another set of studies concerned with the effects of reward and punishment. A significant line of research in the last 20 years has been the mapping of the locations of reward and punishment centers in the mammalian brain. The initial observations on the reward effect were made by Olds and Milner (1954) and on the punishment effect by Delgado, Roberts, and Miller (1954). The experimental subject—typically a rat, cat, or monkey—is prepared with a two-pole electrode implanted so that it remains in its brain, with the tiny, stimulating tip of the electrode aimed at a particular structure of the brain. By means of this electrode, a small electric current can be delivered to that part of the brain surrounding the electrode tip, thereby artificially firing off a probably large population of neural cells in the neighborhood of the electrode tip. In the typical reward experiment, the subject is permitted to operate a switch that delivers brief electric shocks to his brain. If he learns to do this repeatedly, operating the lever at an appreciable rate, then stimulation at that brain site is said to be rewarding. Conversely, if he refrains from stimulating his brain under optimal conditions of learning, the stimulation could be either neutral or punishing. If it is punishing (aversive), then he will learn some response to turn off (escape) the brain shock once it is presented. By means of tests such as these, brain structures may be classified as rewarding, neutral, or punishing.

Upon investigation, it has been found that reward sites are densely and widely

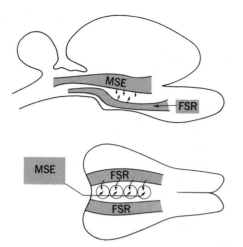

Figure 14.1. Schematic sections of the rat's brain showing locations of major positive and negative reinforcement centers determined by electrical stimulation. The top figure is a sagittal section, slicing fore and aft from the top of the brain to the bottom. The bottom figure is a horizontal section, looking down upon the middle interior of the brain. Pure punishing effects were produced by stimulation of the periventricular system of fibers, here labeled MSE (for midbrain substrate of escape); pure positive rewarding effects were produced by stimulation of the lateral hypothalamic tube, here labeled FSR (forebrain substrate of reward). The nuclei (circled in lower figure) into which both these systems project yield ambivalent—that is, positive-negative—reactions.

scattered throughout the subcortex of the rat's brain. The schematic drawing in Figure 14.1 shows one of the major positive reward systems (labeled FSR for forebrain substrate of reward), a large "tube" of fibers on the lower floor extending from the hindbrain through the midbrain (hypothalamus) forward to the forebrain. Sites in which electrical stimulation produces punishing effects are situated above these reward fibers. They are labeled MSE (for midbrain substrate of escape) in Figure 14.1. These effects depend, of course, on the intensity and other characteristics of the electrical stimulation to the brain. The

intensity of the stimulation must exceed some threshold value before its behavioral effect is seen, and response rate typically increases with stimulus intensity up to some optimal level. Roberts (1958) and Bower and Miller (1958) first reported on electrode placements (in cats and rats, respectively) in which the onset of brain stimulation appeared to be rewarding, but if the stimulation was left on, it apparently became aversive after a few seconds or so. Thus, the animals would learn to perform one response to turn on the stimulus and another response to turn it off. These dual effects apparently arise because, although the electrode tip is located among positive reward cells, there are negative cells in the vicinity, so that during the few seconds of shock the effective site of stimulation spreads out from the electrode tip and activates the negative cells. Some of these ambivalent sites are circled in Figure 14.1. An alternate interpretation is that the electrical stimulus self-adapts to neutrality as the stimulation continues, and it is terminated simply in order to release the system from adaptation and to get another rewarding onset of stimulation. Experiments by Deutsch (1973) make this latter interpretation somewhat more plausible.

A number of interesting features regarding the electrical reward effect in nonambivalent sites have been uncovered. First, the self-stimulating behavior does not satiate, whereas most naturally occurring positive reinforcers do, as in eating or drinking. This absence of satiation is inferred from the fact that animals will continue to stimulate their brains at a high rate for very many hours, until they drop from fatigue. Human patients who have received stimulation to alleged "pleasure centers" of their brains (during experiments done in the course of routine brain surgery) often report the stimulation as joyful or satisfying or relaxing without unpleasant aftereffects, and they willingly take more (Heath & Mickle, 1960). Second, the behavior generally extinguishes very rapidly when the electrical stimulation is shut off, despite the fact that very high response rates had been generated by it. Third, in discrete-trial learning situations (e.g., a runway), performance is generally poorer the longer is the intertrial interval. At many brain sites, the "cooled off" animal must be "primed" with one or more free brain shocks before it goes into its act of rapid self-stimulation. Fourth, the reward effect at some locations appears to depend on the state of one or another motivational (drive) system. Rates of self-stimulation at some sites seem to depend on the animal's hunger drive (i.e., satiation lowers self-stimulation rate), and at other sites to depend on the level of circulating sex hormones (i.e., castration lowers self-stimulation rate). These drive-related effects do not appear at all rewarding sites in the brain. Moreover, many hypothalamic electrodes that elicit motivated consummatory responses—feeding, drinking, or copulation—were also found to be rewarding at somewhat lower intensities (see Caggiula, 1970; Hoebel, 1968). However, these effects were apparently mediated by separate cell groups near the big electrode. A more analytic study by Olds, Allan, and Briese (1970), using micro-electrodes, separated the cells where stimulation produced eating or drinking from nearby cells where stimulation produced only reward effects. The earlier studies had used larger electrodes that stimulated several cell groups, each group responsible for evoking functionally distinct effects.

Deutsch and Howarth (1963) have advanced a theory about brain stimulation reward which attempts to handle many of the pertinent facts. The gist of the theory is that the electrical stimulation in these "reward" experiments is actually serving two functions: reward for the immediate response and motivation for the next response in the series. Each brain shock produces some motivation for the habit which produced the brain shock. The motivation produced by a brain shock decays with the time elapsed since the brain shock, eventually diminishing to zero. The stronger the brain shock, the longer it takes the motivation to decay. The postulated effect of brain-shock reward may be aptly compared with the familiar effect of eating salted peanuts; the behavior is practically self-perpetuating, having a peanut keeps the desire for another going, but the urgency of the want declines with the lapse of time since consumption of the previous peanut.

Deutsch and Howarth present several experimental results consistent with their hypothesis, all essentially showing that the strength of behavior established with a brain-shock reward declines with time since the last brain shock. Gallistel (1966, 1969a) has confirmed and extended these drive-decay findings. He has also found (Gallistel, 1969b) that in rats implanted with two functional reward electrodes, the priming provided on one electrode still injects motivation for getting electrical stimulation (ESB) through the other as well. Since the theory postulates a dual effect of electrical stimulation—excitation of reward and motivational pathways—Deutsch and his associates have investigated means for separating these two effects. Results of a series of experiments are consistent with the assumption that the sensitivity of the two systems differs as stimulation parameters (current intensity, pulse frequency) are varied. Observations in one experiment suggested that the motivational pathway had a lower threshold than the reward pathway. Thus, a brain shock of low intensity could have a motivating but not a rewarding effect. In another experiment, frequency (pulses per second) of the brain shock was manipulated along with intensity. Frequency-intensity pairs found to be equally preferred (rewarding) in a T-maze preference test turned out to be unequally motivating in a simple runway test. This suggests that the reward and motivation pathways are maximally sensitive to different frequencies of electrical stimulation. In another set of experiments (Deutsch, 1964), evidence was adduced for the view that the neural "refractory period" of reinforcement pathways is shorter than that of the motivational pathways. The term *refractory period* refers to a very brief time following the firing of a neuron during which a second stimulus is ineffective and cannot fire the neuron again. By purely behavioral tests, Deutsch inferred that the refractory period for the reward pathway was about four-tenths of a millisecond, whereas that for the motivational pathway was about six- or seven-tenths of a millisecond. This series of experiments certainly provides rather impressive evidence for Deutsch's hypothesis about brain stimulation reward.

NEUROCHEMISTRY OF REWARD AND PUNISHMENT

Research in neurophysiology has proven that transmission of neural impulses is largely a chemical affair. Nerve cells may be thought of as telephone transmission lines that connect with one another at junctures known as *synapses*. Line *A* connects with line *B* across a synapse, and the synapse is responsible for transmitting to *B* any nerve impulse (signal) traveling down line *A*. Nerve *B* has a threshold that the amount of stimulation must exceed in order to make *B* fire. However, several subthreshold impulses from *A* occurring in rapid succession will "temporally summate" in their effects and thus fire *B;* or subthreshold impulses arriving at *B* simultaneously from several different synapses will "spatially summate" to fire *B*. The transmission of a nerve impulse actually results from the impulse in *A* causing a shift in the electrical potential across the membrane of nerve *B* on the other side of the synaptic gap. This model of one neuron connecting to one other is highly idealized; a given neuron may sprout several

thousand dendrites that make synaptic contacts with several thousand other neurons, and a single elongated neuron may receive thousands of contacts from other neurons. Thus, the pattern of influences upon a neuron's firing, and the influences it can have when it fires, are exceedingly complex.

As noted, the transmission of an impulse across a synaptic gap is a biochemical process. It is diagrammed in Figure 14.2 for an idealized cholenergic synapse. An impulse in line *A* releases—literally squirts out at its end—a small amount of a *transmitter* substance, which is acetylcholine (ACh) at this type of synapse. This chemical crosses the tiny gap between *A* and *B* and is absorbed by the membrane of nerve *B*, causing a momentary shift in the membrane potential of nerve *B*. If the shift is large enough, it causes an electrical impulse to be generated and propagated down *B*. Following the firing of *B*, processes come into play that will clear away the residual transmitter substance in the synaptic gap, returning the synapse to its prior state, ready to conduct further signals. At cholenergic synapses, the cleanup process is carried out by the enzyme cholinesterase (ChE), which hydrolyzes (neutralizes) the acetylcholine released at the synapse during transmission. The biochemical reactions here are extremely fast, requiring but a few milliseconds, and the interplay of the ACh and ChE systems is in a synchronized and delicate balance at synapses. Small changes in the availability of, or speed of access to, one or the other chemical could result in malfunctioning, or at least in reduced efficiency in transmission of finely modulated, temporal patterns of neural impulses.

Figure 14.2 illustrates a cholinergic synapse. Neurochemists have discovered 10 to 20 different types of synapses in mammals; each type is associated with different transmitter substances, and more types are suspected. Transmitters identified so far include acetylcholine, the catecholamines (norepinephrine and dopamine), serotonin,

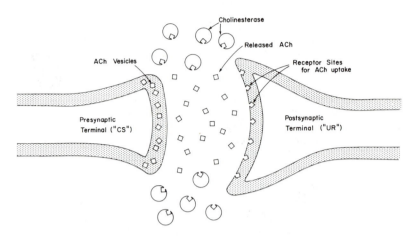

Figure 14.2. Illustration of biochemical events involved in synaptic transmission.

gamma-amino butyric acid (GABA), gly-cine, glutamic acid, aspartic acid, and sev-eral endorphins such as enkephalin. Each has its characteristic locations throughout the nervous system, method of action, and ways of being metabolized. Different trans-mitters are probably associated with differ-ent and anatomically distinct functions of the nervous system, each possibly devel-oped at different times in evolutionary history.

Of particular interest to learning theo-rists is the conjecture by Larry Stein and his co-workers (Stein, 1964, 1969, 1978; Stein et al., 1977) that the major neural circuits underlying reward, punishment, and moti-vated behavior are biochemically differ-entiated, varying in terms of the major transmitter substances utilized in synapses of these systems. Stein infers these biochem-ical properties of the systems by injecting a variety of neurally active drugs and not-ing their effects on thresholds of rewarding self-stimulation and on blocking or en-hancement of rewarding or punishing ef-fects from stimulating electrodes.

Following suggestions in the psychologi-cal literature, Stein first notes that rewards can be identified with events that have

either an exciting arousal function (incen-tive) or a satisfying-gratifying function. These notions are captured in the "drive induction" (arousal) versus the "drive re-duction" (relaxation) theories of reinforce-ment, which are probably both correct but incomplete. Stein argues that the exciting functions of rewards are mediated by brain systems whose primary transmitter is a catecholamine, whereas the gratifying or relaxing functions are mediated by differ-ent brain systems subserved partly by an enkephalin or opiatelike peptides. (A *pep-tide* is a chain of amino acids that serve as building blocks for cell proteins.) Finally, Stein conjectures that the brain systems mediating punishment effects on behavior have serotonin as their transmitter.

The arguments for these theses revolve around many studies of the behavioral ef-fects of drugs. First, rewarding self-stimula-tion is selectively affected by the presence of drugs that influence transmission at cen-tral catecholamine synapses. Thus, a drug like amphetamine, which facilitates the re-lease of catecholamines from presynaptic axons, will facilitate electrical self-stimula-tion; it also causes the brain to be more sensitive to weak rewarding electrical stimulation. On the other hand, drugs that deplete catecholamines or block their action (such as reserpine and chlorpromazine) will suppress electrical self-stimulation at otherwise rewarding sites. Chlorpromazine also makes the animal less sensitive to brain reward, in that higher intensities (amperes) are required before the drugged animal desires the rewarding stimulus. Second, injections of serotonin or a precursor of serotonin intensifies the effect of punishment, whereas drugs that antagonize serotonin lessen the effect of punishment. Punishment effects are typically assessed in a conflict situation in which a rat presses a lever to obtain occasional rewards of sweetened milk; however, each lever press is also punished with a brief foot shock calibrated in intensity to yield a moderate level of lever-pressing. In this situation benzodiazepine drugs (such as Librium and Valium), which decrease the turnover of serotonin, also increase lever-pressing, presumably by decreasing the effect of punishment.

More evidence for Stein's conjectures about reinforcing functions comes from drug-abuse studies in humans and from studies that permit animals to self-administer drugs. An experiment can be arranged in which a rat's lever-pressing causes a tiny drop of some drug like cocaine to be administered directly into a vein by a permanently in-dwelling cannula. (Other drugs may be injected directly into the brain.) In this situation, animals will lever-press to self-administer catecholamine-facilitating agents such as amphetamine and cocaine. Of course, these drugs are also avidly self-administered by humans (under the street names of "speed" and "coke") who report feelings of arousal. These are "exciting" drugs that produce a "rush." On the reverse side of Stein's hypothesis, concerning the relaxing, drive-reducing function of rewards, rats will lever-press to self-administer morphine, as well as a form of enkephalin, in the lateral ventricle of the brain. Morphine and other opiates produce dreamy feelings of quiet pleasure when injected into humans. (Morphine was named after Morpheus, the god of dreams.) Morphine and enkephalin are also both potent painkillers (analgesics).

Further support for Stein's conjecture came from anatomical studies of the mammalian brain. There are three major ascending fiber systems in the brainstem that have a catecholamine (dopamine or norepinephrine) as their primary transmitter, and there is substantial overlap among these catecholamine anatomical systems and those where electrical stimulation is rewarding. In confirmation of Stein's drive-reduction hypothesis, in several tests made so far, anatomical sites that appear rich in enkephalin also yield positive reward when electrically stimulated. Moreover, the drug naloxone, which antagonizes and blocks the action of enkephalin, abolishes the rewarding effect of electrical stimulation in enkephalin-rich sites. Incidentally, naloxone is a morphine antagonist and is used to rescue people who have overdosed themselves on heroin.

Separating the effects of the two catecholamines, dopamine and norepinephrine, is difficult in this work because dopamine is the natural precursor to norepinephrine in neurons, and a given drug usually affects both dopamine and norepinephrine in the same way. But both transmitters seem to play their separate roles in behavioral effects. The important role of norepinephrine was shown in experiments with several drugs (such as disulfiram) that prevent the conversion of dopamine into norepinephrine, and thereby make norepinephrine less available for transmission. Such drugs abolish self-stimulation reward effects; they also inhibit the otherwise facilitatory effect of amphetamines on self-stimulation. While the disulfiram inhibition was in progress, injections of norepinephrine into a rat's brain caused the return of the rewarding effect of electrical stimulation. Such results suggest that norepinephrine is one of the critical transmitters for the reward effect. But there are also reward pathways in which dopamine alone appears to act as the effective transmitter. Baxter and associates (1974) found that rats would avidly self-administer apomorphine intravenously, which stimulates dopamine receptors. This self-administration rate for apomorphine is not affected when the rat is also given a drug which depletes norepinephrine, but it is severely blocked by giving him a drug which antagonizes dopamine. The conclusion is that strong positive reinforcement can also result from dopamine receptor activation. In fact, Stein guesses that the dopamine system underlies the incentive-motive aspects of reward, whereas norepinephrine mediates the memory-strengthening effects of rewards. Teasing apart the influence of these neurochemical systems is a lively topic on the research agenda.

Mood-Altering Drugs

The reader has probably noticed that many of the drugs mentioned above that alter the rewarding or punishing effects of brain stimulation are also commonly used for altering moods of humans, inside or outside the psychiatric setting. Indeed, it is this correspondence that has fueled much theorizing about the neural chemistry of mood and mental illness. In the 1950s, several antipsychotic drugs were found to have profound effects in reducing the psychotic symptoms of schizophrenia, manic-depressive psychosis, and other affective disorders. The phenothiazines (such as chlorpromazine), butyrophenomes (such as Haldol), and rauwolfia alkaloids (reserpine) were effective in relieving symptoms of disorganized thinking, disorientation, blunted affect, withdrawal, and autistic behaviors characteristic of schizophrenia. Many antianxiety drugs were also discov-

ered, such as the benzodiazepines (Librium) and propanediols (Miltown). Many of these drugs affect catecholamine transmission. For example, reserpine prevents storage of norepinephrine in presynaptic sites and chlorpromazine blocks dopamine receptors in the brain, whereas the benzodiazepines decrease the turnover of both norepinephrine and serotonin. Other mood-altering chemicals are imipramine, which facilitates norepinephrine transmission and is used to treat mental depression, and lithium salts, which decrease norepinephrine transmission and are used to treat (endogenous) bipolar manic-depressive psychotics. These drug effects suggest that psychotic depression is caused by a decrease in catecholamines at normally rewarding sites of the brain and/or an excess of serotonin in neurons of the punishment (and anxiety) systems.

Stein and Wise (1971) suggested that schizophrenia might result from disturbance or damage to the brain's norepinephrine neuronal systems. Consistent with this, Wise and Stein (1973) found that an enzyme used in converting dopamine to norepinephrine occurred in lower amounts in the brains of autopsied schizophrenics than in the brains of "normal" controls who died suddenly in accidents or from heart attacks. Unfortunately, that specific result has not been replicated, and so the hypothesis has been discarded. Although no specific hypothesis has yet been proven, the general approach of relating the neurochemistry of reward to mental disturbances and to mood alterations caused by drugs is a significant, lively and fruitful development in investigating the physical basis of mind.

Painkillers in the Brain

The neural circuitry underlying pain perception has been investigated for many years; several circuits have been identified, including one going from the lower brain stem and medulla down through the spinal cord. Two recent discoveries have opened up new horizons in this research area. The first is the discovery of several sites in the brain stem (for instance, the periaqueductal gray matter and the dorsal-lateral funiculus) where electrical stimulation produces a profound analgesia (relief from pain). The stimulation appears to act by inhibiting the upward transmission of pain signals through spinothalamic tracts. The painkilling stimulus also will reduce pain reflexes at lower spinal levels. For example, a rat who normally reacts swiftly when his foot is pinched will show no response if the pinch occurs during brain stimulation of the central gray matter (see Mayer et al., 1971). Also, rats receiving painful foot shock will lever-press in order to receive pain-inhibiting stimulation in the central gray matter. Such electrical stimuli are also described as pain-relieving by human patients who suffer chronic pain from spinal injuries.

The second discovery is that the electrically produced analgesia is mediated by stimulation that causes the release at these sites of several biochemicals collectively named *endorphins* (meaning "internally made morphine"). Endorphins are neural secretions that act like transmitters, and several varieties have been identified (including enkephalin). Endorphins are so called because they mimic the action of morphine in blocking pain. The mimicry is observed in several respects. First, anatomical studies show that morphine and endorphins share similar sites of brain action. Second, injection of minute amounts of endorphin into the brain has the same pain-relieving effects as do tiny injections of morphine at the same sites. Third, naloxone, a drug that blocks opiate-receiving neurons, reduces the analgesia otherwise created either by injecting morphine or endorphin or by electrically stimulating the central gray matter. Fourth, animals become "tolerant" to electrical stimulation of the central gray area because successive bouts of stimulation come to have lesser analgesic effects, much as morphine (or heroin) addicts require larger doses to produce the same effect. Moreover, once an animal has developed tolerance to electrically elicited pain relief, it is found to be tolerant also to morphine injections. This parallel suggests again that electrically produced analgesia acts by the same medium as does morphine and other opiates—namely, brain stimulation releases endorphins.

Such results demonstrate that the brain has developed its own pain-inhibiting system, and that pain and stress cause the release of endorphins in the brain to counteract the pain. Morphine simply mimics the body's own means of pain relief. Like morphine, endorphins also create a euphoric feeling which may be the warm glow of relief that often follows the termination of prolonged stress. (This may be something like the "high" that long-distance runners so often describe.) For the learning theorist, it is interesting to speculate that endorphin release could be conditioned to previously neutral stimuli that precede the onset of pain (if pain causes release of endorphins). This may help explain *placebo effects,* wherein sugar pills labeled as medicinals cause apparent relief of suffering. The view that endorphin release can be conditioned would account for a long-standing puzzle—namely, that animals prefer painful foot shocks that are predictably cued by a CS to similar foot shocks that are unpredictable. If endorphins were released in anticipation of the predictable shocks, then such shocks would be felt as less punishing than the unpredicted shocks.

These questions regarding the neuropharmacology of reward and punishment are being intensively researched, and many new findings are being reported. Major hypotheses and facts will be developing at a rapid pace in the near future.

Arousal and Attention

Electrophysiological studies have brought forth many facts about arousal and attention. The arousal dimension ranges from euphoric excitement, alert attentiveness, and relaxed wakefulness to drowsiness and deep sleep. These states are closely correlated with phenomenal impressions of conscious awareness, as shown by distinctive patterns in the electroencephalogram (EEG) of the subject. We can gauge the depth of sleep from the EEG. The sleeper's EEG proceeds through about four distinct levels as he falls into a deeper sleep, but the sleep EEG then bobs up and down in level in about 90-minute cycles throughout the night. At the top of these cycles, the sleeper enters rapid-eye-movement (REM) sleep for several minutes. During REM, the sleeper is dreaming and moving his eyes as though he were watching a visual scene unfold before him (see Kleitman, 1963).

A host of studies have implicated the reticular activating system (RAS) of the brain stem as of paramount importance in arousal. This system seems to be involved in sleeping, wakefulness, and in fine gradations in attention. Anatomically, this system, which in humans is about the size of the little finger (see Figure 14.3), is located at the core of the brain stem just above the spinal cord and below the thalamus and hypothalamus.

A number of important facts regarding the RAS are well established. First, selected cells of the RAS are aroused or alerted when signals are being transmitted through sensory input cables from the skin, ear, nose, and so on. These sensory input cables send their information to specific "projection" areas in the cerebral cortex, all (except smell) doing so through specific relay nuclei in the thalamus. On the way in, however, these input cables send off collateral branches into the RAS. These collaterals are shown schematically in Figure 14.4. Within the RAS, the collaterals from the various sensory channels are intermingled and lack specificity. Second, the

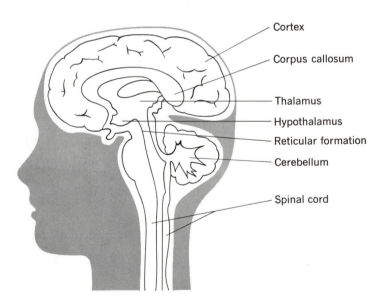

Figure 14.3. Schematic sagittal section of the brain in man. (From D. P. Kimble, 1963.)

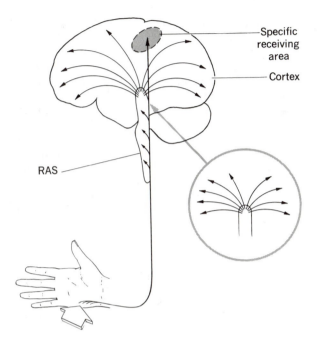

Specific receiving area

Cortex

RAS

Figure 14.4. Schematic drawing showing how a touch stimulus to the hand is relayed to a specific receiving area in the cerebral cortex. The sensory channel also sends collateral branches into the reticular activating system (RAS), which in turn projects alerting stimulation to many areas of the cerebral cortex. The inset shows the cortical projections arising from the forward end (thalamic section) of the reticular formation. (From D. P. Kimble, 1963.)

RAS projects its unspecific messages to broad, diffuse areas of the cerebral cortex (see Figure 14.4). Research has indicated that the probable operation of this system is as follows: new sensory information stimulates the RAS, which relays the presence of some kind of stimulation to various sensory receiving areas of the cortex. This diffuse stimulation alerts the cortex, essentially telling it that some kind of news is arriving. The alerted cortex is then better able to deal with or process the specific information arriving over the specific sensory input channel to the cortex.

This story has been slowly pieced together. The alerting function of the RAS has been inferred from the fact that direct electrical stimulation of the RAS will awaken a sleeping cat and produce EEG brain waves characteristic of alertness and excitement. If the RAS is destroyed, a profound and enduring coma results; for all practical purposes, the animal is reduced to a sleeping vegetable. Anesthetic drugs

that produce unconsciousness appear to act by depressing the RAS. The coma produced by either the ablation or the anesthetic endures despite the intactness of the sensory projection pathways. Though sounds, touches, and lights still evoke definite electrical responses at the cortex while the animal is comatose, the subject is unaware of these inputs because the RAS switch controlling "consciousness" has been turned off. Nonspecific stimulation from the RAS thus apparently prepares the cortex to process the incoming sensory information.

Some indirect evidence of the perceptual efficiency of an alerted cortex is seen in experiments by Lindsley (1958) and Fuster (1958). The Lindsley study showed that the cortex was better able to resolve and discriminate two successive light flashes if it were brought into an appropriate state of alert readiness by prior RAS stimulation. Fuster's study showed that prior RAS activation enabled monkeys to pick up more discriminating information from a very brief glimpse of a visual array.

Sensory Blocking

In recent years a number of experiments have made it clear that the waking brain exerts considerable control over its sensory input channels. An electrical signal coursing inward from a particular receptor may be subject to modulating influences all along its sensory pathway to the primary receiving area at the cortex. These influences may either enhance or inhibit the inward-coursing signal, although inhibition seems to be the predominant mode. Enhancement and inhibition effects may be seen in the changes in the electrically evoked response recorded from various relay stations (synapses) along the sensory input cable. These effects are probably mediated by fibers from the cortex to relay stations near the receptors. A number of sensory inhibition effects can be produced by electrical stimulation in certain parts of the reticular formation.

The main function of these brain-to-periphery neural circuits appears to be that which is ascribed roughly to "attention." By this means the brain can attenuate or "block out" sensory signals that are of no interest to it at the moment, while at the same time amplifying that sensory channel (if any) upon which attention is concentrated. The evidence for this generalization comes from studies of habituation and distraction, and the influence of brain stimulation upon evoked responses to sensory stimulation.

Consider first the phenomenon of *habituation*. When a novel stimulus of sufficient intensity impinges on a receptor, it evokes a strong and definite electrical response in the relays of that input channel, in the primary sensory cortex for that input channel, and in the reticular formation. This is the electrical accompaniment of the orienting reflex discussed by Pavlov and Sokolov (see Chapter 3). However, if the stimulus is repeated in a regular, monotonous series, the evoked response diminishes to a low, stable level, often not even detectable. The response has habituated. This habituation can be seen not only at the cortex but also far downstream, at essentially the first sensory relay station beyond the receptor. Such habituatory control is presumably designed to disengage the high brain centers from dealing with stimuli that have ceased to have any significance for it. The habituation can be temporarily lifted by disturbing the animal (e.g., by electric shock to the feet or an arousing reticular shock). Also, it is released to some extent by making some alteration in the stimulus pattern. The release of habituation seems to follow a regular generalization gradient related to the amount of stimulus change. Also, habituation will not occur if the stimulus is converted through conditioning into a signal of biological importance (e.g., by pairing a click with a painful shock or with food). In fact, the evoked electrical response is even larger than normal in this case. Thus, the significance of an input signal is crudely coded almost at once from the receptor inward.

A second set of observations relates to *selective attention*. It is well known that human adults can attend selectively to one stimulus and ignore others that are concurrently presented. A large number of psychological experiments have been done with such selective attention tasks, and the relevant variables have been reasonably well mapped out (see Moray, 1969, 1970, for reviews). Several EEG studies (using scalp electrodes with human adults) have examined changes in the average cortical response evoked by a given stimulus depending on whether it is or is not attended to. An initial study was done by Spong, Haider, and Lindsley (1965); their subjects were presented with concurrent series of light flashes and of auditory clicks, the two occurring independently in time. When subjects were instructed to attend to and count the light flashes, the evoked responses produced by flashes and recorded from the visual cortex (occipital area) were large, whereas the evoked responses produced by the clicks and recorded from the auditory cortex (temporal area) were small. When the instruction was reversed, and the subjects were requested to count clicks and ignore the light flashes, the magnitudes of the respective cortical evoked responses were reversed. This illustrates selective attention using stimuli of two different modalities. Later, Donchin and Cohen (1967) showed that, by means of instructions, cortical evoked responses could be selectively facilitated to one visual stimulus and inhibited to a second visual stimulus which occurred at different times mixed among the first stimulus and falling on roughly the same retinal locations as the facilitated stimulus. Thus the differential responses at the visual cortex evoked by the two visual stimuli had to result from central mechanisms assigning different weights for the two stimuli according to their relative importance rather than to good or poor peripheral adjustment of the receptor registering the two stimuli.

Consider a third set of observations on *distraction*. Hernandez-Peon, Scherrer, and Jouvet (1956) recorded in a cat the evoked response to an auditory click at the dorsal cochlear nucleus, a low-level relay station in the auditory pathways. Before habituation occurred, presentation of distracting visual or olfactory stimuli (a mouse or the odor of fresh fish) greatly reduced the evoked auditory response produced at that time by the click. A similar effect was produced by a novel smell or sound upon the evoked response to a light flash in the optic pathways. These observations suggest that the novel stimulus attracted the cat's attention, that stimuli in the input channel

attended to were amplified, whereas stimuli in other input channels not attended to were flattened and blocked out. Moreover, this blockage can go on downstream at sensory relay stations near the receptor. Hernandez-Peon and associates proposed that this blockage was carried out by efferent inhibitory fibers from the reticular formation to sensory relays; that is, when input in the visual channel captures attention, the reticular formation sends out impulses that temporarily inhibit neuronal activity in other input channels. However, such results as those of Donchin and Cohen cited above and others (see Eason et al., 1969) show that the alleged inhibition must be quite general for everything except a focal pattern, applying even to unattended complex stimuli in the attended location and modality. Consequently, the selective weighting of stimuli for their importance can probably occur only after some higher-level analysis. That is, it seems unlikely that low-level sensory relays are discriminating and filtering out sensed stimuli (we are ignoring here overt receptor movements).

A standard view of such results is to suppose that sensory information, possibly in degraded form, gets transmitted to central analyzers and is there weighted for its importance or novelty. During habituation, the reduced signal is fed to a higher-level comparator; if the input matches some stored replica or model of recent signals, a diminished evoked response occurs and the efferents sustain their inhibitory influence on that input channel. If the input does not match recent signals, then a difference detector remits the efferent inhibition and may activate the RAS so that the next stimulus in the series evokes strong electrical activity. Depending on the complexity of the input stimulus, the comparison of input to stored replica goes on at different levels of the brain. The assumption would be that the neural structures responsible for habituation to a particular stimulus are at the same level as those required for its discrimination. Deutsch and Deutsch (1963) propose a simple mechanism whereby the more important of a group of signals might be selected for attention. Inputs arriving over this selected channel would then be connected to further learning or motor processes, whereas the remaining signals are not reacted to.

What may we conclude from the studies reviewed? First, it is clear that variations in reticular activation correlate with levels of wakefulness and arousal. Second, the RAS serves a usually facilitatory role in preparing the cortex for processing sensory information. Third, the RAS probably serves as a nonspecific governor or threshold determining the overall level of importance any stimulus must have to attract attention. In sleep or drowsiness, only the most important signals will be reacted to— for example, a baby's cry for its mother. As a parallel example, a sleeping cat will not be aroused by a neutral tone but will be awakened by a slightly different tone that evokes anxiety because of its previous pairing with shock. Fourth, the RAS and other parts of the brain probably exert some control and can modulate afferent inputs by way of a system of efferent networks. This modulation is usually inhibitory, attenuating channel *A* when channel *B* is being attended to. The simplest "downward" influence is that the brain directs the eyes or ears to point at the source of attended stimulation. Effects of learning, or associating significance to a stimulus through conditioning, can be seen at the cortex. This selective enhancement of attended stimuli at the cortex provides some basis for speculation on the perceptual changes that occur during learning, on the attachment of "meaning" to stimuli, and on how stimulation, instead of being passively registered, is selectively edited, discarded, and reworked for the purposes of the waking organism.

LEARNING AND MEMORY

An organism that could not learn might nevertheless behave differentially under various conditions of motivational arousal— for example, it might withdraw from noxious stimuli and continue to react to favored ones. Such behavior produces learning only when change occurs with experience— that is, when past experiences are somehow stored in memory, so that when stimuli are again encountered, reaction to them is altered in light of what went before. Hence we need to supplement the foregoing account of brain activity with what is known about the changes that take place when learning occurs, and about memory storage and retrieval.

Consolidation of Memory Traces

In broad outline, there are basically two kinds of views about the neural basis for the retention of experience or learning. One view supposes that an experience sets up a continuing electrical activity in appropriate neural circuits and that the persistence of these active circuits is coordinate with the persistence of our memory of the experience coded in this way. When this active trace process stops, we lose that memory. We may call this the "dynamic" view of the engram, or long-term memory (LTM) trace. Opposed to it is the "structural" view, that learning consists in some enduring physical, structural, or biochemical change in the nervous system, and that this physical change will persist even when the original neuronal circuits responsible for its having been established in the first place have returned to relative quiescence following the initial experience.

It takes very little thought or experiment to reject the dynamic view of LTM. For example, cooling a hamster down to 5°C causes it to hibernate, during which time very little, if any, electrical activity can be recorded from its brain. However, when warmed up and tested, it still retains whatever old habits were taught it before the hibernation period. As another example, consider the electrical "brainstorms" of *grand mal* epileptic seizures in human patients. Such seizures begin when a local epileptogenic focus (caused by a brain injury or tumor, for example) starts to recruit neighboring clumps of neurons into its abnormal discharge pattern. They fall into lock-step synchrony in firing with the epileptic focus, and then still more areas are recruited. The effective firing area spreads, and soon most of the cortex is being driven in synchrony with the epileptic focus; the seizure is in full swing, with practically all the brain participating in the paroxysmal activity. This full-blown seizure may last for a few minutes. Upon recovery from such a seizure, the patient is not devoid of memories of his past, as the dynamic view would suggest; in fact, it is difficult to detect that the seizure has produced any loss of memory. There are a variety of other lines of evidence that rule out the dynamic view that memory lives in a continual spinning circuit, so this view assumes practically the status of a straw man.

By a process of elimination, then, we arrive at the accepted view that LTM involves a relatively permanent physical or structural change in the nervous system. Though we cannot prejudge what the nature of this physical change is, it may be innocuous to assume that the change takes place over some span of time following the learning experience, possibly even increasing in magnitude with time. If the time span involved is extremely brief—say only a few *milliseconds* is required to complete the change—then the notion of temporal change is irrelevant to behavioral experiments. However, the notion does have behavioral implications of interest if the time span involved is fairly long—say, many seconds, minutes, hours, or days. It is just

this notion that has been pursued under the label of the "consolidation" hypothesis.

One form of such a hypothesis was proposed long ago by Müller and Pilzecker (1900). They suggested that the neural activity responsible for storing a physical change encoding an experience persists for some time after that experience, and as a consequence of the perseverating neural activity, the physical changes become more firmly fixed or of greater magnitude. This progressive fixation with time is called *consolidation*. If this persisting neural activity is soon interrupted by the intrusion of interfering activity, then the physical change is of small magnitude, and retention of the experience should be poor. Hebb (1949) restated this hypothesis and gave a more detailed neurophysiological model for it. The Müller-Pilzecker hypothesis was originally proposed to account for retroactive interference in recall of verbal materials by human subjects. In that context, it was not very fruitful and has been eclipsed by associative interference theory (see Chapter 6), which proved to be more adequate to the factual details in that area. Continuing interest in the consolidation hypothesis stems partly from clinical observations but primarily from experiments with animals. The main evidence for the consolidation theory of memory comes from studies of disturbing or traumatizing the brain shortly after registration of an experience. In theory, this disruption should prevent consolidation of the neural analogue of the memory, so no learning should be demonstrable at a later test.

In this regard, let us consider the striking clinical phenomena of retrograde and anterograde amnesia. After a person receives a hard knock on the head or some traumatic brain injury (such as a combat wound) producing unconsciousness and a coma, he is very likely when he awakens to be somewhat disoriented and confused; although he may respond to simple questions about his life, he is unable to retain for long what events are happening around him. This is called *anterograde amnesia* and means that the victim is amnesic for events occurring soon *after* he awakens from his accident. Further, the victim probably will be unable to recall the events immediately before and just connected with the accident (so-called *retrograde amnesia,* acting on events backwards from the accident). Figure 14.5 schematizes the portions of the life time-series over which the retrograde and anterograde amnesias (shaded areas) are said to spread.

The retrograde period may extend over events many minutes (5 to 60) before the accident and the anterograde period may extend for a similar time after regaining consciousness, with events closer to these two time-markers being more likely to be forgotten. In the more severe and dramatic instances (W. R. Russell & Nathan, 1946), the events preceding the trauma by several hours, days, or months may be lost to recall, and such a patient is said to have amnesia. In most cases, the person eventually recovers his memories for events before the accident, those more remote in time from the injury being recovered first. As recovery continues, events closer in time to the accident can be recalled; yet there usually still remains an unrecoverable portion of those events just immediately prior to the injury. Similar effects in milder degree caused by deep anesthesia, insulin- or metrazol-induced convulsions, and electro-

convulsive shock have been reported in human patients. The consolidation hypothesis would interpret the retrograde amnesia as showing that the injury or trauma prevents the consolidation of recent material and additionally raises the threshold for recall of older memories. Thus, the older memories, having had more time to consolidate, are stronger; and, during recovery, the threshold for recall declines so that the older, stronger memories return first. Later we will consider alternative theories of these facts.

Electroconvulsive Shocks and Amnesia

In the experimental work on amnesia in animals (typically rats), most of the early experiments investigated how learning is disrupted when the subject receives an electroconvulsive shock (ECS) shortly after a learning trial. The convulsion, similar in many respects to the synchronized brainstorm in an epileptic seizure, is readily induced by briefly passing a strong electric current between electrodes clipped to the ears of a rat. Starting with work by Duncan (1949), a series of studies has shown that ECS given to a rat soon after a learning trial interferes with its performance of the appropriate habit when it is tested the next day after recovery from the short-lived convulsion. Moreover, the closer in time the ECS comes to the end of the learning trial, the greater is the disruption in performance that appears in the subsequent test.

The effect can be illustrated by Duncan's initial experiment. Rats were trained on an active avoidance habit at the rate of 1 trial a day for 18 days. The trial started by placing the rat on the "danger" side of a two-compartment box. If it did not cross over to the "safe" compartment within 10 seconds, its feet were shocked until it did. Following its crossing over to the safe compartment, the rat received an ECS. The

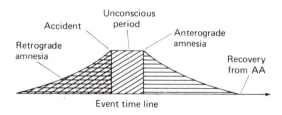

Figure 14.5. Schematic representation of types of amnesia for events surrounding the accident causing unconsciousness.

delay between the response and the ECS was varied for different animals, and was either 20, 40, or 60 seconds, 4 or 15 minutes, or 1, 4, or 14 hours. The ECS treatment was given following each of the training trials. A group of control subjects received no ECS. The effect of the delay between response and ECS is depicted in Figure 14.6, which shows the average number of avoidance responses over the 18 trials for animals given the ECS after each length of delay. The logarithm of the delay before ECS is plotted on the abscissa. Figure 14.6 shows a marked retrograde effect of ECS upon learning. At the shortest interval, 20 seconds, very little learning occurred. As the time before ECS is lengthened, less decrement occurs. With an ECS delay of 1 hour or more, the subjects receiving ECS perform as well as the controls receiving no ECS.

These results may be interpreted as reflecting a process of memory consolidation that goes on over about a 60-minute period following each learning trial. The ECS is assumed to interrupt this process, with the amount learned per trial increasing with the time for consolidation before the process is interrupted by ECS.

Unfortunately, an alternative hypothesis would also explain Duncan's finding—namely, the delay-of-punishment gradient. We might assume that the ECS is aversive, so that it punishes and inhibits responses which it shortly follows, doing so according to a typical delay gradient. This would explain Duncan's findings without requiring the consolidation hypothesis. Later experiments have indeed shown that a series of electroconvulsive shocks begins to act like an aversive event to be avoided; however, relatively little aversion is evident after just one ECS. For this and various other reasons, it is now believed that the best paradigm for showing amnestic effects of ECS is a "one-trial learning" situation into which a single ECS is introduced.

A situation presently in use which meets these requirements is a passive avoidance situation. A rat or mouse is placed upon a small raised platform above a grid floor. If this is done with naive animals, they will step down from the small platform within a few seconds. If they are painfully shocked

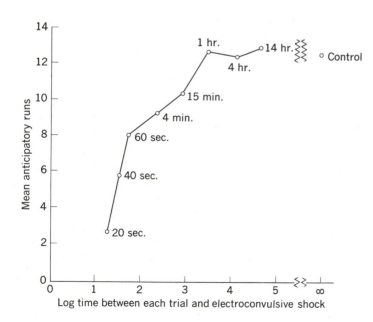

Figure 14.6. The average number of anticipatory runs (avoidance responses) for all 18 trials, related to the logarithm of the delay time between the trial and electroconvulsive shock. Different points on the curve (with delay times indicated) represent different groups of subjects. (From Duncan, 1949.)

from the grid floor when they step down, a later test will show that they now refuse to leave the platform. They have learned a passive avoidance response in one trial. However, animals given an ECS soon after the foot shock seemingly "forget," so that on the next day's test they still step quickly off the platform (e.g., Chorover & Schiller, 1965). A graded amnesia effect is again obtained, although the time constants seem generally lower than those obtained by Duncan. For example, Chorover and Schiller report practically no ECS-induced amnesia when the ECS is delayed as much as 30 seconds following the learning trial; shorter delays (.5, 2, 5, 10 seconds) had stronger amnestic effects. A review of this literature may be found in McGaugh and Herz (1972).

The retrograde effect of ECS has by now been repeatedly observed. Similar amnestic effects have been produced by convulsant drugs, heat narcosis, hyperoxia, and certain anesthetic drugs that produce unconsciousness or convulsions. Over the last three decades, developments have followed three main lines. First, the retrograde amnestic effect has been studied in greater detail yielding deeper empirical knowledge of the phenomenon; in particular, several of the newly discovered facets of retrograde amnesia are difficult to explain using the original consolidation theory. Second, a variety of alternative hypotheses have been offered to explain the amnestic effect of ECS, and these often provoke experiments which try to differentiate the new hypothesis from the old memory-consolidation hypothesis. Third, the search for neurological structures implicated in the amnestic effect has proceeded to finer detail and to more discriminating knowledge of brain events that disrupt consolidation. A few results of each kind will be mentioned here.

Difficulties for the consolidation theory. First, empirical studies have turned up several phenomena in the ECS situation that

create some difficulties for a simple consolidation theory. For one thing, there are frequent reports of ECS-induced amnesia which "spontaneously lifts" with time after the one-trial learning event followed by ECS. But if immediate ECS has really prevented any learning, then there should be no habit to recover over time. However, such recovery is not always obtained; the relevant variables determining recovery are the species (rats recover more often than mice) and, in the passive avoidance situation, the severity of the initial foot shock and of the ECS intensity.

A second embarrassing fact is that different indices of remembering following ECS do not always agree. For example, an animal receiving foot shock followed by ECS may readily "step down" the next day, apparently showing amnesia for the shock, and yet its heart rate will be accelerated in the test situation, indicating some association of fear to the situation (Hines & Paolino, 1970). Or if the animal received foot shock and ECS for stepping down onto the white side rather than the dark side of a two-compartment floor, on the next test day it may step down readily, apparently showing amnesia for the foot shock; yet it will strongly prefer to step down to the side of the nonshocked color, apparently remembering where it received the painful shock the day before (Carew, 1970). These matters could perhaps be handled by supposing that learning involving autonomic responses is more quickly consolidated than is learning involving instrumental responses, although this is clearly ad hoc and unpalatable.

A third discomforting fact for the hypothesis that ECS disrupts consolidation is that memory for the response apparently remains for a few hours after ECS, only to disappear 24 hours later—this test interval is the one typically used in such studies (Geller & Jarvik, 1968; McGaugh & Landfield, 1970). Such findings appear paradoxical for a simple consolidation theory, which would suppose that ECS produces

total forgetting immediately and permanently. Perhaps it is fairer to say that ECS
simply accelerates the rate of forgetting
rather than causing immediate loss of the
experience.

Competing theories of ECS effects. As
noted above, another line of research stems
from testing alternative theories of the
ECS-induced effects. An early one proposed
by Lewis and Maher (1965) was that ECS
should be viewed as an unconditioned stimulus causing unconsciousness and generalized inhibition to become conditioned in
Pavlovian fashion to cues of the situation
paired with ECS. Although this interpretation led to a series of interesting experiments (reviewed in Lewis & Maher, 1965,
and in Lewis, 1969), it has not been generally accepted since it fails to account for
those passive avoidance cases where ECS
produces forgetting which is inferred from
the shocked animal's now *actively* doing
something—namely, stepping down onto
the floor where it had received painful
shock the day before, rather than passively
freezing on the ledge where it is placed like
the control animal who only received foot
shock. A conditioned inhibition theory
would not expect ECS effects to be revealed
in animals actively performing.

A more recent and interesting perspective on effects of ECS or similar brain traumas is that these may involve *retrieval*
difficulties rather than *learning* difficulties
(see Bower, 1972d, pp. 117–20; DeVietti &
Larson, 1971; Lewis, 1969; Nielson, 1968).
One possibility, for example, is that ECS
following a learning event causes memory
for that experience to be repressed, much
as is supposed in the Freudian theory of
repression. Such memories could then be
evoked or assessed later only under special
circumstances. One experiment suggesting
this analysis is by Misanin, Miller, and
Lewis (1968). The critical learning event
was the pairing of a tone with a painful
foot shock to rats. The next day, the group
of rats was presented with the tone followed

by ECS. This delayed experience of tone-
ECS seemed to interfere with memory of
the earlier tone-shock event (despite its
having 24 hours "consolidation time"), for
on the following day the tone did not elicit
much fear as measured by its suppression
of drinking. The idea is that, during the
second day's treatment, the tone at first
reinstated the memory of the tone-shock
pairing; however, the ECS following revival of the tone-shock memory allegedly
caused something like repression or inhibition to become attached to that memory in
such manner as to block its subsequent
retrieval to the tone stimulus. There are
several other results suggesting that ECS
may disrupt retrieval as well as storage of
a memory for an event contiguous to an
ECS (see Miller & Springer, 1973).

Brain correlates of amnestic events. Another line of research on amnesia is concerned with more closely mapping out the
brain events crucial for disrupting memory
consolidation. Some of this research seeks
to specify more precisely the critical brain-
component reaction to ECS or to anes-
thetics that is responsible for producing
graded amnestic effects. For example, findings by Landfield and McGaugh (1972) and
Landfield and associates (1972) suggest that
the degree of ECS-induced amnesia in rats is
correlated with the length of time during
which theta waves are absent in the
hippocampus following ECS. Little or no
amnesia was found for rats for whom
theta activity quickly returned following
ECS. Another kind of research seeks to
interfere with memory consolidation by
applying discrete, localized electrical stimulation to specific brain sites through implanted electrodes. A variety of brain sites
have been found in which single electrical
pulses applied soon after a learning event
will prevent consolidation of a memory.
Such stimulation can be weak and brief
but selectively destructive in contrast to the
"block-buster" devastation produced by a
severe ECS. Interference with learning has

been produced from discrete electrical stimulation to the dorsal hippocampus, the caudate putamen, and the frontal cortex, among other sites, whereas *facilitation* in learning has been obtained from posttrial stimulation in the mesencephalic reticular formation and the ventral hippocampus, among other places (see McGaugh & Herz, 1972, for a review). At present, this research is not particularly illuminating since few experimenters have shown *temporal* gradients of effects, as required by the consolidation hypothesis. Moreover, the studies generally used massed trials, so that posttrial effects of stimulation cannot be easily separated. Thus, for instance, a particular type of brain shock may not prevent learning, but rather its persisting aftereffects may impair sensory discrimination so that the animal performs poorly on trials that follow soon after such stimulation. A psychological analysis of the effects of such brain stimuli can track down in this manner some of the critical structures subserving memory consolidation, but the task is likely to be a long, slow, and probably indefinite process.

Variables Affecting Consolidation Rate

According to the hypothesis of a short-term and a long-term memory store, the input of stimulation supposedly produces "reverberating" neural activity, representative of that experience, which persists for a while. This dynamic neural trace is coincident with our STM. While this reverberatory activity lasts, the permanent structural change underlying the LTM is slowly developing. Once the reverberatory trace dies out, the structural change stops and remains at the level attained. It is plausible, in this theory, to look for variables that influence reverberation rate or the length of time before the short-term trace dies out, since these should affect how much will be consolidated into LTM from a learning trial.

McGaugh (1965, 1968) has investigated two general classes of variables that may be interpreted by this means—namely, drugs and the genetic constitution of the animals. In one line of experiments, he has shown that certain CNS-stimulating drugs such as strychnine, diazamantan, amphetamine, and picrotoxin given in low doses speed up maze-learning of rats when injected either before *or after* the one trial of each day. Such results have by now been replicated many times for several learning tasks (see McGaugh & Herz, 1972). As one example, Davis and associates (1978) found that human adults previously injected with physostigmine (a drug that increases acetylcholine at the synapses) learn to free-recall a list of words faster than do control subjects receiving a neutral saline injection. It is presumed that these stimulants either increase the consolidation rate or prolong the short-term activity trace, which results in more consolidated learning per trial. A standard finding, for instance, is that posttrial injections facilitate learning only if they are given within 15 minutes or so after the day's learning experience.

In the other line of work, McGaugh used genetic strains of rats that had been selectively inbred by Tryon (1942) to be either bright or dull in learning various maze problems. He tested the implications of the idea that the maze-bright and maze-dull strains differ in their neural reverberation rates or times. For example, one implication he confirmed is that in the one-trial learning ECS situation, ECS can be delayed longer yet still produce greater memory deficits in the maze-dull rats. Also, if maze trials are given widely spaced in time, the maze-dulls can learn as fast as the maze-bright rats, the difference appearing only with massed trials. This is understandable if it is assumed that maze-dulls consolidate more slowly and the consolidation of learning from trial n is cut short when trial $n + 1$ starts under the massed condition. Further, it was found that injection of the neural stimulant picrotoxin facilitated massed-trial learning of the maze-dulls (in fact, makes them learn as fast as the maze-brights) more than it facilitates the maze-bright animals. These observations and several others seem consistent with the view that the two genetic strains differ in rate of memory consolidation.

It is proper to note that the short-term and long-term memory distinction used above employs a "conceptual" nervous system to advantage, without specifying the neural circuitry involved. However, there is, to be sure, firm evidence of persisting reverberatory neural circuits in the cortex. For example, Burns (1958) reported that a few electrical shocks applied to an isolated slab of quiescent cortex will produce bursts of neural activity that may persist for minutes (sometimes as long as 30 minutes) after stimulation has stopped. But little is really known of these persisting effects in nonisolated tissue. Nor is much known of the effect on the brain of drugs like picrotoxin which facilitate learning, and we are only now slowly accumulating facts about the neurological effect of ECS upon the metabolism and general functioning of the brain. Our point in noting this is that the consolidation hypothesis derives its major, if not its sole, evidential support from "behavioral" studies, not from the observation of events in the central nervous system.

Although the consolidation hypothesis has proven itself to be a viable theory, a variety of further questions will have to be asked and answered by experiments. What causes differences in the time required to consolidate different learning tasks? Is the change gradual, all-or-none, or gradual with a threshold? How do we distinguish poor storage from poor access to a stored engram? What is the generic nature of the events that disrupt consolidation? How are proactive interference effects on retention to be explained in these terms?

How can animals learn to avoid a place where ECS is delivered if that ECS prevents storage of the memory that it was unpleasant? Does consolidation stop when the short-term trace dies out or does it continue if not interfered with? How do we account for long-term recovery of a memory disrupted by ECS? What are the neural events that are facilitated when posttrial drug injections enhance learning? These and other questions come to mind, and future research will be directed at answering them in detail.

Neurological Patients

Some rather dramatic amnestic results have been obtained from electrical stimulation and selective ablation in the case of human patients undergoing brain surgery for medical reasons (typically, for removal of epileptogenic foci causing frequent seizures). Bickford and associates (1958) and Chapman and associates (1967) have reported that electrical stimulation to the temporal lobe of the brain of the waking patient (during surgery under local anesthesia) produces a temporary retrograde amnesia. The patient may be unable to retrieve events up to 2 weeks past, and the length of this memory gap increases with the duration of the stimulation. The amnesia is temporary, however, with memory being recovered completely a few hours after stimulation. Although the patients were unable during stimulation to retrieve memories several hours or several days old, they were able to perform quite capably on short-term or immediate memory tasks, such as repeating back a short series of digits. Such dramatic findings should be followed up, but require the cooperation of brain surgeons willing to allow some experimentation during the course of very exacting surgery.

The critical role of the hippocampus in memory consolidation has been suggested by the striking disabilities of human patients who have suffered damage or ablation of the hippocampus bilaterally (on both sides of the midline). Although such patients appear to have normal short-term or immediate memory and can recall with some deficit their life before their brain injury, they seem unable to retain new, complex information for any great length of time (Milner, 1966). For instance, such a patient cannot remember a person he met and conversed with only a few minutes before. He will repeatedly introduce himself and ask the same questions as at the earlier encounters, with a perfect confidence that the current meeting is the first one. Such patients, of course, are often quite disoriented as to where they are (in the hospital), how long they have been there, how they came to be there, or what has happened to them or to the world since their brain trauma (see Talland, 1965). For them, the elapsed time and the events which fill that time do not exist; regardless of how long ago they came to the hospital, in their memory it is always "yesterday."

This dramatic syndrome is consonant in certain respects with the dual-memory hypothesis, which proposes a STM and LTM. We might suppose that in these patients the mechanism for transferring representations of experience into LTM has been put out of commission, although their STM is unimpaired, as is retrieval of the long-term memories they had preoperatively. But this cannot be the complete story. Milner (1970) found that her hippocampal-lesioned patient could learn and retain a sensory-motor skill (reverse-mirror drawing) and learn to identify complete pictures of common objects when shown minimal line fragments of them. The patient revealed memory by improving in repeated test performances despite his opinion that a given task was novel and was being encountered for the first time. Others have reported this dramatic inability of amnesic patients to talk about

what they have clearly learned in a non-verbal task (for a review, see Carlson 1977). For example, patients suffering Korsakoff's syndrome (where there is damage to the mammillary bodies, with effects similar to bilateral hippocampal damage) have enough memory to select from an array those pictures seen 18 days earlier, even though they had no awareness that they had ever seen any of the pictures or the experimenter before. Thus, although non-verbal stimuli can be stored by these patients in LTM, their conscious "feeling of knowing" about the material is absent. Also, these patients are poor at retrieving memorized material with cues from another modality; it is as though the hippocampal damage has made the memory extraordinarily literal and specific to the stimulus presented. It should be pointed out that the cues from another modality were verbal, and that these patients show a true deficit in storing verbal messages; apparently their meaning-system for language is quite impaired.

Warrington and Shallice (1972) have described another type of brain-injured patient who has a very defective memory for words presented auditorily (an auditory span of 1 to 2 digits) but who has a fairly normal memory for words presented visually. (His hearing is quite normal.) Such results suggest that memories are coded and stored in part according to their sense modality, and that brain lesions can selectively impair memories from particular modalities.

A Theory of Amnesia

Wickelgren (1979b) proposed an interesting theory to account for the pattern of learning results shown by hippocampectomized patients as well as the anterograde and retrograde amnesia created by ECS treatments. Wickelgren first distinguished between a lower-level type of S-R associative learning and a higher form of configural pattern learning that he calls "chunking," or cognitive learning. (Interestingly, Razran [1971] and Bitterman [1975] have noted that lower species, such as fish and amphibians, show only lower-level conditioning, whereas complex or configural pattern-learning can easily occur only with birds and more advanced animals.) Wickelgren notes that patients with damage to the hippocampus show a similar dichotomy of learning abilities—they can learn simple S-R habits or prime already existing associations, but cannot do higher forms of learning or cognize about it. From this evidence, Wickelgren hypothesizes that in order for a complex memory (bundle of associations) to be formed, diffuse activation from a hippocampal arousal system must be active at the same time as are neurons encoding the specific features of the to-be-learned event pattern.

The basic ideas are shown schematically in Figure 14.7, where nodes stand for neurons (or neuron pools) in the association cortex which represent stimulus features, events, concepts, or ideas, these being activated when those stimuli are presented or thought of. Wickelgren also postulates a large pool of "free" higher-level neurons that have no strong connections initially but which have many weak links to large numbers of lower-level neurons. When the stimulus pattern is presented, its components and structural relations, *a, b, c,* are activated, and activation from them intersects at some higher-level free neuron in the association cortex (denoted *X* here). Associative clusters formed by such vertical associations were discussed at the end of Chapter 6. Wickelgren assumes that the hippocampus serves as an arousal (motivational) system, projecting diffusely to almost every higher-level free neuron. If the stimulus features *a, b, c* activate the node *X* at the same time as it receives arousal from the hippocampus, then a permanent associative cluster starts to grow slowly. That is, the pathways connecting neurons *a, b, c* to neuron *X* increase in efficiency or decrease in synaptic resistance—the analog of association strength. Node *X* thus becomes bound or specified by its strong connections to neurons *a, b, c.* The node *X* then serves as a chunk node, encoding the contiguous association of features or events *a, b, c* in the learned pattern. Node *X* is the physical embodiment of the chunk, or memory, and it basically serves as a switching device for excitation. In particular, presentation of feature *a* could cause the higher-level node *X* to fire, thus firing off neurons *b* and *c,* completing the pattern. Most learning can be represented by way

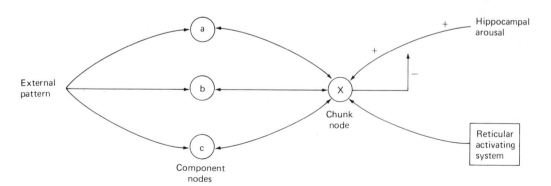

Figure 14.7. Hypothetical diagram of a three-feature stimulus pattern becoming associated into a cortical *chunk node* that receives "learning activation" from the reticular activating system.

of such simple associative structures. To take one example, Tolman would have supposed that the three critical components in Figure 14.7 are the discriminative stimulus, the response, and the rewarding outcome of an event pattern, and that, after learning, the discriminative stimulus alone could evoke the response as well as anticipation of the expected reward.

Wickelgren supposes that a consolidation process ensues for some time after the a-b-c learning event. The a-b-c neurons remain active and fire off cell X in conjunction with hippocampal pulses, all in repetitive cycles. The associative chunk X will be consolidated in case it is preserved from entering into interfering chunks. (Recall that a higher-level node may receive weak input from many lower-level stimulus neurons.) This interfering learning is prevented within the theory, Wickelgren supposes, because of gradual suppression of the linkage from the hippocampus to the bound X cell. That is, during gradual binding of a higher-level chunk, it inhibits and shuts off the link from the hippocampus (see the "minus" link from node X in Figure 14.7); therefore, cell X gets "locked up" to a, b, c and cannot participate in other associative chunks. For arousing the memory trace later, Wickelgren assumes that the cells receive nonspecific activation from some other system such as the reticular activating system, which adds to the sensory arousal from a retrieval cue, a, b, or c.

Wickelgren's theory explains the pattern of learning successes and failures of hippocampal patients, since hippocampal lesions destroy the critical activation link needed to form the higher-level chunks that are required for complex or cognitive learning. Although such patients show long-term memory and some short-term memory (i.e., temporary activation of lower-level event neurons like a or b), they cannot learn new complex memories due to the absence of the "learning pulse" from

the hippocampus. By a similar line of reasoning, the theory accounts for the temporary anterograde amnesia that follows a concussion or ECS. During the unconsciousness and for a while afterwards, the hippocampus has been put out of commission, so no new complex learning can occur during that time. As the convulsion effects wear off, the hippocampal learning link recovers, and so does the subject's learning ability. The theory also accounts for the retrograde amnesia for events near the time of the ECS, because in stopping hippocampal arousal feeding into the higher-level (X) cells, the ECS stops the consolidation of memory for those earlier events. The amount of consolidation would have been larger, the more time that had elapsed between the event-to-be-learned and the ECS.

There is also an extensive literature on the influence of hippocampal lesions on learning in lower animals, typically rats (see reviews by Hirsh, 1974; Isaacson, 1974). The results seem fairly well described by the generalization that hippocampal lesions or disturbances interfere with learning and consolidation of complex configural habits, but not with simple low-level habits. Wickelgren's theory seems to account for all these phenomena in a neat manner, so its detailed evaluation has become an important item on the research agenda. One should note again that Wickelgren's theory largely uses a conceptual nervous system, and although the assumptions are consistent with physiological findings, its validation is entirely based on behavioral observations.

PHYSIOLOGICAL CHANGES IN LEARNING

So far we have managed to discuss the neurophysiology of learning by skirting what is surely the central issue—the nature of the physiological change that occurs during learning. The reason for skirting the issue is simple. The nature of this change is far from being understood. A number of speculative hypotheses have been offered over the years, but the evidence for any one of them is very limited, and little agreement exists even about what are the more promising leads. The hypotheses, such as there are, vary in their degree of elaboration, from one-line "suggestions" to more elaborate systems of postulates; but for none has it been demonstrated that the hypothesis is sufficient to account for a substantial range of the known facts about learning. This is a sorry state of affairs, but one that seems imposed on us by the difficulty of the problem. It certainly cannot be attributed to any lack of industry or ingenuity by experimenters in the field. In this section, we will touch briefly on a diverse miscellany of facts and ideas that are relevant to information storage in the nervous system, and also mention a few of the earlier, more prevalent ideas regarding the physical change in learning, not so much to point to the evidence supporting them but rather to the lack of it.

Let us begin with the example of a Pavlovian conditioned reflex. Next to habituation, classical conditioning is about the simplest context in which to place various notions about the physical change effected by learning. A bell (CS) is paired repeatedly with an electric shock (US) to the forepaw of a dog, eliciting a limb flexion (UR) until, with training, the bell alone serves to elicit the response (CS). When the process is viewed from the anatomical side, at least three classes of structures or cell populations are involved: (a) cells all along the sensory input channel excited by the CS, (b) cells along the sensory input channel excited by the US, and (c) cells along the motor output channel initiating and controlling the response (UR). We will call these multiple struc-

tures the CS, US, and UR sites or centers. Because of innate connections, there already exists a strong tendency for activation of the US center to produce activation of the UR center. Most neurophysiological theories of conditioning employ one or another modified version of the *substitution* notion of conditioning. By virtue of many contiguous pairings of activity in the CS center and the US (or UR) center, the former through some means gets "connected" to the latter so that activation of the CS now transmits effective excitation to the US (or UR) center. Thereupon the CS alone mimics or substitutes in some degree for the action of the US. Various hypotheses are then offered regarding the nature of this functional connection and the processes involved in its formation.

One class of hypotheses has to do with a selective increase in the efficiency of existing neural pathways connecting the CS and US centers, which may be assumed to involve many central synapses linked in a chain. Given good conduction between the CS and US centers, it is conceivable that the CS might fire the US center and thus evoke an anticipatory CR. In this case it is supposed that there is some anatomical or biochemical change at the synapses along such critical pathways. Some possibilities are that the presynaptic axon terminals either swell in size, grow in length, multiply in number to make better contact with the postsynaptic neuron, or that the postsynaptic cell becomes biochemically altered so as to be selectively sensitive to a particular transmitter, thus aiding future transmission across the synapse. There is only small evidence for any of these specific mechanisms in learning. One problem is that normal stimulation across a synapse does not appear to change its efficiency (Brink, 1951). Efficiency can be enhanced, usually for only brief periods (a few minutes), if the synapse is bombarded with a volley of high-frequency impulses (e.g., 400 pulses per second), but the relevance of this particular result for normal learning has not been elaborated.

An alternative idea, proposed by Pavlov and investigated by the Russians, is cortical irradiation of extraneuronal electrical fields. When activated, the cortical sites of the CS and US centers supposedly radiate electrical excitation, spreading out in all directions with diminishing intensity. Because the CS excitation is the weaker of the two, it is supposedly drawn toward the US excitation center by some method unspecified. As a consequence, some kind of cortical pathway (unspecified) would get established between the CS and US center. Beritoff (cited in Konorski, 1948) elaborates on the hypothesis further. However, two immediate problems are encountered by this notion of spreading intracortical electrical fields. First, it is known that animals (dogs) can learn simple conditional reflexes even after the cortex has been totally removed. Second, an experiment by Sperry and Miner (1955) showed that learning was essentially undisturbed in animals whose cortices had been altered by cross-hatching knife cuts or implantation of wires and mica sheets that serve as electrical conductors or insulators. Such devices must have distorted or destroyed any existing or generated electrical fields in the cortex. Yet they did not interfere at all with the learning of fairly complicated CRs.

As noted earlier in our discussion of consolidation, it has been proposed that a sequence of stimulus inputs sets up a short-term activity (memory) trace based on reverberatory neuronal circuits involving elements excited by the CS and US inputs. Neuron *A* excites neuron *B,* which, through some more or less direct path, excites *A* again; hence, the loop of *A* to *B* to *A* activity is alleged to perseverate for a time after the inputs. This persisting reverberatory activity is presumed to induce a more enduring structural change (of unknown nature) so that the *A-B* neural centers will now be aroused as a unit. The fairest statement we can make concerning this notion is that no convincing evidence has been adduced for the existence of reverberatory circuits in the intact brain that (a) are clearly implicated in learning, or that (b) last long enough to have the properties ascribed to them. Although, as mentioned earlier, Burns (1958) did report fairly persistent neural activity following stimulation of the cortex, that was in an isolated slab of material not subject to dissipating forces from other parts of the brain. In any event, the reverberation idea, even if true, still tells us nothing about the nature of the structural change effected by learning.

Model Preparations

Instead of speculating about the neural changes involved in CR learning, the strategy preferred by many investigators is to search for experimental preparations wherein a few neurons modify their behavior in a way that mimics learning. The hope is that by studying a primitive form of information storage or learning at the level of the single neural cell, we may come up with some fruitful hypotheses about the physical changes in learning. In line with this policy, there have been many efforts to devise preparations that show simple learning in a few neurons. We will review two such preparations.

Mirror-focus epilepsy. The first preparation is the *mirror-focus epileptiform phenomenon,* whereby a cluster of normal brain cells learns to behave in an abnormal way. It has been observed that an abnormally discharging group of brain cells in the cortex of one cerebral hemisphere (the primary focus) will fire off a similar discharge in a corresponding area of the opposite hemisphere (the secondary focus). The main links connecting the two foci probably pass through the corpus callosum. The primary focus may be produced by local application of various chemicals (ethyl chloride or aluminum hydroxide) to the brain site or by an injury or tumor (as in epilepsy). Initially, discharge of the secondary focus is dependent upon discharge in the primary focus. However, after a time (about 8 weeks in the monkey), the secondary focus begins abnormally discharging on its own, independently of the primary focus. The primary focus can now be cut out, and the secondary focus continues its pattern of paroxysmal discharging. It has "learned" to discharge in an abnormal way. Moreover, if the secondary focus is neuronally isolated by cutting it away from surrounding tissue (but leaving its blood supply intact) and left in a quiescent state for some months, later stimulation of the tissue will still set off the abnormal discharge pattern. Apparently the tissue slab has "retained" this discharge pattern after months of inactivity. The importance of this preparation is that learning of a primitive sort has been shown to occur in a relatively small group of cortical cells.

Habituation of simple reflexes. Among the model preparations that are proposed as ideal for studying learning processes, mention may be made of three further preparations because of their especial simplicity. One of these is habituation of a flexion reflex of an animal. Typical examples are the flexion of the hind leg of a spinally sectioned cat (see Thompson & Spencer, 1966), the swimming tail-flip of the crayfish (see Wine & Krasne, 1977), or the gill-withdrawal reflex of the mollusk *Aplysia* (see Kandel & Spencer, 1968). These are particularly simple neuronal reflexes, involving a sensory neuron from the skin, a motor neuron to the recorded muscle, and either zero, one, or at most two interneurons (and synaptic connections). Because of their simplicity, it is argued that such preparations are ideal for detailed electrophysiological and biochemical studies of learning phenomena. Habituation, as-

suredly one of the simplest forms of learning (it is comparable to "stimulus recognition" in humans), follows these nine empirical laws in most cases (adapted from Thompson & Spencer, 1966, pp. 18–19):

1. Repeated application of a stimulus results in progressive decrease of the usual response it elicits. This is called habituation.
2. The response spontaneously recovers over time without the stimulus.
3. When habituation series and recovery intervals are repeated, habituation proceeds progressively more rapidly.
4. Generally, the higher the rate of stimulation, the more rapid and extensive is habituation.
5. The weaker the stimulus, the quicker habituation occurs to it. Very intense stimuli may not habituate.
6. The effects of habituation training can proceed beyond the "zero" response level; that is, additional habituation trials given after the response has momentarily stopped will nonetheless cause slower recovery from habituation.
7. Habituation of a response to a given stimulus exhibits generalization to other stimuli.
8. A habituation response can be recovered by momentary presentation of another "surprising" or strong stimulus. This is called dishabituation.
9. Repeated use of the dishabituating stimulus (see 8 above) results in *that* stimulus's losing its dishabituating effect.

These nine characteristics may serve as the operational definition of habituation. Once several of these criteria have been satisfied by a given preparation, the neurophysiological correlates of habituation in that preparation may begin to be studied. Generally, habituation in polysynaptic preparations (like the spinal preparation in cats) is correlated with a decrease in transmission measurable by microelectrodes at interneuronal synapses. In nonsynaptic preparations such as the gill withdrawal reflex of *Aplysia*, habituation appears in attenuated transmission at the presynaptic terminal of the stimulated sensory neuron. Dishabituation occurs by stimulating any sensory neuron that synapses on the same motor unit.

The work on *Aplysia* has used the isolated abdominal ganglion, a cluster of large nerve cells consisting of motor neurons, interneurons, and neurosecretory cells. These cells mediate such diverse behaviors as egg laying, inking (darkening the surrounding water), and gill movement. A few giant nerve cells can be easily seen, stimulated, and recorded from. They show habituation to a repetitive stimulus. They also show nonspecific facilitation ("sensitization") in that repeated firing of a cell by a strong stimulus will "sensitize" the cell so that a weak (previously ineffective) stimulus that reaches the cell by a different synapse will now fire the cell (see Kandel & Tauc, 1965a, 1965b). The period of heightened excitability of the stimulated cell may last from 10 to 30 minutes. This particular phenomenon does not depend on a specific temporal pairing of weak (CS) and strong (US) stimuli; the effect is nonspecific. Whether and how much truly *specific* facilitation can be obtained (requiring CS-US pairings) is still a controversial issue. The plausible models for learning at the single synaptic level have been systematically presented by Kupfermann and Pinsker (1969), with special consideration of the invertebrate evidence.

The problem with studying the physiological substrates of learning or other behavioral phenomena with such simple preparations is that generalization of the results to higher, more complex organisms can be hazardous. Three hurdles must be passed to legitimize the generalization. First, the behavioral properties of learning in the model system must correspond to those found in more complex, intact vertebrates. Second, the neural mechanisms underlying learning in the model system must be simple enough to allow a detailed analysis. Third, the neural mechanisms subserving learning in the model systems must also be demonstrated for learning in the intact higher organism. In their review of such work, Thompson and associates (1971, p. 86) comment as follows: "This fundamental problem of inference is the greatest weakness of the model systems approach—there is no guarantee that the models will yield anything but interesting games quite irrelevant to an understanding of learning in higher vertebrates." In a similar vein, Kupfermann and Pinsker (1969, p. 382) urge, "It cannot be overemphasized that there is an enormous gap between knowledge of the plastic [learning] properties of neurons studied in simple preparations, and knowledge of the physiological basis of reinforcement and learning in intact animals." However, this is an area in which intensive neurophysiological studies may be expected, based on the argument that we have little chance of understanding complex systems unless we can first thoroughly analyze and understand the simple case.

The Neurochemistry of Learning and Experience

One appealing general hypothesis to explore is that individuals differ in their learning capabilities because of differences in the biochemistry of their brains. This is not an implausible supposition to follow up since the transmission of neural signals is largely a chemical affair. Perhaps bright and dull individuals differ in the amount or manner of distribution over the brain of particular essential chemicals, or they may differ in the distribution of antagonistic chemicals that must be maintained in delicate balance for the proper functioning of the mind.

If we seek to discover how brain chemistry is related to behavior, the first questions to be decided are what chemicals to look for and where in the brain to look for them. One approach is to measure the total amount of some chemical in gross areas of the brain—for example, in the whole cortex of a rat. An alternative might be to measure its amount and how it changes in a few neural cells located in specific brain structures implicated in the behavior we are studying. Another line of research uses brain chemistry alternately as an independent variable and as a dependent variable. In the first case, the aim is to find out how behavior varies on some standard task for individuals known to have different distributions of brain chemicals (e.g., because of age or of genetic differences). In the second case, the rearing and learning experiences of animals from a common genetic pool are manipulated, and then we determine whether or not their brain chemistry has been changed as a result of experience. Still another approach is to manipulate neurochemical processes at synapses by injection of centrally acting drugs, and then see whether hypothesized behavior effects follow. In most instances, several approaches are used by the same investigator. In what follows, we shall review one line of work representative of the relatively gross approach to brain chemistry and two that are representative of the synaptic approach.

Enriched environments and brain transmitters. As indicated earlier, one of the transmitters in cortical synapses is acetylcholine. After an axonal impulse releases acetylcholine (ACh) into the synaptic gap (possibly initiating a postsynaptic pulse), cholinesterase (ChE) rushes in to metabolize the ACh and restore the functioning of the synapse.

A group of scientists at the University of California—psychologists Krech and Rosenzweig and biochemist Bennett—carried out a research program on ChE concentrations in rat brains. ChE is used because measurements of it are relatively easy to obtain, whereas reliable assays of ACh are difficult. Over a long period of research, these investigators gradually shifted their emphasis (because of the incoming data) concerning what brain chemistry measure should be used to find re-

liable correlations with behavior. The earliest measure that seemed most discriminating was the ratio of total cortical ChE activity to total subcortical ChE activity, called the *C/S ratio* (for cortical/subcortical). Low values of this C/S ratio are associated with quick learning of maze problems. In one study (Krech et al., 1960), rats reared in an "enriched" sensory environment, one filled with playground toys as well as other rats, had lower adult C/S ratios than rats reared under conditions of relative "isolation," where they were kept in small, enclosed cages devoid of other objects and fellow rats. On later tests of maze-learning (Krech et al., 1962), the "enriched" subjects also learned more rapidly. Within each rearing condition, individual differences in C/S ratio were correlated with errors in the maze-learning problem. The correlation was .81 for animals reared in the enriched environment and .53 for those reared in isolation. This shows a rather strong correlation between brain chemistry and speed of learning.

In other studies, rats of different genetic strains were examined for differences in C/S ratio. A series of studies was carried out with the Tryon maze-bright and maze-dull genetic strains of rats. Examination of the brains of these rats showed that the C/S ratio was lower for the maze-bright than for the maze-dull subjects. This finding is consistent with the previous results —that is, lower C/S ratios make for faster learning. In a genetic experiment by Roderick (1960), rats were selectively bred, some for high cortical ChE levels, some for low. After several generations of inbreeding highs with highs and lows with lows, there was little overlap in the distributions of cortical ChE levels in the two populations. Thus, brain chemistry was shown to be manipulable through genetic selection starting from a common genetic stock.

Although these studies were generally successful in disclosing individual and strain differences in brain chemistry that correlate with learning, the research ran into an interpretative problem. Though the C/S ratio correlated empirically, no one was able to figure out a very convincing explanation for why it did so. Later studies, however, have provided an explanation. The first discovery was that the cerebral cortex of enriched-reared (ER) rats is *bigger* than that of rats in the isolation-reared (IR) condition! Bennett and associates (1964) found that the cortex of the ER rats is both heavier and thicker. Because the increase in cholinesterase activity of the cortex is relatively less than the increase in its weight, the ChE activity per unit of weight decreases in the cortex of the ER rats. The ChE activity of the subcortex remains about the same, whereas the subcortex weight is slightly lower for ER rats, thus making for a higher subcortex ChE activity per unit weight. This explains why the C/S ratio of ChE activity is lower in the ER rats. The second discovery, by Globus, Rosenzweig, Bennett, and Diamond (1973), was that the cortical neurons of ER rats had more dendritic spines, implying more synapses on each cell.

This discovery of a change in size of the cortex and more dendritic growths from cortical neurons came as a complete surprise to those familiar with brain research. Before this, few experts would have believed that the effects of a sensorily enriched environment could induce so "obvious" a change in the brain. But the effects have by now been replicated several times, and are present each time in the ER-IR comparison. The magnitude of the change varies in different areas over the cortex, being largest (about 10 percent by weight) in the visual cortex. But it will be recalled that complexity of visual input is one of the main factors differentiating the two rearing conditions.

In search of a "critical period" for early experience (Rosenzweig et al., 1964), two groups of animals were reared in the same environment, the usual colony room, until they were 105 days of age, making them, roughly, adolescents, and then were separated, some to live in the enriched environment and some in the impoverished environment. After 85 days of such living, the two groups of rats were found to differ significantly in cortical weight and in ChE activity, much as when the differential rearing was done from birth onward. Thus, the brains of rats that have suffered an impoverished early life can be enlarged by placing them in an enriched environment at adolescence. This shows that there is no "critical period" before which the animal must be exposed to the enriched environment in order to produce an increase in the size of its cortex.

These findings instigated a number of follow-up studies investigating individual and strain differences in cortical size and visual learning ability. We need some explanation for (a) how a stimulating environment leads to a selective increase in cortical size and dendritic growth, or (b) why individuals with a slightly larger or more arborescent cortex learn maze problems faster than do their slimmer-brained cohorts. Apparently, we may think of neural tissue much as we think of muscles that increase in size or density with exercise. Such a view would, until recently, have been considered incredible nonsense in any respectable neurological discussion.

Cellular neurochemistry. One active line of contemporary research stems from the hypothesis that the physical basis for memory resides in some relatively enduring change in the biochemical constituents of a neuron which selectively control its response. This would suggest that an engram might be built up by certain biochemical changes occurring selectively in the cells of a neuronal circuit activated by the learning experience.

For various reasons, ribonucleic acid (RNA) was once thought to be the logical candidate to assume this role of the memory molecule. It occurs in abundance in neural cells, it contains within its structure a potentially large storehouse for holding encoded information (explained below), and it determines and controls the specific form of proteins that are synthesized within a cell. RNA is a first cousin of DNA (deoxyribonucleic acid), which has been established to be the gene-carrying hereditary material in the chromosomes of each cell. DNA contains within its complex structure sufficient coded information to specify the genotypic character of an organism (i.e., its appearance), and it exercises its influence by controlling biochemical reactions in complex ways.

RNA is a very large, single-strand molecule (a polymer) consisting of a recurring sequence of a phosphate and sugar pair connected to any one of four bases, adenine, guanine, uracil, and cytosine. One of the four bases followed by a phosphate and a sugar may be considered as one of four types of links used to compose a long, beaded chain. The RNA molecule is very long (probably several thousand units), so that the number of possible sequential combinations of the four bases is very large. To illustrate, suppose each molecule were 2000 links long and at each position any of the four bases could occur. Then the number of different varieties of the molecule would be 4^{2000}, which is indeed a large number. This is important because it shows how much information could potentially be encoded in an RNA molecule. This capacity can be appreciated when it is recalled that Morse code translates a letter of the alphabet into a mere string of four or five binary units (dots and dashes). To compare it to the Morse code, an RNA strand consisting of 2000 units with four alternatives at each unit could encode and store a message about 1000 letters or 200 words long. Whether and how biological information is coded in RNA, and what the code is, are

at present unanswered questions. However, the point here is that RNA has the potential for filling the role of a biological information storehouse.

If this were all there is to say about RNA, then it would have remained merely the subject of idle speculation. But a rash of behavioral evidence appeared to implicate RNA as a possible memory molecule. For one thing, its concentration in human brain cells first increases with age and then decreases, much as learning ability does. It has been reported that adding RNA supplements to the diet of aged persons improves their immediate memory; however, this result has not been obtained in attempted replications. Of more direct relevance is the fact that the concentration of RNA in neural cells increases when they are repetitively stimulated.

When the stimulation is to a cell importantly involved in learning some skill, the RNA in that cell not only increases but also changes its character as indexed by the amounts of the four bases (the "base ratio") found in RNA analysis following learning. In one study by Hydén and Egyházi (1962), rats were trained to balance upon and walk up an inclined tightrope to get a food reward. Following learning, the RNA in the vestibular nucleus was examined. This is a bundle of fibers that relays signals to the brain from the semicircular canals, which are receptor organs involved in maintaining postural balance. RNA in the nucleus of cells at this site was increased by the learning experience, and the dominant species of RNA was of a different kind (different base ratio) than that in control rats subjected to stimulation of their semicircular canals but not given the special training in tightrope balancing and walking. These control rats were instead merely rotated about in a small oscillating cage, movement that stimulates the semicircular canals. An interpretive problem with this study was that no one could figure out the adaptive significance of change in such a low-level sensory relay station.

In a further study (Hydén & Egyházi, 1964), "right-handed" rats were trained to use their left "hands" to grab food pellets from a food dispenser. Neural cells taken from certain layers of the opposite (right) cerebral cortex showed increases in nuclear RNA concentration and changes in the base ratio of the dominant RNA species. The particular cells were taken from cortical areas involved in use of the left hand; this is inferred from the report that destruction of this cortical area would disable the rat from learning the left-handed grasping skill.

A few difficulties arise in interpreting these results. First is the adequacy of the controls. Since stimulation or exercise per se enhances RNA in the neurons involved and the pattern of exercise may alter the type of RNA, the problem is to design the experiment so that the learning subjects and the nonlearning controls receive about the same pattern of input stimulation. The controls typically run are not adequate in this sense. Second, the changes with learning in the dominant species of RNA are confined only to what is found in the cell's nucleus, not in its cytoplasm. Third, the changes in nuclear RNA are found immediately after the animal has been performing in the learning situation, but are no longer detectable if one waits 24 hours after the learning sessions before sacrificing the animal and examining its RNA (see Hydén, 1965); that is, after 24 hours, differences in RNA between the learning subjects and the controls can no longer be detected. Depending on one's attitude, these facts can be interpreted in terms that are either critical of, or sympathetic to, the RNA memory hypothesis.

The memory transfer studies. The lines of evidence offered for the RNA memory hypothesis have been of two sorts: alleged biological transfer of brain extracts containing RNA and memory from one individual to another, and behavioral effects of drugs that inhibit the action of RNA in synthesizing cellular proteins. In the transfer studies initiated by McConnell (1962) and his associates, one subject is trained until she has learned a habit. Then her brain is homogenized, strained, and the biochemical "soup" is injected into a naive subject; thereafter, the naive subject is tested to see whether she too can perform the habit significantly more than can controls who received brain soup from untrained donors. (The soup is a mix of proteins, neural transmitters, RNA, and probably much else.) A transfer effect has been reported for planaria (flatworms), goldfish, rats, and mice (see Gaito, 1966, and Fjerdingstad, 1971, for reviews). The dramatic nature of such transfer effects provoked much subsequent research and a spate of conflicting outcomes. Whether such transfer was found seemed to vary with the species used, exact details of the procedure, methods for extracting RNA and other proteins from the brains of the trained donors, and the site of its injection into the recipient. For example, in rats it is clear that very little of an intraperitoneal injection of RNA actually reaches the brain of the recipient, and such effects as do occur seem dependent on "impurities" rather than the RNA in the soup. The transfer effects are often small, transient, and dependent upon highly specific conditions (see a review of conflicting studies by Chapouthier, 1973). Most neuropsychologists today are skeptical of the transfer findings.

Ungar and associates (1968) reported purifying a polypeptide from brain extracts of trained rats that would transfer a kind of memory to a naive rat. The first animal was shocked in the dark side of a two-compartment box and hence learned to stay on the lighted side (formerly not preferred). Unger reported that naive rats that received the brain extract from trained animals avoided the dark side of the test chamber more than did rats receiving brain extract from unshocked control subjects. Ungar and associates called the purified polypeptide *scotophobin,* meaning "fear of darkness."

An interpretive problem is that the transfer may not be specific to *learning* caused by light-shock pairings. Rather, subjects receiving shock may release some stress hormone that when injected into others causes them to prefer lighter environments. To be categorized as learning, one must show that the result depends critically upon the pairing of darkness with shock. Controls were needed that received noncontingent foot shocks not paired with the light or dark compartments. The critical nature of such controls for nonspecific transfer was shown in an experiment by Frank and associates (1970). Some of their mice were trained on a shock-avoidance task; others were stressed by being rolled around in a jar; others were untouched. Then, all were sacrificed, and biochemical extracts were made from their brains or their livers. These extracts were injected into new mice who learned the same shock-avoidance task. The results demonstrated higher performance on the shock-avoidance task for mice receiving the extracts from either the trained or stressed (jar-rolled) mice, although the latter donors could have learned nothing about the avoidance task. Moreover, the transfer or facilitation of performance was as great when the new learners received injection of a liver extract as when they received brain extracts! Yet, no one would claim that memories are acquired by or stored in the liver. This control experiment suggests that stress alone can release a hormone or neurohumoral agent in a donor's body that may have a nonspecific generalized effect on a recipient's behavior for a while. (An example is the transfer of addictive drugs via placental blood between mother and fetus; the fetus is then addicted for a while after birth.)

The conclusions on this topic have been mired in controversy, conflicting findings, and argumentation. A misfortune of scientific publication policies is that only "positive" findings tend to be reported, so that the studies appearing in the literature are probably a biased sample of all attempts to bring about an effect.

Drugs that inhibit RNA synthesis. In an attempt to affect learning and memory by manipulating availability of RNA at critical synapses, some experimenters have used antibiotic drugs (puromycin, cycloheximides, actinomycin) that inhibit protein synthesis. The hypothesis is that consolidation and maintenance of a memory requires continued protein synthesis (i.e., continued manufacture of neuronal proteins of a special type selected during conditioning), and that disrupting or inhibiting such synthesis should produce some loss of recent memories. For example, mice receiving puromycin injections into the brain before training will learn a maze habit as fast as controls but they appear to forget it much more readily (see Barondes & Cohen, 1966). At a 3-hour retention (relearning) test, for instance, savings were 91 percent for controls as against only 7 percent for the puromycin-injected mice. However, these investigators found virtually no effect on retention from injections of cyclohexamide, a drug similar to puromycin in inhibiting protein synthesis. Cohen, Ervin, and Barondes (1966) suggest that puromycin may be effective on memories whereas cyclohexamide is not because only the former drug induces abnormal electrical activity in the hippocampal region. The other RNA synthesis inhibitor, actinomycin, has had inconsistent effects on learning depending on the task and the species.

The series of studies using puromycin and cyclohexamide have been continually plagued by inconsistencies and uninterpretable results. Two major problems with such research are recognized. First, there is no inhibitor that selectively knocks out only RNA; rather, each drug has a broad range of effects (for example, abnormal EEGs), and performance may suffer due to those side effects. Second, the RNA inhibitors do not completely shut down all protein synthesis (otherwise the animal would die); thus, failure to find amnesia after receipt of an RNA inhibitor could mean that what is left is adequate to do the job. Because of the inconsistent results, many theorists remain skeptical of the basic hypothesis. In reviewing this work, Carlson writes,

> It is impossible to say anything conclusive about these studies. Many investigators believe that protein synthesis is necessary for memory consolidation, but not because of the experimental evidence. . . . Instead, this belief is sustained by our knowledge of the role that proteins play in the biochemistry of structural change. It is quite possible that we will never find a drug that effectively prevents consolidation by general suppression of protein synthesis. Perhaps we will have to find out *which* proteins are involved in consolidation, and how they work, before we can prove their selective inhibition can prevent short-term memories from becoming long-term ones. We may be in for a long wait (1977, pp. 603–4).

Carlson (1977) also reviews research on the enhancement of memory or learning ability by giving drugs (such as magnesium pemoline) that facilitate RNA synthesis. Unfortunately, that research too has yielded no consistent positive results, leading Carlson to write:

> It is fair to conclude that there is no good evidence yet for improvements in learning produced by facilitation of biosynthetic processes involved in physical change (p. 604).

The credibility of the RNA memory hypothesis is further reduced by the absence of a plausible, articulated theory that explains exactly how RNA and memory are, or could be, related. For instance, by what means and by what steps is the RNA in a neuron altered by experience? Since electrical impulses of a particular temporal pattern and frequency are the only information arriving at a neuron, how is this information translated into a biochemical code within RNA? How is this information retrieved? How does the dominant RNA species in the nucleus of a neuron selectively control the transmission properties or responsivity of the cell membrane? These are difficult questions; but the failure to answer them adequately, as well as the conflicting empirical results, has reduced the plausibility of the RNA memory hypothesis.

Efficiency of Cholinergic Synapses

Whether or not RNA changes comprise the biochemical substrate of learning, the most plausible general hypothesis is that learning involves enhanced efficiency of those synapses involved in mediating the successful, learned response. A series of experiments by Deutsch and his associates (reviewed in Deutsch & Deutsch, 1973) has tested a special form of this hypothesis. Specifically, it is proposed that learning experiences initiate processes that cause *cholinergic* synapses in the reinforced neuronal pathways (of the S-R chain) of the brain to produce more effective concentrations of acetylcholine during transmission. Learning is thus identified with the gradual growth in the efficiency of transmission, whereas forgetting is the reverse of this process. Deutsch has investigated this hypothesis by noting the influence on memory of drugs which are known to affect transmission at cholinergic synapses.

The details of the synaptic mechanisms may be explicated by referring back to the diagram in Figure 14.2, which idealizes a single synapse. An electrical impulse traveling down the presynaptic axon causes packets of acetylcholine (ACh) to be released from tiny vesicles of the presynaptic terminal. These move across the synaptic cleft to fit neatly into a population of tailor-made receptor sites on the postsynaptic terminal, each generating small shifts in electrical potential across the postsynaptic membrane. If enough transmitter is absorbed, an appreciable potential shift is integrated so that an impulse will be generated down the postsynaptic neuron. The ACh is neutralized or "eaten up" by cholinesterase soon after it is released. We may think of the cholinesterase molecules as being continuously available in some concentration in the solution surrounding the synapses. If the ACh is produced in excess or is *not* destroyed by cholinesterase, then the UR cell will be "locked up" (hyperpolarized) and unable to fire again until the excess ACh has been cleared away.

By what means can we enhance the ability of the presynaptic terminal (call it the CS) to fire the postsynaptic cell (call it the UR)? One way would be to have the CS terminal release *more* ACh when it is stimulated, so that a previously totally ineffective CS cell now becomes completely effective in firing the UR cell by itself. A second way would be to increase the sensitivity or responsiveness of the postsynaptic membrane to a fixed amount of transmitter released at the presynaptic terminal. This could be done either by increasing the number of effective receptor sites which take up ACh or by lowering the threshold potential required in order to fire the UR neuron.

With this background, let us now consider the action of two types of drugs on this synaptic transmission. First are the anticholinesterase drugs (like physostigmine and DFP) which reduce the cholinesterase in the synapses. This has the secondary effect of increasing the amount of ACh (released by the CS terminal), which then becomes absorbed by the UR terminal. The effect of this increase in effective ACh on

synaptic transmission is not a simple enhancement. If ACh levels are low, then anticholinesterase drugs will increase firing efficiency of the UR cell for a given CS input. But if the ACh levels to CS stimulation are already quite high, then addition of the anticholinesterase increment may cause hyperpolarization ("locking out") with a consequent *lowering* of net synaptic transmission.

Next consider *anticholinergic* drugs such as scopolamine and atropine; these molecules are taken up by receptor sites on the postsynaptic terminal, thus excluding ACh from these sites; yet the uptake of the anticholinergic drugs causes no electrical impulses to be generated in the UR neuron. These are called *blocking* drugs because they block or reduce the normal action of ACh. Their effect on the synapse is to reduce its firing efficiency for a given amount of ACh released by the CS terminal.

Deutsch has used anticholinesterase drugs and blocking drugs to track hypothetical changes over time (following learning) in the efficiency of transmission across a synapse contained in the successful, learned neuronal circuit. The predictions as well as the empirical data may be organized according to the hypothetical diagram in Figure 14.8. This shows effective level of acetylcholine (ACh) transmitter assumed to be released by a CS stimulation, when tested at varying times after initial learning. To explain the various parts of this figure, consider the normal (no-drug) curves first. Following a session of learning experiences, the level of ACh is presumed to accumulate like a STM, then it dissipates over the first day or so. Next, there is increasing consolidation of a "long-term" change in effective ACh at the learning synapses. In Deutsch's view, this consolidation is autonomous and continues over a few weeks. After a few weeks without further use, the ACh substrate of the habit begins to diminish, leading to "forgetting" due to disuse of the habit. The relation be-

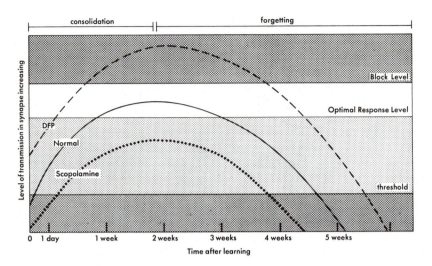

Figure 14.8. The hypothesized changes in "memory" synapses, with time after training and with pharmacological intervention. (Adapted from Deutsch, 1971).

tween effective ACh level and synaptic efficiency is complex, as we noted before: below a lower threshold, there has not been sufficient change in the synaptic efficiency to successfully fire the synapses involved throughout the circuit mediating successful performance of the learned act; above an upper threshold (denoted as the "block level" in Figure 14.8), there is more ACh than can be neutralized by cholinesterase, producing hyperpolarization and "locking up" of the synapse. The behavioral effect in this latter case is alleged to be a weakening of the response or an inability to perform the learned habit. Thus, optimal performance should occur when the effective ACh is in the middle range. The effect of an anticholinesterase drug (DFP or physostigmine) is to elevate the entire curve for "effective ACh" in Figure 14.8, whereas a cholinergic blocking agent (scopolamine) lowers the entire curve. These dashed curves are to be interpreted as the effective amount of ACh released by the CS following the injection of the indicated drug at varying times after initial learning. The amount of shift from

normal in the two cases depends, of course, on the dosage of the drug injected.

This set of interlocking assumptions is quite complex; nevertheless, the data appear to support several of the assumptions. A first set of facts concerns injections of DFP versus scopolamine at varying times after learning. In the typical experiment, a rat is trained in one session with massed trials in a Y-maze to escape electric shock by turning into the lighted arm and avoiding the darkened arm of the maze. Typically, training is carried to a criterion of ten consecutive correct choices. Following a rest interval of either half an hour, 1 day, 3 days, 1 week, 2 weeks, or 4 weeks, a number of rats are injected either with DFP or with scopolamine, and control animals receive an injection of a neutral solution. Different groups of animals are tested at each retention interval, and given one of the three injections. Soon after injection, the animal is tested for retention in the Y-maze, relearning the originally trained habit. The effective retention observed for the three classes of animals is depicted schematically in Figure 14.9. The reten-

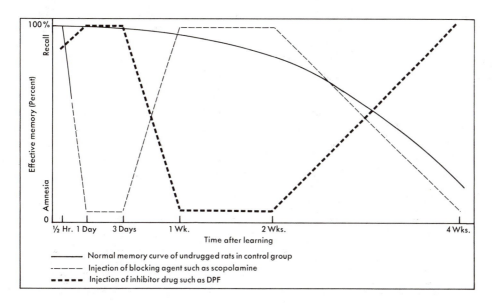

Figure 14.9. The effect of some drugs on memory. Results from rat experiments in Y-mazes show how two types of drugs—blocking agents (scopolamine) and inhibitors (DFP)—can each produce amnesia or recall, depending upon the time of injection after learning. (From Deutsch, 1968.)

tion scores confirm the theory in detail. First, the controls having already learned a strong habit initially show gradual forgetting over time before testing. Animals receiving an anticholinesterase like DFP, which elevates the amount of effective ACh available, show good memory if injected and tested at 1 day and 3 days, poor retention at 1 week or 2 weeks, but good retention if injected and tested after a 4-week delay. Animals receiving the cholinergic blocking agent, scopolamine, show nearly the reverse of the DFP effects: memory is impaired when the scopolamine injection and test occur after 1 or 3 days, is nearly perfect when the injection and test occur after 1 or 2 weeks, but is impaired again when the injection and test occur at 4 weeks after original learning. These effects are those predicted by the hypothetical curves of synaptic transmission in Figure 14.8. For instance, DFP produces poor performance at the 2-week interval because it elevates the amount of effective ACh at the synapse

to above the blocking level, producing hyperpolarization and poor transmission.

In order to check on the consolidation hypothesis of spontaneous memory improvement over time without drugs, animals were undertrained with only a small number of reinforced trials (shock escapes) on the original habit. After a fixed period, varying from 1 day to several weeks, these undertrained rats were returned to the maze to relearn the original habit. As expected, animals tested at 7 or 10 days showed better memory than animals tested after 1 or 3 days, or after several weeks (see Huppert & Deutsch, 1969). Later experiments by Huppert found a similar "reminiscence" effect on appetitively motivated habits reinforced with food rewards.

Further evidence was obtained from animals either undertrained or overtrained on the original habit; we may assume that these differences correspond to different degrees of "consolidation" effected by the end of training. Injections of DFP (or a neutral solution) and testing occurred 5 or 6 days later. For undertrained animals, DFP increased their memory performance above that of the undrugged controls; but for overtrained animals, DFP caused them to perform much worse than their undrugged controls. This is attributable to the blocking (hyperpolarization) of a well-consolidated habit by the excess ACh accumulated when much of the cholinesterase has been inactivated by DFP. A similar result occurs if animals are given a *fixed* number of training trials but with a difficult as opposed to an easy brightness discrimination. Animals learning the easier discrimination should have more consolidated memory after a fixed number of trials than would animals learning the difficult discrimination. Therefore, the prediction is that a DFP injection after 6 days would cause forgetting by the group with the easy, well-learned habit, but an enhancement in performance by the group with the difficult, partially learned habit. This prediction was confirmed.

Deutsch's hypothesis of the efficiency of transmission seems to give a good account of these data, and it promises to be a viable explanation for other research (Deutsch & Deutsch, 1973). However, the details of the results are only now being subjected to systematic replication, and that very necessary step may turn up unexpected findings. One preliminary result, for example, is that these drug effects on memory are easier to demonstrate with rats than with mice (Deutsch, personal communication, 1972), and much exploratory work is required to find the "right" drug dosage for the latter so as to duplicate the effects produced with rats. One disturbing feature of the hypothesis is that it rests very heavily on an analogy between processes occurring at single synapses and the percentage of correct choices made by a rat in a maze. The gap between those two domains is filled with only hopeful promises. Moreover, all the evidence for

the hypothesis rests on drug manipulations of retention. But it is well known that the drugs used by Deutsch have a multiplicity of effects (e.g., scopolamine is often used as a mild sedative or tranquilizer), and it is not known to what extent these other direct and indirect effects influence the results. Another problem is that it is known that many of the synapses in the central nervous system use different transmitters—for example, dopamine and norepinephrine (adrenaline); and these are not affected in nearly the same way as ACh is by anticholinesterase drugs and cholinergic blocking drugs. Since these neurons predominate in the limbic system subserving behavioral reward effects (see the earlier review of Stein's work), Deutsch's biochemical conjectures would not be a plausible description of the alterations in *these* central synapses underlying reward expectancy and incentive motivation. All the tests of the hypothesis to date have used brightness discrimination by rats in a Y-maze, mostly learning to escape shock. Autonomic indices of classical conditioning also need to be studied to see whether they agree with the forgetting assessed from instrumental behavior. A final problem with Deutsch's hypothesis is that it is complex and has a large number of arbitrary parameters or constants. After examining the results of an experiment to be fit by the theoretical curves in Figure 14.8, one can then select a lower threshold, an upper threshold, a "normal" consolidation curve with a peak and flatness as needed, an increment for the DFP-injection curve, and a decrement for the scopolamine-injection curve—all of these selected so as best to fit the observed results. The issue is whether the data can provide a very strong test of the model which has so many arbitrary constants. Apparently so; but it is surely much more difficult to disprove a model with so much flexibility in its quantitative details. Despite these criticisms, however, it is fair to say that Deutsch's work represents some of the more significant and influential extensions available today for the general thesis that learning involves improved efficiency of certain neuronal pathways.

This concludes our brief tour around the fringes of the neurochemistry of learning. This is a young field, full of many surprises, perplexities, and promises. There are major technical difficulties in doing research or theorizing at this level, and progress has to be slow. In order to understand the work at all well, one needs a fairly detailed knowledge of biochemistry, and for this reason not many psychologists are likely to rush into this research area. It should be clear enough that at this early stage of development, no detailed biochemical account can be given for even the simplest learned act. However, we may look forward to major strides in this area in the coming decades.

Learning Changes in Brain Cells

A recent topic of considerable interest is the identification of brain cells that change their response characteristics during the course of a conditioning experiment. The basic procedure is to put an array of microelectrodes into some potentially interesting brain sites, and then to record from them during the several hundred trials of a Pavlovian or instrumental-conditioning session. The hope is to locate a few neurons that change their firing rate over the course of training, and to correlate those changes with the trial-by-trial changes in the behavioral response (the CR) as well as the changes in neurons in other locations. A pioneering study by Jasper, Ricci, and Doane (1960) found changes in the motor cortex and the parietal cortex of monkeys while they were learning to respond with one hand to avoid shock to one visual CS but not to respond to a second, nonshocked visual stimulus. Cells located in the motor cortex

tended to increase their firing rate within each trial just prior to and during the occurrence of the avoidance response, whereas a failure of these cells to increase their firing rate to the CS typically meant no response would occur. Cells in the parietal cortex also tended to increase their firing rate to the CS on trials when the response occurred, but not when it failed to occur to the positive or negative stimulus.

Those early findings set off more detailed investigations by many others, who have examined other brain structures and conditioning arrangements. Some of the most impressive results have been obtained by Berger and Thompson (1978a, b). They used Pavlovian conditioning of the nictitating membrane ("inner eyelid") of a rabbit with a tone CS and an airpuff as US. The animal is strapped down to prevent its movements from disturbing the electrical recordings. In this preparation, the most interesting neural changes during conditioning occur in pyramidal cells in the dorsal hippocampus. Prior to conditioning, these hippocampal cells do not respond to the tone CS, and respond only weakly to the airpuff US. However, within a few CS-US pairing trials, these cells begin to increase their firing rate when the US occurs, and the size of this increment increases steadily over trials. Along with this change to the US, the increased firing rate moves forward in time and occurs to the CS alone in anticipation of the US. The increasing hippocampal firing rate corresponds closely to the increasing amplitude of the behavioral CR to the CS, except the hippocampal increases appear many trials before the behavioral changes become apparent. Thus, the hippocampal recordings are more sensitive than the behavioral response in detecting an early effect of conditioning.

Standardized firing-rate scores for the hippocampal cells are shown in Figure 14.10 plotted over blocks of 13 trials. The

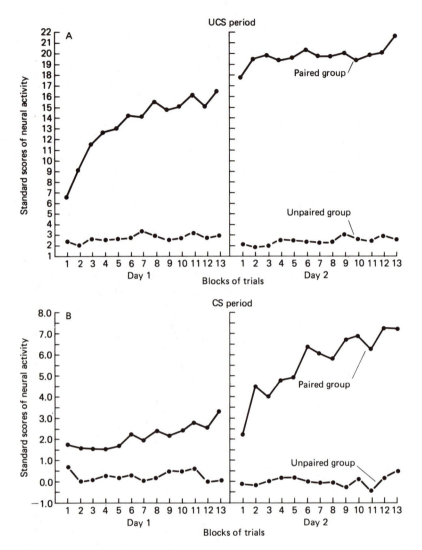

Figure 14.10. Standardized firing rates of hippocampal neurons to the airpuff (UCS, top panel) and to the tone (CS, lower panel) for rabbits receiving the CS and US either paired or unpaired. (From Berger and Thompson, 1978a.)

experimental rabbits received the CS and US paired in time, whereas control animals received explicitly unpaired presentations of tone and puff to measure possible changes from sensitization or pseudoconditioning. The top graph plots the summated firings of the hippocampal cells to the US whereas the bottom graph is for their firing from the onset of the CS to the onset of the US a quarter second later. A number of conclusions are apparent from Figure 14.10. First, explicit pairing of CS and US is necessary to obtain conditioning of the hippocampal responses (as it is for the behavioral response, too). Second, the changes occur sooner to the US than to the CS. Third, the firing rate to the CS and US for the "paired" subjects are both elevated over that for the "unpaired" controls even on the first block of (13) trials. In fact, Berger and Thompson found significant group differences in hippocampal firing after only one or two pairing trials; that is very fast learning, and it shows up in the hippocampus many trials before it appears in overt CRs, a clear example of learning that goes on below a response threshold.

From other data, Berger and Thompson concluded that the latency and amplitude of the hippocampal increase in firing within each trial correlated with the latency and amplitude of the behavioral CR. Thus, the firing rates of these hippocampal cells seemed to be indexing the rabbit's strength of conditioning. Moreover, during a series of unreinforced trials (CS alone), the neural response extinguished in parallel with the eyelid response.

Not all pyramidal cells in the hippocampus show these learning changes. The main cells which do change (80 percent) are those in the dorsal hippocampus that project their axons out through the fornix. Berger and Thompson (1978b) found that similar learning changes could be recorded from cells in the lateral septal region, although it lagged behind the hippocampal changes by many trials. This suggested a projection of the learning changes from the hippocampal cells over precommissural fornical pathways to the lateral septum. No such learning changes were uncovered from nearby cells in the medial septum, or the medial or lateral mammillary nuclei.

Results such as those of Berger and Thompson require careful interpretation. First, it is reasonable that there would be *some* brain changes correlated with the animal's overt response to a CS. At a minimum, cells in the motor cortex controlling the overt CR must necessarily be implicated. The interest of the Berger and Thompson results is that they involve cells from structures that are neither sensory nor motoric. The hippocampus in fact has been often implicated in emotions and in memory. A second point to consider is that the engram may not reside at the cells being recorded, but rather these cells may simply "listen in on" or "relay" the memory activated by the CS. Thus, the CS-US engram may reside in either the brain stem or a sensory association cortex (depending on the complexity of the CS), or both, with parallel projections through the hippocampus to the motor cortex.

Regardless of the exact interpretation to be placed upon such brain-change results, they suggest interesting ways to map out brain circuits implicated in elementary learning. Such data are needed to develop preliminary guesses about how the brain records a particular set of memories.

Localizing Memories

In what parts of the brain are memories stored? About a century ago, it was believed that a memory would be stored at a specific location, perhaps in the association area connected to the dominant sensory cortex aroused by the learning experience. This specific-location hypothesis was questioned by results obtained by Karl Lashley (1924, 1950), who found that a simple light-dark discrimination or a maze habit could be learned by rats almost regardless of which cortical areas of their brain had been removed. Similarly, removal of part of the cortex might cause **temporary loss of a previously learned** brightness discrimination, but the habit was often easily retrained unless the lesion had made the animal blind. After a series of failures to locate a maze habit and a brightness-discrimination habit in the rat's brain, Lashley concluded that a memory is probably established diffusely, throughout all regions of the cortex (or maybe subcortex), that it is multiply duplicated everywhere, involving huge numbers of neurons. As a result, a single neuron would be involved in many thousands of memories, with a memory being represented by a particular pattern or configuration of cortical excitation. On this view, learning of a habit will be slower and retention will be poorer the greater the amount of cortex removed, but removal of any area should have effects equivalent to removal of any other area of the same size. For neuropsychologists, these views about the diffuseness of the memory trace were particularly discouraging.

However, in light of later findings, Lashley's conclusions seem confined to lower mammals and to simple maze habits measured by crude means. Lashley used very simple brightness or spatial discriminations, and it seems likely that these can be acquired by subcortical circuits alone, perhaps involving the lateral geniculate (for vision), the brain stem, and the hippocampus. However, reasonably complex learning, involving many components, difficult discriminations, or complex configural patterns, appears to require "higher" cortical association areas. These conclusions derive from examining the effects of brain damage to humans, monkeys, and chimpanzees. Recent evidence suggests considerable localization of *complex* functions (e.g., language and musical ability), of cognitive skills, and of complex memories in higher animals. The best hypothesis today is probably a modified version of the older theory, that a *complex* memory is localized in the association cortex connected to the sensory cortex that was dominant during that learning experience. In case several sensory modalities are involved (e.g., correlating touch with vision), then the fibers connecting the two association cortices will also be involved in the memory. In addition, memory in the association cortex will be linked to regions of the motor cortex in case movements are involved.

Support for the localized-memory hypothesis comes from many studies, particularly of cognitive functions (e.g., speech) in humans and of visual pattern-learning in primates. Moving inward from the retina, the primate visual system consists roughly of the lateral geniculate, the striate cortex at the back of the brain, the circumstriate belt, and the inferotemporal (visual association) cortex. Simple visual discriminations such as light vs. dark can be learned without any cortex; but the more complex or configured the stimulus patterns to be discriminated, the more probable that "higher" (later) levels of the visual analyzing system will be required before learning can take place. It is a reasonable hypothesis that the recognition of a particular class of visual stimuli (such as your mother's face) is first set up by an assembly or network of cells in the inferotemporal cortex. For example, Gross (1973) found inferotemporal cells in a monkey's brain that responded maximally to rather complex patterns such as a monkey's hand or a brush or a pair of scissors. This makes plausible the idea that visual patterns have discrete, local representations in clumps of cortical cells.

Many theorists have proposed that the visual system is hierarchically organized, with large numbers of low-level feature-detecting neuronal systems being grouped together into significant features (such as lines, edges, angles), which are then configured into still higher-level patterns as the stimulus courses inward and is analyzed further (see Hubel & Wiesel, 1962). Wickelgren's theory of cortical association was of this variety, and the schematic diagram shown in Figure 14.11 will remind you of the basic ideas. Visual stimulation is coded at the retina and lateral geniculate and then excites a number of "feature" cells in the striate cortex (labeled *a, b, c* here) which then converge or intersect at a pattern-synthesizing cell (or clump of cells) in the inferotemporal cortex. Suppose that a concurrent reinforcement in the hippo-

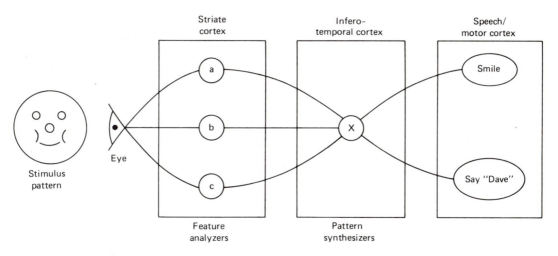

Figure 14.11. Schematic of the synthesis of a visual pattern (*X*) in inferotemporal cortex from features (*a, b, c*) extracted at or before the striate cortex. The diagram is of hypothetical but plausible processes.

campus (limbic system) causes the cells actively grouped at the time to become chunked into the configuration shown. This chunking is basically effected by associating the lower-level features with the chunk node, perhaps by lowering conduction thresholds for these pathways. The *X* cell (or cell cluster) in the inferotemporal cortex would then represent the stimulus pattern (*a, b, c*). We may suppose that the *X* cell acts just like a chunk or associative node in a memory network (see Anderson & Bower, 1973; Wickelgren, 1979a). In particular, later activation of a fragment of the pattern (say, segments *a* and *b*) may activate the *X*-pattern cell, which then via associations will cause downward activation of the absent portion (*c*) of the pattern. For instance, seeing half of a friend's covered face could lead to arousal of his face's pattern cell, which activates lower cells coding the unseen features, thus stimulating visual imagery and expectancies. In fact, the pattern-chunking cell here has been assigned all the properties of the associative bond—namely, as a switching center that groups inputs (like CSs) to-

gether and connects them to outputs (CRs). Thus, the node for the friend's face would be connected to the speech-motor cortex so that the friend could be named. In many learning experiments, the learning of the stimulus-response-reward pattern is indexed mainly by performance of the motor response.

Although the hypothetical chunking idea has been illustrated for visual patterns, it would apply as well to auditory patterns, somesthetic patterns, and so forth. Moreover, the associating mechanism allows cross-modal associations, so that a visual concept node could be connected to a touch or auditory concept node. Humans are adept at such cross-modal associations, especially those that support language, which correlates sights of words and objects, sounds, and speech production.

This general sketch of a chunking model of pattern-learning is similar to D. O. Hebb's (1949) theory of the formation of cell assemblies, and the building up of cell assemblies into regular phase sequences (learned series of patterns or movements). While somewhat plausible, the mechanisms are largely conceptual and conjectural and have not been actually identified. But even an incomplete theory like this can guide the brain researcher and help students organize the material. The actual physiological substrate of a learned circuit will doubtless be much more complex.

The research on the localization of memory traces was boosted by the research of Roger Sperry and his colleagues on the transfer of learning between the two hemispheres of the brain. We turn next to a review of this important work.

TWO HEADS IN ONE SKULL: INTERHEMISPHERIC TRANSFER

One of the more striking features of the vertebrate brain is its bilateral symmetry. Brain structures appear to be duplicated nearly perfectly in homologous positions around the midline of the sagittal plane (i.e., the plane cutting fore and aft from the top of the head to the chin). This bilateral representation of function raises interesting possibilities for research on the localization of the memory trace.

To see some of these possibilities, consider the bilaterality of the visual system in mammals (see Figure 14.12). Visual information is picked up by the retina of each eye and transmitted along separate optic tracts. These tracts meet at a juncture called the optic chiasm. After the juncture, the tracts separate again, the left one coursing through various relay stations to project eventually onto the left cerebral hemisphere, the right one coursing similarly to project onto the right cerebral hemisphere. At the chiasm there is appreciable crossing-over of fibers from the two entering tracts, approximately half the fibers of each tract crossing over to the opposite tract as they emerge from the chiasm juncture. The fibers that cross are those that arise mainly from the half of the retina nearest the nose. Because of this

cross-over of fibers at the chiasm, information from the nose side of the left retina is projected mainly to the right cortex, whereas information from the lateral left retina is projected to the left cortex. Moving on to the cerebral cortex, the two hemispheres are in direct communication with one another through a series of commissures, the fiber bundles that connect homologous structures on the two sides. The largest of these connecting commissures is the *corpus callosum,* a massive bundle of fibers interconnecting many parts of the two hemispheres.

Interocular Transfer and Its Surgical Abolition

Given this anatomical knowledge, let us now consider the phenomenon of interocular transfer of a visual discrimination that an animal (say, cat or monkey) has learned while using one eye. The animal is forced by some means, such as the use of an occluding contact lens, to learn a visual discrimination using only one eye, with the other eye never seeing the discriminative stimuli. Following learning with the use of but one eye, the animal is tested with the opposite eye open and the trained eye occluded. Under normal circumstances, the animal will show practically perfect transfer of the habit from the trained to the untrained eye. A series of experiments by Sperry (1961) and his colleagues makes plausible the assumption that in this case the visual knowledge (or engram) mediating the discriminative performance has been laid down in both visual hemispheres during training, and that during testing with the untrained eye its afferent connections with the brain make contact with either one or both of the trained hemispheres, thus retrieving and using the engram to guide correct responses. Let us begin tracking down the systematic evidence for this interpretation.

Consider first the effect of cutting the

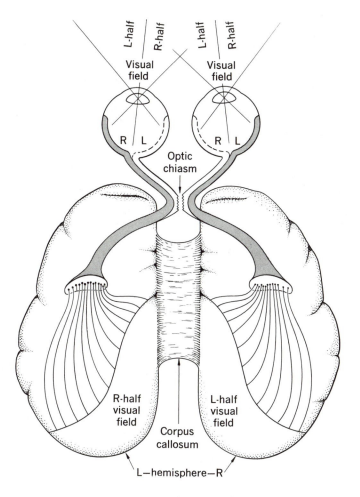

Figure 14.12. Schematic drawing of visual system showing retina, optic chiasm, and projections to visual receiving areas in cerebral cortex. In the figure, the optic chiasm has been sectioned, thus eliminating that half of the visual field normally transmitted by the cross-over fibers from the eye opposite to a cerebral hemisphere. Visual inflow from each eye is restricted to the hemisphere on the same side as the eye. The corpus callosum is shown intact. (From Sperry, 1961.)

optic chiasm in the sagittal plane (as shown in Figure 14.12), in such a manner that each eye projects only to its corresponding visual cortex on the same side. This sectioning of the chiasm produces a hemianopia, which means that when only one eye is used, about half of the visual field (the peripheral edge that projects to the nose side of the retina) is blurred, though all aspects can be seen clearly by moving the eye. Surprisingly, cutting the chiasm in this manner does not affect interocular transfer, regardless of whether the cut is made before or after one-eyed training. Although training has restricted

visual input to, say, the left hemisphere, later tests with the right eye (projecting to the right hemisphere) show that information along that channel in some way makes contact with the engram.

This contact of right eye with engram is made possible in either of two ways. One possibility is that the engram is laid down only in the left hemisphere that gets direct sensory input during training. The right eye and right hemisphere, however, can make use of this engram during testing by virtue of the callosal communication networks connecting the two hemispheres. The other possibility is that while the primary engram is being established in the left hemisphere during training, the connections through the callosum at the same time permit a duplicate or carbon copy of the engram to be laid down in the right hemisphere. The later test with the right eye would then use this carbon-copy engram established in the right hemisphere.

Two experiments indicate that the carbon-copy supposition is more likely the correct one. Suppose that following left-eye training of a chiasm-sectioned cat, we then ablate the visual cortex on the left side. According to the former view, this should disable performance with the right eye because the "informed source" is no longer available to feed information to the naive right hemisphere. But in fact, it is found that animals so treated still show substantial transfer when tested with the right eye. In a second experiment, the callosum is cut following left-eye training of a chiasm-sectioned animal. This should cut the communication lines, so on the basis of the first view we would expect no transfer on tests with the right eye. But such transfer is found. From these experiments, we infer that a duplicate copy of the engram is normally set up via the callosum during one-eyed training of a chiasm-sectioned animal.

With these facts in hand, the reader can readily guess what has to be done to abolish interocular transfer. The effective operation, of course, would be to cut both the chiasm *and* the callosum before the one-eyed visual training begins. And in fact, performing this dual operation before training virtually abolishes interocular transfer; the unseeing eye and hemisphere remain naive about the visual problem learned by the trained eye. This surgical preparation, called the *split brain,* apparently establishes two independent visual systems, one on either side of the brain, and the two sides no longer communicate with one another. For example, by successively occluding one and then the other eye, the animal may easily be trained to conflicting habits to the two eyes—in one case to choose vertical and avoid horizontal stripes when seen by the left eye, and in the other to do the opposite when seen by the right eye. Such conflicting training is extremely difficult for the normal intact animal but is learned with ease by the split-brain cat or monkey. It appears that all of the callosal fibers must be cut to obtain this remarkable independence of visual systems. If even a small portion of callosal fibers are spared, then transfer will still result.

Somewhat similar results have been discovered for transfer of a touch discrimination from one hand to the other, although there are several important differences from the visual system. A touch discrimination (e.g., rough versus smooth surface of objects) learned with the right hand will normally transfer to the left hand. However, if the corpus callosum is cut before the one-hand training, then intermanual transfer is abolished. This is consistent with the anatomical evidence that most somesthetic input lines cross over the midline and are projected to the contralateral hemisphere (i.e., touch on left hand projects to right cortex).

The interhemispheric transfer discussed above has involved, in each case, an active instrumental response, often one controlled by a relatively complicated discriminative stimulus. There is some evidence that conditioned emotional reactions (fear), especially those cued by a simple stimulus (e.g., a change in brightness), can be learned subcortically. Animals learn such CRs despite removal of both cerebral hemispheres. As this suggests, callosal section does not prevent the transfer of such classically conditioned "emotions" (see McCleary, 1960). It is known, too, that simple instrumental brightness discriminations can be learned subcortically—that is, without benefit of cortex. Consequently, it is not too surprising to find that such habits transfer between the eyes despite chiasm and callosal section before one-eyed training (Meikle, 1960; Meikle & Sechzer, 1960). Thus the dramatic absence of transfer from callosal section is seen only for those relatively more complex habits that depend upon a functioning cerebral cortex. This is a small restriction on the generality of the results, but nonetheless a significant one. It tells us that the emotional concomitants of learned instrumental responses are represented subcortically, whereas the refined "knowledge" guiding the selective response is likely to be stored cortically.

The split-brain preparation has illuminated many facts about bilaterality of storage in the visual and somesthetic systems, and the important role played by the corpus callosum in providing the connections that permit making a "carbon copy." Additionally, Sperry (1961) points out the many advantages of the split-brain preparation for the investigation of numerous questions regarding brain functions. For one thing, one brain-half can serve as an effective control when lesions and the like partially incapacitate the other brain-half. For another, radical surgical procedures can be carried out on one side only, when doing these bilaterally would seriously disable the animal as a useful experimental subject. Sperry describes a number of novel and ingenious uses that can be made of this split-brain preparation to investigate age-old problems of how the brain functions.

Split-Brain Humans

Gazzaniga (1967, 1970, 1972) and Gazzaniga and Sperry (1967) have investigated behavioral deficits of several human patients who have had practically all their corpus callosum removed surgically in order to alleviate severe epilepsy. A summary of this research line is in a volume by Gazzaniga and LeDoux (1977). In the visual problems encountered in normal day-

to-day living, these patients appear to perform adequately—but this is because they are able to move both eyes repeatedly over any given visual stimulus. To detect their special deficit, Gazzaniga and Sperry would flash visual stimuli for a fraction of a second, projected to the left (or right) of the visual field. It should be noted that, for split-brain subjects, a stimulus flashed to the left visual field will be relayed primarily to the right cortex (hemisphere), whereas right-field visual stimuli go to the left cortex (see Figure 14.12); this flash procedure is used to "confine" the entry of a visual stimulus to the left or the right cerebral hemisphere. A series of tests carried out by Gazzaniga and Sperry show that the left cerebral hemisphere in split-brain patients is relatively specialized for active speech (e.g., reading, talking, writing), whereas the right hemisphere is more specialized for nonverbal perception and spatial reasoning. The left hemisphere can read words and act upon printed commands, either by speaking or by using the right hand to select named objects by touch. (Recall that the hand is controlled by its opposite cortical hemisphere.) However, the right hemisphere in these split-brain patients appears unable to *say* what word or what picture has been flashed to it; usually the patient says that he saw nothing or maybe "a flash." However, if he is forced to select a word from a small test array, he will unerringly pick the correct item despite his earlier inability to say its name (Gazzaniga, 1970, 1972). Further, the word projected to the right hemisphere may even guide a tactile search (with the left hand) for the correct object (e.g., a spoon) among a collection of objects hidden from the subject's view. Even after picking up in the left hand the object corresponding to the flashed word, the right hemisphere is unable to verbalize the object's name.

Such observations suggest that the right hemisphere has a crude capability for passive visual (verbal) recognition and comprehension; its comprehension, in fact, appears best with pictures, next best with concrete nouns, poorer with verbs, and poorest with abstract nouns derived from verbs (e.g., *painter, trooper*). The observations also suggest a curious form of split consciousness, or dissociation. At one level of awareness, the person is unable to say which test object he is to pick up; however, at another level, he unerringly selects the correct object with his left hand by touch alone. Thus, two behavioral indices of "awareness," or stimulus control, have been effectively dissociated by the split-brain procedure. The paradoxical nature of the dissociated performance rests on the ambiguity of the term "awareness"; we say someone is "aware of" a stimulus (event or state of affairs) either if he can verbally label it or if he behaves in a way which shows that he "takes account of" that event. For example, a person absorbed in a conversation or a radio program while driving a car is aware of the curves and stop signs along the road in the second sense but not in the first. The difference between this common case and that of the split-brain patient is that the patient seems almost incapable of "being aware" in the speech sense of a stimulus pattern projected only to his right cerebral hemisphere.

While somewhat deficient in active speech, the right cerebral hemisphere seems more specialized for handling nonverbal information, such as spatial or geometric figures or musical melodies. For instance, the left hand (controlled by the right hemisphere) is better than the opposite hand in carrying out solutions to puzzles requiring spatial reasoning, or in reconstructing the parts of a block scene or jigsaw puzzle, and so on. A variety of evidence suggests that the left and right hemispheres in man become relatively specialized for perceiving, utilizing, and storing verbal and nonverbal (analogical,

imaginal) information, respectively. A study by Galin and Ornstein (1972) showed that there was relatively greater EEG activity from the left than from the right hemisphere when a person was working on a verbal task (like composing a letter), but the relative EEG activity in the two hemispheres was reversed when the subject was doing a task involving mental imagery. Similar differences in hemisphere-specific EEGs are observed for mental arithmetic (left hemisphere) versus fantasizing (right), and for reading abstract scientific prose versus concrete narrative tales.

Along other lines, papers by Kimura (1963) and Milner (1968) report that patients with brain injury to the left temporal cortex show selective deficits in verbal but not nonverbal memory tasks, whereas patients with injury to the right temporal lobes have nonverbal but not verbal memory deficits. Nonverbal memory was tested by recognition or recall of pictures or melodies presented earlier; verbal memory was tested by recognition or recall of numbers, words, and word pairs. A further note on lateral specialization is that in right-handed children active speech develops primarily in the left hemisphere (the pattern is less clear for left-handed children). If the left hemisphere suffers severe injury or damage before the age of 8 to 14 (the exact critical age is in dispute), the child nonetheless regains adequate speech, but it is represented now in the right hemisphere. However, if the left hemisphere damage occurs *after* the critical age, then speech is grossly impaired and, depending on the extent of damage, only insignificant recovery of speech functions may ever occur (see Lenneberg, 1967). These brain injuries in their differing extents are responsible for the various speech aphasias. A common cause of small, localized aphasias is cerebral strokes, though the damage done in these cases is usually not so extensive as to prevent recovery of normal speech by other parts of the brain.

This whole line of evidence seems to tie up in a reasonably tidy package. We now know a lot about the two cerebral hemispheres, what specialized functions they perform, and how they tend to communicate with one another. This has been an area where much progress has been made, starting with the elementary split-brain preparation devised by Sperry. It illustrates how a physiological finding can ramify into a host of psychological studies (regarding lateralization of function), and can turn up results which clarify fundamental issues regarding perceptual experience and consciousness.

Chemical Dissociation of Cerebral Hemispheres

Bureš and Burešová (1960) and Bureš and associates (1964) have utilized a technique called *spreading depression* through which we may *temporarily* alter the normal functioning of one cerebral hemisphere. This procedure produces an altered animal for a few hours before recovery from the spreading depression occurs. To induce this effect, a small amount of a potassium chloride solution is applied locally through a small hole in the skull to the surface of the dura membrane surrounding the cortex. Within a short time, the normal electrical activity of the treated hemisphere of the cortex becomes depressed. The depression will persist for roughly as long as the chemical solution is applied. When it is removed, normal electrical activity in the depressed hemisphere is soon restored. In the rat, the depression spreads only over that cortical hemisphere to which the chemical has been applied. The effect is not that of a complete anesthetic since even with both hemispheres depressed the animal can still move about; however, it is likely that the animal experiences some numbness and partial paralysis of the legs contralateral to each depressed hemisphere. Of most interest, however, is the finding of Bureš that, while

depressed, a hemisphere gives no sign of retaining habits learned when it was intact. Access to the engram has somehow been blocked by the depression. Of further interest is the fact that an animal whose cortex is functioning normally apparently does not remember events that happened when its cortex was depressed.

The simplest demonstration of this is the absence of interhemispheric transfer of a learned habit. On day 1, a rat is trained to a simple light-shock avoidance habit with, say, its right hemisphere depressed. On day 2, it is tested with either its right or left hemisphere depressed. If the same hemisphere is functioning both days, then the animal shows retention of the habit; if a different hemisphere is functioning on the two days, then it shows little or no retention. I. S. Russell and Ochs (1961) have reported similar results for a bar-pressing habit taught to rats for food reward. The theoretical interpretation is that the hemisphere functioning during the training session stores the engram, while the depressed hemisphere remains naive. On the following test day when the trained hemisphere is depressed, the functioning (but naive) cortex has no access to the engram stored on the depressed side. As with the split-brain monkey, it is also possible, by alternately depressing first one and then the other hemisphere, to train the two hemispheres to conflicting stimulus-response habits, and there is relatively little interference between the two sides and their conflicting habits.

An intriguing question is why the educated hemisphere does not transmit its engram (via callosal connections) to the uneducated hemisphere after its depression has worn off and while the rat is just sitting around in its home cage. The lack of interhemispheric transfer shows that this does not happen. However, it turns out that something like this "cross-callosal tutoring" goes on if the rat is replaced in the learning situation and experiences a few rewarded trials while both hemispheres are functioning. I. S. Russell and Ochs (1961) reported that one trial was sufficient to effect substantial cross-callosal tutoring of the uneducated side; Travis (1964) found less dramatically that four or five trials were needed to get good transfer of an active avoidance habit. These results suggest that stimulation in the learning situation reactivated the engram in the educated cortex, setting up a persisting activity trace, and by way of the callosal links the engram was communicated to and consolidated in the alternate hemisphere.

However, Schneider (1967, 1968) has offered a more parsimonious explanation of these various results with spreading depression—namely, conditioned stimulus generalization. It is assumed that the "state" of spreading depression prevailing during original training—that is, left, right, neither, or both hemispheres depressed (L, R, N, or B)—constitutes part of the total stimulus complex to which the response becomes associated. The most obvious peripheral components of the depressed cortical states are slight numbness and limb paralysis on the side opposite the depressed hemisphere. We may think of the similarity of any two brain states as determined by the overlap in zero, one, or two hemispheres being in the same normal or depressed condition; thus the normal state is equidistant from the state where either the left or the right hemisphere is depressed, but farthest from the state where both are depressed. Similarly, left-depressed is farthest from right-depressed but closer to both-depressed than to neither-depressed conditions. In this perspective, when the animal is tested under a different brain state the habit suffers "stimulus-generalization decrement" due to the changed internal, contextual stimuli. The greater the change in the amount of depression from acquisition to retention, the greater the impairment in test performance—a well-documented fact. Schneider found, for instance, that animals trained when their left hemisphere (L) was depressed retained the most when tested in state L, next most in state B, next in state N, and least in state R. This ordering differs from that expected from the alternate hypothesis that the original habit was confined to the right hemisphere and is available for retrieval whenever that hemisphere is normal. A second fact related to the stimulus-control hypothesis is that animals can be successfully trained to an operant discrimination for which the discriminative stimulus is the presence (versus absence) of unilateral spreading depression.

Schneider explains the "habit-transfer" results of I. S. Russell and Ochs (1961) and Travis (1964) in terms of new acquisition during the so-called transfer trial. In this view, the important relation is between the brain states on the transfer and retention-test trials; the more similar they are, the more stimulus generalization between the two hemispheres will be enhanced by the single transfer trial. To test this prediction, Schneider and Ebbeson (1967) repeated the Russell and Ochs study with an added condition for the transfer trial. Following bar-press training with the left hemisphere L depressed, the transfer trial occurred either with neither hemisphere depressed (N) or with the right hemisphere depressed (R), and later retention for both groups was tested with the right hemisphere depressed (R). The results showed that the single transfer trial produced significant later interhemispheric transfer of bar-pressing for both groups; as expected by the stimulus-control argument, the group receiving the transfer trial in state R showed greater transfer to the later R testing situation than did the group receiving the transfer trial in state N. The alternative hypothesis that the original habit was confined to the right, nondepressed hemisphere has no resources to explain why transfer of the habit to the untrained hemisphere is best when the *trained* hemisphere is depressed, which event should inhibit the habit's retrieval and block its interhemispheric transmission.

These and other results provide rather convincing support for Schneider's stimulus-control theory of effects due to cortical spreading depression. The theory is parsimonious in using familiar concepts; it is also intuitively satisfying since it removes some of the mystical awe surrounding initial reports of dissociated states of consciousness provided by spreading depression. Although Schneider supposes that spreading depression alters the physiological locus of engram storage (from cortical to subcortical mechanisms on the depressed side), his hypothesis is readily understandable in purely psychological terms. A second effect of spreading depression, not reviewed here, is that it can be used, like electroconvulsive shock, as a means of interrupting consolidation of earlier learning experiences (see Albert, 1966). However, there is no need to follow out that line of research here.

Drug-Induced Dissociation

In the split-brain preparation, we have managed to dissociate various parts of the brain from one another. Metaphorically speaking, through the dissociation they are forced to lead separate lives, get educated in different schools, and have separate personalities. A related dissociation or split-personality effect has been reported in a fascinating series of drug studies, starting with observations on curare by Girden and Culler (1937). Later experiments by Overton (1964) showed the effect dramatically, using a different drug and testing somewhat more interesting behavior. His work will be reviewed briefly.

Overton found that the drug sodium pentobarbital produces dissociation in rats. This drug, similar to the popularly known "truth serum," is an anesthetic and, in sufficient dosage, puts the rat to sleep. Depending on the strength of the dose, the animal will begin to awake and become mobile within 15 to 45 minutes following the injection. At this time the animal can be run through various learning tasks; although somewhat lethargic, it will nevertheless learn such simple tasks as to turn left in a T-maze to escape shock delivered to its feet from a grid floor.

Overton reported that habits learned during this drugged state do not transfer to the nondrugged state, although the habit can be reactivated after putting the animal back into the drugged state. The dissociation works as well in the other direction: a habit learned in the nondrugged state is not available to the subject while it is in the drugged state. The habits are drug-state specific. By giving and withholding the drug on alternate days, Overton trained his rats to turn left to escape shock when drugged and to turn right when not drugged. This technique, called *drug-discrimination training*, is one of the most reliable ways to study dissociation between habits learned in the drugged vs. nondrugged states. In Overton's study, the two habits were learned rapidly and independently, with little or no interfering cross-talk between the two states. Overton showed that complete dissociation is only the extreme pole of a graded continuum. He could obtain more or less dissociation depending on the amount of drug given, with larger dosages yielding a greater degree of dissociation. Since Overton's initial experiments, drug discrimination has been investigated with a variety of drugs and species. A book by Ho, Richards, and Chute (1978) reviews much of this work.

With regard to Overton's evidence, the explanation that immediately comes to mind is something like Schneider's stimulus-control hypothesis. In this perspective, the drugged and nondrugged states are differentiated in terms of differences in (a) how external stimuli are perceived, e.g., vision might be blurred in the drugged state, and (b) the presence or absence of distinctive interoceptive stimuli, as in the different "feelings" we have when we feel drowsy or alert or thirsty or whatever. If these kinds of stimuli were radically different in the drug and nondrug states, then the lack of transfer might be explained. The presence and absence of pentobarbital (and its internal effects) come to be discriminative stimuli to which different responses are attached.

Overton anticipated this "state-as-stimulus" interpretation and ran several control conditions to assess its plausibility. Discrimination learning of conflicting habits to presence versus absence of pentobarbital was compared to that obtained with presence versus absence of the following stimuli: the drug Flaxedil (a peripheral muscle relaxant), thirst and hunger, an ambient light over the maze, a light and a tone, and a stronger shock. Only in the last condition did any significant discrimination learning ("dissociation") occur, and then at a markedly slower rate than under pentobarbital.

To this evidence we can react in either of two ways. The first is to stick to the stimulus interpretation and exclaim with wonder at what a strong, effective stimulus a pentobarbital injection is. The other is to reject the stimulus interpretation as ad hoc and barren and to seek alternative explanations. One alternative sketchily advanced by Overton is that by modifying the thresholds and firing patterns of neurons, the drug may cause different neural circuits to become active from those that are active in the nondrug state. In this case the differences might consist in different patterns or timings of neural firing so that different circuits or routes of a complex neural network are used. This hypothesis is speculative and has only the original results to recommend it.

One interesting refinement suggested by Chute and Wright (1973; also Wright & Chute, 1973) is that the important internal state (drugged vs. nondrugged) is the one available during *consolidation* of the memory rather than preceding and during the learning experience per se. These investigators drugged half their experimental rats with sodium pentobarbital immediately *after* their experience in a one-trial passive avoidance task. Later, half these rats were tested in the drugged state, and half in the nondrugged state. Surprisingly, animals showed most memory (i.e., they consistently avoided) when their testing state agreed with their state just after the learning trial. Such results support the state-dependency hypothesis, that retrieval of a memory occurs most reliably when the retrieval state matches that prevailing at the time the learning experience is being consolidated. Unfortunately, this specific result has not been replicated reliably.

There have been several attempts to produce state-dependent learning in humans with different drugs (Swanson & Kinsbourne, 1979). The results have not been completely consistent, perhaps because of variations in the measures of memory used. An important insight came from Eich and associates (1975), who concluded that state-dependent retrieval effects are most likely to be found when there are high demands on the subject to generate her own retrieval cues. Thus, if subjects are required to free-recall a list of words learned several days before, the instruction to "recall that word list," is relatively nonspecific, and demands that the subject generate her own cues (e.g., "What types of words were they?"). This kind of memory performance appears most likely to suffer when the person's drug state is changed between learning and retention testing. On the other hand, if memory is tested by the recognition method (e.g., "Which of these words was on the list—

spoon or *sky?*"), or by providing strong associative or semantic cues to the subject (e.g., "A kitchen utensil"), then the subject does not have to come up with her own retrieval cues. In this case, state-dependent effects are minimal; that is, memory performance is not much affected by the congruence of the retrieval state with the learning state.

An experiment by G. H. Bower, Monteiro, and Gilligan (1978) indicates that the learner's emotional mood may serve as a "state" or context that can produce a state-dependent effect. Using hypnosis, Bower and associates induced their subjects to feel happy while learning one word list and sad while learning another; later, subjects tried to free-recall each word list while happy or while sad. Retention scores averaged 78 percent for the list learned in the same mood as the recall mood but only 47 percent for the different-mood list. The investigators concluded that emotional mood can act as a distinctive context for storage and retrieval of memories. They suggested that mood acts as a constant cognitive element in STM that both stamps itself upon incoming experiences being learned and also biases the direction of associative searches for specific memory targets. This might explain the selective learning and selective recall of sad or negative life experiences by psychiatrically depressed patients; the biases in memory operate in a vicious circle so as to maintain the mental depression.

Overton (1978) has reviewed the major theories as well as the methodological problems in proving a strong form of the state-dependent learning-and-retrieval hypothesis. It is difficult to show consistent state-dependent effects over and above the operation of several simple "main effects." A first simple effect is that material learned while the subject is drugged may be poorly learned; it is often learned slowly, and appears easily forgotten regardless of the state at the time of testing. This is under-standable enough if the drug simply blocks storage or consolidation of material into LTM. For example, two or three stiff drinks of alcohol will significantly retard verbal and pictorial learning (Parker, Birnbaum, & Noble, 1976). Severe intoxication will prevent nearly all consolidated learning, although the drunk person may consciously attend and react (slowly) to events in her world. Second, a drug often has some direct effect on test performance. In some cases this effect is facilitory, as when alcohol reduces excessive fear and enables more efficient performance of an active avoidance response (e.g., eliminates unadaptive "freezing"); in others, the effect can be mildly debilitating, as when alcohol in humans reduces their concentration, motivation, and performance on a recall test.

Deutsch and Roll (1973) have argued that these simple main effects suffice to account for the typical results that are claimed as evidence for state-dependent learning and/or recall under drugs. In those cases where there is a residual "true interaction" between presence versus absence of the drug during training and testing, the stimulus-control hypothesis (see above and Schneider, 1967) may be brought in to interpret the results. That is, it would be supposed that recall is best when the contextual stimuli present during learning are reinstated as completely as possible during the retention test. This is a very old and revered principle in studies of human retention (see Pan, 1926; McGeoch & Irion, 1952). It is used, for example, to isolate interpolated material and prevent it from creating interference in recall of some originally learned material. In an early illustrative study, interpolated learning occurring while the subject was in a hypnotic trance caused little forgetting of an original list that was learned and later recalled in the normal waking state. The reverse sequence of states—original learning and retesting done while the subject was in a trance with interpolated learning occurring while awake—also drastically reduced retroactive interference. These and many other studies illustrate the potent influence on recall of reinstatement of the original context of learning.

In summary, then, the notions of dissociated states and state-dependent learning as unique physiological preparations have not been generally accepted or supported by later research. There are sufficient simple explanations around for the available data, so that parsimony demands that the more "exciting, dramatic" hypothesis of biochemical dissociation of brain states be held in abeyance until new evidence clearly demands something like that hypothesis.

CONCLUDING REMARKS

When we look back over our survey, it is apparent that large-scale advances in neuropsychology have been made over the last few decades. Truly, it is impossible to enter upon a thorough discussion today of such topics as consciousness, set, discrimination, pattern recognition, attention, arousal, drive, reward, and many others without giving a prominent place to the contributions of neuropsychological experimentation to what we know about these subjects. This has indeed been a grand accomplishment, for which praise should be bestowed on hundreds of research workers. However, from the point of view of this book, the most refractory problem of them all for neuropsychology has been our prime topic—learning, or information storage by the nervous system. With a few exceptions, the main lines of neuropsychological research on learning have been touched on here.

When things are viewed in neuronal terms, as we do in this chapter, the central question remains that of identifying the physiological basis for association. Assuming multiple connections between diverse populations of neurons (structures), we know that temporally proximate activity in two of them causes them to become associated in some primitive or basic manner, so that one is now able to excite the other, whereas formerly it did not do so. Several suggestions as to how this might occur have been mentioned. The most likely explanation still is some form of the hypothesis that the "efficiency" of particular neuronal circuits is somehow increased; Deutsch's pharmacological studies suggest further details of this increased efficiency.

A conceptual problem with most neuronal models of conditioning is that they adopt the *substitution* view of the process, whereby the CS comes simply to substitute for the US in eliciting the UR. But that view has been demolished as a *general* account since the mid-1930s. Even lower mammals learn goal-directed actions, not specific responses. For instance, a sheep may be trained to lift his left front foot off a grid floor when a tone sounds that signals an impending electrical shock on the grid. If the sheep is now forced to lie down on its back with its head on the grid floor, and the tone is sounded, the animal will lift its head and shoulders up off the grid floor. The animal does whatever circumstances require to get away from the shock source; he has not learned a stereotyped response elicited by shock to his left-front foot. There are many such demonstrations in the conditioning literature. Tolman summarized these in his hypothesis that organisms learn goal-directed actions, not muscle movements. Clearly, what is needed in these cases is a theory of how an organism's motor-skills apparatus is transferred into any novel situation so that an action to achieve a goal (such as getting off the shock grid) can be executed in a manner sensitive to the constraints of the situation. Hull tried to deal with this issue of response equivalence using his theory of a habit-family hierarchy bound together by an anticipated goal. However, few neurological theories of learning have tried to deal with such complexities. Instead, they have focused on models in which learning consists in alteration of the firing efficiency of specific neuron circuits.

Lest the reader think that our discussion of the role of neurons is too far removed from the behavior in which he or she may be primarily interested, it is apposite to note that appropriate networks of "model neurons" can be easily designed that display rather amazing discrimination and performance capabilities. This general line of theorizing, modeling performance capabilities by designing nerve networks, began with an early paper by Pitts and McCulloch (1947) and has been carried further since then. A book by Culbertson (1962) includes a review of some of the results. Roughly speaking, given any transfer function taking various input information (stimulation) into output information (response), a static nerve network can be designed to yield that transfer function. The hypothetical neurons in such nets all function by the same simple principles, which are derived more or less from neuro-physiological research. Moreover, if certain premises are granted relating to how the efficiency of neural pathways is changed by feedback from the environment (through reward and punishment), then the nerve-net models will show adaptive learning in various situations. Rosenblatt (1958, 1962) shows how orderly discriminative performance can be produced (through reinforcement) by a large neuron network that begins with completely random interconnections. He also gives us the rationale for this general approach to the construction of models of behavior.

By and large, the people who construct nerve-net automata do not claim that their design represents exactly the way that the nervous system achieves what it does in a characteristic performance. They remain content rather with showing that starting with simple neuron elements, networks not obviously contradicted by neurophysiological evidence can be designed to show some of the capabilities of organisms. As such, the automata are "sufficiency proofs," meaning that they prove that interesting behavior *can* be produced out of constellations of simple on-off neural elements. Though the products of such labors are appreciated in some scientific quarters, the fact is that they are not esteemed in others. From the viewpoint of many neurophysiologists, the nerve-net theories ignore too much of what is known about the neuron and the structure of the nervous system. Be that as it may, if neurophysiology is to have an explicit theory capable of making contact with behavioral data, the form of it will be little different from the kinds of schemes presently being designed by those working on nerve-net automata.

The most extensive and interesting theoretical work on neural-net models of learning is being done by Stephen Grossberg (1974, 1975, 1978). Grossberg begins by formulating elementary properties of networks of neurons, assumes that specific stimuli and responses have corresponding neuron pools in the brain, and that learning of stimulus patterns, sequences, or sensory-motor patterns is effected by neuronal equivalents of association formation (e.g., an enhanced synaptic condition along the "correct" circuit). Grossberg formulates the interactions and learning processes with mathematical equations, and derives learning equations and basic mechanisms. (The theory is similar to that of Wickelgren discussed earlier.) Grossberg proceeds to derive a vast number of interesting theorems about classical and instrumental conditioning, motivation and performance, serial learning, the memory span, configural learning, skilled motor performance, attention, feature-detectors, STM, plans, and other phenomena intriguing to learning theories. In each case, the derivations hinge upon representational assumptions about the neural network that will carry out the task, and about how learning and excitation/inhibition processes tune and play upon those network structures. Although the conjectures are made as reasonable and consistent with neurophysiology as possible (though a mathematician, Grossberg has sophisticated knowledge of neurophysiology), the theory basically uses a "conceptual nervous system," with the neural units of the theory being treated much the same way that, say, Estes would treat hypothetical stimulus elements or that semantic-memory theorists treat concept nodes in an associative memory network (see Anderson & Bower, 1973, and Chapter 13). This coalescence of theoretical vocabulary from several diverse approaches is a most welcome event.

Research on the neurophysiology of learning continues at an accelerating pace. Judging from the recent past, its future is likely to be filled with exciting discoveries, the devising of novel techniques, and profound alterations in our conceptions of the nervous system and its relation to behavior. In fact, in few other areas of psychology has there recently been such a high production rate of significant empirical discoveries as in physiological psychology. The pearls are easier to find in a new field than in the older fields that have been intensively cultivated for so many years.

SUPPLEMENTARY READINGS

There are a number of excellent textbooks in physiological psychology, each of which contains a quite detailed review of results on learning. Some of these are:

CARLSON, N. R. (1977). *Physiology of behavior.*

DEUTSCH, J. A., & DEUTSCH, E. (1973). *Physiological psychology.* 2nd ed.

THOMPSON, R. F. (1967). *Foundations of physiological psychology.*

THOMPSON, R. F. (1975). *Introduction to physiological psychology.*

Theoretically oriented treatises on the brain and behavior are:

HEBB, D. O. (1949). *The organization of behavior.*

JOHN, E. R. (1967). *Mechanisms of memory.*

McGAUGH, J. L., & HERZ, M. J., eds. (1972). *Memory consolidation.*

O'KEEFE, J. O., & NADEL, L. (1978). *The hippocampus as a cognitive map.*

PRIBRAM, K. (1971). *Languages of the brain.*

ROSENZWEIG, M. R., & BENNETT, E. L., eds. (1976). *Neural mechanisms of learning and motivation.*

15

APPLICATIONS TO EDUCATION

Any isolation of basic science from applied science, when it persists, is unfortunate. Over the years the advances in science have occurred in intimate relation with advances in technology. The instrument-makers (producing microscopes, telescopes, transistors, computers) have opened new fields of basic research; invention has all along gone hand in hand with scientific discovery. If we were to apply the historical lessons from astronomy, physics, biology (and their related technologies) to the psychology of learning, we would expect an equal intimacy between theory and research in the basic processes of learning and the applied aspects of instruction in the schools. While many students of learning are indeed interested in instruction, this is not universally true. The uneven interest in applications comes about in part through division of labor and specialization of knowledge: there are "pure" science aspects to the study of learning, just as in other fields of inquiry, and the scientist delving into basic problems may not be concerned with applying what he or she knows. Thus one does not expect every geneticist to be interested in the breeding of farm animals, even though what he learns may ultimately be useful to the ani-

mal breeder. While many investigators of learning are interested in pure science, apart from applications, some investigators are very much concerned with the technology of instruction. The range of such interest is reflected in review chapters devoted specifically to the psychology of instruction (Gagne & Rohwer, 1969; Glaser & Resnick, 1972; Wittrock & Lumsdaine, 1977). In this chapter we wish to examine some of the issues that are involved in bridging the gap from the laboratory to the classroom, in the conviction that a sound theory of learning may be validated by its influence upon the arts of practice.

To move from theory to practice is not all that easy. The naive view is that the basic researcher stocks a kind of medicine cabinet with aids to solve the problems of the teacher. When a problem arises, the teacher can take a psychological principle from the cabinet and apply it like a bandage or an ointment to solve the educational problem. It is increasingly recognized that in order to move soundly from basic research to practice we need a detailed analysis of the educational task, the component skills to be taught, and the learning resources of the child and the school system. We must take into account the actual curriculum of the school and the social contexts in which learning occurs.

IDEAS FROM LEARNING THEORY USEFUL IN EDUCATION

While we do not support the medicine-cabinet view of application, the direct application of knowledge from the laboratory to the classroom is not to be entirely rejected. Very often the laboratory knowledge helps us to understand what some of the important variables and influences are, even before these have been formulated in a more prescriptive form. Such principles permit a better analysis by pointing out where to look and what to expect. Students of learning who have not devoted themselves primarily to problems of instruction can still give some very useful advice. Some of this advice comes from those oriented toward S-R theories, some from those who tend more toward cognitive theories, some from those whose concern is with motivation and personality.

1. *Behavioral objectives.* For the behaviorist, the goals of any educational program must be stipulated in concrete behavioral terms—preferably in behaviors that can be measured. Only then can the teacher begin to know how to design a program that will shape the student's behavior towards those goals, and to evaluate the extent to which they have been met. Specifying educational goals in terms of behavioral objectives goes against tradition, which usually states goals in loftier terms of attitudes, analytical skills, understanding, and appreciation of the subject matter. Mager (1961) was an early proponent of writing behavioral objectives for education and wrote an early guidebook on how to translate vague goals into measurable behaviors (see also, Mager, 1972). The translation process itself has a beneficial effect on the teacher and student alike, in forcing the teacher to reflect upon precisely what he or she believes is most important for the student to know, and what student behaviors will comprise evidence for his or her knowing those things. Writing behavioral objectives has become a popular and widespread practice in many school systems as part of the public's concern for accountability of the teaching system. For instance, the parents whose child is taking fifth-grade reading can be told in detail what specific reading competencies the child can be expected to demonstrate by the end of the course. Often, commercial tutoring agencies for reading or math will advertise their programs in specific terms of advancing behavioral objectives of the learner. These changes in stipulating educational goals have largely been brought about by the behaviorists' influence on teaching.

2. *Task or skill analysis.* Implicit in the push for stating educational goals in behavioral terms is the requirement that the educator analyze the criterion task (for example, multiplying two three-digit numbers) into the elementary behavioral components and note how they are organized. This leads, in turn, to assessing the child's initial repertoire and designing an educational program to teach the several components of the criterion skill. For multiplying two 3-digit numbers, the child must be taught, among other things, to write the numbers in column form, to proceed multiplying bottom right to left, to carry the tens digit of one multiplication and add it to the next column, to shift the starting point of the second and third lines of the multiplication over one place, and so on. Such microanalyses reveal just how complex are the skills commonly taught in school. Work by a psychologist, Gagné (1970; Gagné & Briggs, 1974), has been especially helpful in decomposing various educational competencies into a *hierarchy* of subskills, noting how one depends on another. We shall discuss Gagné's work

later in this chapter. The idea of skill analysis has been widely applied in educational research (see Calfee & Drum, 1978, for a task analysis of elementary reading skills).

3. *Shaping.* The analysis of an educational goal into a hierarchy or series of behavioral components implies an educational program. In particular, the fundamental skills are taught first because, according to task analysis, other parts of the criterion competency depend on these. Thus, two-digit multiplication is not taught until the child already can do one-digit multiplication and can add; addition is not taught until the child can identify and use the numbers themselves discriminatively. Thus, a criterion task analysis sets out the *order* in which the component skills should be taught and mastered. This training progression from simple to complex, from a single behavioral unit to a sequence of units, is most like Skinner's *shaping* procedure in which complex skills are taught to animals. One difference is that in shaping animals the trainer must wait for an approximation of the desired response to occur before she can reinforce it, whereas for children the teacher (or text) typically instructs by describing the correct response or by demonstrating it with some examples. Of course, if the children have severe language deficits or consistently fail to attend to the teacher, the teacher must use operant conditioning methods (see, e.g., Lovaas, 1976, on teaching language to nonverbal psychotic children).

4. *Active responding.* Behaviorists have a strong belief that people learn best by actively manipulating the learning material, responding to it, and relating one part to another. Guthrie, Thorndike, and Skinner have emphasized active responding. People are most likely to learn from text if they ask questions about it, then search the text for answers, then actively recite the answers to themselves. A number of verbal experiments (e.g., Bobrow & Bower, 1969; Slamecka & Graf, 1978) have shown that adults better remember information that they have had to connect actively in some prescribed way. For example, adults in experiments by Bower and Masling (1979) showed much better memory for a set of fake correlational statements or empirical laws (e.g., "the rate of schizophrenia increases with family size") if subjects were forced to invent a causal explanation of each within a few seconds. Generating one's own explanation proved much more beneficial than reading an explanation generated by someone else. Further, all reading improvement courses emphasize the importance of readers actively outlining in their minds the contents of what they are reading, then quickly jotting down that outline after first skimming the material. The outline is then to be filled out or corrected as students read over the material at a more deliberate pace.

Another example of active responding is in learning mathematics. Math seems to be taught and learned largely by working through many thousands of example problems. The problems exemplify certain mathematical concepts, operations, or rules. In learning mathematics, we practice doing so many of these examples that we achieve a level where we can perform correctly some time later without being able to state the general rules of mathematics that justify our performance (e.g., the detailed algebraic steps in solving two linear equations in two unknowns). The rules have been translated into automatic habits, or "productions," that are carried out largely without verbalization or conscious effort (see the discussion of productions in Chapter 12).

5. *Recitation and practice.* For most basic academic skills like reading, writing, and arithmetic, there simply is no substitute for repeated practice. Only with much

practice will these habits become automatic and be performed rapidly and effortlessly. Because the habits based on the rules must be general (e.g., multiply *any* three-digit number), one obviously must practice over a variety of specific examples of the rule. The practice is also most beneficial if each response is followed by feedback on whether it is right or wrong, and, if wrong, where the error lies.

Many studies in verbal learning have shown the beneficial influence on later memory of having the subject practice reciting the material to be learned. A classic experiment by Gates (1971) showed that after a necessary minimum time spent passively reading the material to be learned (biographies in one experiment, nonsense syllables in another), students learned more not by reading it over and over again but trying actively to recite the material from memory, prompting or reminding themselves with the text to fill in forgotten details. The findings have held up rather well with other materials over the ensuing years. The value of active recitation is partly motivational, since the subject sets personal recall goals and checks her progress; the value is also partly informative, since her failures in one recitation pinpoint the specific material where learning and retention efforts should be concentrated in the next cycle. Further, it seems that later recall is largely a matter of retrieving the current plan for recitation.

Active recitation is a standard prescription of all guidebooks on study skills, and it is clearly beneficial. After reading a section of her text, the student is urged to outline its main points and to recite that outline and its contents from memory, at several distributed times.

6. *Prescribed study guides.* These rehearse-and-review prescriptions are the last two Rs of the famous SQ3R program for improving study skills (see Robinson, 1961) taught in most schools. The parts of the formula refer to important aspects of reading and assimilating textual material—say, a chapter of a school textbook. The first component is to *Survey* the contents of the chapter by skimming the section headings. The second is to pose some 5 to 10 *Questions* to yourself, questions that can be based on headings in the text. The third is to *Read* the text, seeking answers to the questions posed. The fourth is to *Recite* in your own words the contents of what you have just read and perhaps write it down in outline form. The fifth is to *Review* the outline and reread the chapter to refresh its major points.

The preliminary *Survey* gives the student a framework for organizing the many points about to be read. This outline acts as an *advance organizer* (Ausubel, 1960) that helps the learner categorize, pigeonhole, and interrelate the specific topics of the chapter. The underlying rationale behind advance organizers stems from the early Gestalt psychologists' belief that an array of information is best learned by *understanding* how it fits together, what parts depend upon or support others, and how it is organized. Of course, chapter outlines and lecture outlines do just this. Later research on learning from text (e.g., Meyer, 1975; Kintsch & van Dijk, 1979) has been concerned with the organization of expository texts, how the writer communicates this organization to the reader, and how this communication can be facilitated. Some of this material was reviewed in Chapter 13.

A basic problem with such prescribed study aids is that students find them hard work (more so than passive reading), and so they tend not to take them up nor to continue with them unless some strong incentives (reinforcers) can be built in. Apparently, the student's wish for a high grade is too remote or weak a reinforcer. Most study-improvement programs, therefore, require self-reinforcement contingent on achieving daily study goals.

7. *Reinforcing task-relevant behaviors.* The issue of reinforcing study behaviors is one example of the more general issue of shaping educationally relevant behaviors. The matter comes up in training students not only in self-directed study habits but also in proper "deportment" in the classroom. In elementary grades this usually means that the pupil is to be on time, sit quietly in his or her seat, attend to the teacher, and follow the teacher's instructions on whatever learning task is to be accomplished. These elemental behaviors seem necessary to promote an environment free of continual disruption and distraction, in which tutoring and learning have a chance to occur. In a later section, we will discuss some behavior modification techniques used in classroom management.

Turning to the learning activities themselves, psychologists have learned how to deal with many academic problems created by poor attention, poor concentration, and poor study habits. If a child finds that he cannot concentrate on his reading, the environment can be altered to minimize distractions; the reading material can also be altered to elicit and maintain a high level of concentration. One method devised by Guthrie is to have the student quit studying and leave his desk as soon as he notices his mind wandering from the task at hand. By this technique the desk and books become associated exclusively with studying, not with competing thoughts and daydreams. A more effective method is to ask the child to answer a question after every sentence or two of the lesson and immediately reward his correct answers in some manner. Over trials the number of sentences read before the quiz is increased, and the quiz questions ask for integration of information from several statements. This method may be supplemented with self-instruction (see Meichenbaum & Asarnow, 1979), where the child is taught to recite silently to herself (and follow) a guidance monologue before and during reading. The monologue emphasizes asking questions about the content of the passage, outlining it as one reads, relating one idea to another in the passage or to something else one knows, and so on. Such simple methods prove very effective in dealing with children who have had severe deficiencies in concentration and reading comprehension.

Adult study skills have also been improved through reinforcement procedures (Wark, 1976; Watson & Tharp, 1977). Typical problems occur with high school and college students who have not learned proper study habits. The usual program asks the student to observe and record her study behaviors for a week. Then a reinforcement training procedure is started in which the student studies in only one or two places that are free from distraction, and reinforces herself with some desired privilege (e.g., watching TV) only if she meets certain minimal study goals (usually time spent, pages read, or problems worked) on a given day. Frequently, the student writes her own "contract," specifying what study goals are to be achieved for what rewards to herself. As the program continues, the amount of work required for reinforcement increases, and the reinforcers become more symbolic (e.g., points earned towards a weekend movie). The student continues to be her own "observer and reinforcer" and usually keeps a graph of her cumulative study time on each academic course. The graph of one's self-induced accomplishments (e.g., pages written per day by an author) is frequently more reinforcing than almost any tangible reward. Along with these reinforcement techniques for increasing study time, the teacher also instructs the students on effective study methods such as SQ3R mentioned earlier, and methods for taking notes (on readings or lectures) and reviewing notes for promoting learning.

These reinforcement techniques are effective in overcoming procrastination, the bane of every student's (and professional's) life. The basic idea is to subdivide a large job into many small steps or subgoals, to set oneself just one subgoal at a time, and to reward oneself with a customary privilege (e.g., morning coffee, a pillow at night, reading the newspaper) only if the daily subgoal has been achieved. Getting support for one's program from a group or one's friends helps too, because of the social reinforcement and motivation.

8. *Test anxiety.* Although educators seldom think about test anxiety, students know it can be a problem. Some students panic during crucial exams, their hearts race, their hands shake, their minds go blank; they interpret exam questions in stupid ways, give answers that they later recognize to be wrong, and waste time worrying over the consequences of their behavior. Psychologists consider test anxiety to be just one example of a learned fear, and like other fears, it may be greatly reduced with the right treatment. One successful technique is *systematic desensitization* (see Chapter 3). A procedure developed by Wolpe (1958), who followed Guthrie's idea of counterconditioning, desensitization tries to substitute the relaxation response for the tension and fear the student experiences in the test situation. The student is first taught deep-muscle relaxation, and then in imagination he pairs relaxation with visualized scenes that gradually approximate the test situations that evoke the most anxiety. With repeated practice and visualization, the student extinguishes his fear, and this behavioral state should transfer to the real-life situation. The relaxation procedure should be supplemented whenever possible by having the student relax in the actual room where the exam will occur, take a mock exam, and so on. The student is instructed to relax consciously while taking the exam, and to recite a stream of coping instruc-

tions to himself: "Relax, this isn't so terrible. Concentrate on the problem. Keep cool. Think of alternative problem-solving attacks. Breathe deeply. Let your neck, jaw, and shoulders relax. Work steadily, you'll be done soon" (Meichenbaum, 1977). The student may also be taught specific test-taking skills—how to guess optimally on multiple-choice questions, how to overview a test and budget one's time, how to outline the answer to an essay question before starting to write, and so on. Using these techniques with test-phobic students, psychologists have enabled them to dramatically reduce their anxiety during test-taking and consequently improve their test performances and grades (Osterhouse, 1976).

9. *Goals and interests.* Psychologists have always stressed that learning is best fostered by capturing the learner's *interest* in the subject matter. Interest is a nonanalytic cover term for many factors, but it usually refers either to the reinforcing nature of the material itself (such as cartoon and comic book rewards for children) or to the child's perception that learning the material has a clear instrumental value for attaining some recognizable goal other than a course grade. This linkage of learning and life goals is what is meant by "relevance" in academic subjects. Many school texts and workbooks strongly emphasize the relation between the subject matter and everyday practical problems. Field trips also enhance the relevance of classroom learning. Some university psychology and education classes have students actively apply what they learn by working directly with psychiatric patients, retarded or emotionally disturbed children, drug addicts, and various others. These learning experiences are valuable not only to the students but to the recipients as well. The experiences often significantly increase the students' motivation to learn and use what they are studying in a classroom.

At another level, educators and psychologists have found it most useful to give students more freedom to set their own goals, learn at their own pace, and monitor their own progress (Goodwin & Coates, 1976). However, students can set their own goals only after they have been trained to work responsibly and effectively, and to set goals that correspond to those of the school system—for example, reading at or above a certain level of proficiency. But within this framework, self-directed learners are likely to be happier and better learners; they monitor their work rate, set their subgoals according to what they can realistically demand of themselves, and choose reinforcement schedules or backup rewards that are most satisfying to them. These procedures provide motivation, impart a feeling of ˙success, and increase self-esteem, confidence, and competence. The best feature of self-directed learners, of course, is that they are only minimally dependent on the teacher, and are likely to continue learning when the formal requirements of school are no longer in force. The disadvantage is that self-directed learners create problems with the class schedule, curriculum, and teacher activities. Innovative planning and a change in traditional routines are required to make self-directed learning work.

10. *Perceptual structuring of tasks.* A common prescription from Gestalt psychologists for designing instructional materials is to make the perceptual display highlight the essential features of the problem. Visual aids such as films, pictures, and diagrams can present information organized in space in a manner resembling its conceptual organization. For example, the information in a text passage describing what people belong to what groups, and which groups belong to which organizations, can be depicted as a tree diagram or a network with nodes representing groups, and arrows between nodes representing the "is a member of" relation. The visual aid materially improves memory for the passage itself. Similarly, in presenting physics problems to students, a helpful text will diagram a corresponding physical model or situation with the relevant factors highlighted. These prescriptions for perceptual emphasis are widely known by curriculum and text writers, although they are not always respected.

In teaching complex concepts to children, a frequently helpful strategy (suggested by learning theorists) is to show many close, contrasting negative instances ("near misses") along with a variety of positive instances. Figure 15.1 shows clusters of positive and negative instances for teaching children the concept of the handwritten capital letter *A*. Seeing the handwritten variations within the positive instances enables the child to isolate critical features and their allowable range of variation. The set of near-miss negatives also enables the child to learn which features must be in an *A* (such as a crossbar near the middle of the legs) or must not be there (such as an extra crossbar or vertical line inside the legs). Each near miss highlights a slightly different contrasting feature or relation among parts needed for an *A* pattern, and enables the child to develop a sophisticated rule for this discrimination. These prescriptions, using near misses to teach difficult concepts (e.g., distinguish *tourist* from *immigrant*), strike us as good common sense and second-nature to teachers, yet the rules were in fact suggested by laboratory research on discrimination learning.

11. *Teaching for understanding.* Laboratory research, initially by Gestalt psychologists such as Katona (1940), has demonstrated that material learned by understanding the reasons (or the rules) underlying some phenomenon is better

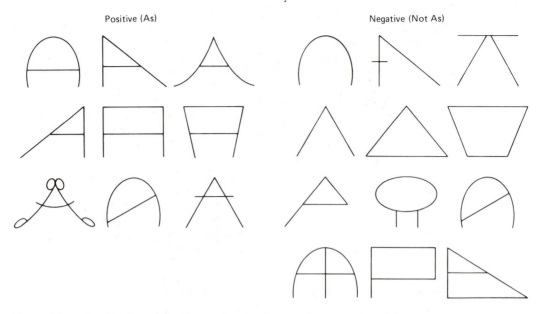

Positive (As)   Negative (Not As)

Figure 15.1. A collection of positive and near-miss negative examples of As.

retained and more easily transferred than is the same material learned by rote memorization. In mathematics, for example, a student is far better off (for later tests) learning the mechanism underlying the generation of the binomial distribution than he is in just memorizing the final formula for the distribution. Similarly, students must learn the sense of a mathematical derivation, such as differentiation of trigonometric functions, rather than just the formula, because later remembering of the sense will allow the student to rederive the formula long after he would have forgotten it from rote memory. The reasons for the rapid forgetting of meaningless statistical formulas are obvious: the many formulas being remembered are similar and interfere with one another, and there is no rule to help sort them out; whereas the concepts underlying the formulas are meaningful, well differentiated, and interconnected in a logical system of rules.

Teachers usually realize that learning by

understanding is preferable (when it is possible), and try to teach pupils to understand concepts, their interrelations, and the basis for operations and rules. Unfortunately, if students fail to understand at the conceptual level, they will often panic and revert to the rote memorization of formulas.

12. *Mnemonic devices.* Over the ages, various showmen as well as teachers have developed a battery of memory aids or mnemonic devices to help themselves or their students learn material of importance to them. A mnemonic device is a method for elaborating some material to be learned, making it more meaningful, relating it to things that are known, and guiding one's recall. The aim is to improve learning and recall. These were briefly reviewed in Chapter 13.

Mnemonics are attempts to solve practical memory problems. The methods vary with the material to be learned and the way in which memory will be tested. The array of methods is laid out in most of the popular books on memory improvement (Furst, 1958; Lorayne & Lucas, 1974). Laboratory tests show that the methods are usually effective, often dramatically so. Let us briefly mention some of the most helpful mnemonic devices.

One technique for learning numbers (say, telephone numbers) is to break them into small groups of 3 or 4 digits, convert each digit to a stock consonant sound (e.g., all 2's are *n*'s, all 4's are *r*'s, and so on), then add whatever vowels you can to make a meaningful word for each group. The code words are then remembered in association with the person having that phone number. The code words are reconverted to the number when it is needed.

A technique for learning a collection or series of items is the pegword method. Examples would be a shopping list, the series of points in a speech you are delivering or listening to, the laws of visual perception, and so on. You first memorize a list of ten or more pegwords using some system, such as the rhymes "1-bun, 2-shoe, 3-tree, 4-door, 5-hive. . . ." These are then used as mental pegs onto which you hang images standing for the successive items you want to recall. The trick is to associate an image of the first pegword with a concrete image of the first item, the second pegword with the second item, and so on through the list. Figure 15.2 illustrates the first five pegs and interactive pictures for the first five items of a shopping list. The interactive scene for each item is to be imagined for about five seconds as the list is presented. Later, when you wish to recall, you cue yourself by reciting the known list of pegwords, asking for each "What did I visualize with the bun? the shoe? the tree? . . ."

Experiments show that the method is very effective, often doubling or tripling recall and ordering it correctly (see Bower, 1970a). Many different lists can be put with the same pegwords, with only slight proac-

tive interference in remembering the most recent list. A comparable method uses mental snapshots of *locations* along a familiar route (say, your route to school) in place of the pegword images; the use of the mental snapshots for memorizing other lists is similar to that for the pegwords, and it yields equivalent benefits for recall. Both methods rely upon imaginal associations of items and a process of cueing oneself to revive each association. The pegword method can be recommended to students who must remember large amounts of arbitrary information, or remember a large collection of things in order. Casting academic materials in a pegword form (for example, translating abstract ideas into a concrete image that will remind you of the idea), will enable students to use the method and thereby improve their memories and test performances in striking fashion. Thus, teachers are well advised to provide mnemonics for the subject matter they want students to remember.

An educationally significant demonstration of mnemonics has been provided by Atkinson (1975; Raugh & Atkinson, 1975) in teaching foreign-language vocabularies to college students. The task of associating, say, a Spanish word with its English equivalent is broken into two steps: first, thinking of an English *keyword* that sounds like all or part of the Spanish word. Thus, *caballo* sounds like "cob-eye-yo," so *eye* would be an appropriate keyword; similarly, *pato* sounds like "pot-oh," so *pot* would be an appropriate keyword. The second stage, depicted in Figure 15.3, is to associate the keyword to the English *translation* of the Spanish word by visualizing some vivid scene of interaction between the two objects. Thus, caballo means "horse"; one can therefore imagine a horse kicking at a large eye, or a horse with a cyclopean eye in its forehead. Pato means "duck," and one may imagine a duck with a pot covering its head. Such bizarre im-

Item Number	Pegword	Peg Image	Item to Be Recalled	Connecting Image
1	bun		milk	
2	shoe		bread	
3	tree		bananas	
4	door		cigarette	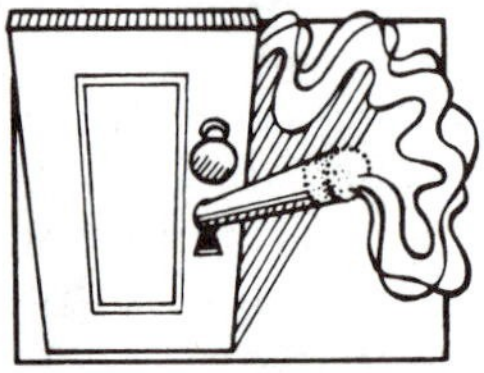
5	hive		coffee	

Connecting images:

1 *Milk* pouring onto a soggy hamburger *bun*
2 A *shoe* kicking and breaking a brittle loaf of French *bread*
3 Several bunches of *bananas* hanging from a *tree*
4 Keyhole of a *door* smoking a *cigarette*
5 Pouring *coffee* into top of a bee *hive*

Figure 15.2. Illustration of use of pegword mnemonic for remembering a shopping list.

CABALLO — eye — HORSE

PATO — pot — DUCK

Figure 15.3. Keyword method for learning Spanish-English vocabulary. (From Atkinson, 1975.)

ages weld together two dissimilar words in memory. Although the two phases have been described separately, they can be taught together, as is done in Figure 15.3. After completing both phases, the learner can go quickly from the Spanish word to the keyword to the translation. This is an example of mediated learning, discussed in Chapter 6.

Atkinson demonstrated that this basic procedure was exceptionally effective in comparison to a control procedure in which subjects learned the vocabulary items without benefits of mnemonics. For example, in one experiment subjects trained with the keyword method learned a Russian vocabulary of 120 items about twice as well as did controls given comparable study time. The advantage was retained as well on a test at the end of six months. The keyword method may set up two-way associations, so that a student who has learned by translating from Spanish to English shows a slight advantage over control subjects when asked to translate from English to Spanish. In other experiments, Raugh and Atkinson (1975) showed that the difficulty of learning a Russian-English pair with the keyword method could be factored neatly into two parts: the probability of remembering the Russian-to-keyword link times the probability of remembering the keyword-to-translation link. Subjects learn better if they make up their own keyword-to-translation link, but they have difficulty devising a useful keyword, and the tutor can be most helpful at this specific point.

The mnemonics program was so dramatically successful in laboratory work that it was used in teaching vocabulary to experimental college classes in elementary Russian and Spanish at Stanford University between 1974 and 1976. The students performed at a superior level, liked the keyword method, frequently asked for keywords when none were provided—in other words, the method was favorably received by students and teachers alike. Not all foreign-language teachers are sympathetic to such mnemonics, however, believing that they complicate what must eventually become an automatic retrieval process. But expert speakers of a language rarely realize how large and difficult a problem vocabulary-learning is for the student; moreover, mnemonics experts assert that the mediators (keywords and images) will drop out with continued use of the words. In any event, the use of mnemonics in foreign-language vocabulary learning is likely to increase in future curricula.

Classroom Management

One recent impact of learning psychology in education has been the introduction of a range of reinforcement techniques to help teachers foster a better learning environment. In order for learning to occur, students must be able to work and study without frequent interruptions and distractions from others. Every classroom teacher, no matter how liberal, still has some set of rules he wants his pupils to follow—for example, to be in class on time, to listen attentively, to refrain from making distracting noise or disturbing others, to sit quietly, and so forth. Problems arise when even one child breaks the rules repeatedly, forcing the teacher to use punitive measures, and turning the classroom into a miniature penal colony.

Starting in the 1960s, a variety of behavior modification procedures based on positive reinforcement techniques were used in experimental classrooms in order to deal with one or two disruptive or aggressive children. In a standard situation, a psychologist would be asked by a teacher to help with a problem child; the psychologist, the teacher, and perhaps the child would then discuss the problem behavior and agree upon an objective way to count and record it. A period of baseline recording then begins, in which the teacher or psychologist tracks the frequency of the child's problem behavior in a specific class for about a week. A reinforcement contingency is then introduced and explained to the child. She can earn the teacher's praise or a certain number of points, tokens, or tangible rewards by displaying specified "good behavior" (e.g., working quietly in her seat), whereas specified bad behavior is either ignored or penalized by the loss of points or tokens. If, after a week or so, the reinforcement program is seen to be not working, certain procedures are altered or adjusted. Perhaps a simpler behavior is targeted, a stronger reinforcer introduced, or unintended reinforcers for undesirable behavior removed; the program continues until its initial goals are met. Then new goals may be set so as to gradually phase out the extrinsic reinforcers while enhancing the quality of the child's attention or work skills; new behavior change programs may then be instituted for these goals.

With variations, such programs have by now been applied to many hundreds of students in hundreds of classrooms, and the results have been dramatically successful (O'Leary & O'Leary, 1972). The techniques have also been applied successfully to other groups (for example, "normal" children, retardates, and delinquents), a wide range of educational levels (from preschool through high school and college), and a variety of institutional settings. Initially, the studies focused on decreasing disruptive behavior—which is obviously necessary for orderly instruction—but later moved on to promote academic behaviors like accurate spelling, math problems, creative verbal descriptions or compositions, novel architectural constructions, and the like.

To give the flavor of these programs, we will review the details of a study by Packard (1970) that illustrates a group-contingent reinforcement procedure. This was a classroom experiment with primary school children in which a general class of behaviors referred to as "paying attention to the teacher's instruction" was shaped through managing reinforcement contingencies. The experiment was carried out by a teacher during each daily 30-minute reading lesson with four different classes (spanning kindergarten to sixth grade).

First, a token economy was instituted in the classroom. The children and teacher drew up a list of reinforcers and agreed upon how many tokens (poker chips) each reinforcer was to cost. Typical reinforcing activities were to be 10 minutes' access to playing with an electric typewriter, sitting next to a friend in the next class, 15 minutes' playtime in the gym, serving as teacher's assistant the next period, or 10 minutes' access to play on a piano. These activities could be purchased with tokens the child

won by "being good,' as stipulated below. The tokens would thus serve as conditioned reinforcers. During this time, the baseline frequency of "inattentive behaviors" by class members was estimated on several occasions, and these were considerable. Attentive behaviors were clearly defined and mainly consisted of sitting quietly, looking at and listening to the teacher, and doing one's lessons; inattentive behaviors included standing up and walking around the classroom, talking to one's neighbor, singing, sleeping, doodling idly, making and throwing paper airplanes, and so on.

Next, the group contingency was instituted and carefully explained to the class; tokens would be given to everyone if the class as a whole were all "paying attention" to the teacher for more than a specified percentage of the 30-minute reading lesson. The specific behaviors that counted as "paying attention" were carefully gone over several times with the children.

Finally, a cue-light prominently displayed on the teacher's desk served to inform the class when the teacher thought they were all paying attention (the green light) as contrasted to when she judged one or more children not to be (the red light). She would flick the light switch from green to red without comment or remarks to the offending pupils. The students knew that as long as the cue-light was green, a recording clock accumulated "attention time" toward their goal for the session; when the cue-light was red, the whole class was losing time and liable not to get their tokens for that day's lesson. The green and red lights served as conditioned reinforcers and punishers, respectively. Needless to say, there were strong group pressures (threats of punishment) brought to bear upon the inattentive member by the others.

Let us call the percentage of the 30-minute lesson during which the whole class was attentive the "percent attentiveness." Initially, the percent attentiveness required for group reinforcement was set very low, but was then advanced to stiffer criteria by means of shaping. In the beginning, each child received, say, three tokens if the percent attentiveness for the group exceeded 40 percent (or 12 minutes of the 30-minute lesson). If the class exceeded that amount by 10 percent, they each received a two-token bonus. Tokens were always delivered at the end of each lesson, and the child could "cash these in" immediately for a low-valued reinforcer or save up several days' worth of tokens for a high-valued reinforcer. After several successful sessions at one criterion, it would be increased so that higher percentages of group attention time were required for token reinforcement; moreover, a group total falling as much as 5 percent below the day's criterion was penalized by taking a token from each child.

This field experiment showed spectacular success in shaping up classroom attention and work habits. Most classes were attending around 90 percent of the time by the end of the procedure; this was judged by independent behavior observers as well as by the teacher. In the experiment, this explicit reinforcement procedure was followed by several others, including simple verbal instructions to pay attention along with repeated reprimands; however, when the token reinforcers were removed, the class attention soon extinguished to around 10 to 20 percent of the time. When token plus backup reinforcers were reinstated, the class's undivided attention to the teacher returned to the 90 percent level. The extinction of attending-to-teacher when extrinsic reinforcers were removed raises the question whether such rewards undermine the children's interest in the classroom material (see Lepper et al., 1977).

This study illustrates principles of shaping, conditioned reinforcers, and punishment for a complex set of behaviors, with contingencies programmed for the group as a whole. The method was so successful that it was adopted by other teachers in the school, despite their earlier resistance to behavior management programs. Clearly, attention to the teacher and good study habits are needed for learning, and their control is obviously important in education. The studies have shown that not only does deportment of the pupils improve but so does their amount of learning of school material. Because the behavior modification program has got them attending, the consequences we normally associate with education—learning, thinking, creativity—begin to appear in greater frequency.

There have been many such illustrations of practical applications of contingency management in schools, institutions, and industries. The techniques have been effective in establishing proper deportment and study skills in even the most difficult situations, often with great benefits to other children and to the community. An example of a serious problem of school life solved by behavior modification programs is violence in the school, gang fights, attacks on teachers, extortion between children and gangs, vandalism, and wanton destruction of school property. In poor, inner-city American schools, violence and vandalism have grown to alarming proportions. Several behavior modification programs for entire classes or schools have been devised to identify and remove the usual reinforcers that maintain violence and vandalism, and to replace them with reinforcers for socially approved or educationally relevant behaviors. For instance, a study by Mayer and Butterworth (1979) with 20 inner-city schools in Los Angeles (grades 4, 5, 6) found that acts of school vandalism and violence in the experimental schools were reduced by more than 50 percent in one year when a school-wide behavior modification program was in use. This reduction occurred over a period during which vandalism at other city schools rose dramatically. An index of difference is that the annual cost of repairs for vandalism at the "untreated" control schools was nearly eight times as great as that at the experimental schools. Moreover, the extent of educationally relevant behaviors in the classrooms of the treated schools increased significantly as did their scores on standard tests of educational achievement.

Such applications of behavioral management techniques are clearly appropriate and are needed on a wider scale. They suggest some of the societal benefits of large-scale applications of behavioralist ideas. These ideas are slowly being extended and applied to industry (to promote safety), to public parks and campgrounds (to reduce littering), to energy conservation (to reduce energy waste in homes and increase car pooling), and so on. Another broad application of behavior theory is to psychotherapy with neurotics and psychotics (see Chapter 9).

GENERAL THEORIES OF INSTRUCTION

The foregoing listing of contributions to education from various theories lacks a coherent framework. Educators have argued that some sort of theory of instruction is needed to guide one's applications, a theory that will recommend or prescribe educational procedures, curricula, and the sequence of topics.

Most of the earlier theories of instruction were embodied in curriculum theory, a discipline within the study of education that seeks to organize the materials of instruction in some orderly manner for effective teaching and learning. It would take us afield to attempt a summary of this literature (e.g., McClure, 1971); our interest is rather in a number of recent developments in which psychologists concerned with learning theory or aspects of cognitive development have turned their attention to improving or optimizing instruction when both subject matter and guided learning

are under scrutiny. What they have developed is, of course, relevant to curriculum, for a theory of instruction is in some sense a theory of curriculum development. At the present time, however, the instructional theories tend to deal with more limited aspects of schooling than do curriculum theories.

The development of programmed learning, in which experimental psychologists played a large part, was one clear instigation for a theory of instruction; however, such a program for schools had to reflect the actual content of school learning and could no longer be limited to artificial laboratory materials. Some educational psychologists who during World War II had been deeply immersed in the actual problems of training airplane pilots, or teaching exotic languages, were eager to see some of the lessons they had learned applied outside the armed services. The upsurge of interest in educational advancements after the Sputnik launching in 1957 had brought scholars from mathematics, physics, biology, and other areas into the design of instructional materials. Professional educators welcomed these new allies, and considerable collaborative work has resulted.

Theory of instruction has not yet settled down into an accepted system refined by the give-and-take of theory, experiment, and dialogue; the best we can do at present is to give some illustrations. For this purpose, we have chosen three approaches, assigned to the three theorists proposing them, no one of whom is committed to a global theory of learning as described in earlier chapters. The approaches are complementary rather than opposed, and they do not deal with exactly the same problems.

Gagné's Hierarchical Task Analyses

Robert M. Gagné is an associationist trained in the verbal learning tradition (see Chapter 6). He turned from the study of basic problems in the laboratory to the practical tasks of training in the air force during World War II, where he worked especially (though not exclusively) on various devices for simulating the task of the pilot. He emerged from this experience concerned with making traditional learning principles more applicable to training tasks. He felt two things were needed for applications. The first was a psychological analysis of the many component skills and their assembly that a student needs in order to perform some complex educational skill. This led to his idea of task-skill hierarchies, to be discussed later, which tell us how to sequence the training of some skills before others. Second, such analyses identify for researchers a number of distinct types of learning, so Gagné set these forth in a list like that in Table 15.1. These are arranged in order of increasing complexity. We have met these types of learning before under other labels; for ex-

ample, Type 1 is classical conditioning, Types 2 and 3 are instrumental conditioning, and Types 4 to 7 are discrimination learning. It is intuitively clear that Gagné, having proposed so many different kinds of learning, should find it relatively easy to describe many kinds of school learning according to one or another of his types.

Perhaps Gagné's greater contribution was in proposing hierarchies of skills and rules in several academic tasks. He has illustrated the hierarchical organization of school instruction, according to his types, for mathematics, science, foreign languages, and English (1965, pp. 175–203; 1970, pp. 246–74).

An example of a skill hierarchy is depicted in Figure 15.4 for a preschooler learning to divide any collection of objects into equal halves, or equal thirds, this skill itself being a prerequisite to understanding sets and other number concepts underlying arithmetic. One asks, what operations and

**TABLE 15.1. Gagné's eight types of learning.
(Modified from Gagné, 1970.)**

Type	Brief Description
1. Signal learning	The classical conditioned response of Pavlov, in which the individual learns to make a diffuse response to a signal.
2. Stimulus-response learning	The connection of Thorndike, the discriminated operant of Skinner; sometimes called an instrumental response.
3. Chaining	Two or more stimulus-response connections are joined together.
4. Verbal association	Chains that are verbal.
5. Multiple discrimination	Identifying responses to stimuli that resemble each other, such that some interferences occur.
6. Concept learning	A common response to a class of stimuli.
7. Rule learning	A chain of two or more concepts; reflected in a rule such as "If *A*, then *B*," where *A* and *B* are concepts.
8. Problem-solving	Thinking is involved; principles are combined according to a "higher-order" rule.

discriminations must a child go through in successfully doing that task? Brief analyses show "that the child must be able to (1) identify two apparently equal subsets of a total group as 'halves' and three such subsets as 'thirds' (a defined concept), and (2) construct actually equal subsets by pairing objects one to each set (a procedural rule)" (Gagné, 1970, p. 253). Analysis of the skill of identifying halves or thirds requires that the child understand the concepts of two and three; analysis of constructing equal subsets suggests prerequisites of "dealing out objects, one to each subset," and "apportioning leftover objects, one to each subset." This hierarchy is like a *recipe* for what must be done to synthesize a complex behavior, and it suggests the progression in which subskills should be taught. Such hierarchies are to be constructed for all such educational skills.

Consider another hierarchy proposed by Gagné (1965), this one for reading (see Figure 15.5). While there is a certain plausibility to such an outline, it is by no means clear that a sequence of instruction can be designed upon it. Also, the basic notion that the lower steps of the hierarchy must be mastered before the higher steps can be learned may not always be the best strategy; there may well be a kind of cyclical development in learning, in which the various stages must be repeatedly expanded and refined (such as vocabulary growth).

Gagné continued to work on these problems, and with Briggs, addressed himself directly to the task of designing instructional sequences (Gagné & Briggs, 1974). In this he dealt explicitly with the problem of the curriculum. He found it useful to refer to a hierarchy of levels, for example, in sequencing a course, a topic within that course, a lesson within that

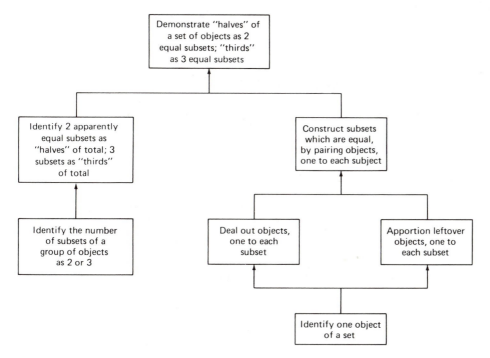

Figure 15.4. A learning hierarchy for a prekindergarten mathematical skill. (From Gagné, 1970.)

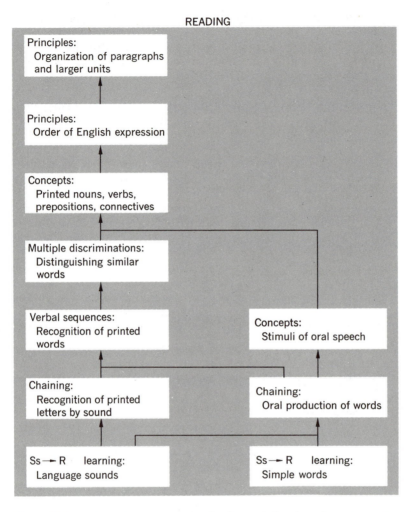

Figure 15.5. A learning structure for the basic skills of reading. (From Gagné, 1965.)

topic, a component within that lesson. None of the steps can be circumvented, whether or not everything is written down in planning the curriculum. To keep this discussion within the context of learning theory, we may consider how he applied sequencing principles to some outcomes expressed as learning outcomes rather than as knowledge specific to some subject matter. One of his summary tables is reproduced as Table 15.2.

It is evident that in any theory of instruction, there must remain a large element of empiricism in the decision as to just how much time and effort must be expended on each step of a sequence. The main point is that Gagné has found the hierarchical principle a useful one for moving from learning principles to the sequencing of instruction. In this sense he has made hierarchy the basis for his approach to a theory of instruction.

TABLE 15.2. Desirable sequence characteristics associated with five types of learning outcome. (From Gagné and Briggs, 1974.)

Type of Learning Outcome	Major Principles of Sequencing	Related Sequence Factors
Motor skills	Provide intensive practice on part-skill of critical importance, and practice on total skill.	First of all, learn the "executive routine" (rule).
Verbal information	For major subtopics, order of presentation not important. Individual facts should be preceded or accompanied by meaningful context.	Prior learning of necessary intellectual skills involved in reading, listening, and so on, is usually assumed.
Intellectual skills	Presentation of learning situation for each new skill should be preceded by prior mastery of subordinate skills.	Information relevant to the learning of each new skill should be previously learned, or presented in instructions.
Attitudes	Establishment of respect for source as an initial step. Choice situations should be preceded by mastery of any skills involved in these choices.	Information relevant to choice behavior should be previously learned, or presented in instructions.
Cognitive strategies	Problem situations should contain previously acquired intellectual skills.	Information relevant to solution of problems should be previously learned, or presented in instructions.

Bruner's Cognitive-Developmental Theory

Jerome S. Bruner is a cognitive psychologist, with primary interests in the development of mental abilities. He had a major impact on the education profession with the publication of his book *The process of education* (1960), which was the outcome of a conference devoted to educational problems, attended by many who had not had strong prior identification with professional education. He later proposed some theorems regarding instruction, illustrated by the teaching of mathematics, and moved further toward a theory of instruction in a subsequent collection of essays (Bruner, 1966). In the latter, he points out that a theory of instruction is *prescriptive* in that it proposes rules for achieving knowledge or skill and provides techniques for measuring or evaluating outcomes. It is also *normative,* in that it sets goals to be achieved and deals with conditions for meeting them.

> . . . A theory of instruction, in short, is concerned with how what one wishes to teach can best be learned, with improving rather than describing learning.
>
> This is not to say that learning and developmental theories are irrelevant to a theory of instruction. In fact, a theory of instruction must be concerned with both learning and development and must be congruent with those theories of learning and development to which it subscribes (Bruner, 1966, p. 40).

He goes on to specify four features that a theory of instruction must encompass:

1. *Predisposition to learn.* A theory of instruction must be concerned with the experiences

and contexts that will tend to make the child willing and able to learn when he or she enters school.

2. *Structure of knowledge.* It must specify the ways in which a body of knowledge should be structured so that it can be most readily grasped by the learner.

3. *Sequence.* It should specify the most effective sequences in which to present the materials.

4. *Reinforcement.* It should specify the nature and pacing of rewards, moving from extrinsic rewards to intrinsic ones.

Each of these points needs elaboration (some of which he provides), particularly with respect to the individual differences among children at any given age, the differences to be expected with growth, the differences in structure within various fields of knowledge, necessary flexibility of sequencing to meet individual differences in rate of learning as well as in preference, and so on. Bruner has taken the position that, with sufficient understanding of the structure of a field of knowledge, something anticipating the later, more advanced concepts can be taught appropriately at much earlier ages. His aphorism has been widely quoted: "Any subject can be taught effectively in some intellectually honest form to any child at any stage of development" (1960, p. 33).

The developmental aspect of Bruner's theory lies in his interest in cognitive development, originally stimulated by Piaget. This has led him to emphasize three modes of representation in a developmental sequence: the *enactive,* the *iconic,* and the *symbolic* (1964b). The enactive mode is learning through action, an essentially wordless learning, such as learning to ride a bicycle. The iconic mode is based on representation through perceptual means (hence the "icon," or image standing for something). A mental map that permits us to follow a route from where we are to where we are going constitutes such an iconic representation. Finally, the symbolic mode enables the translation of experience into words, and these permit eventually

the kinds of transformations that at the later stages become of so much interest to Piaget. In relation to learning theory Bruner notes that much of the conditioning or S-R learning appears appropriate to the enactive mode, Gestalt psychology was concerned very largely with the iconic mode, and the new concern with the symbolic mode brings in the psycholinguists and many others besides Piaget.

As with all of those who become interested in the concrete problems of instruction, Bruner is insistent on the empirical steps necessary before the theory can prescribe the practice. Psychological explanation, at the level of practice, has to account for the ways in which children actually deal with the problems before them; he believes, for example, that Piaget's theory, with its heavy emphasis on epistemology, is too formal to provide a psychological description of the processes of growth (Bruner, 1966, p. 7). Although Bruner's proposals have been interesting and have influenced the attitudes and thinking of educators, they have not been much followed up by research with instructional programs.

Atkinson's Decision-Theoretic Analysis for Optimizing Learning

Richard C. Atkinson came to instructional psychology from an interest in mathematical learning theory (Atkinson, Bower, & Crothers, 1965), which he applied to a form of instructional programming called computer-assisted instruction (CAI). Through actual use of the computer in schools across the country for the teaching of reading and spelling, he became interested in the broader context of instruction, including such practical matters as the amount of time the pupil should spend with the teaching computer and the amount with the live teacher, the costs of computer instruction, and so on. With a number of collaborators, he has worked out several ideas regarding the sequencing of educational tasks and how students should divide their time among tasks (Atkinson, 1972; Atkinson & Paulson, 1972).

Atkinson (1972) proposes four criteria that must be satisfied prior to a precise derivation of an optimal instructional strategy:

1. A model of the learning process.

2. Specification of admissible instructional actions.

3. Specification of instructional objectives.

4. A measurement scale that permits costs to be assigned to each of the instructional objectives.

It is possible at this stage to follow Atkinson's model for rather specific instructional tasks; the collection of such task-specific models should lead to a more general theory of instruction. The model is, in fact, a special case of *optimal control theory* as it has been developed in the mathematical and engineering fields (Kalman, Falb, & Arbib, 1969).

As a first example, Atkinson makes use of data from initial reading instruction in regular classrooms in which CAI supplements the work of the teacher (Atkinson & Fletcher, 1972). The optimizing task that is set is to use the computer most efficiently, granted a specific total amount of computer time available, and in full awareness that not all the pupils are at the same level to begin with or learn at the same rate. The four criteria listed above can be met, at least provisionally. First, several useful models of learning are available: the one-element, or linear-learning, models (see Chapter 6) proved useful for this purpose; the second criterion above, instructional actions, have already been programmed on the computer, so that all that is now necessary is to allocate time on the computer among the pupils in an optimal way; the third criterion, the instructional objective, will be discussed below in more detail; costs and payoffs are readily taken care of because computer time (hence computer cost) is a constant, and the payoff can be defined as the performance on the end-of-the-year reading test.

The instructional objectives for a class, given the individual differences in learning, may not be the same as those for an individual. Atkinson considers four possible objectives:

a. To maximize the mean performance over the class.

b. To minimize the variance in performance over the class.

c. To maximize the number of students who score at or above the average for their grade.

d. To maximize the mean performance without increasing the variance above what it would have been without CAI.

It is very easy to make glib statements about the successes of one school over another, based solely on mean performance on some sort of test. That would rely on objective (a), but note that it *might* mean that the procedures would then favor working with the most promising students, pushing them far ahead and permitting those most likely to fail to end up as failures. Or, in the interests of having everyone come out more or less alike (a romantic interpretation of the democratic ideal), objective (b) might be chosen, with the consequence that the more rapid learners would be held back and all effort spent on the slow learners.

Using the learning rates of students observed in earlier uses of the computer teaching program, it was possible to simulate an experiment on the computer to see what the consequences would be of adopting each of the four objectives, without actually conducting the experiment in the schools. The results are presented in Figure

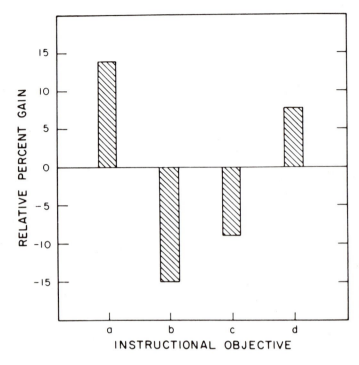

Figure 15.6. Gains or losses to be expected through maximizing each of four objectives. (From Atkinson, 1972.)

15.6, which plots the gains (or losses) through maximizing each objective.

If objective (a) were adopted, calling for maximum mean gain, reading averages would go up about 15 percent by the end of the year, but the variance would also go up about 15 percent. What this means is that the average gain would be at the expense of a greater spread between the more successful and the less successful students—hardly a result to be celebrated. If objective (b) or (c) were chosen, the average performance would be reduced, a consequence of holding back the more rapid learners in order to reduce variability. Objective (d), requiring a program allowing equal time for each student, raises the mean about 8 percent, less than objective (a), but without the unfortunate side effect of increased variability. Hence, in this comparison, objective (d) would seem to be the one to favor. The important point here is to show how a decision-theoretic

model can indeed lead to practical decisions.

As another illustration of the approach in action, we may review briefly a second example from Atkinson (1972): the learning of a foreign language vocabulary (German) by English-speaking college students. Three instructional strategies were employed in an experimental comparison: a *random-order strategy,* in which selected German words are presented in a random order; a *learner-controlled strategy,* in which the learner decides which items require more practice and hence should be presented for study; and a *response-sensitive strategy,* in which the computer was programmed to present materials according to the prior successes and failures of the individual student in line with a decision-theoretic analysis of the task. Roughly, the strategy is to present for study those vocabulary items that the student has been getting wrong and to leave aside the ones he has mastered.

The instruction is controlled by a computer in an instructional session of approximately 2 hours and a briefer delayed-test session a week later. To permit a comparison of the three strategies, the presentation is made as follows. A list of 12 German words (one of seven lists) is displayed, and then one item from the list is selected for test and study. After an item is selected, the student attempts a translation and receives feedback regarding the correct translation. This item can be selected at random, by the learner, or according to the model designed to be optimal. Each subject is assigned to one of these treatment procedures. The delayed test, the same for all students, tests the entire vocabulary of 84 words making up the seven lists. The results, as presented in Figure 15.7, came out as predicted, with the response-sensitive strategy the most successful

on the criterion (delayed) test. The different orders of conditions were as predicted, because the response-sensitive strategy calls for the most practice during the instructional sessions on the items causing most trouble; the learner-controlled strategy is to do something similar to this, but is less efficient; the random strategy totally ignores the specific difficulties of the learner. The optimality of the response-sensitive strategy was derived from a variant of the one-element learning model. The variant is based on the conception that any given foreign-language vocabulary association may be either unknown (state U), in temporary storage in memory (state T), or in relatively permanent memory storage (state P). The learning model accounts precisely for changes from one state to another, and can be used to derive equations for the probabilities of being in each of the states

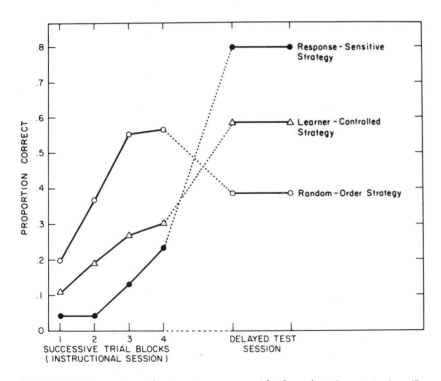

Figure 15.7. Proportion of correct responses with three learning strategies. (From Atkinson, 1972.)

for each of the items at the start of any one trial, given some empirical parameters and the student's response history (Atkinson & Crothers, 1964). The computational procedure is then implemented on the computer.

This example is somewhat incomplete from the point of view of fully practical instructional theory in that it is a little too close to a typical laboratory experiment on learning, being conducted over a short time and with college students not enrolled in a language course. It has the virtue, however, of using school-relevant materials (a foreign language vocabulary), and of testing some theories about instruction by comparing student choice with a systematic choice in sequencing learning. It is clear in this setting that the student is not the most efficient guide to optimize her own learning.

More recent work by Malone, Macken, and Suppes (1979) has dealt with the issue of how to allocate a limited amount of instructional computer time among a group (or class) of students performing and learning at different levels in order to maximize learning of the group. The researchers first fit a mathematical formula to the expected grade placement of each student on performance tests (for math or reading) as a function of the time he or she has had working on the programmed lessons. Individual differences appear in the constants b and c of the power function:

$$\text{GP}(t) = bt^{.45} + c,$$

where t is minutes learning on the computer, $\text{GP}(t)$ is the grade placement level, c is like a beginning level, and b is like a learning rate. The researchers ran a simulation, similar to that leading to the results in Figure 15.6, that investigated the four different criteria mentioned above and the strategies of student allocation of computer time that they dictate. The results were comforting because they showed that within reasonable limits, different ways of assigning computer time to fast versus slow students created relatively little difference in the overall amount of learning for the class. The surest policy with clear benefits was simply to increase the CAI time available to the class as a whole.

Atkinson's theory deriving from work with the computer is, of course, only one among several approaches (the others not dependent upon the computer) to the problem of how to deal effectively with individual differences in learning. Carroll (1963a), for example, proposed a model in which the individual would be allowed enough time to learn what he needed to learn as a background for the next stage, interpreting aptitude for a task as essentially the time required for the individual to master that task. This approach was adopted by Bloom and his associates and developed into an instructional plan known as *mastery learning*, based on the guiding principle that the learner should achieve mastery at one stage before going on to the next (Bloom, 1968; Block, 1971). Another approach has been that known as *individually prescribed instruction* (IPI), developed by Glaser and his associates at Pittsburgh (e.g., Lindvall & Bolvin, 1967; Lindvall & Cox, 1969). Utilizing materials arranged in progressively more difficult units, the school using IPI tries to meet individual differences in mathematics, reading, and science by permitting each student to work with appropriate materials after she has taken a placement test to prescribe the proper unit. Still another approach is *aptitude-treatment interaction* (ATI), which proposes that individual differences be met by different approaches to instruction for students of different aptitude (e.g., Cronbach, 1967; Cronbach & Snow, 1969). Adapting instruction to the individual is a basic problem in the design of the curriculum, and it is to be expected that various approaches will be invented to meet this need. The three theories of instruction presented here (Gagné's hierarchical model, Bruner's cognitive-developmental model, and Atkinson's decision-theoretic optimization model) illustrate contemporary explorations toward a prescriptive theory of instruction. So far, these theories have had relatively little influence upon curriculum design, text writing, or course sequencing in actual school systems.

TECHNOLOGICAL AIDS IN TRAINING AND INSTRUCTION

Teachers have always used such aids to instruction as were available to them: slates, blackboards, libraries, textbooks, workbooks, laboratories, studios, stages, playgrounds. There have been educational innovations over the years, and educational technology, as such, is not new. What is new is the pace at which new devices have been developed. We now have a better opportunity to ask what research tells us about their effectiveness. In turn, because of the clarity with which they proceed, they may also contribute to instructional theory, as in the preceding account of Atkinson's work with the computer.

Simulators

Gagné (1962b) has reviewed the succesful use of machine simulators in user training, not only aircraft simulators for training pilots, but trainers for aircraft controllers and control tower operators, missile guidance operators, and technicians of various kinds. He points out that it is not necessarily the device that is simulated, but the *operations* or *tasks* related to it: procedures, skills, identifications, trouble shooting, and team skills such as communication of information.

He believes that the educational use of simulators should be at fairly advanced stages of instruction, as in the training of

civilian technicians, and perhaps in some kinds of performance assessment (e.g., assessment of automobile-driving skill).

The generalizations, as far as theory of learning is concerned, again bear more upon task analysis than upon learning processes involved, though of course problems of degree of similarity between the simulated and the real situation must be considered. This is essentially a practical matter, however, and is not helped too much by theories of generalization and transfer.

Films and Television

Films and television are similar in that both use animated pictures with sound. Films may of course be presented over closed-circuit television, with some advantage in that room darkening is less necessary and remote projectors or video tape recorders can present the films. Television may also be "live," again either from a remote source or over closed-circuit from near sources, including the lecturer's own desk if he wishes to permit a room full of students to look over his shoulder as he carries out a dissection or performs some other demonstration. We are not interested here in how the equipment can be made more convenient, although that of course has something to do with its use. Instead, our concern is with the kind of teaching that takes place with such audiovisual aids.

In a review of the research on learning from films, Hoban (1960) classified the results of some 400 investigations of teaching films into three zones of certainty with respect to the findings: low, intermediate, and high certainty. To achieve high certainty, results had to satisfy four criteria: (1) they should be intuitively reasonable, (2) they should have been reported by a competent and constructively imaginative investigator, (3) they should be related to some systematic formulation, and (4) the investigation should have been replicated. Other degrees of certainty were attached to those findings which did not satisfy these four criteria. Skipping over the findings of low and intermediate certainty (areas in which more research is urgently needed) we may examine the results that Hoban felt met his high-certainty criteria. These can be stated fairly concisely:

1. People learn from films.
2. Learning from films varies in amount with audience characteristics, such as age and formal education.
3. The amount of learning from films can be increased by the use of one or more of the following tested mechanisms and methods:

   a. *Redundancy.* Filmmakers (and English teachers) make the use of redundancy an uphill fight, according to Hoban, yet repetition of information, even repetition of whole films, can be demonstrated to provide increments in learning.

   b. *Participation.* If student activity, such as answering questions inserted in a film, can be encouraged, learning is enhanced, particularly if there is some feedback so that the student knows whether or not she answered correctly. Experimentation has shown that this is not merely a motivational device (to be sure that the student notices what is going on) but that there is a genuine benefit from making relevant responses.

   c. *Attention-directing devices and methods.* A motion picture can use arrows that appear on a chart (or picture) to call attention to some feature, or in other ways can help the student search out the desired critical information. Such devices and teaching methods appropriate to them produce gains in learning films.

These are not novel findings to learning psychologists; of greater importance is how these principles are embodied in detail, taking into consideration again the structure of what is being taught.

Television came rapidly to the fore as a possible means of teaching after receiving sets became widely available in homes and schools, and after the development of artificial satellites led to the practical possibility of directing programs to widely separated targets, including developing areas where textbooks and teachers might be scarce. In a comprehensive review of studies of the effectiveness of television in instruction, Chu and Schramm conclude:

> . . . it has become clear that there is no longer any reason to raise the question whether instructional television can serve as an efficient tool of learning. This is not to say that it always *does.* But the evidence is overwhelming that it *can,* and under favorable circumstances that it does. This evidence comes now from many countries, from studies of all age levels from preschool to adults, and from a great variety of subject matter and learning objectives (1967, p. 98).

The peculiar advantages which they point out are that television allows a good teacher to be shared by a number of classes, it provides a variety and quality of experiences that would otherwise be impossible, and it can carry teaching to areas in which there are no schools. Educational television programs beamed to remote rural areas have been particularly helpful in the developing third world. Television also frees the local teacher to use available time for working with smaller groups and for giving individual guidance. The chief disadvantage is that it is a one-way system, and in fact there has been some experimentation with call-back or talk-back systems (e.g., Greenhill, 1964), but cost considerations have thus far made them not generally feasible. The best supplement to the TV is a local tutor who can expand upon the points of the TV program, answer questions, and motivate and reinforce work.

The Language Laboratory

The impetus for language teaching started during World War II, and considerable effort was expended on ways to facilitate such learning. Here, if anywhere, we should expect a payoff for education, because language teaching has always been one of the standard school tasks, although there has been some vacillation between teaching the language as something to be spoken or as something to be read. The military training emphasized the spoken language; now the emphasis has shifted within schools and colleges back to the spoken language and away from reading knowledge. This has come about in part because better devices are available for bringing acceptably pronounced utterances to students in smaller schools who might lack teachers fully proficient in the language being taught. The language laboratory was rapidly adopted afer 1945 (Haber, 1963).

A language laboratory is simply a class of devices which allow speech, recorded on electromagnetic tape, to be used in instruction. The more elaborate contemporary devices permit the student to imitate what is heard, and then to listen to her own production or to have the teacher monitor what she has said. The console at which the teacher sits may allow two-way communication with a number of students at once.

Even the best training methods do not eliminate the arduous practice required by adults to learn a second language. In the Army Language School at Monterey, California, a student typically spent nearly all of his time for 8 months working on a language, and 12 months if it was one of the more difficult ones. Even so, many were unsuccessful. In one of the earlier studies of language learning in the armed services, S. B. Williams and Leavitt (1947) reported that 80 percent of those who undertook to learn Japanese dropped out before they completed mastery of the language. There are no easy roads to the mastery of any difficult learning task.

Carroll (1963b), reviewing research on foreign language teaching, gives the impression that we know next to nothing about the effectiveness of the procedures that have been adopted in language laboratories, such as the student's hearing her own speech, practice on particular patterns of speech, and so on. The work on associative learning that could be relevant to vocabulary learning (see the *mnemonic devices* section) is usually not relevant to the usual way language is taught, which emphasizes using novel words in a meaningful speech context.

There have been several comparisons of language laboratories with conventional methods. One study carried out by faculty members at Antioch College compared conventional teaching of 20 students in a class taught six times a week by a regular instructor with teaching in a language laboratory in which 60 students met twice a week with a regular instructor and four times a week with student laboratory assistants (Antioch College, 1960). The experimental procedures saved about 12 hours per week of the time of the regular instructors. The laboratory periods of $1\frac{1}{2}$ hours each were divided into the presentation of audiovisual materials (slides and accompanying tape-recorded sound), individual work in language laboratory booths, and drill and practice in face-to-face contact with the student assistants. In two separate years, achievement tests at the end of the year showed no significant differences to be attributed to the two forms of instruction; because the laboratory method was better liked by the students and saved the time of regular instructors, it still had something to recommend it. Pickrel, Neidt, and Gibson (1958) showed that teachers untrained in Spanish could teach conversational Spanish to seventh-grade students effectively if they based their teaching on tapes prepared by a specialist in Spanish; the children did not differ in oral fluency from those taught by the regular Spanish teacher. Thus the new methods offer promise, but no great revolution in teaching effectiveness. In the study just cited, the groups taught by the Spanish teacher were superior to those taught by tapes on written tests of Spanish.

In his analysis of what is involved in foreign language learning, Carroll (1962) identified the following aspects of foreign language aptitude: phonetic coding, grammatical sensitivity, rote memory for foreign language materials, and inductive language learning ability. It may be noted that ordinary verbal knowledge (tested by vocabulary in the familiar language) is not a good predictor of ability to learn a foreign language, in part because in the first stages of learning a foreign language it is not necessary to master a large vocabulary. In his model of the learning process as it applies to foreign language learning, Carroll (1962, 1963b) proposes that success is a function of the following five elements, the first three of which are qualities of the learner, the final two, of the instructional process:

1. The learner's language aptitude.

2. The learner's general intelligence.

3. The learner's perseverance.

4. The quality of the instruction.

5. The opportunity for learning afforded the student.

Again we note the importance of analyzing the nature of the performance in order both to specify the requisite component abilities and to design an appropriate instructional program.

Programmed Learning

Attention to programmed learning began with the introduction of the teaching machine as a technological aid, although the essence of programming does not reside in the particular kind of equipment used. The first of these machines was developed by Sidney L. Pressey at Ohio State University many years ago (Pressey, 1926, 1927).

While originally developed as a self-scoring machine to facilitate the taking and scoring of objective examinations, the machine soon demonstrated its ability to actually teach. The student reads the question presented in the aperture of the machine, selects an answer from among several alternatives, and then presses the button corresponding to this chosen answer. If she is correct, the next question appears in the slot; if she has made a mistake, the original question remains. The machine counts her errors and the tape does not move on to the next question until the right button has been pressed. Because the student knows that she is correct when the question moves, she has immediate information (reinforcement, feedback) and thus learns while testing herself. Because the machine has counted her errors, her score can be read off as soon as she has finished taking the test. This machine of Pressey's did not become popular, although a number of studies by him and his students showed it to be effective as a teaching device.

A new forward push was given to the idea of automatic self-instruction by the publication of a paper by Skinner (1954), whose operant-conditioning work had already given him authority in the field of learning. The time was now right, and work on teaching machines and programmed learning flourished shortly thereafter. Now it is a very large-scale international scientific, educational, and commercial enterprise. Skinner's machine differed from Pressey's chiefly in that the student was not given alternatives to choose from but instead was asked to write his own response in the spaces provided, and then, as a printed tape advanced, the correct answer appeared for comparison with what he had written. He thus "emitted" his own response to be "reinforced" by the comparison response. A further difference is involved: the material is so planned that it is not essentially a review of partially learned material, but rather a "program" in which the responses of the learner are "shaped" as he learns.

A program is divided into a large number of discrete frames in which some information is presented and some other information is tested for recall. Example frames for teaching the procedure of classical conditioning are illustrated in Figure 15.8. The text and question at the top of the frame is conceived by Skinner as like a complex "stimulus"; the student composes and writes her response at the lower right, and then the correct answer is uncovered to provide immediate corrective feedback. Successive frames in a program develop and elaborate upon a single concept, rule, or procedure. The program often tests new information shortly after it is introduced, tests a given principle in several alternative ways, and reviews concepts and principles learned much earlier in the program. Skinner emphasized immediate reinforcement

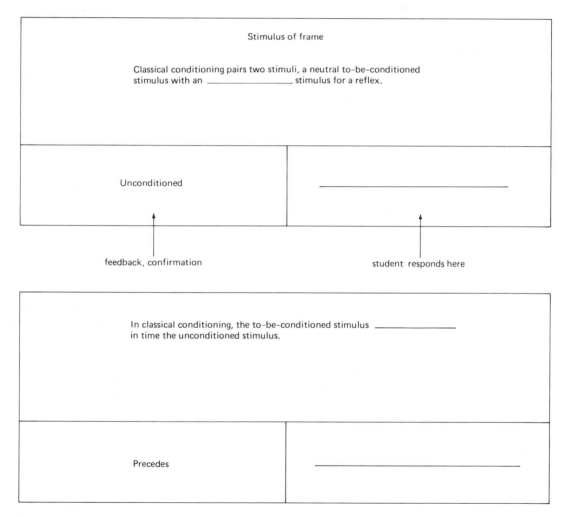

Figure 15.8. Examples of two frames in a program for teaching about classical conditioning. The student reads the question from the top of the frame, writes in an answer, then looks at the correct answer.

for constructed responses, a gradual progression to complex repertoires, fading-out stimulus prompts for answers, discrimination of concepts, and controlling the learner's attention and motivation. More complex instructional devices have been developed beyond those of Pressey and Skinner. Lumsdaine (1959) describes several others. For example, in one arrangement, a step-by-step film projection is used to teach a technician how to operate a piece of electronic equipment. A single demonstrational segment appears on the screen until the learner has mastered it. She then presses the button to bring on the next illustration, and so on, until she has learned the complete operation. Modern electronic computers have been brought into the picture, occasionally to combine slide projection, motion picture projection, and other materials within the program for a single learner, occasionally to allow the management of learning for a group of learners. The flexibility provided makes possible almost any arrangement that the investigator desires, as long as the costs can be met.

The essence of learning by means of a teaching machine lies not in the machinery but in the material to be presented, and it has been found that properly designed programmed books can serve about the same purpose as the simpler forms of teaching machines. The simple machines are sometimes derogated as "mechanical page-turners" because they do little more than the student can do as well for herself. Obviously, the more complex machines go well beyond this, and the belittling of the simple machine is intended to point to the importance of the program over the technology. The programmed text is not to be confused with the earlier "workbook" in common educational use; the workbook was primarily a place to practice on examples of what had been taught by the teacher or a textbook, whereas the programmed text is designed to do the teaching itself.

Hence the program necessarily must begin with what the learner already knows, and it then adds to this by supplying answers that are at first *hinted at* or *prompted* in order to make the correct answers highly probable. These answers, once "reinforced," are then overlearned through their repeated use as new material is grafted onto that already learned. It is evident that the person who constructs a program must be aware of the *organization of knowledge,* both its logical organization and its psychological organization, in order to build knowledge and understanding in this way. The programmer does her best to anticipate what will happen, then in practice she corrects the program through tryout until it can be mastered by its intended learners with a minimum of errors, usually in one run through the program. The result of the learning is then tested by a conventional-type examination to see if the material has indeed been mastered and can be applied appropriately in new contexts.

Skinner (1958) made the case for a similarity between programmed instruction and individual tutoring, as follows:

1. A good tutor begins where the pupil is, and does not insist on moving beyond what the pupil can comprehend.

2. A good tutor moves at the rate that is consistent with the ability of a pupil to learn.

3. A good tutor does not permit false answers to remain uncorrected.

4. A good tutor does not lecture; instead, by his hints and questioning he helps the pupil to find and state answers for himself.

According to Skinner, all these qualities are found in a good program.

Varieties of programming. The type of program advocated by Skinner, that which moves step by step through a single set of materials, has come to be called linear programming. Another type, commonly associated with the name of Norman Crowder, is known as a *branching program.* In the programmed books which use this method (e.g., Crowder & Martin, 1961), multiple-choice answers are provided, and the answer the student selects directs him to a different page in the book. The book is thus a "scrambled one" which is read most irregularly. The correct answer leads to a page on which the next bit of instruction is given, with new alternatives. An incorrect answer is pointed out, with some comments as to why this might have been selected, and then the learner is sent back to make another choice. Crowder believes that students who are ill prepared should always have a way to go back to simpler materials, and those who are well prepared should be able to bypass some of the material; hence his later developments provide for these alternative paths through the material. Linear programs of a more modern sort also provide for some kind of review for those who wish to go back to earlier parts of the program, and some kind of skipping for those ready to go ahead. Computer-based programs provide the maximum amount of flexibility in these respects, including alternative paths and different examples for those who may need them. Thus programming is no more a single line of development than the teaching machine is a single type of equipment.

Much research has been done comparing instruction by programs to traditional lecture methods. Such comparisons show that programmed learning is as good as, and often better than, lecture methods of teaching. Research comparing different variations within programming has proven frustratingly uninformative, as the students seem to learn about as much regardless of what the program requires them to do. Thus, results in a final exam are about the same whether the learning program requires the student to construct his answer versus select or recognize a correct answer, whether the student responds versus merely studies the correct answer to questions, whether the feedback is given immediately versus after a delay, whether the programs follow in a linear order versus branch on errors, and so on (McKeachie, 1974). One suspects all the experiments with null results are due to the low power of the statistical design, and the relatively gross, nonanalytic nature of the "final-exam" criterion. Thus, students may "make up" for a poor program by studying or reviewing on their own for a course grade.

Perhaps the greatest complaint against programmed textbooks, or programs for machines, is that ultimately they are very slow moving, repetitively dull, and boring to bright students. Students taught only with the program feel a real need for contact with a human teacher who will answer questions, help clarify the goals of the course or its organization, and so on. It seems very likely that the teacher contact also supplies much of the social incentives to motivate and sustain the student's continued interaction with the teaching machine. As with TV or radio courses, teaching machines work best when a human tutor is added as a motivator.

Computer-Assisted Instruction (CAI)

Computer-assisted instruction has by now taken on so many dimensions that it can no longer be considered a simple derivative of the teaching machine or of the kind of programmed learning that Skinner introduced. The teaching machine and the linear or branching programs are, to be sure, its immediate ancestors, but it has evolved rapidly.

One great advantage of the computer over other kinds of educational technology is that it can provide a very flexible presentation of materials to the learner and keep track of the progress of a number of learners at the same time. A "readout" from the computer can show where all the learners are at a given time, and what their progress has been from some earlier point of reference.

Several modes of computer-assisted instruction have come into use (Atkinson & Wilson, 1969). The first is the tutorial drill-and-practice procedure, as an outgrowth of programmed learning; this is doubtless the most prevalent mode, and the one used in the systems developed by Atkinson and by Suppes at Stanford. This mode is, of course, commonly used by teachers without the computer; the computer has the advantage of individualizing the activities and of introducing greater learning efficiency through the management of the learning by the computer. A somewhat different method has been used in the teaching of statistics at the University of California at Los Angeles. The student learns a computer language through which she can manipulate large bodies of data, and hence come out of the statistics course able to handle data. Another use is in connection with games that simulate actual problems, whereby complex decisions in relation to metropolitan problems or political control systems can be made and their consequences studied. One such system developed by the Board of Cooperative Educational Services in Westchester County, New York, deals with economic problems through what is called the Sumerian game. The student rules a mythical empire and allocates manpower and other resources; the computer estimates the interactive consequences of her decisions. Even laboratory experiments in chemistry can be carried out without the student's handling equipment and chemicals (Bunderson, 1967). The flexibility of the computer is enormous; hence, any preconception as to the inherent limitations of computer-assisted instruction is likely to be false.

The development of CAI at Stanford University provides a representative case history of the growth of both the technology and the acceptance of CAI. A small system was developed beginning in 1963, and then a large-scale program was undertaken after funds became available under the Elementary and Secondary Education Act of 1965. A system making use of the IBM 1500 was developed jointly by IBM and the Stanford group and became operative in 1966. From the small start of computer drill for 41 fourth-grade children in one school in 1965, the system grew until by 1968 approximately 3000 students received daily lessons in initial reading, arithmetic, spelling, logic, and elementary Russian in seven nearby schools and in locations as far distant from California as McComb, Mississippi, and Morehead, Kentucky. All instruction was controlled by one central computer located at Stanford. In expanded form, the system is still in operation today, run by a commercial computer-instruction company.

The original 1500 Tutorial System for reading instruction had a complex station or terminal at which the student worked, consisting of a screen on which images could be projected from frames randomly accessed under computer control, a cathode-ray tube on which material could be presented, a light pen by which touch-probe responses on the cathode-ray tube could be made and recorded, a typewriter keyboard, a set of earphones, and a microphone (Figure 15.9). This device, a kind of virtuoso of instructional technology, served its purpose in showing what could be done; however, as so often happens with new products, it has gradually become simplified without much loss in effectiveness—see Figure 15.10 (Atkinson & Fletcher, 1972).

The motivational problems with the computer turn out to be different from what might have been expected. Instead of being put off by its formidable mechanical qualities, the student often becomes very fond of the computer because it is responsive. Therefore, one form of motivation may be to deny a student the opportunity to use it, which she will interpret as deprivation or punishment (Hess & Tenezakis,

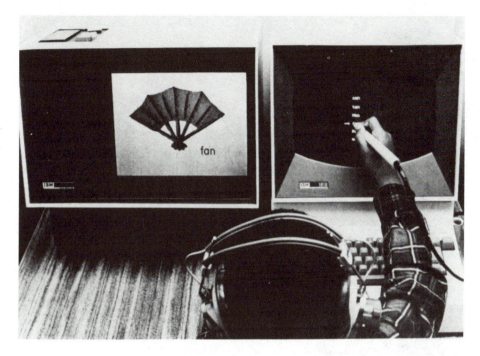

Figure 15.9. Student terminal used for tutorial instruction in initial reading. (Courtesy of R. C. Atkinson.)

1970). Access to the computer lessons is then used to reward other educational exercises.

Such teaching systems have proven very effective; students learn well on them, and the systems can do many of the drill-and-practice lessons and thereby free teachers for more challenging tutoring. Children progress through the instructional program at their own pace, but the amount learned is largely controlled by their time on the computer.

A lingering problem is always that of costs. Economic feasibility depends on sufficient use of the computer to reduce the hourly cost per student. It has been estimated that for a single system serving 500 terminals (enough for a small elementary school, a junior high school, and a high school in close proximity), the cost could be kept to $0.11 per student hour, about

what is now spent on traditionally administered instruction in rural schools (Kopstein & Seidel, 1969). Nonetheless, CAI is widely viewed by school districts as an extravagant luxury they cannot afford in times of tight budgets. When budgets must be cut, innovative hardware seems always to be among the first to go—rather a machine than a teacher who needs the job. Another obstacle to adoption is that not sufficiently diverse CAI programs are commercially available for specific curricula that vary across school districts.

Intelligent CAI

A complaint among those working in artificial intelligence (see Chapter 12) is that standard CAI makes very little use of the real power of the computer, that it is functioning in these applications as an "ex-

Figure 15.10. Simplified terminal later used for instruction in initial reading. (Courtesy of R. C. Atkinson.)

pensive page-turner," and is rather far removed from the qualities of a real tutor. One might as well have the student use a programmed textbook. For example, the student cannot ask questions of the computer or get it to distinguish confusing concepts. The programmer must anticipate all possible puzzles and questions, and try to answer them in her program—an impossible task. The division of "knowledge" into tiny frames seems ad hoc. While the standard CAI program can tell a student his response is wrong and tell him the correct answer, it cannot make hypotheses based on a student's history of mistakes as to where his real misunderstandings or difficulties lie. In present CAI programs, the computer's representation of a student's knowledge is simply the frame number (or lesson number) in the skill-strand

he is working on, as though one's knowledge of physics is simply the set of problems one has been able to work correctly so far.

Carbonell (1970) and his colleagues started a trend toward installing more human-tutoring qualities into CAI systems with their SCHOLAR program, a miniature system for teaching facts about South American geography. The basic goal was to have a computer-based Socratic tutor that would use its knowledge of geography to compose diagnostic questions to ask the student; the tutor could understand and evaluate a student's (typed) complex answers to its questions, diagnose which parts of the student's knowledge were defective and needed learning, and respond intelligently to any unexpected questions the student might ask about geography. These are very advanced goals, indeed, and SCHOLAR and its successors have only partially achieved them; yet they serve as future goals to aim for.

The components of an intelligent CAI system are its *domain expertise* regarding the knowledge it is to impart, a *student model* indicating what the student does and does not know at any moment, and a set of *tutoring strategies* specifying how the to-be-learned information is to be presented to the learner. Additionally, the system must have capabilities for understanding natural language questions and for generating answers in reasonable English. No current system has perfected all these components. Rather, a given researcher will concentrate on developing only one or two components of the larger system—say the question-answering part.

SCHOLAR used a relatively primitive language-understander based on Case Grammar, a semantic network to represent its knowledge of geography, and a set of intersection and search rules to infer answers to questions. A novel feature of SCHOLAR's knowledge representation was *importance tags* that were attached to each fact, indicating what level of detail was being reached about some topic; importance tags were used heuristically to answer questions, especially to focus in on the given level of detail that the student wished to discuss. If asked "Tell me about Peru," SCHOLAR would give only the more important facts. The designers of SCHOLAR (see Collins et al., 1975) noted a number of interesting facts about question answering. One novel distinction centered upon whether the question referred to a "closed set" of a small list of objects (say, countries in South America), or an "open set," where only the more important members of an indefinitely large set are stored explicitly in the knowledge base (e.g., foodstuffs grown in Peru). The nature of the set is tagged in the knowledge base and is used to answer questions.

Let us consider how SCHOLAR uses open and closed tags on a category. If asked "Is Denmark a country of South America?" and it does not know anything about Denmark, it will search its closed set of South American countries and, failing to find Denmark in that set, will answer "Definitely not." If asked whether rubber is a product of Guyana (which fact is not stored explicitly), it reasons to a plausible answer using the fact that a country's products is an open set. In this case, SCHOLAR first would note that other countries that have rubber products list this as an important fact, and since it hasn't rubber among Guyanan products of that importance, it concludes "Probably not, otherwise I would have known such an important fact."

This heuristic method and the many others that are programmed into SCHOLAR for plausible reasoning are fascinating and human-like, and make SCHOLAR an interesting simulation of human question answering. However, while SCHOLAR was an interesting theory of human question answering, it never reached the advanced stage necessary for it to actually tutor geography students.

There have been many fascinating later developments in designing intelligent CAI systems, but only brief mention can be made of them here (see J. S. Brown & Goldstein, 1977, for some review). The WHY system of Collins (1976) and Stevens and Collins (1977) teaches students about systems that have causal relations among concepts, where students often have misconceptions about why processes work as they do. WHY tries to help the student discover the correct causal process by considering a range of simple cases he may already know. For example, in teaching the causes of rainfall, WHY gets the student to first guess a causal rule, then it chooses counter-examples to force successive revisions of the rule, proceeding in a Socratic manner according to several "tutoring rules" to help the student formulate a causal rule of sufficient generality. The tutoring rules of WHY, and the way it follows overall goals of instruction, are very good instructional strategies for any teacher to follow.

Another intelligent CAI program is SOPHIE, developed by J. S. Brown and Burton (1975), which teaches problem-solving skills to engineers. This program focuses on *troubleshooting* in a piece of defective electronic equipment with a known circuit diagram. From known voltage or current measurements of the circuit, students hypothesize "faults," and SOPHIE instructs them on reasonable ways to concoct and evaluate successive hypotheses.

Another example of a troubleshooting program in teaching is BUGGY, also developed by J. S. Brown and Burton (1978), which helps teachers diagnose the underlying causes of a student's errors in doing arithmetic problems. BUGGY was motivated by the belief that many student errors are not random but very systematic, and are created by some basic misconception (some "bug") of how a math operation is to be performed. The effective teacher must be able to diagnose the procedural bug and prescribe precise remediation. The BUGGY program takes some task, such as adding three-digit numbers, represents it as a network of subprocedures (e.g., adding numbers only in same column at one time), and produces examples of what addition errors will occur if one or more subprocedures are defective. When acting as an instructor, BUGGY chooses a procedural bug that students often have, and produces a sample of addition errors with this bug. A teacher examines these examples and hypothesizes what the bug is, as in the SOPHIE system; the BUGGY program will then produce other examples for the teacher to check his bug-hypothesis against. This trains teachers in diagnosis. BUGGY itself can also infer bugs from the pattern of a student's errors; it does this by throwing a bug (error) into some sub-

skill of its procedural network (e.g., carrying a 1 from the first-column sum over to the *third* column), calculating answers for the student's problems to see whether the types of errors and their pattern match, and continuing to try out bugs until some close match is found. In a subtraction test given to 1,325 students in grades 4, 5, and 6, BUGGY was able to find one or another consistent bug in its procedural network (for the subtraction task) that would account for the error patterns of 40 percent of the students; the others presumably were showing some random careless errors or multiple-bug errors. Such diagnostic information is useful in tutoring a specific student, and the frequency of types of bugs in a population of students suggests areas of difficulty where teacher efforts should be concentrated.

These intelligent tutoring programs are clearly in an embryonic stage. Several domains of expertise are being explored and many tutoring strategies are being suggested. Much attention is being given to details of knowledge representation (of the expert) and plausible question answering by the tutor. The systems that now exist are crude prototypes and are a long way from being ready for practical use in the field. However, the thought that goes into intelligent tutors leads to some of the most advanced and sophisticated recommendations or heuristics available for teachers to use in practice. Thus, the actual benefits of the research may not lie so much in practical working programs as in tutoring heuristics that can be taught to human instructors.

Personalized Systems of Instruction (The Keller Plan)

In a seminal article (1968), the psychologist Fred Keller presented a method of course instruction that was designed to do away with lecturing and rigid scheduling and to allow the student to progress at her own pace and demonstrate her grasp of the materials. The program was developed originally for teaching introductory psychology courses in college, but has by now been expanded to any content course at college or high school level. After many years as a college teacher, Keller became convinced (as have many others) that lecturing was an exceedingly poor means of imparting information to students; he believed that if lectures had any justification at all it was to serve as motivators for learning behaviors the students would perform outside of class.

To replace lecture teaching, Keller suggested that the teacher prepare a large number of *learning units* for his course materials. Each learning unit should be associated with some text reading; the teacher's "lecture notes," or discussions of the readings, would highlight points and state emphatically which ones were to be learned. Preparing such units requires teachers to become very clear about exactly what they want their students to learn; they must decide how to divide a subject into many small self-contained units, and how to present them, and how to assess the students' mastery of them. Typical units involve a major topic (e.g., "biological drives") and often coincide with a chapter or chapter section of an introductory text on the subject. A typical course might be divided into 20 or so learning units.

After preparing notes for each learning unit, the teacher allows the students to work at their own pace, starting at the beginning unit. Students must take a short quiz over the essential points of a unit, and they must pass it at a high level of proficiency (usually 90 percent or better) in order to be allowed to progress to the next unit. If they fall short of this criterion on a quiz, a proctor or the teacher reviews the missed material with them; the students review the unit again and return to take a different test on that unit. Unit tests can

be taken at any time students feel they are prepared and below-criterion test performances do not enter into their grades. The proctor records only those unit tests each student has passed, and grades are determined by how many units the student has covered during a standard academic semester or quarter. Lectures may be given, but attendance is optional; the lectures function to enhance interest by live demonstrations, interviews, and films relevant to the units of the course.

This method of instruction is referred to as the *personalized system of instruction* or PSI. From the student's perspective, PSI is personalized in that he proceeds at his own pace, studies and learns largely on his own, receives many quizzes and much feedback on the progress of his learning, and engages in tutorial discussions with a proctor. In comparison with traditional lecture classes with the standard midterm and final exams, students in PSI courses always know exactly where they stand in attaining course objectives and what they have yet to do to attain one or another grade. They can work quickly or slowly, depending on the pressures of other courses or jobs. Some students work so fast that they complete all the required units by midterm of an academic quarter. But PSI teachers are not dismayed by such events. Since they have decided what things must be known to pass the course, they believe that knowledge has been fairly assessed; furthermore, evidence suggests that the quality and retention of information is largely independent of how rapidly it was acquired.

Since the advent of PSI, many studies have compared students' learning by PSI with those learning the equivalent materials in conventional lecture courses. These comparisons have proven extraordinarily favorable to PSI. Students learn as much, often more, under a PSI course; they like the subject matter and the course; and they readily take more PSI courses and tout their benefits. Once skeptical teachers have been converted to its use, whole departments—even whole colleges—have converted to the PSI system. PSI has been shown effective in teaching many types of courses; a paper by Kulik, Kulik, and Carmichael (1974) reviews its success in teaching a broad spectrum of college science courses.

As have most teaching-method packages, many variants of PSI have been tried out, and adopters are constantly experimenting with the format and rules of course operation. Many of these variations, with attendant comparative evaluations, are reported in the *Journal of Personalized Instruction*. One effective variation is the use of many student proctors, often student "graduates" of the course, who tutor their peers currently taking the course. The proctors often learn a tremendous amount themselves (as shown in their advance course work in the field), by preparing oral exams for their student charges or tutoring those who need it. In PSI courses, the definition of a unit is flexible and may include a field trip, performing an experiment, a quiz over several related public lectures, and so on. The proficiency criterion for unit mastery, enabling the student to proceed, has been varied from 70 to 100 percent as required and has had the expected results: a high proficiency requirement for progressing to the next unit causes the students on average to learn more about fewer units in a fixed time. The attractive feature about the PSI framework is that it allows so much individual tailoring of course units and assignments according to the teacher's conception of what is important to be taught.

One obstacle to widespread adoption of the PSI methed is that it demands lots of work from the instructor to set it up the first time it is offered. Many unit notes, teaching aids, manuals, and alternate quizzes must be prepared in advance of offering the course, and this initial effort is more than many teachers wish to make. More-

over, maintaining the course requires constant attention, enlisting the aid of proctors, meeting regularly with proctors and slow students, and arranging for stimulating class demonstrations. If an instructor is to teach a given course only a few times, she may feel this initial effort will not be repaid by the reduced work in catch-up years.

A second obstacle to PSI is that many students, teachers, and administrators feel that a class *must* have live lectures, and any attempt to get away from this may be viewed as teacher negligence and laziness. The virtues of lecturing are often extolled in terms of motivating students, answering their questions, stimulating thought, and spontaneous creativity (not to mention humor). These traditional beliefs persist and override PSI despite evidence that, on the whole, the average live lecture is a poor instructional medium. Obviously, the lecture format is chosen for other reasons and not because it imparts a great deal of on-the-spot learning.

Perhaps the largest problem for PSI programs is that they clash with traditional conceptions of course scheduling and grading, which determine the day-to-day functioning of college (or high school) administrators and students alike. Often a "course room" (like a language lab) must be set aside where any numbers of students may go to study any given lesson—for example, to listen individually to a taped demonstration with slides—or to take any given unit test. But beyond that, the ideas of the unit-mastery system, of multiple retesting without penalty, of letting students continue until they pass as many units as they desire—all raise havoc with traditional grading practices. The most common way of conducting a PSI college course, where grades are determined by how many units a student completes in a semester or quarter, so motivates the students that a huge percentage of them earn *A*s in a course, and most of the remainder earn *B*s.

And these grades are not easily won. Students repeatedly acknowledge that they work much harder and longer on a PSI course than on a conventional lecture course, and believe that they learn much more. But college registrars and deans are bothered by large introductory courses in which the majority of students receive an *A*.

The PSI philosophy involves a new orientation toward education, proficiency, and grades. Grades presumably once told us what percent of the course objectives were attained by a student; but in mastery learning, the students are learning all the important objectives the instructor has specified—if they did not, they could not proceed to the next unit. As everyone is well aware, grades are also used to compare and rank-order students, and it is this comparative function that is being lost when students learn with PSI courses. Grades are used for screening, for selection, for deciding who shall be favored with job offers, admission to professional schools, graduate school fellowships, and the like. Companies or professional schools want the "brighter" students, and they look to course grades to help with that selection. But perhaps it is time for schools to reconsider their true mission instead of blindly filling the evaluative role that has been thrust upon them by society. That mission is to teach, to inform, to satisfy curiosity, to facilitate discovery, to foster the growth of skilled, competent individuals, to promote knowledge, analytic insightfulness, and perhaps wisdom.

PROBLEMS IN APPLICATIONS

We have briefly reviewed several of the teaching devices and innovative instructional methods that have been developed by learning psychologists. It is obvious that each new device, like a simulator or a teaching simulation-game, requires research to develop it, test its effectiveness, vary it, and sharpen and delimit its usefulness. The process requires the cooperation of "applied behavioral engineers" as well as academic psychologists and the instructors or teachers in the field. There is much work to be done of an engineering nature. Once some idea to, say, improve instruction in arithmetic is tried out successfully in the laboratory, it has yet to be incorporated into an experimental curriculum with local sympathetic teachers. Once it passes that test, the curriculum may be sent to more distant schools and to less willing teachers, who will surely not follow the exactly prescribed procedures in administering the system. If, however, the material continues to educate successfully, the next phase is to package it for wider use, to advocate or promote its adoption by local or state school boards, to prepare manuals, to train teachers to use the materials or lessons properly, and so on. Clearly, most learning researchers are ill equipped by talents, temperament, or career goals to engage in many of these phases. Hence, they are most likely to turn their few ideas for educational methods or materials over to an educationalist or curriculum development center. Clearly, the full set of activities needed to get a curriculum idea adopted is a job for a specialist; therefore much of the recent educational funding by the United States government has been for large research centers that develop experimental curricula and test them under field conditions.

The Problem of Educational Innovation

In something as complex as a school system, innovative new methods often encounter obstacles. The best of equipment may lie idle, the best of resources remain unused, the best of techniques sabotaged, unless there is care in introducing the new methods or new materials to all concerned. Once the basic-science principles have been established and the applications validated in practice schoolrooms, their more widespread adoption is by no means guaranteed, nor, if the adoption is forced, is there assurance that the desired results will be forthcoming. Abstractly, the steps of innovation are clear enough: (a) provide a sound research-based program, validated in tryout; (b) have the program packaged in such a way that it is available, as in good textbooks, supplementary readings in the form of pamphlets, films, programs for teaching machines, and guides for the teacher; (c) provide testing materials by which it can be ascertained if the objectives of the program have indeed been realized, with appropriate normative data on these evaluative instruments; (d) provide service training of the teacher to overcome the teacher's resistance to new methods and materials and to gain his enthusiastic acceptance of the program as something valuable, as well as to train him in its use; and (e) be sure there is support for the program from the community, school boards, parents, and others concerned with the schools. To cite one example, the resistance to widescale adoption of PSI teaching methods comes from teachers who do not want to expend the effort, or who love to lecture, and from administrators upset with the high grades of PSI students. Although research results argue for PSI as do students, the obstacles come from other quarters of the academic community.

We have not always appraised our innovative strategies carefully. We have sometimes gone overboard for the novel and untried; at other times we have been very resistant. Commercialism and vested interests enter in unpleasant ways, sometimes supported, unfortunately, by factions of the educational profession itself. Here, then, is a task calling for wisdom and sensitivity. The psychological contributions to the task may come more from social psychology than from the psychology of learning, for the processes are those of social control and attitude change. But unless there is serious concern about the appropriate ways in which to bring about innovation, schools are likely to be the victims of whims, rather than the heirs of the best tradition we can establish through cooperative effort.

There are some specific suggestions that might be given consideration. It would be desirable, for example, for every school system, of whatever size, to have somewhere within it a school building, or at least a set of schoolrooms, devoted to in-service training of teachers and to innovation; these are ongoing matters important at the community level and cannot be left to teacher-training colleges or universities. Both children and teachers could be rotated through these rooms in order to try out innovations before there is firm commitment to them. A few teaching terminals for computer-assisted instruction or some closed-circuit television projectors could be tried out without investing in them for a whole school system. Teachers could have a voice in saying whether or not they wanted the new devices, or in selecting among various possibilities. Usually no harm would be done in waiting for a while if teachers were not ready, for methods imposed on teachers are unlikely to prove successful. Some of the innovations to be tried out might be those of successful local teachers themselves, here given the opportunity to show their colleagues how they do it in their own classrooms. Members of the school board and representatives of the parents could be brought in also to observe such testing. The principles of tryout before acceptance, of choice by those who are to use the method, seem to be sound ones. If the new methods are indeed good, they will find acceptance.

In order to build a sound connection between the experimental studies of learning and the classroom, we need a series of steps, for applied science consists of more than applying principles to practice. The main point is that in the research and development phases, a collaboration is called for between psychologist, subject-matter specialist, and teacher; beyond this, careful consideration must be given to techniques of innovation. If we achieve success in integrating these phases, we will move toward that improvement of education which will be satisfying to us all.

SUPPLEMENTARY READINGS

The following books are helpful in attempting to appraise theories of instruction, educational technology, and educational research.

Theories of Instruction

BLOCK, J. H., ed. (1971). *Mastery learning.*

BRUNER, J. S. (1966). *Toward a theory of instruction.*

GAGNÉ, R. M. (1970). *The conditions of learning.*

KELLER, F. S., & RIBES-INESTA, E., eds. (1974). *Behavior modification: Applications to education.*

HILGARD, E. R., ed. (1964a). Theories of learning *and instruction.*

SKINNER, B. F. (1968). *The technology of teaching.*

Educational Technology

ATKINSON, R. C., & WILSON, H. A., eds. (1969). *Computer-assisted instruction: A book of readings.*

CARNEGIE COMMISSION ON HIGHER EDUCATION (1972). *The fourth revolution: Instructional technology in higher education.*

CHU, G. C., & SCHRAMM, W. (1967). *Learning from television: What the research says.*

LANGE, P. C., ed. (1967). *Programed instruction.*

LEVIÈN, R. E. (1972). *The emerging technology: Instructional uses of the computer in higher education.*

SUPPES, P., JERMAN, M., & BRIAN, D. (1968). *Computer-assisted instruction: Stanford's 1965–66 arithmetic program.*

SUPPES, P., & MORNINGSTAR, M. (1972). *Computer-assisted instruction at Stanford, 1966–68.*

TICKTON, S. G., ed. (1970). *To improve learning: An evaluation of instructional technology.*

Educational Research

CRONBACH, L. J., & SUPPES, P., eds. (1969). *Research for tomorrow's schools.*

GAGE, N. L., ed. (1963). *Handbook of research on teaching.*

GAGNÉ, R. M., & GEPHART, W. L., eds. (1968). *Learning research and school subjects.*

GLASER, R., ed. (1978). *Advances in instructional psychology.* Vol. 1.

SUPPES, P., ed. (1978). *Impact of research on education: Some case studies.*

WITTROCK, M. C., ed. (1977). *Learning and instruction: Readings in educational research.*

REFERENCES

ABERNETHY, E. M. (1940). The effect of changed environmental conditions upon the results of college examinations. *J. Psychol.*, 10: 293–301.

ABRAMSON, L. Y., SELIGMAN, M. E. P ., & TEASDALE, J. E. (1978). Learned helplessness in humans: Critique and reformulation. *J. abn. Psychol.*, 87: 49–74.

ALBERT, D. J. (1966). The effect of spreading depression on the consolidation of learning. *Neuropsychol.*, 4: 49–64.

ALLEN, G. A., & ESTES, W. K. (1972). Acquisition of correct choices and value judgments in binary choice learning with differential rewards. *Psychon. Sci.*, 27: 68–72.

ALLISON, J. (1976). Contrast, induction, facilitation, suppression, and conservation. *J. exp. Anal. of Behav.*, 25: 185–99.

ALLPORT, G. W., & POSTMAN, L. (1947). *The psychology of rumor.* New York: Holt, Rinehart and Winston.

AMAREL, S. (1968). On representations of problems of reasoning about actions. In D. Michie, ed., *Machine intelligence.* Vol. 3. New York: American Elsevier.

AMMONS, R. B. (1962). Psychology of the scientist. II: Clark L. Hull and his "Idea Books." *Percept. Mot. Skills,* 15: 800–802.

AMSEL, A. (1958). The role of frustrative nonreward in noncontinuous reward situations. *Psychol. Bull.,* 55: 102–19.

AMSEL, A. (1962). Frustrative nonreward in partial reinforcement and discrimination learning. *Psychol. Rev.,* 69: 306–28.

AMSEL, A. (1965). On inductive versus deductive approaches and neo-Hullian behaviorism. In B. B. Wolman, ed., *Scientific psychology.* New York: Basic Books. Pp. 187–206.

AMSEL, A. (1967). Partial reinforcement effects on vigor and persistence. In K. W. Spence & J. T. Spence, eds., *The psychology of learning and motivation.* Vol. 1. New York: Academic Press.

AMSEL, A., & WARD, J. S. (1965). Frustration and persistence: Resistance to discrimination following prior experience with the discriminanda. *Psychol. Monogr.,* 79, No. 4 (Whole No. 597).

ANAND, B. K., CHHINA, G. S., & SINGH, B. (1961). Some aspects of electroencephalographic studies in yogis. *Electroencephalography and Clinical Neurophysiology,* 13: 452–56. Also in C. T. Tart, ed., *Altered states of consciousness: A book of readings.* New York: Wiley.

ANDERSON, J. R. (1972). FRAN: A simulation model of free recall. In G. H. Bower, ed., *The psychology of learning and motivation: Advances in research and theory.* Vol. 5. New York: Academic Press.

ANDERSON, J. R. (1975). Computer simulation of a language-acquisition system: A first report. In R. Solso, ed., *Information processing and cognition: The Coyola symposium.* Hillsdale, N.J.: Erlbaum. Pp. 295–349.

ANDERSON, J. R. (1976). *Language, memory, and thought.* Hillsdale, N.J.: Erlbaum.

ANDERSON, J. R., & BOWER, G. H. (1972a). Recognition and retrieval processes in free recall. *Psychol. Rev.,* 79: 97–123.

ANDERSON, J. R., & BOWER, G. H. (1972b). Configural properties of sentence memory. *J. verb. Learn. verb. Behav.,* 11: 594–605.

ANDERSON, J. R., & BOWER, G. H. (1973). *Human associative memory.* Washington, D.C.: V. H. Winston.

ANDERSON, J. R., & BOWER, G. H. (1974). A

propositional theory of recognition memory. *Mem. and Cog.*, 2: 406–12.

ANDERSON, N. H. (1964). An evaluation of stimulus sampling theory: Comments on Professor Estes' paper. In A. W. Melton, ed., *Categories of human learning*. New York: Academic Press.

ANDERSON, R. C., & CARTER, J. F. (1972). Retroactive inhibition of meaningful-learned sentences. *Am. Ed. Res. J.* 9: 443–48.

ANDERSON, R. C., & MYROW, D. L. (1971). Retroactive inhibition of meaningful discourse. *J. ed. Psychol., Monogr. Suppl.*, 62: 81–94.

ANDERSON, R. C., & WATTS, G. H. (1971). Response competition in the forgetting of paired associates. *J. verb. Learn. verb. Behav.*, 10: 29–34.

ANTIOCH COLLEGE (1960). *Experiment in French language instruction: Second report, 1959–1960*. Yellow Springs, Ohio: Antioch Press.

ARNOLD, P. (1976). On the nature of associations. Unpublished Ph.D. dissertation. Stanford University.

ARNOLD, P. G., & BOWER, G. H. (1972). Perceptual conditions affecting ease of association. *J. exp. Psychol.*, 93: 176–80.

ASCH, S. E. (1969). Reformulation of the problem of association. *Amer. Psychol.*, 24: 92–102.

ASCH, S. E., CERASO, J., & HEIMER, W. (1960). Perceptual conditions of association. *Psychol. Monogr.*, 57 (Whole No. 3).

ASHBY, W. R. (1952). *Design for a brain*. New York: Wiley.

ATKINSON, R. C. (1962). Choice behavior and monetary payoffs. In J. Criswell, H. Solomon, & P. Suppes, eds., *Mathematical methods in small group processes*. Stanford: Stanford Univ. Press.

ATKINSON, R. C. (1972). Ingredients for a theory of instruction. *Amer. Psychol.*, 27: 921–31.

ATKINSON, R. C. (1975). Mnemotechnics in second-language learning. *Amer. Psychol.*, 30: 821–28.

ATKINSON, R. C., BOWER, G. H., & CROTHERS, E. J. (1965). *Introduction to mathematical learning theory*. New York: Wiley.

ATKINSON, R. C., & CROTHERS, E. J. (1964). A comparison of paired associate learning models having different acquisition and retention axioms. *J. math. Psychol.*, 1: 285–315.

ATKINSON, R. C., & ESTES, W. K. (1963). Stimulus sampling theory. In R. D. Luce, R. R. Bush, & E. Galanter, eds., *Handbook of mathematical psychology*. Vol. 2. New York: Wiley.

ATKINSON, R. C., & FLETCHER, J. D. (1972). Teaching children to read with a computer. *The Reading Teacher*, 25: 319–27.

ATKINSON, R. C., & PAULSON, J. A. (1972). An approach to the psychology of instruction. *Psychol. Bull.*, 78: 49–61.

ATKINSON, R. C., & RAUGH, M. R. (1975). An application of the mnemonic keyword method to the acquisition of a Russian vocabulary. *J. exp. Psychol.: Human Learning and Memory*, 104: 126–33.

ATKINSON, R. C., & SHIFFRIN, R. M. (1965). *Mathematical models for memory and learning*. Technical Report No. 79, Psychology Series, Institute for Mathematical Studies in the Social Sciences. Stanford: Stanford Univ. Press.

ATKINSON, R. C., & SHIFFRIN, R. M. (1968). Human memory: A proposed system and its control processes. In K. W. Spence & J. T. Spence, eds., *The Psychology of Learning and Motivation*. Vol. 2. New York: Academic Press.

ATKINSON, R. C., & SHIFFRIN, R. M. (1971). The control of short-term memory. *Sci. Amer.* (August), pp. 82–90.

ATKINSON, R. C., & WICKENS, T. D. (1971). Human memory and the concept of reinforcement. In R. Glaser, ed., *The nature of reinforcement*. New York: Academic Press.

ATKINSON, R. C., & WILSON, H. A., eds. (1969). Computer-assisted instruction. In *Computer-assisted instruction: A book of readings*. New York: Academic Press. Pp. 3–14.

AUDLEY, R. J. (1960). A stochastic model for individual choice behavior. *Psychol. Rev.,* 67: 1–15.

AUSUBEL, D. P. (1960). The use of advance organizers in the learning and retention of meaningful verbal learning. *J. ed. Psychol.,* 51: 267–72.

AZRIN, N. H. (1964). Aggression: A speech to American Psychological Association, Sept. 6, 1964, Los Angeles. Title listed in *Amer. Psychol.,* 17: 501.

AZRIN, N. H., HAKE, D. F., & HUTCHINSON, R. R. (1965). Elicitation of aggression by a physical blow. *J. exp. Anal. Behav.,* 8: 55–57.

AZRIN, N. H., & HOLZ, W. C. (1966). Punishment. In W. K. Honig, ed., *Operant behavior: Areas of research and application.* New York: Appleton-Century-Crofts. Pp. 380–447.

AZRIN, N. H., HUTCHINSON, R. R., & HAKE, R. F. (1966). Extinction-induced aggression. *J. exp. Anal. Behav.,* 9: 191–204.

BABKIN, B. P. (1949). *Pavlov: A biography.* Chicago: Univ. of Chicago Press.

BADDELEY, A. D. (1978). The trouble with levels: A reexamination of Craik and Lockhart's framework for memory research. *Psychol. Rev.,* 85: 139–52.

BANDURA, A. (1962). Social learning through imitation. In M. R. Jones ed., *Nebraska Symposium on Motivation: 1962.* Lincoln: Univ. of Nebraska Press. Pp. 211–69.

BANDURA, A. (1965). Vicarious processes: A case of no-trial learning. In L. Berkowitz, ed., *Advances in experimental social psychology.* Vol. 2. New York: Academic Press.

BANDURA, A. (1969). *Principles of behavior modification.* New York: Holt, Rinehart and Winston.

BANDURA, A. (1971a). *Social learning theory.* New York: General Learning Press.

BANDURA, A. (1971b). *Psychological modeling: Conflicting theories.* New York: Aldine-Atherton.

BANDURA, A. (1977a). *Social learning theory.* Englewood Cliffs, N.J.: Prentice-Hall.

BANDURA, A. (1977b). Self-efficacy: Toward a unifying theory of behavior change. *Psychol. Rev.,* 84: 191–215.

BANDURA, A. (1978). Reflections on self-efficacy. *Adv. behav. Res. Ther.,* 1: 237–69.

BANDURA, A., GRUSEC, J. E., & MENLOVE, F. L. (1966). Observational learning as a function of symbolization and incentive set. *Child Devel.,* 37: 499–506.

BANDURA, A., & JEFFERY, R. W. (1973). Role of symbolic coding and rehearsal processes in observational learning. *J. Pers. soc. Psychol.,* 26: 122–30.

BANDURA, A., & MAHONEY, M. J. (1974). Maintenance and transfer of self-reinforcement functions. *Behav. Res. Ther.,* 12: 89–97.

BANDURA, A., & WALTERS, R. H. (1963). *Social learning and personality development.* New York: Holt, Rinehart and Winston.

BARCLAY, J. R., et al. (1974). Comprehension and semantic flexibility. *J. verb. Learn. verb. Behav.,* 13: 471–81.

BARNES, J. M., & UNDERWOOD, B. J. (1959). Fate of first-list associations in transfer theory. *J. exp. Psychol.,* 58: 97–105.

BARONDES, S. H., & COHEN, H. D. (1966). Puromycin effect on successive phases of memory storage. *Science,* 15: 594–95.

BARRETT, R. J., PEYSER, C. S., & McHOSE, J. H. (1965). Effects of complete and incomplete reward reduction on a subsequent response. *Psychon. Sci.,* 3: 277–78.

BARSALOU, L. W. (1979). Ad hoc categories and cross-classification. Manuscript in preparation. Stanford University.

BARTLETT, F. C. (1932). *Remembering.* London: Cambridge Univ. Press.

BASMAJIAN, J. V., KUKULKA, C. G., NARAYAN, M. G., & TAKEBE, K. (1975). Biofeedback treatment of foot-drop after stroke compared with standard rehabilitation technique. *Arch. phys. Med. Rehab.,* 56: 231–36.

BAXTER, B. L., GLUCKMAN, M. L., STEIN, L., & SCERNI, R. A. (1974). Self-injection of apomorphine in the rat: Positive reinforcement by a dopamine receptor stimulant. *Pharm., biochem., behav.,* 4: 611–12.

BEACH, L. R., ROSE, R. M., SAYEKI, Y., WISE, J. A., & CARTER, W. B. (1970). Probability learning: Response proportions and verbal estimates. *J. exp. Psychol.,* 86: 165–70.

BECK, A. R. (1976). *Cognitive therapy and the emotional disorders.* New York: International Universities Press.

BEM, D. J. (1967). Self-perception: An alternative interpretation of cognitive dissonance phenomena. *Psychol. Rev.,* 74: 183–200.

BEM, D. J. (1972). Self-perception theory. In L. Berkowitz, ed., *Advances in experimental social psychology.* Vol. 6. New York: Academic Press.

BENNETT, E. L., KRECH, D., & ROSENZWEIG, M. R. (1964). Reliability and regional specificity of cerebral effects of environmental complexity and training. *J. comp. physiol. Psychol.,* 57: 440–41.

BENTHAM, J. (1789). *The principles of morals and legislation.* London.

BERGER, W. F., & THOMPSON, R. F. (1978a). Neuronal plasticity in the limbic system during classical conditioning of the rabbit nictitating membrane response: I. Hippocampus. *Brain Res.,* 145: 323–46.

BERGER, W. F., & THOMPSON, R. F. (1978b). Neuronal plasticity in the limbic system during classical conditioning of the rabbit nictating membrane response: II. Septum and mammillary bodies. *Brain Res.,* 156: 293–314.

BERGIN, A. E., & GARFIELD, S. L. eds. (1971). *Handbook of psychotherapy and behavior change.* New York: Wiley.

BERNBACH, H. A. (1965). Stimulus learning and recognition in paired-associate learning. Doctoral dissertation, Univ. of Michigan. Also Technical Report No. 05823-7-T under Contract No. AF 49(638)-1235.

BERNOULLI, D. (1738). Specimen theoriae novae de mensura sortis. *Commentari academiae scientiarum imperiales petropolitanae,* 5: 175–92. (Translated by L. Sommer in *Econometrika* (1954) 22: 23–36.

BERSH, P. J. (1951). The influence of two variables upon the establishment of a secondary reinforcer for operant responses. *J. exp. Psychol.,* 41: 62–73.

BEVER, T. G. (1968). Associations to stimulus-response theories of langugage. In T. R. Dixon & D. L. Horton, eds., *Verbal behavior and general behavior theory.* Englewood Cliffs, N.J., Prentice-Hall.

BEVER, T. G., FODOR, J. A., & GARRETT, M. (1968). A formal limitation of associationism. In T. R. Dixon & D. L. Horton, eds., *Verbal behavior and general behavior theory.* Englewood Cliffs, N.J.: Prentice-Hall.

BEVER, T. G., FODOR, J. A., & WEKSEL, W. (1965a). On the acquisition of syntax: A critique of contextual generalization. *Psychol. Rev.,* 72: 467–82.

BEVER, T. G., FODOR, J. A., & WEKSEL, W. (1965b). Is linguistics empirical? *Psychol. Rev.,* 72: 493–500.

BICKFORD, R. G., MULDER, D. W., DODGE, H. W., SVIEN, H. J., & ROME, P. R. (1958). Changes in memory function produced by electrical stimulation of the temporal lobe in man. *Res. Pub. Assoc. for Res. in Nerv. and Ment. Dis.,* 36: 227.

BILODEAU, E. A., ed. (1966). *Acquisition of skill.* New York: Academic Press.

BINDER, A., & FELDMAN, S. E. (1960). The effects of experimentally controlled experience upon recognition responses. *Psychol. Monogr.,* 74, No. 496.

BIRCH, H. G. (1945). The relation of previous experience to insightful problem-solving. *J. comp. Psychol.,* 38: 367–83.

BIRNBAUM, I. M. (1972). General and specific components of retroactive inhibition in the A-B, A-C paradigm. *J. exp. Psychol.,* 93: 188–92.

BIRNBRAUER, J. S. (1976). Mental retardation. In H. Leitenberg, ed., *Handbook of behavior modification and behavior therapy.* Englewood Cliffs, N.J.: Prentice-Hall. Pp. 361–404.

BITTERMAN, M. E. (1975). The comparative analysis of learning. *Science,* 188: 699–709.

BJORK, R. A. (1970). Positive forgetting: The noninterference of items intentionally forgotten. *J. verb. Learn. verb. Behav.,* 9: 255–68.

BLACK, A. H. (1972). The operant conditioning of central nervous system electrical activity. In G. H. Bower, ed., *The psychology of learning and motivation: Advances in research and theory.* Vol. 6. New York: Academic Press.

BLACK, A. H. (1977). Comments on "Learned helplessness: Theory and evidence." *J. exp. Psychol.: General,* 106: 41–43.

BLACK, A. H., & PROKASY, W. F., eds. (1972). *Classical conditioning. II: Current theory and research.* New York: Appleton-Century-Crofts.

BLACK, J. B., & BOWER, G. H. (1980). Story-understanding as problem-solving. *Poetics* (in press).

BLANCHARD, E. B., & YOUNG, L. D. (1974). Clinical application of biofeedback training. *Arch. gen. Psychiat.,* 30: 573–89.

BLOCK, J. H., ed. (1971). *Mastery learning: Theory and practice.* New York: Holt, Rinehart and Winston.

BLODGETT, H. C. (1929). The effect of the introduction of reward upon the maze performance of rats. *Univ. Calif. Psychol.,* 4: 113–34.

BLODGETT, H. C., & McCUTCHAN, K. (1947). Place versus response-learning in the simple T-maze. *J. exp. Psychol.,* 37: 412–22.

BLODGETT, H. C., & McCUTCHAN, K. (1948). The relative strength of place and response learning in the T-Maze. *J. comp. physiol. Psychol.,* 41: 17–24.

BLOOM, B. S. (1968). Learning for mastery. *Evaluation Comment,* 1, No. 2. Univ. of California at Los Angeles. Reprinted in Block (1971), pp. 47–63.

BLOUGH, D. S. (1961). Experiments in animal psychophysics. *Sci. Amer.,* 206 (July): 113–22.

BLOUGH, D. S. (1966). The study of animal sensory processes by operant methods. In W. K. Honig, ed., *Operant behavior: Areas of research and application.* New York: Appleton-Century-Crofts.

BLOUGH, D. S. (1975). Steady-state data and a quantitative model of operant generalization and discrimination. *J. exp. Psychol.: Animal Behavior Processes,* 104: 3–21.

BOBROW, S. A. (1970). Memory for words in sentences. *J. verb. Learn. verb. Behav.,* 9: 363–72.

BOBROW, S. A., & BOWER, G. H. (1969). Comprehension and recall of sentences. *J. exp. Psychol.,* 80: 455–61.

BODEN, M. A. (1977). *Artificial intelligence and natural man.* New York: Basic Books.

BOLLES, R. C. (1970). Species-specific defense reactions in avoidance learning. *Psychol. Rev.,* 71: 32–48.

BOLLES, R. C. (1972). The avoidance learning problem. In G. H. Bower, ed., *The psychology of learning and motivation: Advances in research and theory.* Vol. 6. New York: Academic Press.

BORKO, H., ed. (1967). *Automated language processing.* New York: Wiley.

BOURNE, L. E., DOMINOWSKI, R. L., & LOFTUS, E. F. (1979). *Cognitive processes.* Englewood Cliffs, N.J.: Prentice-Hall.

BOUSFIELD, W. A. (1953). The occurrence of clustering in the recall of randomly arranged associates. *J. gen. Psychol.,* 49: 229–40.

BOWER, G. H. (1959). Choice-point behavior. In R. R. Bush & W. K. Estes, eds., *Studies in mathematical learning theory.* Stanford: Stanford Univ. Press. Pp. 109–24.

BOWER, G. H. (1960). Partial and correlated reward in escape learning. *J. exp. Psychol.,* 59: 126–30.

BOWER, G. H. (1961a). Application of a model to paired-associate learning. *Psychometrika,* 26: 255–80.

BOWER, G. H. (1961b). A contrast effect in differential conditioning. *J. exp. Psychol.,* 62: 196–99.

BOWER, G. H. (1962a). Response strengths and choice probability: A consideration of two combination rules. In E. Nagel, P. Suppes, & A. Tarski, eds., *Logic, methodology, and philosophy of science: Proceedings of the 1960 International Congress.* Stanford: Stanford Univ. Press. Pp. 400–412.

BOWER, G. H. (1962b). An association model for response and training variables in paired-associate learning. *Psychol. Rev.,* 69: 34–53.

BOWER, G. H. (1962c). The influence of graded reductions in reward and prior frustrating events upon the magnitude of the frustration effect. *J. comp. physiol. Psychol.,* 55: 582–87.

BOWER, G. H. (1967a). A descriptive theory of memory. In D. P. Kimble, ed., *The organization of recall.* Vol. 2 of series. New York: New York Academy of Sciences.

BOWER, G. H. (1967b). Verbal learning. In H. H. Helson & W. Bevan, eds., *Contemporary approaches to psychology.* Princeton: Van Nostrand.

BOWER, G. H. (1968 and continuing). *The psychology of learning and motivation.* Vols. 2–13. New York: Academic Press.

BOWER, G. H. (1970a). Analysis of a mnemonic device. *Amer. Sci.* 58: 496–510.

BOWER, G. H. (1970b). Organizational factors in memory. *Cog. Psychol.* 1: 18–46.

BOWER, G. H. (1971). Adaptation-level coding of stimuli and serial position effects. In M. H. Appley, ed., *Adaptation-level theory.* New York: Academic Press. Pp. 175–201.

BOWER, G. H. (1972a). Perceptual groups as coding units in immediate memory. *Psychon. Sci.,* 27: 217–19.

BOWER, G. H. (1972b). Mental imagery and associative learning. In L. W. Gregg, ed., *Cognition in learning and memory.* New York: Wiley.

BOWER, G. H. (1972c). A selective review of organizational factors in memory. In E. Tulving & W. Donaldson, eds., *Organization of memory.* New York: Academic Press.

BOWER, G. H. (1972d). Stimulus-sampling theory of encoding variability. In E. Martin & A. Melton, eds., *Coding theory and memory.* Washington, D.C.: Hemisph. Publ. Corp.

BOWER, G. H. (1973). How to . . . uh . . . remember! *Psychol. Today,* 7, No. 5: 62–70.

BOWER, G. H. (1974). Selective facilitation and interference in retention of prose. *J. ed. Psychol.,* 66: 1–8.

BOWER, G. H. (1975). Cognitive psychology: An introduction. In W. K. Estes, ed., *Handbook of learning and cognitive processes.* Vol. 1. Hillsdale, N.J.: Erlbaum. Pp. 25–80.

BOWER, G. H. (1976). Experiments on story understanding and recall. *Quart. J. exp. Psychol.,* 28: 511–34.

BOWER, G. H. (1978a). Interference paradigms for meaningful propositional memory. *Amer. J. Psychol.,* 91: 575–85.

BOWER, G. H. (1978b). Contacts of cognitive psychology with social learning theory. *Cog. Res. Ther.,* 1: 123–47.

BOWER, G. H. (1978c). Experiments on story comprehension and recall. *Discourse Proc.,* 1: 211–31.

BOWER, G. H., BLACK, J. B., & TURNER, T. J. (1979). Scripts in memory for text. *Cog. Psychol.,* 11: 177–220.

BOWER, G. H., CLARK, M. C., WINZENZ, D., & LESGOLD, A. (1969). Hierarchical retrieval schemes in recall of categorized word lists. *J. verb. Learn. verb. Behav.,* 8: 323–43.

BOWER, G. H., & GLASS, A. (1976). Structural units and the redintegrative power of picture fragments. *J. exp. Psychol.: Human Learning and Memory,* 2: 456–66.

BOWER, G. H., & HOLYOAK, K. (1973). Encoding and recognition memory for naturalistic sounds. *J. exp. Psychol.,* 101: 360–66.

BOWER, G. H., LESGOLD, A., & TIEMAN, D. (1969). Grouping operations in free recall. *J. verb. Learn. verb. Behav.,* 8: 481–93.

BOWER, G. H., & MASLING, M. (1978). Causal

explanations as mediators for remembering correlations. Unpublished manuscript. Stanford University.

BOWER, G. H., & MILLER, N. E. (1958). Rewarding and punishing effects from stimulating the same place in the rat's brain. *J. comp. physiol. Psychol.,* 51: 669–74.

BOWER, G. H., MONTEIRO, K. P., & GILLIGAN, S. G. (1978). Emotional mood as a context for learning and recall. *J. verb. Learn. verb. Behav.,* 17: 573–85.

BOWER, G. H., & SPRINGSTON, F. (1970). Pauses as recoding points in letter series. *J. exp. Psychol.,* 83: 421–30.

BOWER, G. H., STARR, R., & LAZAROVITZ, L. (1965). Amount of response-produced change in the CS and avoidance learning. *J. comp. physiol. Psychol.,* 59: 13–17.

BOWER, G. H., & THEIOS, J. (1964). A learning model for discrete performance levels. In R. C. Atkinson, ed., *Studies in mathematical psychology.* Stanford: Stanford Univ. Press.

BOWER, G. H., & TRABASSO, T. R. (1964). Concept identification. In R. C. Atkinson, ed., *Studies in mathematical psychology.* Stanford: Stanford Univ. Press. Pp. 32–94.

BOWER, G. H., & WINZENZ, D. (1969). Group structure, coding, and memory for digit series. *J. exp. Psychol. Monogr.,* 80, No. 2, Part 2: 1–17.

BOWER, T. G. R. (1965). Stimulus variables determining space perception in infants. *Science,* 149: 88–89.

BOWYER, P. A., & HUMPHREYS, M. S. (1979). Effect of a recognition test on a subsequent cued-recall test. *J. exp. Psychol.: Human Learning and Memory,* 5: 348–59.

BRAINE, M. S. (1963). On learning the grammatical order of words. *Psychol. Rev.,* 70: 323–48.

BRELAND, K., & BRELAND, M. (1951). A field of applied animal psychology. *Amer. Psychol.,* 6: 202–4.

BRELAND, K., & BRELAND, M. (1960). The misbehavior of organisms. *Amer. Psychol.,* 16: 661–64.

BREWER, W. F. (1974). There is no convincing evidence for operant and classical conditioning in humans. In W. B. Weimer & D. S. Palermo, eds., *Cognition and symbolic processes.* Hillsdale, N.J.: Erlbaum.

BRIGGS, G. E. (1954). Acquisition, extinction and recovery functions in retroactive inhibition. *J. exp. Psychol.,* 47: 285–93.

BRIGGS, G. E. (1957). Retroactive inhibition as a function of original and interpolated learning. *J. exp. Psychol.,* 53: 60–67.

BRINK, F., JR. (1951). Synaptic mechanisms. In S. S. Stevens, ed., *Handbook of experimental psychology.* New York: Wiley. Pp. 94–120.

BROADBENT, D. E. (1957). A mechanical model for human attention and immediate memory. *Psychol. Rev.,* 64: 205–15.

BROGDEN, W. J. (1939). Sensory pre-conditioning. *J. exp. Psychol.,* 25: 323–32.

BROWN, J. S. (1969). Factors affecting self-punitive locomotor behavior. In B. A. Campbell & R. M. Church, eds., *Punishment and aversive behavior.* New York: Appleton-Century-Crofts.

BROWN, J. S., & BURTON, R. (1975). Multiple representations of knowledge for tutorial reasoning. In D. G. Bobrow & A. Collins, eds., *Representation and understanding: Studies in cognitive science.* New York: Academic Press. Pp. 311–49.

BROWN, J. S., & BURTON, R. (1978). Diagnostic models for procedural bugs in basic mathematical skills. *Cog. Sci.,* 2: 155–92.

BROWN, J. S., & GOLDSTEIN, I. P. (1977). Computers in a learning society. Testimony before the U. S. House of Representatives' Science and Technology Subcommittee on Domestic and International Planning. October. *U.S. Congressional Record.*

BROWN, J. S., & JACOBS, A. (1949). The role of fear in the motivation and acquisition of response. *J. exp. Psychol.,* 39: 749–59.

BROWN, J. S., KALISH, H. I., & FORBER, I. E. (1951). Conditioned fear as revealed by magnitude of startle response to an auditory stimulus. *J. exp. Psychol.,* 41: 317–28.

BROWN, P. L., & JENKINS, H. M. (1968). Auto-shaping of the pigeon's key-peck. *J. exp. Anal. Behav.*, 11: 1–8.

BROWN, R., & McNEILL, D. (1966). The "tip of the tongue" phenomenon. *J. verb. Learn. verb. Behav.*, 5: 325–37.

BRUCE, D., & PAPAY, J. J. (1970). Primacy effect in single-trial free recall. *J. verb. Learn. verb. Behav.*, 9: 473–86.

BRUCKER, B. S. (1977). Learned voluntary control of systolic blood pressure by spinal cord injury patients. PhD dissertation. New York University.

BRUDNY, J., GRYNBAUM, B. B., & KOREIN, J. (1974). Spasmodic torticollis: Treatment by biofeedback of the EMG. *Arch. phys. Med. Rehab.*, 55: 403–8.

BRUNER, J. S. (1960). *The process of education.* Cambridge: Harvard Univ. Press.

BRUNER, J. S. (1964b). The course of cognitive growth. *Amer. Psychol.*, 19: 1–15.

BRUNER, J. S. (1966). *Toward a theory of instruction.* New York: Norton.

BRUNER, J. S., GOODNOW, J., & AUSTIN, G. (1956). *A study of thinking.* New York: Wiley.

BRUNSWIK, E. (1939). Probability as a determiner of rat behavior. *J. exp. Psychol.*, 25: 175–97.

BUCHANAN, B. G., & MITCHELL, T. M. (1978). Model-directed learning of production rules. In D. A. Waterman & F. Hayes-Roth, eds., *Pattern-directed inference systems.* New York: Academic Press. Pp. 297–312.

BUCHANAN, B. G., MITCHELL, T. M., SMITH, R. G., & JOHNSON, C. R., Jr. (1978). Models of learning systems. In J. Belzer, A. G. Holzman, & A. Kent, eds., *Encyclopedia of computer science and technology.* Vol. 11. New York: Marcel Dekker.

BUCHWALD, A. M. (1967). Effects of immediate vs. delayed outcomes in associative learning. *J. verb. Learn. verb. Behav.*, 6: 317–20.

BUCHWALD, A. M. (1969). Effects of "right" and "wrong" on subsequent behavior: A new interpretation. *Psychol. Rev.*, 76: 132–43.

BUDZYNSKI, T. H., et al. (1973). EMG biofeed-back and tension headache: A controlled outcome study. *Psychosom. Med.*, 35: 484–96.

BUNDERSON, V. (1967). The role of computer-assisted instruction in university education. *Progress Report to the Coordination Board of the Texas College and University System.* Austin: University of Texas.

BUREŠ, J., & BUREŠOVÁ, O. (1960). The use of Leao's spreading depression in the study of interhemispheric transfer of memory traces. *J. comp. physiol. Psychol.*, 53: 558–63.

BUREŠ, J., BUREŠOVÁ, O., & FIFKOVÁ, E. (1964). Interhemispheric transfer of a passive-avoidance reaction. *J. comp. physiol. Psychol.*, 57: 326–30.

BURKE, C. J.; ESTES, W. K., & HELLYER, S. (1954). Rate of verbal conditioning in relation to stimulus variability. *J. exp. Psychol.*, 48: 153–61.

BURNS, B. D. (1958). *The mammalian cerebral cortex.* London: Edward Arnold.

BUSH, R. R., & MOSTELLER, F. (1955). *Stochastic models for learning.* New York: Wiley.

BYKOV, K. M. (1957). *The cerebral cortex and the internal organs.* Translated by W. H. Gantt. New York: Chemical Publishing.

CAGGIULA, A. R. (1970). Analysis of the copulation-reward properties of posterior hypothalamic stimulation in male rats. *J. comp. physiol. Psychol.*, 70: 399–412.

CALDWELL, W. E., & JONES, H. B. (1954). Some positive results on a modified Tolman and Honzik insight maze. *J. comp. physiol. Psychol.*, 47: 416–18.

CALFEE, R. C., & DRUM, P. A. (1978). Learning to read: Theory, research, and practice. *Curr. Inq.*, 8: 183–249.

CAPALDI, E. J. (1966). Partial reinforcement: An hypothesis of sequential effects. *Psychol. Rev.*, 73: 459–77.

CAPALDI, E. J. (1967). A sequential hypothesis of instrumental learning. In K. W. Spence & J. T. Spence, eds., *The psychology of learning and motivation: Advances in research and theory.* Vol. 1. New York: Academic Press.

CAPALDI, E. J., & CAPALDI, E. D. (1970). Magnitude of partial reward, irregular reward schedules, and a 24-hour ITI: A test of several hypotheses. *J. comp. physiol. Psychol.,* 72: 203–9.

CARBONELL, J. R. (1970). AI in CAI: An artificial-intelligence approach to computer-aided instruction. *IEEE Transactions on Man-Machine Systems,* MMS-11(4): 190–202.

CAREW, T. J. (1970). Do passive avoidance tasks permit assessment of retrograde amnesia in rats? *J. comp. physiol. Psychol.,* 72: 267–71.

CARLSON, N. R. (1977). *Physiology of behavior.* Boston: Allyn & Bacon.

CARNEGIE COMMISSION ON HIGHER EDUCATION (1972). *The fourth revolution: Instructional technology in higher education.* New York: McGraw-Hill.

CARPENTER, F. (1974). *The Skinner primer: Behind freedom and dignity.* New York: The Free Press.

CARROLL, J. B. (1962). The prediction of success in intensive foreign language training. In R. Glaser, ed., *Training research and education.* Pittsburgh: Univ. of Pittsburgh Press, Pp. 87–136.

CARROLL, J. B. (1963a). A model of school learning. *Teachers Coll. Rec.* 64: 723–33.

CARROLL, J. B. (1963b). Research on teaching foreign languages. In N. L. Gage, ed., *Handbook of research on teaching.* Chicago: Rand McNally. Pp. 1060–1100.

CARTERETTE, T. S. (1961). An application of stimulus sampling theory to summated generalization. *J. exper. Psychol.,* 62: 448–55.

CATANIA, A. C. (1979). *Learning.* Englewood Cliffs, N.J.: Prentice-Hall.

CAVANAUGH, J. P. (1972). Relation between the immediate memory span and the memory search rate. *Psychol. Rev.,* 79: 525–30.

CERMAK, L. S. (1975). *Improving your memory.* New York: McGraw-Hill.

CERMAK, L. S., & CRAIK, F. I. M., eds. (1978). *Levels of processing and human memory.* Hillsdale, N.J.: Erlbaum.

CHAPMAN, L. J., & CHAPMAN, J. P. (1967). Genesis of popular but erroneous diagnostic observations. *J. abn. Psychol.,* 72: 193–204.

CHAPMAN, L. J., & CHAPMAN, J. P. (1969). Illusory correlation as an obstacle to the use of valid psychodiagnostic signs. *J. abn. Psychol.,* 74: 271–80.

CHAPMAN, L. F., WALTER, R. D., MARKHAM, C. H., RAND, R. W., & CRANDELL, R. H. (1967). Memory changes induced by stimulation of hippocampus or amygdala in epilepsy patients with implanted electrodes. *Trans. Amer. Neurol. Assoc.,* 92: 50–56.

CHAPOUTHIER, G. (1973). Behavioral studies of the molecular basis of memory. In J. A. Deutsch, ed., *The physiological basis of memory.* New York: Academic Press.

CHASE, N. G., & SIMON, H. A. (1973). Perception in chess. *Cog. Psych.,* 4: 55–81.

CHOMSKY, N. (1957). *Syntactic structures.* The Hague: Mouton.

CHOMSKY, N. (1959). Review of Skinner's *Verbal Behavior. Language,* 35: 26–58.

CHOMSKY, N. (1965). *Aspects of the theory of syntax.* Cambridge: MIT Press.

CHOMSKY, N. (1967). Review of Skinner's *Verbal Behavior.* In L. A. Jakobovits & M. S. Miron, eds., *Readings in the philosophy of language.* Englewood Cliffs, N.J.: Prentice-Hall.

CHOMSKY, N. (1971). The case against B. F. Skinner. *N.Y. Rev. Books* (Dec. 30, 1971), pp. 18–24. Also published as "Psychology and Ideology," *Cognition,* 1972, 1: 11–46.

CHOMSKY, N. (1972). *Language and mind.* Enlarged ed. New York: Harcourt Brace Jovanovich. (1st ed., 1968).

CHOROVER, S. L., & SCHILLER, P. H. (1965). Short-term retrograde amnesia in rats. *J. comp. physiol. Psychol.,* 59: 73–78.

CHU, G. C., & SCHRAMM, W. (1967). *Learning from television: What the research says.* Stanford: Institute for Communication Research.

CHUMBLEY, J. (1969). Hypothesis memory in concept learning. *J. math. Psychol.,* 6: 528–40.

CHUTE, D. L., & WRIGHT, D. C. (1973). Retrograde state dependent learning. *Science,* 180: 878.

CLARK, H. H., & CLARK, E. (1978). *Psychology and language.* New York: Harcourt Brace Jovanovich.

COAN, R. W., & ZAGONA, S. V. (1962). Contemporary ratings of psychological theorists. *Psychol. Rec.,* 12: 315–22.

COHEN, H. D., ERVIN, F., & BARONDES, S. H. (1966). Puromycin and cycloheximide: Different effects on hippocampal electrical activity. *Science,* 154: 1157–58.

COHEN, L. H., HILGARD, E. R., & WENDT, G. R. (1933). Sensitivity to light in a case of hysterical blindness studied by reinforcement-inhibition and conditioning methods. *Yale J. Biol. Med.,* 6: 61–67.

COLEMAN, E. B. (1962). Sequential interference demonstrated by serial reconstruction. *J. exp. Psychol.,* 64: 46–51.

COLES, L. S. (1968). An on-line question-answering system with natural language and pictorial input. *Proceedings of ACM 23rd National Conference.* Pp. 157–67. Princeton: Brandon Systems Press.

COLLINS, A. (1976). Processes in acquiring knowledge. In R. C. Anderson, R. J. Spiro, & W. E. Montague, eds., *Schooling and the acquisition of knowledge.* Hillsdale, N.J.: Erlbaum. Pp. 339–63.

COLLINS, A. M., & LOFTUS, E. F. (1975). A spreading-activation theory of semantic processing. *Psychol. Rev.,* 82: 407–28.

COLLINS, A., WARNOCK, E. H., AIELLO, N., & MILLES, M. L. (1975). Reasoning from incomplete knowledge. In D. G. Bobrow & A. Collins, eds., *Representation and understanding.* New York: Academic Press. Pp. 383–415.

COLLINS, A. M., & QUILLAN, M. R. (1969). Retrieval time from semantic memory. *J. verb. Learn. verb. Behav.,* 8: 240–47.

COOK, S. W., & SKINNER, B. F. (1939). Some factors influencing the distribution of associated words. *Psychol. Rec.,* 3: 178–84.

COOMBS, C. H., DAWES, R. M., & TVERSKY, A. (1970). *Mathematical psychology: An elementary introduction.* Englewood Cliffs, N.J.: Prentice-Hall.

COOPER, L. A., & SHEPARD, R. N. (1973). Chronometric studies of the rotation of mental images. In W. G. Chase, ed., *Visual information processing.* New York: Academic Press.

CORNSWEET, T. N. (1970). *Visual perception.* New York: Academic Press.

COTTON, J. W. (1955). On making predictions from Hull's theory. *Psychol. Rev.,* 62: 303–14.

COWLES, J. T., & NISSEN, H. W. (1937). Reward expectancy in delayed responses of chimpanzees. *J. comp. Psychol.,* 24: 345–58.

CRAIK, F. I. M. (1970). The fate of primary memory items in free recall. *J. verb. Learn. verb. Behav.,* 9: 143–48.

CRAIK, F. I. M. (1973). Levels of analysis: A view of memory. In P. Pliner, L. Kranes, & T. M. Alloway, eds., *Communication and affect: Language and thought.* New York: Academic Press.

CRAIK, F. I. M., & LOCKHART, R. S. (1972). Levels of processing: A framework for memory research. *J. verb. Learn. verb. Behav.,* 11: 671–84.

CRONBACH, L. J. (1967). How can instruction be adapted to individual differences? In R. M. Gagné, ed., *Learning and individual differences.* Columbus, Ohio: Merrill. Pp. 23–29.

CRONBACH, L. J., & SNOW, R. E. (1969). *Individual differences in learning ability as a function of instructional variables.* Stanford: Stanford School of Education.

CRONBACH, L. J., & SUPPES, P., eds. (1969). *Research for tomorrow's schools.* New York: Macmillan.

CROTHERS, E. J. (1965). Learning model solution to a problem in constrained optimization. *J. math. Psychol.,* 2: 19–25.

CROUSE, J. H. (1971). Retroactive interference in reading prose materials. *J. ed. Psychol.,* 62: 39–44.

CROWDER, N. A., & MARTIN, G. (1961). *Trigonometry*. Garden City, N.Y.: Doubleday.

CROWDER, R. G. (1976). *Principles of learning and memory*. Hillsdale, N.J.: Erlbaum.

CULBERTSON, J. T. (1962). *The minds of robots*. Urbana: Univ. of Illinois Press.

DALY, H. B. (1969). Learning of a hurdle-jumping response to escape cues paired with reduced reward or frustrative nonreward. *J. exp. Psychol.*, 79: 146–57.

DALY, H. B. (1970). Combined effects of fear and frustration on acquisition of a hurdle-jump response. *J. exp. Psychol.*, 83: 89–93.

DALY, H. B. (1974). Reinforcing properties of escape from frustration aroused in various learning situations. In G. H. Bower, ed., *The psychology of learning and motivation*. Vol. 8. New York: Academic Press.

D'AMATO, M. R. (1973). Delayed matching and short-term memory in monkeys. In G. H. Bower, ed., *The psychology of learning and motivation*. Vol. 7. New York: Academic Press.

D'AMATO, M. R., & WORSHAM, R. W. (1972). Delayed matching in the Capuchin monkey with brief sample durations. *Learning and Motivation*, 3: 304–12.

DAVIDSON, J. M. (1966). Activation of male rats' sexual behavior by intracerebral implantation of androgen. *Endocrinology*, 79: 783–94.

DAVIS, K. L., MOHS, R. C., TINKLENBERG, J. R., PFEFFERBAUM, A., HOLLISTER, L. E., & KOPELL, B. S. (1978). Physostigmine: Improvement of long-term memory processes in normal humans. *Science*, 201: 272–74.

DECECCO, J. P., ed. (1967). *The psychology of language, thought, and instruction: Readings*. New York: Holt, Rinehart, & Winston.

DEESE, J. (1965). *The structure of associations in language and thought*. Baltimore: Johns Hopkins Press.

DEESE, J., & HULSE, S. H. (1967). *The psychology of learning*. 3rd ed. New York: McGraw-Hill.

DEGROOT, A. (1946). *Het Denken van den Schaker*. Amsterdam: Noord-Hollandsche Uitgevers Maatschappij.

DEGROOT, A. D. (1965). *Thought and choice in chess*. New York: Basic Books.

DE LEMOS, M. M. (1969). The development of conservation in aboriginal children. *Internatl. J. Psychol.* 4: 255–69.

DELGADO, J. M. R., ROBERTS, W. W., & MILLER, N. E. (1954). Learning motivated by electrical stimulation of the brain. *Amer. J. Physiol.* 179: 587–93.

DELPRATO, D. J. (1972). Pair-specific effects in retroactive inhibition. *J. verb. Learn. verb. Behav.*, 11: 566–72.

DENIKE, L. D., & SPIELBERGER, C. D. (1963). Induced mediating states in verbal conditioning. *J. verb. Learn. verb. Behav.*, 1: 339–45.

DESMOND, A. J. (1979). *The ape's reflexion*. New York: The Dial Press.

DEUTSCH, J. A. (1954). A machine with insight. *Quart. J. exp. Psychol.*, 6: 6–11.

DEUTSCH, J. A. (1960). *The structural basis of behavior*. Chicago: Univ. of Chicago Press.

DEUTSCH, J. A. (1964). Behavioral measurement of the neural refractory period and its application to intracranial self-stimulation. *J. comp. physiol. Psychol.*, 58: 1–9.

DEUTSCH, J. A. (1968). The neural basis of memory. *Psychol. Today*, 1 (12): 56–61.

DEUTSCH, J. A. (1971). The cholinergic synapse and the site of memory. *Science*, 174 (19 November): 788–94.

DEUTSCH, J. A. (1973). Prolonged rewarding brain stimulation. In G. H. Bower, ed., *The psychology of learning and motivation*. Vol. 7. New York: Academic Press.

DEUTSCH, J. A., & CLARKSON, J. K. (1959). Reasoning in the hooded rat. *Quart. J. exper. Psychol.*, 11: 150–54.

DEUTSCH, J. A., & DEUTSCH, D. (1963). Attention: Some theoretical considerations. *Psychol. Rev.*, 70: 80–90.

DEUTSCH, J. A., & DEUTSCH, D. (1973). *Physiological psychology*, 2nd ed. Homewood, Ill.: Dorsey.

DEUTSCH, J. A., & HOWARTH, C. I. (1963). Some tests of a theory of intracranial self-stimulation. *Psychol. Rev.,* 70: 444–60.

DEUTSCH, J. A., & ROLL, S. K. (1973). Alcohol and asymmetrical state-dependency: A possible explanation. *Behav. Biol.,* 8: 273–78.

DEVIETTI, T. L., & LARSON, R. C. (1971). ECS effects: Evidence supporting state-dependent learning in rats. *J. comp. physiol. Psychol.,* 74: 407–15.

DEWS, P. B., ed. (1970). *Festschrift for B. F. Skinner.* New York: Appleton-Century-Crofts.

DICARA, L. V. (1970). Learning in the autonomic nervous system. *Sci. Amer.,* 222: 30–39.

DICARA, L. V., & MILLER, N. E. (1968). Instrumental learning of vasomotor responses by rats: Learning to respond differentially in the two ears. *Science,* 159: 1485–86.

DINSMOOR, J. A. (1954). Punishment: I. The avoidance hypothesis. *Psychol. Rev.,* 61: 34–46.

DINSMOOR, J. A. (1955). Punishment: II. An interpretation of empirical findings. *Psychol. Rev.,* 62: 96–105.

DOLLARD, J., & MILLER, N. E. (1950). *Personality and psychotherapy.* New York: McGraw-Hill.

DOMJAN, M., & WILSON, N. E. (1972). Specificity of cue to consequence in aversion learning in the rat. *Psychonom. Sci.,* 26: 143–45.

DONCHIN, E., & COHEN, L. (1967). Averaged evoked potentials and intramodality selective attention. *EEG and clin. Neurophysiol.,* 22: 537–46.

DREYER, P., & RENNER, K. E. (1971). Self-punitive behavior—masochism or confusion? *Psychol. Rev.,* 78: 333–37.

DULANY, D. E. (1968). Awareness, rules and propositional control: A confrontation with S-R behavior theory. In T. R. Dixon & D. L. Horton, eds., *Verbal behavior and general behavior theory.* Englewood Cliffs, N.J.: Prentice-Hall.

DUNCAN, C. P. (1949). The retroactive effect of electroshock on learning. *J. comp. physiol. Psychol.,* 42: 32–44.

DUNCKER, K. (1945). On problem-solving. Translated by L. S. Lees from the 1935 original. *Psychol. Monogr.,* 58, No. 270.

DUNHAM, B. (1957). Hull's learning theory. *IBM J. Res. Devel.,* 1: 347–55.

DUNHAM, P. J. (1971). Punishment: Method and theory. *Psychol. Rev.,* 78: 58–70.

DUNHAM, P. J. (1972). Some effects of punishment upon unpunished responding. *J. exp. Anal. Behav.,* 17: 443–50.

DWORKIN, B. R. (1979). Behavioral principles in the treatment of disease. Paper at meetings of the American Psychological Association. New York. In press in *J. behav. Med.*

DWORKIN, B. R., et al. (1979). Baroreceptor activation reduces reactivity to noxious stimulation: Implications for hypertension. *Science,* 205: 1299–1301.

EASON, R. G., HARTER, M. R., & WHITE, C. T. (1969). Effects of attention and arousal on visually evoked cortical potentials and reaction time in man. *Physiol. Behav.,* 4: 283–89.

EBBINGHAUS, H. (1885). *Memory.* Translated by H. A. Ruger & C. E. Bussenius. New York: Teachers College, 1913. Paperback ed., New York: Dover, 1964.

EBENHOLTZ, S. M. (1972). Serial learning and dimensional organization. In G. H. Bower, ed., *The psychology of learning and motivation.* Vol. 5. New York: Academic Press. Pp. 267–314.

EDWARDS, W. (1954). The theory of decision making. *Psychol. Bull.,* 51: 380–417.

EDWARDS, W. (1962). Utility, subjective probability, their interaction, and variance preference. *J. Conflict Resolution,* 6: 42–51.

EICH, J. E., WEINGARTNER, H., STILLMAN, R. C., & GILLIN, J. C. (1975). State dependent accessibility of retrieval cues in the retention of a categorized list. *J. verb. Learn. verb. Behav.,* 14: 408–17.

ELLIOTT, M. H. (1928). The effect of change of reward on the maze performance of rats. *Univ. Calif. Publ. Psychol.,* 4: 19–30.

ELLIS, A., & HARPER, R. A. (1973). *A guide to*

rational living. No. Hollywood, Cal.: Wilshire Book Co.

ELLIS, N. R., DETTERMAN, D. K., RUNCIE, D., MCCARVER, R. B., & CRAIG, E. M. (1971). Amnesic effects in short-term memory. *J. exp. Psychol.*, 89: 357–61.

ELLISON, G. D. (1964). Differential salivary conditioning to trace. *J. comp. physiol. Psychol.*, 57: 373–80.

ELLISON, G. D., & KONORSKI, J. (1964). Separation of the salivary and motor responses in instrumental conditioning. *Science, New York*, 146: 1971–72.

EPSTEIN, W. (1972). Mechanisms of directed forgetting. In G. H. Bower, ed., *The psychology of learning and motivation: Advances in research and theory*. Vol. 6. New York: Academic Press.

ERDELYI, M. H., & GOLDBERG, B. (1979). Let's not sweep repression under the rug: Toward a cognitive psychology of repression. In J. F. Kihlstrom & F. J. Evans, eds., *Functional disorders of memory*. Hillsdale, N.J.: Erlbaum. Pp. 355–401.

ERDELYI, M. H., & KLEINBARD, J. (1978). Has Ebbinghaus decayed with time? The growth of recall (hypermnesia) over days. *J. exp. Psychol.: Human Learning and Memory*, 4: 275–89.

ERICSON, K. A., & SIMON, H. A. (1978). Retrospective verbal reports as data. C.I.P. Working Paper No. 388. Pittsburgh: Carnegie-Mellon University.

ERNST, G. W., & NEWELL, A. (1969). *GPS: A case study in generality and problem-solving*. New York: Academic Press.

ESTES, W. K. (1955a). Statistical theory of spontaneous recovery and regression. *Psychol. Rev.*, 62: 145–54.

ESTES, W. K. (1955b). Statistical theory of distributional phenomena in learning. *Psychol. Rev.*, 62: 369–77.

ESTES, W. K. (1958). Stimulus-response theory of drive. In M. R. Jones, ed., *Nebraska Symposium on Motivation*. Vol. 6. Lincoln: Univ. of Nebraska Press.

ESTES, W. K. (1959a). The statistical approach to learning theory. In S. Koch, ed., *Psychology: A study of a science*. Vol. 2. New York: McGraw-Hill.

ESTES, W. K. (1959b). Component and pattern models with Markovian interpretations. In R. R. Bush & W. K. Estes, eds., *Studies in mathematical learning theory*. Stanford: Stanford Univ. Press.

ESTES, W. K. (1962). Theoretical treatment of differential reward in multiple-choice learning and two-person interactions. In J. Criswell, H. Solomon, & P. Suppes, eds., *Mathematical methods in small group processes*. Stanford: Stanford Univ. Press.

ESTES, W. K. (1969a). Reinforcement in human learning. In J. Tapp, ed., *Reinforcement and behavior*. New York: Academic Press.

ESTES, W. K. (1969b). Outline of a theory of punishment. In B. A. Campbell & R. S. Church, eds., *Punishment and aversive behavior*. New York: Appleton-Century-Crofts.

ESTES, W. K. (1970). *Learning theory and mental development*. New York: Academic Press.

ESTES, W. K. (1971). Learning and memory. In E. F. Beckenbach & C. B. Tompkins, eds., *Concepts of communication*. New York: Wiley. Pp. 282–300.

ESTES, W. K. (1972a). Research and theory on the learning of probabilities. *J. Amer. Statis. Assoc.*, 67: 81–102.

ESTES, W. K. (1972b). An associative basis for coding and organization in memory. In A. W. Melton & E. Martin, eds., *Coding processes in human memory*. Washington, D.C.: V. H. Winston.

ESTES, W. K. (1973). Memory and conditioning. In F. J. McGuigan, ed., *Contemporary Perspectives in Learning and Conditioning*. Washington, D.C.: V. H. Winston.

ESTES, W. K., ed. (1975–1978). *Handbook of learning and cognitive processes*. 5 vols. Hillsdale, N.J.: Erlbaum.

ESTES, W. K. (1976). The cognitive side of probability learning. *Psychol. Rev.*, 83. 37–64.

ESTES, W. K., KOCH, S., MacCORQUODALE, K., MEEHL, P. E., MUELLER, C. G., JR., SCHOENFELD, W. N., & VERPLANCK, W. S. (1945). *Modern learning theory.* New York: Appleton-Century-Crofts.

ESTES, W. K., & SKINNER, B. F. (1941). Some quantitative properties of anxiety. *J. exp. Psychol.,* 29: 390–400.

ESTES, W. K., & STRAUGHAN, J. H. (1954). Analysis of a verbal conditioning situation in terms of statistical learning theory. *J. exp. Psychol.,* 47: 225–34.

EVANS, S. (1936). Flexibility of established habit. *J. gen. Psychol.,* 14: 177–200.

FAHLMAN, S. E. (1974). A planning system for robot construction tasks. *Art. Intell.,* 5: 1–50.

FALKENBERG, P. R. (1972). Recall improves in short-term memory the more recall context resembles learning context. *J. exp. Psychol.,* 95: 39–47.

FALMAGNE, R. (1970). Construction of a hypothesis model for concept identification. *J. math. Psychol.,* 7: 60–96.

FEIGENBAUM, E. A. (1959). An information-processing theory of verbal learning. RAND Corp. Paper, P-1817.

FEIGENBAUM, E. A. (1978). The art of artificial intelligence: Themes and case studies of knowledge engineering. *Proceedings of the Fifth International Joint Conference on Artificial Intelligence* (STAN-CS-77-621). Stanford, Calif.: Computer Science Dept.

FEIGENBAUM, E. A., & FELDMAN, J. (1963). *Computers and thought.* New York: McGraw-Hill.

FEIGENBAUM, E. A., & SIMON, H. A. (1961). Performance of a reading task by an elementary perceiving and memorizing program. RAND Corp. Paper, P-2358.

FEIGENBAUM, E. A., & SIMON, H. A. (1962). A theory of the serial position effect. *Brit. J. Psychol.,* 53: 307–20.

FEINGOLD, B. D., & MAHONEY, M. J. (1975). Reinforcing effects on intrinsic interest: Undermining the overjustification hypotheses. *Behav. Ther.,* 6: 367–77.

FELDMAN, J. (1961). Simulation of behavior in the binary choice experiments. *Proceedings of the Western Joint Computer Conference.* New York: IRE. Pp. 133–44.

FELDMAN, J. (1962). Computer simulation of cognitive processes. In H. Borko, ed., *Computer applications in the behavioral sciences.* Englewood Cliffs, N.J.: Prentice-Hall.

FERSTER, C. S., & SKINNER, B. F. (1957). *Schedules of reinforcement.* New York: Appleton-Century-Crofts.

FESTINGER, L. (1942). Wish, expectation, and group standards as affecting level of aspiration. *J. Abnorm. soc. Psychol.,* 37: 184–200.

FESTINGER, L. (1957). *A theory of cognitive dissonance.* New York: Harper & Row.

FESTINGER, L. (1961). The psychological effects of insufficient rewards. *Amer. Psychol.,* 16: 1–11.

FETZ, E. E., & FINOCCHIO, D. V. (1971). Operant conditioning of specific patterns of neural and muscular activity. *Science,* 174: 431–35.

FIELDS, C. (1970). Instrumental conditioning of the rat cardiac control system. *Proc. Nat'l. Acad. Sci. (USA).* 65: 293–99.

FIKES, R. E., HART, P. E., & NILSSON, N. J. (1972). Learning and executing generalized robot plans. *Art. Intell.,* 3: 251–88.

FIKES, R. E., & NILSSON, N. Y. (1971). STRIPS: A new approach to the application of theorem proving to problem solving. *Art. Intell.,* 2: 189–208.

FILLMORE, C. (1968). *The case for case.* In E. Bach & R. T. Harms, eds., *Universals in linguistic theory.* New York: Holt, Rinehart and Winston.

FISHER, A. E. (1956). Maternal and sexual behavior induced by intracranial chemical stimulation. *Science,* 124: 228–29.

FJERDINGSTAD, E. J., ed., (1971). *Chemical transfer of learned information.* New York: American Elsevier.

FLAVELL, J. H. (1976). *Cognitive development.* Englewood Cliffs, N.J.: Prentice-Hall.

FLEXSER, A. J., & BOWER, G. H. (1974). How frequency affects recency judgments: A model for recency discrimination. *J. exp. Psychol.*, 103: 706–16.

FOWLER, H., & MILLER, N. E. (1963). Facilitation and inhibition of runway performance by hind- and forepaw shock of various intensities. *J. comp. physiol. Psychol.*, 56: 801–5.

FOX, S. S., & RUDELL, A. P. (1970). Operant controlled neural event: Functional independence in behavioral coding by early and late components of visual cortical evoked response in cats. *J. Neurophysiol.*, 33: 548–61.

FRANK, B., STEIN, D. G., & ROSEN, J. (1970). Interanimal "memory" transfer: Results from brain and liver homogenates. *Science*, 169: 399–402.

FREEDLE, R., ed. (1979). *Multidisciplinary approaches to discourse processing.* Hillsdale, N.J.: Ablex.

FREIJA, N. H. (1972). Simulation of human memory. *Psychol. Bull.*, 77: 1–31.

FRIEDMAN, L. (1967). Instinctive behavior. *Behav. Sci.*, 12 (2): 85–108.

FRIEDMAN, M. I., & STRICKER, E. M. (1976). The physiological psychology of hunger: A physiological perspective. *Psychol. Rev.*, 83: 409–32.

FRIEDMAN, M. P., PADILLA, G., & GELFAND, H. (1964). The learning of choices between bets. *J. math. Psychol.*, 1: 375–85.

FROLOV, Y. P. (1937). *Pavlov and his school.* New York: Oxford Univ. Press.

FURST, B. (1958). *Stop forgetting: How to develop your memory and put it to practical use.* Garden City, N.Y.: Doubleday.

FUSTER, J. M. (1958). Effects of stimulation of brain stem on tachistoscopic perception. *Science*, 127: 150.

GAGE, N. L., ed. (1963). *Handbook of research on teaching.* Chicago: Rand McNally.

GAGNÉ, R. M. (1962b). Simulators. In R. Glaser, ed., *Training research and education.* Pittsburgh: Univ. of Pittsburgh Press. Pp. 223–46.

GAGNÉ, R. M. (1965). *The conditions of learning.* New York: Holt, Rinehart & Winston.

GAGNÉ, R. M. (1970). *The conditions of learning.* Rev. ed., New York: Holt, Rinehart & Winston.

GAGNÉ, R. M., & BRIGGS, L. J. (1974). *Principles of instructional design.* New York: Holt, Rinehart & Winston.

GAGNÉ, R. M., & GEPHART, W. L., eds. (1968). *Learning research and school subjects.* Itasca, Ill.: Peacock.

GAGNÉ, R. M., & ROHWER, W. D., JR. (1969). Instructional psychology. *Ann. Rev. Psychol.*, 20: 381–418.

GAITO, J. (1966). *Molecular psychobiology: A chemical approach to learning and other behavior.* Springfield, Ill.: Charles C Thomas.

GALIN, D., & ORNSTEIN, R. (1972). Lateral specialization of cognitive mode: An EEG study. *Psychophysiol.*, 9: 412–18.

GALLISTEL, C. R. (1966). Motivating effects in self-stimulation. *J. comp. physiol. Psychol.*, 62: 95–101.

GALLISTEL, C. R. (1969a). The incentive of brain-stimulation reward. *J. comp. physiol. Psychol.*, 69: 713–21.

GALLISTEL, C. R. (1969b). Self stimulation: Failure of pre-trial stimulation to affect rats' electrode preference. *J. comp. Psychol.*, 69: 722–29.

GANTT, W. H. (1965). Pavlov's system. In B. B. Wolman & E. Nagel, eds., *Scientific Psychology.* New York: Basic Books. Pp. 127–49.

GARCIA, J., & KOELLING, R. (1966). Relation of cue to consequence in avoidance learning. *Psychon. Sci.*, 4: 123–24.

GARDNER, B. T., & GARDNER, R. A. (1971). Two-way communication with an infant chimpanzee. In A. Schrier & F. Stollnitz, eds., *Behavior of non-human primates.* Vol. 3. New York: Academic Press.

GATES, A. I. (1917). Recitation as a factor in memorizing. *Arch. Psychol., N.Y.*, 6 (40).

GAZZANIGA, M. S. (1967). The split brain in man. *Sci. Amer.*, 217 (2): 24–29.

GAZZANIGA, M. S. (1970). *The bisected brain.* New York: Appleton-Century-Crofts.

GAZZANIGA, M. S. (1972). One brain—two minds? *Amer. Sci.*, 60: 311–17.

GAZZANIGA, M. S., & LEDOUX, J. E. (1977). *The integrated mind.* New York: Plenum.

GAZZANIGA, M. S., & SPERRY, R. W. (1967). Language after section of the cerebral commissures. *Brain,* 90: 131–48.

GEIS, G. L., STEBBINS, W. C., & LUNDIN, R. W. (1965). *Reflexes and conditioned reflexes: A basic systems program.* New York: Appleton-Century-Crofts.

GELLER, A., & JARVIK, N. E. (1968). The time relations of ECS-induced amnesia. *Psychon. Sci.,* 12: 169–70.

GENGERELLI, J. A. (1928). Preliminary experiments on the causal factors in animal learning. *J. comp. Psychol.,* 8: 435–57.

GERST, N. S. (1971). Symbolic coding processes in observational learning. *J. Pers. Soc. Psychol.,* 19: 7–17.

GEWIRTZ, J. L., & STINGLE, K. G. (1968). Learning of generalized imitation as the basis for identification. *Psychol. Rev.,* 75: 374–97.

GIBSON, E. J. (1940). A systematic application of the concepts of generalization and differentiation to verbal learning. *Psychol. Rev.,* 47: 196–229.

GIBSON, E. J. (1969). *Principles of perceptual learning and development.* New York: Appleton-Century-Crofts.

GIBSON, J. J. (1966). *The senses considered as perceptual systems.* Boston: Houghton Mifflin.

GIRDEN, E., & CULLER, E. A. (1937). Conditioned responses in curarized striate muscle in dogs. *J. comp. Psychol.,* 23: 261–74.

GLANZER, M. S. (1972). Storage mechanisms in recall. In G. H. Bower, ed., *The psychology of learning and motivation: Advances in research and theory.* Vol. 5. New York: Academic Press.

GLANZER, M. (1978). Commentary on "Storage mechanisms in recall." In G. H. Bower, ed., *Human memory: Basic processes.* New York: Academic Press, Pp. 115–24.

GLANZER, M. S., & CLARK, H. H. (1962). Accuracy of perceptual recall: An analysis of organization. *J. verb. Learn. verb. Behav.,* 1: 289–99.

GLASER, R. (1978). *Advances in instructional psychology.* Vol. 1. Hillsdale, N.J.: Erlbaum.

GLASER, R., & RESNICK, L. B. (1972). Instructional psychology. *Ann. Rev. Psychol.* 23: 207–76.

GLASS, A. L., HOLYOAK, K. J., & O'DELL, C. (1974). Production frequency and the verification of quantified statements. *J. verb. Learn. verb. Behav.,* 13: 237–54.

GLASS, A. L., HOLYOAK, K. J., & SAMTA, J. (1979). *Cognition.* Reading, Mass.: Addison-Wesley.

GLEITMAN, H., NACHMIAS, J., & NEISSER, U. (1954). The S-R reinforcement theory of extinction. *Psychol. Rev.,* 61: 23–33.

GLOBUS, A., ROSENZWEIG, M. R., BENNETT, E. L., & DIAMOND, M. C. (1973). Effects of differential experience on dendritic spine counts in rat cerebral cortex. *J. comp. physiol. Psychol.,* 82: 175–81.

GOLD, B. (1959). Machine recognition of hand-sent Morse code. *IRE Trans. on Inform. Theory,* IT-5. Pp. 17–24.

GOLDFRIED, M. R., & DAVISON, G. C. (1976). *Clinical behavior therapy.* New York: Holt, Rinehart, & Winston.

GOLDMAN, A. I. (1970). *A theory of human action.* Englewood Cliffs, N.J.: Prentice-Hall.

GOLDSTEIN, H., KRANTZ, D. L., & RAINS, J. D. (1965). *Controversial issues in learning.* New York: Appleton-Century-Crofts.

GOODWIN, D. L., & COATES, T. J. (1976). *Helping students help themselves.* Englewood Cliffs, N.J.: Prentice-Hall.

GOSS, A. E. (1953). Transfer as a function of type and amount of preliminary experience with task stimuli. *J. exp. Psychol.,* 46: 419–28.

GOULD, P., & WHITE, R. (1974). *Mental maps.* Middlesex, Eng.: Penguin Books.

GRAY, J. A., ed. (1964). *Pavlov's typology: Recent theoretical and experimental developments from the laboratory of B. M. Teplov.* New York: Macmillan.

GREEN, B. F., JR. (1963). *Digital computers in research.* New York: McGraw-Hill.

GREEN, C. C. (1969a). Application of theorem

proving to problem solving. *Proceedings of the International Joint Conference on Artificial Intelligence*. Bedford, Mass.: Mitre Corp. Pp. 219–40.

GREEN, C. C. (1969b). Application of theorem proving to question-answering systems. Unpublished doctoral dissertation. Stanford: Stanford Univ. Technical Report CS-138, Computer Science Dept.

GREEN, C. C., & RAPHAEL, B. (1968). The use of theorem-proving techniques in question-answering systems. *Proceedings of the 23rd National Conference of the Association of Computing Machinery*. Washington, D.C.: Thompson.

GREEN, D. M., & SWETS, J. (1966). *Signal detection theory and psychophysics*. New York: Wiley.

GREEN, E. E., GREEN, A. M., & WALTERS, E. D. (1970). Voluntary control of internal states: Psychological and physiological. *J. transper. Psychol.*, 2: 132–47.

GREEN, E. J. (1956). Stimulus variability and operant discrimination in human subjects. *Amer. J. Psychol.*, 69: 269–73.

GREENBERG, J. H., ed. (1962). *Universals of language*. Cambridge: MIT Press.

GREENBLATT, G., EASTLAKE, D., & CROCKER, S. (1967). The Greenblatt chess program. *Proceedings of the Fall Joint Computer Conference*. Anaheim, Calif.

GREENHILL, L. P. (1964). Penn State experiments with two-way audio systems for CCTV. *NAEB J.*, 23: 73–78.

GREENO, J. G. (1968). *Elementary theoretical psychology*. Reading, Mass.: Addison-Wesley.

GREGG, L. W. (1972). Simulation models of learning and memory. In L. W. Gregg, ed., *Cognition in learning and memory*. New York: Wiley.

GREGG, L. W., & SIMON, H. A. (1967). Process models and stochastic theories of simple concept formation. *J. math. Psychol.*, 4: 246–76.

GROSS, C. G. (1973). Inferotemporal cortex and vision. In E. Stellar & J. M. Sprague, eds., *Progress in physiological psychology*. New York: Academic Press.

GROSSBERG, S. (1974). Classical and instrumental learning by neural networks. In R. Rosen & F. Snell, eds., *Progress in theoretical biology*. New York: Academic Press. Pp. 51–141.

GROSSBERG, S. (1975). A neural model of attention, reinforcement, and discrimination learning. In C. Pfeiffer, ed., *International Review of Neurobiology*, 18: 253–327.

GROSSBERG, S. (1978). A theory of human memory: Self-organization and performance of sensory-motor codes, maps, and plans. In R. Rosen & F. Snell, eds., *Progress in theoretical biology*. Vol. 5. New York: Academic Press. Pp. 235–374.

GROSSMAN, S. P. (1960). Eating or drinking elicited by direct adrenergic or cholinergic stimulation of the hypothalamus. *Science*, 132: 301–2.

GROSSMAN, S. P. (1967). *A textbook of physiological psychology*. New York: Wiley.

GROSSMAN, S. P. (1975). Role of the hypothalamus in the regulation of food and water intake. *Psychol. Rev.*, 82: 200–224.

GRUSEC, T. (1965). Aversive conditioning and peak shift in stimulus generalization. Unpublished doctoral dissertation. Stanford: Stanford Univ.

GUTHRIE, E. R. (1930). Conditioning as a principle of learning. *Psychol. Rev.*, 37: 412–28.

GUTHRIE, E. R. (1934). Pavlov's theory of conditioning. *Psychol. Rev.*, 41: 199–206.

GUTHRIE, E. R. (1935). *The psychology of learning*. New York: Harper & Row.

GUTHRIE, E. R. (1936). Psychological principles and scientific truth. *Proc. 25th Anniv. Celebr. Inaug. Grad. Stud.* Los Angeles: Univ. Southern California.

GUTHRIE, E. R. (1938). *The psychology of human conflict*. New York: Harper & Row.

GUTHRIE, E. R. (1940). Association and the law of effect. *Psychol. Rev.*, 47: 127–48.

GUTHRIE, E. R. (1942). Conditioning: A theory

of learning in terms of stimulus, response, and association. Chapter 1 in *The psychology of learning*. 41st Yearbook of the National Society for the Study of Education, Part II: 17–60. Chicago: Univ. of Chicago Press.

GUTHRIE, E. R. (1952). *The psychology of learning*. Rev. ed. New York: Harper & Row.

GUTHRIE, E. R. (1959). Association by contiguity. In S. Koch, ed., *Psychology: A study of a science*. Vol. 2. New York: McGraw-Hill. Pp. 158–95.

GUTHRIE, E. R., & HORTON, G. P. (1946). *Cats in a puzzle box*. New York: Rinehart Press.

GUZMAN, A. (1968). *Computer recognition of three-dimensional objects in a visual scene*. MIT Artificial Intelligence Laboratory, Project MAC-TR-59. Cambridge.

GWINN, G. T. (1949). The effects of punishment on cats motivated by fear. *J. exp. Psychol.*, 39: 260–69.

HABER, R. N. (1963). The spread of an innovation: High school language laboratories. *J. exp. Ed.*, 31: 359–69.

HALL, J. F. (1971). *Verbal learning and retention*. Philadelphia: J. B. Lippincott.

HAMBURGER, H., & WEXLER, K. (1975). A mathematical theory of learning transformational grammar. *J. math. Psychol.*, 12: 137–77.

HAMILTON, D. L., & ROSE, T. L. (in press) Illusory correlation and the maintenance of stereotyped beliefs.

HANSON, A. R., & RISEMAN, E. M. (1978). *Computer vision systems*. New York: Academic Press.

HARLOW, H. F. (1949). The formation of learning sets. *Psychol. Rev.*, 56: 51–65.

HARLOW, H. F., & HARLOW, M. K. (1966). Learning to love. *Amer. Sci.*, 54: 244–72.

HARSH, C. M. (1937). Disturbance and "insight" in rats. *Univ. Calif. Publ. Psychol.*, 6: 163–68.

HART, J. T. (1965). Memory and the feeling-of-knowing experience. *J. educ. Psychol.*, 56: 208–16.

HAYES-ROTH, B., & HAYES-ROTH, F. (1979). A cognitive model of planning. Unpublished manuscript. THE RAND Corporation. Santa Monica, Cal.

HAYGOOD, R., & BOURNE, L. E. (1965). Attribute and rule learning aspects of conceptual behavior. *Psychol. Rev.*, 72: 175–95.

HAYS, R. (1962). Psychology of the scientist: III. Introduction to "Passages from the 'Idea Books' of Clark L. Hull." *Percept. Mot. Skills*, 15: 803–6.

HEATH, R. G., & MICKLE, W. A. (1960). Evaluation of seven years' experience with depth electrode studies in human patients. In E. R. Ramey and D. S. O'Doherty, eds., *Electrical studies on the unanesthetized brain*. New York: Harper & Row. Pp. 214–47.

HEBB, D. O. (1949). *The organization of behavior*. New York: Wiley.

HEBERT, J. A. & KRANTZ, D. L. (1965). Transposition: A re-evaluation *Psychol. Bull.*, 63: 244–57.

HEFFERLINE, R. F., & KEENAN, B. (1963). Amplitude-induction gradient of a small-scale (covert) operant. *J. exp. Analy. Behav.*, 6: 307–15.

HEFFERLINE, R. F., KEENAN, B., & HARFORD, R. A. (1959). Escape and avoidance conditioning in human subjects without their observation of the response. *Science*, 130: 1338–39.

HELSON, H. (1964). *Adaptation-level theory*. New York: Harper & Row.

HELYER, S. (1962). Supplementary report: Frequency of stimulus presentation and short-term decrement in recall. *J. exp. Psychol.*, 64: 650.

HENLE, M. (1961). *Documents of Gestalt psychology*. Berkeley and Los Angeles: Univ. of California Press.

HERENDEEN, D. L., & SHAPIRO, M. M. (1971). Classical and DRO discrimination of salivary responding. Paper presented at meetings of the Western Psychological Association, April 1971.

HERENDEEN, D. L., & SHAPIRO, M. M. (1972). A within- and between-subjects comparison of the effects of extinction and DRO on salivary responding. Paper presented at meetings of the Midwestern Psychological Association, May 1972.

HERGENHAHN, B. R. (1976). *An introduction to theories of learning.* Englewood Cliffs, N.J.: Prentice-Hall.

HERNANDEZ-PEON, R., SCHEERER, H., & JOUVET, M. (1956). Modification of electric activity in cochlear nucleus during "attention" in unanesthetized cats. *Science,* 123: 331–32.

HERRNSTEIN, R. J. (1969). Method and theory in the study of avoidance. *Psychol. Rev.,* 76: 49–69.

HERRNSTEIN, R. J. (1970). On the law of effect. In P. B. Dews, ed., *Festschrift for B. F. Skinner.* New York: Appleton-Century-Crofts.

HESS, E. H. (1958). "Imprinting" in animals. *Sci. Amer.,* 198: 81–90.

HESS, R. D., & TENEZAKIS, M. D. (1970). *The computer as a socializing agent: Some socio-affective outcomes of CAI.* Stanford: Stanford Center for Research and Development in Teaching.

HILGARD, E. R. (1931). Conditioned eyelid reactions to a light stimulus based on the reflex wink to sound. *Psychol. Monogr.,* 41: (184).

HILGARD, E. R. (1956). *Theories of learning.* 2nd ed. New York: Appleton-Century-Crofts.

HILGARD, E. R. (Ed.) (1964a). *Theories of learning and instruction.* 63rd Yearbook of the National Society for the Study of Education, Part I. Chicago: Univ. of Chicago Press. Pp. 1–418.

HILGARD, E. R., & BOWER, G. H. (1966). *Theories of learning.* 3rd ed. New York: Appleton-Century-Crofts.

HILGARD, E. R., & BOWER, G. H. (1975). *Theories of learning.* 4th ed. Englewood Cliffs, N.J.: Prentice-Hall.

HILGARD, E. R., & CAMPBELL, A. A. (1936). The course of acquisition and retention of conditioned eyelid responses in man. *J. exp. Psychol.,* 19: 227–47.

HILGARD, E. R., & MARQUIS, D. G. (1940). *Conditioning and learning.* New York: Appleton-Century-Crofts.

HILL, W. F. (1971). *Learning: A survey of psychological interpretations.* Rev. ed., Scranton, Pa.: Chandler.

HINDE, R. A. (1966). *Animal behavior: A synthesis of ethology and comparative psychology.* New York: McGraw-Hill.

HINDE, R. A., & STEVENSON-HINDE, J., eds. (1973). *Constraints on learning.* New York: Academic Press.

HINES, B., & PAOLINO, R. M. (1970). Retrograde amnesia: Production of skeletal but not cardiac response gradients by electroconvulsive shocks. *Science,* 169: 1224–26.

HINRICHS, J. B. (1970). A two-process memory strength theory for judgment of recency. *Psychol. Rev.,* 77: 223–33.

HINTZMAN, D. L. (1968). Explorations with a discrimination net model for paired-associate learning. *J. math. Psychol.,* 5: 123–62.

HINTZMAN, D. L., & BLOCK, R. A. (1971). Repetition in memory: Evidence for a multiple trace hypothesis. *J. exp. Psychol.,* 88: 297–306.

HIROTO, D. S., & SELIGMAN, M. E. P. (1975). Generality of learned helplessness in man. *J. Pers. soc. Psychol.,* 31: 311–27.

HIRSH, R. (1974). The hippocampus and contextual retrieval of information from memory: A theory. *Behav. Biol.,* 12: 421–44.

HO, B. T., RICHARDS, D. W., & CHUTE, D. L., eds. (1978). *Drug discrimination and state dependent learning.* New York: Academic Press.

HOBAN, C. F. (1960). The usable residue of educational film research. In W. Schramm, ed., *New teaching aids for the American classroom.* Stanford: Institute for Communication Research. Pp. 95–115.

HOEBEL, B. G. (1968). Inhibition and disinhibition of self-stimulation and feeding: Hypothalamic control and post-ingestional factors. *J. comp. physiol. Psychol.,* 66: 89–100.

HOEBEL, B. G., & TEITELBAUM, P. (1962). Hypothalamic control of feeding and self-stimulation. *Science,* 135: 375–76.

HOFFDING, H. (1891). *Outlines of psychology.* New York: Macmillan.

HOFFMAN, H. S. (1962). The analogue lab: A new kind of teaching device. *Amer. Psychol.,* 17: 684–94.

HOLLAND, J. G., & SKINNER, B. F. (1961). *The analysis of behavior: A program for self-instruction.* New York: McGraw-Hill.

HOLLAND, P. C., & RESCORLA, R. A. (1975). Second-order conditioning with food unconditioned stimulus. *J. comp. physiol. Psychol.,* 88: 459–67.

HONIG, W. K. (1962). Prediction of preference, transposition, and transposition-reversal from the generalization gradient. *J. exp. Psychol.,* 64: 239–48.

HONIG, W. K., ed. (1966). *Operant behavior: Areas of research and application.* New York: Appleton-Century-Crofts.

HONIG, W. K., & JAMES, P. H. R. (1971). *Animal memory.* New York: Academic Press.

HONIG, W. K., & STADDON, J. E. R. (1977). *Handbook of operant behavior.* Englewood Cliffs, N.J.: Prentice-Hall.

HONZIK, C. H. (1936). The sensory basis of maze learning in rats. *Comp. Psychol. Monogr.,* 13 (64).

HOROWITZ, L. M., NORMAN, S. A., & DAY, R. S. (1966) . Availability and associative symmetry. *Psychol. Rev.,* 73: 1–15.

HOTHERSALL, D., & BRENER, J. (1969). Operant conditioning of changes in heart rates in curarized rats. *J. comp. Physiol. Psychol.,* 68: 338–42.

HOVLAND, C. I. (1937). The generalization of conditioned responses: I. The sensory generalization of conditioned responses with varying frequencies of tone. *J. gen. Psychol.,* 17: 125–48.

HOVLAND, C. I. (1938). Experimental studies in rote-learning theory: III. Distribution of practice with varying speeds of syllable presentation. *J. exp. Psychol.,* 23: 172–90.

HOVLAND, C. I. (1952). A "communication analysis" of concept learning. *Psychol. Rev.,* 59: 461, 472.

HUBEL, D. H., & WIESEL, T. N. (1962). Receptive fields, binocular interaction, and functional architecture in the cat's visual cortex. *J. Physiol.,* 160: 106–54.

HULL, C. L. (1932). The goal gradient hypothesis and maze learning. *Psychol. Rev.,* 39: 25–43.

HULL, C. L. (1934a). The concept of the habit-family hierarchy and maze learning. *Psychol. Rev.,* 41: 33–54.

HULL, C. L. (1934b). Learning: II. The factor of the conditioned reflex. In C. Murchison, ed., *A handbook of general experimental psychology.* Worcester, Mass.: Clark Univ. Press. Pp. 382–455.

HULL, C. L. (1935). The conflicting psychologies of learning—a way out. *Psychol. Rev.,* 42: 491–516.

HULL, C. L. (1937). Mind, mechanism, and adaptive behavior. *Psychol. Rev.,* 44: 1–32.

HULL, C. L. (1938). The goal-gradient hypothesis applied to some "field-force" problems in the behavior of young children. *Psychol. Rev.,* 45: 271–99.

HULL, C. L. (1943). *Principles of behavior.* New York: Appleton-Century-Crofts.

HULL, C. L. (1951). *Essentials of behavior.* New Haven: Yale Univ. Press.

HULL, C. L. (1952a). *A behavior system: An introduction to behavior theory concerning the individual organism.* New Haven: Yale Univ. Press.

HULL, C. L. (1952b). Autobiography. In Carl A. Murchison, ed., *A history of psychology in autobiography.* Vol. 4. New York: Russell & Russell Press.

HULL, C. L. (1962). Psychology of the scientist: IV: Passages from the "Idea Books" of Clark L. Hull. *Percept. Mot. Skills,* 15: 807–82.

HULL, C. L., HOVLAND, C. I., ROSS, R. T., HALL, M., PERKINS, D. T., & FITCH, F. G. (1940). *Mathematico-deductive theory of rote learning.* New Haven: Yale Univ. Press.

HULSE, S. H., DEESE, J., & EGETH, H. (1975). *The psychology of learning.* New York: McGraw-Hill.

HULSE, S. E., FOWLER, H., & HONIG, W. K., eds. (1978). *Cognitive processes in animal behavior.* Hillsdale, N.J.: Erlbaum.

HUMPHREYS, L. G. (1939). Acquisition and extinction of verbal expectations in a situation analogous to conditioning. *J. exp. Psychol.,* 25: 294–301.

HUNT, E. B. (1962). *Concept learning.* New York: Wiley.

HUNT, E. B. (1975). *Artificial intelligence.* New York: Academic Press.

HUNT, E. B., & HOVLAND, C. I. (1961). Programming a model of human concept formation. *Proceedings of the Western Joint Computer Conference.* New York: IRE. Pp. 145–56.

HUNT, E. B., MARIN, J., & STONE, P. (1966). *Experiments in induction.* New York: Academic Press.

HUPPERT, F. A., & DEUTSCH, J. A. (1969). Improvement in memory with time. *Quart. J. exp. Psychol.,* 21: 267–71.

HYDÉN, H. (1965). Activation of nuclear RNA in neurons and glia in learning. In D. P. Kimble, ed., *Learning, remembering, and forgetting.* Vol. 1. *The anatomy of memory.* Palo Alto: Science and Behavior Books. Pp. 170–239.

HYDÉN, H., & EGYHÁZI, E. (1962). Nuclear RNA changes of nerve cells during a learning experiment in rats. *Proc. Nat. Acad. Sci. U.S.,* 48: 1366–73.

HYDÉN, H., & EGYHÁZI, E. (1964). Changes in RNA content and base composition in cortical neurons of rats in a learning experiment involving transfer of handedness. *Proc. Nat. Acad. Sci. U.S.,* 52: 1030–35.

INGLES, J., CAMPBELL, D., & DONALD, M. W. (1976). Electromyographic biofeedback and neuromuscular rehabilitation. *Can. J. behav. Sci.,* 8: 299–323.

ISAACSON, R. L. (1974). *The limbic system.* New York: Plenum Press.

ITARD, J. M. G. (1932). *The wild boy of Aveyron.* Translated by George Humphrey & Muriel Humphrey. New York: Century.

JACKSON, T. A. (1942). Use of the stick as a tool by young chimpanzees. *J. comp. Psychol.,* 34: 223–35.

JACOBY, L. L. (1974). The role of mental continuity in memory: Registration and retrieval effects. *J. verb. Learn. verb. Behav.,* 13: 483–96.

JAKOBSON, R., FANT, C. G. M., & HALLE, M. (1963). *Preliminaries to speech analysis: The distinctive features and their correlates.* Cambridge: MIT Press.

JAMES, W. (1890). *The principles of psychology.* New York: Holt, Rinehart and Winston.

JASPER, H. H., RICCI, G., & DOANE, B. (1960). Microelectrode analysis of cortical cell discharge during avoidance conditioning in the monkey. In H. H. Jasper & G. D. Smirnov, eds., *The Moscow colloquium on electroencephalography of higher nervous activity: Electroencephalography and clinical neurophysiology.* Suppl. 13. Pp. 137–55.

JENSEN, A. R. (1962). An empirical theory of the serial-position effect. *J. Psychol.,* 53: 127–42.

JENSEN, A. R., & ROHWER, W. D., JR. (1970). An experimental analysis of learning abilities in culturally disadvantaged children. Final Report, Contract No. OEO-2404 to Office of Economic Opportunity. Berkley: Univ. Cal. July.

JOHN. E. R. (1967). *Mechanisms of memory.* New York: Academic Press.

JOHNSON-LAIRD, P. N., GIBBS, G., & DEMOWBRAY, J. (1978). Meaning, amount of processing, and memory for words. *Mem. Cog.,* 6: 372–75.

JOHNSON, N. F. (1970). The role of chunking and organization in the process of recall. In G. H. Bower, ed., *Psychology of learning and motivation: Advances in research and theory.* Vol. 4. New York: Academic Press.

JONCÍCH, G. (1968). *The sane positivist: A biography of Edward L. Thorndike.* Middletown, Conn.: Wesleyan Univ. Press.

JONES, E. E., KANOUSE, D., KELLEY, H. H., NISBETT, R. E., VALINS, S., & WEINER, B., eds. (1971). *Attribution: Perceiving the causes of behavior.* New York: General Learning Press.

JUDSON, A. J., COFFER, C. N., & GELFAND, S. (1956). Reasoning as an associative process: II. "Direction" in problem solving as a function of prior reinforcement of relevant responses. *Psychol. Rep.* 2: 501–7.

JUST, M. A., & CARPENTER, P., eds. (1977). *Cognitive processes in comprehension.* Hillsdale, N.J.: Erlbaum.

KAHNEMAN, D., & TVERSKY, A. (1971). Subjective probability: A judgment of representativeness. *Cog. Psychol.,* 3: 430–54.

KAHNEMAN, D., & TVERSKY, A. (1973). On the psychology of prediction. *Psychol. Rev.,* 80: 237–51.

KALMAN, R. E., FALB, P. L., & ARBIB, M. A. (1969). *Topics in mathematical system theory.* New York: McGraw-Hill.

KAMIN, L. J. (1965). Temporal and intensity characteristics of the conditioned stimulus. In W. F. Prokasy, ed., *Classical conditioning.* New York: Appleton-Century-Crofts.

KAMIN, L. J. (1969a). Selective association and conditioning. In N. J. Mackintosh & W. K. Honig, eds., *Fundamental issues in associative learning.* Halifax: Dalhousie Univ. Press.

KAMIN, L. J. (1969b). Predictability, surprise, attention, and conditioning. In B. A. Campbell & R. M. Church, eds., *Punishment.* New York: Appleton-Century-Crofts.

KAMIYA, J. (1962). Conditioned discrimination of the EEG alpha rhythm in humans. Paper presented at the Western Psychological Association Meeting. San Francisco.

KAMIYA, J. (1969). Operant control of the EEG alpha rhythm and some of its reported effects on consciousness. In C. T. Tart, ed., *Altered state of consciousness.* New York: Wiley.

KANDEL, E. R., & SPENCER, W. A. (1968). Cellular neurophysiological approaches in the study of learning. *Physiol. Rev.,* 48: 65–134.

KANDEL, E. R., & TAUC, L. (1965a). Heterosynaptic facilitation in neurones of the adbominal ganglion of *Aplysia depilans. J. Physiol.,* 181: 1–27.

KANDEL, E. R., & TAUC, L., (1965b). Mechanism of heterosynaptic facilitation in the giant cell of the abdominal ganglion of *Aplysia depilans. J. Physiol., Lond.,* 181: 28–47.

KANFER, F. H. (1968). Verbal conditioning: A review of its current status. In T. R. Dixon & D. L. Horton, eds., *Verbal behavior and general behavior theory.* Englewood Cliffs, N.J.: Prentice-Hall.

KANT, I. (1781). *Kritik der reimen Vermunft.* Leipzig: P. Reclam. English ed., *Critique of pure reason.* Translated by J. M. D. Meiklejohn. London: George Bell, 1887.

KAPATOS, G., & GOLD, R. M. (1973). Evidence for ascending noradrenergic mediation of hypothalamic hyperphagia. *Pharm., Biochem. Behav.,* 1: 81–87.

KAPLAN, B. (1973). EEG biofeedback and epilepsy. Paper at meeting of American Psychological Association, Montreal, August.

KASAMATSU, A., & HIRAI, T. (1966). An electroencephalographic study of the Zen meditation (Zazen). *Folio of Psychiatry and Neuropsychology, Japonica,* 20: 315–36. Also in C. T. Tart, ed., *Altered states of consciousness: A book of readings.* New York: Wiley, 1969.

KASWAN, J. (1957). Association of nonsense figures as a function of fittingness and intention to learn. *Amer. J. Psychol.,* 70: 447–50.

KATONA, G. (1940). *Organizing and memorizing.* New York: Columbia Univ. Press.

KATZ, J. (1966). *The philosophy of language.* New York: Harper & Row.

KAUSLER, D. H. (1974). *Psychology of verbal learning and memory.* New York: Academic Press.

KAZDIN, A. E. (1975). *Behavior modification in applied settings.* Homewood, Ill.: Dorsey Press.

KAZDIN, A. E. (1977). *The token economy.* New York: Plenum Press.

KAZDIN, A. E., & WILSON, G. T. (1978). *Evaluation of behavior therapy.* Cambridge, Mass.: Bollinger.

KELLER, F. S. (1968). Goodbye, teacher. *J. app. behav. Anal.,* 1: 69–89.

KELLER, F. S., & HILL, L. M. (1936). Another "insight" experiment. *J. genet. Psychol.,* 484–89.

KELLER, F. S., & RIBES-INESTA, E., eds. (1974). *Behavior modification: Applications to education.* New York: Academic Press.

KELLER, F. S., & SCHOENFELD, W. N. (1950). *Principles of psychology.* New York: Appleton-Century-Crofts.

KELLER, L., COLE, M., BURKE, C. J., & ESTES, W. K. (1965). Paired-associate learning with differential reward. Technical Report No. 66, Psychology Series, Institute for Mathematical Studies in the Social Sciences. Stanford Univ., Sept. 3.

KEPPEL, G. (1968). Retroactive and proactive inhibition. In T. R. Dixon & D. L. Horton, eds., *Verbal behavior and general behavior theory.* Englewood Cliffs, N.J.: Prentice-Hall.

KEPPEL, G., POSTMAN, L., & ZAVORTINK, B. (1968). Studies of learning to learn: VIII. The influence of massive amounts of training upon the learning and retention of paired-associate lists. *J. verb. Learn. verb. Behav.,* 7: 790–96. New York: Academic Press.

KIMBLE, D. P. (1963). *Physiological psychology: A unit for introductory psychology.* Reading, Mass.: Addison-Wesley.

KIMBLE, G. A. (1961) *Hilgard and Marquis' conditioning and learning.* 2nd ed. New York: Appleton-Century-Crofts.

KIMMEL, H. D. (1966). Inhibition of the unconditioned response in classical conditioning. *Psychol. Rev.,* 73: 232–40.

KIMURA, D. (1963). Right temporal lobe damage. *Arch. Neurol.,* 8: 264–71.

KINTSCH, W. (1964). Habituation of the GSR component of the orienting reflex during paired associate learning before and after learning has taken place. *J. math. Psychol.,* 2: 330–41.

KINTSCH, W. (1970). *Learning, memory, and conceptual processes.* New York: Wiley.

KINTSCH, W. (1974). *The representation of meaning in memory.* Hillsdale, N.J.: Erlbaum.

KINTSCH, W. (1975). Memory for prose. In C. N. Cofer, ed., *The structure of human memory.* San Francisco: W. H. Freeman. Pp. 90–113.

KINTSCH, W., & MORRIS, C. J. (1964). Application of a Markov model to free recall and recognition. *J. exp. Psychol.,* 69: 200–206.

KINTSCH, W., & VANDIJK, T. A. (1979). Toward a model of text comprehension and production. *Psychol. Rev.,* 85: 363–94.

KINTSCH, W., & VIPOND, D. (1978). Reading comprehension and readability in educational practice and psychological theory. In L. G. Nilsson, ed., *Memory: Processes and problems.* Hillsdale, N.J.: Erlbaum.

KLEITMAN, N. (1963). *Sleep and wakefulness.* Rev. ed. Chicago: Univ. of Chicago Press.

KLEITMAN, N., & CRISLER, G. (1927). A quantitative study of a salivary conditioned reflex. *Amer. J. Physiol.,* 79: 571–614.

KLING, J. W., & RIGGS, L. A. (1971). *Experimental psychology.* New York: Holt, Rinehart and Winston.

KOCH, S. (1954). Clark L. Hull. In W. K. Estes, S. Koch, K. MacCorquodale, P. E. Meehl, C. G. Mueller, W. N. Schoenfeld, & W. S. Verplanck, *Modern learning theory.* New York: Appleton-Century-Crofts. Pp. 1–176.

KOCH, S. ed. (1959). *Psychology: a study of a science.* Vol. 2. New York: McGraw-Hill.

KOFFKA, K. (1924). *The growth of the mind.* Translated by R. M. Ogden. London: Kegan Paul, Trench, Trubner.

KOFFKA, K. (1935). *Principles of Gestalt psychology.* New York: Harcourt, Brace & World.

KÖHLER, W. (1917). *Intelligenz-prufungen an Menschenaffen.* See Köhler, 1925.

KÖHLER, W. (1920). Die physische Gestalten in Ruhe und in stationären Zustand, Ein naturphilosophische Untersuchung. Braunschweig Verlag. Portions condensed and translated in W. D. Ellis, *A source book of Gestalt psychology.* New York: Harcourt, Brace & World, 1938. Pp. 17–54.

KÖHLER, W. (1925). *The mentality of apes.*

Translated by E. Winter. New York: Harcourt, Brace & World.

KÖHLER, W. (1929). *Gestalt psychology.* New York: Liveright.

KÖHLER, W. (1938). *The place of value in a world of facts.* New York: Liveright.

KÖHLER, W. (1940). *Dynamics in psychology.* New York: Liveright.

KÖHLER, W. (1941). On the nature of associations. *Proc. Amer. Phil. Soc.,* 84: 489–502.

KÖHLER, W., & RESTORFF, H. VON (1935). Analyse von Vorgangen im Spurenfeld. *Psychol. Forsch.,* 21: 56–112.

KONORSKI, J. & MILLER, S. (1937a). On two types of conditioned reflex. *J. Gen. Psychol.,* 16: 264–72.

KONORSKI, J. (1948). *Conditioned reflexes and neuron organization.* Cambridge, Eng.: Cambridge Univ. Press.

KOPSTEIN, F. F., & SEIDEL, R. J. (1969). Computer-administered instruction versus traditionally administered instruction: Economics. In R. C. Atkinson & H. A. Wilson, eds., *Computer-assisted instruction.* New York: Academic Press. Pp. 327–62.

KOTESKEY, R. L. (1972). A stimulus sampling model of the partial reinforcement effect. *Psychol. Rev.,* 79: 161–71.

KRANTZ, D. L. (1971). The separate worlds of operant and non-operant psychology. *J. appl. behav. Anal.,* 4: 61–70.

KRASNER, L. (1958). Studies of the conditioning of verbal behavior. *Psychol. Bull.,* 55: 148–70.

KRASNER, L. (1962). The therapist as a social reinforcement machine. In H. H. Strupp & L. Luborsky, eds., *Research in psychotherapy.* Vol. 2. Baltimore: French-Bray.

KRECH, D., ROSENZWEIG, M., & BENNETT, E. L. (1960). Effects of environmental complexity and training on brain chemistry. *J. comp. physiol. Psychol.,* 53: 509–19.

KRECH, D., ROSENZWEIG, M., & BENNETT, E. L. (1962). Relations between brain chemistry and problem solving among rats raised in enriched and impoverished environments. *J. comp. physiol. Psychol.,* 55: 801–7.

KRECHEVSKY, I. (1932a). "Hypotheses" in rats. *Psychol Rev.,* 39: 516–32.

KRECHEVSKY, I. (1932b). "Hypotheses" versus "chance" in the presolution period in sensory discrimination-learning. *Univ. Calif. Publ. Psychol.,* 6: 27–44.

KRECHEVSKY, I. (1933a). Hereditary nature of "hypotheses." *J. comp. Psychol.,* 16: 99–116.

KRECHEVSKY, I. (1933b). The docile nature of "hypotheses." *J. comp. Psychol.,* 15: 429–43.

KREUTZER, M. A., LEONARD, S. C., & FLAVELL, J. H. (1975). An interview study of children's knowledge about memory. *Child Devel.,* 40 (1), Serial No. 159.

KROLL, N. E. A., PARKS, T., PARKINSON, S. R., BIBER, S. L., & JOHNSON, A. L. (1970). Short-term memory while shadowing: Recall of visually and of aurally presented letters. *J. exp. Psychol.,* 85: 220–24.

KRUMBOLTZ, J. D., & THORESEN, C. E., eds. (1969). *Behavioral counseling: Cases and techniques.* New York: Holt, Rinehart and Winston.

KUHN, T. S. (1962). *The structure of scientific revolutions.* Chicago: Univ. of Chicago Press.

KULIK, J. A., KULIK, C. L., & CARMICHAEL, K. (1974). The Keller plan in science teaching. *Science,* 183: 379–83.

KUO, Z. Y. (1937). Forced movement or insight? *Univ. Calif. Publ. Psychol.,* 6: 169–88.

KUPFERMANN, I., & PINSKER, H. (1969). Plasticity in *Aplysia* neurons and some simple neuronal models of learning. In J. T. Tapp, ed., *Reinforcement and behavior.* New York and London: Academic Press.

LaBERGE, D. L. (1959). A model with neutral elements. In R. R. Bush & W. K. Estes, eds., *Studies in mathematical learning theory.* Stanford: Stanford Univ. Press.

LaBERGE, D. L. (1961). Generalization gradients

in a discrimination situation. *J. exp. Psychol.*, 62: 88–94.

LANDFIELD, P. W., & McGAUGH, J. L. (1972). Effects of electroconvulsive shock and brain stimulation on EEG cortical data rhythms in rats. *Behav. Biol.*, 7: 271–78.

LANDFIELD, P. W., McGAUGH, J. L., & TUSA, R. J. (1972).Theta rhythm: A temporal correlate of memory storage processes in the rat. *Science,* 175: 87–89.

LANGE, P. C. ed. (1967). *Programmed instruction.* 66th Yearbook of the National Society for the Study of Education, Part II. Chicago: NSSE.

LASHLEY, K. S. (1924). Studies of cerebral function in learning: V. The retention of motor habits after destruction of the so-called motor area in primates. *Arch, neurol. Psychiat.*, 12: 249–76.

LASHLEY, K. S. (1950). In search of the engram. *Society of Experimental Biology*, Symposium 4. Pp. 454–82.

LASHLEY, K. S., & BALL, J. (1929). Spinal conduction and kinesthetic sensitivity in the maze habit. *J. comp. Psychol.*, 9: 71–105.

LAWRENCE, D. H., & FESTINGER, L. (1962). *Deterrents and reinforcement: The psychology of insufficient reward.* Stanford: Stanford Univ. Press.

LeDOUX, J. E., WILSON, D. H., & GAZZANIGA, M. S. (1978). Manipulo spatial aspects of cerebral lateralization. *Neuropsychologia,* 15: 743–58.

LEE, C. L., & ESTES, W. K. (1977). Order and position in primary memory for letter strings. *J. verb. Learn. verb Behav.*, 16: 395–418.

LEHNERT, W. (1978). *The process of question answering.* Hillsdale, N.J.: Erlbaum.

LEITENBERG, H., ed. (1976). *Handbook of behavior modification and behavior therapy.* Englewood Cliffs, N.J.: Prentice-Hall.

LENNEBERG, E. H. (1967). *The biological foundations of language.* New York: Wiley.

LEONARD, D. W. (1969). Amount and sequence of reward in partial and continuous reinforcement. *J. comp. physiol. Psychol.*, 67: 204–11.

LEPLEY, W. M. (1934). Serial reactions considered as conditioned reactions. *Psychol. Mon.* 46 (205).

LEPPER, M. R., & GREENE, D., eds. (1978). *The hidden costs of reward.* Hillsdale, N.J.: Erlbaum.

LEPPER, M. R., GREENE, D., & NISBETT, R. E. (1973). Undermining children's intrinsic interest with extrinsic rewards: A test of the "overjustification" hypothesis. *J. Pers. soc. Psychol.* 28: 129–37.

LEPPER, M. R., SAGOTSKY, G., & GREENE, D. (1977). Overjustification effects following multiple-trial reinforcement procedures. Unpublished manuscript. Stanford University Psychology Department.

LESGOLD, A. M., & BOWER, G. H. (1970). Inefficiency of serial knowledge for associative responding. *J. verb. Learn. verb. Behav.* 9: 456–66.

LEUBA, C., BIRCH, L., & APPLETON, J. (1968). Human problem-solving during complete paralysis of the voluntary musculature. *Psychol. Rep.*, 22: 849–55.

LEVIÉN, R. E. (1972). *The emerging technology: Instructional uses of the computer in higher education.* New York: McGraw-Hill.

LEVINE, G., & BURKE, C. J. (1972). *Mathematical model techniques for learning theories.* New York: Academic Press.

LEVINE, M. (1965). Hypothesis behavior. In A. M. Schrier, H. F. Harlow, & F. Stollnitz, eds., *Behavior of nonhuman primates.* Vol. 1. New York: Academic Press.

LEVINE, M. (1969). Neo-noncontinuity theory. In G. H. Bower & J. T. Spence, eds., *The psychology of learning and motivation.* Vol. 3. New York: Academic Press.

LEVINE, M. (1970). Human discrimination learning: The subset sampling assumption. *Psychol. Bull.*, 74: 397–404.

LEVIS, D. J. (1976). Learned helplessness: A

reply and an alternative S-R interpretation. *J. ex. Psychol.: General*, 105: 47–65.

Levy, N., & Seward, J. P. (1969). Frustration and homogeneity of rewards in the double runway. *J. exp. Psychol.*, 81: 460–63.

Lewin, K. (1935). *A dynamic theory of personality.* Translated by D. K. Adams & K. E. Zener. New York: McGraw-Hill.

Lewis, D. J. (1969). Sources of experimental amnesia. *Psychol. Rev.*, 76: 461–72.

Lewis, D. J., & Kent, N. D. (1961). Attempted direct activation and deactivation of the fractional anticipatory goal response. *Psychol. Rep.* 8: 107–10.

Lewis, D. J., & Maher, B. A. (1965). Neural consolidation and electroconvulsive shock. *Psychol. Rev.* 72: 225–39.

Light, L. L., & Carter-Sobell, L. (1970). Effects of changed semantic context on recognition memory. *J. verb. Learn. verb. Behav.*, 9: 1–11.

Light, L. L., Stansbury, C., Rubin, C., & Linde, S. (1973). Memory for modality of presentation: Within-modality discrimination. *Mem. and Cog.*, 1: 395–400.

Lindsay, P. H., & Norman, D. A. (1972). *Human information processing: An introduction to psychology.* New York: Academic Press.

Lindsley, D. B. (1958). The reticular system and perceptual discrimination. In H. H. Jasper et al. eds., *Reticular formation of the brain.* Boston: Little, Brown. Chap. 25.

Lindvall, C. M., & Bolvin, J. O. ((1967). Programmed instruction in the schools: An application of programming principles in "individually prescribed instruction." In P. C. Lange, ed., *Programmed instruction.* 66th Yearbook of the National Society for the Study of Education, Part II. Pp. 217–54. Chicago: NSSE.

Lindvall, C. M., & Cox, R. C. (1969). The role of evaluation in programs for individualized instruction. In R. W. Tyler, ed., *Educational evaluation: New roles, new means.* 68th Yearbook of the National Society for the Study of Education. Pp. 156–88. Chicago: NSSE.

Linton, M. (1975). Memory for real-world events. In D. A. Norman & D. E. Rumelhart, eds., *Explorations in cognition.* San Francisco: W. H. Freeman. Pp. 376–404.

Locke, E. A., Cartledge, N., & Kerr, C. S. (1970). Studies of the relationship between satisfaction, goal setting, and performance. *Org. Behav. hum. Perf.* 5: 135–58.

Locke, J. & Locke, V. L. (1971). Deaf children's phonetic, visual, and dactylic coding in a grapheme recall task. *J. exp. Psychol.*, 89: 142–46.

Loftus, G. (1972). Eye fixations and recognition memory for pictures. *Cog. Psychol.*, 3: 525–51.

Logan, F. A. (1956). A micromolar approach to behavior theory. *Psychol. Rev.*, 63: 63–73.

Logan, F. A. (1959). The Hull-Spence approach. In S. Koch, ed., *Psychology: A study of a science.* Vol. 2. New York: McGraw-Hill. Pp. 293–358.

Logan, F. A. (1960). *Incentive.* New Haven: Yale Univ. Press.

Logan, F. A. (1965). Decision making by rats. *J. comp. physiol. Psychol.*, 59: 1–12, 246–51.

Logan, F. A. (1968). Incentive theory and changes in reward. In K. W. Spence & J. T. Spence, eds., *The psychology of learning and motivation.* Vol. 2. New York: Academic Press.

Logan, F. A. (1969). The negative incentive value of punishment. In B. A. Campbell & R. M. Church, eds., *Punishment and aversive behavior.* New York: Appleton-Century-Crofts.

Logan, F. A. (1970). *Fundamentals of learning and motivation.* Dubuque, Iowa: Brown.

Logan, F. A. (1977). Hybrid theory of classical conditioning. In G. H. Bower, ed., *The Psychology of learning and motivation.* Vol. II. New York: Academic Press. Pp. 203–43.

Logan, F. A. (1979). Hybrid theory of operant conditioning. *Psychol. Rev.*, 86: 507–41.

Logan, F. A., & Ferraro, D. P. (1978). *Systematic analyses of behavior: Basic learning and motivational processes.* Hillsdale, N.J.: Erlbaum.

Logan, F. A., & Wagner, A. R. (1965). *Reward and punishment.* Boston: Allyn & Bacon.

LoLordo, V. M., McMillan, J. C., & Riley, A. L. (1974). The effects upon food-reinforced pecking and treadle-pressing of auditory and visual signals for response-independent food. *Learn. and Mot.,* 5: 24–41.

Lorayne, H., & Lucas, J. (1974). *The memory book.* New York: Ballantine Books.

Lorenz, K. Z. (1952). *King Solomon's ring.* New York: Crowell.

Loucks, R. B. (1933). An appraisal of Pavlov's systematization of behavior from the experimental standpoint. *J. comp. Psychol.,* 15: 1–47.

Lovaas, O. I. (1976). *Language acquisition programs for nonlinguistic children.* New York: Irvington Publishing.

Lovaas, O. I., & Newsom, C. D. (1976). Behavior modification with psychotic children. In H. Leitenberg, ed., *Handbook of behavior modification and behavior therapy.* Englewood Cliffs, N.J.: Prentice-Hall.

Lovejoy, E. (1968). *Attention in discrimination learning.* San Francisco: Holden-Day.

Luce, R. D., Bush, R. R., & Galanter, E., eds. (1963). *Handbook of mathematical psychology.* Vols. 1 and 2. New York: Wiley.

Luce, R. D., Bush, R. R., & Galanter, E., eds. (1965). *Handbook of mathematical psychology.* Vol. 3. New York: Wiley.

Luria, A. R. (1966). *Higher cortical functions in man.* New York: Plenum.

MacCorquodale, K. (1969) B. F. Skinner's *Verbal Behavior:* A retrospective appreciation. *J. exp. anal. Behav.,* 12: 831–841.

MacCorquodale, K. (1970). On Chomsky's review of Skinner's *Verbal Behavior. J. exp. anal. Behav.,* 13: 83–100.

MacCorquodale, K., & Meehl, P. E. (1953). Preliminary suggestions as to a formalization of expectancy theory. *Psychol. Rev.,* 60: 55–63.

MacCorquodale, K., & Meehl, P. E. (1954). Edward C. Tolman. In W. K. Estes, S. Koch, K. MacCorquodale, P. E. Meehl, C. G. Mueller, W. N. Schoenfeld, & W. S. Verplanck, *Modern learning theory.* New York: Appleton-Century-Crofts. Pp. 177–266.

MacFarlane, D. A. (1930). The role of kinesthesis in maze learning. *Univ. Calif. Publ. Psychol.,* 4: 277–305.

Mackintosh, N. J. (1974). *The psychology of animal learning.* New York: Academic Press.

Mackintosh, N. J., & Honig, W. K., eds. (1971). *Fundamental issues in associative learning.* Halifax: Dalhousie Univ. Press.

McCleary, R. A. (1960). Type of response as a function of interocular transfer in the fish. *J. comp. physiol. Psychol.,* 53: 311–21.

McClure, R. M., ed. (1971). *The curriculum: Retrospect and prospect.* 70th Yearbook of the National Society for the Study of Education, Part I. Chicago: Univ. of Chicago Press.

McConnell, J. V. (1962). Memory transfer through cannibalism in planarians. *J. Neuropsychiat.,* 3 (Suppl. 1): 542.

McCrary, J. W., & Hunter, W. S. (1953). Serial position curves in verbal learning. *Science,* 117: 131–34.

McGaugh, J. C. (1965). Facilitation and impairment of memory storage processes. In D. P. Kimble, ed., *Learning, remembering, and forgetting.* Vol. 1. *The anatomy of memory.* Palo Alto: Science and Behavior Books. Pp. 240–91.

McGaugh, J. C. (1968). Drug facilitation of memory and learning. In D. H. Efron et al. eds., *Psychopharmacology: A review of progress, 1957–1967.* PHS publication 1836. Pp. 891–904. Washington, D.C.: U.S. Govt. Printing Office.

McGaugh, J. L., & Herz, M. J. (1972). *Memory consolidation.* San Francisco: Albion.

McGaugh, J. L., & Landfield, P. W. (1970). Delayed development of amnesia following electroconvulsive shock. *Physiol. and Behav.,* 5: 751–55.

McGEOCH, J. A. (1932). Forgetting and the law of disuse. *Psychol. Rev.,* 39: 352–70.

McGEOCH, J. A., & IRION, A. L. (1952). *The psychology of human learning.* Rev ed. New York: Longmans.

McGILL, W. J. (1963). Stochastic latency mechanisms. In R. D. Luce, R. R. Bush, & E. Galanter, eds., *Handbook of mathematical psychology.* Vol. 1. New York: Wiley.

McGOVERN, J. B. (1964). Extinction of associations in four transfer paradigms. *Psychol. Monogr.,* 78 (Whole No. 593).

McGUIGAN, F. J., & SCHOONOVER, R. A. (1973). *The psycho-physiology of thinking.* New York: Academic Press.

McGUIRE, W. J. (1961). A multiprocess model for paired-associate learning. *J. exp. Psychol.* 62: 335–47.

McKEACHIE, W. J. (1974). The decline and fall of the laws of learning. *Ed. Res.* 3: 7–11.

McNEILL, D. (1970). *The acquisition of language.* New York: Harper & Row.

MADDEN, E. H. (1962). *Philosophical problems of psychology.* New York: Odyssey.

MAGER, R. F. (1961). *Preparing instructional objectives.* Palo Alto, Cal.: Fearon Publishing.

MAGER, R. F. (1972). *Goal analysis.* Belmont, Cal.: Fearon Publishing.

MAHONEY, M. J. (1976). *Scientist as subject: The psychological imperative.* Cambridge, Mass.: Ballinger.

MAIER, S. F., & SELIGMAN, M. E. P. (1976). Learned helplessness: Theory and evidence. *J. exp. Psychol.: General,* 105: 3–46.

MALONE, T. W., MACKEN, E., & SUPPES, P. (1979). Toward optimal allocation of instructional resources: Dividing computer-assisted instruction time among students. *Instr. Sci.,* 8: 107–20.

MANDLER, G. (1967). Organization and memory. In K. W. Spence & J. T. Spence, eds., *The psychology of learning and motivation: Ad-*

vances in research and theory. Vol. 1. New York: Academic Press.

MANDLER, G. (1968). Association and organization: Facts, fancies, and theories. In T. R. Dixon & D. L. Horton, eds., *Verbal behavior and general behavior theory.* Englewood Cliffs, N.J.: Prentice-Hall.

MANDLER, J. M., & MANDLER, G. (1964). *Thinking: From association to Gestalt.* New York: Wiley.

MARCUS, M. P. (1977). *A theory of syntactic recognition for natural language.* Unpublished PhD thesis. Cambridge: MIT.

MARLER, P. (1970). A comparative approach to vocal learning: Song development in white-crowned sparrows. *J. comp. physiol. Psychol.,* 71 (2) Part 2 (monograph).

MARTIN, E. (1965). Transfer of verbal paired associates. *Psychol. Rev.,* 72: 327–43.

MASSERMAN, J. H. (1943). *Behavior and neurosis.* Chicago: Univ. of Chicago Press.

MAYER, G. R., & BUTTERWORTH, T. N. (1979). A preventive approach to school violence and vandalism: An experimental study. *Pers. Guid. J.,* 57: 436–41.

MAYER, D. J., WOLFE, T. L., AKIL, H., CARDER, B., & LIEKESKIND, J. C. (1971). Analgesia from electrical stimulation in the brainstem of the rat. *Science,* 174: 1351.

MECHNER, F. (1958). Probability relations within response sequences under ratio reinforcement. *J. exp. anal. Behav.,* 1: 109–22.

MEEHL, P. E. (1950) On the circularity of the law of effect. *Psychol. Bull.,* 47: 52–75.

MEICHENBAUM, D. (1977). *Cognitive behavior modification: An integrative approach.* New York: Plenum Press.

MEICHENBAUM, D., & ASARNOW, J. (1979). Cognitive behavior modification and metacognitive development: Implications for the classroom. In P. Kendell & S. Hollon, eds., *Cognitive behavior interventions: Theory, research and procedures.* New York: Academic Press.

MEIKLE, T. H. (1960). Role of corpus callosum

in transfer of visual discrimination in the cat. *Science,* 132: 1496.

MEIKLE, T. H., & SECHZER, J. A. (1960). Interocular transfer of brightness discrimination in "split-brain" cats. *Science,* 132: 734–35.

MELTON, A. W., ed. (1964). *Categories of human learning.* New York: Academic Press.

MELTON, A. W., & IRWIN, J. McQ. (1940). The influence of degree of interpolated learning on retroactive inhibition and the overt transfer of specific responses. *Amer. J. Psychol.,* 53: 173–203.

MELTON, A. W., & MARTIN, E., eds. (1972). *Coding processes in human memory.* Washington, D.C., V. H. Winston.

MENZEL, E. W. (1973). Chimpanzee spatial memory organization. *Science,* 182: 943–45.

MENZEL, E. W. (1974). A group of young chimpanzees in a one-acre field. In A. M. Schrier & F. Stollnitz, eds., *Behavior of nonhuman primates.* Vol. 5. New York: Academic Press. Pp. 83–153.

MENZEL, E. M. (1978). Cognitive mapping in chimpanzees. In S. H. Hulse, H. Fowler, & W. K. Honig, eds., *Cognitive processes in animal behavior.* Hillsdale, N.J.: Erlbaum. Pp. 375–422.

MERRYMAN, C. T. (1969). Effects of strategies on associative symmetry. Indiana Mathematical Psychology Rep. No. 69-6. Bloomington: Univ. of Indiana Press.

MERRYMAN, C. T. (1971). Retroactive inhibition in the A-B, A-D paradigm as measured by a multiple-choice test. *J. exp. Psychol.* 91: 212–14.

MEYER, B. (1975). *The organization of prose and its effect upon memory.* Amsterdam: North-Holland.

MICHAEL, R. P. (1962). Estrogen-sensitive neurons and sexual behavior in female cats. *Science,* 136: 322–23.

MICHOTTE, A. (1954). *La perception de la causalité.* 2nd ed. Louvain: Publications Univ. de Louvain.

MILLER, G. A. (1956). The magical number seven plus or minus two: Some limits on our capacity for processing information. *Psychol. Rev.,* 63: 81–97.

MILLER, G. A., GALANTER, E., & PRIBRAM, K. H. (1960). *Plans and the structure of behavior.* New York: Holt, Rinehart and Winston.

MILLER, G. A., & McNEIL, D. (1969). Psycholinguistics. In G. Lindzey & E. Aronson, eds., *The handbook of social psychology.* 2nd ed. Vol. 3. Reading, Mass.: Addison-Wesley.

MILLER, N. E. (1944). Experimental studies in conflict. In J. McV. Hunt, ed., *Personality and the behavior disorders.* New York: Ronald Press. Pp. 431–65.

MILLER, N. E. (1948). Theory and experiment relating psychoanalytic displacement to stimulus-response generalization. *J. abnorm. soc. Psychol.,* 43: 155–78.

MILLER, N. E. (1951). Learnable drives and rewards. In S. S. Stevens, ed., *Handbook of experimental psychology.* New York: Wiley.

MILLER, N. E. (1958). Central stimulation and other new approaches to motivation and reward. *Amer. Psychol.,* 13: 100–108.

MILLER, N. E. (1959). Liberalization of basic S-R concepts: Extensions to conflict behavior, motivation and social learning. In S. Koch, ed., *Psychology: A study of a science.* Vol. 2. New York: McGraw-Hill. Pp. 196–202.

MILLER, N. E. (1965). Chemical coding of behavior in the brain. *Science,* 148: 328–38.

MILLER, N. E. (1969). Learning of visceral and glandular responses. *Science,* 163: 434–45.

MILLER, N. E., & BANUAZIZI, A. (1968). Instrumental learning by curarized rats of a specific visceral response, intestinal or cardiac. *J. comp. physiol. Psychol.,* 65: 1–7.

MILLER, N. E., & BRUCKER, B. S. (1978). Learned large increases in blood pressure apparently independent of skeletal responses in patients paralyzed by spinal lesions. In N. Birbaumer & H. O. Kimmel, eds., *Biofeedback and self-regulation.* Hillsdale, N.J.: Erlbaum Assoc.

MILLER, N. E., & DOLLARD, J. (1941). *Social learning and imitation.* New Haven, Yale Univ. Press.

MILLER, N. E., & DWORKIN, B. R. (1974). Visceral learning: Recent difficulties with curarized rats and significant problems for human research. In P. A. Obrist, A. H. Black, J. Brener, & L. V. DiCara, eds., *Cardiovascular psychophysiology.* Chicago: Aldine. Pp. 312–31.

MILLER, N. E., & DWORKIN, B. R. (1977). Critical issues in therapeutic applications of biofeedback. In G. E. Schwartz & J. Beatty, eds., *Biofeedback: Theory and research.* New York: Academic Press. Pp. 129–61.

MILLER, N. E., & DWORKIN, B. R. (1978). Different ways in which learning is involved in homeostasis. Paper presented as US-USSR Symposium on the neurophysiological mechanisms of goal-directed behavior and learning.

MILLER, N. E., & MURRAY, E. J. (1952). Displacement and conflict: Learnable drive as a basis for the steeper gradient of avoidance than of approach. *J. exp. Psychol.,* 43: 227–31.

MILLER, R. R., & SPRINGER, D. D. (1973). Amnesia, consolidation, and retrieval. *Psychol. Rev.,* 80: 69–79.

MILLER, S., & KONORSKI, J. (1928). Sur une forme particulière des réflexes conditionnels. *C. R. Soc. Biol. Paris,* 99: 1155–57.

MILNER, B. (1970). Memory and the temporal regions of the brain. In K. H. Pribram & D. E. Broadbent, eds., *Biology of memory.* New York: Academic Press.

MILNER, B. R. (1966). Amnesia following operation on temporal lobes. In C. W. N. Whitty & O. L. Zangwill, eds., *Amnesia.* London: Butterworths.

MILNER, B. R. (1968). Visual recognition and recall after right temporal-lobe excision in man. *Neuropsychol.,* 6: 191–209.

MINSKY, M. (1961). Steps toward artificial intelligence. *Proc. of Inst. of Radio Engineers,* 49: 8–30. Also reprinted in E. Feigenbaum & J. Feldman, eds., *Computers and thought.* New York: McGraw-Hill, 1963.

MINSKY, M., ed. (1968). *Semantic information processing.* Cambridge: MIT Press.

MISANIN, J. R., MILLER, R. R., & LEWIS, D. G. (1968). Retrograde amnesia produced by electroconvulsive shock after reactivation of a consolidated memory trace. *Science,* 160: 554–55.

MISCHEL, W. (1968). *Personality and assessment.* New York: Wiley.

MISCHEL, W. (1971). *Introduction to personality.* New York: Holt, Rinehard & Winston.

MITCHELL, D., KIRSCHAUM, E. H., & PERRY, R. L. (1975). Effects of neophobia and habituation on the poison-induced avoidance of exteroceptive stimuli in the rat. *J. exp. Psychol.: Animal Behavior Processes,* 104: 47–55.

MOAR, I. (1980a). Directional information in visual images. Unpublished paper. Stanford Psychology Dept. Stanford University.

MOAR, I. (1980b). The nature and acquisition of cognitive maps. In D. Cantor & T. Lee, eds., *Proceedings of the international conference on environmental psychology.* London: Architectural Press.

MOESER, S. D., & BREGMAN, A. S. (1973). Imagery and language acquisition. *J. verb. Learn. verb. Behav.* 12: 91–98.

MOLTZ, H. (1957). Latent extinction and the fractional anticipatory response mechanism. *Psychol. Rev.,* 64: 229–41.

MOORE, B. R. (1973). The role of directed Pavlovian reactions in simple instrumental learning in the pigeon. In R. A. Hinde & J. Stevenson-Hinde, eds., *Constraints on learning.* New York: Academic Press.

MOORE, B. R., & STUTTARD, S. (1979). Dr. Guthrie and *Felis domesticus,* or, tripping over the cat. *Science,* 205: 1031–33.

MORAY, N. (1969). *Listening and attention.* Baltimore: Penguin Books.

MORAY, N. (1970). *Attention: Selective processes in vision and hearing.* New York: Academic Press.

MORRELL, F. (1960). Secondary epileptogenic lesions. *Epilepsia,* 1: 538–60.

MORRELL, F. (1961a). Effect of anodal polarization on the firing pattern of single cortical cells. *Ann. N.Y. Acad. Sci.* 92: 860–76.

MORRELL, F. (1961b). Electrophysiological contributions to the neural basis of learning. *Physiol. Rev.,* 41: 443–94.

MORRELL, F. (1963). Information storage in nerve cells. In W. S. Fields & W. Abbott, eds., *Information storage and neural control.* Springfield, Ill.: Charles C Thomas.

MORRIS, C. D., BRANSFORD, J. D., & FRANKS, J. J. (1977). Levels of processing versus transfer-appropriate processing. *J. verb. Learn. verb. Behav.,* 16: 519–33.

MORSE, W. H. (1966). Intermittent reinforcement. In W. K. Honig, ed., *Operant behavior: Areas of research and application.* New York: Appleton-Century-Crofts.

MOWRER, O. H. (1947). On the dual nature of learning—a re-interpretation of "conditioning" and "problem-solving." *Harv. educ. Rev.,* 17: 102–48.

MOWRER, O. H. (1956). Two-factor learning theory reconsidered, with special reference to secondary reinforcement and the concept of habit. *Psychol. Rev.,* 63: 114–28.

MOWRER, O. H. (1960). *Learning theory and behavior.* New York: Wiley.

MUELLER, C. G., JR., & SCHOENFELD, W. N. (1954). Edwin R. Guthrie. In W. K. Estes, S. Koch, K. MacCorquodale, P. E. Meehl, C. G. Mueller, W. N. Schoenfeld, & W. S. Verplanck, *Modern learning theory.* New York: Appleton-Century-Crofts. Pp. 345–79.

MUENZINGER, K. F. (1938). Vicarious trial and error at a point of choice: I. A general survey of its relation to learning efficiency. *J. genet. Psychol.,* 53: 75–86.

MÜLLER, G. E., & PILZECKER, A. (1900). Experimentelle Beiträge zur Lehre vom Gedachtnis. *Z. Psychol.,* Ergbd. I.

MURDOCK, B. B., JR., (1960). The distinctiveness of stimuli. *Psychol. Rev.,* 67: 16–31.

MYERS, J. L. (1970). Sequential choice behavior. In G. H. Bower, ed., *The psychology of learning and motivation: Advances in research and theory.* Vol. 4. New York: Academic Press.

MYROW, D. L., & ANDERSON, R. C. (1972). Retroactive inhibition of prose as a function of the type of test. *J. educ. Psychol.,* 63: 303–8.

NEIMARK, E. D., & ESTES, W. K., eds. (1967). *Stimulus sampling theory.* San Francisco: Holden-Day.

NEIMARK, E. D., & SHUFORD, E. H. (1959). Comparison of predictions and estimates in a probability learning situation. *J. exp. Psychol.,* 57: 294–98.

NEISSER, U. (1967). *Cognitive psychology.* Englewood Cliffs, N.J.: Prentice-Hall.

NEISSER, U. (1976). *Cognition and reality.* San Francisco: W. H. Freeman.

NELSON, D. L., et al. (1979). Doubts about depth. *J. exp. Psychol.: Human Learning and Memory,* 5: 24–44.

NELSON, T. O. (1977). Repetition and depth of processing *J. verb. Learn. verb. Behav.* 16: 151–71.

NEWELL, A. (1970). Remarks on the relationship between artificial intelligence and cognitive psychology. In R. Banerji & M. D. Mesarovic, eds., *Theoretical approaches to nonnumerical problem solving.* New York: Springer-Verlag.

NEWELL, A. (1973). Production systems: Models of control structures. In W. G. Chase, ed., *Visual information processing.* New York: Academic Press. Pp. 463–526.

NEWELL, A., SHAW, J. C., & SIMON, H. A. (1958). Elements of a theory of human problem solving. *Psychol. Rev.,* 65: 151–66.

NEWELL, A., SHAW, J. C., & SIMON, H. A. (1959). A report on a general problem-solving program. *Proceedings of the International Conference on Information Processing.* New York: UNESCO. Pp. 256–65.

NEWELL, A., & SIMON, H. A. (1956). The logic theory machine. *IRE Transactions on Information Theory,* IT-2. Pp. 61–69.

NEWELL, A., & SIMON, H. A. (1961). Computer simulation of human thinking. *Science,* 134: 2011–17.

NEWELL, A., & SIMON, H. A. (1963). Computers in psychology. In R. D. Luce, R. R. Bush, & E. Galanter, eds., *Handbook of mathematical psychology.* Vol. 1. New York: Wiley.

NEWELL, A., & SIMON, H. A. (1972). *Human*

problem solving. Englewood Cliffs, N.J.: Prentice-Hall.

NEWTON, J. M., & WICKENS, D. D. (1956). Retroactive inhibition as a function of the temporal position of interpolated learning. *J. exp. Psychol.*, 51: 149–54.

NIELSON, H. C. (1968). Evidence that electroconvulsive shock alters memory retrieval rather than memory consolidation. *Exp. Neurol.*, 20: 3–20.

NILSSON, N. J. (1971). *Problem-solving methods in artificial intelligence.* New York: McGraw-Hill.

NISBETT, D., & ROSS, L. (1979). *Human inference: Strategies and shortcomings of social judgment.* Englewood Cliffs, N.J.: Prentice-Hall.

NOBLE, C. E. (1966). Selective learning. In E. A. Bilodeau, ed., *Acquisition of skill.* New York: Academic Press. Pp. 47–98.

NORMAN, D. A., & RUMELHART, D. E., eds., (1975). *Explorations in cognition.* San Francisco: W. H. Freeman.

NOTTEBOHM, F. (1970). Ontogeny of bird song. *Science,* 167: 950–56.

NOTTERMAN, J. M., & MINTZ, D. E. (1962). Exteroceptive cueing of response force, *Science,* 135: 1070–71.

NUTTIN, J. (1949). "Spread" in recalling failure and success. *J. exp. Psychol.*, 39: 60–69.

NUTTIN, J. (1953). *Tâche, réussite et èchec.* Louvain: Publications Univ. de Louvain.

O'KEEFE, J., & NADEL, L. (1978). *The hippocampus as a cognitive map.* Oxford, Clarendon Press.

OLDS, J. (1965). Operant conditioning of single unit responses. *Excerpta Medica, Foundation International Congress Series,* 87: 372–80.

OLDS, J. (1969). The central nervous system and the reinforcement of behavior. *Amer. Psychol.*, 24: 114–32.

OLDS, J., ALLAN, W. S., & BRIESE, E. (1971). Differentiation of hypothalamic drive and reward centers. *Am. J. Physiol.*, 221: 368–75.

OLDS, J., & MILNER, P. (1954). Positive reinforcement produced by electrical stimulation of septal area and other regions of rat brain. *J. comp. physiol. Psychol.*, 47: 419–27.

O'LEARY, K. D., & O'LEARY, S. G., eds. (1972). *Classroom management: The successful use of behavior modification.* New York: Pergamon.

O'LEARY, K. D., & WILSON, G. T. (1975). *Behavior therapy: Application and outcome.* Englewood Cliffs, N.J.: Prentice-Hall.

OLSON, G. M. (1969). Learning and retention in a continuous recognition task. *J. exp. Psychol.*, 81: 381–84.

OLTON, D. S. (1979). Mazes, maps, and memory. *Amer. Psychol.*, 34: 583–96.

OLTON, D. S., & SAMUELSON, R. J. (1976). Remembrance of places passed: Spatial memory in rats. *J. exp. Psychol.: Animal Behavior Processes,* 2: 97–116.

O'NEIL, H. F., JR., ed. (1978). *Learning strategies.* New York: Academic Press.

ORNSTEIN, R. E. (1969). *On the experience of time.* London: Penguin Books.

ORNSTEIN, R. E. (1972). *The psychology of consciousness.* San Francisco: W. H. Freeman.

OSGOOD, C. E. (1949). The similarity paradox in human learning: A resolution. *Psychol. Rev.*, 56: 132–43.

OSGOOD, C. E. (1953). *Method and theory in experimental psychology.* New York: Oxford Univ. Press.

OSTERHOUSE, R. A. (1976). Group systematic desensitization of test anxiety. In J. D. Krumboltz & C. E. Thoresen, eds., *Counseling methods.* New York: Holt, Rinehart and Winston. Pp. 269–79.

OVERTON, D. A. (1964). State-dependent or "dissociated" learning produced by pentobarbital. *J. comp. physiol. Psychol.*, 57: 3–12.

OVERTON, D. A. (1978). Major theories of state dependent learning. In B. T. Ho, D. W. Richards III., & D. L. Chute, eds., *Drug discrimination and state dependent learning.* New York: Academic Press. Pp. 283–318.

PACKARD, R. G. (1970). The control of "classroom attention": A group contingency for complex behavior. *J. appl. behav. Anal.*, 3: 13–28.

PAIVIO, A. (1971). *Imagery and verbal processes.* New York: Holt, Rinehart and Winston.

PAIVIO, A., & CSAPO, K. (1972). Picture superiority in free recall: Imagery or dual coding? Research Bulletin #243. Department of Psychology, University of Western Ontario, Aug. 1972.

PALMER, S. E. (1975). Visual perception and world knowledge: Notes on a model of sensory-cognitive interaction. In D. A. Norman & D. E. Rumelhart, eds., *Explorations in cognition.* San Francisco: W. H. Freeman.

PAN, S. (1926). The influence of control upon learning and recall. *P. exp. Psychol.*, 9: 468–91.

PARKER, E. S., BIRNBAUM, I. M., & NOBLE, E. P. (1976). Alcohol and memory: Storage and state dependency. *J. verb. Learn. verb. Behav.*, 15: 691–702.

PASCAL, G. R. (1949). The effect of relaxation upon recall. *Amer. J. Psychol.*, 62: 32–47.

PASKEWITZ, D. A., & ORNE, M. T. (1973). Visual effects on alpha feedback training. *Science,* 181: 360–63.

PAVLIK, W. B., & CARLTON, P. J. (1965). A reversed partial-reinforcement effect. *J. exper. Psychol.*, 70: 417–23.

PAVLOV, I. P. (1903). Experimental psychology and psychopathology in animals. In Pavlov (1928), pp. 47–60; also in Pavlov (1955), pp. 151–68.

PAVLOV, I. P. (1927). *Conditioned reflexes.* London: Clarendon Press.

PAVLOV, I. P. (1928). *Lectures on conditioned reflexes.* Translated by W. H. Gantt. New York: International Publishers.

PAVLOV, I. P. (1932). The reply of a physiologist to psychologist. *Psychol. Rev.*, 39: 91–127.

PAVLOV, I. P. (1941). *Conditioned reflexes and psychiatry.* New York: International Publishers.

PAVLOV, I. P. (1955). *Selected works.* Moscow: Foreign Languages Publishing House.

PAVLOV, I. P. (1957). *Experimental psychology and other essays.* New York: Philosophical Library.

PERKINS, C. C., JR. (1955). The stimulus conditions which follow learned responses. *Psychol. Rev.*, 62: 341–48.

PETERSON, J. (1922). Learning when frequency and recency factors are negative. *J. exp. Psychol.*, 5: 270–300.

PETERSON, L. R. (1963). Immediate memory: Data and theory. In C. N. Cofer & B. S. Musgrave, eds., *Verbal behavior and verbal learning.* New York: McGraw-Hill.

PETERSON, L. R., & PETERSON, M. J. (1959). Short-term retention of individual verbal items. *J. exp. Psychol.*, 58: 193–98.

PIAGET, J. (1954). *The construction of reality in the child.* New York: Basic Books.

PICKREL, G., NEIDT, C., & GIBSON, R. (1958). Tape recordings are used to teach seventh grade students in Westside Junior-Senior High School, Omaha, Nebraska. *Nat. Assoc. Sec. Sch. Principals Bull.*, 42: 81–93.

PITTS, W., & MCCULLOCH, W. S. (1947). How we know universals, the perception of auditory and visual form. *Bull. Math. Biophys.*, 9 (3): 127–47.

PLOTKIN, W. B. (1976). On the self-regulation of the occipital alpha rhythm. *J. exp. Psychol.: General*, 105: 66–99.

PLOTKIN, W. B. (1979). The alpha experience revisited. *Psychol. Bull.* 86: 1132–48.

POPPEN, R. L. (1968). Counterconditioning of conditioned suppression. Unpublished doctoral dissertation. Stanford: Stanford Univ.

POSTMAN, L. (1961). The present status of interference theory. In C. N. Cofer, ed., *Verbal learning and verbal behavior.* New York: McGraw-Hill. Pp. 152–79.

POSTMAN, L. (1962). Rewards and punishments in human learning. In L. Postman, ed., *Psychology in the making.* New York: Alfred A. Knopf. Pp. 331–401.

POSTMAN, L. (1964). Short-term memory and incidental learning. In A. W. Melton, ed., *Categories of human learning*. New York: Academic Press. Pp. 146–201.

POSTMAN, L. (1971). Transfer, interference, and forgetting. In J. W. Kling & L. A. Riggs, eds., *Woodworth and Schlosberg's experimental psychology*. 3rd ed., New York: Holt, Rinehart and Winston.

POSTMAN, L., & STARK, K. (1969). Role of response availability in transfer and interference. *J. exp. Psychol.*, 79: 168–77.

POSTMAN, L., STARK, K., & FRASER, J. (1968). Temporal changes in interference. *J. verb. Learn. verb. Behav.*, 7: 672–94.

POSTMAN, L., STARK, K., & HENSCHEL, D. (1969). Conditions of recovery after unlearning. *J. exp. Psychol. Monogr.*, 82 (Whole No. 1).

PREMACK, D. (1959). Toward emperical behavior laws: I. Positive reinforcement. *Psychol. Rev.*, 66: 219–33.

PREMACK, D. (1962). Reversibility of the reinforcement relation. *Science,* 136: 255–57.

PREMACK, D. (1963). Rate differential reinforcement in monkey manipulation. *J. exp. anal. Behav.*, 6: 81–89.

PREMACK, D. (1965). Reinforcement theory. In M. R. Jones, ed., *Nebraska Symposium on Motivation: 1965*. Lincoln: Univ. of Nebraska Press.

PREMACK, D. (1969). A functional analysis of language. Invited address to Meetings of American Psychological Association, Washington, D.C.

PRENTICE, W. C. H. (1959). The systematic psychology of Wolfgang Köhler. In S. Koch, ed., *Psychology: A study of a science*. Vol. 1. New York: McGraw-Hill. Pp. 427–55.

PRESSEY, S. L. (1926). A simple apparatus which gives tests and scores—and teaches. *Sch. and Soc.*, 23: 373–76.

PRESSEY, S. L. (1927). A machine for automatic teaching of drill material. *Sch. and Soc.*, 25: 549–52.

PREWITT, E. P. (1967). Number of preconditioning trials in sensory preconditioning using CER training. *J. comp. physiol. Psychol.*, 64: 360–62.

PRIBRAM, K. (1971). *Languages of the brain.* Englewood Cliffs, N.J.: Prentice-Hall.

PROKASY, W. F., ed. (1965). *Classical conditioning: A symposium.* New York: Appleton-Century-Crofts.

PRYTULAK, L. S. (1971). Natural language mediation. *Cog. Psychol.* 2: 1–56.

QUILLIAN, M. R. (1968). Semantic memory. In M. Minsky, ed., *Semantic information processing*. Cambridge: MIT Press.

RACHLIN, H. (1974). Self-control. *Behaviorism,* 2: 94–107.

RACHLIN, H. (1976). *Behavior and learning.* San Francisco: W. H. Freeman.

RACHMAN, S., HODGSON, R. J., & MARKS, I. (1971). The treatment of chronic obsessive-compulsive neurosis. *Behav. Res. Ther.*, 9: 237–47.

RASHOTTE, M. E., GRIFFIN, R. W., & SISK, C. L. (1977). Second-order conditioning of the pigeon's keypeck. *An. Learn. Behav.* 5: 25–38.

RATLIFF, F. (1965). *Mach bands: Quantitative studies on neural networks in the retina.* San Francisco: Holden-Day.

RAUGH, M. R., & ATKINSON, R. C. (1975). A mnemonic method for learning a second-language vocabulary. *J. edu. Psychol.*, 65: 1–16.

RAZRAN, G. (1971). *Mind in evolution: An East-West synthesis of learned behavior and cognition.* Boston: Houghton Mifflin.

REBER, A. S., & MILLWARD, R. B. (1968). Event observations in probability learning. *J. exp. Psychol.*, 77: 317–27.

REDDY, D. R., ERMAN, L. D., FENNELL, R. D., & NEELY, R. B. (1973). The HEARSAY speech understanding system: An example of the recognition process. *Proceedings of the Third International Joint Conference on Artificial Intelligence.* Stanford, Cal.

REIFF, R., & SCHEERER, M. (1959). *Memory and*

hypnotic age regression. New York: International Universities Press.

REIGER, C. J. III (1975). Conceptual memory and inference. In R. C. Schank, ed., *Conceptual information processing.* Amsterdam: North-Holland.

REISS, S., & SUSHINSKY, L. W. (1975). Undermining extrinsic interest. *Amer. Psychol.,* 30: 782–83.

REITMAN, J. S. (1971). Mechanisms of forgetting in short-term memory. *Cog. Psychol.,* 2: 185–95.

REITMAN, J. S. (1976). Skilled perception in Go: Deducing memory structures from interresponse times. *Cog. Psychol.,* 8: 336–56.

REITMAN, W. R. (1964). Information-processing models in psychology. *Science,* 14: 1192–98.

REITMAN, W., & WILCOX, B. (1978). Pattern recognition and pattern-directed inference in a program for playing Go. In D. A. Waterman & F. Hayes-Roth, ed., *Pattern-directed inference systems.* New York: Academic Press. Pp. 503–24.

RESCORLA, R. A. (1966). Predictability and number of pairings in Pavlovian fear conditioning. *Psychon. Sci.,* 4: 383–84.

RESCORLA, R. A. (1968). Probability of shock in the presence and absence of CS in fear conditioning. *J. comp. physiol. Psychol.,* 66: 1–5.

RESCORLA, R. A. (1969a). Conditioned inhibition of fear. In N. J. Mackintosh and W. K. Honig, eds. *Fundamental issues in associative learning.* Halifax: Dalhousie Univ. Press.

RESCORLA, R. A. (1969b). Pavlovian conditioned inhibition. *Psychol. Bull.,* 72: 77–94.

RESCORLA, R. A. (1972). Informational variables in Pavlovian conditioning. In G. H. Bower, ed., *Psychology of learning and motivation: Advances in research and theory.* Vol. 6. New York: Academic Press.

RESCORLA, R. A. (1973). Second-order conditioning: Implications for theories of learning. In F. J. McGuigan & D. B. Lumsden, eds., *Contemporary approaches to conditioning and learning.* Washington, D.C.: V. H. Winston.

RESCORLA, R. A. (1976a). Pavlovian excitatory and inhibitory conditioning. In W. K. Estes, ed., *Handbook of learning and cognitive processes.* Vol. 2. Hillsdale, N.J.: Erlbaum. Pp. 7–35.

RESCORLA, R. A. (1976b). Stimulus generalization: Some predictions from a model of Pavlovian conditioning. *J. exp. Psychol.: Animal Behavior Processes,* 2: 88–96.

RESCORLA, R. A. (1978). Some implications of a cognitive perspective on Pavlovian conditioning. In S. H. Hulse, H. Fowler, & W. Honig, eds., *Cognitive processes in animal behavior.* Hillsdale, N.J.: Erlbaum. Pp. 15–50.

RESCORLA, R. A., & SOLOMON, R. L. (1967). Two-process learning theory: Relationships between Pavlovian conditioning and instrumental learning. *Psychol. Rev.,* 55: 151–82.

RESCORLA, R. A., & WAGNER, A. R. (1972). A theory of Pavlovian conditioning: Variations in the effectiveness of reinforcement and nonreinforcement. In A. Black & W. F. Prokasy, eds., *Classical conditioning: II. Current research and theory.* New York: Appleton-Century-Crofts.

RESTLE, F. (1955). A theory of discrimination learning. *Psychol. Rev.,* 62: 11–19.

RESTLE, F. (1957). Discrimination of cues in mazes: A resolution of the "place-vs.-response" question. *Psychol. Rev.,* 64: 217–28.

RESTLE, F. (1962). The selection of strategies in cue learning. *Psychol. Rev.,* 69: 329–43.

RESTLE, F. (1964a). Sources of difficulty in learning paired associates. In R. C. Atkinson, ed., *Studies in mathematical psychology.* Stanford: Stanford Univ. Press.

RESTLE, F. (1964b). The relevance of mathematical models for education. In E. R. Hilgard, ed., *Theories of learning and instruction.* 63rd Yearbook of the National Society for the Study of Education. Chicago: Univ. of Chicago Press.

RESTLE, F. (1965). Significance of all-or-none learning. *Psychol. Bull.*, 64: 313–25.

RESTLE, F. (1970). Theory of serial pattern learning: Structural trees. *Psychol. Rev.*, 77: 481–95.

RESTLE, F. (1971). *Mathematical models in psychology: An introduction.* Baltimore: Penguin Books.

RESTLE, F., & BROWN, E. (1970). Organization of serial pattern learning. In G. H. Bower, ed., *The psychology of learning and motivation: Advances in research and theory.* Vol. 4. New York: Academic Press.

RESTLE, F., & GREENO, J. (1970). *Introduction to mathematical psychology.* Reading, Mass.: Addison-Wesley.

RESTORFF, H. VON (1933). Analyse von Vorgangen in Spruenfeld. I. Über die Wirkung con Bereichsbildungen im Spruenfeld. *Psychol. Forsch.*, 18: 299–342.

REVUSKY, S., & GARCIA, J. (1970). Learned associations over long delays. In G. H. Bower, ed., *The psychology of learning and motivation: Advances in research and theory.* Vol. 4. New York: Academic Press.

RICHARDSON, A. (1969). *Mental imagery.* London: Routledge & Kegan Paul.

RIESBECK, C. K. (1975). Conceptual analysis. In R. C. Schank, ed. *Conceptual information processing.* Amsterdam: North-Holland. Pp. 83–156.

RIESBECK, C. K. (1978). An expectation-driven production system for natural language understanding. In D. A. Waterman & F. Hayes-Roth, eds., *Pattern-directed inference systems.* New York: Academic Press. Pp. 399–415.

RILEY, D. A. (1958). The nature of the effective stimulus in animal discrimination learning: Transportation reconsidered. *Psychol. Rev.*, 65: 1–7.

RILEY, D. A. (1963). Memory for form. In L. Postman, ed., *Psychology in the making.* New York: Alfred A. Knopf. Pp. 402–65.

RILLING, M. (1977). Stimulus control and inhibitory processes. In W. K. Honig & J. E. R. Staddon, eds., *Handbook of operant behavior.* Englewood Cliffs, N.J.: Prentice-Hall. Pp. 432–80.

RIZLEY, R. C., & RESCORLA, R. A. (1972). Associations in second-order conditioning and sensory preconditioning. *J. comp. physiol. Psychol.* 81: 1–11.

ROBBINS, D. (1971). Partial reinforcement: A selective review of the alleyway literature since 1960. *Psychol. Bull.*, 76: 415–31.

ROBERTS, W. A. (1972). Short-term memory in the pigeon: Effects of repetition and spacing. *J. exp. Psychol.*, 94: 74–83.

ROBERTS, W. W. (1958). Both rewarding and punishing effects from stimulation of posterior hypothalamus of cat with same electrode at same intensity. *J. comp. physiol. Psychol.*, 51: 400–407.

ROBINSON, E. S. (1927). The "similarity" factor in retroaction. *Amer. J. Psychol.*, 39: 297–312.

ROBINSON, E. S. (1932). *Association theory today.* New York: Appleton-Century-Crofts.

ROBINSON, F. P. (1961). *Effective study.* Rev. ed. New York: Harper & Row.

ROBINSON, J. A. (1970). An overview of mechanical theorem proving. In R. Banerji & M. Mesarovic, eds., *Theoretical approaches to non-numerical problem solving.* New York: Springer-Verlag.

RODERICK, T. H. (1960). Selection for cholinesterase activity in the cerebral cortex of the rat. *Genetics,* 45: 1123.

ROHWER, W. D., JR. (1970). Mental elaboration and learning proficiency. In J. P. Hill, ed., *Minnesota Symposium on Child Psychology.* Vol. 4. Minneapolis: Univ. of Minnesota Press.

ROSENBLATT, F. (1958). The perceptron: A problablistic mode for information storage and organization in the brain. *Psychol. Rev.*, 65: 386–407.

ROSENBLATT, F. (1962). *Principles of neurodynamics.* Washington, D.C.: Cornell Aeronautical Laboratory, Report 1196-G-8.

ROSENZWEIG, M. R. (1962). The mechanisms of

hunger and thirst. In L. Postman, ed., *Psychology in the making*. New York: Alfred A. Knopf.

ROSENZWEIG, M. R., & BENNETT, E. L., eds. (1976). *Neural mechanisms of learning and motivation*. Cambridge: MIT Press.

ROSENZWEIG, M. R., BENNETT, E. L., & KRECH, D. (1964). Cerebral effects of environmental complexity and training among adult rats. *J. comp. physiol. Psychol.*, 57: 438–39.

ROSS, B. H. (1980). The more the better? Number of decisions as a determinant of memorability. Unpublished manuscript. Stanford University. Dept. of Psychology.

ROSS, B. H., & BOWER, G. H. (1980). Comparison of models of associative recall. Unpublished manuscript. Stanford University. Dept. of Psychology.

ROSS, R. R. (1964). Positive and negative partial-reinforcement effects carried through continuous reinforcement, changed motivation, and changed response. *J. exp. Psychol.*, 68: 492–502.

ROTTER, J. B. (1954). *Social learning and clinical psychology*. Englewood Cliffs, N.J.: Prentice-Hall.

ROWLAND, V. (1968). Cortical steady potential (direct current potential) in reinforcement and learning. In E. Stellar & J. M. Sprague, eds., *Progress in physiological psychology*. Vol. 2. New York: Academic Press.

ROZIN, P. (1965). Specific hunger for thiamine: Recovery from deficiency and thiamine preference. *J. comp. physiol. Psychol.*, 59: 98–101.

ROZIN, P. (1967). Specific aversions as a component of specific hungers. *J. comp. physiol. Psychol.*, 64: 237–42.

ROZIN, P., & KALAT, J. W. (1972). Learning as a situation-specific adaptation. In M. E. P. Seligman & J. L. Hager eds., *Biological boundaries of learning*. New York: Appleton-Century-Crofts.

RUBIN, E (1921). *Visuelle wahrgenommene Figwren*. Copenhagen: Gyldendalske.

RUJA, H. (1956). Productive psychologists. *Amer. Psychol.*, 11: 148–49.

RUMELHART, D. E. (1977). *Human information processing*. New York: Wiley.

RUMELHART, D. E., LINDSAY, P. H., & NORMAN, D. A. (1972). A process model for long-term memory. In E. Tulving & W. Donaldson, eds., *Organization of memory*. New York: Academic Press.

RUNDUS, D. J. (1971). Analysis of rehearsal processes in free recall. *J. exp. Psychol.*, 89: 63–77.

RUNDUS, D. J., & ATKINSON, R. C. (1970). Rehearsal processes in free recall: A procedure for direct observation. *J. verb. Learn. verb. Behav.*, 9: 99–105.

RUSINOV, V. S. (1953). An electro-physiological analysis of the connecting function in the cerebral cortex in the presence of a dominant area. *Communications at the XIX International Physiological Congress, Montreal*.

RUSSELL, I. S., & OCHS, S. (1961). One-trial hemispheric transfer of a learning engram. *Science*, 133: 1077–78.

RUSSELL, W. R., & NATHAN, P. W. (1946). Traumatic amnesia. *Brain*, 69: 280–300.

RYLE, G. (1949). *The concept of mind*. London: Hutchinson.

SACERDOTI, E. D. (1974). Planning in a hierarchy of abstraction spaces. *Art. Intell.* 5: 125–35.

SACERDOTI, E. D. (1975). *A structure for plans and behavior*. Menlo Park, Cal.: A. I. Tech. Note 109, Stanford Research Institute.

SACKETT, G. P. (1967). Some persistent effects of different rearing conditions on preadult social behavior of monkeys. *J. comp. physiol. Psychol.*, 64: 363–65.

SALZBERG, P. M., PARKS, T. E., KROLL, N. E. A., & PARKINSON, S. R. (1971). Retroactive effects of phonemic similarity on short-term recall of visual and auditory stimuli. *J. exp. Psychol.*, 91: 43–46.

SAMUEL, A. L. (1959). Some studies in machine learning using the game of checkers. *IBM J. Res. Devel.*, 3: 210–29. Also reprinted in E. A. Feigenbaum & J. Feldman, eds., *Computers and thought*. New York: McGraw-Hill, 1963.

SAMUEL, A. L. (1967). Studies in machine learning using the game of checkers: II. Recent progress. *IBM J. Res. Devel.*, 11: 601–17.

SASMOR, R. M. (1966). Operant conditioning of a small-scale muscle response. *J. exp. anal. Behav.*, 9: 69–85.

SCHACHTER, S. (1971). Some extraordinary facts about obese humans and rats. *Am. Psychol.*, 26: 129–44.

SCHACHTER, S., & SINGER, J. E. (1962). Cognitive, social, and physiological determinants of emotional state. *Psychol. Rev.*, 69: 379–99.

SCHANK, R. C. (1972). Conceptual dependency: A theory of natural language understanding. *Cog. Psychol.*, 3: 552–631.

SCHANK, R. C., ed. (1975a). *Conceptual information processing.* Amsterdam: North-Holland.

SCHANK, R. C. (1975b). The structure of episodes in memory. In D. G. Bobrow & A. Collins, eds., *Representation and understanding.* New York: Academic Press.

SCHANK, R. C., et al. (1975c). SAM—a story understander. Research Report 54. New Haven, Conn.: Yale University, Dept. of Computer Science.

SCHANK, R., & ABELSON, R. P. (1977). *Scripts, plans, goals, and understanding.* Hillsdale, N.J.: Erlbaum.

SCHANK, R., & COLBY, K. M., eds. (1973). *Computer models of thought and language.* San Francisco: W. H. Freeman.

SCHLOSBERG, H. (1937). The relationship between success and the laws of conditioning. *Psychol. Rev.*, 44: 379–94.

SCHNEIDER, A. M. (1967). Control of memory by spreading cortical depression: A case for stimulus control. *Psychol. Rev.*, 74: 201–15.

SCHNEIDER, A. M. (1968). Stimulus control and spreading cortical depression: Some problems reconsidered. *Psychol. Rev.*, 75: 353–58.

SCHNEIDER, A. M., & EBBESON, E. (1967). Interhemispheric transfer of lever pressing as stimulus generalization of the effects of spreading depression. *J. exp. anal. Behav.*, 10: 193–97

SCHOEFFLER, M. (1954). Probability of response to compounds of discriminated stimuli. *J. exp. Psychol.*, 48: 323–29.

SCHOENFELD, W. N. (1970). "Avoidance" in behavior theory. In P. B. Dews, ed., *Festschrift for B. F. Skinner.* New York: Appleton-Century-Crofts. Pp. 351–56.

SCHOENFELD, W. N., ANTONITIS, J. J., & BERSH, P. J. (1950). A preliminary study of training conditions necessary for secondary reinforcement. *J. exp. Psychol.*, 40: 40–45.

SCHULL, J. (1979). A conditioned opponent theory of Pavlovian conditioning and habituation. In G. H. Bower, ed., *The psychology of learning and motivation.* Vol. 13. New York: Academic Press, Pp. 57–90.

SEGAL, E. (1977). Toward a coherent psychology of language. In W. K. Honig & J. E. R. Staddon, eds., *Handbook of operant behavior.* Englewood Cliffs, N.J.: Prentice-Hall. Pp. 628–53.

SELFRIDGE, O., & NEISSER, U. (1960). Pattern recognition by machine. *Sci. Amer.* (Aug.) 203: 69–80.

SELIGMAN, M. E. P. (1970). On the generality of of the law of learning. *Psychol. Rev.*, 77: 406–18.

SELIGMAN, M. E. P. (1975). *Helplessness.* San Francisco: W. H. Freeman.

SELIGMAN, M. E. P., & MAIER, S. F. (1967). Failure to escape traumatic shock. *J. exp. Psychol.*, 74: 1–9.

SEWARD, J. P., & LEVY, N. J. (1949). Sign learning as a factor in extinction. *J. exp. Psychol.*, 39: 660–68.

SHAPIRO, D., CRIDER, A. B., & TURSKY, B. (1964). Differentiation of an automatic response through operant reinforcement. *Psychon. Sci.*, 1: 147–48.

SHAPIRO, D., & SURWIT, R. S. (1976). Learned control of physiological function and disease. In H. Leitenberg, ed., *Handbook of behavior modification and behavior therapy.* Englewood Cliffs, N.J.: Prentice-Hall. Pp. 74–123.

SHAPIRO, M. M. (1961). Salivary conditioning in dogs during fixed-interval reinforcement contingent upon lever pressing. *J. exp. anal. Behav.*, 4: 361–64.

SHAPIRO, M. M., & HERENDEEN, D. L. (1975). Food reinforced inhibition of conditioned salivation in dogs. *J. comp. Physiol. Psychol.*, 88: 628–32.

SHEFFIELD, F. D. (1949). Hilgard's critique of Guthrie. *Psychol. Rev.*, 56: 284–91.

SHEFFIELD, F. D. (1954). A drive-induction theory of reinforcement. New Haven: Yale Univ. Mimeographed manuscript.

SHEFFIELD, F. D. (1961). Theoretical considerations in the learning of complex sequential tasks from demonstration and practice. In A. A. Lumsdaine, ed., *Student response in programmed instruction*. Washington, D.C.: National Academy of Sciences–National Research Council, Pub. 943. Pp. 13–32.

SHEFFIELD, F. D., (1965). Relation between classical conditioning and instrumental learning. In W. F. Prokasy, ed., *Classical conditioning: A symposium*. New York: Appleton-Century-Crofts.

SHEPARD, R. N. (1964). Review of computers and thought. *Behavioral Sci.*, 9: 57–65.

SHERRINGTON, C. S. (1906). *The integrative action of the nervous system*. New Haven: Yale Univ. Press.

SHETTLEWORTH, S. J. (1975). Reinforcement and the organization of behavior in golden hamsters. *J. exp. Psychol.: Animal Behavior Processes*, 104: 56–87.

SHIMP, C. P. (1969). Optimal behavior in free-operant experiments. *Psychol. Rev.*, 76: 97–112.

SHIMP, C. P. (1975). Perspectives on the behavioral unit: Choice behavior in animals. In W. K. Estes, ed., *Handbook of learning and cognitive processes*. Vol. 2. Hillsdale, N.J.: Erlbaum.

SHORTLIFFE, E. (1976). *Computer-based medical consultation: MYCIN*. New York: Elsevier.

SIDMAN, M. (1960). *Tactics of scientific research: Evaluating experimental data in psychology*. New York: Basic Books.

SIEGEL, S. (1961). Decision making and learning under varying conditions of reinforcement. *Ann. N.Y. Acad. Sci.*, 89: 766–83.

SIEGEL, S. (1978). Tolerance to the hyperthermic effect of morphine in the rat is a learned response. *J. comp. physiol. Psychol.*, 92: 1137–49.

SIMMONS, R. F. (1970). Natural language question-answering systems: 1969. In R. Banerji & D. Mesarovic, eds., *Theoretical approaches to non-numerical problem solving*. New York: Springer-Verlag.

SIMMONS, R. F., BURGER, J. F., & LONG, R. F. (1966). An approach toward answering English questions from text. *Proceedings of the Fall Joint Computer Conference*. Pp. 357–63.

SIMON, H. A. (1972). Complexity and the representation of patterned sequences of symbols. *Psychol. Rev.*, 79: 369–82.

SIMON, H. A., & BARENFELD, M. (1969). An information-processing analysis of perceptual process in problem-solving. *Psychol. Rev.*, 76: 473–83.

SIMON, H. A., & FEIGENBAUM, E. A. (1964). An information-processing theory of some effects of similarity, familiarization, and meaningfulness in verbal learning. *J. verb. Learn. verb. Behav.*, 3: 385–96.

SIMON, H. A., & HAYES, J. R. (1976). The understanding process: Problem isomorphs. *Cog. Psychol.*, 8: 86–97.

SIMON, H. A., & KOTOVSKY, K. (1963). Human acquisition of concepts for sequential patterns. *Psychol. Rev.*, 70: 534–46.

SIMON, H. A., & SIKLOSSY, L. (1972). *Representation and meaning: Experiments with information processing systems*. Englewood Cliffs, N.J.: Prentice-Hall.

SKAGGS, E. B. (1925). Further studies in retroactive inhibition. *Psychol. Monogr.*, 34: (161).

SKINNER, B. F. (1936). The verbal summator and a method for the study of latent speech. *J. Psychol.*, 2: 71–107.

SKINNER, B. F. (1937a). Two types of conditioned reflex: A reply to Konorski and Miller. *J. gen. Psychol.*, 16: 272–79.

SKINNER, B. F. (1937b). The distribution of associated words. *Psychol. Rec.,* 1: 71–76.

SKINNER, B. F. (1938). *The behavior of organisms: An experimental analysis.* Englewood Cliffs, N.J.: Prentice-Hall.

SKINNER, B. F. (1948a). *Walden two.* New York: Macmillan.

SKINNER, B. F. (1948b). Superstition in the pigeon. *J. exp. Psychol.,* 38: 168–72.

SKINNER, B. F., (1950). Are theories of learning necessary? *Psychol. Rev.,* 57: 193–216.

SKINNER, B. F. (1951). How to teach animals. *Sci. Amer.,* 185: 26–29.

SKINNER, B. F. (1953). *Science and human behavior.* New York: Macmillan.

SKINNER, B. F. (1954). The science of learning and the art of teaching. *Harvard educ. Rev.,* 24: 86–97.

SKINNER, B. F. (1957) *Verbal behavior.* Englewood Cliffs, N.J.: Prentice-Hall.

SKINNER, B. F. (1958). Teaching machines. *Science,* 128: 969–77.

SKINNER, B. F. (1968). *The technology of teaching.* Englewood Cliffs, N.J.: Prentice-Hall.

SKINNER, B. F. (1969). *Contingencies of reinforcement: A theoretical analysis.* Englewood Cliffs, N.J.: Prentice-Hall.

SKINNER, B. F. (1971). *Beyond freedom and dignity.* New York: Knopf.

SKINNER, B. F. (1974). *About behaviorism.* New York: Knopf.

SKINNER, B. F. (1976). *Particulars of my life.* New York: Knopf.

SKINNER, B. F. (1979). *The shaping of a behaviorist.* New York: Knopf.

SLAMECKA, N. J. (1964). An inquiry into the doctrine of remote association. *Psychol. Rev.,* 71: 61–76.

SLAMECKA, N. J., & CERASO, J. (1960). Retroactive and proactive inhibition of verbal learning. *Psychol. Bull.,* 57: 449–75.

SLAMECKA, N. J., & GRAF, P. (1978). The generation effect: Delineation of a phenomenon. *J. exp. Psychol.: Human Learning and Memory.* 4: 592–604.

SLOBIN, D. I. (1971). *Psycholinguistics.* Glenview, Ill.: Scott, Foresman.

SMALLWOOD, R. D. (1962). *A decision structure for teaching machines.* Cambridge: MIT Press.

SMALLWOOD, R. D. (1971). The analyses of economic teaching strategies for a simple learning model. *J. math. Psychol.,* 8: 285–301.

SMITH, C. B. (1956). Background effects on learning and transposition of lightness discriminations. Unpublished doctoral dissertation. Univ. of Texas.

SMITH, E. E. (1976). Theories of semantic memory. In W. K. Estes, ed., *Handbook of learning and cognition.* Vol. 5. Hillsdale, N.J.: Erlbaum.

SMITH, S., & GUTHRIE, E. R. (1921). *General psychology in terms of behavior.* New York: Appleton-Century-Crofts.

SNYDER, M., & CANTOR, N. (1979). *Testing theories about other people: Remembering all the history that fits.* Unpublished manuscript. Univ. of Minnesota.

SOKOLOV, E. M. (1963). Higher nervous functions: The orienting reflex. *Ann. Rev. Physiol.,* 25: 545–80.

SPEAR, N. E. (1978). *The processing of memories: Forgetting and retention.* Hillsdale, N.J.: Erlbaum.

SPENCE, K. W. (1936). The nature of discrimination learning in animals. *Psychol. Rev.,* 43: 427–49.

SPENCE, K. W. (1937). The differential response in animals to stimuli varying within a single dimension. *Psychol. Rev.,* 44: 430–44.

SPENCE, K. W. (1942). The basis of solution by chimpanzees of the intermediate size problem. *J. exp. Psychol.,* 31: 257–71.

SPENCE, K. W. (1947). The role of secondary reinforcement in delayed reward learning. *Psychol. Rev.,* 54: 1–8.

SPENCE, K. W. (1956). *Behavior theory and conditioning.* New Haven: Yale Univ. Press.

SPENCE, K. W. (1960a). The roles of reinforcement and nonreinforcement in simple learning. In *Behavior theory and learning: Se-*

lected papers of K. W. Spence. Englewood Cliffs, N.J.: Prentice-Hall. Chap. 6.

SPENCE, K. W. (1960b). *Behavior theory and learning: Selected papers.* Englewood Cliffs, N.J.: Prentice-Hall.

SPERRY, R. W. (1961). Cerebral organization and behavior. *Science,* 133: 1749–57.

SPERRY, R. W., & MINER, N. (1955). Pattern perception following insertion of mica plates into visual cortex. *J. comp. physiol. Psychol.,* 48: 463–69.

SPONG, P., HAIDER, M., & LINDSLEY, D. B. (1965). Selective attentiveness and evoked cortical responses to visual and auditory stimuli. *Science,* 148: 395–97.

STAATS, A. W. (1968). *Learning, language and cognition.* New York: Holt, Rinehart & Winston.

STAATS, A. W. (1975). *Social behaviorism.* Homewood, Ill.: Dorsey.

STAATS, A. W., & STAATS, C. K. (1963). *Complex human behavior.* By permission of the author.

STADDON, J. E. R., & SIMMELHAG, V. L. (1971). The "superstition" experiment: A re-examination of its implications for the principles of adaptive behavior. *Psychol. Rev.,* 78: 3–43.

STALNAKER, J. M., & RIDDLE, E. E. (1932). The effect of hypnosis on long-delayed recall. *J. gen. Psychol.,* 6: 429–59.

STEA, D. (1964). The acquired aversiveness of a cue contiguously associated with the removal of positive reinforcement. Unpublished doctoral dissertation. Stanford Univ.

STEIN, L. (1964). Reciprocal action of reward and punishment mechanisms. In R. G. Heath, ed., *The role of pleasure in behavior.* New York: Hoeber. Pp. 113–39.

STEIN, L. (1969). Chemistry of purposive behavior. In J. T. Tapp, ed., *Reinforcement and behavior.* New York: Academic Press.

STEIN, L. (1978). Reward transmitters: Catecholamines and opiod peptides. In M. A. Lipton, A. DiMascio, & K. F. Killam, eds., *Psy-*chopharmacology: A generation of progress.* New York: Raven Press. Pp. 569–81.

STEIN, L., & WISE, C. D. (1971). Possible etiology of schizophrenia: progressive damage to the noradrenergic reward system by 6-hydroxydopamine. *Science,* 171: 1032–36.

STEIN, L., WISE, C. D., & BELLUZZI, J. D. (1977). Neuropharmacology of reward and punishment. In L. I. Iverson, S. D. Iverson, & S. H. Snyder, eds., *Handbook of psychopharmacology.* Vol. 8. New York: Plenum. Pp. 25–53.

STERMAN, M. B. (1973). Neurophysiologic and clinical studies of sensorimotor EEG biofeedback training: some effects on epilepsy. *Seminars in Psychiatry,* 5: 507–25.

STERNBERG, S. (1969). Memory scanning: Mental process revealed by reaction-time experiments. *Amer. Sci.,* 57: 421–57.

STEVENS, A. L., & COLLINS, A. (1978). Multiple conceptual models of a complex system. Tech. Report No. 3923. Cambridge: Bolt, Beranek & Newman. To appear in R. Snow, P. Federico, & W. Montague, eds., *Aptitude, learning, and instruction.*

STONE, C. P., & NYSWANDER, D. B. (1927). Reliability of rat learning scores from the multiple T-maze as determined by four different methods. *J. genet. Psychol.,* 34: 497–524.

STRASSBURGER, R. C. (1950). Resistance to extinction of a conditioned operant as related to drive level at reinforcement. *J. exp. Psychol.,* 40: 473–87.

STRATTON, G. M. (1919). Retroactive hypermnesia and other emotional effects on memory. *Psychol. Rev.,* 26: 474–86.

SUITER, R. D., & LoLORDO, V. M. (1971). Blocking of inhibitory Pavlovian conditioning in the conditioned emotional response procedure. *J. comp. physiol. Psychol.,* 76: 137–44.

SULZER-AZAROFF, B., & MAYER, G. R. (1977). *Applying behavior analysis procedures with children and youth.* New York: Holt, Rinehart, and Winston.

SUPPES, P., ed., (1978). *Impact of research on education: Some case studies.* Washington, D.C.: National Academy of Education.

SUPPES, P., & ATKINSON, R. C. (1960). *Markov learning models for multiperson interactions*. Stanford: Stanford Univ. Press.

SUPPES, P., & DONIO, J. (1967). Foundations of stimulus-sampling theory for continuous-time processes. *J. math. Psychol.*, 4: 202–25.

SUPPES, P., & GINSBERG, R. (1963). A fundamental property of all-or-none models. *Psychol. Rev.*, 70: 139–61.

SUPPES, P., JERMAN, M., & BRIAN, D. (1968). *Computer-assisted instruction: Stanford's 1965–66 arithmetic program*. New York: Academic Press.

SUPPES, P., & MORNINGSTAR, M. (1972). *Computer-assisted instruction at Stanford, 1966–68: Data, models and evaluations of the arithmetic program*. New York: Academic Press.

SUPPES, P., ROUANET, H., LEVINE, M., & FRANKMANN, R. W. (1964). Empirical comparison of models for a continuum of responses with noncontingent bimodal reinforcement. In R. C. Atkinson, ed., *Studies in mathematical psychology*. Stanford: Stanford Univ. Press.

SUSSMAN, G. J. (1975). *A computer model of skill acquisition*. New York: American Elsevier.

SUTHERLAND, N. S., & MACKINTOSH, N. J. (1971). *Mechanisms of animal discrimination learning*. New York: Academic Press.

SWANSON, J. M., & KINSBOURNE, M. (1979). State-dependent learning and retrieval. In J. F. Kihlstrom & F. J. Evans, eds., *Functional disorders of memory*. Hillsdale, N.J.: Erlbaum.

TALLAND, G. A. (1965). *Deranged memory: A psychonomic study of the amnesic syndrome*. New York: Academic Press.

TAYLOR, C. (1964). *The explanation of behavior*. London: Routledge & Kegan Paul.

TEITELBAUM, P., & EPSTEIN, A. N. (1962). The lateral hypothalamic syndrome. *Psychol. Rev.*, 69: 74–90.

TENENBAUM, J. M., & BARROW, H. G. (1977). Experiments in interpretation-guided segmentation. *Art. Intell.*, 8: 241–74.

TERRACE, H. S. (1963a). Discrimination learning with and without errors. *J. exp. anal. Behav.*, 6: 1–27.

TERRACE, H. S. (1963b). Errorless transfer of a discrimination across two continua. *J. exp. anal. Behav.*, 6: 223–32.

TERRACE, H. S. (1964). Wavelength generalization after discrimination learning with and without errors. *Science*, 144: 78–80.

TERRACE, H. S. (1973). Classical conditioning. In G. S. Reynolds, C. Catania, & B. Schard, eds., *Contemporary experimental psychology*. Chicago: Scott, Foresman.

TERRACE, H. S. (1979a). How Nim Chimsky changed by mind. *Psychol. Today*, 13: No. 6, (Nov.), 65–76.

TERRACE, H. S. (1979b). *Nim*. New York: Knopf.

TERRY, W. S. (1976). The effects of priming US representation in short-term memory on Pavlovian conditioning. *J. exp. Psychol.: Animal Behavior Processes*, 2: 354–70.

TERRY, W. S., & WAGNER, A. R. (1975). Short-term memory for surprising vs. expected unconditioned stimuli in Pavlovian conditioning. *J. exp. Psychol.: Animal Behavior Process*, 1: 122–33.

THOMPSON, R. F. (1967). *Foundations of physiological psychology*. New York: Harper & Row.

THOMPSON, R. F. (1975). *Introduction to physiological psychology*. New York: Harper & Row.

THOMPSON, R. F., PATTERSON, M. M., & TAYLOR, T. J. (1972). The neurophysiology of learning. *Ann. Rev. Psychol.*, 23: 73–104.

THOMPSON, R. F., & SPENCER, W. A. (1966). Habituation: A model phenomenon for the study of neuronal substrates of behavior. *Psychol. Rev.*, 73: 16–43.

THOMSON, D. N., & TULVING, E. (1970). Associative encoding and retrieval: Weak and strong cues. *J. exp. Psychol.*, 86: 255–62.

THORNDIKE, E. L. (1898). Animal intelligence: An experimental study of the associative processes in animals. *Psychol. Rev., Monogr. Suppl.,* 2 (8).

THORNDIKE, E. L. (1903). *Educational psychology.* New York: Lemcke and Buechner.

THORNDIKE, E. L. (1911). *Animal intelligence.* New York: Macmillan.

THORNDIKE, E. L. (1913). *Educational psychology: The psychology of learning.* Vol. 2. New York: Teachers College.

THORNDIKE, E. L. (1922). *The psychology of arithmetic.* New York: Macmillan.

THORNDIKE, E. L. (1931). *Human learning.* New York: Century. Paperback ed., Cambridge: MIT Press, 1966.

THORNDIKE, E. L. (1932a). *The fundamentals of learning.* New York: Teachers College.

THORNDIKE, E. L. (1932b). Reward and punishment in animal learning. *Comp. Psychol. Monogr.,* 8: (39).

THORNDIKE, E. L. (1933a). A proof of the law of effect. *Science,* 77: 173–75.

THORNDIKE, E. L. (1933b). An experimental study of rewards. *Teachers Coll. Contr. Educ.,* No. 580.

THORNDIKE, E. L., (1935). *The psychology of wants, interests and attitudes.* New York: Appleton-Century-Crofts.

THORNDIKE, E. L. (1949). *Selected writings from a connectionist's psychology.* New York: Appleton-Century-Crofts.

THORNDIKE, E. L., et al. (1928). *Adult learning.* New York: Macmillan.

THORNDIKE, E. L., & WOODWORTH, R. S. (1901). The influence of improvement in one mental function upon the efficiency of other functions. *Psychol. Rev.,* 8: 247–61, 384–95, 553–64.

THORNDYKE, P. W. (1976). The role of inferences in discourse comprehension. *J. verb. Learn. verb. Behav.,* 15: 437–46.

THORNDYKE, P. W. (1978). Pattern-directed processing of knowledge from texts. In D. A. Waterman & F. Hayes-Roth, eds., *Pattern-directed inference systems.* New York: Academic Press. Pp. 347–60.

THORNDYKE, P. W., & HAYES-ROTH, B. (1979).

The use of schemata in the acquisition and transfer of knowledge. *Cog. Psychol.,* 11: 82–106.

THORNTON, J. W., & JACOBS, P. D. (1971). Learned helplessness in human subjects. *J. exp. Psychol.,* 87: 369–72.

THUNE, L. E., & UNDERWOOD, B. J. (1943). Retroactive inhibition as a function of degree of interpolated learning. *J. exp. Psychol.,* 32: 185–200.

TILTON, J. W. (1939). The effect of "right" and "wrong" upon the learning of nonsense syllables choice arrangement. *J. educ. Psychol.,* 30: 95–115.

TILTON, J. W. (1945). Gradients of effect. *J. genet. Psychol.,* 66: 3–19.

TIMBERLAKE, W. (1980). A molar equilibrium theory of learned performance. In G. H. Bower, ed., *The psychology of learning and motivation.* Vol. 14. New York: Academic Press.

TIMBERLAKE, W., & ALLISON, J. (1974). Response deprivation: An empirical approach to instrumental performance. *Psychol. Rev.,* 81: 146–64.

TINKLEPAUGH, O. L. (1928). An experimental study of representative factors in monkeys. *J. comp. Psychol.,* 8: 197–236.

TOLMAN, E. C. (1932). *Purposive behavior in animals and men.* New York: Appleton-Century-Crofts. Reprinted, Univ. of California Press, 1949.

TOLMAN, E. C. (1939). Prediction of vicarious trial and error by means of the schematic sowbug. *Psychol. Rev.,* 46: 318–36.

TOLMAN, E. C. (1942). *Drives toward war.* New York: Appleton-Century-Crofts.

TOLMAN, E. C. (1951). *Collected papers in psychology.* Berkeley: Univ. of Calif. Press.

TOLMAN, E. C. (1959). Principles of purposive behavior. In S. Koch, ed., *Psychology: A study of a science.* Vol. 2. New York: McGraw-Hill. Pp. 92–157.

TOLMAN, E. C., & BRUNSWIK, E. (1935). The organism and the causal texture of the environment. *Psychol. Rev.,* 42: 43–77.

TOLMAN, E. C., & GLEITMAN, H. (1949). Studies in learning and motivation: 1. Equal reinforcements in both end-boxes, followed by shock in one end-box. *J. exp. Psychol.*, 39: 810–19.

TOLMAN, E. C., & HONZIK, C. H. (1930a). "Insight" in rats. *Univ. Calif. Publ. Psychol.*, 4: 215–32.

TOLMAN, E. C., & HONZIK, C. H. (1930b). Introduction and removal of reward, and maze performance in rats. *Univ. Calif. Publ. Psychol.*, 4: 257–75.

TOLMAN, E. C., RITCHIE, B. F., & KALISH, D. (1946). Studies in spatial learning: II. Place learning versus response learning. *J. exp. Psychol.*, 36: 221–29.

TOLMAN, E. C., RITCHIE, B. F., & KALISH, D. (1947). Studies in spatial learning: V: Response learning vs. place learning by the non-correction method. *J. exp. Psychol.*, 37: 285–92.

TRABASSO, T. R., & BOWER, G. H. (1964). Component learning in the four-category concept problem. *J. math. Psychol.*, 1: 143–69.

TRABASSO, T. R., & BOWER, G. H. (1968). *Attention in learning: Theory and research.* New York: Wiley.

TRAPOLD, M. A. (1962). The effect of incentive motivation on an unrelated reflex response. *J. comp. physiol. Psychol.*, 55: 1034–39.

TRAPOLD, M. A. (1970). Are expectancies based upon different positive reinforcing events discriminably different? *Learn. and Motiv.*, 1: 129–40.

TRAVIS, R. P. (1964). The role of spreading cortical depression in relating the amount of avoidance training to interhemispheric transfer. *J. comp. Psychol.*, 57: 42–46.

TROWBRIDGE, M. H., & CASON, H. (1932). An experimental study of Thorndike's theory of learning. *J. gen. Psychol.*, 7: 245–58.

TRYON, R. C. (1942). Individual differences. In F. A. Moss, ed., *Comparative psychology.* Englewood Cliffs, N.J.: Prentice-Hall.

TULVING, E. (1962). Subjective organization in free recall of "unrelated" words. *Psychol. Rev.*, 69: 344–54.

TULVING, E. (1966). Subjective organization and effects of repetition in multi-trial free recall learning. *J. verb. Learn. verb. Behav.*, 5: 193–97.

TULVING, E. (1968). Theoretical issues in free recall. In T. R. Dixon & D. L. Horton, eds., *Verbal behavior and general behavior theory.* Englewood Cliffs, N.J.: Prentice-Hall.

TULVING, E. (1969). Retrograde amnesia in free recall. *Science*, 164: 88–90.

TULVING, E. (1972). Episodic and semantic memory. In E. Tulving & W. Donaldson, eds., *Organization of memory.* New York: Academic Press.

TULVING, E., & DONALDSON, W., eds. (1972). *Organization of memory.* New York: Academic Press.

TULVING, E., & PEARLSTONE, Z. (1966). Availability versus accessibility of information in memory for words. *J. verb. Learn. verb. Behav.*, 5: 381–91.

TULVING, E., & PSOTKA, J. (1971). Retroactive inhibition in free recall: Inaccessibility of information available in the memory store. *J. exp. Psychol.*, 87: 1–8.

TULVING, E., & THOMSON, D. N. (1971). Retrieval processes in recognition memory: Effects of associative context. *J. exp. Psychol.*, 87: 116–24.

TULVING, E., & THOMSON, D. N. (1973). Encoding specificity and retrieval processes in episodic memory. *Psychol. Rev.*, 80: 352–73.

TVERSKY, A. (1977). Features of similarity. *Psychol. Rev.*, 84: 327–52.

TVERSKY, A., & KAHNEMAN, D. (1971). Belief in the law of small numbers. *Psychol. Bull.*, 76: 105–10.

TVERSKY, A., & KAHNEMAN, D. (1974). Availability: A heuristic for judging frequency and probability. *Cog. Psychol.*, 5: 207–32.

TVERSKY, A., & KAHNEMAN, D. (1978). Causal schemata in judgments under uncertainty.

In M. Fishbein, ed., *Progress in social psychology*. Hillsdale, N.J.: Erlbaum.

Tversky, A., & Sattath, S. (1979). Preference trees. *Psychol. Rev.*, 86: 542–73.

Uhr, L., & Vossler, C. (1963). A pattern-recognition program that generates, evaluates, and adjusts its own operators. In E. A. Feigenbaum & J. Feldman, eds., *Computers and thought*. New York: McGraw-Hill.

Ulrich, R. E., & Azrin, N. H. (1962). Reflexive fighting in response to aversive stimulation. *J. exp. anal. Behav.*, 5: 511–20.

Underwood, B. J. (1957). Interference and forgetting. *Psychol. Rev.*, 64: 49–60.

Underwood, B. J. (1966). *Experimental psychology*. 2nd ed. Englewood Cliffs, N.J.: Prentice-Hall.

Underwood, B. J., & Postman, L. (1960). Extra-experimental sources of interference in forgetting. *Psychol. Rev.*, 67: 73–95.

Ungar, G., Galvan, L., Clark, R. H. (1968). Chemical transfer of learned fear. *Nature*, 217: 1259–61.

Uster, H. J., Bättig, K., & Nägeli, H. H. (1976). Effects of maze geometry and experience on exploratory behavior in the rat. *An. Learn. Behav.*, 4: 84–88.

Uster, H. J. (1977). "Analyse des Explorationsverhaltens von Ratten in Labyrinthen unterschiedlicher komplexitaet." Unpublished doctoral dissertation. Zurich, Switzerland: Eidgenoessischen Technischen Hochschule.

Van Lawick-Goodall, J. (1971). *In the shadow of man*. Boston: Houghton Mifflin.

Verhave, T. ed. (1966). *The experimental analysis of behavior: Selected readings*. New York: Appleton-Century-Crofts.

Verplanck, W. S. (1962). Unaware of where's awareness: Some verbal operants—notates, monents, and notants. In C. W. Eriksen, ed., *Behavior and awareness*. Durham, N.C.: Duke Univ. Press.

Vitz, P. C., & Todd, R. C. (1967). A model for simple repeating binary patterns. *J. exp. Psychol.*, 75: 108–17.

Vitz, P. C., & Todd, R. C. (1969). A coded element model of the perceptual processing of sequential stimuli. *Psychol. Rev.*, 76: 433–49.

Voeks, V. W. (1948). Postremity, recency, and frequency as bases for prediction in the maze situation. *J. exp. Psychol.*, 38: 495–510.

Voeks, V. W. (1950). Formalization and clarification of a theory of learning. *J. Psychol.*, 30: 341–63.

Voeks, V. W. (1954). Acquisition of S-R connections: A test of Hull's and Guthrie's theories. *J. exp. Psychol.*, 47: 137–47.

Von Neumann, J., & Morgenstern, O. (1944). *Theory of games and economic behavior*. Princeton: Princeton Univ. Press.

Wachtel, P. L. (1977). *Psychoanalysis and behavior therapy*. New York: Basic Books.

Wagner, A. R. (1963). Conditioned frustration as a learned drive. *J. exp. Psychol.*, 66: 142–48.

Wagner, A. R. (1966). Frustration and punishment. In R. N. Haber, ed., *Research on motivation*. New York: Holt, Rinehart & Winston.

Wagner, A. R. (1976). Priming in STM. In T. J. Tighe & R. N. Leaton, eds., *Habituation*. Hillsdale, N.J.: Erlbaum. Pp. 95–128.

Wagner, A. R. (1978). Expectancies and the priming of STM. In S. H. Hulse, H. Fowler, & W. K. Honig, eds., *Cognitive processes in animal behavior*. Hillsdale, N.J.: Erlbaum.

Wagner, A. R., & Rescorla, R. A. (1972). Inhibition in Pavlovian conditioning: Application of a theory. In R. A. Boakes & M. S. Holliday, eds., *Inhibition and learning*. New York: Academic Press.

Wagner, A. R., Rudy, J. W., & Whitlow, J. W. (1973). Rehearsal in animal conditioning. *J. exp. Psychol. Mon.*, 97: 407–26.

Walter, W. G. (1953). *The living brain*. New York: Norton.

Wang, H. (1960). Towards mechanical mathematics. *IBM J. Res. Devel.*, 4: 2–22.

Wang, H. (1965). Games, logic, and computers. *Sci. Amer.*, 98–107.

WARK, D. M. (1976). Teaching study skills to adults. In J. D. Krumboltz and C. E. Thoreson, eds., *Counseling methods.* New York: Holt, Rinehart & Winston. Pp. 454–61.

WARREN, H. C. (1921). *A history of association psychology.* New York: Scribner's.

WARRINGTON, E. K., & SHALLICE, T. (1969). The selective impairment of auditory verbal short-term memory. *Brain, 92:* 885–96.

WARRINGTON, E. K., & SHALLICE, T. (1972). Neuropsychological evidence of visual storage in short-term memory tasks. *Quart. J. exp. Psychol.,* 24: 30–40.

WATERMAN, D. A. & HAYES-ROTH, F., eds., (1978). *Pattern-directed inference systems.* New York: Academic Press.

WATKINS, M. J. (1974). When is recall spectacularly higher than recognition? *J. exp. Psychol.,* 102: 161–63.

WATKINS, M. J., HO, E., & TULVING, E. (1976). Context effects in recognition memory for faces. *J. verb. Learn. verb. Behav.,* 15: 505–18.

WATSON, D. L., & THARP, R. G. (1977). *Self-directed behavior: Self-modification for personal adjustment.* 2nd ed. Monterey, Cal.: Brooks-Cole.

WATSON, J. B. (Kinesthetic and organic sensations. Their role in the reactions of the white rat to the maze. *Psychol. Monogr.,* 8: (33).

WATSON, J. B. (1914). *Behavior, an introduction to comparative psychology.* New York: Holt, Rinehart and Winston.

WATSON, J. B. (1916). The place of the conditioned reflex in psychology. *Psychol. Rev.,* 23: 89–116.

WATSON, J. B. (1919). *Psychology from the standpoint of a behaviorist.* Philadelphia: J. B. Lippincott.

WATSON, J. B. (1924) *Behaviorism.* New York: Norton.

WAUGH, N. C., & NORMAN, D. A. (1965). Primary memory. *Psychol. Rev.,* 72: 89–104.

WEAVER, G. E., DUNCAN, E. M., & BIRD, C. P. (1972). Cue-specific retroactive inhibition. *J. verb. Learn. verb. Behav.,* 11: 362–66.

WEBB, W. B., & NOLAN, C. Y. (1953). Cues for discrimination as secondary reinforcing agents: A confirmation. *J. comp. physiol. Psychol.,* 46: 180–81.

WEISS, J. M. (1971a). Effects of coping behavior in different warning conditions on stress pathology in rats. *J. comp. physiol. Psychol.,* 77: 1–13.

WEISS, J. M. (1971b). Effects of punishing the coping response (conflict) on stress pathology in rats. *J. comp. physiol. Psychol.,* 77: 14–21.

WEISS, J. M., GLAZER, H. I., & POHORECKY, L. A. (1975). Coping behavior and neurochemical changes: An alternative explanation of the original learned helplessness experiments. In *Relevance of the pyschopathoolgical animal model to the human.* New York: Plenum Press.

WELFORD, A. T. (1976). *Skilled performance: Perceptual and motor skills.* Glenview, Ill.: Scott, Foresman.

WENDT, G. R. (1937). Two and one-half year retention of a conditioned response. *J. gen. Psychol.,* 17: 178–80.

WERTHEIMER, M. (1923). Untersuchung zur Lehre von der Gestalt, II. *Psychol. Forsch.,* 4: 301–50. Translated and condensed as "Laws of organization in perceptual forms," in W. D. Ellis, *A source book of gestalt psychology.* New York: Harcourt, Brace & World. 1938. Pp. 71–88.

WERTHEIMER, M. (1945). *Productive thinking.* New York: Harper & Row.

WERTHEIMER, M. (1959). *Productive thinking.* Enlarged ed. New York: Harper & Row.

WEXLER, K., & CULICOVER, P. W. (1980). *Formal principles of language acquisition.* Cambridge: MIT Press.

WHITEHEAD, A. N., & RUSSELL, B. (1925). *Principia mathematica.* 2nd ed. Vol. 1. Cambridge, Eng.: Cambridge Univ. Press.

WHITLOW, J. W. (1975). Short-term memory in habituation and dishabituation. *J. exp. Psy-*

chol.: *Animal Behavior Processes,* 1: 189–206.

WHITMAN, J. R., & GARNER, W. R. (1962). Free recall learning of visual figures as a function of form of internal structure. *J. exp. Psychol.,* 64: 558–64.

WHYTT, R. (1763). *An essay on the vital and other involuntary motions of animals.* 2nd ed. Edinburgh: J. Balfour.

WICKELGREN, W. A. (1977). *Learning and memory.* Englewood Cliffs, N.J.: Prentice-Hall.

WICKELGREN, W. A. (1979a). *Cognitive psychology.* Englewood Cliffs, N.J.: Prentice-Hall.

WICKELGREN, W. B. (1979b). Chunking and consolidation. *Psychol. Rev.,* 86: 44–60.

WICKENS, D. D. (1973). Classical conditioning, as it contributes to the analyses of some basic psychological processes. In F. J. McGuigan & D. B. Lumsden, eds., *Contemporary approaches to conditioning and learning.* Washington: V. H. Winston. Pp. 213–44.

WILENSKY, R. (1978). Understanding goal-based stories. PhD Thesis. A. I. Research Report # 140. New Haven, Conn.: Yale University Computer Science Dept.

WILKS, Y. (1973). An artificial intelligence approach to machine translation. In R. Shank & K. Colby, eds., *Computer models of thought and language.* San Francisco: W. H. Freeman.

WILLIAMS, D. R. (1965). Classical conditioning and incentive motivation. In W. F. Prokasy, ed., *Classical conditioning.* New York: Appleton-Century-Crofts.

WILLIAMS, D. R., & WILLIAMS, H. (1969). Automaintenance in the pigeon: Sustained pecking despite contingent non-reinforcement. *J. exp. anal. Behav.,* 12: 511–20.

WILLIAMS, G. F. (1971). A model of memory in concept learning. *Cog. Psychol.,* 2, 158–84.

WILLIAMS, S. B., & LEAVITT, H. J. Prediction of success in learning Japanese. *J. appl. Psychol.,* 31: 164–68.

WINE, J., & KRASNE, F. (1978). The cellular analysis of invertebrate learning. In T. Teyler, ed., *Brain and learning.* Stamford, Conn.: Greylock Publishing. Pp. 13–31.

WINOGRAD, T. (1972). Understanding natural language. *Cog. Psychol.,* 3: 1–191.

WINOKUR, S. (1976). *A primer of verbal behavior.* Englewood Cliffs, N.J.: Prentice-Hall.

WINSTON, P. H. (1970). *Learning structural descriptions from examples.* Cambridge: MIT Artificial Intelligence Laboratory, Project MAC-TR-231.

WISE, C. D., & STEIN, L. (1973). Dopamine-β-hydroxylase deficits in the brains of schizophrenic patients. *Science,* 181: 344–47.

WISEMAN, S., & NEISSER, U. (1971). Perceptual organization as a determinant of visual recognition memory. Paper presented at the meetings of the Eastern Psychological Association, New York City.

WITTROCK, M. C., ed. (1977). *Learning and instruction: Readings in educational research.* Berkeley, Cal.: McCutchan.

WITTROCK, M. C., & LUMSDAINE, A. A. (1977). Instructional psychology. In M. R. Rosenzweig & L. W. Porter, eds., *Annual review of psychology.* Vol. 28. Palo Alto, Cal.: Annual Reviews. Pp. 417–59.

WOLFE, J. B. (1934). The effect of delayed reward upon learning in the white rat. *J. comp. Psychol.,* 17: 1–21.

WOLFLE, D. L. (1936). The relative efficiency of constant and varied stimulation during learning: III. The objective extent of stimulus variation. *J. comp. Psychol.,* 22: 375–81.

WOLMAN, B. B., & NAGEL, E., eds. (1965). *Scientific psychology.* New York: Basic Books.

WOLPE, J. (1958). *Psychotherapy by reciprocal inhibition.* Stanford: Stanford Univ. Press.

WOODS, W. A. (1970). Transition network grammars for natural language analysis. *Communications of the Association for Computing Machinery,* 13: 591–606.

WOODWARD, A. E., BJORK, R. A., & JONGEWARD,

R. H. (1973). Recall and recognition as a function of primary rehearsal. *J. verb. Learn. verb. Behav.*, 12: 608–17.

WOODWORTH, R. S. (1918). *Dynamic psychology.* New York: Columbia Univ. Press.

WOODWORTH, R. S. (1958). *Dynamics of behavior.* New York: Holt, Rinehart & Winston.

WOODWORTH, R. S., & SCHLOSBERG, H. (1954). Experimental psychology. Rev. ed. New York: Holt, Rinehart & Winston.

WRIGHT, D. C. & CHUTE, D. L. (1973). State-dependent learning produced by posttrial intrathoracic administration of sodium pentobarbital. *Psychopharmacologia*, 31: 91.

WRIGHT, J. C. (1960). Problem-solving and search behavior under noncontingent reward. Unpublished doctoral dissertation, Stanford Univ.

WULF, F. (1922). Über die Veränderung von Vorstellungen (Gedächtnis and Gestalt). *Psychol. Forsch.,* I: 333–73. Translated and condensed as "Tendencies in figural variation," in W. D. Ellis, *A source book of gestalt psychology.* New York: Harcourt, Brace & World, 1938. Pp. 136–48.

WYRWICKA, W., & DOBRZECKA, C. (1960). Relationship between feeding and satiation centers of the hypothalamus. *Science,* 123: 805–6.

WYRWICKA, W., & STERNMAN, M. B. (1968). Instrumental conditioning of sensorimotor cortex EEG spindles in the waking cat. *Physiol. & Behav.* 3: 703–7.

YERKES, R. M. (1927). The mind of a gorilla: I. *Genet. Psychol. Monogr.* 2.

YNTEMA, D. B. & TRASK, F. P. (1963). Recall as a search process. *J. verb Learn. verb. Behav.,* 2: 65–74.

YOUNG, M. N., & GIBSON, W. B. (1966). *How to develop an exceptional memory.* Hollywood, Cal.: Wilshire Press.

YOUNG, R. K., HAKES, D. T., & HICKS, R. Y. (1965). Effects of list length in the Ebbinghaus derived-list paradigm. *J. exp. Psychol.,* 70: 338–41.

ZEAMAN, D., & HOUSE, B. J. (1963). The role of attention in retardate discrimination learning. In N. R. Ellis, ed., *Handbook of mental deficiency.* New York: McGraw-Hill. Pp. 159–223.

ZEILER, M. D. (1963). The ratio theory of intermediate size discrimination. *Psychol. Rev.,* 70: 516–33.

ZENER, K. (1937). The significance of behavior accompanying conditioned salivary secretion for theories of the conditioned reflex. *Amer. J. Psychol.,* 50: 384–403.

ZIMBARDO, P. G., ed. (1969). *The cognitive control of motivation.* Glenview, Ill.: Scott, Foresman.

ZIRKLE, G. A. (1946). Success and failure in serial learning: I. The Thorndike effect. *J. exp. Psychol.,* 36: 230–36.

Acknowledgments

Permission to reprint the following is hereby gratefully acknowledged:

Figures 2.3 and 2.4. Tilton, J.W. (1945) Gradients of effect. *J. Genet. Psychol.*, 66: 3–19. By permission of The Journal Press, Provincetown, Mass.

Table 3.1. Kimble, G.A. (1961) *Hilgard and Marquis' conditioning and learning*, 2nd ed. By permission of Prentice-Hall, Englewood Cliffs, N.J.

Figure 9.1. DiCara, L.V. Learning in the autonomic nervous system, 222:30–39. Copyright © 1970 by Scientific American, Inc. All rights reserved. By permission.

Quote on page 187. Azrin, N.H., & Holz, W.C. (1966). Punishment. In W.K. Honig, ed. *Operant behavior: Areas of research and application*. By permission of Prentice-Hall, Englewood Cliffs, N.J.

Figure 11.11. Menzel, E.W. Chimpanzee spatial memory organization. *Science*, 182:943–45. Copyright 1973 by the Amer. Assoc. for the Advance. of Science.

Figure 15.3. Atkinson, R.C., & Raugh, M.R. An application of the mnemonic keyword method to the acquisition of a Russian vocabulary. *J. Exp. Psychol.: Human Learning and Memory*, 104:126–33. Copyright 1975 by the Amer. Psychol. Assoc. Reprinted by perm.

Figures 15.9 and 15.10. Reprinted courtesy of R.C. Atkinson.

Figure 4.1. Fowler, H., & Miller, N.E. Facilitation and inhibition of runway performance by hind- and forepaw shock of various intensities. *J. Comp. Physiol. Psychol.*, 56:801–5. Copyright 1963 by the Amer. Psychol. Assoc. Reprinted by perm.

Figure 3.10. Shettleworth, S.J. Reinforcement and the organization of behavior in golden hamster. *J. Exp. Psychol.: Animal Behavior Processes*, 104:56–87. Copyright 1975 by the Amer. Psychol. Assoc. Reprinted by perm.

Figure 11.10. Olton, D.S., & Samuelson, R.J. Remembrance of places passed: Spatial memory in rats. *J. Exp. Psychol.: Animal Behavior Processes*, 2:97–116. Copyright 1976 by the Amer. Psychol. Assoc. Reprinted by perm.

Figure 11.3. Roberts, W.A. Short-term memory in the pigeon: Effects of repetition and spacing. *J. exp. Psychol.*, 94: 74–83. Copyright 1972 by the Amer. Psychol. Assoc. Reprinted by perm.

Figure 11.4. Supplementary report: Frequency of stimulus presentation and short-term decrement in recall. *J. Exp. Psychol.*, 64:650. Copyright 1962 by the Amer. Psychol. Assoc. Reprinted by perm.

Figure 13.3. Peterson, L.R., & Peterson, M.J. Short-term retention of individual verbal items. *J. Exp. Psychol.*, 58: 193–98. Copyright 1959 by the Amer. Psychol. Assoc. Reprinted by perm.

Figures 11.8 and 11.9. Levine, M. Human discrimination learning: The subset sampling assumption. *Psychol. Bull.*, 74:397–404. Copyright 1970 by the Amer. Psychol. Assoc. Reprinted by perm.

Figure 6.9. Martin, E. Transfer of verbal paired associates. *Psychol. Rev.*, 72:327–43. Copyright 1965 by the Amer. Psychol. Assoc. Reprinted by perm.

Figure 6.10. Briggs, G.E. Retroactive inhibition as a function of original and interpolated learning. *J. Exp. Psychol.*, 53:60–67. Copyright 1957 by the Amer. Psychol. Assoc. Reprinted by perm.

Figure 6.12. Briggs, G.E. Acquisition, extinction and recovery functions in retroactive inhibition. *J. Exp. Psychol.*, 47:285–93. Copyright 1954 by the Amer. Psychol. Assoc. Reprinted by perm.

Figure 6.11. Barnes, J.M. & Underwood, B.J. Fate of first-list associations in transfer theory. *J. Exp. Psychol.*, 58:97–105. Copyright 1959 by the Amer. Psychol. Assoc. Reprinted by perm.

Figure 6.13. Postman, L., Stark, K., & Henschel, D. Conditions of recovery after unlearning. *J. Exp. Psychol. Monogr.*, 82 (Whole No. 1). Copyright 1969 by the Amer. Psychol. Assoc. Reprinted by perm.

Table 8.2. Schoeffler, M. Probability of response to compounds of discriminated stimuli. *J. Exp. Psychol.*, 48:323–29. Copyright 1954 by the Amer. Psychol. Assoc. Reprinted by perm.

Figure 8.4 and 8.5. Estes, W.K. Statistical theory of spontaneous recovery and regression. *Psychol. Rev.*, 62:145–54. Copyright 1955 by the Amer. Psychol. Assoc. Reprinted by perm.

Figure 9.2. Miller, N.E., & Banuazizi, A. Instrumental learning by curarized rats of a specific visceral response, intestinal or cardiac. *J. Comp. Physiol. Psychol.*, 65:1–7. Copyright 1968 by the Amer. Psychol. Assoc. Reprinted by perm.

Figure 13.5. Ellis, N.R., Detterman, D.K., Runcie, D., McCarver, R.B., & Craig, E.M. Amnesic effects in short-term memory. *J. Exp. Psychol.*, 89:357–61. Copyright 1971 by the Amer. Psychol. Assoc. Reprinted by perm.

Figure 13.6. Rundus, D.J. Analysis of rehearsal processes in free recall. *J. Exp. Psychol.*, 89:63–77. Copyright 1971 by the Amer. Psychol. Assoc. Reprinted by perm.

Figures 15.6 and 15.7. Atkinson, R.C. Ingredients for a theory of instruction. *Amer. Psychol.*, 27:

921–31. Copyright 1972 by the Amer. Psychol. Assoc. Reprinted by perm.

Figures 13.15, 13.16, 13.17. Bandura, A. SOCIAL LEARNING THEORY. Copyright 1977, pp. 23, 79, 80. By permission of Prentice-Hall, Englewood Cliffs, N.J.

Quote on p. 464. Bandura, A. SOCIAL LEARNING THEORY, © 1977, p. 23. By permission of Prentice-Hall, Englewood Cliffs, N.J.

Figure 8.1. Hergenhahn, B.R. (1976). Estes's model of how stimulus elements change from the unconditional state to the conditioned state. In *An introduction to theories of learning*. By permission of Prentice-Hall, Englewood Cliffs, N.J.

Figure 10.8. Norman, D.A., Rumelhart, D.E. & the LNR Research Group. Explorations in Cognition. W.H. Freeman and Co. Copyright © 1975.

Figure 13.14 and Table 13.3. From an article by Kintsch, W. in THE STRUCTURE OF HUMAN MEMORY ed. Charles N. Cofer. W.H. Freeman and Co. Copyright © 1976.

Figure 2.5. DeNike, L.D., & Spielberged, C.D. (1963). Induced mediating states in verbal conditioning. *J. Verb. Learn. Verb. Behav.*, 1:339–45. By permission of Academic Press, Inc. New York, N.Y.

Figure 9.7. Blough, D.S. Steady-state data and a quantitative model of operant generalization and discrimination. *J. Exp. Psychol.: Animal Beh. Proc.*, 104:3–21. Copyright 1975 by the Amer. Psychol. Assoc. Reprinted by perm.

Figure 13.13. Collins, A.M., & Quillan, M.R. (1969) Retrieval time from semantic memory. *J. Verb. Learn. Verb. Behav.*, 8:240–47. Academic Press, New York, N.Y.

Figure 14.10. Berger, W.F., & Thompson, R.F. (1978). Neuronal plasticity in the limbic system during classical conditioning of the rabbit nictitating membrane response: I. Hippocampus. *Brain Res.*, 145:323–46. By permission of Elsevier, Amsterdam, The Netherlands.

AUTHOR INDEX

Hypothalamus, 479, 480, 481, 483, 484, 490
Hypothesis theory (Levine), 342–44

Iconic representation (Bruner), 556
Identifiability, stimulus, 36
If-then rules, 397 (*see also* Productions, systems of)
Illusory correlation, 441–43
Imitative behavior (*see* Observational learning)
Importance tags, 571
Imprinting, 12
Incentive motivation: Estes's theory of, 234; and habit strength, 339; Logan's theories of, 121–22, 127–30, 346–47; Spence's theory of, 119–22
Incentives, 99
Incremental reinforcement (Mowrer), 112, 113
Incremental vs. all-or-none learning, 143
Individually prescribed instruction (IPI), 560
Inference: insightful, 337–38; theorists' dependency on, 15; Tolman on, 328, 340
Inference rules, 397, 399 (*see also* Conceptual dependency analysis)
Information hypothesis regarding aftereffects, 37, 38–44
Information-processing (IP), 8, 15, 353–415; concepts and models of, 355–60; evaluation of, 409–415; language-processing programs, 399–409; learning programs, 360–64; pattern recognition in, 364–85; problem-solving programs, 385–96; specialist knowledge programs, 396–99
Information retrieval, programming, 400
Inhibition: in classical conditioning, 52–57; of delay, 61; Gibson on, 141–42; in Hull's theories, 100–101; proactive and retroactive, 145; reciprocal, 87
Inhibitory blocking, 280
Inhibitory conditioning, 58–62
Input, 355; and invariance problem, 364–65
Insight: Guthrie on, 93; Köhler's experiments on, 300–302; not considered by Skinner, 199; and problem solving (Gestalt theory), 319–21; Thorndike on, 47–48; Tolman on, 337; vs. trial and error in problem-solving, 16
Insight learning, 301
Instance Selector, 362, 363

Instinct (*see* Species-specific behavior)
Instruction (*see also* Education): Atkinson's decision-theoretic analysis for optimizing learning, 556–61; Bruner's cognitive-developmental theory, 555–56; Gagné's hierarchical task analyses, 551–55; theories of, 551–61
Instrumental conditioning, distinguished from classical conditioning, 64–65, 200–202
Intelligence, artificial (*see* Artificial intelligence)
Intelligent planner programs, 395–96
Intentional action vs. involuntary response, 419
Intentions (Guthrie), 81–82
Interest, learner, 542–43
Interference: associative, 78; with meaningful text, 162–64; proactive, 157–62, 228, 285; retroactive, 148, 228
Interference theory, 10, 152–57; main shifts in, 164
Interhemispheric transfer, 524–34
Intermediary responses, peripheral vs. central, 15
Interoceptive conditioning, 58
Interocular transfer, 524–27
Interpolation, 10
Intertrial reinforcement (ITR), 276
Intervening variables (Hull), 95–96, 97, 98
Intervention plan, behavior modification, 289, 290
Intrinsic interest, undermining of, 204–205
"Intuitive statistician" view, 441, 442
Invariance problem in input, 364–65
IPI (*see* Individually prescribed instruction)
Irradiation, cerebral, 53, 55, 56
Isometric behaviors, 354
Item learning vs. order learning, 138
ITR (*see* Intertrial reinforcement)

Jasper-Ricci-Doane study of learning changes in brain cells, 519
Jensen's theory of serial position effect, 139–40
Johnson-Laird study of levels of processing, 435
Journal of Personalized Instruction, 574
Judson-Cofer-Gelfand experiment on problem solving, 194–95

Kamin's theory of surprisingness, 282
Kamiya's experiment on biofeedback, 264

Kant's theories, 4, 5, 7, 12
Kapatos-Gold experiment on hunger, 479–80
Kaplan study of biofeedback and epilepsy, 266
Kaswan's experiment on good continuation principle, 306–307
Katona's experiments on understanding, 318
Keller-Schoenfeld analysis of chaining, 178–79
Keller's personalized systems of instruction (PSI), 572–75
Keppel-Postman-Zavortink experiment on interference theory, 160
Keyword mnemonic method (Atkinson), 545, 547–48
Kimble's classification of conditioned reflexes, 64
Kimmel's results on inhibitory conditioning, 60–61
Kimura report on split-brain patients, 528
Kinesthesis (Watson), 75, 77
Kintsch-van Dijk hypothesis of text coherence, 457–59
Kintsch-Vipond reading model, 459
Knowledge: acquisition of, 8; as a labeled graph structure, 449–52; and memory, 1–2; organization of, 329, 556
Knowledge specialists, 396–99
Koffka's theories, 302
Köhler's theories: on forgetting, 317; on insight, 300–302; on memory, 311
Krechevsky's experiments on expectancy theory, 342, 344
Krech-Rosenzweig-Bennett studies of brain cholinesterase, 509–510
Kreutzer-Leonard-Flavell metamemory knowledge concept, 425
Kuno's Harvard Multiple-Pass Syntactic Analyzer, 402–403
Kupfermann-Pinsker view on neuronal models, 508

LaBerge's neutral-elements rule, 222
Laboratory technology, 188–95
Landfield-McGaugh experiment on ECS-induced amnesia, 499
Language (*see also* Verbal behavior): acquisition, 6–7, 13, 68; computer, 356, 360; foreign, 545, 547–48, 558–60, 562–64; laboratory, 562–64; and maturation, 13
Language-processing programs, 399–409; conceptual dependency analysis, 404–406; goal-plan-action analysis, 406–409;

META–DENDRAL program, 397–98
Metamemory, 425
Methodology, behaviorist, 169–70
Michael's experiment on sexual behavior, 481
Michotte's experiment on causality, 5
Micromolar theory (Logan), 121, 127–30
Miller-Banuazizi experiments on visceral conditioning, 256–59
Miller-Brucker clinical application of biofeedback, 259
Miller-Dollard experiments using cybernetic analysis, 109
Miller-Konorski example of instrumental conditioning, 64
Miller's (G. A.) theory of memory chunks, 427, 436
Miller's (N. E.) theories, 107–109, 185–86
Milner's reports on memory disabilities of neurological patients, 502, 528
Mirror-focus epilepsy, 506–507
Mirror-image strings, 418
Misanin-Miller-Lewis experiment on ECs effects, 499
Mitchell-Kirschbaum-Perry experiment on cue novelty, 71
Mnemonics, 143–44, 313, 438–39, 544–48
Modeling, behavior modification, 291–92
Model preparations, neurophysiological studies, 506–508
Models (see Information-processing, concepts and models; Mathematical learning models; Simulation of human behavior; Stimulus sampling theory)
Moeser-Bergman experiment on grammar induction, 401
Molar vs. molecular description of behavior, 327
Mood-altering drugs, 488
Moore's report of species-specific reactions, 204
Motivation, 14, 43; biological, 478–82; CAI responsiveness providing, 568–69; in cognitive theories, 467–69; deficit, 285; Gestalt position on, 322; Guthrie on, 81, 92; incentive, 119–22, 339; neurological mechanisms, 478–82, 484–85; Skinner on, 199; Spence on, 119–22; in stimulus sampling theory, 232–34; Tolman on, 341
Motoric reproduction skills (Bandura), 465–66
Mowrer-Estes's stimulus-response scanning mechanism, 344–45
Mowrer's theories, 109–113, 344–45
Müller-Pilzecker memory consolidation hypothesis, 495

Multiple baselines research design, 189
Multiple schedules research design, 189–90
MYCIN program, 397, 399

Native response tendencies, 11–12 (see also Species-specific behavior)
"Near misses," 543, 544
Need reduction (Hull), 99, 102
Negative recency effect, 226
Negative transfer, 138
Neimark-Shuford experiment on probability-learning, 225
Neophobia, 71
Nervous systems, types of (Pavlov), 56
Network, semantic, 449, 450–51
Neural-net models, 535–36
Neurochemistry: of learning and experience, 508–19; of reward and punishment, 485–89
Neurological patients, experimentation on, 501–502
Neuronal conditioning, 263
Neurons, 476
Neurophysiology of learning, 475–536; interhemispheric transfer, 524–34; learning and memory, 494–504; motivation, arousal and attention, 478–85; Pavlovian, 54–57; technical developments in, 477–78
Neurosis, 286 (see also Phobias): behaviorist's view of, 288, 289; experimental, 57; Skinner's theory of, 198
Neutral-elements rule (LaBerge), 222
"Never-right" experiment (Estes), 40–44
Newell-Shaw-Simon Logic Theorist (LT), 363, 385–87
Newell-Simon theories: and General Problem-Solver (GPS), 390–92, 410; on inference in simulation, 411; on means-ends analysis, 396; on simulation advantages, 413–14
Nonreinforcement, effect of, in hypothesis-testing theory, 342; and nonreward (see Frustrative nonreward)
Nonreward: Amsel's frustration theory of, 274; and latent learning, 339–40; recent interpretations of, 273–77
Nonsense syllables, 134, 142

Obesity, 479–80
Observational learning, 462–67; Skinner's weakness on, 206
Olds-Allan-Briese study of ESB reward, 484
Olds-Milner experiment on ESB reward, 482

Olds's experiment on neuronal conditioning, 263
Olton-Samuelson experiment on short-term spatial memory, 347–48
Omission training (Sheffield), 202
One-element model of SST, 235–40
One-factor theory of reinforcement, 202
One-trial learning, 78, 88; Guthrie on, 88
Operant conditioning, 64, 169–211 (see also Skinner's theories): applied with biofeedback, 259–62; applied to teaching, 539; of autonomic responses, 255–59; and classical conditioning, 171, 202–203; differentiation in, 177–78; discrimination in, 173–77; drive affecting, 184–86; emotion in, 186; experiments on, 174–77, 178, 183–84, 185, 186, 194–95, 200–205, 255–59; and laboratory technology, 188–95; law of, 255; neuronal, 263; punishment in, 187–88; reinforcement in, 172, 177, 179–84; response chains in, 178–79; studies of, 172–73; and traditional viewpoints, 209–211
Operant and respondent behavior, distinction, 170–71, 199–203, 255
Operants, 200
Order learning, vs. item learning, 138
Organization: of knowledge (Tolman), 329; and memory, 436–40; perceptual, laws of (Gestalt theory), 302–309
Orienting reflex (OR), 13, 492
Osgood's transfer surface theory, 146–48, 149, 150
Osmoreceptors, 480
Outcome expectations, 476
Output, computer, 355
Overshadowing, 420, 442
Overton's dissociation studies, 531–32, 533

Packard's study of group-contingent reinforcement, 549–50
Pain perception, 488–89
Paired-associates learning (PAL), 134, 141–44, 236–40, 368–71
Paivio's theories of mental imagery, 440
Pandemonium (parallel processor), 366
Paradoxical conditioned responses, 261–62
Parallel processor, 365, 366–67
Parsing systems, 401–404, 452–53
Partial reinforcement extinction effect, 126, 341–42, 346
Participant modeling, 470–71

324, 436–48; and repetition, 446

Recency: effect in STM, 430–31; of experience, 4; judgments, 445–46; law of (Watson), 75; principle of (Guthrie), 76

Reciprocal induction, 56

Reciprocal inhibition, 87

Recitation, value of active, 539–40

Recognition-action cycles, 399

Recognition memory, 231, 244–47, 434

Recover (see Spontaneous recovery)

Reductionism, 2–3

Reductive system (Hull), 102–103

Reflection, empiricist, 3

Reflexes (see also Classical conditioning): conditioned (CR), 49, 75, 76; innate, 254; orienting (OR), 13, 492; unconditioned (UR), 49

Reflexive aggression, 186

Refractory period, 485

Rehearsal: elaborative vs. maintenance, 434, 435; hypotheses of (Thorndike), 37–38; intensity of, 283; intention to learn effect on, 135; mode of, and symmetry (Merryman), 36; overt, 429–31; in STM, 426–31, 432, 434

Reiger's inference generation program, 405

Reinforcement (see also Second-order conditioning): anticipation of, 466; conditioned, 109, 183–84; vs. contiguity, 16, 17; correlated, 128; decremental (Mowrer), 112, 113; differential, 466; differential (Logan), 128; drive-reduction hypothesis of, 107, 113; effect of, in hypothesis testing theory, 342; gradient of (Hull), 102, 104–105; Guthrie on, 82; in Hull's theory, 98–99, 102, 103; incremental (Mowrer), 112, 113; intermittent, 179; and latent learning theory, 339, 340; law of, 267; negative (Skinner), 172; in observational learning, 466; one-factor theory of, 202; in operant conditioning, 172, 177, 179–84; partial, and extinction effect, 273–77, 341–42, 346; Pavlov on, 50–52; positive (Skinner), 172; in programmed learning, 564, 565–66, 568–69; recent developments in study of, 267–73; relativity of, 267–70; response-deprivation theory of, 270–73; secondary, 183–84, 268, 329;

Skinner on, 172, 177, 179–84; in stimulus sampling theory, 217–18, 234; teaching, 541–42, 548–50; Tolman on, 329, 341–42; two-factor theory of, 199–200; in verbal learning tradition, 135–36

Reinforcers: Skinner on, 172, 184; trans-situational generality of, 267

Reiss-Sushinsky experiment on undermining intrinsic interest, 205

Reitman's study of pattern-recognition ability, 389–90

Relational responding (Spence), 114–17

Remembering, 2, 135, (see also Memory)

Remote associations (Ebbinghaus), 136–37

REM sleep, 490

Repetition, 10; improvement through, 77–78; and recall, 446

Rescorla's experiments: on generalized enhancement, 280–81; on inhibitory conditioning, 59; on second-order conditioning, 62–64

Rescorla-Wagner theory of conditioning of elements within compounds, 278–81, 282, 442

Research designs, single-subject, 188–90

Respondent and operant behavior, distinction, 170–71, 199–203, 255

Response (see also Classical conditioning): by analogy (Thorndike), 28–29; anticipatory goal (Hull), 103–4; availability (Thorndike), 36–37; bias, 244; chains (Skinner), 178–79; conditioned (CR), 49, 97; contiguity of cue and, 76–81; differentiation of, 37, 173, 177–78; elicited, 170, 200; emitted, 170, 200; intermediary, 15; involuntary, 254–59; latency in stimulus sampling theory, 229–30, 231; learning, 37; paradoxical, 261–62; probability, 143; pure observing, 203; rate of, 170, 229, 230–31; stationarity, 236; stereotypy, 88–89; in stimulus sampling theory, 229, 230–31; strength, net, 97; variation (Thorndike), 27; voluntary, 65, 254

Response connections, 216–17

Response-scanning mechanism, 344–45

Response-sensitive strategy (Atkinson), 558, 559

Response unit specificity, 418–19

Restle-Brown experiments on law of common direction, 308

Restle's mathematical model of discrimination learning, 336–37

Restle's theory of stages of all-or-none pocesses, 240

Retention, 9, 10, 464

Reticular activating system (RAS), 490–92, 493–94

Retrieval: ECS disruption of, 499; encoding and, 446–49; rule, 310

Retrieval cues, 9, 10, 314–15

Retrieval scheme, 439

Retroactive inhibition, 145–46

Retroactive interference, 148, 228

Reverberatory loop of activation (Estes), 249

Reversal design, 188–89

Reversibility of behavioral phenomena, 210

Revusky-Garcia experiment on conditioned bait shyness, 420

Reward: acquired, 183; automatic, 31–33, 44–46; by brain stimulation, 482–85; in connectionism, 26, 30–33, 35, 37–46; effect of, vs. punishment, 30–31; Estes on, 87, 213; expectancy, 334–35; extrinsic, 204–205; gradient of (Spence), 102, 104; Guthrie on, 82–84; in Hull's theory, 98, 99, 102; informational hypothesis of, 37, 38–44; neurochemistry of, 485–88; Sheffield on, 86–87; Skinner on, 199; in spread of effect testing, 31–33; Tolman on, 341

Ribonucleic acid (RNA), 510–14; RNA memory hypothesis, 512–14

Riesback's syntax parser program, 402

Rilling's experiment on errorless discrimination learning, 176–77

Rizley-Rescorla experiments on second-order conditioning, 63

RNA (see Ribonucleic acid)

Robert's experiments: on ESB dual-effects, 438; on forgetting in STM, 332, 333

Robinson's theories on retroactive inhibition, 145–46, 150

Robots, 353–55, 392–96

Roderick's experiment in selective breeding, 509

Ross's criticism of "levels of processing" framework, 435–36

Ross's experiment on frustration, 124–26

Rote memorization, 317–19, 323, 544

Rotter's expectancy-reinforcement theory, 345

Valences (Tolman), 328, 329, 334, 340–41, 345
Value propositions, 423
Ventromedial nucleus, 479–80
Verbal behavior, 192–95
Verbal conditioning, 44–46
Verbal learning tradition (*see also* Paired-associates learning (PAL); Functionalist approach; Serial learning): associationism in, 133, 134, 135, 141, 165–67; characteristics of, 164–65; criticisms of, 167–68; experimental testing in, 154–64, 167; forgetting in, 144–64; origins of, 133–34; paradigms, 134; reinforcement in, 135–36; theory in, 134–36, 165; transfer in, 144–64
Verplanck's experiment on behavior shaping, 411–12
Vicarious trial-and-error behavior (VTE), 344–45
Visceral conditioning experiments, 256–59
Vividness of experience, 3–4
Voeks's experiments on response acquisition, 89–91
Voluntary control, 45–46 (*see also* Autonomic conditioning; Biofeedback)
Von Restorff effect, 317
VTE (*see* Vicarious trial-and-error behavior)

Wagner's experiment on frustrative nonreward, 123

Wagner's model of habituation, 283–84
Wagner's theory on surprise intervention with rehearsal mechanism, 283
Walter's Machina speculatrix, 353
Warrington-Shallice description of selective impairment of memory, 502
Watkins-Ho-Tulving report on context effects in recognition memory, 448
Watson's theories, 15, 74–76, 301, 412, 439; and behavioristic revolution, 4; and Guthrie's theories, 75–76, 77, 93; and Pavlov's theories, 57, 75, 76
Weber's law, 333
Weiss's experiments: on coping with stress, 286; on learned helplessness, 287
Wertheimer's theories: on camouflage, 309; laws of perceptual organization, 302–309; on productive thinking, 321–22
Wexler-Culicover induction algorithm, 401
Whitlow's tests of STM theory of habituation, 284
WHY program, 571–72
Wickelgren's theories: of amnesia, 502–504; of cortical association, 522
Wilensky's goal-plan understanding program, 408
Williams's concept learner model, 373–74

Williams's experiment on incentive motivation, 119–20
Williams-Williams experiment on autoshaping, 204
Winograd's language parsing and understanding program, 403–404, 449
Winston's scene analysis program, 378, 379–81, 452
Wolfe's experiment on gradient of reinforcement, 104
Wolfson's thesis on salivary secretion, 49
Wolpe's theory of systematic desensitization, 79–80, 542
Woods's syntax parser program, 402, 403
Woodward-Bjork-Jongewald experiment on levels of processing, 434
Work decrement, 101
Working memory, 363, 421, 422
Wulf's theories of forgetting (Gestalt), 316–17

Yoga, and biofeedback, 264

Zeiler's transposition theory, 117
Zen, and biofeedback, 264
Zirkle's theory of spread of effect, 35